To the children of this and future generations.

Important Information

EMERGENCY PHONE NUMBERS

Emergency Medical Service (EMS) _____

Hospital emergency room _____

Ambulance _____

Fire department _____

Police _____

Poison Control Center _____ 24-hour taxi service _____

Gas company _____ Electric company _____

Father's work # _____ Pager or cellular phone # _____

Mother's work # _____ Pager or cellular phone # _____

School # _____

Other _____

INFORMATION TO PROVIDE WHEN CALLING FOR EMERGENCY HELP

Your name / Type of emergency (*poison, broken bone, loss of consciousness, gaping wound, etc.*)

Your address _____ Apartment # _____

Major intersection or notable landmarks nearby _____

Phone # you're calling from _____

PHYSICIANS

Family physician _____

Phone # _____ Office hours _____

Dentist _____

Phone # _____ Office hours _____

Other physicians

Dr. _____ Phone # _____

Dr. _____ Phone # _____

Dr. _____ Phone # _____

Dr. _____ Phone # _____

RELATIVES

Name _____ Phone # _____

Name _____ Phone # _____

Name _____ Phone # _____

Name _____ Phone # _____

Name _____ Phone # _____

Name _____ Phone # _____

PASTORS, COUNSELORS, ATTORNEYS

Name _____ Phone # _____

Name _____ Phone # _____

Name _____ Phone # _____

Name _____ Phone # _____

MEDICATIONS AND PRESCRIPTIONS

All-night pharmacy phone # _____

Prescription-service phone # _____

Frequently used medications _____

_____

_____

_____

HEALTH INSURANCE

Health insurance agent _____

　　Health insurance phone # _____ Policy # _____

　　Phone # for verification of coverage _____

　　Address for sending claims _____

_____

Health insurance agent _____

　　Health insurance phone # _____ Policy # _____

　　Phone # for verification of coverage _____

　　Address for sending claims _____

_____

An encyclopedia of information. A dictionary of definitions. A bedside companion for parents of all ages and stages. Mothers and fathers need help in the most important mission they will ever undertake—parenting healthy children. This book is a great resource!

ELISA MORGAN
President and CEO
MOPS International

The Complete Book of Baby and Child Care is the most helpful and comprehensive book on the subject that I have ever read. It not only provides an abundance of information regarding the physical development of our children from conception through college, but it also gives useful insight toward the process of helping our children develop emotionally and spiritually. I highly endorse this book and will use it in raising my daughter.

STEPHEN ARTERBURN, M.ED.
Cofounder and Chairman
New Life Clinics

Finally we have an authoritative, biblically based, and medically reliable guide for parents to raise their children according to Christian principles. I know our members will be prescribing this exciting resource to their patients!

DAVID STEVENS, M.D.
Executive Director
Christian Medical and Dental Society

I am eager to recommend this book as widely as possible. In addition to its value as a medical manual, it is a spiritually valid and balanced discussion of such subjects as discipline of children, single-income families, a parent's guide to teen sexuality, and how to select caregivers for children when both parents work. Wonderfully practical, this excellent book has Bible-based counsel as its keynote.

KENNETH N. TAYLOR
Translator of *The Living Bible*
Author of *Everything a Child Should Know about God* and other children's books

As a congressman with a special interest in adolescent health, a family physician, and a father of three grown children, I am excited to finally find a comprehensive book on parenting that includes realistic advice on parenting adolescents. *The Complete Book of Baby and Child Care* not only covers issues about the first few years of life, but it also deals with preparing your child for adulthood. The special sections talk candidly about issues such as teenage sexuality, sexually transmitted diseases, depression, suicide, and addictive behaviors. I strongly recommend this book as a resource for new parents and experienced parents alike.

THOMAS A. COBURN, M.D.
Member of Congress

The Focus on the Family®
Complete Book of Baby and Child Care

FOCUS ON THE FAMILY®

COMPLETE BOOK OF

Baby &
Child Care

THE
FOCUS ON
THE FAMILY
PHYSICIANS RESOURCE
COUNCIL, U.S.A.

PRIMARY AUTHOR:
Paul C. Reisser, M.D.

MANAGING EDITOR:
Melissa R. Cox

EDITOR:
Vinita Hampton Wright

Tyndale House Publishers, Inc.
WHEATON, ILLINOIS

The information contained in this book provides a general overview of many health-related topics.
It is not intended to substitute for advice that you might receive from your child's physician,
whether by telephone or during a direct medical evaluation. Furthermore, health-care practices
are continually updated as a result of medical research and advances in technology.
You should therefore check with your child's doctor if there is any question about
current recommendations for a specific problem.
No book can substitute for a direct assessment of your child by a qualified health-care professional.

Visit Tyndale's exciting Web site at www.tyndale.com

Library of Congress Cataloging-in-Publication Data

Reisser, Paul C.
   The Focus on the Family complete book of baby and child care /
The Focus on the Family Physicians Resource Council ;
primary author, Paul C. Reisser.
      p.   cm.
   Includes bibliographical references and index.
   ISBN 0-8423-0889-X (hardcover, alk. paper)
   ISBN 0-8423-3512-9 (softcover)
   1. Pediatrics—Popular works.   2. Child care.   3. Child development.
I. Focus on the Family Physicians Resource Council.   II. Title.
RJ.R4165   1997
618.92—dc21   97-23617

Printed in the United States of America

05   04
10   9   8

Table of Contents

Foreword
by Dr. James Dobson

If you've picked up this book, it is likely that you are a parent, soon to be one, or know someone who is. Maybe you and your spouse are expecting your first child. Pregnancy has been an experience more precious and indescribable than you could ever have imagined. Ultrasound photos, despite their blurry resolution, provide incontrovertible evidence of your baby's developing hands and feet, the shape of his or her head, the not-yet-seeing eyes. As this fragile life takes shape, you can't help being filled with wonder at the intricate, unfolding miracle of God's handiwork.

Perhaps your scenario is not so idyllic. Maybe you are not yet out of high school. The father of your baby conveniently excused himself when he learned of your condition. You've lived at home with your mom and dad throughout your pregnancy, or perhaps in a halfway house with other girls in crisis pregnancies.

Or your grown daughter has rejected her own baby, and now you're being asked to bring up your grandchild. Or you're a single dad trying to find your way in a world that fails to recognize that sometimes daddies have to be mommies too. Perhaps your baby is no longer a baby at all, but a troubled teen flirting with drugs and premarital sex—what do you do? This book was written with you in mind too.

Under the best of circumstances, rearing kids is a challenging assignment. As a parent, you will be called on to don a variety of hats, among them teacher, doctor, psychologist, friend, and pharmacist. As you contemplate the challenges ahead, you may feel overwhelmed by the responsibility. How can you nurture healthy self-esteem in your children? How can you teach them to protect themselves from unhealthy ideas, attitudes, habits, and associations? How can you build within them discernment and self-discipline? How can you develop in them, day by day, the values that are so basic to their well-being? And—one of the toughest questions of all—how can you guide them into independence until they themselves are walking with God in wisdom and truth, rather than simply following you?

The most discerning, vigilant, and competent parents ultimately find themselves feeling inadequate to accomplish these important tasks. A parent must have support, guidance, and encouragement—from other parents, from friends and family, from physicians and pastors. And we believe that, ultimately, each child must be entrusted to the care, love, and protection of Jesus Christ. I urge you not to shortchange your children by underestimating the importance of biblical precepts—either in the values you teach or in the way you conduct your own life. The stakes are simply too high.

Here at Focus on the Family, we recognize that parenting a child involves the care and nurture of the whole person—body, mind, *and* soul. That's why I'm particularly excited to be able to introduce to you this wonderful new offering from Tyndale House Publishers, *The Focus on the Family Complete Book of Baby and Child Care.* This comprehensive, well-researched volume offers detailed advice from more than fifty of the country's most highly respected physicians and medical authorities. Some have appeared as guests on the *Focus on the Family* broadcast, and many are members of Focus's prestigious Physicians Resource Council. This book is full of practical, specific guidance on every aspect of the child rearing process—from infancy through the teen years and beyond. Additionally, the book contains over four hundred topical definitions, as well as charts, graphs, illustrations, and resource listings.

And what truly sets this book apart is the spiritual guidance and encouragement woven throughout its pages. You will find countless helpful hints for instilling in your little ones the timeless truths of Scripture—and the foundation of faith upon which rest our ultimate hope and salvation.

You yourself may have gotten a rough start in life. You may not have received the nurturing and encouragement you deserved as a child. Maybe you've struggled with issues of low self-esteem and feelings of rejection from your own parents. If that's your story, I have good news for you: Starting here, you *can* do better by your own child. It begins with dedicating yourself and your baby to the care of the only truly perfect parent—the Lord Jesus Christ.

Whatever your parenting situation—be it by choice or by chance, whether the circumstances are ideal or heartbreaking, whether yours is a background of poverty or privilege—it matters not. What does matter is that you have been charged by God with a profound and sacred trust: that of shaping and nurturing a human life. Handle it with care. God bless you!

James Dobson

Acknowledgments

In many ways, the preparation of this book has resembled the process of parenting a child from infancy to adulthood. Our "baby" was born in enthusiastic brainstorming sessions, during which exciting and formidable proposals were set in motion. During the book's infancy, as the first chapters and reference topics were written, we slowly began to appreciate the amount of time, effort, and patience that would be required before our "young adult" would be ready to meet the world.

But there was no turning back. We eventually hit our stride over a period of months as more chapters and topics were written, reviewed, debated, revised, and reviewed again—often as many as nine or ten times over the course of several months. Our "child" grew and matured and received ongoing prayer, loving attention, and correction until another rite of passage arrived: an "adolescence" of sorts, when hundreds of pages of manuscript were presented to Tyndale House Publishers. More questions, suggestions, and insights from Tyndale's team led to further refinements, sometimes after spirited (but inevitably fruitful) discussions.

Finally graduation day has arrived, and our offspring is now vacating the nest and beginning an independent life, one that we pray will enhance and assist your family.

This project is the result of a diligent and cooperative effort of many talented individuals over a period of nearly three years. To all of them we are deeply indebted. While we cannot fully acknowledge the full length and breadth of their contributions, the following is our attempt to give credit where it is most certainly due.

First of all, a standing ovation is due to the members of the Physicians Resource Council review team, who spent endless hours in conference calls and many days in sometimes cramped quarters reviewing literally every letter of the manuscript. We thank you for your dedication, perseverance, patience, professionalism, and commitment.

THE FOCUS ON THE FAMILY
PHYSICIANS RESOURCE COUNCIL REVIEW TEAM
AND CONTRIBUTING EDITORS

Marilyn Maxwell Billingsly, M.D.
INTERNAL MEDICINE/PEDIATRICS—ST. LOUIS, MISSOURI

Douglas O. W. Eaton, M.D.
INTERNAL MEDICINE—SAN BERNARDINO, CALIFORNIA

J. Thomas Fitch, M.D.
PEDIATRICS—SAN ANTONIO, TEXAS

Patricia O. Francis, M.D.
PEDIATRICS—MORAGA, CALIFORNIA

Gaylen M. Kelton, M.D.
FAMILY MEDICINE—INDIANAPOLIS, INDIANA

Richard D. Kiovsky, M.D.
FAMILY MEDICINE—INDIANAPOLIS, INDIANA

Robert W. Mann, M.D.
PEDIATRICS—ARLINGTON, TEXAS

Paul Meier, M.D.
PSYCHIATRY—RICHARDSON, TEXAS

Mary Anne Nelson, M.D.
FAMILY MEDICINE—CEDAR RAPIDS, IOWA

The remaining members of the Focus on the Family Physicians Resource Council, in both the United States and Canada, also contributed to this project in a variety of ways.

UNITED STATES

John P. Livoni, M.D. (chair)
RADIOLOGY—SACRAMENTO, CALIFORNIA

Peter F. Armstrong, M.D.
ORTHOPEDICS—SALT LAKE CITY, UTAH

Reed Bell, M.D.
PEDIATRICS—GULF BREEZE, FLORIDA

Robb Blackwood, M.D.
FAMILY MEDICINE—CHESAPEAKE, VIRGINIA

Eugene Diamond, M.D.
PEDIATRICS—CHICAGO, ILLINOIS

Thomas E. Elkins, M.D.
OBSTETRICS/GYNECOLOGY—BALTIMORE, MARYLAND

W. David Hager, M.D.
OBSTETRICS/GYNECOLOGY—LEXINGTON, KENTUCKY

Walter Larimore, M.D.
FAMILY MEDICINE—KISSIMMEE, FLORIDA

Alan A. Nelson, M.D.
PSYCHIATRY—REDSTONE, COLORADO

Claudia Nelson, M.D.
PEDIATRICS—REDSTONE, COLORADO

Donald Nelson, M.D.
FAMILY MEDICINE—CEDAR RAPIDS, IOWA

Jeffrey B. Satinover, M.D.
PSYCHIATRY—WESTON, CONNECTICUT

Curtis Stine, M.D.
FAMILY MEDICINE—DENVER, COLORADO

Morton Woolley, M.D.
GENERAL SURGEON—LOS ANGELES, CALIFORNIA

CANADA

Margaret Cottle, M.D. (chair)
PALLIATIVE CARE—VANCOUVER, BRITISH COLUMBIA

Ron Calderisi, M.D.
GENERAL SURGEON—VANCOUVER, BRITISH COLUMBIA

Stephen Genuis, M.D.
OBSTETRICS/GYNECOLOGY—EDMONTON, ALBERTA

Jim Gilbert, M.D.
GENERAL SURGEON—PEMBROKE, ONTARIO

Rosemarie Gilbert, M.D.
FAMILY MEDICINE—PEMBROKE, ONTARIO

Ron Jarvis, M.D.
FAMILY MEDICINE—DUNCAN, BRITISH COLUMBIA

Tim Kelton, M.D.
FAMILY MEDICINE—NORTH YORK, ONTARIO

Peter Nieman, M.D.
PEDIATRICS—CALGARY, ALBERTA

Dickson Vinden, M.D.
FAMILY MEDICINE—CANNINGTON, ONTARIO

Peter Webster, M.D.
RESPIRATORY MEDICINE—TORONTO, ONTARIO

In addition to the members of the Physicians Resource Council, we would like to thank the many contributors who provided research, written material, and reviews of topics in their fields of expertise:

Jane Anderson, M.D.
PEDIATRICS—SAN FRANCISCO, CALIFORNIA

Karl Anderson, M.D.
UROLOGY—SAN FRANCISCO, CALIFORNIA

Brian L. Burke Jr., M.D.
PEDIATRICS—GRAND RAPIDS, MICHIGAN

Robin Cottle, M.D.
OPHTHALMOLOGY—VANCOUVER, BRITISH COLUMBIA

Sarah Chandler, M.D.
FAMILY MEDICINE—LUBBOCK, TEXAS

M. C. Culbertson Jr., M.D.
PEDIATRIC OTOLARYNGOLOGY—DALLAS, TEXAS

William G. Culver, M.D.
ALLERGY-IMMUNOLOGY—LOVELAND, COLORADO

Joyce Fischer, M.D.
PEDIATRICS—BLUFFTON, INDIANA

Russell Engevik, M.D.
EMERGENCY MEDICINE—JULIAN, CALIFORNIA

Linda Flower, M.D.
FAMILY MEDICINE—TOMBALL, TEXAS

Lawrence P. Frick, M.D.
FAMILY MEDICINE—CHILLICOTHE, OHIO

Stanley Hand, M.D.
OPHTHALMOLOGY—ORLANDO, FLORIDA

John Hartman, M.D.
FAMILY MEDICINE—KISSIMMEE, FLORIDA

Gerald Hough, M.D.
PEDIATRICS—BRANDON, FLORIDA

Duke Johnson, M.D.
FAMILY MEDICINE—TUSTIN, CALIFORNIA

W. Kip Johnson, M.D.
FAMILY MEDICINE—IRVINE, CALIFORNIA

Ronald Jones, M.D.
PEDIATRICS—SPRINGFIELD, MISSOURI

Paul Liu, M.D.
PEDIATRICS—PHOENIX, ARIZONA

Margaret Meeker, M.D.
PEDIATRICS—TRAVERSE CITY, MICHIGAN

Carl Meyer, D.O.
PEDIATRICS—GREENVILLE, PENNSYLVANIA

Michael C. Misko, M.D.
FAMILY MEDICINE—HOLDEN, MISSOURI

D. Brett Mitchell, M.D.
FAMILY MEDICINE—DENISON, TEXAS

John Moyer, M.D.
PEDIATRICS—DENVER, COLORADO

Steve Parnell, M.D.
FAMILY MEDICINE—FAIRMONT, MINNESOTA

Jan Payne, M.D.
PATHOLOGY—ST. PAUL, ALASKA

John C. Rhodes, M.D.
FAMILY MEDICINE—LAS VEGAS, NEVADA

David Sadowitz, M.D.
PEDIATRIC HEMATOLOGY/ONCOLOGY—CAMINUS, NEW YORK

Bodo Treu, M.D.
FAMILY MEDICINE—OMAHA, NEBRASKA

G. Scott Voorman, M.D.
OTOLARYNGOLOGY—THOUSAND OAKS, CALIFORNIA

James C. Wilkes, M.D.
PEDIATRICS/PEDIATRIC NEPHROLOGY—LEXINGTON, KENTUCKY

Franklin D. Wilson, M.D.
ORTHOPEDICS—INDIANAPOLIS, INDIANA

Gentry Yeatman, M.D.
ADOLESCENT MEDICINE—TACOMA, WASHINGTON

We would like to thank the following individuals for reviewing segments of the completed manuscript for accuracy:

Mary Beth Adam, M.D.
ADOLESCENT MEDICINE—TUCSON, ARIZONA

Stephen Apaliski, M.D.
PEDIATRIC ALLERGY—FORT WORTH, TEXAS

Sarah Blumenschein, M.D.
PEDIATRIC CARDIOLOGY—FORT WORTH, TEXAS

Paul Bowman, M.D.
PEDIATRIC HEMATOLOGY/ONCOLOGY—FORT WORTH, TEXAS

Preston W. Campbell, M.D.
PEDIATRIC PULMONOLOGY—NASHVILLE, TENNESSEE

James Cunningham, M.D.
PEDIATRIC PULMONOLOGY—FORT WORTH, TEXAS

Mary Davenport, M.D.
OBSTETRICS/GYNECOLOGY—BERKELEY, CALIFORNIA

Mary A. Eyanson, M.D.
PEDIATRICS—CEDAR RAPIDS, IOWA

David Michael Foulds, M.D.
PEDIATRICS—SAN ANTONIO, TEXAS

Roni Grad, M.D.
PEDIATRIC PULMONOLOGY—SAN ANTONIO, TEXAS

W. Wayne Grant, M.D.
PEDIATRICS—SAN ANTONIO, TEXAS

David Gregory, D.Ph.
PHARMACOLOGY—NASHVILLE, TENNESSEE

Lyn Hunt, M.D.
PEDIATRIC GASTROENTEROLOGY—FORT WORTH, TEXAS

Vernon L. James, M.D.
DEVELOPMENTAL MEDICINE—SAN ANTONIO, TEXAS

Cheryl Kissling, R.N.
LACTATION CONSULTANT—CEDAR RAPIDS, IOWA

Mary Kukolich, M.D.
GENETICS—FORT WORTH, TEXAS

Risé L. Lyman, D.D.S.
GENERAL DENTISTRY—SAN ANTONIO, TEXAS

Everett Moody, M.D.
PEDIATRIC OPHTHALMOLOGY—ARLINGTON, TEXAS

Britt Nelson, M.D.
PEDIATRIC INTENSIVE CARE—ARLINGTON, TEXAS

Amil Ortiz, M.D.
NEONATOLOGY—SAN ANTONIO, TEXAS

Steve Phillips, M.D.
PEDIATRIC NEUROLOGY—SACRAMENTO, CALIFORNIA

Judith L. Pugh, M.D.
PEDIATRIC NEPHROLOGY—SAN ANTONIO, TEXAS

S. DuBose Ravenel, M.D.
PEDIATRICS—HIGH POINT, NORTH CAROLINA

Brian Riedel, M.D.
PEDIATRIC GASTROENTEROLOGY—NASHVILLE, TENNESSEE

James Roach, M.D.
PEDIATRIC ORTHOPEDICS—FORT WORTH, TEXAS

Mark Shelton, M.D.
INFECTIOUS DISEASES—FORT WORTH, TEXAS

Glaze Vaughn, M.D.
PEDIATRIC SURGERY/UROLOGY—FORT WORTH, TEXAS

Teri Walter
PHYSICAL THERAPY—ARLINGTON, TEXAS

Paul Warren, M.D.
BEHAVIORAL PEDIATRICS—PLANO, TEXAS

Rick Weiser, M.D.
ADOLESCENT MEDICINE—PLEASANTON, CALIFORNIA

Also, this project would not have been possible without the immeasurable support of our loving spouses, Alan Cox and Teri Reisser. Your love, patience, and endurance literally kept us going. This project is not only ours but yours. We appreciate and love you!—Melissa R. Cox, Paul C. Reisser, M.D.

EDITORIAL STAFF

PRIMARY AUTHOR: Paul C. Reisser, M.D.
MANAGING EDITOR: Melissa R. Cox
TYNDALE EDITOR: Vinita Hampton Wright

FOCUS ON THE FAMILY

Bradley G. Beck, M.D. MEDICAL ISSUES ADVISOR
Lianne Belote, ADMINISTRATIVE ASSISTANT
Lisa D. Brock, RESEARCH EDITOR
Bob Chuvala, RESEARCH EDITOR
Kathleen M. Gowler, ADMINISTRATIVE SUPPORT
Karen Sagahon, ADMINISTRATIVE SUPPORT
Keith Wall, RESEARCH EDITOR

Special thanks to:

Glenn Bethany   Mark Maddox
Kurt Bruner   Dean Merrill
Charmé Fletcher   Craig Osten
Anita Fuglaar   Mike Yorkey
Al Janssen   Rolf Zettersten

TYNDALE HOUSE PUBLISHERS: EDITORIAL

Meg Diehl, PROJECT MANAGER
Vinita Hampton Wright, EDITOR
Peter Bodnar, PROOFREADING SUPERVISOR
Jan Pigott, COPY EDITOR
Anisa Baker, ADMINISTRATIVE SUPPORT

Special thanks to: Ron Beers

TYNDALE HOUSE PUBLISHERS: PRODUCTION

Julee Schwarzburg, PROJECT MANAGER
Catherine Bergstrom, ART DIRECTOR
Judy Wireman, TYPESETTER/DESKTOP PUBLISHER
Christina Fox, PRINT BUYER

GRAPHICS/ILLUSTRATIONS

BOOK DESIGN: Catherine Bergstrom
ASSIGNMENT EDITOR: Melissa R. Cox

MEDICAL ILLUSTRATIONS:
Jeff Lane, pages 50, 65–68, 74, 95, 127, 142, 149,
744–745, 750–753, 756–759, 778
Vincent Perez, pages 6, 62, A6–A15

NONMEDICAL ILLUSTRATIONS:
Will Chittick, pages 768, 770–775
Alan Flinn, pages 763, 821–822, A18–A19
Rick Johnson, pages 52, 128–131, 140, 158,
160, 163, 806–815, 817–819

ART REVIEWERS:
Bradley G. Beck, M.D.
John Livoni, M.D.
Curtis Stine, M.D.

GESTATIONAL PHOTOGRAPHY:
Lennart Nilsson, pages A3–A5

COVER PHOTOS:
Susan Andrews

CHAPTER PHOTOS:
Scott Barrow, page 33
Blaine Harrington, pages 241, 365
Mark Kozlowski, pages 59, 187
James McLoughlin, pages 1, 113, 211, 329, 389
SW Productions, pages 477, 503
Camille Tokenrud, page 155
TSM/Jeff Zaruba, page 613

PHOTO BUYER:
Marlene S. Muddell

COMMISSIONED PHOTOGRAPHY:
Reg Francklyn, pages A16–A17

MEDICAL PHOTOGRAPHY:
Stanley Hand, M.D., pages A28 (conjunctivitis,
corneal abrasion), A29 (hyphema), A31
(sty, subconjunctival hemorrhage)
Victor Newcomer, M.D., pages A27–A31

BACK COVER TEXT:
Alan G. Cox

Introduction

The Focus on the Family Complete Book of Baby and Child Care has been designed to assist you throughout the course of the most rewarding and challenging job of your life: parenting. Whether you are expecting your first baby in the near future or have years of parenting experience, we hope that you will find this book helpful—not only as a useful resource but also as a source of inspiration, especially when the going gets a little tough (or extremely difficult).

This book is divided into two major sections:

The first section is a detailed chronological tour of a child's life from conception through infancy, toddlerhood, preschool and school years, adolescence, and finally the release of a young adult to independent living. Chapters in this section are intended to be read in their entirety, but you may also benefit from reviewing specific topics contained within them. The chapters include:

- details about physical, mental, and emotional development at each age
- practical information about basic topics such as feeding, sleep, safety, and common illnesses
- suggestions for building strong bonds with your child, providing appropriate discipline through a balance of love and limits, and instilling moral and spiritual values
- encouragement for strengthening marriage, meeting the special challenges of single parenting, avoiding burnout, managing conflicts, and, in general, surviving and thriving through the entire journey of parenthood

The second major section is a health-care reference containing over 400 entries, arranged alphabetically, including:

- definitions or brief descriptions of a wide variety of medical conditions
- explanations of many health-related terms
- more extensive reviews of common health problems in childhood (for example, sore throats, headaches, and allergies) or of conditions affecting specific parts of the body (for example, the eyes and teeth)

This book contains a number of additional features:

- **Special Concerns** dealing with topics that are important to parents of children in all age-groups: adoption, discipline, conflicts within the family, educational issues, the impact of divorce on children, and many others

- an overview of a number of **orthopedic conditions** (those related to muscles, bones, and joints), from congenital deformities to everyday bumps and bruises
- a section devoted to **emergency care** and **first aid**
- an **atlas of the human body,** with charts detailing skeletal and muscular landmarks as well as the major organ systems
- more than 35 **photographs** of common skin conditions
- a listing of **resources,** including addresses and/or phone numbers of organizations that can assist you in gathering additional information about specific problems

As you begin to use *The Focus on the Family Complete Book of Baby and Child Care,* it is important that you keep these cautionary points in mind:

- This book is intended to serve as a road map to help orient and guide you through your parenting journey. It does not provide detailed directions for every conceivable situation you might encounter along the way, nor is the advice it contains cast in concrete. The basic principles set forth in this book must be molded and adjusted to fit you and your own child.
- This book is not intended to serve as a substitute for specific input that you will receive from your child's physician. You will be encouraged many times throughout these pages to contact a doctor or (if the situation is urgent) to take your child directly to a medical facility, for a variety of specific problems. *No book can substitute for a direct assessment of your child by a qualified healthcare professional.*
- Despite our best efforts to include the most up-to-date information, in the field of health care the "current wisdom" changes continuously, especially in areas such as immunization guidelines. What was hot news when this book went to press may be outdated in a matter of months. This is another reason to check with your child's doctor if you have any questions about a particular situation you might encounter.

For the physicians who serve on the Focus on the Family Physicians Resource Council, this book has indeed been a labor of love. Having spent countless hours over the past three years preparing the information and advice contained within this book, our heartfelt desire is that it will be a valuable resource for you while enhancing the life of your child(ren) for many years to come.

May you find joy in your parenting journey,
JOHN P. LIVONI, M.D., M.P.H., Chair
Focus on the Family Physicians Resource Council

Preparing for Parenthood

*"For I know the plans I have
for you," declares the Lord,
"plans to prosper you and not
to harm you, plans to give
you hope and a future."*

JEREMIAH 29:11

Preparing for Parenthood

Whether you are just beginning to think about starting a family

    . . . or have just learned that you are going to be a mother or a father in a few months

    . . . or are a day or two away from a trip to the delivery room

    . . . or are planning an adoption

    . . . or have a baby (or two) in your arms

    . . . or have a house full of toddlers, school-age children, adolescents, or a combination of all ages

    . . . or are proud grandparents,

this book is dedicated to enhancing the journey you have started.

Parenting is an adventure, a source of incredible fulfillment, and a unique privilege. It's a voyage of discovery, a humbling responsibility, and a learning curve. On many occasions, it brings both laughter and tears. It is, above all, a gift from God—one that deserves to be received with joy and treated with the utmost respect.

Many people enter parenthood unexpectedly, at times even suddenly, often in a state of panic. Nearly everyone who accepts the assignment develops qualms at some point. You may have already progressed from "Am I really ready for all the responsibility of bringing up a child?" to "What am I going to do if _____ happens?" to "How in the world did I get into this?"

If any of those questions have passed through your mind, take heart, and remember some fundamental truths of parenting:

- ◆ You're not alone. Many millions have traveled the path before you.

♦ You probably know a lot more than you think.

♦ It's never too late to learn, to mold your attitudes and refine your skills.

Whether you're aware of it or not, the process of becoming a mother or a father actually begins well before the doctor announces, "It's a boy!" or "It's a girl!" It begins before conception. In fact, it begins before the physical intimacy that sets the biological marvel of reproduction in motion.

And for an event of this importance, it's nice, as much as is humanly possible, to be prepared. This chapter is all about getting ready, but it's worth reading even if a lot of water has already passed under your parental bridge.

FEARFULLY AND WONDERFULLY MADE: HOW A BABY DEVELOPS

Many authors and poets, after hearing the cry and seeing the first flailing movements of tiny arms and legs at the moment of birth, have declared that the process of coming into the world is a miracle.

But while childbirth is truly awe-inspiring, the real miracles began long before this transition of the baby from one environment to another. If you are expecting an arrival in the near future, be assured that wondrous and marvelous events have already taken place in the warm sanctuary of the womb. For it was there that a tiny cluster of 64 to 128 cells embedded in the thickened lining of the uterus, just six days after the meeting of egg and sperm. Within seventy-two hours of establishing a temporary residence, this new human being sent a powerful hormonal signal to override the mother's monthly cycle, preventing the shedding of her uterine lining.

Then began the astonishing process of differentiation, as new cells took on particular shapes, sizes, and functions, aligning themselves into tissues and organs, eyes and ears, arms and legs. Each of these cells contained all of the information needed to make *any* of the multitudes of cell types in the body. Yet during the process of constructing and organizing, integrating and communicating with one another, individual cells began to express unique qualities in very short order, but in a seamless and orderly pattern. The intricacy and timing of these events are nothing less than masterpieces of planning and engineering.

See color insert for photos of fetal development, page A3.

Before the end of the first six weeks of life, your child's heart has started to beat, eyes are developing, the central nervous system is under construction, most internal organs are forming, and small buds representing future arms and legs have sprouted. One cell created by the union of egg and sperm has now become millions, and your new daughter or son has reached the length of one-quarter of an inch.

By the end of eight weeks, the fingers and toes have been formed. Heart, lungs, and major blood vessels have become well developed. Taste buds and the apparatus needed for the sense of smell have appeared. Tiny muscles have generated body movements, which at this point a mother cannot feel.

When twelve weeks of growth have ended, your baby has reached a length of three inches. The heartbeat can be heard using an electronic listening device. All of the organs and tissues—including heart, lungs, brain, digestive system, kidneys, and reproductive organs—have been formed and are in place. The only necessary remaining ingredient is time: six more months for growth and maturation.

Sixteen weeks after conception, eyebrows and hair are growing. Your baby, now measuring six to seven inches and weighing nearly as many ounces, kicks, swallows, hiccups, wakes, and sleeps. Soon the mother can begin feeling movement inside, an important milestone still referred to as "quickening."

Four weeks later, with weight now approaching one pound, your baby can hear and react to sounds, including Mom's heartbeat and stomach rumblings, as well as noise, music, and conversations outside the uterus. (Whether any of these sounds are recognized or become part of early memories is uncertain.)

At twenty-six weeks of life, breathing movements are present, although there is no air to be inhaled. Depending on their weight, babies born prematurely at this time have a 50 to 75 percent chance of survival with expert care, although complications are common. With each additional week that passes within the mother's womb, the baby's likelihood of surviving a premature delivery improves, the risk of long-term complications declines, and the medical care needed after birth usually becomes less complex.

The final fourteen weeks are the homestretch, during which your baby grows and gains weight very rapidly. By the end of *thirty-two weeks,* the bones are hardening, the eyes are opening and closing, the thumb has found its way into the mouth, and the arms and legs are stretching and kicking regularly. Your baby is twelve to sixteen inches long and weighs about three pounds. Over the next four weeks, the weight nearly doubles, and you will feel all sorts of kicks, prods, and pokes much more strongly. A baby born at this age will need some assistance with feeding and keeping warm and could still develop more complicated medical problems as well. However, the vast majority of those born a month or so ahead of schedule do very well.

You created my inmost being; you knit me together in my mother's womb.

PSALM 139:13

Finally, after a few more weeks of rapid weight gain (about half a pound per week during the last six weeks of gestation), your baby is fully developed and ready to meet you.

Every mother and father awaits the birth of a child with a mixture of anticipation, excitement, and anxiety. Who will this new person be? Will this be a son

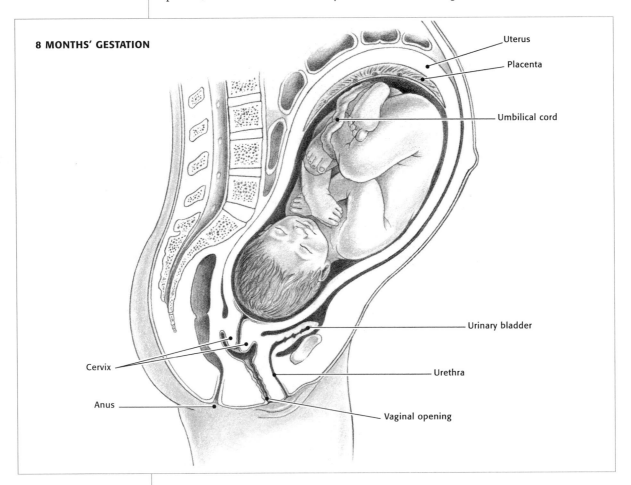

8 MONTHS' GESTATION

Uterus

Placenta

Umbilical cord

Urinary bladder

Cervix

Urethra

Anus

Vaginal opening

or a daughter (or more than one)? Will she have her mother's eyes? Will he have his father's chin? Will everything be in the right place? Could there have been any problems that occurred silently during the passage from conception to birth?

No one can answer all these questions until the moment of birth. Furthermore, a baby may have some initial problems that clear up quickly and easily, while a more serious disturbance may not be apparent until a number of days, weeks, or even months have passed. Obviously, everyone involved in the debut of a new life is hoping, praying, and working toward the safe arrival of a healthy baby to a healthy mother. While no one can guarantee this happy outcome, there are many positive steps and basic precautions that can dramatically increase the likelihood of a joyful "special delivery."

Planning Ahead: Lifestyle and Health Questions for the Mother- (and Father-) to-Be

In a very real and practical sense, parenting begins well before the news arrives that a new family member is on the way. The state of the union of the parents-to-be and particularly the health of the mother *before* pregnancy strongly affect her health *during* pregnancy, which in turn, plays a vital role in the baby's well-being both before and after delivery.

If you are planning to begin a family, or even if your pregnancy is well under way, you would be wise to review the following list of self-assessment questions. Much of what follows is directed toward the mother, but the ongoing health and habits of *both* parents are very important. (Expectant fathers, please read on.)

> *One important note:* This book is not intended to be a comprehensive resource on pregnancy and childbirth. The information given in this and the next chapter is intentionally limited to parenting before the delivery room—matters that specifically affect the health of the baby to be born. This is not to imply that a mother's health is any less important, or that her well-being and her child's are not intimately connected. Nevertheless, the length, breadth, and depth of pregnancy care are beyond the scope of this book. If you are pregnant (or may be soon), it is very important that you find a physician who will not only guide you through pregnancy but also recommend books and other materials from which you can learn more about this miraculous process.

How well are you taking care of your (one and only) body?

Imagine what would happen if a strict law were passed declaring that you could buy only one automobile in your lifetime. Suppose the law also included a stiff penalty for riding in anyone else's vehicle. If your car ever became seriously damaged or fell apart, you would have to walk—everywhere. How well would you take care of your one and only car if the only alternative would be a pair of very sore feet? Would you fill its tank with the cheapest grade of no-name gas or find the highest-octane premium fuel on the market? Would you get the oil changed, engine tuned, and wheels aligned on a regular basis or wait for rumbles, rattles, and warning lights to appear before heading for the service station? When you weren't using it, would you keep the car snug in the garage or let the elements beat on it mercilessly day and night?

The analogy to your one and only body should be obvious: If it deteriorates and malfunctions, you can't borrow anyone else's. *And neither can your baby.* Poor nutrition, smoking, and the use of alcohol and drugs can have a serious impact on your baby's development, especially during the first eight weeks when the vital organs are under construction. But your pregnancy may not even be confirmed until this period has already passed. Therefore, *the habits you develop well before you even think about having a child are very important.*

So how are you treating yourself? Specifically:

How's your nutrition?

Contrary to what talk shows and tabloids say, good nutrition does not involve magic formulas, rigid restrictions, or tackle boxes full of vitamins and supplements. In fact, you are probably familiar with the basic principles of healthful eating that continue to be reinforced by research and consensus: variety, moderation, and proportion in selecting from the primary food groups. The U.S. Department of Agriculture and the Department of Health and Human Services have developed the Food Guide Pyramid to illustrate these concepts, updating the traditional idea of the "basic four" food groups (see Pyramid, page A18).

The pyramid illustrates guidelines for the relative number of servings of various types of foods (the amounts should be adjusted for pregnancy). Remember that the concept of a serving is a simple tool that you can use to help track your general intake. It will vary depending on the type of food being considered.

The goal is not to become obsessed with meticulous counts of servings or calories but to understand which foods should be emphasized on an ongoing basis. If the "four food groups" in your current diet are burgers, soft drinks, doughnuts, and chips, you need to do some serious revision—primarily shifting to the lower-fat, higher-quality grain, vegetable, and fruit groups.

If you are a vegetarian, you should be able to continue through an entire pregnancy without difficulty, provided that you include a wide variety of foods. If you eat absolutely no animal products, such as milk, eggs, or cheese, you may become shortchanged on protein and calories, as well as on iron, calcium, vitamin B$_{12}$, and zinc. Vitamin and mineral supplementation would be advisable, as would some consultation with a dietitian.

Theoretically, a woman who eats a variety of fresh, high-quality foods in the rough proportions of the pyramid should not need to take supplemental vitamins and minerals. But certain substances are so critical to a healthy pregnancy that most physicians will prescribe **prenatal vitamins** to make up for any deficiencies in the mother's diet. Remember, however, that *supplements do not make up for careless eating habits.*

There is evidence that taking supplemental **folic acid** will reduce the likelihood that the newborn will have one of several types of major problems known as **neural tube defects.** Within the first month after conception, a tubelike structure forms from which the brain and spinal cord develop. If the tube does not close properly, serious abnormalities of these vital structures can result. Unfortunately, neural tube defects may occur before you know you are pregnant. Therefore, the U. S. Public Health Service now recommends that *all women of childbearing age take 0.4 mg of folic acid daily* to reduce the risk of a neural tube defect occurring in an unexpected pregnancy. If you have already had a child with a neural tube defect, a higher dose of folic acid—4 mg per day—is recommended for a month prior to the time you plan to become pregnant and should be continued through the first three months. (This amount of folic acid requires a doctor's prescription.) You can, of course, obtain folic acid through foods such as dark leafy vegetables, cereals, whole grain breads, citrus fruits, bananas, and tomatoes. However, in light of the research favoring supplementation, you should check with your physician about the amount of folic acid recommended for your pregnancy.

A pregnant woman needs additional **iron,** both for her increased blood volume as well as for the growing tissues and iron stores within her baby. Iron is necessary for the formation of **hemoglobin,** the protein within red blood cells that binds to oxygen, thus allowing red cells to deliver oxygen to every cell in the body. If the supply of iron in a mother's food is inadequate to meet this increased need, iron deficiency anemia will eventually result. This can cause her to feel extremely tired—more so than she would normally expect from the pregnancy itself.

An intake of about 30 mg of elemental iron per day will meet the need of most pregnant women. (Those who are already iron deficient may require 60 mg or more to correct this problem.) Since a typical diet provides only 5 or 6 mg of elemental iron per one thousand calories of food, and because consuming five thousand calories per day would be both unwise and impractical, iron should be included in your prenatal vitamin regimen. Absorption of iron is improved when foods containing vitamin C are eaten at the same time.

A woman's daily **calcium** intake normally should be 1,000 mg per day during the childbearing years, but should increase to 1,200 to 1,500 mg per day during pregnancy because of the new skeleton under construction inside her uterus. Dairy products are a rich source of calcium—300 mg are available in a cup of milk and 450 mg in a cup of nonfat yogurt—so this added requirement is usually readily obtained from foods. If you can't tolerate dairy products, your doctor may recommend that you take calcium supplements, since prenatal vitamins alone typically do not include the full amount. Calcium carbonate or calcium citrate are the forms that are most easily absorbed.

Do you weigh enough or too much?

Obesity is a health hazard for many reasons, all of which are heightened during pregnancy. Excessive weight during pregnancy is a risk factor for **high blood pressure** and **diabetes,** both of which can lead to significant problems for mother and baby. The aches and pains (especially in the lower back) that are so common during the later stages of pregnancy can become intolerable when there is already an extra burden of several pounds on muscles and joints. Recent evidence suggests that overweight pregnant women are more likely to have babies with neural tube defects, regardless of folic acid intake.

But being underweight before or during pregnancy is no great advantage either because the nutritional needs of the baby may be compromised. This can result in a baby of low birth weight who is at risk for a variety of problems, including difficulty maintaining normal temperature or blood-sugar level after birth.

If you have had a history of erratic nutrition habits or even a full-blown eating disorder (such as **anorexia** or **bulimia**), you and your baby will benefit greatly from ongoing counseling and coaching from a dietitian before, during, and after pregnancy. Similarly, if you are struggling with excessive weight, a gradual process of reduction (ideally under the guidance of a dietitian) *prior* to becoming pregnant would be wise. Attaining a stable weight prior to pregnancy will help prevent rapid regaining of weight after pregnancy begins. If you are already pregnant, however, a weight-loss program is not a good idea because the nutritional needs of both you and your baby could be jeopardized. Pregnancy would be a good time, however, to modify eating habits toward healthy patterns that will serve you well for the rest of your life.

Are you exercising your muscles, heart, and lungs?

A sedentary lifestyle—that is, one without deliberate exercise—has been specifically identified as a health risk for both women and men. Unfortunately, despite the numerous and well-publicized benefits of regular exercise, a majority of Americans still do not take part in any form of planned physical activity. But a regular habit of exercise established now will serve as an investment in long-term health and also improve the way you feel throughout pregnancy.

Several normal changes during pregnancy put new physical demands on your body. Aside from a normal weight gain of twenty-five to thirty-five pounds, your heart will be dealing with a 50 percent increase in blood volume. Muscles and ligaments in the back and pelvis will be stretched and subjected to new tensions and strains. Unless you have a scheduled cesarean section, you will also go through the rigors of labor—which is aptly named—and the birth itself. These are physically challenging events, and those who are well conditioned will usually fare better. In fact, their labor may even be shortened.

The increased stamina and muscle tone resulting from regular exercise will also increase your energy level, improve sleep, reduce swelling of the legs, and probably reduce aches and pains in the lower back. If you are on your feet all day, it may seem ridiculous to spend precious time for additional muscle motion. But unless you are a professional athlete, it is unlikely that your daily activities, no matter how exhausting, will specifically condition your heart and lungs. The good news is that you don't need to become a marathon runner to see some benefit in your health.

If you are not used to exercising, a goal of thirty minutes three or four times per week is reasonable. It is always better to do light or moderate exercise on a regular basis than heavy exercise intermittently. While stretching and muscle strengthening are worthwhile, aerobic conditioning—in which increased oxygen is consumed continuously for a prolonged period of time—has the greatest overall benefit.

The most straightforward and least costly aerobic activity is walking. No fancy equipment, health-club membership, or special gear (other than a pair of comfortable, supportive shoes) is needed. Pleasant and safe surroundings, a flat surface, and agreeable weather are advisable, however, as well as a companion. Another person (whether your husband, an older child, a relative, a friend, or another pregnant woman) will add accountability to the process, and the conversation can be enjoyable and help the time pass quickly. Gentle stretching for a few minutes before and after is a good idea, in order to warm up and then cool down leg and back muscles.

Alternatives to walking include:

◆ A home treadmill. Advantages: No concerns about weather, aggressive dogs, or finding someone to watch your children. You can be flexible about the time of day to use it. Disadvantages: Cost, size, and noise.
◆ An exercise video or book geared to pregnant women. Advantages: Same as above, with less cost. Disadvantage: Repetition could become boring.
◆ A prenatal fitness class at a local hospital or health club. Advantage: Interaction with instructor and other women can be helpful and motivating. Disadvantages: Cost. Also, scheduling and child-care needs may be complicated.
◆ Swimming. Advantage: Good aerobic conditioning involving many muscle groups, with no added strain on sore muscles and joints of the lower back and pelvis. Disadvantage: You need access to a pool.
◆ Stationary cycling. Advantage: Good aerobic conditioning and (depending on your anatomy) probably less strain on your lower back than from walking. Disadvantage: Many women become increasingly uncomfortable on this equipment as pregnancy progresses.

If you are already well conditioned, you should be able to continue using your specific exercise routine. If you are already a confirmed jogger or an accomplished tennis player, you can probably continue these activities through the early months of pregnancy. Snow skiing, surfing, waterskiing, and horseback riding all pose specific risks during pregnancy because of the possibility of falls—especially as your center of gravity shifts and your balance becomes less reliable as the uterus enlarges. All of these activities should be reviewed with your physician throughout the course of your pregnancy. Note: Scuba diving is not recommended at any time during pregnancy.

A few special precautions about exercise during pregnancy:

◆ Pregnancy is *not* a good time to take on a new, intense form of exercise, especially if it involves jumping, jerking, high-impact motion, or sudden changes in direction.
◆ Exercise should not be so vigorous or prolonged as to cause exhaustion, overheating, or dehydration. During pregnancy your heart rate should stay below 140, regardless of the type of exercise you are doing.
◆ After the twentieth week of pregnancy, you should avoid exercises that require you to lie on your back.
◆ Exercise should not continue if any of the following pregnancy-related problems develop: preterm rupture of membranes; poor growth of the

baby (**intrauterine growth retardation**); vaginal bleeding; high blood pressure; preterm labor; and cervical incompetence, a condition in which the cervix or "neck" of the uterus isn't strong enough to prevent a premature delivery. Exercise may also be limited if you are pregnant with more than one baby.

◆ If you have specific health problems such as heart disease, high blood pressure, irregular heart rate, epilepsy, fainting episodes, asthma, arthritis, or anemia, review any exercise plans with your physician, whether or not you are pregnant.

In addition to aerobic activity, a variety of gentle stretching and muscle-conditioning activities can help prepare your body for the changes of late pregnancy and labor. Your doctor and/or childbirth class instructor will have a number of suggestions for such exercises.

Are you taking or inhaling any substances that might harm you or your baby?

As a result of widespread public-health announcements, most people are aware that smoking cigarettes, drinking excessive amounts of alcohol, and using illicit drugs are risky and destructive, especially during pregnancy. Yet it's often difficult to believe that "this could happen to me"—that we might actually suffer the bad effects we hear about. Furthermore, even if one is convinced of the dangers of these substances, gaining freedom from their grip can be a real uphill battle. If you need any additional reasons to separate yourself from cigarettes, alcohol, or illegal drugs, or some extra resolve to remain free of these unhealthy habits, consider carefully the following facts:

Cigarette smoking. This is a form of legalized drug addiction that is harmful to the smoker, those around the smoker, and especially the baby growing inside the smoker. Thousands of chemicals in cigarette smoke flow directly from the mother's lungs into her bloodstream and then directly into the baby. Nicotine specifically causes constriction of blood vessels in both the placenta and the baby, thus reducing the baby's supply of vital blood and oxygen. Carbon monoxide in smoke binds tightly to red blood cells and displaces oxygen. The overall effect is a recurrent choking of the baby's oxygen supply, resulting in smaller (by an average of half a pound) and shorter babies. Unfortunately, these infants (whom doctors refer to as "small-for-dates") are more likely than their normal counterparts to have a variety of medical problems after birth.

The smoker's baby is more likely to be born prematurely or to be stillborn. The tragedy of **sudden infant death syndrome (SIDS)** occurs twice as frequently when the child's mother has smoked throughout pregnancy, and the risk increases drastically if there is continuing exposure to secondhand smoke after birth. According to a study published by researchers at the University of California, infants exposed to smoke from ten or fewer cigarettes per day are more than twice as likely to die of SIDS than babies in smoke-free environments. When the exposure involves more than twenty cigarettes per day, the risk soars to more than twenty times that of infants not exposed.[1]

Exposure to cigarette smoke after birth is linked to colds, ear infections, and asthma. And the child who sees Mom and Dad smoke is also much more likely to pick up the habit than are his peers who live in homes where there are no smokers.

Let's not forget smoking's effect on the mother. Aside from the long-term risks of chronic lung disease, heart disease, ulcers, and diseased blood vessels, she is more likely to have unexpected vaginal bleeding during her pregnancy.

The only good news about smoking is that *quitting early in pregnancy reduces the baby's risk of problems to the level of a child born to a nonsmoker.* For many women, the emotional impact of a threat to the baby is powerful enough to override the compulsion to light up, and a pregnancy usually lasts long enough to help temporary abstinence become a smoke-free life.

But cigarettes are so powerfully addictive that additional support may be necessary to kick the habit. If you are a smoker, it's never too late—or too early—to stop. A successful decision to quit usually requires:

- A well-defined list of reasons that have some emotional power. ("I don't want to starve my baby of oxygen" or "I want to live long enough to see my kids grow up.") Since resistance to quitting often hinges on an emotional attachment to cigarettes, your reasons for giving up smoking should likewise motivate you on an emotional level.
- A specified quitting date that is announced to family, friends, and coworkers. Some gentle peer pressure can be a powerful motivator.
- Participation in a stop-smoking class. These are available in most communities through nearby hospitals or local chapters of national organizations (American Lung Association, American Heart Association, American Cancer Society).

- A firm declaration that your home, car, and workplace are smoke-free zones. Nobody, but nobody—spouse, in-laws, guests, visiting heads of state—lights up in your airspace.
- If you are not yet pregnant, you may wish to consider using nicotine patches or chewing gum to assist you through the withdrawal process. These are now available on both a prescription and nonprescription (or over-the-counter) basis. If you have any questions or concerns about their proper use, you may want to discuss them with your physician. You should not smoke while using nicotine patches or gum, and you cannot use them during pregnancy.

Alcoholic beverages. Daily consumption of alcohol during pregnancy, with or without binge drinking, may lead to a complex of problems in the baby known as **fetal alcohol syndrome.** Babies with this disorder may have a variety of abnormalities of the head, face, heart, joints, and limbs. In addition, the central nervous system can be affected, causing mental retardation, hyperactivity, and behavioral problems. The damage appears to be directly related to the amount of alcohol consumed, especially during the early months of pregnancy.

A woman who enjoys an occasional drink may wonder how much alcohol might be safe during pregnancy. Some studies suggest that even two drinks a week may lead to a mild withdrawal syndrome in the newborn, with increased irritability and stomach disturbances. The simplest and safest course is to abstain from alcohol altogether during pregnancy. You would be wise to abstain or consume no more than two alcoholic drinks per week if you are not yet pregnant but might become so in the near future. If drinking is not an ingrained habit, this should not be difficult. But if you find it hard to stay away from alcohol or control how much you drink at any given time, total avoidance is even more important. It is likely that you will need outside help to do so, whether in a group setting such as a church support group or Alcoholics Anonymous, or individually with a professional counselor.

Illegal drugs. The use of illegal drugs continues to be a fearsome epidemic in our culture. The popular term *recreational drug use* is a contradiction because the word *recreation* implies an activity that has a positive, restoring, re-creating effect on mind and body. These substances, however, have just the opposite effect, draining away the resources, health, and, ultimately, life from their users. When the user is a pregnant woman, two lives (at least) are being damaged.

Regular **marijuana** users may deliver prematurely and even at term are more likely to have smaller babies. **Cocaine** use during pregnancy can cause not only a miscarriage or premature labor but also the eventual delivery of a small, irritable baby who may have serious, lifelong problems. Aside from any difficulties that might arise from premature delivery, cocaine itself can damage the infant's central nervous system, urinary tract, and limbs by constricting their blood supply. Increased irritability during the newborn period, developmental delays, and difficulty with learning and interacting with others may also be attributable to cocaine use by the mother. (Frequently other substances such as alcohol and tobacco have been used as well, complicating the question of identifying specific consequences of cocaine.)

A mother's use of narcotics such as **heroin** or **methadone** throughout her pregnancy may subject the baby to a difficult withdrawal after birth. Symptoms, which usually begin during the first day or two after birth, can include increased irritability, tremors, a high-pitched cry, constant hunger, sweating, and sneezing. In severe cases, seizures, vomiting, diarrhea, and difficulty with breathing can occur. Furthermore, if these drugs are taken intravenously (that is, injected into the veins), there is an additional risk of acquiring HIV, which eventually causes **AIDS.** This will not only shorten the mother's life drastically, but could infect her baby as well.

As serious as all these health concerns are, they do not encompass the vast waste of resources and the chaotic lifestyle that so often accompany the use of illegal drugs. Chronic drug abusers are usually unable to deal consistently with the daily demands of child care. Food preparation, safety in the home, and basic health practices are likely to be compromised. Run-ins with the law and difficulty maintaining steady employment are not uncommon. Healthy relationships with friends and family members may be in short supply. The disturbances and distractions of chronic drug use seriously compromise a parent's ability to bring up healthy children. Whether or not you are pregnant, the time to stop using any of these toxic substances is *now,* and seeking help to do so should be an immediate priority.

Caffeine. This stimulant abounds in everyday beverages such as coffee, tea, and soft drinks, as well as some headache remedies and pain relievers. A daily intake of up to 200 mg (the amount in one or two five-ounce cups of coffee) is widely considered safe during pregnancy. Larger amounts (over 500 mg per day) will keep both you and your baby awake, and his or her increased activity levels before birth may lead to a lower birth weight. If you consume coffee by the potful or sodas by the six-pack, you should begin cutting back to the 200 mg limit (see table) before you become pregnant or reduce immediately if you are already expecting. Decreasing the brewing time for coffee or tea will also cut caffeine content.

Prescription and over-the-counter (OTC) drugs. In general, you should try to avoid using any type of medication that isn't specifically prescribed or approved by your physician. *Always be sure to inform any physician who treats you that you are or might be pregnant, since this could have a significant impact on medication(s) he or she might recommend.*

CAFFEINE CONTENT OF FOODS AND BEVERAGES		
Food Source	*Amount*	*Caffeine Content*
Regular coffee	8 oz	100–500 mg
Instant coffee	8 oz	80–100 mg
Decaf coffee	8 oz	3–5 mg
Tea	8 oz	60–65 mg
* Regular cola	6 oz	36 mg
Diet cola	6 oz	18 mg
Chocolate bar	1 oz	20 mg

* Read labels to determine the presence of caffeine in specific soft drinks, such as Mountain Dew, Dr. Pepper, etc.

The fact that you can buy a drug off the shelf at the supermarket doesn't necessarily mean that it is wise to use it during pregnancy. Pain relievers, cold tablets, laxatives, and other medications, as well as vitamin, herb, and food supplements, may seem harmless merely because they are easily accessible or advertised as "natural." A number of these are, in fact, quite safe during pregnancy, but you should consult your physician, who is familiar with your medical history and the details of your pregnancy, before using any of them. Common examples of OTC medications include the following:

Pain relievers. Acetaminophen (Tylenol, Panadol, and various others) is generally recognized as safe for both mother and baby during pregnancy when used in the recommended dosage, but it can be toxic to the liver in an overdose. This drug reduces aches, pains, headaches, and fever. Both aspirin and the various brands of the anti-inflammatory drugs ibuprofen (Advil, Motrin, Nuprin, and others), naproxen (Aleve), and ketoprofen (Orudis KT and others) may increase the risk of bleeding in both mother and baby, especially around the time of birth. Anti-inflammatory medications taken late in pregnancy also may inhibit the onset of labor. Furthermore, they can cause a structure in the infant's heart known as the **ductus arteriosus** to close, resulting in potential circulatory problems after birth. While such complications are very unusual, you should avoid these medications during pregnancy (especially during the final weeks) unless they are recommended for a specific purpose by your physician.

Cold tablets. Decongestants, antihistamines, cough syrups, and nasal sprays are sold in a bewildering array of combinations and preparations. All are intended to relieve symptoms, but these drugs rarely have a direct effect on the course of an upper-respiratory illness. Some of the ingredients in cold remedies are considered safe during a normal pregnancy, but you should check with your physician and pharmacist before using any of them. Rest, fluids, and time will take care of the vast majority of these infections. However, you should also contact your doctor if your runny nose, sore throat, or cough continues for more than a week; if you are producing thick, discolored drainage from nose or chest; or if you are running a fever over 100°F. If the doctor you speak with is not the one who is caring for your pregnancy, be sure that he or she knows you are pregnant.

Antacids. Many pregnant women develop heartburn and indigestion because of changes in the intestinal tract produced by the growing uterus. Antacids are generally considered safe during pregnancy when used in recommended doses, but they may provoke diarrhea and can interfere with the absorption of prescription drugs.

Laxatives. Constipation is common during pregnancy, but chemical laxatives are not the preferred method of treatment. Lots of fluids and juices, additional fiber in the diet (whether directly from food sources or psyllium-seed supplements such as Metamucil or Citrucel), and regular exercise are the best first-line remedies. If you are not able to have a bowel movement for a few days at a time, you should review additional options with your physician.

Are you exposed to any environmental hazards?

During the course of your pregnancy, and especially during the first three months, you should minimize your exposure to **X-rays** (also called **ionizing radiation**). Exposure to very large doses during the early weeks when the baby's tissues and organs are under construction could lead to birth defects. Fortunately, the X-ray exposure involved in common medical examinations is a tiny fraction of the amount generally considered risky. If you have had one or more diagnostic X-rays and then discover you were pregnant at the time, it is extremely unlikely that your baby will be affected. Nevertheless, if this occurs you should review with your physician what procedures were done.

Some reasonable precautions to minimize your (and your baby's) exposure to X-rays include these steps:

- If X-rays (including those in the dentist's office) have been recom-mended, be sure to tell both your physician and the X-ray technician if you are or might be pregnant.
- If at all possible, postpone X-rays until after the baby is born, or at least wait until the first three months of pregnancy have passed. Procedures that do not utilize ionizing radiation, such as **ultrasound** or **magnetic resonance imaging (MRI),** may be alternative options that can supply the necessary diagnostic information. (It is currently assumed but not proven that an MRI study is safe in early pregnancy.) If X-rays are needed in an emergency situation, techniques that limit exposure (such as shielding the abdomen with a lead apron or limiting the number of films taken) may be utilized. (It is generally recommended that a woman of reproductive age have her abdomen shielded when she has *any* type of X-ray.)
- If you work around sources of ionizing radiation (for example, in an office or hospital area where X-rays are taken), be sure to follow carefully the occupational guidelines in your facility for minimizing and measur-ing any ongoing exposure.
- Depending upon location, dose, and timing during pregnancy, radiation therapy for cancer may—or may not—pose a significant hazard to a developing baby. The difficult problem of managing a cancer arises only in about one in one thousand pregnancies. Should this occur, however, the benefits and risks of any proposed treatment—as well as the conse-quences of postponing treatment—must be reviewed in detail, and decisions made after careful deliberation and prayer.

Over the past several years concerns have been raised about the effects of ex-posure of pregnant women to **nonionizing radiation**—microwaves, radio waves, electromagnetic fields (such as those associated with power lines), and infrared light. Thus far, problems arising from these forms of radiation have not been clearly demonstrated. Specifically, research has not shown an increased risk of birth defects among pregnant women who work at video display terminals (VDTs) such as computer monitors for several hours per week. Similarly, adverse effects of living near power lines have not been established.

Some concerns have been raised about prolonged exposure to high tem-peratures in **hot tubs, whirlpools,** and **saunas.** A body temperature elevation to 104°F or beyond during the first three months of pregnancy may increase the risk of a baby having a neural tube defect (see page 9). Because a maximum safe amount of exposure to high temperature cannot be established with complete certainty, it is best to avoid hot tubs or extremely hot baths altogether during the course of your pregnancy (and especially during the first three months).

Do you have any medical problems that need to be addressed?

Before 1900, a pregnant woman typically had only one prenatal visit with a physician prior to her delivery, during which her due date was determined—and little else. When next seen, she might be near term and in perfect health—or severely ill with an infection or a complication of her pregnancy. One of the major advances in public health in the early twentieth century was the recognition that a number of health problems that affect both mother and child could be detected, and in many cases corrected, through screening during pregnancy.

Many experts now not only advocate starting prenatal care as soon as possible after a pregnancy is diagnosed but even recommend a preconception visit for those who are thinking about starting a family. Whether before or during pregnancy, a thorough history and physical examination, including a review of important areas such as family background, habits, lifestyle, and general health, are wise. Some basic laboratory tests may also be done. Since all these areas can affect the health of a pregnancy and thus the quality of a baby's start in life, an ounce or two of prevention and protection can save several pounds of costly cure. Areas to consider include:

Family background. If there is a history of any diseases that are passed by inheritance (such as diabetes, cystic fibrosis, sickle-cell disease, or Tay-Sachs disease) within the family of either parent-to-be, genetic counseling can help to determine the potential risk of having a baby with a similar problem. This information can in turn guide decisions about having certain tests done during pregnancy to detect possible problems in the child (see Special Concerns, page 93).

Previous pregnancies. If you have had a prior pregnancy loss, a complication during labor or delivery, or a child born with a congenital problem of any type, specific tests and preparations may be in order before or during another pregnancy.

General health. Pregnancy is not a disease, of course, but it does have a significant impact on the way a woman's body functions. Furthermore, a number of medical problems can have a profound effect on her pregnancy and the health of her baby. The most important of these are diabetes, high blood pressure (hypertension), epilepsy, heart disease, asthma, kidney disease, and the so-called autoimmune disorders such as rheumatoid arthritis or systemic lupus erythematosus. Any of these problems should be addressed and controlled, if at all possible, *before* becoming pregnant or as soon as possible after pregnancy is confirmed.

Infections and immunity. Most acute illnesses (such as colds) that might occur during a pregnancy are weathered without difficulty by both mother and baby. However, some types of infections in a pregnant woman can have adverse effects on her unborn child. When one of these occurs, the ultimate outcome will depend on (among other things) the type of organism, the severity of the infection, and the stage of pregnancy during which it occurs. While the more troublesome infections are uncommon, it is well worth taking some basic precautions in order to avoid them.

Rubella (**German or three-day measles**, see photo on page A31) is a viral infection that causes fever, aches, and a rash for a few days. If a woman becomes infected with rubella during the first month of pregnancy, her baby will have a 50 percent risk of developing one or more serious defects, which together are known as **congenital rubella syndrome.** These can include delayed growth, mental retardation, eye disorders, deafness, and heart disease. If the infection occurs in the third month or later, the risk drops to 10 percent.

Any woman who might become pregnant should have a blood test to see if she is immune to this disease. A vaccine against the rubella virus has been avail-

LAB TESTS COMMONLY DONE DURING PREGNANCY

- A complete blood count (CBC) to check for anemia and other abnormalities of blood components.
- A urinalysis to check for infection, protein (which normally is minimally present in urine), blood, or other signs of disease.
- Blood type and Rh factor. This is important because differences between your blood type or Rh and the baby's could lead to complications in the newborn. For women who do not have the Rh factor (that is, they are Rh-negative), additional screening is done later in the pregnancy.
- A blood test for immunity to rubella (German measles).
- Tests for syphilis, hepatitis B, and HIV, and possibly cultures for chlamydia and gonorrhea (see Special Concerns, page 77).

- Blood glucose to check for diabetes.
- A Pap smear to check the cells of the cervix (the opening of the uterus) for abnormalities, including cancerous or precancerous cells.
- Screening for bacterial and viral infections in the vagina and cervix is often performed during the second half of pregnancy. Specifically, testing to detect bacterial vaginosis, which could increase the risk for premature rupture of membranes and subsequent labor, and a culture for group B streptococci, which can infect and harm the newborn after delivery, may be done during your pregnancy.
- Other tests may be appropriate, based on your history or exam findings. For example, if you have high blood pressure, an assessment of kidney function and other tests may be necessary.

able since 1969, so most young women have had one or even two MMR (measles/mumps/rubella) injections during childhood—but *this does not guarantee that they are protected.* If the blood test does not detect antibodies to rubella, she should have an immunization *before* she becomes pregnant. Most experts recommend waiting for three months after the injection before becoming pregnant, although congenital rubella syndrome has not been reported even when the injection has been accidentally given during pregnancy. (If a woman is breast-feeding, the rubella vaccine can be administered without any apparent risk to the nursing child.)

Chicken pox (varicella, see photo on page A27) is another viral infection that usually occurs during childhood, although susceptible adults (including pregnant women) can also develop this illness—often with a more difficult course than their younger counterparts experience.

A developing baby can be infected with the mother's chicken pox, and the consequences will depend on the timing of the illness. During the first twenty weeks of pregnancy, there is about a 2 percent risk of developing a congenital varicella syndrome, which may include any of several defects of eyes, heart, and limbs. There is no way to determine whether the baby has been affected at the time of the mother's infection. Unfortunately, women who are infected with chicken pox during the first half of pregnancy may be told that they should have an abortion without being told that the risk of a congenital problem is quite low.

After twenty weeks of pregnancy, chicken pox in the mother does not result in harm to her baby unless the infection occurs from five days before to two days after delivery. (Before birth, the baby can be infected through the mother's blood via the umbilical cord. If the mother is infected shortly after giving birth, the baby can contract the illness by direct expsoure.) When this occurs, a severe infection can result, because the baby may acquire the virus without also receiving any of the mother's protective antibodies. If this occurs, the baby should receive an injection called varicella-zoster immune globulin (or VZIG), which provides a temporary protective dose of "borrowed" antibody.

If you are pregnant and do not believe you have had this disease, you should be careful to avoid any child who has, or might have, chicken pox, as well as any adult who develops shingles, which can spread the same virus. If you are uncertain whether or not you have had chicken pox in the past and wish to find out prior to or during pregnancy, your doctor can order a blood test that detects antibodies to the virus.

Group B streptococci are bacteria that are present in the vagina of approximately 20 to 25 percent of pregnant women and can infect the baby during birth, especially if labor is premature or if the woman's membranes (the "bag of waters") are ruptured for more than eighteen hours prior to delivery. Overall, about one of every one thousand infants is infected during birth, often with severe consequences including pneumonia and meningitis. Your doctor may recommend a culture to detect this bacteria at some point during your pregnancy. Of the 20 to 25 percent of women who carry this bacteria, only 1 to 2 percent of their babies will be *infected.* Therefore, antibiotics can be administered to the mother during labor to decrease the rate to 0.5 percent.

Toxoplasmosis is an infection caused by a parasite that may contaminate undercooked meat or dead animals and thus can appear in the feces of cats that eat rodents and decaying meat. If a woman develops toxoplasmosis during pregnancy, her baby has about a one in three chance of becoming infected, and of those, about one-third will show some signs of the disease. Significant problems in these infants can include premature delivery, a small head (microcephaly), encephalitis (inflammation of brain tissue), weak muscles, an enlarged liver and spleen, and inflammation of the retina. If recognized in mother and/or infant, toxoplasmosis can be treated with antibiotics. Unfortunately, this infection can be difficult to diagnose, and treatment doesn't usually change the outcome.

The most important take-home lesson about toxoplasmosis is that prevention is possible through two simple measures. First, any meat you consume during pregnancy, or *any* time, should be well cooked. Second, you should avoid any contact with cat droppings if you are pregnant or might be in the near future. This means staying away from the litter box and avoiding close contact with cats, especially if they spend much time outdoors.

Parvovirus causes an infection, seen commonly in schoolchildren but also in other age-groups, called **erythema infectiosum,** or "fifth disease." Typically seen in winter and spring months, fifth disease is most well known for producing a so-called slapped-cheek rash on the face, although a lacy eruption may be seen on the arms, legs, and upper body as well. Adults who are infected may develop the rash but also typically develop aching joints. However, both children and adults can become infected without any symptoms at all. Unfortunately, this disease is contagious for up to three weeks *before* the rash breaks out, so it is virtually impossible to prevent exposure of other family members.

If a woman becomes infected with parvovirus during pregnancy, it's very likely (better than an 80 percent chance) that there will be no adverse effects on her baby. However, sometimes the mother's infection results in a severe anemia in the baby, which in turn can cause congestive heart failure. Therefore, a pregnant woman who is exposed to this infection should have a blood test to determine whether she is immune to it. If she is, there should be no cause for concern. If not, testing may be recommended later in the pregnancy to determine whether she has become infected.

If infection with parvovirus appears to have taken place during pregnancy—with or without symptoms—the baby should be monitored with ultrasound exams prior to birth for signs of heart failure resulting from anemia. Should either or both of these develop, the baby may require medication, early delivery, or even a transfusion prior to birth (one of the many forms of medical intervention now available for the preborn).

Cytomegalovirus (CMV) has the dubious distinction of causing the most common congenital infection in the United States while being both untreatable and rarely (if ever) preventable. Fortunately, significant CMV disease in newborns is very uncommon. Approximately 1 to 2 percent of pregnant women experience a primary (first-time) infection with CMV, but the vast majority have no symptoms. About 30 to 40 percent of infected mothers transmit the virus to their babies, but only about 10 to 15 percent of infected infants will have some form of noticeable disease at birth. The overall risk of any infant having serious disease related to CMV (that may involve the central nervous system, vision, hearing, pneumonia, or liver disease) is between one in ten thousand and one in twenty thousand.

At the present time, pregnant women are not screened for their susceptibility to CMV because there is no effective treatment for this infection. However, if a woman develops an illness during pregnancy that resembles mononucleosis—with fever, sore throat, enlarged lymph nodes in the neck, and marked fatigue—her physician may at some point request blood tests or even cultures to help determine if CMV might be involved. If this diagnosis is made, she will need careful and accurate counseling regarding the risk of the baby having congenital disease.

Approximately twenty different **sexually transmitted diseases (STDs)** pose significant risks to both mother and baby. Many STDs are passed during intimate contact with people who look perfectly well and have no signs of illness. *Unfortunately, the first indication that an infection has taken place may be the birth of a very sick baby, a miscarriage or stillbirth, or even a woman's inability to become pregnant.* The Special Concerns on page 77 has details about STDs and pregnancy, including descriptions of their symptoms, risks to an unborn child, treatment, and prevention. Even if you consider yourself at low risk for having a sexually transmitted disease, you would be wise to review this information. (An in-depth look at the impact of STDs on adolescents and young adults is contained in a Special Concerns section on page 573.)

Personal and Spiritual Preparations: What Sort of World Will Your Child Live In?

As important as it is to have a safe and satisfactory childbirth, in the long run the most critical assignments of parenthood involve much more than preparing for the delivery date. Once the cord is cut and the first breaths of air are taken, your child's world has permanently and dramatically changed. If she is going to thrive, and not merely survive, that world needs to be safe, stable, and loving, especially during the first three years of life.

It is a tragedy that the world at large is anything *but* safe, stable, and loving. It is full of "many dangers, toils, and snares," to quote the writer of the hymn "Amazing Grace," so much so that some young adults are not sure they are willing to bring a child into a world so torn by upheaval and uncertainty.

But for children (especially the very young), the world they experience is primarily the creation of the people around them. The sights, sounds, and touches of parents and family and a general sense of order, comfort, and predictability can be an island of love and sanity, even when the culture outside the front door is volatile or even violent. The reverse is also true: The prettiest home in the nicest neighborhood may be hell on earth for a young child, who will carry the aftermath of damaging experiences into adulthood.

Whatever else you do as you bring up your child, you must convey a crucial message that she can hear, see, and *experience* in hundreds of different ways, especially when she is young:

> You are loved, you are important, and you always will be, no matter what happens. I care enough about you to provide for you, stand with you, coach you, correct you, and even die for you if necessary. My commitment to you is not based on what you do or don't do, how you look, whether your body is perfect or handicapped, or how you perform in school or sports. It is based on the fact that I am your parent and you are my child, a priceless gift that God has loaned to me for a season. Eventually I will release you to live your own life, but while you are growing up, I consider caring for you an assignment of utmost importance.

Obviously, a newborn baby will not understand these words, and even an older child will not fully grasp their meaning. But embracing these words as a mind-set and a fundamental attitude toward your child will shape thousands of interactions that ultimately convey its message. Indeed, most of the other details and techniques of child rearing—feeding, toilet training, education, and the

The task of parenting is too scary on our own, and there is not enough knowledge in the books to guarantee the outcome of our duties. We desperately need divine help to do the job properly!

THE NEW DARE TO DISCIPLINE

rest—pale in comparison to the importance of communicating this attitude to your child, week in and week out for years.

The question to ponder, therefore, is this: Are you ready to deliver this message to your child and to strive to make your child's world safe, stable, and loving?

This is certainly a more complicated question to answer than "Are you smoking cigarettes?" or "Is your blood pressure too high?" The answer has a lot to do with how *you* were brought up and with the decisions you have made up until now. The answer is also tied up in how you see yourself in relation to the baby, to any other children you may have, to your mate, to your own parents, to the world in general, and, ultimately, to God. To get a better grasp on this issue, consider carefully the following questions, perhaps writing down your thoughts in a journal for future reference:

- What did your mother and father teach you about love, safety, and security? Did you see them express affection for one another? Did they build one another up or barrage one another, and everyone else, with criticism? (If you were reared by one parent, the same questions apply in connection with that parent or other caregivers.)

- Did you hear and feel that you were loved unconditionally? Were consistent limits set and enforced? Was discipline administered in a context of teaching and love, or did unpredictable punishments occur in outbursts of anger? Were you abused as a child—or as an adult?

- Are you expecting your baby to give you love? Are you hoping to derive significance from the role of being a mother or a father? Or do you already feel loved and believe that your life is significant and useful?

- How do you feel when
    you are interrupted frequently?
    someone needs you constantly?
    you have ongoing responsibilities?
    sudden changes rearrange your plans?
    you don't get enough sleep?

The messages you received from one or both parents can have a profound impact on the messages you in turn give to your own child. If your world was safe and secure, and if you felt loved and accepted by the most important people in your life—even when you were being corrected or disciplined—you are more likely to transmit that same sense of belonging and security to your own child. If the opposite was true, you may have a difficult time communicating that message to a child because you are probably still seeking it yourself.

You may be looking for love, acceptance, and significance from the role of being a mother or a father (and the recognition from others that ideally should come with the role) or even directly from your child. *But for babies or small children, nearly all of the loving and caring flows in a one-way direction: from you to them.* The newborn baby in particular is totally incapable of offering any affection before the first genuine smile appears at about the age of one month. His or her crying—especially if there is a lot of it—may sound downright hostile to the mother or father who is looking for a little appreciation for all the effort, pain, and sleepless nights.

If you are not sure—or are not happy—about your answers to these questions, you are not alone. No one has had perfect parents, and no one has lived a life free of mistakes and bad decisions. We are all on a learning curve, especially with parenting, and it's never too late to make course corrections. Here are some ways to get started:

Tap into a support team. By seeking guidance and input from your pastor, a professional counselor, a relative, or someone with parenting experience whom you respect, you can gain valuable encouragement and support. Many churches have ongoing small-group studies available for young parents, and these can be water in the desert during some of the challenging periods of child rearing. A counselor may be efficient at sorting through your particular personal issues, but a great deal can also be accomplished with a person (or a couple) who is willing to serve as a mentor. If you have been verbally, physically, or sexually abused as a child (or adult), it is particularly important that you work with someone who is qualified to help you in the process of healing the wounds that are an inevitable consequence of such experiences.

Take advantage of books, audio cassettes, and videotapes that can be utilized at your own pace. There is an abundance of materials that can educate and inspire you or supplement counseling about a particular problem.

Maintain a regular quiet time. Setting aside time to read Scripture, reflect, and pray elevates the entire project of child rearing to a different plane. However, if you already have one or more small children at home, sitting down for a peaceful quiet time may seem about as easy as flying to Mars. Some planning, creativity, and perseverance will definitely be necessary. (For example, this activity may have to take place during nap time or after the children are in bed, assuming you can stay awake and ignore whatever mess needs to be picked up. Or you may try to think and pray while taking a walk around the block, with or without a stroller.) Whatever effort is spent carving out some time for personal renewal will definitely pay off—perhaps in ways you may not appreciate until months or years have passed.

God is clearly presented in both Old and New Testaments as the perfect parent: not only our Creator but a loving, patient, wise Father who cares enough to guide and correct His children on a daily basis. When we truly begin to grasp the lengths to which God has gone in expressing His love for each of us and His desire to be involved in the details of our lives, our ultimate sense of identity, security, and significance takes on a whole new meaning. If we were brought up in an atmosphere of inconsistency, neglect, or hostility and violence, God is willing and able to parent us, even as adults. And that in turn leads us into a new capacity for loving and cherishing our own children.

Prayer forges powerful links not only to God but also to those we most care about. It's never too late to give thanks for our children, to release the health and well-being of each child to God's provision since they ultimately belong to Him anyway, and to pray for those who will influence that child in the future— friends, teachers, pastors, and eventually, a mate.

For the parent who is married: Cultivate your relationship with your spouse. Kids whose parents are openly affectionate, do kind things for one another, and respect one another will feel secure indeed. *Your relationship with your husband or wife cannot be put on hold when children begin to arrive.* Eventually they will leave the nest, and you will want to have a healthy and thriving marriage, with a long-lasting supply of conversation and worthwhile projects, after they are gone.

Some thoughts for the expectant and new father

As your wife progresses through her pregnancy, your original commitment to "love, honor, and cherish" will take on some important new dimensions. She is going through some significant physical changes, including radical variations in hormone levels, which can affect energy, appetite, and mood. At any given time, she may feel tired (especially if there are other small children at home), nauseated, ungainly, and unattractive. After your baby is born, she may feel terrific, but she could also feel exhausted or depressed. Unfortunately, for all of these reasons, pregnancy and the months that follow are when there may be an increased risk of infidelity. Your job, therefore, is to honor the commitments you made at the altar on your wedding day and to say and do things that communicate a consistent message:

> You are loved, you are important, and you always will be, no matter what happens. I care enough about you to provide for you, stand with you, protect you, and even die for you if necessary. My commitment to you is

not based on how you look, whether your body is perfect, how much you accomplish, or whether we can have sex. It is based on the fact that I am your husband and you are my wife and that our union is a priceless gift that God has so graciously provided. I consider looking out for your well-being to be an assignment of utmost importance as long as we live.

Sound familiar? Cultivating this attitude toward your wife is the foundation for communicating the same message to your child. Some practical suggestions include:

Take the time to communicate. If you have been separated from your wife all day, debriefing with her is far more important than browsing through the evening paper or watching the six o'clock news. This is particularly important if she is caring for small children at home, since most women crave adult conversation after a day full of toddler talk. Ask: "How are you feeling?" "Are you tired?" Say: "You look great." "You're not fat—you're pregnant."

Learn how to listen. If she's had a bad day, hear her out. It's more important to let her ventilate and find out what she needs rather than to try and "fix" everything.

Offer to take on some tasks that might not normally be your "turf" at home. Better yet, just do them without saying anything about it. Shoo her out of the kitchen, clean up the kids' mess, or offer to do the grocery run if you're not doing so already. Give her the opportunity to go out for a few hours to do something she enjoys or simply let her put her feet up or take a warm, uninterrupted bath.

Maintain (or start) a "date night" every week or at least twice a month. Spending a lot of money is not the object—but spending time together is. She needs to know that she is still desirable and that you appreciate her.

Unexpected flowers and cards always make an amazingly positive impact, as they have for generations.

Pray regularly for, and with, your wife.

On the warnings and cautions side, remember the following:

Learn to deal with conflict constructively. Most people do not automatically know how to discuss differences of opinion, especially strong ones, in a manner that is mutually respectful. If you find that discussions are generating more heat than light, take the time and effort to work with a pastor or counselor on your specific issues. Better yet, find a husband-wife team you both respect and who would be willing to serve as mentors, particularly in improving the basic way you approach disagreements.

Choose your timing carefully when you discuss conflicts and problems. If you are both tired, distracted, or irritated, the conversation will likely be unproductive.

Eliminate from your vocabulary words and phrases that insult or degrade your wife. If common courtesy would prevent you from saying them to a coworker or a complete stranger, you have no business saying them at home.

Never, under any circumstances, strike, shove, or in any way make physical contact with your wife as an expression of anger or an intention to injure her. There is never justification for taking this type of harmful action, but it is particularly destructive when she is pregnant. If you are angry and have run out of words, walk away from the situation and calm down. If you have hit your wife (or any woman in your life) in the past or feel the urge to do so, seek help from a pastor or counselor; such problems don't get better by being ignored or denied.

For the mother-to-be who is single

All of the recommendations mentioned earlier—finding a support team, taking advantage of helpful books and tapes, and establishing a quiet time—are especially important for you and perhaps worth reading again. It is a courageous but often very difficult task to raise a child on your own, and you should not hesitate to seek whatever help is available within your family, church, or community at large. Most significantly, on many occasions you will also need to remember that God is keenly aware of all your needs and that He will be your "silent partner," standing beside you during those times when you feel you've reached the end of your resources.

At the same time, you will need to be careful with your attitude about your child. Watch out for the dangerous but all too common feeling that he is a burden, a hassle, or an obstacle to what you *really* would like to do with your life. (This viewpoint isn't unique to single mothers, by the way.) Because you might not have someone to share the workload, the time your child is dependent upon you may seem like an eternity. In fact it is but a season, and one that will never return. It may take effort to do so, but remember—especially when what you want most is a good night's sleep, one that isn't interrupted by crying—to cherish this new person in your life.

So . . . Are You Ready
to Bring Up a Child?

This is a trick question.

As important as it is to plan ahead and prepare for parenthood, it is impossible to be *completely* ready. Even those who feel ready, willing, and able, who have had all their checkups, have gone to the childbirth classes, and have decked out the nursery to look like a designer showcase may be thrown a major curveball with the arrival of their new baby. An unexpected physical abnormality, a sudden medical problem during or after delivery, or perhaps a difficult temperament in an otherwise normal child can turn the lives of the most well-equipped parents inside out.

For most parents, there is never a perfect time to have a baby. There will *always* be problems and circumstances to deal with: education, career paths, money, living space, health problems, and most of all, the basic maturity to nurture a child—especially the first one. Unfortunately, our culture has become so fixated on idealized notions of what constitutes a "wanted" pregnancy that in the United States there is one abortion for every three babies born.[2]

Many women have not actually been trying to become pregnant when they find out they are carrying a child, and a number are in difficult circumstances. This is a particularly acute issue when the mother is young, single, and limited in resources. Those who need help dealing with the circumstances surrounding their pregnancy should not have to fend for themselves. Over the past decade, hundreds of independent crisis pregnancy centers have been established across North America, all dedicated to helping pregnant women (both single and married) and those close to them tackle challenges of pregnancy and parenthood. Their services, all given without charge, range from locating a shelter and medical care to providing baby supplies and single-parent support groups.

The bottom line is that circumstances will *never* be perfect. No pregnancy, childbirth, or newborn baby will be flawless. But one major advantage of having nine months between conception and delivery is that it allows both Mom and Dad time to adjust and prepare for this major change in their lives. With time to reflect and draw on inner resources and assistance from family and community, the most turbulent beginnings of parenthood can ultimately have a successful outcome.

NOTES
1. H. Klonoff-Cohen et al., *Journal of the American Medical Association* 23 (March 8, 1995).
2. "Abortion Surveillance: Preliminary Data—United States, 1993," *MMWR* 45 (Washington, D.C., GPO, 1996): 235–238.

CHAPTER 2

Developing a Birth Plan

*My husband told me one night with his
hand on my tummy that he gave the
baby over to God. That was comforting.
We're not alone in our journey.*
LOVING YOUR PREBORN BABY

Developing a Birth Plan
and Preparing the Nest

Just as every child is a unique and irreplaceable creation, each baby's entry into the world is a one-of-a-kind event. No two births are alike, even for parents who have had a number of children and feel like old pros. One critical aspect of childbirth never changes: Everyone involved in this momentous process wants the same outcome—a healthy baby and a healthy mother. Whether everything has moved like clockwork or nothing has gone as planned, this outcome is what matters most. This goal must be kept in mind during all phases of planning and experiencing birth and must override every other consideration.

There are many possible routes to the destination called "healthy baby–healthy mother." A number of choices must be made along the way, although some parents may have more options than others. Who will provide the prenatal and delivery care? What type of childbirth-preparation classes are available? Who will be present at the delivery, and who will serve as coach? Will medications or anesthesia be used to relieve pain? Who will check on and follow the baby after delivery? Will the baby stay with Mom constantly or spend time in the nursery? What about breast feeding versus bottle feeding?

You may have strong convictions about all of these topics, or they may seem like a bewildering array of details to sort through when all you care about is getting everyone through the big event safe and sound. No doubt you will receive, if you haven't already, an earful of opinions from friends and relatives. There is no shortage of books, magazine articles, videotapes, and other materials available containing information and opinions about childbirth and all that follows it.

Like everything else in parenthood, wisdom about childbirth begins by avoiding extremes. Ignoring the inevitable due date and "letting it happen" without any preparation could result in a truly unpleasant experience, if not a full-blown disaster. But holding rigid expectations about every detail of the "perfect" birthing experience could lead to disappointment and frustration—or even skirmishes in the labor-and-delivery area. Either of these approaches will get the parent-child relationship off to a shaky start.

Instead, thoughtful consideration of the following questions will help you formulate a sense of direction as you approach the due date. Write down some of the things you would like—and not like—to be part of your birthing experience, as well as the areas about which you are uncertain. Seek advice from a few mature people who have been down the road before you and don't be dismayed if you hear differences of opinion. Be sure to review these topics with your health-care provider, preferably before the first contractions of labor begin!

WHO IS GOING TO PROVIDE YOUR CARE DURING PREGNANCY AND CHILDBIRTH?

Depending upon the community in which you live and the type of health-care coverage you have, you will be dealing with one or more of the following types of providers:

An **obstetrician/gynecologist (ob/gyn)** has completed four years of medical school, followed by at least four years of residency training specializing in the female reproductive system. An ob/gyn is prepared to handle both routine and problem deliveries and can perform cesarean sections. Some have additional training in treating infertility. A **maternal-fetal medicine specialist** is an ob/gyn who has expertise in dealing with unusually difficult or high-risk pregnancies. Perinatologists may follow a pregnancy from beginning to end or may serve as consultants to other ob/gyns in their community.

Many **family physicians (FPs,** also called **family practitioners)** provide care for pregnant women. (In Canada, FPs take care of most uncomplicated deliveries.) Following medical school, an FP completes a three-year residency that encompasses the gamut of health care, including adult internal medicine, pediatrics, ob/gyn, and surgery. A family physician can provide routine obstetric care and baby and child care as well. Most do not take care of women with high-risk pregnancies or complicated deliveries, so FPs will routinely have an ob/gyn available for backup if trouble arises.

While most obstetricians and family physicians hold the familiar M.D. degree, a number of doctors who hold a **D.O. (Doctor of Osteopathy)** degree are equally qualified to serve as primary-care physicians during pregnancy and childbirth. However, this is not the case with chiropractors, naturopaths, and other alternative practitioners, whose training does not qualify them to provide prenatal care or deliver babies.

Nonphysician providers of prenatal care include the following:

A **certified nurse-midwife (CNM)** is a registered nurse who has additional hospital experience in labor and delivery and a year of training in midwifery. After passing a certification exam and obtaining a state license, a CNM can follow a normal pregnancy through delivery. The practice patterns of midwives in a given community will vary, depending upon the facilities and medical backup available to them. In a best-case scenario, they collaborate actively with ob/gyns and FPs, providing care for patients in hospitals and/or adjacent birth centers that handle uncomplicated deliveries.[1]

In some physicians' offices, a **nurse-practitioner** or **physician's assistant** may provide basic prenatal care under a doctor's supervision but will not actually deliver the baby.

WHO IS GOING TO PROVIDE CARE FOR THE BABY?

Your options for the baby's health-care provider may include the following:

Pediatricians have a medical degree and have taken at least three years of residency training in the care of infants, children, and adolescents. Like family physicians and ob/gyns, pediatricians are considered **primary-care physicians**—that is, they serve as the point of entry into the health-care system. They provide routine checkups and manage the vast majority of illnesses and other health problems of children. Some spend additional years developing expertise in subspecialty fields such as pediatric cardiology, neurology, and gastroenterology. (These physicians normally serve as consultants for specific problems, rather than providing primary care. In Canada pediatricians generally function as consultants.) A **neonatologist** specializes in the care of premature infants and sick newborns, usually in an intensive-care unit.

Family practitioners (whether holding M.D. or D.O. degrees) care for all age-groups, including infants and children. Depending upon their practice setting, FPs may request consultation from pediatricians or subspecialists when dealing with more difficult cases.

Pediatricians and family physicians may also employ **nurse-practitioners** and **physician's assistants,** who are trained to provide basic services in an office setting. They can carry out routine exams, treat common medical problems, and

If any of you lacks wisdom, he should ask God, who gives generously to all without finding fault, and it will be given to him.

JAMES 1:5

prescribe medication under the supervision of a physician. Some parents wonder whether they get their money's worth if they do not actually see a doctor during their visit. But often these **allied health professionals,** as they are called, are actually able to spend more time answering questions and working through common problems.

Choosing Health-Care Providers for Mother and Baby

This is a very important issue because the qualifications of your health-care providers and the quality of your relationship with them can have a major impact on your childbirth—and child rearing—experiences. Ideally you will be working with someone (or a team) who

- ◆ is competent. The greatest bedside manner in town can't compensate for lack of knowledge or poor judgment.
- ◆ treats you with respect. Courtesy, willingness to answer questions and explain clearly what is going on, and a feeling of collaboration rather than condescension are essential to good health care.
- ◆ is available. Whether you are dealing with a solo practitioner or a multi-specialty group, you should be able to make contact with someone who can answer questions or respond to a problem within a reasonable period of time. That person may be the doctor, a colleague on call, an office nurse, a nurse-practitioner, or a physician's assistant.
- ◆ shares, or at least respects, your basic value system.

Finding all of these qualities in a practitioner may be easier said than done. Depending on their community and health insurance coverage, some families will have more choices than others. If you have options—for example, a list of preferred providers available through your insurance—don't hesitate to make inquiries. Most hospitals have referral lists of physicians who are permitted to admit patients to their facility. This will tell you that they have passed some level of scrutiny regarding their basic competence but not much else about their practice patterns or office routines.

If you already know someone in the medical community—a longtime family physician or a neighbor who is a nurse, for example—ask for recommendations. Take an informal poll of families with children in your church or neighborhood to see which names are mentioned most often. Families with pro-life convictions often prefer to see physicians who do not perform abortions. Local crisis pregnancy centers or other pro-life organizations usually maintain a list of these physicians.

If you have narrowed your list but aren't sure of your choice, you may want to set up a meet-the-doctor session. Such a visit should allow you to:

See how you are treated on the phone. Does the person at the other end of the line sound friendly, pleasant, and willing to talk, or harried and hostile?

Check out the office itself. Do you (or any of your children, if they are going to be seen there) feel comfortable and welcome? Is the waiting area tidy or a wreck? Does it feel like a bus station, a funeral parlor, or a nice place to relax? If children are going to be seen, are there things for them to do or look at?

Meet the doctor. If you make it clear up front that you want to talk briefly and not become a patient yet, you can also ask whether there will be a consultation fee. You may not be charged, in which case you shouldn't expect a half-hour conference. If you have a lot of questions about the practice, someone on the office staff may be able to answer them for you. A large, multidoctor practice may even have a designated patient-relations representative who will be more than happy to answer questions and show you around. Whatever you do, don't set up a get-acquainted visit and then suddenly ask, "By the way, can you look in Johnny's ear?" If you want medical attention, ask for it ahead of time and sign in as a patient.

Questions you may want to ask the physician who is going to take care of you during pregnancy and childbirth:

- What is the routine for prenatal visits?
- With whom does he or she share after-hours coverage? Ideally you should have a chance to get to know any and all of the people who might deliver your baby.
- What will happen when labor begins? Are there routines, such as electronic fetal monitoring, that are expected as a part of every childbirth? Any problems with moving around during labor? If you want to have an unmedicated childbirth, will the physician support that decision? If you desire pain relief, what options will be available? What is the physician's approach to an **episiotomy** (an incision to widen the opening of the birth canal just before delivery)?
- Don't be afraid to bring up the *M* word—*money.* How much will the prenatal and delivery care cost? How much more will it cost if a cesarean section is necessary? Is a checkup afterward included? How much will be

covered by the insurance plan? (Before this discussion takes place, you would be wise to become familiar with the extent of your health insurance coverage.)

♦ How long should you expect to stay in the hospital after the delivery?

Questions you may want to ask of the physician who is going to care for the baby:

♦ How soon after birth will the baby be examined? If there is a need for cesarean delivery, will another doctor be called to care for the baby? (Some hospitals allow only pediatricians to tend to the newborn at the time of a cesarean birth. In these facilities, if a family practitioner had originally been designated as the baby's physician, he or she would usually assume care after the baby's condition has been judged stable.)

HOW TO HAVE A GREAT RELATIONSHIP WITH YOUR DOCTOR

The best relationships between physicians and their patients, both young and old, are built on two basic qualities: mutual respect and flexibility. From the health-care provider's side, these are manifested by listening to you (and your child), providing understandable explanations, answering questions, and being willing to discuss options and alternatives to normal routines. From the patient's side, respect and flexibility involve acknowledging the value of the provider's training and experience, being willing to change course (especially during labor and delivery) if things are not going the way you had expected, and understanding that no one can guarantee a perfect outcome.

If you find yourself seeing a doctor who insists on "my way or the highway," who talks down to you like a schoolteacher addressing a misbehaving child, who races in and out of the exam room like the White Rabbit in *Alice in Wonderland,* or who won't give your questions the time of day, you might consider choosing another practitioner.

Assuming that you have a decent working relationship with your health-care provider, you can get even more out of your visits by following a few basic suggestions.

♦ DO let the doctor know at the outset of your visit what you want to talk about. If you have a number of concerns and want to make the most of your time, give him a list of your questions, letting him know what's most important to you.

♦ DO make friends with the nurses and other office staff. They'll often be able to help you solve problems more quickly than the doctor will.

♦ DO respect your doctor's off-call boundaries. If you run into him at church or in a supermarket, don't ask for medical advice.

♦ DON'T utter the dreaded phrase "by the way . . ." at the end of the visit. That new problem may need more time than the other things you've already discussed.

♦ DON'T bring surprise patients. ("While I'm here, could you look at Billy's throat?")

♦ DON'T insist you will "talk with the doctor and no one else," except in very unusual or highly confidential situations. Many physicians rely heavily on a nurse to screen calls and questions, and refusing to talk with her may delay getting your problem solved.

♦ DON'T challenge every recommendation he makes. Good dialogue is healthy, but if you find yourself arguing more than agreeing, you should probably seek care from someone else.

- What are the physician's views regarding breast or bottle feeding? Will you receive support for either decision? Any opinion regarding feeding on demand as opposed to attempting to establish a schedule?
- What is the routine for checkups and immunizations after the baby is born?
- Does he or she have strong opinions about discipline? (This topic may be too far-reaching to cover during a visit of this type, although it should be brought up as the baby approaches the toddler months.) Are there any books or other materials regarding child rearing that he recommends? (This may provide you a glimpse of the practitioner's worldview and approach to basic values.)

WHERE WILL YOUR BABY BE BORN?

While interest in birth centers and home deliveries has waxed and waned over the past few decades (see page 43), in North America hospitals remain the most widely utilized birth setting for a number of reasons. The first and most obvious is that most pregnant women seek care from obstetricians and family practitioners—all of whom are trained, and for the most part continue to practice, in hospitals.

But a more compelling reason, and the overwhelming advantage of a hospital delivery, is the availability of definitive care for both mother and baby if something goes wrong. This is particularly important when a pregnancy is known to be complicated by medical problems such as diabetes, high blood pressure, prematurity, twins or multiples, or an unusual position of the baby in the uterus. Even a straightforward pregnancy can have a stormy conclusion, especially if it is your first, and the rapid availability of a full range of medical, surgical, and pediatric services is a reassuring safety net.

In addition, more options for pain relief, if needed, are available within the hospital than in other settings.

Some expectant parents have concerns about interventions and procedures they might experience during a hospital delivery, perhaps wondering if they leave their autonomy and options at the door when they check in. But over the years most hospitals have revised their maternity-care policies to become much more parent-friendly.

In response to patients' desires (and common sense), most hospitals have drastically altered their maternity-care areas to create **labor/delivery/recovery (LDR) rooms.** Traditionally, women in hospital maternity-care areas have labored in one room, delivered the baby in another, recovered and stabilized in a third, and finally spent one or more days in a regular hospital room. In contrast, LDR rooms are usually large and nicely decorated (often with a couch, TV, and ample space for family members). The entire labor-and-birth process can proceed without the disruption of moving in and out of four different rooms.

In some facilities, mother and baby remain in the LDR for the duration of their stay, in which case the room is called an **LDRP,** the *P* standing for *postpartum,* meaning "after delivery." Because they combine the best of both worlds—a family-friendly environment with high-tech capabilities—LDRs (or LDRPs) in hospitals have enjoyed wide acceptance by both parents and health-care providers. In addition to the more pleasant surroundings, labor-and-delivery policies in most hospitals have also shifted to a more family-friendly, flexible, collaborative approach.

You can take a number of steps to become better prepared for a birth experience at a hospital:

Visit the facility and become acquainted with the labor-and-delivery area. Familiarity with the environment and the staff can greatly increase confidence and comfort during labor. Most hospitals host prenatal classes, tours, maternity teas, and other outreach activities. Hospital staff enjoy caring for women in labor, so get to know them, look things over, and feel free to ask lots of questions.

See if the hospital has specific policies regarding the number of people allowed in the delivery area. A husband's participation is almost always desired by the hospital, but you may wish to have other family members or close friends present as well. Are there any restrictions?

Find out what will happen to your baby after the birth. Will your baby stay with you? Is "rooming in" the rule or the exception? What routines are part of the baby's care? Is the hospital equipped to handle medical problems of the newborn? If your baby is premature, has an infection, or needs intensive care, will he be transferred to another facility?

Ask about the kind of teaching and assistance available after delivery. Does the staff provide "basic training"? If you have trouble nursing, is there a consultant available to help?

Take care of the paperwork ahead of time. Most hospitals allow you to preregister, check insurance coverage, and deal with other business details so this won't be a distraction during labor. Also, find out from your insurance carrier how many days in the hospital they will cover, assuming there are no unexpected problems. Some policies are more restrictive than others, and your doctor should be aware of any financial constraints you may have.

What Type of Childbirth Classes Will You Take?

Notice that the question was not *whether* you will take childbirth classes. The normal process of moving a baby from the womb to the outside world is called labor for a reason—it's work. One reason so many women were heavily sedated

WHAT ABOUT BIRTH CENTERS AND DELIVERIES AT HOME?

Some hospitals have established **birth centers** on or adjacent to their campus, staffed by midwives, family physicians, and/or obstetricians who are affiliated with the hospital. These facilities are geared toward women with low-risk, straightforward pregnancies, offering pregnancy-and-delivery care in one location. Usually prenatal visits are carried out in the same location and by the same health-care providers as the childbirth. The cost of birth-center care may be significantly less than the formal hospital setting. There is a relaxed familiarity to the surroundings and typically few surprises for the parents-to-be. Should a significant problem develop, however, mother and baby can be moved quickly into the main hospital for definitive care.

A number of **freestanding birth centers** operate independently and geographically separate from hospitals, offering similar services but with one distinct disadvantage: If a major problem should arise, mother and baby must be transferred to the nearest hospital. This process can be upsetting, time-consuming, costly (if an ambulance is needed), and potentially risky.

One study analyzing the outcomes of more than twelve thousand births at eighty-four freestanding birth centers in the United States showed a satisfactory safety record for low-risk pregnancies—although one out of four women delivering her first baby required transfer to a hospital. Since only 7 percent of women who already had one or more vaginal deliveries required transfer, *freestanding birth centers would be best utilized only for low-risk pregnancies in women who have already had at least one child.*

Furthermore, it is imperative that the health-care practitioners not only be well trained in normal childbirth but also be capable of recognizing significant problems and be willing to transfer you promptly from the facility should the need arise.

Home birth is usually chosen by those with a fervent conviction that this is the most natural and least intrusive way to bring a child into the world. But home birthing compromises safety for the sake of a particular style of birth experience. If a serious problem develops suddenly—an unfortunate but very real possibility in maternity care—the home team is at a major disadvantage, and a catastrophe could occur in the time it takes to pack up and move to the nearest hospital. Even if a problem is less severe or develops more slowly, resources at home are extremely limited. Because home birth is not considered mainstream health care in our society, it may attract fringe practitioners whose credentials and skills are questionable.

If you are thinking about having your baby at home, you should carefully review your reasons and ask whether several hours of convenience and comfort at home are really worth the potential for a lifetime of damage—or a loss of life. All things considered, choosing to proceed with a home birth is not a wise decision.

In the final analysis, if you really have your heart set on a nonhospital type of delivery, a birth center directly affiliated with an adjacent hospital would be the better option—assuming, of course, that your pregnancy is uncomplicated.

during childbirth a few decades ago is that few were adequately prepared for what would happen once labor started. As the contractions of the uterus became more uncomfortable, fear and anxiety would multiply the pain until virtually all control would be lost. In 1944 the groundbreaking book *Childbirth without Fear* by British physician Grantly Dick-Read introduced the concept that a woman who understood what was happening during labor and learned how to work with it could have a calm, controlled, and far more comfortable birth experience.

Over the next several years, a variety of prepared childbirth approaches and techniques were developed as the goal of having a "natural" childbirth gained popularity and acceptance. Some advocates of natural childbirth campaigned for labor and delivery completely devoid of any medical intervention, at times putting expectant parents who subscribed to these ideas at odds with their physicians. In response, many doctors complained about "natural childbirth fanatics" who challenged every detail of the hospital routine. But over time, physicians observed that well-informed couples working as a team had a much better experience—and usually had an easier time from a medical perspective—than terrified, unprepared patients who spent the entire labor and delivery in a state of panic and uncontrolled pain.

Childbirth classes are now considered a routine component of prenatal care. They come in all shapes and sizes and may be presented in hospitals, homes, or community centers. Instructors may emphasize one or another school of thought or blend ideas from several sources. Needless to say, some classes will be more organized and detailed than others. The leader should be a certified childbirth educator. Your doctor will probably have a referral or two, but you would be wise to ask some parents who have recently experienced childbirth for their recommendations as well.

Some hospitals or large medical groups also offer early-pregnancy classes dealing with nutrition, exercise, and general self-care. If available, these are well worth attending.

Normally you will begin childbirth-preparation classes during the sixth or seventh month of pregnancy, with a goal of being finished two weeks before the baby's due date. Most meet one evening per week for eight to twelve weeks, though in some communities late starters can take a crash course in one or two weekends. Childbirth preparation is intended to be a team effort of the mother and another person who will be available for the entire course, including the birth itself. Usually this team will be a husband-wife pair, but in some situations (especially with a single mother), a relative or close friend may be serving as the teammate.

The following areas should be covered as part of the curriculum:

- What happens during pregnancy and childbirth: basic anatomy and physiology, including the development of the baby, changes in the mother, and the stages of labor and birth.
- Basic self-care: nutrition, exercise, sexuality, and maintaining a healthy lifestyle.
- Managing the contractions: relaxation, breathing, and pain-control techniques; positions during labor; and the final pushing stage.
- Details of the birth setting: when and where to go, what will happen in the labor-and-delivery area (or birth center), how the labor will be monitored, possible interventions, and pain-medication options if and when needed.
- Possible problem areas and their treatment: failure to progress, fetal distress, premature labor, prolonged rupture of membranes, or cesarean section and its aftereffects.
- Preparing for the first days of baby care, including feeding techniques.

The approach most commonly taught in childbirth classes is the **Lamaze method** or some variation of it. This method was introduced by French obstetrician Fernand Lamaze in his 1958 book *Painless Childbirth*. In America, Lamaze's techniques have been called **psychoprophylaxis** (literally, "mind protection"), and the organization that accredits its teachers is the American Society for Psychoprophylaxis in Obstetrics, or ASPO. Along with other information, ASPO/Lamaze teaches a technique of distracting the mind from pain by using special breathing patterns and actively focusing attention on an external object.

ATTENTION FATHERS: BE AVAILABLE WHEN THE TIME ARRIVES

As has already been mentioned, fathers are no longer routinely shuttled off to a smoke-filled waiting area while their children are being born. They are now encouraged to play an active role in the delivery process through attending childbirth classes and acting as coaches (or at least loving supporters) during labor. But one additional, very practical detail involves being careful with the calendar.

The last month of your wife's pregnancy is probably not the best time to schedule several double work shifts or back-to-back business trips to the other side of the country. Obviously, no one can know for sure the exact due date, but it's a shame to work diligently through the preparation process and then miss the actual event. This may require giving your employer a fair amount of advance notice about the upcoming delivery and your desire to be present for it. The same type of advance planning is also important for the person who serves as coach for a single mother during her labor.

Another widely utilized method was launched in 1965 when Denver obstetrician Robert Bradley published *Husband-Coached Childbirth.* Along with stressing the involvement of the mother's husband as a coach (a term men could relate to), the **Bradley method** teaches deep relaxation techniques rather than focusing attention away from the body. Of these two approaches, the Bradley method tends more to discourage pain medications and other interventions.

Some childbirth educators teach their own homegrown blend of both approaches. Regardless of the method you choose, the object of your preparation should not be to become a walking encyclopedia, reform the entire health-care system, or nurture unrealistic expectations of a problem-free childbirth experience. Training should combine a broad base of general knowledge, adequate time to practice pain-reducing techniques, reassurance that you can handle both normal and unexpected developments, and a healthy dose of reality.

If you truly desire an unmedicated childbirth but find that you can't manage the pain, accepting medication is not a moral failure.[2] If you forget some of the finer points of your breathing technique during the heat of the moment, you're not the first to do so. If an uneventful labor suddenly takes a surprise detour at the last minute, you need to be ready to ask intelligent questions, weigh the options, make an informed decision, and remain calm if things don't turn out the way you expected. *Remember: A healthy baby and a healthy mother are ultimately more important than a perfect childbirth experience.* You want to be as prepared as possible, and you should work diligently toward a controlled labor and joyous delivery, but you're not going to be graded on your performance.

As was already mentioned in chapter 1, this book does not contain step-by-step information about the childbirth process. You should be learning those details through your physician and childbirth classes.

WHAT DOES THE NEW ARRIVAL NEED AT HOME?

As important as it is to prepare for the birth itself, there are some important and practical details to consider about life *after* your baby's arrival. New parents-to-be are often concerned about the amount of clothing and equipment they will need when their son or daughter finally arrives—and how much it will cost. If you have the financial resources to outfit a designer nursery and a four-season infant wardrobe, you will find no shortage of catalogues and showrooms to accommodate you. But most young couples with growing families are stretching their pocketbooks in several directions. You should be relieved to know that it is possible to meet a new baby's needs exceptionally well without creating a new-born penthouse. After all, infancy is the one stage in a child's life when he is not interested in material things. The newborn doesn't care where his clothes and equipment came from. Modest surroundings that are rich in parental love and tenderness will yield far better results than showcase environments that are emotionally impoverished. Remember—the greatest person who ever lived was born in a stable.

Actually, it is extremely unlikely that you will have to buy everything you need and want for the new baby. If you have older children, or friends and relatives with children, a number of items can usually be borrowed or handed down for the new arrival. Friends may throw a baby shower or two for you before the delivery and, after the big event, indulgent grandparents and other well-wishers will perhaps descend on you with all manner of gifts. If you are a single parent or you have had to deal with opposition and obstacles to your pregnancy, your local crisis pregnancy center (CPC) can assist you with a variety of baby supplies. Many new parents are able to obtain needed supplies at a fraction of the original cost by visiting local garage sales and thrift shops. Babies and children outgrow their clothes so quickly that many secondhand items that have been worn very little (and look brand-new) can be purchased for a few dollars. Used nursery furniture and equipment can also be picked up at bargain prices, but make sure that whatever you buy meets current safety standards, especially if it is more than a few years old (see page 50).

SHOULD YOUR CHILDREN WATCH THE BABY BEING BORN?

A few decades ago, only doctor and nurses welcomed the vast majority of American newborns into the world. Once the "husband barrier" was broken and fathers became active in the delivery process, some couples wanted childbirth to become a family affair. Why not let the other children watch the birth of their new brother or sister?

Some enthusiasts describe positive experiences with children as young as four years of age watching siblings being born. But the likelihood of an emotional jolt for the children, the potential distraction for the adults, and the issue of violating the boundaries of modesty within a family are all good reasons to keep your kids out of the delivery room. A better option would be to have the children prepared to see their new sibling soon after delivery—when both mother and baby appear to be okay and have had a few minutes to allow things to settle down.

If you choose to video the delivery for future viewing by your children or other family members, consider carefully who ought to see what. A living-color, full-frame shot of Mom's pelvic region isn't exactly appropriate viewing for the general public. There are lots of other interesting things to capture (especially facial expressions) during childbirth, and it would be prudent to talk over your wishes with whoever is shooting your video for you. If your video does indeed directly view the moment of birth, consider creating an edited G-rated version for the kids to see later on. This might include, for example, shots of the birth from a vantage point looking over the mother's shoulder.

It's a good idea to create your need/wish list *before* you start purchasing items for the nursery. You can use your list to keep track of what you've already acquired so that shopping trips for baby gear will be shorter and more focused. The goods you will need, commonly referred to as a **layette,** will fall into the following basic categories:

Clothing

While there is no magic formula for deciding how many of each type of garment to acquire, the following list covers the basics:

- Small, lightweight (receiving) blankets—3 or 4
- Sleeper sets with feet—3 or 4
- Light tops (gowns or sacques)—2 or 3
- T-shirts or undershirts—3 or 4
- Socks or booties—3 or 4
- Sweaters—2 (heaviness depends on climate)
- Hats—2 (level of protection depends on climate)
- Infant sleeping bag (bunting)—1

As you acquire clothing for your baby, remember three important principles:

Think ahead. Most newborns outgrow newborn-size clothes in a very few weeks, if not days, so favoring somewhat larger sizes for much of the wardrobe is a wise idea. This is especially true for those cute but costly dress-up outfits that may hang idly in the closet after a few outings. If you receive a number of these as gifts, don't remove the tags and boxes and consider doing some discreet trades for bigger sizes at the store where they were bought. If you are buying outfits for the next few months, consider what the future may hold weather-wise.

Think safety. Be sure that no garment is too snug around your baby's neck, hands, and feet and completely avoid any accessory such as a necklace or a long ribbon that could become tangled around the neck. Buttons, beads, and other small objects attached to shirts or pants may be a hazard if they can become detached and find their way into little hands, mouths, and airways; it's a good idea to reinforce buttons and bows, which requires only some time, a needle, and thread. Snaps are safer and handier. Infant and toddler clothing should be flame-retardant—a safety feature that will be stated on the label. Prewash the baby clothes you buy, whether secondhand or fresh from the department store. Use detergents without perfumes or other ingredients that might irritate the baby's skin. Many brand names offer such products (such as Tide-Free); this information will appear on the label. This will assure not only that used garments are sanitary but also that new clothing is free from any detergents or other chemicals used during the finishing processes.

Don't worry about shoes at this point. Not only are they unnecessary before a baby can walk, but they may interfere with normal growth of the feet.

Think convenience and comfort. Since diaper changing is a frequent activity with babies, easy access is preferable to a complicated, multilayered outfit when cleanup is necessary.

Diapers

You will need to decide whether you want to use cloth or disposable diapers, or at least which you would like to start with.

Disposable diapers are abundant in every supermarket and most notable for their convenience. When it's time for a change, take them off, dump any solid waste into the toilet, fold them up, and throw them away. Manufacturers also compete with one another to see who can create the most leak-proof diaper by combining superabsorbency with cleverly engineered plastic linings that prevent urine or stool from escaping onto bedding or furniture. For all of these advantages, however, disposable diapers have their drawbacks. Not only are they more costly than cloth diapers, but their plastic liners do not disintegrate, raising environmental concerns. (Over two thousand diapers enter dumps and landfills every year for each baby using disposables.)

Cloth diapers are less expensive, even when you use a diaper service. But they must be laundered by someone. If that someone is you, wash them separately from other clothing after rinsing them out in the toilet. Use hot water and a double rinse and avoid fabric softeners and scented additives, which can provoke rashes on some infants' skin. Since newborns will soil as many as ten or more diapers a day, you will need a stockpile of three or four dozen. You will also need pins or clips (unless you use the newer models with Velcro fasteners) and some type of waterproof protective covering, unless you buy the all-in-one versions.

Diaper services bring the convenience level of cloth diapering nearly up to that of disposables and still at less cost. Shop around for prices, delivery schedules (twice weekly is typical), and policy regarding whether you rinse first or simply toss the diaper, waste and all, into the pail the service provides. The price of the service should be weighed against the cost of laundry supplies and utility bills when you do the job yourself, as well as your time and energy, which may be in very short supply. While cloth diapers may appear kinder to the environment, it should be noted that diaper services (or parents at home) must consume con-

A relationship that is characterized by genuine love and affection is likely to be a healthy one, even though some parental mistakes and errors are inevitable.

THE STRONG-
WILLED CHILD

siderable amounts of water and energy to clean them. Ultimately your choice between disposable and cloth diapers should be compatible with your family's time and budget constraints.

CRADLE

CRIB

$2\frac{3}{8}''$

Furniture and other hardware

This is where your biggest onetime expenses may lie and where some judicious borrowing of equipment from friends and family will be helpful.

A **cradle** or **bassinet** is a portable sleep space, allowing you the convenience of changing your newborn's sleeping quarters relatively easily. In some families, a cradle whose gentle rocking has calmed restless infants for many decades is handed down from generation to generation. Bassinets don't sway, but they do have the advantage of being portable. Be certain that the legs of the bassinet are stable and sturdy so it cannot accidentally collapse.

If you want the new baby right next to your own bed or elsewhere in the house, a cradle/bassinet will allow you more flexibility. However, within three or four months your baby will outgrow it, and he will need to graduate to a crib.

A **crib** can be the newborn's sleeping place from day one and will be in use for two to three years. Since your baby will spend time in a crib without direct supervision, this must be a completely safe environment. In order to prevent falls and other types of accidents, cribs manufactured over the past several years have had to comply with a number of safety requirements. If your baby is going to be using an older model, you will need to check the following:

◆ The **slats** in the crib should be no wider than two and three-eighths inches apart.
◆ Unless they are supporting a high canopy, **corner posts** that extend above the rails are a potential hazard because they may entangle loose clothing. They should be unscrewed or cut off.

- **Paint** on an old crib may contain lead, and any flakes of paint accidentally swallowed by a curious baby could cause lead poisoning. When in doubt, sand off the old coat (taking care not to inhale it yourself) and apply some high-quality enamel in its place.
- The **headboards** and **footboards** should be solid and without decorative cutouts that could trap a head, hand, or foot.

In addition, you should check the following before you place your baby in any crib, new or old:

- The **mattress pad** should fit snugly into the frame. If you can wedge more than two fingers between the pad and the crib side, the mattress pad is too small. Remove any extraneous tags and thin plastic wrappings. If you use a mattress cover, be sure it is made of thick plastic that, ideally, can be zipped around the pad. Don't place pillows or any soft bedding material other than a fitted sheet under the baby. His head or face might become accidentally buried in the soft folds, especially if he happens to be face down, which could lead to suffocation. (This may be one of the conditions leading to the tragedy of sudden infant death syndrome, or SIDS. See sidebar, page 172.) Sheepskin, down mattresses, feather beds, and wavy water beds pose similar risks.
- **Bumper pads,** securely tied into place, should line the inside of the crib. When your baby can pull up to a standing position, the pads should be removed, since they can assist a baby's attempts to climb over the rail. The same is true of large stuffed animals that a toddler might use as a soft step or launching pad for a trip over the side.
- The **side rails** should latch securely in place, with the release mechanism out of reach of exploring fingers. When fully raised, the rails should extend at least twenty inches above the top of the mattress. As your baby grows and eventually stands up, the mattress will need to be lowered.
- If you hang any **mobiles** above the crib, be sure they remain out of reach a few months from now when your baby begins to move toward (and grab for) interesting objects.
- For many reasons—sun exposure, shades, cords, and, worst of all, the possibility of a disastrous fall—never put a crib next to a window, whether open or shut.

A **changing table** can be a convenient one-stop location for diaper duties at home. But it is also notorious for being the place from which a baby takes his first fall. If you use a changing table:

◆ Never step away, turn around, or otherwise divert your attention from the job at hand unless you pick up the baby to do so. Babies seem to choose this moment to show off their new ability to roll over—and then take a fast trip to the floor. Never answer the phone or the door if it means walking away from your baby.

◆ To reduce the likelihood of such a fall, make sure you have all the changing gear—new diaper, wipes, etc.—within reach before you start.

◆ The table should have a two-inch guardrail around its edge and a safety strap to help you secure the baby. However, these should not be considered a substitute for your undivided attention when your infant is on the changing table.

◆ Don't distract an older baby by letting him handle a can of baby powder (which he might accidentally unload into his or your airspace), play with a disposable diaper (whose plastic liner he might rip off and choke on), or suck on some other miscellaneous object on the changing table.

Car seats

Unlike a changing table, a **car seat** is an absolute necessity. Automobile accidents are a leading cause of death in children, and proper use of car seats could prevent hundreds of tragic losses every year. As a result, every state has passed laws requiring their use. Most hospitals will not allow you to take your new baby home without one, and many will loan or rent you a seat if you cannot buy one.

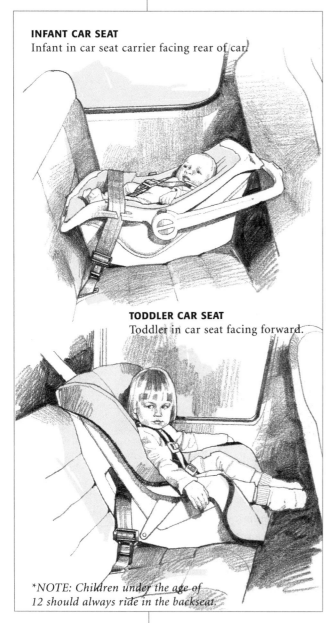

INFANT CAR SEAT
Infant in car seat carrier facing rear of car.

TODDLER CAR SEAT
Toddler in car seat facing forward.

NOTE: Children under the age of 12 should always ride in the backseat.

Each infant, toddler, and young child must be properly secured into an appropriate car seat *every* time he rides in a car—*no exceptions.* Holding a baby in your lap, even if you are wearing a seat belt, can cause him to be crushed between you and the dashboard in an accident—assuming that he hasn't been thrown through the windshield first. Even if the time needed to buckle everyone in place will be far longer than the drive itself, *do it anyway,* because most accidents occur within a few miles of home at speeds below thirty miles an hour. The death of a child for any reason is always a horrendous loss for a family, but the pain is greatly magnified when that loss could have been prevented.

The car seat for a newborn should be either an infant or convertible model manufactured since 1982, the year federal safety regulations were enacted. Because the newborn has no head control, he must face backward to prevent dangerous, rapid forward movement of the head during a sudden stop. The seat should position him so that his upper body is angled upward but not sitting upright, since he can't keep his head from flopping forward. You may need to use small rolled-up towels or diapers to pad the seat and keep him from slouching. The center of the backseat is the safest location for him, and thus you should avoid putting him in the forward passenger seat. This means that, should he start to fuss, you will have to resist the temptation to turn around and tend to him while your vehicle is in motion.

An infant car seat can have the distinct advantage of doubling as a carrier or even a comfortable napping spot for a small baby when you're not in the car. However, the reverse is not true: You should never use an infant carrier as a car seat. Once your baby outgrows the infant car seat (usually between nine and twelve months of age, or about twenty pounds), it will have little use until another baby enters your life. A convertible seat can be reconfigured to face forward when your baby reaches his first birthday and will accommodate him until he weighs forty pounds. It will be, however, too heavy and cumbersome to serve any other purpose.

It is very important to read directions carefully, to make certain the seat can be anchored securely in the car(s) that will carry your baby, and to see that any prospective chauffeurs (grandparents, for example) know how to use the seat properly.

Other safety measures to consider in regard to baby car seats include:

- (For information about older children, air bags, and car seats, see page 406.)
- *If your car has a passenger-side air bag, you should never place your baby in the forward passenger seat.* As was just noted, even without the air bag, the backseat is a safer location for an infant seat. But if an air bag is present, it can cause serious or even fatal injuries to a baby if the bag inflates during an accident.

◆ When your car is sitting in the sun, cover the infant seat with a towel, since plastic and metal parts can become hot. Even if a towel has been used, check the temperature of the seat, belts, and buckles with your hand to be sure you're not depositing your baby into a veritable frying pan.

◆ At some time (or perhaps most of the time), your baby will wail indignantly when put into the car seat. Make sure there is nothing physically annoying him (such as a hot buckle or a stray toy poking his leg), talk or sing sweetly to him, and press on. But do not give in and take him out of the seat to restore calm to the car. If for some reason your baby's crying has reached an unusually distracting pitch, pull off the road and tend to his needs. But then buckle him in before you continue.

◆ *Do not, under any circumstances, ever leave your baby—or any children— unattended in your car.* Amazing and terrible things can happen while you "just dash into the cleaners for thirty seconds." Aside from physical risks to your baby, such as becoming overheated on a warm day or chilled when it's cold, there's always the exciting possibility that an older child will discover how to release the brake—or at least find the horn. And, while we would rather not think about such horrific possibilities, children left unattended in a car present a prime opportunity for a predator who is seeking his next victim to abduct and abuse.

Baby carriers—front and back

See color insert for photos of baby products, page A17.

Many parents find front and back carriers extremely helpful during the first several months of a child's life. They allow a parent to tend to a variety of activities with hands free and baby close and secure. Front carriers are most useful for the first three to six months, after which a baby's increasing size, weight, and activity may begin to strain a parent's back and shoulders. Carriers may be configured so the baby is in an upright position with legs dangling through leg holes (like a backpack worn backwards) or in a "sling" arrangement in which the baby can lie horizontally as in a hammock. Of the two, the sling is somewhat more versatile; the baby can be placed in a variety of orientations (not merely staring at Mom's or Dad's chest), the weight can be adjusted or shifted to either shoulder, and some parents are able to continue carrying babies this way comfortably well past the first birthday. One variation on the sling is configured to allow an infant four months or older to be carried on one hip, an arrangement some parents find more comfortable.

When buying a front carrier, you may want to wait until you can take your baby with you and then "try him on for size." Pay attention to these details:

- How would you rate the padding, distribution of weight, and general comfort? Would you be able to walk around for extended periods of time with your baby in this particular carrier?
- How easy (or difficult) is it to put on and adjust, or remove, the carrier?
- How well supported are the baby's head and body?
- Does your baby seem contented in this arrangement? Some babies will be more calm and comfortable in a sling, while others may seem to prefer a vertical carrier.

If you choose a front carrier, you may find that carrying your baby for extended periods of time in a front pack is convenient for you, soothing for your new baby, and a bonding experience between the two of you. Some parents whose babies seem to cry a great deal if not held may find that a comfortable front carrier calms the infant—and maintains the parents' sanity. However, *you must not use a carrier when you are driving or riding in a car.*

A back carrier is most useful after a baby has gained steady head control, at which point you won't need to worry about the position and support of the head (which you cannot see). If both parent and passenger find the carrier agreeable, it may remain in service through the toddler months. As with front carriers, it is a wise idea to try on various models with the baby in place. One potential disadvantage of this arrangement is that you can't see or talk directly to the baby. This may become a bigger problem if he is irritable or begins to shift himself around by pushing against the frame. When using a back carrier you must also remember to bend your knees if you are tending to something close to the ground. If you bend at the waist, the baby may topple out of the carrier.

Carriages and strollers

These familiar items are useful when you have some distance to cover with your baby and you don't want to carry him. They come in a variety of shapes, sizes, and prices, some plain and simple and others loaded with bells and whistles. There are convertible models that can be changed from a carriage to a stroller when a baby becomes mobile and jogging (or even racing) strollers for those who want to do some serious exercise while the baby comes along for the ride (see color insert).

Unfortunately, according to the U.S. Consumer Product Safety Commission, there are more than ten thousand emergency-room visits every year involving children under five who have been injured in carriages or strollers. If you acquire one of these now or during the coming months, look beyond price and durability to these safety features as well:

- Look for a wide base that will not tip over easily.
- Check the seat belt. Is it securely attached to the frame? Is it strong? Is it easy for you to fasten and unfasten?
- Check the brakes. Do they securely lock the wheels? Are there brakes on two wheels rather than on just one? Are they easy to use? Will they be out of reach of inquisitive fingers when your baby becomes a curious toddler?
- If there is a basket that holds your supplies or parcels, for stability it should be placed low and in front of or directly over the rear wheels.

Your safety awareness will need to continue as you utilize a carriage or stroller for months into the future:

- Make sure the equipment is appropriate for the baby's size. Once a baby can sit up on his own, it won't be long before he can fall out of a carriage, so he must graduate to a stroller into which he can be more securely fastened.
- Always use the seat belt, even if your baby (or older child) protests.
- Don't hang a purse or shopping bag over the handle—the leverage may tip the carriage or stroller backwards.
- Keep older children away from the stroller as you fold or unfold it.

"READY OR NOT, HERE I COME!"

In a few short years you will probably hear your child call out this familiar phrase during some energetic neighborhood game. But now as you await your baby's arrival, you will also hear (and feel) the same message as your baby begins the inevitable passage from the womb to the outside world. Ready or not, your daughter or son will soon be arriving.

We hope that well before the delivery date you will have the time (and energy) to make some of the important physical, financial, emotional, and spiritual preparations that have been outlined in this and the previous chapter. If you haven't yet, and the due date is fast approaching, don't panic. You can jump on the learning curve at any time—even well after your baby has been born.

Speaking of births, the time has come to shift our focus to that exciting first meeting with your baby and the first eventful days of your child's life.

NOTES

1. *Lay midwives* do not have a nursing degree. They may or may not have formal training, a state license, or physician backup. Skill levels vary, and health-care professionals generally have serious qualms about their capabilities should any problem develop.

2. One approach that relieves pain while allowing you to remain awake and alert is the **epidural anesthetic,** which may be given either by the obstetrician (if he or she is trained to do so) or an anesthesiologist. This involves the injection of pain-relieving medication through a small plastic catheter into the space just adjacent to the fibrous sack that surrounds the spinal cord. Pain is dramatically reduced without paralysis of the lower half of the body, and the ability to push during the final stage of labor is usually not affected. The catheter can be left in place if more medication is needed, and if a cesarean birth takes place, this medication can provide a great deal of nondrowsy pain relief.

The Moment Arrives

*We don't have to seek
miracles anymore:
The miracle has found us!*
CARRIE HEIMAN

The Moment Arrives

After months of anticipation, some emotional highs and lows, and (usually) a number of hours of labor, the waiting will finally be over. All your hopes and preparations are about to culminate in the arrival of the tiny new person (or perhaps more than one!) whom you will soon be holding in your arms. Without question, your first look, touch, and embrace of this newest member of your family will be an intense experience, one that we hope will be joyous and fulfilling as well. What can you expect to see?

WHAT HAPPENS DURING THE FIRST FEW MINUTES AFTER BIRTH?

The moment your baby exits the birth canal (or the uterus in a cesarean delivery), she will begin a rapid and radical transition from the warm liquid "inner space" of amniotic fluid—in which the placenta efficiently provided for all her needs by way of the umbilical cord—to the outside world. Within seconds she must begin breathing for herself, within minutes begin regulating her own temperature, and within hours begin actively taking nutrients.

As soon as her body is out (or sometimes when the head alone has just been delivered), her nose and mouth will be gently cleared of fluid. The umbilical cord will be clamped and then cut. (By prior arrangement, Dad may be offered this privilege.) In order to prevent heat loss and a drop in body temperature, the baby will be dried quickly, often while being checked to be sure she is breathing adequately. The mild rubbing that occurs during drying will actually stimulate breathing. (No one swats a newborn on the fanny after birth, by the way.) You may hear a little whimper, a continuous noisy howl of protest, or something in between during these exciting first few moments.

How quickly you are able to hold your newborn will depend on your condition and the baby's. In many uncomplicated births, the baby practically makes a nonstop flight from birth canal to mother's chest. In others, the need for some immediate attention to deal with a problem will delay this initial moment of contact. If the delivery was particularly difficult or was a cesarean birth, the mother may not have as much freedom or may be too preoccupied to attend to her baby. If the baby's breathing is slow to start or sluggish and inadequate, she will be quickly placed on a warmer. Further gentle stimulation

**FULL-TERM BABY
PRIOR TO DELIVERY**

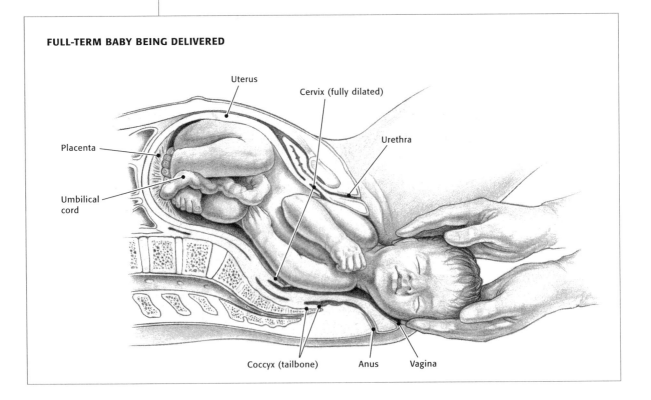

FULL-TERM BABY BEING DELIVERED

Uterus

Cervix (fully dilated)

Placenta

Urethra

Umbilical
cord

Coccyx (tailbone)　　Anus　　Vagina

will continue, and if needed, oxygen or assistance with a bag and mask will be given until the problem stabilizes.

Some babies need more attention to the vocal cords and airway because of the presence of **meconium** in the amniotic fluid. Meconium is a thick, tarlike material that accumulates in the baby's intestines starting at about the fourth month after conception. Normally it is not seen until after birth, but 10 or 15 percent of babies will pass some beforehand. Meconium is usually harmless to a baby, even if swallowed. But if a large amount is present before delivery, and if she makes any breathing or gasping attempts before birth or during delivery, meconium may have been inhaled into her airway. This can cause a number of respiratory problems, and thus if your baby exits the birth canal amidst some meconium-stained fluid, her airway should be cleared of this material as soon as possible. (While the need for these sorts of interventions is the exception rather than the rule, the possibility of an unexpected respiratory problem in the newborn is one of the reasons most health-care providers prefer not to deliver babies away from the hospital.)

Assuming things go smoothly, you should have an opportunity to spend time with your new baby immediately after birth. While keeping her warm and covered, both mother and father can gently touch and caress her, check out the tiny details of her hands and feet, allow her to grasp their fingers, and look into her eyes if they are open. This is a close, emotional time, and you should feel free to laugh, cry, say a prayer of thanksgiving, or just be silent and savor the moment.

The baby may or may not be interested in trying to nurse right away, but you need not be in any hurry. She has plenty of extra fluid in her newborn system, and you may want to try the first feeding later when you are a little more comfortable. The doctor will usually be attending to some after-birth details—collecting a sample of blood from the umbilical cord, delivering the placenta, checking for and repairing any damage, and generally cleaning up, so this may not be the ideal setting in which to get positioned for the first nursing.

The baby's first report card and other details

At one minute and five minutes after birth, a nurse or doctor will do a quick survey of your baby and then assign an **Apgar score.** This simple point system was devised by anesthesiologist Dr. Virginia Apgar during the early 1950s as a tool to predict which infants might need closer observation or more intense care after birth. A baby is given zero, one, or two points on each of five variables: appearance (specifically color), pulse rate, response to stimulation, activity (including muscle tone), and respirations.

Few babies receive a perfect ten at five minutes because most have some dusky or bluish coloration of the hands and feet. (Note that references to pink or blue coloration in the table have nothing to do with the racial or ethnic origin of the baby.) If the score is six or less at five minutes, the baby will be given closer attention. It serves as a cue or a red flag for the level of care a baby may need immediately after birth.

APGAR SCORECARD			
	Score		
Sign	0	1	2
Appearance	pale or blue	body pink, extremities blue	completely pink
Respirations	absent	slow and irregular	good, crying
Pulse	not detectable	below 100	above 100
Reflex irritability	no response to stimulation	grimace	cough, sneeze, or cry
Muscle tone	limp, or weak movement	some movement	active motion

Scores determined for each sign are totaled. The highest possible score is 10. By five minutes of age, most healthy babies have scores of at least 7. A score less than that indicates that the baby warrants careful watching.

Eventually the health-care staff will weigh and measure your baby, take footprints, apply an armband, and carry out a few other standard procedures. There is no reason your baby should be unceremoniously carted off to the nursery for these details two minutes after birth. On the other hand, you don't need to be upset if you are separated from the baby for a few minutes once you've had a comfortable time to get acquainted.

Soon after the baby is born, the nurse will bathe her to remove the thick, whitish material called **vernix,** which served as a protective covering for her skin while she was in the womb. The baby will also receive three routine medical treatments:

- One dose of **antibiotic eye ointment or drops.** Eye infections caused by gonorrhea or chlamydia acquired during birth can be serious enough to cause blindness. These are effectively prevented by this treatment. Even if you feel certain that you could not possibly carry these organisms, all states by law require this treatment.

- A shot of **vitamin K.** Newborn infants have a relatively low level of this vitamin, which is necessary for normal blood clotting. Rarely, the level is so low that the baby may be at risk for internal bleeding that can cause significant damage (a syndrome known as **hemorrhagic disease of the newborn**). A single injection of vitamin K prevents this problem.

- A **plastic clip** on the remnant of the umbilical cord. The clip will be removed before discharge or will be left in place and removed at the doctor's office during a follow-up visit.

A closer look: physical appearance and behavior of your newborn baby

Your newborn will not look like the smiling image you have seen beaming from a jar of baby food. (The "newborns" you see in movies and TV-show delivery rooms are nearly always a few weeks old.) She, in fact, will have a unique appearance immediately after birth. Be sure to take plenty of pictures—this phase will be very short.

Depending on the course of labor, her head may develop an oval shape known as **molding,** resulting from compression of the soft bones of the skull during the trip through the birth canal. This may be accentuated if her head is large and if labor was long. Pressure against her mother's pelvis may also produce some puffiness of the scalp. If blood vessels break under the skin, a collection of blood called a **cephalhematoma** will form, although it may not be obvious for a day or two after birth. Normally all these conditions resolve without difficulty or any specific treatment. However, a cephalhematoma may take months to disappear and may harden in the process.

MOLDING AFTER VAGINAL BIRTH

When you gently run a finger over the top of a newborn's head, you will feel the **fontanelles**—the two indentations where the bones of the skull have not yet joined. These so-called soft spots, the largest of which will be felt toward the front of the skull, are actually covered with a thick protective membrane. They are usually flat, but they may bulge slightly when the baby cries or pushes out a bowel movement. If you watch the hair on the scalp covering her anterior (or forward) fontanelle, you may even see some gentle pulsations.

A newborn may be nearly bald, be endowed with thick hair, or have an amount in between. Don't be too impressed (or upset) with the hair you see; color, texture, and amount will usually change to some degree during the first year. You may also notice some soft, thin, fuzzy hair called **lanugo** along the back and shoulders. Lanugo is more obvious in some babies than others, but if at first it looks conspicuous, you need not worry about your newborn growing a fur coat. This will disappear within several weeks.

Her face, and especially her eyelids, will be puffy. A closer look at the eyes usually reveals some shade of blue gray or blue brown in Caucasian babies, or brown in dark-skinned infants. Unless she is born with dark brown eyes, the final color of her eyes may not be known for at least six months. The newborn can focus on and follow a slowly moving object at close range and may be particularly attentive to a nearby face. Some of the most emotional moments in parenting occur when a new baby and a loving parent gaze into one another's eyes. Because her brain will need some time to assemble these visual images into meaningful patterns, your smile will not be returned for a while. (She will begin this direct socializing at four to six weeks of age.) You may notice some bright red spots on the white portion (the **sclera**) of one or both eyes. These are areas where tiny blood vessels ruptured during labor. They are not a sign of damage and will disappear on their own in several days.

CEPHALHEMATOMA

Periosteum

Accumulation of blood

Periosteum

Bone

A newborn has well-developed hearing and will appear startled (with sudden jerking movements) in response to a sudden loud noise. While her environment doesn't need to be hushed like a library, it is a good idea to keep the sounds around a new baby at a comfortable level. If a noise is loud enough to annoy you, it will certainly not be pleasant for her. Soothing voices, humming, singing, and soft music are definitely welcome in her world of new sounds.

THE MOMENT
ARRIVES
67

The newborn's nose is relatively flat, and her nasal passages are quite narrow. Since she breathes primarily through her nose rather than her mouth, you may often hear a noisy, snorting type of breathing, especially if she is excited. Furthermore, she may sneeze from time to time, in order to clear mucus out of her nose. This by itself does not mean that she has a cold. However, if you notice mucus draining from the nose, or if you are not sure whether the breathing sounds are normal, ask the doctor to check it. You may also hear your baby hiccuping, as she may have done inside the womb. This does not require any specific treatment.

The skin of the newborn is usually smooth, but in postmature (late arriving) babies it tends to appear more wrinkled. Some (or much) of her skin may be covered by vernix, especially in the creases of the arms and legs. This material, which helped protect the skin while she floated in amniotic fluid, will be much more noticeable if she is premature. Many babies have areas of dry, flaky skin, especially on the hands and feet. These do not need to be treated with lotion, but dryness will persist if a baby is bathed too frequently. She may have a dusky color for the first few minutes until her newly functioning lungs send blood with higher levels of oxygen through her circulation. As this process continues, she will "pink up," although hands and feet may maintain a bluish tinge for a longer period of time. Some babies develop a ruddy coloration or may appear flushed when they cry. In nonwhite infants, the dusky color will be more pronounced, but lips, tongue, and fingernails will appear pink once the blood is carrying more oxygen.

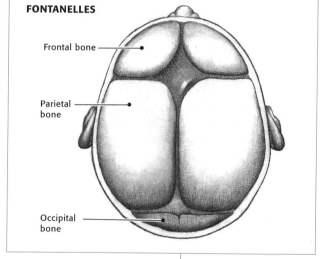

FONTANELLES

Frontal bone

Parietal bone

Occipital bone

When you have had time to inspect her from "stem to stern" in more detail, you may notice some unique markings on her skin. A small red **salmon patch** (some may call it a "stork bite") occurs on the nape of the neck in 50 percent of all infants. One or more of these may also appear on the eyelids or on the forehead between the eyebrows. Eyelid patches will disappear by three to six months of age, while those on the neck will fade but may last for years. Areas of increased pigmentation known as **mongolian spots** (see photo on page A29) are common on the back and buttocks of dark-skinned newborns, although they may be found in all racial and ethnic groups. These spots may even have a greenish or bluish tinge like a bruise and will disappear gradually over a few years' time. Tiny cysts known as **milia** (see photo on page A29) appear on the nose, cheeks, and forehead of many newborns. (The same type of cysts are nearly always seen on the roof of the mouth and have been dubbed **Epstein's pearls.**) Between one and two days of life, many newborns develop a number of red spots with a slightly raised pale center. This eruption, unique to newborns, is known as **erythema toxicum,** but it is not a sign of any illness or toxicity. Both milia and erythema toxicum disappear without treatment.

In baby boys the testicles will normally be present in the scrotum, having made a short but important journey from within the abdomen to the scrotal sac during the final weeks of pregnancy. When one (or both) has not moved into position at birth, the baby is said to have an undescended testicle, a condition that will be evident at the time of the first exam. This occurs in approximately 3 percent of full-term male infants and is more common in premature newborns. Fortunately about 80 percent of undescended testes will enter the scrotum by the end of the first year of life.

The scrotum of a baby boy may appear puffy or even swollen, a change that normally resolves within a few days. In about 10 percent of male infants, a collection of fluid called a **hydrocele** may persist for six to twelve months. A hydro-

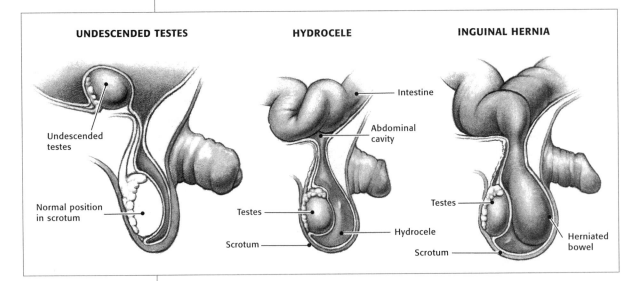

UNDESCENDED TESTES

Undescended testes

Normal position in scrotum

HYDROCELE

Intestine

Abdominal cavity

Testes

Hydrocele

Scrotum

INGUINAL HERNIA

Testes

Herniated bowel

Scrotum

cele normally resolves on its own, but sometimes it is accompanied by a swelling in either groin that often appears during crying or straining. This is a **hernia,** a sac that may contain a small portion of bowel. If you feel that your infant may have a hernia, have his doctor check this area during an office visit. If one is indeed present, it will need to be corrected surgically. Rarely, the contents of a hernia sac become stuck (or **incarcerated**) in the abdominal wall, restricting blood flow and causing increased swelling and pain. Emergency surgery may be needed to prevent damage to the bowel. If your infant's groin becomes markedly swollen or tender (provoking crying when touched), you should call the doctor immediately.

The baby girl's genital area—specifically the **labia** or "lips" at the opening of the vagina—may also appear swollen. In addition, a little mucus, or even a small amount of blood, may drain from the vagina during the first few days of life. Both are caused by sudden changes in hormone levels after birth and will disappear on their own. (For more information, see *genital care and concerns*, Reference.)

While a newborn is awake, his legs will tend to be flexed frog-style, with fists closed and drawn toward the face. In fact, he may accidentally scratch himself. Some newborn shirts enclose the hands to prevent scratching, but if necessary long nails can be carefully trimmed. A newborn's feet will tend to be turned inward and the legs bowed. During sleep, arms and legs will relax and unfold.

As you watch his arms and legs move around, don't expect any purposeful movements. A newborn cannot deliberately reach for anything, kick in a specific direction, or turn the head toward a sound. However, he does have a number of reflex behaviors that are already programmed into the nervous system at the time of birth. When you gently stroke one of his cheeks, he will turn his head in that direction. This is called the **rooting reflex,** and it helps the baby locate his food source. Place a nipple (or fingertip) in his mouth, and he will begin to suck on it. This **sucking reflex** will in turn set off the **swallowing reflex.** These nourishment-seeking behaviors are necessary for survival.

The **Moro** or **startle reflex,** on the other hand, is not. If a newborn is startled or if his head or body moves suddenly downward, his arms will quickly arch over his chest, as if trying to embrace the nearest solid object. The Moro reflex will disappear after the first few months of life. The **grasp reflex** is easy to demonstrate: Place your finger in a newborn's hand, and he will grasp it tightly for a short period of time. This reflex will disappear around the age of two months, but shortly thereafter he will be deliberately grabbing everything within reach.

GETTING FURTHER ACQUAINTED WITH YOUR BABY: THE BONDING PROCESS

Over the past several years, much has been written about the importance of bonding with a newborn, especially in an era when family structures and commitments have seemed so shaky. What exactly establishes the deep emotional ties with a child that will cause a parent to spend untold hours feeding, bathing, rocking, changing, and attending to the seemingly unending needs of a new baby? Is the bond locked into the genetic code of mothers and set loose by the flow of hormones during pregnancy? Is it biologically preexistent in fathers, or does it develop through watching role models in his family, as an extension of his love for his wife, or by an act of the will? Does it spring to life when the baby is first seen at the moment of birth? And what secures the attachment of a newborn to his mother and father?

Some have suggested that there is a critical time in the baby's first hours of life when a special connection will be made, especially between mother and child, that will affect the quality of their relationship for years to come. But this assumption raises a troubling question: What happens when mother or baby (or both) have special medical problems and cannot be together during those early hours or days? What if the new mother has a cesarean delivery and thus only momentary contact with her baby after birth, not to mention the potential distraction of pain during her recovery? What if the baby is born prematurely and must spend weeks in a high-tech hospital setting?

The answers hinge on the fact that human behavior is highly complex and not rigidly stereotyped or predictable like a computer program. As a result, bonding is a process that begins well before the baby is born and continues for years thereafter. It is certainly influenced by biology, hormones, and genetics. But it is also shaped by the upbringing of the new mother and father, their personal and spiritual values, their commitment to one another, and some everyday decisions they must make. Furthermore, human babies are not like newly hatched ducklings that attach themselves to the first object they see.

Throughout this book we will be looking at the process of building and nurturing the bonds between parents and children and suggesting practical ways to carry out this important assignment. Here are several specific ideas for during childbirth and the time immediately following it:

If at all possible, keep sedating medications to a minimum during the hour or two before delivery. It is indeed nice if both mother and baby are awake and alert when they meet for the first time. However, it is not a sign of moral failure to request pain relief during labor (especially in the later stages when discomfort can become much more intense). If you in fact receive medication that produces drowsiness immediately after birth, you will have plenty of opportunity to begin enjoying and interacting with your baby in very short order.

Stop, look, listen, and touch. Whether immediately after birth, a few hours later, or (better yet) many times over the next several months, take the time to sit quietly and enjoy your new family member. Study his features. Let him grip your finger. Smile and talk and sing to him. Count his toes. Marvel at the handiwork of God's creation and thank Him for loaning this child to you for a season.

Look into rooming in. Continuous contact with the baby in her room can give a new mother more practical and realistic preparation for the first few days at home. A pattern for nursing can be established, problems can be talked over with the nurses and other staff members, and (more important) there is more time for everyone to get acquainted with the new baby. Most hospitals today are flexible about these postdelivery arrangements, and some will assign a single nurse to attend both mother and child in a more coordinated fashion.

Some mothers prefer a variation on this theme, in which the baby spends most of the day rooming in and goes to the nursery during the late-night and early-morning hours. This can be particularly helpful for a mother who has had a long, exhausting labor. Occasionally when one or more small children are waiting at home and Mom already knows the basics of feeding and newborn care, she will actually prefer *not* to have full-time responsibility for the new baby, in order to get a time-out and rest for a day or two. However, this relatively quiet interlude should include a generous amount of one-on-one time with the newborn, since the other children will want some attention once everyone arrives home.

In one sense, it might seem easier to spend time forming attachments with the new baby by getting out of the hospital and returning home as soon as possible. But home is also where your responsibilities are. Someone needs to prepare meals, do laundry, feed the dog, maintain order, and tend to any other children in the family, all of which could compete with your attention to your newborn. Ideally, prior arrangements can be made with husband, relatives, friends, or live-in help to take on some of these daily assignments. Preparing for this phase of childbirth can be every bit as important as all the classes and exercises during the last months of pregnancy.

Feeding and bonding. There are numerous advantages to breast feeding, which will be elaborated on in detail in the next chapter. One that many mothers have described is a feeling of special closeness and nurturing that comes from a com-

Children have been loaned to us temporarily for the purpose of loving them and instilling a foundation of values on which their future lives will be built. We will be accountable through eternity for the way we discharge that responsibility.

THE STRONG-
WILLED CHILD

bination of skin-to-skin contact with the baby, the satisfaction of providing him nutrients and watching him grow as a result, and possibly the release of hormones triggered by nursing. For these and many other reasons, breast feeding is the form of nourishment preferred by medical authorities (at least for the first few months).

Because of the unique relationship between mother and baby during breast feeding, fathers may feel that they have less to offer, at least for the first several weeks. On the contrary, there are plenty of hours left in the day when the baby can be held, rocked, talked to, and generally enjoyed by his father. In addition, while Dad may be tired from hours of coaching, he will not have suffered the same physical exhaustion from the childbirth process that Mom did, and he should be given the opportunity to tend to their newborn child as often as possible.

If you cannot or choose not to breast-feed, you need not lose sleep wondering whether your bonding with your child is going to be impaired. For one thing, both parents can interact with the baby during bottle feeding. And remember that feeding is only one of many components of the attachment process.

What about bonding after a cesarean delivery?

The need to deliver the baby by cesarean section may arise suddenly, or it may be known for some time in advance. The reasons this surgery may be recommended and the techniques used to carry it out will not be detailed here. (They should be covered in detail in your childbirth classes.) However, in most cases there should be time to carry out an **epidural anesthetic,** which allows the mother to be awake and alert during the delivery. Furthermore, the father or coach is typically allowed to sit at the head of the operating table, near the anesthesiologist. Only a small minority are so-called "crash" surgeries, in which an emergency requires that a general anesthetic be given.

When your baby is delivered by cesarean section, as soon as her cord is clamped and cut, she will be taken to a warmer for a brief examination. (While this is going on, the obstetrician and an assistant will check your uterus and abdomen, then begin the process of closing the multiple layers of tissue between the uterus and skin.) If all appears satisfactory, the baby will be brought to the head of the table where you can look at and touch her briefly. Unfortunately, the logistics of a cesarean delivery make a prolonged time with her difficult, and any attempt to nurse immediately after birth is impossible. After the surgery, you will go to a recovery area, where you may have further contact with your baby.

The first minutes (or even hours) after a cesarean delivery are usually not what most couples hoped for as a postchildbirth bonding experience. But catching up can be done over the next few days. Here are a few suggestions to help the process go more smoothly.

Explore your pain-relief options. A cesarean is major surgery, and pain control will be necessary for the first few days. The traditional injections of meperidine (Demerol) or other narcotics every few hours can cause wide swings between drowsy relief and wide-awake discomfort, either of which can interfere with your interaction with your baby. If at all possible (and if available at your hospital), consider having the analgesic (pain-relieving) medication given through a **patient controlled analgesia (PCA)** pump. This is an intravenous system that delivers the medication at a rate you control, within specified limits. The effect is smoother, without extremes of pain or sleepiness. Some anesthesiologists will leave the small tube for the epidural block in place, allowing for very effective pain relief without any drowsiness at all.

Don't give up on nursing. Breast feeding after a cesarean delivery is challenging because the usual positions for holding the baby can be quite uncomfortable. But it can be done and is worth the effort (see chapter 4, page 121).

Try to recruit some extra help at home. The discomfort and fatigue that are so common in the wake of major surgery can turn the most basic tasks at home into major projects, leaving little energy (or enthusiasm) for the pleasantries of bonding. If your husband can't take extra time away from work to be home, consider having someone lend a hand for a few hours a day or even serve as a live-in to take care of some of the daily necessities. This person could be a relative (perhaps one of the baby's grandmothers), a volunteer from church, or someone specifically hired for this job. (Some insurance plans will help fund this assistance through a home-health agency.)

ADDITIONAL EVENTS BEFORE GOING HOME

The newborn examination. Sometime during the first twenty-four hours after birth, your baby's pediatrician or family physician will carry out a formal examination. (Of course if problems are apparent at birth, an evaluation will be carried out immediately.) Unless you go home within a few hours, a second checkout exam may be done before discharge. You should receive feedback from these checkups, especially if there are any problems. In addition, you may have questions about basic care and follow-up visits. You will get more out of these conversations if you write your questions down ahead of time.

Routine blood tests. Most states require that your baby be screened for certain congenital metabolic disorders that can cause major problems if not detected very early. These include **phenylketonuria (PKU),** which can cause mental retardation; **galactosemia,** which can lead to brain, liver, and kidney damage, as well as cataracts; **congenital hypothyroidism,** which, if untreated, can affect growth and intelligence; and **sickle-cell disease,** an abnormality of red blood cells that can cause a variety of problems in black children or children of Mediterranean ancestry.

Screening is usually done on a small sample of blood obtained from the baby's heel. Occasionally borderline abnormal results will require that the test be repeated, especially in a premature infant. If one of these uncommon metabolic problems is detected, your baby's physician will provide further information regarding the next steps to be taken.

Circumcision. Circumcision is the removal of the foreskin, the half inch of skin that covers the head of the infant's penis. It has been a religious and cultural tradition in many parts of the world for thousands of years and was the norm for newborn boys a generation ago. More recently, some consumer groups and professional organizations have questioned the wisdom of routine circumcision.

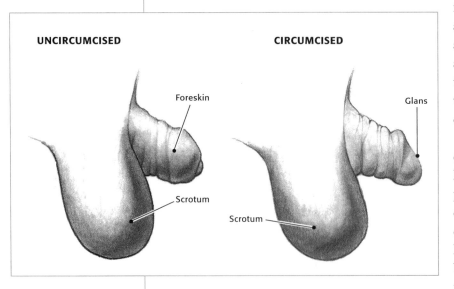

UNCIRCUMCISED   CIRCUMCISED

Foreskin

Glans

Scrotum

Scrotum

The advantages of circumcision are primarily hygienic. The circumcised penis is easier to keep clean, whereas uncircumcised boys and men must learn to retract (gently pull back) the foreskin to clean the head of the penis. Otherwise, the accumulation of debris and bacteria may lead to an inflammation known as **balanitis.** Some evidence suggests that uncircumcised children are at higher risk for infections of the urinary tract. In older men, cancer of the penis (a relatively rare disease) occurs almost exclusively in the uncircumcised.

On the other hand, circumcision is a minor surgery and thus carries with it a very slight risk of complications, specifically moderate bleeding, infection, or even injury to the penis. If there is a family history of bleeding problems, the procedure should not be done until the baby's clotting status has been checked. Babies who have not had a vitamin K injection (sometimes the case when the baby was born at home) tend to bleed more freely after the procedure. (Interestingly, the biblical mandate for circumcision of male babies in the nation of Israel called for the procedure to be done on the eighth day—which, prior to the use of vitamin K, was precisely the time clotting-factor levels would peak, thus reducing the risk of bleeding.)

Typically, circumcision is done by the baby's pediatrician or family doctor, or by Mom's obstetrician, before the baby leaves the hospital, although it can be arranged anytime during the first few weeks. It should not be done if there is any question about the newborn's stability, especially during the first twenty-four hours. Some physicians use a local anesthetic to relieve pain, although the baby will normally stop crying immediately after the procedure is finished. Circumcision is generally carried out when the infant's stomach is empty, but he can be nursed immediately afterwards. A small dressing will be applied to prevent bleeding, and it will fall off on its own within a day or two. The head of the penis will appear somewhat raw, and a small amount of petroleum jelly will keep it from sticking to the inner surface of his diaper. If the circumcision has been done with a device called a Plastibell, the small plastic bell will fall off on its own in about three or four days, leaving a healed surface.

If a baby boy is not circumcised, the foreskin should be left alone until it can be retracted easily, which may occur anytime before puberty. Occasionally problems with the foreskin develop later in life, and in some cases a circumcision becomes a medical necessity for an older child or adult.

Whether or not to have a baby boy circumcised is a straightforward decision for some families and a quandary for others. Despite some potential health advantages, there is no medical consensus specifically supporting or condemning routine infant circumcision. For many families, religious or other traditions are the main considerations. In others, the father or an older brother has been circumcised, and the parents want everyone to look alike. Foreskin uniformity in the family, however, is not really necessary for a child's emotional well-being.

If you are uncertain about your decision, take some time to discuss the pros and cons with the baby's physician and (assuming you are married) with your spouse. The bottom line is that you can and should be comfortable with your decision.

WHEN DOES THE BABY GO HOME?

After a hospital birth, it is not uncommon for mother and baby to return home in one or two days following a vaginal delivery and three or four days after a cesarean. Obviously this will change if mother or baby needs further care. If the newborn is premature or develops an unexpected problem that requires a longer stay, most hospitals are prepared to offer parents as much ongoing contact with the baby as possible.

Whether after a few hours, a day or two, or an extended stay, the gathering together of mother, father, baby, other family members, and your assorted new baby gear (including flowers, balloons, gifts, and other items that may have suddenly appeared after the delivery) for the trip home is a true graduation, a family commencement. Savor the moment and make sure someone captures it in pictures or on video. You are about to begin the next great adventure in parenting.

Sexually Transmitted Diseases (STDs): Their Impact on You and Your Unborn Child

Syphilis is caused by a spiral-shaped organism known as a **spirochete,** which easily passes from mother to baby during pregnancy and can cause serious problems in many of the baby's organs or even stillbirth. Fortunately, the infection can be detected by a blood test, which is normally obtained as part of the first prenatal visit. If the test is positive, additional tests are necessary to confirm the diagnosis. If a woman becomes infected later in her pregnancy, however, the diagnosis might be missed, with disastrous consequences for the baby. Many of the problems caused by syphilis can be avoided if this infection is promptly diagnosed and treated (usually with penicillin).

Gonorrhea is a bacterial infection that continues to infect more than one million Americans every year. A pregnant woman with an active infection can transmit it to her baby during childbirth. The eyes of the newborn are extremely sensitive to this bacterium, and severe damage or even blindness can result if they become infected. For this reason antibiotic eye ointment or drops (required by state law) are given to every newborn, regardless of the mother's history. Gonorrhea prior to or during pregnancy can be treated with antibiotics; the type of antibiotic, dose, and length of treatment will depend on the extent and severity of the infection.

Chlamydia is an organism that has risen from relative obscurity in the 1970s to become the most common bacterial STD in the United States. As with gonorrhea, a chlamydia-infected woman may pass the organism to her baby during delivery. Not only may the baby's eyes become infected, but a stubborn pneumonia can also develop. When an infection with chlamydia is diagnosed, treatment with antibiotics can and should be carried out.

Herpes simplex virus (HSV) is notorious for a property it shares with a number of other organisms: Once a person is infected, HSV remains for life. HSV type 1 typically causes eruptions known as cold sores or fever blisters around the mouth or nose, although it can also cause genital infections through oral-genital contact (see photo on page A28).

A baby born to a mother with HSV could be infected during vaginal delivery if there is a herpes outbreak on the mother's genital area. The risk of transfer is much higher (50 percent) if this is the mother's first outbreak rather than a recurrence (3–5 percent). For the newborn, an HSV infection can be disastrous. About one-third of infected infants will have surface (skin and mucous membrane) involvement only. In the other two-thirds, the virus spreads throughout the body and central nervous system, with a strong likelihood of major consequences including blindness, seizures, mental retardation, and death.

If you have a history of genital herpes, it is important to inform your physician, and both of you should be watchful for any recurrences. If there is an outbreak within a week before birth, your physician will probably recommend a cesarean delivery to minimize the risk of contact between virus and newborn. While cold sores around the mouth are less likely to cause trouble, you should be cautious if one is present when you give birth. You should avoid touching your mouth, wash your hands frequently, and wear a surgical mask over your mouth when handling your baby until the sore heals. (Be sure to check with your doctor to confirm that you are dealing with an HSV outbreak.)

Genital warts are caused by the **human papilloma virus (HPV).** This infection is extremely common among sexually active individuals. HPV causes soft, wart-like growths in the genital area. During pregnancy these may grow dramatically, and surgery, cautery, or laser treatment may be needed to remove them. Fortunately HPV transmission from mother to newborn during delivery appears to be extremely uncommon; however, if it does occur, it causes recurrent growths on the vocal cords. Of greater concern is the association of HPV with cancer of the mother's cervix (the opening of the uterus). Any woman who has ever had one or more genital warts or has ever had sexual intercourse should have regular Pap smears to detect early changes that might be caused by HPV infection in the cervix, which can be treated before developing into a cancer.

Bacterial vaginosis is an overgrowth of bacteria in the vagina that can be (but is not always) sexually transmitted. Because this condition can increase the risk of premature rupture of membranes, screening for it may be performed during the second half of pregnancy.

Acquired immune deficiency syndrome (AIDS) is caused by the **human immunodeficiency virus (HIV).** The vast majority of HIV infections are transmitted during sexual contact, through contaminated needles and syringes used during the injection of illegal drugs, or by transfer from infected mother to baby during pregnancy. (Transmission of HIV during blood transfusions is now extremely rare.) A small number of cases in infants have been attributed to nursing from an infected mother.

After gaining access to the body, HIV multiplies quietly within the immune system over a period of many months or years, gradually destroying its ability to deal with invading microorganisms. The eventual result is full-blown AIDS, in which a person becomes vulnerable to a variety of devastating infections and some forms of cancer. Although this condition has been almost universally fatal, the development of new drug regimens may extend the life span and improve the quality of life for those with this disease, while researchers continue to seek a cure. Pregnancy does not increase the progression of HIV infection to AIDS but can worsen the disease in a woman who is already severely ill.

A pregnant woman infected with HIV has a 25 to 35 percent risk of transmitting the virus to her baby. If she has progressed to active AIDS, the risk can be as high as 60 to 70 percent. About one in five infected newborns will develop AIDS-related illness by one year of age and die from overwhelming infection before another year passes. The rest develop AIDS later in childhood, with the risk increasing by 8 percent each year. (For a more detailed look at the child with HIV/AIDS, see *HIV infection/AIDS,* Reference 699.)

Screening tests for HIV detect a person's antibody response to the virus and not the virus itself. If such screening indicates that one has the HIV virus (is HIV positive), further investigation will be necessary to determine the status of the infection and guide treatment decisions. It is strongly recommended that testing for HIV be carried out as part of routine prenatal screening for the following reasons:

- ◆ A woman can become infected with HIV even if she has not been involved in a high-risk lifestyle. A single sexual encounter with an infected individual or a onetime experiment with intravenous drugs can transmit the virus.

◆ The signs and symptoms of HIV/AIDS may not appear for years after the initial transmission, so a woman may have no idea that she is infected.

◆ Medical treatment of an HIV-infected pregnant woman may decrease her odds of transmitting the virus to her baby to less than 10 percent.

Hepatitis B is a viral infection of the liver that is transmitted through the same mechanisms as HIV. The majority of cases resolve completely following a flulike illness with fever, nausea, and **jaundice** (a yellow discoloration of skin). However, about 5 percent develop a chronic infection that can lead to **cirrhosis** (scarring) or even cancer of the liver. Furthermore, chronic carriers—of which there are about one million in the United States—can transmit the virus to sexual partners or from mother to baby during pregnancy or delivery. Most babies who are infected at birth become chronic carriers as well and risk developing long-term complications.

A blood test for hepatitis B surface antigen should be a part of routine prenatal screening. If it is positive, further testing can determine if a woman has a new infection, an old infection that has resolved, or a chronic infection. Depending on the results, appropriate plans can be made to help protect the newborn with an antibody injection if needed, along with the routine hepatitis B vaccine normally given shortly after birth.

A final word on STDs

Sexually transmitted diseases can have lifelong and life-threatening consequences both for parents and their children. Yet they are definitely preventable for those who are willing to commit to a "no-risk" sexual lifestyle. In a best-case scenario, this means that a man and a woman abstain from sexual relations until marriage and then remain strictly monogamous in a mutually exclusive relationship. Medically, this eliminates a significant number of risks, and greatly enhances the stability of the environment for raising children.

The threat of HIV/AIDS has sparked an ongoing national campaign for safe sex, which has placed a heavy emphasis on condom use to prevent the spread of STDs. But while condoms offer some degree of protection some of the time, they are far from foolproof. Condom failure rates for preventing pregnancy are widely reported to be 10 percent or higher per year, meaning that at least one out of ten sexually active women using condoms as their only form of birth control will be pregnant within a year. But a woman can become pregnant only two or three days per month, while STDs can be transmitted *every day*. Furthermore, some

STDs, such as syphilis, herpes simplex, and human papilloma virus (HPV) infection, can occur on areas of the genitals that are not covered by condoms. Most authorities, even those who strongly advocate condom use, consider condoms to offer little, if any, protection against infection with HPV. If you are unmarried, it would be wise to remain abstinent until you enter a permanent, monogamous relationship.

If you have had one or more sexual partners prior to marriage, you should discuss STD screening with your physician. This is especially important if you are pregnant, because so many STDs have more serious consequences for the baby if they are acquired during pregnancy. In addition, it is important for a pregnant woman to be both candid and thorough in reviewing her sexual history—including any prior symptoms of vaginal discharge, pelvic discomfort, or surface changes in the genital area—with her physician, because important screening tests may be recommended based on this information.

The Adopted Child

Approximately fifty thousand native-born and many more foreign-born children are adopted every year in the United States. Each of these adoptions represents a unique set of circumstances in which the paths of adults and children who (with rare exception) do not share biological ties converge. Adopting a child can fulfill a couple's most cherished dreams and desires while meeting a child's deepest needs for love and stability. But as honorable, compassionate, and joyous as this process might be, it is also rarely accomplished without considerable effort, significant (but surmountable) challenges, and occasional heartaches.

Because this book is primarily concerned with rearing children, most of the issues and details of events prior to bringing an adopted child home will not be discussed here. Concerns related to adoption agencies, attorneys, regulations, foreign governments, finances, paperwork, the home study,[1] and, above all, the endless patience often required of adoptive parents-to-be are all very important but ably covered in a variety of other books and materials. One topic that *will* be addressed is the nature of the relationship between the adoptive parents and the birth parents[2] (especially the mother), assuming that one or both of the birth parents are involved in the adoption process, since their interactions can have a significant impact on the child's upbringing.

CLOSED AND OPEN ADOPTIONS

When a pregnant woman decides that she is going to release her baby for adoption, two basic scenarios may occur, each having many variations. In what is called a **closed adoption,** the birth mother has very little (if any) contact with her infant immediately after delivery, and no contact with the adoptive parents. Confidentiality regarding the parties involved in the adoption prevents future interactions between them. Closed adoptions were the norm in previous generations (and remain so in Canada) and are still carried out in significant numbers in the United States. Those who favor this approach feel that it brings about more timely and effective closure for all concerned, allowing the birth mother to move on with her life and the adoptive parents to focus their attention exclusively on the baby. Others raise concerns that closed adoption may leave the birth mother with a significant emotional crater to fill, as she can only imagine what her child's life will be like during the ensuing months and years. Also, unless specific arrangements have been made (as is done in Canada and in some adoption agencies in the United States through a registry system), the child of a closed adoption would be unable to fill an important gap in his own personal history if he should desire to meet his birth mother when he is an older adolescent or adult.

In recent decades the partially or completely **open adoption** has become more common. This means that there is some degree of interaction between the birth mother or both birth parents and the adoptive family. In many cases, the birth mother actually selects who will rear her child from a number of potential candidates presented by an adoption agency. The couple may then become involved with the birth mother through an extended period of her pregnancy, and one or both adoptive parents might even attend the birth of the baby. The birth mother or both birth parents may relinquish the baby directly to the adoptive parents at the hospital or shortly after the birth in a physical gesture of release. Such a relationship can be fulfilling for all concerned, and it will also offer the adoptive parents more knowledge of the baby's prenatal care and family health history. But it is not without potential pitfalls. Childbirth and adoption are emotionally charged events, and open adoption raises the possibility for complications in both the immediate and distant future. If you are going to be involved in an open adoption, consider the following:

The relationship between the adoptive parents and the birth mother, and everyone's expectations for the future, should be carefully considered and discussed before the baby is born.

For example, if the prospective parents offer a generous amount of attention and affection (and even material goods within the legal limits set by the state) to the birth mother prior to the delivery, they might satisfy some deep needs in the birth mother's life. But once the baby arrives, the parents' attention quite understandably shifts dramatically to the infant. The birth mother may then feel like a nonentity, someone who was valued only because she was carrying the prized baby inside her. Depression, bitterness, even second thoughts about the adoption decision could result from this turn of events. If the adoptive parents do not want or intend to have an ongoing relationship with the birth mother after the birth, they should be careful about the signals they send beforehand.

It is very important that expectations be clarified regarding the amount of contact between mother and adoptive family once the baby is born. The birth mother may want to visit her baby, which can help her develop a clear mental picture of the setting in which her child will be brought up. But ongoing visits might also become uncomfortable for the adoptive parents if they begin to feel that they are "on trial" when the birth mother is present. These visits can also be emotionally difficult for the birth mother, who sees her baby relating to another woman as "Mommy."

What about long-term contact between the birth mother and the adoptive family? In some cases regular visitation continues for years, but it is more common for interaction to be limited to pictures and an update from the adoptive parents once or twice a year. For many birth mothers, the need for closure leads them to a decision to walk away both physically and emotionally, bringing ongoing contact with their child to an end. Many experts in this field argue that long-term contact can be unhealthy for the birth mother because it could prevent her from moving forward with her life. Furthermore, the birth mother's continued involvement in her child's life might become disruptive if she interferes with decisions the adoptive parents must make on a day-to-day basis. Everyone must have a clear understanding that the adoptive parents *are* the parents and that they have the final say in the way the child is brought up. Honest conversation and counseling will help clarify expectations and minimize the risk of conflict.

Everyone involved in an adoption must understand that the birth mother will undergo a significant grieving process that normally lasts many months, even under the best of circumstances.

It is very important for the birth mother to receive competent and compassionate counseling before—but especially after—the birth, to work through the grieving and releasing process. It is not enough for an agency or an attorney to say that counseling is available "if she needs it" and then leave it up to the birth mother to initiate the process. Adoptive parents would be wise to see to it that counseling takes place and to cover its cost if necessary. Not only does this ensure that the birth mother's emotional needs are taken seriously, but it also reduces the likelihood of a reversal—a heart-wrenching event in which the birth mother decides after a few weeks or months that she wants to keep her baby after all. All too often the seeds of a reversal are sown when the normal grieving process leads the birth mother to think that the adoption choice was a mistake.

All of these concerns, especially the need for counseling before and after the baby's birth, most certainly apply to the biological father also, assuming that he remains involved and is engaged in the ongoing decision making.

Sometimes the adoption process takes place much more rapidly, and adoptive parents may find themselves meeting a birth mother or both birth parents for the first time at the time of birth. While there might not be much opportunity for building a relationship on such short notice, the exploration of everyone's expectations should still take place, even if in a somewhat condensed time frame.

What If an Adoption Falls Through or Is Reversed?

Two of the most emotionally charged events related to the adoption process are the "failed placement" (the placement that has been arranged with considerable effort, but then falls through for whatever reason) and the reversal (the baby has actually arrived in the adoptive parents' home for several days, or even a few months, only to be taken away when one or both biological parents have a change of heart before their legal rights to the baby have been terminated). Both of these situations (especially the reversal) can be extraordinarily difficult and will generate virtually the same full force of grief that would occur with the loss of any child. *The severity of the loss must be acknowledged, and the need for grieving not ignored.* (Although some may try to lessen your pain by saying or implying, "This wasn't really your child, after all," your loss is real, and lack of biological ties has nothing to do with it.) Counseling, whether individually or through a support group, can be very helpful, especially when the question of trying to arrange another adoption is to be broached.

Common Concerns of Adoptive Parents

Parents who are considering adopting a baby or a child often have a number of qualms and concerns, most of which are quite normal (and similar to those of parents anticipating caring for their own new baby).

Will I be able to love this child as if he were my own flesh and blood (especially if I already have one or more biological children)? The process of adding children to any family raises similar questions ("Is there enough love in me for this new baby on the way?"). But God is able to open a parent's heart to "make room" for the newcomer. After a very short while it becomes virtually impossible to imagine life in the family without him.

Will I be able to treat each child in my family the same way, especially if I have both biological and adopted children? Actually, no two children in any family can be treated in exactly the same way because each child is a unique creation. Remember that no child is perfect, that all children will give you grief at some point, and that one child will probably cause more overall difficulty than another. The issue isn't treating everyone exactly the same way, but rather being firmly committed to each child's well-being and surrounding each one with both unconditional love and appropriate limits.

Can I discipline a child who has been abused or abandoned? Absolutely—in fact, not doing so is a worse form of abandonment. Discipline does not merely consist of negative consequences or punishment imposed for misbehavior; it encompasses the entire process of building a child's character and imposing appropriate limits. (See Special Concerns, page 289.)

Am I up for this? Doubts and feelings of inadequacy about parenting are normal. (Even if you believe that you have child rearing completely figured out, the next bundle of joy God sends will most likely change that opinion.) However, if you feel major persistent qualms about your ability to parent, by all means spend time with a qualified counselor to sort through your specific concerns.

Special Issues in Caring for Adopted Children

The most basic needs of an adopted child are the same as those of any other child: physical, emotional, and spiritual nurturing in an environment where love, stability, and appropriate limits are clearly evident. Nearly all of what you will read in this book or other resources about parenting will apply to your adopted child. However, several specific concerns that may arise during or after the adoption process are worth a brief review.

Unity of purpose on the home front

While in nearly every case the prospective parents share equally the desire to adopt a child, occasionally one may be less enthusiastic about this undertaking than the other. It is unwise for one person to merely "go along" with an adoption primarily to please one's spouse. The commitment of both parents to the adopted child should be as strong as if he were biologically their own.

What if there are one or more other siblings at home at the time of the adoption? Ideally, they should be prepared in the same manner they would be if Mom were expecting a new baby. Tell them the facts in basic language they can understand and describe the adoption in a positive light. There will be a new brother or sister who will be sharing in the love of the family and who will be treated with the same love and respect that everyone at home receives. If the adopted child has any special problems or will be of different racial or ethnic origin, discuss this in a matter-of-fact way. It should go without saying that parents in such situations will need to be both fair and abundantly affectionate to all the children, striving to see that no one feels left out or is treated with favoritism—just as in any family where more than one child is present.

Nursing an adopted baby

Believe it or not, it is not necessary for a woman to bear an infant in order to nurse one. A woman who would like to breast-feed an adopted baby may be able to produce her own milk through a combination of medication that stimulates lactation and repeated stimulation of her breasts, either by using a pump prior to the adoption or allowing the baby to nurse after he arrives.

This process is usually more successful with infants younger than eight weeks of age, although it can also be attempted with an older baby. While nursing an adopted child can yield many of the benefits that breast feeding affords to infants and mothers (see chapter 4, page 122), it will also require considerable commitment and effort. Furthermore, it is very likely that the adoptive mother's production of milk will be less than adequate to meet all of the growing baby's nutritional needs. Supplementation with formula will thus be necessary in such cases. Needless to say, plans to nurse an adopted baby should be discussed in advance with a knowledgeable physician or lactation consultant.

Adopting an older baby or child

Parents of newborns are normally concerned about the process of bonding with their new baby, often wondering if even brief periods of separation will interfere with it. But what if you are going to begin parenting a baby who has lived with someone else for several weeks, months, or years—perhaps one who cannot even understand your language?

In such circumstances you cannot necessarily expect an instantaneous bonding experience or a picture-perfect first meeting where a child throws his arms around your neck in a display of unrestrained gratitude. In fact, in some cases the initial contact will be strained. A baby might be frightened, fussy, fidgety—or oddly quiet, especially if he has been raised in an environment where crying yielded little response from his adult caretakers. An older child who has not had a stable environment or who has been ignored or mistreated in the past might be reserved or even sullen. Any parent adopting such a child should be aware that neglect, trauma, or abuse early in that child's life may have resulted in long-term or even permanent developmental and relational problems. Children who are not nurtured and stimulated as infants sometimes have great difficulty ever attaching to other people, no matter how much those people express love and affection for them. In addition, a baby or child arriving from a foreign country may be tired, poorly nourished, and literally overloaded by the entire experience. Whether coming from across town or halfway around the world, he may actually show signs of grieving for whatever familiar faces and environment he has left behind.

Getting acquainted with, and then getting close to, an older adopted child will take time and a fair amount of patience. Obviously it is helpful if information about the child's background and previous experiences is available. If you have not yet had a child, you would be wise to read about the normal developmental milestones for the age of the child you will be adopting. In general, voices that are calm and reassuring, touch that is soft and soothing, and sensitivity to the cues given by the child will go a long way toward a harmonious adjustment. If all your best efforts to form a mutually satisfying attachment seem to be a resounding failure, don't hesitate to seek help from your child's physician, the adoption agency (assuming that one was involved), or a counselor, preferably one who has experience with adoptive parents and children.

Adopting a child with a physical, mental, or emotional handicap

A special-needs child can be a great blessing to a family, but it is important to have a clear understanding of problems that are likely to arise during his life. (In some cases a handicap may require special education and care well into the child's adulthood.) Support services, including other parents who have raised a child with similar problems, should be consulted both before and after the adoption.

Medical concerns

You should obtain as much information as possible about the medical history of the baby or child you are planning to adopt. Details of the family history, the mother's pregnancy and delivery, congenital problems, illnesses, and immunizations are helpful, if available. However, in some cases you may not even be certain of your child's birth date, and some evaluation based on physical and behavioral characteristics will be necessary. (This may not be easy if the child has been malnourished or raised in a deprived setting that has delayed his growth and developmental milestones.)

If your adopted child appears to be well, you might want to wait for several days (or even a few weeks) before taking him for a medical evaluation, so that he can become comfortable with you before entering the unfamiliar realm of the doctor's office. A child from a foreign country may require a more extensive examination soon after arrival—even if he has been examined before leaving his country of origin—because of the possibility that he might have acquired one or more infections (such as tuberculosis, hepatitis B, or intestinal parasites) that are more common in other areas of the world, or conditions (such as particular forms of anemia) seen in certain racial and ethnic groups. If the child appears ill upon arrival, he should be evaluated as soon as possible.

Cross-cultural and cross-racial adoptions

From an infant's standpoint, his ethnic background is not initially a major source of concern, although the adoptive parents might need to deal with occasional inappropriate reactions such as "Why would you adopt a child of a different race?" As the child becomes older, however, you will need to deal with questions raised by differences in appearance within the family. Most can be handled during the ongoing process of talking to him about his adoption (see next section). Exploring your child's racial or ethnic heritage as a means of enhancing his overall understanding of his "story" would be beneficial to both you and your child. Your child should be encouraged to develop and maintain friendships within his minority community. This will make him more comfortable moving in and out of his own subculture. Keep in mind, though, that your child's basic sense of identity should focus primarily on qualities of character and bonds of love that have been established in your family over a period of years.

TALKING TO A CHILD ABOUT HIS ADOPTION

In bygone generations it was common not to reveal to a child his status as an adopted child, apparently out of fear that this would cause him undue pain or alienation. Unfortunately, this approach usually had the opposite effect. Very often it was during adolescence—a time already full of great upheaval, self-doubt, and issues of an emerging identity—that he would learn of his adoption, often by accident (such as a relative's careless slip of the tongue). And so, with all the other concerns of this age-group already in full swing, he would now have to contend with harrowing questions such as "Why did my mother abandon me?" and "What else don't I know about my family?"

Just as children should be given information about sexuality on a need-to-know basis that is age appropriate, so should the adopted child's unique question "Where did I come from?" be met with answers that are straightforward, tactful, and truthful. Ideally, a child should not grow up remembering a time when he did not know that Mom and Dad were not his biological parents. *The events leading to his adoption should be described as a unique and positive story.* The decision of his birth mother very often can be understood as one born out of love and concern rather than an act of abandonment. But even if the child was abandoned by his birth mother, he can be told, quite truthfully, that *God did not abandon him and never will.* Whatever the circumstances might have been, a child can be led to understand that God not only "knit him together in his mother's womb" but also entrusted him to his adoptive parents, who are continually joyful that he has become an important member of their family.

Some adoptive families put together a scrapbook that tells the child's story. This might include pictures of the birth mother, if available, and if possible a note from her to the child explaining what she did, her feelings about him, how happy she was about the family that was adopting him, and so forth. Baby pictures, documents, a map of his country of origin if he came from a foreign land, and any other such memorabilia are of great interest to children, who will look through them over and over as they grow up.

What if an older child or teenager expresses a desire to meet one or both of his birth parents? These feelings are not unusual or inappropriate, and in most cases they should not be squelched.[3] In many cases, meeting one or both biological parents could take some of the mystery out of his origins and identity and also help him appreciate his adoptive parents. If there have been ongoing contact and friendly relationships over the years, a meeting may not be terribly difficult, either logistically or emotionally. However, if contact has been lost, this will be difficult to arrange without a fair amount of detective work. If you know that a birth parent is unstable or involved in a lifestyle you disapprove of, it might be prudent to forestall such a meeting until the child is mature enough to deal with it. This may not occur until he is a young adult.

NOTES
1. A home study is a detailed assessment of the prospective parents and their home, required by all adoption agencies in an effort to ensure that an adopted child will be brought up in a safe and nurturing environment.
2. Throughout this section the term *birth mother* will be used to designate the woman who is giving birth to the child. *Birth parents* refers to both the birth mother and the biological father.
3. An exception would be a situation in which an adopted teenager who is struggling against parental ground rules believes that "things would be better if I could be with my *real* mom." A grass-is-greener fantasy should not be the primary motivation for contacting a birth parent, and this process should not move forward until the issues at home have been resolved.

Birth Defects and Prenatal Testing

Every parent-to-be anticipates the arrival of a new son or daughter with a strong sense of anticipation and excitement but also with a certain level of concern in the back of his or her mind: *What if there is something wrong with my baby?* For some, a known family risk of a particular disease or a child already born with a birth defect usually brings this concern to the forefront of prenatal considerations: *How can we find out ahead of time whether or not this baby will be normal?*

WHAT ARE BIRTH DEFECTS?

Birth defects, also called **congenital disorders,** are abnormalities that are present at birth, whether or not they are diagnosed at that time. According to the March of Dimes Birth Defects Foundation, some type of birth defect is present in one out of every twenty-eight newborns. More than three thousand specific birth defects have been identified, ranging from conditions that are barely noticeable to some that are catastrophic. (Birth defects are the most common cause of infant death in the United States, claiming more than eight thousand lives every year.[1]) These disorders sometimes involve visible changes in one or several parts of the body, or they can affect the baby on a less visible metabolic or microscopic level.

WHAT CAUSES BIRTH DEFECTS?

While the underlying causes of many types of birth defects are understood, *in roughly two out of three cases the specific reason is unknown* and thus assumed to be the result of a complex interaction of genetic and nongenetic factors during the intricate process of the baby's development within the womb. Birth defects in which a specific cause can be identified fall into the following categories:

Genetic abnormalities

Genetic abnormalities, which arise directly from the transmission of genetic information from one generation to the next, account for 20 to 25 percent of all birth defects. In what is truly a marvel of engineering, all of the information necessary to form and maintain a human being is coded on long strands of the spiral molecule known as **deoxyribonucleic acid,** or **DNA.** An extended segment of DNA that serves a specific function (such as providing the blueprint for a certain protein) is called a **gene,** and an estimated fifty to one hundred thousand of these genes govern the physical attributes of each individual. Rather than being randomly dispersed throughout the cells whose functions it governs, DNA is packed into forty-six dense bodies known as **chromosomes,** all of which easily fit within the nucleus of a cell. Our forty-six chromosomes consist of twenty-three pairs, of which twenty-two are known as nonsex or **autosomal,** while one pair consists of the sex chromosomes designated X and Y.

Each of our 60 trillion cells contains *all* of our genetic code, with the exception of egg and sperm cells, which contain only a single set of twenty-three chromosomes. At the time of conception, twenty-three chromosomes from the mother's egg and twenty-three from the father's sperm combine to begin a new human being. These include an X chromosome contributed by the egg, and either an X or a Y chromosome from the sperm. If the final product contains two X chromosomes, the baby will be a girl, while an XY combination of chromosomes will result in a boy.

While this extraordinarily complex activity normally proceeds without mishap, at times it does not function as originally designed. This might result in profound abnormalities in the number or structure of the chromosomes, such that the fertilized egg may fail to divide properly, may not implant within the mother's uterus, or may not develop beyond a very early stage. In such cases a woman will have an early miscarriage or the new life will end without her ever being aware that it had started. However, a number of genetic abnormalities do not end this way, and the pregnancy may continue to term. There are two main types of genetic abnormalities:

Single-gene abnormalities involve a defect in a particular strand of DNA, which in turn causes a specific malfunction within the body. These abnormalities are further subdivided into three categories: dominant, recessive, and X-linked. These variations arise from the fact that genes are paired—that is, the genes on a chromosome inherited from the mother have a corresponding gene on the chromosome provided by the father. The effect of one gene may override the other, or they might make an equal contribution to a particular trait.

A **dominant genetic disorder** (for example, Huntington's-chorea) needs only one gene (which can come from either parent) to be manifested. If one parent is affected, there is a 50 percent chance that his or her child (of either gender) will have the same abnormality. Some dominant disorders run in families, while others result from a mutation that occurred in an individual egg or sperm.

A **recessive genetic disorder** (for example, cystic fibrosis) is one that will occur only when an abnormal gene that causes it is contributed by both parents. A child who receives an abnormal recessive gene from only one parent usually will not manifest that defect, although he or she will be a *carrier* of the disorder. If both parents of a child are carriers of a recessive disorder, the child has a 50 percent chance of being a carrier, a 25 percent chance of having two normal genes, and a 25 percent chance of being affected. Recessive genetic defects often cluster in particular racial, ethnic, or geographic groups.

X-linked genetic disorders (for example, hemophilia) are carried only on the *X* chromosome and may be dominant or recessive, although the latter are more common. Females with an abnormal X-linked gene usually are not affected by the problem because they typically have a normal gene on their other *X* chromosome, which will override the abnormal gene.

GENETIC MAPPING

Dominant Disorders
D Dominant gene (altered)
d Recessive gene (normal)

Normal   Affected

Affected   Normal   Affected   Normal

Recessive Disorders
R Dominant gene (normal)
r Recessive gene (altered)

Unaffected   Unaffected
Carrier   Carrier

Normal   Unaffected   Unaffected   Affected
              Carrier   Carrier

X-Linked Recessive
X X Chromosome (normal)
X X Chromosome (recessive)
Y Y Chromosome (normal)

Unaffected   Normal
Carrier Mother   Father

Normal   Normal   Carrier   Affected
Daughter   Son   Daughter   Son

Chromosomal abnormalities involve significantly larger amounts of genetic material than do single-gene defects. Either part or all of a chromosome may be missing or duplicated. Often the results are not compatible with development of the fetus within the womb, and a miscarriage results. (It is estimated that half of all miscarriages that occur during the first three months of pregnancy are caused by chromosomal abnormalities.) The abnormality may be passed on from one or the other parent or may occur during the development of egg or sperm.

The risk of a child having a chromosomal abnormality increases steadily with the age of his mother. The risk of a twenty-five-year-old woman having a baby with Down syndrome—the most common disorder of this type—is 1 in 1,250, and the risk for all significant chromosomal disorders is 1 in 476. At age thirty-five, the numbers are 1 in 378 for Down syndrome and 1 in 192 for all chromosomal disorders. At age forty-five, those numbers drop to 1 in 30 and 1 in 21 respectively.[2]

Infections

Infections that are passed from mother to baby prior to birth account for about 3 to 5 percent of all birth defects and are discussed in detail in chapter 1.

Medical problems in the mother, such as diabetes, high blood pressure, and heart disease, can affect the development of the baby growing within her. Detecting and managing any maternal conditions are key factors of prenatal care and a major reason regular visits with a qualified physician are so important during pregnancy.

Substances that pass from mother to baby

While the uterus, placenta, and amniotic fluid are usually very effective in providing a safe environment for the growing baby before birth, certain chemical compounds that enter the mother's bloodstream are capable of causing harm to her preborn child. The degree of damage can vary enormously depending upon the amount of the substance involved and the stage(s) of development at which the exposure to the unborn child takes place. These substances include:

- Drugs—prescription and nonprescription, legal and illegal
- Alcohol and tobacco
- Chemical and occupational pollutants

The use of drugs, alcohol, and tobacco is discussed in detail in chapter 1 (see page 13). The gamut of potential environmental exposures, especially in the workplace, is well beyond the scope of this book. However, if you are pregnant (or might become so in the near future), you should become knowledgeable about any chemical compounds to which you are exposed on a regular basis.[3]

How Are Congenital Defects Identified Prior to Birth?

A few decades ago, an expectant mother had little to inform her about her baby's condition other than the size of her abdomen, the movements that she felt inside it, her own sense of well-being or illness, and some very rudimentary input from her doctor. Advances in medical technology have changed that situation dramatically so that even the most uneventful pregnancy is now likely to be assessed with one or more prenatal screening tests.

This section will briefly describe a number of screening and diagnostic procedures utilized during pregnancy, along with their potential benefits and risks. Their role and significance in *your* pregnancy will depend upon your personal and family history as well as how far your pregnancy has progressed. You should be aware that tests will vary in their accuracy and predictive value. *Depending upon the procedure, abnormal results may not predict defects with absolute certainty, nor do normal results guarantee a problem-free baby.*

Ultrasound

Ultrasound (also called **diagnostic ultrasonography** or **sonogram**) is an extremely useful tool that utilizes high-frequency sound waves to create images of a woman's uterus and the baby growing within it. Sound waves are sent through a handheld transmitter called a transducer that is gently applied to a woman's abdomen or early in pregnancy may be placed inside the vagina using a narrow probe. (Placing the ultrasound transducer inside the vagina does not pose any risk for either mother or baby.) The sound waves reflect back to the transducer from internal structures in patterns that vary depending upon their shape and density. The images are displayed on a monitor and may even be recorded on videotape. (Some of the images may be printed for the expectant parents to take home as their first "baby picture.")

When is it performed? Ultrasound may be carried out during any stage of pregnancy. The timing for this procedure will depend to some degree upon its purpose, the state of your pregnancy, any problems that are developing, and your physician's approach to following a normal pregnancy. Many doctors recommend routine ultrasonography between the sixteenth and twentieth weeks of pregnancy, at which point many details (including the chambers of the baby's heart) can be visualized.

How is it performed? A woman having an ultrasound will normally be instructed to drink a few glasses of water and hold off on voiding until the procedure is completed because a full bladder serves as a useful landmark. (A full bladder is not necessary for a vaginal ultrasound.) A conducting gel will be applied to the abdomen and the transducer then gently pressed against it in a number of locations. A basic evaluation, which can be carried out in the doctor's office, will usually not take more than twenty minutes, while a more detailed (sometimes called level two) study could take an hour or more. The latter might be done if there is concern about an abnormality for which more detailed information and sophisticated equipment are needed.

Normally you will be able to see the monitor during an ultrasound, and the technician or physician will usually point out a variety of highlights of your "tour" of the uterus and its occupant. Parents are often delighted and deeply moved by the first sight of their new child and may be surprised by the amount of movement if the baby is active at the time of the procedure.

Is it safe? Ultrasound has never been reported to cause harm to mother or baby, even during the earliest stages of pregnancy. No X-rays are involved, and the mother's skin is not punctured. Sometimes there is mild discomfort when the transducer is pressed against a full bladder.

What information does it provide? This test can provide a great deal of information:

- Verification that pregnancy is in fact under way within the uterus. A tiny sac can be visualized three weeks after conception, and a week later the baby's body can be seen within it. Ultrasound is also useful in diagnosing an **ectopic pregnancy** (one that is growing in an abnormal location).
- An accurate determination of the age of the baby and whether or not more than one baby is present.
- An assessment of the growth rate and movements of the baby.
- Detection of major structural abnormalities of the head, spinal cord, chest, abdomen, or limbs.
- The location and appearance of the placenta and the amount of amniotic fluid.

- Identifying structures (such as the placenta) that are important to diagnostic tests such as amniocentesis and chorionic villus sampling (see page 101).

Maternal blood tests: Alpha-fetoprotein, beta-HCG, and estriol

These tests are known as the "triple screen," and they are considered *screening* tests because:

- They are relatively easy and inexpensive to perform.
- While they detect pregnancies in which the baby may be at higher risk for certain problems, they do *not* make a specific diagnosis.
- They can be carried out on large numbers of pregnant women to determine who might benefit from more complex diagnostic testing.

Screening for **alpha-fetoprotein** (or **AFP**) is the most widely used test. Alpha-fetoprotein is one of two major proteins that circulate in the blood of the developing fetus. The other protein, **albumin,** is found also in the bloodstream of adults, while AFP is unique to the fetus. Normally during pregnancy a small amount of AFP finds its way into the **amniotic fluid** (fluid surrounding the fetus in its closed sac) and from there into the mother's bloodstream. A certain amount of AFP can thus be measured in the mother's bloodstream, and the level gradually rises during the first twenty weeks of pregnancy. A number of conditions can increase the amount of AFP that passes from fetus to mother at any given point in the pregnancy:

- A leak of fetal blood into the amniotic fluid or a defect in the placenta that allows more AFP to pass into the mother's bloodstream.
- Twins, because the two fetuses produce more AFP than one.
- An abnormality in which some of the fetus's internal tissue is exposed, allowing an increased amount of AFP to escape into the amniotic fluid. Examples of such conditions are open neural tube defects (anencephaly or spina bifida), which expose nerve tissue at the top or bottom of the spinal column (see page 9), or abdominal wall defects (omphalocele or gastroschisis) in which part of the intestinal tract may be present outside of the abdomen.

The screening test for a mother's blood level of AFP is quite sensitive: 80 to 85 percent of fetuses with neural tube defects can be detected through elevated levels of this protein in the mother's blood. However, the test is not very specific, since so many other conditions also cause the AFP to be elevated. As a result, out of one hundred cases in which maternal AFP is abnormally high, more than ninety-five will prove to be false alarms in which no neural tube defect or other significant problem is identified.

How is the screening done? AFP is measured in a sample of blood drawn from the mother. The screening is most accurate if done between sixteen and eighteen weeks after the last menstrual period, but it can be carried out between fifteen and twenty weeks. Because of the steady rise of AFP during pregnancy, *accurate dating of the pregnancy is very important for a meaningful interpretation of this test.* In addition, the mother's age, weight, and race are taken into account when determining what level of AFP should be considered normal.

What if the AFP level is abnormally high? Your physician may want to repeat the test to confirm that the results are definitely abnormal. Even when the lab results are consistently high, however, a high AFP does not necessarily mean that the baby has a significant problem. Usually the next step will be an ultrasound examination, which can help specifically to

- confirm the accuracy of the date of the pregnancy. One of the most common reasons for an unexpectedly high level of AFP in a mother's bloodstream is that her pregnancy is actually farther along than was originally estimated.
- determine whether there is a multiple pregnancy (twins or more).
- detect abnormalities such as neural tube defects.

If the ultrasound study does not provide an explanation for the high AFP level, an amniocentesis (see below) may be carried out to determine the level of AFP in the amniotic fluid. This test is much more accurate than maternal AFP levels at predicting the presence or absence of neural tube and abdominal wall defects. But a serum-AFP and ultrasound may be adequate to make the diagnosis. A combination of normal amniotic fluid AFP and normal ultrasound would indicate that one of these problems is extremely unlikely. (However, an elevated AFP not caused by an open neural tube defect or twins has been associated with a greater chance of late-pregnancy complications.)

What if the AFP is abnormally low? A low AFP might indicate an increased risk of Down syndrome, although this is not a highly accurate test. (It will identify only about 20 to 30 percent of fetuses with Down syndrome in pregnant women under age thirty-five.) However, some confirmation of this risk may be obtained from two other maternal blood tests, which can be carried out at the same time. **Estriol** is an estrogen hormone whose level in the mother will be affected by the status of both the fetus and the placenta. **Beta-HCG (human chorionic go-**

nadotrophin) is a hormone produced by the placenta soon after conception, rising to levels that are detectable by the time the first menstrual period is missed.

If a low maternal AFP is present in combination with a low level of estriol and a high level of beta-HCG, the likelihood that the baby will have Down syndrome is definitely greater than if the AFP alone is abnormal. The results of these tests are combined with the mother's age to determine the probability that her baby will have Down syndrome. Remember, however, that *these tests cannot actually make this diagnosis.* This requires other studies, which will be discussed shortly.

Amniocentesis

Amniocentesis is the withdrawal of a small amount of amniotic fluid from the sac that surrounds the fetus. Both the contents of the fluid and the fetal cells that are present within it can be studied to diagnose a variety of problems before birth.

How is it done? When used to diagnose birth defects, amniocentesis is usually carried out between the fourteenth and twentieth weeks of pregnancy. Whether done in a physician's office or in a hospital, an ultrasound is routinely done first to assess (among other things) the size and position of the fetus, the location of the placenta, and the amount of amniotic fluid present. Then an appropriate site is selected on the mother's abdomen, antiseptic solution is applied, and often a local anesthetic is injected. (However, the anesthetic cannot numb the wall of the uterus, so a brief stinging or cramping pain might be felt when it is punctured.) Under ultrasound guidance, a long needle is inserted through the abdominal wall and into the amniotic fluid. Between 15 and 30 ml (or 1/2 to 1 ounce) of fluid is removed before the needle is withdrawn.

What kind of information is obtained from studying amniotic fluid?
- *Chromosome analysis.* Fetal cells within the fluid are cultured for one to two weeks and then specially treated so the chromosomes within them can be identified and studied. Extra or missing chromosomes are seen in disorders such as Down syndrome, in which the nucleus of each cell contains three chromosome 21s rather than the usual two. The analysis can also provide advance notice of the baby's gender, although amniocentesis will not be done strictly for this purpose. Results of chromosome analysis may not be ready until four weeks after the procedure.

◆ *Measurement of alpha-fetoprotein (AFP) in the amniotic fluid,* when screening tests done on the mother's blood reveal abnormal levels of this protein, as just described.

◆ *Identification of genetic markers* for certain diseases (for example, cystic fibrosis) where there is a family history or increased risk.

◆ *Assessment of the maturity of the baby's lungs.* This is evaluated toward the *end* of pregnancy in situations where a need to induce labor must be weighed against the possibility that the baby's lungs will not be mature enough to function normally once out of the womb. The compounds lecithin and sphingomyelin are measured within the amniotic fluid, and when the **lecithin/sphingomyelin (or L/S) ratio** is more than 2, the baby can be expected to breathe adequately on his or her own after birth.

What kinds of birth defects will amniocentesis not detect?

◆ Specific, isolated structural abnormalities that do not have genetic or chromosomal causes. Examples would be cleft lip or palate, club foot, absent fingers or limbs, or heart defects.

◆ Disorders in the fetus arising from alcohol, tobacco, or drugs used by the mother.

What are the risks of amniocentesis? The mother might experience mild cramping for a few hours after the procedure. Occasionally local infection or leaking of amniotic fluid occurs at the puncture site. Unfortunately, the risks for the baby due to amniocentesis are more significant. Between one in 200 and one in 400 amniocentesis procedures in early pregnancy will result in a miscarriage. The risk of this complication occurring in a specific pregnancy will depend upon a variety of factors, including the size of the baby and the experience of the physician who performs the test. Miscarriage most commonly results from damage to the placenta, which may bleed and separate from the uterus, or from infection, which can begin if bacteria are accidentally carried by the needle into the amniotic fluid. Rarely, amniocentesis provokes early labor.

In what situations might amniocentesis be recommended for detecting a birth defect?

◆ When a woman has had another child with a chromosomal abnormality.

◆ When either parent has a chromosomal abnormality.

◆ When the mother's alpha-fetoprotein screening or triple screen is abnormal and the reason cannot be determined by ultrasound alone.

◆ When there is an increased risk of a genetically transmitted disorder for which additional information may be provided through analysis of amniotic fluid or the cells it contains.

♦ When a pregnant woman is over thirty-five years old. At this age, the chances of finding a chromosomal abnormality (one in 378 for Down syndrome, one in 192 for all chromosomal defects) are roughly equal to the risk of a miscarriage from the amniocentesis. This is the most common reason that amniocentesis might be recommended during the first half of pregnancy. Unfortunately, in some instances a woman may be given the impression that she *must* have amniocentesis if she is over age thirty-five and that the pregnancy *must* be terminated if an abnormality is found. However, there is no requirement, legal or otherwise, that this test be carried out, regardless of a pregnant woman's age, and certainly no situation in which an abortion is mandated.

Chorionic villus sampling

Chorionic villus sampling (CVS) is a procedure in which cells are taken from tiny, fingerlike projections of the placenta (called villi, which means literally "shaggy hairs"). These cells contain the same genetic material as the baby and can be cultured for chromosomal analysis and other genetic tests.

When and how is it done? CVS can be carried out between the ninth and twelfth weeks of pregnancy. Using ultrasound for guidance, a needle is introduced through the abdominal wall into the uterus to the edge of the placenta, where a small amount of tissue is aspirated. An alternative procedure involves the insertion of a small catheter into the vagina and through the cervix (the opening of the uterus) to the placenta, from which the cells are withdrawn.

What information can be obtained from CVS? The cells obtained from chorionic villus sampling can be cultured and then analyzed for chromosomal and genetic abnormalities, yielding information similar to that gained from amniocentesis. However, this procedure can be carried out more than a month earlier than amniocentesis, and more cells are available at the outset, so results can be ready within a week to ten days. But CVS cannot diagnose neural tube defects because it does not obtain amniotic fluid. Also, while normal results can be considered highly reassuring, when abnormal results are obtained there is a 5 to 10 percent chance that the baby will in fact be normal. (This can occur because of chromosomal changes in the placenta that are not present in the fetus.) Thus when tests run on a CVS specimen are abnormal, a follow-up amniocentesis later in the pregnancy may be considered to verify these results.

What are the risks of CVS? As with amniocentesis, the mother may experience some cramping as well as pain at the puncture site if the specimen is obtained through the abdomen. (The vaginal approach is generally painless.) Vaginal bleeding and local infection are possible complications of the abdominal approach. Of greater concern is the risk of miscarriage, which occurs after about one in 100 procedures—at least twice the rate for amniocentesis. In addition CVS has been linked to limb abnormalities (missing or undeveloped fingers and toes) in the baby and cases of severe infections in the mother's uterus.

These risks, along with the slight but not insignificant possibility of a false positive result (that is, one that suggests an abnormality when the baby is in fact normal), raise particular concerns about CVS. The presumed advantage of this test over amniocentesis is that it allows for an earlier identification of the baby's genetic status—and thus an earlier abortion if the mother has decided that she will end her pregnancy if the baby is abnormal. If abortion is not an option that she intends to exercise, however, there would appear to be little purpose to expose her and her baby to this procedure's risks.

How Do I Decide Whether or Not to Have Chorionic Villus Sampling or Amniocentesis to Look for a Birth Defect?

Make this decision carefully, prayerfully, and with all the facts you can possibly gather. You should be properly counseled and fully informed regarding the following:

- What potential birth defect(s) will the procedure help to identify?
- How high is the risk that the baby might be affected with a particular defect?
- How does the risk of the baby's having the abnormality compare with the risk of the procedure? It would be of questionable value to perform any procedure if the chance of provoking a miscarriage was significantly greater than the likelihood of identifying a problem, and it would be undeniably sad to lose a normal baby under such circumstances—especially in situations where infertility has been a problem.

- What have the complication rates been for the specific physician or medical center that would be performing the procedure? CVS, in particular, requires special expertise and experience.

- What would be the specific benefits of having information about the defect prior to birth? Are there interventions available that might help the baby while still within the uterus? Would preparations be needed for expert care at the time of delivery or shortly thereafter? Would it help the parents to learn about the condition ahead of time and make their own adjustments to cope with it?

- Is the primary purpose of the procedure to determine whether or not to continue the pregnancy? CVS is done to identify genetic abnormalities early in the pregnancy so that an abortion, if chosen, might be carried out with less difficulty. Amniocentesis, on the other hand, in a number of situations provides information that can improve the care of the baby either before or after delivery. There could thus be instances in which a woman who knows she would not have an abortion might nevertheless benefit from having an amniocentesis. (See page 566 for further discussion of abortion.)

- What costs would be involved with this procedure? These would include not only physician fees but also laboratory costs and other expenses incurred at the facility where the procedure is to be performed.

With this information clearly in mind, you need to consider not only the medical aspects of the decision but also the personal and ethical dimensions. Your own values will significantly affect your response to the information you receive from prenatal testing—or whether you decide to have one or more procedures done in the first place.

In particular, you should consider ahead of time how you might respond to the unsettling news that your baby might have a birth defect. This is an extremely difficult question, even for those who value human life at all stages and in all conditions. How do you currently view people who have a significant physical, intellectual, or emotional handicap? How would you feel if such a person were your own child, living with you and depending on you for his daily needs, possibly for many years?

On a much broader scale, how do you view adverse events that occur in your life? Are they the meaningless cruelties of a mechanical universe? Are they divine punishment for something you have or haven't done? Or are they the fallout from a broken world, trials that God nevertheless can redeem and even use for a greater purpose in your life—and perhaps in the lives of many others?

These might seem rather weighty considerations to bring into a discussion of the pros and cons of a few medical tests, but these questions apply profoundly to the realm of prenatal evaluation of the baby. If you feel that a baby who will be born with one or more significant defects represents a biologic mistake—a life that shouldn't be lived—and that caring for him would be an exercise in futility, this viewpoint will seriously influence your response to any bad news you hear from your physician. Your reaction to such news could be quite different if you believe that life's trials are not pointless or punitive and that (to quote the apostle Paul) "we also rejoice in our sufferings, because we know that suffering produces perseverance; perseverance, character; and character, hope. And hope does not disappoint us, because God has poured out his love into our hearts by the Holy Spirit, whom he has given us" (Romans 5:3-5).

Undoubtedly, some people undergo prenatal testing in order to identify a significant disorder in time to abort the fetus. However, depending on the specific condition, there may be other measures that can help the less-than-perfect child (and the parents) before the birth. In certain situations knowledge that a baby will be born with a particular defect will allow physicians to prepare for his arrival and begin corrective measures in a timely manner. Advances in medical and physical therapy may also change the long-term outlook for a child with a particular defect.

WHAT IF THE RESULTS OF PRENATAL SCREENING OR DIAGNOSTIC TESTS ARE ABNORMAL?

Your response will, of course, depend on the test that was done and the specific defect that may be involved. It is important, first of all, to have a clear understanding of the reliability of the test(s) and the implications of the results. Was the test a screen, such as the alpha-fetoprotein blood test, that could prove to be a false alarm after further testing? Is there more than one possible explanation for the results? Does a repeat test or follow-up study need to be done to confirm the diagnosis? All of these questions should be reviewed carefully after receiving the news of abnormal results on any test.

Assuming that a birth defect has been identified with some certainty, what else might you do upon receiving this information? Again, this will depend significantly on the type of problem and its long-term implications. The diagnosis of Down syndrome, for example, which has a relatively normal life expectancy, is vastly different from anencephaly, in which most or all of the brain is missing and death follows very soon after birth. You will, in fact, need to deal with news of a birth defect on a number of levels.

Your *emotional response* will probably be intense and will need to be acknowledged and expressed among those whom you love and trust. Don't be surprised if you experience a wide range of feelings, including:

- Shock
- Denial—*This can't be happening.* Accepting the diagnosis might be extremely difficult, even when the same diagnosis is given by further testing or another consultant.
- Sorrow and grief—over many losses: the loss of hopes and dreams for a normal child or for the baby's life itself if the defect is one that will seriously shorten her life.
- Anger—at oneself *(What did I do wrong?)*, at someone else, or even at God *(Why have You allowed this to happen?)*
- Impatience—wanting more information, answers to difficult questions, and perhaps more testing immediately.

This is the time for solidarity and teamwork between husband and wife. Blaming or finger-pointing is a luxury no one can afford.

Your *practical and problem-solving response* should be to find out more about the defect. What does it involve? Can anything be done to correct or improve it before or after birth? Reading about it, doing research in the library or on the Internet, or talking with other parents who have dealt with the same problem can help you understand more clearly what you may be dealing with later on.

Your *support-gathering response* is extremely important. An impending birth defect is not the type of problem that is discussed easily. Those with whom you are closest among family, friends, and church members need to be brought up to speed on your problem. You will need shoulders to lean (and cry) on, open ears and hearts, and knees ready to bend in prayer for you and your child.

Finally, your *spiritual response* is crucial. During this time you may wonder if God is making any sense or if He hears your cries and prayers. Don't be surprised (and try not to get upset) if you hear simplistic or unkind "answers" from well-meaning individuals; don't let such responses prevent you from drawing near to God, who really does care about this situation more than you can imagine. Indeed, its ultimate significance—what it will mean, how it will affect you and your family, what you will learn from it, and how this difficulty and sorrow will be redeemed—may not be clear for many years or even during this lifetime.

A Special Encouragement

You might feel a great deal of pressure to end a pregnancy by means of abortion, especially if the defect is severe. You wonder if it wouldn't be more merciful to all concerned if this imperfect life and all the trials that will accompany it would not be brought into the world in the first place.

We certainly don't want to trivialize the sorrow, difficulty, and expense involved when a child has a serious defect. But it is important to remember that no child you bear will be free of defects and imperfections. Even if all the body parts and systems are completely normal when a baby is born, other profound problems could develop later in life. A "normal" child might suffer injuries and illness after birth or break your heart eventually by making poor lifestyle choices. On the other hand, a baby who is malformed or destined for subnormal intelligence or a very short life could become the greatest blessing of your life.

NOTES
1. While not minimizing the untold sadness that such a loss brings to a family, it is of some comfort to know that the number of deaths caused by congenital disorders represents a very small fraction of the approximately 3.5 million births that take place every year in the U.S.
2. The American College of Obstetricians and Gynecologists, *Planning for Pregnancy, Birth, and Beyond* (New York: Signet, 1994), 94.
3. The Occupational Safety and Health Administration in Washington, D.C., which has established standards designed to reduce the likelihood of work-related injury or harm, requires that information be made available to any employee regarding potentially harmful compounds present in the workplace. In order to arrive at a "bottom line" that reduces risks to your (and your unborn child's) health, you may need some help from your physician in interpreting the Medical Safety Data Sheets (MSDS) or any other input you receive regarding harmful materials to which you may be exposed.

Baby Blues,
Postpartum Depression,
and Postpartum Psychosis

Many mothers who have just had a mountaintop experience in the delivery room are often dismayed to find themselves in a dark, turbulent emotional valley during the first weeks after the baby is born. Between 50 and 60 percent of women are affected by a temporary emotional slump commonly known as "baby blues," while 5 to 10 percent suffer from a more severe disturbance known as postpartum (literally, "after the delivery") depression. A much less common—but far more severe—disturbance known as postpartum psychosis occurs after about one in 1,000 deliveries.

When one considers all of the intense physical and psychological changes that accompany the birth of a new baby, it's actually surprising that storm clouds aren't a part of *every* mother's emotional weather after childbirth.

There are a number of physical factors that can affect the emotions of a new mother:

- Dramatic shifts in the levels of a number of hormones (estrogen, progesterone, prolactin, cortisone, and others) after delivery. No one has identified which one (or perhaps a combination) might play a dominant role. There are probably differences in the sensitivity of women to changing hormone levels, as occurs in premenstrual syndrome.
- Physical exhaustion following the demands of labor.
- Blood loss during and after delivery.
- Pain after childbirth, especially following a cesarean section. Drugs that may be needed to kill pain can also affect mood and energy level.

- Loss of sleep, perhaps starting with an all-night labor and continuing with the round-the-clock needs of a newborn.
- Genetic factors. Depression, anxiety syndromes, panic attacks, and even more severe disturbances have a definite biochemical component. Because vulnerability to these syndromes can be inherited, they may run in families, much like diabetes, heart disease, or other medical problems.

Personal and family issues that could also affect the emotions include:

- A difficult labor and delivery during which very little went according to plan.
- Problems with the baby. These might include a complex medical concern such as prematurity or a normal baby with feeding problems or unusual irritability.
- A mismatch of expectations. The amount of time and effort involved in caring for a newborn may come as a shock to some (especially first-time) mothers, who may have never experienced being on call twenty-four hours a day.
- Lack of family support. If Dad is gone most of the day (or there is no dad in the picture) and relatives are not available to lend a hand, taking care of a newborn can be overwhelming. This will be worsened if a marriage is shaky or if a new mother is getting negative input: "Why are you so tired? I've been working hard all day—all you've had to do is sit around with the baby!"
- Perfectionism. With a new baby (or even with one or more older children) it is not possible to be the Mother of the Year, keeper of the showcase home, rising young executive, and amorous wife. Childbirth and baby care bring one's limitations into striking and sometimes distressing focus.
- Financial pressure. Budgets are often tight in new families, and the expenses surrounding childbirth will add new stress to the family finances.
- Feelings of being stuck or trapped in the new role. A woman who has been pursuing a rewarding career or who is accustomed to a relatively carefree lifestyle might begin to feel that nonstop responsibility for a helpless newborn is a ball and chain—especially if family support or financial resources are limited.

POSTPARTUM BLUES

Baby blues, the most common mood problem related to childbirth, usually develops during the first week after delivery. Symptoms can include irritability, tearfulness, anxiety, insomnia, lack of energy, loss of appetite, and difficulty concentrating. This emotional and physical slump typically resolves by itself within two weeks. However, it should not be met with an attitude of "ignore it and it will go away." Support and reassurance from husband, family, and friends are very important. In addition, help with the baby, housekeeping, and other practical details can make a major difference.

POSTPARTUM DEPRESSION

While many of its symptoms are very similar to those of baby blues, **postpartum depression (PPD)** is a more serious condition. Not only does it last longer, but its impact on both mother and baby is more profound. A mother with PPD may be so intensely depressed that she has difficulty caring for her baby, or she may develop extreme and unrealistic anxiety over the infant's health. Furthermore, ongoing disruption of mother-child interactions can have adverse effects on the infant's long-term development.

PPD can begin at any time during the first six months after childbirth. While two out of three mothers recover within one year, this problem should not be left to run its course. Like a major depression occurring at any other time in life, PPD is not a situation in which a little "attitude adjustment" is all that is needed. If symptoms such as those listed above for baby blues continue for more than two weeks, professional help should be sought. Treatment might involve extended counseling, the use of antidepressant medication, or both. Medication is sometimes very helpful in normalizing biochemical mechanisms in the central nervous system that affect mood, sleep patterns, and fatigue. However, if a mother is breast-feeding, input from the baby's doctor will be needed if medications are being considered.

POSTPARTUM PSYCHOSIS

In the relatively rare but very serious disorder called **postpartum psychosis,** a woman experiences not only a disturbance in mood but also a break with reality. At some time during the first month after delivery, she may become confused and experience hallucinations and delusions. She may even consider harming herself or her baby. A woman who develops postpartum psychosis must be evaluated immediately by a qualified psychiatrist, although it might be difficult to convince her that this is necessary. This condition can and should be treated with appropriate medication. There is, however, a one-in-seven chance that it will recur with a subsequent pregnancy.[1]

It is important to note, however, that postpartum depression and psychosis can occur without warning. A woman's mood during her pregnancy does not necessarily predict how she will feel after the baby comes home. However, if a woman has a history of depression or other significant emotional problems or if they have occurred in her immediate family, those close to her should be alert for signs of turbulence during the days and weeks following childbirth. *A mother who has suffered postpartum psychosis in the past must be observed carefully for any signs of recurrence after future deliveries.*

PREVENTING EMOTIONAL PROBLEMS AFTER CHILDBIRTH

The first chapter of this book includes a section (see page 27) that contains recommendations for parents anticipating the birth of their child. These include tapping into a support team, maintaining a personal quiet time, and (for married couples) building the relationship with one another. All of these are important *after* the baby is born as well. Fathers should pay particular attention to the items under "Some thoughts for the expectant and new father." Expressions of love and respect, help with the daily tasks of living, and ongoing prayer for (and with) a new mother can certainly help prevent an emotional upheaval during the weeks after a baby arrives.

NOTES
1. D. A. Bright, "Post-partum Mental Disorders," *American Family Physician* (1994): 50.

The First Three Months, Part One

We are born helpless.
As soon as we are fully
conscious, we discover loneliness.
We need others physically,
emotionally, intellectually;
we need them if we are to know
anything, even ourselves.
C. S. LEWIS

The First Three Months, Part One: Family Adjustments, Feeding the New Arrival, and Dealing with Basic Health Concerns

Now that the efforts of labor and delivery are over, within a few hours or a few days after your baby's birth (with rare exception), you will be bringing your son or daughter home. If this is your first child, you will most likely have some apprehensions about the coming weeks—or, for that matter, about the first night. Will he get enough nourishment? How often should he be fed? Where should he sleep? Will *we* get any sleep? What if he starts crying—and won't stop? If there are other children at home, how will they respond to the new arrival?

Many of these questions have already been addressed in a childbirth- or parenting-preparation class. And if you have older children at home, you have already dealt with most of these concerns before and may not feel the need for any further "basic training." But just in case you didn't get all the bases covered, the following two chapters will cover the ABCs of new baby care.

Before we begin, remember:

- The information in this book assumes that your baby is full-term, has been examined, and is basically healthy. If he was born prematurely or has medical problems that require special care, you should follow the specific directions of your physician.
- In the coming months you will be getting all sorts of advice from friends, relatives, and other resources. Much of it will be helpful and appropriate, at least for most babies. But if something you read or hear doesn't make sense or doesn't work, don't be afraid to get a second opinion. And if you get conflicting advice, don't panic. Newborns are much

more sturdy and resilient than you might think, and there are very few mistakes that loving, attentive parents might make that cannot be straightened out later on.

◆ While it is normal to feel some anxiety over the responsibility of full-time care for a new baby, the process of parenting a newborn should not be dominated by fear and uncertainty. Be confident that you and your baby can and will survive and thrive, even while all of you are learning. Since every parent-child combination is unique, some adjusting and improvising will be a necessary part of the process. But it is neither necessary nor wise to wade through the first months or years purely on blind instinct.

First Things First for Couples: Mom and Dad's Partnership

With all the excitement and changes that come with the role of parenting, whether for the first time or with a new addition, *it is extremely important that mother and father continuously reaffirm the importance of their own relationship.* For many reasons, it is common for a new baby to take center stage and for parents, especially new ones, to put the maintenance of their marriage at the bottom of the daily priority list. Remember that the two of you became a family with the exchange of vows, before children were in the picture. You will remain a family after the children have grown and left your home. While they are under your roof, a rock-solid partnership, continually renewed and refreshed, will be the foundation for the security of any and all children you add to your original family of two. Your new baby is to be loved and cherished, but he must not, for his own sake, become the permanent center of gravity around which everything else in your home revolves.

Preventing turmoil in the nest

You might assume that the awe and wonder of having a newborn at home would automatically forge a powerful bond between the proud parents. But it is also quite possible for the new demands of baby care to generate some unexpected friction, resentment, or jealousy in the marriage.

If the new baby is breast-fed rather than bottle-fed, much of a young mother's time and energy will be occupied with feeding, not to mention the many other details of infant care. (This can also occur, of course, when a baby is bottle-fed, although in this case others can take turns with feeding sessions.) As a result, a father might begin to feel left out and could even resent a nursing child who seems to have displaced him from his wife's affections.

This may be aggravated by unspoken assumptions about mothers' and fathers' roles, especially with newborns. If one parent believes that tending to a baby is "women's work" and that Dad need not report for duty until his son can throw a ball or his daughter is ready to ride a bike, a wedge can develop between mother and father. He may become weary of seeing her attention directed toward meeting the newborn's seemingly endless needs. She may become irritated if he isn't pulling his weight at home, especially if he seems to expect her to meet a lot of his needs when she is thoroughly exhausted.

How can you prevent a newborn nest from becoming a "house divided"?

Hot tips for Mom: Make sure your husband knows that he hasn't been relegated to the back burner of your affection and interest. Beware of total and absolute preoccupation with your new baby, as normal as that desire might seem to you. If you nurse, carry, rock, caress, and sleep with your baby twenty-four hours a day without offering some attention to your mate, before long your marriage may be a shadow of its former self.

Whenever possible, try to freshen up if you haven't seen your spouse for several hours—even if you're pooped. It's important that you take care of yourself even in these early days of motherhood, because from now on it will be tempting to neglect yourself when there are so many needs and tasks surrounding you. Certainly your husband will appreciate seeing you take steps to maintain your health and appearance. But for your own sake it is important to cultivate good feelings about who *you* are by giving some priority to your personal needs and interests. Taking care of yourself, even in small ways, can help you avoid baby-care burnout—not only now but also in the days and seasons to come.

Hot tips for Dad: Pay lots of attention to your newborn, for whom you can do all sorts of things (such as cuddling, rocking, and changing). Wives tend to become very enamored with husbands who clearly cherish their babies. Don't expect to be treated like another child at home, waiting for a weary housekeeper to fix your meals, do your laundry, and clean up your messes. Roll up your sleeves and pitch in. Finally, take another look at the material in chapter 1 entitled "Some thoughts for the expectant and new father" (page 28). Your commitment to "love, honor, and cherish" has no expiration date.

Patterns you establish now in your marriage may well continue as your new baby and other children at home grow to maturity. Ultimately their sense of security will rise or fall with the visible evidence of stability, mutual respect, and ongoing love of their mother and father for one another. Overt demonstrations of affection not only fulfill deep and abiding needs between husband and wife, but they also provide a strong, daily reassurance for children that their world will remain intact. The same can be said of time set aside by parents for quiet conversation with one another *before* the children have gone to bed.

Equally significant is a regular date night for Mom and Dad, which should be instituted as soon as possible and maintained even after the kids are grown and gone. These time-outs need not be expensive, but they may require some ongoing creativity, planning, and dedication. Dedication is necessary because child-care needs, pangs of guilt, and complicated calendars will conspire to prevent those dates from happening. But the romance, renewal, and vitality they generate are well worth the effort.

Special note to single parents

Taking care of a new baby is a major project for a couple in a stable marriage. For a single parent—who usually, but not always, is the mother—the twenty-four-hour care of a newborn may seem overwhelming from the first day. But even without a committed partner, you *can* take care of your baby and do it well. The job will be less difficult if you have some help.

Hopefully, before the baby was born you found a few people who would be willing members of your support team. These might be your parents, other relatives, friends, members of your church, or volunteers from a local crisis pregnancy center (CPC). By all means, don't hesitate to seek their help, especially during the early weeks when you are getting acquainted with your new baby. If your parents offer room, board, and child-care assistance, and you are on good terms with them, you would be wise to accept. Or if a helpful and mature family member or friend offers to stay with you for a while after the birth, give the idea careful consideration. (Obviously, you should avoid situations in which there is likely to be more conflict than help.)

Even after you have a few weeks or months of parenting under your belt, at some point you may need a brief time-out to walk around the block, or advice on calming a crying episode. But no one will know unless you ask. Many churches and CPCs have ongoing single-parent groups in which you can relax for a few hours on a regular basis, swap ideas, and talk with others who know first-hand the challenges you face.

Preparing other children for the new arrival

Parents often worry about how the arrival of a new baby will affect other children in the family. Children's responses are as different as the children themselves. Some siblings will struggle with jealousy for a while; others welcome the new baby excitedly, eager to be "big sister" or "big brother." But most children, especially if they are younger than age six or seven, will experience a range of emotions: happiness, jealousy, possessiveness toward the baby, protectiveness, fear of being forgotten by the parents, fear that there won't be enough love in the family to go around. While parents can't prevent the onset of these emotions, they can do much to prepare children for an additional person in the family.

Talk about the baby's coming well in advance. When Mom's stomach begins to grow, the other children may ask about it; this is a good time to begin talking about the new sister or brother to come. Allow your other children to enjoy the anticipation along with you.

Include your other children in discussions about the baby. Let big brother or sister join in the conversations about names for the baby and preparations for the nursery. Involve them in as much of the process as you can.

Be careful about how much the arrangements for the baby will impinge on other children's space in the house and schedule. Be sure to prepare children if they are going to get moved out of a bedroom or if their possessions are going to be displaced. Don't disturb their routine any more than necessary, both in preparation for the new baby and after the baby has come home.

Make plans for other relatives to pay attention to the other children. Since Mom and Dad are going to have their hands extra full the first several weeks after the baby comes home, arrange for Grandma or some other relative to do some special things with the other children. And make sure Mom and Dad are relieved of baby duty part of the time so they can spend time with the other children.

Pay attention to signs of jealousy or other forms of upset. Don't take lightly difficult emotions your children may be experiencing. Respond to them, talk to them, let them know they are still important, and continually assure them of your love for them.

Small children are quite capable of harming infants, often without realizing the seriousness of their actions. If a child is acting angry or jealous toward the new baby, don't leave them alone together.

Direct visitors' attention to the other children. Visitors will ooh and aah over the new baby and often neglect siblings. Bring big brother or sister into the circle. Praise their accomplishments. Talk about how well they help you with the baby.

Remember that much of the negative emotion young children feel toward a new baby is rooted in their own fear of being forgotten or not loved by you. As long as you continually express your love for them and their importance to your family, most of their jealousy will subside with time.

LIFE WITH A NEWBORN: WHAT CAN YOU EXPECT?

If you are bringing home a new baby for the very first time, you have probably been wondering what your life will be like on a day-to-day basis. Perhaps you have envisioned your new parenthood as a tranquil scene from a greeting card or a TV commercial: a contented mother and father sitting by the fireside, smiling softly at the tiny cherub who sweetly coos her love in return. Or you may have heard tales of misery from family or friends, describing endless sleepless nights, relentless fatigue, and no life at all away from the seven-pound tyrant who demands attention every moment. Some young mothers arrive at parenthood believing that caring for their new baby will be like bringing a puppy home from the pet store. If you already have children, you know that none of these visions accurately encompass the breadth and depth of caring for a newborn.

In one sense, a newborn has a relatively simple agenda: eating, sleeping, crying, being quietly alert, and eliminating urine and stool, repeated over and over each day. Therefore, it wouldn't seem all that difficult or complicated to care for her. After all, she won't be feverishly exploring every cupboard in the house, struggling with overdue homework assignments, or arguing with you over rights to the car.

But there are countless variations on these basic activities and some unpredictability in the way each baby behaves from day to day. If you have had two or more children, you are already aware that, as unique human beings, each of your offspring has displayed various differences from the others since day one, or even *before* day one.

Furthermore, the first few days of life at home may seem unsettled for both you and your baby. You may be coping for the first time with the profound reality of being responsible for a tiny, helpless human twenty-four hours a day and wondering if you will ever "have a life" again. It may take several character-building days for both baby and parents to establish a predictable pattern of eating and sleeping—or to become used to the absence of a predictable pattern. In response to her new surroundings, your baby may also be more fussy or sleepy after she first arrives home.

For all these reasons, cookbook approaches to baby care, with step-by-step directions for every situation, are unrealistic. Instead, as we look at the elements of your new baby's daily routine, we will outline some basic facts and principles that you can then adapt and fine-tune to your family's unique circumstances. Above all, try your best to relax and trust that you and your baby will in fact eventually settle in (and settle down) together.

FEEDING YOUR NEWBORN

For a new baby and her parents, feeding time represents far more than "open mouth, insert milk." In the course of receiving life-sustaining calories, nutrients, and fluids from multiple feedings every day, your baby is also having a series of important multisensory experiences. The receptors of sight, hearing, touch, taste, and smell are all actively gathering information during feedings. More important, emotional bonds are forming as the discomfort of hunger is repeatedly ended by a loving parent. As you become more familiar with your baby and more relaxed, you can look forward to each feeding as a special, satisfying, and relaxing event rather than a time-consuming chore or a source of anxiety. Like so many other aspects of parenting, how you approach and prepare for this activity will have a major impact on its success.

The vast majority of newborn babies are ready, willing, and able to take in the milk offered to them. As mentioned in the last chapter, they come equipped with rooting, sucking, and swallowing reflexes that are quite efficient at transporting milk from nipple to stomach. While babies may show differences in feeding styles and some may seem more adept than others at the outset, you should assume from the beginning that you and your baby are very capable of working together to accomplish this important goal.

Breast or formula?

Over the past few decades a mountain of scientific evidence has validated what is, in fact, a very straightforward observation: Human mothers are beautifully designed to feed their own babies. Breast milk, with extremely rare exception, is the best—and should normally be the complete—source of nutrition during the first months of a child's life, without additional water, juice, cereal, or other foods.

While there is clear medical consensus that breast feeding is the preferred source of fuel for the newborn, it should not be viewed as a sacred rite. If you need or choose to bottle-feed, you can do so with assurance that your baby will do well physically and emotionally. There are a variety of formulas available that will meet a baby's nutritional needs quite adequately, and both Mom and Dad or a single parent can provide a warm, nurturing experience while feeding an infant from a bottle.

Whether you feed your baby breast milk or formula (or a combination of the two), it is important to understand that *she does not need other types of food or fluids during the first three to four months.* Juice, cow's milk from the dairy case, cereal, fruit, and other solids are all unnecessary and/or inappropriate for your baby at this stage of her life.

Details about formula feeding begin on page 139. However, if you are planning to use formula but have the option to breast-feed or if you are not sure which approach to use, take time to consider carefully the following information before you make your final decision.

What are the advantages of breast feeding?

Human milk is uniquely suited to human babies. It is not only nutritionally complete and properly balanced, but it is also constantly changing to meet the needs of a growing infant. The fat content of breast milk increases as a feeding progresses, creating a sense of satisfied fullness that tends to prevent overeating. Furthermore, the fat and cholesterol content of breast milk is higher in the early months, when these compounds are most needed in a baby's rapidly growing brain and nervous system. The primary proteins in all forms of milk are whey and casein, but in human milk, whey, which is easier to absorb, predominates. Compared to cow's milk, the carbohydrate component of breast milk contains a higher percentage of lactose, which appears to play an important role in both brain development and calcium absorption.

Vitamins and minerals are adequately supplied in mother's milk. No supplements are needed for the normal breast-fed infant, although additional vitamin D may be recommended by your baby's physician if you live in a climate or geographical area where sunshine is rare. Trace elements, such as copper and zinc, are present in the right amounts, and iron is present in breast milk in a form that is easier to absorb than in any other type of milk.

Breast milk is absorbed extremely efficiently, with little undigested material passing into stool. Experienced diaper changers are well aware that formula-fed infants tend to have smellier stools, a by-product of the nutritional odds and ends (especially certain fats and proteins) that are not thoroughly absorbed on their trip through the bowel.

From day one, breast milk contains antibodies that help protect babies from infections. The first product of the breast after birth, known as **colostrum,** is particularly rich in antibodies known as **immunoglobulin A,** which help protect the lining of the intestine from microscopic invaders. As the mother comes in contact with new viruses and bacteria, her immune system generates the appropriate microbe-fighting antibodies and passes them on to her baby, thus reducing—but by no means eliminating—the newborn's risk of becoming infected. This is particularly important in the first several months of life, when the newborn's immune system is less effective at mounting a defense against microscopic invaders. While formula manufacturers have labored mightily to duplicate the nutritional mixture of breast milk, they cannot hope to supply any of these complex immune factors. Breast-fed infants thus tend to have fewer infections (including ear and intestinal infections) as long as they are given breast milk than their formula-fed counterparts.

Breast milk is free. It is clean, fresh, warm, and ready to feed, anytime and virtually anyplace. It does not need to be purchased, stored (although it can be expressed into bottles and frozen for later use), mixed, or heated.

Stimulation of a mother's nipples by a nursing infant releases a hormone called oxytocin, which helps her uterus contract toward what will become its nonpregnant size. The hormonal response to nursing also postpones the onset of ovulation and the menstrual cycle, providing a natural—though not foolproof—spacing of children. Nursing mothers also tend to reach their prepregnancy weight more quickly.

Breast feeding lends itself to a sense of closeness, intimacy, and mutual satisfaction. The skin-to-skin contact, the increased sensory input for the baby, and the mother's satisfaction in being able to provide her child's most basic needs can help establish strong bonds between them.

As a mother comforts her child, so will I comfort you; and you will be comforted over Jerusalem.

ISAIAH 66:12-13

Are there any reasons not *to breast-feed?*

There are a few medical situations in which breast feeding poses a risk for the baby. HIV, the virus responsible for AIDS, has been reported to be transmitted from infected mother to noninfected infant through breast feeding. A mother with active hepatitis B or tuberculosis should not nurse her baby. Obviously, a serious illness in the mother may make breast feeding extremely difficult or even unsafe for both mother and child. Furthermore, virtually all medications show up to some degree in breast milk, and some are potentially harmful for infants. If one or more drugs that may be unsafe for a baby are needed to preserve the mother's life and health, formula feeding should be used. Careful consultation with both mother's and baby's physicians is in order when making this decision.

Previous breast surgery may affect a mother's ability to nurse. A biopsy or local lump removal in the past normally will not cause difficulty. Even after a mastectomy it is possible to feed a baby adequately using the remaining breast. Breast-reduction surgery, however, may result in an inadequate milk supply if the majority of milk-producing tissue has been removed. Previous breast-enhancement/implant surgery should not cause a problem for nursing unless the ducts that carry milk to the nipple were cut during the procedure.

Infants born with phenylketonuria (PKU) or galactosemia, rare metabolic disorders that are detected by routine screening tests after birth, must be fed special formulas to prevent a variety of serious consequences. Congenital problems such as a cleft lip or palate, heart disease, and Down syndrome can create special challenges for nursing. However, the benefits of mother's milk for these infants are usually well worth the extra effort needed to provide it for them, even if they cannot obtain milk directly from the breast. A team effort involving parents, physicians, and a lactation consultant will be necessary.

A number of nonmedical concerns might cause a woman to be reluctant to breast-feed or to consider abandoning it too quickly. These are worth some review and reflection.

A previous bad experience. "I had a baby who wouldn't nurse/couldn't nurse/didn't want to nurse. She wouldn't stop crying until we gave her a bottle. After days of frustration, tears, and sore nipples, I felt like a total failure."

If you had difficulty nursing a baby in the past, remember that each newborn is different. There is no rule that says history must repeat itself, and there are, in fact, very few women who simply are unable to supply enough milk to sustain their offspring.

Physical problems. "My breasts are too small/too big. My nipples are flat/dimpled/inverted."

Your milk is supplied by **mammary** (milk-producing) **glands** whose function is not related to breast size. In response to large amounts of hormones circulating during pregnancy—especially prolactin (literally, "for milk"), estrogen, progesterone, and human placental lactogen (which, as its name indicates, is secreted by the placenta)—the mammary glands enlarge, mature, and become capable of producing milk. However, the actual process of creating milk is held in check during pregnancy by these same elevated hormone levels. When your baby is born and the placenta delivered, the abrupt loss of placental hormones allows milk production to begin in earnest—whether you plan to nurse or not. This interplay between multiple hormones and structures within the body is intricately designed, and you can assume that it will function as intended.

Nipples may vary in shape, and some may be easier for infants to grasp and suck than others. Those that clearly protrude may look like better nursing candidates than those that are flat, dimpled, or inverted. What matters most, however, is what happens when the infant attempts to latch on and suck. To get a preview, gently squeeze *behind* the nipple using thumb and index finger.

When properly attached, a baby will grasp the entire **areola** (the dark area surrounding the nipple) and not just the nipple itself. If your nipple clearly extends outward in response to this squeeze, your baby should have little difficulty. If your nipple flattens or inverts further, however, you may have tiny adhesions under the skin that are preventing it from extending outward. Normally, changes in the breast related to pregnancy will help correct this problem. However, if the squeeze test is still yielding a flat or inverted nipple by the last trimester of pregnancy, a **breast shell** may help. This is a simple plastic device, worn inside the bra, that exerts constant gentle pressure on the areola and gradually helps the nipple protrude. If help is needed after birth, shells can be worn between feedings.

Don't try to toughen up your nipples by pulling or rubbing them before or during pregnancy. Not only will this fail to prevent any soreness during nursing, but it might stimulate the release of hormones that can cause the uterus to contract or even begin labor prematurely. (Nursing an older child may also cause premature contractions. If this happens, the child must be weaned immediately.)

Lifestyle issues. "I don't want to be the only one who can feed the baby. I've seen women whose babies are like appendages stuck permanently on their chests. They have no life—they can't go anywhere or do anything without their baby."

Breast feeding does take more of Mom's time, but it need not be a ball-and-chain experience. After nursing has become a well-established routine, milk can be expressed into a bottle and stored for Dad, grandparents, or baby-sitters to use at a later date. And if you need to get away for a long evening or even overnight, it won't harm your baby to have a formula feeding or two if you don't have enough of your own milk in the freezer. Don't forget that nursing means being free from the hassle of buying formula; preparing it; and dealing with nipples, bottles, bottle liners, and other items.

Keep in mind that it is hardly a major setback if nursing slows your life down for a while. Your body needs time for rest and restoration after accomplishing the formidable tasks of completing pregnancy and childbirth. Do you really need to accelerate immediately back into the fast lane of your prepregnant lifestyle? This very dependent season of your child's life—whether she is breast- or bottle-fed—is relatively short, and it would be beneficial for both of you if you could settle back and enjoy it as much as you can. (This applies whether or not you need to return to a full- or part-time job outside the home or have other children making demands on your time.)

Returning to work. "I need to return to my job in two months, and I don't see how I can spend eight or ten hours in the office at the same time I'm trying to nurse."

Even one or two months of nursing are worth doing, and believe it or not, with some planning, creativity, and assistance on the home front, it is possible for a breast-feeding mother to return to work. The adjustments will vary considerably with the age of the baby, the location of the job, and the hours involved.

BREAST-FEEDING BASICS

As mentioned in chapter 3, your new baby may be nursed for the first time immediately after delivery or some time later if you or the baby has medical needs that require immediate attention. A newborn is alert and most ready to nurse during the first two hours after birth; therefore many physicians recommend that a mother offer the breast during that time if at all possible. However, even if your first feeding must be delayed several hours or even days, you can still get off to a good start.

Whenever you begin, you and your baby should be able to find a position that not only is comfortable but also allows him to latch on to the breast properly. This occurs when his mouth closes over the areola and forms a seal with his gums. His tongue should be positioned against the underside of the nipple and then with wavelike motions, compress it, emptying the milk-containing ducts just below the areola.

If he repeatedly clamps down on the nipple only and not the areola, you will probably develop some major pain and cracking in the nipple before long—and have a frustrated baby as well because he won't get much milk this way. Some babies at first seem more interested in licking or nibbling than in grasping the breast properly. While it is a good idea in general to avoid bottle feedings during the first several days unless absolutely necessary, it is particularly important that these "lick and chew" newborns stay away from formula and pacifiers until they catch on to latching on.

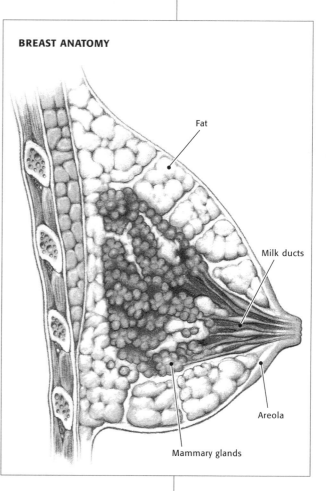

BREAST ANATOMY

Fat

Milk ducts

Areola

Mammary glands

If you nurse immediately after delivery, it will usually be easiest to lie on your side with the baby's entire body facing you, stomach to stomach. This position will also be very useful in the days following a cesarean delivery, in order to prevent the weight of the baby from pressing on your sore abdomen. In this position you will need to lift your breast with the opposite hand to move the areola next to his mouth. More common is the sitting cuddle position, in which the infant's head is cradled in the bend of your elbow with your forearm supporting his back and your hand holding his bottom or upper leg. An alternative sitting position, called the football hold, places your baby's body at your side supported by your arm with your hand holding his head. This is another helpful position if you have had a cesarean birth, since it minimizes pressure on your incision site. It is also useful for mothers of twins who wish to nurse both babies simultaneously.

Once you are positioned comfortably, gently lift your breast and stroke your baby's cheek or lower lip with your nipple. This will provoke his rooting reflex. When his mouth opens wide, gently pull him to you so that your areola enters his mouth. You will need to make this move relatively quickly before his mouth closes. Be sure not to "meet him halfway" by leaning forward, or else you will have a very sore back before long. It helps to compress your breast slightly between thumb and palm or between two fingers in a scissorlike position, using your free hand, but stay a couple inches behind the areola when you do so.

When your baby begins sucking, nerve endings in the nipple send a message to the pituitary gland at the base of your brain. The pituitary in turn secretes the hormone prolactin, which stimulates more milk production, and **oxytocin,** which causes tiny muscles that surround the milk ducts to squeeze milk toward the areola. This event is called the **let-down reflex,** which you will probably feel as a change of pressure or, less commonly, as a tingling within the breasts. Some women, however, can't feel the let-down reflex at all. Once your milk has come in, you may notice anything from a slow drip of milk to a full-blown spray during let-down. Many women will experience let-down not only in response to their baby's sucking but also when their baby—or someone else's—begins to cry. During the first days after delivery, you will also feel contractions of the uterus in response to the oxytocin released by the pituitary gland. While these might be uncomfortable, they are carrying out the important function of reducing the size of your uterus.

**NURSING POSITION—
SIDE**

The let-down reflex may be inhibited by certain drugs, as well as by smoking. Let-down also may not function as well if you are upset or tense. It is therefore important that your nursing times be as relaxed and calm as possible. You might consider setting up a comfortable "nursing corner" at home, where your favorite chair (very often a rocker) and a table with soft light, a few key supplies, soft music, and even something to read are within easy reach. A small stash of healthy snack food and some water or juice may be a welcome addition as well. If you live in a multistory setting, you may want to set up one of these "nursing stations" on each floor. Take the phone off the hook and savor these moments, not worrying about whatever else you think you should be doing. Watch your baby, caress him, talk or sing softly to him, or take some time to pray quietly. These can be sweet times of reflection and meditation during otherwise busy days.

Remember that for the first three or four days you will be producing **colostrum,** the yellowish, high-protein liquid full of antibodies and white cells. With rare exception, this is all your baby will need, since he was born with extra fluid in his system that compensates for the relatively low fluid volume of colostrum. When your milk supply begins to arrive, you will notice some increased fullness, warmth, and probably tenderness. During this process your breasts are said to be **engorged,** and they may actually swell so much that your baby will have trouble latching on to them. Should this occur, you can gently express some milk from each breast, softening it so your baby can grasp more easily. To express milk, grasp the edge of the areola between thumb and fingers and then repeatedly squeeze while pushing gently toward your chest. (A warm compress or hot shower may be needed to get the milk flowing.) Engorgement typically lasts only a day or two (see page 133).

NURSING POSITION—CUDDLE

Nursing patterns

Each baby has a unique style of nursing, and yours may mesh easily with your milk supply and lifestyle or may require that you make some adjustments. Some infants get right down to business, sucking vigorously and efficiently without much hesitation. These "barracudas" contrast sharply with the "gourmet" nursers, who take their sweet time, playing with the nipple at first, sampling their meal, and then eventually getting started. Some babies vary the gourmet approach by resting every few minutes, as if savoring their feeding, or even falling asleep one or more times during the nursing session. The "suck and snooze" types may exasperate a mother who feels that she doesn't have all day to nurse. While it's all right to provide a little mild stimulation (such as undressing him) to get Sleepy back on task and complete his feeding, some downsizing of your expectations for the day's activities may be necessary to prevent ongoing frustration.

Newborns also vary in the frequency with which they need to nurse. A typical span between feedings will be two to three hours or eight to twelve times per day, but during the first days after birth, the interval may be longer, with only six to eight feedings in a twenty-four-hour period. The baby will feed more often than usual during growth spurts. The time involved in a feeding will also vary, but a typical feeding will take ten to fifteen minutes per breast.

As with nearly every aspect of life, what is said to be "typical" may not match with what happens in reality—especially with newborns. For example, your first nursing experiences in a hospital setting may be somewhat confusing, especially if you are not rooming in. Many hospital nurseries still adhere to the tradition of bringing out all the babies to their mothers for feeding on a fixed schedule. But most babies don't automatically synchronize to Nursery Standard Time and may be sound asleep for these nursing "appointments." The result is repeated frustration for mothers whose zonked-out newborns seem to have little interest in latching on, let alone sucking, during the first few days after birth. In a worst-case scenario, a baby who hasn't been ready to nurse with Mom might wake up and sound off when he's parked in the nursery, only to have his crying ignored or answered with a bottle. Many hospital nurseries now bring newborns to their mothers when they're hungry rather than in fixed shifts. Overall, however, rooming in gives everyone a better chance to get acquainted and, more important, nurse when the baby is awake and hungry.

NURSING POSITION—
FOOTBALL HOLD

Don't worry if your baby doesn't seem terribly interested in frequent nursing during the first few days. That will change, often just after you bring him home. The early phase of sleepiness that occurs as he adjusts to the outside world will usually give way to more active crying and nursing—sometimes every few hours—after the first week. Some parents are aghast when this happens. The mellow baby they enjoyed in the hospital suddenly seems wired and insatiable just a few days later. Don't panic. Instead, look at this as a time to hone your nursing skills with a very willing partner.

The newborn baby normally will announce his desire for milk very clearly, with some insistent crying every two to four hours. When this occurs, it is appropriate to tend to him promptly, change him if necessary, and then settle in for a feeding. Some infants make sucking movements or fuss for a while before overtly sounding off. There's no point in waiting for full-blown crying before offering the breast. For five to ten minutes you will notice him swallowing after every few sucks, and then he will shift gears to a more relaxed mode or even seem to lose interest.

At that point he can be burped, either by lifting him and placing his head over your shoulder, or by sitting him up with your hand under his jaw and gently patting him on the back. You can also place him face down across your lap, with head supported and chest a little higher than abdomen, and gently pat his back.

Once he burps, he may show interest in the other breast. (If he doesn't burp and yet he appears comfortable, you can still proceed with the feeding.) Since the first side may be more completely emptied during the feeding, it is wise to alternate the breast from which he starts. (A small pin or clip that you move from one side of your nursing bra to the other can help remind you where to begin next time.)

Relatively frequent nursing is typical after the first days of life, and it will help stimulate your milk production and let-down reflex. A newborn who seems to be very content with infrequent feedings (more than four hours apart) should probably be checked by your physician to confirm that his activity level is satisfactory. He may in fact need to be awakened to feed every three hours to ensure adequate weight gain during the first two or three weeks.

Problems and concerns with nursing

"How do I know if she's getting enough?" During the first few days after birth, this concern often prods new mothers toward bottle feeding, where they have the security of seeing exactly how much the baby is consuming. Remember that the quantity of milk you produce during a feeding will start with as little as half an ounce (15 ml) of colostrum during the first day or two and increase to an ounce (30 ml) as the milk supply arrives by the fourth or fifth day. After the first week, your milk output will range from two to six ounces per feeding. Obviously, there is no direct way for you to measure how much your baby is

*NOTE: It is important to maintain proper head control of the child.

BURPING BABY OVER SHOULDER   **BURPING BABY UPRIGHT**   **BURPING BABY OVER LAP**

sucking from your breast, but other signs will indicate how the two of you are doing:

- When the room is quiet, you will hear your baby swallowing.
- Once your milk has arrived, you may notice that your breasts soften during a feeding as they are emptied of milk.
- After the first four or five days, you should be changing six to eight wet diapers each day. In addition, you will notice one or several small, dark green stools—sometimes one after every feeding—that become lighter after the first (meconium) stools are passed. As your milk supply becomes well established, your baby's stools will take on a yellowish color and a soft or runny consistency. Later on, stools typically become less frequent.
- Tracking your baby's weight will give you specific and important information. *It is normal for a baby to drop nearly 10 percent of her birth weight (about eleven or twelve ounces, for example, for a seven-pound baby) during the first week.* Usually she will have returned to her birth weight by two weeks of age, and thereafter she should gain about two-thirds to one ounce per day. Obviously you can't track these small changes at home on the bathroom scale. Instead, it is common to have a checkup during the first week or two after birth, during which your baby will be weighed on a scale that can detect smaller changes. If there is any question about appropriate weight gain, your doctor will ask you to return every week (or more often, if needed) to follow her progress.

One of the most important—and hardest—things to remember if you are concerned about the adequacy of your nursing is to *relax.* If you approach every feeding with fear and trembling, you may have difficulty with your let-down reflex. Furthermore, newborns seem to have an uncanny sense of Mom's anxiety, and their jittery response may interfere with smooth latching on and sucking. Remember that for many women, breast feeding requires time, effort, and learning. Even if your first few feedings seem awkward or your baby doesn't seem to be getting the hang of it immediately, you should be able to make this process work. Take a deep breath, take your time, and don't be afraid to ask for help if you are truly having trouble getting started.

"It hurts when I nurse!" No one wants to spend a good portion of the day in misery, and a strong dose of pain with every feeding can demoralize even the most dedicated breast-feeding mother. Some tenderness during the baby's first few sucks of each feeding is not unusual for a few days after birth while a callus is being formed.

Many mothers also feel aching during the let-down reflex, and some may even notice a brief shooting pain deeper in the breast after nursing as the milk supply is refilling. For some women the engorgement of the breasts prior to each nursing session can be very painful. It is possible, in fact, to have intense pain with engorgement even when your nursing technique is correct and nothing specific is wrong with your breasts. Some mothers who are unprepared for such severe discomfort may give up on nursing too soon. But becoming comfortable with nursing may, in fact, take a few days or even a few weeks as your baby learns and your body adjusts to this new function.

In most cases, pain serves as a warning that should not be ignored. If you have significant, ongoing pain with nursing, you should review this with your doctor and attempt to identify one of the causes that can and should be treated.

Intense discomfort can arise from traumatized, cracked, or inflamed nipples, which, of course, are sensitive areas to begin with. If the nipple is irritated at the tip, it is probably entering your baby's mouth at an upward angle and rubbing on her palate. During the latching-on process, try holding your breast so the nipple points downward. This is often easier if you are sitting, using the cuddle or football hold.

If the nipple is more tender at the base, it is more likely being chewed during feedings. Remember that your baby needs to take the entire areola into her mouth when she latches on, so your nipple lies against her tongue. If she won't open her mouth fully or slides off the areola after latching on, your nipple will be gummed continually while you nurse. To add insult to injury, your baby may not get enough milk when this occurs. The combination of miserable mom and crying newborn is often enough to send Dad out into the night in search of formula.

To help your baby latch on to the whole areola (and not just your nipple), wait for her to open her mouth wide enough and then gently pull her to the breast. If you are engorged and she is having difficulty forming a seal around the areola, you can express or pump some milk so that area will be softer. You may have to utilize the football hold (see page 127) to give your hand better control of her head and thus keep her from sliding off the areola. If she seems to lose her position during the feeding, don't be afraid to pull her gently from the breast and then reattach. If she has a strong hold, you should first loosen it by pulling downward gently on her chin or inserting a finger into the corner of her mouth to release the vacuum seal formed by her gums.

Other causes of painful irritation of one or both nipples, or even full-blown inflammation known as **dermatitis,** include:

- Overzealous use of soap and water that can remove the skin's own moisturizers. Rinse your breasts during your normal shower or bath but keep soap away from your nipples.

- Continuous moisture on the skin surface. This can occur when the breast is not allowed to dry off after a feeding or when the pads of a nursing bra are moist. Air drying for a few minutes after nursing is the simplest solution, while making certain that your nursing bra is dry as well.

- An allergic reaction to breast creams or oils. Paradoxically, traditional remedies for breast soreness such as vitamin E preparations or impure lanolin may make the problem worse if they provoke an allergic dermatitis. If your nipple develops redness, swelling, and a burning sensation, stop using any nipple cream. If the problem persists or worsens, see your doctor. You may have to use a mild anti-inflammatory prescription cream for a few days to calm this problem down more quickly.

- An infection with the yeast organism known as **Candida albicans,** which will also be present in the baby's mouth. In this case the irritation may not only burn but also itch. Candida may appear sometime after you have been nursing without any problems. A tip-off is the presence of small, white patches inside your baby's cheeks. Candida infection in the baby's mouth (also known as **thrush**) is not a dangerous condition, but it can be a persistent annoyance.

  Candida infections usually respond to treatment with an antifungal cream (check with your doctor). At the same time, your baby should be given antifungal drops by mouth. If both of you are not treated concurrently for several days, the infection may bounce back and forth between you. Furthermore, in order to prevent reinfection, you will need to change nursing pads after every feeding. If your baby is receiving any feedings from a bottle or is using a pacifier, you will need to boil the rubber nipples and pacifiers every day until the infection clears.

- Rarely an ongoing **eczema** problem that has appeared on other parts of your body will erupt on the breast during nursing. You will want to consult with your doctor about appropriate treatment, which may involve the short-term use of a mild anti-inflammatory cream.

- A potentially more serious cause of pain is **mastitis,** an infection caused by bacteria that gain entry into breast tissue, usually through a cracked nipple. Symptoms include pain, swelling, heat, redness, and tenderness in a localized area of one breast, accompanied by generalized aching and fever. If there is no fever, it probably is a plugged duct and does not require antibiotics. Should this problem develop, it is important to contact your physician. Antibiotics that are safe for both mother and baby will normally be prescribed, and acetaminophen may be used to reduce both pain and temperature. The use of warm, moist compresses can assist in the treatment. *In addition, it is important to continue nursing,* although you may be more comfortable with more frequent, shorter sessions. Your baby will not become ill by nursing from an infected breast, and emptying the breast of milk helps clear the infection. Ice cubes can be applied directly to the breast (at first in quick, short strokes) above and below the infected area. This can help reduce pain and swelling.

Aside from some of these specific treatments for breast and nipple pain, how else do you spell *relief* until the cracking or irritation heals?

- Don't attempt to toughen your nipples, either before or after the birth, by rubbing, stretching, or pinching them.
- Acetaminophen (or ibuprofen) may be taken thirty to sixty minutes before you nurse. Of course, it is wise to take medications only when necessary while nursing, but a short-term pain reliever that helps you continue nursing will be a worthwhile exception.
- Take some measures to "move things along" during your feedings. Express a little milk before your baby latches on and then gently massage your breasts while nursing to help them empty more quickly. Think in terms of shorter but more frequent feeding times.
- Air dry your nipples for several minutes after you nurse. Some mothers find that ice applied to the nipple just before nursing may reduce pain when the baby latches on. Many traditional remedies such as breast creams, oils, vitamin E capsules, or even tea bags have fallen out of favor, especially since some may actually increase the irritation. However, a *pure* lanolin preparation applied after nursing may help restore normal skin moisture and decrease pain.
- If your baby forms a strong suction with her gums, be sure to release her grip before you pull her from your breast.
- If all else fails, consider pumping your breasts and allowing your baby to accept your milk from a bottle while your nipples are healing, especially if they have been bleeding. This is less desirable during the first several

days while she is still learning the ropes, but it's better than giving up on nursing altogether.

Remember that a temporary time-out from breast feeding to allow for healing or for any other reason (for example, an illness affecting either mother or baby) does not mean that you cannot resume nursing when things calm down. Pumping your breasts at feeding time will help you maintain your supply. Furthermore, even if your baby has spent a fair amount of time with a bottle, she can learn (or relearn) to obtain nourishment successfully from your breast.

"My baby wants to nurse all the time. I'm getting sick of being a human pacifier." All babies derive comfort and satisfaction from sucking, but some are true enthusi-

PUMPING AND STORING BREAST MILK

There will likely be at least a few, if not many, times during your breast feeding when you will not be able to nurse your baby for several hours (or days) at a time. These occasions might involve anything from an evening out for dinner, an unexpected trip, a time-out to allow irritated nipples to heal, or even the desire to supply breast milk to a premature infant who must be fed by tube. Nursing mothers who begin or resume work outside the home may have to contend with daily absences of several hours from their babies. While formula can be a satisfactory substitute in these situations, it is also possible to maintain your baby's nourishment with your own milk.

GUIDELINES FOR EXPRESSING MILK—FOR IMMEDIATE OR FUTURE USE
- First, hands should be thoroughly washed with soap and water each time you collect milk. (The breasts do not need to be washed, however, but should be free of any lotions or creams.)
- Next, before any milk is expressed, each breast should be gently massaged. Using the palm of the hand, stroke several times from below, above, and sides of the breast toward the nipple, applying gentle pressure.
- After massaging, milk can be expressed from each breast, either by hand or with the assistance of a breast pump. Either method is acceptable, and the choice of one or the other approach can be based on effectiveness, convenience, and cost.

- As with the first days of nursing, you may find it easier to begin expressing milk for three to five minutes at a time and then gradually progress to ten- or fifteen-minute sessions if you are collecting milk on a regular basis.

To express by hand. Sit in a comfortable position and lean over the container into which you will be collecting the milk. Place the thumb and index finger of one hand about an inch to either side of the nipple and then press toward your chest while gently squeezing the fingers toward one another. At first, you may see a few drops, a literal spurt, or nothing at all.

When the milk stops flowing, release your fingers, rotate to another position around the nipple, and squeeze again. If you don't see much milk, keep trying and don't give up—becoming adept at expressing milk may take practice. You may find that massaging again improves your flow. It may also be helpful to alternate between breasts, rather than expressing all the milk from one before moving to the other.

To express using a breast pump. Breast pumps utilize a funnel or bicycle-horn-shaped apparatus that is placed against the breast. A vacuum is created, either by manually moving a piston or by an electrically powered device, and milk is sucked into an appropriate container. Electrical pumps are more expensive but may be more efficient, especially for a mother who needs to express asts who would be more than happy to turn every nursing session into a ninety-minute marathon. You may be happy with this arrangement, but more likely it can lead to sore nipples and a gnawing concern that your entire existence has been reduced to being a mobile restaurant. Fortunately, you are not without options.

A healthy newborn, properly attached to the breast and sucking continuously, will empty about 90 percent of the milk available on each side within ten minutes. You can usually hear and feel the transition from intense sucking and swallowing to a more relaxed, pacifying sucking after five to ten minutes on each side, at which point you can decide how long you want to continue. If you're both feeling snugly and comfortable, relax and enjoy it. But if it's the middle of the

(continued)

milk on a regular basis. (Some models can pump from both breasts simultaneously.) It is usually possible to rent one from a medical-supply company, hospital, or other local resource in order to confirm its usefulness before actually buying one.

To make an airtight seal between the pump and your breast, a little water or milk can be applied to the skin where contact is made. The apparatus should be applied snugly enough to make a good seal but not pressed so tightly to restrict the flow of milk. Pumping can continue until after the milk has stopped flowing for a minute or so. After you are finished, use soap and water to wash whatever components of the pump came in contact with the milk and then allow them to air dry. (Check the manufacturer's directions for specific details about cleaning and proper handling of the equipment you are using.)

COLLECTING AND STORING MILK

Your milk can be collected in a clean baby bottle or a nurser bag that attaches directly to a nipple assembly. Your baby can immediately drink what you have just expressed (which would be the case, for example, if you are expressing milk while sore nipples are healing), but you can also store milk for future use.

Remember that breast milk is a perishable food. Here are some guidelines for handling it so it will maintain its nutritional value and not become contaminated:

- If you plan to refrigerate or freeze milk, do so as soon as you have finished collecting it. Label and date it.
- You may feed a baby fresh breast milk that has been left at room temperature for up to six hours, after which the milk should be discarded.
- Breast milk that has just been expressed may be kept in the refrigerator for seventy-two hours, but any that is thawed from the freezer must be used within twenty-four hours.
- Various time limits for safe storage of breast milk in the freezer have been recommended; they range from two weeks to six months. A reasonable guideline would be to store milk no longer than one month. Mark each bottle or plastic bottle liner with the date you collected it and use the oldest milk first.
- You can combine the milk from both breasts into a single bottle or plastic bottle liner. If a particular pumping session has not yielded enough milk, you can freeze it and then add more cooled milk to the same container later—but don't change the date on your label.
- When you want to feed your baby expressed milk, thaw it by placing the bottle or bottle liner in warm water. Heating milk in a microwave is not recommended because of the potential formation of hot spots in the milk that could burn the baby's mouth.

night and you need sleep, or other children need your attention, or you're getting sore, you won't destroy your baby's personality by gently detaching her.

A problem can arise, however, if your baby sounds terribly unhappy and indignant when you decide enough's enough. How do you respond? The answer depends on how far along and how well established you are in your nursing relationship. In the earliest days when milk is just arriving or you're not sure whether she is truly swallowing an adequate volume, it is probably better to give her the benefit of the doubt and continue for a while longer. This is especially true if you are blessed with a casual "gourmet" or "suck and snooze" baby who may not empty your breast very quickly.

But watch the various indicators of your progress: good swallowing sounds, frequent wet diapers, weight gain, and softening of your breast after feeding. If these are going well and you feel you have developed a smooth nursing routine after two or three weeks, you can consider other calming maneuvers, including the use of a pacifier (see sidebar). *If your soothing maneuvers aren't working, however, or your baby doesn't seem to be gaining weight, contact your baby's doctor for further evaluation and recommendations.*

PACIFIER POINTERS

Some parents say they could not have survived their baby's infancy without these gadgets, while others (and some breast-feeding advisers) see them as an abomination. While they are not exactly a threat to world peace, pacifiers can be overused. They are definitely not good for very young infants who have not established stable and efficient nursing patterns. The feel, texture, taste, and smell of a pacifier are clearly different from that of Mom's nipples, and sucking a pacifier too soon may interfere with a baby's learning the real thing. But after two weeks or more, assuming nursing is going well, a pacifier can help calm a baby who

- is already fed and full, but still wants to suck;
- doesn't have anything else, such as a wet diaper, bothering him; and
- will suck on it with apparent satisfaction.

Inserting a pacifier in an infant's mouth must not be a substitute for normal feeding, parental nurturing, or checking to see if something is wrong.

If you decide to use a pacifier, make sure you get a one-piece model with a soft nipple—either the straight bottle shape or the angled "orthodontic" type. Never use the nipple assembly from a feeding bottle as a pacifier because the nipple can come loose and choke your baby. Make sure you have the right size for babies younger than six months and that it is designed to survive boiling or trips through the dishwasher. For the first six months, you will need to clean pacifiers frequently in this way to reduce the risk of infection.

Babies are unable to replace pacifiers that fall out of their mouth, so you will have to do this for them. *Do not, under any circumstances, tie a pacifier to a string or ribbon around a baby's neck to keep it in place. Your solution to the wandering pacifier could strangle your baby.*

If you find a pacifier that your baby likes, buy several. They have a knack for disappearing into the sofa, under the car seat, or into the bottom of the diaper bag, so lots of backups are a good idea.

Some mothers make the mistake of assuming that every sound from a baby should be answered with nursing, when something else (or nothing in particular) may be bothering her. If, for example, she has just finished a good feeding thirty minutes ago and begins to fuss after being put down for a nap, it is reasonable to wait and listen for a while, since she may settle down on her own, rather than trying to nurse her again. Otherwise you may find yourself spending nearly every minute of the day and night with your baby attached to your breast. As the days pass, you will become more discerning about the meaning of your baby's various crying messages.

A final note: If you are having a significant problem with breast feeding—whether it be latching on, anatomy problems, sore nipples, sluggish nursers, slow weight gain, or anything else—seek out a **lactation consultant** for some additional help. This is a health-care professional whose wealth of knowledge and practical suggestions can help both mother and baby succeed at breast feeding, even when the going gets very tough. Your baby's doctor or a local hospital should be able to give you a referral.

BOTTLE-FEEDING BASICS

Choosing a formula

First things first: *For the first year, do not feed your baby cow's milk from the dairy section at the store.* Cow's milk that has not been specifically modified for use in infant formulas is not digested well by human infants; it contains significant loads of protein that your baby's kidneys will have difficulty processing, and it contains inadequate amounts of vitamin C and iron. It also contains inadequate amounts of fat, which provides 50 percent of the calories in human milk and formula. Furthermore, the new baby's intestine may be irritated by cow's milk, resulting in a gradual but potentially significant loss of red blood cells. Finally, some of the protein in cow's milk may be absorbed through the baby's intestine in a way that can lead to allergy problems later in life.

The vast majority of bottle-fed infants are given commercial formulas, whose manufacturers have gone to great lengths to match mother's milk as closely as possible. The most commonly used formulas are based on cow's milk that has been *significantly* altered for human consumption. Among other things, the protein is made more digestible and less allergenic, lactose is added to match that of human milk, and butterfat is removed and replaced with a combination of other fats more readily absorbed by infants.

Soy formulas, which are based on soy protein, do not contain lactose, which is the main carbohydrate in cow's milk. These are used for the small percentage of infants who cannot digest lactose and who develop excessive gas, cramps, and diarrhea when they consume regular formula. In addition, bottle-fed infants who have diarrhea resulting from a viral or bacterial infection may develop a temporary difficulty processing lactose. During their recovery, these babies often tolerate soy formulas better than cow's milk formulas. Infants from families with a strong history of cow's milk allergy have traditionally been started on soy formulas as a precautionary measure, but many of these may be allergic to soy formula as well.

BOTTLE-FEEDING BABY

There is a variety of formulas that have been designed for special needs. Infants who are allergic to both cow's milk and soy formulas may use what are called **protein hydrolysate** formulas, in which the proteins are essentially predigested. Special formulas are also available for babies with phenylketonuria (PKU) and for premature infants.

Check with your baby's physician regarding the type(s) of formula he or she recommends. Once you have made your choice, you can stock up with one or more of the three forms in which they are normally sold:

- **Ready-to-feed** is just that. Put it into a bottle if it isn't already packaged in one, make sure the temperature is right, and you're all set. While extremely convenient, this format is also the most expensive.
- **Concentrate** must be mixed with water in the exact amount recommended by the manufacturer. If it is too diluted (mixed with too much water), your baby will be shortchanged on nutrients. But if it is too concentrated (mixed with too little water), diarrhea and dehydration may result. The unused portion of an opened can of concentrate may

be sealed and stored in the refrigerator for twenty-four hours, after which it should be discarded.

- **Powdered formula** is the least expensive form and must be mixed exactly as recommended, using the measuring scoop provided.

If you cannot afford formula and do not have access to community resources, it is possible to mix your own using evaporated (*not* condensed) milk, corn syrup, and sterile water. However, you must talk to your doctor about the specific combination of ingredients as well as additional vitamin supplementation.

You can prepare a day's worth of bottles at one time, storing the ones you don't immediately need in the refrigerator for up to twenty-four hours. The good news for today's bottle-feeding parents is that the laborious process of boiling water and sterilizing bottles, which consumed a great deal of time and energy in previous generations, is (with a few exceptions) usually not necessary to prepare formula safely today. However, these basic precautions will prevent your baby's formula from being contaminated by potentially harmful bacteria:

- Wash your hands before you begin handling formula, water, bottles, and nipples.
- If the formula you are using comes from a can, wipe the top before you open it. Use a separate can opener specifically designated for this purpose, and clean it on a regular basis.
- Unless there has been a recent flood, earthquake, outbreak of bacterial infection, or other local calamity, tap water is usually safe to use in mixing formula. (Check with your baby's doctor for a recommendation regarding whether your water should be boiled first.) Running the cold-water tap for a minute or two will decrease the amount of lead or other impurities that might have collected within the pipes. *Well water should be checked for bacterial contamination or excessive mineral content and should always be boiled before you use it.* If you have any doubts or concerns, use bottled water.
- After each use, bottles and nipple assemblies can be washed in the dishwasher or by hand with hot, soapy water, using a bottle brush to clean the inside thoroughly. Follow with a good rinse.

It's not necessary to warm a bottle, although younger babies prefer tepid or room-temperature formula. To warm a bottle you've stored in the refrigerator, let it sit for a few minutes in hot water. Warming the bottle in a microwave is *not* recommended because uneven heating may cause pockets of milk hot enough to scald a baby's mouth. Before feeding, shake the bottle well and let a drop or two fall on your hand. It should be barely warm and definitely not hot. Also check the flow rate from the nipple. An ideal flow is about one drop per second when the bottle is held upside down. If the nipple allows milk to flow too quickly, your baby may choke on it. If it flows too slowly, he may swallow air while he tries to suck out his meal.

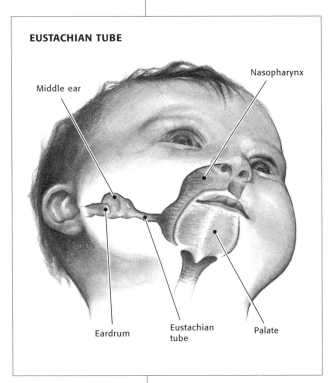

EUSTACHIAN TUBE

Middle ear

Nasopharynx

Eardrum

Eustachian
tube

Palate

You can use four- or eight-ounce bottles made from plastic or glass. (Later on, however, when he can hold his own bottle, glass bottles should be replaced with plastic.) Many parents prefer the nurser style in which formula is poured into a plastic bag that attaches to a plastic shell and nipple assembly. Babies tend to swallow less air from the bags, but they cost more in the long run. It is important not to use the bags to mix concentrate or powder because you cannot measure accurately with them.

As with breast feeding, bottle feeding should be relaxed and unhurried, preferably in a comfortable and quiet area of your home. Hold your baby across your lap with his upper body slightly raised and his head supported. A flat position during feedings not only increases the risk of choking but also allows milk to flow into the passageways, called **eustachian tubes,** that lead into the middle ears. Frequent ear infections may result. Stroke the nipple across his cheek or lower lip to start the rooting reflex, and be sure to keep the bottle elevated enough so the milk completely covers the inside of the nipple. Otherwise, he may start sucking air.

The fact that milk is flowing from a bottle does not mean that the feeding should switch to autopilot. Take time to lock eyes with your infant, talk or sing softly to him, gently caress him, and pray about this new life with which you've been entrusted. Your baby should not be left unattended with a bottle propped in his mouth. This practice puts your baby at an unnecessary risk for ear infections or choking.

Formula-fed newborns typically will consume two or three ounces every three or four hours, gradually increasing to a routine of taking about four ounces every four hours by the end of the first month. A general rule of thumb is that a normal baby will need between two and two and one-half ounces of formula per pound of body weight each day (up to fifteen pounds). Normally he will give crying or fussing cues when he is hungry and turn his head away or push the nipple out of his mouth with his tongue when he is full. If the bottle isn't empty, don't force the issue. However, during the first few weeks it is wise to awaken him to feed if he is sleeping for stretches of more than four hours during the day.

When (if ever) should the baby's formula be changed?

Most doctors will recommend that bottle-fed infants begin with an iron-fortified cow's milk formula, and if doing well with it, use it through the first year of life. (Iron is not absorbed as efficiently from formula as from breast milk, and the amount added to iron-fortified formula ensures that your baby will get what he needs.) Like their breast-fed counterparts, babies in this age-group do not need other vitamin supplementation.

One of the headaches that most bottle-feeding parents eventually face is figuring out whether irritability, especially if accompanied by gas or loose stools, means that baby and formula are not getting along. There are no clear-cut answers to this dilemma.

If you think your baby might be having a problem with the current formula, discuss it with his physician. It may be appropriate to try another brand, or even a different form of the same brand, and observe the results. Sometimes persistent crying, irritability, and poor sleep at night—definitely one of the most disturbing situations for new parents—will provoke a switch to soy-based formula. If it seems to help, stay with it. Beware of making changes too quickly or attributing every one of your baby's problems to his current formula, because you won't be able to sort out cause and effect, and you may overlook some other cause of his discomfort. Occasionally there may be such frustration and expense associated with finding a tolerated formula, that relactation may be considered. A lactation consultant can assist even if several weeks without nursing have passed.

HEALTH AND SAFETY CONCERNS: CHECKUPS AND IMMUNIZATIONS

Your pediatrician or family physician will ask that you follow a specific routine of well-baby visits; there is a definite purpose to this plan that involves monitoring the baby's progress and administering immunizations that are very important to her health. If you have been sent home from the hospital within twenty-four hours of your baby's birth, your baby should be checked within the next twenty-four to forty-eight hours. If all is going smoothly, you can expect to take your baby back for a checkup between two and four weeks of age and then again at two months.

During these visits, the baby will be weighed and measured and the results plotted on a standardized growth chart, which allows the health-care provider to track her progress over time. You will be asked how she is feeding, sleeping, and eliminating urine and stool. At the one- and two-month visits, specific behavioral milestones such as smiling and head control will probably be discussed. The baby will be examined from head to toe, so be sure to put her in an outfit that can be removed easily.

It is important that you bring up any problems or concerns you have, no matter how minor they seem. If you have a number of questions, write them down and present them at the beginning of the visit so the practitioner can see what's on your mind. Don't suddenly pull them out as a list of by-the-way items after everything else is done. If the examiner seems rushed and uneasy about taking time to deal with your concerns, find out how and when you can go over them. Some large practices have well-trained nurses or other health educators who can answer most of the questions you might have.

Your baby will most likely receive her first **hepatitis B** immunization either at birth or during the first two months of life. The second dose will be given one month after the first. At the two-month visit, it is customary for babies to receive their **DTaP (diphtheria/tetanus/pertussis), OPV (oral polio)** or **IPV (inactivated polio)**, and **hemophilus B** immunizations.

Many parents are anxious about the prospect of their tiny baby receiving these vaccines, and some have read literature suggesting that they are dangerous or ineffective. But the overwhelming evidence indicates that these shots do indeed drastically reduce the risk of these terrible diseases and that the odds of having a problem from any of the vaccines are far less than the odds of contracting the disease if no vaccine is given. (See page A26 for an immunization chart for children newborn to sixteen years of age.)

All the infections that vaccines guard us against can be very serious or even lethal. Some, such as diphtheria and polio, terrorized entire communities a century ago but have become extremely uncommon through widespread vaccination efforts. On the other hand, the bacteria that cause whooping cough and tetanus are still very prevalent, and quite ready, willing, and able to infect those who have not been adequately vaccinated. These illnesses can be prevented for a very modest amount of discomfort and cost and with an extremely low risk of any significant complications. Unfortunately, because of concerns over the expense, risks, or appropriateness of vaccines, some parents neglect, avoid, or even actively oppose immunization programs. This is unwise and places children in needless peril. If you have any concerns over the safety or effectiveness of any vaccine recommended for your child, be sure to discuss them with her physician.

What about side effects of immunizations?

Of these routine immunizations, pertussis (the *P* in DTaP) traditionally has caused the most side effects when given in the original DPT format. Now most children are receiving the so-called "acellular" form of pertussis (abbreviated *aP*),

---

WHAT DO DTAP, OPV/IPV, HEMOPHILUS B, AND HEPATITIS B VACCINES PREVENT?

Diphtheria is a serious bacterial infection that causes a thick membrane to form in the nose, throat, or airway. The membrane is attached to underlying tissues, so that attempting to remove it causes bleeding. Diphtheria bacteria within the membrane produce a toxin that can damage heart, liver, kidney, and nerve tissue. Paralysis and death may result. Because of widespread vaccinations, fewer than five cases occur in the U.S. each year.

Pertussis (whooping cough) causes severe coughing, often to the point of choking; it can last for months. It is particularly rough on infants and small children and can lead to pneumonia, seizures, and death. This disease is highly contagious and much more common than diphtheria. About four thousand cases are reported each year, half of which involve children less than a year old.

Tetanus results from a toxin produced by bacteria that enter the body through contaminated wounds. The toxin causes painful, spasmodic contractions of muscles (which gave rise to the colloquial term *lockjaw* for this disease) and can lead to death.

Polio is a viral infection that damages the central nervous system; it can cause mild or serious paralysis and results in death in 5 to 10 percent of the cases.

Hemophilus B is a type of bacteria that can cause, among other things, pneumonia and meningitis (an infection of the membranes that enclose the brain and spinal cord). Since the introduction of hemophilus B vaccines during the past decade, the number of cases of meningitis in young children caused by this bacteria has fallen dramatically.

Hepatitis B is an infection of the liver caused by a virus that is most commonly transmitted in three ways: from an infected mother to her infant, (later in life) through sexual contact with an infected person, or by exposure to infected blood. However, a large number of cases occur without a history of any of these events, which is one reason health officials recommend universal vaccination against this virus.

Fortunately, most people infected with hepatitis B recover without any long-term effects. In a small percentage of cases, however, the immediate illness can be severe enough to cause death. In others, prolonged active infection with the virus occurs, a process that can lead eventually to cirrhosis and cancer of the liver. While hepatitis B is not a common childhood disease, children are at a higher risk for developing long-term complications if they should become infected. Immunization of all children has been recommended as the most effective means to reduce the total number of cases of this disease over the next several years.

which causes far fewer problems. Local soreness and fussiness after the injection, if present, may be treated with a dose of acetaminophen infant drops. These can be given at the time of the immunization or shortly thereafter in order to relieve discomfort. For babies weighing less than twelve pounds, the appropriate amount is one-half a dropper (or 0.4 ml) of the standard infant solution (which contains 80 mg per 0.8 ml). For infants who are heavier than twelve pounds, a full dropper (or 0.8 ml) may be used. For doses in older children, see chart on page 638. Fewer than one in one hundred infants will develop a persistent cry (lasting longer than three hours); about one in three hundred may get a high fever (ranging as high as 105°F); while about one in one thousand may develop an unusual, high-pitched cry. *More severe neurologic complications following the DTaP vaccine, such as a prolonged seizure or change in consciousness, are extremely rare—and may not be directly related to the vaccine at all.* All things considered, these are reasonable risks to take in exchange for protection against a very disruptive and potentially lethal illness.

Oral polio vaccine (OPV) contains live virus, which can very rarely cause the disease in someone receiving it. According to the Centers for Disease Control (CDC), the odds of this occurring are practically infinitesimal: one case in 1.5 million first doses, and one case in 30 million subsequent doses. Some virus may be excreted in the baby's stool after the vaccine is given, and this could cause an infection in someone whose immune system is defective (for example, a person receiving cancer chemotherapy or an individual with AIDS). People with these conditions should avoid close contact with a baby who has just received OPV vaccine, or as an alternative, the baby may be given the inactivated polio vaccine (IPV). Although it is permissable to use all oral or all injectable polio immunization, many physicians are now choosing to use a sequential schedule of IPV/OPV in hope of reducing the number of cases of vaccine associated paralytic polio (VAPP). This would consist of two doses of IPV followed by two doses of OPV.

If your baby is ill at the time of the visit, the vaccines will usually be postponed, because it may be difficult to determine afterwards whether a problem, especially a fever, has been caused by the illness or by the vaccine. If your baby has only a minor case of sniffles, the vaccines will usually be given. If you have any doubt or questions about vaccinations, be sure to get all your questions answered before any immunization is given to your baby.

What if the baby becomes ill?

Because newborns normally receive a healthy donation of Mom's antibodies through the umbilical cord blood supply prior to birth, they usually escape common illnesses such as colds and flu during the first several weeks, as long as they are well nourished and their environment is kept reasonably clean. Nursing infants have the added advantage of ingesting their mother's antibodies at every feeding.

This is indeed providential, because an illness in a baby younger than three months of age is a completely different situation from one in an older baby. For one thing, your new baby has very few ways to notify you that something is wrong. You will not have the luxury of language and specific complaints ("My ear hurts" or "I have a headache") to guide you. You won't have months or years of experience with this particular child—or, if this is your first baby, perhaps with any child—to sense what is "normal" for her.

In addition, your baby's defense system is still under construction, and her ability to fight off microscopic invaders will not be fully operational for a number of months. As a result, a seemingly minor infection acquired during the first several weeks can turn into a major biological war.

Also—and this is the most unsettling reality of all—an illness can go sour much more rapidly in a newborn than in older children. If bacteria are on the move, they can spread like wildfire. If fluids are being lost through vomiting or diarrhea, dehydration can develop over several hours rather than days.

These warnings are not meant to generate undue anxiety but rather to encourage you to notify your baby's health-care provider if you think something is wrong, especially during the first three months of life. You can also reduce your newborn's risk of infection by keeping her out of crowded public places, preventing, if possible, direct contact with individuals who are ill with contagious infections, and minimizing group child-care situations, especially during the first few weeks after birth.

What are the signs that a baby might have a problem?

Some of the danger signals in infants are similar to those that will alert you to problems later in life. But in newborns, several of these signals are more critical and require a more immediate and detailed evaluation than in older babies and children. Here are some important newborn distress signals:

Fever. There will be many occasions in the coming months and years when your child will feel hot, and the thermometer will agree. In babies over three months of age, this may or may not be cause for alarm, depending on what else is going on. *Remember, in a baby under three months of age, a rectal temperature over 100.4°F should be considered cause for an immediate call to the doctor's office.*

(If your baby seems perfectly well, his temperature is slightly above 100.4°F, and there is a possibility that he was overdressed or in a hot environment, you can remove some clothing and try again in thirty to forty-five minutes. A temperature that is closer to normal will be reassuring—but you should run the story by your baby's physician anyway. Do not give the baby acetaminophen (Tylenol) or a tepid bath in this situation, because you need to know whether the fever will come down on its own. Besides, the fever itself is not dangerous. It is the possible causes of the fever that you need to worry about.)

If there is no doubt about the presence of fever, your baby needs to be evaluated right away, either by his own physician or at the emergency room. You may be surprised or even alarmed by the number of tests that may be requested after your baby is examined. The problem is that a newborn fever can indicate a serious bacterial infection that could involve the lungs, urinary tract, or the tissues that surround the brain and spinal cord (these tissues are called **meninges**). Bacteria could also be present in the bloodstream, in which case the baby is said to have **sepsis**.

It is not unusual for a doctor to recommend that a newborn with a fever undergo blood tests, an evaluation of the urine, and a lumbar puncture (or spinal

TAKING AN ACCURATE TEMPERATURE

You cannot accurately judge your baby's temperature by placing your hand on her forehead or anywhere else. *Skin temperature strips are no better.* Furthermore, you cannot get an accurate reading using an oral thermometer in babies and small children because they can't cooperate in keeping the little bulb (whether mercury or electronic) under the tongue. Electronic ear thermometers will give you a ballpark number, but results may vary somewhat depending on your technique. Therefore, even in these days of slick and expensive electronic equipment, an old-fashioned, low-tech rectal mercury thermometer remains the standard when you need to know what's going on with a very young infant. (While mercury has been used in glass thermometers for decades, some now utilize a different silver-colored liquid that behaves the same way. We will use the term *mercury* to refer to the contents of all glass thermometers.)

You should get two or three of these at the drugstore, since they have a habit of breaking or disappearing just when you need one. A rectal thermometer has a short rounded mercury bulb at one end, while an oral thermometer has a longer straight bulb (see diagram on next page). If you're not experienced with a mercury thermometer, you may want to practice reading the temperature

before the moment of truth arrives. Hold the end opposite the mercury bulb between thumb and index finger and slowly rotate the thermometer back and forth. You should be able to see the squared-off end of the mercury column next to the temperature markers. When you read the result, be sure not to confuse numbers such as 100.2° (which lies just above 100°) with 102°, which is quite a bit higher.

Before taking the temperature, shake the thermometer until it reads below 98.6° by grasping the end opposite the bulb and snapping your wrist a few times. Make sure your fingers aren't slippery, and stay away from tables and counters.

Your baby should be lying tummy-down on a bed or crib, or across your knees if he is very small. Keep one hand firmly in control of his lower back and don't try to take the temperature while he is actively squirming or resisting you. Lubricate the mercury tip of the thermometer with petroleum jelly and put a little around the baby's anus as well. Then gently insert the thermometer into the child's rectum about one inch. *Do not force the thermometer into the rectum.* Hold it for about three minutes, then remove it and read the temperature. Afterwards cleanse and rinse the bulb end, shake it down, and put it in its case—which should be labeled as a rectal, not oral, thermometer.

tap), all of which obtain specimens to be cultured for bacteria. A chest X-ray may be ordered if there is any question about pneumonia. In addition, the baby may be admitted to the hospital for two or three days so antibiotics can be given intra-

THERMOMETERS

(rectal)   (oral)

**INSERTING
RECTAL THERMOMETER**

venously (that is, through a vein) while the cultures are growing in the laboratory. If he is doing well and no bacteria are growing in the cultures, he will be sent home.

All of this may seem rather drastic in response to a simple fever, but babies in this age-group are more vulnerable to the spread of bacteria—especially into the bloodstream and meninges. If left untreated, the results could be disastrous.

Feeding poorly. Lack of interest in nursing, poor sucking, or failing to awaken for feeding well beyond the expected time could be an important indicator of a medical problem. If you contact a physician with a concern that your newborn is ill, the physician will want to know, among other things, how the baby appears to be feeding.

Vomiting. As will be discussed later in this chapter, you will need to distinguish between spitting up and vomiting, since the latter is much more significant in a newborn (see page 153).

Decreased activity or alertness. A baby who is listless—with eyes open but little spontaneous movement, an indifferent response to stimulation, or very floppy muscle tone—may be quite sick. Believe it or not, a vigorous protest by a baby during an examination is a reassuring finding. At this age, remaining quiet and disinterested while being poked and prodded by the doctor is not a sign of being a "good" patient but rather an indication of probable illness.

Nonstop crying. As will be described in the next chapter, many babies enter a "crying season" between two weeks and three months of age, without any specific medical cause. But you can't assume that prolonged, inconsolable crying is normal until the baby has been evaluated by his physician.

Abnormal movements. Unusual jerking of arms, legs, or head, especially if sustained for several seconds, may represent a seizure or other significant problem affecting the nervous system. Contact your baby's doctor immediately for further advice if you observe this type of activity.

Unusual color. A pale or mottled color of the skin or bluish discoloration of the lips could indicate a change in normal circulation patterns.

HOME MEDICAL SUPPLIES
FOR BABY'S FIRST THREE MONTHS

- rectal thermometers
- bulb syringe for clearing nostrils
- cotton swabs, cotton balls
- acetaminophen infant drops
- topical ointment for diaper rash
- humidifier/vaporizer

COMMON MEDICAL PROBLEMS DURING THE FIRST THREE MONTHS

Jaundice is a yellow orange discoloration of skin caused by the buildup of a substance called **bilirubin** in the bloodstream. Bilirubin is a by-product of the breakdown of red blood cells, which normally circulate for about four months until they wear out. (New red cells are constantly produced within the bones in tissue called **marrow.**) Removing and recycling the contents of red cells require the liver to process bilirubin, which before birth is largely managed through the mother's circulation. After birth, the newborn's liver takes a few days to gear up for this job, and the level of bilirubin in the bloodstream will increase by a modest amount. If a significant backlog of bilirubin develops, the baby's skin will take on a yellow orange hue, beginning with the head and gradually spreading toward the legs.[1]

Whether or not jaundice is significant will depend upon several factors, including the level of bilirubin, how soon and how fast it has risen, the suspected cause, and whether the baby was full-term or premature. In some instances, extremely high bilirubin levels can damage the central nervous system, especially in the premature infant. *Therefore, if you notice that your new baby's skin color is changing to pumpkin orange, or the white area of the eyes is turning yellow and/or your baby is feeding poorly, see your doctor.*

If there is any concern, the doctor will order blood tests to check the bilirubin level, and other studies may be done to look for underlying causes. Normally the jaundice will resolve on its own, although some healthy babies will carry a slight yellow orange tint for weeks. Occasionally a little extra help is needed. This may involve five approaches, as directed by the baby's physician:

- Treat any underlying cause (such as an infection), if possible.
- Increase the baby's fluid intake by feeding him more often.
- Expose the baby to *indirect* sunlight—that is, undressed down to diapers in a room bright with sunlight *that does not directly shine on his sensitive skin.* Since indirect sunlight has only a modest effect on clearing bilirubin, don't use this approach unless you are sure that your baby won't become too hot or cold in the room you use.
- In some cases of jaundice, an enzyme found in mother's milk may interfere to a modest degree with the clearing of bilirubin. Occasionally your health-care provider may ask you to stop breast feeding briefly and use formula until the problem improves, after which nursing can resume. In such a case, it is important that you continue to express milk so your breasts will continue to produce it and will be ready when your baby is able to resume breast feeding. This should *not* be an occasion to stop nursing altogether.
- A treatment called **phototherapy** may be utilized if the bilirubin level needs to be treated more actively. Under a physician's direction, the baby, wearing protective eyewear, lies under a special intense blue light like a

sunbather at the beach. In addition, or as an alternative, a baby can lie on a thin plastic light source called a **Bili Blanket.** Whether carried out at a hospital or at home (using equipment provided by a home-health agency), phototherapy usually reduces bilirubin gradually within two or three days, if not sooner.

Colds and other respiratory infections are relatively uncommon in this age-group. The breathing patterns in a newborn baby, however, may cause you some concern. He will at times move air in and out noisily, with snorting and sniffing sounds emanating from his small nasal passages, even when they are completely dry. Some sneezing now and then isn't uncommon, but watery or thick drainage from one or both nostrils is definitely abnormal. A call to the doctor's office and usually an exam are in order when this "goop" appears in a baby under three months.

If your newborn has picked up a cold, you can gently suction the excess nasal drainage with a rubber-bulb syringe, since a clogged nose will cause some difficulty breathing while he is feeding. *Do not give any decongestant or cold preparations to a baby this young unless given very specific directions—not only what kind, but exactly how much—from your baby's physician.* (In general, experimental evidence has suggested that such medications are not terribly effective in babies and young children.)

Even when his nose is clear, your baby's breathing rate may be somewhat erratic, varying with his activity and excitement level. A typical rate is thirty to forty times per minute, often with brief pauses, sighs, and then a quick succession of breaths. If he is quiet and consistently breathing fifty or more times per minute, however, he may have an infection or another problem with his lungs or heart. Flaring of the nostrils, an inward sucking motion of the spaces between the ribs, and exaggerated movement of the abdomen with each breath suggest that he may be working harder than usual to breathe. An occasional cough probably doesn't signal a major problem, but frequent or prolonged bouts of coughing should be investigated, especially if there are any other signs of illness.

Infections of the middle ear (known as **otitis media**) may complicate a cold in any baby, including a newborn. There are, however, no specific signs of this important problem in a young baby. (At this age, movement of the hands around the side of the head are random, and your baby cannot deliberately point to or try to touch any area that is bothering him.) Furthermore, an ear infection can be much more serious in this age-group. If he is acting ill, irritable, running a fever, or all of these, he will need to have his ears checked by his doctor.

Some babies always seem to be overflowing with tears in one eye. This is caused by a narrowing of the duct near the inner corner of each eye, which acts like a drain for the tears that are produced constantly to keep the eye moist. Aside from causing a nonstop trail of tears down one side of the face, this narrowing can lead to a local infection, manifested by goopy, discolored drainage, crusting, and if more widespread, a generalized redness of the eye known as **conjunctivitis** (see photo on page A28). The crusting and drainage will need to be removed gently using moist cotton balls, which should be promptly thrown away after being used, since they may be contaminated with bacteria. In addition, the baby's health-care provider will probably prescribe antibiotic eye drops or ointment for a few days. He or she may also suggest that you gently massage the area between the inner corner of the eye and the nose to help displace and move any mucous plug that might have formed.

Usually the clogged tear duct will eventually open on its own, but if it continues to be a problem after six months, talk to your baby's doctor, who may refer you to an ophthalmologist.

Spitting up breast milk or formula is not uncommon during the first weeks of life, and some babies return a little of their feedings for months, sometimes if they are not promptly burped. As long as he is otherwise doing well—gaining weight and making developmental progress—this can be considered a temporary annoyance that will correct itself. However, if a baby in this age-group begins **vomiting,** with stomach contents returning more forcefully, some prompt medical attention is in order.

If there is also a marked increase in the amount of stool (usually indicating that an infection in the intestinal tract has developed), the baby will need careful observation for signs of dehydration. These signs include poor feeding, a decrease in urine output (manifested by fewer wet diapers), sunken eyes, decreased tears or saliva, persistent fussiness or listlessness, and cool or mottled skin. A baby under three months of age with any of these problems should be evaluated immediately.

Projectile vomiting is an alarming event in which the stomach's contents fly an impressive distance. A young baby with this problem should be checked promptly. In a few cases forceful vomiting is caused by a thickening muscle in the portion of small intestine known as the **pylorus,** just past the stomach, which can begin to cause trouble after the second week of life. This condition, known as **pyloric stenosis,** has been traditionally considered a problem of firstborn males, but a baby of either gender or any birth-order position can be affected. In a young baby with forceful vomiting, a combination of an examination with an ultrasound or an X-ray study of the stomach will usually clarify the diagnosis. If pyloric stenosis is present, surgical correction is a must and should be carried out as soon as possible. The surgery is relatively simple, however, and is very well tolerated by the vast majority of infants.

Settling in at home and getting a good start with your baby's feeding are important accomplishments during the first few weeks of life. But there are other concerns to deal with and new learning curves to master as you and your baby become better acquainted. In the next chapter we will look at your baby's other important behaviors, especially sleeping and crying; a number of guidelines and ground rules for commonsense baby care; and some survival skills for new parents.

NOTES
1. Why jaundice progresses from the head downward rather than evenly over the entire body is unknown, but this peculiarity can give an examiner a rough idea of its severity.

CHAPTER 5

The First Three Months, Part Two

Definition of a baby:
That which makes the home happier,
love stronger, patience greater, hands busier, nights
longer, days shorter, purses lighter, clothes
shabbier, the past forgotten,
the future brighter.
MARION LAWRENCE

The First Three Months, Part Two: Sleeping, Crying, and Other Newborn Pursuits (. . . and Survival Skills for New Parents)

From the moment you see, touch, and begin to live with your new baby, one basic reality will become abundantly clear: She can do nothing to meet her own needs. She can't feed herself, lift her head, change position, or scratch where she itches. She can—and will—let everyone know when she is unhappy, but she can't communicate exactly what is bothering her.

The fact that she is totally dependent on those who care for her may not sink in until your first day and night at home. Assuming that your baby was born in a hospital, it is likely that nurses and other health-care personnel provided some, if not most, of her care. Now you're on your own with this little person who needs you for everything. Don't feel strange if this thought creates a sense of mild anxiety or near panic. Almost every parent has felt the same sense of inadequacy.

For many young parents, a combination of grandparents, other relatives, and friends who are baby veterans is available to lend a hand, a few helpful hints, and a shoulder to lean on during these first weeks. Remember, however, that some of the advice you receive from others may not be medically accurate. Grandparents and other relatives may suggest—perhaps with considerable enthusiasm—approaches to baby care that differ from your own or even from your doctor's advice. Many of these are more a matter of style than substance, but if any differences of opinion seem significant, seek input from your baby's physician.

If you are isolated from your family or are a single parent, you may feel as if you're drowning in this new, nonstop responsibility. Most likely your discouragement won't last long, especially as you get used to the basic routines of baby care. *But don't be afraid to seek help if you feel that you are going under for the third time.* Your church, a local crisis pregnancy center, or even the social-services department of the nearest hospital should be able to provide both emotional and practical support.

Remember that your baby's need for total care has a time limit. Indeed, one of the most important tasks of your child's first two decades will be the gradual process of becoming completely independent of you. As she develops new skills, she will need and want you to do less and less for her—and she'll probably be quite vocal about telling you so. All too soon you will face the ultimate challenge of releasing her to live on her own. During those times of emerging independence, you will find yourself thinking back, perhaps misty-eyed, to the time when she needed you so much.

HOLDING A NEWBORN PROPERLY
Hold infant with your hand protecting the child's neck from sudden movement.

SPECIAL CONSIDERATIONS OF A NEWBORN'S TOTAL DEPENDENCE

Your baby's total dependence on you has a number of practical, as well as emotional, ramifications that should be kept in mind as you begin your first weeks of parenthood.

Controlling the head

Because a newborn's head is so large relative to his body size—more so than it will ever be in the future—and because his neck muscles are not strong enough to control it, his head must be constantly supported. Allowing it to flop freely in any direction could injure both his head and neck. Always pick him up with two hands, one of which should support and control the baby's head. Once you have picked him up, you can cradle him in one arm with his head resting in your hand. Never pick him up quickly, especially if you don't have control of his head, and *never shake him for any reason, because this can cause brain damage.*

Temperature and clothing

A newborn is less capable of regulating his body temperature than he will be in just a few months. This doesn't mean that he should be bundled in arctic gear twenty-four hours a day or that your thermostat at home should be set at greenhouse levels. Keep his environment at a temperature that's comfortable for you, and dress him in about the same number of clothing layers that you would want for yourself, with a light receiving blanket added during the first few weeks. Typically this will involve a diaper and an infant T-shirt covered by a gown or sleeper set. If the weather is hot and you don't have air-conditioning, you can dispense with everything but the diaper and T-shirt. In cold weather, extra layers will be needed if you take him outside. Because he can lose a considerable amount of heat from the surface of his head, keep it covered when he is outside in chilly weather.

When dressing or undressing your young baby, be careful with his head and hands. Don't pull a shirt or sweater over his head in a way that drags the material forcefully past his skin, ears, and nose. Instead, use your hand to spread the shirt's neck wide open, and then maneuver it over his head so there's little if any pressure of the garment against his skin. Once his head is through, don't try to push his hands through the narrow opening of the sleeves. Instead—one sleeve at a time—reach through the opening, gently grasp his hand, and carefully pull the sleeve over it. When removing a top, reverse the procedure, pulling the garment over the hands first and then his head.

DIAPER DUTY

Before your child passes her final exam in Toilet Training 101, you can look forward to changing about five thousand diapers. (Actually the number may seem more like about 43 trillion, especially if you have more than one baby in diapers at the same time.) Since your newborn will need to be changed eight to ten times a day, you'll have plenty of opportunities to practice this skill.

As discussed in chapter 2 (Developing a Birth Plan and Preparing the Nest), you'll need to decide whether your baby will spend most of her time in disposable or cloth diapers. You'll also need supplies to clean up dirty bottoms, either small washcloths that can be moistened with warm water or commercial baby wipes, which are convenient when you are away from home. Some babies' skin may be sensitive to fragrances or irritated by the alcohol contained in some wipes, but fragrance-free and alcohol-free varieties are also available. Baby powder isn't necessary and can be left out of the changing procedure altogether unless your baby's health-care provider recommends it for a moist rash. If you do need to use powder, shake a little into your hand and then apply it directly to the infant's skin. Don't shake out clouds of powder, which can be irritating if inhaled. And keep the powder can out of the reach of older babies and children.

DIAPERING STEPS
Place baby on diaper with tabs facing up.

Pull diaper between baby's legs.

Make sure diaper is secure, fasten tabs, and fold top edge down to the baby's waist.

You'll want to check your baby's diaper for moisture or stool every two or three hours when she's awake. You don't need to rouse a sleeping baby if you notice a wet diaper unless you are trying to calm down a rash. Urine alone is normally not irritating, although stool left in contact with skin can provoke a rash because of its acidity.

When it's time to change a diaper, gather all your supplies before you begin. This is particularly important if you are using a changing table.

Remember—you must not walk away from a baby lying on a table or, for that matter, on any open surface above the floor. Unfasten the diaper while you gently grasp her feet by the ankles and pull them upward to expose the genital area. Use the diaper to remove the bulk of any stool that remains on the baby's skin and then use your washcloth or wipe to clean the skin. Be careful to cleanse the creases between legs and upper body, then lift up her ankles again to slide the new diaper under her bottom, and fasten it into place. A baby girl's bottom should be cleaned from front to back to avoid spreading bacteria from her rectal area to the vagina or urinary tract, and you don't need to wipe between the labia (the folds of skin that border the opening of the vagina) unless stool is present. If you are using diaper pins, keep your finger between the cloth and her skin. If the pin strays, you'll tolerate the point far better than your baby's sensitive abdomen will.

Changing diapers certainly isn't anyone's favorite activity, and the job shouldn't be left solely to Mom. Dad can and should learn to become adept at this task, along with any preadolescent or teenage children at home. Even if you're squeamish about cleaning up stool, avoid making a "yuck" face and groaning at every mess you find. As often as they occur during the day, diaper

DEALING WITH DIAPER RASH

Nearly every baby will develop diaper rash at some point. Causes can include:

- Prolonged exposure to urine or stool, especially after solid foods are started.
- Chemical or fragrance irritants in baby wipes, detergents used to wash diapers, or soaps used during bathing. Some babies will even react to the material used in a specific brand of disposable diaper.
- Infections with bacteria or, more commonly, yeast (candida). Yeast infections tend to cause a more intense irritation, often with small extensions or "satellites" around the edges of the rash.

Steps you can take to calm a diaper rash include:

- Change the diaper as soon as possible after it becomes wet or soiled. Once a rash develops, ongoing contact with urine and stool can irritate it further. Super-

absorbent diapers, while more convenient, tend to be changed less frequently, which may unintentionally increase contact of urine with skin.

- Try to eliminate other types of irritants. Change to fragrance- and alcohol-free wipes. If you are washing your own cloth diapers, use soap rather than detergent (this will be marked on the label) and double-rinse. If using disposable diapers, try another brand.
- Let your baby's bottom air dry after it is cleaned. If you feel particularly adventurous, leave it open to the air for a while before putting on a new diaper.
- Ointments such as Desitin or A&D may have a soothing effect. If the rash is severe, your baby's physician may prescribe a mild cortisone cream for a few days. If yeast appears to be involved, an antifungal cream, either alone or in a blend with cortisone, will usually calm the rash within a few days.

changes should be times when you communicate love and reassurance, not re-pulsion (even in fun). Some babies routinely put up a howl during these cleanup sessions, but with rare exception they eventually get used to the process. After two or three months, your baby may even coo at you during diaper changes.

BATHING YOUR BABY

Aside from daily cleansing of the diaper area, newborns and young babies don't need to be bathed more than two or three times a week. Before the umbilical remnant falls off, don't immerse your baby in water. Instead, give him a simple sponge bath, using a soft washcloth and a basin of warm water (comfortable to your touch) containing a small amount of a mild baby soap.

The remnant of your baby's umbilical cord may generate some goopy material, and for the first several days the area around the umbilical stump should be kept clean and dry. Use a cotton swab moistened with rubbing alcohol to wipe away any moist debris that accumulates until the cord falls off. The remnant of the cord will shrivel and fall off within two or three weeks. You may notice small spots of blood at the umbilical site for a few days.

Occasionally, local bacteria will get a foothold at the stump site, generating pus, tenderness, and redness. Contact your baby's physician if this occurs or if there is any persistent swelling and moisture several days after the stump is gone. This area will normally be examined during the first few routine check-ups, but be sure to bring it to the practitioner's attention if you don't like the way it looks.

If your baby was circumcised, he may have a small dressing wrapped around the area from which the foreskin was removed. The dressing will normally fall off within a day or two, and it does not need to be replaced. If a Plastibell was used for the circumcision, it will begin to separate after a couple of days. Don't try to pull it off; let it come loose by itself. A small dab of lubricating jelly applied to any moist or raw surfaces will prevent them from sticking to the diaper. Later on, you can use a soft, warm, moist washcloth to remove (gently) any debris that remains on the penis.

You can sponge-bathe your baby while he lies on any surface that is adequately padded. To keep him from losing body heat, cover him with towels, except for the area you are washing. Start with the head, using water only (no soap) around the eyes and mouth. Then, using the washcloth dipped in soapy water, work your way down, saving the diaper area for last. Be sure to cleanse the skin creases of the neck, behind the ears, under the arms, in the groin, and beneath the scrotum in boys.

After the umbilical stump is dry, you can bathe your baby in a "bathinette" specifically designed for this purpose or even in the sink. As with the sponge bath, water should be comfortably warm but not hot (test with your elbow or wrist) and no more than a couple inches deep. Make sure you have all your supplies (washcloth, soap, shampoo, towel) ready before you undress your baby. If you have forgotten something you need or the phone rings, pick your baby up out of the water and take him with you. *Never leave a baby unattended in a bath, even with only one or two inches of water.*

If he has a dirty diaper at the time you undress him, clean the area as you normally would *before* he goes into the water. You may choose to give him a sponge bath just as you did before the umbilical cord remnant fell off and then rinse him off in the bathwater. If you plan to use shampoo (not necessary with every bath, especially if he isn't endowed with a lot of hair), be sure to control his head so the shampoo and water used to rinse it don't get in his eyes, nose, or mouth.

BATHING NEWBORN

Your baby will have no interest in rubber ducks or other bath toys at this age. Some babies fuss when put into water, but usually the sensation of warmth and rubbing by a pair of loving hands will have a calming effect. At this age, long baths are neither necessary nor wise, since the effect of prolonged contact with water may dry out his skin and cause rashes. (This is also the reason he should not be bathed every day.) In a few months, as he comes to enjoy splashing and playing in water, baths can extend beyond the time it takes to be cleaned.

Because he can lose body heat so quickly when he's wet, be ready to wrap him in a towel as soon you bring him out of the water. This will also improve the stability of your hold on him. The last thing you want is to have a wet, wiggly baby slip out of your hands.

A Newborn's Skin

See color insert for color photos of skin conditions.

A new baby's skin is so sensitive that at times looking at her cross-eyed may seem to provoke a new rash. You will see spots and splotches come and go, especially in the first several weeks, but most don't need special treatment.

The characteristics of newborn skin and some common conditions including erythema toxicum, milia, and salmon patches were mentioned in chapter 3. In addition, during the first few weeks many babies develop pimples on the face, neck, and upper back, which in some cases look like acne. (A full-blown eruption is sometimes referred to as **neonatal acne,** see photo on page A30.) These pimples most likely are a response to some of mother's hormones acquired just before birth, and with rare exception they will resolve without treatment. If they become progressively worse, however, have them checked by your baby's healthcare provider.

Another common skin problem in early infancy is **seborrheic dermatitis** (see photo on page A31), an inflammation of those areas of skin where the oil-producing sebaceous glands are most abundant: the scalp, behind the ears, and in the creases of the neck and armpits. The most striking form is **cradle cap,** a crusty, scaly, oily eruption of the scalp, which may persist for months. Fortunately, cradle cap is neither contagious nor uncomfortable, but you can help shorten its appearance with a few simple measures. Washing the hair with a gentle baby shampoo every two or three days, followed by gentle brushing, will remove much of the scaly material. Baby oil applied for a few minutes before shampooing may help soften more stubborn debris, but use it sparingly and be sure to wash all of it off. In more severe cases, your baby's doctor may recommend an antidandruff shampoo. A mild cortisone cream or lotion may also be prescribed, especially if there are patches of seborrhea on other parts of the body.

Another common rash appears on the chin and upper arms and is caused by excessive heat. **Heat rash** produces tiny red bumps rather than overt pimples and can usually be remedied by removing excess clothing.

A newborn's skin is easily dried out by excessive exposure to water, so if her skin seems dry or flaky, you may use a little baby lotion on the affected areas. Stay away from baby oil, which plugs pores and can actually provoke rashes. Keep your new baby completely out of direct sunlight because even very brief exposure can cause sunburn.

A NEWBORN'S BEHAVIOR PATTERNS

As you settle into your routines with a new baby, you'll begin to notice patterns developing in a number of his behaviors. Although a newborn has only a few basic activities that occupy his first days and nights, he will carry them out in ways that are uniquely his. Mothers are often aware of differences between their children well before birth, as they feel the kicks and prods inside. The initial cry, the first waving of arms and legs, the attachment at the breast, and the willingness to cuddle will be some of the first strokes of a unique signature for this person you have brought into the world.

While every child is one of a kind, there are certain common threads and trends in behavior that have been observed in many newborns. Harvard pediatrician T. Berry Brazelton, M.D., who has studied and written extensively about newborn behavior, has described three basic types of babies, which he has dubbed "quiet," "active," and "average."

Quiet newborns sleep a lot—up to eighteen hours a day, even while nursing. They may sleep through the night very early and snooze through daytime feedings. They fuss or cry for about an hour each day and may communicate their needs quietly by sucking on their hands or wriggling in their cribs.

Active newborns behave quite differently. They sleep about twelve hours a day and spend half of what's left crying and fussing. They seem extremely sensitive to the environment, arouse easily, and may be slow to calm. When they're hungry, everyone will know about it. When it's time to nurse, they may clamp onto the breast or bottle frantically, gulping and swallowing air and then burping back a partial refund on whatever went down.

Average babies fall into the middle ground, sleeping fifteen hours or so each day, crying and fussing for about three hours a day. While more reactive to light and sound around them than quiet newborns are, they may calm themselves back to sleep if aroused. They'll let you know whenever they're hungry, but they usually settle fairly quickly when fed.

These are thumbnail sketches rather than detailed portraits, and no baby's behavior will fit precisely into one category or another. Furthermore, these characteristics are not necessarily previews of permanent coming attractions. During their first few days at home, many newborns go through a transition period that is marked either by seemingly endless sleeping or nonstop fussing. They may then shift gears after the first week, behaving quite differently as they adjust to their new surroundings. The newborn who is more active for the first weeks or longer may become much calmer later on, and vice versa.

What is most important for parents to know is that *these patterns are all in-born variations of normal behavior, not the result of child rearing techniques, the phase of the moon, or the virtues or sins of the parents.* Some newborn behaviors, however, may be altered if drugs or alcohol was used by the mother during pregnancy.

These characterizations of babies should not be taken as value judgments. Because the quiet baby may not seem very demanding, it could be tempting to think of him as "sweet," "good-natured," or "mellow." On the other hand, the active baby might bring to mind a different vocabulary: "a handful," "high-strung," "a real pistol," or "exhausting." In fact, the weary parents who were not prepared for an active baby may find themselves bleary-eyed at 3 A.M., wondering if their child is still under warranty and whether it's too late to trade for another model.

Parents should not waste too many hours gloating over their angelette who sleeps peacefully all the time or reminiscing about the good old days before their baby kept them up for hours every night. The quiet baby may become lost in the shuffle, especially in a house already busy with the activities of older children, unless parents deliberately take the time and effort to interact with him. Worse, his low-key nursing style could lead to an inadequate intake of calories and poor weight gain. If you have a quiet baby, you and the doctor will need to keep a close watch on his weight and possibly deliberately awaken him (at least during the day) to nurse at more frequent intervals. The active baby, on the other hand, for all of his intensity, will tend to be more social and interactive when he's not fussy. He may seem like a "taker" much of the time, especially during the first three months of life, but he will also give back quite a bit to those who hang in there with him.

"SLEEPING LIKE A BABY"

This timeworn phrase is reinforced whenever we behold a baby in deep, relaxed sleep. Wouldn't it be nice if we could sleep like that?

Well, not exactly.

During the first three months of life, a baby's sleeping patterns are quite different from those she will experience the rest of her life. A newborn sleeps anywhere from twelve to eighteen hours every day, but this is not unbroken slumber. Her small stomach capacity and her round-the-clock need for nutrients to fuel her rapid growth essentially guarantee that her life will consist of ongoing three- or four-hour cycles of feeding, wakefulness, and sleep. Like it or not, two or three feedings will be on the nighttime agenda for the first several weeks.

Furthermore, the patterns of brain activity during sleep are unique in a newborn. All of us experience cycles of two different types of sleep—rapid eye movement, or REM, and non-REM—throughout the night. During REM sleep, the brain is active with dreams, manifested by movements of the eyes and frequently other body parts as well. We may twitch, roll, or thrash, and we may be more easily awakened if the bed is cold, the bladder full, or the environment noisy. Non-REM sleep, during which little, if any, dreaming takes place, passes through phases of light, deep, and very deep sleep. There is less movement, deeper and slower breathing, and increasing relaxation of muscles when we pass through these stages in repeated cycles throughout the night. Adults spend about one-fourth of their sleep time in REM sleep and the rest in non-REM.

Babies also manifest these types of sleep but spend equal time in each, alternating about every thirty minutes. During non-REM, or quiet, sleep they will appear very relaxed, breathing regularly, and moving very little. During REM or active sleep, they seem to come to life, moving arms and legs, changing facial expressions, breathing less regularly, and perhaps making a variety of sounds. They may be experiencing their first dreams during these periods.

Adults and children older than about three months pass through the increasing depths of non-REM sleep before they enter a REM phase. *But newborns reverse this pattern,* starting with a period of REM sleep before moving into non-REM stages. As a result, the new baby who has just fallen asleep may be easily awakened for twenty minutes or more, until she moves into her non-REM phases.

This accounts for those character-building situations for some parents in which they feel they are dealing with a little time bomb with a short fuse. A fed, dry, and apparently tired baby fusses and resists but finally succumbs to sleep after prolonged cuddling and rocking. But when placed ever so gently into the cradle or crib, she suddenly startles and sounds off like a fire alarm. The cycle repeats over and over until everyone, baby included, is thoroughly exhausted and frustrated. The problem is that this baby isn't getting past her initial REM phase and happens to be one who is easily aroused out of it. If all else fails, the problem usually will resolve itself by the age of three months, when she shifts gears and enters non-REM sleep first.

Helping a new baby enter the slumber zone

For those parents who don't want to wait twelve weeks, there are two basic, but quite different, approaches to helping this baby—or, for that matter, any baby—fall asleep. Each approach has advocates who tend to view their ideas as vital to a

Ultimately, the key to competent parenting is being able to get behind the eyes of your child, seeing what he sees and feeling what he feels.

THE STRONG-WILLED CHILD

happy, stable life for both parent and child, while seeing the other as producing troubled, insecure babies. In reality, both have something to offer, and neither will work for every baby-parent combination.

One method calls for parents to be intimately and directly involved in all phases of their baby's sleep. Proponents of this approach recommend that she be nursed, cuddled, rocked, and held continuously until she has fallen asleep for at least twenty minutes. She can then be put down in her customary sleeping place, which may be Mom and Dad's bed. The primary advantage of this approach is that it can help a baby navigate through drowsiness and REM sleep in the comfort and security of closeness to one or both parents. Those who favor this approach claim that a baby does best when she has more or less continuous contact with a warm body, having just exited from the inside of one. Those who challenge this approach argue that she may become so accustomed to being "manipulated" into sleep that she will not be able to fall asleep on her own for months or even years. Every bedtime or nap time will thus turn into a major project, and parents (or whoever is taking care of the baby) will be hostage to a prolonged routine of feeding and rocking well into the toddler years.

The other approach suggests that a baby can and should learn to "self-calm" and fall asleep on her own. Rather than nursing her to sleep, she can be fed thirty to sixty minutes before nap or bedtime and then put down before she is asleep. She may seem restless for fifteen or twenty minutes or even begin crying but will likely settle and fall asleep if left alone. Proponents of self-calming feel this approach frees Mom and Dad from hours of effort to settle their baby and allows the baby to become more flexible and independent, without her security being dependent on their immediate presence at all times. Critics argue that leaving her alone in a bassinet or crib represents cruel and unusual treatment at such a young age. Some even suggest that this repeated separation from parental closeness leads to sleep disorders (or worse) later in life.

You may be relieved to know that neither of these methods was carved in stone on Mount Sinai along with the Ten Commandments. You should tailor your approach to your baby's unique temperament and style and to your (and your family's) needs. Whatever you do will probably change over time as well. What works for your first baby may fail miserably for the second, and what helps this month may not the next. When dealing with newborns and very young infants, a fair amount of adjusting and pragmatism are not only wise but necessary.

"Let's see if this works" is a much more useful approach than "We *have* to do it this way," except for a few ground rules dealing with safety.

Most babies give clues when they are ready to sleep—yawning, droopy eyelids, fussiness—and you will want to become familiar with your child's particular signals. If she is giving you these cues, lay her down in a quiet, dimly lit setting and see if she will fall asleep. If she is clearly unhappy after fifteen or twenty minutes, check on her. Assuming that she is fed and dry, comfort her for a while and try again. If your baby is having problems settling herself, especially during the first few weeks of life, do not attempt to "train" her to do so by letting her cry for long periods of time. *During the first few months of life, it is unwise, for many reasons, to let a baby cry indefinitely without tending to her. Babies at this stage of life cannot be "spoiled" by adults who are very attentive to their needs.*

If you need to help your new baby transition into quiet sleep, any of these time-honored methods may help:

- Nursing (or a bottle, if using formula) may help induce sleep, especially at the end of the day. However,

    (a) Don't overfeed with formula or, worse, introduce solids such as cereal at this age in hopes of inducing a long snooze. A stomach that is too full will interfere with sleep as much as an empty one. Solids are inappropriate at this age and will not lengthen sleep.

    (b) Never put a baby to bed with a bottle propped in her mouth. Not only can this lead to a choking accident, but it also allows milk to flow into her eustachian tubes (which lead into the middle ears), increasing her risk of ear infections.

- Rocking gently while you cuddle your baby can calm both of you. If this works for your baby, relax and enjoy it. A comfortable rocking chair is a good investment, by the way, if one hasn't been handed down from earlier generations of your family.

- One alternative to the rocking chair is a cradle—again, rocked smoothly and gently. Another alternative is a baby swing, but it must be one that is appropriately designed for this age-group.

- Many new babies settle more easily if they are swaddled—wrapped snugly in a light blanket.

- Quiet sounds such as the whirring of a small fan (not aimed toward the baby), a tape or CD recording of the ocean, or even small devices that generate monotonous "white noise" may help settle your baby and screen out other sounds in the home. For the musically inclined, there are several lovely anthologies of lullabies, quiet classical music, or gospel songs and hymns that might soothe a fussy baby.

- A gentle touch, pat, or massage may help settle a baby who is drowsy in your arms but squirmy in her bed.
- Many babies routinely fall asleep when they are continuously jostled during a car ride. Occasionally a frustrated parent who is dealing with a wakeful baby during the night may take her out for a 3 A.M. automobile trip—although this does not guarantee that she will stay asleep once the ride is over. Since staggering out into the night isn't much fun, especially in the dead of winter, some high-tech baby catalogues offer a device that attaches to a crib and simulates the motion of a car. Needless to say, both of these measures should be considered only as last-resort maneuvers for a very difficult sleeper.

All of the above, except for the white noise and the swaddling, involve ongoing parental activity to help settle a baby. In some situations, however, prolonged rocking, jostling, patting, and singing may be counterproductive, keeping a baby awake when she needs *less* stimulation in order to settle down. If a few weeks of heroic efforts to induce sleep don't seem to be working, it may be time to take another look at self-calming. Steps that may help the self-calming process when a baby has been put down but is not yet asleep include the following:

- Guide a baby's flailing hand toward her mouth. Many infants settle effectively by sucking on their hand or fingers.
- Identify a simple visual target for the baby's gaze such as a single-colored surface; a small, nonbreakable mirror in her crib; or a nearby window or night-light and place her in a position where she can see it. (Complex visual targets such as moving mobiles or busy patterns may not be as useful for settling during the earliest weeks, especially when a baby is very tired.)
- But make sure she is on her back before falling asleep.

What about sleeping through the night?

Newborns do not typically sleep in long stretches during the first several weeks of life, nor do they know the difference between day and night. By two months, however, they are capable of lasting for longer periods without a feeding. Most parents will go through the pulse-quickening experience of awakening at dawn and realizing that the baby didn't sound off in the middle of the night. "Is he okay?" is the first breathless concern, followed by both relief and quiet exultation: "He slept through the night!"

By three months of age, much to their parents' relief, a majority of babies have established a regular pattern of uninterrupted sleep for seven or eight hours each night. However, some will take longer to reach this milestone. A few actually drift in the wrong direction, sleeping peacefully through most of the day and then snapping wide-awake—often fidgeting and fussing—just when bleary-eyed parents are longing for some rest. If you have a baby who favors the wee hours, you will want to give him some gentle but definite nudges to use the night for sleeping:

- Make a specific effort to increase his awake time during the day. Don't let him fall asleep during or right after eating, but instead provide some gentle stimulation. Talk or sing to him, lock eyes, change his clothes, play with his hands and feet, rub his back, or let Grandma coo over him. Don't make loud noises to startle him, and do not under any circumstances shake him. (Sudden movements of a baby's head can cause physical damage to the brain.) Let him nap only after he has been awake for a while after nursing. This can also help prevent a baby from becoming dependent on a feeding to fall asleep.

- If your baby is sleeping for long periods during the day and fitfully at night, consider gently awakening him while he is in one of his active sleep phases when a nap has lasted more than three or four hours.

- By contrast, make nighttime interactions—especially those middle-of-the-night feedings—incredibly boring. Keep the lights low, the conversation minimal, and the diaper change (if needed) businesslike. This is not the time to party.

- Remember that babies frequently squirm, grunt, and even seem to awaken briefly during their REM sleep phases. Try to avoid intervening and interacting with him during these times, because you may unknowingly awaken your baby when he was just shifting gears into the next phase of sleep. This may require some adjusting of your sleeping arrangements.

- If your baby tends to awaken by the dawn's early light and you don't care to do likewise, try installing shades or blinds to block out the first rays of sunlight. Don't assume that his rustling around in bed necessarily means he is waking up for good. Wait for a while before tending to him, because he may go back to sleep. Sometimes, however, he will wake up with the local roosters no matter what you do, at which point you may want to consider adjusting your schedule to follow the famous "early to bed, early to rise" proverb until a few more months pass.

Where should your baby sleep?

By the time your baby arrives home for the first night, you will have had to address a basic question: Will she sleep in her own room, in a cradle or bassinet next to your bed, or in your bed right next to you? There are advocates for each of these arrangements.

Those who espouse sleeping with your baby point out that this is widely practiced throughout the world and that it gives the newborn a sense of security and comfort she won't feel in a crib. Critics of shared sleeping raise concerns about parents accidentally rolling over and crushing the baby; however, the risk of this is remote. The more immediate concern is the potential disruption of parental sleep, intimacy, and privacy.

New babies don't quietly nod off to sleep at 10 P.M. and wake up calmly eight hours later. They also don't typically sleep silently during the few hours between feedings. As they pass through their REM sleep phases, they tend to move around and make all sorts of noises, often sounding as if they're waking up. All of this

---

SAFE SLEEP: REDUCING THE RISK OF SUDDEN INFANT DEATH SYNDROME (SIDS)

Sudden infant death syndrome (SIDS), also called **crib death,** has been the subject of intense research for a number of years. While the exact cause is uncertain, SIDS involves a disturbance of breathing regulation during sleep. It is relatively rare, occurring in two or three out of every thousand newborns, most often between the first and sixth months, with a peak incidence between the second and third months. It is more common in the winter months, the reason of which remains unknown.

SIDS is more common in males with low birth weight and in premature infants of both sexes. Breast-fed babies, on the other hand, may have a reduced risk. In addition, some potential contributing factors to SIDS can be minimized by taking a few basic preventive measures:

- *Stay completely away from cigarettes during pregnancy, and don't allow anyone to smoke in your home after your baby is born.*

- *Lay your baby down on his back.* For decades, childcare guidebooks recommended that new babies sleep on their stomachs, based on the assumption that this would prevent them from choking on any material they might unexpectedly spit up. However, recent evidence suggests that this position might be a risk factor for SIDS. *Therefore, it is now recommended that a newborn be positioned on his back to sleep.*

Exceptions to this guideline are made for premature infants, as well as for some infants with deformities of the face that might cause difficulty breathing when lying face up. In addition, your doctor may advise against the face up position if your baby spits up excessively. If you have any question about sleeping position, check with your baby's doctor. Sometime after four months of age, your baby will begin rolling activity isn't easy to ignore, especially for new parents who tend to be tuned in and concerned, if not downright worried, about how their new arrival is doing. Unless you learn to screen out these distractions and respond only when she is truly awake and in need of your attention, you may find yourself woefully short on sleep and patience within a few days.

The other issue to consider is the effect on the mother and father's relationship. If Mom and Dad are equally enthused about having a new bedmate, great. But many young couples aren't prepared for the demands a new baby may place on them and especially on a mother who may have little energy left at the end of the day for maintaining her relationship with her husband. A father who feels that his wife's attention is already consumed by the baby's needs may begin to feel completely displaced if the baby is in his bed too.

Many parents prefer to have their baby sleep in another room but wonder whether they will hear her if she needs them. They need not worry. An infant who is truly awake, hungry, and crying during the night is difficult to ignore. And new parents, especially moms, are uniquely tuned in to their baby's nighttime vocalizing and will normally awaken at the first sounds of crying, even after sleeping through louder sounds such as the rumble of a passing truck.

(continued)

over on his own, at which point he will determine his own sleeping positions. By this age, fortunately, SIDS is extremely rare.

• *Put your baby to sleep on a safe surface.* Don't place pillows or any soft bedding material other than a fitted sheet under the baby. His head or face might become accidentally buried in the soft folds (especially if he happens to be face down), which could lead to suffocation. Sheepskin, down mattresses, and feather beds pose a similar risk. For similar reasons don't put your baby to sleep on a wavy waterbed or beanbag chair. Even on one of these plastic surfaces, a baby whose face shifts to the wrong position could suffocate.

• *Don't overbundle your baby.* Overcompensating for the cold of winter by turning up the thermostat and wrapping a baby in several layers of clothing should be avoided. If he looks or feels hot and sweaty, start peeling off layers until he appears more comfortable.

A few parents experience the terror of seeing their baby stop breathing, either momentarily or long enough to begin turning blue. It is obviously important in such cases to begin infant CPR and call 911 if he does not start breathing on his own (see Emergency Care, page 811). A careful evaluation by your doctor or at the emergency room is mandatory. It is also likely that this baby will be sent home with an **apnea monitor,** which will sound off if a breath is not taken after a specified number of seconds.

Parents who have suffered the loss of an infant for any reason must work through a profound grieving process. When SIDS is the cause, they may also feel a great sense of guilt as well as great anxiety over the safety of their other children. It is important that they obtain support from family, church, and if available, a local support group for families who have dealt with such a loss.

The advantage of this arrangement is that parents will be less likely to be aroused repeatedly through the night by their baby's assorted movements and noises during sleep. They will also avoid intervening too quickly during a restless period, which can accidentally interrupt a baby's transition from active to quiet sleep. Having your baby sleep in another room may also increase her nighttime adaptability, allowing her to go to sleep in a variety of environments.

If you are truly concerned about hearing your baby when she first begins to cry, you can purchase an inexpensive electronic baby monitor, which will broadcast sounds from the baby's room into yours. However, you may find that you are hearing (and possibly being kept awake by) a lot of "false alarms" as your baby stirs and makes a variety of sounds without actually awakening. On the other hand, it would be unwise to leave your baby in a place where you would be totally unable to hear her and then rely on a monitor to be your electronic ears. If the monitor failed for some reason, your baby might lie uncomfortable, crying, and unattended for an extended period of time.

Many parents prefer to place their newborn in a cradle next to their bed. In order to get any sleep, however, they will have to filter out the baby's assorted nocturnal noises that do not need a response. Nevertheless, this arrangement may be useful with a newborn who has a difficult time settling during the night. If she is in another room, one or both parents may begin to feel like a yo-yo, circulating in and out of bed in response to repeated bouts of crying or fussing. These infants and their parents may have an easier time if they sleep in close proximity, so that Mom and Dad can offer nursing and comfort as often as needed without having to get up several times throughout the night.

As with the techniques you choose to help your baby settle down to sleep, you will need to determine which sleeping arrangements work best for your family and be flexible about the various possibilities. Moreover, it is important that parents keep their communications about this subject open with each other. If Mom is the one getting up to nurse a fussy baby and as a result spends more hours in the baby's room than in her own bed, Dad may need to assume a larger share of the nighttime duties. He could, for example, bring the baby to Mom for nursing and then return her to her crib when the feeding is done. Similarly, if Dad is feeling an increasing distance from Mom because of a baby in their bed, Mom may need to be willing to empty the nighttime nest of offspring.

One of the tricky issues for parents who share their bed with one or more children is deciding when and how to reclaim their bed for themselves. Most children are more than happy to sleep with Mom and Dad well into or beyond their toddler years, and making the transition to their own bed may be easier said than done. Parents who routinely allow one or more babies and children in bed with them for months or years should regularly take stock of the effect this custom is having on their marriage. Regaining sexual intimacy after the birth of a child normally requires some time and effort for both parents. It may be far more challenging if there are more than two bodies in the marriage bed.

CRYBABIES: WHAT HAPPENS WHEN THE TEARS WON'T STOP?

One of the greatest mental and emotional adjustments new parents must make is sorting out the meanings of, and their responses to, the new baby's crying. In most cases, crying is a clear signal that a stomach is empty or a diaper full, and the appropriate response will quiet it. Even in these routine circumstances, however, the newborn cry has distinct qualities—insistent, edgy, and downright irritating. Indeed, it can sound almost like an accusation—"I don't like the care you're giving me!"

If your new baby's cry gives you a twinge of discomfort or even annoyance, don't panic; your response is quite normal. If you're a mother acutely short on sleep and sore in body (especially if you've had a cesarean delivery), with hormones shifting in all directions, you may find yourself harboring some troubling thoughts about your crying newborn. These feelings can enter the minds of even the most dedicated parents.

How should you feel about and deal with your baby's crying? First of all, it's important to understand the function of crying. Remember that a newborn baby is totally helpless and cannot do *anything* for himself other than suck on a breast or bottle given to him (or one or two of his own fingers that have accidentally found their way into his mouth). Unless someone meets his most basic needs on an ongoing basis, he will not survive. Crying is his only means—but a most effective one—of provoking a parent into action. It's *designed* to be annoying and irritating, to create all sorts of unpleasant feelings, especially among those closest to him. The responses that usually stop the crying—food, clean diapers and clothing, cuddling and cooing—are what keep him alive.

During these first three months of your baby's life, assume that when he cries, it's for a good reason. His crying is definitely *not* a deliberate effort to irritate you, manipulate you, or test parental limits. Therefore, it is appropriate to take action in response to your baby's crying, as opposed to ignoring it and hoping it will go away. *You cannot spoil a baby at this young age,* and for now it is far better to err on the side of giving too much attention than too little. He needs

O Lord, you are our Father. We are the clay, you are the potter; we are all the work of your hand.

ISAIAH 64:8

comfort, open arms, and ongoing love from those around him, even though he cannot express any signs of gratitude or even pleasure in response to all you give him. This is not the time for any misguided attempts to "train, mold, and discipline" your child. (In several months you will begin to have plenty of opportunities to carry out that important assignment.)

What is your baby trying to tell you when he cries? Most likely, one of these things:

- He's hungry and wants to be fed.
- He has a wet or dirty diaper.
- He's wet, hot, cold, or uncomfortable in some other way.
- He wants to be held.

At some point, usually between two weeks and three months, there will be at least one occasion when you suspect that *something has gone terribly wrong*. Just a day or so ago you could comfort your baby regularly and predictably. A feeding every few hours, dry diapers, and a little rocking and cooing would end crying fairly quickly. Now, however, he starts fussing late in the afternoon or early in the evening, and nothing works for an hour . . . or two . . . or three. Or he suddenly lets out an ear-piercing wail or screams for no apparent reason in the middle of the night. What's going on? You may never know for sure. But it may help if you understand that many babies cry like this now and then, some do it every day, and a few seem determined to set a world's record for the longest crying episode in history.

Dealing with colic

According to a long-standing definition, if your baby cries three hours a day three days a week for three weeks, and he's between two weeks and three months of age, he has **colic.** A simpler definition, without counting hours and days (and more to the point), is "a whole lot of crying that doesn't calm down with the normal measures, and the doctor says there's nothing really wrong with him." True colicky episodes tend to occur around the same time each day, usually in the late afternoon or evening, and are marked by intense activity on the baby's part, such as flailing about or pulling his knees to his chest. From all appearances, he acts like he's feeling a lot of discomfort—and undoubtedly he is.

The classic theories about the cause of colic have assumed that the baby's intestinal tract is at fault—that it goes into uncontrollable spasms, perhaps because of immaturity or a reaction to something in Mom's milk or the current formula. Other proposed explanations include a problem interacting with parents, often assuming that Mother is tense or high-strung, and as a result the baby is also. But changing feeding patterns or formulas may or may not help, and colicky babies may land in families that are intact or disjointed, relaxed or uptight. Basically, a universal cause for colic has yet to be determined.

If your baby begins having long stretches of crying, you will need to address two basic concerns:

1. Does he have a medical problem?
2. How is everyone—baby included—going to get through this?

The first question needs to be answered relatively quickly, because a medical illness can be a much more serious problem during the first three months of life than when the baby is older. Some indicators of a disturbance that might need a physician's care include:

- Any fever over 100.4°F taken with a rectal thermometer (see sidebar, page 148)
- Poor sucking at the breast or bottle
- Change in color from normal pink to pale or bluish (called **cyanosis**) during feeding or crying
- Overt vomiting, as opposed to spitting up. (When a baby spits up, the partially digested food burps into his mouth and dribbles down his chin and clothes. When he vomits, this material becomes airborne.)
- A marked increase in the amount and looseness of bowel movements
- Unusual jerking movements of the head, eyes, or other muscles that you don't recall seeing before

If any of these occur, you should contact your physician, and your baby should be checked—especially if he has a fever. If he is crying up a storm but seems okay otherwise, he should still have a medical evaluation, either as part of a routine checkup or at an appointment specifically for this purpose. The more specific information you can give the doctor, the better. When did the crying start? How long does it last? Does anything seem to set it off? Is it improved or worsened after a feeding? Are there any other symptoms?

Assuming your baby is doing well otherwise (gaining weight, arriving at his developmental milestones more or less on time, showing no apparent signs of medical illness), your primary tasks during his crying episodes are to *be there* for him and to make ongoing efforts to comfort him. *You are not a failure, and you should not give up if your measures do not succeed in stopping the crying.* Eventually each crying episode will end, and the crying season overall will come to a close, in nearly all cases by the third to fourth month of age.

So what do you do for a colicky baby, assuming that he is fed, dry, and not sick? You can try any or all of the following, once or many times. If a particular measure helps one time but doesn't the next, don't panic. You may get impressive results today with something that failed miserably last week.

Soothing movements. Gentle rocking or swaying in someone's arms is a time-honored baby comforter. Unfortunately, when a baby is wailing at full volume, you may unconsciously begin moving faster or more forcefully—but you should *avoid rapid, jerky movements,* which not only make the problem worse but may even injure the baby. Cradles and baby swings that support the body and head can also provide this type of movement.

Soothing sounds. Provide humming, gentle singing, white noise, or pleasant recorded music.

Soothing positions. Some colicky babies respond to being held tummy-down against your forearm like a football or across your thigh. Others seem to calm down while being carried close to Mom's or Dad's body in a baby sling. Swaddling in a light blanket and resting on one side or the other might help.

Soothing environments. Spending time in a quiet, dimly lit room can help calm a baby who may be in sensory overload at the end of the day. Turn down the TV and unplug the phone if you have to.

Soothing trips. A ride in the car or a stroller may provide the right mix of gentle movement and sound to soothe the crying.

Soothing touch. Gentle touching or stroking of the back, stomach, or head may help.

Soothing sucking. Nursing may seem to calm the crying, even if he just had a feeding. A pacifier may also work. If your baby doesn't seem satisfied by *any* of your feedings, you should check with his physician and possibly a lactation consultant as well. This is particularly important if he's not gaining adequate weight, because the problem may be that his hunger is never satisfied. If your colicky baby is formula-fed, you may at some point want to try a different brand or a different type of formula—for example, switching from cow's milk to soy-based formula. (Check with your baby's health-care provider on this.) Sometimes a change will bring about some noticeable improvement.

Self-soothing. Sometimes all the rocking, singing, touching, and pacifying maneuvers unwittingly overload the baby's capacity to handle stimulation. The self-soothing measures mentioned in the previous section on sleep (page 170) may work wonders when everything else has failed.

What can you do for yourself while all of this is going on?

Keep reminding yourself that "this too will surely pass." You will deal with crying problems for only a short period of your child's life. Believe it or not, before you know it there will come a time when you'll wonder where all those baby years went.

If you find yourself reaching the end of your rope, *don't take it out on the baby.* Mounting frustration and anger are indications that you need a brief time-out. If that time arrives, don't allow yourself to become a martyr or a child abuser. Sounding off verbally at the baby will accomplish nothing, and *you must not carry out any physical act of anger*—picking him up or putting him down roughly, shaking him, hitting him, or anything else that inflicts pain or injury—no matter how upset you may feel. Instead, put him in his cradle or crib and *walk away* for fifteen or twenty minutes until you have a chance to collect your thoughts and calm down. It won't hurt him to cry by himself for that period of time, and you can then try comforting him again. He may have expended enough energy to become more responsive to calming efforts at this point. If necessary, call a friend or relative and get your frustration off your chest, or let someone else come look after your baby for a while (see sidebar, page 180).

If at all possible, husband and wife should pass the baton during a prolonged crying episode. Let Dad hold the baby while Mom takes a walk around the block and vice versa. Single moms—and for that matter, married ones—shouldn't be embarrassed to seek help from an experienced relative or friend. If Grandma wants to help you for a while during a rough evening, by all means let her do it. She may have a few tricks up her sleeve that aren't in any book.

Try to find some humor in all this to maintain your perspective. Pretend you are the next Erma Bombeck and jot down some of your observations. If you have one or more books that have made you laugh out loud, by all means keep them close at hand.

Try to maintain "self-preservation" activities as much as possible. A quiet time for reflection and prayer may have to occur during a feeding, but it will provide important perspective and strength. Having a world-class wailer is a humbling experience, and it is during these rough times that special intimacy with God often develops. The question to ask Him isn't "Why did You give me such a fussy baby?!" but "What do You want me to learn about myself and life in general through this experience?" You may be surprised at the answer.

If you have "gone the distance," repeatedly trying every measure listed here (and perhaps a few others as well) without success, check back with your baby's doctor. Be prepared to give specific information—for example, how many hours the baby has been crying, not just "He won't stop!" Depending upon your situation and the baby's crying pattern, another medical evaluation may be in order.

MILESTONES AND MEMORIES

Even though nursing, sleeping, and crying may dominate the landscape during the first several weeks, you'll be happy to know that your baby will also be taking in all kinds of information and learning new ways to respond to it. Young babies manifest six different levels of consciousness: quiet sleep, active sleep, drowsiness, quiet alertness, active alertness, and crying.

Quiet alertness occupies about 10 percent of your baby's time at first, but you will want to watch for these moments of calm attentiveness, during which you can begin to have some genuine interaction. Enjoy them, file them in your memory bank, and if you have time, you may want to jot your impressions in a

TO GRANDPARENTS AND OTHER PARENT SUPPORTERS: THE GIFT OF TIME

If you have experience as a parent, whether recently or in the more distant past, one of the greatest gifts you can offer a relative or friend with a fussy baby is a brief respite. This is particularly important for single moms, but even a married mother may have a husband who isn't much help when the baby is having full-throttle colic. And a baby who cries nonstop can wear out both Mom and Dad before much time has passed.

The sound of someone else's baby crying is not nearly as nerve-wracking as it is for the mother or father of the child. You may also be able to model some perspective, a reminder of the preciousness of this new life, by cooing and fussing over a baby who may not seem very lovable to her parents at this particular moment.

Take the initiative in asking a new parent how life with the new arrival is going, and in particular if there are any problems with fussing and crying. If you have time, energy, and child rearing skills, offer to look after the baby for a while. You might suggest a specific time ("How about if I come over tomorrow or Wednesday night around six, so you can get out for a couple of hours?") rather than something vague ("Let me know if I can help you"), which may be more difficult to accept without sounding utterly desperate. Your offer to provide a time-out for a frazzled parent may be far more valuable than any baby-shower gift.

personal journal. As the weeks pass, you will begin to notice that your baby is spending more time in calm and active alertness, during which you will see several wonderful developments in a variety of areas:

Vision. During the first few weeks, a baby focuses best on objects eight to fifteen inches from her face. You may find her staring intently at the fist at the end of her outstretched arm, which happens to be in her focusing range. She will prefer to study plain, high-contrast, black-and-white images such as stripes, checks, or spirals, or a simple drawing of a face. She may gaze intently into a small, unbreakable mirror attached to the inside of her crib. But her favorite subject to scrutinize will be the face of another person, about a foot away from hers. She will not respond directly to a smile for a few weeks, but a lot of smiles are what she should see.

Your baby will be able to follow an object with her eyes only momentarily at first. You can give her some practice at this ability by moving your face or a brightly colored object slowly from side to side across her field of vision. Around two months of age she will be able to coordinate her eye movements to stay locked on an interesting visual target that passes through a semicircle in front of her. She will also be interested in more complex shapes and patterns and will be able to hold her head steady enough to fixate on simple, high-contrast objects hung from a mobile over her crib. By three months of age her distant vision will be increased to the point that she will recognize you halfway across a room.

Responses to color also develop over the first several weeks. At first she will pay attention to objects with bright, strongly contrasting colors. Ironically, the soft colors that are so often used in decorating a baby's room won't be particularly interesting to her at first. It will take a few months before her color vision has matured enough to distinguish a full palette and varieties of shades.

From time to time all babies will briefly cross their eyes as they develop their tracking skills. But if she frequently appears to have crossed eyes as she approaches the age of six months, she should be checked by her physician and an ophthalmologist.[1]

Hearing. Newborns will vary in their sensitivity to sounds. Some infants seem capable of sleeping through a violent thunderstorm, while others appear to startle when a cat crosses the street a block away. If a young infant is placed in a very noisy environment, he may appear to "shut down," markedly reducing his activity level. This is a protective mechanism, an internal withdrawal from a situation that is overloading him. While you don't need to maintain a hushed silence around your newborn, you should try to keep the noise level around him at a comfortable level—no more than, for example, the intensity of pleasant conversation between two or three people. If you want to go to a ball game or a concert where the crowds and sounds are pumped up, leave the baby at home.

Within a few weeks, he will appear to pay attention to certain sounds, especially the voices of those who regularly care for him. By two months of age, he may begin to shift his eyes and head toward your voice. He may also show some movements and expressions indicating that he recognizes this familiar and comforting sound. As he continues toward three months of age, you will notice him starting to turn toward other interesting sounds, such as a tinkling bell. If the sound is repeated over and over, however, he will tune it out and stop responding to it.

Smell. A very young baby is capable of responding to a variety of smells and can distinguish the smell of his mother's breast from those of other nursing mothers by the end of the first week of life.

Touch. All of us are strongly affected by touch, but babies are particularly sensitive. They will startle in response to scratchy surfaces, rough handling, or sudden temperature changes—especially when their skin makes contact with something cold. Cuddling, caressing, and stroking may help calm a crying episode, but these shouldn't be used merely to stop tears. Touch is an important expression of love and will nourish her emotions before she can understand any words. It should be as routine a part of her day as her feedings.

These developments set the stage for your baby's first true **socializing,** which will probably begin just as you are starting to wonder whether all the nursing and diapers and nonstop caregiving are worth it. You may first notice a brief flicker of a grin after a feeding. Was that a smile or a gas pain? Maybe it was both or maybe neither, but it felt like a puff of fresh air on a hot day. Suddenly—at about the age of four to six weeks—it will be unmistakable: You will lock eyes with your baby, and a big grin will flash across her face. It will be an unforgettable moment, and the next time she smiles will be equally rewarding because you'll know that this milestone was for real.

Over the next month, you will catch smiles in response to your own grinning, cooing, talking, or singing to your baby. You may notice special enthusiastic body movements in response to familiar voices and the turning of eyes and head to seek them out. Even more pleasant are your first "conversations." At about two months your baby will begin to coo, often in response to your speaking to her in soft, soothing tones. At this age, she will not understand the words you speak, but the tone of your voice will communicate volumes.

Even at this young age, your baby may show some selectivity in her responses. Not everyone will necessarily receive the big grin and happy sounds. More often than not, it will go to the most familiar faces and voices. Your baby is already starting to sort out who is important in her life, and so whoever wants to be included in that category will need to log some time with her. This is particularly important for fathers, who may find it harder to interact with a squirmy two-month-old than an older child who likes to "wrestle" on the carpet or play catch. Mothers who are weighing decisions about work outside the home also need to ponder how much time the baby should spend with other caregivers.

Growth and movement. Babies lose and then regain several ounces (about a tenth of their birth weight) during the first ten days of life. From then on, you can anticipate a weight gain of about two-thirds to one ounce per day, or one to two pounds per month. Your baby will add between one and one and a half inches in height each month as well. These amounts will vary, of course, depending on your baby's feeding patterns and on genetics, which will affect whether this growing body will ultimately resemble a ballerina or a fullback. During each medical checkup, your baby's height, weight, and head circumference will be measured and then plotted on a growth chart. Tracking your baby's growth will be an important tool for her health-care provider to confirm how well she is doing.

During the first three months, you will see dramatic changes in your baby's movement patterns. At birth her arms and legs flail and jerk, her chin may twitch, and her hands may tremble. Many of her movements are reflexes, such as rooting, sucking, and grasping. In addition, you may see her do a "fencing" maneuver known as the **tonic neck reflex:** If her head is turned in one direction, you may see the arm on that side straighten and the other arm flex, as if she were about to enter a sword fight. In addition, if you gently hold her body upright, supporting her head, and then lower her gently until her feet touch a firm surface, she will begin stepping motions. This has nothing to do with how soon she will begin walking, and this so-called **stepping reflex** will be gone by the age of two months. However, she will kick her legs quite vigorously when awake and active while lying on her back or stomach.

Hand and arm movements will gradually become less jerky and almost appear purposeful. Between two and three months, she will begin to spend more time with her hands open rather than clenched and will bring them toward her mouth or in front of her face, where she may appear to study them. She still won't have the coordination to reach directly for something that interests her, although she will tightly grasp a small object placed in her hand. In fact, you may have to help her let it go.

At two months she will have developed enough control of her neck muscles to hold her head in one position while lying on her back. When lying on her stomach, she will be able to raise her head briefly, just long enough to turn it from one side to another. But her head control overall will not be secure until three to four months of age, so you must support her head whenever you hold or carry her.

Other people in your baby's life

Just as it is important for you to handle your newborn carefully and appropriately, any older brothers or sisters in the family will need to be supervised during their interactions with the baby. They should have been given plenty of advance warning, in language they can understand, about the new brother or sister who is on the way, and perhaps will have had a chance to say hello to him while Mom was still in the hospital. For very young children, fascination with the wiggly little person will be mixed with an overriding concern about whether there is enough love to go around.

With everyone oohing and aahing over the new baby, your toddler or preschooler may conclude that the best way to get attention is to act like the baby. You may notice him trying to climb into the baby's crib or suddenly forgetting all his potty-training skills. Rather than spending a lot of energy rebuking this behavior, take time to affirm his capabilities and point out some of the advantages of being older. ("You're such a big boy now—you can go to the park and ride on the swings! The baby is too little to do that.") He needs reassurance that he is special and unique, and he needs one-on-one time with Mom and Dad. If Mom is worn out or recovering from surgery, Dad or a grandparent should be prepared to take on this assignment.

Equally (if not more) important is the need to ensure the new baby's safety around children who are not likely to be well versed in the details of newborn care. Toddlers and preschoolers who want to touch and caress the new baby must be shown how to do so gently, avoiding the baby's eyes, nose, and mouth and clearly told that they can only touch the baby while Mom or Dad is there watching them. They should not be allowed to carry a new baby, play any of their physical games with the baby, or touch the baby with anything but their hands that have just been washed. If they have runny noses or a cough, they'll need to wait until the illness is gone before getting near the baby.

If you see an older sibling talking or acting aggressively toward a new baby, immediately separate the two, find out what's going on, and make certain the issue (usually jealousy) is settled before allowing any further contact. Small children, especially if they are upset (for whatever reason), are quite capable of injuring babies, whether or not they fully realize what they are doing. Toddlers and two-year-olds are particularly incapable of processing the moral and physical reasons they should not act aggressively toward a baby, although it is appropriate to define limits for them in this as in other arenas (see chapters 7 and 8, pages 225, 259). Parents and other caregivers will thus need to remain constantly on guard to protect a young infant from the older sibling—who was himself a baby not long ago.

The same rules about colds and acute illnesses apply to relatives and friends who may want to handle your baby. Because her immune system is not as competent as it will be in a few months, you should be careful to expose her to as little risk of infection as possible. This means that, at the risk of upsetting a well-meaning friend or relative, you may need to be firm about keeping your new baby away from anyone with an acute infection, especially one involving sneezing and coughing (which can easily spread contaminated droplets). Adults and older children will have a much easier time getting over their temporary disappointment than your newborn will have recovering from an acute infection. Your protective stance for the first two to three months of your baby's life should also include keeping her out of crowds in general and group nurseries in particular, unless it is absolutely necessary to do otherwise.

Don't hesitate to ask well-wishers to come back at a later date if you are feeling overwhelmed by all your new responsibilities. If the baby is fussy and you're running on empty with too little sleep, keep visitors to a minimum, place a polite sign on the door asking not to be disturbed, and let the answering machine take care of incoming calls so you can get some extra rest. You'll have plenty of time to socialize and show off your pride and joy in the coming months.

NOTES
1. If the position of her eyes is constantly presenting two images instead of one to her brain, she will shut down the information arriving from one eye or the other, resulting in **amblyopia,** or "lazy eye."

CHAPTER 6

Three to Six Months: Expanding Horizons

Don't forget that compared to a grown-up person every baby is a genius. Think of the capacity to learn! The freshness, the temperament, the will of a baby a few months old!
MAY SARTON

Three to Six Months: Expanding Horizons

As your baby grows and slowly graduates from the newborn stage, you will find yourself entering a phase of increased enjoyment and satisfaction in parenting. During these months your baby will progress from being a pure "taker" of your love and energy to a "giver" as well, someone who can flash a smile and carry on irresistible interactions with nearly anyone who will give him the time of day. For a baby these months are full of intense exploration. No longer restricted to crying as his only method of gaining attention, your baby is now finding all sorts of new ways to investigate and affect what goes on around him. While he isn't exactly capable of propelling himself out the front door while your back is turned, his wondrous new skills will create some safety challenges.

PHYSICAL DEVELOPMENTS: ARMS, LEGS, AND BODIES IN MOTION

During his first three months, one of your baby's major accomplishments was simply learning to keep his head still enough to focus on an object and track a moving object with his eyes. Now he is starting to use larger muscle groups that will eventually allow him to sit up on his own. This begins with more decisive head control, which you will notice when he is lying on his stomach while awake. He will make a more deliberate effort to keep his head elevated so he can see what's going on in front of him. You can encourage the exercise of these upper back and neck muscles by placing a small toy or brightly colored object—or your smiling face—in front of him while he is in this position.

He will then progress to lifting his entire upper chest, with or without help from his arms. When he combines this with vigorous kicking, you will see surprisingly active rocking, and by five or six months, the right combination of movements will send him rolling over front to back. Rolling back to front will not be far behind. (A few babies roll back to front first.) Invariably, he will accomplish this skill for the first time when you least expect it, so never leave him alone on any elevated surface such as a bed or changing table, or he may add free-falling to his new movement experiences.

At this stage he will enjoy being propped on pillows in a sitting position, although he must be watched because he can easily topple forward. He will soon figure out how to "sit" in a hunched position with one or both hands on the floor, precariously maintaining his balance. He can still topple easily, so make sure his landing will be on a soft surface. At six months of age at the earliest, he will be able to maintain a sitting position without using his hands, although he is still a few months away from maneuvering himself into a sitting position.

Another adventure for him at this age is being held by the upper body and "standing" in someone's lap. Most babies love to flex their legs and bounce up and down, as if ready to bear their weight in a standing position. They are, of course, nowhere near achieving this milestone, and the playful bouncing won't bring it along any sooner. But it also won't cause any harm to growing muscles and bones. However, you should not suspend or lift a baby's full weight by holding his hands or arms.

Your baby's ability to use his hands will develop dramatically during these three months. As a newborn he spent most of his time with his little fists clenched and could only respond with a tight reflex grip to objects placed in his hands. Now he will spend more time with open palms, and more important, he will begin to reach deliberately toward interesting things that catch his eye. He will grasp as if his hand were in a mitten, thumb against the other fingers, or rake an item into his hand. (Independent use of the fingers and the ability to pick up an object between the thumb and index finger will not develop until about nine months of age.) You will not be able to tell whether he is right- or left-handed at this point, since this characteristic is not clearly manifested until about the age of three years.

But even without fine tuning, your baby will become a first-class grabber by the age of six months. Not only will he reach for toys in his immediate vicinity (or his own feet), but when someone holds him, he will expertly seize hair, earrings, or the pen in Dad's shirt pocket. Furthermore, all of these items will be inspected carefully and fearlessly, not only with eyes and fingers but invariably with his mouth. You will now need to enter a state of perpetual vigilance for small objects that you would rather not see entering his mouth, either because they are incredibly gross or because they might be accidentally swallowed and/or block his airway.

As his reaching and grasping skills become more developed, he will also discover the joy of "letting go." During these three months you will see him transfer an object from one hand to the other, which requires that one hand release what the other hand takes. At some point he will also discover gravity, as he begins to drop things and observe what happens as a result. In later months this may become a serious pastime as toys, food, and other unidentified nonflying objects are released from various heights (such as crib or high chair) in order to watch them careen or bounce or even shatter. All of this activity is exploratory and not a sign of a destructive streak or a future career in sports. But he will eventually need to be taught what items can be tossed and where.

Vision and hearing

During these three months your baby will continue to gain in the ability to see and hear what's going on around her. By six months she will be able to focus on people or objects several feet away and follow movement in all directions. She will show interest in more complex patterns and subtle shades of color, so this is a great time to hang a mobile over her crib. She will also find stroller rides stimulating times to take in a passing parade of new colors and shapes.

She will become more skillful at localizing the source of sounds and turning her head in the direction of your voice or an interesting noise in her vicinity. In addition, you will begin hearing a wider range of sounds—babbles, belly laughs, bubbling noises, and even a screech or two for good measure. Sometimes she will even alter her "speech" patterns, raising and lowering her voice as if giving an oration in a language only she understands. Rather than parroting back her assorted sounds, which is often irresistible, you can begin to transform some of her favorite syllables into simple words such as *baby, doggie, Mommy,* and feed them back to her. By seven months of age, she should begin imitating sounds you make.

SOCIAL DEVELOPMENTS: THE JOYS OF INTERACTING

For many parents, this stage of a baby's life is one of the most pleasant they will experience, a time when a true personality emerges from the seemingly endless cycles of feeding, sleeping, and crying during the first three months. All of her new skills in movement, vision, hearing, and noisemaking seem to converge and

Spiritual training should begin before children comprehend what it is all about. They should grow up seeing their parents on their knees before God, talking to Him. They . . . will never forget what they've seen and heard.

PARENTING ISN'T
FOR COWARDS

complement each other as she shows off for family, friends, and complete strangers. When her face lights up for Aunt Mary, she'll likely get a big grin and a lot of sweet talk in return. When she babbles and gurgles for Grandpa, she'll probably hear a few new funny noises in response. Even older brothers and sisters will enjoy making the new baby smile.

In all of these encounters, your baby is finding out what kind of world she lives in. What sights and sounds envelop her and what happens when she tries to make an impact, in her own way, on her surroundings? Does she see smiles and bright colors, hear laughter and pleasant voices, and feel hugs, kisses, and cuddling? Is she in a place that is safe physically and emotionally? Even during her first stirrings of independence, she is still completely helpless, depending on the adults around her for her physical needs and her most basic sense of security. She may not be able to understand your words, but she'll get a strong message about her importance to you and your family.

Everyone who cares for your baby plays a role in this process. It is particularly important for Dad to interact with her at this point. Playing with a baby this age isn't all that difficult. With rare exception, your baby can now be entertained simply by laying her across your lap and playing with her hands and feet, making faces, and giving her interesting objects to handle. She will love to wave rattles and toys that make sounds or musical tones. She will enjoy looking at books or magazines with bright pictures. She will like touching and squeezing soft toys, especially if they have an interesting texture.

There will probably be grandparents and favorite uncles and doting aunts around who will also enjoy these simple pleasures. Sometimes a relative who hasn't had all the day-to-day responsibilities and interrupted sleep for the past few months can give you a fresh perspective on your baby, a reminder that tending her is not only worthwhile but a source of enjoyment. This is especially important if you are a single parent, because you will need the break from being on call twenty-four hours a day and the reassurance that raising your child is worth the effort.

FEEDING: NEW ADVENTURES

If your baby is nursing, he will typically need to fill his tank about five times a day and soon should be skipping the late-night feeding(s) if he isn't already. By six months, if he is waking up two or three times during the night, it is far more likely to be for reasons other than hunger (see page 198).

Some mothers who are breast-feeding quite successfully will, for a variety of reasons, begin to think about shifting from breast to bottle before their baby reaches six months of age. If at all possible, however, continue nursing during these months, for all of the reasons outlined in chapter 4 (page 122). If you need to start or resume employment outside the home and cannot nurse your baby during work hours, you do not necessarily need to switch your baby entirely to formula. Depending upon your schedule and your baby's feeding patterns, you may be able to nurse before and after work and even express milk (which can be used at a later feeding) during the time you are away from home. (If you intend to shift from breast to bottle feeding, see sidebar, page 232.)

A formula-fed baby will similarly be consuming five bottles every day, each containing five to eight ounces of formula, depending on his weight. You can discuss the amount with your physician at the four- and six-month checkups, but a ballpark amount for a given feeding is an ounce of formula for every two pounds of weight. By the way, it's too early to begin drinking from a cup at this age. That adventure can begin after your baby reaches the six-month mark.

Parents of babies in this age-group often wonder if this is a good time to introduce solid foods. Thirty years ago, physicians routinely advised parents to begin feeding their babies rice cereal at two months and then speedily progress to other types of foods. Your baby's grandmother may have started you on cereal practically from day one, and perhaps one of your friends has announced with some satisfaction that her baby is already taking all sorts of fruits and vegetables at two months of age. But consuming solids is *not* a sign of advanced intelligence or motor skills. In fact, there are reasons you don't need to be in any hurry to introduce solids before your baby is six months old:

Breast milk or formula can supply all of the calories and nutrients your baby needs for his first six months of life, and it is more easily digested than other foods. The efficiency of the intestinal tract in absorbing other foods increases significantly between the fourth and sixth months.

Babies who are fed solids early may develop food allergies. If there is a strong history of allergies in either parent or other family members, you would be wise to wait. After six months infants are better equipped to process a variety of foods without this risk.

Solid foods are best managed by a baby who has some basic developmental skills in place. (See sidebar page 194.)

First experiences with solid foods

While you don't need to be in a rush to start solids, most babies are given their first taste of foods other than breast milk or formula between four and six months of age. Like many other everyday concerns in child rearing, directions for introducing solids to babies were not included in the Ten Commandments. Families have made this transition for thousands of years in thousands of ways. What follows are basic guidelines to help you navigate this passage smoothly, along with a few cautions about certain foods and feeding practices that would best be avoided.

Before you decide to let your baby try something other than milk, think about your timing. First, she should be ready developmentally (see sidebar).

The other timing question to consider is the specific setting of your baby's first experience with solids. Pick a time when you aren't going to be rushed or hassled, and take the phone off the hook for good measure. Your baby shouldn't be tired, cranky, ravenously hungry, or completely full. Give her part of a feeding of breast milk or formula before you try the new stuff. *Remember that when you begin solids, they will only supplement milk feedings, not substitute for them,* so the normal feeding should be finished after whatever solid food she has eaten.

What should you start with? The general consensus is that rice cereal specifically formulated for babies is best. It is well absorbed, contains iron, and rarely causes allergic reactions. Whether premixed in a jar or prepared by you with water or formula, it can be adjusted to whatever thickness your baby prefers. You should feed her from a small spoon and not a bottle with an enlarged hole in the nipple. If she sucks solids out of a bottle, she may get too much volume and become obese if this is done repeatedly. And she will delay learning how to swallow solids without sucking.

DEVELOPMENTAL SIGNS THAT YOUR BABY IS (OR ISN'T) READY FOR SOLID FOOD

- While sucking at the breast or bottle, the newborn first protrudes her tongue, pushing it against the nipple as she sucks and swallows. This tongue-thrusting reflex, which gradually subsides over the first six months, interferes with the process of taking food from a spoon and moving it to the throat, where it can be swallowed. A baby who repeatedly pushes her tongue against your spoon probably isn't ready for solids.

- Accepting food from a spoon is much easier for a baby who can control her head position, a skill which will be far better developed after six months than at three or four. A young baby whose head flops everywhere if not supported should be given more time with just breast or bottle.

- By six months of age your baby will be happily grabbing everything in sight and putting whatever she finds into her mouth, an indication that she will find a spoon worth exploring as well.

- If a couple of teeth erupt before six months of age (the usual time of the first appearance of teeth), this in itself is not a sign that your baby is ready for pizza. Your baby won't use her teeth to chew food yet for some months. In fact, even if she still doesn't have teeth at the six-month mark, she will be quite able to swallow the mushy solids you'll be feeding her.

Offer her about half of a small baby spoonful (or use a small coffee spoon if you wish), which should total about a quarter teaspoon. She may not know what to do with your offering and may even appear to reject it with a grimace. Talk to her in soothing tones through the entire process. When she gets the hang of swallowing this amount, she will begin opening her mouth in anticipation of more. Aim for a total of about one tablespoon once a day, gradually increasing to two or three tablespoons per feeding once or twice per day. If she simply refuses or repeatedly tongue-thrusts, don't force her. This is not a moral issue or a contest of wills. Simply wait and try again in another week or two.

When two or three tablespoons are going down smoothly at one feeding, you can try other cereals. Oats and barley are good for the next round, but check with your baby's doctor before trying corn or wheat cereals, which may provoke digestive problems in some infants. After cereals have been successfully consumed for a few weeks, you can think about adding other foods to the mix. Either vegetables or fruits may be the next category you try, but vegetables may hold an advantage because they will not condition your baby to sweet tastes. Fruits can be added later, and meats should be introduced last. By the time your baby is eating from three or four food groups, she will probably be eating three times per day. You may choose to raise a vegetarian and not introduce meats to your baby at all, but if you do, be sure that you are adequately informed so your baby won't be deprived of any necessary nutrients.

Let your baby try each new food (one to three tablespoons' worth) for a few days before introducing another. Observe for any signs of a reaction: diarrhea, irritability, runny nose, coughing or wheezing, or a rash, especially around the face. If there is any possibility that a reaction has occurred, withdraw the food, wait for the problem to calm down, and try again. If you see the same response, put that food aside for several weeks and then run the story by your baby's doctor before serving it to her again. Of course, if any feeding is followed by a more severe reaction, such as an immediate rash or difficulty breathing, contact the doctor immediately. Fortunately, sudden and intense reactions to foods are very uncommon at this age.

You can obtain many foods for your baby in prepackaged forms at the store, or you can prepare them yourself. Commercial baby foods have the advantage of convenience, especially if you are traveling or are short on time for food preparation. Unlike their predecessors of a few decades ago, most are free of sugar, salt, and artificial flavorings—they contain just the straight food in a mushy consistency, ready to feed. When opening a baby-food jar, make sure the safety button in the middle of the lid pops up. If it doesn't, return the jar or throw it away.

Don't feed your baby directly out of the jar because the enzymes and bacteria from her saliva may degrade or contaminate the food she doesn't finish. Instead, spoon a small amount on a plate and refrigerate what remains in the jar; it will be good for a day (or a month if left in the freezer). Whatever she doesn't finish from her plate should be thrown away.

Foods do not need to be hot; room temperature or slightly warm is just fine for most babies. If you need to warm something from the refrigerator, use the microwave with extreme caution—if at all—because of the possibility of uneven temperatures and hot spots within the food that could burn the baby's mouth. Food that is microwaved should be thoroughly stirred so the heat is distributed evenly throughout. If heating food in a baby-food jar, you can place the jar in a pan of warm water for a few minutes.

Don't become a clean-plate fanatic with your baby. When first sampling solids she will take only small amounts—one or two tablespoons at a time—and then gradually increase her intake over time. Watch for signs that she is no longer hungry—turning her head, getting fussy, or general disinterest in what you are offering from the spoon. Trying to force her to eat a prescribed amount is not only an exercise in futility but may also set up a bad habit of eating when she has no appetite.

THE DEBUT OF TEETH

During these months you may notice that your baby is doing a fair amount of drooling. This does not necessarily mean that the appearance of her first teeth is imminent. The ongoing flow of saliva serves partly to protect the mouth from being traumatized by the various objects, including her feet, that your baby will stick in her mouth. Antibodies in saliva may also help prevent bacteria and viruses on those objects from gaining a foothold in her throat or intestinal tract.

Somewhere in the neighborhood of six months, the first two lower front teeth, called the central incisors, will poke through the gums. (However, don't worry if you don't see any teeth for the first year. After that, if none have appeared, check with your baby's doctor.) The central incisors will be followed sometime later by the four upper incisors and then by two more lower incisors. Your baby may ease through this or display a lot of fussiness. She may drool somewhat more than usual and may also try to gum the nearest firm object. Contrary to popular belief, teething does not generate a temperature over 100.4°F taken rectally. If your baby has a fever something else is wrong.

Rubbing your finger against the gum through which the tooth is erupting may help the pain, or she may prefer a teething ring—which should not come from the freezer because it will be too hard. Acetaminophen (Tylenol and others) can help, but topical preparations that are supposed to numb the gums don't usually provide impressive relief because they can't remain in place for long.

A few additional cautions about foods and feeding

Do not feed honey to your baby. Infants younger than twelve months of age who eat honey may develop **infant botulism,** a form of food poisoning that can cause serious damage to the nervous system or very rarely can be fatal. Infant botulism has also been linked to corn syrup.

Keep your baby on breast milk or infant formula (fortified with iron) rather than milk from the dairy case. Infants who drink cow's milk before their first birthday are more likely to develop an allergy to the protein it contains. Cow's milk may also interfere with the absorption of iron contained in other foods.

Steer clear of fruit juices, punch, or other sweetened drinks. Some babies can become so enamored with sweet liquids that they will favor them over more nutritious sources of calories. They may also become hard to separate from their beloved juice bottle, which unfortunately will keep their new teeth continuously bathed in cavity-provoking sweet liquids. A good time for your baby to begin enjoying juices is when she can drink them from a cup.

Don't feed your baby foods with added salt or sugar or with spicy flavors. She needs to become accustomed to the basic, unadulterated taste of high-quality foods.

Don't let your baby become a "grazer." Some parents respond with food (breast, bottle, or snacks) whenever their baby utters any sound remotely suggesting displeasure. The result is nonstop eating by a baby who is never actually hungry or completely satisfied, and who may gain excessive weight.

Remember not to put your baby to bed with a bottle of milk. If she falls asleep with anything other than water in her mouth, bacteria can damage her incoming teeth. A baby who drinks from a bottle while lying flat will also be at greater risk for developing middle-ear infections. If your baby truly seems to sleep better after a bedtime snack, be sure all of it is swallowed.

SLEEP: IS IT TIME TO ESTABLISH A ROUTINE?

Between the fourth and sixth months, your baby will probably have settled into a sleeping routine that is more predictable and easier on everyone during the wee hours. Two naps during the day, one in the morning and one in the afternoon, are a good habit to encourage and maintain. These may last from one to three hours, and at this age you need not awaken your baby from a long nap unless it seems to be interfering with his sleep at night. (Some infants continue to catnap during this period.) Between two and four months or shortly thereafter, your baby should be skipping a night feeding. By sixth months, he should well be able to handle an eight-hour stretch without being fed unless he was premature or is exceptionally small. But whether this translates into uninterrupted sleep will depend on both your baby and your sleeping arrangements.

If he's down for the night by 8 P.M., he may be genuinely hungry at 4 A.M. But at that hour, unless he's sounding off with a sustained howl, you may want to wait a few minutes to see if he might go back to sleep. Delaying his bedtime may help extend his and your uninterrupted sleep in the morning, but a decision to allow him to stay up later must be weighed against other family needs. Ideally, before he is put to bed, there should be some time to wind down with quiet activities—a feeding, some cuddling, some singing, and perhaps a bath. With repetition of a routine, he will begin to associate these particular activities with bedtime and a surrender to sleep. If at all possible, have different people walk through this process with him so he won't come to expect that Mom or Dad is the only person in the world who can bring the day to a close.

Now is a good time to let him learn to fall asleep on his own if he hasn't been doing so already. When he is drowsy but not yet asleep, lay him down, pat him gently, and leave the room. Make sure there's a night-light on so he can see familiar surroundings. If he fusses for more than a few minutes, you can come back for a brief reassurance (perhaps offering some gentle patting on the back) but not a full-blown recap of the nighttime routine. If he persists, let a little more time go by before you return. If there's no end in sight to the crying and you can't stand to let it continue, do whatever works to bring on sleep, and then try again at a later date, perhaps on a weekend night when you have some flexibility in your evening and morning schedules.

If he isn't able to fall asleep by himself by six months of age, the window of opportunity for learning this skill may not be open again for several months. After six months, he is likely to begin a normal phase known as **separation anxiety,** in which a mighty howl may erupt when you or his closest caregivers are out of his sight, especially at bedtime. As a result, if after six months he's still used to being nursed, held, and rocked through several rounds of "Hey Diddle Diddle" until he's sound asleep, you can plan on repeating this ritual for months on end unless you are prepared to endure a vigorous and prolonged protest.

Remember that your baby's nighttime activity may include one or more awakenings that do not necessarily need your attention. If you rush into your baby's room to feed, cuddle, and rock him with every sound he produces, he will become quite accustomed to this first-class room service, and you may find that he is rather reluctant to give it up. Obviously, if he sounds truly miserable and is keeping everyone awake, do whatever is necessary to comfort him and calm things down. At this age it is still better to err on the side of too much attention than too little. After a few more months pass, however, you can become more hard-nosed if he seems intent on having a social hour several times a night.

CRYING: MORE THAN JUST HUNGER OR A WET DIAPER

Your baby's growing list of skills for interacting with her surroundings also includes new expressions of displeasure, and you will notice that a "language" of sorts is developing in her cries. The sounds she makes when she is hungry will be different from those she makes when she is undressed on the doctor's examining table and very different from her reaction to an immunization. Unlike the newborn's intense, almost primitive, crying in response to any and all forms of discomfort, after four months a baby may also cry in order to get attention or other action from the adults in her life. Watch and listen carefully, and you will learn to distinguish a cry that says, "I need to be fed" from one that says, "I'm bored" or "I want that toy I just threw on the floor."

Learning to discern the various intensities and inflections of her cries will also help you decide whether you need to tend to her immediately, or whether she can wait a little while you finish what you are doing. Indeed, as she progresses in her social skills through the first year, she will also need to discover that she is not the center of the known universe. If you know that she is fed, dry, and comfortable, you may want to delay a bit your response to the cry that seems to say, "I want some attention *right this minute.*"

HEALTH AND SAFETY ISSUES: SOME REMINDERS

As your baby begins to show his first signs of mobility and starts inserting everything he can grab into his mouth, you are but a few short months away from the exciting project of keeping him and your possessions safe when he wants to check out *everything in sight.* There will be much more on this topic in the next chapter, but a few basic ground rules are worth stating and repeating.

Don't leave your baby alone on any surface such as a changing table, kitchen counter, or sofa. He will invariably pick that moment to demonstrate his ability to roll over.

Don't leave your baby unattended even for a few seconds while he is in water, whether bathing in the sink, infant tub, or adult bathtub. He can drown in an inch or two of water.

Everyone in your house, including young children, should know how to dial 911 in case of an emergency. All adults and children over twelve should be trained in infant CPR. Local hospitals normally conduct CPR classes on a regular basis.

Be extremely cautious about leaving one of your older children in charge of your baby, even for a few minutes. This assignment should be considered only for a responsible sibling more than twelve years of age who has been observed handling the baby appropriately for a number of weeks. He or she must have explicit information about your whereabouts, instructions about what to do if the baby cries or has any other type of problem, and names and phone numbers of people to call for help if needed.

Always buckle your baby securely into his car seat, no matter how short the ride. Through the sixth month he will still be sitting backward, unless he is well ahead of schedule in size (more than twenty pounds) and in control of his head. The center of the backseat is the safest location for him; thus you should avoid putting him in the forward passenger seat. This means that, should he start to fuss, you will have to resist the temptation to turn around and tend to him while your vehicle is in motion. *If your car has a passenger-side air bag, you should never place your baby in the forward passenger seat.* If the air bag inflates during an accident, it can cause serious or even fatal injuries to a baby.

Never carry your baby while you are also holding a cup of hot liquid. One strong wiggle could result in a scalding injury to one or both of you.

Keep a watchful eye for small objects scattered around your living space. These would include older children's Legos, marbles, action figures, and other toys that might come within your baby's reach and therefore go into the mouth. If your baby is going to spend time on the floor, put your face on his level and scan the horizon. Look for stray coins, paper clips, pieces of dry pet food, plastic wrappers, electrical cords, or unstable objects that might fall on your baby if given a gentle shove.

Beware of parking your baby in an infant swing or doorway jumper and then turning your attention elsewhere. After four months, a baby with enough wiggle power may be able to squirm out of a swing or even bring the whole thing down.

Keep your baby out of walkers, which are responsible for thousands of accidents every year. These devices will not teach him how to walk or speed up his motor development. Instead, they give your active baby the opportunity to propel himself to the edge of the stairs, investigate whatever is sitting on your coffee table, or flip the walker over when he bumps into an obstruction.

Extremely vigorous play (such as tossing a baby a few inches into the air and catching him) is not a good idea at this age. Rapid accelerations and changes in direction, however playful, can have the same effect as shaking a baby, risking injury to his neck and brain.

A baby's skin may become sunburned after as little as fifteen minutes of direct exposure to the sun. Don't allow your baby to have prolonged exposure to direct sunlight (even on a hazy or overcast day), especially between the hours of 10 A.M. and 3 P.M. This is particularly important at higher altitudes or around lakes and seashores where the sun's ultraviolet light (which provokes the burn) can reflect off sand and water. Furthermore, sunscreens containing PABA (the most commonly utilized ultraviolet-absorbing ingredient) shouldn't be used on your baby's skin before he is six months old. If you take your baby outdoors for any length of time, keep him in the shade or use an umbrella and make sure his skin is covered with appropriate clothing (including a hat or bonnet) even if he is in the shade.

Medical checkups and immunizations

If all goes well, your baby will have just two encounters with her doctor during this time period: a well-baby check at four months and another at six months. During these visits, you should be asked questions about your baby's feeding and sleeping patterns, developmental milestones, and indications that she is seeing and hearing well. Some of the practitioner's assessment of your baby's progress will hinge more on observations you have made rather than the actual examination in the office. It will help a great deal if you can offer information about your baby's head control, her use of her hands, rolling over, tracking objects with her eyes, responses to sounds, and her other activities.

Concerns you might have about whether she is "ahead" or "behind" schedule in these areas must be put in perspective because there can be a wide variation in the time when babies accomplish various tasks. In most cases, what matters more is whether your baby is making steady progress overall. If you have questions and concerns about development—or any problems you have encountered—be sure to ask about them during these checkups. It will help if you write them down. If your list contains more than two or three items, let the doctor or nurse know at the beginning of the visit.

Your baby's height, weight, and head circumference will be measured and plotted on a growth chart. At the six-month check, it is likely that she will have doubled her birth weight. During each visit the examiner will look "stem to stern," noting how your baby moves and responds during the entire process. Unless there are specific reasons to do otherwise, your baby should receive DTaP (diphtheria/tetanus/pertussis) and hemophilus B immunizations at both four- and six-month checkups, and the OPV (oral polio vaccine) or IPV (inactivated polio vaccine) at the four-month exam. Your baby's doctor may recommend a third dose of polio vaccine at the six-month check or a later date. If she received her first hepatitis B vaccination at birth and her second at one month, she may receive her third and final dose at the six-month check-up. (Some physicians may delay the third dose until the age of twelve to eighteen months.) If she is on a different timetable, of course, you will have to confirm the date of the follow-up hepatitis injection. Be sure to let the doctor or nurse-practitioner know if your baby had an unusual response to any prior immunizations.

When your baby is ill: common medical problems

You now have a more sturdy, immunologically competent baby than you had three months ago. Infections are not as likely to get out of control and turn into a major medical event or a catastrophe. Unlike the first three months of life, a fever over 100.4°F rectally is no longer a cause for an immediate trip or call to the doctor's office or emergency room. But all of her exploring with hands and mouth is certain to introduce some new viruses and bacteria into her body, and some of these will gain enough of a foothold to cause trouble.

Invaders in the air passages. By far the most common illness you will see will be an **upper respiratory infection** (URI in medical shorthand or colds to everyone else), involving the nose, ears, throat, and upper airway. The most obvious symptoms will be a runny nose and cough, with irritability and disturbed sleep likely as well. Remember, your baby can respond to a sore throat or headache only by fussing and crying. It will be many months before you have the luxury of your child being capable of telling you what hurts. Fever may or may not be present, and you should get in the habit of checking your baby's temperature if she appears ill. Don't rely on

your sense of touch to decide whether the temperature is normal, but take the extra time to use a thermometer. If you need to discuss the illness with your baby's
doctor or nurse-practitioner, he or she will want to know whether a fever is part of
the problem (see sidebar, page 148).

If the cause of this infection is a virus—and there are at least a hundred different varieties of the **rhinovirus,** which is the usual culprit—your baby's immune system will normally deal with it within a week and return things to
normal. During these few days, your baby will want and need more cuddling and
comforting. Her appetite may be less enthusiastic than usual, or she may want to
nurse more often. You do not need to withhold feedings unless there is a significant airway problem, which is rare. Remember to wash your hands regularly,
since you can't avoid contact with drool and drainage, and these infections are
spread more commonly by contaminated hands than through airborne droplets.
Your fingers, which could be hosting some unfriendly organism, make more trips
every day to your eyes, nose, and mouth than you think.

Acetaminophen may be helpful for relieving aches and pains for a few hours
at a time. It can also help reduce but not eliminate a fever, a capability that is useful only because it can make your baby more comfortable. Although it is an important symptom during an illness, fever rarely causes problems in and of itself,
and you do not need to embark on a crusade to drive it away. If you use acetaminophen at this age, your baby will take a dose of 40 mg (0.4 ml of the infant
drops that contain 80 mg per 0.8 ml) if she weighs less than twelve pounds and
80 mg (0.8 ml of the infant drops) if she weighs more than twelve pounds.

Review with her doctor or nurse-practitioner about whether to give your
baby a cold remedy or cough syrup to relieve symptoms. There are scores of different brands, combinations of ingredients, and dosage schedules on the market,
but not many are geared for babies, and some may cause more problems than
they solve. Depending on your baby's sensitivity, the ingredients in these medications (decongestants, antihistamines, cough suppressants, and even alcohol)
may cause sedation, which could be confusing and worrisome. Is she getting
worse, or is it the medication? Or these medications may cause her to be more irritable and wakeful.

The antihistamines in many cold preparations may also thicken the secretions in the nose or airway, making them harder to clear. (In addition, controlled
studies of these medications have suggested that they are not likely to be effective
in children.) But if coughing and drainage are making your baby miserable and
if your baby's doctor recommends it, one of these products, whether a single-
ingredient decongestant or a combination cold-and-cough reliever, may be tried.

Be careful, and watch yourselves closely so that you do not forget the things your eyes have seen or let them slip from your heart as long as you live. Teach them to your children and to their children after them.

DEUTERONOMY 4:9

If it seems to help for a few hours and doesn't cause any problems, you can continue to use it as needed. Since most colds are caused by viruses, and viruses are not affected by antibiotics, don't be surprised if your baby's doctor doesn't prescribe one of these medications. (Do not pressure the doctor to use them if they're not really needed.)

Remember that you can use a rubber-bulb syringe to suck excessive secretions from your baby's congested nose. Saline nose drops may be helpful in cleansing nasal passages. Three or four drops of nasal saline solution may be instilled in each nostril (one at a time) and then suctioned out. This simple procedure may relieve congestion that is interfering with feeding. A cool-mist vaporizer may also help soothe the nose. However, a vaporizer must be cleaned and rinsed daily to prevent mold and bacteria from growing in it and then being sprayed all over the room the next time it is used. In addition, if everything in the room, including the baby, is perpetually damp from the vaporizer, you're probably using it too much.

Unfortunately, not all colds go away peacefully in a few days. Some allow bacteria to gain a foothold, producing a variety of illnesses for which your baby will need medical attention. One sign that bacteria have invaded is that the nasal drainage not only refuses to disappear after a week or two but turns and stays thick and discolored (gray, yellow, or green). If a cold persists more than two weeks or thick discolored discharge continues more than a few days, give your doctor a call—especially if there is a fever. (This isn't a sinus infection, by the way, because at this age the sinuses are not fully formed.) Antibiotics may be necessary to help your baby deal with these invaders.

The anatomy of a baby's nose and ears may allow bacteria to travel into the middle ear by way of the eustachian tubes. The resulting infection of the middle ear—that is, the air-filled space behind the eardrum—is known as **acute otitis media**. Usually an ear infection will cause pressure to build up behind the eardrum or irritate the drum directly, producing a great deal of discomfort and often fever. Therefore, a baby with a cold who becomes increasingly irritable should definitely be checked, especially if fever is present. Untreated, a middle-ear infection could cause local damage or spread to surrounding structures. Otitis media normally responds to an antibiotic, but *once started, the medication should be continued for its full course.* If your baby reacts to the antibiotic in some way—for example, with a rash or diarrhea—contact the doctor's office for further instructions.

Any virus or bacteria that infects the nose or throat can find its way into the linings of one or both eyes (known as the **conjunctivae**). These eye infections, known as **conjunctivitis** (or pinkeye, see photo on page A28), produce a reddish discoloration along with a discolored drainage. When this material dries overnight, the eyelids may be stuck together with a crusty debris you will need to remove gently with a warm, wet washcloth. Your doctor will normally prescribe antibiotic drops or ointment, which can be a little challenging to instill in the eyes of your wiggly, unhappy patient for a few days. Careful hand washing is a must for anyone handling a baby with conjunctivitis because the organisms involved have a knack for spreading to others by hitching a ride on unsuspecting fingers.

Coughing will not be hard to miss, but the ultimate source may not be quite as obvious. Mucus draining into the throat from the nose (postnasal drip) can provoke coughing, as will any infection involving the larynx (vocal cords), trachea (airway), bronchial tubes, or lungs. If the very upper portions of the airway are involved, you will notice a barking sound with the cough, in addition to hoarseness and noisy respirations. This syndrome, known as **croup,** is uncommon before the age of six months.

Bronchiolitis is an inflammation of the very small tubes that lead to tiny air sacs called **alveoli** where oxygen is transported into the bloodstream. It may be caused by any of several types of viruses but is most commonly attributed to the Respiratory Syncytial Virus (RSV). Bronchiolitis is usually restricted to infants and young children under the age of three and may become serious enough to require hospitalization. Coughing may actually be less obvious than wheezing and difficulty breathing. **Pneumonia** is an infection of the air sacs themselves and may be caused by bacteria or viruses or, rarely, by aspiration of some foreign material such as water or food. The baby with widespread pneumonia will usually appear quite ill, with fever, rapid respirations, and signs that breathing has become hard work: grunting, flaring of the nostrils, and retracting (sucking inward) of the muscles between the ribs. Sometimes, however, the pneumonia will be so localized to a certain section of lung that coughing and shortness of breath will not be evident. Fever and irritability may be the only symptoms.

If you have any concerns about your baby's well-being during a cold or other respiratory illness, don't hesitate to call your physician for advice or an assessment. A number of situations definitely deserve a call, although the timing and urgency of your contact will depend on the condition of your baby.

If your three- to six-month-old baby is active and feeding well, you can wait to call during office or daytime hours for

- coughing that persists more than a week or is persistent enough to interrupt sleep;
- fever under 103°F accompanying a cold or cough;
- thick, discolored drainage, redness, and/or crusting from the eyes;

- watery discharge from the nose that lasts more than seven to ten days, or thick discolored drainage for more than a few days;
- discolored drainage from one or both ears; this indicates that your baby not only has had an ear infection but has had a spontaneous rupture of the eardrum. This event is not a disaster. In fact, it relieves pressure and pain in the ear, but antibiotics are usually prescribed.[1]

You should call, regardless of the hour, for

- any signs of difficulty breathing other than nasal congestion; rapid respirations (more than forty per minute) or evidence of labored breathing (grunting, flaring of the nostrils, or retracting of the spaces between the ribs) should be evaluated by a physician. If your baby seems to literally gasp for breath, take her immediately to the nearest emergency room, or, if you are unable to do so, call 911;
- relentless crying or listlessness, especially with a fever;
- poor color—pale, bluish, dusky, or mottled skin;
- rectal fever of 103°F or more, especially if your baby is very irritable or lethargic.

You should be aware that many viruses can generate a high fever that a baby over four months of age can tolerate surprisingly well. If your baby is active, feeding well, and in reasonably good spirits despite the fever, your doctor may advise a check during office hours rather than the middle of the night.

Digestive-tract disturbances. As in previous months, you will want to keep a close watch on your baby if he begins to throw up or if his stools increase in frequency and volume. Some babies at this age may still routinely spit up some breast milk or formula after any given feeding and may even seem worse than a few weeks ago. That's because the muscles at the lower end of the esophagus may be looser than they were before. If height, weight, and developmental milestones are still on track, however, the primary focus can remain on minimizing the amount of spitting up. Eventually the problem should correct itself. Helpful measures in the meantime include

- more frequent, smaller feedings;
- more frequent burping during the feeding;
- enlisting gravity's assistance by keeping your baby in an upright position for a half hour after a feeding.

But if your baby's vomiting is forceful, you'll need to watch him carefully. If he is lethargic, running a fever, and/or pouring out loose stools, call the doctor's office for advice and probably a weigh-in and exam, since babies in this age-group can become dehydrated very quickly, especially if they are losing fluids from both ends.

If he throws up once but seems otherwise normal and in good spirits, you can see what happens over the next hour or two. If all is well, you can nurse him for a couple of minutes, watch him again for ten or fifteen minutes, and repeat this process for an hour. If there are no further signs of trouble, resume your normal feeding routine. The same can be done with a bottle-fed baby, except that re-hydrating solutions such as Pedialyte or Ricelyte should be tried instead of formula.

A similar approach holds for diarrhea. One or two loose stools in an otherwise happy and active baby need not generate a lot of concern. It happens from time to time, and you won't necessarily know why. If your baby is formula-fed, check to see if his most recent batches of formula have been correctly measured and mixed. If stools are frequent and watery but not accompanied by vomiting or signs of dehydration (see page 208), breast-fed babies can continue nursing as usual because Mom's milk is easy on the intestinal tract. Formula-fed babies, however, should be given a rehydrating solution until the stools begin to slow down and firm up. Plain water will *not* be absorbed nearly as well, and carbonated soft drinks (with or without the fizz) or juices will not contain the ideal blend of electrolytes such as sodium and potassium to replace what has been lost in the stool. Babies who are already taking solids can try some foods that are mildly constipating such as rice cereal, applesauce, or banana.

After your baby has experienced an intense bout of diarrhea, your physician may suggest using a lactose-free formula, since the illness may temporarily cause lactose intolerance. *Medications used to control diarrhea in adults, such as diphenoxylate (Lomotil) or loperamide (Imodium), should generally not be given to young infants.* They don't actually treat the cause of the loose stools, and they may cause the extra stool to accumulate in the bowel rather than pass into the diaper. This could lead to a false sense of security because it *looks* as if your baby has stopped the diarrhea.

If diarrhea lasts more than one or two days, especially if a fever is present, call your baby's doctor—even if the baby seems to be doing well. He should be evaluated if he is listless, passing blood with the stool, or having vomiting episodes along with the diarrhea.

Whether brought on by mild or moderate vomiting, diarrhea, or both, you should be aware of signs that **dehydration** (loss of body water) is becoming significant. A decrease in activity level, fewer wet diapers than usual, and fewer tears with crying suggest mild to moderate dehydration. If these occur, call your health-care provider for advice, which may include a doctor's evaluation.

Signs of more severe dehydration—indicating a much more urgent need for a trip to the doctor's office or emergency room—include the following:

- Dry mouth and no tears
- No urine for five to six hours, indicating that your baby is working hard to conserve his fluids
- Sunken eyes
- A sunken fontanelle (the soft spot in the skull)
- Skin texture that is no longer elastic, but more like bread dough
- Persistent fussing, especially if it is more of a moan or whine than a vigorous cry
- Cool and/or mottled skin
- Marked listlessness, with lack of interest in play or feeding. A baby this age who lies still while awake, shows little interest in people or things

---

WHAT CAUSES VOMITING AND DIARRHEA IN INFANTS?

Vomiting can be provoked either by an intestinal infection or by illness somewhere else in the body. When vomiting and diarrhea begin suddenly at the same time, the problem is usually **gastroenteritis** (or stomach flu), most often caused by a virus. Occasionally bacteria or even parasites are at fault.

Vomiting may also signal a problem elsewhere: an ear infection, pneumonia, urinary tract infection, or even meningitis. Because of the number and variety of possible causes of persistent vomiting, a medical examination will nearly always be needed, especially in a baby less than a year of age.

Diarrhea, with few exceptions, indicates a problem focused in the bowel. Usually this is an infection—most commonly viral, especially in the winter when an unsa-vory character known as rotavirus makes its rounds—but bacteria and parasites may have to be ruled out by taking samples of stool to a local laboratory for culturing and other tests. Contaminated food can be a cause of infectious diarrhea in older babies and children.

Antibiotics are a notorious cause of diarrhea in infants and children because they directly irritate the bowel or wipe out the normal bacteria in the intestine and allow less friendly organisms to multiply.

Food allergy, lactose intolerance, or a problem with formula may also provoke loose stools, though without other signs of illness such as fever or lethargy. Some detective work with your health-care provider may be needed if your baby has persistent loose or watery stools but is otherwise doing well.

around him, and has markedly reduced movements of arms and legs may be in serious trouble and should be evaluated immediately.

Please note: Detailed information about each of these illnesses, including treatment principles and options, can be found in the Reference Section.

FOR MORE INFORMATION

Turn to the Reference Section for more detailed information on:

- colds   page 668
- vomiting   page 740
- diarrhea   page 676
- ear infections   page 678

ARE WE HAVING FUN YET?

As you progress toward the halfway mark of your baby's first year, you will probably find yourself increasingly "settled in" with this new person in your life. Feeding and sleeping should become generally more ordered and predictable, so you can spend less time in maintenance mode and more in playful and pleasant interactions with him. You don't yet have the challenge of keeping track of a crawler/cruiser/toddler who is fervently seeking to explore every nook and cranny of your home. This child has yet to look you in the eye and communicate in his own unique way, "I know what you want, and I'm not giving it to you—what are you gonna do about it?"

Obviously not every infant approaching six months of age is a complete joy, and some will still be spending a lot more time fussing than cooing. But, if at all possible, this would be a good time for you to take a deep, slow breath and marvel at the wondrous gift God has entrusted to you. This project called parenting should include times when you momentarily lay aside your quest to catch up with the bills, laundry, projects brought home from work, dishes in the sink, and general clutter. At least once every week take the phone off the hook, sit back in a comfortable chair, place your baby on your lap, and take a good long look at him. Watch his eyes; see how he is beginning to use his hands; catch the details of his toes. If you can elicit a few sounds from him, carry on a little "conversation." Jot down in a notebook some thoughts about what you now behold. In a few short years, long after you have forgotten whatever cares and annoyances were floating through this particular day, these memories will linger in your mind like a sweet song.

NOTES
1. Before the development of antibiotics, as a therapeutic measure physicians deliberately made small incisions in the drums of infected ears to relieve pressure and allow drainage.

CHAPTER 7

Six to Twelve Months: Explorers

A child more than all other gifts
That earth can offer to
declining man
Brings hope with it, and
forward-looking thoughts.
WILLIAM WORDSWORTH

Six to Twelve Months: Explorers

During the six months prior to her first birthday, your baby will begin a momentous transition. As Sir Isaac Newton might have put it, she will change from a "body at rest" to a "body in motion." Her blossoming ability to control arms and legs will enable her to propel herself from point A to point B, usually by way of points C, D, and E. This exciting development will also set in motion a series of conflicts that you and your child will reenact in thousands of ways over the next two decades.

She will want to investigate everything she can get her hands on but will be completely clueless about risks and consequences. And, though fervently desiring to explore whatever she can see, she will also be afraid of separation from familiar faces, voices, and hugs. Your challenge will be to protect her—and her environment—while allowing her to stretch her wobbly legs and find out how the world works.

Before the end of the first year, she will also need to discover that, contrary to her own belief, she is not the center of the universe. She will need to learn about limits, that she cannot have or do whatever she wants, whenever she wants. She will need to discover that someone is in charge, and it isn't her. Your job will be to introduce her to these realities in a way that is loving, firm, consistent, and respectful.

Welcome to a whole new chapter of parenting!

DEVELOPMENTAL MILESTONES: FROM SITTING TO "CRUISING" AND CLIMBING . . .

Between six and nine months, your baby will be figuring out how to sit up and remain steady. First she will need support from pillows or the nearest adult. Then she will begin to prop herself up using her outstretched hands in a "tripod" posture. Eventually she will sit up for minutes at a time without toppling. By nine months, half of all babies are able to maneuver themselves into a sitting position from any other posture. This will give her considerable satisfaction, because her hands will be free to examine interesting objects while she remains upright.

Once your baby discovers the wonders of her world that are visible from a few inches off the floor, she will develop a keen interest in moving herself closer to whatever she spies across the room. Whether she eventually tries to roll, slither, scoot, or crawl toward them and when she first makes the attempt will be impossible to predict. If she takes to crawling, her skill will peak between seven and ten months, at which point you will be amazed at the speed with which she can cross the floor. She may use the traditional hands-and-knees approach, scuttle sideways like a crab, or inch forward military-style.

Some babies rarely or never crawl, and crawling doesn't actually appear on standard charts as a developmental milestone. Babies don't need to learn to crawl before they walk, and there is no correlation between this skill and future athletic or intellectual ability. Learning to crawl is not necessary for visual development, hand-eye coordination, or learning to read later in life. If other skills are moving ahead and your baby's doctor confirms that all else is going well, don't panic if she decides to skip crawling and move on to bigger and better things.

At around nine months of age, she will make another discovery: Standing upright is really, really fun. Usually someone in the family will pull her to a standing position next to the sofa or a soft chair, and she will gleefully remain there, using her hands to hold her position. Eventually she will figure out how to pull herself to her feet, using any available object that appears tall enough. Next comes the ultimate prewalking thrill of "cruising" from one place to another while holding on to whatever will keep her upright.

There will be three potential problem areas during this phase of exploration. First, expect a minor commotion if she pulls herself to a stand but can't figure out how to let herself down. You can teach her to bend her knees and lower herself to the ground without a fall, a skill that will save her a few bruises and spare you several trips to wherever she has become hung up, including her crib.

Second, your baby will have no ability to judge the stability of whatever she sees around her. If she decides to pull herself up using a wastebasket, a petite end table, a houseplant, or a floor lamp, both she and her unsteady support may end up on the floor. The results can be unpleasant if she pulls down a loose tablecloth on which sits your favorite china, or dangerous and disastrous if she applies her weight to an object that is both unstable and heavy such as a wobbly bookcase.

The third problem arises from a variation on cruising—climbing. Some babies find the lure of heights irresistible and will startle you with their ability to scale low-level furniture, stairs, or even combinations of pillows and stuffed animals to explore the upper atmosphere of the room. A few climbers will carry out remarkable acts of problem solving in their efforts to gain increased elevation. Unfortunately, their interest in heights will not be matched by an appreciation of the discomforts caused by a fall.

If your budding cruiser is going to be turned loose in a room, take a quick visual survey or a brief tour at her level to make certain that she won't find out about the force of gravity the hard way. Particularly important is keeping her off the stairs, which she will find irresistible once she discovers them. After her first birthday, she can begin to learn, with your direct supervision, how to get herself downstairs backwards. But until she is clearly "stair safe" many months from now, you will need to consider getting one or more barricades if her activity areas include potential access to a flight of stairs. These barricades should be the sturdy, horizontal gates with narrow slats (two and three-eighths inches or less apart), not the old-fashioned accordion-style, wood-slat barriers, which are less stable and are potential traps for inquisitive heads.

Letting her suffer some bruising consequences to "teach her a lesson" is a bad idea at this age. Not only will this risk unnecessary injury, but she is in fact not yet capable of understanding and judging the risks involved in her explorations. (She won't start on this learning curve until she is about fifteen months of age.)

Standing and walking

As your baby continues his relentless efforts to stay upright, he will at some point let go of his favorite support and stand on his own for a few seconds. At the same time or shortly thereafter, he will take a few shaky steps, perhaps with one or both parents cheering him on. Within a week he likely will be purposefully walking from one end of the room to the other, with or without a few unscheduled drops to the floor along the way. His legs will be bent and toes pointed outward, giving a thoroughly precarious appearance to his efforts. But all the lurching and plopping, which you may find nerve-wracking to watch, won't slow him down at all. (Don't forget to grab the camera so you—and he—can enjoy seeing it later.)

When will all this ambulating begin? Depending upon his size, center of gravity, genetic code, and temperament, anywhere between eight and fourteen months of age. If he is on the hefty side, he may have more difficulty hoisting his weight and maintaining his balance. The timing of his first steps has nothing to do with his future batting average or his chances of getting into college, but if he arrives at his first birthday and cannot stand even while being supported, your health-care provider—who will be doing a routine checkup at this age anyway—should be consulted.

What about shoes? Shoes serve little purpose prior to the onset of walking other than to decorate the feet for a family portrait. Once your baby starts to walk routinely, however, you may want to get shoes to protect his feet if he will be walking somewhere—such as the backyard or a park—where terrain is more likely to contain objects that are unfriendly to little soles.

Shoes should be big enough to allow a half inch of space between his toes and the tip of the shoe, and since his feet will be growing rather rapidly, there is no sense in blowing the family budget on designer footwear. A simple pair of tennis shoes with a sole that grips will suffice. Unless prescribed by a qualified health-care professional to remedy a specific problem, he shouldn't need wedges, heel lifts, or other hardware in his shoes. He won't need arch supports because his arch is covered by a fat pad that will gradually recede over two to three years.

Furthermore, you may notice that while his toes point outward when he walks (because of looseness of the hip ligaments), his feet will tend to point inward (pigeon toes) when he lies down. Both of these situations should straighten out by the time he is about eighteen months old. If any positioning of feet or legs seems extreme or not symmetrical, have your baby's doctor (or, if necessary, an orthopedist who deals with young children) take a look. If you see your baby limp, whether now or in the future, a medical evaluation should be carried out as soon as possible. *Limping is never normal,* and it may indicate that any number of significant medical problems is occurring.

Eyes and hands

By seven or eight months of age, your baby's visual capabilities will have matured to the point that she can focus on people and objects across the room, though not quite with the clarity with which she sees things directly in front of her. She may find a mirror entertaining, as she watches the interesting little person who responds exactly to her own movements. She will be more attentive to a variety of colors and shapes and will be rapidly absorbing visual information about the world around her. You will at times notice her staring intently at something across the room. More often she will become fixated on, and apparently fascinated by, some tiny object directly in front of her—a wad of lint, a stray Cheerio, or a little bug.

Her increased visual skills will be matched by new abilities with hands and fingers. By nine months she will have progressed from the mitten or rakelike grasp (using four fingers as a unit against the thumb) to the more precise "pincer" grasp between thumb and one finger. She will also begin cooperative efforts between her two hands such as picking up toys, passing an object from hand to hand, or smacking two items together to enjoy the sound they produce.

Over the next three months, these investigations with hands will become more sophisticated. She will discover the joy of releasing something from her hands, or actually throwing it, and watching what happens. She will turn it around and look at it from a variety of angles, rub it, and shake it. If it has a hole, she'll poke a finger into it. If it has parts she can move, she'll push, pull, twist, or spin them. Toward the end of the first year she will enjoy dumping small objects out of a container and then putting them back in, one at a time. She will knock something over and then set it upright, over and over. And, of course, she will bring *everything* directly to her mouth for examination by lips, gums, and tongue.

Sounds, syllables, and speech

One of the most pleasant developments between six and twelve months is watching your baby begin to make all sorts of new sounds. After six months he will begin imitating various syllables, primarily with vowels at first. By nine months, gurgling and babbling will be replaced by sounds with consonants such as "baba" or "dada," either in short bursts or repeated at length. He will probably not assign these sounds to a particular person (for example, "mama" for his mother) until twelve months or after.

As he progresses toward his first birthday, his "speech" will sound more sophisticated, though without much obvious meaning. Your one-year-old is likely to utilize a vocabulary of a few words, along with some wonderfully modulated babbling that rises and falls with the inflections of real speech. You can almost imagine that he is a visitor speaking a foreign language. He will also begin to communicate with gestures, such as pointing to something he finds interesting, waving bye-bye, or shaking his head to signify no. You may also hear exclamations such as "Uh-oh!"

While his speaking vocabulary may not be lengthy at his first birthday, he can understand quite a bit more (in fact, far more than you probably realize) well

Two distinct messages must be conveyed to every child during his first forty-eight months: (1) "I love you more than you can possibly understand" and (2) "Because I love you I must teach you to obey me."

DR. DOBSON
ANSWERS YOUR
QUESTIONS ABOUT
RAISING CHILDREN

before that date. After nine months he will begin responding to his own name and may show recognition of familiar people, pets, or objects. He will likely (we hope) respond to the word *no* before he starts using it himself. He may turn his head toward a person or toy you name, and before long he will surprise you by following a simple command.

You can make a major contribution to your child's language development during these months, even if you're not yet having much conversation. All day long you can name objects that you both see, talk in simple terms about what you are doing, and even look through simple picture books together. Try to keep your vocabulary straightforward and consistent, and don't expose him to hours of convoluted baby talk. Instead, coo and fuss and caress with your voice to your heart's content—using real words. His little computer will be processing all of this input, associating objects and pictures with words that you provide, and he might as well get it right the first time.

As cute as you will find his babbling, resist the temptation to repeat back his garbled versions of new words. If he points to a truck and says, "Guck!" be sure to say, "That's right, truck!" rather than leading him to believe that he has truly seen a guck. (One exception: Grandparents almost always proudly assume the names given to them by the first grandchild, such as "Nana and Papa," "Gomba and Bumpa," etc.)

Now is a good time to think about the kinds of sounds your baby will be imitating. Does everyone in the family speak in calm, pleasant tones, or do conversations sound loud and confrontational? Are compliments or complaints exchanged across the kitchen table? Is your baby likely to learn "Shut up!" before he says "I love you"? Is he hearing more words from the adults in his life or from the TV set droning in the corner? If you don't like what your baby is hearing, hold a family meeting and prayer time to help launch some new conversation patterns (and perhaps lower noise levels) at home.

Gestures and games

In addition to imitating your words and speech patterns, your six- to twelve-month-old will also begin to mimic gestures and movements. You will be pleasantly surprised one day to see him holding his toy telephone to his ear rather than banging it on the floor, or stroking his toy brush across his hair rather than gumming it. By one year of age, he will also enjoy a number of gesture games, such as peekaboo, pat-a-cake, and "so big." ("How big is Tyler?" Tyler's hands will imitate yours reaching for the sky, as you say, "So-o-o-o big!")

You can have fun with your baby and watch some developmental milestones being reached as he develops his sense of **object permanence.** At four or five months of age, if something is out of sight, it's also out of mind. If he pushes his rattle off the edge of the sofa, he won't pursue it with his eyes. But at about nine months of age, he can keep an image of something fixed in memory long enough to look for it after it disappears.

Take one of his toys, show it to him, and then hide it under a small cloth. Voila! He will pull the cloth away to reveal the toy, much to everyone's delight. As he practices this skill, you can try putting two or more obstacles between him and the toy. With increasing maturity of his sense of object permanence, he will be more persistent in finding it. To make the game even more exciting, you can "hide" yourself behind a chair or around a corner and then let him "find" you. (You may need to leave a foot in view or peek around the corner the first time until he gets the idea.)

Other games you can play (which for your baby are actually explorations of the world around him) include rolling a ball back and forth, building a small tower out of plastic blocks and letting him knock it over, and plopping all sorts of smaller objects into a large container and then dumping them out. There are, indeed, very few fancy gadgets that babies this age will appreciate any more than simple, inexpensive toys (or, for that matter, household items): all sizes and types of plastic containers, lightweight unbreakable bowls and cups, balls of all sizes (as long as they are too big to fit into his mouth), building blocks, toy telephones, and plastic cars, trucks, and planes (whose edges aren't sharp and whose parts won't come loose).

SAFETY MEASURES: CURIOSITY, CHAOS, AND CAUTIONS

All of these activities with eyes and hands are not random or meaningless. On the contrary, they are vital to your baby's development. Her brain and nervous system are assimilating information at a rapid pace, and all of the staring, touching, and gumming are providing important input about how things are and the way they work. By nine months of age, your baby's curiosity will be insatiable. She will not be content to merely inspect every item within her reach. She will also be itching to get her hands on all those interesting shapes that she's been seeing for weeks on end from across the room. Her intense curiosity will thus become a driving force in advancing her motor skills.

This normal—and necessary—development will generate extra work and worry for everyone in your baby's life. Her explorations should be encouraged, but they will inevitably require some adjustment of your living arrangements. You'll need to balance your baby's healthy curiosity against her need for a safe environment and your need for some semblance of order.

Avoiding extremes is important. Confinement for hours on end in a playpen, which might be convenient for the grown-ups, will impair the flow of information to baby's developing brain. But giving her unlimited access to all parts of the home without some thoughtful preparation is an invitation to harm or disaster. *Furthermore, attempting to train a baby at this age by subjecting her to a nonstop*

SPECIAL TOYS, AND TOYS TO AVOID

Short attention spans and nonstop investigation of one item after another mean that you don't have to spend a lot of money on a special toy, since your young explorer probably won't spend any more time with it than with the box containing it. However, if Uncle John really wants to unload some cash on a toy for his nephew, you could steer him toward the following:

- Push toys, especially if they have a low center of gravity that allows your baby to cruise or "walk" behind them.
- Busy boxes with all sorts of switches and levers to push and noises to make.
- Bath toys that can be emptied and filled (a few plastic cups may suffice for this) or toys that float, squeak, and squirt.
- Sturdy picture books with thick cardboard "pages"; your baby will probably get less of a charge out of the pictures than he will from moving the pages back and forth, since they function as a colorful hinge, and many babies at this age are hinge fanatics.

Toys to think twice about or avoid altogether at this age include:

- Stuffed animals. That's right, stuffed animals, especially for the baby younger than nine months who has no idea who Barney or Mickey Mouse is or has any interest in finding out. These toys can collect dust, aggravate allergic noses, shed hair and stuffing, and lose plastic eyes and noses that might end up in someone's airway or even in an older toddler's nose. If the stuffed toys accidentally get in the line of fire when your baby spits up, they'll reek for weeks. As your baby passes the nine-month mark and separation anxiety becomes more evident, a soft something may be enlisted for duty as a transitional object to help keep him calm when you are out of the room or out for the evening. Whatever is used must be sturdy enough to survive lots of handling and washing and must not be adorned with little decorative items that might come loose.
- Anything with sharp edges, little parts, or big parts that might easily become little parts.
- Balloons. Aside from scaring the daylights out of your baby when they pop, those little rubber fragments are very easy to choke on.
- Toys that are supposed to "educate" your baby about abstract concepts such as letters and numbers. It will be some time before your baby will comprehend this type of symbolism, and efforts to introduce him to the ABCs and 1-2-3s are unnecessary at this point in his life. Right now your baby's education is going on during every waking hour as he handles, gums, bangs, and drops everything in sight and as he listens to older people talk to him.

*torrent of No's! and hand-slapping while she is merely trying to find out what's what
in her world will make everyone miserable and exhausted.*

Some reasonable baby-proofing and commonsense precautions will spare
everyone a lot of toil and grief.

**Take a child's-eye tour of whatever living space will be available to your crawler/
cruiser/walker.** Are there any top-heavy items—chairs, tables, floor lamps, book-
shelves—that might fall if pulled by your baby? Any electrical cords or outlets
within reach? (Install plastic plugs to block unused outlets from inquisitive fingers.) Do you see any wires with frayed insulation? These are a hazard to everyone, not just the baby. What about cords dangling down from a curling or steam
iron resting on a counter or ironing board? A yank on one of these could cause
not only a hazardous bonk on her head or body but also a very painful burn.

Are there any small objects lying around that, upon entering her mouth,
might end up in her airway? Your vigilance regarding small objects will be a daily
concern if you have older children at home, because their toys and games tend to
have lots of tiny parts and pieces that have a way of dispersing throughout your
home. How about cords attached to draperies and blinds? These should be
looped or tied on a hook well out of reach to prevent the baby's getting tangled
in them.

**Don't leave your prized china or other valuable breakables within reach of a newly
mobile baby and then demand that she not touch them.** She will have no concept
of the difference between a cup made by Wedgwood and one brought home from
Wendy's, except, perhaps, the sound they make when they hit the floor. Your expensive collectibles should be displayed (or stored) out of reach during this season of your child's life.

**While some recommend that your kitchen be kept off-limits to little explorers, this
will probably not be a realistic option.** Most parents and older children traverse
the kitchen many times each day, and dealing with a barricade every time is a major nuisance. Lots of family interactions take place in kitchens, and your baby will
not want to be left out.

This will mean, however, relocating cleaning compounds and other chemicals to higher ground. Bleach, furniture polish, and drain cleaners are particularly hazardous, and automatic-dishwasher powder can be extremely irritating if
it gets into the mouth. Sharp objects, which of course are abundant in kitchens,
must also be kept out of reach at all times. If you have an automatic dishwasher,
be sure to keep the door latched when you are not loading or unloading it. A

wide-open dishwasher door is not only an irresistible climbing spot but also a gateway to all sorts of glassware and sharp utensils.

Many families set aside a low cupboard for "baby's kitchen stuff"—a collection of old plastic bowls, cups, spoons, lids, and other safe unbreakables that she can examine and manipulate to her heart's content. (By the way, she will probably spend a fair amount of time moving the cupboard door back and forth on its hinge.) You may want to steer her toward this particular cupboard and away from the others (this will take lots of repetition) or make the arrangement more formal by installing plastic safety latches in the cupboards and drawers that are off-limits.

While kitchens are difficult to barricade, bathrooms are another story. Like kitchens, they are full of potential hazards: medications, cleaners, and, most important, bodies of water. Any medications (prescription or over-the-counter, including vitamins and iron) and cleaning substances must be stored well out of reach and returned to their secure spot *immediately* after each use (see sidebar).

Never leave a baby unattended in the bath, even at this age, and be certain to empty the tub as soon as you're done with it. Open toilets are an irresistible destination for a cruiser. The possible consequences of a baby's investigation of an unflushed toilet are both unsafe and stomach turning. More important is the possibility that a top-heavy toddler might lean over far enough to fall in.

Never leave hair dryers, curlers, or other electrical devices plugged in after you use them. For that matter, no one should be using any of these items when the baby (or anyone else) is in the bathtub, unless you have a very large bathroom with a lengthy distance between appliance and water. If your baby or an older child tries to take the hair dryer for a swim, *even if it's turned off but plugged in*, the resulting shock could be lethal.

Unlike most kitchens, bathrooms have doors that can be shut to prevent unsupervised entry. If an enterprising explorer learns to turn door handles, an additional high latch may need to be installed.

Survey your home for "what's hot and what's not." Radiators, heaters, floor furnace grills, and fireplace screens can all become surprisingly hot, and a protective barrier between these surfaces and little fingers will be needed, at least at some times of the year.

Never leave pots cooking with their handles extending over the edge of the stove, since one healthy pull could result in a severely scalded child. Some stoves also have exposed knobs that babies and toddlers might love to twist and turn. If these are easily detachable, you may want to remove them between meals.

A similar reminder applies to hot liquids such as soups and gravies near the edge of your dining table, especially if they sit on a tablecloth that could be pulled from below. Avoid carrying your wiggly explorer and a cup of hot coffee or tea at the same time. One sudden twist on her part could fling hot liquid over both of you.

Set your hot water heater temperature below 120°F to minimize the risk of an accidental scald from the tap.

How about those houseplants? Infants and toddlers can be quite adept at doing some impressive pruning on your prized houseplants if they are within reach. A more worrisome possibility is that these young children might choose to sample the leaves and stems, which may be irritating to the lining of the mouth or even overtly toxic. Now is the time to move the plants out of reach, unless you know for certain that they are nontoxic and you don't care if they get mangled sometime during the next few months. In order to prevent your explorer from having a close encounter with the dirt around any plants that remain at floor level, you can cover the soil with screen mesh.

Finally, think about your baby's introduction to the great outdoors. When the weather's nice and the family gathers in the backyard, what interesting but hazardous items might cross her path? Once again, make a baby's-eye survey of any area that she might reach (if she's a skilled crawler, keep in mind how fast she can move while your attention is diverted).

If you have a swimming pool, make sure that a childproof fence surrounds it. (Some states by law require this safety barrier.) If your yard contains a spa, it should be securely covered when not in use. Pool and hot-tub drain covers should be checked periodically to make sure they are properly in place. If not, a child's hand or even hair could be pulled into the outlet by the suction created by the pump, and she might be unable to break free. Children have drowned in such circumstances. As a backup precaution, make sure that the pump's on-off switch is readily accessible.

Check the lawn for mushrooms, and if you are not absolutely certain they are nontoxic, get rid of them, because anything your baby finds at this age is likely to go straight into her mouth. Are there any garden tools, insecticides, fertilizers, or other unfriendly items lying around? The more potential dangers you can eliminate from her immediate access, the more you can enjoy your time outdoors with her.

One other outdoor hazard you must not ignore is the sun. A baby's skin is very sensitive to the ultraviolet (UV) light generated by the sun, and at peak times of the day (between 10 A.M. and 3 P.M.) as little as fifteen minutes of direct exposure can provoke an unpleasant burn. This is a particular problem at higher altitudes, where UV light is more intense, and around lakes and oceans, where UV can reflect from water and sand. Sunburns can also occur on hazy or overcast days because UV light penetrates both haze and cloud cover.

If your baby is going to be experiencing the great outdoors for any length of time, try to avoid the 10 A.M. to 3 P.M. time of peak intensity, keep her in the shade as much as possible, and utilize appropriate clothing (as well as a hat or bonnet) for protection. An explorer who is going to be in and out of sunlight will benefit from a sunscreen with a sun protection factor (SPF) rating of at least fifteen, applied an hour before she ventures forth. If you are going to take her with you into the pool, use a waterproof version and reapply it after you are done. Occasionally a baby will react to the common UV-protecting ingredient known as PABA, which is used in many sunscreens. If your baby has very sensitive skin, you might take your sunscreen for a "test drive" by applying some to a small area of her skin (an inch or so wide) for several hours to see if any reaction develops.

Parental vigilance . . .

Many of these guidelines represent passive restraints—fixed barriers between child and hazard. But you cannot anticipate every possible risk or create enough safeguards for a 100 percent-safe environment, unless you want to turn your home into a padded cell. You will need to take more active measures as well, involving both your own surveillance and some basic training for your baby.

From your standpoint, perpetual vigilance is the price of child rearing, at least for now. You must develop an ongoing sense of your child's whereabouts, a third eye and ear that are tuned in to him, even when he is in a confined and seemingly safe space such as his crib. You will need to monitor his activities constantly to see what new perils might cross his path in the immediate future.

The riskiest times will be those when you are distracted, frazzled, or just plain weary. You may be in the middle of a project involving hazardous tools or materials—a long overdue deep cleaning, for example. Suddenly the phone rings, or someone is at the door, or another child cries out in another room. Before you drop everything to attend to the new situation, look at what might be open, exposed, or available to your baby. Could he get to any of it? You may have to delay your response for a few moments while you ensure there is no way your baby in motion can get his hands on something dangerous.

Beware of those times in the day—especially the late afternoon—when your energy may be low, your mind preoccupied, and your patience short. One or more other children may be irritable at this time, competing for your attention. But don't lose track of your youngest crawler/cruiser/toddler, who may have just discovered something interesting that was dropped under the kitchen table.

Sometime in your parenting career, you may reach a point of such sheer exhaustion that you just have to lie down for a little while. Do you let an older child watch the baby or let him roam around your bedroom while you close your eyes for a few precious minutes? Think hard before you stretch your safety boundaries. Some cautions about using older children as baby-watchers were brought up in the previous chapter, but you must be even more wary when you have a new explorer. An older child is more likely to become distracted by a friend or toy, and a major problem could develop during a few moments of inattention. If you are really that tired, see if a trusted adult such as a friend, neighbor, or relative might relieve you for one or more hour's respite.

. . . and baby's boundaries

The other side of the safety coin involves your child. As her first birthday nears, she must learn that there are some boundaries in her world, even if she has been given access to a substantial amount of your living space. Of course, she will have no way of knowing what is okay to touch and what is off-limits until she is given that information. And give it you must, remembering that—for now—her driving force is nearly always her intense curiosity rather than a specific desire to put you and your limits to the test. At this stage of development, in fact, you can take advantage of her curiosity, along with her short attention span, to help shift her interest away from the things you want her to avoid.

Keep in mind that your limit setting will require a lot of legwork because you can't use much verbal "remote control" until she's a few months older. If she is

He who spares the rod hates his son, but he who loves him is careful to discipline him.

PROVERBS 13:24

examining something that is unsafe or inappropriate, it is extremely unlikely that she will understand the command ("Emily, don't eat that bug!") you issue from across the room. The tone of your voice may get her attention and perhaps stop the deed momentarily. But you will also have to separate the offending item from her fingers (or mouth) while making a simple and concrete statement about it. ("No, no—not for Emily" or "Don't touch the stove—ouch!")

Will she understand what you are saying? Probably not at first, although she will pick up your reaction about what she has been doing. More important, her amazing little computer is continually processing information about "What happens when I _____?" and you definitely want to provide a lot of the input. In particular, when setting boundaries, your tone of voice should communicate that you mean business. (You can't project much of a warning or a sense of authority if you sound like the Lullaby Lady.) On the other hand, yelling, haranguing, or (worse) sounding off without taking any action will definitely work against you. Sometimes a verbal and physical response at the same time can turn your statement into an object lesson: "Don't touch the curtains" will make more of an impact while you are physically removing her from them.

Her short attention span will usually allow you to distract her focus elsewhere after you have made your point. Most likely she will forget about whatever she found interesting if you offer her something else that is equally intriguing. But she may also forget whatever you were originally trying to tell her. If she is really intent on pursuing her investigation, she may promptly head back to the shiny knobs on the stereo or the ill-tempered cat's flopping tail, even when you have just taken her away from it—for the seventh time.

When your mobile baby seems determined to override your intentions and repeatedly bears down on the forbidden target, *don't back away from the limits you have set.* Take action *every time,* making your statement by using an increasingly firm tone of voice (which won't be difficult). One approach to consider when she crosses your line over and over again is to remove her completely from the temptation zone. A time-out in a crib or playpen, where her roaming privileges are temporarily curtailed for a few minutes, may be appropriate at this point.

At some point, however, you may need to take more direct and immediate action, especially if she is repeatedly reaching for something that is dangerous. A quick thump on the hand (not hard, but enough to get her attention) may need to accompany your verbal warning, but this should be done only if

- you are certain that she understands what you want (which is not likely before nine months of age);

- her safety is on the line; and

- you have no other way to separate her from the hazard.

The point of your response is not to lash out in anger and frustration but to change behavior for her benefit and protection. If she is bent on playing with the handle on the oven, for example, the brief sting of your rebuke will be far less painful than a burn on her fingers. When she cries as a result, take a moment to comfort her and talk things over. While she won't understand a lecture on burn prevention, some simple input such as "Mommy said not to touch this" will usually be understood by a baby approaching the first birthday.

Indeed, at this age your objective is not to teach great moral principles or the whys and why nots of home safety. Later when her language and reasoning skills are more sophisticated, you will carry out that assignment on an ongoing basis. In the meantime, she must assimilate some reasonable house rules into her ever increasing fund of knowledge about how her world works. Your consistent enforcement of boundaries, even at this preverbal stage, will establish that you are in charge and position you to handle the more overt challenges to come.

If it hasn't become apparent by now, you will soon become acutely aware that you cannot guarantee the absolute safety of your child. In addition to loving, comforting, teaching your child, and taking appropriate safety precautions where you live, now is the time to renew your commitment to pray for her as well. Remember that she is on loan, entrusted to your care for a season, and her Creator ultimately knows and loves her far better than anyone can imagine. Acknowledging that fact and seeking His wisdom on a daily basis—even for the everyday routines of parenting—will help keep your concerns in perspective and tap into strength and insight that extend far deeper than your own.

FEEDING: SOLID FOODS—BEYOND THE BASICS

During these six months your baby will make another important transition as he becomes nourished primarily by solid foods. Chapter 6 described the process of introducing your baby to solids in some detail (page 192), and if you are just now beginning to offer your baby any food other than milk, you should review that information.

Chapter 6 also mentioned some reasons not to begin solids too early (before four months of age), but you don't want to wait too long either. As your baby passes the sixth month, breast or formula feeding alone will fall short of providing the calories and nutrients he needs. Between six and nine months he may be more willing to try a variety of foods than after the one-year mark. Your goal at six months will thus be to begin solids if you haven't by now and then to expand his food horizons gradually and steadily.

By the end of the first year, the general outline of his eating patterns should resemble your own, except for amounts and textures. This raises the question of where you will take your baby nutritionally. If your family's eating habits are chaotic and your diet loaded with fat, salt, and sugar, do you want your baby to reach the same endpoint? This may be a good time to reevaluate and reconfigure your own food choices.

By nine months you will see some side-to-side chewing movements that signal readiness for foods with a thicker texture. This is a good time to begin trying some mashed or chopped food from the family meal and some finger foods that your baby can feed himself. The latter include items such as small pieces of soft fruit (peaches or pears, for example), little squares of bread or toast, unsalted crackers, pieces of pancake or soft waffle, and cooked soft pasta.

Don't become a clean-plate fanatic with your baby. When first sampling

INTRODUCING YOUR BABY TO SOLID FOODS

1. After three tablespoons of rice cereal are going down smoothly at one feeding, you may want to try other cereals such as oats and barley. Check with your baby's doctor before trying corn or wheat cereals, which provoke digestive problems in some infants.

2. After cereals have been established on the menu for a few weeks, you can introduce either fruits or vegetables. Vegetables may hold an advantage because they will not condition your baby to sweet tastes. Fruits can be added later, and meats introduced last. You may choose to raise a vegetarian and not introduce meats to your baby at all, but if you do so, be sure that you are adequately informed so your baby won't be deprived of any necessary nutrients.

3. Remember to let your baby try each new food (one to three tablespoons' worth) for a few days before introducing another. Observe for any signs of a reaction: diarrhea, irritability, runny nose, coughing or wheezing, or a rash, especially around the face.

If there is any possibility that a reaction has occurred, withdraw the food, wait for the problem to calm down, and try again—unless the reaction is severe; then consult your baby's doctor. If you see the same response again, put that food aside for several weeks, and tell your baby's doctor before serving it to her again. If there's a more severe reaction, such as an immediate rash or difficulty breathing, contact the doctor immediately. Fortunately, sudden intense reactions to foods are very uncommon at this age.

4. Once your baby is taking food from different groups (for example, cereal and vegetables), you can feed her solids twice daily and expand to three times daily when three or more types of food are part of her daily routine. In addition, her daily intake should include about sixteen to thirty-two ounces of breast milk or formula. (A rule of thumb is that one nursing session at this age delivers six to eight ounces of milk.)

solids he will take only small amounts—one or two tablespoons at a time—and then gradually increase his intake over time. Watch for signs that he is no longer hungry—turning his head, getting fussy, or general disinterest in what you are offering from the spoon. Trying to force him to eat a prescribed amount is not only an exercise in futility, but may also set up a bad habit of eating when he has no appetite.

Chapter 6 listed a number of cautions about foods and feeding. Because of their potential impact on your baby's health, these caveats will be repeated here along with some additional notes for the more experienced solid-food consumer.

- *Do not feed honey to babies under the age of twelve months* because of the risk of infant botulism, a form of food poisoning that can cause serious damage to the nervous system, or very rarely can be fatal. Corn syrup has also been found to cause infant botulism.
- Keep your baby on breast milk or infant formula (fortified with iron) until he reaches the age of twelve months. Infants who drink cow's milk

---

(continued)

Once she has become well acquainted with solids, for most feedings you'll probably want to offer breast milk or formula *after* your baby has had other foods. (Milk can also be given between meals and at bedtime.) Solids won't hold much interest if her tank is already full of six or eight ounces of milk.

A FEW REMINDERS ABOUT FOOD PREPARATION: If you are using commercially prepared baby food from a jar, make sure that the safety button in the middle of the lid pops up when you open it. If it doesn't, return the jar or throw it away. Don't feed your baby directly out of the jar because the enzymes and bacteria from her saliva may degrade or contaminate the food she doesn't finish. Instead, spoon a small amount on a plate, and put what remains in the jar into the refrigerator, where it will be good for a day (or a month frozen). Whatever is left on her plate should be thrown away.

You may prefer to prepare your own foods rather than (or in addition to) using commercial baby-food products. At first, keep them simple: adequately cooked and then pureed in a blender or baby-food grinder or mashed with a fork. Fruits other than bananas should be cooked rather than served raw.

Avoid salty, sugary, and spicy concoctions as well as foods that might provoke allergic reactions. When your baby has had her fill of a particular item, you can store any extra in the refrigerator. However, before serving rewarmed food to your baby at a later meal, inspect and smell for any signs of spoilage. If in doubt, toss it out.

Solid foods do not need to be hot; room temperature or slightly warm is just fine for most babies. If you need to warm something from the refrigerator, use the microwave with extreme caution—if at all—because of the possibility of uneven temperatures and hot spots within the food that could burn the mouth. Microwaved food should be thoroughly stirred so the heat is distributed evenly throughout. If heating baby food in a jar, you can place the jar in a pan of warm water for a few minutes.

before their first birthday are more likely to develop an allergy to the protein it contains. This may lead to the loss of small amounts of blood from the intestine. Cow's milk may also interfere with the absorption of iron contained in other foods. Both of these could lead to a shortage of red blood cells (anemia). After twelve months, when you do begin to offer cow's milk, use whole milk, not low-fat or nonfat, because your baby will need the extra fat to construct his growing central nervous system.

♦ Keep your baby away from chocolate, peanut butter, shellfish, egg whites, citrus fruits, strawberries, and tomatoes before his first birthday; these can induce future allergies. Some physicians also add wheat and corn to this off-limits list for the same reason.

♦ Even more risky to your baby are foods that might cause a choking accident. Avoid any foods that are small and hard such as seeds, nuts, small candies, uncooked peas, and popcorn. Also keep your baby away from foods that are sticky, chewy, stringy, or small and round. Peanut butter and hot dogs are thus off-limits, along with grapes, uncooked vegetables, raw apples, and dried fruit. In a nutshell, foods that can't be smushed by gums or easily dissolved in saliva or that might fit snugly into a small airway don't belong in your baby's mouth.

♦ Don't feed your baby foods with added salt or sugar, or with spicy flavors. He needs to become accustomed to the basic, unadulterated taste of high-quality foods. Offer fruit for dessert rather than calorie-drenched sweets such as custards and puddings. Don't let your baby develop a taste for soda, punch, or other sweetened drinks.

♦ Keep up the variety. If your baby seems to ignore everything but one or two foods—crackers and bananas, for example—don't be frightened or blackmailed into allowing him to establish a major food rut. Hold these items and offer him a variety of alternatives from the other food groups instead. If he refuses, don't panic. When he's hungry, he'll eat what you've offered, especially if he hasn't filled his tank with milk before mealtime.

♦ Don't let your baby become a "grazer." Some parents respond with food (breast, bottle, or snacks) whenever their baby utters any sound remotely suggesting displeasure. The result is nonstop eating by a baby who is never actually hungry or completely satisfied and who might acquire a long-term habit of turning to food for comfort. You would be wise to avoid feeding patterns such as this that might result in overeating, especially if obesity is a problem on either side of your family.

Between six and nine months, you can establish mealtime routines: breakfast, lunch, and dinner, with midmorning and midafternoon snacks if you and your baby desire. But when meals are over, let them be over.

- Don't put your baby to bed with a bottle of milk or juice. If he falls asleep with anything other than water in his mouth, bacteria can damage his incoming teeth. A baby who drinks from a bottle while lying flat will also be at greater risk for developing middle-ear infections. If your baby truly seems to sleep better after a bedtime snack, be sure all of it is swallowed and then carry out a gentle toothbrushing with water (if he has any teeth) before going to bed.

- Don't let your baby become a "juiceaholic." Some become so enamored with the sweet taste of juices that they will favor them over more nutritious sources of calories, including milk. Furthermore, juices sucked from bottles may stay in contact longer with the teeth and lead to early decay. Juice bottles have a way of becoming an entrenched habit.

  Hold off on juices until he can drink them from a cup. Once he has started drinking them on a regular basis, set a four-ounce daily limit, or dilute four ounces with an equal amount of water if you want to offer them more often. Since citrus fruits may provoke allergic responses during the first year, you may want to hold the orange juice until after the first birthday. (Check with your baby's doctor.)

Avoiding high-chair hazards

As your baby begins to spend more time with solids each day, you may find it easier to feed her in a high chair. As with all baby equipment, a few simple precautions will help prevent unpleasant or even serious accidents.

- As with bathtubs and car seats, rule number one with high chairs is *never leave your baby unattended while she is sitting in it.*

- Make certain that the chair has a broad base so it cannot be easily tipped over. Grandma's high chair might be a venerated family heirloom, but if it doesn't sit rock solid on the floor, use a newer one. If you use a chair that folds, make sure it is locked into place before your baby gets in.

- Take the few extra seconds to secure your baby with the chair's safety straps. This will prevent her from wiggling and sliding out of position or standing up to survey the horizon, both of which could result in a serious injury.

- Before your baby is seated, make sure the chair is at a safe distance from the nearest wall or counter. Otherwise, a healthy shove from your young diner might topple her and the chair to the floor.
- Don't let other children play under or climb on the high chair.
- Clean food debris off the chair and tray after each meal. Your baby may have no reservations about sampling any leftovers—in various states of decay—that are within finger range.

If you use a portable baby seat that clamps onto a table when you travel or eat out, observe a few additional precautions:

- Make sure the table is steady enough to support both chair and baby and that the chair is securely clamped to the table before your baby gets in. Card tables, glass tops, tables supported only by a center post, and extension leaves are not strong or stable enough for this job.
- Position the chair so your baby can't push against one of the table legs and literally "shove off" for a voyage to the floor.

MAKING THE TRANSITION FROM BREAST TO BOTTLE?

If breast milk has been your baby's primary nutrition source through the first six months of life, you will need to introduce her to solids during the coming months (if you haven't started already) as has just been described.

But should you switch to formula feeding as well? The answer depends entirely on you and your baby. On one hand, if the two of you are a smoothly functioning nursing team and everyone is quite happy with this arrangement, there's absolutely no need to change. If a well-meaning relative thinks you're "getting a little carried away with this breast-feeding thing" because you're still nursing a baby who is nearly a year old and perhaps starting to walk, you can let her know, without any embarrassment, that this arrangement is working very nicely for you. In other words, at this point in your baby's life, "if it ain't broke, you don't need to fix it."

On the other hand, baby or mother (or both) may be ready to make a change during the months approaching the first birthday. As babies become more mobile and

fascinated with the world around them, they may also become squirmy and distracted during nursing sessions—especially during the day when they are wide-awake and their hunger is being satisfied by other foods. They may suck a few times and then display body language that says, "Sorry to eat and run, Mom, but I got things to do!" To add injury to insult, some babies may absentmindedly chomp into a nipple with their newly erupted teeth.

Many moms have their own reasons to wean a baby from nursing to formula between six and twelve months of age. Perhaps they feel the need to devote more of their time and attention to other people and activities within the home, to educational pursuits, to outside employment, or to a combination of these interests. Some begin to long for "having my body back," especially if nursing is starting to feel more like alligator wrestling. There may be a budding (or even full-grown) desire to pursue weight reduction and physical conditioning without worrying about affecting a baby's nutritional well-being.

- The chair should attach to the bare surface of the table, not a tablecloth or place mat that can slide off.
- Don't let older children play under the table and/or seat, since they might accidentally bump and dislodge it.

Dining area or "mess" hall?

Some babies are quite content to let you feed them one spoonful of food after another, while others can't wait to take matters literally into their own hands as soon as possible. When your ten-month-old reaches for the feeding spoon, she is primarily interested in it as an object to investigate and manipulate—just like everything else she touches. It is quite unlikely that she will use it to transfer food into her mouth with any consistency until she has passed the fifteen-month mark. Instead, she will probably bang her spoon against the nearest hard object, fling it to the floor, or perhaps dip it into her food—before she bangs and flings it.

(continued)

Even more fundamental and important for many mothers is the realization that an inevitable passage is arriving: The totally helpless and dependent newborn, who derived all of her sustenance from her mother who carried and nursed her, is now taking the very first steps toward independence. She now needs more nourishment than she can obtain from milk. She is starting to move in all directions under her own power. She most certainly needs to be loved and cherished and must have plenty of Mom's attention if she is going to thrive, but her direct physical attachment to her is coming to a close. Whether it occurs now or sometime after the first birthday, allowing this brief season of intimate dependence to end is but one of hundreds of ways in which she will need to be released, step by tiny step, over the next eighteen to twenty years.

Whatever your reasons might be, if you are ready to move from breast feeding to a bottle or cup:

- Substitute the bottle or cup for a feeding in which your baby tends to be distracted or not interested in a long nursing session. (Usually this is one in the middle of the day.) Each week add a bottle substitution to a different feeding. Usually bedtime nursing is the last to go.
- Eliminate nursing for reasons other than nourishment. If you need to comfort your baby, caress and rock her rather than using the breast as a pacifier.
- Cut down the duration of nursing sessions. If your baby wants a "hit and run" session, don't try to keep her at the breast longer than she seems interested.
- If your breasts are becoming engorged and uncomfortable as your baby nurses less often, express just enough milk to stay comfortable. If you empty them fully, they will produce larger quantities of milk.

A final note: If you have second thoughts during this transition and decide to maintain your nursing relationship for a few more months, you can reverse the process by having your baby nurse longer and more often. Your milk supply will increase accordingly.

Many babies could care less about the spoon, no matter who is holding it, and simply want to turn every solid into a finger food—or an unidentified flying object. Either scenario will serve as an impressive illustration of the word *mess*. After a prolonged mealtime with a self-feeder in this age-group, food may be every-where—from head to toe on the baby, scattered over a radius of several feet around her high chair, and perhaps decorating a few walls, people, and pets as well.

One theoretical advantage of giving your baby free rein in feeding herself before her first birthday is that her prowess with the spoon might develop more quickly. However, it is questionable whether early spoon practice really matters in the long run. A more realistic benefit of self-feeding is that she'll tend to reg-ulate her own food intake. She'll get down to business (eating and making a mess in the process) when she's truly hungry, then shift into other activities (making a mess full-time) when her appetite is satisfied. The end result is a baby who stops eating when she's no longer hungry, an eating habit that will serve her well the rest of her life, making it less likely that she will turn to food for needs other than hunger or unwittingly overeat on a regular basis. In contrast, a baby who happily accepts any and all food offered to her, even after she is no longer hungry, is at risk of becoming overweight.

The major disadvantage of a do-it-yourself feeding at this age, of course, is the extra cleaning effort needed to round up the wayward food. To protect floors and carpets, some parents buy special "splash mats" at stores that sell baby para-phernalia or even set up an empty plastic wading pool around the high chair. Unfortunately you can't haul all this gear to a restaurant or a friend's house, and you may grow tired of hosing off the high chair after every meal. Furthermore, just as imposing some limits on your baby's explorations is necessary for safety and sanity, imposing some semblance of order at mealtimes is a reasonable and worthwhile goal.

Some parents go to the opposite extreme, trying to control and orchestrate every bite taken by the baby. If this is your intention, keep an eye on your blood pressure, because you'll be repeatedly going to the mat with your child over the fine points of what she will or won't eat. *Whatever else you do, don't attempt to force a baby to eat when she's not hungry and don't let your concern over her lack of interest in a particular food escalate into trench warfare.* If she doesn't like ba-nanas, for example, find some other fruit she does enjoy.

A balanced approach is for you to manage the spoon with the gooey stuff—the cereal and strained foods—for the first several months, until she is able to handle this assignment herself with a minimum of mess making. You can let her handle a spoon all she wants, of course, without getting food involved. As she passes her first birthday, see if she will imitate you as you show how it's used. At the same time, let her have some of the self-contained finger foods described above, either before or after spoon feeding. Pay attention, however, to the signs that she isn't hungry: turning her head, not accepting the spoon, getting restless in the chair, or tossing the finger foods overboard. If she doesn't want to eat, don't try to feed her, but don't let her play with the food.

Cup control

Another skill to work on in the high chair is drinking from a cup. Since this project involves hand control, new swallowing skills, and liquid that might go anywhere and everywhere, take your time. The cup you choose for your baby may be easier to handle if it has two handles or, depending on his preference, no handles. A weighted bottom will help keep it oriented topside up, and sturdy construction is a must. The pretty china cup illustrated with Beatrix Potter characters might be nice to look at, but for everyday use unbreakable plastic is the only way to go. You may wish to get a transitional cup that has a lid with a small spout, but when it's time to use the real thing, he may not know whether to sip or suck. The spouted version might best be used for the baby who resists the cup in favor of his beloved bottle.

After he's gotten the hang of taking food from a spoon, you can try putting a little water in his cup. When you first put it to his lips, he will probably not know quite what to do. After you let a few drops enter his mouth, he may swallow, or let it run down his chin, or some of each. Be patient. Only one in four babies will master this skill by the age of nine months, and it may be an additional six months before most of the liquid goes where it belongs.

Overall, it's better to start cup training earlier rather than later. A one-year-old who is a confirmed bottle user or who has been exclusively breast-fed may take a dim view of this plastic contraption you are handing him. Some babies, left to their own devices, become attached to their bottles as an ongoing source of comfort and security. You will definitely want to avoid having a toddler (or a preschooler!) who wanders around all day with a bottle in his mouth.

HEALTH ISSUES: MEDICAL CHECKUPS

During this six-month period your baby will not need as many routine checkups as he did during the first six months of life. Normally, visits are carried out at six months, nine months, and one year. Your baby's doctor will, as before, measure progress in height, weight, and head circumference. A review of developmental milestones and a check from head to toe will also be on the agenda. You should feel free to ask questions about feeding or behavior problems that might concern you, and check for any specific guidelines about the introduction of solid foods. You can expect some input about safety at home as well, including directions about appropriate action to take in case your baby accidentally swallows a toxic substance or an overdose of medication (see Poisoning, page 800).

As noted in the previous chapter, the third DTaP (diphtheria/tetanus/pertussis) and hemophilus B immunizations will be given at the six-month check. The third hepatitis B vaccination may be given now if the series was started at birth, although some physicians may delay the third dose until the age of twelve to eighteen months. If for any reason your baby has fallen behind on his basic immunization schedule, talk to the doctor about a timetable for catching up. Now that he has reached the six-month mark you may be tempted to slack off on vaccinations, especially if your budget is tight. But you should press on and complete this process because the illnesses that you may prevent can be devastating (see chapter 4, page 143). If you are short on funds, check with your local health department about the availability of low-cost immunizations. Many communities have vaccination programs that are carried out on a regular basis throughout the year.

Between a baby's ninth and twelfth months, some health-care providers administer a skin test to detect any possible exposure to tuberculosis. At the one-year checkup your baby may have blood drawn to check for **anemia** (a shortage of red blood cells) or exposure to lead. If anemia is present at this age, it usually indicates a need for more iron in the baby's diet. Your doctor will give you specific recommendations if this is the case.

Common illnesses in infancy, including upper respiratory infections (colds), ear infections, intestinal upsets, and other disturbances were discussed in chapter 6 in the section entitled "When Your Baby Is Ill: Common Medical Problems." These will not be repeated here, but if you need a quick review, turn to page 202.

SOCIAL DEVELOPMENTS

While no two babies interact with the rest of humanity in exactly the same way, there are distinct trends you will likely notice during this very eventful six-month period.

At six months of age and for the next two or three months thereafter, babies tend to socialize easily with the world at large. As you walk by a seven- or eight-month-old who is peering over someone's shoulder in the church foyer, flash a grin and you'll probably get one in return. This sunny responsiveness—to just about anyone—is pleasant and certainly endearing, but it won't last forever. It also does not mean that a baby is equally attached to every grown-up on the planet. All the attention and care that have been given at home have been making a profound impact, and the bonds of attachments for the immediate family will continue to strengthen during these important months.

Strangers and separation

As early as six months of age, but usually between eight to twelve months, a new phase will develop. Your baby, who may have seemed so comfortable around everyone, will begin showing anxiety among unfamiliar people. The approach of someone new or someone she hasn't seen for a while will provoke a wide-eyed stare, usually followed by wailing and clinging to you for protection. This is called **stranger anxiety.**

This behavior may bother Aunt Mary, who hasn't seen your baby yet and was expecting a warm embrace from her newest niece. Since fear of strangers is virtually universal as the first birthday approaches and continues well into the second year, both you and Aunt Mary should relax about it. In fact, a simple strategy can help her and your baby get acquainted.

First, Aunt Mary shouldn't try to touch, kiss, or hold the baby right away. In fact, even a direct return of your baby's stare may set off a healthy cry. Instead, you should chat with Aunt Mary as if nothing else is going on. Let your baby see that this is someone you are comfortable with, and let her get used to the sight of this new person in your home. After a while, some simple exchanges of looks, touches, and eventually play will likely begin as Aunt Mary becomes one of the gang.

The flip side of stranger anxiety is **separation anxiety,** an increased unwillingness to be separated from the main caregiver—usually (but not always) Mom. Your baby may begin to cry when you simply step into another room for a moment or put her into her crib for a nap. If and when she's about to be left with a relative or a sitter, the crying may escalate into a wailing and clinging session of spectacular proportions.

Separation issues can turn into an emotional upheaval for parents and baby alike. On one hand, it's nice to know that your child thinks so highly of you, so to speak. But having your baby/toddler cling to you like superglue, or hearing a prolonged chorus of protest every night at bedtime, or wondering whether you can't have a night (or weekend) away without massive guilt can begin to feel like a ball and chain.

Your approach to this development should be, first of all, to avoid extremes. Some parents, especially with the first baby, feel that their supreme calling in life is to prevent their child from having one minute of unhappiness. Whatever it takes to prevent crying they will do, and whatever the baby seems to want they will provide, immediately and without question. But this is an exercise in futility, and a setup for creating an overindulged, selfish, and miserable child. Conversely, parents who take a very controlling approach to child rearing may not be very concerned about separation anxiety. But they also run the risk of being inattentive and neglectful of a young child's emotions in general. Both approaches stake out a path of least resistance that may seem to work for now but may also exact a terrible price in the future.

Since you are no doubt sensitive to your child's emotions but probably don't want to feel entirely controlled by her cries and moods, you'll be relieved to know that separation anxiety is a normal phase of development. It's virtually inevitable, but you can buffer its impact. For example, if a sitter is coming to your home, take an approach similar to the one just described for Aunt Mary. Have your sitter arrive a half hour early so she can get acquainted with your baby in an unhurried manner. If you are dropping the baby off at a place that is new to her, try to stick around for a while to allow your baby time to explore and get accustomed to the new environment. When it's time for you to depart, don't stoke the emotional fires with a hand-wringing send-off. Let your baby get involved in an activity with the caregiver, say a short and sweet good-bye, and then leave. (If your baby or toddler is going to spend time with a favorite set of grandparents or an aunt and uncle whom she knows well, you may find that your departure barely provokes any response at all.)

The separation process will be much more unpleasant if your baby is tired or hungry. If you can schedule your departure after a nap or a meal, it may go more smoothly. There is no harm in finding a so-called transitional object to serve as a comforting reminder of things that are familiar to her. (It can also help at bedtime—see next page). This can be a soft toy or small blanket, much like the world-famous security blanket belonging to Linus in the "Peanuts" comic strip. Once this object has been picked out by your child, you may want to buy a duplicate (or in the case of a blanket, tear it in half) to have on hand if the original is lost or in the washer. Tattered, stained, and probably a little smelly, this item may become a treasured souvenir of your child's early years.

Separation and sleeping

For some babies separation becomes a major issue at bedtime. As was mentioned in the previous chapter, if your baby isn't used to falling asleep on her own by eight or nine months of age, you may be in for some stormy nights ahead if you try to revise her routine. If she wakes up during the night, not only will she sound off, but she may also pull herself to a stand in her crib and rattle it vigorously until you tend to her. (Make sure you have adjusted the mattress and side rails of the crib so she can't tumble out.) Even a baby who originally was doing very well at bedtime may start resisting the process, crying and clinging to you when it's time to go to sleep.

You can still work toward bringing her into a state of drowsiness (but not quite asleep) using a little nursing or formula, rocking and singing, augmented perhaps by her favorite soft object. Then lay her down, pat her gently, reassure her, say good night, and leave. The same approach should be used if she begins awakening during the night. If this is a new behavior for her, check to be sure she isn't ill, grossly wet or soiled, or tangled in her blanket. Tend to these concerns if needed, but keep your visit quick, quiet, and businesslike and then say good night. She shouldn't need any middle-of-the-night feedings at this point; if you continue offering them well after the six-month mark, you'll only be providing room service and bleary-eyed companionship, not meeting any nutritional needs.

If you have an infant older than nine months who is still routinely rousing everyone from sleep two or three times a night, even after you have been providing a boring response for weeks, you may want to consider more deliberate measures to bring this behavior to a close. This would involve picking a time—usually on a weekend—when you can say good night and then resolve not to return until the next morning—if you can handle it—no matter how often and how long the crying goes on. *Keep in mind that returning to your baby after a prolonged bout of crying may convince her that endurance pays off.* Obviously, you would not want to try this "commando" approach with a child who is sick, or on a hot summer night when the windows are open, or when you need to be wide-awake the next day, or (most important) if *both* parents are not wholeheartedly ready for it.

You should greet your baby in the morning with smiles, hugs, and reassurance. Yes, indeed, you love her as much as the day is long, but nighttime is for sleeping. Normally after three, or at most, four nights, she will get the picture and sleep through the night thereafter (unless, of course, something else is wrong). Obviously, if interrupted sleep doesn't bother anyone, you may choose to leave things alone.

Eventually your child will sleep through the night on her own—but with some children it may take many more months before this occurs spontaneously.

Relationships and security

This six-month period of your baby's life begins an extremely important phase in development, not only for his motor skills but for his intellectual and social abilities as well. The intense curiosity and exploration described earlier isn't limited to the world of objects. It also includes a huge amount of information gathering about the people around him. He will make the transition from having limited forms of communication—crying when he's uncomfortable or hungry and random babbling when he feels good—to owning a wide array of sounds, gestures, and body movements.

As he exercises these abilities, he will be learning how his parents, siblings, and others around him respond. If he is uncomfortable and cries as a result, does anyone come to make him feel better? Does this happen when he makes different kinds of sounds? Does crying evoke a response more often than other behaviors? If he can't get to something he wants and cries (or makes other sounds), will someone get it for him? What happens when he touches or plays with various objects he finds? If he seems unhappy when he is taken away from a particular object, is your response consistent? Who makes him feel warm and comfortable? Who smiles and makes pleasant sounds—and who doesn't?

Your baby won't be formulating these questions (he hasn't the words for them yet), but he will be paying close attention to your reactions and responses, and he will be taught by them.

He will need to know that he is deeply and consistently loved. He will flourish when someone responds to his sounds of frustration or pleasure and comes to assist him or to share in the joy of a particular discovery. Paradoxically, he will also develop some security when he learns that those who love him don't necessarily come "right this instant" every time he calls out. A little delay in getting what he needs—and not always getting what he wants—will not harm him when it occurs in a setting where there is an abundance of smiles, caresses, and sweet conversation. On the contrary, it will teach him that he is secure in your love, even when you are not immediately present or even when your love for him causes you to overrule his immediate desires.

CHAPTER 8

Twelve to Twenty-Four Months

Oh, that our home on earth might be to them the pathway, the gate to the Father's home in heaven! Blessed Father, let us and our children be Thine wholly and forever. Amen.
ANDREW MURRAY

Twelve to Twenty-Four Months: Declarations of Independence

During the first twelve months of life, your baby will have undergone an incredible transformation—from a totally helpless newborn to a mobile explorer who is interacting vigorously with everything and everyone around him. During the next year of life, the physical changes you see in your child from month to month will not appear nearly as dramatic. You will, however, start the year with a "baby on wheels" and end it with a small child whose mind and body have, in fact, undergone some very significant developments.

Because of his mobility, your one-year-old will keep you hopping during nearly all of his waking hours. Track shoes, a sense of humor, and a little tolerance for disorder are a must from here on. Striving to ensure that he (and everything in his path) stays in one piece will be a full-time project, and you would be wise to review carefully the cautions regarding safety and sanity set forth in the first half of chapter 7 (page 213).

But as much attention as this assignment rightfully requires, a common mistake made by parents of toddlers is to enter a maintenance (or, in some cases, raw survival) mode and never move beyond it. As much as they need food, safety, endless cleanups, and diaper changes, toddlers also need the important grown-ups in their life to be *fascinated* with them. "Lord, give me the strength to get through this day" may be the repeated cry of the parent's heart (usually about 5 P.M.). But with it should come a postscript: "Lord, help me understand, appreciate, and marvel at this incredible creation You have loaned to me." Your toddler is no less "fearfully and wonderfully made" now that he is tearing all over the house than he was while he was being knit together in his mother's womb.

Your need for both of these prayers may become more intense, at least at times, as your child begins to demonstrate a reality that is painfully obvious to parents and often ignored by the most learned philosophers: Little children aren't inherently virtuous. They are not born brimming with selfless instincts and kind gestures. They have no concept of other people's viewpoints or needs. In fact, they are not even morally neutral "blank slates" who will readily follow whatever direction you give to them. They come hardwired with a will, boundless energy to express their interests, and powerful emotions to display if they aren't satisfied at any given moment. They don't need to be taught to grab, fight, howl in anger, or bluntly defy you (or anyone else caring for them). If you have any doubt that humankind is a fallen race (as painfully set forth in Genesis 3 and demonstrated in every generation thereafter), you have yet to spend any length of time in close quarters with a toddler.

Your response to this reality should be, as much as possible, measured, loving, calm (at least most of the time), and, like everything else, governed by an avoidance of extremes. If you don't believe that your sweet, innocent baby could ever challenge you ("Not *my* boy, whom I love so dearly . . ."), you're in for a rude shock this year. And if you aren't prepared and willing to meet him confidently when he does, you may find yourself living with a miserable, demanding two- or three-year-old, or even a full-fledged miniature tyrant.

However, if you are bound and determined to meet every departure from perfect decorum with harsh words and an iron fist, your opportunities to shape his will, impart moral standards, and serve as a role model will be squandered. Whatever good behavior you see will be based on raw fear and, once soured with a few years of resentment, will be spectacularly discarded at the first available opportunity.

During these next several months—which will pass more quickly than you might imagine—you will enter into some crucial interactions with your child. By the end of this year he needs to know and understand that you love him fervently and unconditionally and, at the same time, that you are in charge and he isn't. *If either or both of these messages are not clearly established by the second birthday (or within the few months that follow), your child rearing tasks during the following years are likely to be far more difficult.* His patterns of relating to you and any other people close to him, whether generally pleasant or continually combative, are likely to become more firmly entrenched by the third birthday and may continue for years thereafter.

You don't need to do everything perfectly this year to bring up a healthy, delightful child, however. An isolated mistake or even getting on the wrong track for a number of weeks isn't going to ruin his life. God has granted parents a good deal of time on the learning curve and children a great deal of resiliency. So take a deep breath, fasten your seat belt, stay on your knees (not just when you're picking up toys), and amid all the challenges, don't forget to step back once in a while to marvel at this little person you are nurturing.

PHYSICAL DEVELOPMENTS

Height, weight, and other physical progress

If you haven't already done so during one of your child's well-baby checkups, take a look at the growth curve that should be in her medical chart. Better yet, ask the doctor or office staff for a copy you can continue updating on your own. You'll notice that the average rate of growth during the second year is slower than it was during the first twelve months. A normal one-year-old will have tripled his or her birth weight but then will gain only three to five more pounds by age two. Similarly, regardless of gender, your child will add roughly four inches of height between the first and second birthdays, less than half the height gained during the first year. Interestingly, while your child's head will increase in circumference only about an inch over the next twelve months, by age two it will have reached 90 percent of its adult size.

The percentile curves shown on the growth charts begin to diverge more noticeably after the first twelve months. In other words, the differences in height and weight between a child who is at the 90th percentile (that is, larger than 90 percent of the children his age) and one of the same age who is at the 10th percentile will become more dramatic after the first birthday. For most children, position on the growth chart depends largely on genetics, with a height and weight trajectory that will be fairly predictable after the first eighteen to twenty-four months of life have been tracked, barring an unusual problem or chronic illness. If your child is "falling off" a curve—that is, she has been at a certain percentile of weight and height for a number of months and then appears to shift to a significantly lower level during subsequent checkups—a medical or nutritional problem may be present, and your health-care provider may recommend further evaluation.

See growth charts in the insert, page A20.

Even though she will not be making drastic changes in height and weight, the baby look will begin to fade away between her first and second birthdays. With more muscle motion, her arms and legs will look longer and leaner and the abdomen less prominent. Her face will gradually shift from the round, nonspecific but universally appealing look of a baby to more well-defined features that will give you a preview of her future appearance. As you watch her enthusiastically attempting to blow out two birthday candles, don't be surprised if you find yourself wondering, "Where did my baby go?"

As described in the previous chapter, the debut of walking may already have occurred two or three months before the first birthday, or it may be a few months away. By eighteen months, your child should have this skill down pat. While early starters won't have any long-term advantage over the late bloomers who are otherwise normal, they will be somewhat ahead of the game in maturity of their gait. It takes a few months to progress from the broad-based, lurching, hands-up, toes-out, frequent-faller "toddling" walk to a smoother, more narrow-based gait with fewer falls, improved maneuvering, and—a big thrill for many kids—the ability to use hands to carry things while on the move.

Parents watching a toddler careen around the room may wonder about the alignment of the legs: Are they turned outward too far? Does one foot point in a different direction from the other? During the first several weeks of walking, this may be impossible to answer. If you see an obvious, consistent difference in the orientation of the legs, however, you should have your toddler's health-care provider watch her move up and down the office corridor. He or she may want an opinion from an orthopedist to determine whether specific intervention is in order.

The treatment for the vast majority of toddler gait concerns is "tincture of time"—they resolve as weeks pass and coordination improves. However, an obvious limp or a toddler's sudden unwillingness to walk after she clearly knows how is always abnormal and should be evaluated medically as soon as possible.

Vision, hearing, and language

The average one-year-old can see well enough to spy small objects across the room or planes flying overhead. By the age of two he will probably approach normal vision, although it is difficult to measure accurately at this age. If he seems to be squinting a lot or bringing objects right up to his face before he interacts with them or doesn't seem to be tracking objects with his eyes, an exam by an ophthalmologist (a physician who specializes in eye problems) would be a good idea.[1] This should also be done if you see obvious crossing of his eyes (even temporarily) or if they don't seem to be moving in the same direction.

While major visual problems are uncommon in one-year-olds, hearing can become impaired if ear infections and colds—which are not at all unusual in this age-group—leave persistent thick fluid behind one or both eardrums (see *ear care and concerns,* Reference). If the problem persists untreated for weeks or months, your child's ability to understand and generate language can be delayed.

If you have any concerns about hearing loss (see sidebar), by all means have his ears and hearing checked—the sooner the better. While your health-care provider can usually determine whether there is fluid behind the eardrum or identify other physical problems, a detailed assessment of hearing in this age-group requires special training and equipment. A relatively new and painless test with the intimidating name "brain stem evoked response audiometry" can test hearing without your child's cooperation, but you may have to travel some distance to have it done. If your toddler's physician recommends this test or a consultation with an ear, nose, and throat (ENT) specialist, don't hesitate to do so.

Assuming that hearing is intact, your child will probably have a speaking vocabulary of a few words at his first birthday and about ten times that many at his second, some of which he may combine into two- or three-word sentences. What he can *understand,* however, will become much more impressive as the year progresses. As he moves past the eighteen-month mark, he will point to all sorts of things—people, objects, body parts—when asked about them ("Where is your nose?" "Where's Auntie Linda?"). By the second birthday, the unintelligible strings of sounds that sounded like a foreign language at the beginning of the year will be honed down to simple statements or even questions. Even more amazing is seeing your walking baby, who not long ago lay helpless in a crib, following a simple command such as "Go get the ball."

Over the next several months, you will have the unique and important opportunity to help expand your child's language skills. You won't need a teaching credential, a master's degree, or special training in child development to do this. Instead, you will simply need to "be there" when you are with him. Keep your an-

---

WHEN MIGHT YOU SUSPECT YOUR ONE-YEAR-OLD HAS A HEARING PROBLEM?

- He doesn't turn in response to sounds or ignores you when you call him. Many parents have had the humbling experience of repeatedly disciplining a toddler for failing to respond to them, only to find out later that he really couldn't hear them.
- He isn't using any single words (such as *mama*) by the age of twelve to fifteen months, or his speech is unintelligible by the age of two. Babies and toddlers normally love to experiment with all sorts of

sounds, and one who seems to be specializing in making noises he can feel (such as gargling or growling) may not be able to hear his own vocalizations.

- His responses to sounds seem to be selective. While you might suspect that he is choosing to pay attention to some and not others, he may be hearing low-pitched sounds better than high-pitched ones, or one ear may be affected but not the other.

tennae up and be ready to give him dozens of little doses of your attention and conversation throughout the day.

Take advantage of his curiosity. When he approaches you with an object or points to something and makes a sound (which may rise at the end like a question—"Car?"), you've got his attention. Name the object and say something simple about it ("Yes, that's Daddy's car"). He doesn't need a lecture about auto mechanics, of course, but don't be afraid to aim your comment a little beyond what you think he might understand.

Talk to him while you're doing everyday chores. Folding clothes may be boring to you, but if he's watching, it doesn't take any extra time to name the items or say what you're doing with them. Remember, his little computer is on all the time.

Read to him. Reading simple stories to your child, especially at bedtime, is an extremely worthwhile activity to begin this year, if you haven't already. (Be sure to let him see what you are reading and to identify for him anything he finds interesting in the pictures.) His interest and understanding will increase dramatically over the course of the year. By age two, in fact, he may be able to fill in the blanks in a story he knows well, anticipating and saying one or more words at favorite spots along the way.

A few cautions about language:

Remember to speak to your child using clear, meaningful words. Use a pleasant tone of voice, but avoid baby talk, and don't repeat his unique mispronunciations of words, even if they *are* cute (see page 217).

Don't make reading to him an issue if he's not interested at the particular story time you have in mind. Usually you won't meet much resistance at bedtime when children are attentive to just about anything that delays lights-out, but they may not be as interested during daylight hours.

Don't expect Big Bird, Bert and Ernie, and the rest of the gang on *Sesame Street* to take care of your child's language development or other learning experiences. Even if he pays attention (which at this age he probably won't do for any length of time), live humans who are paying attention to *him* do a much better job.

Hands, minds, and safety

This year your toddler will continue the process of exploring whatever she finds around her. Her ability to pick up and manipulate objects both large and small will become much more refined and coordinated during the coming months. By her second birthday, she will enjoy scribbling with crayons (preferably not on the walls), stacking four or five items and then knocking them over, playing with clay, and sticking pegs of various shapes into similarly shaped holes. Many toddlers also become fascinated with things that go around. Wheels that spin on toy cars, pedals on bicycles, a lazy Susan you don't need anymore, or a saucepan lid turned upside down on the kitchen floor may become objects of your child's greatest affection.

Between eighteen and twenty-four months of age, most toddlers also become enamored with balls; holding, rolling, tossing, watching them bounce around, and then chasing them hold endless interest and delight. Beware, however, of small round objects (such as marbles) that might be put in the mouth and then accidentally inhaled. Best bet: Buy your toddler her own inexpensive inflatable twelve- to eighteen-inch beach ball. It's quiet, it can't do much damage, she can carry it around when she doesn't want to throw it, and it's easy to replace.

By her second birthday, you may get a preview of your child's preference for using the right or left hand. But she may also use the spoon with her right, scribble with her left, and throw a ball with either. Don't try to push the use of one hand over the other and don't worry about speeding up the process. She'll sort out her handedness in due time.

This year your child will significantly increase her grasp of the way things work. Her sense of object permanence—the idea that something is still present even if she can't see it—will become more sophisticated. Not only will she learn to search for a toy she saw you place under two or three blankets or pillows, but she will also become a whiz at little hide-and-seek activities. If she sees you stick a toy in your pocket, she won't forget where it went.[2]

Brief episodes of playacting and imitation will become more sophisticated over the course of the year. Watch her hold the toy phone to her ear (or yours), try to brush her hair, rock her "baby," or turn the steering wheel on a toy car. As the months pass, she will try to engage you in some of these scenarios. If you can stop for a few moments to pretend to drink out of the toy cup she offers you or talk on her phone, you'll make her day. Finding the right balance between responding to these overtures often enough to satisfy your child but without endless interruption to whatever you're trying to get done is an art in parenting (see Social and Emotional Development: The "First Adolescence" later in this chapter).

Children cannot raise themselves properly. There is no substitute for loving parental leadership in the early development of children.

DR. JAMES DOBSON
ANSWERS YOUR
QUESTIONS ABOUT
MARRIAGE AND
SEXUALITY

Because of your child's maturing motor and problem-solving skills, your vigilance for her ongoing safety must not only continue but become more sophisticated. Her developing fine-motor coordination will also include new abilities that can lead to new hazards: turning doorknobs, manipulating latches, flipping switches, and pushing buttons. Turn your back for a moment and she may be locked in the bathroom or out the door and down the street, peering over the edge of Grandma's swimming pool. Her interest in climbing to precarious new heights may increase, along with her ability to find new and clever ways to get to them.

Her tendency to "gum" everything as a means of gathering information will wane, but she may not hesitate to place small objects in her mouth. Remember to stay vigilant for any such items that might cause choking if accidentally inhaled. She may very well take a swig or a bite of *anything* that looks interesting. Medicines, plants, cleaning products, dog food—you name it—nothing is off-limits for an oral sampling. You cannot assume that a bad taste will keep her from guzzling the furniture polish or anything else. This year and the next are the most risky for your child's having an accidental ingestion of a dangerous substance.

If you haven't done so by now, buy a small bottle of **syrup of ipecac,** a drug that may be used to induce vomiting if your baby eats or drinks something that might harm her. *You should give a dose of ipecac only if you are told to do so by the doctor, the emergency department, or a poison-control center.* Ipecac should *not* be used with many substances, especially caustic materials (such as drain cleaner) or petroleum products (such as gasoline or furniture polish) because they can do as much or more damage on the way up as they have done on the way down. For medications and other items, however, you may be instructed to use ipecac to empty the stomach. In a child over one year of age, one tablespoon (15 cc) followed by two glasses of water will induce vomiting, normally within fifteen to twenty minutes (see "Time to Buy Ipecac," page 222).

FEEDING: ESTABLISHING PATTERNS FOR EATING

By her first birthday, your toddler should have a working knowledge of a variety of foods from the well-known groups in addition to her milk. Remember that while cow's milk may be introduced after the first birthday if your child doesn't demonstrate any allergy to it, *whole* milk—not low-fat or nonfat—should be on the menu. Cholesterol is not an issue at this age, and the fat in whole milk is useful in building a number of tissues, including the central nervous system. Beware, however, of allowing a budding milkaholic to push her milk consumption past sixteen to twenty-four ounces (one to one and one-half pints) per day. Not only will this curb her interest in other types of food, but large amounts of milk may also interfere with the absorption of iron from other foods, which in turn can lead to anemia (a deficiency in red blood cells).

During this year you will want to establish a routine with meals and snacks if you haven't already. Three meals and two small snacks at generally consistent times are far preferable to nonstop grazing, which trains a child to eat for all kinds of reasons other than hunger, scatters food everywhere, and may lead to a choking accident if a toddler stumbles with food in her mouth. This is a good time to establish a routine of sitting down at the table before eating, which actually is beneficial for adults and older children as well.

A fair amount of the food she eats at a meal can consist of small portions of whatever the rest of the family is having, as long as it

- isn't too hot in temperature;
- isn't too hot in seasoning, or overly salty, sweet, or swimming in butter or grease—which isn't so great for the rest of the family either;
- is either mushy or cut into small, easily chewed pieces. Continue to avoid foods that could easily lodge in the airway: hot dogs (that aren't cut into bite-size pieces), nuts, seeds, hard candy, grapes, popcorn, peanut butter, raw vegetables, dried fruit, etc., as described in chapter 7 (see page 227).

One development on the food front that catches many parents off guard is the erratic appetite of the toddler. She may eat voraciously one day and show little interest in food the next, or consume a sizable breakfast and then quit after only a few bites of the day's other meals. With her nonstop activity during waking hours, this apparent inconsistency in fueling patterns may not make sense, but it is not uncommon. In fact, at this age her intense curiosity and compelling desire to explore the world around her will tend to limit her interest in food to two primary activities: eating it if she's hungry and examining it if she isn't. If either of these isn't happening at the kitchen table, she'll probably want to move on to more interesting pursuits. Also remember that growth is not as rapid now as it was during the first year, and that the average toddler needs only about one thousand calories a day—not a huge amount of food—to meet her nutritional needs.

Your goal should be to offer her a variety of foods in modest amounts each day. If she turns you down, don't turn your mealtime into a battle zone. Attempting to force a toddler to eat anything is an exercise in futility, and insisting that she can't leave the table or have another meal until she has finished every last speck of her vegetables (which might get a few days old while you wait) will lead to miserable, exhausting times around the dinner table.

Don't panic and then offer your toddler something she really likes out of fear that she won't get enough to eat. This may turn into a subtle form of dietary extortion and is a surefire way to create long-term food habits that may be nutritionally inadequate. If she doesn't want much now, put the plate back in the fridge and warm it up for the next meal. When she's hungry, she'll eat. If you are worried about her food intake, write down what she has eaten over a week's time and run it by her doctor. If she is active, showing developmental progress, and gaining on the growth chart, she's getting enough. Remember: No normal child will voluntarily starve herself.

You should discuss with your health-care provider whether or not your toddler should be on vitamin supplements. Some use these routinely, while others feel that well-balanced food intake essentially eliminates the need for vitamins. Fluoride supplements may be recommended, however, based on the content of your local water supply. Your child's doctor or local pediatric dentist should have this information, or you can obtain it from the agency that supplies your water.

Weaning

As the year progresses, you will see improving skill in your toddler's use of the cup and spoon, which will enable you to turn more of the feeding assignment over to her. With increasing cup proficiency (see chapter 7, page 235), you can begin phasing out bottles. This process may meet with some resistance but should be started by the first birthday and accomplished by the fifteen-month mark. Plan on substituting cup for bottle one meal at a time (or all three at once, if you're adventurous), and then do likewise for her snacks. Usually a bottle before bedtime is the last to go, since it has a way of becoming part of the nighttime routine. Remember: No milk or juice should ever be given to your baby while she is lying down and falling asleep, because this practice (which is all too easy to start as a last resort during a restless night) can lead to dental cavities and ear infections. A little snack just before bed and before brushing teeth is fine, but food should not be part of any middle-of-the-night activity at this point (see page 239).

Once you've decided to bid the last bottle feeding farewell, your best bet is to pack all of them away when your toddler is asleep. If she begins to ask (or cry) for her "baba," be matter-of-fact and upbeat: "Your bottles are gone! And you're so big, you don't need them anymore!"

If your baby is still nursing at this point and has never used a bottle, she can graduate directly from breast to cup and avoid bottles altogether. As mentioned in the previous chapter, you should still introduce your baby to drinking from a cup even if most of her fluids are coming directly from Mom. If you wait too long, you may face resistance when it's time to stop nursing.

With solids, you will need to decide how much mess you can tolerate. Some postmeal cleanup will be necessary while your child learns the fine points of hand-spoon-mouth coordination, but you shouldn't confuse the pitching of food and fluids in all directions with her self-feeding learning curve (see chapter 7, page 233). One way to minimize the mess is to keep the serving sizes small. A typical balanced menu for a one-year-old equals measured quantities of half a cup of a fruit or vegetable, two to three ounces of meat, or a slice of bread made into a half-sandwich. (Remember, of course, that your toddler on any given day may eat less or more than these amounts.)

MENU FOR TODDLERS

◆ breads and cereals	*4 servings per day*
◆ milk	*2–3 cups per day*
◆ vegetables and fruit	*4 servings per day*
◆ meat/poultry/fish, eggs, beans	*2 servings per day*

A child's serving is generally one-fourth the size of an adult serving.

Keep in mind:
- Children will often consume a lot in the bread and grains group. As long as they are eating from other food groups as well, this is usually not a problem.
- Too much milk will add fat to a child's diet and replace valuable nutrients from other food groups.
- Too much fruit or fruit juice will add sugar to a child's diet and lessen the appetite for other necessary foods.

Depending upon everyone's schedule, make an effort to include your toddler at the family table for at least one meal per day. Traditions and timetables will vary, of course, but for many families, a shared meal (usually dinner) may be the one occasion when everyone at home can share conversation as well as food. (Shutting off the TV and perhaps taking the phone off the hook will enhance this experience.) While not exactly participating at the same level as everyone around the table, your one-year-old will be watching and listening and will become accustomed to being included in these gatherings. Let her see the family pause for a blessing. Indeed, it would be well for her to hear brief words of thanks before her other meals too, a practice that will prepare her for that time in the near future when she begins to understand the meaning of prayer.

SLEEPING: ESTABLISHING A ROUTINE

By his first birthday, your child should have been sleeping through the night for some time. If not, remember that by now his nocturnal awakenings aren't the result of any nutritional needs. Instead, he has become accustomed to the fact that having company or a snack feels good during the night. Why go back to sleep after awakening momentarily in the wee hours when there are other pleasantries to enjoy?

If you really don't mind working the nursery night shift, you may choose to put off dealing with the inevitable protest that will break forth when you cancel room service. But if he is otherwise well, you can usually establish uninterrupted

WHEN SHOULD I WEAN MY TODDLER FROM BREAST FEEDING?

Some authorities discourage nursing as a frequent daily activity after a toddler reaches 12 to 15 months of age. Others (especially members of nursing advocacy groups) encourage a completely open-ended approach, noting that in some cultures mothers may nurse a newborn on one breast and a child as old as five on the other. If you are pondering this question, remember that there are both nutritional and behavioral aspects to consider.

Unlike the first months of your baby's life, nursing does not serve a life-sustaining function after solids have been introduced. In fact, at this age if frequent trips to the breast are substituting for solid foods, your toddler may become anemic or even gradually undernourished. The role of nursing thus becomes increasingly social and emotional as the months (or years) pass, especially after eighteen months of age. This can be a source of ongoing nurturing, closeness, and even relaxation between

mother and child. If all else is going well, there may be no compelling reason to bring it to a close in the immediate future.

On the other hand, nursing for an extended period of time could cause or prolong problems such as:

- A toddler who is overly dependent on or demanding of Mom. If she is clinging to you and your breast day and night and not spending much time exploring the world around her, she needs to expand her horizons. If she wants to nurse whenever she's unhappy or bored, she needs to learn how to find comfort in other ways (such as cuddling without the oral intake). If she refuses to take liquids from any other source but Mom, parental activities are going to be stifled. If you are still nursing because your toddler throws a tantrum whenever she can't have access to sleep for everyone within one or two days, typically over a weekend, once you decide to take the plunge (see chapter 7, page 239, for details).

Even a seasoned all-night sleeper, however, may depart from his pattern during an illness, while on a trip, after a move, or perhaps because of a bad dream. Under these circumstances, you'll need to provide care and comfort (though not snacks, unless you have been specifically directed by the doctor to push fluids when he is sick) until things settle down, then nudge him back toward his old habits.

For many toddlers the Good Ship Slumber may be rocked in other ways. At some point, you're likely to run into bedtime resistance, manifested either by winsome appeals (requests for another kiss, one last drink, and in subsequent months, answers to riddles of the universe) or by outright rebellion against getting or staying in bed. Some of this may arise from separation anxiety, from negativism, or simply from the fact that other people are up doing interesting things, and lying in a crib or bed seems awfully boring by comparison. You may be tempted to take the path of least resistance and let him decide when he's ready to sleep—in other words, when he eventually collapses from sheer exhaustion. This is a bad idea for a number of reasons:

(continued)

your breast, you are under siege. In this case, you may need to curtail nursing simply to gain control of your (and her) life.

- A mom who is overly dependent on the toddler. As was mentioned in the last chapter (see sidebar, page 232), the intimacy of nurturing a dependent young infant occurs for a special but brief season. Acknowledging that it is over is a necessary step for both mother and child. If you feel that your meaning and purpose in life are going to evaporate if you are not nursing, you may need to explore some more basic issues relating to your identity and importance as an individual. This may be worked out informally in conversations with other mothers, but more formal counseling may be appropriate as well.

- Friction in the marriage. If your husband is beginning to feel that personal and physical intimacy with you

is hampered by the ongoing presence of one or more children at your breast, the duration of nursing should be open for discussion.

- Modesty problems. A small child burrowing under Mom's blouse can be an awkward event at the mall or in the neighbors' living room, and appropriate limits must be set for the location of nursing an older toddler. A preschooler who is still accessing Mom's breast may well be crossing modesty boundaries, even in the privacy of the home.

If one or more of these problems have developed, it may be time to get the weaning process under way. There is rarely, if ever, a need to do a "cold turkey" approach, however, and a gradual phaseout is likely to provoke less turmoil. The principles for shifting from nursing to bottle or cup described in the previous chapter (see sidebar, page 232) apply at this age also.

◆ You need to spend time with older children (if you have any) without an increasingly tired and irritable toddler wandering around.

◆ You need to spend time with your mate or by yourself without *any* children wandering around.

◆ Your toddler needs the sleep—a good ten or eleven hours at night, which probably won't happen if he's staying up until your bedtime.

If not already in place, establishing a fixed bedtime routine and a fixed bedtime will be an important task this year. Even if his vocabulary is limited, you can talk him through the steps you choose: bath, jammies, story, song, prayer, for example, carried out in a manner that winds him down. A raucous wrestling match or chasing the dog right before bedtime probably won't help set the stage for turning in. Keep in mind that whatever bedtime routine you establish (including one that takes one or two hours to complete) may become entrenched and expected every night for years to come.

As with a blessing before meals, your child will learn the routine of a short bedtime prayer before he understands the words or the theology. Over the coming months and years, however, this brief but important moment should take on new meanings and should not become a singsong patter repeated every night for no apparent reason other than long-standing habit.

As happened (hopefully) when he was an infant, your toddler should be placed in his crib or bed sleepy but not asleep. If he becomes accustomed to falling asleep on the sofa, floor, or your bed, he is more likely to resist signing off on his own pillow—both at bedtime *and* during the night.

Parents who have maintained a "family bed" through the first year should take the baby's first birthday as an occasion to review the current sleeping arrangements. Does your child need a parental body next to him to fall or stay asleep? (If one or both parents were to go away on a retreat for a night or two, would there be a problem?) More important, how is the presence of a much larger and more mobile baby affecting your sleep and your intimacy? Mother and Father should be in complete agreement about this situation or seek to resolve any difference of opinion if they are not—even if counseling is needed. Serious and damaging rifts in a marital relationship can develop if one spouse feels displaced physically and emotionally by a child who is taking over an ever increasing area of bed space. In general, if either Mom or Dad feels that it's time for the baby to sleep elsewhere, the other parent should oblige—not only out of respect for the other's feelings but in recognition that the marital relationship needs to be nurtured and preserved.

At the first birthday, most children are still logging three to four hours of daytime sleep, usually in two naps. The amount of daytime sleep will decline to two or three hours over the next year, and as a result, the morning nap will eventually phase out. When your toddler shifts to a one-nap-per-day routine, don't start too late in the afternoon or you may increase his bedtime resistance. (Who wants to go to bed after just getting up?) And, though he may seem intent on playing through the entire afternoon, don't be conned into eliminating nap time altogether, even if he resists it. Without daytime sleep, afternoons will probably be more notable for combat than for companionship.

SOCIAL AND EMOTIONAL DEVELOPMENT: THE "FIRST ADOLESCENCE"

During the second twelve months of life, your child will display a gamut of behaviors and emotions that, depending on your frame of mind, you may find confusing, amusing, or downright exasperating. A little preparation and some insight into the emerging worldview of the one-year-old can help you sort out and manage this important developmental passage.

First and foremost, keep in mind that above all else your baby/toddler needs to know that she is loved, accepted, and "at home" with you and that you are on her side without reservations—even when you won't give her everything she wants. She needs kind and loving words and actions all day long, and she will come to you frequently for them.

Expect overtures of all sorts, often with arms outstretched, many times during the day as your toddler seeks

- cuddling and hugs;
- comforting after a bump or bruise;
- reassurance after being frightened;
- help with a problem, such as getting something out of reach or fixing a misbehaving toy;
- your enthusiastic reaction to something she has brought to you;
- a response to a simple question (or sounds that resemble a question);
- relief from being hungry, thirsty, or having a wet or dirty diaper;
- an invitation to role-play (at her direction)—pretending to talk on her toy phone, for example;
- confirmation that you are still "there" when she has not seen you for a few minutes.

These approaches for comfort, input, and help will not last forever, and to the best of your ability they shouldn't be ignored. For a toddler they provide some critical fact-finding about how things work, how to get help, and who cares about her. They probably will also have a major impact on the way she interacts with the world at large in subsequent years. In a very real sense, you are her "launching pad," and after determining that her base of operations is safe and secure, she will be able to explore an expanding world around her.

You may find it difficult or impossible to stop whatever you're doing and respond immediately every time your toddler comes or calls to you. In fact, a little wait at times won't hurt: She needs to learn that she is important, but not Queen of the Domain. If you're on the phone or up to your elbows in dishwater, it's quite all right to acknowledge one of her overtures with "I hear you, and I'll help you in a few minutes."

AVOIDING TODDLER-CARE BURNOUT

There is no getting around it: Bringing up a toddler requires a seemingly limitless supply of time and energy. If you have other children at home, especially if one or more of them are under five, the demands on your attention may seem even more overwhelming. Simply maintaining some semblance of order can be a daunting task, and worrying about such niceties as a child's language development may sound like a fantasy if you feel immersed in total chaos.

There may be other pressures too. The parent who elects to stay at home (usually the mother but not always) may feel that her brain is rapidly turning to mush and that the stimulating worlds of education and career are passing her by. ("I've got a degree in history, and all I'm doing is changing diapers and listening to babbling.") If both parents work or if a single parent is rearing a toddler, much of the work may need to be done at home after a full day working elsewhere.

Because so much is going on in your toddler's life, he needs meaningful attention and input from the most important people in his life. If you feel that you're just marking time, becoming demented, or enduring in a state of slave labor, consider the following antiburnout ideas:

- There should be some time during your day when things become quiet. This usually can occur only after little people are in bed. You cannot collect your thoughts or anything else if kids are up until all hours of the night. Early bedtime for small children is not only good for them but necessary for you.
- Some of this quiet time should be real quiet time, designated for reflecting, reading, praying, and journaling. A daily devotional will provide not only refreshment but perspective on how your parenting tasks fit into the big picture of who Jesus is and what He's doing.
- Don't feel as if you are wasting your time and education to focus your primary attention on your children at this age. Believe it or not, the world isn't passing you by, and there will be plenty of time to make your mark in it later on. This doesn't mean that you have to put your brain in neutral, however, or that all outside activities must come to a screeching halt.
- Try to remember that this particular period of your child's life is not only extremely important but, in fact, highly interesting. Many people take sophisticated classes and earn advanced degrees to understand what is unfolding in front of you every day.

As with everything else in parenting, extremes are best avoided. If your toddler is clinging to you every minute of the day or whining and crying if you pay attention to anything or anyone else, she may be *too* attached to you and not spending enough of her day exploring and learning about other parts of the known universe. In this case, you may need to be more assertive about delaying your response to her when you need to tend to other business. On the other hand, if you find yourself issuing a steady stream of brush-offs, uh-huhs, or irritated sighs ("What is it now?!"), take a few minutes to review your own state of mind or think about some ways to recharge your batteries (see sidebar).

Exploring: pushing the boundaries and the advent of negativism

At some point during the second year of life, usually between fourteen and sixteen months, your child will begin a phase that may seem exasperating but is

(continued)

You can, in a very real sense, become a student of child development and the human condition in your own living room by being an observer as well as a caregiver. You may even want to consider doing some additional reading about this phase of your child's life.

◆ Take time for yourself. If you are a full-time parent at home, you will need regular time-outs—not merely for errands but for personal refreshment. These might include exercise workouts, walking in the park or strolling through the mall by yourself, or meeting a friend for lunch. Yes, you will need someone to watch your offspring while you do this, but it's worth the trouble and expense.

◆ Don't become starved for adult communication. When you reunite with your mate at the end of the workday, the first order of business should be some unhurried and attentive conversation between the two of you. Your child(ren) should see you do this and should be informed (as often as necessary) that this is "your time" together and "their time" will arrive shortly. Not only will this help maintain your marriage, but children who see their parents regularly connecting and showing affection will feel much more secure about the stability of their world.

◆ Married couples should also maintain their date night, once a week if possible. Important news for fathers: Never stop courting your wife, especially now. Notes, flowers, and unexpected gifts speak volumes and breathe new life into your relationship.

◆ Build relationships with other parents who have young (or even older) children. Many parents meet regularly in small groups, whether assembled spontaneously or organized by their church.

Hundreds of local groups affiliated with MOPS—Mothers of Preschoolers—meet on a regular basis across the United States (and in a number of other countries as well), offering support, conversation, and pleasant activities for mothers and their small children. (For the location of a MOPS group in or near your community, call 1-800-929-1287.) Local crisis pregnancy centers often put together single-moms' groups and activities. In the setting of such a get-together, you can share wisdom and woes, find support and encouragement, release laughter and tears, and even receive exhortation, if necessary.

quite normal. Up until this point, his explorations of the world will have been fact-finding missions. He has been finding out "what happens when I eat the mashed banana, turn the knobs on the stereo, push my toy car across the floor, flip the light switch, pull the cat's tail, bounce the ball, laugh, cry, yell, babble . . ."

Some of these acts have results that are interesting or feel good, some tweak little fingers, some get attention, some make the big people laugh or get upset, some are still under investigation. If the important people in his life have responded consistently, he will have figured out many of the ground rules of his world or at least have a good sense of the odds that a particular consequence will follow a certain deed.

Now, however, he will take his explorations a step further and up the ante. Instead of merely observing cause-and-effect relationships, he will want to find out how much power he wields. What will happen if he pushes the limits? Who's really in charge here? Mom may have said not to do this or touch that, but did she really mean it? Older sister's dolls are supposed to be off-limits, but will anyone do something about it if I carry one away?

During the months that follow, most, if not all, of the limits you have set will be challenged. At times they will receive a spectacular full-frontal assault. To call him "oppositional," a developmental term applied to this period, may be an understatement. By eighteen months, his favorite word may well be *no* followed by three exclamation points. What parents usually find astonishing, and at times humorous, is the extent and irrationality of this negativity:

"Would you like some water?" you ask innocently, holding his cup.
"No!"
You put the cup on the counter.
"Waaber!" he cries, reaching for it.
You fill it and give it to him.
"No!" He pushes it away.
You put the cup on the counter.
"WAABER!!" he howls.
You offer him the cup.
"NO!!" He swipes at the cup, nearly knocking it out of your hand.

What fuels this temporary insanity is, in fact, a very simple premise: If it wasn't his idea, he won't have anything to do with it.

Another startling variation on this theme is his disobeying a rule you have made abundantly clear—and making sure you're there to see it broken. This is not what was going on at eleven or twelve months, when his insatiable curiosity would override his very short memory, so he might explore an object after you have told him to leave it alone—seven times.

By eighteen months he can understand simple rules very well. Furthermore, the toddler in this phase won't always operate in stealth mode, a routine practice for older rule breakers. Instead, he may trot right over to the curtains you just told him not to touch, wait until you're watching, look you in the eyes (perhaps with a grin to boot), and give them a healthy tug. He is extremely interested in your response, and it is crucial that you give him one with more substance than "Isn't he cute. . . ." Dr. James Dobson has described the appropriate parental response in a memorable adage: "If he's looking for a fight, don't disappoint him." This doesn't refer to taking part in a literal brawl, of course, but to taking a consistent posture of standing your ground when your authority has been clearly challenged.

The duration and severity of this oppositional stage will vary, but you can count on manifestations of it for at least six months. Some children who are particularly agreeable and compliant won't give you much to write home about. (There aren't too many of these.) Others who are especially strong-willed seem to put on the war paint and push the boundaries on a daily basis.

To some degree, this behavior represents an important developmental milestone for your toddler. He is developing a budding sense of identity, an awareness that it is possible to make things happen, and a compelling need to find out how far his newfound capabilities can take him. At the same time, of course, he is emotionally volatile, lacking in wisdom, and extremely primitive in his handling of relationships. And when there is a conflict, any attempt at reasoning is usually an exercise in futility.

These characteristics are, indeed, strikingly similar to some seen in another age-group—teenagers. You might think of this phase of your child's life as a preview of adolescence, a turbulent but universal passage for which there is, thank goodness, light and sanity at the end of the tunnel. As with adolescence, some parental wisdom can keep the family boat from rocking too hard. Aside from the fact that a teenager is a lot bigger than a toddler, there is one crucial difference in the way you manage these two periods of your child's life. During the teen years, your goal will be to let go, to escort your son or daughter to independent, responsible adulthood. But with a toddler, it is critical that he understand without any doubt that you are in charge.

If this fact is not established with absolute certainty (though always with an abiding sense of love and respect) by twenty-four to thirty months of age, your child may be very unpleasant to live with for months—or even years—thereafter. Indeed, for many children the "terrible twos" are but an extension of the "ornery ones," only with more horsepower. But a child who comes through this developmental stage knowing he is surrounded by unshakable love and consistent limits will generally be happier and more civilized throughout the rest of childhood.

How do you make it clear to your toddler that you are in charge? Some basic approaches and specific techniques of discipline—the word literally refers to teaching and molding, not merely corrective action or punishment—are discussed in detail in Special Concerns, page 289. How to deal with tantrums, breath holding, head banging, and other spectacles is included in that section.

Relationships with other children

Very often two or more sets of parents who have toddlers of similar ages will have the bright idea of getting their offspring together for a little fun and group playtime. After all, isn't this a good time to learn how to get along and make new friends?

Believe it or not, the answer is "probably not," *especially* if the children are closer to one than to two years old.

With rare exception, a one-year-old is incapable of playing cooperatively with children her own age. Her universe is centered around herself, and she cannot comprehend such niceties as understanding the viewpoint or feelings of someone else. Parents and other adult caregivers are important to her, of course, but another small child will generate little more interest than another toy—except when each is interested in the same item.

If there's one concept that is foreign to the toddler's outlook, it is sharing. She cannot grasp the idea that one of her toys can be "borrowed" or used by someone else and still remain hers, or vice versa. She lives in the here and now, and "waiting a turn" is a meaningless phrase. Her outlook has been summarized quite amusingly by child-development expert Dr. Burton L. White:

THE TODDLER'S CREED
If I want it, it's mine.
If I give it to you and change my mind later, it's mine.
If I can take it away from you, it's mine.
If I had it a little while ago, it's mine.
If it's mine, it will never belong to anyone else, no matter what.
If we are building something together, all the pieces are mine.
If it looks like mine, it's mine.[3]

Therefore, if you turn more than one toddler loose in the same room, keep a close watch and plan to serve as referee. Having plenty of toys available will help, of course, but you will need to be ready to intervene at the first sign of combat. This is important not only as a means of keeping the flow of tears to a minimum but also to prevent physical consequences. All too often if a desired item can't be pulled easily out of the grip of another child, pushing and hitting will follow.

Should this occur, separate the opponents with a clear rebuke ("No hitting!"), tend to any wounds, and then administer consequences. In this case, immediate withdrawal of a privilege (such as access to the toy she wanted) or a time of isolation from the others and the toys is an appropriate response.

If the skirmish includes biting, you will need to take decisive action to reduce the risk of a repeat performance, because human bite wounds carry a significant risk of infection. The biter should be removed from the scene and given a firm, eyeball-to-eyeball order: "Do not bite Amanda or anyone else! Biting hurts very much." A long lecture about manners or infections isn't necessary, but you may want to maintain a steady (but not painful) grip on the upper body to prevent any wiggling or movement for a minute or so. A toddler normally becomes quite unhappy after a very short period of this restraint, and continuing it for fifteen to thirty seconds after she begins to complain will reinforce your point. (Say it again before you let go.) Do not shake or slap her and never bite the biter in an effort to show "how bad it feels."

Along with maintaining zero tolerance for your child's biting anyone, consider some preventive measures as well. If you hear a conflict brewing between two toddlers, don't wait for them to negotiate through their disagreement because they can't (and won't) at this age. Distract, separate, take whatever is in dispute out of the picture, or simply call it a day if it looks as if everyone is tired and cranky.

Depending upon the spacing of your children, conflict between a toddler and other siblings is virtually inevitable. If your children are spaced less than two years apart, the older at first will be wary of the attention being showered on the younger and may even regress to babylike behavior in an effort to regain center stage. Once she is assured of her place in your affection, however, she probably will pay little attention to the baby—until he becomes mobile. Once this happens, the insatiable curiosity of the new explorer will inevitably lead to an invasion of big sister's possessions. If your older child isn't yet two and a half, don't expect her to embrace any high-minded ideals about sharing. Try to keep your

The rod of correction imparts wisdom, but a child left to himself disgraces his mother.

PROVERBS 29:15

older child's prized possessions out of harm's way, and in return, make it clear that any hitting or other physical action taken against the younger sibling will have unpleasant consequences.

Even with very basic ground rules, however, some combat is inevitable. Furthermore, when it erupts, you may not always be able to figure out who did what to whom or who was at fault. This problem often gives parents considerable grief, and you will need plenty of wisdom, prayer, and patience to deal with it. In general, your response will have to depend on the age of the children involved. With very young children, separation from one another and whatever they were fighting over will be your most common tactic. Remember that this age-group is not terribly responsive to logic and reason. Later on, more sophisticated ground rules, "rules of evidence" when stories contradict, and consequences that fit the crime will need to be carried out.

If there is a difference of a few years or more between children, the likelihood of conflict with a toddler will be reduced. Not only will the older child have her own circle of friends and interests, but depending on her age, she may serve, at least at times, as a caregiver. She should not, however, be given disciplinary authority or responsibilities that belong to you alone.

Health Issues: Checkups and Immunizations

Your toddler should have a routine exam at age one, at fifteen and eighteen months, and at age two. As before, along with the normal gentle poking and prodding, his measurements will be taken and charted, and his developmental milestones (walking, etc.) should be reviewed. Remember to bring something to entertain your toddler in case you have to wait before the visit.

Don't expect a great deal of cooperation from your toddler during these exams. Typically the same physician who was greeted with coos a few months ago will now elicit howls of terror. Most of the exam will need to be done with your child sitting on your lap, and at times (such as when his ears are being checked) you will need to hold him still, pinning arms and head to your chest in an affectionate hammerlock. Occasionally, a more prolonged look into the ears will be needed, especially when wax needs to be cleared, and you may be asked to help keep your screaming and thrashing patient quite still on the exam table while this is going on. You will be impressed at how strong he is, how upset he sounds, and how guilty you feel. Remember, however, that he is experiencing far more fright than pain.

Everyone will have an easier time at the doctor's office if you can maintain a cheerful and confident demeanor throughout the visit. If your toddler senses that you are apprehensive or ambivalent about what is going on, his fright level may increase tenfold. When he cries or resists, don't plead with him to stop. Keep your voice mellow and reassuring, and your grip tight.

Between twelve and fifteen months of age, your child should receive his MMR immunization, which protects him from measles, mumps, and rubella. He may develop a fever or even a slight rash after seven to ten days, but more serious reactions are extremely unlikely. *If your child has shown a severe allergic reaction to eggs, notify the doctor ahead of time, since the production of the vaccine involves the use of egg products.* If necessary, consultation and testing by an allergist may be needed before the vaccine is given. If you are pregnant, it is safe for your child to receive the vaccine, as there are no reported cases of rubella being transmitted from toddler to mother as a result of the toddler's being immunized.

At fifteen to eighteen months, another diphtheria/tetanus/pertussis (DTaP) immunization will be due. In addition, he will probably receive another immunization against hemophilus influenza B bacteria. (The timing will depend on the particular type of vaccine used.) Between twelve and eighteen months your child's physician may also recommend a vaccine against chicken pox (varicella). Finally, if the third dose of polio or hepatitis B vaccine has not yet been given, it should be given between twelve and eighteen months.

Is It Time to Start Potty Training?

Probably not.

Some children may show signs that they are ready to learn this skill before the second birthday, and you may begin the process of training them if you desire (see chapter 9, page 341). But most toddlers are still in the throes of discovering their place in the world and dealing with their emotions during this eventful year, and adding any pressure to get rid of diapers and use the toilet may create even more turmoil. Take your time.

NOTES
1. Ideally this would be a pediatric ophthalmologist—a physician who specializes in children's eye problems—although many ophthalmologists deal with all age-groups. Unless specially trained and equipped, your primary-care physician will not be able to determine the visual acuity of a one-year-old.
2. Don't try to fake her out with some sleight of hand, by the way. "Magic tricks" where items appear or disappear unexpectedly will confuse the toddler's budding sense of object permanence. Save the disappearing ball and card tricks for the older kids.
3. Burton L. White, Ph.D., *Raising a Happy, Unspoiled Child* (New York: Simon and Schuster, 1994), 161.

When Your Child Has a Fever

In order to function properly, the human body is intricately designed to maintain its internal (also called **core**) temperature within very narrow limits. The normal human core body temperature is 98.6°F (or 37°C), but temperatures as low as 96.8°F (36°C) or as high as 100.4°F (38°C) are not necessarily abnormal. Normal variations in body functions brought about by a child's biological clock can cause temperatures to be lower in the early morning and higher in the later afternoon and evening. A child who has been in vigorous perpetual motion will have a higher body temperature than one who has been resting quietly.

The control center for regulating temperature is in the **hypothalamus,** a structure at the base of the brain that governs a number of critical bodily functions. The hypothalamus monitors body temperature and balances heat production and heat loss to maintain the temperature within very narrow limits. This **set point** is much like the desired temperature that you set on your thermostat at home. Heat is increased by shivering and by constriction of blood vessels at the body surface, and it is lost through sweating, breathing more rapidly, and dilation of surface blood vessels.

WHAT IS FEVER, AND WHAT CAUSES IT?

A fever is an abnormal elevation of core temperature. Most medical practitioners define a fever as a temperature higher than 100.4°F taken rectally in an infant and in a toddler up to three years of age.

There are several important points to remember about fever:

◆ *A fever is not a disease in itself* but a sign that the body's regulation of temperature has temporarily changed. Fever in children is most commonly a response to infection, and it is now known to serve a useful purpose by stimulating activity of white blood cells and other functions in the immune system.

◆ While it is a significant sign of an illness in progress, *fever itself is rarely dangerous for an infant or child.* A persistent temperature of 106°F or higher can be harmful, but this level occurs only in unusual circumstances such as in an extremely hot environment or during a heatstroke. Fever generated by the hypothalamus in response to an infection only occasionally exceeds 105°F, but essentially never rises above 106°F. Even at this level a fever will not cause damage except in very unusual circumstances, although it will usually be accompanied by some general discomfort (especially headache or body aches).

◆ *The height of the temperature does not always indicate how serious the problem is.* An infant with roseola, for example, will typically be quite active and cheerful even with a temperature climbing past 104°F. Conversely, a baby or child can be gravely ill with a temperature that is much lower.

◆ Whether or not a fever is specifically treated, it may go up and down several times during the course of an illness. Some parents mistakenly fear that a fever will climb relentlessly if they don't take active measures to lower it.

Body temperature is elevated in three ways:

◆ *Elevation of the body's internal thermostat.* This is by far the most common mechanism. Chemical factors released by the body in response to invasion by viruses or bacteria can raise the set point of the hypothalamus, provoking shivering and other mechanisms that raise body temperature. Rare causes of a rise in set point are certain cancers (for example, leukemia) and illnesses such as arthritis syndromes, which generate inflammation within the body but are not infections.

◆ *Heat production exceeds heat loss.* This can occur if heat loss mechanisms are thwarted by high environmental temperature or even when a child is wearing too many layers of clothing. Uncommon disorders such as hyperthyroidism or an overdose of certain types of drugs (for example, aspirin) may cause the body to generate excessive heat.

♦ *Malfunction of the body's normal heat-loss mechanisms.* This may result
from an overdose of certain drugs or from the syndrome known as **heat-stroke** (see Heatstroke, page 799). This is also an uncommon reason for a
child's fever.

WAYS TO MEASURE A CHILD'S TEMPERATURE

There will be many occasions during your child's life when you will need to
determine her body temperature as accurately as possible. Even though the
touch of your hand might suggest that your child is "burning up" or "cold
and clammy," this impression based on surface temperature can be very mis-leading. Most fevers below 102°F cannot be detected this way, and children
who feel warm to the touch are as likely to have a normal temperature as an
elevated one. Plastic liquid-crystal strips placed on the forehead aren't much
better and may miss a fever entirely. To obtain a reliable core temperature
measurement, your best bet is to use a thermometer in one of these loca-tions:

♦ *Rectal* temperature most accurately and reliably reflects core tempera-ture, especially in infants and young children. It is typically 0.9°F (or
0.5°C) higher than oral temperature. *Measuring temperature rectally is
specifically recommended for infants under three months of age,* for whom
significant medical decisions may hinge on the numbers that are
obtained.

♦ Taking an *oral* temperature is usually more convenient than a rectal
temperature in older children (preschool age and older), assuming they
can cooperate. It will be less reliable if the child is breathing through her
mouth or has taken hot or cold liquids within ten minutes prior to the
reading.

♦ Temperatures taken using a thermometer whose tip is held in a child's
armpit (also called **axillary readings**) are not as reliable as those prop-erly taken rectally or orally. However, they may be more accurate than a
temperature taken improperly in an uncooperative child.

♦ *Ear* temperatures taken with special electronic thermometers are both
quick and convenient, but they may be less accurate in infants and
toddlers (see next page).

When talking to your physician, tell him the exact temperature and method used. Do not add or subtract a degree because this could make a significant difference in the care of your child, depending on his age.

TYPES OF THERMOMETERS

Glass (mercury) thermometers are inexpensive ($3 or $4), have no batteries that need replacing, and when properly used can provide a very accurate temperature reading. However, they don't work as quickly as digital or ear thermometers, and some people find them difficult to read. They also must be shaken down and cleaned with alcohol after each use.

Rectal glass thermometers, which have a short bulb-shaped tip, are used with infants and small children, while oral glass thermometers (with an elongated tip) are appropriate for children who can cooperate when the tip is placed under their tongue.

Digital thermometers use battery-driven heat sensors and take about thirty seconds to arrive at a reading (usually signaled by a beep), which is displayed on a small screen. They can be used to take temperatures orally, rectally, or under the arm. Typically costing about $10 or less, they come with a package of disposable polyethylene sleeves. A new sleeve should be used each time a temperature is taken, so you will need to maintain a supply of these if a digital thermometer is your preference.

Ear (tympanic membrane) thermometers can give an estimate of core temperature instantly by measuring the energy emitted from tiny blood vessels within the eardrum. Many doctors' offices and clinics utilize them because of their speed (less than two seconds to get a reading) and convenience, since very little cooperation is required from the child. In fact, these thermometers can be used when a child is asleep. However, the readings may be less accurate, especially in infants and toddlers, because of the children's smaller external ear canals; the reliability of the reading can also be affected by the position of the thermometer's tip within the ear. Another disadvantage of these devices is their cost of $60 or more.

TAKING A CHILD'S TEMPERATURE

When taking a rectal temperature, the infant or young child should be placed stomach-down across your lap. Lubricate the metallic tip of the thermometer with petroleum jelly and also put a little around the child's anus. Then gently insert the thermometer into the child's rectum about one inch. *Do not force the thermometer into the rectum.* Leave the thermometer in place for two or three minutes or until the temperature stops climbing in a mercury thermometer; then remove it and read the temperature.

When using an oral thermometer, the tip should be placed under the mid or back portion of either side of the tongue. The child should hold the thermometer steady with her lips and fingers, not with her teeth. Be sure your child is not biting down on the thermometer, which could cause it to break. The mouth should be closed, so she will need to breathe through her nose for two to three minutes until the mercury is no longer rising. (If her nose is extremely congested, she may need to take intermittent mouth breaths, or you might want to consider using a different method of checking her temperature.)

If you use an ear thermometer, be sure to follow the manufacturer's directions for proper use, being especially attentive to the position of the tip in your child's ear. During its first few uses you may want to compare your reading with a simultaneous temperature taken by a glass thermometer, in order to confirm that you are obtaining consistent readings.

If you are taking an armpit temperature, first make sure that this area is dry. (If damp, the reading could be inaccurately low.) Place the thermometer tip in the center of the armpit and hold the child's elbow against her chest until you hear the beep (for a digital thermometer) or for three minutes if using a glass thermometer.

WHAT TO DO IF YOUR CHILD HAS A FEVER

First, stay calm—which may be easier said than done if your child is very young—and then assess the situation. The actual height of the temperature is important, but equally significant are *the age of your child and what else is going on.* Before calling the doctor, determine if there are other symptoms such as coughing, runny nose, sore throat, rash, or (in children who can communicate) pain in some location.

Even more important is *the way your child is acting,* which will help you determine how urgent the problem is. A normal child will usually become somewhat irritable, less active, more clingy, and less hungry when a fever is present. (This shouldn't be surprising if you remember how you felt the last time you had a significant fever.) In a typical acute illness such as a cold, your child may act like her old self again when the fever subsides. With more serious infections, however, changes in behavior tend to be more profound, and if one or more of these are present, call the doctor immediately.

Most acute illnesses that generate a fever in infants and children are caused by viruses and will disappear on their own, while some illnesses may involve bacteria that will respond to specific antibiotic treatment. (Certain viral illnesses, such as influenza, may also improve more rapidly with treatment.) If the fever persists for more than twenty-four hours, a call to your child's physician and possibly an evaluation may help determine the problem. In addition, there are some other general measures that may be helpful.

Dress your infant or child in light clothing and keep her room at a comfortable temperature. Turning up the heat at home or bundling her up in hot clothes will not speed recovery, and doing so may actually keep her temperature elevated. If she is shivering, give her a light blanket for comfort. (Remember, though, that shivering is a process that will raise the body temperature.)

Give your sick child fluids of all kinds, since some body fluids will be lost during sweating. Appetite is typically reduced during an illness in which fever is present. Large or fatty meals should be avoided, since fever tends to slow movement of food through the digestive tract.

Your child does not need to be strictly confined to bed, but activities should be kept on the quiet side, since vigorous exertion might increase her temperature. If the illness is potentially contagious (and most viruses are), she should be kept away from other children or anyone (such as an elderly person) whose health might be jeopardized by an acute infection.

Sponge bathing an infant or child to bring down a fever is *not* necessary, except in unusual situations (such as heatstroke) where temperatures exceed 106°F. However, sponging might help her feel more comfortable, especially if her temperature is higher than 104°F. It is helpful to give a dose of acetaminophen or ibuprofen (see next page) at least thirty minutes before doing so to lower the set point of your child's thermostat. (Otherwise, she will simply shiver back to her original temperature.)

Set the child in an inch or two of lukewarm water (85°F to 90°F, which should feel just slightly warm to the touch). *Do not use cold water,* which will make her shiver (and thus raise her temperature), and *do not use rubbing alcohol,* which can be dangerous when absorbed through the skin or inhaled. Use a sponge or washcloth to keep body surfaces wet for thirty to forty-five minutes, during which time she will lose heat as water evaporates from her skin. You do not have to bring her temperature down to normal—lowering it a couple of degrees will help her feel better.

Using Medications
to Lower Temperature

Three medications that are available without prescription can help reduce an infant's or child's fever. Before using them, keep these things in mind:

- The primary reason to give these drugs will normally be to make your child more comfortable. They will not make an infection disappear more quickly. If your child has a fever but is otherwise contented, you don't need to give her anything to make the fever go away.
- *The fever's response to any of these medications is not an indication of the severity of the illness.* One dose may only reduce the fever 2° or 3°F over a couple of hours, or it may merely limit the height of an upward temperature "spike." Don't panic if the thermometer reading doesn't drop right away or if it rises again after a few hours.
- *Do not give medication to lower fever to a baby under three months of age without contacting your physician.* In this age-group, determining the *cause* of the fever is far more important than lowering the temperature itself.

There are several medications on the market that can help lower fever:

- Acetaminophen (Tylenol, Panadol, Liquiprin, Tempra, and other brands) is available in a variety of oral and rectal suppository preparations and may be given every four hours as needed. While this medication has been widely and safely used for a number of years, an accidental overdose can be potentially dangerous (see *acetaminophen,* Reference).

  Most acetaminophen products list recommended doses based on age, but if possible, it is better to determine the dosage based on weight, especially if your infant or child is above or below average (see dosage chart under Acetaminophen, page 638).
- Ibuprofen (Children's Motrin, Children's Advil, and other brands) has the potential advantage of a longer-lasting effect—six to eight hours per dose, as opposed to acetaminophen's four to six.

- Aspirin is effective in lowering temperature and relieving aches and pains *BUT it is not recommended for this purpose in anyone younger than twenty-one years of age* because of its link to an uncommon but serious disorder called **Reye's syndrome** (see Reference, page 719).

FEBRILE CONVULSIONS

Febrile convulsions—seizures precipitated by fever—occur in 2 to 5 percent of children sometime between four months and five years of age. These seizures often begin early in an acute illness, usually during the rapid upswing of a fever (which doctors refer to as a **spike**). In fact, an infant or child whom you find hot and cranky with a 104°F temperature is *not* likely to have a seizure in the immediate future because with rare exception she has already arrived at the high temperature without incident. (Temperature spikes tend to occur so quickly that it is unlikely that you will be able to take a temperature while one is actually taking place.) (See *seizures*, Reference.)

Caregivers: Who Will Care for Your Child While You Are Away?

Even if you are the most dedicated and attentive parent(s) on earth, you cannot (and indeed should not) provide hands-on care for your child twenty-four hours a day, seven days a week, from the delivery room to the college dormitory. Many times during your child rearing career you will need to release her to the temporary care of another person. Whether this involves an occasional time-out to run errands or a routine of several hours every workday, transferring responsibility for your child to someone else raises many questions:

- How do you choose a caregiver?
- Is it better for your child if the caregiver comes to your home, or is it okay to take her elsewhere (such as to another home or day-care center)?
- How long is it appropriate for you to be away from your child?

Without question these are extremely important topics. Like many other concerns of parenting (such as discipline), there is no surefire formula that will apply to every family or even to one family through the development of all its children. What follows therefore are a few basic—but very important—overriding principles.

Child-care issues overall cluster around two major situations:

- Extended periods of child care on a regular basis, usually occurring when both parents (or a single parent) are employed outside the home.
- Short-term or episodic care, commonly referred to as baby-sitting, which is discussed at the end of this section (page 287).

The first of these concerns—and the question of whether the mother of one or more young children should be employed outside of the home—is by far the more complicated, emotional, and controversial of the two.

Working in and out of the Home

Whether you are a young couple enthusiastically welcoming the first baby to your nest, seasoned parents with a home full of children of all ages, a blended family, or a single mom or dad, you must deal with some of the following issues:

- How much income does the family need, and where will it come from?
- How will we divide labor in the home? Will one parent be the main income producer while the other's primary role is caring for children? Or will both parents share more equally in these tasks?
- How will bringing up one or more children mesh with one or both parents' work schedule, not to mention education and career plans?
- Is it wise for both mother and father to work outside the home? If this is done, who is going to take care of the child(ren)?
- How can a single mother or father best cope with the simultaneous demands of earning a living and rearing children?

Every family will have different circumstances that affect the answer to these questions:

- Age, abilities, and temperament of each child
- The state of the marital union or the absence of a marriage partner
- Educational background
- Job/professional skills
- Financial resources
- Relationships with immediate and extended family members
- Involvement with a church community
- Goals, plans, and dreams for the future

For some parents there will be many ways to approach these questions. For others, options are very limited and the answers will be defined by current circumstances. Most single parents, for example, have the daunting dual role of primary income provider and full-time parent. There is no standard solution that will work for every family or even for one family throughout its entire lifetime. But when thinking through these very important and often emotionally charged questions, it is important to keep some broad perspectives and reality checks in mind.

Faulty expectations, identity, and the "end of life" test

Much discontent over the question of balancing child rearing and career(s)—for both mothers and fathers—can arise from several powerful but faulty expectations:

The expectation that rearing one or more children won't require considerable effort or many changes in lifestyle. An infant cannot be fed and changed and then left to her own devices, nor can an older child be expected to grow up on her own. Not only must a child's basic health and safety be assured, but her intellectual and emotional development requires continuous monitoring and frequent interaction with adults who are deeply committed to her.

The expectation that a certain lifestyle is necessary for happiness. With rare exception, whatever standard of living young parents envision for themselves in the immediate or distant future will probably require more income than expected. Remember Murphy's Law of Money: Everything costs more than you expect—both to purchase and to maintain. The belief that a particular home or car, travel, and certain experiences are necessary for contentment in life can push the budgetary limits to the point that a second income becomes a necessity. But this could have the ultimate effect of trading irreplaceable interactions with one's own children for material goods that will eventually be worn out and discarded.

The expectation that mother can be Supermom, effortlessly managing a career, nurturing children, and experiencing extraordinary marital satisfaction—all with great style and finesse. TV commercials and magazine ads have helped create this fantasy, which more often than not leads to frustration, guilt, and, most of all, fatigue. There may be a few true Supermoms around, but the other 99 percent who are more earthbound usually realize that they must accept a number of compromises at home and/or work in order to survive.

An issue more often but not always for women: The expectation that being at home will result in the evaporation of one's intellect and ambition. Women have received this message from numerous voices, including popular media, friends and acquaintances who work outside the home, even insensitive husbands and family members who either don't understand or have forgotten what is involved in running a household and nurturing children. The decision to remain at home is often made at considerable sacrifice, and many women find themselves disadvantaged later when they try to reenter the outside marketplace after a few years' absence from it. However, to assume that staying home with the children will erode a woman's mental or professional powers is to subscribe to an extremely narrow view of life.

The rewards of participating significantly in a child's development cannot be measured. A parent who chooses to stay home is aware that her children will only be home for a season and that her impact on their intellect, development, and values will probably continue for decades. Rearing children is a career that requires a host of skills as well as insight, patience, and wisdom.

The world of work is changing to accommodate parents who have decided to spend more time with their children. An increasing number of options for working part-time or from a home office are making it possible for both moms and dads to be with their children more often and more consistently. Many women for whom an outside career or interest is important have created satisfying professional options for themselves from within the home setting. These are encouraging developments, both for women who want to pursue a career outside the home (whether now or in the future) and for women who are content to make home their career but who want to pursue artistic or community interests.

An issue more often but not always for men: The expectation that the career track defines identity and that all other concerns pale in comparison. Men are notorious for defining themselves in terms of their occupation and position. (How often do you hear a father answer the question "What do you do?" with "I'm Trevor and Amanda's dad"?) But the danger of this orientation is that the demands of a career and the "pursuit of excellence" at work can result in rampant absenteeism from home and mediocrity in parenting. Many fathers and mothers buy into the myth that a few minutes of time spent with one's children every day is just fine, as long as it's "quality time." But will a one-ounce steak be satisfying because it is "quality steak"? Or (perhaps more relevant for men) will sex every six months be adequate because it is "quality sex"?

Both mothers and fathers need to think very carefully about these issues. The truth is, *a true and lasting sense of worth, identity, and satisfaction comes ultimately from being present and accounted for in God's family and going about His business every day.* In the final analysis, these qualities are not derived from the initials after one's name, the title on one's door, the plaques on the walls, or the money in the bank. They do not come from being CEO of Universal Widget or having a home that is the envy of the neighborhood—or having kids who are perfect. Parents must beware of the "If only . . ." syndrome: "If only ____, then I'd be satisfied/content/happy." These are the longings of those who are perpetually restless and discontented, who never fill the gaping hole remaining in their lives, no matter how often they successfully accomplish last month's "If only . . ."

The "end of life" test. Parents who are making decisions about who will rear their children should ask themselves an important question: When you are staring down death's corridor, what in your life will really matter? Will you look back fondly at the hours spent at the office and pine over the fact that you weren't there longer? You may be the world's greatest Monopoly player—on the game table or in the real world—but eventually you will have to fold up the board, put the money back in the box, and put it in the closet. No one will remember for very long who won the game, but those who were at the table with you will long recall whether their time with you was pleasant or miserable.

More specifically, will your children arrive at your bedside and thank you for all the career goals you accomplished? They will probably remember most fondly and thank you for the times you spent with them—rocking them, listening to them, wrestling on the carpet, having lunch at their favorite restaurant, going fishing, walking on the beach, or helping them out of a jam. At that moment, what will matter most will be the people you care about, the lives you have touched, and the prospect of hearing, "Well done, my good and faithful servant."

Best and second best

These considerations are not intended to incite great pangs of guilt nor to say that careers launched from within or outside the home are somehow evil. They are, however, meant to raise serious questions about priorities, about what *really* matters, and to lay the foundation for the following observations.

While children are growing up, they should be cared for primarily by people who are *passionately and sacrificially committed to them.* In the vast majority of cases, the people who best fit this description are their own parents. However, grandparents, other relatives, or close friends may feel this way too.

People who are hired to take care of other people's children can and should be responsible, mature, kind, and attentive—but they will rarely be passionately and sacrificially committed to those children. Most paid caregivers are probably not going to develop a deep emotional bond or a relationship with a child that will last for years.

If at all possible, then, it is most desirable for children to spend the majority of their waking hours with one of their own parents or with someone else who has an equally intense commitment—especially during the first few years of life when children are dealing with basic issues of security and trust.

This will not always be possible for a variety of reasons. If it isn't and your child is going to spend a significant amount of time in the care of others, your energy should be expended not on guilt but on finding the best possible caregiver arrangements, a process that will be reviewed in the next section. As much as possible, continually seek ways to arrange schedules and time commitments that will maximize parental time with each child at home.

SEEKING A CAREGIVER

Assuming that your child is going to be spending time on a regular basis with a caregiver other than one of her parents, what options are available?

In-home care: the caregiver comes to your child

This person might be a relative such as a grandparent, a nanny that you hire for an extended period, or perhaps a college student or *au pair* from another country who provides care in exchange for room and board. There are several advantages of in-home care:

- Your child remains in a completely familiar environment—with access to his own crib or bed, toys, yard, etc.
- Assuming that the same person comes to your home regularly, there will be greater stability and consistency in your child's life.
- The caregiver's attention is focused specifically on your child(ren), rather than on a larger group.
- There is no exposure to contagious diseases from other children. If your child becomes ill, care does not have to be interrupted or rearranged.
- Convenience is maximized—there is no need to transport your child and the items she needs to another home or facility.
- Depending upon the caregiver's availability, there may be more flexibility in this arrangement; your home doesn't have "closing hours."

 Disadvantages of in-home care are as follows:

- If you are hiring the caregiver, in-home care is likely to be more costly. In this case, the individual will in effect be your employee, so you will need to be aware of possible tax implications and even liability concerns. (For example, who pays the bills if the caregiver is injured in your home? Your homeowner's insurance may or may not cover such expenses.)

◆ What do you do if the caregiver is ill or can't come for some other reason? You will always need to have Plan B ready in case such a problem arises.

Family child care: your child stays in the caregiver's home

In this arrangement, an individual (or perhaps a couple) provides care in his or her home for a number of children who may be of similar or widely variable ages. (If the caregiver is a devoted relative who is responsible only for your child(ren), this situation may be essentially the equivalent of in-home care.) The advantages of family child care include:

◆ Your child remains in a home rather than a "facility" environment. If the family is someone you and your child already know, there will be some familiarity (and perhaps less separation anxiety).
◆ As with the in-home arrangement, having the same caregiver every day will provide consistency in your child's experiences.
◆ There are likely to be fewer children than in a day-care center, and thus less exposure to contagious diseases.
◆ Costs are sometimes less than for in-home care or a day-care facility.
◆ As with care in your own home, there is often more flexibility with hours.

Disadvantages of family child care include the following:

◆ There may be no licensing requirements for family caregivers in your state. In this case, you will need to rely more heavily on your own assessment of the caregiver and the home environment to determine if all is safe and sound. (Obviously, it is helpful if you know the family beforehand.)
◆ Plans may have to be rearranged (sometimes without warning) if the caregiver becomes ill, has an unexpected family problem, or simply goes on vacation.
◆ If the caregiver is responsible for several children, you will need to determine if she or he can give adequate attention to your child and not become overwhelmed.

Facility child care: your child stays at a day-care center operated by a church, university, or commercial entity

There are several advantages to this type of child care:

◆ These are normally licensed and thus accountable to regulations regarding the facility and the staff. These places may have extremely well-trained employees, age-appropriate learning programs, and physical resources (such as playground equipment) not available in homes.

- ◆ Facilities normally have predictable staffing and hours of operation. You will not need to make sudden adjustments because a caregiver is ill or unavailable.
- ◆ If care is provided by a church whose beliefs you share, your child might be exposed to songs, stories, and other input that build spiritual and moral values.

The disadvantages of facility child care include:

- ◆ Day-care centers sometimes have relatively large child-to-staff ratios so that individual attention for your child is in short supply.
- ◆ If the facility does not offer competitive wages, it might not attract well-trained or attentive staff. Staff turnover in some centers can be rapid, leading to unpredictable relationships between the children and their adult caregivers.
- ◆ Infections are spread much more easily among groups of children who are interacting at close range and handling the same toys. Both upper-respiratory infections (including middle-ear infection) and diarrhea are more frequent among children in day-care centers.
- ◆ While hours of operation are more predictable, they might not be very flexible. What happens if you are stuck in traffic or experience some other delay at the end of the day?

All things being equal, if care is provided on a regular, ongoing basis by someone other than a parent, the order of preference for choosing a caregiver would be as follows:

1. One or more relatives, either in your home or in theirs
2. A nonrelative in your home, such as a nanny or a live-in
3. Nonrelatives in a home setting
4. Large-group day care in a facility

This ranking is based on several key assumptions:

- ◆ A relative is more likely to be attached and attentive to your child than a nonrelative would be.
- ◆ A stable, predictable situation is more desirable than one in which there is constant change.

- If there are fewer children for each caregiver, your child is likely to receive more individual attention.
- Infections are less common among small numbers of children than in large-group settings and even less frequent in your own home.

As with so many other parenting concerns, there are always exceptions to these guidelines. For example:

- A conscientious nonrelative is preferable to an irresponsible family member.
- A large day-care center that is well maintained and staffed by adults who love children is preferable to a home setting that is unsanitary and poorly supervised.
- A caregiver that you hire to stay in your home may not necessarily devote herself to your child's well-being while you are gone.

If you need, but do not yet have, child care available, ask some trusted friends or coworkers for suggestions or referrals. Your church might have references or a bulletin board listing caregivers in your community. Newspaper and yellow-page listings are also possibilities, although with these you do not have the advantage of a specific recommendation. Ultimately you must survey the options available to you and then consider carefully which might best meet your family's needs. In doing so you will need to keep three factors in balance:

1. Is your child likely to thrive in this situation? How closely will the care duplicate (or at least resemble) the way *you* care for your child at home?
2. How well will the availability and location of the caregiver mesh with your own schedule and daily logistics?
3. Are the child-care arrangements affordable?

There are also specific considerations for infants and toddlers. A baby's physical and intellectual development, as well as emotional security, requires *ongoing* adult attention. Infants need mental, emotional, and physical stimulation; they should not be left lying or sitting for hours in a crib or playpen. They need to be changed when wet, comforted when crying, and played with when awake and comfortable. They should be hand-fed; propping a bottle in an infant's mouth creates a risk of choking and of ear infections. (If you are looking into a center that provides care for infants, check to see if there are a number of comfortable chairs in which adults can hold and feed babies.)

Mobile babies and toddlers need room to explore—safely. They can neither be confined to a small enclosure nor allowed to roam far and wide without supervision. Their attention can shift as rapidly as their mood, and they are not capable of playing cooperatively with other children.

In order to give adequate attention to the needs and development of infants and toddlers, there should be:

- at least one caregiver for every three children younger than two years of age. If at all possible each infant or toddler should have a main caregiver— that is, someone with whom she has an ongoing and consistent relationship.
- at least one caregiver for every four children between two and three years of age.
- at least one caregiver for every eight children between three and six years of age.

With these basic principles clearly in mind, you must also evaluate several aspects of any potential child-care arrangement, including short-term (baby-sitting) care:

The person or people involved (This is the most important.) *You should get to know those who are going to be responsible for your child's welfare.* Don't hesitate to request one or more interviews, and take the time to observe the caregiver's interactions with your own child as well as with other children.

- Does the caregiver appear comfortable, relaxed, and pleasant with children?
- How well does the caregiver interact with *you?*
- What prior experience does the caregiver have?
- Are references available?

If you are dealing with group care in a home or day-care center, ask the following questions about the staff before you make your decision:

- Who is in charge, and what are her or his credentials?
- What is the ratio of children to caregivers?
- If assistants are used, are they at least fourteen years old and properly supervised?
- Is everyone trained in child CPR?

The child-care setting (assuming it is not your own home) Before choosing the best facility for your situation, look at the following:

- Is it clean, cheerful, and attractive to you and your child?
- Do tables, chairs, and other equipment appear to be in good repair?

- Are there any potential safety problems?
- Are electrical outlets covered?
- Are smoke detectors and fire extinguishers present?
- Are heating, air-conditioning, and overall ventilation adequate?
- Are cleaning supplies, medications, and other hazardous products inaccessible to children?
- Are appropriate toys available?
- Is the outdoor play area properly fenced and secured?
- Are enough mats, cots, cribs, or beds available for naps?
- Is there an area specifically designated for diaper changing? Is it cleaned after each use? Is it anywhere near where food is prepared?
- Are pets present? Are they child-friendly? Is your child allergic to animals?

Philosophy, policies, and programs (in day-care centers or group home care)
Consider the following when choosing your facility:

- Are there written policies and procedures you can review?
- Is the basic worldview of the caregiver or facility compatible with yours?
- Will the values you teach at home be honored?
- Is there any spiritual input for older children?
- What is the caregiver's outlook on training and discipline?
- Are the disciplinary policies delineated and followed by all caregivers?
- Does there appear to be an appropriate balance between love and limits in dealing with behavior problems?
- What types of measures are used to maintain order?
- Is disciplinary spanking ever carried out, and if so, under what circumstances?
- Is disruptive or destructive behavior handled appropriately?
- If you observe a child's behavior being corrected, is it done with respect?
- Are children adequately supervised at all times?
- What kind of food is offered to children?
- Are activities planned and available for older children?
- Do these activities enhance learning and overall development?
- Are arts and crafts available?
- Is there excessive reliance on TV or other passive activities?
- Are there opportunities for physical exertion and outdoor play?
- What happens when a child is ill?
- Do children who are sick remain in contact with those who are not?

- Are the caregivers willing and able to give prescribed medications to infants and children?
- Are parents encouraged to drop in at any time to see how things are going? (*This is very important.* Be wary of any place where your access to your child or the facility is discouraged or restricted.)
- Is the caregiving situation appropriately secure?
- Are there clear policies regarding releasing children to adults who are not their parents?
- Can the facility prevent unauthorized individuals from entering?

RED FLAGS

While stable and nurturing child care is desirable, *safe* child care is an absolute necessity. Injuries resulting from adult carelessness, physical or sexual abuse, or assaults on a child's emotions are a parent's nightmare—and all are unacceptable in any setting. Unfortunately, signs of neglect or wrongdoing may not be especially obvious, and even if they are, it can be impossible to prove that the caregiver was at fault. Nevertheless, you will need to keep your eyes and ears wide-open for any of these potential indicators of trouble:

- Does your child become unusually upset or fearful about being left with a particular caregiver?
- Does the caregiver appear impatient, irritable, or stressed?
- Has your child become more withdrawn or shown other signs of not being herself after spending time with a caregiver?
- Have you discovered unexplained bruises, welts, or other marks on your child's body?
- Has your child exhibited inappropriate language or sexual behavior?
- Do you feel uneasy whenever you leave your child with a particular caregiver?
- Are you discouraged from dropping in on the caregiver unannounced?
- If you have made an unexpected visit, have you found things in disarray, children improperly supervised or extremely upset?

If you observe one or more of these red flags, you should strongly consider removing your child from that situation until you can determine with greater certainty what is best in the long run. You may need to speak candidly to the caregiver about what you have observed and see if the response you receive is appropriate, evasive, or overtly hostile. If you believe that your or someone else's child has been abused in a child-care setting, you should contact your nearest child-protection agency and explain your concerns. Even if you are not certain whether abuse has actually taken place, it is their job to investigate more fully and take appropriate action if needed.

Baby-sitters

While it is vitally important to be diligent regarding the choice of a long-term caregiver for your child, it is also important to be careful about your choice of baby-sitters, even though the time your child spends in their care may be considerably shorter. During the first six months of your child's life, it is best to leave her in the hands of experienced relatives or other adults. As your child grows older, however, younger baby-sitters can be utilized. Indeed, some of the best baby-sitters you may find will be students in high school or middle school. (Most states require that a baby-sitter be at least twelve years old if he or she is going to be unsupervised. Check your local statutes.) In many communities, hospitals or other organizations offer short courses (including CPR training) for baby-sitters, and those who have completed such a program could be excellent candidates for you to consider.

It is best to build a roster of trustworthy baby-sitters before you actually need one. Ask other mothers of young children whom they recommend and why. Responsibility, experience, and good rapport with young children are important qualities to seek. You might find some excellent sitters and have a chance to see them in action in the church nursery or Sunday school.

Once you have potential candidates, it is helpful to spend time with each one in your home. If possible, have him or her watch your child while you do some other work at home. This will give you a chance to observe how the sitter interacts with your child; it will also allow your child time to become familiar with the baby-sitter, thus reducing separation anxiety (if the child is old enough to manifest it) when you leave.

When you leave your child with a sitter, always leave the address and phone number of the location(s) where you can be reached, along with the number of your doctor, the local hospital, and another relative or friend who will be home in case you can't be reached. You might want to invest in a pager to allow you more geographical flexibility.

Let the baby-sitter know when you expect to be home and what you expect to happen while you're gone—including feeding, bathing, and bedtime routines. If a child needs medication, make sure the baby-sitter knows exactly how much and when to give it. The sitter should also know any other family rules, such as those applying to TV or video watching, as well as any reliable ways to comfort your child when you leave. The baby-sitter should allow no visitors into your home unless you have made prior arrangements. If it helps you feel comfortable, check in with the sitter by phone after you've been gone awhile to find out how things are going.

Make sure that your pay rate is clear from the start. Ask a friend what the going rate is for each age-group and don't hesitate to offer more for the best sitter on your list. If you would like the sitter to clean up dishes or straighten up elsewhere in the home, offer to pay a little extra.

If your child is old enough to understand, tell her that you are leaving and you will be back. Don't sneak out when she isn't looking, and don't be pulled into a long, emotional parting scene. Your child will survive and, with rare exception, will calm down shortly after you leave. Enjoy the night out!

A Final Note: Who Will Provide Care If You Are Gone . . . for Good?

Planning for a disaster is never enjoyable. But an accident during even the most routine errand might unexpectedly leave your child(ren) without one or both parents. If such a tragedy were to take place, who would care for your children, and how would their material needs be met?

All parents must consider this possibility, carefully decide whom they would want to care for their children—along with a number of other financial, practical, and spiritual considerations—and then express their desires in a legally binding document. The specific steps involved in the preparation of a will or a living trust are beyond the scope of this book and should be reviewed with an attorney who is well versed in estate planning.

What matters most is that parents not succumb to the notion that "it can't happen to me/us" but instead take the proper measures to provide for their children should the unthinkable happen.

Principles of Discipline and Training: Balancing Love and Limits

Discipline: Training and instruction that is intended to produce a specific pattern of behavior, character development, and moral or mental improvement. (From the Latin *discipulus:* "pupil," derived from *discere:* "to learn.")

Mention the word *discipline* in connection with rearing children, and images of various forms of punishment may come to mind. *But discipline encompasses the entire process of shaping and molding a child's attitudes and behaviors over the years that he or she is entrusted to your care.* This project is deserving of your diligence, fervor, humility, and prayer.

Training your children cannot be approached in a careless or haphazard manner because, left to their own devices, children rarely gravitate toward virtuous behavior, selfless attitudes, and responsible decisions. If these are not learned at home during thousands of interactions with parents and other family members, they may never be learned at all—to the detriment of the child and everyone around him.

But you don't need to live in a state of constant anxiety, wondering whether one false move on your part will unleash a career criminal years later. The discipline of children involves an overall mind-set rather than a cookbook full of behavioral recipes ("If he does this, you should do that"). Discipline can include a variety of techniques and approaches that vary depending upon the child's age and temperament. And what brings about a desired result with one child may prove to be a dismal flop with a sibling. While you will want to have an overall plan in mind, you will have to improvise along the way.

The subject of training and discipline often raises a lot of questions, concerns, and even controversy. For example:

How do I sort out all the input and advice I get, including the impact of my own upbringing? Your approach to discipline will be influenced significantly by your own experiences as a child or adolescent. You may even overcompensate for extremes that have affected you. If you were treated harshly as a child, you may tend toward being permissive, and vice versa. You will also receive plenty of advice (some more worthwhile than others) from relatives and friends, books and magazines, sermons, radio and TV programs, child rearing classes, and your child's physician. You will have to choose wisely from these resources, separate the wheat from the chaff, and try to avoid becoming a "Method of the Month Club" parent.

Am I too rigid or too lenient? If you don't worry about this question once in a while, you may be at risk for extreme or unhealthy discipline patterns.

How early can or should discipline begin? Based on developmental milestones, you can't expect a baby under eight months of age to follow directions, although certain behaviors (such as day and night sleeping patterns) may be shaped by parents. As your baby becomes mobile, you will need to begin establishing and enforcing limits through a variety of approaches. If you haven't started some basic molding and training of your child by eighteen months, you're off to a late start.

Why is it so difficult? And why does my child keep challenging me? Sometimes (or perhaps most of the time) bringing up children seems at best loaded with uncertainty, at worst a perpetual uphill struggle. Why? Because each child is a unique creation, a person with a mind, spirit, and will of his own. Children are not built like cars or computers; they do not arrive with instruction manuals that guarantee that *B* will happen if you do *A*. Nor do they enter your life as "blank slates" whose thoughts and actions are completely determined by whatever input you provide at home. While many of their behaviors are predictable in general terms, they are not little robots who will automatically yield to your direction.

Some children who are endowed with a particularly strong will seem bent on bucking everyone who crosses their path—beginning in the delivery room. If you have been blessed with one of these children, don't panic, and don't give up. You won't be the first parent in your neighborhood to bring up a strong-willed child, and as you continue to shape that powerful will, you may well see not only an adolescent who resists peer pressure but later a young adult who has become an effective leader.

What about disciplinary spanking or other physical punishment? This question, which will be reviewed in some detail later on, has become increasingly controversial in recent years. Some parents use spanking (a form of corporal punishment) too frequently, too severely, and too long into childhood. A few parents abuse their children in the name of discipline. In response to these harmful extremes, many authors and organizations have concluded that *all* physical discipline, including disciplinary spanking, is inappropriate. But this position is also extreme. At the right time, for the right reasons, and with the right safeguards, spanking can be a useful tool in rearing young children.

EXTREMES IN DISCIPLINE: WHAT NOT TO DO

No mother or father disciplines children with absolute perfection, and like every other parent in the world, you will make mistakes. You may say or do something that you later regret, or you may neglect one or more worthwhile aspects of the training process. But parenting involves a long learning curve, and children brought up in an environment where it is clear that they are deeply loved will be resilient in the face of numerous parental errors. Nevertheless, stay away from patterns of missteps and omissions that could have a lasting negative impact on your child. If any of the following have taken root in your home, remember that it's never too late to make midcourse corrections.

Physical abuse. Punching, slapping, whipping, burning, and other horrors inflicted upon children are *not* discipline. They are abuse and have no place in the rearing of a son or daughter. They do not serve to benefit the child in any way; they do serve as unhealthy ways for a parent to vent anger. These behaviors indicate a basic defect in the parent's communication skills, the parent's lack of respect for the child's body and emotions, and a gross misunderstanding of a parent's responsibilities. If this type of violence has occurred in your home, seek counseling immediately to prevent further damage. Such help is especially important if you received this sort of treatment as a child, because abusive patterns may continue through generations unless someone has the courage to break the cycle.

Verbal thrashing. Even if you don't throw sticks and stones or break any bones, your words can hurt your children. Harsh, degrading, insulting language—"You are so stupid," "I'm disgusted with you," "You little jerk"—burns its way into the memory and emotions of a child. While physical abuse scars the body, verbal abuse scars the mind and heart, and neither is a proper exercise of parental authority. It is important to seek counseling to rein in these verbal beatings and stop the abuse.

Authoritarianism. This rigid micromanagement of childhood behavior stresses pure obedience without any understanding or internalization of principles. There may be times when you need to declare, "Because I'm the mom, that's why!" But demanding knee-jerk submission in every detail of life will wear thin as the years pass. You can probably impose this regime on your children when they are younger, but as they reach adolescence, their rebellion will be a certainty—and probably will be spectacular.

Management by yelling and screaming. Some parents arrive at the mistaken conclusion that their children will respond to them only when they raise their voices in anger. This idea usually develops over time through many repetitions of a scenario in which a parent's direction is ignored by a child—and nothing is done about it. When this pattern is fully developed, a child will have learned to gauge accurately when Mom or Dad is likely to take action.

Typically, after five or six requests or orders have been ignored, the parent's voice becomes more forceful, words are clipped, and the child's middle name is used: "John Patrick Smith, you get into that tub NOW!" The child has calculated that something unpleasant is likely to occur at this point and heads for the bathroom. The parent comes to believe that anger got the desired results, and he or she may resort to it more frequently. In fact, it wasn't the anger, but *action* (or the likelihood of it) that got the child moving.

Eventually, if action doesn't always follow the angry words, a child may learn to ignore even the most intense outbursts. This not only dilutes the effectiveness of all other communication within the family but may lead to a disaster in an emergency. (Imagine a child chasing a ball into the street unaware of the truck bearing down on him and ignoring, as always, his parent yelling at him to stop.)

Idle threats. Many parents attach threats of dire consequences to the orders they give a child: "You'd better not _____, *or else!*" But if the child repeatedly disobeys and *"or else"* never happens, she will learn that a lot of what Mom or Dad says is just hot air. This may escalate to some form of home terrorism; a frustrated parent whose warnings aren't taken seriously may increase the verbal artillery to abusive levels or become enraged to the point of finally making good on some extravagant threat. As with "management by yelling," it is action and conse- quences early in the game, and not threats alone, that motivate children to follow directions.

Laissez-faire parenting: little or no adult input or involvement. This occurs when one or both parents are too busy, overwhelmed, tired, or indifferent to set and enforce consistent limits. A child who is left more or less to his own devices will probably not be very relaxed and happy, but rather quite unsettled, because the boundaries that provide security are missing. Even though most kids push and shove against limits, they will become surprisingly anxious if few or none are present.

Nonstop bribery. Rewards have a definite place in training children, but parents should not haggle or make deals over every direction they give a child—espe- cially those that are not negotiable. It would be quite inappropriate to say, "I'll give you a cookie if you get in your car seat." A child should not become used to the idea that virtue is only worthwhile if there's a prize attached. Moral values eventually need to be internalized, not merely bought and sold.

"Democratic" parenting. One of the great cultural follies of our times is the belief (often expressed with humanitarian fervor) that parents and children should have equal say in all matters and that a mother or father has no right to exert any parental authority over a child. A variation on this theme occurs when a parent is unwilling or unable to override a child's drives and desires, usually out of fear of rejection, an unwillingness to deal with conflict, or the mistaken notion that anything that causes an infant or child to become upset is terribly harmful.

But conflict is inevitable in any long-term human relationship, including the one between parent and child. Misguided attempts to keep a child from experi- encing any unhappiness by routinely giving in to her every desire will ensure that she is miserable and unpleasant. Respect for a child's identity and feelings is im- portant. But someone needs to be in charge while she is growing up, and for ev- eryone's sake, it should not be the child.

Overt permissiveness. This is a more extreme and naive version of democratic parenting; it is assumed that children are born bundled with "virtue software." They are thus seen as innocent little "clean slates" who may even possess moral qualities their elders have lost. According to this misguided viewpoint, while they might be corrupted by a negative environment, children in a nurturing setting do not need correction. Some parents tolerate a great deal of disrespectful and destructive behavior in their young children based on the assumption that they are "getting it out of their system." Unpleasant surprises during late childhood and early adolescence await those who adopt this approach.

Six Basic Principles of Discipline

1. Balance love and limits.

Balance expressions of love—physical affection, kind words, comfort, help—with appropriate boundaries and consequences. Children cannot survive without experiencing consistent and unconditional love. From the first day of life through her journey into adulthood, your child must know that your love is rock solid, the foundation from which she can safely and confidently explore her world. Chapter 1 contained an important statement about a crucial message that your child needs to hear, see, and experience in hundreds of different ways from the moment she is born through the day you release her to live on her own. This message summarizes the essence of unconditional love and bears repeating here:

> You are loved, you are important, and you always will be, no matter what happens. I care enough about you to provide for you, stand with you, coach you, correct you, and even die for you if necessary. My commitment to you is not based on what you do or don't do, how you look, whether your body is perfect or handicapped, or how you perform in school or sports. It is based on the fact that I am your parent and you are my child, a priceless gift that God has loaned to me for a season. Eventually I will release you to live your own life, but while you are growing up, I consider caring for you an assignment of utmost importance.

Children also need, and actually fervently seek, boundaries and ground rules. Expressing love and enforcing limits are not contradictory but intimately related. Allowing a child to have her way without any restraint is not an expression of love. At the other extreme, harsh, rigid, or authoritarian treatment of children, even if it produces apparent model citizens, isn't an appropriate exercise of limit setting either.

2. Parents must assume leadership in the home.

For a variety of reasons—whether the nonstop attention required to rear infants and small children, fatigue, distractions, or one or more strong-willed children at home—it is possible for parents to find themselves struggling simply to maintain order and manage the demands of daily life. After a few or several years, the children may set the family's agenda and even drift into a general disrespect or disregard for the parents' authority. This is an unhealthy state of affairs for three reasons:

- Children lack the wisdom, knowledge, experience, and capabilities to train and nurture themselves.
- Children will not gain the skills and responsibility to live independently as adults without ongoing direction from parents who require that the children learn and do things that don't come naturally.
- Children want to know and will ask in a variety of ways, "Who's in charge here?" If the answer is "I guess I am," the result will be uncontrollable, disruptive, and generally unhappy children.

The critical importance of establishing your right to lead is central to the next two principles.

3. Distinguish among normal behavior, childish irresponsibility, and willful defiance—all of which need your guidance and correction but in different ways.

- The normal explorations of infants and toddlers should be encouraged—but in a manner that is safe for themselves and their surroundings.
- Throughout your child's years at home, you will have to deal with numerous episodes of childish irresponsibility—knocking over the milk, leaving your saw out in the rain, losing her new gloves, forgetting his lunch, not feeding the cat, leaving toys strewn all over the living room.

  These actions need correction, but they usually do not represent a direct challenge to your authority. A steady diet of rewards, consequences, and lots of patience will gradually introduce your child to responsible behavior over a period of several years.

- On specific occasions (with some children, on a regular basis), however, the issue will be willful defiance. This can begin surprisingly early (between fifteen and eighteen months of age), may continue through adolescence, or become relatively rare by the grade-school years.

  Willful defiance takes place when your child (1) knows and clearly understands what you want (or don't want) to happen, (2) is capable of doing what you want, and (3) refuses to do so.

  Whether passive or "in your face," the child's defiance is asking several questions: Do Mom and Dad really mean business? What's going to happen if I don't do what they want? Are they tough enough to make me? Who's really in charge here?

When confronted with such a situation, act clearly and decisively, meeting the challenge head-on. Not only must your child not have his way, but his attitude about what he has done must be turned around as well. When the conflict is over, you should be on the same team once again. You don't need to be harsh or hostile, but you must not back down. If you do not establish your right to lead early in the game (by the age of two or three at the latest), your ability to influence or control your child later on will be seriously compromised.

At times it may be difficult to tell whether your child is being defiant or irresponsible. Did he hear you? Did he understand clearly what you wanted? Can he actually accomplish it? Failing to get straight A's is not defiance. But refusing to shut off the TV and sit down with the books after being told to do so probably is. When dealing with willful defiance, the child's attitude is the central issue. As Dr. James Dobson has noted in a memorable adage, "If he's looking for a fight, don't disappoint him." This doesn't refer to having a literal brawl with your child, of course, but rather to a consistent posture of standing your ground when your authority has been clearly challenged.

4. Accept the fact that conflict between parent and child is inevitable.

Whether dealing with a full-blown showdown or managing a series of minor irritations, it is impossible to avoid conflict with your child at some point. Effective, loving parenting is characterized not by the absence of conflict but by the resolution of conflicts in ways that maintain both your leadership and your child's dignity.

5. Love and concern for the child's best interests must be your final guide.

The effort required to give good discipline is a continuous expression of love, and that love may take you in some unexpected directions. It may lead you to allow a child to suffer some consequences for his irresponsibility, even when you might easily bail him out. If he repeatedly forgets to take his lunch to school, letting him feel hunger for a couple of hours (rather than running the wayward sack over to the school office every day) will change his behavior far more than reminding him sixteen times over the breakfast table. You may both hurt while the consequence is playing out, but the final outcome—a learning experience with long-term benefits—will serve his best interests.

On the other hand, love may also lead you to overlook the specifics of a child's transgression based on his intent. If he makes a mess in the kitchen while trying to fix breakfast for you, the motive of the heart should overshadow whatever has been spilled on the counter and floor. (He can, of course, be asked cheerfully to participate in the cleanup chores—another good learning experience.)

Love will also cause you to examine your own motives as you deal with different child rearing situations. Are you responding harshly to whining because you're tired or overwhelmed? Are you giving in to demands and tantrums from a two-year-old because you were the victim of excessive punishment as a child and don't want to overreact? If you're upset over her messy room, are you concerned about her attitude toward her possessions or what your relatives will think if they see it? If you feel that your motives are unclear and your actions unpredictable, spend some time with an older parent whose child rearing results you respect, or meet with your pastor or a counselor to discuss what has been taking place.

6. Stay on your knees.

If you think you've got parenting wired because your firstborn was a compliant, relentlessly pleasant child, cheer up. You will probably be blessed with a miniature tornado next time around, and whatever you did with Number One won't begin to manage Number Two. Similarly, if you've read books (including this one) and feel you've got the discipline situation figured out and reduced to a formula, brace yourself—something thoroughly humbling will probably cross your path in the near future. There is only one Parent who completely understands all sons and daughters on the face of the earth, and seeking His wisdom on a daily basis should be a priority for all who train and nurture children.

TOP TEN GROUND RULES OF DISCIPLINE

Here are some building blocks, the brick and mortar of the process of training children.

1. Keep your primary goals in mind.

If you plan to take the assignment of training children seriously, it is important to have a firm grip on your basic goals. What are you trying to accomplish? The following, listed in order of increasing sophistication, should be on your child rearing agenda.

Keeping the child safe. Many limits you place on your child, beginning as soon as he can move himself from point A to point B, will be designed to keep him from harm. Early in his explorations he will have no idea whether an object in his world is friend or foe. He should not find out primarily through painful trial and error. As the months and years pass, he should gain an increasingly sophisticated understanding of cause and effect and consequences.

Preventing harm to others.

Preventing damage to property (whether the child's or someone else's).

Teaching respect for those in legitimate positions of authority. This must begin with you, the parent, and later extend to other designated caregivers. Soon after her first birthday, your child will make clear that she wants to know who's in charge here. If you haven't established your authority and your right to lead very early, you will be in for a bumpy ride later on. Establishing your authority does not mean that you need to be harsh, vindictive, or dictatorial. Instead, you are preparing her for the reality that *everyone* at various times of life must submit to someone else.

Eventually a child's respect must encompass teachers, coaches, law-enforcement officers, employers, and so on. Ultimately, she must also learn to recognize God's authority over her life—and understand that this authority is motivated by love and a boundless desire for her (the child's) well-being. Whether you realize it or not, your child's concept of God will be affected to a significant degree by her experiences with you during her years at home.

Teaching internal controls for actions and words. The ability and willingness to delay gratification are not programmed into children, who usually want what they want when they want it, which is *now*. Learning to wait one's turn and to put off the reward until the work is done isn't merely an exercise for toddlers and grade-school children. This training received in childhood has ample application to adult life as well, in arenas as diverse as education (plowing through years of course work to earn a degree), finances (waiting to buy something until one can afford it), and sexuality (delaying the pleasure of intercourse for the wedding night).

Furthermore, what comes "out of the mouths of babes" (as well as older children) often isn't particularly delicate or thoughtful. While not enforcing a repressive notion of children being seen but not heard, one of your most important projects over the years will be teaching your child to engage the mind before putting the tongue in gear.

Teaching basic civility. Manners, politeness, and general decorum are not inborn behaviors in children. Not only should saying please, thank you, and other details of civilized life be taught at an early age and repeated until they become automatic, but as a child passes through the grade-school years, the *attitudes* of respect and selflessness that underlie the habits will become habits as well. Ideally, both the attitudes and the behaviors will be modeled consistently at home—but this does not guarantee that your example will be followed, and specific instruction will usually be necessary.

Preventing negative behavior patterns and more serious long-term consequences. Selfishness, dishonesty, disrespect, poor impulse control, aggression, and destructiveness are annoying and disruptive in a four-year-old. In a fourteen-year-old they can lead to devastating or even lethal outcomes, not only for a teenager but for his family and an ever widening circle of people who must deal with the consequences of his words and actions.

Teaching internalized values. Honesty, responsibility, compassion, perseverance, loyalty, self-discipline, courage, and faith are admirable qualities in a grade-school child. In an adult they lead to a life of productivity and service. People demonstrating these qualities often emerge as leaders in their circles of influence.

2. Discipline should be appropriate for the child's age and capabilities.

A baby under the age of seven months is unable to act in a self-conscious manner or to carry out more than a handful of specific acts. Thus, efforts to make baby "mind" at this age are futile and ill advised. If she cries or wiggles during a diaper change, there is no point in attempting to "discipline" her to do otherwise.

If she develops a world-class episode of colic, she isn't doing it to ruin your day, assert her independence, or challenge your authority. She doesn't feel right, and crying is the only way she can express that discomfort. However, some shaping of behavior (such as reversing day and night sleep patterns by stimulating her during the day) is possible at an early age, as discussed in earlier chapters of the book.

Between a baby's eighth and fifteenth months, some limit setting must begin as a baby becomes more mobile. However, as detailed in chapters 7 and 8, *an intense desire to explore her surroundings is normal, and her fierce determination should not be interpreted as defiance.* She may crawl toward the same plant fifteen times, not because she is trying to take charge, but because it looks terribly interesting, and her memory is very short. The primary methods to utilize at this age are baby-proofing and distraction, which are preferable to a steady diet of No's! from parents and older children.

After fifteen months, episodes of true clashing of wills are likely to begin. She will not only be more mobile but increasingly capable of actions that can be annoying, damaging, or dangerous. Her improving memory prevents distraction from being effective in turning her attention away from the things you want her to avoid. And while she is also capable of understanding simple directions, overt defiance and negativism are also likely to be displayed.

During these months (up to about age three), your expectations for behavior that your child can control should focus on her safety, as well as on preventing her from harming people or damaging the world around her. Specific goals for her should include coming when called, responding to simple directions (such as not touching or manipulating things that are off-limits), and not hitting or biting anyone—including you.

On the other hand, you cannot expect a child this age to sit still for long periods of time (such as in church or at a movie), to be affectionate with someone (a visiting relative, for example) on cue, or to show much interest in formal learning activities. It is futile to force a child this age (or any other) to consume whatever food you have placed before her. Remember that you determine what kinds of food are on the plate; she determines how much she'll eat.

As your child progresses into grade school, your expectations will become more sophisticated, encompassing both moral behavior and increased levels of responsibility. Be careful, however, about imposing consequences upon a child for physical or intellectual shortcomings that are beyond her control (see sidebar).

3. Constantly praise what your child does right.

Praise and positive feedback are a critical cornerstone for training children. The positive things you say to a child should normally outnumber the negative by a wide margin. This may seem difficult when you're dealing with a toddler who is constantly into everything throughout the house or with an adolescent for whom you feel time is running short for corrective action at home. But at both ends of childhood, and in between as well, actively watch for and applaud behaviors that are praiseworthy ("I really liked the way you helped your brother put away his toys"). As part of an effort to "accentuate the positive," let him overhear you when you compliment one of his accomplishments or a virtuous behavior to a friend or relative. The well-worn advice to "praise in public, criticize in private" is particularly applicable to children, who can be profoundly affected by what they hear said about themselves in the presence of others. Remember also that saying complimentary things about his appearance ("I just love your curly hair") may be nice during a cuddle session, but this won't necessarily improve his behavior.

Rewards and special privileges are perfectly appropriate ways to bring about desirable results, especially in situations where you are trying to increase effort or responsible behavior. For example, many parents set up systems in which points are awarded for activities such as getting out of bed on time, keeping a room clean, or taking out the trash. When a certain number of points are accumulated, an appropriate reward (such as a trip to the park or a small toy) is given. A variation on the theme (especially for children with a shorter attention span) involves offering a treat that will begin as soon as one or more tasks are completed. ("When everyone's toys are picked up, the back porch is swept, the animals fed, and dishes put away, we can all go out for frozen yogurt.") Or money may be offered for completing extra work such as weeding the yard. And, yes, it's okay to offer a reasonable premium for a certain number of A's or B's on the report card, especially if this inspires a child to put forth more effort on schoolwork.

Some parents might argue that rewarding children is merely bribing them for things they should do anyway. It's true that you should not use rewards on a

---

BEHAVIORS THAT SHOULD NOT NORMALLY BE SUBJECT TO PUNISHMENT

- *Normal exploratory behavior in infants and toddlers* (as discussed in chapters 7 and 8).
- *Toilet training.* It will happen when she's ready.
- *Bed-wetting.* This is a physiological event that is not under conscious control and will rarely (if ever) respond to rewards or punishment (see *bed-wetting*, Reference).
- *Speech problems.* These need professional assessment, and a lot of work may be needed at home, but delayed or garbled speech is not a character-development issue.
- *Accidents.* An older child can be involved with cleanup, repair, and restitution, especially if carelessness was involved.
- *Irritability and negativity specifically related to illness or extreme fatigue.*
- *Report cards that fall short of perfection.* Children should not be punished for failing to bring home straight A's, but you can set up appropriate ground rules for the effort a child puts forth at home, such

as doing homework before fun and games. If a child's school performance is falling short of her capability, the problem may be a need for more self-discipline, but specific learning problems may be involved as well.

- *Attention deficit/hyperactivity disorder (ADHD) problems.* A child with ADHD may have a great deal of difficulty with impulse control and learning from mistakes, even when she wants to do the right thing. However, among many other things (including perhaps medication), she still needs discipline and training to make progress and survive in the world. Parenting a child with ADHD is an art and a true test of one's patience and stamina. (See *attention deficit/hyperactivity disorder*, Reference.)
- *Performance in sports.* Dropping the ball in center field or failing to make a team shouldn't provoke disciplinary measures at home. In fact, parental support and encouragement at such times are extremely important.

nonstop basis, especially for nonnegotiable behavior such as brushing teeth or coming when called. But few adults go to work every day purely out of the goodness of their heart, and a paycheck is as concrete a reward as anything you might concoct for your child. There is nothing wrong with allowing a child to strive toward tangible goals as long as they are not fostering overt greed or materialism.

4. Limits and expectations must be defined clearly by parents and understood by their children.

For discipline to be effective, especially during the early years, a child needs to know and understand what you want and what will happen if he doesn't comply. By the time he arrives at the preschool years or soon thereafter, he should be able to repeat back to you both the limit and the consequence of breaking it. If he misbehaves but truly appears not to have known that what he did was wrong, an explanation is more appropriate than punishment. (However, if a mess was made or damage done, he should take part in the cleanup and restoration process.)

When discussing consequences, don't make threats that are outright lies ("If you do that again, the police will come and take you away" or "If you don't stop that, the doctor will give you a shot!" A child who has been told that an immunization or any other medical treatment is a punishment is not only misinformed but may come to resent the doctor or nurse as well.) Cooperation during future visits may be jeopardized, and the child might become reluctant to say something about an important symptom for fear of being "punished" by the doctor again. Furthermore, don't issue a warning involving a consequence you are not actually willing to carry out. "If you don't stop arguing, we're going to cancel our trip to the lake!" is either an excessive or an idle threat, especially if the trip has been planned for six months, with reservations and a deposit already mailed. After several grandiose warnings that never come true, your children will catch on and not pay attention to you. But if you're truly willing to blow an entire vacation over an argument in the backseat, you need to reconsider whether your punishment really fits the crime.

How many rules and regulations you actually spell out will depend on your child. He should learn that the basic moral principles you have taught him apply to the world at large and not just to his immediate family. But you may have to make these connections explicit. For example, even if it seems self-evident to you, you may have to make it clear that the statement "Don't take things that don't belong to you" includes what is in the neighbor's garage as well as what is in his sister's toy chest.

As you begin to increase a child's responsibilities at home, your expectations will generally need to become more detailed. It probably won't occur to him to hang his shirts in the closet rather than throw them on the floor, for example, so if you want him to do this (and he's capable), he will need specific directions.

One fundamental expectation deserves special mention: Your child should learn to follow your directions whether or not you decide to give reasons and explanations. If you find yourself haggling and debating with your child every time you ask or tell him to do something, it's time to tighten the reins. Present a plain-spoken declaration of your right to lead ("I'm the parent, you're the child, and what I say goes. Period!"), along with a warning that further arguing will lead to unpleasant consequences.

Remember, however, that while you have the right to expect your child's obedience, you also have the responsibility to lead in a manner that is reasonable and has his best interests at heart. Like adults, children and adolescents care passionately about what is fair, and they become agitated when consequences seem to appear out of thin air. The New Testament warns parents not to exasperate their children, and a steady stream of arbitrary or unjust punishments will not only exasperate them but reap a bitter harvest years later.

You will need to exercise particular wisdom in situations where you really didn't give specific directions, even if you feel they shouldn't have been necessary. He might insist that "Nobody said I couldn't jump off the roof!" and you might feel justified in retorting with equal fervor (as you head for the emergency room to treat his twisted ankle), "You should have known better!" But these frustrating episodes can actually be rich opportunities to teach broad principles (looking before leaping, thinking before acting), which will be more effective than merely generating more detailed rules.

5. Consequences must occur consistently and in a timely manner.

Ideally, your child should respond to any specific direction you give ("Please pick up your toys now") without delay, distraction, or argument. In reality, many parents would faint if their child actually obeyed them right away, without some fussing or complaint. But this goal can be achieved if the following principles are put into action:

When appropriate, give a little advance notice if you intend to interrupt something your child is doing. ("Tyrone, in ten minutes I want you to head upstairs and start your bath. I'll set the buzzer so you'll know when it's time." Or "Monique, when your video is finished, I need you to set the table.") Make sure your directions are understood.

If and when your child doesn't do what you have asked, take action and explain why.
("I see you're still sitting here twenty minutes after I told you to start your bath.
Tyrone, it's very important that you do exactly as I tell you. To help you remember next time, you're going to bed a half hour early tonight." "Monique, I let you finish your video, but you didn't set the table when it was done. I respected what you were doing, but it's very important that you respect me by following my directions. I want you to set the table now, and to help you remember to do what I ask, you're not going to watch any videos for a day.")

You don't have to get angry or raise your voice. You don't have to complain or make threats. Just take appropriate action, making sure that what you do will be meaningful but not harsh and that you will follow through with the action. If Monique shrugs and says she isn't going to watch any videos tomorrow anyway, extend the ban for as many days as needed to get her attention.

Make certain that your response to a child's misbehavior is *timely*. A toddler will not remember what you were upset about an hour ago, and an older child should not be kept in suspense all day waiting for some undefined but worrisome punishment to be delivered.

Be sure to enforce your rules and limits *consistently*. Not only should your children know that you will back up your words with action every time, but they should also know that your response won't waver to any great degree. The same transgression shouldn't bring about a soft reminder one night and a harsh punishment the next. On-again, off-again discipline is confusing, and it generates disobedience and unhealthy fear. In a two-parent family, both parents should strive to dispense consequences in a similar manner. "Wait till your father gets home" is a phrase you should never have to use, because Mom and Dad should deliver the goods with equal conviction.

All of these principles are important because most children become experts at the game called "What happens if . . . ?" They spend a lot of time observing cause and effect and can usually predict with some accuracy when parental action is likely to occur. In many families, the odds depend upon which parent is playing the game, what else is going on, time of day, tone of voice, and numerous other factors. If a child hears a lot of talk about what he should or shouldn't do but little of it is backed up with action, he will probably pay little attention (unless he is extremely sensitive to tone of voice or verbal disapproval alone). The bottom line is that if and when your child challenges your leadership (whether actively or passively), respond with action—calmly, respectfully, quickly, decisively, and consistently.

6. The consequence should be appropriate for the transgression.

In most situations, **words** are all the response you will need. For toddlers and small children, **a disapproving look** and **a tone of voice** that says you mean business will often promptly change behavior or even bring tears and the need for comfort. Remember that what you say should be appropriate for the age-group. For the toddler, simple statements such as "Don't touch the stove," especially when accompanied by physically lifting him away from it, are appropriate. For older children, reaffirming the reasons for your limits is worthwhile as well. And if you make it a point to sound pleasant and relaxed most of the time, your more serious tone of voice will be far more effective when you choose to use it.

Withholding a privilege can be effective from toddlerhood through adolescence. If your toddler bangs a toy against the coffee table despite your clear direction to stop, put the toy away for a while. If you've told your first-grader to put his bike in the garage but it remains on the front lawn all night, a day without it will help remind him next time. If your adolescent has ignored specific instructions about being home by a certain hour, a week without phone or driving privileges can be a meaningful way to get her attention.

Time-out can be useful with toddlers, preschoolers, and early grade-school children, especially when emotions need to cool down. This involves isolating the child in a playpen, in his room, or simply on a chair—without toys or other entertainment—for a specified period of time. Usually one minute of time-out per year of age is appropriate, although if the child hasn't calmed down, more time may be necessary. This approach is usually effective—assuming, of course, that the child is willing to cooperate. If he refuses to stay on the chair or starts trashing his room during a time-out, more direct physical intervention may be necessary.

Restitution is an important principle of discipline that can and should be used, especially with older children and adolescents. If your child makes a mess, he cleans it up. If he causes someone else's property to be damaged or destroyed, whether directly or through passive negligence, he participates in the repair and restoration. He may have to work to repay all or part of the costs involved.

Not all acts of restitution necessarily involve property. If your daughter lies to someone, for example, she should confess to that person. If she has broken a promise or failed to honor a commitment, she will need to apologize to the person(s) involved. These acts of humility are often far more difficult—but also more character building—than enduring any time-out or loss of privilege.

Allowing consequences to play out is a potentially powerful approach to discipline, especially during the school-age years. The basic principle is this: Look at childhood mistakes as learning opportunities, and avoid rushing in to rescue your child from natural consequences (provided, of course, they are merely unpleasant and not potentially dangerous). For example:

- If he leaves his bike on the front lawn and someone steals it, don't replace it immediately. He'll be more careful with the next bicycle he owns.
- If she forgets to bring home her permission slip for the field trip, let her miss it. She won't forget the next time.
- If he plays roughly and carelessly with his new toy and breaks it, don't go straight to the store to buy a new one. Let him mourn the loss and talk with him about taking better care of his possessions in the future.
- If she dawdles every morning and then misses the school bus, let her deal with the fallout from the unexcused absence.

Your motivation should not be anger or spite, and your tone should not be "I told you so," "Now you'll listen to me," or "That'll teach you!" If anything, this process should be painful for you; you should provide emotional support and comfort while you resist the urge to bail him out. Whatever you choose to teach during one of these episodes need not come with a flood of reprimands because he has already felt the sting of wrongdoing.

Why should you and your child endure these unpleasant experiences, especially when it is often within your capability to end them quickly and easily? Because what he learns from an uncomfortable episode as a child may save him from a disastrous or even lethal miscalculation as an adolescent. A child who is allowed to become an expert on consequences will be more likely to think through the outcomes of his actions later on when the stakes are higher. Going without his lunch won't kill him, but getting involved with illegal drugs or premarital sex might. Furthermore, if he is repeatedly spared the consequences of his misbehavior throughout childhood and adolescence, he may never learn self-control or exercise good judgment as an adult.

Physical punishment (specifically, disciplinary spanking) is a tool that can be useful in specific circumstances. However, some voices in our culture condemn all spanking, based on claims that it teaches violence, perpetuates abuse, damages a child's dignity, and doesn't change behavior. These criticisms are valid for abusive forms of corporal punishment such as slapping, kicking, beating, and in cases of spanking when it is used excessively or inappropriately, such as when representing an expression of anger and frustration, causing injury.

But when utilized with appropriate guidelines, spanking can and should be neither abusive nor damaging to a child's physical or emotional well-being. With toddlers and preschoolers, a controlled swat on the behind may be appropriate to bring a confrontation to a timely conclusion. A disciplinary spanking should be administered only in response to an episode of willful defiance characterized by a clear, appropriate parental directive that the child understands and is capable of following; a direct challenge from the child, especially with a disrespectful or hostile tone; or persistent and blatant refusal to cooperate.

In such situations, attempts to reason with a hotly defiant toddler or to "share your feelings" with a disrespectful preschooler are likely to be futile. Allowing a child to call you names, spit at you, throw objects, take a swing at you, or damage your home is inappropriate and unhealthy, does not help him "get it out of his system," and virtually guarantees more of the same destructive and obnoxious behavior in the future. And if the conflict continues to boil or escalate, your anger and frustration may reach a flash point at which hurtful words or actions may result.

Any physical action you take in such circumstances should not be an outpouring of anger or an act of revenge, but rather a tactic to turn your child's behavior around and bring the rebellion to a swift conclusion. A spanking of one to three quick swats should provide a brief, superficial sting to the buttocks or the back of the upper thighs. It should be just hard enough to get the child's attention, bring on some tears, and break through the defiance.

Many parents wonder whether a disciplinary spanking should be administered with a neutral object or with the palm of a hand. One might argue that a child should not experience the touch of a parent's hand as a painful event and that a mother's or father's hands should be used exclusively for holding, caressing, or comforting. Furthermore, if a spanking is administered with a neutral object—a thin flexible switch, for example—a brief time will elapse while it is located, decreasing the likelihood of lashing out impulsively in the heat of the moment.

On the other hand (no pun intended), any object that extends more than a few inches from the hand can gain surprising momentum during a spanking, especially when the wrist is in motion at the same time. Since a neutral object, unlike the hand, cannot "feel" the force of its impact, it may be difficult to know whether a spanking is producing an appropriate superficial sting or much more severe pain.

The bottom line is this: Whether the hand or a neutral object is used in a spanking, it should not cause bruising or other damage to the skin. (You should try your method of choice on your own skin first.) Unfortunately, some misguided or abusive parents utilize fearsome hardware during spankings—razor straps, heavy belts, belt buckles, canes, or worse—that virtually guarantee injury to the child. This type of punishment, as well as face slapping, punching, hair pulling, or any other form of violence, is completely inappropriate and has no place in the rearing of a child.

A disciplinary spanking should be carried out in private, between parent and child (and not in front of the rest of the world or wide-eyed siblings). It must be followed by reconciliation, comforting, reassurance, and simple teaching about how to avoid such an episode in the future. *You should not need to take this course of action more than a few times during your child's life.* Once you have established clearly that you are in charge, many (if not most) defiant episodes can be settled using other measures such as verbal reprimands, time-outs, or restriction of privileges. If you have a particularly strong-willed child, however, more than a few disciplinary spankings may be necessary. But if you find yourself taking this type of action on a daily or weekly basis, you should reevaluate your basic approach to discipline. Perhaps you are taking too harsh a response to childish irresponsibility or not communicating clearly to the child what you expect. Or it is possible that for various reasons your child is not capable of understanding or following your directives. If spankings have become a frequent occurrence in your home, in order to prevent physical, emotional, or even spiritual damage to your child, you should consider seeking alternative approaches and other help from a counselor or pastor who shares your basic values and views on child rearing.

Disciplinary spanking should not be carried out

- if you feel extremely angry, highly stressed, or emotionally unstable;
- if you were abused as a child, unless you have worked through your past hurts (and the issue of corporal punishment of your own children) with a professional counselor;
- if you are not clear about the difference between childish irresponsibility and willful defiance, either in general or in the specific situation at hand;
- if both parents are not in agreement about its appropriate use;
- after a child reaches the age of ten. Disciplinary spanking should occur infrequently after the age of five or six;
- by anyone other than a child's parent, except under specific circumstances (such as a prolonged period of care by another person in the parent's absence) in which explicit permission and ground rules have been laid down.

7. A unified approach to discipline, carried out regardless of who is in charge of a child at any given time, should be a firm parental goal.

If other caregivers are involved in your child's upbringing, they should be brought up to speed on your viewpoint and techniques of training and discipline. If a child's mother and father are divorced, every effort should be made to maintain the same standards in each parent's household. Without such unity, children will learn to play one parent or caregiver against the other ("Mom said no, so let's ask Dad").

An honest disagreement about principles and practices should not be discussed in front of the children. Under no circumstances (except an imminent threat to a child's life or health) should one parent openly contradict or overrule the instructions of the other. This is not only disrespectful, but it also undermines the other parent's authority. If necessary in the heat of the moment, parents should call a time-out and discuss their issues behind closed doors before taking further action.

8. Don't restrict teaching of values to times of confrontation.

In many families, the only time moral principles are discussed is during corrective action resulting from an episode of wrongdoing. But this will tend to leave children with a stunted or even repressive sense of values. Be on the lookout for "teachable moments," those conversations during which you can give your child a broader and deeper understanding of right and wrong. Chapter 10 (pages 385–388) contains a number of helpful suggestions.

9. When appropriate, allow your child to make choices that will give her a growing sense of competence and individuality.

During the preschool years, this can involve simple decisions such as which pajamas she wants to wear or which story she wants to hear at bedtime. As the years pass, the range and significance of the options should increase—which summer camp to attend, which musical instrument to play. The gradual granting of increased independence and responsibility, which is one of the fine arts of parenting, is discussed in more depth in chapter 13.

Don't offer choices or begin haggling over issues for which there should be no negotiating: for example, sitting in the car seat, bathing, visiting the doctor.

10. Remember that children learn a great deal about appropriate behavior from what they see modeled by the adults in their lives.

You can talk about virtues and work diligently to instill values in your children, but like water seeking its own level, their moral sensibilities aren't likely to rise above whatever goes on in front of them at home. At least for the first several years of life, you as a parent are their authority on just about everything. Your words and actions provide hundreds of little vignettes that can teach them about responsibility, kindness, honesty, faith, and perseverance—or the opposite of these virtues. The beginning of wisdom in providing training and discipline for your children is an honest, ongoing appraisal of your own life and values. No matter how busy or tired you might feel, don't shrink from this important and worthwhile process.

Child Abuse and Neglect

In 1960 when the term *battered child syndrome* was first introduced into the medical literature, it was estimated that fewer than 750 children were significantly abused every year in the United States. Fourteen years later, about 60,000 incidents of child abuse were reported. That number soared to 1.1 million in 1980 and to 3.9 million in 1995. Investigation by child-protection agencies substantiated nearly 1 million of these reports. These statistics suggest that about 1.5 percent of children in the United States are abused every year. Of these, more than 1,200 die as a result of their mistreatment. About half of these victims are babies younger than one year of age, and more than 85 percent are younger than five.[1]

This dramatic increase in the number of reported cases of child abuse over the past three decades is partly the result of increased awareness of the problem combined with mandatory reporting requirements for health-care professionals, teachers, and others who work with children. In addition, the breakdown of families, the escalation of violence in many communities, and, most important, the overall deterioration of moral values (including loss of respect for all human life) in our culture undoubtedly play a significant role as well.

There is but one small bit of comfort to be found amidst these alarming statistics and trends: While without question all parents make mistakes and fall short of perfection—including saying or doing things that they later regret and might even apologize for—the vast majority do not repeatedly act in a way that could be considered abusive, and likewise the vast majority of children are not victims of abuse. Unfortunately, however, when mistreatment does occur, the abuser most often is a parent, relative, or someone who has an ongoing relationship with the child. It is uncommon for a child to be harmed by a total stranger.

Without a doubt the most sobering aspect of abuse statistics is that they represent large numbers of individual babies and children—with names, faces, voices, desires, and needs—who have suffered intense and often horrifying pain, usually at the hands of those who should have been nurturing and protecting them. What is equally troubling is the enormous damage that child abuse produces: deep physical and emotional wounds (which may not heal for years, if they ever do), tortured memories, distorted relationships, and the likelihood that history will repeat itself when the abused child grows up and has his or her own children. Those who mistreat children—whether out of ignorance, irresponsibility, uncontrolled emotions, or actual intent and planning—cannot begin to understand the extent of these repercussions.

There are four basic types of child abuse: physical, sexual, and emotional abuse, and neglect. Of the confirmed instances of abuse, roughly 50 percent involve some form of neglect, 30 percent involve physical abuse, and 20 percent involve sexual abuse. Neglect is more readily recognized in children under four years of age, who are unable to provide for their most basic needs. And while physical abuse can occur in children of all ages, life-threatening and fatal injuries are seen more commonly in children under age three. All forms of abuse can occur individually or concomitantly, and emotional abuse can be assumed to exist when any other type of abuse is present.

Physical Abuse

Physical abuse is perhaps the easiest form of abuse to recognize, but its definition varies among doctors, health professionals, parents, and states. Spanking a child one time on the buttocks, for example, when done in a controlled and loving fashion, may be an appropriate form of discipline to one parent but perceived as abuse by another.

Physical abuse often occurs when a parent (or other adult) who is stressed and upset strikes out at a child in anger and frustration. Adults who are at higher risk for this type of behavior include those who

- were abused themselves as children;
- have relationships with other adults (often their spouse) in which physical violence recurs;
- are stressed by financial, employment, or marital problems;
- are isolated from other adults who might provide emotional support, companionship, accountability, or a break in child-care responsibilities;

- have limited knowledge of the normal behavior of infants and children and highly unrealistic expectations of what is required to care for them properly;
- have a limited repertoire of responses when a child is disruptive or disobedient;
- use alcohol and drugs to the extent that their inhibitions are reduced and their judgment is impaired.

In addition, children with the following problems and characteristics are at higher risk of being abused:

- Babies who are irritable or demanding—sensitive to the environment, easily aroused, and slow to calm.
- Premature infants.
- Children with behavioral or learning problems. Attention deficit/hyperactivity disorder (ADHD) may create a particular risk when the child is very hyperactive (see *attention deficit/hyperactivity disorder,* Reference).
- Children with mental retardation.

Physical abuse often results in distinct patterns of injuries that are not typical for everyday childhood accidents. For example, marks or bruises over the back, buttocks, abdomen, or cheeks might indicate abuse because these areas of the body aren't usually injured during normal childhood activity. Skin markings or welts in the shape of a hand, belt, rope, or buckle could be signs of intentional injury. Unusual fractures (especially in infants), bite marks, and symmetrical or patterned burns are often identified in emergency rooms or physicians' offices as possible signs of abuse. Health-care professionals (including doctors and dentists), teachers, and counselors are required by law to report even a remote suspicion of abuse to local child-protection services. While not under legal obligation to do so in most states, neighbors or family members may at times have to consider the difficult decision of bringing their concerns to the attention of the appropriate community agency.

Unfortunately, some accidental bumps and bruises might be mistaken for abuse. For example, toddlers and active children often bang their shins and fall on their foreheads during normal play and may have bruises in those areas. A false accusation of child abuse can be a devastating experience for parents; therefore, adults who care for children in any setting must be knowledgeable about normal patterns of injury versus those inflicted by abuse and not make accusations lightly. On the other hand, it would be more harmful (or even fatal) for a child to experience ongoing physical battering merely because those who were concerned about him were afraid to take appropriate action to protect him.

Remember that it is not the job of the person reporting a suspicion of abuse to be absolutely certain that harm is being inflicted. Uncovering the truth about a child's injuries can be extremely difficult, and those who work in child-protection agencies must often make very tough decisions, weighing the potential risk to the child against the trauma that can result from taking action when in fact no wrongdoing took place. A judicious blend of common sense, compassion for all concerned, and courage to intervene when necessary is required of anyone who must deal with child abuse.

SEXUAL ABUSE

Sexual abuse is so psychologically complex for the victim that its true incidence is difficult to ascertain. Shame and embarrassment heavily shroud this form of abuse, and many victims fail to report it. However, current estimates suggest that as many as 20 percent of children will be sexually abused in some way before they reach adulthood.[2]

It is important to understand that sexual abuse can take a variety of forms. The common denominator is that a child or adolescent is used in some way for the sexual stimulation of another person who is an adult or at least significantly older than the victim or someone who holds power or control over the victim. **Sexual contact** involves any form of physical touch that is intended to provoke sexual arousal of the abuser or the victim. This can include:

- Direct genital contact with the victim, including penetrative intercourse (vaginal, anal, or oral), whether or not overpowering force was used.
- Fondling, rubbing, touching, or manipulating genitals or breasts, including simulated intercourse.
- Kissing or touching clothed or unclothed areas of the victim's body for sexual stimulation or arousal.

Sexual interactions do not involve direct physical touch and may be more difficult for the victim to interpret, but they are no less abusive. These can include:

- Visual interactions in which the perpetrator deliberately watches a naked child or adolescent or exposes the victim to sexual imagery—whether pornographic literature or videos or an exhibition of his or her own

body—to obtain sexual arousal. Very often exposing a child to pornographic material is intended to desensitize the child to more overt sexual
contact.

- Verbal interactions in which inappropriate sexual or suggestive comments
  are made about the child or adolescent, usually in a degrading or seductive manner.
- Psychological interactions in which a child or adolescent becomes a
  confidant in an adult's highly personal or even sexual matters. In such
  cases a child may become a surrogate spouse or partner with whom the
  abuser shares deep and intimate secrets that violate appropriate boundaries between adult and child.

While some of the situations listed above might sound less severe than others, *every form of sexual exploitation is destructive and degrading, an assault on the
body and soul of the victim.* Even in situations where a child or adolescent is se-
duced into apparent compliance with ongoing sexual activity, this is never a vic-
timless crime. The consequences are not only damaging physically—involving at
least pain and at worst injuries and/or exposure to sexually transmitted disease—
but emotionally and spiritually as well. Children who are sexually abused are at
risk later in life for various forms of self-destructive behavior, distorted or impaired long-term relationships (including difficulty with marital commitment
and sexuality), addictions, and overall feelings of shame and worthlessness.

Sexual abuse occurs at all socioeconomic levels. As with physical abuse, instances of sexual abuse involving a total stranger are far less common than those
in which the perpetrator is someone the child knows—in a worst-case scenario,
one of his own parents. Risk factors for the child include the absence of the natural father at home, parental discord, poor relationship with one or both parents,
a parent who was sexually abused as a child, and general lack of supervision.
However, even children who are raised by attentive parents in an intact family
might be victimized by a relative, a neighbor, a caregiver, or an adult in a position of authority over them, such as a camp counselor or a youth leader.

This violation of a child's trust by someone in a close relationship—a person
who is supposed to be looking after his welfare and protecting him from harm—
is extremely damaging to a child's basic understanding of the world. One of the
saddest assignments of parenting is to warn children about the possible risks "out
there" and to help them become streetwise about the dangers they might encounter as they grow up and become more independent. Being sexually abused
by someone who isn't "out there" but who instead is in a child's circle of trusted
family, friends, or acquaintances sends a very powerful message to the abused:

There isn't any place in the world that is safe, and you can't trust anyone. This mind-set is a major mental and emotional handicap, and years of counseling could be required to overcome it.

Children who have been sexually abused can be difficult to identify since most children are too afraid or embarrassed to disclose it. The power of secrecy is profound, particularly when the abuser is a family member. Very often the perpetrator either seduces a child into silence ("This is just our little secret") or threatens the child with emotional or bodily harm if anyone finds out what has happened.

There are several signs of sexual abuse that parents might look for:

- Sexual knowledge or speech that is not appropriate for the child's age (excluding normal bathroom fascination and humor in the early grades).
- Overtly sexual behavior or demonstrations. While children fantasize frequently, the content of normal fantasy does not include adult sexual acts.
- Depression, including suicidal behavior.
- Disturbed sleep and nightmares that are more frequent than usual.
- Refusal or extreme reluctance to go to a particular place or spend time with a particular person.
- Fear of being left alone.
- Physical complaints such as abdominal pain or headaches.
- Vaginal discharge or pain on urination. Recurrent urinary tract infections in girls or boys, while usually *not* indicative of sexual abuse, can occur because of it.

Sexual abuse is so abhorrent for children as well as parents that denial of its existence by either party is not only common but often doggedly persistent. Often mothers fail to recognize it in their daughters. Even when the abuser is not a family member, parents might not believe a child's story or, while acknowledging the abuse, may downplay its effects on the child. One of the most devastating scenarios for a child or adolescent is to be subjected to ongoing abuse because everyone looks the other way instead of coming to his rescue.

In many cases, the accuracy of a younger child's testimony regarding sexual abuse is called into question or even flatly challenged. However, in light of their concrete thinking patterns, it is almost impossible for young children to concoct sexual scenarios about which they should have little or no knowledge unless the events have actually occurred. In fact, since sexual abuse embodies tremendous shame, even children with physical signs of abuse frequently deny its occurrence.

Parents must be strong enough to listen carefully, face the fact that abuse may indeed have occurred, and then support their child or adolescent through its aftermath. This includes the process of physical evaluation (which can be highly threatening and uncomfortable for a child, even in the best of hands), as well as appropriate psychological and spiritual counseling, which will need to extend for months or possibly years to repair the damage.

It is also critical to take appropriate action to protect the child from the perpetrator. Aside from the obvious step of ensuring that the abuser does not have further access to the child, appropriate legal action should be taken. There may, however, be considerable reluctance to put a child through the trauma of interrogation by police, testimony in court, and so forth, especially if the abuser is known to the family. But it is also critical that the child knows that this violation is not going to be ignored or taken lightly. Furthermore, taking action could prevent other children from being victimized by the same perpetrator.

Neglect

Neglect is a more passive but no less devastating form of abuse. *Nearly half of all child-abuse deaths result from neglect.*[3] Caring for infants and children is a time-consuming and labor-intensive responsibility, and some parents (or other caregivers) are unable or unwilling to put forth the effort necessary to carry out this task. In neglect's most severe forms, a child's most basic needs for food, clothing, shelter, and nurturing are not met, resulting in a syndrome known to health-care workers as **failure to thrive.**[4] Infants and children living in such circumstances exhibit diminished subcutaneous fat, poor growth, and inadequate weight gain. While any child could suffer neglect, children are at greatest risk if born to mothers with a history of substance abuse or to those living in situations where parents or other caregivers are overwhelmed by chaotic lifestyles, intense emotional turmoil, and scarce resources. If the neglected child's plight is not discovered so that corrective action can be taken, delays in growth and development—physical, psychological, and spiritual—can have significant long-term repercussions.

Other forms of neglect are no less significant. A child who lives in an unsanitary environment, who is infrequently bathed, or who rarely receives medical care will be at risk for a variety of infections. Lack of adequate supervision, especially for toddlers, puts children in harm's way for injuries related to accidents, contact with hazardous materials, and even trauma inflicted by other children. Indifference to a child's education, while not immediately life-threatening, can seriously hinder his future quality of life.

EMOTIONAL ABUSE AND NEGLECT

Emotional abuse, which accompanies all other forms of abuse, can be difficult to define, since psychological coping mechanisms vary in children. Technically, emotional abuse is any parental behavior that is harmful to the emotional well-being of a child. Verbal attacks and emotional abandonment are perhaps the most common forms of this abuse, leaving a child starving for attention, love, and affirmation. In order to develop and thrive, infants and children need not only physical sustenance and safety but also ongoing emotional nurturing. Such nurturing is not optional but a basic ingredient of well-being. Parents must acknowledge and accept their God-given responsibility for meeting a child's emotional needs for love, security, and affirmation. Failing to satisfy the deep emotional needs of a child could result in psychological instability (manifested as severe anger outbursts and depression), developmental delays and retardation, and physical failure to thrive.

Emotional abuse of children takes various forms:

- **Harsh, degrading language:** "You are such an idiot," "I'm sick of you," "You little jerk," and other insults that can't be printed here burn into the memory and emotions of a child for years, if not for a lifetime. The effect is magnified when these insults are hurled in the presence of other family members. Verbal abuse scars the mind and heart.
- **Inconsistency:** The child never knows whether to expect hugs or harassment from one day (or hour) to the next.
- **Indifference:** One or both parents are too busy, overwhelmed, tired, or disinterested to pay attention to the child, show affection, or set consistent limits.
- **Authoritarianism:** Every detail of a child's behavior is sternly micromanaged, stressing pure obedience in the name of "discipline" or even "raising godly children." Little or no allowance is made for childish mistakes or exploration.
- **Nonstop criticism/unwillingness to give praise or approval:** This is the fraternal twin of authoritarianism, causing a child to believe that whatever he does is never good enough, no matter how hard he tries.

WHAT CAN BE DONE?

The response to any situation in which children are abused or neglected must involve the following components:

The problem must be recognized and acknowledged.

A number of signs and symptoms that might be observed in a child or adolescent who has been abused have been listed earlier in this section. Many of these (such as depression) are not specific for abuse, although they could represent a general response to a traumatic event. A few, such as the presence of a sexually transmitted disease, provide airtight proof that abuse has taken place.

When one or more worrisome findings or behaviors are observed in one's own child—or in certain instances, someone else's—a parent or other responsible adult may have to ask, at an appropriate time, some nonthreatening, open-ended questions: "You've looked kind of sad since the camp-out last weekend. Can we talk about it?" "That's an interesting mark on your tummy—can you tell me how you got it?" "Is there anything that bothers you about going over to Uncle John's and Aunt Mary's?" The response most often will be reasonable, but if it sounds evasive or doesn't ring true, you may need to probe a little more specifically: "Did something happen last weekend that upset you?" "Has anyone touched you in a way that made you feel bad or uncomfortable?"

Attentive and compassionate listening, and not interrogation, is extremely important when such sensitive questions are being raised. Above all, make sure the child understands that you will not become angry with her over what she tells you. *Even more critical is the reassurance that any abuse that has taken place, especially sexual molestation, is not her fault.* Victims of abuse are often burdened with the idea that they were responsible for whatever happened to them, that they are "bad" or "dirty," and that their parents will reject or punish them if they tell what happened.

If in fact you hear some unpleasant or even horrifying details from a child, you will need to remain calm and focus on both comforting her and making her feel safe. Try to avoid venting any strong emotions of your own (especially anger over what has happened) in a way that might bring more discomfort to the child. However, you will want to talk in private with a mature, trustworthy individual in order to process what has happened, pray about it, and make appropriate decisions regarding the next steps to be taken. Even if you are not under legal obligation to report abuse, if you suspect that a child you know is being victimized or neglected, seek input from a trained counselor, your pastor, or the nearest child-protection service.

The child must be protected from further harm.

In some cases, this may require taking the child out of the home, at least temporarily, either because it is clear that she is in immediate danger there or because concerns have been raised that are so serious that her safety must be ensured while the situation is investigated. Such an action can be traumatic for all concerned, even for the child who has been abused at home, but in most cases the ultimate goal of those who must make this type of decision is to keep families together, not break them apart.

If the abusing individual does not live at home, usually it is less difficult—but no less important—to see that the child is protected from further risk. This usually will involve keeping her away from any situations in which abuse may have taken place. Your commitment to her security should be made abundantly clear, especially if any threat has been made by the abuser.

If a child's basic needs are not being met at home, decisions regarding her future must be tailored to the individual family. Obviously, if a neglected child has significant medical problems, dealing with those will be the first order of business. Ideally, multiple resources will be brought to bear on the situation. Perhaps members of the extended family can take care of the child while other individuals or organizations work with the parent(s) to stabilize the home. In many cases, families that are very distressed or barely getting by will derive great benefit from community volunteer groups, including local churches, which can provide more multifaceted support. In a best-case scenario, this would include not only help with material needs but also ongoing interactions with individuals who could teach basic parenting skills, encourage, troubleshoot, and, if needed, exhort the parents toward more constructive and stable lifestyles.

The abuser's behavior must change, and he or she must be prevented from harming anyone else.

Dealing with the person(s) alleged or proven to be abusing a child is a difficult, emotional process, which to a large degree will (and should) be managed by child-protection and law-enforcement personnel. In many cases, physical abuse occurs when someone whose parenting skills are limited and whose personal problems are overwhelming lashes out at a child in the heat of the moment. Very often there was no premeditated intention to do harm, and the primary need is for assistance in resolving problems at home, learning different coping skills, or gaining a new and basic understanding of handling infants and children. Depression, anxiety, or substance-abuse problems might need to be addressed, and ongoing accountability will be critical.

In cases of sexual abuse, the action taken will depend greatly on the circumstances and the age of the perpetrator. A young adolescent who discovered some pornographic material and then acted out his fantasies with a child may be extremely remorseful and more in need of rehabilitation than imprisonment. A career pedophile, on the other hand, is someone from whom society and its children must be protected at all costs.

With rare exception, confronting a perpetrator is extraordinarily difficult, especially if the individual is a relative, family friend, or someone who has been in a position of responsibility and trust. On many occasions raising the issue of abuse will be met with adamant denial on the part of both perpetrator and victim, especially if the child is fearful of repercussions. Parents who have been abusing their children virtually always know that their actions are wrong, but fear of losing their children and shame in facing their own behavior may prevent them from seeking help. Breaking through the denial is necessary for restoration of physical, emotional, and spiritual health. Loving friends or family members who recognize abuse may be able to convince and reassure the parent involved that restorative help is available and critically important.

If you yourself have abused your own or someone else's child(ren) or have had some close calls in which you felt an impulse to harm a child, it is urgently important that you deal with this problem. You will need to broach the subject with a responsible adult to whom you have ongoing accountability, such as your pastor, your physician, or a counselor. The process of acknowledging any wrongdoing to God and to those who have been harmed, owning up to its painful consequences, understanding its origins, and preventing recurrences will not take place overnight. Be prepared for a long and probably difficult process, but also be encouraged by the fact that no one is beyond hope. No matter what has happened, no matter how much pain must be processed, it is possible—one step at a time—to learn to function in a more healthy and loving way. But it is vitally important that you not attempt such a difficult journey alone. If you are confronting and dealing with your own abusive behavior, allow trustworthy people to come alongside you, both for support and accountability.

NOTES
1. C. T. Lung and D. Daro, "Current Trends in Child Abuse Reporting and Fatalities: The Results of the 1995 Annual Fifty-State Survey." Chicago, Ill.: National Committee to Prevent Child Abuse.
2. "American Medical Association Diagnostic and Treatment Guidelines on Child Sexual Abuse," *Archives of Family Medicine* 2 (January 1993): 20.
3. C. T. Lung and D. Daro, "Current Trends."
4. *Failure to thrive* is a term encompassing problems arising from a variety of situations, including but not limited to abuse and neglect.

Sexual Identity in Childhood

In most deliveries, no one can be certain whether to announce "It's a girl!" or "It's a boy!" until *all* of the baby has emerged from the birth canal. Over the next several months, a baby's gender is signaled to the outside world primarily by the way he or she is dressed and possibly by the way the hair is fixed (assuming there is enough to fix). As the toddler becomes a preschooler and then enters the school-age years, indicators of maleness or femaleness begin to encompass more than clothing and hairstyles.

During these early years nearly every parent sends a multitude of messages and cues that suggest, or even explicitly state, what it means to be a boy or a girl. At the same time parents begin to look for behavior patterns that suggest their child has accepted his or her sexual identity. Considerable worry can develop if one or both parents start to wonder whether their child is getting the picture about what it means to be male or female. They may think, *My boy likes to play store and draw pictures all day, and he can't throw a ball three feet—what kind of sissy is he turning into? My girl plays football better than the boys next door and never wants to wear a dress—is she ever going to settle down and become more feminine?* Beneath such questions runs an anxious concern, especially regarding the older child: *Is this behavior an indication that my child is not going to have normal relationships with the opposite sex later in life?* What parents may or may not realize, however, is that what shapes healthy identification with one's sex as male or female is not merely the kind of toys children are given to play with or even specific efforts to direct them toward masculine or feminine pursuits. The process involves a number of factors as well as deeper currents in a child's life.

There is not absolute agreement among child-development experts regarding the factors that establish a child's gender identity and ultimate sexual orientation. This section does not set out to define the subject of homosexuality versus heterosexuality in any comprehensive fashion. But there are certain factors that are fairly easy to recognize and assess, and parents who want to bring up children who have a healthy acceptance of their sex can make some basic additions to their parenting awareness and skills in this area.

Every human is born with what might be called a "father vacuum" and a "mother vacuum"—an explicit need for attention and approval from a loving adult of each sex. If children grow up with an abundance of love (expressed both verbally and physically), positive attention, and discipline from both a father and a mother, they will develop a basic sense of trust, self-worth, and a healthy comfort with their sex. Our sexual identity is established in early childhood, especially between the ages of two and six. Quality time spent with affirming adults of both sexes is particularly crucial for a child during those years.

What happens if one of those vacuums isn't filled? While we may think of a vacuum in terms of a parent's physical absence, many children who develop gender-identity problems have significant male and female adults in their lives, but one or both of those adults are absent emotionally, if not abusive emotionally and/or physically.

Much damage to a child's identity is inflicted by ongoing rejection and criticism from the parent of the same sex. This is particularly true if the negativity focuses harshly on the child's expression of sexual identity.

For example, suppose that Shawn is a physically slight and shy six-year-old in a family where manliness is embodied in contact sports and aggressiveness. He wants to look at books rather than wrestle, draw rather than throw a ball, and dress up his stuffed animals rather than bang his toy trucks into his blocks. His father, who lettered in varsity football and continues to enjoy an informal scrimmage in the vacant lot across the street, envisions throwing passes to a strapping son and daydreams about someday watching him score a key touchdown in the city playoffs. Shawn's younger brother Bret loves rough-and-tumble play and at the age of four already seems to have a head start on athletic skills.

As Dad sizes up his sons, he has a very important decision to make. He could apply a narrow grid of expectations to Shawn and drown him in negativity. He can constantly make fun of the "little girlie" things Shawn likes to do. He could repeatedly compare Shawn unfavorably to Bret: "Why can't you be like your brother?" Dad could withdraw and ignore his older son altogether. In this situation, Shawn's identity as a boy will be challenged and berated. Later in life, there may be an increased risk that he will have difficulty sorting out his sexual impulses, since these will have become mixed with unfulfilled longings for a father he never really knew.

But there is a more positive way for Dad to respond to his son. While still enjoying Bret's budding physical prowess, Dad could also get involved in Shawn's world of books, drawings, and stuffed animals, making it clear to his son that these are also "cool things for guys to do." In this case, Shawn will become secure with the idea that he is definitely male, and at the same time, will not have to spend years of his life seeking masculine love and approval.

This example illustrates a very important principle: *Children should be affirmed as male and female as they are, even if their form of expression doesn't fit whatever their parents might have envisioned as a truly masculine boy or feminine girl.* Even if it requires considerable parental effort and self-control, the child must be protected from relentless criticism, especially about something so sensitive. *This is a particularly important assignment for the parent who is the same sex as the child,* because it is likely that persistent negative or even hostile input from that parent will create a craving for attention and affection from an adult of the same sex. If this intense need eventually finds fulfillment in a same-sex relationship that includes intimate physical contact, a long-term homosexual orientation may develop.

There are limits to unquestioning acceptance of a child's behavior, whether it relates to sexual identity or anything else, and appropriate course corrections may be necessary from time to time. If a boy has decided to see how he might look in a dress and makeup, for example, parents can and should calmly set house rules about attire, just as they do about other everyday activities. If a daughter's interests don't mesh with those of other girls in the neighborhood, she may need help finding some friends with whom she can share common pursuits. If a child's behavior or mannerisms are so eccentric that they alienate or draw fire from others, especially in areas involving sexual identity, it is definitely appropriate to initiate changes to prevent the child from developing an ongoing sense that he or she is different from, and perhaps not accepted by, others. (This painful sense of being marginalized during childhood can play a role in the development of a homosexual identity later in life.) Just as in every other area of shaping and molding a child's behavior, this should be done without browbeating or sarcasm.

Although sexual abuse certainly doesn't lead to a same-sex orientation all or even most of the time, it may contribute to the process. If, for example, a young boy has one or more sexual experiences with an older boy or man, he may derive some physical pleasure from these activities and thus decide early on that he is homosexual. He will probably not understand that sexual response can be automatic and that the presence of physical pleasure does not mean that a certain act establishes his sexual identity. In another scenario, a girl who is sexually abused by one or more men might avoid relationships with males later in life and then eventually turn to other women for emotional and physical intimacy. Sexual (or physical or emotional) abuse that breaks down any child's trust in people of the same *or* opposite sex can have a very damaging impact on that child's understanding of sexuality.

Single parents have reason to be concerned that their children interact during those early, critical years with responsible, loving adults of both sexes. What if a boy who is being reared by a single mother has very little interaction with adult males during the years from age two to six? If his craving for male attention remains unfilled, he may have homosexual temptations as a teen or an adult. His deepest need isn't for sex, but rather to love and be loved by his father. Unfortunately, circumstances and interactions (including sexual molestation) at critical moments in his life could lead to a "sexualizing" of these needs, where their fulfillment becomes associated with intimate physical contact with another male. Or an insecure sense of masculinity might push him toward heterosexual promiscuity as a means of proving himself.

This does not mean that every boy raised by a single mother is destined for turbulence over his sexual expression. In most cases he will receive enough attention from one or more significant males that will help fill the vacuum and secure his identity as a boy during those early, formative years. Among boys raised by single mothers, positive male role models are also very important for their civilizing effects: keeping unruly behavior in check, instilling respect for Mom and others in the family and neighborhood, encouraging consistent efforts at school, and so forth. Developing a deep personal relationship both with God and with mature heterosexual males in the family, at his local church, or elsewhere can help a boy secure not only his identity (including its sexual component) but also his understanding of right and wrong.[1]

What about the more unusual situation of a two- to six-year-old girl who is raised by a single father and who spends very little quality time with a female authority figure? She may have sexual-identity issues similar to those of her male counterpart who is raised without a father figure. Her deep need for female attention to fill the mother vacuum might draw her toward a lesbian relationship later in life or result in multiple heterosexual encounters to overcome a need to prove her femininity to herself. Indeed, if her experiences with men were particularly unsatisfying or even hurtful—a likely possibility if they involved casual sex—this could increase the odds that she *will* find a physically intimate and more fulfilling relationship with a woman.[2]

More extreme cases in which a child has a definite and persistent unwillingness, even intellectually, to accept his or her sexual identity ("I am not a boy; I don't want to be a boy") are uncommon and need formal evaluation by a professional who is qualified to deal with behavioral and identity issues in children. Some of these situations arise when one or both parents have strongly desired a baby of the opposite sex from the one who was born. There is a risk in such situations that the child will be given all sorts of input and cues, some more overt than others, that in essence push him or her toward fulfilling the role of the sex that the parents desired. In extreme situations, a parent may actually bring up and identify the child as a member of the opposite sex—for example, consistently dressing a boy in girl's clothing for at least the first few years of life. While few parents attempt to meet their own needs in such a drastic and inappropriate manner, it is important for parents to recognize and deal with any such longings so that mixed or negative messages about sexual identity are not broadcast to a child—especially during the critical years between ages two and six.

In summary, the development of sexual identity and its later expression is a complex process that can be directed and redirected in a variety of ways. Like so many other aspects of child rearing, there are no simple formulas that can guarantee a healthy outcome in this area. Nevertheless, three principles mentioned in this section bear repeating. In essence they are exhortations to cherish each child as a unique gift from God. Implementing these principles will contribute to a stable sexual identity for your child and greatly benefit his or her general well-being.

Whether brought up in a one- or two-parent home, a child needs loving and affirming attention from both male and female adults. This is particularly important in early childhood (especially between the ages of two and six), but it is never too late for a child, or even an adolescent, to begin fulfilling this need. If his own mother or father cannot carry out this assignment, relatives, friends, or fellow church members should reach out in love to help meet that need.

While allowing for appropriate course corrections, the worth of children should be affirmed based on who the children are, not on what others think they should be.

Parents should be careful not to send messages of rejection if their children don't seem to fit certain expectations of masculinity and femininity.

A child must be fully accepted and cherished as a boy or a girl, as determined by his or her physical sex, even if one or both parents had hoped for a child of the opposite sex.

NOTES
1. In minority communities where a significant percentage of children are raised by single mothers, extended families and church communities often play a prominent role in supplying positive male role models.
2. A healthy relationship between a young child and the parent or a loving adult of the opposite sex is no less important, but in different ways. A two- to six-year-old female with an attentive mother but an absent or emotionally distant father will usually have a normal sexual identity, but she may crave male attention. If the vacuum left from the lack of a father's love (or adequate male substitutes) remains unfilled as she grows up, her desire for emotional intimacy may leave her vulnerable to sexual advances from males in high school. Similar dynamics with regard to sexual identity and relationships with the opposite sex may arise when a boy is raised by an attentive father but an absent or emotionally distant mother.

Two-Year-Olds: Movers and Shakers

*What feeling is so nice as a child's hand
in yours? So small, so soft and warm,
like a kitten huddling in the shelter of
your clasp.*
MARJORIE HOLMES

Two-Year-Olds:
Movers and Shakers

"Give me an army of two-year-olds, and I can conquer the world."
—*Bill Cosby*

Although you have probably heard the phrase "terrible twos" more often than you care to remember, the birthday cake with two candles on it shouldn't create a feeling of impending doom. True, your two-year-old may be working through the negativism of his "first adolescence" in all its defiant glory. Yes, you will have days when he runs headlong away from you when you call him, then later clings to you like Velcro when you want to leave him with a trusted caregiver for an hour. And, yes, your two-year-old is bigger, stronger, and faster than he was six months ago, and he is probably turbocharged with energy much of the day. And, to be sure, if you have a new baby who is starting to be more mobile and is becoming a bigger blip on your two-year-old's radar screen, you can count on some fireworks erupting between them.

But while you have your work cut out for you in many respects, you will also have the privilege of watching some incredible developments in language, thinking, and creativity unfold during this twelve-month period. The transition from infant to child will be completed by the third birthday, and with this transition will come the joy of having more complex interactions and sustained companionship with him.

As has been stressed already (and will be repeated throughout this book), during the next twelve months it is extremely important that your child know how deeply committed you are to him, how much you truly love him, and how secure his home base really is. At the same time, he must also know that you are in charge and that the limits you set down will be enforced consistently. As the year progresses, you will be able to help him understand the reasoning behind a number of the rules you have made, especially those that have to do with his safety. Giving him some whys won't be a sign of weakness; what you say will still go, whether or not he buys your logic. Instead, these explanations will begin to build an internal moral foundation that should become a mighty fortress as the years pass. (This process is described in Special Concerns page 289.)

PHYSICAL DEVELOPMENTS

A weight gain of about four pounds and two-and-a-half to three-and-a-half inches in height can be expected this year. A popular notion holds that your child will have reached half of his adult height by the age of two. While you may get a general idea of his ultimate altitude by doubling his height at twenty-four months, don't start buying his high school wardrobe quite yet. Differences in nutritional and hormonal patterns may hand you a surprise during the teen years, especially if the onset of puberty is either quite early or delayed.

The gradual change in the overall shape of your child's body that began last year will become more obvious. The size of his arms, legs, and upper body will increase much more than his head as he loses the top-heavy proportions of an infant. His posture will become more erect and stable, his abdomen less prominent, and his back straighter. Baby fat will continue to disappear, replaced by more grown-up contours.

His body movements, which are already perpetual, will also become much more sophisticated. By the third birthday he will be able to run, jump, climb up or down stairs while holding your hand or the rail, stand on one foot (if you demonstrate), and do any number of things with his hands while walking. During the course of this year he will discover the pleasure of maneuvering up and down a small slide, kicking a ball, and pedaling a small tricycle.

As his capacity for vigorous activity continues to increase, you will want to find a pleasant and safe outdoor environment where he can discharge some of his boundless energy every day. But whether in your own yard, a greenbelt, or a local park, you must continuously keep track of his activities and explorations and not merely turn him loose without supervision. Indeed, he will be delighted if you join him in whatever tumbling, chasing, or piggyback pursuits he enjoys.

As during his first months of crawling and toddling, his judgment at this age will be no match for his physical capabilities. This is especially true around bodies of water such as spas and swimming pools, which must be securely gated or otherwise inaccessible. *Never* underestimate the ability of your two-year-old to climb onto, into, or under whatever hazardous place he can find.

Along with his full-body activities, his coordination of hand, wrist, and finger movements will also improve. Given a pencil or crayon, he will be happy to scribble at age two and will add circular motions to his artistic repertoire by age three, even attempting to represent some object on the page. Be sure to ask him what it is and be prepared for some wonderful and unique explanations. Write down what he says on the back of his masterpiece, along with the date. After a decade or so passes, these small treasures will spark sweet memories.

Your child will learn to turn the pages of a book one at a time, a skill he will enjoy demonstrating (along with more focused attention) during story time. New abilities with grip and wrist motion will allow him to turn doorknobs and handles, as well as to unscrew lids—and the tops of medicine bottles—by the end of this year. He will also begin to enjoy stacking blocks or even use them to build little structures such as towers or corrals. He will probably derive equal if not greater pleasure out of knocking these creations over, sometimes with wild abandon. Some guidance and ground rules about the proper handling of building blocks and similar toys, including respect for what playmates or siblings may be creating with them, will not only prevent damage from flying objects but also preserve peace in the playroom.

LANGUAGE: A BLOSSOMING OF WORDS

During the next twelve months, you can expect an enormous increase in the number of words your child can speak and understand. You should be aware, however, that normal children will vary significantly in the use of language at this age. Some will seem to pick up new vocabulary day by day, while others may say little for weeks, then surprise you with a complete and quite expressive sentence. As a general estimate, your child will arrive at her second birthday with the ability to use about fifty words, some of which will be connected in two-word sentences ("Doggy jump!"). She will, however, *understand* about three hundred words. By the third birthday, roughly one thousand words will be in her memory bank, and sentences of four to six words (including pronouns such as *I* or *you*) will be forthcoming.

Many parents become unnecessarily concerned about their child's progress in language skills when they compare notes with other parents. Remember that the child who seems to be a walking dictionary is not necessarily more intelligent or gifted than the one who speaks less frequently. Check with your child's health-care provider, however, if her speech seems garbled or unintelligible by two and a half years of age or if she persists in using grunts and gestures rather than words to express her desires. Potential problems such as hearing loss will need to be ruled out, and an assessment by a speech therapist can help clarify whether there is a difficulty with comprehension, expression, or both.

In addition to learning the meanings of hundreds of new words, your child will also begin to pick up other important information about how words are assembled and in what tone of voice they are used. Are your family's conversations calm and laced with respectful and soothing phrases, or do they sound like a cross between a barracks and a back alley? If you don't believe your child is tuned in to your language, wait until she repeats some choice comment she overheard last week—just when the pastor stops by for a visit.

Is your family's vocal volume roughly equal to that of a jet engine? If so, is it because everyone must sound off in order to be heard over the noise of the TV, radio, or CDs blaring in the background? Young children naturally tend to use "outdoor voices" whether they are playing in the backyard or sitting at the dinner table, and most will need to be reminded on more than one occasion to turn down the volume. But such training can be seriously undermined if the opposite is demonstrated every day by everyone else at home.

A more subtle but important aspect of communication with your two-year-old—and with older children as well—may be lost in the day-to-day business of living. Much of your day will be spent taking care of her basic needs, keeping her out of harm's way, and picking up whatever is strewn in her wake. In the process, most of your conversations with her will gravitate toward admonitions: "Don't touch the . . . ," "Watch out for the . . . ," "Get down from the . . . ," "Eat your . . . ," or even "Good girl!"

As necessary as these communications are (especially the positive statements), your child will blossom when you show interest in what *she* is doing or thinking. "Tell me about your cars" or "What do think that bird is trying to do?" or "Look at all these ants on the sidewalk—I wonder where they're going" are the kinds of comments that tell your two-year-old she is interesting and important. As her ability to express herself becomes more sophisticated, her responses to these overtures from you will become some of your most cherished memories. Her mind is a fascinating place, and your genuine interest in what is going on inside of it should be cultivated and exercised from now on.

Sleeping

Two-year-olds generally need nine to thirteen hours of sleep, most of which (eleven hours or thereabouts) occur during the night, with about a two-hour nap at midday. Some will still do best with two shorter naps, while others will regularly fight nap time with a vengeance. How long you continue a daytime sleep routine will depend upon its impact on your child. If he resists but eventually falls asleep for an hour or two, most likely a nap is worth maintaining. Similarly, if he turns into a three-foot-tall tyrant by the end of the day whenever he skips his nap, you should overrule his objections to a siesta. The time to phase out naps—whether this year or later—will arrive when he can regularly make it through the entire day without having a prolonged attitude meltdown.

Your more important assignment will be to maintain a bedtime routine in the face of increasing resistance, which in some children can become impressive. Some of the turbulence you may encounter at bedtime or during the night can arise from the following issues:

It's not his idea. The recurring cry for many two-year-olds will continue to be a heartfelt rendition of Frank Sinatra's theme song "My Way." If the all-important question "Who's in charge here?" has yet to be settled, bedtime can be one of the great battlegrounds in a contest of wills between you and your child. You will certainly want to make sure that bedtime is a calm, relaxing, reassuring time of day and that other concerns are dealt with (see below). But ultimately someone will have to decide when it's bedtime, and it shouldn't be your two-year-old.

Separation anxiety. As independent as he may want to be, he may not feel that he's gotten quite enough time and attention by the end of the day. Or he may be unsettled about being away from you, even in the familiar surroundings of your home. Often this can be resolved by making sure that the bedtime routine isn't rushed, by providing security/comfort objects (a favorite toy or blanket), by playing quiet, soothing music in his room, or by leaving the door to his room open—provided that other sounds in the home won't keep him awake. If he hears the family having noisy fun without him, he will have little interest in lying down and closing his eyes.

Other fears. Your child is reaching an age at which he may become worried about scary sounds he hears, funny shapes in the closet, or darkness itself. A night-light in his room or light from the next room coming through an open doorway is likely to be a necessary fixture at this age and for a number of years to come. Unexpected loud noises, such as a cat fight outside his window, a siren passing nearby, or a booming thunderstorm, may frighten a small child and require some hands-on comforting.

Your two-year-old may also be unsettled about what went on during the day. Noisy arguments between parents are alarming, even when he can't understand their content. A move to new living quarters, a new baby in the house, the first trip to a preschool or day-care facility, or changes in family routines related to one or both parents' job schedules may also rock his sense of security. Ongoing overtures for attention at bedtime may signal a need for more (or more reassuring) attention during the daylight hours.

Night terrors. These unpleasant events, which affect up to 2–4 percent of children (more commonly boys), scare the daylights out of everyone who sees them. During the middle of the night a confused, wild-eyed child will suddenly begin screaming, kicking, thrashing, sweating, moaning, and jabbering incoherently. His heart will be pounding and his breathing rapid—and so will yours. He may climb out of bed, stumble around and injure himself, and if he is older, try to run out of the house. What is especially unsettling during a night terror is that your child won't respond to you or even seem to know you. When you attempt to calm him, he may thrash more violently and try to push you away.

Despite all of the wild activity, children do not actually awaken during a night terror. They are instead having a disordered arousal from deep (non-REM) sleep. (See chapter 5, page 166, for a brief review of REM and non-REM sleep.) The first episode occurs between the ages of two and four years, and other family members may have done the same thing during their toddler years.

Your job during a night terror is to sit tight through the interminable ten to thirty minutes, provide soothing reassurance that you're there and that he's okay, hold him if he'll let you, and most of all prevent him from hurting himself. You may also need to calm down any older children who have been awakened by the commotion and are witnessing this wild event. *Don't leave him alone,* because

---

BEDTIME CASSETTES

An alternative to quiet music at bedtime is a cassette tape of a parent or grandparent singing or reading favorite stories. You can create a "library" of these by turning on a portable recorder while you sing or read to your child. If you capture some of his cooing and comments, these tapes will become precious keep-sakes after he is grown. One drawback: If the cassette player won't reverse itself, your child may become unhappy if he isn't asleep by the end of the tape. Like any routine, if he becomes used to the tapes he may eventually have a difficult time falling asleep without them.

there is a very real risk of injury, and *don't try to wake him up.* He is actually in a state of sleep that does not readily progress to wakefulness, and shaking or speaking forcefully to him ("Wake up! Wake up!") will only compound his (and your) agitation. Furthermore, if you succeed in bringing him to full consciousness, he will be unhappy and irritable and may have difficulty going back to sleep. Instead, if you sit tight and stay cool, you will be surprised at how quickly the night terror ends once it has run its course. Your child will suddenly fall back to sleep, and in the morning he will have no memory of the previous night's uproar. You, on the other hand, may stare at the ceiling for a while as your adrenaline surge calms down.

Your child may have only one night terror, or you may have to endure many episodes before he outgrows them. Identifying a cause may be difficult, although it is possible that a sudden pain, such as a cramp in the abdomen, during the wrong phase of sleep may set off a night terror. In rare cases, night terrors may be frequent enough to require preventive medication prescribed by a physician.

Nightmares. These are different from night terrors in all respects. They are scary dreams, occurring during active (REM) sleep late in the night or very early in the morning. In contrast to the bug-eyed thrashing of the night terror, a child who cries out after a nightmare will be wide-awake, aware, and responsive to your presence and comfort. Instead of the sudden return to sleep that follows a night terror, a nightmare may leave a child unwilling or unable to fall back to sleep.

Whether or not he can tell you about the dream will depend upon his age and vocabulary. Even if he can't fill you in on the details, it's safe to assume that whatever he experienced was frightening and that his need for comfort is genuine. In particular he will need your reassurance that the dream was not real, a difficult concept to grasp at this age. A few moments of prayer can also help impart the idea that Jesus is truly in charge and looking after your child whether he's asleep or awake. Be sure, however, that you are not contributing to the problem by reciting "Now I Lay Me Down to Sleep." This poem's infamous lines "If I should die before I wake, I pray the Lord my soul to take" are not only alarming and inappropriate for children (and adults) but have no basis in Scripture or anywhere else.

How you deal with nightmares will depend on your perception of what is going on. A child who suddenly awakens at 4 A.M. crying and frightened will need conversation and cuddling. When he was younger, you may have worked diligently to end routine nighttime awakenings by holding back on "room service" during the wee hours (see chapter 7, page 239). But after a real nightmare, this approach should be set aside.

Rarely you may find it expedient to let him fall asleep in your bed if he won't calm down any other way. However, if he repeatedly wanders into the family room a half hour after bedtime and calmly announces that he "had a bad dream" or crawls into your bed night after night using "nightmare" as the password, he may be trying to change the bedtime ground rules, and a more businesslike approach will be needed.

Unlike night terrors, nightmares are influenced far more by daytime input. The old adage about turning off the scary movie because "it might give you nightmares" is certainly appropriate for small children, who cannot readily distinguish reality from fantasy. Because television, videotapes, and video games can bring hair-raising images before your toddler's undiscerning eyes, you will need to exercise nonstop vigilance in this area. Even films such as *Pinocchio* or *Snow White,* widely considered to be childhood classics, contain sequences that could definitely scare a toddler.

New sleeping quarters. One of the important transitions most two-year-olds must navigate is the move from crib to "real bed." This will become necessary when the side rail of his crib reaches to less than three-quarters of his standing height (usually at about thirty-six inches), since the risk of scaling the rail and falling out increases after this point. The arrival of a younger sibling may also prompt the move.

The move to a bed can be a happy occasion, an indication that he is a "big boy" and no longer a baby. If he is unhappy about leaving the crib, affirming how grown-up he is may help change his opinion. You may help him gain more enthusiasm for moving to a bed if you let him help pick it out (assuming you are shopping for one) or at least choose fun sheets and pillowcases to adorn his new sleeping quarters.

One potential drawback of a bed is that it allows your toddler to get up and "come calling" if he doesn't want to stay put. A more unsettling possibility is that your toddler may decide to wander around the house—or even go outside—when everyone is asleep. You may be able to limit these nighttime explorations (and certainly prevent accidental falls from bed) by installing a simple safety rail. However, a determined toddler can easily climb around the rail and get out of bed. For this reason, if size and circumstances permit, it may be wise to maintain the crib until he is closer to three years of age and possesses a little more wisdom and training. If you aren't already doing so, keep all doors and windows locked.

Bedtime confrontations

All the factors just described can add up to bedtime confrontations. If your toddler is no longer in a crib, not feeling the least bit sleepy, unhappy about missing out on grown-up company, worried about bad dreams, or in a challenging mood, he may try to get up several times after he's been tucked in. Another drink of water, another trip to the potty if he's toilet trained, curiosity, boredom, interesting aromas from someone's late snack, a "tummy ache," a claim of a "bad dream" (probably bogus if he just went to bed), or anything else he might think of may all be reasons he feels compelled to exit his bed and his room.

As in every other area in which you are shaping your child's behavior, a consistent response—loving but firm—will be necessary. Once he has been through the bedtime routine, any further interactions should be calm, brief, and businesslike. "It's time for bed" should be your monotonous response, and his return to bed should be enforced without any further fun, games, food, or ceremony. The problems come when there's a lot of variation at bedtime, or if one or both parents feel guilty about the kind of interactions they've had with him during the day. But the time to remedy the need for more quality time with your two-year-old shouldn't be at 11 P.M. If you give in and let him fall asleep on the couch or agree to a snack or another story, be prepared for more of the same tomorrow night.

If your two-year-old is a late-night or early-morning explorer, you may need to install a barricade (the same type of folding gate used to keep toddlers off the stairs) across his exit route. Otherwise, you may awaken to find him finger painting on the walls, dumping flour on the floor, or worse—turning on appliances, leaning precariously over the toilet bowl, or perhaps checking out the garage.

Finally, if you have been "cosleeping" with your child, now is a good time to end this practice. When you decide that moving day has arrived, carry out the transition with some advance notice. Talk about how great it is to have "your own bed" or "your own room." If possible, let him help you prepare the new sleeping place. At this age, he most likely would like to have a say in the choice of his bed, if you're buying one, or at least in the decor of the new surroundings—sheets, pillowcases, night-light, or even wallpaper if you feel ambitious. Some parents graduate their toddler to a futon or sleeping bag near their bed and then gradually move it closer to the ultimate destination. And most of all, reassure him that snuggle times aren't over.

You will also need to decide what to do if your toddler occasionally slips into your bed in the middle of the night. If you feel too weary to escort him back to his room or you don't mind the extra sleeper when you're already conked out,

Parental warmth after discipline is essential to demonstrate that it is the behavior— not the child himself—that the parent rejects.

THE NEW DARE TO DISCIPLINE

you may choose not to make this an issue. But if you decide that your bed is off-limits except by special invitation, enforce your policy consistently, no matter how tired you might feel. One approach to consider is designating some special snuggle times—for example, on weekend mornings.

FEEDING: FOODS AND SNACKS

Many of the recommendations about foods and snacks presented in chapter 7 (page 227) apply to your two-year-old as well, and reviewing them now would be a good idea. The variations on the basic themes are as follows:

Offer a few more calories, but not from fat. As was the case a year ago, your two-year-old does not need a huge number of calories to grow and fuel her full-throttle engine. Roughly 1,200 to 1,400 calories per day—which won't seem like much—will do, spread out over three meals and one or two snacks. One change from last year is that fat intake should drop to 30 percent of the total each day rather than 40 percent. In other words, 360 calories out of 1,200 should come from fat.

In order to reduce the amount of fat calories coming from milk, now is the time to switch from whole milk to lower fat (2 percent) or nonfat. She will need about sixteen ounces (one pint) of milk or an equal amount of other dairy products per day for her calcium intake. There is no benefit, by the way, in putting a toddler on a nonfat diet. She still needs at least 25 percent of her total calories to arrive in the form of fats to continue building her central nervous system and other vital structures. Overall, maintain a wide-ranging balance of the four basic food groups, which should duplicate what the rest of the family is eating.

Avoid bringing up a junkaholic or a food hermit. Over the next year and thereafter, your child will be exposed to a whole new world of foods with more sugar, salt, and fat than she should eat on a regular basis. She will probably like at least some of these concoctions, and her inclinations will be supported by clever ads on TV (if you let her watch the tube) and colorful packages at the store. In light of this reality, you will need to avoid two extremes.

First, don't let her sway your food-preparation choices by persistent requests or demands for Chocolate Frosted Gonzo Flakes, Cheddar-Ecstasy Dip Chips, or Super-Zapper Sodas. Stick with the basics when you buy and serve foods, and then stand your ground. On the other hand, don't become a dietary diehard, a purist who won't allow your child to go anywhere that doesn't serve food that is hand-grown, organically fertilized, homemade, unrefined, and 100 percent free of sugar. Your child can't live in a nutritional glass bubble, and it won't kill her if she has a couple of french fries or some birthday cake at a friend's party.

Utensils will be under better control, but not all foods are safe. During this year your child will master the use of both spoon and fork, relieving you completely of the duty of transferring food from her plate to her mouth; she will become adept at using a cup with one hand. However, she still isn't free from the risk of choking on the same foods that were hazardous last year: seeds, nuts, grapes, popcorn, celery, and little hard candies. Hot dogs and carrots should also be off-limits unless cut into bite-size pieces.

Avoid mealtime power struggles. If there is one arena in which a two-year-old has nearly as much autonomy as she would like, it is in eating. If she won't swallow it, you can't make her, and you shouldn't try. There are more important battles to win.

For the next several months you may wonder if your child is getting enough to eat, because often she may refuse to consume foods you place in front of her. But a child at this age may be an eager eater at only one meal a day. If she doesn't take much at lunch, she'll probably make up for it at dinner or the following day. Don't ruin a meal by nagging, bribing, or punishing a toddler who isn't interested in food.

Don't be extorted into preparing a separate toddler meal containing food that is different from everyone else's unless your family favors spicy dishes. Your job is to serve your two-year-old modest servings of wholesome foods that cover the gamut of the major food groups. Your child's job is to decide how much she'll actually eat. If she begins to push you for something else, hold the line. She won't starve.

If you are truly worried about your child's nutritional well-being, write down what she eats for a few days and then take this list to her physician. A check of height and weight and a brief exam will usually clear the air. A child who is in trouble medically usually shows other signs of illness: fever, diarrhea, lethargy, or poor weight gain, for example. A child who "won't eat" but is otherwise very active is most likely getting enough food.

TOILET SKILLS AND PHASING OUT DIAPERS

For many families, seeing a child graduate to a diaper-free lifestyle is as important a milestone as his unassisted first steps across the room. Like walking, toilet skills can't and won't happen until your child is good and ready. But unlike standing up and stepping out, the sequence of steps needed to send urine and stool from child to toilet isn't programmed into a toddler's brain. It needs to be taught by someone—usually one or both parents, although in large families older children sometimes teach the younger quite effectively.

When is it time to start this process? Some kids begin to master toilet skills between eighteen and twenty-four months of age, but it is uncommon for children to be diaper-free during the day by age two. The majority can be trained by thirty-six months, but for some children, daytime control may not be accomplished until the fourth birthday. Staying dry through the night may occur at the same time, but more often (for physiological reasons) dry mornings may not arrive until several months or even years later. Most children will learn to control bladder and bowel at the same time. However, for some, bowel control is easier to achieve, while for others, bowel control may lag several months behind.

Aside from his age, you should be on the lookout for indications that your child is ready to learn bladder and bowel control:

- He demonstrates some awareness that elimination (especially of stool) is going on. When a bowel movement is on its way, he may squat, grunt, grimace, or try to manipulate his diaper. Afterward he may be more insistent about getting cleaned up.
- The time between wet diapers is increasing. This indicates that a specific spinal-cord reflex, which automatically empties an infant's bladder whenever a certain amount of urine accumulates, is now being inhibited by signals from the brain. *No amount of training can speed up this neurological development.*
- He is able to understand and carry out two or three simple commands in sequence.
- He tries to imitate some of the things you do every day. You will want to take advantage of this normal behavior of two-year-olds during the toilet-training process.
- He is not embroiled in negativism. If his favorite word is still *no* and you're still neck deep in a daily struggle with him over who's in charge, this is not the best time to start a venture that requires as much cooperation as using the toilet.

In addition to your two-year-old being ready to learn, you must be ready to teach. While you undoubtedly would have been thrilled to see the last diaper disappear yesterday, be prepared to offer some patient, persistent, but relaxed attention to this project for as long as three to six months. This means that you should *not* be working under time pressure. All too often potty training turns into a do-or-die crash course because one or both parents want their toddler in a preschool or day-care setting where diapers are off-limits. If you feel that somehow time is of the essence and find yourself impatient over your toddler's bathroom progress and exasperated when he has an accident, you may need to take a deep breath and reconsider your priorities.

If patience is not your virtue, you may want to start training later rather than sooner, when your child will have better comprehension, be more cooperative, and have fewer accidents. If you tend to be more laid back, you may be able to try your luck with a younger trainee. You may find it easier to begin when the weather is warmer and there are fewer layers of clothing to worry about.

Once you feel that everyone is ready for the first day of potty school, you can begin a series of steps that will work most of the time. These may be stretched out over a period of several weeks or, for adventurous families with an agreeable toddler, compressed into a few days. Be prepared to adapt, revise, and adjust as you see fit. Above all, make sure you praise every step he takes in the right direction and don't show disappointment, dismay, or anger if he doesn't quite get what you're driving at. Punishment or harsh reprimands are counterproductive in teaching a child to use the toilet and should not be used.

Start talking about the process in an upbeat way. You will need to choose your vocabulary for these conversations with a little caution, since any particularly colorful words you use may be broadcast by your child in public, usually when least expected. Most families manage quite well with terms such as "pee," "peepee," or "tinkle" for urine and "poop" or "poopoo" for stool, with "going potty" designating the process of eliminating either. In most settings these terms won't raise any eyebrows but will communicate a child's needs with reasonable precision.

While you're changing a diaper, mention that soon he won't need diapers anymore and that he'll be using a potty just like Mom and Dad, older siblings, etc. You may want to read a children's book about becoming potty trained (there are a number on the market) if you find it appropriate.

Let him become familiar with the sight of his own potty seat. If you buy one, let him help you pick it out. At the outset, a toddler-sized seat that allows him to push against the floor while having a bowel movement is preferable to one that attaches to the big toilet but requires him to dangle his feet. You can make this item a familiar sight in the bathroom, although for safety reasons, your toddler should not be spending time there by himself if he has just turned two. As an alternative, it can be part of the furniture in his room for a while before he begins to use it.

Invite him to sit on the potty chair. If he's willing, let him take this "test drive" without his pants and diaper on. If he's wary and reluctant, let him sit on it while still dressed. If you don't mind the temporary intrusion on your own bathroom time, you might have him sit on his throne while you sit on yours. For the sake of orienting him to some ground rules for modesty in the family, this part of the process would best be done with the parent of the same gender. Sharing potty time should be skipped if either parent (or the toddler) is uncomfortable with the idea.

A quick story might make the process more interesting to him. After he has done this several times and appears comfortable with it, have him sit on the toilet *without* his pants or diaper on. You don't need to prolong this exercise, but make it pleasant.

Let him see you empty stool from a soiled diaper into the receptacle of his potty chair, while you explain that soon he will let his own "poop" drop in without the diaper. You may want to demonstrate how you flush his product down the toilet— but then again you may not, because your progress may become sidetracked by riddles of the universe ("Where does it go?"), deep concerns, or utter fascination with the loud noise and rushing rapids. Or (believe it or not) toddlers have been known to resist the idea that "part of them" suddenly just disappeared before their wondering eyes.

When you're ready to "go for it," put him in loose pants that are easy to remove (or if you're feeling adventurous and can confine him to floors that are easy to wash, let him go bare). Watch for his telltale signs that a stool is coming 'round the bend, being especially vigilant thirty to sixty minutes after his biggest meal of the day. This takes advantage of the **gastrocolic reflex,** through which the stomach notifies the colon to get things moving because more digested food is on the way.

If you're not getting any obvious signals, place him on his potty every hour or two and encourage him to do his business. Take your time, look relaxed, chitchat, or even read part of a story if you'd like. If he succeeds, give him lots of praise. If he doesn't, don't worry about it—and don't become aggravated if he goes right after you get him off his potty. If he seems completely clueless about the whole project or you find yourself getting increasingly frustrated, go back to diapers for a while and try again later. Usually urine will be released at the same time as stool, so both boys and girls typically learn to pass urine while sitting down. Sometime later, after control is well established, a boy can be shown (usually by Dad or an older brother) how to void while standing up.

Even though he has succeeded several times, you can continue to give him potty prompts during the day: when he gets up, after meals, before naps, on your way out the door, before bedtime—basically every couple of hours throughout the day. As he becomes more adept at this process and you are changing fewer moist or dirty diapers, you can graduate to training pants during the day and eventually during naps as well. If you so desire and both of you are ready, he can move to a kid-sized training seat on the big toilet. When using this equipment, it will be easier for him to push during a bowel movement if you place a small stool under his feet.

Remember to instill some hygienic routines as part of your training program. Little girls should be taught to wipe from front to back for both urine and stool, in order to reduce the risk of bladder infections. Washing hands with soap after using the potty should become a habit. When he uses public facilities, show him what he can and can't touch, and how to use the faucet/soap/paper towels/hand dryers after he has done his business.

Eventually he will use the potty at bedtime and wake up dry the next day, then triumphantly empty his bladder into the potty or big toilet. Give him lots of praise when this happens, but don't be discouraged if history doesn't repeat itself with total consistency.

The time it will take before you can count on dry diapers and then dry sheets every morning will vary enormously among children. For some, a combination of very deep sleep, weak inhibition of the bladder reflex, and other physiological factors will delay nighttime bladder control for years. Getting him up at night to stagger into the bathroom and use the potty in a dead sleep will not hasten the process. *Do not reprimand, humiliate, or punish a child who has trouble in this area because it is completely out of his control.* Not only will such measures fail to bring about the desired results, but they burden a child with needless shame, frustration, and ultimately resentment. Indeed, punishing him for wetting the bed is about as fair as punishing him when it rains outside during the night (see *bedwetting*, Reference).

Toilet troubleshooting

Despite everyone's best intentions, your student in Toilet Training 101 may not follow the curriculum you've set forth. Some possible glitches include the following:

"He just doesn't get it" or "He just isn't interested." He probably isn't ready. Take a deep breath, back off, and don't appear disappointed or angry with him. "That's okay, we'll try the potty again later on" is a lot better than "Aren't you *ever* going to get rid of those diapers?" This is a developmental and physiological issue, not one involving laziness, lack of intelligence, disobedience, or contest of wills. It's important that your child—and you—not feel like a failure over toilet training.

Make sure the problem isn't your own time pressure, perhaps manifested by nonstop nudging about "getting rid of those diapers." You need not worry that he's going to enter first grade in diapers, no matter what the in-laws or neighbors say. However, if you have been working with your child for a few months and you're not getting anywhere or he's reached his third birthday with no control in sight, talk this over with his physician.

"He was doing well for quite a while, but now he's back to wetting or soiling his pants." There are a number of possible causes for bathroom backsliding. Has there been a significant change in his life? A move to a new house or even a new room can rock his boat enough to disrupt the plumbing control. Even more challenging is the arrival of a new baby, who may suddenly become the center of attention. He may have come to the conclusion that doing what the baby does is a good way to recapture adult interest. Take some time with him—perhaps at bedtime or during an outing to get a special treat—to sound him out. Is he worried about something or someone? You may be surprised by his answer, and the time you spend with him might solve the problem.

Another possibility is that he is becoming so engrossed in play (especially with new toys or neighborhood cohorts) that he ignores nature's call until the last second—and then it's too late to get to the toilet. You may need to reinstitute some reminders about using the bathroom throughout the course of the day.

A possibility that is less likely but should not be overlooked is a bladder infection. Because their urine travels a shorter distance from the bladder to the outside world, this type of infection is more common in little girls. Clues that might suggest this problem include vague complaints of discomfort in the lower abdomen, an unusual and unpleasant odor arising from the urine, unexplained fever, or the appearance of urine in the underwear. The classic adult symptoms such as burning, stinging, and the need to void frequently are not commonly expressed by children. If you can't figure out why your toilet-trained child suddenly isn't making the grade, consider having the urine checked at the doctor's office.

Sometimes soiling his pants is a sign that he is constipated, with liquid stool leaking around a solid plug that is stuck in his rectum. Read on.

"He complained that his bowel movements were hurting, and now he won't go at all."
Take some irritation of the anal area, combine with stool that's a little firm, add
a touch of apprehension about all of this toilet business, and you have a recipe
for full-blown toddler constipation. If that last bowel movement was painful, you
can guarantee that he won't be interested in trying again. What may turn this
common scenario into an ordeal is mounting pressure from all directions. He is
getting more uncomfortable, especially after he eats, because the colon is squeezing down on increasingly hard and bulky stool. He is hearing from you that he
needs to sit on the potty and let the "poopoo" out so he'll feel better. He wants to,
but he doesn't, and to top things off, he needs for it to be his idea.

To break the mounting tension, you will want to help the next few stools exit
as painlessly as possible. A little lubricating jelly gently applied to his anal area
two or three times during the day and perhaps some anti-inflammatory ointment prescribed by his doctor (if there is local irritation that needs to be calmed
down) will make the passage of stool less risky for him. You will have to sell him
on the idea, however, before he tries again.

In order to "prime the pump" and start the bowels moving, you might consider letting him use diapers again for a few days, especially if he's a new convert
to using the potty. The diaper may seem a safer place to let the poop come out,
but let him know that he'll be able to use the potty again soon (see *constipation*,
Reference).

**"We know he's ready to use the toilet—in fact, he's done it a few times—but he re-
fuses to cooperate, and we know he's not constipated."** Make sure there aren't any
unexpected reasons for his resistance. You might take him step-by-step through
the motions by playacting with a stuffed animal who "needs to learn to go potty"
and see if he'll talk to you about what the animal is thinking. Perhaps he is worried about falling into the big toilet and being flushed away. Or maybe he saw a
commercial or cartoon in which some creature came out of the toilet. Whatever
it is, don't laugh at him, but calmly separate worry from reality.

If there are indications that "all systems are go" but he won't, and the problem appears to be flat-out balking, you may want to give him a friendly nudge in
the right direction. When he comes to you wanting to have his diaper changed,
for example, take your sweet time before you attend to this chore, and when you
do, make it cool and businesslike. On the other hand, if his diaper has been dry
after a few hours, make a pleasant fuss about it and exclaim how grown-up it
would be to use the potty and not need diapers anymore. It may help to offer a
pleasant incentive (some stickers, new underwear, or an outing he would enjoy,
for example) in exchange for a designated period of daytime potty cooperation.

CARE OF THE TEETH

Between eighteen and thirty months of age, all twenty of the **primary ("baby")** **teeth** (see illustration on page A15) will have arrived. Although they will all be replaced, **secondary (permanent) teeth** (see illustration on page A15) won't appear for a few more years, so primary teeth deserve attention and care. (If a tooth becomes injured, see a dentist immediately. Sometimes it is possible to save damaged teeth.) Their biggest enemy will be decay **(caries),** which affects many children by the age of three. If damage from caries is severe enough to cause the loss of any primary teeth, proper alignment of the permanent teeth may be affected later on.

There are four ways to reduce the likelihood of decay.

Check with your child's health-care provider about the use of fluoride. This decay-retarding substance may already be present in your local water supply, or it may be given in the form of an oral supplement, with or without vitamins. It is important that your child not receive too much fluoride, however, because it can cause discoloration of teeth.

Introduce your child to a dentist who sees children (pedodontist). This should be done no later than the third birthday. Special preventive measures such as topical fluoride treatment or sealants may be recommended, and you can also check about the use of supplemental fluoride.

Your toddler won't be adept at handling a toothbrush, so you will need to do the honors with a soft brush at least once a day, usually at bedtime. To remove any plaque, which can start the process of decay, take enough time to brush both front and back of all the teeth. This process may go more smoothly if the child's head is leaning against you or resting on your lap. If she doesn't like toothpaste, just use water. If you use fluoride-containing toothpaste, do so sparingly, because it is likely that some will be swallowed, and a surprising amount of fluoride can be absorbed this way. A pea-sized amount of toothpaste is all that should be used. There is enough fluoride in a strip of toothpaste covering the length of the bristles to cause eventual discoloration of a child's teeth if a substantial amount is swallowed regularly.

Finally, don't let your toddler become hooked on foods that will provide a playground for destructive bacteria. Gummy candy, dried fruit, toffee, or caramel, which leave residue stuck on teeth for hours, are not only bad for teeth but also present a risk of choking incidents at this age. Keep these items away from your two-year-old.

SAFETY CONCERNS: SPECIAL CAUTIONS FOR YOUR TWO-YEAR-OLD

Your two-year-old is as intensely curious about the world around her as she was last year, but her methods of gathering and processing information are now more sophisticated. At this point she should be moving well beyond random touching, grabbing, banging, and gumming everything in sight. Instead, her efforts will become more focused and purposeful as she spends more time manipulating objects with her mind as well as her hands.

As this year progresses, she will be able to switch toys on and off; put together simple puzzles; and match objects by size, shape, and color. Her expanding memory will allow her to understand both time sequences ("This happens before that") and cause-and-effect relationships ("If I push this, it falls over") and to apply them to new situations. This does not, unfortunately, give you much breathing room for safety concerns, especially at the beginning of this year. While she can understand more sophisticated prohibitions ("Don't chase your ball into the street"), her impulse control and judgment have a long way to grow. She also is unlikely to comprehend the ultimate risks of violating your warnings. To make matters worse, if she's in a limit-challenging mood, she may decide to create a contest over one of your safety rules. Therefore, constant vigilance must be main-

PREVENTING BATH-TIME COMPLICATIONS

Normally you would expect the only result of a bath to be a clean and pleasant-smelling child. However, occasionally bath time may play a role in provoking vaginal irritation and discharge as well as bladder infections in young girls. Irritation at the tip of the urethra—the small tube through which urine passes—may also be a bath-time-related problem in boys. The culprit very often is bubble bath, soap, or shampoo in the bathwater. Some simple preventive maneuvers include the following:

- Avoid bubble baths altogether.
- Keep bath times relatively short—fifteen minutes or less.
- If a child wants to play around in the bath for a

while, let her do so before any soap or shampoo enters the water. As soon as the cleansing/hair washing is done, get her out.
- The genital area is sensitive and should be washed with water alone, not soap.

Remember—if a child is having problems with recurrent urinary tract infections or ongoing vaginal discharge, a thorough medical evaluation should be undertaken. Other measures may be recommended, including emptying the bladder immediately after exiting the tub (if the child is toilet trained) or switching to showers (see *urinary tract care and concerns,* Reference).

tained throughout the next several months and years, with particular attention to the following areas:

Traffic hazards. Because she can run more swiftly and dart into the nearest street, she must be monitored at all times when she is in an area where there are no barriers separating her from traffic.

Harmful substances. Medications must remain completely inaccessible, especially if they happen to be liquid and pleasantly flavored. Not only is she more skillful with the use of her hands, but her pretending games or imitation—new and important behaviors at this age—may include scenarios of playing doctor or taking medicines to get well. Make sure you have a fresh supply of ipecac to use if instructed to do so, in case of an accidental ingestion of medication (see sidebar, page 222).

Car-seat struggles. She may become more vocal in protesting the use of her car seat, or she may actually figure out how to get out of it at some choice moment. Don't give an inch on your insistence that the seat be used for every ride in the car, no matter how short.

Dangerous "grown-up toys." Never underestimate her ingenuity in getting her hands on appliances, tools, or other hardware that she has seen you use. Imitation may come into play here as well.

The bathtub. She is still too young to be left in a bathtub unsupervised. The physical prowess that now makes shallow water seem less hazardous also enables her to turn on the faucet, leading to a possible scalding injury or even an overflowing tub. (Lowering the temperature of your water heater below 120°F will reduce the risk of this type of injury.) She might also decide to see what happens when she jumps up and down in the water—and in so doing, slip and fall.

Water hazards. Nonstop watchfulness is an absolute necessity whenever your two-year-old is near a swimming pool or any other body of water. Curiosity is abundant and caution scarce at this age, and a child can make a beeline toward a body of water in just a few moments while you are distracted with something else. If you have a pool at home, it is essential that a fence with a childproof gate surrounds it. A spa or hot tub must be covered when not in use. If your child is playing in water, she must be observed by a responsible individual—ideally by someone who is in the water with her—*at all times.*

Do not rely on inner tubes, water wings, or other flotation devices to keep your child safe.

Sibling skirmishes. Be on the lookout for impending aggression toward siblings, both older and younger. Whether or not your two-year-old is the one who initiates the conflict, her ability to inflict damage is ever increasing.

Special concerns: imitations and attitudes

One of the fascinating developments of a two-year-old's emerging intellect is the capacity for imitation, role playing, and make-believe. Watch her be a mommy to one of her dolls or pretend to drive her toy car around the carpet or collect some of her animals into a miniature zoo, and you can learn a lot about what she's thinking.

A normal and important component of this phase is imitating parents, especially the one of the same gender. Listen to her give an exhortation to her favorite stuffed animal, and you may hear words, phrases, and even vocal inflections that sound amazingly familiar. You may even see a little mirror of yourself in a young child's stride or in her hand gestures. This imitation is, in fact, normal and healthy—provided, of course, that what your child sees is worth copying. Remember that the little computer is always on, and now the data going into the memory banks isn't just the names of objects around the house. Character traits that are on display at home—whether respect, courtesy, stability, and love, or their opposites—are all being watched and assimilated, no matter who is modeling them.

Parents often wonder whether they should try to influence the type of role playing their child carries out. In bygone generations some might have fussed and fumed, usually in vain, if Johnny played house and Susie pretended to be a train engineer. Today some cultural forces push parents and preschools—with equal fervor and futility—to keep children "gender neutral" in their play roles. In fact, at this age kids will gravitate toward the types of toys and play activities *they* find interesting, no matter what you do. Later on, however, there may be some potential concerns regarding play patterns and sexual identity (see Special Concerns, page 323).

You should monitor more closely the *attitudes* that are being manifested in the pretending. Are you generally seeing and hearing pleasant themes and variations on your family's activities and interests? Or are you noticing some disturbing trends, focusing more on violence and destruction? If you don't like what you're seeing, you may want to take stock of the material to which your two-year-old is exposed.

This is the time to become particularly attentive to the role of television in your child's life, not to mention your own. A year ago your walking baby didn't show much sustained interest in the tube. But two-year-olds can become captivated by the stories and images they see on the flickering screen and by age three can become TV addicts. Furthermore, a huge variation exists in the quality and appropriateness of network and cable programming geared toward children. While you may find material that is nourishing to your child's mind and heart, far too much children's TV is deplorable—violent, occultic, manipulative, dumb, and dumber. As noted earlier in the discussion of nightmares, many classic films for children are far too intense for two- or three-year-olds. Without being paranoid or overly legalistic, now is the time to get a firm grip on what you allow into your home and your child's mind.

SUGGESTIONS FOR TAMING THE TUBE

- Decide what, when, and how long your child will watch TV. Specifically:

    (a) Set definite limits on time and content.

    (b) Monitor what's going on, and be prepared to remove your toddler from the viewing area (or shut the program off) if things are getting too intense.

    (c) Talk to your child about what she just watched. Even a program with elements or a message you don't like can be a teaching springboard if you put your spin on its content. ("That boy didn't speak very nicely to his mom, did he?")
- Be discerning about children's videos. Watch them yourself before showing them to your child. While many worthwhile stories utilize fantasy or supernatural elements, some G-rated cartoons contain messages that may undermine or contradict the spiritual values you cherish and teach at home.
- Be even more discerning about video games. Even though a toddler won't have much luck manipulating the controls, she may watch with rapt attention while the older kids battle monsters, space aliens, or other humans—and she may view some grisly and disturbing images.
- Don't get into the habit of using the TV as an electronic baby-sitter. After a long day it is extremely tempting to park the kids in front of the screen so

you can pick up the clutter, get a meal started, or simply put your feet up for a few minutes. If you need a time-out, put on a specific video you know to be worthwhile or at least search for wholesome children's programming. But don't leave the TV on for hours on end or allow older children to channel surf, because you will lose control of those powerful images and sounds entering the minds of the most important people in your life.
- Ask yourself periodically whether television viewing is replacing conversation in your family. Consider declaring your home a "TV-free zone" one or more evenings every week in order to encourage reading, games, or other activities. Don't allow the TV to become a routine guest (or intruder) at any family meal.
- If you are having trouble controlling the broadcast material coming into your home, consider disconnecting the cable or antenna and relying strictly on videocassettes that you buy and/or rent, choosing material based on quality, age appropriateness, and family-friendly values.
- If TV watching is getting out of control and the tube is exerting far more influence in your family's life than you feel is appropriate, consider as a last resort giving the television a new home for a while—unplugged in the garage.

Social Developments: Interactions
with Other Children

One obvious setting in which you will want to keep track of your two-year-old's playing and pretending is in the company of other children. Remember that as a one-year-old it would have been unusual for your child to engage in interactive play with another toddler her age. They might have played alongside one another, noting any potential threats to their possessions (which for each included everything in the room), but cooperative ventures would have been rare indeed.

As she passes her second birthday and moves toward her third, however, the possibility for more cooperative, interactive play with peers definitely increases. Ideally this will include situations in which she sets the pace ("Let's play with this now . . .") and others in which she follows another child's lead. Whether or not she can strike a healthy balance between leading and following other children will depend, in part, on the flavor of her relationships at home. If she is consistently loved and respected, she will be more likely to feel confident and friendly with other children and content to interact with them in a variety of ways. But if she has received the messages that she isn't worth much and that the world in which she lives is dangerous and unpredictable, she may shy away from dealing with other children or may be easily bullied. In the same way, seeing the adults at home overpowering others with loud voices and threatening actions may inspire her to adopt a similar, aggressive approach to her peers or younger children.

If she believes that she rules the world (or at least everyone who crosses her path), her interactions with peers will probably be stormy, unless the others are willing to play servants while she continues her starring role as Queen of Everything. But when she has learned about meaningful limits and knows that she can't get her way through whining, yelling, hitting, grabbing, or other negative behaviors, she'll be less likely to try these out on other children.

But no matter how flawlessly she has been reared, the virtue of sharing with peers—or anyone else—will probably *not* become part of your child's repertoire until sometime around the third birthday. Sharing is still not an easy concept to grasp at this age for a number of reasons: The inborn, primitive self-centeredness of infancy and toddlerhood doesn't wane easily; patience is in short supply at age two; and it takes a while to grasp the idea that something given up now can be retrieved later.

While you shouldn't let your two-year-old act like a playroom tyrant, you may not see any lightbulbs go on while you give an inspirational message about being unselfish or invoke the famous admonition, "How would *you* feel if someone did that to you?"

When you intervene in a squabble over a toy or book, you can divert the combatants' attention to something else or demonstrate the concept of taking short turns (five minutes or less) by using a little timer: "Jared can have the book until the buzzer goes off, and then Samantha gets to look at it." In this way she can experience sharing (however reluctantly) and even make it a habit of sorts, under your direction. Save your oration about the virtues of sharing until next year, when she can better understand what you're talking about and retain the basic idea.

What about nursery schools and play groups? Don't feel pressured to enroll your child in nursery school to give her an academic "head start." Child-development experts generally agree that formal schooling at this age rarely brings about any long-term educational benefit. Burton L. White, for example, in his classic work The First Three Years of Life notes that "no nursery school curriculum yet devised has been shown to bestow any lasting educational advantage on children, not even superiority in social adjustment."[1] Furthermore, you should also resist any push to start her in a nursery school because "she needs to learn to socialize." Most children won't get much out of structured socializing until at least two and a half years of age, at which time there are two basic reasons to consider this option:

1. If she's ready, your child will probably enjoy it.
2. If you're ready, you'll probably enjoy a short break in your child-care routines during the week.

Under normal circumstances, the foundations for healthy, productive interactions with others will be laid at home, and in low-key, informal play with friends under your supervision. As it is, children at this age tend to play one-on-one rather than in true group activities, and yours can learn how to get along with others quite nicely without attending any structured program for toddlers.

If you and your child are ready and willing to try nursery school/play-group experiences, look ahead to the next chapter (page 385) for suggestions and cautions.

If you are bringing up a young Mozart or a prodigy in some other area, special programs to encourage her skill may be appropriate. But be careful of highly regimented training or undue pressure to perform that can rob her of her childhood.

If your child's physician or a consultant has identified learning problems or delays in development, early intervention may help prepare her for her formal school years. The form this might take, of course, will vary greatly, depending upon the type and severity of the problem, the programs available in your area, and your own resources. Most states have instituted programs to provide special help for children as young as three (or in some locations, during infancy); the professional who counsels you should be able to make an appropriate recommendation.

Dealing with a two-year-old's emotions

Many parents approach this period of their child's life with a mixture of eager expectancy and dread. There's a real person emerging here, and it's exciting to see how he's going to develop. But in reflecting on the nonstop activity and the limit testing that went on during the previous year, you may be less than enthusiastic about the prospect of both perpetual motion and perpetual *e*-motion.

Like the adolescent, the two-year-old is undergoing major changes in his body and mind; he is still learning about the limits of his power and independence, and he tends to *feel* intensely about nearly everything. If he likes something, he can be ecstatic about it. If he loses or breaks it, the world might as well be coming to an end. If some task or toy frustrates him, he may fly into a rage. If he wants something and you won't let him have it, you may be shocked by the intensity of his reaction.

You might be reassured (or dismayed) to know that this is not only common but is, in fact, a warm-up for similar events—with a much bigger child—ten to twelve years from now. Even if you were consistent in contending with his negativism last year and have established a clear understanding that you care deeply about him but you are in charge, you still need to be prepared for some flare-ups. If he is still entrenched in a major power struggle with you as he passes his second birthday, you should make it a top priority to set up your boundaries in love—and concrete.

One of the arts of parenting a two-year-old is finding the right balance in responding to this changing emotional weather. Obviously, when he's cheerful or happily excited, you can for the most part enjoy the moment with him. Your only caution may have to be a reminder to contain his exuberance if it's getting a little rowdy, especially indoors. But when he's upset or you see a storm broiling on the near horizon, you'll have to make some judgment calls about the causes and effects and what course to take. Some examples:

If it's the end of a long, active day and he's becoming increasingly irritable (and irritating), getting him fed and to bed will probably do the most good.

Children are incredibly vulnerable to rejection, ridicule, criticism, and anger at home, and they deserve to grow up in an environment of safety, acceptance, and warmth.

THE NEW DARE TO DISCIPLINE

If he's trying to do something that's beyond him and the frustration is mounting, your job will be to provide a good-natured reality check. If the project looks to you like it's impossible for him—stacking fifteen blocks one upon the other, for example—put it away and tell him "you'll do better with this later." It won't be the last time you offer this advice.

If he's having a hard time getting along with a younger sibling, don't be shocked. If a new baby has arrived, we hope your two-year-old has been well prepared (see chapter 4, page 119). However, don't expect him to buy the idea that "we have so much love for you that we wanted to share it with your baby sister."

A better approach would be to let him know that the new baby *does* need lots of attention, but that as an older child he has some special privileges. Make sure that he gets his own time with each parent without the baby in the vicinity. Otherwise, if he observes that the baby is getting all the adult attention, logic will dictate that he should act like the baby (or act up in general) in order to get some attention of his own. Also avoid constantly sending him messages that say the newcomer is more important ("Be quiet! You'll wake the baby!" or "I can't help you right now—the baby needs me"). Of course, he must be taught what is okay and what isn't in touching or handling a new baby: no poking eyes and ears, shaking, or any rough treatment.

As the novelty wears off and the new baby becomes part of the furniture, she will eventually be of less concern to your two-year-old until she starts crawling, toddling, grabbing his stuff, or even grabbing *him*. It is nearly impossible for a two-year-old to handle this intrusion on his space and possessions without some friction. Plan on several episodes in which you hear yelling and crying from another room, find one or both children in tears, and then have no idea who did what to whom. (Don't always assume that the older has attacked the younger. Some young toddlers can really dish it out to older siblings.) You may have to break up a few skirmishes without justice being served because you won't have enough evidence to arrive at a verdict. Comfort the wounded, separate the combatants, and perhaps remove an object of contention for a while. If consequences are due, be sure they are delivered to the guilty party.

Don't cave in to emotional outbursts that are clearly designed to manipulate you or change a decision you've made. Many young parents have been held hostage by a two-year-old who throws a tantrum in the grocery store when he can't have a cookie or who whines long enough to wear down their resistance. Once you've drawn your line ("We're not buying a toy today"), don't budge, and don't allow requests, begging, or demands to continue. In a firm, calm voice, eyeball-to-eyeball, take your stand: "I've said no and I mean it—don't say anything more about it."

However, as he progresses toward his third birthday, it will give your toddler great satisfaction if you allow him to make some simple decisions. "Do you want the red or the blue shoes today?" "Would you like to visit the park or the pet shop?" Remember that you will be gradually releasing control over to him during the next several years and that giving him appropriate (and not terribly taxing) choices will serve to remind both of you of this reality.

Dealing with a full-blown tantrum. When actually faced with one of these episodes, you will need to determine what works best for you and your child. This will depend to some extent on the cause. If it appears that the blowup has been brought on by factors such as fatigue, hunger, lack of sleep, or perhaps too much stimulation for one day—for example, an outburst at the end of a long afternoon at an amusement park—you should try to not only deal with the spectacle in front of you but also look for ways to cool off what is fueling it. (This may be easier said than done, especially in the heat of the moment.) Depending upon your assessment, calm but firm measures such as getting him to a quiet place or putting him down for a nap may be helpful. If your child's emotional fuse always seems to get short under specific circumstances—perhaps at a certain time of day such as late afternoon or before a meal or at the end of a long car ride—you may want to adjust activities to reduce the likelihood of a repeat performance.

If the tantrum is born out of frustration with a toy or game whose proper use is beyond him, your best bet is to put the offending object away and try to distract your toddler with something else. But if the angry outburst is primarily an attempt to influence you to do something or to change your mind, you must be firm in your resolve to never allow any decision to be altered by a tantrum. If you give an inch, you can plan on many repeat performances.

Whatever is provoking and fueling a tantrum—whether physical factors beyond your child's control, the frustrations and conflicts of toddlerhood, or a deliberate attempt to manipulate the nearest adult—you still have to deal with it. Some have argued that a tantrum needs an audience and that ignoring it will therefore serve to remove fuel from the fire. If the outburst is at home and you can walk away, this approach may work. Make it clear that you will talk to him when he quiets down and not before. A variation on this theme suggests isolating the tantrum thrower in his room until he calms down.

But in some situations, ignoring the tantrum won't be appropriate. If he is sounding off in the church foyer, turning away will prolong a disturbance that is disruptive to others. In this case, bodily removal to a quiet and private area followed by a more direct intervention is appropriate. If he is clearly trying to manipulate or goad you, a judicious swat or two on the behind followed by a calm explanation of how the problem can be avoided in the future will be more likely to bring the incident to a conclusion (see Special Concerns, page 289, for more information on discipline). On the other hand, if he is beside himself, flailing wildly and out of control, containing him in a bear hug, which you won't release until he calms down, may be more appropriate. Whatever action you take, you must not allow the threat or eruption of a tantrum to torpedo your plans, whether in church, a restaurant, the mall, or anywhere else.

Another situation in which you cannot ignore a tantrum thrower is when he is causing damage. You might put him in his room to cool down, but what if he starts kicking the door or smashing the furniture? Or what if he delivers a swift kick to the dog or yanks his sister's hair? Once again, some form of direct intervention will be necessary. Trying to have a rational conversation in such situations is fruitless, negotiating is inappropriate, and asking or pleading for him to stop is disastrous. Protection of people and property and swift action to bring the episode to a close (including administration of consequences) take the highest priority. Discussions should begin only when the child is back under control.

If your two-year-old suddenly seems to be having tantrums more frequently with little or no provocation, consider having his health-care provider take a look at him to rule out a medical problem.

Another less dramatic but equally important form of emotional output is the verbal insult or disrespectful gesture. If you have a disagreement with your two-year-old and he lets fly with a choice comment such as "I hate you!" or "You're a doodoo head," you should not punish him the *first* time. At this age he does not fully grasp the power of language, and it's your job to provide his first lessons. Sit him down, lock eyes with him, and explain clearly why such statements will be off-limits from now on. Let him know that it hurts you if he says he hates you, and that you will not allow him to call you names like "doodoo head" or "dummy." The same should go for sticking out the tongue or other disrespectful gestures aimed in your direction.

Your two-year-old needs to begin learning the ABCs of what is, in fact, a sophisticated skill: how to express anger appropriately. Right now, virtually all of your input on this subject will be focused on what *not* to do—not to hit, bite, kick, throw or destroy things, launch a tantrum, or spew insults. When he is a little older, you can give him a basic but critically important message: *The way to express anger is in words that are not disrespectful to another person.*

It will take him years—perhaps his entire life—to learn not only how to control his impulses (both physical and verbal) when he is upset but also how to say the right words at the right time and in the right way when he needs to vent his anger. For example, he needs to learn that it is appropriate to tell another person that "I'm angry with you" or "I'm angry about what you said/did," rather than use hurtful words such as "I hate you." If this is a problem area in your own life or perhaps in your entire family, by all means get some counseling and go to work on it, because your child will learn far more (for good or ill) from your example than from your admonitions about what he should or shouldn't do.

HEALTH CONCERNS: MEDICAL VISITS

Beginning at age two, routine medical checkups will take place every year. Whether or not your two-year-old will remain calm or combative during the exam will depend on his temperament and his memory. One way to ease his apprehension is to bring a favorite stuffed animal or doll. Not only will this serve as a little piece of familiar landscape in a strange environment, but the doctor or nurse-practitioner may be willing to "examine" the toy along with your child. This will show him what's coming and provide some reassurance as well ("Goofy's heart sounds fine; now let's check yours"). If he wants to sit on your lap for the exam, let him. By next year, he'll probably be eager to climb up on the table by himself.

Remember to be completely straightforward about any shots or other procedures that your child may not like. If something is going to hurt, don't say it won't or your child won't believe you next time. He should know that it's okay to cry but that he needs to hold still. *Never say that the doctor is going to give him a shot if he doesn't behave.* It is vital that your child understand that medical procedures will never be done as a punishment but only because you and the doctor care about him.

PARENTAL MAINTENANCE: FATIGUE, RELATIONSHIPS, AND THE MEANING OF LIFE

This year you will wonder at times why God didn't install roller skates on parents' feet, and you will perhaps wish you could get a transfusion of your child's energy. Indeed, ongoing fatigue is often an unwelcome companion during the eventful years of bringing up young children.

This energy deficit is particularly common among mothers of toddlers. For whether or not she stays at home with her young children, and whether or not she has a supportive husband who shares in the work of child rearing, much of the responsibility for caring and nurturing a young child will tend to fall on Mom. Furthermore, if there is a new baby in the family, Mom will be recuperating from the physical changes of pregnancy and childbirth and, more likely than not, nursing as well. In this case, her need for stamina may seem even more profound.

The following comments about fatigue are therefore directed to mothers. They are, however, in no way intended to overlook the importance of fathers in rearing small children, nor to slight those fathers who are carrying the primary child-care load, whether married or single. We hope they, too, will find this material useful.

Mothers who stay at home with one or more kids under the age of three may find themselves suffering from lack of sleep, lack of adult conversation, and (most important) lack of recognition for the job being done. All of these can sap huge amounts of energy from the most talented, motivated, and dedicated moms.

If you are in this position, you may begin to suspect that the only milestones in your life are those achieved by your children and that you are a fool for staying home while your childless friends are busy earning advanced degrees or accomplishing great things in their glamorous careers.

If you feel that there is no end to your day's work and that life has been reduced to an endless, draining, and monotonous routine, wake up and smell the coffee, because life is *not* passing you by. On the contrary, you are at the center of the action. You are shaping and molding the very core—the attitudes, the faith, the future—of one or more young lives. *Very few careers offer anything resembling this opportunity and none to the depth that is possible as a parent.* Believe it or not, your friends who are navigating the freeways by the dawn's early light may actually envy you.

This is a time to renew your fascination with your child and to remind yourself that you have him on loan for but a few short years. An attitude of deep thanksgiving—even in the midst of toys strewn all over the house, piles of laundry yet to be done, crayon marks on the walls, and little hands frequently pulling at your sleeve—is not only appropriate but invigorating.

While it may seem as if the current responsibilities will last forever, there will in fact be many years ahead to pursue education and career, if that's your calling. Who said that you had to check your mind at the door of the maternity ward or that your reading must forever be limited to *The Runaway Bunny* or *The Cat in the Hat*? There is no law against ongoing learning while children are young, whether through informal study or more formal courses (even one at a time) taken at a local college or other continuing-education resource.

The arrival of your child's second birthday is also an important time to take stock of the parental "state of the union." Is there still a strong sense of teamwork, shared goals, communication, and intimacy? Or are mother and father moving through the months on different tracks, which may be parallel but more likely are diverging? Without taking deliberate steps to maintain your marriage, drift-

SUGGESTIONS FOR FATHERS OF SMALL CHILDREN: HOW TO HELP YOUR WIFE AT HOME

- As demanding as your day may be, never harbor the delusion that rearing children at home isn't real work. If you need convincing, send your wife away on a retreat and take full charge of your child(ren) for a weekend. Note how utterly relieved you feel when she returns.
- When you arrive home after your long, tiring day, remember that your wife has had an equally long, tiring day. She needs, most of all, two things:

    (a) Adult conversation, including expressions of appreciation for what she has been doing.

    (b) An adult pair of hands to pitch in, take charge of one or more children, wrangle dirty diapers or other debris, or begin any other activity that will lighten her load.
- Do not expect to be taken care of like another child in the house. Pick up your own clothes and toys.
- Don't expect much sexual response if your wife is exhausted and you haven't done much to lighten her load during the course of the entire evening. Remember that sex begins in the kitchen—with meaningful conversation, compliments, acts of kindness, and some elbow grease applied to helping reduce her to-do list.
- Get involved in or even take over the process of getting your kids ready for bed. As they get older, you will hear thoughts and questions at bedtime that won't be expressed at any other time of the day. Be ready to listen and be amazed.
- Maintain the habit of a regular date night—a meal (fancy or otherwise), a concert, a walk, whatever your imagination and budget can manage—in which the focus is conversation and companionship. Make it a point to keep your wife current on your day's activities and find out about hers.
- If your hours at work seem to be getting longer, take an honest stock of your attitude. Do you really need to work through dinner every night? Is that trip necessary? Are you listening to the siren song that says your career is a lot more fulfilling than the tasks awaiting you at home? Think again, long and hard, if your hours are gradually turning your wife into a single parent. And if you are going to be later than expected on any given day, be sure to let her know.
- Take her away for a romantic weekend, or even dinner and an overnight stay, at a pleasant location where her daily responsibilities are temporarily suspended. (With planning and creativity, this need not be expensive.) Another worthwhile activity is a marriage-enrichment weekend such as a Family Life conference (1-800-FL Today), which can serve as a therapeutic time-out and an opportunity to renew and deepen your commitment to one another.
- Call her during the day to touch base, offer an encouraging word, or simply say, "I love you."
- Flowers and gifts for no particular reason speak volumes.

ing in different directions is all too easy. Both husband and wife must take part in keeping their marriage fresh and strong.

As important as it is to maintain communication within your marriage, your spouse may not be able to meet all your needs in this area. Regular times of grown-up conversation with other adults of the same gender who share your values can help keep the demands of each day in perspective.

Time-outs for personal refreshment—not just for running errands but for exercise, coffee with a friend, treating yourself to an unscheduled afternoon out, or a time to be alone with God—are both legitimate and necessary. Track down the best baby-sitters in your area and reward them well. If cash is short, consider utilizing a baby-sitting co-op with people you know well, where child care is swapped among several people on a barter system. If you are blessed with loving grandparents nearby, give them the opportunity to spoil the kids for a few hours (or even overnight) while you take a break.

Mothers who work outside of the home, whether single or married, face additional generators of pressure and fatigue. Fulfilling the responsibilities of a job requires that the demands and details of parenting be carried out during fewer hours—often at the end of a workday when a great deal of energy has already been expended. You may feel guilt-ridden over the time you have to be away at work or concerned about the adequacy of your day-care arrangements ("Are they

---

SUGGESTIONS FOR STAY-AT-HOME MOTHERS OF SMALL CHILDREN: HOW TO HELP YOUR HUSBAND FEEL HAPPY TO BE HOME

- Let him know that you're happy to see him. Don't greet him with a laundry list of complaints or "honey-do's" before he has crossed the threshold. Start the evening's agenda with a heartfelt embrace. Give him a few moments to unwind if possible.

- Don't neglect your own grooming and appearance. Like it or not, even the most committed and principled male is still affected by what he sees. A fashion statement isn't necessary, but freshening up before the evening arrives will make more of an impact than you might realize.

- If you are overdue for time alone with your husband, *you* can take the initiative to clear a night, arrange

child care, and make some plans. You don't have to wait for him to get the ball rolling.

- Do you know what's happening at his workplace? He'll be affirmed if you're as interested in his day's events as you would like him to be in yours.

- While you don't want to be faking or participating with teeth firmly gritted, remember that your husband is strongly affirmed by a positive sexual response from you, just as you are by thoughtful gestures from him throughout the day. He will feel loved and honored in his own household when you initiate sex, especially if he realizes that you've had to plan carefully for intimate time with him at the end of a very busy, tiring day.

doing as good a job as I would?"). Worries over income, especially for single moms, may add to the burden.

All these issues might tempt you to abandon reasonable limits that your child(ren) needs or to spend money you don't have to make up for any shortages in your time and attention. Whatever you do, don't allow a child to play the guilt card in order to get his way or con you into buying something for him. *Remember that consistency in expressing love and enforcing reasonable limits is far more valuable to your child in the long run than a lot of material goods.*

If both parents work outside of the home, cooperation, communication, and sharing responsibilities will be even more important. The suggestions already listed for homes in which one parent (usually the mother) is at home definitely apply to you as well, with slight modification.

Single parents have the challenging and important job of being both mother and father to their children and creating an environment for them that is safe and stable. If you are a single parent, you may at times wonder whether you can really carry out all these obligations adequately, especially if hours are long and income is limited. The answer is that you can, especially if you stay with the basics: love and limits for your children, lots of prayer, and a little help from your friends. As mentioned in previous chapters, you should maintain and tap into your support team (family, friends, church groups, crisis pregnancy centers) for ongoing camaraderie, attitude adjustment, troubleshooting, and adult conversation. Maintain a stable attitude with your children, and in future years they will rise up and bless you, marveling at what you accomplished without a mate. (A helpful resource is the magazine *Single Parent Family,* published by Focus on the Family, which deals with all aspects of the challenging undertaking of rearing children as a single mother or father. A subscription can be obtained by calling 1-800 A FAMILY.)

NOTES
1. Burton L. White, Ph.D., *The First Three Years of Life* (New York: Fireside Books/Simon and Schuster, 1995), 342.

Three- and Four-Year-Olds

*If a child is to keep alive
his inborn sense of wonder,
he needs the companionship
of at least one adult who can
share it, rediscovering with him
the joy, excitement, and mystery
of the world we live in.*
RACHEL CARSON

Three- and Four-Year-Olds: Windows of Opportunity

An extraordinary period awaits you during the next several months as baby days and toddlerhood become more distant memories. For a number of reasons, the two years leading to the fifth birthday are a unique and critical period, during which you can shape the entire gamut of your child's attitudes and understanding. Developments in his intellect and speech will enable you to communicate with him in much more sophisticated ways. He will still be intensely curious about the world around him and is now better equipped to learn about it. More important, he will also want to understand how *you* see things both great and small and what is important to you. Whether the topic is animals, trucks, the color of the sky, or the attributes of God, he will be all ears (even though his mouth may seem to be in perpetual motion) and deeply concerned about what you think.

This wide-eyed openness will not last forever. While you will greatly influence his thinking throughout childhood, during the coming months you will have an important window of opportunity to lay foundations that will affect the rest of his life. No one can do this job perfectly; therefore generous doses of humility and much time in prayer are definitely in order for this phase of parenting.

PHYSICAL DEVELOPMENTS

During the next twenty-four months, your child's growth should maintain a steady, if not spectacular, pace. You can expect gains of two and a half to three inches and four to five pounds each year. He will continue his gradual physical transition from toddler to child: More baby fat will disappear, his abdomen will no longer protrude, and arms and legs will slim down to the point of looking almost scrawny. Don't be too concerned if his limbs look a bit delicate, since muscle development will catch up in due time. Indeed, if a chunky look persists well past the third birthday, ask his health-care provider to check how he's doing on the height and weight chart. (By the way, the flat foot you saw when he was a toddler should be developing an arch.)

Your child's medical checkups at ages three and four will probably be rather uneventful, but he shouldn't skip them. Aside from checking growth and developmental milestones and giving a head-to-toe exam, his health-care provider may recommend giving him his DTaP (diphtheria/tetanus/pertussis) and polio vaccinations (boosters) if he has passed his fourth birthday. He will probably also receive his second dose of MMR (measles/mumps/rubella) at age four to six.

The third birthday is a good time to begin recording your child's growth milestones in a way that everyone in the family can follow. A scroll marked with numbers to measure height can be attached to the wall of his room, or you can even make some marks on the back of his door if you're careful not to wash them off or paint over them. You can enlist your child's eager cooperation by making the measuring process a special event twice a year—on each birthday and then six months later. Make sure that his feet are flat on the floor, he is standing straight, and his head isn't tilted up or down. Mark the spot using a ruler or other flat surface that rests across the top of his head and is perpendicular to the surface you're using. As he grows, he will take special pleasure in seeing how much he has changed from year to year.

His walking, running, and jumping movements should become increasingly smooth and will be joined by tiptoeing, hopping, spinning, and standing on one foot. By age four he will also climb up and down stairs without holding a rail or your hand. He will enjoy pedaling a tricycle and throwing a ball, although his ability to catch a ball with any reliability will develop somewhat later. He will, however, be thrilled if he succeeds in snagging any soft object that you gently toss right to him. If you take him to a local park, he will relish his time on small-scale swings, slides, tunnels, climbing gear, and sandboxes.

Although he won't career randomly from one place to another as he did as a toddler, don't be surprised when he decides to charge ahead of you in the park, church, mall—or at the end of the sidewalk. At this age enthusiasm and the desire for independence are far more abundant than are wisdom and judgment.

Keep your eyes peeled and a good grip on your child's hand when you are approaching traffic, near a pool, or walking through a crowd.

You may have to deal with peer pressure for the first time as your child's social skills and interests in other children begin to blossom. A child who normally is cautious about taking risks may suddenly decide he wants to climb on, jump off, or crawl under something that is off-limits—in response to the tempting, teasing, encouragement, or example of other children. As a result, during the coming months you will need to begin teaching your child, in very simple terms, the "why" of your rules, along with the "what and where" (or more often the "what not" and "where not").

At this age it is likely that he will push you a little or even wear you out with "Why . . . ?" questions. This isn't necessarily an attempt to start an argument but more likely a sign of growth and simple curiosity about the "whys" in his world—including your limits and ground rules. Try to use the reason "Because I'm the mom, that's why!" sparingly. You are now building your child's value system, precept upon precept, as well as his ability to link actions with consequences. At this age, he is beginning to understand and is capable of appreciating the reasons for your rules. Take advantage of his openness by explaining them whenever you can.

His accomplishments with hands and fingers over the next two years will please him and you as well. When drawing with a pencil or crayon, he will begin to use a more sophisticated grip, with thumb on one side and fingers on the other, rather than grasping with his fist. Watch for his first wonderful drawing of a person—with arms and legs extending directly from the head. After he turns four, his "people pictures" will begin to include details such as facial features (eyes, nose, ears) and eventually a body to which the arms and legs are attached. When not creating his own images on paper, he may enjoy tracing or reproducing geometric shapes.

Budding three- and four-year-old artists also delight in using brushes, clay, paste, and finger paints—materials that are much more fun for everyone if clothes, furniture, and carpets aren't in jeopardy. Wearing grubby clothes and setting up shop in the yard (or laying down lots of newspapers indoors) is a good idea. Kid-safe, blunt-ended scissors are also a big hit with this age-group, but be sure everyone is clear on what is to be cut and what is to be left alone. Finding your bank statement converted into tiny geometric shapes or little sister's locks shorn can be a jarring experience at the end of a long day. A less messy but surprisingly satisfying activity for many preschoolers is "painting" the front steps or a corner of the back patio using a brush and a can of water.

There are qualities in your special youngster that may not have been seen before. Find them. Cultivate them. And then give God time to make something beautiful in his little life!

PARENTING ISN'T
FOR COWARDS

Whatever arts and crafts your child works with, be sure to relax, enjoy, and, most of all, show interest in what he is producing. Groaning over the messy hands and clothes, trying to "correct" what he creates, or plunging headlong into lessons for the genius-in-the-making are less worthwhile at this age than asking some open-ended questions ("What's happening in the house you drew?"). You'll have plenty of time to get him involved in formal training in later years if he really has a knack for a particular craft.

Your child will also develop new skills manipulating other types of objects: jigsaw puzzles with a few pieces, fasteners and buttons for his own or his toys' clothes, and building blocks, among other things. Meals should generate less cleanup as he becomes more adept at using his fork and spoon. Since some accidents and spills are inevitable, you may want to wait another couple of years before adding glassware to his dining equipment.

FEEDING: SPEAKING OF MEALTIMES . . .

During the coming months, your child will continue to show wide variations in her desire for food. A ravenous appetite one day followed by picking and dawdling sessions the next won't be at all unusual. Just as when she was two, your job will be to provide an appropriate mix of healthy options; her job will be to decide how much of each (within reason) she will consume. If you need a calorie estimate of her needs, figure about forty calories per pound per day. A thirty-five-pound child, for example, will consume about fourteen hundred calories per day, spread over three meals and two snacks. Between 25 and 30 percent of the total should be in the form of fats. Milk should be kept to a maximum of sixteen ounces (one pint) per day. Vitamin supplements are not necessary at this age, but if you have any concerns, check with your doctor.

In the coming months, you will want to pay more attention to patterns of your child's food intake than to the details of what she eats at any particular meal. Specifically, keep the following in mind:

Emphasize variety and freshness. The average North American supermarket contains a dazzling selection of vegetables, fruits, grains, and meats—available in any season. Children should be exposed to this rich diversity at an early age, whether or not they partake of it. In general, fresh foods are more nutritionally intact than frozen items (though not by much), and both fresh and frozen foods are better nutritionally than canned foods. Dishes prepared using raw ingredients are more likely to be more wholesome and economical than prepackaged microwave concoctions—although time pressures for many families have made meals from scratch increasingly uncommon.

Resist the encroachment of sugar, salt, and grease. Your child may be getting the good stuff at home, but advertising and slick packaging are working desperately to woo her taste buds in other directions. A few trips to the local Burger Ecstasy franchise or a bowl of Cocoa Frosted Flakes at a friend's house may create a permanent and demanding customer. At this point, you have control over what lands on her plate, a responsibility and opportunity that will not last long. Do what you can to mold her tastes, and don't let her manipulate you into buying products that aren't nutritional.

Don't allow food to become an accompaniment to a whole gamut of other activities. Eating is a good thing to do when she's hungry or when the family sits down together for a meal. Period. It should not become a cure for boredom, a pacifier for a stubbed toe, or a bribe for doing something you want.

Don't turn meals into power struggles. If you provide a wholesome selection of foods at a meal and she isn't interested, don't fight over it, make it the main subject of conversation, or force her to sit for hours at the table until she eats it. Put her plate in the refrigerator, and take it out again when she's hungry. Don't be badgered into preparing something specifically for her at every meal, and don't allow her to become stuck in a rut of three or four foods that are "the only things she ever eats." She won't starve if you hold your ground.

While busy schedules may rule out formal dining three times a day, at least one meal a day should pull the family around the table at the same time. Dinner is most often the choice, but for many children breakfast is the biggest meal of the day, and socializing at that time may be more productive than at other times. For some families, one or two meals per week—perhaps Saturday breakfast or Sunday dinner after church—serve as the special time everyone can come together. At such times, the atmosphere should be relaxed and inviting. The TV should be off, the phone unplugged if necessary, and the conversation should draw everyone into the event.

A preschooler is old enough to learn some basic table manners: keeping the volume of her voice reasonable, chewing with her mouth closed, saying please and thank you, using a napkin, and waiting until everyone is seated and a blessing is offered before beginning to eat. If she is done with her meal and conversation among the adults is extending beyond her interest and attention span, don't insist that she sit indefinitely. But before she gets up, she should ask to be excused. After she departs, don't let her crawl around under the table with the family pets.

GRADUATE-LEVEL POTTY SKILLS

By the third birthday or soon thereafter, it is likely that your child will be well versed in the basics of using the toilet. If you are still working through this process, review the previous chapter, page 341.

Your next assignment in this area will be to teach the skills necessary for solo trips to the toilet, which will be desirable if preschool is on the horizon and necessary for kindergarten. These skills include:

- Learning how to get clothes and underwear out of the way and then reassembled afterward. Obviously, easy-on, easy-off garments are desirable. Boys at this age are still a little young for zippers, which have a way of getting stuck or (worse) accidentally pinching the penis when zipped up.
- Learning how to wipe clean after a bowel movement. Girls need to be taught to wipe front to back to reduce the risk of moving bacteria from the anus to the opening of the vagina and bladder, where the bacteria can gain access to the bladder and start an infection.
- Learning to finish the job by flushing and then washing hands with soap.
- For little boys, learning to urinate standing up.
- Learning to use rest rooms out of the house. You'll need to give directions during visits to public facilities, pointing out things of interest such as the appropriate gender sign on the restroom door, the flush handle (if it's different from the ones at home), faucets/paper towels/hand dryers, and so on. (Even after these skills are well established, you should continue to escort your child on any trip to a public rest room. At this age he is by no means ready to handle a chance encounter with someone whose behavior might be inappropriate or abusive.)

Your child may not be waking up dry in the morning at this point. In fact, by the age of five, at least 10 percent of children occasionally or regularly wet the bed. For some children this problem persists for years, and often in such cases there is a family history of this problem. *Rewards, (or worse) reprimands, humiliation, and punishment have no place in dealing with bed-wetting because the problem is one of physiological maturity and is completely out of a child's control.* The best solution in nearly all cases is patience, continued use of diapers or training pants to contain the nocturnal flood, a lot of reassurance, and a few more birthdays (see *bed-wetting,* Reference).

If your child has been dry through the night for a number of months and then begins to lose bladder control, a physical problem such as a bladder infection or an emotional upheaval such as a move or a new sibling might be the cause. A visit to the doctor would be a good idea if this occurs.

Private Parts and Decent Exposure

During or before toddler days, your child undoubtedly discovered that touching the genital area felt good, and you may have been dismayed to see little hands exploring inside the diaper zone (whether clean or otherwise) on a number of occasions. This type of exploration is common and quite normal in young children, as is an ongoing curiosity about body parts. Questions about where they (or their siblings) came from are part of the same package. When it comes to dealing with such sensitive areas and topics, you have a number of important assignments:

Make it clear that *you* are the prime source of information about these matters—and not the kid next door or some other unreliable source. Be levelheaded, honest, calm, and straightforward when you name body parts and explain what they do. Using actual terms *(penis* and *vagina)* and not more colorful vocabulary may save some embarrassment later on if your child happens to make a public pronouncement. This information by itself doesn't jeopardize your child's innocence.

Instill respect for the body your child has been given, the Creator who made it, and the functions it performs. This means that you should not communicate a sense of shame or repulsion about any part of your child's (or your own) anatomy. It also means that you need to teach what, where, when, and how it is appropriate to touch or talk about these areas.

Your child needs to know that these are things to discuss at home with Mom and/or Dad and not with other kids in the neighborhood. If you discover him and a playmate checking out each other's pelvic area, don't panic. This is also normal curiosity at work, and he just needs a brushup on the ground rules. Remind him that these areas of his body are just for himself, his parents, and his doctor to see, and not other people. Tell your child that if someone else tries to touch those areas, he should protest noisily, get away, and tell you as soon as possible. He must know that you will not be angry or upset with him if this should happen.

If a child makes comments, gestures, or body movements that suggest exposure to or experience with sexual activity, further evaluation will be needed.

Other signs of potential sexual abuse include age-inappropriate sexual behavior or demonstrations, depression, disturbed sleep, fear of being left alone, or pain on urination (see Special Concerns, page 314, for more information on sexual abuse). You will need to review what you have seen and heard with your physician, who will investigate and/or refer you to an appropriate professional for further evaluation.

Release information on a need-to-know basis. Your child does not need to hear everything about reproduction in one sitting and will be overwhelmed (or bored) if you try to explain too much at once.

Respond forthrightly with a minimum of fluster when your child cuts loose with offensive language that he didn't hear from you. Our culture is flooded with off-color messages and images that degrade the beauty and wonder of sexuality, and you will not be able to keep your child completely insulated from such negative input. As a result, your child may pick up some R-rated expressions in the neighborhood, even at this young age. (Be sure, by the way, that what you say or the language you allow in your home isn't in any way inspiring this unpleasant verbiage.)

If this occurs, stay calm. It is unlikely that he even understands what he just said, as a simple quiz ("Do you know what that means?") will often confirm. He is far more likely to be interested in the power of words to create a stir than in actually expressing some specific sexual or crude sentiment. Without sounding alarmed or flustered, explain that the words he just used are not ones that you use in your family and that he needs to stop saying them in your home or anywhere else. You should emphasize that such words and expressions put down other people and can make them feel upset or even afraid.

If your child's new expressions include casual or inappropriate use of the words *God* or *Jesus,* a simple explanation about the importance of respecting those names will be needed as well.

Once you have stated your case, be sure to take appropriate action if you hear a repeat performance. If he persists after one or two reminders, let him know that a consequence will follow next time and then carry it out if needed. If your child begins using harsh or obscene language, you need to not only retrain his vocabulary quickly and decisively but also have a frank conversation with whomever you determine to be the source.

Sleeping Routines and Monster Patrol

Most three- and four-year-olds will sleep about twelve hours each night. A day-time nap may continue to be part of your child's routine, but don't be surprised when it is phased out during the next several months. If you are struggling with your child over bedtime, read again the section on sleep in the previous chapter (page 335). This is also a good time to review the management of nightmares (and their less common counterparts, night terrors) described in that same section.

Remember that bedtime should be early because your child needs the sleep and you need time with other children, your spouse, or yourself. During the middle of summer, this can be a challenge. The sun may still be shining, and all sorts of activity may still be going on outside at what is normally bedtime. You will need to decide how much to bend your routines to match the seasons, or perhaps invest in heavy window shades if you need to darken your child's room at this time of year. You may also need to exercise sensible flexibility to accommodate family work schedules.

The activities that surround getting tucked in should become a familiar and quieting routine. At this age, bedtime can be a delightful, enlightening experience. You can introduce your child to some wonderful stories, including books with several chapters that can create eager anticipation for the next night's installment ("I wonder what's going to happen to Pooh and Piglet tonight. Better get ready for bed so we can find out!"). Your child's desire to keep the lights on and you in the room as long as possible will usually cause her to be remarkably transparent and receptive.

Expect to hear some of her private thoughts or to tackle some riddles of the universe ("Are there cats in heaven?" "Where did the sun go?"). Without being manipulated *too* much, allow enough slack in your day so you can relax during these wide-eyed sessions. You will probably have many more opportunities at bedtime to talk about God and the values you care about than during family devotions or even at church, Sunday school, or other formal religious teaching sessions. The lyrics of the following song illustrate the importance of spending quality time with your child:

TAKE THE TIME
It's nine-fifteen, and bedtime took too long, once again—
Another drink, another glass of water, and then
The questions come, the hands hold tight, and the eyes are opened wide,
And something in me whispers, "Now's the time."

"Mommy, why did Muffy die? Daddy, where's the sun?"
"Are there cats in heaven? And why did Jesus come?"
And though a whole day's dishes wait, and bills are piled high,
Something in me whispers, "Take the time."

Take the time, while they're right here by your side,
Take the time, while their arms are opened wide.
Teach them how to love the Lord with all their heart and mind.
Oh, they're only home a season, take the time.

Riding off to Narnia upon a lion's back,
Chubby fingers close the book and add it to the stack.
"Aslan didn't kill the witch—oh Dad, why did he die?"
And something in me whispers, "Now's the time."

Her baseball game's tomorrow, but so's my interview.
How can I play Scrabble, when there's so much to do?
Little faces plead with me to put my work aside,
And something in me whispers, "Take the time."

Take the time, while they're right here by your side,
Take the time, while their arms are opened wide.
Teach them how to love the Lord with all their heart and mind.
Oh, they're only home a season, take the time.

For one day they'll want to spend time alone.
One day they'll need to be on their own.
Next week their hugs may not seem quite the same—
Oh Lord, may they honor Your name.

It's nine-fifteen, and bedtime took too long, once again—
Another drink, another glass of water, and then
The questions come, the hands hold tight, and the eyes are opened wide,
And something in me whispers, "Now's the time."

Take the time, while they're right here by your side,
Take the time, while their arms are opened wide.
Teach them how to love the Lord with all their heart and mind.
Oh, they're only home a season, take the time.
—*1985, Paul and Teri Reisser*

You will also need to deal with some childhood fears when it's time to tuck in. Monsters in the closet, under the bed, or outside the window may need to be banished. Be sure to ask what your child has in mind—is the creature something from a book or video, or perhaps a tall tale spun by an insensitive adolescent next door? Are we talking about space aliens, Brothers Grimm concoctions, or something from the nightly news that is in fact a reality somewhere in the world or the community? Are there tensions at home creating a need for reassurance?

Very often the beast in question doesn't exist except in someone's imagination. In this case it can be tempting to give a lighthearted, direct inspection ("I don't see any monsters in your closet—just a lot of junk!"), but you may leave the impression that there are monsters or aliens running around *somewhere*—they just don't happen to be here at the moment. For these fears, more decisive reality checks are important ("Bigfoot isn't under your bed or anywhere else").

When the issue is burglars or other villains who actually *do* exist out there, you will need to be more specific about the safeguards in your home: You are present (or if you are going out, someone whom you trust will be there), the doors are locked, and perhaps you have a dog or an alarm system that adds to your home's security. In addition, remind your child that God is keeping watch over her twenty-four hours every day. What your child really wants is reassurance and confidence that things are under control.

If a fearful bedtime resistance persists or escalates, take time to find out if something else is bothering her. Did your child see a disturbing image on TV or a video? Did she hear an argument the other night? Did something else frighten her? Once you have spent time exploring the problem, it's okay to make some minor adjustments to reduce the anxiety level: leaving a light on in the hallway or the door open a little wider, for example. But don't get pulled into more elaborate or manipulative routines, such as her insisting on falling asleep in your bed or on the living-room floor when she claims that she's afraid of something. She needs to know that she will be just as safe and sound in her own bed as anywhere else.

LANGUAGE: MASTERING THE MOTHER TONGUE

Your child arrived at her third birthday with a vocabulary of about five hundred to one thousand words. During the next two years, you can anticipate a dramatic increase to about twenty-five hundred words. At age three, these will be gathered into sentences of five or six words, and from here on the assembly of words into phrases and sentences will gradually become more sophisticated.

Watch and listen carefully, and you will witness a miracle.

As she has grown from baby to toddler, you have heard your child's babbling, her mimicry, her one- or two-word exclamations, and her first simple statements. And you have seen how much more she could understand than what she could say. In the coming years, your child will be revealing her ideas, her rhymes and music, her fantasies, her questions, and her fears. Language will be a window into her soul and spirit—and the most obvious evidence that you are dealing with a unique human being.

Whether she is very verbal or more conservative with her narrations, don't let your brain slip into neutral when she is chirping away about anything and everything. Listen, learn, and marvel. At the same time, you can help her develop this most incredible gift of speech.

She will soon be using personal pronouns (I, you, he, she), and you can speed up her process of sorting them out by using them correctly yourself. As natural as it may seem to refer to yourself and your child in the third person ("Mommy wants Jamie to get into the tub"), this is the time to begin using the words *I* and *you* instead. When she mixes them up ("Me want a cookie"), be careful that your correction doesn't create further confusion. (If you say, "You mean, '*I want a cookie*,'" she may think that you want one too. A correction such as "*Jamie, you should say, 'I want a cookie'*" would work better.)

Pronouns won't be the only verbal mistakes you will hear. Other mispronunciations will be abundant, although you (or anyone else) should be able to understand what she is trying to say. Your friends should not need an interpreter when she speaks, and if she is truly unintelligible at this age, she should have a formal speech evaluation.

At times her comments may remind you more of Tweety Bird ("Da kitty went up da twee!") than the Queen's English, and you will have to decide how many times per day (or hour) you will want to offer corrections. Some friendly input in response to her most obvious mistakes can help move her speech in the right direction. But badgering her or correcting every last syllable will exasperate her while she's trying to get the hang of this complex new skill.

The best approach is to spend plenty of time speaking clearly to her. Just as you avoided using endless baby talk when she was starting to vocalize, in general you should not parrot back her creative pronunciations, no matter how cute they might be. Write them down as a keepsake in her baby book, and then persist in using words and sentences properly.

One common language glitch at this age is stuttering or stammering, which may cause some concern when you first hear it. Before you call a speech therapist, however, understand that one in twenty preschool children manifests this on a temporary basis, especially when tired, excited, or upset. This may be a case of too many words in the assembly line between the thought and the actual expression. The opening syllable or even the first couple of words in a sentence may trip repeatedly on the tongue before moving on to the rest of the thought. "Um" or "uh" may show up midword or midsentence if she loses track of where the idea was going.

Don't worry about this if it occurs on an occasional basis over a month or so. Avoid showing impatience or disapproval while she's trying to get through her sentence. Also, don't try to fish the words out for her, complete her thoughts, or add any pressure to the situation. If anything, her stuttering may be a signal that the speed and pitch of everyone's conversation at home needs to calm down a bit. Normally this situation will resolve itself. However, if your child is having an ongoing problem getting her sentences launched, looks tense, twitches and grimaces, or is definitely upset by her stuttering, she should be evaluated by a speech therapist.

Other things you can do to help your child's language blossom include:

Read to her and with her. Don't limit storytelling to bedtime. Go to the library regularly and help her fall in love with books. Have her sit next to you while you read so she can study the pictures and watch the words as you say them. Don't be in a rush to get to the last page. If she wants to linger over a picture and point out a few highlights, by all means, stop and enjoy the scenery.

The object here is not to produce a four-year-old who is ready to enter high school. Driving and drilling for early academic achievement may actually backfire, especially if she begins to feel pushed and anxious about her progress in learning letters or words. Reading at this age should forge emotional bonds—not only to books but also to *you.* This lasting benefit, by the way, cannot happen in front of a TV screen.

Listen. This is a skill you may have to learn (or relearn), especially if you feel as though all you do is listen to chattering throughout the day. At least once each day—and much more often if possible—consciously stop, look, and listen to what your preschooler has to say. Lock eyes, uncross your arms, and acknowledge what you hear ("Wow! That's pretty exciting! What else happened?") as if you were sitting with a friend over a cup of coffee. This simple activity is one of the

Provide your children with many interesting books and materials, read to them and answer their questions.

THE NEW DARE TO DISCIPLINE

most important ways to validate your child's identity and significance, and its impact will last throughout her lifetime.

Carry on conversations. This flows from taking the time to listen to your child but adds the dimension of a thoughtful exchange. Decades ago one of the most successful television programs was Art Linkletter's *House Party,* and its most popular segment was called "Kids Say the Darndest Things." Linkletter simply conversed with children in a calm and friendly manner and was rewarded with responses that were incredibly candid and funny. His skill was in showing interest in children, without worrying for those few minutes whether they had clean hands or tidy rooms. He didn't correct, rebuke, scold, or exhort, and what he heard in return was extraordinary.

As a parent, your job is to be concerned about the daily welfare and training of your child. You can't run your home like a TV talk show, but for a few minutes each day, try settling back and simply talking with your child, even pretending for a moment that you are interviewing her. You may be surprised when you hear what's on her mind. And if you show that what she says is worthy of your attention, it is likely that she will return the favor. While you're at it, her language skills will grow in leaps and bounds.

Try to answer questions. You'll hear them from dawn till dusk, and if you can give a simple but meaningful answer, not a mumbled "I dunno" or a disinterested shrug, your child will learn language, information, and values. Your child's questions will also provide you with priceless opportunities to talk with her about God. Okay, so you don't know exactly why the grass is green or how airplanes fly, or you may become frustrated when your brilliant response is met with a sudden change in her train of thought, as if she paid no attention to what you said. But she *does* care very much what you think about life and the world, a state that won't last forever. All through the first years of your child's life, the little computer is on all the time, waiting eagerly for someone to provide input. No one is better qualified than you. If you need a break, instead of becoming frustrated, use a timer for a "quiet moment." Tell your child that you will talk again after the buzzer goes off.

SOCIAL DEVELOPMENTS: MIND, HEART, AND RELATIONSHIPS

Language is not the only territory your preschooler will be striving to explore and master. At this point he is sorting out not only words but reality itself. He is now well past the basic "see-touch-taste-drop it" method of exploration that served him in his toddler days. By age three or shortly thereafter, he has come to understand that he is an individual separate from you. By now he should know—without any doubt whatsoever—that he is deeply loved and respected, that his welfare is your highest priority, and that he doesn't rule either the universe or your family. (Special Concerns, page 289, can help you in the area of training and discipline.)

With this foundation firmly established, your child is free to launch out into the world and learn about it with curiosity and confidence rather than with fear and trembling. Taking part in conversations within the family, asking questions, and falling in love with books are important basic components of his exploring process. Other components include:

Mimicry and imitation. This was mentioned already in the previous chapter on two-year-olds, and it becomes more obvious (and potentially more fun, if you're patient) during the preschool years. If you are working in the garden, he'll want to dig and rake along with you. If you're sorting laundry, he may be surprisingly good at finding the matching socks. If you're painting or pounding nails, guess who will want his own brush or hammer. If you're setting the table, he is quite capable of learning what goes where and eventually can carry out this everyday task on his own.

Try not to look at his efforts to participate as a hassle that will bog you down. Rather, see them as giving you an opportunity to chat with him during everyday activities, and he can practice some basic skills in the process. Not only does he need your praise and affirmation for wanting to help, but it is healthy for him to experience the act of serving someone else, even if his attention span is rather short.

Don't forget that imitation can include negative behaviors as well. If you hit your finger with a hammer, guess who will learn some new words if you don't watch how you react. If you use harsh or unkind words when there's a disagreement, guess who is learning a nonproductive way to solve problems. If you slam your fist on the table when you become frustrated, guess who will be scared or do the same thing when he feels the same way.

What may be a little frustrating during this stage of your child's life is that you may hear him mimic the words and tone of voice that you use when you're blowing off steam, yet not see a whole lot of evidence that he is imitating your positive role modeling. Mom and Dad may speak to one another with consistent respect and kindness—a worthy goal, by the way, whether or not children are in the room—yet hear a blistering exchange between brother and sister over a toy that each wants. *Where did* that *come from?* you might wonder.

Before you become discouraged, keep two facts in mind. First, your child really *is* taking in the flavor of your habits and conversations at home. They form the foundation of his expectations and assumptions about life: what he is used to, what he considers normal, what he will carry with him throughout his life (including the family he starts himself in another twenty or thirty years). Believe it or not, your attitudes are being caught.

Second, a healthy and wholesome family environment does not override the core of self-centeredness that is present in every human being from birth. The manifestations of willfulness and negativity that you saw in your child as a toddler and a two-year-old probably have been contained by now, but they sprang from deep roots that never completely disappear. Therefore, you need to not only demonstrate virtues but teach them as well, including "lab exercises" when appropriate. Saying please and thank you (and later understanding a depth of meaning in these words), waiting one's turn, and telling the truth need to not only be observed but also talked about and practiced on an ongoing basis.

Role playing and fantasy. This staple activity of childhood will get into full swing during the preschool years. Whether in your home, at a play group, or among other children in the neighborhood, you can bet the children will play variations on "let's pretend" with great fervor. Your child will undoubtedly try everything from copying domestic roles (the traditional "playing house") to trying out occupations (bus driver, nurse, airline pilot), setting up play situations (store, airport, hospital, church), or assuming the roles of characters (human and otherwise) he has seen in books or videos. Costumes and props will be imagined and constructed from things at hand, although toy manufacturers have been eagerly supplying ready-made accessories for generations.

In general, this is not only normal but healthy. Pretending to be Moses or Batman, setting up a store or a ranch on the back patio, and devising their own adventures exercise language and the imagination far more than staring at a TV screen will. Children can learn to plan, solve problems, and cooperate with one another during these projects. For the most part, you can not only encourage these activities but also capture some of them on video for future enjoyment (and a little watery-eyed nostalgia). In fact, your child(ren) will be ecstatic if you occasionally enter into the adventure yourself for a while. If you happen to see a procession of kings and queens in the hallway, you might enjoy serving lunch as a dignified servant, using your hammiest British accent. If your child announces that she is a world-famous doctor, tell her you have a symptom or two and see what she diagnoses.

You can generally allow these make-believe sessions to proceed with a minimum of parental intrusion, but keep your eyes and ears open for a few situations that might need some revision of the script:

- *Inappropriate characters.* While someone may want to play Captain Hook or Goliath to round out the characters in a make-believe story, role-playing options shouldn't include serial killers, vampires, or other relentless evildoers. Suggest more heroic or more neutral characters.

- *Destructive scenarios.* Action and conflict drive many adventures, from knights in armor to Wild West and outer-space fantasies. But if your child's pretend characters do nothing but Ninja-kick, wave laser sabers, fire toy guns, and generally inflict make-believe (if not real) damage, you may want to suggest some less violent alternatives. If he is allowed to watch TV, he's probably reenacting some rough (and dumb) stuff from the tube. Do everyone a favor and muzzle the electronic beast (see chapter 11, page 413).

- *Toxic fantasy.* This is a tough call in some cases, because fantasy elements of many stories (such as C. S. Lewis's Chronicles of Narnia) can serve to convey some very positive values. But role playing that involves "pretend" occult practices (such as séances or Ouija boards) or elaborate spell casting could whet young appetites for more hazardous practices later on.

- *Hurt feelings.* When the pretending is orchestrated by older children, younger or less popular participants may become stuck with roles no one else wants or receive lots of "make-believe" abuse that starts to feel like the real thing. If you see that someone seems to be getting the short end of the stick consistently, suggest alternative casting as well as caution about the kinds of things that are said, even when pretending.

- *Too much of a good thing.* Preschoolers can become so enthused about pretending to be Superman or Pocahontas that they may not want the game to end, or they may try to use their character to gain power or attention. When your call to get into the tub is met with a resounding refusal ("X-Wing pilots don't need baths!"), you'll have to decide whether to have your way by playing along ("Your bath orders come directly from your squadron leader!") or by calling for an intermission.

- *Early adolescence.* Little girls love to play "lady dress-up" with old hats, costume jewelry, and gloves. However, if your four-year-old insists on putting on nail polish and frilly dresses for every occasion or becomes overly infatuated with the teenage social life of a popular doll, you might encourage her to broaden her horizons.

Making friends. Unlike the parallel play of younger children—in which "playing together" means playing side by side without actually interacting except to squabble over a mutually favored toy—preschoolers are usually ready for some genuine cooperative play. The concepts of sharing and taking turns can now be understood and usually put into action, but reminders and supervision will still be necessary.

Some children enter a bossy phase during this period (especially when they are four), which can make things unpleasant for younger or less assertive children in their vicinity. If your child begins to sound like a miniature dictator, take him aside for a gentle reminder about basic kindness and manners. Also be sure to give him lots of praise when he plays well with other children. Specific information helps: "I like the way you let Megan have the ball so nicely when she asked for it."

Along with the make-believe and role-playing activities, your child will begin enjoying a variety of interactions with other children. These might include simple games, puzzles, and assorted play "projects" such as creating buildings, roads, and unidentified objects with blocks and other construction toys.

Before long, your child will enjoy inviting a friend over for playtime or a meal and will most likely receive a similar invitation in return. You will, of course, already have some idea of the ground rules of the other family, and vice versa, before this "cultural exchange" takes place. Obviously, your child can't live in a glass bubble, but it would be desirable if the basic standards and values you hold dear aren't undermined by playmates at this young age. If he brings home words or attitudes from a friend's house that rub you the wrong way, talk to him about what you find troublesome, and then see if you can influence the other child and his family in a more positive direction. If you can't make any headway with a playmate who is having a negative impact on your child, you may need to direct your child's attention to other children.

Where can you find prospective companions for your preschooler? If your circle of friends or immediate neighborhood doesn't include any families with children the same age, check the ranks of your church. Assuming child care is provided, you might see if he hits it off with someone while you're attending the service. Another potential source of friends for your child (and for Mom as well) is a local MOPS (Mothers of Preschoolers) group. These regular get-togethers provide structured play for the kids and a time-out for mothers, who have their own program (which may involve a speaker, discussion, or other activities). To locate the nearest MOPS group, call (800) 929-1287.

You may wish to enroll your child in a preschool or other structured play group for a specified amount of time each week. While the term *preschooler* is used widely (including in this chapter) as a synonym for three- and four-year-old children, whether your child actually attends preschool is completely up to you. This experience is not a requirement for future academic achievement or necessary for proper social development. If he's ready, he'll enjoy it, and you may find the break in child care a welcome change of pace during the week.

Keeping the faith. Some parents have bought into the idea that their child's spiritual development is such a "personal" matter that no attempt should be made to

---

WHAT TO LOOK FOR IN A NURSERY SCHOOL OR PLAY GROUP

As in any situation in which you leave your child in someone else's care, your primary concern for a potential nursery-school experience will be that it is safe, beneficial for your child, and basically enjoyable. To improve the likelihood of this happening, consider the following:

- What is the basic outlook/worldview of the school? Do the teachers and administrators share your values, or will what you teach at home be undermined by the day's events at school?
- Do the teachers have special training in working with small children? How long have the teachers been employed there? (A high turnover rate of staff should raise some concerns. If teachers don't stay long, there may be a worrisome reason.)
- How many children will be assigned to each teacher? In general, the smaller the classes or groups are, the better.
- Are the facilities safe and sound? Are staff members trained to handle an emergency? Is there a reasonable level of cleanliness? If the school accepts children who are not toilet trained, are the changing areas adequately separated from other activities, especially food handling?
- Is the school endowed with an adequate supply of toys, games, crafts, and other equipment? Does the day's schedule include free playtime as well as structured activities?

- What is the school's policy regarding children who are ill? Do you notice kids with runny noses and hacking coughs running around with the others? If sick children are not sent home, you might see a dramatic increase in the number of colds and other illnesses your child develops.
- What is the school's approach to discipline? What measures will be taken if your child misbehaves? Do you agree with them?
- Does your child know any of the children in the school? Sometimes a familiar face can make a transition into an unfamiliar environment much easier for your child.
- Does the staff have any problem if you drop in to see how things are going? Do they encourage parents to be involved with the school? Think twice if a school is resistant to parental visits or participation, which should be welcomed. A school and a child's parents should be teammates, not competitors.
- Do you know other families who use the school? Some candid input from graduates of the facility can be very useful when you are making a decision whether or not to send your child there.
- Do you sense a real heart for children among the administrators and teachers? Fancy learning programs are far less important at this age than a genuine interest in *your* child's well-being.

influence the direction the child chooses. This is a serious mistake. While your child must ultimately decide on her own whether or not she will begin and nurture a relationship with God, you have not only an opportunity but a responsibility to teach and demonstrate the spiritual principles that are the foundation of your family life (see chapter 14, "Passing the Baton," page 615).

So how do you communicate spiritual truths and moral values to a three- or four-year-old? Can she conceive of an infinite God or understand theology or sit through a religious service? Both Old and New Testaments address this quite plainly:

> Hear, O Israel: The Lord our God, the Lord is one. Love the Lord your God with all your heart and with all your soul and with all your strength. These commandments that I give you today are to be upon your hearts. Impress them on your children. Talk about them when you sit at home and when you walk along the road, when you lie down and when you get up. Tie them as symbols on your hands and bind them on your foreheads. Write them on the doorframes of your houses and on your gates.
> —*Deuteronomy 6:4-9*

> But Jesus called the children to him and said, "Let the little children come to me, and do not hinder them, for the kingdom of God belongs to such as these. I tell you the truth, anyone who will not receive the kingdom of God like a little child will never enter it."
> —*Luke 18:16-17*

First, we are to talk to our children about God as we go about our daily business. As important as regular observances can and should be, spiritual matters shouldn't be confined to a specified religious time slot once a week. Conversations about God should be as routine and natural as those about any other subject. Our children should see us pray about the issues of our lives, give thanks for our food (and everything else), and acknowledge God's leadership in our decisions. In dealing with more formal teaching or family devotions, simple stories will communicate volumes to preschoolers. The Scriptures are filled with them, and Jesus often told stories to get His point across.

Second, small children appear uniquely qualified to understand intimacy with God in ways that may elude them later in life. Perhaps it is their utter trust in their earthly parents (which can be expanded to include a heavenly Father) or their lack of cynicism or their openness or their uninhibited joy and enthusiasm for the objects of their love that draw them to the God they cannot see. Whatever else they do, parents and the other adults who care for children must not hinder them from trusting in God, which seems to come naturally to them.

One important job for parents who care about the spiritual lives of their preschoolers is to help them distinguish not only right from wrong but truth from fantasy. This means that you will have to make some careful decisions about dealing with a few popular traditions in our culture. The crux of the matter is this: If your child is going to take you seriously when you talk about the God who made heaven and earth, you don't have the luxury of deliberately bending the truth (or tying it in knots) in other matters. Whatever else you do, never mislead your child when she asks you point-blank for the facts about mythical personalities or anything else.

On a day-to-day basis, you will also have a responsibility to help your preschooler understand the difference between truth and make-believe in her own life. At an age when there is so much to learn about the world and so much imagination at work in your child's head, the boundaries between reality and fantasy will wear thin at times. If you hear a breathless report that there are giant spiders crawling around her room, and it appears that her main interest is in gathering attention or reassurance, explain what can go wrong if she makes up alarming stories. A brief recounting of the fate of the boy who cried wolf may be in order.

If she tells a whopper of a tall tale to explain why her dollhouse is now caved in on one side ("A big gorilla climbed through my window and jumped on it!"), you will need to coax the truth out with some finesse. In particular, she must understand that telling a lie to escape punishment is far more of a concern than the actual misdeed itself. The first offense in this area should be treated more with explanation than with punishment, but repeated episodes will require specific and meaningful consequences. Otherwise a habit of lying will eventually undermine every relationship in her life.

Needless to say, you cannot afford to demonstrate any "white lies" of your own. If your child hears you say, "Tell him I'm not here" when an obnoxious caller is on the phone, for example, whatever you are trying to teach about truth and lies will be wasted breath.

This is an appropriate time to present your child with her own Bible (age-appropriate and containing lots of pictures), which can provide a rich source of input and topics for conversation. Should your preschooler memorize Scripture? Some are able to commit Bible verses to memory quite easily before their fifth birthday, and for these children the words will be "hidden in their hearts" for the

The spirit of a child is a million times more vulnerable than his will. It is a delicate flower that can be crushed and broken all too easily (and even unintentionally).

THE STRONG-WILLED CHILD

rest of their lives. For others, attempts to memorize are like pulling teeth, and if you force the issue, you may create a distaste for Scripture rivaling that for broccoli and brussels sprouts.

A more effective way to "hide the Word" in a child's heart when she doesn't memorize easily is to use songs. Many tapes, CDs, and videos communicate spiritual principles and Scripture verses to children (and their parents) through music. The best of these not only teach and entertain but leave both parent and child humming uplifting tunes—sometimes for years to come. Few investments pay such rich dividends.

Ages Five through Eleven

So long as we are loved by
others, I would almost say we
are indispensable; and no man is
useless while he has a friend.

ROBERT LOUIS
STEVENSON

Ages Five through Eleven: Life Lessons

Check the books lining the shelves of the child-care section of the library and you'll see a crateload of titles dealing with birth and infancy and nearly as many devoted to toddlers and preschoolers. Just down the aisle you'll find another impressive collection dealing with teenagers. What happened to those in-between years? You might ask the same question of this book. It took us ten chapters to arrive at the fifth birthday, but after this chapter we move on to a lengthy discussion about adolescence. Doesn't anything happen between preschool and junior high?

Actually, plenty is going on: physical growth, maturing emotions, the acquisition of a host of intellectual and physical skills, the shaping of moral values, and, yes, the gradual approach to that eventful transition to adulthood known as adolescence. All of these changes are important and need plenty of parental guidance, prayer, and input. This is no time for Mom and Dad to put their parenting skills on autopilot as their child cruises through the elementary grades. Indeed, the attention you give your child during these years may significantly reduce the stress and difficulties of adolescence.

Many themes recur without major variations between the ages of five and eleven. Relationships with family and friends, and school, sports, and other group activities dominate the landscape. Parents usually don't feel they have been thrown onto a steep and slippery learning curve or breathlessly wonder what's coming around the next bend as they do during a child's infancy and teen years. The child's emotional weather tends to be at a lull. The tides of toddler rebellion subside somewhat, and truces are usually forged in any conflict between the generations.

There are, of course, exceptions. You may feel that the first five years were wonderful but that you have now entered a time of turmoil. Perhaps you have been dealing with a strong-willed child whose "terrible twos" have persisted and developed into "fighting fives" or "struggling sixes." Even if your child's grade-school years prove to be smooth sailing, you will probably encounter some turbulence before your parenting assignment is over.

But these years should be deeply gratifying, a time to enhance and deepen your relationship with your son or daughter—who will not remain a child for long. While you may have thought you would never see your child graduate from infancy and toddlerhood, the grade-school years pass with incredible speed. Keep your eyes, ears, and heart open so you don't arrive at her high school graduation wondering where these years went.

Growth and Development

Changes in size and shape occur at a predictable rate from year to year for most children between the ages of five and eleven. And yes, growth really does take place in spurts rather than in a slow and steady climb. Both boys and girls typically gain two inches in height and six to seven pounds each year. This may vary, of course. Your child's doctor will continue to mark her progress on a growth chart to confirm that she is maintaining an appropriate rate from year to year; this will also alert the doctor to any significant changes. As mentioned in previous chapters, you can get a rough idea of your child's eventual adult height from the growth curve on her medical chart.

One development that might catch you off guard during this period is the beginning of **puberty.** You might not suspect that your fifth grader is poised at the dawn of her reproductive years, but the first event of this process for girls—the appearance of breast buds—occurs, on average, at age ten. This could happen as early as age eight, or it may wait until thirteen. The first menstrual period, which signals that the intricate hormonal interplay between central nervous system, ovaries, and uterus has completed its first cycle, typically takes place about two years after the appearance of breast buds. In boys, the onset of puberty occurs, on average, a year later than in girls.

The stages of this remarkable process will be reviewed in detail in chapter 12. You might want to look over that information now if your child is approaching the age at which pubertal changes might begin. Ideally, you will not only be prepared to answer questions about these important events when they occur but will anticipate their arrival so they and many other concerns can be discussed ahead of time. Some suggestions for preparing your child for adolescence will be discussed later in this chapter.

Sometimes the timing of birth dates and growth spurts will place children of noticeably different sizes in the same grade-school classroom. Children can become quite self-conscious if they are the tallest or shortest among their peers. They can also be incredibly unkind to one another over differences in body size or shape. If your child is clearly at the extreme for his age in either height or weight, keep track of his emotional well-being as well as his growth chart while he progresses through school. If he is accumulating a collection of unflattering nicknames ("Moose," "Shrimp," "Beanpole"), you should definitely intervene because the impact of this verbal assault on his emotions and spirit can be profound. The overweight child is particularly vulnerable to scorn and rejection. Likewise, you must not allow any nicknames for your child that have even remotely negative connotations to take root in your family. What you or his siblings might consider playful and harmless fun could painfully chip away at his sense of worth for months on end and shape his image of himself for years to come.

Your response to any significant variations from average height or weight will depend on the particular problem. Discussions with a doctor, dietitian, teacher, and even school principal may be in order, along with evaluations of bone structure, hormonal status, food intake, and progress in school, if appropriate. For example, a short child, especially a boy, without a treatable medical problem may do better if he delays starting school for a year so he is on more even terms (heightwise) with his classmates. But if height really doesn't bother him and he is on equal terms emotionally and intellectually with the taller classmates, it might cause more harm to hold him back. If being grouped with younger students were to stigmatize him as "slow" or "dumb," the impact could be more negative than being shorter than everyone else. As you consider various options, be sure to bring your child into the decision-making process.

An obviously overweight child may need ongoing supervision of food choices and specific measures to increase his physical activity. If your child is overweight, or if his health-care provider raises a concern that his weight is excessive for his height, you will need to address this issue with both tact and diligence. Consultation with a qualified dietitian is definitely advisable because weight loss in children isn't a simple matter of "just eat less." Food choices must take into account ongoing growth, the child's likes and dislikes, family eating patterns, and long-term planning. At times parent and child may have different ideas about what "ideal" weight should be, or a preadolescent may be so worried about body image as to be at risk for an eating disorder in the near future. If there are emotional undercurrents and unrealistic expectations relating to food and appearance, a dietitian can serve as a professional source of reliable information, as well as a neutral party to help sort out any disagreements within the family. Once a dietary course is set, a child may need some ongoing supervision of food choices and perhaps encouragement toward appropriate physical activity.

Classmates may need some exhortation, either as a group or individually, regarding the way they treat others who are different. If you learn that your child has been making cutting comments about another child's appearance, seize the opportunity for friendly but firm discussion about the importance of respect for others' feelings.

Above all, your child will need ongoing reassurance that you are on his team, that you care about his problem, and that you will be a steadfast ally while it is being solved (see Special Concerns, page 430).

Food and Nutrition

Despite the significant change in your child's body size and weight in the coming years, your role in fueling that growth will be remarkably similar to what it was during the past few years: providing a variety of wholesome foods from the major food groups. Your child's job will be to decide how much of it to eat.

Appetites will vary greatly from meal to meal and day to day. Your best overall check of adequate intake will be tracking your child's weight over time. (See page 340 for notes on dietary habits that also apply here.)

Your biggest nutritional challenge during these years will be to stem the cultural tide of fast foods, soft drinks, candy bars, and salty snacks that compete with better quality foods. As he grows older and more independent, your child may have more access to junk foods through contact with friends, increased mobility on his bicycle, and some allowance money burning a hole in his pocket. And at this age he is still likely to be influenced by clever advertisements designed to mold his nutritional preferences.

Your other major difficulty will be in fostering regularity of eating habits. If your child has an early school bus to catch, breakfast may be lost in a blur as he runs out the door. If you don't make his lunch, he may choose cafeteria food based more on taste preference than nutritional content. If he has all kinds of activities after school and you have a full agenda as well, dinner may be a survival-of-the-fittest exercise, with the refrigerator serving as the hunting ground. Even with complex activity schedules, for the sake of communication and cohesiveness it's still beneficial to gather the family for a meal together at least two or three times per week, if not more often. Whether you are a whiz in the kitchen or prefer to occupy it as little as possible, plan on plugging away at the following during the next several years:

Don't skip breakfast. He doesn't need a three-egg omelet and a rose on the table, but he does need some reasonable fuel to start the day. Cereal, toast, and juice can be prepared with a minimum of fuss and will launch the day properly.

If you don't pack his lunch, find out what's on the menu at the school cafeteria and guide his choices. If you make his lunch, get him involved in the process and make sure he's eating it. Kids are notorious for swapping or ignoring foods they don't really want, so why waste your money and time on things he won't consume?

Continue leading the charge for less fat, more fiber, less sugar, more complex carbohydrates, and less salt in your family's everyday food choices.

Check with your child's doctor about vitamin supplements. Truly picky and erratic eaters may need them, but most children in this age-group will not.

Make sure your child receives two to three servings of calcium-rich foods daily.

MEDICAL CHECKUPS AND IMMUNIZATIONS

Your child's checkups at ages three and four were probably uneventful, at least from the child's perspective. At five, however, school is on the horizon, and specific screening and immunization updates are due. Find out about local school entrance requirements and your health-care provider's routine for this exam, because a little preparation may soften some of the "sticker shock." You don't have to go into the gory details, but you might mention that this is a special visit and that the doctor is going to make sure that your child is ready for school.

Aside from the normal height, weight, vision, and hearing screening, and a head-to-toe exam, what else may happen?

- A **urinalysis.** A number of problems can be detected by an evaluation of urine, so make sure your child doesn't urinate just prior to the visit.
- A **blood test** (usually by finger stick) to check for anemia.
- A **skin test for tuberculosis** (which may depend on school requirements, your location, and your child's risk for exposure to this disease). This has probably been done at least once at a previous checkup, but your child

may not remember it. The small prick on the forearm must be checked by the doctor if a firm bump develops at the site of the injection after forty-eight to seventy-two hours. A local reaction may indicate that your child has had contact with the bacteria that cause tuberculosis, although he may not have an active infection. Further testing will usually be necessary.

◆ **Diphtheria/tetanus/pertussis (DTaP)** and **oral polio (OPV)** or **inactivated polio (IPV)** vaccinations. Your child probably received his initial series of these immunizations as an infant, and a booster around eighteen months. A final dose will ensure he is not at risk for any of these serious diseases later in childhood. After the seventh birthday, the pertussis component of DTaP is no longer given. (The sidebar on page 143 in chapter 4 summarizes these infections.)

◆ **Measles/mumps/rubella (MMR)** vaccine. After the initial dose at twelve to fifteen months of age, a second dose should be given prior to entering school. For those children already in school, a second dose should be given prior to the age of eleven to twelve years.

Many five-year-olds have heard unpleasant things about shots, so plan on meeting some resistance when the moment arrives. Don't be tempted to pass on this part of the visit because you don't want to cause him pain when, you may think, he isn't likely to be exposed to any of these infections.

Think again. First, your local school district will require that immunizations be current. More important, just because he has reached this age without having contracted any of these illnesses doesn't mean he is out of the woods. Measles epidemics still break out from time to time and can cause serious complications. The bacteria that cause tetanus most likely reside in the soil outside your back door. And whooping cough (pertussis, the *P* in DTaP), while not nearly as risky at age five as during infancy, can produce an extremely annoying and persistent cough. For these and many other infections, an ounce of vaccine prevention is worth far more than several pounds of misery and expensive treatment.

Let your child know that the shot will help him stay well, that you know it will hurt and may even ache for a day or two afterward, and that he can say "Ouch" and even cry—as long as he holds still. If he can't or won't, you may have to take charge and hold him (or at least his arm) steady for the person giving the injection. Stay calm but firm. If you look apprehensive, upset, or guilty, the procedure will be much harder for everyone. When the visit is over, you may want to do something that he enjoys to honor the occasion.

After your child reaches age five, his physician will want to see him for routine checkups annually or every other year, depending on a variety of considerations. *Quick exams for camp or sports, especially those done assembly-line style on large groups of children, should not substitute for more comprehensive physicals by your regular health-care provider.* His vision will be screened as part of some or all of these checkups, and if there is any concern, a visit to an ophthalmologist may be recommended. A formal eye exam would be wise if your child is squinting, complaining of blurry vision, having difficulty seeing the blackboard at school, or bringing objects close to his face in order to see them (see *eye care and concerns*, Reference). Dental checkups should be carried out at least every twelve months or as recommended by your child's dentist.

OTHER IMMUNIZATIONS DURING THE SCHOOL YEARS

In addition to the diphtheria/tetanus/pertussis (DTaP), polio (OPV/IPV), and measles/mumps/rubella (MMR) vaccinations, the following may be recommended by your child's physician:

- **Chicken pox (varicella)** The vaccine for this common childhood disease was introduced in 1995 and is frequently given to infants between twelve and eighteen months of age. If your child has never had chicken pox or the vaccine, a single dose before age thirteen (or two doses, four to eight weeks apart, after age thirteen) will prevent the disease or reduce its severity should it occur. Chicken pox tends to be more severe, and at times dangerous, in teenagers or adults. Varicella vaccine may be given at the same time as an MMR and/or Td injection. If varicella and MMR are not given simultaneously, an interval of at least a month should separate the two.
- **Hepatitis B**. If your child has not yet been vaccinated against this virus, which can cause significant and long-lasting inflammation of the liver, talk to the doctor about beginning the three-injection series. This disease is most often transmitted through sexual contact, intravenous drug use, or other contact with the blood of an infected person, making it uncommon in children. But a significant number of cases in both children and adults occur without this

history. Because the vaccine is safe and effective and hepatitis B is potentially very serious or lethal, immunization of all children and adolescents is now recommended.

- **Hepatitis A.** If your family travels extensively, especially to rural or impoverished areas of foreign countries, you may want to have everyone vaccinated against this virus, which is transmitted through contaminated food and water. The hepatitis A vaccine provides long-term, specific, and effective immunity. (For more information about these and other forms of hepatitis, see *hepatitis*, Reference.)
- **Influenza.** This virus makes an annual appearance in most communities during the winter, provoking fever, aches, and coughing that are often more intense than a garden-variety upper respiratory infection. While most children recover from influenza after a few days of rest, fluids, and acetaminophen or ibuprofen for their aches and pains, those with significant medical problems such as heart disease, diabetes, or chronic respiratory disturbances (especially asthma) may suffer severe complications. These children normally are given influenza vaccine each year in the fall. Because new strains of this virus appear annually, a new vaccine must be prepared each year (see *influenza*, Reference).

Common Symptoms and Health Concerns

Not all of your child's medical visits will be for routine checkups. Certain common problems, both acute and chronic, are worth mentioning briefly. (Most of these are reviewed in detail in the Reference section of this book.)

- **Headaches.** A little effort may be needed to separate the annoying but harmless ones from those that need medical attention.

  (a) Tension-type (often called muscle-contraction) headaches, the most frequent in children and adults, have a typical pattern of pain across the forehead, often accompanied by a feeling of tightness around the head and/or neck like a rubber band. These may be a physical response to hunger, stress, or worry and usually respond to simple treatment: acetaminophen, a snack if he's hungry, a brief rest in a quiet environment, and a cool washcloth across the forehead.

  (b) Migraine or vascular headaches involve changes in the diameter of blood vessels, typically cause more severe, throbbing pain on one or both sides of the head, and are often accompanied by nausea and vomiting. A migraine in children often improves dramatically after throwing up. Often a child can tell when a headache is about to begin, and a prompt dose of a nonprescription pain reliever may stop or relieve it. (Check with your child's physician.)

  (c) Headaches caused by colds and sinus infections are usually accompanied by a runny nose, congestion, and pressure in the face. Decongestants may help relieve this discomfort, and your child's doctor may prescribe antibiotics if a sinus infection appears likely.

  (d) Headaches frequently accompany any illness that generates a fever, such as a sore throat, upper respiratory infection, or chicken pox. The headache will typically wax and wane with the temperature. If the pain is severe and relentless, and especially if it is accompanied by a stiff neck or change in behavior such as confusion or marked drowsiness, a medical evaluation should be carried out immediately to rule out a more serious infection such as meningitis.

- **Colds, ear infections, and other upper-respiratory infections** will typically occur less frequently now, but they will be easier to diagnose and treat because your school-age child is better able to describe his symptoms.

  (a) More than one hundred types of viruses can cause **colds,** with their characteristic runny nose, scratchy throat, and hacking cough. Rest, fluids, a cool-mist humidifier, and seven to ten days (or less) for the immune system to banish the invaders are usually all the treatment needed. Over-the-counter cold and cough remedies may ease symptoms for a few hours, although they have a better track record in adults. If one of them helps your child feel better, you may use it as needed in the appropriate dose. (Common ingredients in the medications are listed in *colds,* Reference.)

Acetaminophen or ibuprofen can help reduce aches, pains, and fever. Remember that the reason for reducing your child's fever is comfort, not medical necessity, except in rare circumstances (see Special Concerns, page 267). Antibiotics are useless in treating a cold, but your child's physician may prescribe them if bacteria complicate the picture. Signs that bacteria could be part of the problem include symptoms persisting for more than ten to fourteen days, the appearance of discolored (yellow or green) drainage from the nose or phlegm from the chest for more than a few days, or fever that begins or worsens after several days of illness.

(b) **Ear infections** occur less often because bacteria must travel a longer distance through the eustachian tubes now than when your child was an infant and toddler. An infection usually causes persistent, sometimes severe, pain and usually is treated with antibiotics. Because fluid can accumulate in the middle-ear space during and after an infection, a follow-up visit to check both ear and hearing may be recommended. Intense, continuous ear pain may also be caused by an infection in the outer ear canal or even by inflammation in the throat. Any ongoing ear pain should be checked as soon as possible.

During a cold, your child may complain of intermittent ear pain that may disappear when he swallows or yawns. He probably has a congested eustachian tube. Time and possibly decongestants should resolve the problem, but the ear(s) should be checked by your doctor if the pain is severe, fever is present, or if there is any hearing loss or drainage from the ear. Occasionally, irritation of the joint where the jawbone connects with the skull produces what seems to be an earache. A medical checkup will be necessary to determine what is wrong.

(c) **Sore throats** are generally caused by viruses, although postnasal drainage down the throat during a cold can provoke discomfort. In a limited number of sore throats, the culprit is a form of **streptococcus** (called group A beta hemolytic strep), which can generate a more serious illness. If your child's throat is sore, inflamed, and accompanied by fever and headache, the doctor may do a strep test and/or a throat culture. If the test is positive, antibiotics will be necessary.

♦ If your child is prone to **allergies** and/or **asthma,** you will probably know well before he reaches his fifth birthday. Nevertheless, some children who have had little trouble with the nose or chest may start to sniff, sneeze, or cough on an ongoing basis, raising concerns that "He's sick all the time" or "She's had a cold for two months." These symptoms are often caused by newly developed allergies. Reactive airways that twitch and spasm sometimes provoke frequent coughing or overt wheezing, especially after exercise. Because allergies are often provoked by specific environmental factors (for example, house dust and mold), they can often be treated more effectively after you and your physician or an allergist have done some detective work. If symptoms are frequent or continuous, it's a good idea to seek medical assistance for managing allergies, rather than relying strictly on over-the-counter antihistamines or decongestant-antihistamine combinations. Helpful approaches for dealing with allergies are discussed in the Reference section under *allergies in children.*

♦ **Abdominal pains** (stomach aches) will be felt occasionally by nearly every child, but in some they are a more frequent complaint (see sidebar). Sorting out the source of abdominal discomfort, whether a new event or an ongoing problem, will require some investigation at home and possibly in the doctor's office. For common patterns of pain and their possible causes, see *abdominal pain,* Reference.

♦ **Orthopedic (bone and joint) problems** are common in school-age children. As they develop greater body weight and stronger muscles, and then throw themselves enthusiastically into neighborhood games or organized sports, opportunities to sustain sprains, strains, or fractures increase dramatically. Depending upon your child's enthusiasm for rough-and-tumble play, you may become well acquainted with a local orthopedist during these years. Safety precautions for outdoor activities will follow later in this chapter (also, see Home Safety: Outdoors, page 823).

Another orthopedic concern is pain in an arm, leg, pelvis, back, or some other area of bone or muscle for no apparent reason. In general, bone/muscle/joint discomforts that need medical attention include:

♦ Pain that persists in one specific area for more than a day or two

◆ Pain that is intense enough to interfere with normal activities
◆ Pain associated with local redness, swelling, tenderness, or inability to move a joint through its normal range of motion*
◆ Limping or refusal to walk or run because of pain*
◆ Fever, nausea, rash, or other generalized symptoms associated with any of the above*

The last three items marked with an asterisk (*) should be evaluated as soon as possible to avoid serious complications such as destruction of a joint or uncontrolled infection. These symptoms could indicate that serious trouble is brewing, including inflammation or infection of a bone or joint, an unsuspected fracture, or even a destructive process including the very rare instance of a tumor involving a bone or soft tissue.

THE RIDDLE OF RECURRENT STOMACH ACHES

Recurrent abdominal pain is the most common and vexing type of chronic pain problem in school-age children. It occurs most frequently between the ages of eight and ten and nearly twice as often in girls than in boys. Fewer than 10 percent of children with this syndrome have a clear-cut medical reason for their discomfort. Despite research, no single mechanism has been identified to explain it. Symptoms will end within a few weeks in roughly half of those affected, but many have problems into adulthood.

Pains may be sharp or dull, high or low in the abdomen, widely spread or somewhat localized. Nausea, vomiting, dizziness, and sweating may also occur. After one to three hours, the pain will disappear. While these episodes may interfere with a variety of daytime activities, they rarely awaken the child from sleep. Very often there appears to be no obvious relationship to food or time of day, and there are no other signs of illness such as fever, weight loss, severe diarrhea, or blood in the stool.

A variety of causes for recurrent abdominal pains have been suggested, including irritation of the stomach's lining, irritability and cramping of the small or large intestine, intolerance to foods, and a psychological response to stress. In many children the problem is constipation—not unusual in this age-group—which can result in a painful abdominal cramp shortly after a meal. The cramp may be relieved following a bowel movement or may stop on its own in a few minutes (see *constipation*, Reference).

A less straightforward problem occurs when the pains seem to be related to stress, whether the everyday variety (getting ready for school) or more significant events such as abuse by a school-yard bully or the uncertainty generated by a stormy parental relationship. A medical evaluation may need to be accompanied by some sensitive questions about what currently resides within a child's worry zone. While you should not assume that these discomforts are imaginary or manufactured to escape responsibility, judgment will be needed to gauge a child's tolerance to pain in general and the severity of these pains in particular.

If diagnosing recurrent abdominal pain is a challenge, treatment is an art. Reassurance, passage of time, mild pain relievers, stool softeners, avoidance of certain foods (especially dairy products), and some troubleshooting of the issues of life may be on the agenda. If the problem is particularly vexing, your child's physician may recommend an evaluation by a specialist.

It's not uncommon for children in this age-group to mention occasionally that a leg or some other area hurts. If none of the above red flags are present, a wait-and-see approach is reasonable. Usually the pain will calm down on its own within a short time and be forgotten. Some particularly vigorous play, for example, can cause overuse injuries such as minor muscle strain or irritation where a muscle attaches to bone (**tendonitis**). Temporary aching in one or both legs late in the day or during the night has traditionally been called **growing pains,** although the cause is uncertain. No specific treatment is needed other than your TLC, perhaps accompanied by gentle massage, heat, stretching, and acetaminophen or ibuprofen.

PHYSICAL FITNESS AND SPORTS

Your child may have seemed like a perpetual-motion machine during his toddler and preschool years, and perhaps you looked forward to when he might slow down a little. Now you may be facing a very different problem. Many school-age children shift gears into a sedentary lifestyle, especially if you allow TV and video games to encroach on time once spent outdoors. Studies of physical fitness in children over the past two decades have shown a gradual decline in strength and endurance with a concurrent rise in percentage of body fat.

For better or worse, habits developed early in life are likely to continue for decades into the future. The benefits of maintaining regular exercise throughout life include a reduced risk of coronary artery disease and other medical problems, improved energy and sense of well-being, and better stress management. Your child isn't going to be motivated by concerns over heart attacks and diabetes that may occur forty years from now. But he may be interested in activities, sports, and games that involve muscle motion if they are part of your family's way of life. Exercise and fitness need to be modeled, not just talked about.

Children and their parents can exercise in countless ways. The most basic is a twenty-five to thirty-minute walk four or more times a week, an activity that many adults choose for fitness. Children may enjoy being part of a brisk family stroll, especially on a balmy summer evening, but over the long haul they are more likely to prefer more vigorous and/or competitive pursuits. Bicycling, swimming, roller-skating or in-line skating, and skiing can offer excellent conditioning, provided that appropriate safety precautions are taken. And these activities can be enjoyed by your child for many years.

At age five or six, some children enter organized team sports programs, especially soccer and T-ball (or later Little League baseball). Others become active in individual competitive sports such as swimming, gymnastics, or skating. In some families, children become involved in archery, bowling, sailing, or horseback riding. There are few athletic or physical skills that children cannot begin to learn during these years, with these exceptions:

- Collision sports such as football or hockey should be postponed until age fourteen unless they are specifically noncontact forms of these games. Sports with a potential for physical contact such as soccer or basketball may be intimidating for children under age eight. A child who is younger, smaller, or less aggressive than his fellow players may find these activities too intense.
- Because of its potential for causing damage to the brain, boxing should be avoided completely.
- Exercise caution and discernment if your child wants to join a martial-arts program. Martial-arts classes for children and adolescents are more popular than ever, and they can help build confidence as well as skills in self-protection. But some guidelines are in order. Make sure that the emphasis is on building balance, coordination, and restraint, not on thrashing an opponent—you don't want *your* child to become the neighborhood bully. Check out the safety guidelines in the classes. For example, breaking boards should not be part of the curriculum before the age of twelve because of the risk of damage to bones, tendons, and ligaments in the hands and feet. Also watch out for any religious or mystical component that might be incompatible with your faith.

Participation in sports and competition can have many benefits for children: developing strength and coordination, acquiring self-discipline, learning cooperation and sportsmanship, and building friendships. But these activities also have the potential to cause physical injury; generate considerable stress or permanent emotional scars; and nourish a host of negative attitudes, including elitism, hostility, and an obsession with winning. To maintain balance and build positive experiences through sports, revisit the following questions on a regular basis:

- Is your child really interested in this activity? You may have loved Little League, but your child may prefer soccer.

Children love daily routine activities of the simplest kind. You can turn the routine chores of living into times of warmth and closeness if you give a little thought to them.

DR. DOBSON
ANSWERS YOUR
QUESTIONS ABOUT
RAISING CHILDREN

- Is your child physically and emotionally ready to practice and compete in the sport?
- Is the proper protective equipment available and used at all times?
- Do the coaches and trainers enjoy working with children, including the least skilled? Are they focused on the right attitudes and values (see below), or do they appear driven to win at all costs? Are they competent?
- Do you have the resources and time to support your child through the tryouts, practices, and events?
- How heavily is your child's—or your own—self-concept dependent on his success? Does the emotional weather at your home rise and fall with the fortunes of the team or your child's ranking at the last swim meet?
- Are positive values being taught and modeled by all concerned? Is unsportsmanlike conduct tolerated? Are parents who watch the events behaving themselves?
- *Are we having fun yet?* The vast majority of children will not become professional athletes or Olympic contenders, so the experiences of sports and competition should be enjoyed, not endured. If the sport becomes a thorn in your child's side or constantly drains her of energy and joy, reconsider goals and priorities.

WHEN IS IT OKAY TO QUIT?

Your daughter begged you to let her begin gymnastics classes, but now her muscles are sore, and it's clear that it is hard work—much harder than she thought it would be. Furthermore, she's not as good as the other girls, and more than a couple of times she's landed with a painful thud on the mat. She's had enough, but you've spent ninety-five dollars for a class that will continue for another six weeks. Do you let her bail out or make her continue to the bitter end—perhaps quoting the adage that "winners never quit and quitters never win"?

The answer will depend on your child and her track record. If she has a habit of making enthusiastic false starts and rarely bringing any project to completion, she will probably benefit from the experience of struggling to complete the course she started. This reality therapy will be especially important if you have funded the classes after she promised to finish them. In this case,

being true to her word is the issue rather than the classes themselves.

When the activity in question is something that other family members enjoy together, such as skiing or skating, some positive encouragement to struggle through the learning process in order to enjoy a lifelong payoff would be appropriate.

If she has been consistently involved in other long-term activities but is clearly miserable in this one, you may want to let her quietly retire. Make sure the problem isn't a mismatch of child and coach or a mistaken entry into a group that is too advanced. At times a change of venue, trainer, or team can make a significant difference. However, if the activity proves to be a dead end, don't berate her for it. Allowing her to maintain her dignity will accomplish far more than any trophy on the family shelf.

MUSIC, DANCE, ART, CLUBS,
AND OTHER PURSUITS

Between the fifth and twelfth birthdays, many children begin to play musical instruments, start dance lessons, or join scouting or other programs that offer a variety of valuable experiences. As with athletic programs, your child will take to some of these more fervently than to others, and the benefits and costs of each should be evaluated on a regular basis. Pay particular attention to your child's level of interest, enjoyment, progress, and commitment as well as to any signs of stress or distress.

In general, this should be a time for a child to sample a variety of activities and interests. What does he do well? Where does she fit in? He may not be a whiz with a ball and glove but have a knack with a trombone or a special touch with animals. Finding her niche(s) in life will require trying a number of activities on for size. Some will fit better than others, and she needs to be able to see what works for her without the threat of rebuke or humiliation—although some activities that you consider central to your family's identity, such as attending church, will not be open for negotiation.

If you are bringing up a child with unusual gifts, whether in athletics, music, or some other arena, the training and discipline required for him to develop his fullest potential may be demanding for everyone in the family. Focused and prolonged practices, unusual schedules, and intense competition will need to be balanced against the other needs of a growing child, including friendships, play, and a broad-based education.[1]

The other potential pitfall during these important years is the problem of "too much of a lot of good things." Some children who have school, Little League, music/dance lessons, Scouts, and church activities have calendars that make a corporate president look like a slacker. If two or more children in the same family are in this busy loop, juggling schedules, transportation, and phone calls can crowd out such basic activities as sharing a meal together or attending the same church service. It may become necessary to evaluate the impact of a child's commitments on the family as a whole and not merely on the child himself.

As with group sports activities, in artistic, social, and even church group settings there is always the potential for cliques, unhealthy comparisons, and excessive emotional pressure, which are especially harmful for younger or shyer children. Pay attention to your child's response to his extracurricular activities. If he is gifted or interested in a particular pursuit, he will probably not only thrive but also survive the occasional bad day, tedious meeting, less-than-stellar performance, or spat with his cohorts. But take heed if you see ongoing crying complaints, withdrawal, or even aggression. A good way to keep tabs on these activities is to get involved yourself where you can—perhaps serving as a chaperone, assistant, snack provider, or even occasional teacher of something you do well.

Earlier we listed some questions to keep in mind in order to promote balance and positive experiences with sports. A similar list applies to other group activities:

- Is your child truly interested in this activity? You may have been an Eagle Scout, but he might hate camping and hiking. Piano may be your forte, but she might prefer the electric guitar.
- Are the adults in charge responsible, competent, caring toward children, and acceptable as role models? Do they promote and demonstrate moral and ethical behavior? Are they more worried about how well a performance or project turns out or about making sure that everyone involved has a positive, growing experience?
- Are the attitudes of the other children involved in the group having a positive or negative impact on your child? Is there general acceptance of everyone as one of the gang, or do cliques and pecking orders abound?
- Do you have the time and resources to support your child through the meetings, rehearsals, performances, excursions, fund-raisers, or other components of the group? (The schedules involved in some performing-arts activities can become daunting as curtain time draws near.)
- Is your child's, or your own, self-concept strongly dependent upon her abilities, acceptance, and accomplishments in one or more activities? If she doesn't get a solo or a part in the play, do the storm clouds roll in?
- Last but not least, is everyone enjoying the activity or merely enduring it? Is it enhancing your family's life and providing some cherished memories or sapping energy and joy from child and parent alike?

PHYSICAL SAFETY, INDOORS AND OUT

During the next several years, your child will generally not require the type of nonstop surveillance that was necessary to keep her safe as a toddler and preschooler. However, you will now have the responsibility and privilege of teaching your child habits that will increase the likelihood that she remains safe and healthy. The following areas are particularly important:

Automobiles and other machines that have wheels and motors. Automobile accidents are the most common cause of death in this age-group, so make sure that each person in the car wears a seat belt/shoulder harness, even if you're going just a few blocks. The rule must be that the car doesn't move until everyone is properly secured and that the car stops if someone unfastens her belt. Period. Furthermore, teach your child to buckle up whenever she rides in someone else's car, even if that person's rules are more lax than yours.

In addition, practice these safety guidelines:

- Children under twelve years of age should not sit in the front seat of a car that has a passenger-side air bag, according to the National Highway Traffic Safety Administration. Even in a low-speed accident, the sudden inflation of an air bag (which moves at about 200 mph) can injure or even kill a child.
- Never allow your child to ride in the cargo area of a station wagon, van, or truck. She may find the novelty exciting, but in an accident, she could be thrown from the vehicle or crushed.
- Don't let preteen children operate motorcycles, motorbikes, all-terrain vehicles (ATVs), or off-road vehicles. They lack the coordination and judgment to drive them without risking accident and injury.
- Don't give your child driving lessons out on a deserted stretch of country road or in your quiet neighborhood. Let her learn when and where it's legal and after she's had the appropriate driver's-training class.
- Be wary of allowing your child to ride as a passenger on any open vehicle such as Uncle John's motorcycle or the neighbor's dune buggy. Helmets are a must, and the operator should be mature and prudent, without any inclination to show off or give your child a high-velocity thrill. Be a party pooper proudly and fervently for the sake of your child's safety.

Bicycles, skateboards, roller skates, and in-line skates. The right equipment and the right habits can prevent falls, bruises, fractures, head injuries, or worse.

- Make sure that the bicycle is the right size for your child. The balls of your child's feet should touch the ground when he sits on the seat. When he stands, there should be an inch of clearance between the center bar and his crotch. Don't be tempted to buy a bike that is too big for him so he can grow into it because he will have trouble controlling it. Hand brakes should be used only when his hands are strong enough to use them effectively.
- No one (including Mom or Dad) rides a bike or uses a skateboard or in-line skates without a properly fitting helmet that meets the standards of the American National Standards Institute (ANSI) or the Snell Memorial

Foundation. Critical injuries to the skull and brain can occur during a bicycle accident, and *a helmet can reduce the severity of damage by as much as 90 percent*. As your child grows, the helmet will need to be sized upward accordingly and replaced if it is damaged in a crash. The same helmet should also be worn while using a skateboard or roller skates/blades, along with knee pads and wrist guards.

◆ Teach your child the rules of the road, stressing that he has the same responsibilities as the operator of any other vehicle. Riding in the street should be a privilege reserved for those over six years old who can demonstrate that they have full control of the bicycle and understand how to maneuver it properly, whether or not cars are in the vicinity. Darting in and out of driveways, ignoring traffic signs and signals, riding on the wrong side of the road, or showing off with tricks or stunts (such as riding two on a bike) should be corrected immediately, and if necessary, a temporary restriction of riding privileges should occur if there are repeat performances.

◆ Children should not ride bicycles at night.

◆ Skateboarders and roller skaters/bladers should stay out of the street and avoid homemade ramps and jumps.

Pedestrians. Not all of the risks in traffic belong to those on wheels.

◆ Teach your child how to use crosswalks and interpret traffic and pedestrian signals. Show him how to look both ways and double-check before crossing the street, even when the signal says he has the right-of-way. Supervise his street crossing until he is at least seven.

◆ Talk to your child until you're blue in the face, if needed, about darting into the street. Remind him that the ball he is trying to save from being run over can always be replaced, but he cannot.

Bodies of water. With or without swimming lessons, your child is not ready to use a pool or enter any other body of water without adult supervision. No adult, no swimming. Don't overestimate your child's ability or endurance in water. Drowning is the second most common cause of death in this age-group, so consider being trained to give CPR. Local hospitals or Red Cross chapters routinely offer training.

◆ Your backyard pool should be surrounded by a high fence, and entry access should be locked if an adult is not present.

- Floating toys or rubber rafts do not provide adequate flotation safety for a child who cannot swim. If the toys deflate or overturn, he could drown.
- Don't allow your child to swim in a river or canal. If he wants to wade into the water at the beach, wade with him and stay close by. If there's any undertow, get out and play in the sand instead. Your child must understand that rivers, lakes, and oceans do not behave like a backyard pool, and they should be treated with the utmost respect.
- No one dives without knowing how (hands striking the water first, not the head) and knowing how deep the water is. Diving should take place only from a true diving board at a pool full of water. Diving off a dock or platform at a lake could lead to a disastrous head or neck injury if the water is not sufficiently deep.
- When in a boat, every child under twelve years of age should wear a personal flotation device, and one should also be available for each older passenger. In addition, a harness (which attaches the child to Mom or Dad) may be appropriate to limit the explorations of children under the age of five.[2]
- No one swims during an electrical storm.

Fire hazards and firearms. The bottom line is to separate your child from things that burn, ignite, explode, or discharge.

- Make sure that your home has properly installed and functioning smoke detectors. Replace the batteries every six months. Consider getting a carbon-monoxide detector as well.
- Teach your child what to do in case of a fire (see sidebar, next page).
- Never underestimate your child's fascination with things that burn. School-age children can be incredibly creative with matches or leftover Fourth of July fireworks. Tell your child in no uncertain terms that playing with fire in any way is strictly off-limits and that they should steer clear of—and report—other children who are doing so.
- Think very carefully before bringing or keeping guns in the home. Children rarely have a sense of their destructive power or a grip on the fact that real people who are shot don't just get up and walk away (or show up unscathed in the next episode). If you own one or more guns, the unloaded weapon(s) should be under lock and key and the ammunition locked elsewhere. Talk to your child candidly about the real dangers of firearms, and make it clear that under no circumstances is he to handle any gun—yours or anyone else's—on his own. Furthermore, if

another child appears to have a real gun, your child should get away immediately and notify you or the nearest responsible adult.

Promoting Emotional, Moral, and Spiritual Health

As a baby, toddler, and preschooler, your child needed—and demanded—your attention. When she was a hungry newborn, no one could sit still while she was crying at full volume. As a toddler, when she wanted something, most likely everyone heard about it—over and over—until she got a response.

But your school-age child won't behave this way. She won't be coming to you one hundred times a day needing a little problem solved or looking for a hug. As she becomes more involved with school, friends, and various activities outside the home, you may begin thinking of her as self-sufficient and no longer needing the time and attention you provided during her first five years of life. But she still needs your ongoing attention, input, and guidance. She cannot and should not play the role of parent to herself. In addition, she also deeply craves your ongoing acceptance and affirmation. If she can't get these from you, she'll seek attention elsewhere, and those who might give it to her may have agendas radically different from yours.

FIRE-SAFETY PREPARATIONS FOR YOUR CHILDREN

We hope you will never have to deal with a major fire in your home, but some basic preparation will prevent all-out panic if one should occur. Some details to cover with your children include:

- How to use 911 and/or other emergency numbers
- Stay low to the ground when smoke is present
- Avoid opening any doors that are hot to the touch
- How to escape through a window (including use of chain ladders if needed)
- How to stop, drop to the ground, and roll if clothing is on fire
- What firefighters may look like in their full gear (Children might be frightened by the bulky shapes

with face masks and axes or other tools and run away from them.)
- Get help from neighbors
- Agree on a meeting place after escape
- Family fire drills

While you are talking about your family's response to a fire, you should also go over contingency plans for any possible natural disaster (such as an earthquake, flood, tornado, hurricane) that might occur where you live. Include instructions as to whom you or your children might contact in case communications are disrupted. (It may be easier to get in touch with a relative across the country who could serve as a communication dispatcher for the family.)

This can be a hazardous time in a family's development. During a child's school years, parents often become deeply embroiled in their own career development or other pursuits. But if one or both parents are careening through the week with schedules and deadlines bearing down relentlessly every day and on weekends, who will have time to play a game of Scrabble or talk about a problem? If parental energy is consumed by achievement and acquisition, who will have the interest to sort through this week's math problems or walk up the beach and chat about what makes people tick?

Right now, your child's eyes and ears and heart are likely to be as open to your input as they will ever be in her life. Once she begins adolescence, this will probably not still be the case—at least for a while. As these next few years pass, therefore, you will need to create some margin in your life, some reserve of time and energy, so you can *be there*—both physically and emotionally—for your school-age child.

What specific areas of her life should you be paying attention to?

Instilling basic moral values

During the next few years, your child will need to make an important transition. She will need to shift from being good because you told her so to becoming civilized and virtuous on her own. Whatever you choose to call it—internalizing values, assimilating moral principles, buying into what you've told her, developing good habits, or as Scripture describes it, having the law written on the heart—encouraging this process is the most important responsibility of your parenting career. Of course, no one will be 100 percent successful at it because no one will ever arrive at moral perfection. But while recognizing everyone's limitations, you will want to track your child's progress in acquiring a number of important assets:

- An active, meaningful faith in God that is applied to everyday life experiences and influences attitudes and decisions.
- Respect for others within and outside the family, regardless of age, race, gender, appearance, or behavior.
- Submission to those who are in proper authority, beginning with parents and extending to teachers, coaches, law-enforcement officials—and ultimately to God Himself.
- Respect for the property and possessions of others, while at the same time understanding that happiness ultimately does not arise from the material things a person might acquire.

◆ A commitment to honesty and integrity, with a consistent, internalized habit of telling the truth.

◆ Self-control, self-discipline, and an understanding of the importance of delaying gratification while working toward future goals.

◆ Refraining from using language that is offensive, obscene, or profane.

Obviously your child will not develop these virtues overnight. She may do the right thing repeatedly out of obedience to you, but growing in wisdom and exercising moral values is a lifetime project, and most values are understood more clearly through example and modeling. She will learn a lot about faith when she hears you pray, about respect for property when she sees you pay for something you accidentally break, and about relationships when she sees you apologize when you've done something wrong. She will be all ears as you respond to annoying situations and people, and like it or not, whatever language you use or attitudes you have she will consider okay for her to use under similar circumstances. She may not

WHAT IF YOU AND YOUR CHILD ARE PERPETUALLY IN TURBULENT WATERS?

All this talk of spending time to share affirmation and values with your school-age child may sound like so much hot air if you are still embroiled in a nonstop trench war. Are you dealing with a son or daughter who is constantly irritable, negative, or disruptive? Do you spend most of your time simply trying to maintain some semblance of order? Are your requests or directives routinely met with passive indifference or outright rebellion? Do you feel a major sense of relief when you get away from your child for a while?

If so, some basic evaluation and course corrections are in order. Among other things, you may be dealing with one or all of the following:

◆ *A medical problem.* Many chronic conditions (for example, allergies, recurrent headaches, sinusitis, or anemia to name a few) can cause a child to feel poorly enough to provoke ongoing irritability. Acute illnesses (such as the flu) or injuries (especially a blow to the head) can do likewise. In either case there are usually more specific symptoms or an event to suggest a medical problem. Nevertheless, a review of the situation by your

child's physician can help determine whether a medical problem is responsible for your child's behavior.

◆ *Medications and drugs.* Antihistamines or decongestant/antihistamine combinations may cause irritability, although usually the connection between the drug and the mood change is readily apparent. Drugs which themselves are intended to change behavior (for example, Ritalin or Dexedrine for attention deficit disorder) can sometimes backfire and worsen negative behavior. Illicit drugs and inhalant abuse now penetrate the school-age population in many parts of the country, and their effect on behavior can be very significant. (Drug abuse is discussed in Special Concerns, page 579.) If you are concerned about a possible connection between your child's mood and medications or drugs—whether prescribed, over the counter, or bought on the street—a physician's evaluation is wise.

◆ *A neurochemical disturbance* such as attention deficit disorder (see *attention deficit/hyperactivity disorder*, Reference).

understand or appreciate how hard you work to provide food, clothing, shelter, and other necessities and niceties of life. But when you demonstrate courage, kindness, appreciation, and charity, your actions will be deeply embedded in her memory.

Most of these interactions can't be planned or crammed into a few minutes of "quality time" every day. Many opportunities to teach or demonstrate moral values may catch you off guard and will be gone in the blink of an eye. In order to seize the moment, you have to be there to do the seizing.

Monitoring the input to mind and heart

In the mid-1950s, no television had more than twelve channels, the content of movies was constrained by a code of strictly enforced values, the top ten songs on the radio dealt with "moons and Junes," and the most provocative game in the toy store was Monopoly. Today scorching language, gut-wrenching violence, casual nudity, mind-boggling sexual acts, and general disrespect for life and tradi-

---

(continued)

- *A significant emotional disturbance.* Children can suffer clinical depression, for example.
- *An innately strong-willed child* who is going to challenge your leadership until the day he sets out on his own as a young adult.
- *A problem in consistent limit setting* during the first few years of life—perhaps brought on by parental turmoil, burnout, illness, or divorce—which now needs to be corrected.
- *Abuse*—by other children or by an adult in your child's life. Children who have been abused emotionally, physically, or sexually will often demonstrate drastic changes in their behavior around other people, even those they love and trust. Withdrawal and ongoing hostility could be signs of a problem in this area.
- *Your own behavior as a parent.* Could your words, attitudes, or actions be contributing to your child's current behavior? Is your parenting style either excessively controlling or overly permissive? Are your responses to him unpredictable and disrespectful of his feelings? Is he getting enough of your time and attention, or could his negativity actually be a cry for more of it? A wise parent will periodically carry out

prayerful self-examination, and a significant behavior problem in a child is certainly an appropriate occasion for this task.

Your problem-solving approach will depend on your child and the resources available to you. An evaluation by your child's physician would be a good start and, if appropriate, a referral for family counseling with someone who shares your values. Personal reflection and prayer, consultation with your pastor, and support in a group of parents with children of similar ages would be wise as well. Repair work in relationships takes time, and you can expect this project to continue for a number of months.

Review the Special Concerns section (page 289), which outlines the basics of balancing love and meaningful limits. In addition, specific books that deal in more depth with problems of childhood behavior include:

The New Dare to Discipline and *The Strong-Willed Child* by Dr. James Dobson (Wheaton, Ill.: Tyndale House Publishers, Inc., 1992 and 1978 respectively).

Making Children Mind without Losing Yours by Dr. Kevin Leman (Old Tappan, New Jersey: Fleming H. Revell Company, 1984).

tional values are readily accessible to anyone, including children. Words and images that are inappropriate for children (or anyone else) can literally flood a home that does not take deliberate steps to stem the tide.

And while you may be careful about the types of things you allow your children to see, neighbors up the street may be careless about the images flickering on their TV screen or who is in the room to see them. To make matters worse, school-age children are intensely curious about "adult" matters and consider it a badge of honor to have had a look at something you've declared off-limits. And while violent or sexually explicit sights and sounds create profoundly strong and disturbing memories, repeated exposure has a desensitizing effect that can seriously warp attitudes and erode respect for the human body—and life itself. Unless you cut your family off from civilization altogether, you will need to be perpetually vigilant about the material your child sees and hears and be prepared to deal with whatever leaks past your defenses.

Your options in dealing with this problem include:

- A simple but rather austere approach: no TV, movies, videos, video games, or Internet. If everyone will go with this flow and you can provide plenty of other forms of stimulation (such as reading, music, games played between human beings, and good old-fashioned, interesting conversation), you may bring up the smartest and most literate kids in town. But if you take too rigid an approach, including strict social restrictions to maintain your rules, sooner or later rebellion is inevitable. It is likely that your child will secretly seek and find some rotting forbidden fruit and ingest it without your knowledge or input.
- At the other extreme, a hang-loose, anything-goes mentality abdicates important responsibilities. Don't become so intimidated by the swarm of media mosquitoes that you shrug your shoulders and take down your protective netting.
- Somewhere in between lies a limited-access approach, which demands time and energy but is potentially rewarding. In this case, the various media are regarded as neutral tools through which either positive or negative material may flow. Specific standards must be set for your family as well as for individual members based on age and maturity. Viewing is planned and limited, both in time and content. Previewing and choosing material that children may watch is an important part of the process. Most worthwhile are the opportunities to discuss what has just been seen and to teach some critical thinking. What take-home

lessons were depicted? What positive values were portrayed? If negative material was present, what was wrong with it?

Even if you succeed in limiting your child's diet of movies, TV programs, videotapes, and electronic games to material that is wholesome and nourishing, you will still have to deal with too much of a good thing. School-age children can easily become TV addicts, and there are good reasons to limit the hours they spend each day staring at the electronic cyclops:

- TV watching is mentally passive. The images, sounds, and ideas generated by the programmers (including blatant sales pitches) are actively pouring into your child's mind, while thinking, reasoning, imagining, or creating—and homework—come to a screeching halt.
- TV watching is physically passive. Young viewers who sit for hours are not running, climbing, cycling, or moving muscles in any meaningful way. Obesity and poor physical fitness are common among avid TV users.
- TV watching can become the centerpiece of family life. Group staring can replace talking, working, playing, eating, or praying together.

To prevent the tube from taking over your child's world, set specific ground rules for everyone:

- Preplan how much, when (after homework and other responsibilities are done), and what will be viewed.
- Invest in a VCR and blank videocassette tapes. If something particularly worthwhile is going to be broadcast at an inopportune time, tape it for viewing later. While videocassette recorders can lure families to rent more movies than they need, when used prudently they are a great investment and time-saver; ultimately they give you more options with more control over content and scheduling.
- Think twice before installing a TV in your child's room. You'll lose control of the viewing activity, and your child will be isolated from the normal flow of family life.
- Think carefully before subscribing to a cable or satellite service that includes access to unedited films. You'll not only be more likely to waste hours watching something obnoxious that just happens to be on, but your child may become acquainted with objectionable material when you aren't around.

Whatever is true, whatever is noble, whatever is right, whatever is pure, whatever is lovely, whatever is admirable— if anything is excellent or praiseworthy —think about such things.

PHILIPPIANS 4:8

◆ Don't let the tube baby-sit your child, especially during the Saturday morning "kidvid" marathon.

TV won't be the only potential media hazard in your child's path during the next few years. You will need to be vigilant in a number of other areas as well:

◆ Be sure to check reviews carefully before taking your child to a movie. While you can click off objectionable TV images, motion pictures on big screens have a greater sensual impact, especially in theaters with bone-rattling sound systems. Remember that even films with the PG rating may contain material that can jolt a child's mind for months. And even movies geared to children may contain supernatural or occultic themes that can collide with your family's faith or subtle messages that can undermine values you have been teaching. Whether a film proves to be a wonderful experience or ninety minutes of nails on the chalkboard, talk to your child about it. What made it good or awful? Were any values taught? Was this a cautionary tale, and if so, what lessons were on display?

◆ Video games (whether played on home computers or on game systems that connect to the family TV set) are enormously popular with children in this age-group and can consume vast amounts of their time and money. If you have video-game equipment of any kind at home, set specific time limits that can be spent playing with them. Also be careful about the types of games your child buys, borrows, rents, or plays at the local arcade. While many are good, clean fun, some consist of nonstop fighting, and a few contain vivid images of carnage or overtly antisocial themes.

◆ While you might think of fantasy/role-playing games as a healthy alternative to TV and video, beware of those in the Dungeons and Dragons genre. Older children can become deeply enmeshed in one or more roles they assume in these games, spending huge amounts of time in complex scenarios that often are pervaded by destructive supernatural themes and violence.

◆ Few parents would object to seeing their child engrossed in reading. But some of the most popular books for children eight and older are designed to scare the daylights out of them. A series of paperback horror stories for kids, often written in first person, regularly adds new titles and exposes young readers to imagery and situations that would have been unthinkable in children's books a generation ago. You would be wise to steer your child toward books that are better written and more edifying.

◆ You must supervise your child's use of computer on-line services as carefully, if not more so, as his film, video, or TV viewing. *Don't leave him alone in his room for hours on end playing with a computer and a modem.* You might be pleased to think that your budding genius is becoming proficient with modern communications technology, but he could be tapping into extraordinarily explicit and perverse sexual material, antisocial and violent text and images, and chat rooms where the on-line conversations get very raunchy and inappropriate. *Make it clear that your child should not give his name, address, phone number, or any other personal information to someone on-line or agree to go somewhere to meet any new "friends" he might have spoken with by modem.* (Pedophiles and other criminals have discovered on-line services to be fertile ground for finding unsuspecting prey.) Most on-line services have mechanisms that allow you to limit your child's access to certain areas, and new software can to some degree serve as an electronic "nanny" that will terminate inappropriate material. But these tools are imperfect, and you would be wise to require that all your child's on-line activities take place *only* when you are home and *only* on a computer you can directly monitor.

Sex education: meet the faculty

For decades movies and sitcoms have presented a caricature of the sweaty-palmed, birds-and-bees conversation in which Dad stammers through a convoluted description of sex to a preadolescent child—who, it turns out, knows all of the details already. The humor arises from the tension most parents feel about discussing sex with their kids. ("What if we tell him too much?" "Will this rob him of his innocence?" "What if he starts asking about what *we* do?")

What isn't so funny is the reality that too many children learn about sex from everyone *but* their parents. Playground slang and obscenity, a distorted description of intercourse from the tough kid up the street, or worst of all, a look at some pornographic pictures or videos often provides a child's first jarring glimpse of sex. What should be seen as the most beautiful, meaningful, and private communication between a married couple becomes a freak-show curiosity. "Mom and Dad did *that??* More than once?!"

Efforts by public schools to correct misinformation from the street and lack of information from home often leave out a critical ingredient: the moral framework within which the facts about reproduction should be presented. Without an ethical context, sex education becomes little more than basic training in anatomy, physiology, infectious diseases, and contraception.

Many churches have made laudable efforts to teach biblical principles of sexuality to their youth groups. But these important concepts are not always accompanied by accurate medical information or refusal skills. Furthermore, youth-group presentations usually begin late in the game (i.e., during the teen years) and rarely involve an ongoing dialogue about this subject.

The best place for a child to learn about sexuality is at home from those who care most about him. Anyone can teach the basic facts about reproduction in an hour or two (or they can be read in any of several reference books), but you are in the best position to put this information in the proper context and give it the right perspective over a period of years. There are no cut-and-dried formulas for carrying out this assignment, but keep the following principles in mind:

Giving a child facts about reproduction, including details about intercourse, does not rob him of innocence. Innocence is a function of attitude, not information. A school-age child who understands the specifics of sex, while seeing it as an act that, in the proper context, both expresses love and begins new life, retains his innocence. But a child who knows very little about sex can already have a corrupt mind-set if he has been exposed to it in a degrading, mocking, or abusive context.

If you feel squeamish or inhibited about broaching this subject with your child, reflect for a moment about your own attitudes. Do you harbor any feelings that sexual activity, even within the context of marriage, is somehow base or something that God really doesn't approve of?

Don't wait to tell your child everything you know about sex during a single, intense marathon session. Doing so risks either waiting until it's too late or dumping more in the child's lap than he can process. Instead, information should be released gradually during many conversations over a period of several years.

In many instances, you will be giving information on a need-to-know basis. Your five-year-old is probably going to want to know how the baby inside Aunt Susie is going to get out. But your child may not think to ask how the baby got there, and you don't need to broach the subject at that time. On the other hand, if you haven't yet had any discussions about reproduction with your ten-year-old, you will need to take the initiative to start some conversations. She has already heard all sorts of things on the playground and needs to hear from more reputable and mature sources.

What if your child asks you questions you can't answer? Be honest, and then do some research. You gain far more stature in your child's eyes by showing candor than by bluffing. You may not have a detailed knowledge of the intricacies of the menstrual cycle or the developmental stages of puberty, but you're never too old to learn. (You could brush up on some of these topics by reading the sections in the next chapter regarding adolescent growth and development.)

Sex education: the curriculum

As you ponder the process of communicating to your school-age child about sex, remember that the primary message you need to give him—more important in the long run than the specific facts and figures—is the importance of respect:

- Respect for the body each of us has been given and for the Creator of that body
- Respect for the wonder of reproduction
- Respect for privacy in sexual matters, not only his own, but parents', friends', and others'
- Respect for his future and an understanding that sexual activity can have a profound effect on his health and happiness for the rest of his life
- Respect for marriage as the appropriate context for sexual expression

Think in terms of a gradual and relaxed release of information to your child, beginning with the basic naming of body parts and a general understanding of where babies come from during the preschool years and progressing to full disclosure of the reproductive process before puberty begins.

Young children should know the correct names of their body parts (usually learned during bath time) and gain a basic sense of privacy and modesty for the "bathing suit" areas of the body. While understanding that their genitals are not "bad" or "dirty," they should also know that they are not intended for public display. Now that diaper days are over, your child should learn that the genital area should be touched only by the child himself, a doctor or nurse during an exam, or a parent for a specific reason. Tell your child that if someone else tries to touch those areas, he should protest noisily, get away, and tell you as soon as possible. He must know that you will not be angry or upset with *him* if this should happen.

It is extremely likely that before age five, and possibly later as well, your child will engage in some form of genital show-and-tell with a sibling or another small child. If and when you discover this in progress, your response should not be overblown. Don't tell him that you are shocked and terribly ashamed of him, but instead clearly reinforce the privacy rule and remind him about respect for himself and the other child. The same should happen if your child streaks through the house or yard when others are present or exposes himself to someone else to get a reaction. More significant consequences should follow, of course, if you have talked to him about this behavior but he repeats it anyway. Here, however, the issue is obedience more than the specific act itself.

At some point he may barge into the bathroom when you're in the shower or even wander into the bedroom at a highly inopportune time. Again, don't overreact, but calmly ask him to leave. Later let him know that there is nothing bad about what he saw, but that it is meant to be private and that he should knock on the door first before coming into your room. Incidentally, once the toddler years have passed, grown-ups should abide by a dress code when the kids are at home: If you're not wearing enough to be seen by adult houseguests, you're not wearing enough to be seen by your children.

Along with learning the names and addresses of body parts, younger children will also be interested in the big picture of reproduction. Questions will undoubtedly come up if you are expecting a new baby in your family, and this event can provide a nice long window of opportunity to talk about the entire process of pregnancy and birth. With or without a nine-month object lesson at home, a straightforward explanation that a baby grows inside the mother and that at the right time he or she comes into the world through the mother's vagina will satisfy the need-to-know concerns for many children through the first or second grade.

Some will want to know more: How could the baby get through that small hole? Does it hurt to have a baby? Does Daddy help the baby come out? Matter-of-fact answers can alleviate a lot of concern: Yes, it can be uncomfortable when the baby is born, but a doctor helps the baby come out and can give medicine to help the mother feel better. Moms who are going to have babies go to special classes, usually with the dads, so they'll be ready when the time comes.

Eventually, one way or another, the Big Question will come up: Why and how does a baby start to grow inside a mother? (Another common scenario: Once your child is old enough to appreciate a reading of the Christmas story, you may need to explain what a virgin is.) You should avoid mythology (storks) or pseudotheology ("God sends the baby to the mother") or misleading euphemisms ("The mother and father sleep together, and then the baby begins to grow inside the mother"). Some parents talk about mothers and fathers having a very special kind of hug, just for the two of them, which starts the baby growing, but even that explanation may be unclear. Indeed, all of these explanations suggest that pregnancy is a random or unpredictable event.

Only you can judge the readiness of your child, but in most cases when the question needs to be answered, offer a very simple but straightforward explanation. You can talk about how a mother makes a tiny egg inside her body every month, and if there is some sperm from the father to join with the egg at the right time, a baby will begin to grow.

When you get more specific about the process that brings the man's sperm and the woman's egg together, remember to stress context: A man and woman who are married and love each other very much have a special time, just for the two of them, when they get very close to each other—in fact, so close that the man inserts his penis into the woman's vagina. After a while he releases his sperm inside her. Younger children will usually find this idea rather strange, and you can stress that when the man and woman love each other very much, they feel very good while this is going on.

You will need to supply a name for this activity: "Having sex" is probably the most direct without being vulgar; "making love" is a little vague; and "sexual intercourse" is rather clinical, although children should know that this is the term they'll be hearing later in life. Throughout, stress how good sex is—provided it occurs at the right time, with the right person, and in the context of marriage.

Sooner or later, you will also need to talk about situations in which single adults are pregnant or raising children without a partner. You may be having these conversations with your children as a single parent. Children will need to know that some people have sex even though they are not married and that a baby may begin to grow inside a mother as a result. Or they may be married when the baby starts to grow but not married later on.

Whether you will want or need to delve more deeply into the complexities of adult life will depend upon your situation and the age of your child. A young child is going to be more concerned about basic information and his own security with you, whether married or single. A child approaching puberty will probably need more details: What happens when a single woman becomes pregnant? Do they all have their babies? Why do some mothers and fathers split up?

These may be emotional questions to tackle, especially if you have been involved in a divorce or are rearing one or more children on your own for whatever reason. But without condemning others or justifying irresponsibility, this can be an appropriate time to talk about the fact that sexual activity should not be taken lightly. You may want to mention that the Designer of human beings laid down some rules about sex for good reason—not to be a killjoy but to max-

The wise in heart are called discerning, and pleasant words promote instruction.

PROVERBS 16:21

imize our enjoyment of it and to prevent painful consequences. Sex experienced within those boundaries—between one man and one woman, maintained within a marriage relationship to which both are committed for the rest of their lives—is not only right but the safest and most pleasurable.

Preparation for the onset of puberty

As your child approaches puberty, you are going to have to shift gears from talking about sex in general to more specific briefings on his or her own sexuality. Whether you make this a specific discussion or include it as part of a more extensive explanation of what lies ahead during the adolescent years, you will want your child to be ready for the physical changes that are about to take place.

Girls need to know about breast development, new hair growth, and the reproductive cycle. The first menstrual period should be viewed in a positive light, as a passage into adulthood rather than a burden or a "curse of women." Some parents honor the occasion by taking their daughter to dinner at a nice restaurant or presenting a special gift. This event is usually the final stage of pubertal development. If you and your daughter stay in communication about the changes she is experiencing, you can usually anticipate and discuss what she can do if her first period begins when she's away from home.

Similarly, boys should be aware that changes are on the horizon, such as deepening of the voice, enlargement of the genitals, and new hair growth. They should also know about the likelihood that they will have an unexpected emission of seminal fluid during the night (the "wet dream"), and that this is not a sign of disease or moral failure.

Parents will need to discuss with their child the increasing interest in the opposite sex. The boy or girl will also need to be prepared to deal with attention from the opposite sex if and when it occurs. This is an important time to review specific guidelines, and perhaps a little street wisdom, about relationships and physical contact. While reinforcing the importance of saving sex for marriage, what will you say about other kinds of affectionate touching?

Your preadolescent child will most likely wonder if you're going overboard in broaching this subject. "Dad, I'm not going to jump into bed with people, okay? What's the big deal?" But he or she must understand that we are all designed in such a way that physical contact, once started, naturally progresses to increasing intimacy. Indeed, sex is like a car that begins rolling down a hill. At first the hill is nearly flat, but then it becomes progressively steeper. The farther you go, the harder it is to stop. That in itself isn't bad or wrong but simply the way we're made. Since the right time to have sex will be some years away, it will be important to make sure that the car doesn't roll very far before the wedding night. This means that your child will want to have a clear idea what his or her boundaries are and how to maintain them effectively, well before the first socializing with the opposite sex begins.

At some point (probably more than once) during these years, you will need to deal with the subject of **masturbation.** As children approach adolescence, you will have to make a judgment call on what to say about the significance of self-stimulation after puberty arrives. It is extremely likely that masturbation leading to sexual climax will occur at some point, especially for a male. If he is racked with guilt about it and repeatedly vows never to let it happen again, he will probably expend a lot of energy feeling like a moral failure and worrying about his spiritual welfare.

But when masturbation becomes a routine and frequent habit, especially when accompanied by vivid sexual fantasies or, worse, the viewing of pornography, it can be damaging to sexual and emotional health. In essence, a young man may have hundreds of sexual experiences associated with unrealistic or overtly distorted imagery, reinforced with the extreme pleasure of sexual release. At the very least, when he marries, his real-life sexual partner may seem disappointing by comparison, and his physical and emotional bonding with her may be impaired. This problem will be more significant if there have been many actual sexual partners before the wedding night. At worst, he may come in contact with violent or degrading images and associate his own sexual release with them.

Your approach to this issue will need to be both tactful and realistic. *A bottom line worth stressing is that masturbation should not play a major role in your child's life, either as a source of relentless guilt or as a frequent and persistent habit that displaces healthy sexual relations in the future.* If it happens once in a while, it happens. But it should not be pursued as a form of recreation, especially while viewing sexually provocative material, and should never be allowed to occur with other people.

Who should deliver these messages to your growing child? In many families, everyone will feel more comfortable if mothers talk with daughters and fathers with sons. It may be more fruitful in the long run, however, if both parents participate in many of the discussions of sexuality, where mother and father can each offer specific perspectives, and one can pick up the thread if the other draws a blank in a particular area. This also solidifies the notion that sex is a matter for couples who are committed to one another and provides your child with two sources of appropriate information rather than one. In single-parent families in which the child is of the opposite sex from the parent, a trusted friend, relative, or youth pastor may need to fill in some gaps in sensitive areas.

While it may be useful to have both parents involved in discussions of sexuality, it will usually not be wise to talk to more than one child at once. This is especially important when you are dealing with your child's own sexuality rather than with less personal topics. A ten-year-old girl who is learning about very personal changes that will be taking place in her body should not have a wisecracking eight-year-old brother in the room. If necessary, take her to a place where you can ensure privacy before you bring up these subjects.

Preparing for Adolescence: Painting the Big Picture

While discussions about your child's sexuality can help ease the arrival of puberty, there is much more to the upcoming adolescent years than surging hormones. Many children enter the preteen and teen years unprepared for the gamut of changes and challenges that await them. As a result, a grade-schooler may enter adolescence happy and well-adjusted and within a few short years emerge battered, bruised, and thoroughly discouraged—along with the rest of the family.

Your school-age child is likely to be much more interested now in what you have to say than she will be later. Once she enters the adolescent years, it may seem as if she has temporarily changed the frequency of her mental tuner so she won't receive your broadcasts. While you may now feel as though you've got her number, in a few years you might hear a busy signal.

Years ago, Apollo astronauts would pass behind the moon as part of their normal flight plan. But during those tense minutes, communication between the spacecraft and mission control would be impossible. When they emerged from the dark side of the moon, contact would resume. You may face a dark-side-of-the-moon experience in the coming years, during which a cool head and lots of prayer will be needed while you wait for your child to emerge from the other side. But you may avert or shorten it by walking your child through the trajectory called adolescence before the rocket takes off.

Ideally, you should plan on having a series of conversations with your prepubertal child at age nine or ten for a girl, and perhaps a year or two later for a boy. Some parents plan a special weekend away from home, perhaps in the mountains or at a pleasant hotel, in order to have some undistracted, one-on-one time during which these discussions can take place. If possible, both parents should be involved in this process. If you are a single parent, don't feel that you can't deal with most (if not all) of the topics involved in this preadolescent briefing. As was mentioned in the previous section regarding connection with sexuality, if you feel uneasy talking about the physical transition to adulthood with your prepubertal child of the opposite gender, you may want to enlist a trusted friend, a relative, or your youth pastor to help with this particular topic.

Before you embark on this series of discussions, you may want to brush up on information about this upcoming period of your child's life. Feel free, though, to mine your own memories for illustrations and recollections about how you felt when you were growing up. If you know any cautionary tales about people who made some unwise decisions, don't hesitate to tell them. Your child will probably remember such stories long after these conversations are over and may even pass them on to her children.

To gather additional details for this task, you may want to read ahead in this book to the chapters regarding adolescence. Another excellent resource is Dr. James Dobson's book and tape series entitled *Preparing for Adolescence,* which is directed specifically toward the child who is about to embark on this voyage toward adulthood. Some parents have found it helpful to listen to the tapes with their children and then discuss them, while others digest the materials on their own and adapt them to their own child's specific needs and personality.

During this preparation, you will want to talk about the following subjects, among others:

The physical changes that will be taking place in the near future. Along with hormonal and sexual developments, there will be rapid growth of bone and muscle, although the timing and rates may vary greatly among children. As a result, an eighth-grade gym class may contain skinny boys with alto voices who are competing and taking showers with peers who are hairy, muscular, and highly intimidating. Remind your child that, whatever his particular timing might be, the transition to adulthood will indeed take place. (How many men with boys' voices has he seen recently?)

The emotional weather forecast. The transition from childhood to adulthood is usually marked by times of intense emotions, especially during the early teen years. When things are going well, she may feel ecstatic. When there is a problem, the world will seem to be coming to an end. Relationships with her peers may swing wildly from love to hate and back again—within the same day.

The valley of the shadow of lack of confidence. Your child needs to know that all who pass through this period feel unsure of themselves. This goes for the most popular, attractive, athletic, intelligent students as well—they *all* desperately crave acceptance and approval. It also holds true for the tough, mean, sarcastic types who make everyone else miserable.

The herd instinct. Because everyone wants desperately to be accepted and avoid ridicule during adolescence, the opinions of peers can carry incredible and sometimes ridiculous weight. Your child must understand the importance of standing her ground, even in the face of intense pressure, when she is being pushed to say or do something she knows to be wrong. The obvious areas to stress are those that might threaten life and health: smoking, drinking, illegal drugs, sex, breaking the law. But a few seemingly less dangerous concessions to peer pressure can also set long-term negative habits in motion. Under the influence of a poorly chosen friend, your child might sample the following:

- Music with antisocial or amoral lyrics
- Films, videos, or Internet sites with violent or pornographic content
- Occultic or death-oriented games
- Obscene, profane, or simply disrespectful language
- Counterproductive attitudes about school, church, and family

Explain to your child that anyone who might pull her in any of these directions simply does not have her best interests in mind. Getting into something that violates the standards you have set at home in order to impress a friend or win someone's approval is like throwing her most prized possession down the toilet.

As will be discussed in the following chapters, you will need to pick your battles in the area of conformity to the crowd. If peer standards call for everyone to wear white socks and sneakers, and anyone who wears dark socks and dress shoes is declared a geek, let her wear the official footwear. Within reason, she shouldn't have to suffer ridicule in areas that do not involve ethical or moral standards.

The process of picking a husband or wife. What kind of person will your child be looking for? You will want to spend some time with this one, stressing the importance of shared faith and values, character, and the ease of making conversation with anyone who may become a marital partner. Good looks and the buzz of romantic chemistry are nice frosting on the cake, but they aren't enough to serve as the foundation for a lifelong journey. Remind your child that you will be praying for that special person, whoever he or she might be. If you haven't done this before, now is a good time to start.

Reassure her that these growing pains will not last forever. Remind her also that, in contrast to the fluctuations of her emotions, the whims of the peer group, and whatever is "hot" and "not" during the coming years, some things will last: your love for her, her place in your family, and above all, the care and involvement of God in her life.

NOTES
1. This issue is presented with considerable insight in the film *Searching for Bobby Fischer,* a true story of a child with extraordinary skill in chess. Parents of children who possess unusual gifts would benefit from watching this film and thinking carefully about the importance of developing character along with talent.
2. State laws may vary, but the American Academy of Pediatrics (AAP) recommends that children under twelve years of age wear a flotation device.

Eating Disorders

While the majority of the world's children suffer from a chronic lack of adequate food to sustain normal growth and development, the most common nutritional disorder among children and adolescents in developed countries is an excess of body fat. In some ways, this is not surprising. When food is abundant, it is not unusual to eat more than is really needed to relieve hunger. Furthermore, eating will occur for a host of reasons that have little to do with appetite, such as providing emotional pleasure and comfort. Eating is also a common response to excitement, boredom, anger, depression, or simply an accompaniment to virtually any form of relaxation or social gathering.

Our bodies are designed primarily for surviving the ebb and flow of an unstable food supply. When more food arrives than is immediately needed, intricate biochemical processes see to it that the leftovers are stored as fat for use during the next famine. If a famine never arrives, the excess fat becomes a permanent resident and continues to accumulate.

Modern technology has provided a multitude of labor-saving devices and beguiling passive entertainments, all of which promote much more sitting and watching than active muscle motion. A great many grade-school children, adolescents, and adults have thus moved from the perpetual motion of their toddler years to a sedentary lifestyle that does not maintain even a basic level of exercise. As a result, excessive body fat is a continuing physical and emotional problem for millions of children and adolescents.

At the same time, powerful cultural forces provoke behaviors that pose even more serious threats to the young. We are saturated night and day with powerful images of beautiful, shapely, impossibly sleek women or buff, tight-muscled masculinity. This leads many, especially prepubertal and adolescent girls, into dangerous thinking: *If only I could look like* that, *my problems would be over.* Often this fantasy fuels a deeply felt desire for physical perfection that collides rudely with the imperfect appearance of a very real body seen in the mirror. The conflict can lead not only to erratic eating habits and dieting, which are not without some risks, but also to the more severely disordered eating patterns known as bulimia and anorexia nervosa, which can rob an adolescent of health or life itself.

While the issues relating to excessive weight and eating disorders cannot all be covered in depth in this book, this section will review key concepts that can help children and adolescents—and their parents—begin moving in the right direction if one of these problems is already present.

DEALING WITH EXCESSIVE WEIGHT

Twenty to 30 percent of American children and adolescents are estimated to be **overweight,** which is traditionally defined as 10 to 20 percent over "ideal" (a better term would be "appropriate") weight[1] for age and height or **obese** (more than 20 percent over appropriate weight). It is important to understand that the significance of a given weight depends not only upon age and height but also on general build and percentage of body fat. For example, a muscular, well-conditioned athlete may technically weigh more than the ideal amount for his height, but his percentage of body fat may be normal or even low.

Normally height and weight are entered on a growth chart as part of routine physical examinations, and very often a look at the pattern of these measurements over a period of time can clarify concerns about a child's weight. If your child or adolescent is more than 20 percent overweight, a medical evaluation is appropriate, whether as part of a regular checkup or during a special visit. While it is unlikely that the doctor will find a treatable disease that is responsible for the weight problem, it is most important to seek help and begin to work with the child on this problem for the following reasons:

◆ Eating and weight patterns established in childhood tend to persist into adulthood. The longer the problem continues, the more the odds against reaching a normal adult weight worsen. One in four obese children entering adolescence will eventually reach a normal weight, but only one in twenty-eight who are obese at the end of adolescence will accomplish this goal.[2]

- Long-standing obesity is associated with a host of health problems later in life, including elevated blood pressure, stroke, diabetes, gall bladder disease, and painful destructive changes in joints.
- Even more significant for obese children and adolescents is the cruel and relentless psychological (and at times even physical) abuse that they nearly always receive from peers. Name calling, isolation, and other forms of social brutality are the order of the day for the overweight child, leaving emotional wounds that could take years to heal—if they ever do.

Once medical causes and/or effects of obesity in a child have been assessed, specific nutritional guidelines should be obtained from a qualified professional. If at all possible, this input should be provided by a registered dietitian who works with young people, since weight management for children and adolescents who are still growing is not a simple matter of "just eat less" or "just go on a diet." *Indeed, food restrictions that leave a child constantly hungry are potentially harmful, both physically and emotionally.* Even if you or some other member of the family has benefited from a specific eating plan or weight-loss program, do not impose that program on your child or adolescent. Her physiology and situation are unique, and any program she undertakes should be under the guidance of a physician and/or nutrition counselor. The amounts and types of foods must be adequate to meet her ongoing needs for growth and development, while at the same time allowing either for gradual loss of weight, holding it level, or slowing its rate of increase. Mapping out the appropriate changes requires some expertise.

A dietitian might ask you and your child to keep a detailed food diary for two or three weeks before attempting any dietary modifications. This can provide insight into the relationship between eating patterns and the current weight. Often the overweight child or adolescent is not consuming more calories than her lean counterpart, and this observation will need to be considered in the course of nutritional planning. The diary may also reveal specific food choices that are contributing to the weight problem.

How parents can help their overweight child

Once reasonable goals have been set and a basic course mapped out, there are a number of contributions parents can make to help their child achieve a proper weight:

Be supportive and matter-of-fact about what needs to be done. *The last thing an overweight child or adolescent needs is another critic.* Whatever insults she hasn't heard from an insensitive cohort at school she has probably said to herself. Harping on the weight problem not only adds to the shame, guilt, and self-loathing, but it may even push her toward more extreme and destructive eating behaviors.

Instill the concept of making wise food choices for life, rather than for just "going on a diet." A diet has a lot in common with a jail sentence—a time of deprivation resulting from a crime (eating too much). When the sentence is served, very often it's back to business as usual. Furthermore, after the body has been deprived through a diet, it may become even more efficient at storing fat. As a result, the dieter can actually gain back more weight than she lost.

Give your child as much responsibility as possible in her food choices, appropriate with her age. You can only push the right food choices for so long. Eventually she will need to make the process her own and enforce her own decisions. The sooner this happens, the better, especially if she has already entered adolescence.

Model healthy eating habits. Leading by example is much more effective than giving a lot of directions. Because of genetics, lifestyle, or both, it is not unusual for more than one family member to be struggling with extra pounds. The choices that benefit the overweight child or adolescent will most likely be helpful for everyone else around the table.

Help your child avoid temptation. It's easier to make healthy food choices when healthy foods are the only kinds available. If the shelves at home are stocked with calorie-dense, high-fat snacks and sweets, don't expect any great progress. Are there family habits or traditions, such as eating continuously while watching a video or playing a game, that are contributing to the problem?

Encourage and model physical activity. Many overweight children and adolescents are also very inactive. The goal should be to find an activity such as walking, cycling, jogging, swimming, or basketball that increases oxygen consumption continuously for fifteen to thirty minutes most days of the week. If this means converting some time spent in front of TV and video games into exercise, all the better for both body and mind. Needless to say, all of your encouragement to "go outside and get some exercise" will be much more meaningful if you are doing likewise.

EATING DISORDERS

While eating and body image are sources of concern or exasperation for millions of people, for some they become the focus of extreme and potentially dangerous behavior. According to the American Psychiatric Association, at any given time roughly a half million people in the United States are affected with an eating disorder. Of these, 95 percent are young women between the ages of twelve and twenty-five, most from middle- or upper-income families. (These conditions are rarely seen in developing countries.) Athletes, models, dancers, and others in the entertainment industry are at particular risk, usually because of intense concern over maintaining a particular, often unrealistic, appearance or level of performance.

The two most common eating disorders, other than obesity, are **anorexia nervosa** and **bulimia nervosa.**

Anorexia nervosa

Anorexia nervosa is a condition of self-imposed starvation that eventually leads to a body weight at least 15 percent below the expected level for an individual's age and height. It is characterized by an extreme fear of gaining weight and a striking disturbance of body image; the anorexic who appears grossly emaciated will look in the mirror and see herself as overweight. This distorted perception typically is stubbornly resistant to feedback from families, friends, and health professionals, even in the face of serious physical and medical consequences.

As more weight is lost, the fear of gaining weight intensifies rather than diminishes, leading to nonstop preoccupation with eating and weight. Behaviors that are called **obsessive-compulsive** often attend this disorder. What little food is eaten will usually be derived only from "safe" low-calorie sources, often measured out in precise quantities and then consumed in an exacting, almost ritualistic manner. Food might be cut into tiny pieces and then arranged and rearranged on the plate to give the impression that some of it has been eaten. Anorexics may obsess over the number of calories they consume from medication or even from licking a postage stamp. Often they carefully monitor body measurements such as upper arm circumference. The fervor with which calories are restricted is frequently applied to burning them as well, and an anorexic individual might exercise vigorously for hours every day. Other efforts to rid the body of calories may include "purging" behaviors, such as self-induced vomiting, which are seen more commonly in bulimia nervosa (see below).

It should come as no surprise that medical consequences, most arising from the body's attempt to conserve energy, become more serious as starvation and weight loss continue. With loss of fat and circulating estrogen, the intricate hormonal interplay of a woman's monthly cycle shuts down. (The absence of three consecutive menstrual periods is one of the diagnostic criteria for anorexia nervosa.) This, combined with an ongoing inadequate intake of nutrients and calcium, leads to loss of bone density, which can cause stress fractures, especially in the presence of intense exercise.

Starvation leads to reduced capacity of the stomach, delays in its emptying of food, and constipation, all of which may be falsely interpreted by the anorexic as gaining weight. Dry skin, thinning of the scalp hair, and development of a fine hair growth on the body called **lanugo** typically occur. Loss of fat stores and metabolic energy conservation lead to a lower body temperature, often causing the anorexic individual to wear more layers of clothing to keep warm. More serious complications arise from the heart, which typically slows its contraction rate and decreases in size in response to efforts to conserve energy. Heart rhythm might become irregular, sometimes to a degree that is life-threatening, especially in the presence of purging behavior, which depletes the body of potassium.

For all these reasons, anorexia nervosa should be considered a very serious condition with lethal risks. Between 5 and 20 percent of anorexics die from starvation, cardiac arrest, or suicide. (The higher death rates are observed among those with a long duration of anorexia, more severe weight loss, poor family support, and multiple relapses despite treatment.)

Bulimia nervosa

Bulimia nervosa is characterized by behavior known as **binging** and **purging,** which may continue for decades. During a binge, an individual quickly consumes an enormous amount of food containing many thousands of calories, often without even chewing or tasting it. The resulting physical and emotional discomfort will then provoke a purge, usually involving self-induced vomiting. Bulimics often use laxatives and diuretics (so-called water pills, medications that increase urine output)—sometimes in dangerous quantities—in a misguided belief that the medications will somehow help rid the body of the food that isn't lost through vomiting. The binging and purging cycles may occur a few times a week or, in severe cases, several times daily.

Bulimia is much more common than anorexia, but it frequently goes undetected because most episodes take place in secret and typically do not lead to significant weight loss. (However, some individuals with anorexia may engage in binge-and-purge behaviors.) Nevertheless, bulimia can have many serious medical consequences. The repeated exposure of teeth to stomach acid (during vomiting) can erode enamel, cause a yellowish discoloration, and lead to decay. The throat and esophagus might become chronically inflamed, and the salivary glands—especially the parotid glands that lie directly in front of the ears—can become enlarged in response to continuing episodes of vomiting. Repeated use of laxatives can lead to severe constipation, while heavy diuretic use may have an adverse effect on kidney function.

Potentially dangerous disturbances in heart rhythm can arise from the repeated loss of potassium from vomiting, as well as from excessive ingestion of diuretics and laxatives. Other equally serious (but fortunately uncommon) events include bleeding and even rupture of the esophagus or stomach from frequent vomiting. Food aspirated into the airway during vomiting can cause choking or pneumonia.

WHAT CAUSES EATING DISORDERS?

What influences cause such seemingly unrewarding and even dangerous behaviors? While each case is unique, potential contributing factors include the following:

- *Cultural factors.* In developed countries, advertisements, films, videos, and TV programs continually display images of bodily perfection, especially for females. Those who are shapely, sleek, and most of all *thin* are seen as successful, sophisticated, desirable, and apparently free of emotional or personal pain. A vulnerable individual who desperately desires these attributes but cannot attain them through normal means may buy into this and thereby set in motion unhealthy and extreme behaviors.
- *Personality and psychological factors.* A typical profile of an anorexia patient is a perfectionistic, high-achieving, adolescent female. She may be seen as a compliant, "good" girl by her parents (one or both of whom might be perfectionistic also), and she usually does not rebel or even have much of a social or dating life. While excelling in many areas, she may berate herself over any performance that falls short of perfection. Some researchers theorize that refusing to eat may serve as a form of rebellion or that it may represent one area of her life over which she can exercise total control. Bulimics, on the other hand, are less predictable in personality and attributes, although alcohol or drug abuse may be a

concurrent issue. In nearly all individuals with either type of eating disorder, anxiety and depression play a significant role.

♦ *Biochemical factors.* Chemical messengers in the brain called neurotransmitters are known to be associated with mood, emotional stability, appetite, and sleep. Many people are genetically vulnerable to changes in neurotransmitter levels, which can lead to overt depression and anxiety disorders, as well as a condition called **obsessive-compulsive disorder (OCD)**—performing certain repetitive acts or ritualistic behavior to relieve anxiety. Neurotransmitter imbalances appear to play a role in the origin of eating disorders, and many features of anorexia bear a striking resemblance to those of OCD.

Because eating disorders can put health and even life in serious jeopardy, they should be taken very seriously. Initiating treatment can be difficult for the bulimic, because so much of her disordered behavior goes on in secret, and for the anorexic, who may stubbornly deny that she needs help or may undermine therapeutic efforts.

In order to be effective, treatment must address a variety of issues and will often require a team approach. A thorough medical evaluation is extremely important and will sometimes reveal a variety of problems that need attention. Counseling will be needed on a long-term basis and should involve the entire family. Antidepressant medication that normalizes neurotransmitter levels can help stabilize mood, relieve depression, and reduce the obsessive component of anorexia. A dietitian should be involved to provide nutritional input and accountability. Pastoral counseling should be sought in an effort to work through issues of guilt and shame, as well as to provide a reorientation to life from God's perspective. In severe cases of anorexia, hospitalization and medically supervised refeeding may be necessary to prevent a fatal outcome.

How parents can help

It is impossible to predict who might develop an eating disorder, but it is possible for parents to reduce an adolescent's risk in the following ways:

Beware of perfectionism, especially in regard to a child's weight or physical appearance. Your child must understand that her worth and your acceptance of her are not based on physical beauty or perfect performance; your love and acceptance are, in fact, unconditional. If you have difficulty expressing this idea to your child or adolescent, you might need to address this issue in counseling on your own.

Beware of demands on an adolescent to "make weight" for an athletic team, slim down for a cheerleading or dance team, or in some other way subject the body to stringent dietary restrictions.

Help your child understand that body shape and build have a strong genetic basis and that few are capable of attaining cover-girl status, even with intense effort.

Eliminate from your own and your family's conversations jokes or other demeaning comments about the appearance of others.

Point out to your children how advertising and other media put forth images of beauty and body image that are out of reach for nearly everyone.

Be a good role model in your own eating and exercise habits, and be careful about openly criticizing your own body appearance.

Focus on relationships and building emotional intimacy in your family, rather than on food-related issues. Be aware of the purposes beyond relieving hunger that food might be serving in your home. Is it used for comfort or reward? Is it used to relieve boredom? Be careful not to use food as a substitute for hugs and saying, "I love you."

NOTES
1. While the term *ideal weight* is commonly used in many charts and other resources, it carries some negative baggage. First it implies that there is an exact weight that is "just right" for *everyone* at a given age and height. More important, it implies that anyone who doesn't achieve this standard is "less than ideal," an attitude that can contribute to disordered eating behaviors.
2. Ellyn Satter, *Child of Mine* (Bull Publishing, 1991).

Education Issues

The human capacity to receive information, store it, process it, retrieve it, alter it, and then apply it to new situations is a profoundly complex process and a unique gift from God. It should inspire awe whether we are beholding an infant's recognition of a face, a school-age child's first comprehension of a multiplication table, or a college student's completion of a senior thesis. Developing this capacity to its fullest is a lifelong project, but it is particularly important during childhood and adolescence. The benefits of doing so for individuals and for society at large have long been recognized, leading to mandates for compulsory education in most developed countries.

The educational process does not suddenly begin when a child reaches the age of five and enters kindergarten.

Vast amounts of information about the world and how it works are assimilated during the first several months of life through an infant's interactions within the family. The infant examines objects with eyes, hands, and mouth, bangs them together, and drops them on the floor while observing what happens. The toddler eagerly explores anyplace his wobbly legs will take him. Preschoolers are persistently curious about how (and why) things work as they do and are eager for input from adults and older siblings.

Parents can encourage all of these learning processes and, in so doing, prepare their children for formal education in very simple ways:

Interact constantly with your child during the early years in ways that are appropriate to his age. Talk to your baby a lot, even before he is using words himself, so that he can hear and learn words and phrases. Ask him about what he sees and hears when he is old enough to communicate with you. Let him watch you carry out simple tasks in your home, and talk about what you are doing. (Let him help you, if possible.) Don't delegate this responsibility to the television or other forms of passive entertainment. Your child needs input from people, not electronic devices.

Read to your child and instill in him a love of books, starting at a very early age. A child who is just forming his first words can benefit from sitting on a lap, looking at the pretty pictures in a book, and hearing the soothing words that accompany them. Toddlers and preschoolers become enthralled with stories and want to hear favorites dozens or even hundreds of times. Even a child who is an excellent reader benefits from hearing stories read aloud at home, especially when they inspire interesting conversations. (Actually, this delightful activity can continue long after the kids are completely grown.)

Take your youngster places. Young children love to explore, and virtually any outing you devise can be turned into an adventure. Help him fall in love with the local library. Let him become acquainted with zoos, museums, and other types of exhibits. Take him to an airport, a train station, a harbor, a dairy farm, or a factory where they make something interesting. Let him hear live music or watch a parade from the curbside rather than through the narrow window of a TV screen. You might learn a few things yourself during these outings.

Once the process of formal education begins, parents must remain active participants and not mere bystanders.

It is a major miscalculation to assume that you can drop your child at the schoolhouse door at the age of five and expect others to take over the total responsibility of educating him for the next thirteen years. You must play an active, ongoing role in selecting the school, tracking his progress, encouraging, coaching, and troubleshooting when problems arise. No school "owns" your child while he is on their grounds, and any school your child attends is accountable to you—not the other way around. You may even choose to provide some or most of your child's education at home. Whatever approaches you and your child follow, remember that you should be in charge and that you are ultimately responsible for the outcome.

WHAT TYPE OF SCHOOL SETTING
SHOULD A CHILD ATTEND?

The answer is *whatever works best for him and the family.* Your child may thrive in the public school system from kindergarten through senior high. Or he may learn better at home or may thrive best spending various amounts of time in different educational settings. Input from friends, relatives, and others in your community can help you clarify your options, but you should not be pressured into an educational decision that doesn't best fit your child's needs and your capabilities.

Public schools are attended by the majority of children between the ages of five and eighteen.

Advantages of public schools include:

- They are available without tuition in every community. (If the nearest facility is some distance from your home, transportation is normally available at no or minimal cost.)
- They are likely to have resources, equipment, and programs that are difficult to duplicate in other settings.
- In many communities public schools maintain a commitment to excellence and achievement that can help a child reach his fullest potential.

Disadvantages of public school (which vary greatly between school districts and individual facilities) include the following:

- Large class sizes might minimize individual attention to a child's particular needs or strengths.
- Social environments in some schools are disruptive to learning, oppressive, or even dangerous.
- Prayer and religious teaching are not allowed in the public school classrooms.
- Some schools or teachers may promote agendas that contradict values taught at home. (For example, teaching about sexuality may stress condoms and contraception while ignoring or minimizing the importance of responsibility, abstinence, and connecting sexuality to a value system.)

If your child attends public school, there are several things you as parents can do to help him achieve successful learning there:

- Get involved with the school in a supportive way. Take part in school functions, join the PTA/PTO, and, if possible, become a classroom volunteer. Make friends with the teachers and administrators, pray for them, and let them know how much you appreciate what they are doing. They have an incredibly challenging and often stressful job, and they would appreciate any words of praise. Assume that you and the school's faculty are on the same team, unless ongoing problems convince you otherwise. A great way to support your child is through a mother's prayer group—Moms In Touch International, (619)486-4065.

- Talk to your child on a regular basis about what is going on at school. Keep track of the materials your child is bringing home, not only to make sure he is keeping up on his schoolwork, but also to note any trends or issues in the curriculum about which you might have concerns.

- If your child is having run-ins with teachers or other students, gather all the information you can before arriving at any conclusions. If it does appear that your child is being treated unfairly by a teacher or harassed by other students, you will need to lend him some assistance. But if *your child* is acting up in class and causing problems for the teacher or other students, the school might need you to back their efforts to maintain order (see chapter 13, page 535).

- If you disagree with something that is being taught or promoted at school, deal with your concerns in a gracious, stepwise approach. Make sure your facts are straight. (Perhaps your child didn't give you the "big picture" or he misunderstood what was being said.) Talk about your concerns with the teacher or appropriate administrator without making emotional accusations or threatening to take your issue "all the way to the school board." If you feel that there is a need for a significant change in the curriculum, your best bet is to join forces with other like-minded parents and work for change within the system. Remember that while the school is ultimately accountable to you, its staff has enough problems on its hands without being bullied or browbeaten.

Private schools may range from new and limited operations to well-endowed academies with histories stretching back for centuries.

There are several advantages of a private school:

- In most cases private schools have smaller classes; this allows for more individual attention for each child.
- Academic standards are sometimes higher and more rigorously encouraged than in public-school settings.

- There is likely to be stronger control over the social and classroom environment.
- Private schools are free to include religious teaching as part of the curriculum as well as prayer and promotion of moral values that support those taught at home. In Christian academies, teachers can help students integrate a biblical worldview into any and all areas of study.

The disadvantages of private schools include:

- Unless your state has a voucher system in place, it could cost a significant amount of money for tuition and other fees for private education. This may well be worth the extra effort, but for many families the extra expense is simply beyond the reach of the family budget.
- The school may have limited resources for programs such as athletics, the arts, or science (for example, laboratory facilities).
- The school may not be equipped to deal with children who have special needs or learning disabilities.

If your child is going to attend private school, all of the parental recommendations noted earlier for public school apply. In addition, parents can do the following:

- Find out if the school is properly accredited and learn about the teachers who are on staff. What kind of credentials do they hold? Is there a high turnover rate (a bad sign), or do the teachers tend to stay at the school for a number of years?
- Ask about the school's curriculum and approach to academics. Will your child learn basic reading, writing, and mathematical skills? Can he move forward at a faster rate if he is capable? Will he get extra help if he needs it?
- Find out about the school's approach to discipline and maintaining order in the classroom. What are the policies and procedures if a child misbehaves?
- If the school is church-based or has commitments to teaching biblical content and values, how is this carried out? Is class time or special assemblies devoted to this task?

Home schooling has gained considerable momentum over the past several years, and it is definitely not a "fringe" approach to education.

Between 600,000 and one million children are now home schooled in the United States.[1] There are several advantages to home schooling:

- Parents can educate their children within the context of the family and all of the security, love, and guidance it affords.
- Home schooling provides maximal flexibility. The content, pace, approach, and style of the curriculum can be adjusted to each child's ability. In addition, home-schooling families can schedule the educational process according to the family's needs, rather than adhere to a fixed academic calendar.
- Home-schooled children have been found in general to learn as well as, if not more quickly and efficiently than, their counterparts in more structured settings.
- While home schooling is most widely carried out among children in elementary and middle-school grades, curriculum is available for all age-groups through high school.
- Parents can freely integrate values and faith into their child's curriculum.

Disadvantages of home schooling include:

- Home schooling is a significant undertaking for one or (ideally) both parents, and someone needs to be home to do it. A great amount of time and effort is needed to obtain curriculum, map out the activities and assignments, review work and progress, and so forth. If both parents must work outside the home, or if a single parent is supporting the family, the demands of earning a living will make home schooling extremely difficult.
- Parents involved in home schooling may have to consider and possibly adjust their parenting style when they are functioning as teachers. Low-key, less demanding parents sometimes have difficulty being assertive about imposing assignments and deadlines. Those who are prone to be more controlling and impatient may exasperate their children with excessive structure and workloads.
- Curriculum for adolescents (especially in languages, math, and science) might reach a level of complexity that exceeds a parent's education, comprehension, or resources. Outside help will be needed in these situations.
- As with private schools, resources and facilities for certain activities or special needs may not be available within the local home-school community.

If you are planning to become involved in home schooling, there are several things you can do:

- Get in touch with (and possibly join) a local home-school association or support group. In some communities these are highly organized, offering not only information about local and state educational requirements but also an impressive array of activities and guidance regarding curriculum. Some home-school groups organize special classes (for example, in science, math, or languages), field trips, athletic teams, and graduation ceremonies.

- Don't try to reinvent the wheel (unless you really want to). A variety of curricula is available for all age-groups that can provide you with a basic outline and study materials for virtually any subject.

- Be patient and flexible. Part of the advantage of the home-school environment is that you do not need to stay locked into a particular approach if it isn't working for you and your child.

What If My Child Isn't Doing Well in School?

Every parent dreads the prospect of discovering that his child is falling behind or utterly failing in one or more subjects in school. Whether the news is delivered by a teacher or suspected when a child is having difficulty in a home-school environment, it is very important to work diligently to find out what is (or isn't) going wrong and then seek to correct it or at least make improvements as soon as possible. The emotional distress of falling behind, of feeling overwhelmed, or of being singled out as "stupid" or a "retard" can be devastating to a child and can start him on a downhill spiral with disastrous consequences. The child who decides that school isn't for him and isn't worth the hassle will "check out," first emotionally and then literally, charting his first steps on a course toward low-paying, unskilled labor or even unemployability because of inadequate job skills. In a worst-case scenario, the frustrated child or adolescent will find others who share his lack of regard for school, increasing his risk for destructive or even criminal activity.

Because learning is such a complex process, simple answers and quick fixes for such problems are rarely, if ever, available. Furthermore, any number of conditions may interfere with school performance, and in some children more than one factor may be involved.

A problem with vision or hearing. The eyes and ears are the primary entry points for information that the brain must receive and process. If a child cannot see or hear adequately, the demands of school will eventually overwhelm his ability to compensate for these deficits. Usually both vision and hearing are evaluated at a child's five-year medical checkup, but gradual changes might take place over a period of years. Periodical checkups are important and should be scheduled.

Emotional or personal turmoil. A child who is besieged by personal issues (such as parental divorce, frequent moves, or loneliness) may be too distracted to attend to school-related tasks. If anxiety and depression interfere with concentration and memory, your child may need specific medical intervention as well as counseling (see Special Concerns, page 601).

Attention deficit/hyperactivity disorder (ADHD). This important condition is discussed in detail in the Reference section, beginning on page 653.

Learning disabilities. These are disorders of the complex mechanisms in the brain that are responsible for processing written or spoken material. They are estimated to affect 7 to 10 percent of children and adolescents and often run in families. Children with learning disabilities by definition have normal or above-average intelligence, yet have significant problems with one or more of the following activities: reading, writing, listening, speaking, concentration, or performing mathematical computations. (This does not mean, incidentally, that all children with problems in a particular subject area have a learning disability.)

In most cases, the reason for a learning disability is unknown. However, these difficulties are sometimes associated with prematurity, exposure to toxins (such as alcohol or illicit drugs) prior to birth, infections of the central nervous system, or head injuries. Another contributing factor in some children is a lack of appropriate stimulation during the early years of life, resulting from extremely impoverished or chaotic conditions at home.

A child's medical history might provide clues to the origin of a learning disability, but frequently risk factors and early signs of trouble are not detected during routine physical exams. While a physician's evaluation can be helpful in ruling out other problems, the diagnosis of a learning disability usually requires specific educational and neurodevelopmental testing by a professional who is experienced in this field. Once the problem is identified, treatment could involve a variety of approaches, including new learning strategies, speech therapy, specialized instruction, and curriculum modifications. Coping with a learning disability will require ongoing effort by the child and coaching by professionals and parents for many months or possibly years.

Alternative or unconventional solutions such as dietary modification, megavitamins, special eyeglasses, eye exercises, or "vision training" have failed to pass scientific muster. Resorting to such methods that offer the tantalizing hope of a "cure" for the learning disability will only delay the assistance the child truly needs and may also cost significant sums of money.

Chronic illness. Usually the presence of a chronic illness is already known to the child's parents and physician, and special efforts must be made to minimize absences and their impact on the educational progress.

Mental retardation. Significant retardation is usually diagnosed during infancy or preschool years, but milder forms may not be apparent until a child begins having difficulty in the early grades of school. Appropriate testing by a qualified psychologist can identify this problem, which should be managed in such a way as to maximize the child's educational potential.

Miscellaneous factors. These could include motivational difficulties, learning styles that do not accommodate well to standard classroom activities, and issues of personality and temperament that conflict with school activities.

Helping a child who is having difficulty at school will require both parents and professionals working with the child as a supportive team. If there are family issues at home causing significant anxiety or distraction, counseling may be needed to sort them out and regain equilibrium. A physician's evaluation related to this specific problem is a wise idea. Testing and guidance from an educational psychologist, a developmental expert, and/or a special-education teacher will probably be necessary. Sometimes a child needs help with the basic tasks of setting up a work environment at home: turning off the TV, sitting down in a quiet spot, pulling his materials together, and getting started. This can be done gently but firmly through parental guidance.

In general, parents of a child who is having difficulty in school will need to protect him from ridicule, praise the things he does well, and provide ongoing encouragement and exhortation to do the work that needs to get done. Having a learning disability or other difficulty does not mean that a child can't be challenged in a positive way to work on his basic skills and, in so doing, improve his prospects for the future.

NOTES
1. Tom Hess, "Home Education Is on the Move," *Focus on the Family Citizen,* 1996.

Divorce and Its
Effect on Children

"What God has joined together, let no man put asunder."

In spite of this solemn admonition that concludes most wedding ceremonies, more than half of all marriages are eventually "put asunder" in the United States, which currently has the highest divorce rate in the industrialized world.[1]

Not too many decades ago, couples having significant marital conflict frequently saw children as a reason to stay together. Many would postpone divorce and strive to maintain the appearance of normalcy at home until their children were grown and gone. But in the wake of many cultural shifts of the 60s and 70s, children have come to be seen as beneficiaries of divorce and less often as an obstacle to it: "The children will be better off if we're not arguing/we're not in a loveless marriage." In other words, "everyone will be better off if we go our separate ways." The advent of no-fault divorce laws, beginning in California in 1969 and spreading to 45 states within five years and to all 50 states by 1985, was accompanied by a 34 percent increase in divorce rates between 1970 and 1990.[2]

The Pain Inflicted by Divorce

After more than two decades of widespread dissolution of marriages, research suggests that, in general, children of divorce are *not* as well off as those who grow up in intact families. According to the Family Research Council:

- Three out of four teen suicides are committed by adolescents from broken homes.

◆ Children of divorce are 70 percent more likely to have been expelled from school and are twice as likely to drop out of school, compared to their peers who are in intact families.

◆ Seven out of ten preteens and teenagers in long-term correctional facilities come from broken homes.

Author Judith Wallerstein reported in *Second Chances: Men, Women, and Children a Decade after Divorce* that in a study of sixty families divorced between 1971 and 1981, ten years after the breakup of their parents the children felt "less protected, less cared for, less comforted" and still had "vivid, gut-wrenching memories of their parents' separation." A comprehensive analysis known as the California Children of Divorce Study found that more than a third of the children studied were dealing with moderate to severe depression five years after their parents' divorce. According to Wallerstein, almost all of the adolescent girls in the study "confronted issues of love, commitment, and marriage with anxiety, sometimes with very great concern about betrayal, abandonment, and not being loved."[3] Recent research also suggests that parental divorce may have long-term physical consequences for children. A seventy-year longevity study reported in the *American Journal of Public Health* in 1995 indicated that individuals who were younger than twenty-one years of age when their parents divorced were more likely to have a shorter lifespan than those whose families remained intact.

Even when Mom and Dad's relationship has ongoing conflicts, from a child's perspective the breakup of the family is the end of life as she knows it. Depending upon the age and personality of the child, several immediate and long-term reactions are virtually inevitable, even when the divorce is amicable. These are likely to include fear, insecurity, sadness (in some cases overt depression), anger, and guilt. Younger children are particularly vulnerable to the idea that they were somehow at fault and that "Mommy and Daddy wouldn't have split up if I had been better." Older children and adolescents are often as angry as they are sad; in some cases they act out that anger, especially if the divorce is going to force them to move or cause some other significant change in their normal activities.

Divorce has such serious consequences for all concerned, especially children, that it should be considered an extreme measure. Sometimes there may be no alternative, such as in a marriage that has been severely damaged by repeated and unrepentant infidelity. A partner cannot be forced to stay in a marriage if he or she has decided to leave it—no matter how fervently the other partner desires to seek solutions and prevent divorce.

A commitment to avoid divorce at all cost does not mean that marital partners should drift silently through years of discontent without taking appropriate action when needed. In many ways a marriage is like a house—it needs a solid foundation, ongoing maintenance, intermittent repair, and perhaps major remodeling. Too many couples look at a marriage that needs a lot of repairs and conclude—often too quickly—that it can't be fixed, that they want to move out, or that they never wanted to live there in the first place. But when one or more children have grown up in this family and see it as the center of their world, the process of leaving it is traumatic.

A detailed look at the process of marriage mending is beyond the scope of this book, but numerous resources—including books, seminars, support groups, and couples retreats—are available to help with this task. Most important, a couple whose marriage is in trouble should enlist the help of a counselor whom they trust and with whom they can work over a period of months or years if necessary. This process should also include a spiritual inventory. If both husband and wife have committed their lives to Christ, each should seek to submit to Him daily and consciously place the marriage under His authority. If one or both have not yet established a personal relationship with Christ, there can be no more crucial time to do so than during major marital reconstruction.

Additional accountability to a pastor, other couples (especially those who have built solid marriages over some years), or even mature relatives, assuming they are not contributing to the problem, may be necessary. In a society that seeks a quick fix for everything from cars to children, making a commitment to an arduous process of restoring a marriage—especially when the possibility of a satisfying finished product seems hopelessly out of reach—may require both a leap of faith and a lot of small steps. But when we consider the damage that divorce inflicts upon children, this effort should become a couple's first priority. Ending the marriage should be considered only as the very last resort.

What If Divorce Is Already in Progress?

If a divorce is indeed going to take place, now is a crucial time for you to put your children's welfare ahead of your own emotions. *The divorce process itself can be brutal for children if parents do not make very deliberate choices about their behavior—especially in regard to legal matters.* The following basic decisions can help keep the damage to a minimum.

Settle as many issues as you can outside the courtroom.

The adversarial nature of legal proceedings and the determination of attorneys to deliver the best outcome for their clients can bring out the worst in people, especially if there are many unresolved conflicts between the parents. One or both members of a divorcing couple may feel justified in attacking and blaming the other for what has happened or even taking revenge in a public courtroom for hurts that have been suffered. You owe it to your children to resolve as many issues as you can without turning the process into an endless nightmare of fights and name-calling, lawsuits and countersuits, and meetings with lawyers and judges.

Not only is this type of open warfare between Mom and Dad traumatic for their children to watch, but it ultimately imposes a major financial burden on a family already beset with a great deal of stress. Do you really want to spend your children's future college funds on unnecessary and avoidable legal fees? No matter how much hurt a spouse may have inflicted, it is unwise to finance your retaliation with your children's (and your) future. When decisions have been reached by mutual agreement, expensive enforcement procedures are less likely to be needed in the future.

A competent professional mediator or a divorce attorney who places a high priority on fairness and maintaining civility in family relationships may be able to help a couple come to an agreement without the pain and cost of a bruising legal battle. If a spouse is determined to "play dirty" in court, you will probaby have no choice but to defend yourself—but don't assume that your only recourse is to "fight fire with fire." Your children will likely be burned in the process.

Do not ask your children to take sides.

When you feel you have been wronged by your estranged spouse, it is natural to want those closest to you to sympathize with your cause. But you must consider very carefully what is appropriate for your children to hear about your difficulties with the other parent. Even if it is clear that you have not been treated respectfully or fairly, telling your children all about your spouse's misdeeds may help you feel better for a while, but it could be devastating for them.

If you are going through a divorce, your children are already struggling with how to relate to both parents in a situation that feels very unnatural and threatening to them. It is inappropriate—and blatantly unfair—for them to be called upon to choose sides, to relay messages between warring parents, or to hear unpleasant details that are neither their responsibility nor under their control.

Children are born with the need and desire to love both parents. It is not your prerogative to isolate them from their other parent's love, even when that person has hurt you. In some situations it will be necessary for children to have limited (or no) access to a parent whose lifestyle is unhealthy or dangerous. Even then, however, in many cases the children may be able to maintain a relationship within certain boundaries.

Do not allow your conflicts with a spouse to interfere with your responsibility for the children.

A skillful attorney might be able to win a settlement that is more favorable to one party than it is fair. But a loving parent may have to consider relinquishing a few "points" in the divorce negotiations if doing so means that the children will receive better care and resources adequate to meet their needs.

A frightening number of otherwise reasonable adults become neglectful after a divorce settlement, and in doing so, act in a way that defies God's principles for caring for their families. If you owe child support, it is important—and right—to pay it when due. Furthermore, you need to make certain that your child's medical needs are properly met, even if doing so involves contributing more than is required of you. Your former spouse may be struggling to pay bills and provide a decent home for your children. Strive to be helpful and supportive in such a situation, rather than add to the problem.

Do not turn to your children for emotional support.

As vulnerable as you may feel while your marriage is ending, it is your responsibility to be the emotional anchor for your children—and not the other way around. While you can't avoid allowing them to see your sadness or even anger at times, you will need to make extra efforts to provide stability for your children at a time when their world feels very unsafe to them. Providing stability will include repeated reassurances that the divorce is not their fault and ongoing confirmation that they are still loved by both parents.

Above all, it is not their job to take care of you or become your confidant, even if they appear to be adjusting well to the divorce. Make every effort to find the emotional support you need through relationships with other adults.

WHAT IF DIVORCE HAS ALREADY TAKEN PLACE?

Even when a marriage has ended, it is critical to remember that parenting responsibilities have *not* ended. In the best situations, children of divorced parents should be able to continue a meaningful relationship with both mother and father, even if one has primary custody and the other's contact is more limited.

In reality, this does not always occur. One parent may abandon the other (and the children), move away, adopt a destructive lifestyle, or behave in an abusive manner. In such cases the other parent will need to carry on alone but supported by other adults who can help fill some of the gaps left by the parent who is gone.

Maintain a civil and cooperative relationship with your former spouse.

Assuming that both parents remain involved with the children, every effort should be made to agree upon policies that affect the children. Curfews, spending money, after-school jobs, trips, driving privileges, and disciplinary measures should be handled in a similar manner in both households. This can occur, of course, only if the parents cooperate. Unfortunately, it only takes one parent to create conflict for a child by making new rules, abandoning the old ones, or disregarding the other parent's concerns or wishes. Parents may consider seeking the help of a counselor to help them arrive at appropriate mutual guidelines.

Help your child work through her emotions about life after divorce.

Children will need help processing the emotions that are an inevitable response to the divorce, as unpleasant as those feelings may be. Don't hesitate to connect your child with an appropriate resource—a counselor, youth pastor, or a trusted relative—who can help her sort through her feelings.

Ongoing insecurity and sadness may cause a child to become overly dependent or even "clingy" with the parent who is providing the majority of the care. The parent might even reciprocate, allowing a child to assume the role of a confidant or surrogate spouse. This may extend as far as allowing (or even inviting) a child past toddlerhood to sleep in the same bedroom (or bed) with the parent, which is detrimental to the emotional health of both. As hard as it may be in the emotional storms that follow divorce, it is important for a parent to *remain* a parent—loving, affirming, compassionate, but also setting and maintaining appropriate limits for the child and boundaries for their relationship.

Keep discipline and order intact.

Children need structure when life is stable and going well; in the wake of a parental breakup the security of loving boundaries is more important than ever. Parents are often tempted to "ease up" on children in the interest of relieving sadness or guilt. But abandoning your house rules and failing to take appropriate action when your child misbehaves will only compound the problem.

You may find it especially difficult to maintain discipline if the other parent becomes lax, because the children will be more than willing to point out the differences during a time of conflict ("Dad doesn't make us go to bed this early"). If at all possible, meet with your former spouse and attempt to establish consistent disciplinary policies. If the other person is in fact lackadaisical or inconsistent in this area, don't lower your own standards—but don't try to overcompensate by becoming more strict.

Take care of yourself.

Because of the significant physical and emotional consequences following divorce, men and women who have undergone this process should be mindful not only of their children's well-being but also of their own health. Basic self-care— a sensible diet, regular exercise, adequate sleep, and a balance of work and recreation—is a starting point. To this should be added the support of a network of friends, involvement in a church (if possible, one that has an active ministry for divorced individuals), and, above all, a day-by-day walk with God, who is the ultimate source of life and health.

What about Remarriage and Blended Families?

Forty percent of all marriages are actually remarriages for one or both parties, and approximately one in three Americans is a stepparent, stepchild, stepsibling, or in some way a member of a stepfamily. The formation of a new marital partnership in which children from one or both prior relationships come together under the same roof is no small undertaking. Idealized, "Brady Bunch" interactions are a sitcom fantasy, and in the worst situations conflicts between stepsiblings or between children and stepparents can undermine the remarriage or destroy it completely.

At the same time, there is the potential for building a new family that is loving and productive. This is possible with time, patience, and a lot of communication. Some principles to keep in mind include the following:

Remarriage should be preceded by effective counseling to prevent history from repeating itself.

Why did the previous marriage(s) fail? Was there anything that could or should have been done to prevent it? What understanding of God and moral values is each member bringing to this new partnership? What about goals, priorities, and expectations? What are the child rearing styles of each parent? Does one tend to be more permissive or more authoritarian than the other? Will each person plan to discipline the other's children, and if so, how? All of these questions, and many more, need to be addressed in detail before wedding plans are made.

Beware of sexual involvement during this exploratory process. Not only can it cloud your judgment, but it will send any older children or adolescents at home a mixed message ("Sex outside of marriage is OK for me but not for you"). Sexual entanglement outside of marriage is as bad an idea for adults as it is for adolescents (see Special Concerns, page 541).

The transition from acquaintance/friend to marriage partner and co-parent of someone else's children cannot be made overnight.

Depending upon their ages and experiences, children may manifest intense—and at times contradictory—responses to the prospect of Mom or Dad (or both) getting involved with a new partner. The idea of having a "whole family" again can be appealing, especially if it seems to be making the child's own parent happy. But there will also be anxiety or even agitation over a potential competitor for the parent's affection and attention. Becoming friendly with a new adult in the parent's life might bring up confusing feelings of divided allegiance—*if I like Mom's new boyfriend, does that mean that I'm not being loyal to Dad?* Children of divorce often maintain a fantasy that Mom and Dad will get together again, and remarriage to someone else will end that dream abruptly. Thus, another adult in the parent's life may be greeted by responses that are cool, if not hostile, from the children who are watching developments with great interest and concern.

The plot thickens when remarriage brings into focus the lines of authority. Should the new stepparent begin giving out orders or disciplining the partner's children? What happens when the child has a conflict with the stepparent and comes to the natural parent for support and comfort? All of these potential complications should be anticipated and talked over before a remarriage takes place.

Even when this is done, the nuts and bolts of daily life will create new issues that must be worked through over many months.

At the outset, it is often best for each parent to handle disciplinary matters for his or her own children, while serving as backup and support for whatever the other parent decides to do. A stepparent's sudden application of rules that the children have not been used to can lead to serious conflict. Each parent can learn something from the other, and in doing so, strengthen his or her own child rearing skills. A unified parental front in a blended family is every bit as important as in an intact family.

When children from two different families are combined through remarriage, be prepared for some turbulence.

During the initial "getting to know you" process, sweetness and light may prevail. But some degree of conflict is inevitable. For example, a child who has to share his room with a new stepsibling may resent the sudden lack of privacy and will probably be very territorial about his possessions. Issues will arise over who uses the bathroom when, who picks up what, or who does which jobs around the home. Be sure that house rules, assignments of chores, administration of consequences, and granting of privileges are carried out in ways that are scrupulously fair and open to respectful discussion. Children become extremely indignant if they feel there is favoritism or injustice from either parent.

Be prepared to seek counseling when two families become one.

Given the number of potential conflicts within a blended family, you would be wise to see a counselor to expedite problem solving and troubleshooting. Depending on the damage incurred by the loss of the original family, whether through divorce or death, children in particular may need help adjusting to a new family. This should never be seen as strictly the child's problem but as an issue for the entire family. Family counseling can provide a safe forum in which every family member can share and be heard and, in turn, hear how the others feel.

You, as parents, will need outside support as well. A church family or local support group might provide this, but don't hesitate to see a counselor or pastor for more focused aid if you need it.

NOTES
1. It should be noted that this number is skewed somewhat by those who marry and divorce more than once.
2. "Divorce Reform," in *The Whole Family Catalog: 25 Policy Planks for a Pro-Family Future* (Family Research Council, 1996).
3. Judith S. Wallerstein and Sandra Bleakeslee, *Second Chances: Men, Women and Children a Decade after Divorce* (New York: Ticknor and Fields, 1989).

Conflict within the Family—
Parental Disagreements
and Sibling Rivalry

Conflict between parents and their children is inevitable. The toddler's foot-stomping negativity, the preschooler's refusal to pick up his toys, the school child's disinterest in homework and chores, and the adolescent's adamant declarations of independence from parental restrictions are but a few variations on this universal theme. But conflicts within families are not limited to differences of opinion (or pitched battles) between parents and children. Parents normally disagree with one another about any number of concerns, even in the most harmonious marriages. Furthermore, if they have more than one child, strife between offspring is so common that it has achieved a well-worn title: sibling rivalry. Thus for any family the question isn't so much *whether* discord will arise, but *how to manage it* in a way that will build up rather than tear down relationships.

A variety of age-specific suggestions for handling conflicts between parents and children are set forth throughout the chapters and Special Concerns of this book (see particularly Special Concerns: Principles of Discipline and Training, page 289). This section is concerned primarily with conflicts between members of the same generation—between parents or between children.

WHEN MOM AND DAD DISAGREE

It is a sad fact that *few people have the opportunity to observe their parents resolve a conflict in a positive and mutually satisfying manner.* Instead, disagreements within a marriage all too often deteriorate into one of several unhealthy scenarios:

- *Suppression.* Fear of conflict causes husband or wife (or both) to allow issues to smolder and simmer—sometimes for years—into a stew of resentment. There may not be any fireworks in the home—but not much happiness either.
- *Repression.* One person dominates the other, winning every conflict through physical or verbal intimidation.
- *Guerrilla warfare.* Conflicts are manifested through quick jabs—indirect put-downs, subtle insults, sly sarcastic comments—that chip away at the other person without ever dealing with any issues directly.
- *Character assassination.* One person is subjected to name-calling, harsh remarks about appearance or intelligence, or ongoing scorn for his or her opinions or motives by the other. Continuing direct assaults on an individual's identity and value create wounds that can take years to heal, and such behavior indicates that the relationship is in serious trouble.
- *Dredging up past grievances.* This tactic is manifested by counterproductive phrases such as "You *always* do this . . ." or "Here we go again . . ." or "This is just like that time when . . ." It is virtually impossible to settle today's issue when baggage from the past is continually dragged out of the closet.
- *All-out war.* Yelling, abusive language, shoving, and hitting are clear signs that the marriage is seriously damaged.

Children who have repeatedly observed one or more of these destructive responses to conflict are likely to be ill equipped to manage disagreements that will inevitably arise in their own marriages. Unhealthy patterns may thus be perpetuated—either duplicating what was demonstrated by the older generation or perhaps moving toward opposite extremes. For example, someone who has lived through many intense and painful arguments may decide to ignore or sidestep issues to avoid the threat of an unpleasant altercation. But this course of inaction can allow anger and resentment to fester for years, leading ultimately to a sour—or dead—marriage.

If parents hope to demonstrate healthy conflict resolution for their children, they will need to practice—both before and after children are born. Some couples will have broached this subject during premarital counseling. Virtually every marriage could benefit from working on it in more formal settings—in small groups organized through churches (assuming they are properly led), in couples' communication classes, or in private counseling. While it is not possible to detail in this book all of the principles involved in settling disagreements in marriage, the following basic concepts can serve as a foundation for parents who desire to work on this important area.

Mutual respect is an absolute necessity. Without respect on both sides, any relationship will ultimately deteriorate or become destructive. With mutual respect, it is possible to have an intense disagreement with another person without causing damage to a relationship or those who are affected by it. Respect acknowledges the ultimate worth of the other person—as established by God and not by any other attributes or accomplishments—and affirms that worth in attitudes, words, and actions.

If parents do not respect one another or if respect flows only in one direction, attempts to resolve issues are likely to be unsuccessful or hurtful. This fundamental problem must be addressed—usually in a counseling setting—if a marriage is going to survive and thrive through the years of raising children and beyond.

When a disagreement arises, conversation should focus on the issue and not the person. If Mom feels she needs more help with the kids in the evening, it isn't productive to begin the discussion with the statement "You care more about that TV than your own children!" If Dad is getting worried about the family budget, he won't get very far by saying, "All you ever do is spend the money I work so hard to bring home!" Once the issue is defined (How do we care for the kids when we're both tired? or How can we keep better track of our finances?), the focus can shift toward generating and evaluating a potential solution.

When an issue needs to be discussed, pick an appropriate time and place. Not at the end of the day when energy is low and fuses may be short; not right before bed; not when anger is at a fever pitch; not when there isn't time to work through it; not when the TV is on, the phone is ringing, the kids are crying, and the dog is barking. If it is clear that an issue needs to be addressed, it's quite all right for either person to call time and say, "This isn't a good time to discuss this" or "I don't feel like talking about it right now"—as long as a specific time is set to talk about it in the very near future. The best time to talk is when both parties are rested, focused, and attentive. It's helpful to work through an issue in a place that is relatively free of distractions and interruptions. This may be a particular room, somewhere out in the yard, or a place away from home. Many couples do their best negotiating at a coffee shop or on a long walk.

Pray together before discussing the issue. Laying the issue before God can help keep it in perspective and reinforce your common ground. Be careful not to use this prayer time unfairly to express your viewpoint or claim God's backing for your side of the conflict. Prayer should be an exercise in humility, not a power play.

Each person must be able to express his or her viewpoint fully, without interruption. A key element of respect is listening carefully to what the other person is saying, without thinking about one's own response. One technique that encourages attentive listening involves picking an object (such as a pen) and stipulating that whoever holds it is entitled to speak without any interruption. The other person cannot say a word until the pen is passed, and the pen will not be passed until the person receiving it can summarize what was just said to the speaker's satisfaction—without argument, rebuttal, or editorial comment. If the listener doesn't get it right, the pen doesn't pass. This approach may at first seem awkward and ritualistic, but it is surprisingly effective at improving listening skills.

Get in the habit of checking frequently to be sure that you understand what the other person is saying. "I hear you saying that . . ."

Avoid "You . . ." statements—especially those containing the words *always, never, should,* or *shouldn't*. Replace them with statements that express your own feelings. "You never spend any time at home anymore!" essentially demands a rebuttal ("That's not true!"). In contrast, "It seems as if the kids and I are spending more evenings by ourselves than ever before, and it makes me feel lonely" is a straightforward observation and an expression of a genuine feeling. Similarly, a statement such as "You shouldn't make commitments for both of us without talking to me first!" is likely to provoke a defensive response. The one way in which a "you" statement can legitimately enter a conversation is in this form: "When you say (or do) _____, I feel _____ ." (For example, "When you make commitments for both of us without talking to me first, I feel as if my opinion doesn't count.") This type of statement can help one person understand how specific words or actions are affecting the other person.

Avoid "Why . . . ?" questions—especially those (once again) containing the words *always* or *never*. "Why do you always leave the back door open?" can be answered in only one of two ways: defensively ("I don't either!") or sarcastically ("Because I'm an idiot!") "Why . . . ?" questions immediately and automatically turn a discussion into a battle.

Avoid dragging events from the distant past into the current issue. "Here we go again. . . !" or "This is just what you did on our vacation in 1990, when you . . ." If current problems are indeed related to grievances from the past, then those specific concerns need to be discussed and resolved apart from any current problems.

Name-calling and other forms of insults are disrespectful and should be banned from all conversations within a family (or anywhere else). Verbal insults live in everyone's memory long after apologies have been made. One of the most powerful lessons your children can learn from you is how to disagree or be angry with a person without labeling, name-calling, or insulting them in other ways. Remember that body language (sighing, rolling the eyes, etc.), gestures, and tone of voice can communicate disrespect as powerfully as the most explicit insult.

The discussion of an issue should eventually arrive at a point of exploring possible courses of action. "What can I do to help you not feel so tired at the end of the day?" or "How can we make Sunday morning less hectic?" It may help to list a number of possibilities and then talk through the pros and cons of each one.

Realize that on a number of issues you may have to "agree to disagree," and that in doing so, the other person's viewpoint is not to be subject to constant ridicule. This will mean compromising in some cases. There is usually, however, some solution that will allow for each person's needs to be met.

If your discussions of issues frequently deteriorate into shouting matches or glum stalemates, get some help. It takes courage and maturity to go to a counselor or to a mature couple whom you know to be experienced in conflict resolution, in order to determine what goes wrong when disagreements arise in your home. Constructive suggestions from an unbiased third party, if acted upon consistently, can drastically improve the quality and outcome of these conversations.

SHOULD WE HAVE DISAGREEMENTS IN FRONT OF THE CHILDREN?

Parental modeling of respectful disagreements can be a powerful and useful life lesson for children to observe, provided that a few cautions are kept in mind:

Consider your audience. The child(ren) should be old enough to comprehend what you are talking about and emotionally mature enough to grasp the concept that you can disagree with someone whom you deeply love and respect. Preschoolers and early-grade-school children can become terrified by the thought that Mom and Dad don't like each other and may misinterpret a spirited parental exchange as the unraveling of their world. They probably should rarely, if ever, witness a serious parental disagreement. Older children and adolescents, on the other hand, can benefit from seeing how two mature people can settle an issue in a positive way.

Play by the rules. If kids are going to watch or listen, you should be well versed in healthy conflict resolution, resolve to keep the tone of conversation respectful, and strive to come to a positive solution of your issue.

Consider demonstrating how you settled an issue. If you have had a particularly fruitful conversation about a problem, think about reenacting it for your children to show how you dealt with it. You might even demonstrate some right and wrong ways to deal with an issue—especially if your children are having some problems in this area themselves.

Beware of voicing a disagreement in front of a child who is the subject of the disagreement. Parents should be united, even if they are not in total agreement, when dealing with basic issues of child rearing—especially those relating to limits and discipline. A child must never get the idea that if Mommy says no, he can go talk to Daddy, or that one parent will veto the other's disciplinary measures. However, with some concerns that are not fundamentally important, an older child might benefit from hearing different viewpoints, as long as they are expressed appropriately. (For example, the pros and cons of going to a summer camp or joining an athletic team could be an excellent topic for discussion among child and parents, even if there is not total agreement about the best decision.)

Declare a cease-fire, if necessary. If your discussion is deteriorating into a shouting match and children are within earshot, *call it off* until you can continue in private—after you have cooled down. It is devastating—and inappropriate—for children to hear their parents yelling, insulting one another, or being physically aggressive. If your disagreement reaches this level, you should not only isolate it from your children but seek counseling as soon as possible.

When Siblings Engage in Combat

This section does not begin with the word *if* because siblings *will* have conflicts—sometimes with shocking ferocity. In some families the nonstop bickering and pummeling that goes on in the backseat of the car, at the kitchen table, around the TV set, or in any other location where two or more children are gathered, is enough to cause mothers and fathers to want to turn in their resignation from parenthood. This is particularly exasperating when the parents have not modeled antagonistic or harsh behavior. *Where does all this awful hostility come from? Where did we go wrong?*

What generates so much conflict between brothers and sisters? With rare exception, it is not the result of poor parenting. Much of it is an expression of basic human nature. There is nothing in the human genetic code that spontaneously brings forth from children concern for the rights and needs of others—including their closest family members. This (and nearly all other values) must be taught and modeled by parents, relatives, teachers, and other civilizing influences as children grow up.

A number of other factors may contribute to sibling combat. Recognizing them and working to reduce their impact can go a long way toward maintaining peace in your home:

Desire for parental attention. *There's only so much of Mom or Dad to go around— how do I know that I'm still loved and important?* This isn't merely the unspoken question of a toddler when a new baby comes home. Regardless of the number and the ages involved, if there is more than one child in the nest there may be some serious concerns about (and competition for) a parent's attention. Ironically, in some cases children may instigate a fight merely to get an adult involved with them—even when the consequences are unpleasant. But even if the attention-seeking behavior is annoying, the basic questions are the same: *Who cares about me? Am I significant to anyone? Does what I think or do really matter?*

To avoid endless guilt, you need to acknowledge that you have limits—that you can't be all things to one child, let alone many. Nevertheless, amidst all the basic responsibilities of daily living; maintaining a home; generating income; and pursuing church, educational, or community projects, *some time and energy must be available for individual attention to each child on a regular basis.* If your schedule is particularly busy, you should consider setting a regular date with each child, during which he will have your undivided attention. This need not be elaborate; a walk in the park or an outing for an ice-cream cone can be a memorable occasion, provided that the parent isn't distracted by thoughts about all the other things that need to be done at home.

Comparisons. When two children first meet, comparisons are an immediate and normal occurrence: Who is older, bigger, and faster? If there is a disagreement, who is tougher? What toys does one have that the other doesn't? Depending on the situation, these questions may be minor points of interest that do not affect a budding friendship, or they may prove to be a source of major conflict.

Within the close quarters of a family, comparisons between children will be an inevitable daily reality and may become a source of ongoing friction. What happens if one child is a prodigy in school and her brother has learning disabilities? What if one is gifted in sports and another literally can't get to first base? What if the first two children are relatively compliant but the third has a will of steel and a limitless capacity to tell everyone where to get off?

Parents of more than one child will regularly have to exercise a delicate responsibility: recognizing and praising each child's unique skills, strengths, and accomplishments without implying that one sibling is somehow better than another. In some cases, you may have to look a lot harder to find what is praiseworthy, but it is that child who will most need your affirmation. Whatever you do, avoid negative comparisons such as "Why can't you throw a ball like your brother?" or "You'll go a lot farther in life if you buckle down to your schoolwork like your sister does!" These kinds of comments are virtually guaranteed to stir resentment.

Invasion of privacy. While sharing is a virtue that should be encouraged during and after the preschool years, no child—or adult—appreciates having his possessions pawed through, broken, strewn on the floor, or taken to places unknown. This often becomes a point of contention when a child becomes mobile and begins exploring (and trashing) the fascinating toys belonging to older siblings. It is quite appropriate to help an older child safeguard her belongings when there is a toddler on the loose, perhaps by providing closet or shelf space for her that is inaccessible to the younger child, keeping the older child's bedroom door closed, or limiting the range of the toddler's explorations. Unfortunately, older children and adolescents can also thoughtlessly raid a sibling's (or a parent's) possessions, often provoking surprisingly harsh responses.

You need to caution your children about becoming overly attached to and emotional about their possessions. But you also need to instill in them a healthy respect for the possessions of others, especially within your own home.

Oppression. Older children can be merciless in their physical and emotional torment of younger siblings, and parents must be prepared to intervene when this type of behavior is going on. But sometimes younger children can harass and irritate older siblings, and they should not be given free rein to do so simply because they are smaller.

Injustice. "He did it!" and "She started it!" are common "not guilty" pleas of siblings who are asked to account for a mess, a broken toy (or window), or a fight. Many times you will have to sort out who did what to whom, and at times you will need the wisdom of Solomon to dispense justice in the face of conflicting testimony or inconclusive evidence. While children may fervently seek to escape punishment, they care desperately about fairness. Don't play favorites. The fact that one child is normally more compliant than another doesn't mean that he isn't capable of instigating wrongdoing.

In addition to your efforts to minimize these hot spots for sibling rivalry, here are a few more general principles to keep in mind:

Don't get pulled into every conflict. Sometimes children will start an uproar in a misguided attempt to gain adult attention. Ignoring their efforts will reduce the odds of a repeat performance. Even if that isn't their motivation, in some situations it's reasonable to give children a chance to sort out their own conflicts.

AVOIDING CONFLICT WHEN THE NEW BABY COMES HOME

Of all the situations in which a child might be concerned about getting parental attention, few are more acute than when Mom brings a newborn home from the hospital. A preschooler or grade-school child who has peer-group friends and other interests will usually take this event in stride. She may be not only fascinated with the new baby but also willing to help with simple tasks related to newborn care.

Very often, however, the older sibling is a toddler, who may take a dim view of this squirmy creature who now monopolizes so much of her mother's time. Not being able to express her feelings in words yet, she may regress in behavior, forgetting toilet-training skills, asking for a bottle, trying to climb into her old crib, or whatever else seems like a possible way to get back to the way things used to be. Simple preparations can help prevent behavior meltdown when the newborn comes home:

- As Mom's abdomen enlarges during pregnancy, talk to your older child about the new baby who is soon going to be born. She may be fascinated to feel the baby's kicking and other movements, but she may not be able to comprehend that this bumpy thing will soon occupy the bassinet or crib that used to be hers. Nevertheless, make it clear that there will be a new baby here soon (a picture book about new babies may help), that the baby will need a lot of Mom's attention, but that this will not mean that Mom cares any less for her.

- Wrap up inexpensive gifts for the older child that can be given to her at opportune times after the baby is born (such as when relatives bring gifts for the newborn). Remember, though, that the attention that comes with the gift—especially when someone is interested in playing with her and whatever she has unwrapped—is usually going to be more important than the item itself.

- If she seems to regress in her behavior, talk to her about all the advantages of being older and bigger: she doesn't have to wear a diaper, she can go to the park with Grandpa, she can eat big kid's food, she can look at books, etc.

- If her hands are clean (and she isn't fighting the latest cold virus), let her gently touch the baby *under your direct supervision.* Remind her that this is done only when you're watching and that she can't poke or jiggle the baby as she would a toy.

- As much time and energy as caring for a newborn takes, seize any opportunity to give your toddler individual attention. When the baby's feeding habits are well established, read or tell a story to the older child every day during one of the baby's feeding sessions. This can communicate graphically that the new arrival is adding to your family life and not merely taking away attention that was once hers.

Don't let conflicts get out of hand. If the children are not arriving at an appropriate solution, if someone is being bullied, or if insults (or fists) are flying, call a time-out for tempers to cool down.

Repeatedly teach the principle of mutual respect and its implications. Just as marital conflicts must be settled within a framework of mutual respect, so also must disagreements between children. This is the basis for curbing insults and not allowing arguments to escalate into physical combat.

Administer disciplinary measures privately. The embarrassment of being disciplined in front of other people—especially other children who may secretly take pleasure in watching the punishment—is both painful and counterproductive and more likely to lead to resentment than improved behavior.

Discourage tattling. If one child tells you about the misdeeds of another, the second child's behavior must be dealt with, assuming that the story is true. But if the first child seemed smug or gleeful while reporting to you what his sibling did or appeared to gloat over the other child's discipline, he needs to be reprimanded too. The issue isn't that he reported the wrongdoing; at times such information may prevent an accident or injury. What you want to discourage is the attitude of tattling that derives satisfaction or pleasure from another's "crime and punishment."

Remember that "this too will surely pass." It is often difficult to believe that children who have squabbled so intensely for so many years can actually have civilized relationships later in life. Yet in the vast majority of cases, a child's passage into adolescence and adulthood ends sibling warfare and replaces it with pleasant camaraderie, deepening friendship, and (most surprisingly) fervent loyalty.

Helping Children
Cope with Death

Death is a reality not easily grasped by children (or, for that matter, by adults). Between the ages of three and five your child will begin to realize that nothing lives forever, and from then on you can expect him to have many questions, fantasies, and fears about death. He may or may not express these directly, but as he grows through the preschool years and beyond, he will certainly be aware of them. In a variety of ways through the course of childhood and adolescence, he will need to work through his concerns and adjust his understanding of life so that it encompasses and eventually comes to terms with death.

In many ways, talking to a child about this subject poses many of the same problems as talking about sexuality. Both topics are very important matters of the human condition, but they are sensitive, emotional, and difficult to broach with children. Furthermore, most children receive a great many impressions, ideas, and messages—often grossly inaccurate or wrongheaded—about both topics from the media, their friends, and conversations they happen to overhear. Just as a child's knowledge and attitudes about sexuality should not be left to develop by chance, neither should those related to dying and death. The same principles of "decent exposure" described in chapter 11 (see page 419) apply to both of these topics.

Tell the truth.

Misrepresentations or lies about anything, including death, ultimately cause far more harm than good. Tact and gentleness are important, of course, but they should not stray into the realm of fantasy or falsehood. Statements such as "Grandpa went away on a long trip" may sound soothing at the moment, but they will cause problems later as your child attempts to get a grip on what actually happened. *It is very important for a child to know that you will not mislead him, even if the facts aren't comfortable for either of you.* This also means that you will need to prepare him if a loved one is seriously ill or near death. Secrets and hushed conversations do more to raise a child's anxiety than a candid appraisal of the situation expressed in simple terms he can understand.

Provide information on a need-to-know basis.

While telling the truth is imperative, your child's ability to deal with the explicit details of illness or death will definitely depend on his age and maturity. Your preschooler doesn't need to know the pathological details about cancer or the gruesome details of the injuries sustained in an auto accident, especially when it involves someone he has known and loved. On the other hand, a high school student might not be satisfied with generalities, and more specific information would be appropriate.

Be aware of your child's concerns related to death, and address them accordingly.

While every child approaches this subject with a unique set of experiences, some conceptions and concerns are common in particular age groups. When discussing death with a child, it is very important to understand what he is thinking about, a process that may require gentle questioning, open ears, patience, and the willingness to respond respectfully to whatever you hear.

Younger children (roughly ages three through six) are still in the process of sorting out real versus make-believe, and their understanding of death may include a variety of fantasies or magical beliefs. For example, they may have seen a TV or movie actor die and then show up next week in another show. Many children have watched E. T. die and then come back to life, and cartoon characters routinely survive severe pummelings. These exposures can cause children to have difficulty understanding the *finality* of physical death, the fact that someone who has died won't come back sometime later.

Younger children may also have problems with cause-and-effect relationships related to death. A child may conclude that something he did, said, or merely thought caused a loved one's death. He may feel terrible guilt and even believe that he can or should do something to bring that person back. Or he might make some frightening connections related to the circumstances of the death. For example, if Grandpa developed a bad cough and then died a week later, someone else's cough could cause a lot of concern: *Daddy has a cough—is he going to die too?*

Older children (ages seven through twelve) are more likely to grasp the realities related to death, but as a result they may also be very prone to worry excessively about those they love. If Mom is a half hour late getting home from choir rehearsal, dire images might come to mind: *What if she had an accident? What would I do without her?*

Adolescents dealing with the death of a loved one, or perhaps a classmate whose life has been lost to accident or illness, will undoubtedly have a variety of strong feelings to sort through. *What if that had been me? How can I go on without _____?* They will need to talk, to be heard and taken seriously, and probably to be held and comforted at some point.

Remember that your child's ideas and attitudes about death are likely to mirror yours.

If you are very anxious about death—as evidenced perhaps by how quickly you attempt to dismiss it or by your reluctance to feel or express grief—your child will pick up on these cues and may well join in your fear. But when the inevitable occasions arise, if you model an open, honest grief that is coupled with your faith, he is likely to adopt that approach.

DEATH OF A PET

Whenever your family acquires a pet, whether a fifty-cent goldfish or an expensive thoroughbred, you can count on two realities: (1) Your child will form an attachment to it, whether or not you do, and (2) except in unusual circumstances, the pet's life expectancy will be shorter than your child's passage into adulthood.

Depending on the type of animal and the age of the child, it is quite likely that your child will think of a pet as a family member. This is especially true if the pet has been in your home from the time your child was an infant or toddler. Activities and experiences with a pet, especially one that is very affectionate, can become an integral part of a child's earliest recollections and often carry deep emotions. The death of a beloved pet can thus represent a major loss to a child or adolescent.

Do not be surprised if your child becomes upset over the death of even a hamster or a bird. And if the pet was cuddly and deeply loved, the response will probably be much more emotional. A parent's immediate impulse may be to try to make the hurt go away, either by downplaying the loss ("C'mon, Evan, it was only a *cat*, for Pete's sake!") or by replacing the departed pet as quickly as possible. But it is important to give your child a chance to grieve, to cry and sob and say how much he misses the pet. (The same process will nearly always occur, by the way, when a pet is lost or runs away and does not return home.)

Very often the loss of a pet will be the first time a child is confronted at close range with the reality of death. As emotional as this will be, it presents an opportunity not only to comfort but also to walk your child through the process of dealing with the loss of a loved one. Depending on the age of the child(ren) involved, if the pet is going to be sorely missed you may want to set aside a brief time to acknowledge his passing, either in conversation around the kitchen table or in a brief "memorial service," perhaps in the backyard. This will not only validate everyone's feelings about the pet but also allow them to remember and give thanks for the good times everyone had while he was alive. It provides an opportunity to interact with your child about this difficult subject and especially to correct (gently) any misconceptions or fantasies about what happens when an animal—or a human—dies.

It is likely, in the course of your conversations, that your child will ask where the pet is now. Don't worry about being too precise with your theology when talking to younger children. They can be reminded how Jesus taught that not even a sparrow can fall to the ground without God knowing about it—and that God certainly knows about the death of your family pet. If your child asks if the pet is in heaven, be truthful and say that the Bible doesn't tell us—but that it does say quite a bit about the importance of *our* being with God after we die. You might take a few moments to pray together, thanking God for the time the pet was part of your family, and talk to your child about the most important aspects of your faith.

DEATH OF A FAMILY MEMBER

The death of a family member—especially a grandparent, a brother or sister, and most of all a parent—is a grievous blow to a child of any age. A very young child (before the age of about two and a half) may not feel or be able to verbalize his response the way an older child will, but it will affect his life nonetheless. To best help a child deal with that emotional blow, maintaining heart-to-heart communication is the overriding principle from which all else follows.

Be aware of components—not stages—of grief.

You may have heard about the stages of grief: denial, anger, bargaining, depression, and acceptance, or some variant of these. But the idea that grief unfolds in fixed stages is oversimplified. More commonly, the emotions of grief will vacillate rather wildly from one component to another. In some children, one of these elements may predominate for a long time, or more than one may coexist. When acceptance is experienced, it is rarely fixed and permanent. Rather, as the storm slowly abates, moments of acceptance will eventually extend for longer periods of time. Only after considerable time has passed and a measure of healing has occurred does acceptance of the loss predominate.

Stay with your child.

How do you relate to your child as she experiences a seemingly unending storm of terrible—and terrifying—feelings? The most important point is to comfort her in her grief, but not to squelch or discount those feelings. This will never be easy, especially when you are dealing with intense emotions of your own. While there are no formulas for this process, the following are a few examples of a child's various expressions of grief at the death of her mother, and her father's comforting responses. These could apply to a variety of situations.

- *Anger:* "I hate her, I hate her! Why did she have to go?"
  Response: "We all get mad when people leave us when we don't want them to. I do too. But Mom wanted to stay with you so much. She just couldn't."
- *Denial:* "I know that Mom is just going to come back after she has a rest."
  Response: "You know, sometimes I feel as though Mom is just in another room, and that I'll walk through the door and there she'll be. It hurts so much when she isn't."
- *Bargaining:* "Daddy, if I promise to be really, really good and stop hitting Jimmy, maybe Mommy will come back."
  Response: "Sweetheart, you didn't do anything wrong that made Mommy die."

The most natural expression of our loving concern is to try to make the hurt go away as quickly as possible. But grief is a process that will be measured in months rather than in hours or days. This is especially true if a parent has died, because his or her absence will continue to be felt throughout childhood. Indeed,

complete healing of this emotional wound may not come until well after a child
has reached adulthood.

Try to recognize disguised reactions.

Children will often react to death in ways that serve to protect them against their
terrible feelings of loss. Some of these reactions include:

Indifference. A child may become listless and emotionless, displaying a degree of
indifference to her loss that seems inappropriate. Children who suffered a major
loss (for example, one or both parents) may go through the funeral this way,
without tears and seemingly intent on returning to their usual activities as
quickly as possible—yet without relish. This may even aggravate other family
members: *Doesn't she care about what has happened?* If your child reacts this way,
it is important not to try to jolt her into a more "genuine" reaction. Instead, make
yourself available to her, spend lots of time together in an atmosphere of caring.
Don't pressure her. In time, she will most likely open up and collapse in your
arms, pouring out grief that was not apparent immediately after the death occurred.

Acting out. Sometimes instead of talking about their grief, anger, and depression, children will become agitated and irritable, seeming to look for opportunities to misbehave or lash out. While this might appear both insensitive and
disrespectful, it may in fact be much easier for a child to do battle with someone else than to deal with the terrible pain that is bottled up inside. While you
will need to enforce appropriate rules and limits as consistently as ever, redou-
ble your efforts to initiate nonthreatening conversations during which you can
ask some questions. Sometimes you will see with great clarity how a particular
misbehavior is directly tied to an unexpressed feeling of loss. Use these moments to take your child aside and explain how you too feel angry at times because of this death, and that you'd like to lash out as well. Perhaps you won't get
an immediate acknowledgment, but more often than not you'll see tears begin
to well up—and the behavior improve.

Depression. A child may develop a clinical depression after a parent or other
loved one dies. A depression, as opposed to normal grief, is manifested in some
or all of these ways:

- Unusually persistent and severe grief, showing little or no sign of resolution after a few months and interfering with the child's ability to carry
  out normal activities.

- Difficulty falling or staying asleep, or the opposite—persistent oversleeping.
- Change in appetite, with unusual weight loss or gain.
- Suicidal thoughts.
- Expressed feelings of hopelessness about the future.
- Withdrawal from normal activities.
- Inability to experience and express pleasure in any activity.
- A sudden change in friends or, in adolescents, drug abuse or sexual activity.

Since normal grief and clinical depression often are so similar in appearance, you may need the counsel of your pastor or a professional to help sort things out. Formal intervention—which could include counseling and, when appropriate, the use of medication—may be necessary and should not be withheld or delayed out of a mistaken notion that "she's young—she'll get over it." Depression is a very real and potentially dangerous disturbance among children and adolescents and should not be ignored (see Special Concerns, page 601).

WHAT ABOUT FAITH IN THE FACE OF DEATH?

Few events in life bring spiritual concerns into focus as powerfully as the death of a friend or loved one, an event that forces those left behind to face the reality that everyone's life on earth must eventually come to an end. For better or worse, the role that your faith plays in the days and weeks that follow the death of a loved one can have a profound impact on your child. Your child should see God's love and care manifested in you and many others during this intense and difficult experience. The following suggestions might help bring this about:

Think carefully about how you describe God's role in death.

A few generations ago, children and adults alike were surrounded by the cultural and religious beliefs that God routinely struck people down, either as punishment or for no apparent reason ("The Lord gave, and the Lord hath taken away"). Today we are more likely to hear about a God who kills with kindness—"God loved Jenny so much that He wanted her to be with Him, so He took her to heaven." It is certainly wise to have a healthy respect for God as the One who holds our lives in His hands, and it is very comforting to know that God has welcomed the loved one who has just died. But a child might be reluctant to draw near to Him if she believes that He can hardly wait for her to die—whether as judgment for one or more transgressions or as an act of love. *(If God loved Jenny so much that she died, does that mean that I'm going to die because God loves me?)*

Pay attention to the messages you and others give your child about God, and don't hesitate to check in with her to see how these ideas have affected her.

Be honest when you don't have all the answers.

Often it isn't possible to make sense out of a particular death. The question "Why would God let this happen?" has for centuries challenged young and old alike whenever illness or accident ended young and apparently innocent lives. The risk in such situations is to offer shallow or pat answers or in bitterness and frustration to reach the devastating conclusion that God either "isn't there" or "doesn't care." What parent and child need to grasp is that God does indeed care very deeply for each of us, but that we aren't always going to be allowed complete (or even partial) understanding of every event that occurs during our lifetime. (This important concept is discussed in detail in Dr. James Dobson's book *When God Doesn't Make Sense.*)

Don't underestimate your child's ability and willingness to trust in God during difficult times.

Children typically desire and understand intimacy with God in ways that may elude adults, especially during a crisis. Quite simply, if they believe in you and trust in your love, so too will they believe and trust in the love of God. In the emotional upheaval of your own grief, be careful not to hinder a child from finding comfort in God, which often will come naturally to a child.

CHAPTER 12

The Adolescent Years, Part One

*Our sons in their youth
will be like well-nurtured plants,
and our daughters
will be like pillars
carved to adorn a palace.*
PSALM 144:12

The Adolescent Years, Part One: Bodies in Motion

Adolescence: The period of physical and psychological development from the onset of puberty to maturity. (From the Latin *adolescere:* "to grow up.")

Between the twelfth and twenty-first birthdays, your child will undergo rapid and intense physical, psychological, and social changes, and at the end of this period she will no longer be a child. Just as you probably approached the "terrible twos" (sometimes called the "first adolescence") with a combination of eager anticipation and a little apprehension, you may now have a similar mix of positive expectation and growing concern as the "real thing" arrives. Without a doubt, adjustments and challenges are ahead for everyone in the family.

Indeed, the years to come may at times feel like a canoe trip down a mountain river. The scenery is constantly changing; the ride is always interesting and often pleasant; but choppy waters, roaring rapids, and an occasional waterfall may await you around the next bend. Your job will be to stabilize the family canoe as much as possible, and by all means, prevent it from turning over before your adolescent reaches the calmer waters of adulthood. Dr. James Dobson has aptly stated that "parenting isn't for cowards," and the coming years may well serve up the greatest tests of your parental fortitude.

It won't be all trials and turbulence. These are highly rewarding years for many families, full of accomplishments, commitments to worthwhile causes, and experiences that aren't possible until children are grown and more mature. You can't expect your two-year-old to appreciate a basketball game, a performance of

Les Miserables, or a great sermon, but your sixteen-year-old can share these experiences with you and be as interested or enthralled as any adult.

This chapter will focus on the physical aspects of this remarkable transformation from child to adult, while emotions, relationships, and other growing pains will be discussed in the chapter to follow. Both chapters will begin with a survey of normal development and then review potential pitfalls, preventive measures, and positive goals for parents and their rapidly growing children. Fasten your seat belt, hold on tight, and enjoy the ride.

PHYSICAL GROWTH AND DEVELOPMENT

From a physical standpoint, the main event of adolescence is puberty, which serves as the physiological bridge between childhood and adulthood.

> *Puberty:* The stage of maturation in which an individual becomes physiologically capable of sexual reproduction. (From the Latin *puber:* "adult.")

Rapid growth and body changes during these years are to a large degree brought about by interactions between several **hormones,** biochemical compounds that are created in one part of the body and sent via the bloodstream to have a specific effect somewhere else. These chemical messages provoke an impressive number and variety of responses throughout the body. All of the hormones and the glands that secrete them are collectively known as the **endocrine system.** Not all hormones, however, are related to reproduction. Thyroid hormone, for example, plays an important role in the body's metabolic rate. Insulin, secreted by the pancreas, escorts glucose (or blood sugar) into the cells that need and use this basic fuel. Growth hormone, as its name implies, is necessary for the attainment of normal adult height.

Speaking of growth hormone, a major growth spurt is one hallmark of adolescence, usually occurring between the ages of ten and fourteen in girls, and twelve and sixteen in boys. (Perhaps "spurt" isn't the most accurate term for this event, which actually lasts between two and three years.) The rate of growth can vary, but it tends to be the fastest during spring and summer. Weight increases as well, and bones progress through their final stages of maturation. In addition, the percentage of body fat increases in girls and decreases in boys.

Pubertal development in boys

A number of marvelous changes take place as a boy's body grows into that of a man's. Male sexual development usually begins between the ages of ten and thirteen (the average age is eleven), and the process is usually completed in about three years, although it can range anywhere from two to five years. The timing and speed of bodily changes can vary greatly between boys of the same age, and the slow developer may need extra encouragement and continued reassurance that he will eventually reach the goal of manhood. (He can be gently reminded that he probably hasn't seen any men walking around lately with high, squeaky voices.) A boy should be checked by his physician, however, if he begins to show pubertal changes before age nine or has none of these developments underway by age fourteen.

The first physical sign of puberty in boys is enlargement in the size of the testicles and thinning of the scrotum. Hair appears on the face, chest, under the arms, and in the genital area. The voice starts to deepen, although it may pass through an awkward phase of breaking, especially when he is excited or nervous.

The testicles begin manufacturing sperm, which are transported through a structure called the **epididymis** (one of which sits adjacent to each testicle) and then onward to the penis through a pair of flexible tubes called the **vas deferens.** The **prostate** begins to produce seminal fluid, which carries sperm out of the body during ejaculation. The newly functioning sexual equipment will at times unexpectedly carry out its functions during the middle of the night in what is called a **nocturnal emission** or "wet dream," a normal event that an uninformed adolescent might find alarming. Along the same lines, boys may be concerned or embarrassed by unexpected erections, which can occur at very inopportune times (for example, just prior to giving a report in front of a class). Neither of these should be interpreted as a sign of impending moral failure. In fact, we hope you will have briefed your son about these normal events before puberty arrived.

If you are a single mother who feels uncomfortable discussing these matters with your son, consider seeking help from an adult male who not only shares your values but has enough rapport to talk with him about these topics.

Some boys develop a small, button-sized nodule of breast tissue directly under the nipple. This is a common response to changing hormones, although it may cause a minor panic when first discovered ("Is this a tumor?" "Am I going to develop breasts like a woman?"). This area may become a little tender but should return to normal within twelve to eighteen months. If you have any questions, or if breast tissue appears to be increasing in size (a phenomenon known as **gynecomastia**), have it checked by your son's doctor.

Pubertal development in girls

While pubertal development and the reproductive process are relatively straight-forward in boys, the changes that take place as a girl progresses to womanhood are in many ways much more complex. (As you will see, they also take quite a bit longer to explain.) Not only does she undergo significant changes in her outward appearance, but inside her body a delicate interplay of hormones eventually leads to a momentous occasion: her first menstrual period (also called **menarche**), announcing her potential to reproduce.

The first visible sign of puberty in girls is the development of **breast buds,** which usually appear about two years before the first menstrual period. Each breast bud is a small, flat, firm buttonlike nodule that develops directly under the areola (the pigmented area that surrounds the nipple). This tissue eventually softens as the breasts enlarge. Occasionally a bud will develop on one side before the other, which might lead to the mistaken impression that a tumor is growing. But the passage of time and (if necessary) a doctor's examination will confirm that this growth is in fact normal.

As the breasts continue to develop, hair begins to grow under the arms, on the legs, and in the genital area. The contour of the hips becomes fuller, and the internal reproductive organs grow and mature. Glands within the vagina produce a clear or milky secretion, which may appear several months before the onset of menstrual bleeding. Finally, at the conclusion of an intricate sequence of hormonal events, the first menstrual flow arrives. This typically occurs around twelve years of age, with a range between nine and sixteen.

As with boys, girls who begin this process earlier or later than average will need some information and reassurance. In general, a girl should be checked by her physician if she develops breast buds before age eight or has her first period before age nine. At the opposite end of the spectrum, the absence of pubertal changes by thirteen or menstrual periods by sixteen should trigger a medical evaluation.

For many adolescents (and their parents), the menstrual cycle is a complex mystery or even a source of some anxiety. While this event may not be a routine topic of conversation over Sunday dinner, you might want to refresh your memory or learn about it for the first time well before the first stirrings of puberty in your offspring. Your daughter(s) at some point will have questions and concerns about the monthly flow: What is normal and what isn't? How often should this occur? What if there's a lot, very little, or none at all? What about cramping?

While the menstrual flow will be the focus of your adolescent's attention, it is only a single event in an elaborate process that prepares her physically each month for the possibility of bearing a child. It is therefore both practical and wise for you and your daughter(s) to understand the basics of a woman's reproductive cycle.

Furthermore, in the course of learning how to treat the women in his life with care and respect, a boy also should learn basic information about the female reproductive cycle. How and when he gains this information, however, will depend both on timing and his maturity level. In order to protect boundaries of modesty (and prevent potential embarrassment), be careful about what is said and who is listening when discussing what is going on inside the body of your teenager. Generic comments ("When a woman is having her menstrual period . . .") are more appropriate than naming names ("When Jessica is having her menstrual period . . ."). When in doubt, conversations about such matters with adolescents, who are likely to be extremely self-conscious, will feel safer if carried out in private or at least with boys and girls separately.

A single father who feels out of his element discussing the female reproductive cycle with his adolescent daughter may want to request help from a woman who is mature, is comfortable communicating this information to adolescents, and holds similar values regarding sexuality.

The Menstrual Cycle

In case your memory is a little fuzzy from health-education or childbirth classes, the following section is a primer on the menstrual cycle. If your adolescent is ready and interested, she or he may read along.

What goes on during the menstrual cycle?

Under normal circumstances, each month a woman's body performs a three-act play entitled *Preparing for a Baby*. What you are about to read is a summary of the essential characters and plot. (As with many other aspects of human physiology, there are thousands of other details that will not be spelled out here and thousands more yet to be discovered. The design of this process is indeed exquisite.)

The main characters in the play are:

+ The **hypothalamus:** a multifaceted structure at the base of the brain that regulates basic bodily functions such as temperature and appetite. It also serves as the prime mover in the reproductive cycle.

- The **pituitary:** a small, punching-bag-shaped structure that appears to dangle from the brain directly below the hypothalamus. It has been called the "master gland" because it gives orders to many other organs. But it also takes important cues from the hypothalamus.

- The **ovaries:** a matched pair of organs in the female pelvis that serve two critical functions—releasing one or more eggs (or ova) each month and secreting the hormones **estrogen** and **progesterone.** At birth the ovaries contain about 2 million eggs, a woman's lifetime supply. During childhood, the vast majority of these gradually disappear, and by the time she reaches puberty only about 300,000 will be left. During her reproductive years, she will release between three hundred and five hundred eggs; the rest will die and disappear.

- The **uterus:** a pear-shaped organ consisting primarily of muscle, containing a cavity where a baby grows during pregnancy. This cavity is lined with delicate tissue called **endometrium,** which changes remarkably in response to estrogen and progesterone produced by the ovaries. The uterus, also called the womb, is located at the top of the vagina and positioned in the middle of the pelvis between the bladder and the rectum.

- The **fallopian tubes:** a pair of tubes, about four to five inches long, attached to the upper corners of the uterus and extend toward each ovary. Their job is to serve as a meeting place for egg and sperm and then to transport a fertilized egg to the uterus.

Act I: Preparing an egg for launch (the follicular phase). The hypothalamus begins a reproductive cycle by sending a message called **gonadotrophin releasing hormone** to the pituitary gland just a short distance away. The message says, in effect, "Send out the hormone that prepares an egg to be released by the ovary." The pituitary responds by secreting **follicle stimulating hormone** (or FSH) into the bloodstream. Each egg within an ovary is covered with a thin sheet of cells, and the term **follicle** (which literally means "little bag") refers to the entire package of egg and cells together. Under the influence of FSH, eight or ten follicles begin to grow and "ripen." Usually only one becomes dominant and progresses to full maturity.

This follicular phase of the cycle lasts about two weeks, during which the dominant follicle fills with fluid and enlarges to about three-quarters of an inch. The egg contained within it will soon be released from the ovary. At the same time, this follicle secretes increasing amounts of estrogen, which (among other things) stimulates the lining of the uterus to proliferate and thicken. This is the first stage of preparation of the uterus for the arrival of a fertilized egg.

Act II: The egg is released (ovulation). As in Act I, this part of the story also begins in the hypothalamus. In response to rising levels of estrogen, the hypothalamus signals the pituitary to release a brief but intense surge of **luteinizing hormone** (or LH) into the bloodstream. This hormone sets off a chain reaction in the ovary. The dominant follicle enlarges, its outer wall becomes thin, and finally it ruptures, releasing egg and fluid. This mini-eruption called **ovulation** takes only a few minutes and occurs approximately thirty-eight hours after the peak of the LH surge. Sometimes a tiny amount of blood oozes from the ovary as well. This may irritate the lining of the abdomen, producing a discomfort known as **mittelschmerz** (German for "middle pain," because it occurs about halfway through the cycle).

Act III: The voyage of the egg and the preparation of the uterus (the luteal phase). The egg is not left to its own devices once it is set free from the ovary. At the end of each fallopian tube are structures called **fimbria** (Latin for "fingers"), whose delicate tentacles move over the area of the ovary. As soon as ovulation takes place, the fimbria gently escort the egg into the tube, where it begins a journey toward the uterus. The cells that line the fallopian tube have microscopic hairlike projections called **cilia,** which move in a synchronized pattern that sets up a one-way current through the tube. If sperm are present in the outer portion of the tube, and one of them is successful in penetrating the egg, fertilization takes place and a new life begins. The fertilized egg will incubate in the tube for about three days before arriving at its destination, the cavity of the uterus, where it floats for about three more days before implanting. On about the seventh day it "rests," so to speak, implanting in the cavity of the uterus. If the egg is not fertilized, it will live only twelve to twenty-four hours and then disintegrate or pass through the tube and uterus into the vagina. (Since sperm live for forty-eight to seventy-two hours, there are three or four days in each cycle during which intercourse could lead to conception.)

Meanwhile, much activity takes place in the ovary after ovulation. The newly vacated follicle has another job to do: preparing the uterus to accept and nourish a fertilized egg should one arrive. The follicle turns into a gland called the **corpus luteum** (literally, "yellow body" because cells lining the inside of the follicle develop a yellowish color), which secretes estrogen and, more important, progesterone. This hormone, which dominates this luteal phase of the cycle, promotes growth and maturation of the uterine lining. This layer of tissue eventually doubles in thickness and becomes stocked with nutrients. Progesterone not only prepares the uterine "nursery" for a new arrival but also relaxes the muscles of the uterus, decreasing the chance of contractions that might accidentally expel its guest. Progesterone also temporarily stops the preparation of any other eggs within the ovaries.

If a fertilized egg successfully implants and continues its growth within the uterus, it secretes a hormone called **human chorionic gonadotrophin** (or HCG), which sends an important message to the corpus luteum: "Keep the hormones flowing!" The corpus luteum obliges and for nine or ten weeks continues to provide the hormone support that allows the uterus to nourish the baby growing inside. After ten weeks, the **placenta** (the complex organ that connects the baby to the inner lining of the uterus) takes over the job of manufacturing progesterone, and the corpus luteum retires from active duty.

If there is no fertilization, no pregnancy, and no HCG, the corpus luteum degenerates. Progesterone and estrogen levels fall, resulting in spasm of the blood vessels that supply the lining of the uterus. Deprived of the nutrients it needs to survive, the lining dies and passes from the uterus, along with blood and mucus, in what is called the menstrual flow (also referred to as the period or **menses**).

While the menstrual period might seem to be the end of the story, the first day of flow is actually counted as day 1 of a woman's reproductive cycle. For while the flow is taking place, the three-act play is starting over again as a new set of follicles begins to ripen in the ovaries. This "circle of life" will thus normally continue month after month throughout the reproductive years until menopause unless interrupted by pregnancy or a medical condition that interferes with this cycle.

What is normal during menstrual periods?

The words *menstrual* and *menses* are derived from the Latin word for "month," which refers to the approximate frequency of this event. A typical cycle lasts from twenty-seven to thirty-five days, although for some women normal menses occur as frequently as every twenty-one days or as infrequently as every forty-five days. Most of the variability arises during the first (follicular) phase leading up to ovulation. Assuming that a pregnancy does not begin, the luteal phase (from ovulation to menses) is nearly always fourteen days, with little variation.

During the first year or two after her first menstrual period, an adolescent's cycles may be irregular because of **anovulatory cycles,** meaning an egg is not released. If ovulation does not take place, the cycle will remain stuck in the first (follicular) phase. Estrogen will continue to stimulate the lining of the uterus until some of it becomes so thick that it outgrows its blood supply. The shedding of this tissue resembles a menstrual period, but it is unpredictable and usually occurs with very little cramping. When ovulation finally takes place, the lining of the uterus will mature and then be shed all at once if a pregnancy has not started.

After her first menstrual period, several months may pass before a girl's endocrine system matures to the point of producing regular ovulation. During this time it is not unusual for her to skip two or three months between cycles. Since cramping doesn't normally occur unless ovulation has taken place, menstrual pains may not be noticed for months (or even one or two years) after the first cycle.

Menstrual flow normally lasts three to six days, although very short (one-day) or longer (seven- or eight-day) periods may be normal for some women. One to three ounces of blood is usually lost during each cycle, although more or less than this amount may be a regular occurrence without any ill effects.

Virtually all normal activities can be continued during a menstrual period. Bathing or showering is not only safe but advisable in order to minimize any unpleasant odor. Feminine hygiene sprays and deodorant pads and tampons may irritate delicate tissue, and douching is unnecessary and should be avoided. Any persistent drainage that is discolored, itchy, painful, or foul-smelling should *not* be treated by douching but rather be evaluated by a physician.

What can go wrong with menstrual periods?

Menstrual cramps (also called dysmenorrhea) most often are a by-product of the normal breakdown of the lining of the uterus (endometrium) at the end of a cycle. Chemicals called **prostaglandins** are released into the bloodstream by the endometrium, often with unpleasant effects. The most obvious response is a series of contractions of the muscles of the uterus, which may actually be as forceful as contractions during labor. During a strong contraction, blood may be inhibited from circulating through all of the uterine muscle and, like any other muscle temporarily deprived of oxygen, will sound off with genuine pain. Prostaglandins may affect other parts of the body during a menstrual period, causing diarrhea, nausea, headaches, and difficulty with concentration. One bit of good news in connection with menstrual cramps is that they do not predict what level of pain a woman will feel later in life during childbirth. In other words, a teenager with severe menstrual cramps is not necessarily going to have equally severe labor pains.

Menstrual cramps can be relieved in a variety of ways:

- ◆ Heating pads or warm baths are often helpful, for reasons that are unclear. (These may increase blood flow within the pelvis, improving the supply of oxygen to uterine muscle.)
- ◆ Exercise and good general physical condition are often helpful in reducing cramps. Walking is a good exercise during this (or, for that matter, any) time of the month.
- ◆ Specific prostaglandin-inhibiting medications work well for many adolescents and older women alike. These were formulated to reduce the pain and inflammation of arthritis but were found to also have a significant effect on menstrual cramps. Several are now available without prescription: ibuprofen (Advil, Motrin, Nuprin, and other brands), naproxen (Aleve) and ketoprofen (Orudis KT and others). These anti-inflammatory drugs should be taken with food to decrease the chance of irritating the stomach. They are most effective if they are taken at the first sign of cramping and then continued on a regular basis (rather than "here and there" in response to pain) until the cramps stop. Your daughter's physician may recommend one of these medications (sometimes

PADS OR TAMPONS?

From the very first to the final reproductive cycle, either tampons or external pads may be used to absorb menstrual flow. Each has its specific advantages and disadvantages.

External pads may be more comfortable for a young adolescent who feels uneasy about inserting a foreign object into her vagina. However, pads may cause heat and moisture to be retained around the external genital area (especially in hot or humid climates) and increase the likelihood of local irritation or infection.

Tampons allow more freedom of activity (especially for vigorous exercise or swimming) and less chance of contributing to external irritation. Some parents may worry about tampons causing damage inside or at the opening of the vagina. However, inserting a tampon does not tear the hymen (the ring of soft tissue just inside the labia at the entrance to the vagina), although difficulty inserting tampons may be the first indication of an abnormality of this structure. Very rarely, small vaginal ulcerations may result from

improper tampon insertion. Occasionally a tampon may disappear into the vagina and cannot be located by the wearer. This is not a dangerous situation, although if left behind for more than a day or two, a stray tampon can generate a powerful odor and discharge. A doctor or nurse-practitioner can retrieve it without much difficulty.

Of more concern is the association of tampon use with **toxic shock syndrome (TSS),** a condition caused by a toxin produced by the bacterium staphylococcus aureus. A number of cases in the early 1980s occurred in connection with a particular type of tampon that appeared to foster the growth of staphylococci in the vagina and irritate the vaginal lining. This tampon was taken off the market, but subsequent evidence has indicated that a primary risk factor for the development of TSS is the *amount of time a tampon is left in the vagina.*

Most of the symptoms of this problem are nonspecific: fever, chills, vomiting, diarrhea, sore throat, and with a dosage schedule different from what is written on the package) or prescribe one of several anti-inflammatory medications. Individual responses vary. If one type doesn't work well, another may seem like a miracle.

- Other pain-relief medications that may be helpful include:

    (a) Acetaminophen (Tylenol and others), which does not inhibit prostaglandins but can be quite effective nonetheless. Some women have found that alternating medications is helpful—for example, starting with ibuprofen, using acetaminophen for the next dose a few hours later, then switching back, and so on.

    (b) Midol, which combines acetaminophen with the antihistamine pyrilamine (which may be mildly sedating). Depending on the particular formulation, Midol may include ibuprofen or a mild diuretic (to decrease fluid retention).

    (c) Stronger pain relievers may be prescribed by a physician if the discomfort of menstrual cramps cannot be controlled by other measures.

(continued)

faintness (caused by a drop in blood pressure). A more specific sign is a sunburnlike rash on the palms and soles. When severe, toxic shock syndrome is treated in the hospital with large doses of antibiotics as well as fluids given intravenously to maintain blood pressure. The development of flulike symptoms and light-headedness—feeling faint or actually passing out, especially associated with standing up or other changes in position—may be very significant if they occur during a menstrual period. These symptoms should be evaluated by a physician *as soon as possible.*

Fortunately TSS is rare. (Some staphyloccal infections are associated with TSS and may have no involvement with tampon use; thus they can occur in men and women, for example, a postoperative wound infection.) Most physicians feel that tampons are safe for both adolescents and older women, although fifteen- to nineteen-year-olds are at the most risk for developing toxic shock syndrome from tampon use. Simple precautions can markedly reduce this risk:

- First, and most important, *don't leave a tampon in place for more than six hours.*
- Follow the manufacturer's instructions closely.
- Insert (and remove) a tampon carefully.
- Store tampons in a clean, dry place.
- Wash hands thoroughly before inserting or removing tampons.
- Use tampons with the least absorbency necessary to control the flow. Tampons are now graded for absorbency as follows:
    (a) Junior
    (b) Regular
    (c) Super
    (d) Super plus (not recommended for use by adolescents)
  Less absorbent tampons are smaller and less likely to irritate the lining of the vagina. If a tampon is difficult to remove, a smaller size should be used.
- Consider alternating tampons and pads during the same menstrual period. (For example, use tampons during the day, pads at night.)

If menstrual cramps are disruptive and unresponsive to home remedies and nonprescription medications, it is important that they be evaluated medically. Abnormalities of the cervix (the opening of the uterus) or the uterus itself or a syndrome called **endometriosis** (in which tissue that normally lines the uterus grows in other parts of the body, usually in the pelvis) can on rare occasions be the cause of significant menstrual pain in an adolescent. If the medical examination is normal, the physician may suggest one or both of the following prescription medications:

- **Diuretics** decrease fluid retention but do not directly relieve cramps; however, discomfort may be less annoying if any fluid retention is relieved (see Premenstrual Syndrome later in this chapter).
- **Birth control pills** (oral contraceptives) may be helpful in reducing or eliminating significant cramps that are not adequately controlled by other means. In fact, for many adolescents this may be the only type of medication that is helpful in reducing severe cramps that regularly interfere with normal activity. Each four-week cycle of pills provides three weeks of estrogen and progesterone in a specified amount. This prevents the LH surge and ovulation and also usually results in less proliferation of the lining of the uterus than occurs during a normal cycle. During the fourth week, no hormones are present in the pills, so during this time the lining is shed as in a normal cycle. However, the smaller amount of tissue involved usually generates less cramping.

A decision to use birth control pills should not be made casually. A medical evaluation to rule out other causes of pain may be necessary. Nausea, headaches, bloating, and/or worsening of acne are unpleasant side effects experienced by some users. The pills must be taken consistently each day to be effective.

In addition, the use of birth control pills may raise parental concern: Could taking them for menstrual cramps (or any other therapeutic purpose) indirectly lower your adolescent's resistance to sexual activity? If you don't know the answer to this question, now is the time for candid conversation about sexuality. It would be unfortunate to withhold a treatment that might reduce debilitating pain because of a parent's vague mistrust of an adolescent who is actually fervently committed to remaining abstinent. Furthermore, the decision to postpone sex until marriage should be built on a strong, multilayered foundation. If the absence of contraceptives is the only reason she is avoiding intercourse, she needs to hear and understand many more reasons. (See Special Concerns, page 541, for more information on this important topic.)

Irregular menstrual periods may be a cause for concern if they are

- too rare, occurring every three or four months after more than a year has passed since the first period;
- too frequent, with bleeding or spotting occurring throughout the month;
- too long, lasting more than seven or eight consecutive days;
- too heavy, soaking through more than six to eight pads/tampons per day.

For any of these problems, a medical evaluation is usually indicated to discover the underlying cause. In many instances the diagnosis will be anovulatory cycles resulting from an immature endocrine system. But other physical or even emotional events can also interfere with the complex interaction of hormones that brings about the monthly cycle. These include:

- *Medical disorders.* These could include malfunctions of the endocrine system (including pituitary, adrenal, or thyroid glands) or abnormalities of the ovaries, uterus, or vagina.
- *Significant changes in weight.* Obese adolescents can generate enough estrogen in their fat cells to impact the lining of the uterus. At the opposite extreme, stringent diets or the severe reduction in food intake seen in anorexia will effectively shut down the menstrual cycle (see Special Concerns, page 429).
- *Extreme levels of exercise.* Female athletes with demanding training programs may have infrequent periods or may stop their cycles altogether.
- *Stress.* Stormy emotional weather is no stranger to the adolescent years, and personal upheavals can cause a teenager to miss one or more periods.
- *Pregnancy.* In some cases an unexpected absence of menstrual cycles indicates that an unplanned pregnancy has begun.

It is important that extremes in menstrual flow (whether too much or too little) be evaluated. Not only may the underlying cause have great significance, but the menstrual irregularity could have damaging consequences of its own. For example:

- Very frequent or heavy bleeding may outstrip an adolescent's ability to replenish red blood cells, leading to iron deficiency, **anemia**. Often there is an inadequate amount of iron in the diet to keep up with what is being lost each month. Anemia can cause ongoing fatigue, poor concentration in school, light-headedness, or even fainting episodes.

◆ Absence of menstrual periods related to a continual failure to ovulate may result in months or years of nonstop estrogen stimulation of the uterus. Without the maturing effect of progesterone, the lining of the uterus may be at increased risk for precancerous abnormalities.

◆ Adolescents who stop their cycles because of weight loss or intense physical training (or both) may suffer an irreversible loss of bone density, known as **osteoporosis.** Normally a problem faced by women much later in life (typically well after menopause), osteoporosis can lead to disabling fractures of the spine, hips, wrists, and other bones.

It is impossible to state a single course of action that will resolve all the various forms of menstrual irregularity. However, if there appears to be no underlying disturbance that needs specific treatment and the problem is determined to be irregular ovulation, a doctor may recommend hormonal treatment to regulate the cycle. This may take the form of progesterone, which can be given at a defined time each month to bring on a menstrual period. Or birth control pills may be recommended to restore some order by overriding a woman's own cycle and establishing one that is more predictable. As mentioned earlier, the decision to use this type of medication in an adolescent must be made with particular care and discernment.

PMS and related problems. **Premenstrual tension** is experienced by as many as 90 percent of women, while 20 to 30 percent experience more severe symptoms called **premenstrual syndrome (PMS).** This is *not* the same problem as menstrual cramps, which are associated with the monthly shedding of the lining of the uterus. Rather, premenstrual discomforts specifically occur between ovulation and menstruation. They may occur for a day or two prior to menses or extend over the entire two-week period following ovulation.

A specific cause for PMS has not been identified, but the effects are all too familiar for many women, including adolescents. Physical symptoms can include bloating and fullness in the abdomen, fluid retention (with tightness of rings and shoes), headaches, breast tenderness, backache, fatigue, and dizziness. More dramatic are the emotional symptoms: irritability, anxiety, depression, poor concentration, insomnia, difficulty making decisions, and unusual food cravings. These can occur in various combinations and levels of severity. The most striking feature is usually the instability and intensity of negative emotions, which can send other family members running for cover. Some teenagers and older women feel like Dr. Jekyll and Ms. Hyde—calm and rational for the first two weeks of the cycle and out of control for the second two weeks, with dramatic improvement once the menstrual flow is under way.

A few decades ago PMS was considered primarily a psychological event, an "adjustment reaction" to reproductive issues or life in general. This is no longer the case. PMS should be taken as seriously as any other physical issue. While no quick-fix remedies or lifetime cures exist for PMS, a number of measures can help your adolescent (and others at home) reduce its impact:

- *Make sure the emotional and physical symptoms are, in fact, PMS.* Adolescent emotions are often intense and variable, and other life issues (involving school, friends, etc.) may be at the heart of the problem. If there is any question, symptoms can be charted on a calendar, along with menstrual periods, for two or three months. You should see an improvement for at least a week following menses. Symptoms that continue well after a period is over or throughout the cycle involve something other than (or in addition to) PMS.

- *Keep the lines of communication open and plan ahead.* A teenager whose cycle is well established will be able to predict when the more troublesome days are coming. This may give others at home a little advance "storm warning," and they will be able to respond with an extra measure of TLC or at least a little slack. This is particularly important if more than one person at home has difficulty with PMS, since the collision of two unstable moods can be quite unpleasant. If your daughter is currently irritable because of the time of the month and a change for the better is likely in the immediate future, you would be wise to postpone any conversations about emotionally charged issues for a few days if possible. It is important to acknowledge the reality of PMS symptoms without allowing them to become a blanket excuse for blatant disrespect, acting out, or abandonment of all responsibilities.

- *Encourage sensible eating and exercise.* Frequent, smaller meals and avoidance of overtly sugary foods may help keep blood glucose levels (and mood) a little more stable. Avoiding salt can reduce fluid retention. Caffeine may increase irritability, so decaffeinated drinks (and medications) are more appropriate. All-around physical conditioning through the entire month can improve general well-being and help her navigate more smoothly to the end of a cycle.

Parents should guard against comparative statements that routinely favor one child over another. This is particularly true in three areas: physical attractiveness, intelligence, and athletic abilities.

THE STRONG-
WILLED CHILD

In addition, a variety of remedies, nutritional supplements, and medications have been recommended at one time or another for this problem. Some have a more consistent track record (and better scientific support) than others, and your adolescent should consider getting advice from her physician before trying any of these. Ultimately the bottom line for any PMS treatment will be an honest assessment of the effectiveness, safety, and side effects for the individual taking it.

◆ *Nonprescription medications* such as acetaminophen or ibuprofen to reduce aches and pains may be of some help.

◆ *Dietary supplements,* especially vitamin B_6, magnesium, and calcium have been suggested, although results in patients have been somewhat mixed. Megadoses of any vitamin or mineral that exceed RDAs (recommended daily allowances) are not recommended for this condition.

◆ *Prescription medications* that are most widely used for PMS fall into three basic categories. Obviously, the use of any of these will require evaluation and follow-up by a physician.

(a) *Diuretics.* For many women, much of the discomfort from PMS arises from bloating and fluid retention, so the use of a mild diuretic (or "water pill") to maintain normal fluid levels during the second half of each cycle can be effective.

(b) *Antidepressants.* Many PMS symptoms essentially duplicate those seen in depression, and some women with severe PMS fight milder forms of the same emotional symptoms through the entire month. It is possible that the fundamental physiological problem in PMS involves changes in the levels of biological messengers in the brain known as neurotransmitters. New research has shown significant reduction in PMS symptoms with this type of medication, although in order to be effective, daily dosing for an indefinite period of time is necessary. These drugs are safe and not habit-forming, but individual responses and side effects vary considerably.

(c) *Hormonal manipulations* have been utilized with variable success, although they are not commonly prescribed for adolescents with PMS. Women who take supplemental progesterone during the second half of the menstrual cycle may report marked improvement, a worsening of symptoms (especially depression), or no effect at all. Hormonal preparations should be utilized in adolescents only after thoughtful consideration of the pros and cons by patient, parent, and physician.

MEDICAL EXAMS AND EVALUATIONS DURING ADOLESCENCE

During the next few years, your teenager will probably need medical input on a number of occasions. Screening exams for sports, camp, and general health assessment will need to be done. Injuries arising from sports or other vigorous activities may need attention. Problems related to menstruation may require medical evaluation and intervention. In addition, a variety of symptoms and emotional concerns may arise during these years.

Adolescent health-care guidelines recommend yearly visits to the doctor for assessment, screening, and guidance, even if there have been evaluations during the year for other medical problems. Quick exams for camp or sports, especially those done assembly-line style on large groups of adolescents, should not substitute for more comprehensive physicals by your regular health-care provider. If there are special health problems, more frequent exams may be necessary. Most doctors will talk with parent and teen together during the visit, but part of the time will be spent without the parent present. This is usually done in order to increase the likelihood that the doctor is receiving accurate information, with an assumption that many teenagers might feel uncomfortable answering sensitive questions in front of their parents. It is customary during this time alone for a physician to assure the young patient of the confidentiality of their conversation.[1] *It is therefore extremely important that you consider carefully who is going to provide health care for your adolescent.*

In an ideal situation, you will be dealing with someone

- who is medically competent;
- whom your teenager trusts and can talk with comfortably;
- who knows you and your family;
- whom *you* trust, and who shares your basic values.

The last qualification is particularly significant because of the near certainty that your teenager will eventually be in a one-on-one situation with the physician. Your son or daughter may feel more comfortable discussing sensitive topics with a doctor than with you, even if you have an extremely close and honest relationship. You will want to be certain that the advice and counsel given behind closed doors, especially regarding sexual behavior, will not contradict or undermine principles you have been teaching at home. During these critical years, everyone needs to be on the same team.

Although adolescents usually have an interest in discussing a variety of topics with their doctors, they may feel embarrassed to broach certain subjects. The physician should have the interest (and time) to ask some probing questions and then offer sound input based on the response. (There is no guarantee, of course, that a teenager will tell "the whole truth and nothing but," even when confidentiality is assured.) Along with questions about past history and any current symptoms, specific topics that are usually on the physician's agenda (if not on the patient's) include:

- Growth and development. Younger adolescents are particularly concerned about whether they are normal, especially if pubertal changes are taking place earlier or later than in their peers.
- Physical safety, including the use of seat belts, bicycle or motorcycle helmets, and appropriate sports equipment
- Current dietary practices. Are they healthy, erratic, or extreme in any way?
- Vaccination history
- Exercise and sleep. Is there enough of each?
- Tobacco use
- Alcohol and drug use
- Sexual activity
- Relationships at home and school
- The emotional weather. Are there any signs of depression?
- Sexual or other physical abuse. A physician who is attentive to an adolescent's physical well-being and demeanor may be the first to detect signs of abuse. By law the physician is required to report any concerns about abuse to the appropriate local social-service or law-enforcement agency.

In addition to the usual elements of a medical exam (ears, throat, neck, chest, heart, abdomen), a few other areas are important:

- Blood pressure. While not common in adolescents, **hypertension** (elevated blood pressure) must be evaluated further if it is detected.
- The spine. Special attention is given to **scoliosis,** a sideways curvature of the spine. There are specific guidelines regarding the degree of curvature that help determine whether treatment is needed, and if so, what methods might be appropriate.
- The groin area should be checked for **hernias** (primarily in boys).
- The testes should be checked for appropriate development and for any masses. Testicular cancer is unique for its prevalence among young men, and teenagers should get in the habit of a brief monthly self-check for unusual growths in this area.
- The breasts in both sexes.

When should a girl receive her first internal pelvic exam? Most medical authorities recommend that this be done

- if there is a symptom or concern about disease: vaginal discharge, pelvic pain, or other symptoms in this area normally cannot be diagnosed by history alone;
- if a girl has become sexually active;
- if she is going to be married in the near future;
- if she is in her late teens or early twenties, even when there are no specific concerns;
- if she is going to start on birth control pills.

Needless to say, no adolescent (or any older woman) is excited about having a pelvic exam, especially if there is discomfort in this area to start with. It is important that whoever does the exam explain step-by-step what is going to happen and then talk her through it while it is being done. She should be reassured that it is normal to feel nervous and awkward and that while the exam is not particularly comfortable, it shouldn't be extremely painful either. Both patient and parent should understand that a pelvic exam does not terminate a girl's virginity. Sexual morality is not violated by a medical procedure whose purpose is to help assess, diagnose, and treat a physical problem.

A young girl should feel free to tell her physician when and where it hurts and know that the exam will be modified if she is having a lot of pain. Many teenagers feel more comfortable if the exam is done by a physician they know and trust, regardless of gender, while others specifically prefer that it be done by a female health-care provider. In either case, the examiner should be accompanied by a female attendant.

Normally during a pelvic exam, the external genitals are briefly inspected, and then a speculum (the "duckbill" instrument) is gently inserted. A narrow speculum should be available for younger patients, and this should pass through the **hymen** (the ring of soft tissue just inside the labia at the entrance to the vagina) without tearing it. The vaginal walls will be checked, and a **Pap smear** is normally done. During a Pap smear, some cells are gently obtained from the cervix and then transferred to a slide. The cells are examined microscopically for evidence that might indicate that a sexually transmitted disease, a cancer, or a precancerous condition is present. Tests for specific sexually transmitted diseases may also be done. Then the examiner will insert one or two fingers into the vagina while the other hand gently presses on the lower abdomen. Much information can be obtained from this simple maneuver, including the size of the uterus and ovaries and the location and intensity of any tenderness. A rectal examination may also be done at this time.

Some additional tests may be done during a basic physical exam. These could include:

- ◆ Vision and hearing screening
- ◆ Urinalysis
- ◆ Blood tests, especially:
  (a) a blood count to check for anemia (especially in girls)
  (b) cholesterol and other circulating fat molecules (called lipids) if there is history of elevated cholesterol or heart attack before age fifty-five in one or more family members
- ◆ A screening test for tuberculosis may be put on the arm. A temporary local reaction (a firm bump at the injection site) within two or three days indicates a past exposure to tuberculosis. If this occurs, further evaluation will be necessary to determine the appropriate course of action.

A number of immunization updates are usually given during the adolescent years:

- ◆ A **tetanus and diphtheria (Td) booster** should be given ten years following the last injection, which in most cases will have been at four or five years of age. Thus Td is typically given at a fourteen- or fifteen-year-old checkup, unless an injury prior to this age required an earlier booster. Remind your adolescent that this is normally repeated every ten years for the rest of his life. A booster may be given after five years if he sustains a wound that results from a puncture, crush injury, burn, or frostbite, or one that is contaminated with dirt, feces, or saliva. In addition, some physicians give a tetanus booster if five years have elapsed since the last one and the adolescent is going on a wilderness expedition or to a foreign country where vaccine might not be available.
- ◆ **Measles/mumps/rubella (MMR) vaccine** should be given if your child has had only one injection thus far. It is unwise to count on a single immunization during infancy to protect against these infections throughout adolescence and adulthood. (Many colleges now require proof of two doses of MMR prior to entrance.)
- ◆ **Hepatitis B vaccine** should be given if the series has not been completed already. Parents who are aware that this infection is transmitted primarily through sexual contact and intravenous drug use may feel it is unnec-

essary to subject their son or daughter to a three-dose vaccine. ("My kid won't do those things—why does he need these shots?") But a significant proportion of hepatitis B cases occur among people who are not involved in any risky behavior and who have no clear-cut exposure history. Since this infection can potentially be lethal or cause significant chronic illness, the vaccine is a good investment.

- If your adolescent has never had **chicken pox (varicella)** and has not been previously immunized against it, vaccination against this virus would be advisable, especially because infections in teenagers and adults tend to be more severe than in younger children. Prior to the thirteenth birthday, only one dose of varicella vaccine is needed, while after age thirteen two doses should be given four to eight weeks apart. Varicella vaccine may be given at the same time as an MMR and/or Td injection.

HEALTH PROBLEMS, HYPOCHONDRIA, OR CRIES FOR HELP?

You may at times become frustrated by ongoing physical complaints from your adolescent, especially those that sound very compelling in the morning and seem to evaporate by midafternoon or weekends. How do you know whether to offer TLC and bed rest or to escort him out to the bus stop despite his complaints? The answer isn't always easy. More than once you may struggle with guilt after discovering he *was* sick after you overruled his protests and sent him to school. On other occasions, you may be compassionate in the morning, then feel like you've been had when he takes off on his bike at the end of the day.

If symptoms are frequent, ask your health-care provider to help sort things out. To get the most out of this consultation, spend time before the visit talking over the problem with your teenager, listing the problems (fatigue, headaches) and their characteristics (how often, how long, what helps, what makes it worse).

While you're at it, try to get a feel for the social weather at school, in the neighborhood, or at church. Questions with no obvious right or wrong answer ("Who do you like to hang around with?" or "What's your least favorite class?") may open the window to some current events and possibly tip you off about pressures that might be contributing to the symptoms.

Ultimately, your teen's doctor will need to ask questions, including, perhaps, a little gentle probing into the issues of the patient's daily life. If the medical evaluation uncovers a specific diagnosis, be sure that both you and your adolescent understand what should be done about it—including the parameters for going to school versus staying home. If the problem doesn't appear to be an ongoing physical illness, all of you together should develop a game plan for dealing with mornings when he doesn't feel well and agree on the ground rules for school attendance.

If you do indeed uncover personal issues that are contributing to physical symptoms, don't back away from working toward solutions. Whether it's a hard-nosed teacher, local bullies, an acute absence of friendships, or some other emotion-jarring problem, your teenager needs to know that you're on his team and that you weren't born yesterday. Making progress in one or more of these areas will usually go a long way toward shortening his symptom list.

However, if varicella and MMR are not given simultaneously, an interval of at least a month should separate the two.

As discussed in the previous chapter, vaccinations against influenza and hepatitis A may also be appropriate for your adolescent under specific circumstances (see page 397).

Check with the doctor's office if you have any questions about the advisability of these immunizations. This is particularly important if your adolescent has a significant medical problem, especially one that affects the function of the immune system (for example, leukemia, symptomatic HIV disease, pregnancy, or a cancer under treatment with chemotherapy). In addition, be sure to inquire about precautions or potential side effects of any vaccine that he or she might be given.

TAKING ON THE TOUGH TOPICS: SEX AND SUBSTANCES

If parenting an adolescent required only providing guidance through growing pains, schoolwork, mood swings, and preparations for independence, the assignment would still be challenging. But unfortunately we live in an unsettled day and age, a time when various unhealthy choices are often more accessible to teenagers than ever before.

Indeed, the next several miles of your adolescent's highway of life contain several potential road hazards, including premarital sexual activity and its consequences, alcohol, tobacco, and drug use. In many places, no guardrails exist, and steep cliffs await those who swerve a short distance off course. To make matters worse, seductive billboards along the way proclaim that veering toward those cliffs is exciting and pleasurable and that everyone else is doing it.

Like it or not, you don't have the luxury of sending your adolescent off on a journey into adulthood without warning him about destructive detours and deadly cliffs. He should be hearing some of the same advisories from responsible adults at school, church, or within your family, but you can't count on them to do this job for you. You may need to muster enough courage to tell him about poor decisions that turned out costly in your own life. At some point, you may have to help him navigate back from a bumpy side road or even pull him out of a ditch.

We all hope that your adolescent will, like many others, avoid these hazards and their consequences. In order to encourage healthy choices and offer effective help when it's needed, you would be wise to be well informed about these important topics. They are discussed in detail in the following Special Concerns sections, and we encourage you to read them carefully:

- ◆ A Parent's Guide to Teen Sexuality, page 541
- ◆ Sexually Transmitted Diseases (STDs) among Adolescents, page 573
- ◆ Tobacco, Alcohol, and Drug Abuse—Resisting the Epidemic, page 579

While knowledge of these topics is very important, it will be of little value if not utilized in ways that will help mold attitudes and decisions. Finding the best approaches to talking with your adolescent(s) about sensitive subjects requires forethought and patience. The following ideas can help you lay the groundwork for this task.

TALKING TO TEENS ABOUT RISKS: NINE BASIC PRINCIPLES

1. It's easier to talk about sensitive or difficult subjects if you have good rapport with your child about the easier ones. Time spent building relationships during the preteen years usually pays major dividends later on.

2. Parents often worry that if they discuss certain topics (especially sex) in any detail, it will "give the kids ideas." Here's a late news flash: The kids *already* have plenty of ideas, and now they need to hear your viewpoint about them. However, they probably won't ask you, so you need to take the initiative.

3. Warnings about behaviors that threaten life and limb will be more effective if they aren't diluted by nagging about less serious matters. Accentuate the positive, and what you say about the negative will carry more weight.

4. Don't expect to communicate your values in a few marathon sessions. Brief but potent teachable moments crop up regularly throughout childhood and adolescence. Seizing these opportunities requires spending enough time with a child to allow them to take place.

5. It's easier for an adolescent to stay away from the dangerous detours if the main highway is clearly marked, well lit, attractive, and enjoyable. Encourage and support healthy goals, commitments, friends, and activities—all of which are strong deterrents to destructive behaviors.

6. Your actions will reinforce (or invalidate) your words. The misguided commandment "Do what I say, not what I do" has never worked and never will. However, this doesn't mean that mistakes, miscalculations, and reckless behavior in your past invalidate what you say today. Some parents worry that they can't legitimately warn their kids not to do what *they* did as teenagers. Heartfelt confessions, cautionary tales, and lessons learned at the University of Hard Knocks can have a profound impact on young listeners. As long as you're not setting a hypocritical double standard ("It's okay for me but not for you"), don't be afraid to share what you've learned the hard way.

7. Don't shift into "lecture gear" very often, if at all. Your teenager's desire for independence and his heartfelt need to be treated like an adult (even if his behavior suggests otherwise) will cause eyes to glaze and attention to drift if you launch into a six-point sermon on the evils of _____. If you feel strongly about these issues (and you should), say what's on your heart without beating them into the ground.

One way to communicate your view indirectly but effectively is through cassette tapes. You might bring one or more taped messages on a car trip and play them at an appropriate time, perhaps mentioning that they're interesting but not necessarily announcing that you want your adolescent to pay close attention. It helps, of course, if the speaker is engrossing and your teenager isn't plugged into his own portable tape player.

8. Don't give up if your efforts to broach tough topics aren't greeted with enthusiasm. Even when your tone is open and inviting, you may find that a lively conversation is harder to start than a campfire on a cold, windy night. Your thoughts may be expressed honestly, tactfully, and eloquently, but you still may not get rapt attention from your intended audience. Be patient, don't express frustration, and don't be afraid to try again later. If your spouse has any helpful suggestions about improving your delivery of the messages you care about, listen carefully and act accordingly.

9. While you state your principles about sex, drugs, and other important matters with consistency, conviction, and clarity, your adolescent also must understand that he can come to you when he has a problem. If your teenager is convinced that "Mom and Dad will kill me if they find out about _____," you will be the last to find out about _____. But if he knows you are a source of strength and help when trouble comes, you will be able to help him contain the damage if he makes an unwise decision. And indirectly, you may show him the attributes of God, his ultimate refuge and strength.

NOTES
1. When abuse is suspected, however, the health-care provider must notify the appropriate local social-service agency. In addition, if there appears to be an imminent threat of suicide, referral to a qualified counselor, psychiatrist, or a mental-health facility will be necessary.

The Adolescent Years, Part Two

I am the Lord, your God,
who takes hold of your
right hand and says to you,
Do not fear; I will help you.
ISAIAH 41:13

CHAPTER 13

The Adolescent Years, Part Two: Hearts and Minds in Motion

For centuries teenagers have routinely challenged and at times exasperated their parents. Public and private turmoil about what to do about the younger generation is not unique to our moment in history, nor are most of the fundamental concerns that a child will encounter during her eventful passage into adulthood. This chapter will deal with many aspects of that important process, along with a number of parenting attitudes and strategies that can help an adolescent navigate through it in a positive and productive way.

When your child was a newborn, coping with short nights of sleep, dirty diapers, and crying spells may have hampered your ability to marvel at the incredible little person before you. When she was a turbocharged and at times defiant toddler, the nonstop effort required to keep her (and your home) safe and sound may not have given you much time to appreciate her rapidly developing abilities. Similarly, when your adolescent experiences normal growing pains and emotional turbulence (and possibly a crisis or two) during the coming years, it may be all too easy to lose sight of a number of very encouraging and gratifying developments.

Yes, there will be a lot of problems to solve, arriving in all shapes and sizes (often when you least expect them). You will need to guide, monitor, and sometimes intervene to keep the cultural wolves a respectable distance from your teenager's door. You may have to put out some fires or even an occasional four-alarm blaze. Hopefully, through it all you will be able to recognize and appreciate in your adolescent many of the positive attributes that are common in this age-group. (Be sure to praise them for these.) How and when these qualities will be expressed will vary with each individual, but be on the lookout for them:

- Energy and enthusiasm
- Idealism
- Concern for the needs of others—often coupled with a willingness to offer help in ways that adults might find risky or "unrealistic"
- A desire for meaningful relationships
- A sense of humor that can be witty and insightful
- A concern for fairness and justice
- An interest in other cultures and countries
- Development of new skills in athletics, the arts, crafts, the use of tools, writing, and speaking—often with extraordinary achievements
- Curiosity—not only about the *way* things work in the world but *why*
- Willingness to commit to worthwhile causes and to back up that commitment with specific actions
- Ability (and attention span) to appreciate sophisticated music, drama, films, and artwork
- A deep desire for a relationship with God and a willingness to make a lifelong commitment to serve Him

Despite the relatively few years separating one generation from the next, most adults seem to have amnesia about their own adolescence. Parents who have already "been there, done that" may have difficulty recalling how they felt and thought between the ages of twelve and twenty-one. As you read through the stages of adolescent development in the next few pages, try to recall what you were experiencing during those years. Whether your effort brings fond memories, a lot of pain, or merely a sigh of relief that you don't have to go through *that* again, you will connect more smoothly with your teenager(s) if you can remember what it's like to walk a mile in their sneakers.

Since many important differences exist between a twelve-year-old seventh-grader and a college student, it is helpful to divide the adolescent years into three developmental phases:

- Early adolescence—ages twelve through fourteen (junior high)
- Middle adolescence—ages fifteen through seventeen (senior high)
- Late adolescence—ages eighteen through twenty-one (college/vocation)

Each adolescent's life will run on a unique track, of course, and all sorts of variations on the basic themes occur during each phase. Some junior-high students may appear intellectually and emotionally ready for college, while some college students behave as though junior high were still in session. Some thirteen-year-olds are immune to the opinions of their peers, and some twenty-one-year-olds' convictions change with each day's companions. But some familiar trends and behaviors about each of the three phases are generally recognizable.

Throughout these years, a number of important developmental tasks are under way:

The task of achieving independence from parents

With rare exception, adolescents develop a powerful drive to become independent, to be in charge of their daily affairs and their future. As a result, bucking the limits, challenging authority, and resisting constraints imposed at home and school are pretty much par for the course. Just as in the first adolescence of toddler days, the extent of willfulness and the lack of good judgment can at times be spectacular. And while it may sometimes seem outrageous, some degree of struggling against parental control is a normal and necessary part of growing up.

Your job in helping your adolescent complete this task is to release your grip in a controlled and reasonable manner. You still have the right and responsibility to make house rules. But when you impose (and defend) them, you need to do so calmly and respectfully. "Because I'm the Mom, that's why!" may have worked with your two-year-old, but it will rarely be appropriate anymore. Few things exasperate and discourage a teenager more than being treated like an immature child, even if it may seem appropriate (to you) at the time.

Even more important is linking your adolescent's blossoming independence to the realities and responsibilities of adult life. He will need hundreds of age-appropriate reality checks before he leaves your nest, and you are in the best position to provide them. (See chapter 14, "Passing the Baton.")

The task of accepting and respecting one's body

Your adolescent is (or soon will be) in the midst of intense physical changes, especially during the early years of this period. Virtually all systems in the body are involved, but those affected by new surges of hormones will generate the most attention and concern. Three issues will dominate the landscape:

What's happening to me? If your adolescent has not received some advance warning about the changes of puberty, a friendly and factual huddle about this subject will be most reassuring. (Review chapter 11, pages 480–483, and chapter 12.) Even if your teenager already appears quite mature physically, the impact of hormones and rapid growth on emotions, energy, and various parts of the body may not be clear to her—or you. Your input and, if needed, her physician's can calm many concerns.

Do I like this body? Adolescents are keenly interested, at times seemingly obsessed, with body image—both their own and everyone else's. As a result, comparisons with others are always in progress. Whoever holds the winning ticket in the physical sweepstakes—the most attractive features, the knockout figure, the well-sculpted muscles, the athletic prowess—will nearly always reign supreme where teens gather. But even Studley Dooright, the campus megahunk, and Barbie Dahl, the queen of the prom, will be plagued by doubts about their appearance and worthiness.

No matter how well assembled your teenager might appear to you and others, from her perspective someone will always seem to have a better package. Negative comparisons with that person—sometimes amazingly unrealistic—are likely. And an adolescent with an obvious physical deficit may be cruelly taunted by peers and develop a lifelong preoccupation with appearance. Accepting one's body and taking appropriate care of it are important tasks to be accomplished during this transition to adulthood.

Your job here is a delicate one. Your teenager will need generous doses of reassurance that worth is not dependent on appearance, even when the culture around her says otherwise. You will have to endure the fact that any positive comments you make about looks, temperament, accomplishments, or inherent value may not be met with expressions of thanks. It may appear that what you say doesn't count, but it does—in a big way.

One challenge for parents will be to find the fine line between making constructive suggestions and being a nag. Your adolescent's preoccupation with looks may not necessarily translate into specific actions to improve them or to appear pleasing to adults. In fact, at times the opposite will be true. The current "dress code" at junior high, for example, may decree an extremely casual, semi-unkempt look in order to appear "normal." As will be discussed later, within limits, generational differences in clothing and hairstyles may not be worth a family battle.

But sometimes you may need to take the initiative. If he suffers from acne, he'll need your help and some professional input to bring the blemishes under control. If she is clueless about clothes, Mom or a savvy relative may need to help rehabilitate the wardrobe, a project that does not need to be expensive. If weight is a problem, tactful efforts to move the scale in the right direction may improve your adolescent's self-image and general health. These efforts should be positive, stressing healthy foods and activities for everyone in the family, without focusing all the attention on one person. If there is a major problem related to food—whether an unhealthy obsession with thinness or weight that is far above the norm for an adolescent's height—professional help should be sought from a physician, dietitian, counselor, or all of the above (see Special Concerns, page 429).

Will I respect this body? Whether or not they are comfortable with their physical appearance, adolescents must decide how they will care for themselves. Lifestyle and habits established at this age may continue well into adulthood, and it is never too early to establish a healthy respect for the one and only body they will ever occupy. Prudent eating habits can be modeled and encouraged, and you can also point out that exercise isn't merely something to be endured during P.E. class but is also worth pursuing (in moderation) for its own sake. Unfortunately, some teenagers who harbor a mistaken belief that "nothing can happen to me" choose to engage in substance abuse, sexual misadventures, and other risk-taking behaviors that could establish long-standing negative habits or leave permanent physical (not to mention emotional) scars.

Your work in this arena should have begun years ago, and if this took place, your child's concept of respect for his or her body will have roots dating from the preschool years. Even so, reasonable vigilance, good role modeling, and forthright and open conversations about risky behavior will need to be on your agenda until your adolescent has completed the transition to full independence. (Risky activities involving the body were discussed in the previous chapter, and you would be wise to review this material if you haven't just done so.)

The task of establishing healthy peer relationships

The impact of peers on adolescents cannot be underestimated. The right people crossing their path at critical times can reinforce positive values and enhance the entire process of growing up. The wrong individuals can escort them into extremely negative detours or literally suck the life out of them.

Your job is to pray with utter abandon for the friends your adolescent will make over the next several years. Without being too pushy about it, make every effort to make friends with your teenager's friends. If your home is the most teen friendly in the neighborhood, chances are the troops will gather under your roof or in your backyard and respond to your influence in the process.

Because peers can play such a serious role for good or ill in your teen's life, you will need to be forthright and directive about where and with whom her time is spent—especially in the early years. If the drama club, 4-H, Scouts, or athletic teams provide a consistently healthy niche, by all means encourage them. But if a new "friend" who manifests an abundance of toxic language and behavior enters your adolescent's life, don't hesitate to take some defensive measures.

This may include insisting that they spend time together only under your roof with an adult on the premises (and no closed bedroom doors). If it becomes apparent that your teenager is being swayed toward destructive habits, however, reasonable measures to keep them separated will be necessary.

If your church has a strong and active youth group, do everything you can to support it and your teen's involvement in it. But if your youth group has gone stale or has become a clique zone, find another one. The program should honor your family's faith and values, of course, but should also accept all comers, build positive identities, and be fun as it promotes spiritual growth.

The task of developing a coherent identity

Whether they are National Merit Scholars or total nonconformists (or both), adolescents are fervently searching for a clear sense of identity. Whatever the guise or getup, the questions they continually ask boil down to these: *"Who cares about me?"* and *"What can I do that has any significance?"*

If the answers are "my God, my family, and my close friends" and "impacting the world in a positive way," your main task—and it usually will be a pleasant one—will be serving as cheerleader and sounding board as your son or daughter finds the best track on which to run.

If the answers are "my friends (and hardly anyone else)" and "having fun (and hardly anything else)," the ultimate outcome could be more unpredictable. Most adolescents with this mind-set eventually grow up and find a productive niche, while some stay in this shallow, meandering rut well into adulthood. Some also drift into drug use or sexual activity in their search for the next diversion—and ultimately pay dearly for it.

For the teenager whose answers are "no one" and "nothing," if different answers are nowhere on the horizon, the consequences may be more serious: depression, acting out, even suicidal behavior (see Special Concerns, page 601).

Obviously, it is important that your child enter adolescence with some clear and positive answers to the questions of caring and significance. During the coming seasons, she will probably ask them often and in many different ways—some of which may catch you way off guard. Even if she has lost her bearings or abandoned common sense, you will still need to communicate that your love and her significance are unshakable. As in earlier years of childhood, you will need to enforce limits and help her make some course corrections until she is on her own. But she must always know that your fundamental love for her will never change, regardless of grades, clothes, a messy room, dented fenders, or more serious issues.

The task of discovering personal gifts, interests, and passions

One of the most important and life-enhancing aspects of adolescence is the process of looking at a variety of activities and interests. If her childhood interests in Scouts and piano lessons don't continue into the teen years, don't count your time spent in those activities as wasted. She may want to explore drama or gymnastics for a while, and they may become her new passions—or she may discover that the piano really is her true love after all. Your encouragement for her to find and develop her strengths and perhaps to overcome what she (and you) might have considered her weaknesses will pay off in many ways. Not only might she find a niche of true excellence and accomplishment, but all of these activities—even the ones that don't pan out as permanent interests—will broaden her fund of knowledge and experience. Furthermore, your support during these efforts will repeatedly affirm her value.

This is also a time during which many young people develop and hone a social conscience. Altruism often peaks during the teen years, and she may find considerable satisfaction in helping others solve problems and in volunteering to serve in worthy causes. Teenagers can be surprisingly empathetic to the suffering of others, and they may go to great lengths of energy and time to lend someone a helping hand. You will obviously want to encourage selfless and sacrificial behavior—at times you may find your own conscience stirred by your adolescent's willingness to love the unlovely.

You should model practical concern for the needs of others and at the same time offer guidance as to the parameters of your teen's involvement. For example, your daughter might want to rescue a friend from an abusive family situation by inviting her to stay at your home. Perhaps you are able to offer a safe haven—certainly an honorable and meaningful action—but you will also need to walk your daughter through some of the realities and details that may not have occurred to her in the rush to help. If you have a particularly generous and tenderhearted teen at home, you will have to pass along a little street wisdom to help prevent her charitable instincts from being soured by encounters with users and abusers who might take advantage of her.

The task of developing a worldview

The adolescent years are a crucial period in an individual's development of a worldview—the basic (and often unspoken) assumptions that govern attitudes, decisions, and actions—and young people often make decisions during their teens that will literally set a course for the rest of their lives. Many make permanent spiritual commitments at church, camp, or other events and continue to

Above all, love each other deeply, because love covers over a multitude of sins.

1 PETER 4:8

mature in their faith as the years pass. But these are also years during which fundamental questions about God and the universe are asked, and parents may find their own beliefs (or lack thereof) held up for inspection.

Many teens feel the need to chart a different spiritual course from their parents during these years, a development that can make parents feel very uneasy. *What if he turns away from God and all we have taught him over the years?* Before you lose too much sleep over this question, remember that your child must eventually make his own decision whether or not to follow God. You can't do it for him. In fact, to some degree an examination of what he has heard as a child is a healthy process, because he must understand eventually how his faith applies to adult situations and problems.

Your primary job will be to keep your *own* relationship with God thriving—which should include meaningful time in prayer for your child(ren) on an ongoing basis. Spiritual vitality that manifests genuine joy, peace, and other positive expressions on a consistent basis will ultimately communicate more to your adolescent than a lot of clever (or convoluted) answers to his questions. In matters of faith (and in other arenas as well), teenagers are particularly responsive to honesty and integrity and turned off with equal fervor by hypocrisy.

If his need to assert his independence from you spills into the spiritual realm, you may need to entrust his growth in this area to other adults (or even peers) who can positively influence his view of God, faith, and the world in general. Youth leaders, teachers, young couples or single adults, or other friends of the family can often "stand in the gap" for you in this area. Do what you can to encourage these contacts and interactions (without being pushy about it) and then leave the results in God's hands.

Early Adolescence: Life in the Trenches

Take an informal poll of one hundred adults about what years of their lives they would never want to repeat, and you will probably hear "junior high" most often. All too frequently, a relatively well-adjusted, good-natured twelve-year-old enters the seventh grade and two or three years later emerges emotionally (if not physically) battered and bruised. What turns these years into such a war zone?

First, the tides of puberty are likely to be flowing at full speed. Among other things, these generate much concern and self-consciousness about physical changes that are (or aren't yet) under way. Such worries are intensified by the marked variations in development at this age. Within the same class will be skinny thirteen-year-old boys with squeaky voices standing next to hairy hulks who appear qualified for the defensive line of the high school football team. Similarly, flat-chested girls who have yet to experience their first menstrual cycle are mingling with fully developed counterparts who could pass for women several years older. The inevitable comparisons and insecurities can become more acute at the end of gym class if many classmates shower together.

Second, wide mood swings and strong emotional responses to the ups and downs of life are the order of the day. Physical and hormonal components contribute to this stormy weather in both sexes, although the biochemistry of the monthly cycle can accentuate the mood swings in girls.

Like the two-year-old, the young adolescent experiences life in extremes. If she gets a friendly smile from a guy she thinks is cute, everything is coming up roses. If he finishes last in the fifty-yard dash, the whole world stinks. Today two girls declare their undying friendship; tomorrow they announce they hate each other. Last summer he campaigned passionately for a new guitar; today it gathers dust in his room.

Emotional reactions to life's twists and turns, even in a stable home environment, can provoke physical responses as well, especially headaches, abdominal pains, and fatigue. While any of these may be caused by the daily strain of growing up, they should be evaluated by a physician if persistent or disruptive. Insomnia, withdrawal from activities that were once enjoyed, irritability, and a marked change in appetite could signal full-blown depression, a more significant problem that should be taken seriously and treated appropriately (see Special Concerns, page 601).

In addition to these physical and emotional upheavals among individual adolescents, bringing many of them together (as occurs every school day) creates a social stew containing large doses of these volatile ingredients:

- An intense need for acceptance by peers.
- An equally intense concern about looking dumb, clumsy, or at all different from the surrounding herd of other early adolescents—who themselves are intensely concerned about looking dumb, clumsy, or at all different from everyone else.
- An ongoing struggle with self-confidence or overt feelings of inferiority, even among those who are the most attractive and talented (or tough and hostile).
- A surprising—and at times shocking—intolerance for anyone who looks or behaves a little unlike everyone else.
- A limitless capacity for creative (and often obscene) insults, put-downs, and jokes directed at nearly everyone—but especially the one who is

different. This is particularly and sometimes painfully obvious in group settings. Kids who can be quite civilized on a one-to-one basis or who pledge their allegiance to virtue and values at their Sunday-night youth group can unleash a torrent of crude slurs during a slumber party or a school-yard basketball game. In some cases, nonstop verbal harassment can escalate to physical confrontations or violence.

Consequently, school represents more than classroom activities and homework for many adolescents. It can be a daily social gauntlet—unpleasant at best, a barbaric ordeal at worst—requiring every ounce of effort and energy just to complete the round-trip back to home base. As a result, if *any* physical symptom is present when the alarm clock goes off—a headache, a minor cold, too little sleep the night before, some menstrual cramping—you may encounter major resistance when you try to pry your junior higher out of bed (see sidebar, page 499).

While you might expect your young adolescent to come to you for aid and comfort or take cover from the daily shellings at school, the opposite may take place. The budding (or broiling) urge for independence, combined with mood swings, extreme self-consciousness, and intolerance for anything that strikes them as "stupid" or "lame," may begin to drive an alarming wedge into your relationship.

This is the age at which kids may decide that their parents are hopelessly naive, out of touch with reality, or terribly short on intelligence. Your adolescent may avoid sitting with you at church. You may hear criticism of your clothes, musical tastes, and opinions. And don't even think about wearing that slightly weird hat or doing something a little unusual (such as humming your favorite tune a little too loud) in a public place—especially the mall. You may be strongly rebuked for this "embarrassing" display, especially if (heaven forbid) someone she remotely knows might possibly see it. Her concern, of course, will not be for your reputation but hers.

This apparent detachment from you and the family may extend to cutting other moorings to the past. One day your son may suddenly pack up his action figures, shove his baseball cards into a drawer, and insist that you replace the race-car wallpaper that was painstakingly installed in his bedroom just a few years ago. Your daughter's dolls and figurines may suffer a similar fate. Some adolescents also choose this time to abandon cute childhood nicknames in favor of more grown-up-sounding names. Don't be alarmed and certainly don't smirk or ridicule if you are told one day that Suzie wants to be called Susan or that Skipper is now Jonathan. Such sudden announcements that childhood is over may catch

ADOLESCENT
YEARS,
PART TWO
515

you off guard, provoking a lump in the throat or even a few tears. But welcome the transition as best you can. Pack up the toys and memorabilia they don't want, and save them for their own children.

During this period, early adolescents typically form and maintain strong same-sex friendships, even as interest in members of the opposite sex is growing more intense. Infatuations and crushes are to be expected, but intense romances and dating are not good at this age for a number of reasons.

As already mentioned, friends and peers can play a major role in reinforcing or undermining the values that matter to you. You may become frustrated by the fact that a classmate's half-baked opinions seem to matter more than all the common sense you've imparted over the years. But choose wisely if you decide to intervene, because the more you complain about her newfound friends, the more vigorously she may defend them. Some streetwise vigilance, ongoing prayer, and evenhanded but candid conversations about who's hot and who's not on the current friendship list (and why) should be regular agenda items for your busy week.

While the value of your parental stock may seem to be falling by the hour, you may be surprised (and perhaps a little hurt) to see your adolescent form a powerful attachment to another adult. A teacher, choir director, favorite aunt, coach, or youth leader can become the object of intense admiration and attention. This common turn of events can be a blessing if the object of this affection is an ally who shares your values and goals and who moves her in positive directions. But someone with a less constructive agenda can have a significant negative impact.

Middle Adolescence: Peace and War

For many adolescents and their parents, senior high brings a breath of fresh air after the suffocating social environment of junior high. By now the most significant transitions and transformations of puberty are well under way or completed for nearly everyone. The apprehensive question "What's happening to me?" is replaced by the more reflective "So *that's* what was happening." Physical attributes and attractiveness are still major concerns, but obvious differences in development among members of this age-group are far less common.

Opposite-sex relationships are likely to move beyond crushes and awkward nonconversations into friendships and romances that can displace the same-sex and group camaraderie of the past. The issue of appropriate expressions of physical affection should be candidly broached. If you brought up this topic a couple

The right to criticize must be earned, even if the advice is constructive in nature. . . . you are obligated first to demonstrate your own respect for your child as a person.

DR. DOBSON
ANSWERS YOUR
QUESTIONS ABOUT
CONFIDENT,
HEALTHY FAMILIES

of years ago, it may well have seemed like a philosophical question. But when real-life relationships are involved, it becomes a very practical one.

While peer influence remains strong, many of the extreme, often ridiculous herd instincts of two or three years ago have begun to fade. No longer does everyone need to look, dress, and talk exactly alike to avoid nonstop ridicule. In fact, many adolescents now pride themselves on their tolerance and acceptance of all manner of eccentricities among their cohorts. (This does not necessarily extend to adults, however.)

Teens in this age bracket tend to find at least one group they identify with and that provides friendships, fun, and a sense of identity. Church and service organizations, athletics, performing arts (music, drama, dance, film), academics, and even political/social activism will bring kindred spirits together. Idealism may flourish during these years, and commitments made to God and basic values can be fervent and life-changing. If you share one or more of these interests, you can cement deep and satisfying bonds with your teenager.

For many families, however, these years bring a crescendo of conflict. The urge for independence that provokes detachment and verbal criticism from junior highers can deteriorate into a Grand Canyon–sized rift or all-out war at this age. Now, however, you're not dealing with a foot-stomping two-year-old or a misbehaving grade-school child. He may no longer be intimidated by your size or stern look. In order to demonstrate his separation from your influence, he may undergo extreme alterations of appearance, including weird haircuts and hair colors, body piercing, tattoos, and clothing that looks like it came from another planet. If you have a major blowup over some issue, he may take off for parts unknown. He may have access to transportation (his own or someone else's) and may be able to crash temporarily at a friend's place if things aren't going well at yours.

Furthermore, adolescents at this age are capable of carrying out acts with far more serious consequences. Their quest for self-determination or outright rebellion can be combined and energized by an unspoken belief in their own power and immortality. As a result, risky behavior involving alcohol, drugs, and motor vehicles, as well as other physical feats of daring and stupidity, are more likely now. If the social niche that satisfies longings for identity happens to be a gang, crime and violence may enter the equation. Furthermore, intense sexual drives, sensual imagery in films and music, peer pressure, and increased opportunities for intimacy markedly increase the risk for sexual encounters—often with disastrous results. These can indeed be the times that try parents' souls.

For the vast majority of teens, a rebellious phase will eventually end. Only a small percentage will doggedly continue in antisocial and self-destructive paths. Usually a combination of maturing emotions, stabilizing identity, and unpleasant consequences brings an unruly adolescent to his or her senses. As the years pass and the School of Life dishes out hard lessons and reality checks, parents seem to gain intelligence in the eyes of their maturing offspring. In a few decades many of today's rebels will be asking their parents for advice about their own teenagers' uprisings. If you have been tearing your hair out over an adolescent's behavior, don't despair; more likely than not, within a few years you and your grown child will be back on the same team.

DEALING WITH BEHAVIOR MELTDOWN

What do you do when a child declares war on your family, the neighborhood, or the entire civilized world? One teenager who goes off the deep end can, without question, rock a lot of boats in the community. Social workers, doctors, lawyers, police, and clergy may all be in the loop, while Mom and Dad endure an avalanche of pain, frustration, guilt, and expense.

If you find yourself embroiled in a civil war at home or confronted by a teenager who is making some dangerously bad decisions, you need to keep these principles in mind:

Take the bull by the horns. Don't tolerate flagrant disrespect, destruction of your home or other property, criminal activity, or abuse from one of your children. Drastic action may be necessary to keep this type of behavior from tearing your family to shreds. Use your allies including other parents, counselors, clergy, and the police. If more conservative measures aren't working, you may need to consider informing him that he cannot remain under your roof if these acts continue. Living at home would then become a privilege to be earned on your terms, with some critical minimum requirements: no drugs, no booze, no stealing, no sex, and no verbal or physical abuse of anyone in the family.

If he breaks the law and is arrested, depending on the circumstances you may need to choose not to bail him out, as painful as this decision would be. In doing so you would have but one purpose: allowing him to experience the brunt of his bad decisions and to come to his senses.

Don't live with false guilt. Perhaps you have made mistakes (who hasn't?) in raising your prodigal offspring. But even those who work diligently to "bring up a child in the way he should go" (to quote Solomon in the book of Proverbs) can find themselves in the midst of a parent's nightmare. Each child is an independent being with a free will who decides if he will proceed in the "way he should go" or "depart from it." Even this famous verse is not an ironclad guarantee but a statement of the way things generally happen.

Don't underestimate the depth of your adolescent's emotions. Serious problems are not "just a phase he's going through," and often disruptive behavior on a child's part is the manifestation of real suffering and inner turmoil. By all means seek professional help, and if possible try to engage your adolescent in the process of determining what type of counselor or program would be most appropriate in the current situation. For help, call The New Life Treatment Centers, 1-800-NEW LIFE, or a treatment center near you.

Pray without ceasing, and don't give up. Even if you have to allow him to reap the bitter harvest of his choices, continue praying for his safety and return to sanity. More often than not, even the most die-hard prodigals eventually get tired of the pigsty and trudge home.

LATE ADOLESCENCE: THE ART
OF DE-PARENTING

The conclusion of the teen years and the beginning of the twenties often bring stability to a number of areas but also raise new issues. Physical appearance is rarely the ongoing concern that dominated early adolescence, and efforts to improve looks will not only be more common but generally more productive. Direct peer-group manipulation of opinions and actions will be less obvious, although attitudes about the issues of life are not likely to be set in concrete.

Your advice and values will be more readily accepted, acknowledged, or at least tolerated by your older adolescent. By now your offspring will probably be wiser and perhaps sadder as well. While active rebellion is likely to subside as the twenties arrive, some consequences of unwise behavior during the past few years may not go entirely away. Hopefully, however, your teenager will arrive at this final phase without having made any difficult detours, or at least without obtaining any serious or painful scars. But whether the past few years have been smooth sailing or stormy weather, the dawn of independent adult life now looms on the horizon. Your parenting job isn't over until you have escorted your grown child across this threshold into the world of grown-up rights and responsibilities. In a real sense, you will work yourself out of a full-time job.

This process includes a number of transitions that may prove as challenging for you as for your teenager. You must progress

- from parent to caring friend and confidant;
- from gravy train to career guide;
- from being in charge to giving friendly advice—if asked;
- from bailing out and mopping up to allowing some consequences to be suffered.

As in all previous parenting tasks, extremes should be avoided. Give a teenager too much independence too early and he may suffer serious harm on the campus of the School of Hard Knocks. But hold the reins too tight for too long, and you may endure one of these equally painful scenarios:

- A strong-willed young adult who literally tears himself out of your sphere of influence, leaving gaping emotional wounds.
- A compliant "good boy" who never learns how to make his own decisions or earn his own way in the world.
- A rebellious and reckless adolescent/young adult who repeatedly gets into hot water and is always promptly bailed out by concerned and

caring parents. Remember that the father of the prodigal son didn't rescue him from the pigpen. The son had to suffer the consequences of his foolishness and then come to his senses by himself.

- The adult child who hangs out at the happy homestead long after his formal education has come to an end and sees no urgency in seeking his own means of support.

There are a number of reasons parents might feel reluctant to release their grown children to stand on their wobbly feet:

- The world seems a lot more treacherous than it was a generation ago. Parents who deeply desire that their children maintain spiritual commitments and ethical standards into adulthood are genuinely concerned about turning them loose into a culture that has lost its moral compass.
- The prolonged educational process required for many careers can keep young adults in a state of dependence on their parents for years. If you're paying those college bills and perhaps offering room and board (or more) during a graduate program, it is difficult not to keep some strings attached along the way.
- The costs of living independently—a place to live, transportation, food, clothing—can be awfully steep, keeping kids in the nest long after they are grown. Young married couples who are struggling to make ends meet may even be tempted (or forced) to move back in with Mom and Dad.
- A child with a significant physical, intellectual, or psychiatric handicap may need parenting well into the twenties or beyond. Even in these difficult situations, however, it is healthy to release as much responsibility and foster as much independence as possible.
- Parents may have invested so much of their lives into their children's formative years that the dawning of adulthood strikes them with apprehension or even dread: "What will we do when they're gone?!"

This difficult task of letting go can be accomplished by keeping the big picture in mind literally from the moment you hear that first cry in the delivery room. Your child is priceless, but she is only on loan to you for a season. Furthermore, while she can't do anything for herself as a newborn, from that time forward you will be in an ongoing process of transferring more responsibilities and decisions to her. Your two-year-old should be feeding herself, your five-year-old tying her own shoes, and your eight-year-old picking out what to wear to school—even though you can do it more neatly, quickly, or skillfully.

As the adolescent years pass, your teenager needs to hear repeatedly that you will always love her (whatever paths she chooses) but that your parenting role will be coming to an end much sooner than she realizes. Your public-service announcements are as important for the strong-willed fifteen-year-old who is stomping her feet and demanding more freedom ("I'm not a child anymore!") as they are for the laid-back eighteen-year-old who needs to know that the free meal ticket won't be issued forever. The responsibilities you transfer will become more complex—driving a car, balancing a checkbook, and (scariest of all) picking a spouse, among many others. But by walking with your adolescent through these processes step-by-step, your final release will seem like a small step rather than a plunge off a cliff.

PARENTAL SURVIVAL SKILLS

Without a doubt, the adolescent years are a crucial and eventful period—not only for your child but for you as well. Working through it successfully requires

WHAT IF YOUR GROWN CHILD DOESN'T LEAVE THE NEST?

For all their chomping at the bit, when the moment of truth arrives, many adolescents aren't so eager or willing to leave Mom and Dad. If a grown child remains at home after the age of twenty-one or so, two important principles should be observed.

First, the arrangement must be mutually agreeable. It's one thing to let the kids know the porch light will always be on, but they also need to know that having a key to the door is a privilege, not an eternal right.

Second, and more important, the relationship between parent and adult child must be redefined. This means that you will need to insist subtly (and sometimes not so subtly) that she function as an adult. She must treat you and your property with respect, assume responsibility for her own expenses and perhaps some household expenses, do her own laundry and clean up her messes. In other words, she must live in your house more or less with the status of an adult boarder. Treating her as though she were still in junior high school will stifle her emotional maturity and ultimately frustrate everyone under your roof.

But requiring that she take on adult responsibilities at home also means you can no longer be in charge of her decisions. You can't set curfews, tell her what to wear, or pass judgment on her friend(s). You do have the right, however, to ask—not insist—that she keep you posted on her whereabouts as a matter of common courtesy.

You also have the right—and responsibility—to set and enforce codes of conduct under your roof. If your postadolescent offspring is making bad decisions about smoking, drinking, sex, or disorderly conduct, you can insist she do it elsewhere. You are under no obligation to facilitate self-destructive or antisocial behavior.

If house rules are respected and there is a deliberate shift from a parenting to a "benevolent landlady" mode, the situation can be both pleasant and mutually beneficial. You might even develop a nice, grown-up friendship with your child—something that usually requires not only time but a little physical distance between you.

wisdom, finesse, attention to detail, and above all, prayer. Prayer is particularly important because you cannot predict the future or know for certain how your children will respond to the challenges and opportunities that cross their paths.

It is inevitable that we will make mistakes. We will miss important signals from our children about their desires and needs and overreact to others based on *our* desires and needs. We may at times become too distracted, tired, overcommitted, or swamped with other responsibilities to do much more than attempt to put out fires. For the single parent raising one or more teenagers, every aspect of this job may seem overwhelming. With all that is on the line at this critical time, we dare not float through these years without coming before God every day, seeking His wisdom in the face of our inadequacies.

With that important perspective in mind, here are some basic principles that can serve as guideposts for your teen-rearing efforts. The exact paths that you and your family travel will be uniquely your own.

Know thyself.

Among the things you most want for your adolescent in the coming months and years are good health, success in school, meaningful friendships, a positive impact in the community, spiritual vitality, and a loving spouse. Your teenager probably would agree with most of these, at least in principle. But when it comes to the details and the means of accomplishing these goals, you can count on differences of opinion and plenty of them. Furthermore, it is likely that your basic assumptions about what matters in life and what doesn't will be challenged, sometimes vigorously, during the process of rearing a teenager. How you react will probably be driven by your own needs and desires as much as by any consideration of what's best for your child.

The familiar phrase "Know thyself" is no empty cliché when you are parenting adolescents. As one or more of your children approach the teen years, you need to take stock of a few important issues of your own:

Where are you looking for fulfillment and contentment? Do these rise or fall with your adolescent's appearance, grades, social life, performance in sports, or other accomplishments? If things don't go well in one of these areas, how much will this rock your boat and why? Are you more concerned about his well-being and future or your own? Has your sense of significance been built upon the rock of a solid relationship with your Creator or on the shifting sand of your teenager's performance or opinion of you?

The answers will affect whether you can accept and appreciate your teenager on a day-to-day basis, warts and all, or whether there will always be another hurdle he must clear to earn your favor. It is not your teenager's responsibility to enhance your image in the community, duplicate your successes, atone for your failures, or provide you with vicarious pleasures.

Equally important, your feet will need to be firmly planted on solid emotional ground if and when your adolescent enters a phase of annoying negativity. If you begin to sense that your viewpoints or your company is at the moment no longer valued, you will need the internal strength to ward off pangs of rejection or a flush of resentment. Recognizing that this is a common adolescent phase will help, of course. You may find some comfort in the following wry observation:

> When I was a boy of fourteen, my father was so ignorant I could hardly stand to have the old man around. But when I got to be twenty-one, I was astonished at how much the old man had learned in seven years.
> —*Mark Twain*

Above all, knowing that your worth doesn't hinge on the ebb and flow of teenage opinion will help you avoid angry reactions (which can create a much more serious rift in your relationship), while allowing you to deal forthrightly with any disrespectful behavior or comments.

Does your life have any margin? Is your calendar jammed? Are you physically, emotionally, and financially spent most of the time? Do you have any spare time or energy to deal with a problem at school or an adolescent crisis (there will be plenty of them) or simply to get to your teenager's performance in the school play?

Many parents arrive at midlife neck deep in responsibilities and commitments—just as their kids are entering and passing through adolescence. The burden doesn't suddenly arrive on the doorstep one day, of course. It gradually accrues over the years as the career track accelerates, monthly expenses (and debt) mount, and volunteer positions at church and in the community expand. At the same time, parents may find themselves taking care of *their* parents, whose health or faculties may be failing. All of these cares and concerns can be so overwhelming that a teenager's anxiety about a weekend date or an overdue homework assignment may seem trivial.

Retreating from a marginless, stressful, chronically tiring lifestyle requires a number of conscious decisions, and perhaps some sacrifices, from everyone at home. But it also is a powerful act of love, especially when it allows for more time and energy to be spent on building relationships within the family. *Years from now, your grown children will not care nearly as much about your accomplishments, career track, or net worth as they will about the quality of relationship they had with you while growing up.*

Are you invested too heavily in your growing children? Are they the intellectual and emotional center of your life? Will there be a gaping hole in your life when the last young adult leaves the nest? Many parents—especially moms who have poured themselves without reservation into their children's lives—underestimate how emotional the process of letting go will be. Feelings of abandonment and depression may arrive unexpectedly as the last child departs. In some situations, one or both parents become inappropriately embroiled in the details of a grown child's life.

While your children must be a priority in your life, remember that two of you became a family before you had any babies, and that basic unit will continue after they are grown and gone. Maintaining your marriage, lifelong learning, and worthwhile projects are as important for parents as for kids.

Are you nurturing your marriage? As you approach your child(ren)'s adolescent years, are you still on the same team as your spouse? Do you build one another up in front of the kids, or do you unleash verbal attacks for all to witness?

An intact, stable marriage in which affection and mutual respect are openly demonstrated is a valuable asset for raising teenagers. Adolescents learn volumes about relationships from watching interactions at home. When the teen weather is stormy, a united parental front will be very important in restoring calm and maintaining limits. There will be many occasions when one parent can help quiet a conflict between a teenager and the other parent—not by contradicting his or her mate but by supporting and reaffirming him or her. If either partner believes that your marriage needs a tune-up, by all means set aside whatever time is necessary to work with a counselor or pastor.

Are you thinking about walking out on your marriage? Do you think that this would be a good time to escape and start over, now that the kids are older and can "handle it better"?

Think again. With all the physical, emotional, and developmental changes of adolescence in full swing, losing a parent to divorce at this time is a major blow. No matter how skillfully you may offer reassurances that "things will be okay—in fact, probably better" or pledge your undying love and interest in your child's life, with very rare exceptions a divorce will create a profound sense of loss and insecurity. All hands are needed on deck during these important years.[1] If your marriage is in a preterminal condition, find a good counselor, roll up your sleeves, and get to work repairing it.

Fathers, do not exasperate your children; instead, bring them up in the training and instruction of the Lord.

EPHESIANS 6:4

If you are bringing up one or more adolescents as a single parent, are you maintaining a healthy balance between love and limits? Are you overcompensating for the demands on your time, any lack of resources, or perhaps guilt over your marital situation by being too permissive or overly strict? Do you have a relative or good friend you can call upon to lend a hand when conflicts arise?

Rearing teenagers is a major undertaking for two parents and a far tougher assignment if you are on your own. Without the balance provided by another adult, you may find yourself drifting toward one or another extreme in your parenting style. You may need to be particularly careful about becoming so emotionally attached to your child that he or she becomes a surrogate spouse. This state of affairs is unhealthy for both of you.

If at all possible, enlist another mature person (such as a relative or perhaps a member of a support group) to spend time with your teenager. Someone who knows you and your child(ren) well can be particularly helpful in providing another vantage point if you reach an impasse with an adolescent.

Are you modeling behavior that you don't want your teen to imitate? If you are a smoker, don't be surprised if your daughter becomes one also. If you use alcohol on a regular basis, especially as a means to blow off steam or "party hearty," your son may very well follow in your footsteps. If you believe that adolescent sex is no big deal as long as everyone is "protected" or if you carry on sexual relationships outside marriage, don't expect your teenager to remain sexually abstinent.

The adage about actions speaking louder than words is the gospel truth with teenagers. If you're going to talk the talk about health and morals, be prepared to walk the walk as well.

Show genuine interest and respect.

Adolescents despise being treated like little kids. They hate being talked down to. They bristle when orders are dished out and there's no room for discussion. They shut down if they try to express a heartfelt thought and no one listens or someone ridicules it. More often than not, their tempers flare and feelings are hurt because of the *way* something is said—disrespectfully—rather than because of the actual issue.

In other words, they are just like adults.

Even though your teenager may be light-years away from grown-up maturity and responsibilities, you will build strong bonds and smooth your path over the next few years by talking to her as you would to another adult you respect. This, like anything else in life that is worthwhile, takes time and energy. Specific ways to build and maintain a relationship with your teenager include the following:

Take her out for a meal, one-on-one, on a regular basis. Ask questions about what she's interested in and listen carefully to what she says.

Take advantage of common interests. Does he love to ski? Take some time off work and head for the nearest mountain that has snow and ski trails on it. Is she an avid movie- or theatergoer? Go with her and talk about what you've seen. Is he crazy about baseball? Take him out to a ball game and be sure to show up to watch if he's on a team. Does she enjoy chess, Scrabble, or other games? Become a willing (but not too aggressive) opponent.

Ask your teen's opinions about things going on in the world, your community, and your family. If she says something that isn't exactly well informed, don't jump in and "straighten her out." You can gently guide her in the right direction during the natural flow of conversation without making her feel like an idiot after opening up about her views.

When she wants to talk, put down the paper, turn off the TV, look her in the eyes, and pay attention.

Find things to praise—even when there's always much more that you might criticize—and do it often.

If you commit a genuine offense—whether a stray comment that is sarcastic or hurtful, an action that causes your teenager genuine embarrassment or pain, or some other error in judgment—have the courage to apologize. If there has been an argument and both you and your adolescent have said things you later regret, you may need to be the first one to admit that you were wrong. You will not lose face by doing so, but instead you will gain great respect (although you may not hear about it until a few years have passed).

At unexpected times, express satisfaction or outright joy that she is your daughter or he is your son. If you have trouble with this, ask yourself why. It could be that you are breaking new ground here, modeling unconditional acceptance that wasn't explicitly stated when you were growing up.

Know who (besides you) and what is influencing your teenager.

While you as the parent have the primary assignment in shaping your adolescent's journey to adulthood, many other people, institutions, and social forces will have supporting roles. But not all of them will have your teenager's best interests at heart.

Two generations ago the general drift of our culture encouraged basic virtues: honesty, responsibility, sobriety, and the expression of sex within marriage, among others. If a teenager used drugs, was promiscuous, or openly defied authority, he was considered a juvenile delinquent. Today that is no longer the case. Even a casual look at the music, videos, and films geared to adolescents is a harrowing experience. Themes of casual or predatory sex, drug use, violence, death, and despair are not only commercially successful but readily accessible in virtually any home via cable, video rentals, or the Internet. And even public-service and educational messages created for teenagers in the interest of health and safety assume that premarital sex (hetero or otherwise) is the norm, and that condoms should be present and accounted for in every wallet or purse.

These voices, and those of many peers and even educators, sing a lethal siren song every day of the week: "No standards or values are absolute. Anything goes. You are the center of your moral universe."

Unless your family lives in an extremely isolated area, it is virtually impossible to keep these harmful messages and influences away from your adolescent. In fact, a child who is kept in a social vacuum for eighteen years and then suddenly leaves for college, the job market, or the military won't know what hit him when

THE IMPORTANCE OF OPPOSITE-GENDER RELATIONSHIPS

In many families fathers have more interests in common with sons and mothers with daughters. But the importance of nurturing father-daughter and mother-son relationships cannot be overstated.

The tendency in father-son and mother-daughter relationships is for the parent to compare (with some anxiety) the progress of the child to memories of his or her own adolescence. Thoughts such as *He's not doing as well as I was at this age* or *I don't want her to make the same mistakes I did while growing up* can cloud your appreciation of your teenager's uniqueness and your enjoyment of his or her company. Since Dad was never a girl and Mom never a boy, these ongoing comparisons and concerns aren't as likely in opposite-gender relationships.

For a girl, Dad is usually *the* man in her life for many years. How he treats her will affect her relationships with men throughout her teenage and adult years. She will be looking to him for affection, respect, and affirmation of her femininity and will usually expect the same

type of treatment from the males in her life later on. If she has lived with neglect, criticism, and abuse, she may spend years enduring the same from men who are basically perpetually self-centered, irresponsible, and predatory. But if she has been treated with courtesy and respect, she isn't likely to tolerate men who treat her otherwise.

For a variety of reasons, mothers and daughters may butt heads more often during the adolescent years than at other times in their lives. A father's input can help de-escalate conflicts and build Mom's image in the mind of his frustrated daughter.

Mothers can also have a unique relationship with their sons who are nearly grown. While Dad can and should instill standards for behavior with members of the opposite sex, Mom can usually better serve as an adviser regarding matters of the heart. If a son is struggling with a relationship that is tying his emotions in knots, a woman's perspective can offer both insight and comfort.

he gets a taste of what's out on the street. You can and should, therefore, keep your eyes open and be prepared to talk about whomever and whatever you think might be having a negative impact on your teenager's mind and emotions. Specifically, you should note:

Friends. The importance of peers has already been described, especially for early and middle adolescents. As much as you can, get to know and even make friends with your teenager's friends. Listen to what they have to say. An adolescent who likes and respects you will be less likely to encourage your own teenager to disregard your opinions. You may help smooth out a conflict between him and his parents. You might even learn a thing or two about your own child. As you get to know your teen's friends, you can also pray for them.

If you can't connect and it appears that one or more friends are pulling your teenager in directions that are destructive or dangerous, you may have to take the social bull by the horns. Calmly, rationally, and carefully present your concerns. Very often your teenager may be relieved to have a reason to disengage from one or more relationships. In a *worst-case* scenario, you may have to insist that one or more friends are off-limits, which will probably generate a fair amount of protest. Obviously you can't patrol the corridors at school, but you need to make it clear that freedom and privileges will be seriously restricted if she refuses to cooperate. Keep in mind that this plan of action should be reserved for situations in which your child's health and welfare are clearly on the line and not for isolating your teenager from friends whom you find merely annoying.

Music. With a few exceptions, contemporary music plays a prominent and intense role in the life and thought processes of adolescents; this has been true for generations. Today, however, this is not particularly good news.

Over the years most parents have complained about the music their kids enjoyed. During the 1950s and early 1960s, the content of most popular music focused on teen romance, the joys of surfing, and an occasional novelty item such as the "Purple People Eater" or "Alley Oop". Obviously, these songs were hardly masterpieces, and many of them celebrated unrealistic or even silly notions about love and relationships. However, their shortcomings pale in comparison to the malignant cultural tide that rolled in during the late 1960s, when drugs and rebellion began to be celebrated more openly.

The realms of heavy metal and rap teem with obscenity, violence (including rape), sexual anarchy, death, and despair. In bygone days rebellion was at least supposed to be fun. Now it's glum at best and murderous at worst. Slick and hyperkinetic videos that accompany rock hits often add a visual punch to the audio assault.

Depending on your teenager's musical tastes, at some point you may need to square off against the rock juggernaut.[2] There is simply no way that relentlessly negative and destructive lyrics can pound into anyone's mind without making an impact. The issue, by the way, is *content,* not style. Some music that is grating to your ears may actually contain lyrics that challenge the listener to a better lifestyle or tell a cautionary tale.

If you hear something that turns you off throbbing through the walls or headphones, call for a joint listening session. Get the liner notes if possible (and a magnifying glass to read them), then review the CD, cassette, or video together with your teenager. Talk about what the lyrics are saying and how she feels when she listens to them. (You may hear, by the way, an argument that "I just like the beat and the music. I don't listen to the words." Don't buy it. More often than not she can recite lyrics.)

You'll need courage to separate your adolescent from music that is toxic, an open mind to endure the stuff that isn't, and wisdom to know the difference. You should also be prepared to suggest alternatives. For families with Christian commitments, there is a thriving world of contemporary music available in a breadth of styles—including pop, rock, rap, metal, and alternative—that specifically (if noisily) promotes positive values.[3] In addition, a little research will uncover secular music that, while not including overtly biblical phrases or themes, combines high-quality musicianship with family-friendly themes.

Movies, TV, and videos. If you haven't read it recently, review the material in chapter 11 entitled "Monitoring the input to mind and heart" (page 413). As your teenager grows older, you will need to reassess your ground rules for managing these media. You still have a responsibility to oversee the viewing choices in your home, but you may not be able to govern what he watches at a friend's house. Ideally, ongoing conversations about the content of films and TV programs have already instilled some standards and accountability. If you've nurtured a healthy regard for quality and values, he will feel uneasy if he is exposed to trash and stupidity.

Conflicts may arise when "everyone" has seen a certain R-rated film, and he wants to go, too (at the ripe old age of fourteen), or watch it on videocassette. You will need to set and maintain your own family's standards, but at some point you may want to introduce him to more grown-up subject matter under your supervision. Do some homework and read the write-ups (especially in family-oriented magazines). Sometimes an otherwise excellent film receives an

R rating for a brief spurt of bad language or for one or two quick sequences that can be bypassed using the fast-forward button on the remote control. Likewise, a film bearing the milder PG or PG-13 rating may actually be loaded with obnoxious and offensive material.

Whatever you and your teenager see, talk about tone and content. Is this film or program selling a viewpoint, and if so, what is it? If something struck you as offensive, why? Was there a positive message involved? What was it? Before he's finally living on his own, he's going to need to learn discernment. Otherwise, while you may succeed in keeping every scrap of offensive material off his mental radar screen while he's in high school, he's eventually going to be exposed to it later on—but without your preparation or guidance.

Other electronic media. The potential hazards of unrestricted access to video games and computer on-line services (including the Internet) have been discussed in chapter 11. To review them, turn back to page 413.

Literature and nonliterature, including pornography. While you want to encourage reading as an alternative to TV watching, pay attention to the material your adolescent brings home from the library or bookstore. Much of what lands on current best-seller lists is truly pulp fiction, laced with vivid scenes of horror, violence, and sex that are far more explicit than the contents of most R-rated films. Even the so-called romance novels, whose covers are emblazoned with bare-chested hulks looming over bodice-busting sirens, generally contain an abundance of vivid and immoral sexual material. If your teenager is engrossed in a steady diet of books focused on bloodletting, body counts, and bawdy situations, offer some alternatives of better content and quality. (By the way, what books are on your nightstand?)

A more dangerous influence, one that encompasses a variety of media including books, magazines, and videos, is pornography. Twenty years ago someone who wanted to see a dirty movie had to travel across town and sneak into a seedy theater where no one would recognize him. Since then, an explosion of new technologies has given pornography access to nearly every home. Most cable services offer not only unedited feature films on various "premium" channels but also specific channels whose programming consists entirely of sexual material. Nearly every video store has a back room full of hard-core stuff on cassette, available for two or three dollars per night. Most major hotel chains offer pay-per-view movies in every room—including a selection of idiotic "adult" films. Now the Internet has become a lawless Dodge City in which extraordinarily harsh and perverse material can be viewed and captured by any adolescent with a computer and a modem. And all of this doesn't include *Playboy, Penthouse*, and the other spin-offs that have cluttered newsstands and bookshops for decades.

Unlike the general run of films and TV, there is no gray zone for pornography. This is not harmless recreation, especially for an adolescent, and certainly not an appropriate source of information about human sexuality, for a number of reasons:

- Pornography paints a distorted picture of human sexuality as nonstop, careless, and meaningless copulation.
- Pornography degrades women, depicting them as brainless sex toys. Some of it sells the rape myth—that women who say no to a man's sexual advances really mean yes and actually enjoy being raped.
- Pornography is highly addictive for some adolescents (and adults). Consumption of this material might continue into adulthood as a compulsion, contaminating relationships and interfering with a healthy sexual experience during marriage.
- Pornography is progressive for many who become addicted to it. Once someone has seen all the genital gymnastics that a man and woman can do, the search for new excitement may lead to viewing grotesque behavior, sexual violence, and even murder. A few cross the line of sights and sounds to actual participation and criminal behavior.

As your child approaches the teen years, talk about pornography and explain why this material is destructive. Needless to say, there shouldn't be any lurking in your own bedroom. If you as an adult have difficulty staying away from pornography, you should seek counseling from someone who is experienced with this problem.

Nevertheless, it is likely that your teen will stumble upon soft-core material, and perhaps something worse, at some point in his teen years. But what if you are looking through his closet or turning his mattress and stumble onto some sleazy material? Your best approach is neither to ignore it nor to fly off the handle and preach at him for two hours. Instead, plop the magazine (or whatever) in plain view in his room so he knows you found it or casually bring it out when you're ready to talk to him (one-on-one) about your discovery.

Most likely he *knows* that it isn't good to look at it and has dealt with a strong mixture of interest and guilt already, so a low-key approach will be quite effective. (A little humor might even relieve the tension: "Say, this is pretty interesting stuff here! Mom and I were thinking about getting a subscription!") Let him know that *you* know that curiosity about female anatomy is normal at his age, but remind him that this type of material is inappropriate, exploits women, can be as addictive as a drug, and (by the way) is very offensive. Make it clear that you don't want any more of it in your home and give him the honor of dumping it into the trash. It is impossible to know for sure whether he will refrain from looking at pornography somewhere else, of course, but keep your lines of communication open.

If you find material that includes more ominous themes such as homosexuality, violence, or child pornography, you will need to go a step further and get him involved in counseling with a qualified individual who shares your basic views on sexuality.

School and its curriculum. It goes without saying that your teenager's schoolwork should include the basics: reading, writing, math, history, and so forth. In general, it's reasonable to assume that your local schools are staffed by men and women who take their job seriously and have their students' best interests at heart. If your teenager is having problems understanding the material or getting the work done, you will want to review some basic strategies in Special Concerns, page 439.

But what if the problem isn't academics but personality or ideology? What if a particular teacher seems to have it in for your son or daughter, or a class appears to be pushing a political or social agenda that disagrees with yours? What if the family-life or sex-education unit is contradicting everything you have been teaching at home? And, more important, what if your adolescent is subjected to ridicule for expressing a contrary point of view?

Once again, a calm but purposeful approach is in order. You shouldn't abandon your teenager to fend completely for herself. But you should avoid charging into any situation at school with righteous indignation and verbal guns blazing.

First, get all the facts. Find out what "My teacher doesn't like me!" really means. What exactly was said? Is there a pattern? Can you get some written material from the class to look at? Is it possible that your teenager is primarily at fault because of disrespectful or inattentive behavior? It may help to talk to someone else in the same class to get confirmation that a problem really does exist.

You may be able to coach your adolescent through the situation by suggesting ways to de-escalate a conflict (including apologizing, if necessary). If the problem involves a clash of viewpoints, it may in fact be character building for her to deal with differences of opinion in an open forum. In this case you may choose to help her review the facts to bolster her viewpoint or find someone who can provide the input she needs. Remember—it won't hurt her to think through and defend what she believes.

Think carefully before you demand or choose to have her opt out of a controversial activity. This may seem a noble gesture on your part, but it might generate a lot of unnecessary ridicule from peers. For example, if someone gives a skewed presentation on sexual behavior (stressing condom use over abstinence), it may be appropriate for her to hear it—and then have an open discussion and review at home afterwards. This may also be a starting point for you to influence the future curriculum in a more positive direction. On the other hand, if you have advance warning that extremely offensive material is going to be used, exercise the opt-out choice—and then work diligently to change what happens next year.

If it looks as though the situation is out of hand (for example, your teenager is obviously upset, developing physical symptoms, or doesn't want to go to school because of the pressure) or the deck is stacked (points and grades in the class appear to depend on agreement with a teacher's ideology), you'll need to enter the arena.

Schedule an appointment with the teacher to get his or her perspective on the situation. Ask an open question: "Teresa seems to be having some problems in your class. I wonder what we can do to smooth things out?" If you begin with "Why are you picking on my daughter?" or "You're out of line, and I'm taking this all the way to the school board!" there won't be any discussion at all.

Perhaps you haven't gotten the whole story. Maybe some evenhanded give-and-take on controversial issues has been encouraged, and your teenager didn't present her views very well. If so, building bridges rather than lighting fires would be a better course of action.

If, however, it is clear that certain beliefs and viewpoints aren't welcome or are subject to ridicule in the class, and friendly persuasion isn't making any headway, you may have to pursue your teenager's right to a hassle-free education. A meeting of other like-minded parents with the teacher in question, a conference with the principal, and if necessary, a transfer to another class may be appropriate. Your bottom line should not be a tirade that "this school is leading our youth down the road to ruin," but rather the simple notion that school should be a neutral ground for mastering basic material, not pushing a specific social or political agenda.

You can't spend all your time and energy trying to fend off potentially negative influences in your adolescent's life. Aside from your own input, you will also want to identify several allies who can encourage your teenager to move in positive directions. These might include:

- ◆ A relative (aunt, uncle, cousin, grandparent, or even a much older sibling) who shares your values. Someone older than your teenager but younger than you may connect well and not seem so old-fashioned.
- ◆ A teacher, coach, youth pastor, or other person in an authority role who also deals effectively and constructively with areas that adolescents care about.
- ◆ A physician, nurse, or counselor who has professional expertise and supports your value system. Someone with stature and authority can have a major impact on your teenager, especially if he or she has known her for a number of years. Since health exams—and potentially sensitive discussions—will be on the agenda during the next few years, find out if the physician or nurse-practitioner who may be involved is committed to the standards that you promote within your family.
- ◆ A positive peer group. Even one friend who shares your adolescent's values can help her resist a negative tide of peer pressure. A thriving church group can take her well beyond merely holding her ground and involve her in making a positive impact among her peers and in your community.
- ◆ The parent of one of your teenager's friends. Someone who doesn't have an emotional stake in your adolescent but shares your views on morals and behavior may be able to serve as a positive sounding board for topics that your teenager doesn't feel comfortable discussing with you.
- ◆ Films, videos, or music with positive, affirming, or redemptive messages.

You should make every effort, without being too pushy or manipulative, to connect your adolescent with any and all of these resources. But remember, if your efforts are too blatant, your teenager may resist merely because it isn't her idea.

Pick your battles carefully.

Differences of opinion with a growing adolescent on a variety of subjects are inevitable. Even the teenager who is compliant and agreeable will lock horns with you eventually—or become expert at quieter ways to demonstrate her opinions. When you are challenged on a rule at your home or you see or hear your teenager doing something you don't like, you'll need to heed these principles:

Don't argue with your teen. Don't subject him to perpetual threats and finger-wagging accusations and insulting indictments. And most important, don't nag him endlessly.

THE STRONG-
WILLED CHILD

To quote the apostle Paul, "Do not exasperate your children" (Ephesians 6:4). If you choose to comment, nag, or nudge about *everything* she does that isn't up to your standards, be prepared for several years of misery. Yes, she needs your guidance. The choices she makes now can have significant consequences, and she still has lots of room for improvement. But if she hears about her deficits constantly, she will become frustrated and eventually hostile. And guess who she *won't* want to talk to if there's a *real* problem. If all the nitpicky stuff arouses nonstop criticism at home, she can only imagine what will happen in response to a major mistake.

Think through your rules. Ask yourself regularly, "Why am I making this rule?" Does it truly have an impact on your adolescent's well-being? Or does it merely reflect the way things were done when you were growing up?

Don't be afraid to negotiate in some areas. If your teenager respectfully suggests an alternative to a rule or restriction you've imposed, listen carefully. If it's reasonable, seriously consider letting the decision go her way. You will gain some major points and demonstrate that you are truly listening rather than reacting.

Do go to the mat when necessary. There will be issues regarding health, safety, moral principles, and attitude that will require you to state your case and hold your ground. You must still be friendly. You can discuss the reasons and suggest alternatives. You can remind your teenager that her total independence is not too many years away, but that for now you're still in charge in a few key areas. You must reinforce your love for her and treat her with respect. But even though you may risk a temporary decline in popularity, when it's time to take a stand, don't shirk your duty.

Teach and release responsibilities.

The importance of escorting your adolescent into the realm of adult independence and responsibilities has already been discussed at length. With rare exception she will be very eager to have as much of the first and as little of the second as possible. Ideally, she should be experiencing similar amounts of each. Keep in mind that this includes an introduction to many of the mundane tasks you take for granted every week.

Does she want her own car? If you help her obtain one, she needs to be involved in the whole package. What does the registration cost? What about the insurance? How about maintenance? The use of an automobile should rarely be unconditional. Reasonable school performance, trustworthiness, and probably some contribution to expenses (perhaps the insurance, the upkeep, or even saving up for a percentage of the whole purchase) should be part of the bargain. If she gets a ticket, she's going to have to pay for it. Let her look over the registration bill every year as well. This isn't much fun, but she'll have to do it eventually when she's out of your nest.

Another useful reality check is escorting your teenager on a guided tour of your monthly bills. Let her see what you pay for mortgage, taxes, utilities, and the other things she takes for granted every month. Better yet, let her fill out the checks and the register with you during a bill-paying session. She'll learn about a few significant nuts and bolts of everyday life and save you some time as well. Help her open her own checking account and show her how to balance it every month.

It also should go without saying that everyone at home should have specified duties in maintaining household cleanliness and order. Be sure to hand out age-appropriate housekeeping assignments (which may be daily, weekly, or both), with the understanding that the children should do their chores automatically without requiring nonstop nagging and reminders. If you hear whining about this being an imposition, slave labor, etc., remind the complainer that this is merely the way civilized, responsible grown-ups live.

If your adolescent's behavior causes any harm or damage, whether accidental or otherwise, make sure she participates in the restitution and repairs. If you automatically bail her out of every consequence, you will succeed only in perpetuating childish irresponsibility. Indeed, one of the most significant parting gifts you can provide for a grown child is a practical, working knowledge of consequences. Adulthood often involves asking sober questions about a future course of action: "If I do _____, what is likely to happen? What things might go wrong with my plans? What do I need to do to prepare for the possibilities?"

When she has a red-hot idea for an activity or a project, enjoy her enthusiasm but also coach her through the potential problems she may not have thought about. You can do this, by the way, without raining on all of her parades. At times she may think you're a party pooper for bringing up the negatives, but reassure her that you're only doing so because she's almost an adult—and that's what adults do.

Go to bat when necessary.

While you want your adolescent to become increasingly self-reliant as the years pass, there will be times when a problem simply overwhelms him. If it looks like he's going down for the count, don't sit on the sidelines.

School problems, whether academic or ideological, have already been mentioned as an area where you may have to take part in the conflict. A more common situation in which he may need help is in dealing with harassment, especially in junior high. The social swamp at this age breeds amazing verbal and physical abuse, and your young adolescent may not be up for the battle—especially if he displays any vulnerability. Always ask about hassles from other kids if he repeatedly looks distressed, depressed, haggard, or literally beat up. A little persistence may be needed to get to the core of the problem (and the

WHAT IS AND ISN'T WORTH A BATTLE?

Some things that bother you may not be worth a major conflict with your teenager. Think carefully before starting a war over the following:

- A mess in his or her own room (unless the health department pays a visit). Remember: dirty-room syndrome is a self-limited and nonfatal illness.
- Length of hair
- Earrings (for either gender)
- Style of music
- Sound level of music
- Choice of everyday clothing
- Fast food
- Sleeping in when there's not a specific need to arise for school or work
- How, when, and where homework is done—as long as it is getting done

On the other hand, there are a number of areas (some related to the list above) in which you will need to state your case and hold your ground, or at least have some family summit conferences to resolve your differences:

- A mess that is not confined to his or her room. Everyone who is old enough to walk and understand plain English needs to pick up his or her own clothes, trash, dishes, soft drink cans, and other debris. If you are constantly gathering up your teenager's (or one or more friends') stuff from every room, it's time for retraining. Let everyone (including your spouse, if needed) know that you have resigned from unpaid janitorial duties. Furthermore, after one or two reminders, valuables will be confiscated for an unspecified period, and trash may end up in the owner's bed. You can declare your intentions humorously, of course, but be sure to follow through.

- Extreme alterations of hair. A heart-to-heart talk is in order if your adolescent plans to adopt a totally bizarre hairstyle (such as giant green spikes) that will blatantly announce to the world, "I don't care what anybody thinks of me!" Important issues of acceptance and rejection lie below the surface of outlaw or alien appearances and deserve thoughtful exploration rather than ridicule.
- Body piercing. Aggressive body piercing (nose, tongue, navel, etc.) should be discouraged, perhaps with a reminder about respecting and valuing one's body as well as a check on the current status of peer pressure. In addition, if an infection arises from any of this hardware, removing it can be quite uncomfortable.
- Tattoos. Despite a rising acceptance of "body art" in many circles, your adolescent needs to know that it is extremely unwise to do *anything* with permanent physical consequences when his life is in a state of flux. This is particularly important if he seems intent on embedding negative or offensive images in his skin. It will cost him a lot of money and discomfort if he wants them removed later on, which is likely. He should also be aware that infections such as hepatitis B or HIV can be spread by contaminated tattoo needles. A makeshift "tattoo parlor" in a friend's garage should be avoided. Tell him that he can have all the tattoos he wants—after he is eighteen and living on his own. By then his interest in body alterations may well have passed.
- Content of music, as was discussed earlier in this chapter.
- Sound level of music. If your adolescent's music is keeping everyone at home (or the entire neighborhood) awake at night, or if you can hear it across the room—when he's wearing headphones—you will need to insist that the volume come down. Ongoing exposure to extremely loud noise can cause permanent hearing loss.

name of the perpetrator) because kids in this age-group desperately fear ridicule or reprisals.

The solution to harassment, by the way, is not preparing your son for a fist-fight after school. Instead, swift and decisive (but nonviolent) action from one or more adults normally is quite effective. Most schools are ready and willing to put the heat on anyone who is causing this sort of problem—but they will need

(continued)

- Choice of everyday clothing. If garments contain images or words that are violent or offensive, they don't belong on your adolescent. You will also need to veto female attire that is blatantly sexually provocative.
- Extremes in food choices—either excessive or limited in variety or amount. Obesity in adolescence is not only a social issue but may set in motion lifelong health problems. Anorexia and bulimia are obsessions with food that can have very serious consequences as well. In a nutshell, being extremely overweight tends to create medical trouble later in life; anorexia can literally be lethal in a few months. Both deserve focused attention and help from your health-care provider. Anorexia may require psychiatric hospitalization because it can be very difficult to treat. (See Special Concerns, page 429.)
- Toxic friends, as was discussed earlier in this chapter. (See pages 509–510 and 527.)
- Tobacco, alcohol, and street drug use, as is discussed in Special Concerns, page 579.
- Sexual activity—see chapter 11 and accompanying Special Concerns, pages 541 and 573.
- Disappearing. In any home it is a common courtesy—and may be critically important in an emergency—for family members who live under the same roof to be notified of each other's whereabouts. Your teenager needs to understand that this doesn't mean you're treating him like a child. It is childish and irresponsible to take off for hours at a time—especially at night—without keeping the home front posted. If he's going to be at a friend's house for the evening, it's not unreasonable for you to get a name and number. If he's going to go somewhere else, you need to know the destination.

  As he progresses through high school, let him

know that you intend to give him more latitude about the time he is expected home, if he is trustworthy in this area. Remind him that this expectation applies to everyone in your home, parents included.
- Disrespectful comments and actions. Much has been said earlier about treating your adolescent with respect. The same should be expected of his behavior toward you. This does not mean that he isn't allowed to disagree with you or even become angry. In fact, there may be times when he is quite upset with you and perhaps for good reason. He needs to know that you are willing to hear his point of view on anything, even if he is angry, as long as he says it respectfully.

  Occasionally a comment uttered in the heat of battle, a roll of the eyes, or a door that closes a little too hard will strike you as inappropriate. It may not have been deliberate, but you need to let him know how it came across and suggest other ways for him to make his case.

  If you are definitely on the receiving end of sarcastic or even abusive language—or you hear it being dished out to your spouse—you need to bring the conversation to an immediate halt. Explain as calmly as possible that the issue now is no longer whatever you were talking about but the unacceptable way in which the ideas are being expressed. You may get a blank stare, and you may need to spell out what you found objectionable. If there is an appropriate retraction, you can proceed—and you will have provided an object lesson for your adolescent in how to handle issues later in life.

  If your teenager will not back away from comments that are out of line or the problem escalates, more drastic action will be necessary (see sidebar, page 517).

names. If this doesn't work, consider arranging a meeting with the perpetrator and if possible one or both of his parents in a school official's office. Look him in the eye and make it abundantly clear that even one further episode will bring disastrous consequences and that you expect his parents to cooperate.

If the problem involves risks of extreme violence or gang activity, you will need to seek advice from law-enforcement as well as school officials. In a worst-case scenario, a change of school (or home schooling) may be necessary to bring your adolescent through this situation in one piece. *Do whatever it takes (within the bounds of the law) to protect his safety and self-respect.*

A less dangerous (but still very painful) situation that may require your strong arm around a slumped shoulder is loneliness or repeated rejection by peers. If your adolescent can't seem to make or keep any friends, don't shrug and tell her that she'll get over it. She may not. Try to find out what's going wrong and help her make whatever changes are necessary to alter this course.

If she needs to work on grooming, lend a hand (or find someone who can). If you overhear her talking to others in a way that is an obvious turnoff, coach her on conversational skills. Encourage her to invite a friend over for an evening or a special outing. Work with her to find a niche in the community where healthy friendships can develop. And if all else fails, go out of your way to be her best friend until other candidates cross her path.

There will be times when you won't be able to be all things for your adolescent, and other supportive adults in your child's life may need to lend support. Single adults, church youth workers, neighbors, and relatives can fill in a number of gaps and provide a rich, meaningful influence for years to come. Try to keep your son or daughter in contact with different types of people who might have a positive impact. (You might invite them to be guests around your dinner table, for example.)

Keep them busy, within reason.

Without jamming her schedule to the gills, encourage worthwhile activities—a job, church-related projects, sports, performing arts, for example—to add structure to the hours that aren't involved in education. As long as she's not overcommitted and exhausted, these can make her life more well rounded, add to her social network, and (usually) reduce the risk of her getting into trouble.

Stay on your knees.

This section on parental survival skills began with this admonition, and it is worth briefly repeating. You are not omniscient, omnipotent, or omnipresent.

(That is, you can't know everything, do everything, or be everywhere.) But your adolescent's Creator is. Talking to Him regularly about your young adult in the making will therefore help you maintain your perspective, sanity, and strength. These times of prayer can also be opportunities to acknowledge and thank God for the incredible growth and changes that you are witnessing as your child approaches adulthood.

A FINAL THOUGHT: LOOKING AHEAD

As you invest your time and energy into shaping the life of your adolescent, keep the ultimate goal, the prize at the end of this marathon called parenting, firmly in mind. Picture the baby you introduced to the world not too many years ago living as a responsible, self-sufficient, productive, and morally integrated adult. Imagine walking and talking together, swapping ideas and insights over a cup of coffee, enjoying a concert or a film (perhaps with your child paying for your ticket!), fighting back tears as he or she stands at the wedding altar, and ultimately, watching your child start a family.

In the midst of raging hormones and overdue homework assignments, this may seem like an impossible fantasy. But your child will indeed reach adulthood, and we anticipate that, through all of the sweat, tears, and laughter, you will emerge as friends and allies.

Few rewards in your life will be more satisfying.

NOTES
1. The exception to this scenario occurs when it is necessary to escape from a spouse whose behavior is continuously abusive and destructive. Even then, separation may provoke a crisis that brings about the first steps toward change and ultimate reconciliation. But by no means should you allow yourself or a child (of any age) to be subjected to harassment, violence, or molestation.
2. *The American Heritage Dictionary* defines *juggernaut* as "a belief or institution that elicits blind and destructive devotion, or to which people are ruthlessly sacrificed" and "an overwhelming and irresistible force or movement."
3. Parents who want to stay abreast of the music scene without directly wading through it should consider subscribing to *Plugged In,* an informative newsletter that analyzes current offerings from a traditional-values perspective. This material is available from Focus on the Family, Colorado Springs, Colorado (1-800-232-6459).

A Parent's Guide to Teen Sexuality

PART ONE: PRESERVING THE GIFT

This section will focus repeatedly on an important principle: *It is appropriate, wise, and potentially lifesaving to teach your kids to save their sexual activity for marriage.*

God designed sex to bring new life into existence, to generate a powerful bond between a husband and wife, and to be intensely pleasurable. It is a wonderful, extraordinary, and powerful gift that deserves to be treated with great and abiding respect. In the context of a permanent and public commitment, it can be savored, explored, and nurtured without guilt or fear of serious consequences. But at the wrong time with the wrong person, sex can bring disappointment, disease, and derailed life plans and purposes.

Your adolescent, who is curious about and highly interested in sex, needs a clearheaded understanding of its benefits and risks in order to make a serious commitment to remain sexually pure until marriage. Maintaining such a commitment won't always be easy.

Why is it so challenging to preserve the gift of sex for marriage?

Inner drives. Normal adolescents—even yours—have sexual interests and feelings. They also deeply need love and affirmation. As a result, they can become emotionally and sexually attracted to others around them and drawn toward physical intimacy. But they also enter adolescence with a sense of modesty that tends to inhibit sexual explorations.

These realities were clearly recognized just a few generations ago, when modesty was encouraged and more formal boundaries were set between unmarried members of the opposite sex. Today many would call such efforts stuffy, inhibited, and puritanical. But our ancestors were in many ways more "streetwise" about adolescent sexuality and made it somewhat easier for their sons and daughters to resist sexual pressure. Our culture, on the other hand, practically drowns them in temptation.

Seductive messages. A half century ago, Western societies generally supported the concept that marriage was the appropriate arena for sexual activity. During the late 1960s, a cultural upheaval sometimes called the sexual revolution assaulted traditional sexual ground rules. Virtually all popular media (movies, TV, videos, music) as well as educational, health-care, and governmental organizations were affected by this moral free fall. As a result, by the time your child arrives at puberty, he or she will have heard the following destructive messages many, many times and in a variety of ways:

Four Fantasies of the Sexual Revolution

1. Sex is okay any which way with whomever, as long as there is mutual consent, no one gets pregnant (unless she wants to), and no one gets hurt.
2. Sex is usual and customary if you are attracted to someone.
3. Sex unrelated to marriage is normal, natural, expected, and inevitable, so carry a condom.
4. If you are postponing sex until marriage, you must be incredibly unattractive, a social disaster, or a religious fanatic.

Unless they live in complete isolation, adolescents are regularly exposed to sexually provocative material that expresses immoral viewpoints, fires up sexual desires, and wears down resistance to physical intimacy. Even in the "safe" confines of the classroom, a teenager's natural modesty may be dismantled during explicit presentations about sexual matters in mixed company. Limiting your adolescent's contact with destructive input is reviewed in chapter 13 (page 525).

Lack of supervision. Because of fragmented families, complex parental work schedules, easier access to transportation, and at times, carelessness among adults who should know better, adolescents today are more likely to find opportunities to be alone together for long stretches of time. In such circumstances, nature is likely to take its course, even when a commitment has been made to wait until the wedding night for sex.

Overbearing, overprotective supervision. Adolescents who are smothered in a controlling, micromanaging, suspicious environment are strong candidates for rebellion once the opportunity arises. When restraints are tightly enforced in an atmosphere of ongoing mistrust, kids may be tempted to become sexually involved simply to "get it over with," to see what all the fuss is about, and to assert their independence. Ironically, a big (and dangerous) rebellion may represent an effort to break loose from an overabundance of trivial constraints. As will be discussed later in this section, parents can set appropriate boundaries while still entrusting adolescents with increasing responsibility to manage themselves and their sexuality.

Peer pressure. This ever present influence comes in three powerful forms. If two or three of these are present at the same time, resistance to premarital sexual activity may be worn down quickly:

A general sense that "everyone is doing it except me." Movies, TV, videos, and popular music nurture this idea. Conversations with friends or even offhanded comments overheard between strangers bring the idea closer to home. Your child's school health-education presentation will confirm the suspicion if it emphasizes contraception and condom use but barely mentions abstinence. "These professionals know more about this than I do. I must be the only seventeen-year-old in town who hasn't had sex."

Personal comments from friends and acquaintances:

- "You've been with him for six months and haven't slept together yet? What's wrong?"
- "Hey, guys, check out Jason, the last American virgin!"
- "Did you do it/score/get lucky last night?"

Direct pressure from another person who wants a sexual experience or an invitation from a willing potential partner. Come-ons, smooth talk, whining, haggling, and outright coercion by men who want sex with a woman are timeworn negative behaviors. Resistance to them may be lowered by a need for closeness and acceptance and the mistaken belief that physical intimacy will secure a man's love.

In recent years a turnabout has become common: A young man is informed by his girlfriend (or a recent acquaintance) that she wants to have sex with him. Personal convictions that sex is intended for marriage will be put to the ultimate test by a situation like this, especially if some physical contact is already underway. All the admonitions he has heard and the moral code he embraces may suddenly seem terribly abstract, while the intense pleasure that is his for the taking is very real. Which will prevail?

Lack of reasons (and desire) to wait. Some adolescents are determined to have sex, regardless of the risks. Others are unshakably committed to the goal that their first and only sex partner will be their spouse. In between these opposite poles live a large number of teenagers who keep an informal mental tally of reasons for and against premarital sex. Inner longings and external pressure pull them toward it, while standards taught at home and church, medical warnings, and commonsense restraints put on the brakes.

For many teenagers (even those who intend to abstain until marriage), decisions about sex tend to be made based on the drift of this internal "vote count." When the moment of truth arrives, the tally may be close—or a landslide in the wrong direction. Adolescents with a shaky or negative self-concept may be particularly vulnerable to sexual involvement when one of the reasons is the possibility of winning approval from one or more VIPs (Very Important Peers). Therefore, without being overbearing or obsessive, make an effort to have ongoing dialogues with your teenager about the many compelling reasons to postpone sex until the wedding night. (It should go without saying that you should be talking to your teenager about many things besides areas of concern and danger. If your communication is smooth in other less volatile areas, it will likely flow more easily with a sensitive topic such as sexuality.) The following list of reasons to wait may help you formulate and express your thoughts during these important conversations.

Reason to wait #1: STDs

Thirty years ago the typical high school health-education class discussed two sexually transmitted diseases (STDs): syphilis and gonorrhea. They were described as potentially hazardous but nothing a little penicillin couldn't handle. But the sexual playground that opened during the late 1960s has resulted in an STD epidemic unprecedented in medical history, teeming with exotic, dangerous, and often incurable infections.

More than fifteen significant diseases can be transmitted by exchange of body fluids or skin to skin during sexual activity. Some are fatal, a few are relatively harmless, and many have long-term physical and emotional consequences. A few can be successfully treated with antibiotics—but without creating any memory in the immune system. As a result, infections such as gonorrhea and chlamydia can be acquired over and over by the same individual. (For more information on STDs and teens, see Special Concerns, page 573.)

Reason to wait #2: Sex is how babies get started

Each year one million teenagers will become pregnant, resulting in more than four hundred thousand abortions and nearly a half million births.[1] (Approximately 10 to 15 percent of teen pregnancies end in miscarriage.) The vast majority of the pregnancies are unplanned, and a sizable percentage begin even though a contraceptive is used. Two out of three teenage mothers are unmarried (as opposed to 30 percent in 1970).[2] Altogether, four out of every ten adolescent girls will become pregnant by the age of nineteen.

These statistics do not begin to communicate the profound effects of a pregnancy on a young woman's life. Whatever the circumstances of the sexual encounter that began it, a pregnancy cannot be ignored, and whatever is done about it will have a permanent impact on the young mother's life. Once she becomes pregnant, she will never be the same. Only two outcomes are possible: The baby will be born, or the baby will die before birth, whether through deliberate or spontaneous abortion (miscarriage).

Neither of these events is easy to deal with. There's no quick fix where human life is concerned, no way to "rewind the tape" and start over as though nothing happened.

If an unmarried teenager bears and brings up her child, her life (and probably the lives of other family members) will be affected for years to come. She must deal with the many challenges that all young mothers face, but nearly always with some additional difficulties. Her educational plans are likely to be postponed or significantly rearranged. Economic opportunities will probably be limited, and dependence upon welfare is common. Unless she has considerable help and support, a teenage mother will risk difficulties with parenting, difficulty in a future marriage relationship, and more unplanned pregnancies.

In some cases, one or both of the mother's parents choose to take on primary care of their grandchild.[3] This situation can serve to forge new bonds in the extended family, allowing the baby to grow up loved and well cared for in his family of origin, while Mom manages part of his care and continues her schooling or vocation. But the added strain of such arrangements can take a significant toll on a family, and some families are simply too dysfunctional or lacking in material resources to provide adequate care for a new baby.

If a young mother gives up her child for adoption—an act of considerable courage—she will help bring about what is often a relatively positive combination of outcomes. Her baby will be reared by people who are usually better prepared to provide the time, attention, and resources. Then she can make a fresh start with her education and social life. But even this solution will not exempt her from pain. Her baby will never be forgotten, and a sense of loss, sometimes profound, will be felt for the rest of her life.

Women with unplanned pregnancies often feel a burning need to do something as quickly as possible. They may find the options of bringing up or giving up a baby highly uncomfortable, at least at first glance. For a teenager, a nine-month detour from normal activities may seem like an eternity. These and other factors (especially pressure from a boyfriend or parents) may lead to the wrong conclusion that abortion is the best alternative, one that offers a quick resolution, fewer personal complications, far less financial cost compared to having a baby, and usually confidentiality as well. (Many teenagers obtain abortions without parental involvement or consent.)

But abortion is not a completely risk-free procedure. Damage to the uterus that could jeopardize future pregnancies (or even require major surgical repair), infection, bleeding, future infertility, and even more serious events (including death) are possible complications. Furthermore, even if an abortion is carried out without any apparent hitch, a different type of pain may develop months or years later. Because they want so desperately for the crisis to go away, many women will undergo an abortion even though they are knowingly violating their own moral standards. Many come to realize later in life that a human being—a son or a daughter, not a shapeless wad of tissue—was destroyed through abortion. For these and other reasons, many women live with significant, long-term regrets after an abortion, especially if they have difficulty becoming pregnant later in life.

Reason to wait #3: The risk of infertility

An estimated 10 to 15 percent of couples (about 10 million people) have difficulty conceiving, and more than a million couples seek treatment for infertility each year in the United States. Statistics cannot begin to reflect the intense distress this problem creates in a couple's life. Dealing with infertility can be complicated, time-consuming, stressful, and expensive—when the process of starting a pregnancy is designed to be pleasurable and free. Unfortunately, a significant number (but not all) of these infertility problems arise as a consequence of sexually transmitted diseases and thus could have been avoided if both husband and wife had postponed sex until marriage. (For more information on the impact of STDs on women and unborn children, see Special Concerns, page 77.)

Reason to wait #4: "Safe(r) sex" isn't

In spite of a relentless epidemic of sexually transmitted diseases and unplanned pregnancies, far too few people are willing to accept the obvious: These problems and the heartaches accompanying them could be eliminated if adolescents (and single adults) would postpone sex, find and marry one partner, and remain mutually faithful for life. This idea is considered unrealistic by an influential cadre of individuals and institutions that, in response to the AIDS epidemic, began promulgating the notion of "safe sex." When it became clear that only mutually exclusive sex within marriage was truly safe, the concept was redubbed "safer sex."

Presentations that promote safer sex (including those geared to adolescents) usually advocate three precautions:

Myths of safer sex

Myth 1: *If I limit the number of partners with whom I have sex, I'll be safe.* It is true that having fewer partners means fewer chances for exposure to disease. But it only takes one contact to become pregnant or to be infected with a significant or lethal infection if that person has had other partners.

Myth 2: *If I know something about a potential partner's sexual history and I avoid having sex with someone who has had many partners, I'll be safe.* This sounds reasonable, but in fact taking a sexual history is tricky, even in a doctor's office. A prospective partner is often not willing to tell the truth if it means a pleasurable evening might be called off as a result. It is virtually impossible to discover the sexual history of the prospective partner's previous partners, or those partners' partners, and so on. *From an infectious-disease standpoint, one has sex not with just one person but with all of that individual's sexual contacts, and all of their contacts' contacts, and so on.* Furthermore, a significant number of people who are infected with STDs have no symptoms and do not know they are infected.

Myth 3: *If we use a condom every time, I'll be safe.* True, using a condom correctly (a multistep procedure) during each act of intercourse will reduce the risk of pregnancy and some STDs. But condoms are not a terribly effective form of birth control, with failure rates commonly estimated at 10 to 15 percent.[4] This means that out of one hundred women who are sexually active, ten to fifteen will be pregnant within a year if condoms are the only form of contraception used. *Among adolescents, these failure rates are generally higher* for a variety of reasons. Not only are they more likely to forget or mismanage some of the fine points of proper condom use (including having one available in the first place) during the heat of the moment, but many teenagers, and older men as well, simply resist wearing them. Even if used correctly and consistently, condoms can break, leak, or fall off during intercourse.

These failure rates are even more alarming if one remembers that intercourse can lead to pregnancy only on a few days each month, while STDs can be transmitted *every day of every month*. Furthermore, infections such as syphilis, herpes, and human papilloma virus (HPV) are often spread through contact between skin surfaces that a condom cannot cover. (Condoms give almost no protection in preventing the transmission of HPV.)[5]

Reason to wait #5: Devalued sex

Advocating that sex be kept within the boundaries of marriage is not based on notions that intercourse is "dirty" or "unholy" but on a true appreciation for sex as God's fine art. If the original Mona Lisa were entrusted to you for a month, you wouldn't leave it in your backyard, use it as a TV tray, or line a birdcage with it. Similarly, sex deserves more respect than our culture gives it.

- What truly devalues sex is the idea that intercourse is no more meaningful than a good meal or a drive in a fast car.
- What stifles sexual satisfaction is casual copulation with little or no emotional involvement.
- What people miss in nonmarital sex is the opportunity for enjoyment far greater than the immediate sensual experience.

While movies and television often portray casual sex as the epitome of sensual excitement, a healthy, long-term marital relationship is actually the best setting for satisfying sexual experiences. The security of commitment can free both husband and wife to relax rather than "perform," and their familiarity over a period of years allows them to please and excite one another with ever increasing expertise and finesse. In a growing and deepening marriage relationship, sexuality can encompass far more than the superficial, bumper-sticker mentality of merely "doing it." Sex becomes a comfort, a natural stimulant (or relaxant), a playground, a special means of communication, and a bridge that can connect individuals to one another after a difficult day or season. Short-term relationships provide few, if any, of these benefits, and those involved in casual sex cannot approach (or in some cases even comprehend) them.

Reason to wait #6: Distorted relationships

Adding sex to a nonmarital relationship, especially when adolescents are involved, is like throwing a one-thousand-pound weight into a rowboat. The center of gravity drastically shifts, forward motion becomes difficult, and the whole thing may eventually sink. Sex *never* enhances a teenage romance but almost always overwhelms and stifles it. Arguments, secrecy, stress, and guilt usually replace laughter, discovery, and meaningful conversation.

Indeed, sex has a way of wrecking good relationships and keeping bad ones going long after they should have ended. After a sexual relationship is broken off, there is likely to be a sense of loss (sometimes severe), regret, and awkwardness whenever the other person is encountered. Condoms can't prevent a broken heart, and antibiotics can't cure one.

When one or both partners have had prior sexual experience, what's to guarantee that tonight's coupling isn't just another notch on the belt? Trust has become so foreign to the sexual playground that the phrase "trust me" has become the caricature come-on, the phrase uttered by the predator who hopes the intended prey is too dumb not to burst out laughing. Compare this with the experience of two people who have waited until marriage to initiate their sexual experience. For them the wedding night can be an ecstatic time of discovery and bonding, and whatever they might lack in technique can be learned pleasantly enough at their own pace. Additionally, prior sexual experiences create memories that may interfere with bonding and sexual intimacy in a future marital relationship.

Reason to wait #7: Damaged goods

An important warning for adolescent females: In the sexual revolution, women have been—and still are—the big losers:

- The woman virtually always pays a far bigger price than her partner when an unwanted pregnancy occurs.
- With the exception of syphilis and AIDS, many sexually transmitted diseases have more serious consequences in women.
- When women accept the "playboy" philosophy of "sex as recreation," they trade a number of sexual encounters for nothing. No ongoing relationship, no security, no commitments, no love, and possibly no children in the future (if they acquire a pelvic infection from a partner).

Early sexual experiences never enhance self-esteem but usually leave a strong feeling of having been used, violated, and devalued. Instead of learning from experience and refusing to be burned again, the sexually experienced adolescent is likely to say, "What does it matter now? I might as well just go ahead the next time." Without specific counseling to counteract this damaged-goods mentality, resistance to continuing sexual activity may be seriously weakened—especially in adolescents who have had one or more pregnancies, whether ending in abortion or childbirth. This devaluation of both self and sexuality, while generally more common and profound in girls, certainly occurs in boys too.

Reason to wait #8: The moral high ground

Despite the rising tide of sexual anarchy in our society, a great many people still believe the words *right* and *wrong* apply to sexual behavior. Even someone with a casual exposure to traditional Judeo-Christian values should pick up an important message: The Designer of sex cares a lot about when it's done and with whom. Sex outside of marriage can be dangerous to one's physical, emotional, and spiritual health. Even for those who do not follow specific religious precepts, basic decency and concern for the well-being of others should curtail the vast majority of sexual adventures, which so often are loaded with selfish agendas.

Unfortunately, some adolescents who have had ongoing church experiences and explicit teaching about sexual morality may still become involved with premarital sex, which does nothing for spiritual growth. Intimacy with God on Sunday morning (or any other day) will be seriously impaired when there has been illicit physical intimacy.

WHAT CAN PARENTS DO TO REDUCE THE RISK OF PREMARITAL ADOLESCENT SEX?

Plenty. First, reread "Talking to Teens about Risks: Nine Basic Principles" (page 501). Then seriously consider the following measures (all are long-term projects):

Be aware of these specific risk factors for teen sex:

Alcohol and drug use. Aside from reflecting problem attitudes (rebellion, poor self-concept, invulnerability) that make sex more likely, intoxication also clouds judgment and weakens resistance to sexual overtures.

A steady boyfriend or girlfriend. Strong attachments and feelings of exclusivity invite nature to take its course, especially when physical expressions of affection begin early in the relationship. *This is a particular risk in a situation where the boy* *is more than two or three years older than the girl*. Ideally, a take-it-slow approach to relationships can be encouraged and set in motion through conversations both before and during the adolescent years. (This process is discussed at length later in this section.) If a teen romance appears to be getting hot and heavy and a lot of physical contact is already displayed, you will have a more delicate task. You will need to speak with both boy and girl diplomatically but candidly about the physical process they are setting in motion. If you're too easygoing about it, you will do little to discourage further progress down the road toward intimacy. On the other hand, if you come down too hard, you may drive the young lovers closer together, emotionally and physically. Forbidding further contact (which is much easier said than done) should be reserved for situations in which it is clear that the relationship is damaging, dangerous, or abusive.

Little parental monitoring. Adolescents aren't likely to remove clothing and get horizontal if parents are in the next room. Leaving them alone for hours at a time or not requiring accountability is a setup for sex.

A parental belief that adolescent sex is appropriate. If you think nonmarital sex is okay, your adolescent will too and will act on that belief.

A parental belief that adolescent sex is inevitable. Many parents who disapprove of teen sex have also concluded that it is as certain as death and taxes. Their approach to the subject will thus be double-edged: "Don't do it, but in case you do, use this condom." A few take their daughters to doctors or family-planning clinics to obtain birth control pills—*even if they have not become sexually active.* But in sexual matters, the venerable motto "Be prepared" communicates not merely precaution but expectation: "I know you're going to do it." Adolescents will get *that* message loud and clear and are likely to act accordingly.

Low grade-point average/low attachment to school. While school performance is affected by a variety of factors, a basic desire to do well in school reflects (among other things) a more hopeful outlook on the future and a willingness to put off immediate gratification for long-term goals. Teen sex, on the contrary, is a here-and-now event, usually reflecting ignorance of or little regard for consequences. This doesn't mean, of course, that every scholar is a bulwark of morality or that all who are not academically oriented are destined to be promiscuous. What ultimately matters is a person's commitment to basic values such as responsibility, respect for self and others, and concern about the effect of today's decisions on the future.

A history of physical or sexual abuse. These acts against children and adolescents violate their bodies, minds, and hearts. Sexual abuse creates a grossly distorted view of sexual behavior, destroys boundaries, and drives a deep sense of worthlessness into the emotions. Whether the abuse occurred in the distant or recent past, adolescents with this history need ongoing support, counseling, and prayer to help them develop healthy attitudes about sex and about themselves.

Frequent family relocations. Moving generally stresses both parents and adolescents (especially if the kids resent the decision). This can erode parental authority and distract parents from involvement with their children. Bonds to social supports such as church groups that help prevent sexual activity are severed by multiple moves. Loneliness and loss of friendships may lead some teenagers to use sexual activity to gain social acceptance. These issues should be considered by parents who are thinking about a possible relocation.

Only one parent in the household. Parenting was meant to be a team effort, and some risks will naturally increase when one parent is left to do all the protecting and monitoring alone. Some studies do indicate that adolescents living with a single parent are more likely to become sexually active than those living with both parents. Work and household demands can prevent single parents from being as involved and attentive as they need and want to be. And the divorce and desertion that sometimes lead to a one-parent home can make teens uncertain about the value of marriage as the setting for sexual activity and about the role of sexuality in parental relationships.

This increased risk does not mean that adolescent sex is inevitable in single-parent families. But it does place an additional responsibility on single parents to send their teenagers clear and consistent messages about sexuality. And it is one more reason for single parents to enlist as much support as they can.

Understand these specific factors that lower the risk for teen sex.

- Studies have shown that religious commitment consistently lowers the likelihood of adolescent sexual behavior.
- Educational accomplishment/commitment to school.
- Friends who have a similar commitment to abstinence.
- Presence of both parents in the home, especially the biological father. Positive involvement of a father with his teenage offspring has been shown to be an effective deterrent to early sexual activity.

- Parental and community values that support sexual abstinence until marriage and making them clearly known.
- A host of other interesting activities and passions. Adolescents who have other burning interests—such as earning academic honors; starting on a certain career path; traveling abroad; participating in ministry; or excelling in music, drama, sports, or other areas—will be less likely to allow premature sexual involvement to derail their plans and dreams. If they belong to a stimulating family that serves as a launching pad for fulfilling and fun activities, they will be less vulnerable to the boredom, purposelessness, and impaired self-concept that can sweep an adolescent toward unhealthy relationships.

Be a role model for the kinds of relationships you want your kids to develop with members of the opposite sex.

Parents should make every effort to keep their marriage intact and to nourish, enrich, and celebrate it, demonstrating respect and affection for each other on an ongoing basis. This gives adolescents a sense of security and a strong attachment to your values.

Fathers have a particularly important role to play. A boy who sees his father treat his mother with physical and verbal courtesies (which may range from fine points such as opening doors for her to broader strokes such as regularly seeking her opinions and advice and listening to and praising her) and is taught to do likewise will be more likely to carry this behavior and attitude into his own relationships with women. Girls who are consistently affirmed, cherished, and treated respectfully by their fathers aren't as likely to begin a desperate search for male affection that could lead to sexual involvement. Furthermore, they will expect appropriate behavior from the other men in their lives.

Single parents who are bringing up teenagers must repeatedly affirm them and create as stable a home life as possible. Values concerning nonmarital sex should be practiced as well as preached. A sexually active single parent or one who has a live-in partner is proclaiming in no uncertain terms that this activity is all right for teenagers as well.

Do your best to give your teen(s) a strong, positive sense of identity.

Teenagers who feel incomplete, inadequate, and unappreciated are more likely to seek comfort in a sexual relationship. But those with a life rich in relationships, family traditions, activities, interests, and—most of all—consistent love and affirmation are less likely to embark on a desperate search for fulfillment that could lead to unwise sexual decisions. Those who see their future as promising are more likely to protect themselves from physical or emotional damage arising from sexual activity. Those who have a healthy, productive faith in God are more likely to have deeply rooted reasons to respect and preserve the gift of sex and to respect rather than exploit others.

Create a special occasion to talk about abstaining from sex until marriage.

Early in your child's adolescence, plan a special evening (or a weekend away from home) during which the importance of preserving sex for marriage is the central focus. This time, shared by the teen and both parents, could culminate in the presentation of a special token—a necklace, ring, or key, for example—which symbolizes commitment to an abstinent lifestyle. It can be very meaningful if this item is carried or worn by your adolescent for years and then presented to his or her marriage partner on their wedding night.

If your adolescent has already had sexual experiences, make it clear that it is never too late to make a commitment to reserve sex for marriage.

This important concept is called "secondary virginity" and should be strongly encouraged among adolescents who have been sexually active. Some churches and parachurch organizations have formal programs organized specifically to promote the decision to remain sexually abstinent until marriage.

Continue sending healthy messages about sexuality throughout your son's or daughter's adolescent years.

The best time to build a solid foundation about sexuality is before puberty (see chapter 11, page 424, for more details). But even if you've never discussed the subject directly, you still send all kinds of signals about your attitudes over the course of time.

- ◆ Your adolescent needs to know you are comfortable with the subject. If you seem embarrassed, flustered, ashamed, or unapproachable whenever the topic comes up, your teenager will look elsewhere for input.
- ◆ Don't hesitate to broach the subject yourself. Adolescents are reluctant to bring up sexual subjects with their parents, and your chances of having one or more conversations may be nil unless you take the initiative.

Remember that the facts of sexuality are morally neutral. Anyone (even you) can teach them, but you have the opportunity to put the proper perspective on the subject.

- Be careful how you talk about someone else's sexual issues. News of a crisis pregnancy in another family can provide a powerful teachable moment, for good or ill. If you give a clear signal that the nonmarital sex was wrong but respond with compassion (and prayer) for the people involved, you make it clear that you can be approached if anyone at home has a problem. But if your response sounds something like "Don't you *ever* do something as stupid/shameful/evil as this," you could block potentially critical communication in the future. Crisis pregnancy centers routinely find that many of their most difficult clients are the daughters of good, moral, upright, churchgoing parents. "I can't tell Mom and Dad—it'll kill them (or they'll kill me)" is their common refrain as they head for the abortion clinic.

Talk about healthy and unhealthy relationships, and train your adolescent to avoid situations that increase the likelihood of a sexual incident.

Make them streetwise about the general course of relationships, dating, risky situations, and the ugly reality of date rape.

Encourage supervised, structured, nonpressuring group activities with the opposite sex as opposed to single dating situations, especially for adolescents in junior high and early high school. The object should be to learn how to talk and have fun without romantic expectations or sexual pressure. Group activities such as a church picnic or youth group outing are generally healthier than dances or other situations in which pairing up is necessary.

Talk to your adolescent about the qualities that ultimately matter in a relationship with a person of the opposite sex. Shared values (especially spiritual orientation), mutual respect, easy conversation, and enjoyment of everyday activities count far more heavily in the long run than good looks, money, popularity, or intense romantic attraction. Indeed, the best romances and marriages often come from relaxed friendships that progress gradually, with lots of conversations about everything under the sun. Accordingly, dating activities should be seen as experiences that are pleasant, enriching, and relaxing, not times of perpetual emotion.

Talk to your adolescent about unhealthy relationships, and have the courage to speak honestly if you see one developing:

- Relationships that ride a roller coaster of emotions—being madly in love one day, fighting like cats and dogs the next, crying and making up over and over—distract and drain a couple's time and energy and wear out everyone else for miles around. They also turn into difficult marriages.
- Relationships in which one person is intensely needy for the other, and thus clingy and smothering, are parasitic and draining. For example, a teenager who claims, "I'd kill myself if you ever left me" is putting unhealthy pressure on the other person.
- Relationships that have ongoing verbal disrespect in one or both directions are doomed.
- Relationships in which physical abuse occurs must be terminated immediately.

An important note: Unhealthy relationships carry a significant risk for sexual involvement.

Talk to your adolescent about physical demonstrations of affection. This is a natural desire when two people like each other, but how much (and how far) is okay? What about handling the desire—or some pressure—to push physical boundaries? You can lay down rules and regulations, but your adolescent needs a rationale for making good decisions without you. Here are some ideas that may help your teenager.

Set up your expectations and ground rules about dating in advance—well before your teenager asks if he or she can go out with someone.

Each family will have to set its own standards, but extremes are best avoided. Rigid parental control through high school and beyond (including selecting a limited number of "acceptable" candidates for courtship) stifles growth and independence and virtually guarantees rebellion. But a lax, anything-goes approach without parental guidelines is like handing the car keys to someone who has had no driver's training.

Think seriously about adopting a stepwise approach, especially for your adolescent's first socializing experiences with the opposite sex. Many parents have a policy that if someone wants to spend time with their son or daughter under age eighteen, the first step will be an evening at home with the family or joining in a family activity such as dinner and a movie or a ball game. This gives everyone a chance to get acquainted and broadcasts an important message: "The one you want to spend time with is deeply cherished by a family to whom you are accountable. We are happy to welcome you aboard, but nothing less than respectful and honorable behavior will do." Your expectation should be to make friends with the person, not to carry out a third-degree interrogation. In fact, you may develop a friendship that lasts long after your son or daughter has become interested in someone else. If anyone refuses or is extremely reluctant to spend time with the family in this way, however, consider it a red flag—and put further socializing with this person on hold.

If the first step goes well, group dating can be a good way to continue this process, assuming the other people involved are trustworthy. Many parents give the green light to single dating at age sixteen if there is ongoing evidence of maturity and responsibility and if the relationship appears basically healthy.

HOW MUCH TOUCH IS OKAY?: GUIDELINES FOR TEENAGERS ON DATES AND OTHER OCCASIONS

Establish clear and unequivocal respect for your body, your life, and your future. Decide *before* the conversation, *before* the date, *before* the relationship gets more serious that physical intimacy is reserved for the wedding night.

Respecting yourself (and the person you're with) means setting your own limits for physical contact. Stick to them, and be ready to defend them if necessary. Sexual pressure can become a major problem if you are unclear about your boundaries, if you are afraid of rejection, or if you are worried about being called a prude because you won't go past a certain point.

Physical contact—even something as simple as holding hands—may be interpreted in ways you don't intend. What to you means "I like you" or "I think you're okay" might be received as "I'm madly in love with you" or "I want to go further." It's better to express how you feel in *words,* rather than through unclear and potentially powerful physical messages.

Remember that the events that lead to sex are progressive. Think of a car gaining momentum as it coasts down a steep hill. Once a given level of intimacy has been reached, it is very difficult to back up to a more conservative one. Also it is more difficult to defend a boundary in the heat of the moment.

You are much better off setting very conservative limits for expressing affection (holding hands and perhaps a brief embrace or kiss) and progressing slowly, both emotionally and physically, in a relationship. This isn't old-fashioned but smart and realistic. More intense kissing, lying down together, touching personal areas, and increasing the amount of skin-to-skin contact sets off increasingly intense responses that are designed to lead to sexual intercourse—even when neither person intended this conclusion.

If you're not sure whether what you're doing physically is appropriate, ask yourself if you would be comfortable doing it in front of either set of parents or your pastor. Remember that the person you are with now will probably not be the person you will marry. Would you feel comfortable doing what you're doing in front of that person's future husband or wife?

If resisting physical intimacy is becoming more difficult, don't tempt fate. Stay away from situations where the two of you are alone together. Deliberately plan to be around other people or in places where nothing can happen. (It's difficult to have sex at a coffee shop.) Don't lie down on the sofa together to watch a video, and don't watch movies or videos with overt sexual content. Don't banter sexually provocative comments back and forth on the assumption that talk is safer than sex. Remember that your most important sexual organ is your mind, and where it goes your body will follow. (In some school sex-education programs, erotic conversations are actually recommended as an alternative to intercourse. Perhaps this idea works—on another planet.)

Whenever this activity begins, you have the right and responsibility to know specifics *every time* about the intended companion(s), the activity and its location, who's providing transportation, etc. Have a clear agreement about the expected time to arrive home. Whatever time you set, talk about the importance of letting you know if they're going to be home later than planned. *Consistency and reliability about keeping you posted should be a bigger issue than abiding by an absolute time limit.*

While they may complain outwardly about some of these ground rules, most adolescents will feel more secure when you are appropriately involved in the socializing/dating process. This should extend beyond setting limits to offering some encouragements as well, such as quietly offering a little extra cash to help enhance a special occasion. Even more important is making it abundantly clear that your teenager can call you anytime, day or night, from anywhere, if any help is needed—including a ride home from a date that has gone sour.

Talk candidly to your daughter(s) about the unpleasant topic of date rape and how best to avoid it.

The odds are at least one in ten (some researchers say one in four) that a woman will be coerced into unwanted sex at some point in her life. In four out of five cases, the rapist is someone the woman knows—a fellow student, a business acquaintance, a neighbor, and (all too often) a date.

For your part, aside from issuing specific recommendations and warnings (see sidebar, page 560), set some policies that will reduce the risk of a sexual catastrophe. First, veto any dating relationship between your adolescent daughter and someone who is more than two or three years older. The majority of teenage pregnancies involve relationships with men in their twenties or older. Object vigorously to her dating anyone who might have a position of authority or leverage over some part of her life, such as an employer, teacher, family friend, or business associate of yours. These situations are a setup for potential date rape.

Here are some additional cautions to pass along:

Talk explicitly to your son(s) about respect for members of the opposite sex and about sexual responsibility.

Your mission is to embed some very important values deeply into his mind and heart, not only for the teen years but for the rest of his life:

- *Never become a sexual predator.* A male who specifically sets out to maneuver women into sexual encounters might be called a playboy, red-hot lover, or Don Juan, but he's basically a jerk. If and when you see this behavior depicted in a movie or TV program or displayed by someone you know, let your son know that this is no way to treat any woman.

- *Never push a woman's physical boundaries.* If she says no to anything, even holding hands, that statement is final and not to be questioned.
- *Respect and maintain a woman's body, integrity, and future, even if she is inviting intimacy.* Without question one of the most difficult challenges for a healthy teenage male is to hold his ground when a desirable female flashes a bright and explicit green light. *Talk through this situation, including what he might say and how to walk away from this situation immediately.* It is important that he not be flustered or embarrassed and that he be able to decline the invitation in a way that expresses a desire to protect each person's health and future.
- *Approach any activity or relationship with the opposite sex with the intention of enhancing the other person's life and not leaving a wake of regrets.* Thinking in terms of protecting the other person's long-term well-being rather than merely satisfying immediate needs or desires is a sign of maturity. Some thoughtful conversations between parents and sons can help establish these grown-up attitudes.

Part Two: Sexual Crisis Situations

What if—despite your best intentions, careful conversations, and earnest efforts—your adolescent slips, slides, plunges headlong, or is coerced into sexual experiences long before his or her wedding night? How will you respond?

As unpleasant as it might seem, it is important to think about the possibilities ahead of time. Parents would be wise to spend some time alone together (or single parents with a trusted and mature friend) talking through these difficult and emotional "What if . . . ?" questions.

What If You Discover Your Adolescent Is Sexually Active?

Many contemporary resources for parents of teenagers make the wrong assumption that premarital sex is inevitable and recommend that parents help their kids make "mature" sexual decisions—by which they mean wearing condoms and taking other contraceptive precautions. Some parents respond by bringing their teenage (or even preteen) daughters to a doctor or a family-planning clinic for various birth control measures and insisting that no one goes out for the evening without a supply of condoms.

These actions may seem responsible and open-minded to some parents, but giving tacit approval to teenage sex is foolhardy for many reasons: the risks of STDs, distorted relationships, damaged identities, and disrupted marital bonding later in life, not to mention the moral issues involved.

For a reality check, consider whether a responsible parent would carry out this sort of damage control in response to other risky adolescent behaviors:

- If your twelve-year-old starts smoking, would you teach him to buy low-nicotine brands?
- If your fourteen-year-old wants to move out of your home and get an apartment with a bunch of adolescent friends, would you pay the rent?
- If your sixteen-year-old begins downing six-packs every weekend, would you include a few intoxicated practice sessions as part of her driver's training?
- If your eighteen-year-old decides to try IV drugs, would you supply sterile syringes and make sure he understands sterile injection techniques?

Each response would theoretically reduce risks but would also enable and promote misguided decisions.

PROTECTING YOURSELF FROM DATE RAPE

- You are much better off dating someone you know fairly well rather than someone who is a casual or chance acquaintance.
- In general, multicouple or group activities are less risky (and more fun) than single dates.
- Single dates—especially the first time with someone—should take place in public places. An invitation to a play or a sporting event is far preferable to "Come to my place to watch a video." Be especially leery of the suggestion that it would be nice "to go someplace private to talk." Enjoyable and meaningful conversation can happen anyplace where two people can hear each other's voices.
- Consider accepting a blind date only if the person carries a strong endorsement from someone you trust. Even then, this should not be a single date.

- Bring your own money. Paying your own way in the early stages of a relationship can help establish your independence. Even if your date picks up the tab, you might need cash for transportation home if things get out of hand.
- Stay sober. Alcohol and drugs cloud judgment and put you off guard and off-balance.
- Never leave a restaurant, party, or other get-together with someone you just met.
- Trust your instincts. If you don't feel right about the way the date is progressing, bail out. A little awkwardness is far better than a sexual assault. Call home at any time, and a parent will come get you, no questions asked.
- Avoid situations in which you do not feel on equal footing with your companion. If you feel unequal, intimidated, awestruck, or indebted to your date in

If facilitating adolescent sex is a bad idea, so is ignoring it. Equally unproductive is blowing up, finger wagging, lecturing, or name-calling. This is a significant family problem deserving a loving and thoughtful response. The goal is to contain the damage and coach your adolescent toward more healthy and rational decisions. Therefore:

Think before you react. It is normal to feel upset and disappointed, and you will probably need a couple of days to settle down. Setting a time to talk about what has happened may be more appropriate than risking a more volatile, spur-of-the-moment confrontation. Ultimately, emotions should fuel appropriate action rather than ongoing angry outbursts.

Ask open-ended questions ("Can you tell me about your relationship with _____ ?") rather than judgmental ones ("How could you have done this?" or "What in the world were you thinking?"). *Listen* to the whole story (or as much as you are given) before offering your viewpoint. Eye rolling, crossed arms, finger drumming, and editorial comments will shut off communication in a hurry.

Put the emphasis on the big picture. You want your son or daughter to have a long life, good health, meaningful relationships, and freedom from unnecessary turmoil. Premarital sexual activity jeopardizes all of those goals. Be prepared to ex-

(continued)

some way, your willingness to assert yourself may be weakened or delayed. Unhealthy situations include relationships with men more than two or three years older than you, an employer, a teacher, or someone to whom you or your family owes a debt.

◆ Beware of expensive gifts and lavish dates. Too many guys still carry the Neanderthal notion that picking up the tab for a nice evening entitles them to a sexual thank-you. If your date presents that message, don't hesitate to straighten him out. Declining a present that appears to have strings attached is a healthy way to set boundaries.

◆ Look out for the control freak, someone who insists on his way and ignores your likes and dislikes. If he shows contempt for your tastes in restaurants, movies, and music, he may also have little regard for your physical boundaries.

◆ Beware of the person who tries to isolate you from your other friends and your family or who constantly bad-mouths them. If he is extremely possessive and wants you all to himself, chances are he will eventually want all of you sexually as well.

◆ Steer clear of guys who tell raunchy jokes, listen to sexually explicit music, enjoy pornography, or make degrading comments about women. These men have an attitude disease about women and sexuality, and they don't belong in your life.

◆ Don't waste your time with anyone who won't accept your limits; who begs, pleads, and haggles for physical contact; or who trots out worn and pathetic lines such as "If you loved me, you'd do it" or "Trust me. . . ." Anyone who pressures you for sexual favors is a loser and an abuser and most certainly doesn't love you.

plain why. If you aren't convinced, review the reasons to postpone sexual involvement outlined on pages 544–550. Based on your broader range of experience and knowledge, you must tackle one of the most important jobs of parenting—opening young eyes to life's many consequences.

Don't tear down the teenager's sense of worth with comments such as "I am so ashamed of you" or "How could you act like such a jerk/tramp/lowlife?" This kind of rejection and judgment is what drives a lot of adolescents to sexual activity. A strong sense of identity and a conviction that one's future is worth protecting are deterrents to reckless or immoral behavior.

Stress the importance of new beginnings. Many teens who have been sexually active are willing to commit to secondary virginity, postponing any further sexual relationships until marriage. Actively encourage such a decision. Otherwise the feeling that "it doesn't matter anymore" may lead to more bad decisions.

Get medical input. A doctor's evaluation should be on the agenda to check for STDs (and for girls, to obtain a Pap test or perhaps a pregnancy test). *Choose your provider carefully.* It won't help your adolescent choose abstinence if he or she has a doctor who feels that teens can't control their sexual urges and who therefore emphasizes methods of contraception.

Strongly consider getting your son or daughter (and yourself) into counseling. A counselor whom you trust may be able to talk more candidly to your son or daughter about sexuality while promoting the decision to remain abstinent. Sexual activity may be a symptom of more basic problems that need ongoing work. Be prepared to put in time with the counselor yourself to deal with the causes and effects of this problem within your family.

Be prepared to take action appropriate for the situation and the age of your adolescent. Sexual activity in the elementary or middle-school grades deserves a highly concerted effort from parents, physicians, counselors, and others (a trusted youth-group leader at church, for example) to deal with the behavior and with underlying issues. A sexually active twelve- or thirteen-year-old has experienced a serious breach of physical and emotional boundaries, and considerable work will be needed to repair the damage.

You may need to have one or more candid conversations with your adolescent's partner(s) and, possibly, with the parents of the other individual(s) as well. More often than not, this will lead to one or more relationships being terminated and implementation of much tighter supervision and accountability. Parental schedules may need to be rearranged. If the situation involves an adult having sexual contact with a young adolescent, legal action may be necessary. (At the very least, the adult's sexual activity with a minor must be reported as required by law. Any indications of coercion and abuse must also be reported.)

Sexual activity in high school is no less significant, but the response (including medical and counseling input) should represent more of a parent-directed collaboration between the adolescent and the teachers, counselors, and physicians involved in his or her life. This does not mean abandoning efforts to curtail sexual contact but using strategies that stress a mature assessment of consequences. Dating and other socializing patterns that may have increased the chances for intimacy should be reassessed and restructured.

After the age of eighteen, as has been discussed in more detail in chapter 13, you are essentially dealing with a young adult. This will necessarily modify your approach because your position of authority has changed somewhat, especially if your son or daughter is beyond adolescence. However, you can and should offer your input and concerns, and you have the right to stipulate what behavior is appropriate under your roof. If you are still paying the bills for an older adolescent/young adult, you have the right to decide whether such support will continue if it is helping to finance a lifestyle that runs counter to your basic values.

WHAT IF YOUR ADOLESCENT DAUGHTER BECOMES PREGNANT?

Before considering how you might respond to the news that your unmarried teenager is pregnant, take a brief tour of the emotions and thought processes that are likely to be swirling through her mind and heart.

Your daughter's experience

Fear is an overriding emotion in nearly every teen pregnancy. "I can't tell my parents. They'll kill me!" "How can I finish school when I'm pregnant?" "My boyfriend will take off if I don't have an abortion." The adolescent with a crisis pregnancy probably sees nothing but loss on the horizon—loss of love, time, education, and physical health. Fear of one or more of these losses propels most of her other responses.

Denial is common, especially during the early weeks of pregnancy when the only indication might be one or more missed periods, a little fatigue, possibly some nausea, or even a positive pregnancy test. The longing for things to be "the way they were" may delay acknowledging the problem and seeking appropriate help for weeks or even months.

Ambivalence about being pregnant may cause fluctuating emotions. One day the only solution may appear to be an abortion, while the next the prospect of a cuddly baby may seem appealing. Time spent with a friend's crying newborn may jolt the emotions in yet another direction. Indecision and apparent lack of direction in such an overwhelming situation are common.

Guilt. When a pregnancy results from the violation of moral values held since childhood, an adolescent will usually feel ashamed and worthless. Her growing abdomen becomes a constant reminder of her failure.

Pressure to have an abortion. This may come from several directions. A teenager may be weighing what appears to be a dismal future of hardship and remorse against a quick and relatively inexpensive procedure. "No one needs to know, and I can get on with my life." A boyfriend (who may be dealing with his own fear and guilt, along with concerns about future financial responsibilities) may exert considerable pressure to abort, even offering to pay the bill. He may also threaten to bail out of the relationship if the pregnancy continues. Some parents, worried about their daughter's future or perhaps their own reputation in the community (or even the prospect of being responsible for the actual child rearing), may also find abortion attractive.

The "cuddly doll" mentality. Some unmarried teenage girls see their pregnancy unrealistically as an escape from a difficult and unpleasant home situation. They may envision a baby as a snuggly companion who will require roughly the same amount of care as a new puppy, not realizing the amount of energy a newborn will take from her without giving much in return (especially during the first few weeks). Teens with this mind-set need to adjust their expectations of child rearing—not to drive them to abort but to help them make more appropriate plans. If adoption is not chosen as a solution, some careful groundwork should be laid to prevent serious disappointment and even the mother's abuse of the baby.

Your experience as parent(s)

If a pregnancy is an upheaval for a teenager, it is also no picnic for her parents. Discovering that your adolescent daughter is pregnant is a trial like few others, and reactions—fear for her future, denial, guilt—may parallel hers with equal intensity. Parents are likely to feel anger in a number of directions—anger toward their daughter for being careless, not taking their advice, not using good judgment, and disobeying both them and God. They may be angry with the boy (or man) involved, who has violated their trust and their daughter's well-being. They may be angry with themselves for any number of reasons: They were too narrow or too permissive, too busy or too tired to tune into their daughter's world for the past several months—and now look what has happened.

Anger is such a classic parental response that the daughter may try to keep her pregnancy a secret. In fact, many states allow minors to obtain abortions without parental consent or knowledge, based on the presumption that the mother and/or father will be so disruptive and unreasonable that the teenage daughter can better deal with her pregnancy without them.

Your most difficult (and character-building) task is to show how much you really love your daughter, even though you don't approve of what she has done. The classical Chinese symbol for the word *crisis* has special meaning in this situation. It consists of two symbols: one representing *danger,* the other, *opportunity.* The danger is that your response to the pregnancy may open wounds in your family that will take years to heal, if they ever do. Your opportunity is rising to the occasion in such a way as to earn your daughter's lifelong respect and gratitude.

Your mission is to remain calm when panic is in the air and to be more concerned about her embarrassment than your own, which may be enormous. It is to be comforting when you feel like saying, "I told you so!" It is to help organize everyone's conflicting impulses into a thoughtful plan in which the family can work as a team. It is to guide the baby's father into responsible participation if he is willing, when you would just as soon enlist him in the Marines. Most of all, it is to channel your intense feelings into productive outlets—through planning, prayer, vigorous exercise, and blowing off steam to a tolerant friend rather than at your child.

Your daughter will need help, and lots of it, but not a total rescue. She must make a fast transition to adulthood, a state about which you know a great deal more than she does. You must resist the temptation to throw her out or keep her stuck in childish irresponsibility by making all of her decisions. She needs to face all the tough decisions and demands of pregnancy but with you at her side as a confident ally.

You may have one very critical decision of your own to make. What role do you intend to take in the child's upbringing? If the mother-to-be is very young, you may see another parenting job on the horizon and perhaps resent the idea. Or you may be excited about having the nest occupied for several more years.

Your feelings on this issue need to be sorted out, and your course of action planned accordingly.

In the midst of your family's deliberations, be sure ample consideration is given to adoption. A pregnant teenager may be torn by the thought that "if I had the baby, I couldn't handle giving her away." But adoption can provide a livable solution for all parties involved. The baby is raised by a couple who intensely desire to be parents, and the birth mother can pick up and move on to complete her education and career goals, postponing her own parenting until she is ready.

You will also need to address the question of abortion. Many voices will be calling your daughter to the abortion clinic, claiming this simple procedure will bring the crisis to a swift and straightforward resolution. Some parents may be tempted to give this option serious consideration for similar reasons. But before lending encouragement to ending the pregnancy this way, return to the first chapter in this book and read the description of the first weeks of life after conception.

Abortion is not a procedure like an appendectomy that eradicates a piece of diseased tissue. It ends a human life that is designed to develop in a continuous process from conception through birth and beyond. Because this life is unseen for now, its identity and significance may pale in comparison to the problems and concerns of the moment. That developing person, whose life is in the hands of her mother and those influencing her, cannot speak for herself. Like it or not, even under the most trying circumstances, that new person is not better off dead.

Your daughter should consider making an appointment with a local crisis pregnancy center (CPC) in order to sort through the issues, gather information, and consider her options in a compassionate setting. Even if she has strong opinions about what her course of action should be, a CPC can be an extremely valuable resource. Services available at most CPCs include a realistic assessment of the long-range impact of each option, ongoing counseling support, assistance with medical and other referrals, and maternity clothes and baby supplies. Many CPCs also provide some on-site medical services such as prenatal screening exams. All of these services are normally provided at no charge. (For the name and location of a CPC in your area, contact 1-800-A FAMILY.)

It is important that capable and compassionate medical care be maintained throughout the pregnancy. Many pregnant teens delay or avoid seeking appropriate care for a variety of reasons. *But adolescents have higher rates of complications related to pregnancy and childbirth compared with older women.* Most of these problems can be significantly reduced (or at least anticipated) with consistent prenatal visits and appropriate medical follow-up.

WHAT IF YOUR ADOLESCENT SON IS INVOLVED IN A PREGNANCY?

If your son has had a sexual relationship from which a pregnancy has resulted, remember that he will probably be experiencing many of the same emotions as his girlfriend, including fear, guilt, and ambivalence. In addition, he will feel considerable conflict and confusion over the role he should play.

Usually the relationship with the mother-to-be has not, until this point, involved any long-range plans. Now he must make a decision about the level of commitment he intends to assume, and the issues are significant. What does he owe this young woman? Can he walk away from this situation? Should he make a lifelong commitment to her because of this unplanned pregnancy?

He does not bear the biological consequences, of course, and the mother of the baby has the legal right to have an abortion or carry the pregnancy to term with or without his input. This may leave him with the impression that he has no control over the unplanned pregnancy and therefore no responsibility for it. As his parents, you are one step further removed from the situation and may have similar questions about the role you should play.

Above all, your son will need encouragement and guidance to assume the appropriate level of responsibility for his role in the pregnancy. He should not be allowed to abandon his girlfriend with a cavalier, hit-and-run attitude. "It's her problem now" or "She should have protected herself" or even "She should just get an abortion" are shallow and disrespectful responses to a serious situation. Pushing for a quick marriage may seem honorable but is probably unwise. Teenage matrimony carries with it very short odds of long-term success, and the combination of immaturity, lack of resources, and the intense demands of a newborn baby will usually strain an adolescent relationship to the breaking point.

In a best-case scenario, the families of both participants will cooperate to find a productive balance among several tasks: facing the consequences of the sexual relationship, accountability of adolescents to the adults in both families, short- and long-term planning, and mature decision making.

Your son will need encouragement to acknowledge his responsibility to the girl's family and to accept with humility their response, whether it is measured or angry. All of you may have to face the possibility that the other family will choose to deal with the pregnancy on their own, even if you are willing to participate in the process. And if that decision includes forbidding your son to have further contact with someone about whom he cares very deeply, he will have to find the strength to abide by the other family's wishes. If he is allowed to continue their relationship and support her when the going gets tough, clear ground rules (including abstaining from sexual contact) will need to be established and respected.

Having a pregnant girlfriend is tough and painful. But it also can be an opportunity for your son to mature, to find out what he is made of. In the long run, the pregnant adolescent girl isn't the only one who has to make important choices.

WHAT IF YOUR ADOLESCENT ISN'T SURE OF HIS OR HER SEXUAL ORIENTATION?

Few parenting concerns during adolescence generate as much emotional turbulence as the possibility that one's child might have a homosexual orientation. For many parents, especially those deeply committed to traditional values, the thought of a child becoming involved in homosexual relationships raises unsettling moral questions. For some, reactions to homosexuality extend into the darker emotions of hatred and loathing.

In contrast, many influential voices in media, government, and health care state that sexual orientation is inborn and unchangeable; however, that has never been proven. In their view, if your child is destined to be attracted to members of the same sex, nothing can or should be done about it other than to accept it. Gay and lesbian activists proclaim that adolescents who feel same-sex inclinations should explore, embrace, and celebrate their homosexual identity and that their parents should celebrate it along with them.

The vast majority of parents, while neither hating homosexual individuals nor applauding homosexuality, deeply desire to see their adolescents eventually bear and rear children. They anticipate the joys of watching the next generation's courtships, marriages, and family life. Therefore, contemplating a child's involvement in homosexual acts and in unconventional relationships for decades into the future is enough to provoke considerable concern, if not ongoing insomnia.

What should you do if your adolescent's sexual orientation is uncertain or if he or she has had one or more homosexual experiences?

Don't assume that characteristics that fall outside your gender expectations indicate homosexual tendencies. A boy who has a slight build and prefers painting over pitching or fabrics over football may disappoint a father who envisioned bringing up a burly, athletic hero. A daughter who isn't shapely or petite and who excels at basketball rather than ballet may not fulfill a mother's expectations of magazine-cover femininity. But both need unconditional affirmation of their worth from parents who accept and encourage their particular strengths as appropriate.

What may drive a teenager toward same-gender sexuality is *ongoing rejection* from parents or peers. Cutting remarks about a child's or teenager's size, shape, or other attributes merely reinforce the idea that "I'm different from everyone else." If genuine acceptance is eventually offered by someone with a homosexual orientation, the teenager may conclude that "I'm different, so that must mean I'm gay—and furthermore, I've always been this way."

Remember that adolescents may feel transient confusion about sexual identity, especially if they have had a sexual experience with someone of the same gender. Whether as a phase of rebellion and experimentation or as the result of sexual abuse in childhood, your child may have one or more same-sex encounters, which may raise questions in an adolescent about his or her ultimate sexual destination. It is therefore important for children and teens who have had such experiences to receive appropriate counseling that (among other things) will clarify the fact that these events have not destined them to a lifelong homosexual orientation.

If you discover that your child has had one or more homosexual encounters, whether coerced or voluntary, you need to remain his strongest ally. A child or young adolescent who has suffered sexual abuse needs to know that what happened was not his fault and that you are not in any way ashamed of him. He will need comfort, reassurance that his physical boundaries are now secure, and time to sort out his experiences, both with you (which will be very uncomfortable) and with a professional counselor. It is crucial that the damage done by the abuser to a child's sexual identity and sense of self-worth be contained.

If the activities involved one or more peers and were not the result of coercion, your response should parallel what was outlined in connection with premarital heterosexual activity (see page 559). You will need to make a particular effort to maintain a balance between taking a clear stand for moral principles and demonstrating that you and your adolescent are still on the same team. Harsh expressions of revulsion and condemnation are counterproductive, will probably confirm an adolescent's feelings of alienation, and may very well provoke more of the same behavior. At the same time, a resigned and passive nonresponse ("Nothing can be done about this, so I might as well get used to it") squanders an opportunity to bring about change. As with other early and midadolescent sexual activity, conversation and counseling with someone who shares your values is in order.

If your late adolescent moves into adulthood and becomes overtly involved in a homosexual lifestyle, your balancing act will become even more delicate—but no different from the approach you must take to any other of your grown child's choices that you find ill advised or contrary to your values. It is possible and necessary—but at times also very difficult—to express love and acceptance without condoning the behavior. You have the right and responsibility to insist that sexual activity be off-limits under your roof. But decisions about a number of other situations will be tough. For example, should your adult offspring's homosexual lover be included at the family Thanksgiving dinner?

You must commit to patience, prayer, and perseverance. You may shed rivers of tears, but you must not allow animosity or bitterness to take root in your emotions. Most of all, you will need generous amounts of wisdom, because you may be the only voice expressing love while encouraging your child to begin the difficult process of disengaging from ongoing homosexual behavior.

WHAT IF YOUR DAUGHTER IS THE VICTIM OF A SEXUAL ASSAULT?

In the sidebar on page 560, several recommendations were made that could reduce an adolescent's risk of date rape. But even when appropriate precautions have been taken, it is possible that your daughter will be the victim of a sexual assault. The odds are at least one in ten (some researchers say one in four) that she will be coerced into unwanted sex at some point in her life. As unpleasant as it may be to discuss this topic, she should know what (and what not) to do if this occurs, whether the attacker is an acquaintance or a stranger.

First, she should get to a safe place as quickly as possible and then contact a family member and the police *immediately*. In the emotional aftermath of an assault, the urge to deny what has happened may cause a victim to wait days or weeks to report it. But doing so reduces her credibility and makes prosecution of the attacker more difficult. Reporting the assault right away can help her regain a sense of control, obtain proper medical care, and guarantee personal safety. Furthermore, it is important that all physical evidence of the attack be preserved. She should not shower, bathe, douche, or even change clothes, even though it is normal to feel an overwhelming urge to rid herself of every trace of the attack.

Because of embarrassment, fear of reprisal, or apprehension over dealing with police, doctors, and attorneys, only 5 to 10 percent of rapes are reported. The attacker has assumed that he could have his way without any consequences, and he must not be allowed that unjust satisfaction. He has committed a serious crime and deserves punishment for it. Furthermore, most rapists are repeat offenders, and taking action may help prevent someone else from being assaulted.

The officers who take the report will need to ask about specific details of the rape that may be painful to answer but are necessary for proper documentation of the crime. It is important that your daughter be completely honest and candid about what happened, even if she feels that she made a mistake or even violated her own moral standards prior to the rape. If her story changes later on, the case against the attacker will be weakened.

The police will advise that a medical evaluation be carried out, even if your daughter does not believe she was injured. A thorough examination is necessary to assess her physical condition, to collect important evidence, and to provide counseling regarding the possibility of pregnancy or sexually transmitted disease. This should be done in a hospital emergency room where the physicians and staff are equipped to deal with rape victims or in a rape treatment center (assuming that its services include appropriate medical evaluations).

As with the police report, parts of this examination will be difficult and uncomfortable, especially if she has not had a pelvic exam before. But cooperation with the physician and nurses is important, and the temporary discomfort will be worth the long-term benefits of proper medical care.

Finally, your daughter should receive counseling from an individual who is qualified to deal with the impact of the rape experience on her life. This event cannot be ignored and will not be forgotten. She will need both time and support to recover from the physical, emotional, and spiritual aftereffects of a sexual assault. Many powerful emotions must be sorted out, including guilt or mistaken feelings of blame.

It is important that your own anger and frustration not boil over and cause more damage. This is not the time for comments such as "I told you so" or "How could you have let this happen?" Even if your daughter used extremely poor judgment or flatly disobeyed your explicit instructions, she in no way "asked for" or deserved a sexual assault. She will need your help to rebuild her sense of dignity and worth. Without this important repair work, she will be vulnerable to sexual pressure and abuse in the future.

WHAT IF YOUR SON IS THE VICTIM
OF A SEXUAL ASSAULT?

The vast majority of information and advisories regarding rape are directed toward women, who are most commonly—but not always—the victims of sexual assault. In a less frequent (but no less serious) situation, an adolescent or young adult male may be the sexual target of one or more other men. Should this happen to your son, you will need to muster all the same strength and support you would offer a daughter who had been attacked.

In particular, it is critical that appropriate medical assessment, evidence collection, preventive measures for sexually transmitted diseases, and counseling be provided in a timely fashion, just as in the case of a female victim. If possible, the perpetrator(s) should be identified, arrested, and prosecuted. Even if a parent learns about an assault months or years after it took place, medical care and counseling should be provided. It is particularly important that such an event not be allowed to confuse an adolescent's sense of sexual identity or integrity.

NOTES
1. R. M. Cavanaugh, "Anticipatory Guidance for the Adolescent: Has It Come of Age?" *Pediatrics in Review* (1994): 15.
2. B. D. Whitehead, "The Failure of Sex Education," The Atlantic Monthly, October 1995, 73.
3. On occasion, the father's parent(s) may assume this responsibility.
4. D. R. Mishell, "Contraception," *The New England Journal of Medicine* 320 (1989): 777–787.
Elise F. Jones and Jacqueline D. Forrest, "Contraceptive Failure Rates Based on the 1988 NSFG," *Family Planning Perspectives* 24, no. 1 (January/February 1992): 12–19.
5. William Cates, Jr., and Katherine M. Stone, "Family Planning, Sexually Transmitted Diseases and Contraceptive Choice: A Literature Update—Part I," *Family Planning Perspectives* 24, no. 2 (March/April 1992): 78, table 1.

Sexually Transmitted Diseases (STDs) among Adolescents

In the United States, 12 million people are newly infected with STDs each year, and more than 60 percent of these are younger than age twenty-five.[1]

One in five Americans between fifteen and fifty-five is infected with one or more sexually transmitted viruses.[2] Many of these people are unable to rid themselves of the virus(es) they have acquired, and some are plagued with recurrent, prolonged, or even lethal manifestations of their infection.

Pelvic inflammatory disease (PID), in which one or more sexually transmitted organisms invade the uterus, tubes, ovaries, pelvis, or all of these, is diagnosed in more than one million women in the United States each year. More than 75 percent of the infections occur in women younger than twenty-five, and at least one in five cases involves an adolescent—and the rate at which teenagers are affected continues to rise. Teenagers do not respond as well to oral antibiotic therapy as older women, and more than two hundred thousand women require hospitalization for PID each year in the U.S. at an estimated cost of $5 billion.[3]

At least 10 to 12 percent of women become infertile after a single significant episode of PID, usually because of scarring of the fallopian tubes. Repeated infections increase this risk dramatically.

Adolescent girls are particularly susceptible to STDs. *A fifteen-year-old is ten times more likely to develop PID than a twenty-four-year-old involved in the same type of sexual behavior.* This vulnerability is the result of two physiologic realities. First, the cervix (opening of the uterus) in a teenager is covered by a lining of cells called **ectropion** that is more fragile, produces more mucus, and is more easily invaded by organisms that cause STDs than is the lining in an older woman. After a woman has had a baby or reaches her twenties, the ectropion is replaced by a tougher lining that is more resistant to infection. Second, during the first several months after the onset of menses, many menstrual cycles occur without ovulation. This causes the mucus in the cervix to be thinner and thus a friendlier environment for STD organisms.

When STDs are discussed in health-education classes and public-service messages geared to teenagers, the emphasis is on preventing the transmission of HIV/AIDS. As serious as this epidemic is, a number of other significant predators should not be ignored.

Syphilis is caused by a spiral-shaped organism known as a spirochete. It is usually curable with penicillin, but resistant strains are now emerging. The initial sign of infection is a single painless ulcer, or **chancre,** which appears in the genital area (or wherever the initial point of contact was made). The chancre heals in two to six weeks without treatment and may even go unnoticed by the infected individual. A secondary phase occurs in six weeks to six months, producing a mild (and nonspecific) rash or more serious changes in various parts of the body. If untreated, a third stage may develop years later, with life-threatening heart disease and central nervous system disturbances, even insanity. Syphilis can be detected by a blood test. If the initial screen is positive, additional tests will be necessary to confirm the diagnosis and determine the proper course of treatment.

Gonorrhea is a bacterial infection that affects more than one million Americans each year. Symptoms in males tend to be dramatic: a thick discharge from the penis accompanied by significant pain during the passage of urine. Many infected women have no symptoms, while others experience problems ranging in severity from mild discharge to abscesses in the pelvis requiring surgical treatment. In some cases extensive scarring of a woman's tubes may occur. Depending upon the extent of damage, infertility may result.

Once uniformly responsive to penicillin, gonorrhea strains resistant to penicillin are now present in all fifty states.

Chlamydia infection has risen from obscurity in the 1970s to become the most common bacterial STD in the United States. Estimates of infection rates range from 20 to 40 percent of sexually active singles, with the highest rates among teenagers. Assuming it is detected (which may not always occur because symptoms may be subtle or nonexistent), a chlamydia infection normally responds to antibiotics.

In men chlamydia often causes a discharge from the penis that tends to be more watery and less profuse than with gonorrhea. Pain with the passage of urine is also less severe. In women chlamydia may produce vague pelvic discomfort, pain with urination, or no symptoms. Whether or not symptoms are present, chlamydia can infect and damage a woman's reproductive organs and create a significant risk of infertility later in life. A single teenage sexual encounter that transmits chlamydia may cause untold emotional pain and major medical bills years later if a woman is unable to bear children.

Herpes simplex virus (HSV) is notorious for a property it shares with a number of other viral organisms: Once it enters a person's body, it has the capacity for reoccurrence, although the manifestations of this prolonged infection may vary considerably from person to person. HSV type 1 typically causes cold sores or fever blisters around the mouth or nose (see photo on page A28), although it can also cause genital infections through oral-genital contact. HSV type 2 is most commonly spread by genital sexual contact.

The first outbreak of genital herpes is usually the worst, with an irritating, sometimes painful, cluster of blisters that gradually crust and fade over ten to fourteen days. Men usually see an eruption on the penis, although they may not realize its significance because it resolves without treatment. Women are frequently unaware of the infection, but some suffer extreme discomfort in the genital area. The virus is sometimes transmitted through the skin or mucous membranes *even when no blisters are present.* This undoubtedly contributes to its high prevalence. About one in three sexually active single people are infected.

At least 70 percent of those infected will have recurrent outbreaks for months or years. Stress, intercourse, or other local irritation of the genital area (even from tight clothing) may trigger an outbreak, although these normally are not as severe as the first episode. Recurrences may occur several years after the initial contact, often causing concern and consternation in a subsequent relationship. For many the primary discomfort from a herpes infection is psychological, arising from the knowledge that this virus can never be eradicated and that any future sexual partner will probably become infected as well.

Antiviral medications such as **acyclovir** (Zovirax), **valcyclovir** (Valtrex), and **famcyclovir** (Famvir) can limit the severity of the first or subsequent herpes outbreaks, assuming that they are started at the outset of the eruption. When taken on a daily basis, they can reduce the frequency of recurrences, although this treatment can become expensive on a long-term basis.

Herpes outbreaks are rarely life threatening for adults. Unfortunately the same cannot be said for newborns. A baby born vaginally to a mother with HSV may be infected during delivery if there is a herpes outbreak on the mother's genital area, especially if it's her first HSV infection. If the newborn is infected with HSV, the results can be disastrous. About 20 percent of infected infants will have surface (skin and mucous membrane) involvement only. In the other 80 percent, the virus spreads throughout the body and central nervous system, with a strong likelihood of major consequences including blindness, mental retardation, and death.

Genital warts are caused by the **human papilloma virus (HPV).** This is one of the most common sexually transmitted diseases in the United States. (One study of sexually active college females who visited the student health center showed an HPV infection rate of over 40 percent.) Like herpes and many other STDs, HPV can be transmitted by an individual who has no visible signs of disease. *Condoms offer little, if any, protection against HPV, a fact that has not been widely publicized.*

Many who are infected with HPV never have any problem with it. However, the virus frequently causes soft, wartlike growths in the genital area. Small growths, which are usually the most common, respond to topical chemical treatment, but they can become quite large in size, requiring laser or other methods to remove them.

Of greater concern is that HPV has been clearly demonstrated to be the underlying cause of most cervical cancer and is implicated in cancers of the vulva, vagina, and penis. While the male cancer is rare, cancer of the cervix causes more than five thousand deaths each year. This cancer risk is specifically increased by early onset of sexual activity and contact with multiple partners. The cancer is also more aggressive among teenagers than in older adults; a disturbing recent trend has been an increasing number of precancerous abnormalities of the cervix among adolescent women. The aggressiveness of HPV appears to be enhanced by nicotine—yet one more reason to avoid smoking. Any woman who has had genital warts (or for that matter, any woman who has been or is sexually active) should have regular Pap smears to detect early changes in the cervix, which can be treated before they develop into a cancerous growth.

Acquired immune deficiency syndrome (AIDS) is caused by the **human immunodeficiency virus (HIV).** The virus is transmitted through semen, vaginal secretions, blood, and breast milk. Most HIV infections are transmitted during sexual contact (in all forms—heterosexual or homosexual, vaginal, oral, or anal), through accidental injection of infected blood, contaminated needles, or by transfer from infected mother to baby during pregnancy. A small number of cases in infants have been attributed to nursing from an infected mother. Some early cases of HIV resulted from transfusions of blood from infected donors. Revised blood-bank procedures and scrupulous screening of donors have reduced the likelihood of this happening to less than one in one hundred thousand.

At highest risk for this disease are people who have many sexual partners (especially male homosexuals) and/or who are intravenous drug users. But HIV infections are not limited to those with high-risk lifestyles. *The virus can be transmitted during a single sexual encounter,* even to someone having sex for the first time. For a variety of reasons, the rate of new HIV infections has been steadily rising among heterosexuals, especially adolescents.

After causing an initial flulike illness, HIV multiplies quietly within the immune system for years. The infected individual may feel perfectly well during this period but will be capable of transmitting the disease to others. Eventually the virus destroys the competence of the immune system, resulting in full-blown AIDS. Without adequate defenses, the body becomes vulnerable to a variety of devastating infections and some forms of cancer.

Screening tests for HIV detect a person's antibody response to the virus, not the virus itself. Once HIV enters the body, it will take a minimum of three weeks, and in some cases many months, to generate a detectable antibody response. An infected individual whose blood tests remain negative for HIV can still transmit the virus to others.

Hepatitis B is a viral infection of the liver transmitted through the same mechanisms as HIV. The majority of cases resolve completely following a flulike illness with fever, nausea, and jaundice (a yellow discoloration of skin caused by a buildup of a compound called bilirubin, which an inflamed liver does not process normally). However, about 5 percent develop a chronic infection that can lead to cirrhosis (scarring) or even cancer of the liver. Chronic carriers—there are about one million in the United States—can transmit the virus to sexual partners or from mother to baby during pregnancy or delivery. Most babies infected at birth become chronic carriers as well and risk developing long-term complications if not treated.

Hepatitis B is the only STD for which a reliable vaccine has been developed. Because efforts to vaccinate those at highest risk did not substantially reduce the number of new cases and because many cases of hepatitis B occur in people who do not have a history of risky behavior, current recommendations call for immunizing all infants, children, and adolescents against this virus.

In the midst of an enchanted evening at a secluded rendezvous, with romance in the air and hormones in high gear, it's easy to forget (or ignore) the unpleasant facts about STDs—including how prevalent they are. In most instances, an infected sexual partner will show absolutely no evidence of any illness. He or she may be a wonderful, intelligent person—dressed for success, impeccably groomed, attractive, and well mannered—but still capable of transmitting an organism that can impair health or threaten life itself. In other words, there is no way to look at a potential partner and determine if sex with that person might be safe or not. Furthermore, as is discussed in the section entitled "Safe(r) sex isn't" (page 547), the protection offered by condoms is far from foolproof. When dealing with these diseases, the only sex that is safe takes place within a mutually exclusive relationship with an uninfected life partner.

NOTES
1. U.S. Public Health Service, *Healthy People 2000: National Health Promotion and Disease Prevention Objectives* (Washington, D.C., U.S. Department of Health and Human Services, GPO, 1990).
2. P. Donovan, *Testing Positive: Sexually Transmitted Disease and the Public Health Response* (New York: The Alan Guttmacher Institute, 1993).
3. G. R. Newkirk, "Pelvic Inflammatory Disease: A Contemporary Approach," *American Family Physician* 53 (1996): 112–135.

Tobacco, Alcohol, and Drug Abuse— Resisting the Epidemic

Not too many generations ago, our ancestors regularly watched in horror as bubonic plague, diphtheria, smallpox, and other lethal epidemics swept through their towns and families, taking rich and poor alike to the grave. Today, the consumption of alcohol, tobacco, and a host of addicting drugs has become a modern-day plague ravaging many of our youngest citizens.

Like the scourges of old, the drug epidemic spreads without regard to economic, racial, geographic, educational, religious, or family boundaries. More recently, it has become particularly aggressive among preteen children, dipping freely into the primary grades for new consumers. While all of us should work and pray toward ending this blight in our nation and our communities, we must ultimately be concerned about preventing it from moving across our own doorsteps.

No child whom you bring into the world will be automatically immune from the drug epidemic. Therefore you must work diligently over the years to "drugproof" your child(ren). This project involves various tasks that cannot be tackled haphazardly. First, you must understand what draws kids toward drugs. You also need basic information about the substances that are currently prowling your neighborhood. You should become familiar with the signs that a drug problem might be developing in your home. Finally, and most important, you must be prepared to take long-term preventive measures and to respond appropriately if one or more of the toxins should breach your family's defenses.

WHY DO KIDS START (AND CONTINUE) USING DRUGS?

Four factors set the stage for adolescent drug use:

- *Attitudes of parents* toward tobacco, alcohol, and other substances. Children learn what they live. Smoking, drinking, and other drug-related behaviors among parents will usually be duplicated in their children.
- *Attractiveness of drugs.* Smoking and drinking are widely promoted as habits enjoyed by sophisticated, fun-loving, attractive, and sexy people— what most adolescents long to become. Illegal drugs are "advertised" by those using them in an adolescent's peer group.
- *The high induced by drugs.* If drug use wasn't pleasurable, it would be relatively easy to keep kids and harmful substances separated. But the reality is that many kids enjoy the way they feel on drugs—at least for a while.
- *Availability of drugs.* Finding drugs is not difficult for children and adolescents in most communities, but tougher local standards can help keep drugs out of less-determined hands.

Once the stage is set, the following factors exert a more direct influence on who will and who won't try drugs. The consequences of early experiences (whether pleasant or disagreeable), the drug used, and one's genetic predisposition will determine whether a problem is nipped in the bud or blossoms into addiction.

Peer pressure. Peers play a huge role at each stage of a child's or adolescent's drug experience—whether resisting them, experimenting, becoming a user, or confronting withdrawal and recovery. The need for peer acceptance is especially strong during the early adolescent years and can override (or at least seriously challenge) the most earnest commitments. "Just say no" may not mean a whole lot when smoking, drinking, or taking drugs determines who is included in highly esteemed ranks of the inner circle.

There are three obvious implications:

- *It is important that kids find their niche in the right peer group(s),* among friends who are not only committed to positive values (including drug-free lifestyles) but also involved in worthwhile and enjoyable pursuits.
- *You may have to intervene if your adolescent (especially in the early teen years) is hanging out with the wrong crowd.* This is discussed in detail in chapter 13 (see page 509).

◆ *Children and adolescents with a healthy, stable identity and an appropriate sense of independence will be more resistant to peer pressure.* This will be discussed later.

Curiosity. Unless your family lives in total isolation, your child will be aware of smoking, alcohol, and drug use well before adolescence from discussions at school, watching TV and movies, or direct observation. Some curiosity is inevitable: *What do these things feel like?* Whether this leads to sampling and whether an experiment progresses to addiction will depend on the individual's mind-set and physical response.

Thrill seeking. This desire for excitement is in all of us to some degree and propels us toward all kinds of activities: skydiving, roller coasters, movies (where sights and sounds are "bigger than life"), fireworks displays, sporting events, and so on. Some of these are more risky than others, but none require chemical alteration of the senses to be satisfying. Unfortunately, many children and adolescents seek drug experiences to produce thrills that normal consciousness can't duplicate.

Rebellion. Wayward children may engage in smoking, alcohol, and drug use as a show of "independence" from family norms and values.

Escape from life/relief from pain. This is often the driving force in drug use. If everyday life seems boring, meaningless, oppressive, or painful (physically and/or emotionally), alcohol and drugs may appear to offer a powerful time-out. The strongest resistance to drug abuse therefore arises from an ongoing sense of joy and contentment that transcends circumstances. These attitudes are usually acquired, not inborn. Early positive experiences in the family and an active, wide-awake relationship with God play the most important roles in molding such attitudes.

THE "GATEWAY" DRUGS: TOBACCO, ALCOHOL, MARIJUANA, AND INHALANTS

Few children and adolescents start a career of drug use by snorting cocaine or injecting heroin. The path usually begins with products from the corner store—tobacco, alcohol, or household products that are inhaled—or with marijuana, which some mistakenly consider safe.

Tobacco—the smoking gun

No drug habit has a greater negative impact on our national health than tobacco, which is implicated in more than four hundred thousand deaths in the United States each year. The list of disorders caused or aggravated by tobacco is staggering. Among these diseases are cancers of the lung, mouth, vocal cords, and other organs; chronic lung disease; asthma; ulcers; clogging of the vessels that supply blood to the heart and other organs, causing heart attacks, strokes, amputations, and premature deaths. Babies and children who breathe smokers' exhaust at home are at risk for respiratory infections, asthma, and sudden infant death syndrome (SIDS).

The vast majority of diseases related to tobacco take their toll later in life after subjects have had years of exposure. So why is adolescent tobacco use such a major concern?

Nicotine is extremely addictive. Nicotine's hook is set quickly and, once in place, is extremely difficult to remove. Some research indicates that smoking as few as two to four cigarettes during adolescence imparts at least a 66 percent risk for becoming a regular smoker. A few hits of nicotine produce a unique combination of relaxation and alertness, and withdrawal produces unpleasant physical and psychological symptoms. As a result, fewer than 10 percent of smokers can limit their habit to five cigarettes or fewer per day.

Almost every long-term smoker first lights up during adolescence. Nearly 30 percent of any high school graduation class are regular smokers, as are more than 70 percent of their peers who dropped out of school. Over the past two decades, the average age at which tobacco use begins has dropped from sixteen to twelve. The younger one becomes nicotine dependent, the more cigarettes will be smoked as an adult.

A huge amount of money is spent every year to make smoking appear glamorous and exciting. The tobacco industry's annual multibillion-dollar advertising budget is supposedly intended to encourage adults to switch brands, but the cartoon characters, sexy young couples, macho men, and liberated women in cigarette ads have clearly been shown to influence children and adolescents. Heavy visibility of these ads at sporting and cultural events also sends definite signals that tobacco is hot stuff. Warnings issued in health-education class pale in comparison. In one survey of high school smokers, more than 95 percent were aware of health risks, but 70 percent claimed they were not concerned enough to stop.

Cigarettes keep very bad company. Smoking is associated with significantly poorer school performance and a higher likelihood of sexual activity. Because the use of alcohol and marijuana is significantly greater among adolescent smokers, tobacco is identified as a "gateway" drug—one that increases the odds of using even more dangerous substances. It is the last of these points that should sound the alarm for parents of adolescent smokers. If your teenager is smoking cigarettes, he is eight times more likely to be using illicit drugs and eleven times more likely to be drinking heavily than his nonsmoking counterparts.[1]

Smokeless (chewing and snuffing) tobacco, which has been made highly visible (and glamorized to some degree) by users who are professional athletes, is not a safe alternative to cigarettes. The use of smokeless tobacco has nearly tripled in the past twenty years, with a dramatic increase among adolescents. A 1990 report published by the Centers for Disease Control included a survey that showed that nearly 25 percent of white, male high school students acknowledged current use of smokeless tobacco. Usage rates are even higher in many Native American populations. Chewing tobacco is clearly associated with damage to the gingiva (the soft tissues surrounding the teeth) and with aggressive cancers of the mouth. Furthermore, both chewing and snuffing deliver powerful jolts of nicotine. A 1993 report from the National Institutes of Health indicates that a typical dose of snuff contains twice the amount of nicotine in a cigarette, while a wad of chewing tobacco contains *fifteen times that amount.* Needless to say, addiction to these substances is very common, as are withdrawal symptoms when use is stopped.

Alcohol—the most dangerous gateway drug

In all fifty states, it is illegal to sell alcoholic beverages to anyone under age twenty-one. This is no accident, because for teenagers alcohol is a gateway to a lot more than other drugs.

Alcohol causes more deaths among adolescents than any other substance. About 40 percent of all deaths in sixteen- to twenty-year-olds result from motor-vehicle crashes, and half of these are alcohol related. Overall, driving under the influence is the leading cause of death for people between the ages of fifteen and twenty-four. Alcohol also frequently plays a role in adolescent deaths from other causes: homicides, suicides, drownings, and motorcycle and bicycle accidents.

In addition, alcohol plays an important role in adolescent crime, sexual promiscuity, and date rape. According to research compiled by Mothers Against Drunk Driving (MADD), 95 percent of violent crime on college campuses is alcohol related, and 90 percent of reported campus rapes involve alcohol use by the assailant, the victim, or both. In one study cited by MADD, 60 percent of college women diagnosed with a sexually transmitted disease were drunk when they became infected.

Another sobering reality about drinking is the early age at which it frequently begins.

- According to the American Academy of Pediatrics, about one in seven fourth-graders has already experienced alcohol intoxication. Two out of three eighth-graders and nine out of ten twelfth-graders have tried alcohol at least once. One in three eighth-graders and half of all twelfth-graders have used alcohol within a given month.
- More alcoholic products that specifically appeal to kids are hitting the marketplace. Wine coolers are increasingly popular with younger drinkers, as are a new wave of alcoholic concoctions billed as "thirst quenchers," often containing lemon or other fruit flavors.

A significant number of drinkers (about 20 percent) develop full-blown alcohol addiction and struggle with it for years. Ironically, the person who prides himself on the ability to "hold his liquor" is at the greatest risk for alcoholism. If large quantities of alcohol must be consumed to produce intoxication, he is demonstrating a *tolerance* for alcohol—something all alcoholics have in common—and addiction is likely to develop. Tolerance of alcohol and the risk of addiction are thought to be genetically predisposed and usually run in families. *Adolescents with family members who have had alcohol-abuse problems must be warned that they are at higher risk for becoming addicted to alcohol if they ever start drinking.*

Marijuana—inhaled intellectual impairment

Parents who experimented with marijuana during the 1960s may not be terribly concerned about this drug. But what kids are smoking today bears little resemblance to what flower children were inhaling three decades ago. The average batch of marijuana in the 1960s contained 0.2 percent delta-9-tetrahydrocannabinol (or THC for short), its main mood-altering chemical. Today's vintage contains at least 5 percent THC, or twenty-five times the old concentration, which—along with four hundred other assorted chemicals—adversely affects the brain, lungs, heart, gonads (ovaries or testes), and immune system. In preteens and young adolescents, heavy use of marijuana can also impair growth and development.

Most kids who use marijuana or take THC capsules experience a sense of euphoria, relaxation, and calm. Some feel it enhances perception. The reality is that it impairs intellectual function, specifically concentration, memory, judgment, and motor skills. Short-term fallout can include injuries and death from motor-vehicle accidents or other trauma as well as sexual misadventures resulting from loss of inhibition and rational thinking.

Long-term users are known for an "amotivational" syndrome in which goals and self-discipline and the activities that require them (especially school performance) literally go up in smoke. During the teen years a child should be learning how to think and act more maturely, but frequent marijuana use can halt that process. Worse, it introduces kids to the harrowing world of illegal drugs and the criminals who produce and distribute them.

Inhalants—cheap (and dangerous) thrills

This form of substance abuse is particularly hazardous because:

- The materials involved are inexpensive and readily available in any garage or hardware store. Model glue, contact cement, gasoline, lacquers, paints, toiletries, cosmetics, and dozens of other aerosol and volatile products can have mind-altering effects if inhaled deeply.
- Substance inhalers are generally very young. The age of peak use is typically fourteen or fifteen, with first experiences as early as six to eight years of age.
- Abuse of these products is increasing. An estimated 15 to 20 percent of adolescents have abused inhalants at least once before graduation from high school. The practice is especially prevalent among Hispanic and Native American children and teens.
- The potential effects are disastrous. The most serious by-product of chronic use is permanent damage to the brain and nervous system, causing loss of intellectual function and coordination. In addition, a variety of products can be lethal during or after inhalant use. One study of inhalant deaths revealed that over 20 percent occurred among first-time users. One consequence known as **sudden sniffing death syndrome** can occur when a user is surprised or suddenly frightened during the act of inhaling. Many inhalants temporarily increase the sensitivity of the heart muscle, and an abrupt adrenaline surge in response to being startled can provoke a lethal irregular heart rhythm.

Depending upon the substance used, several deep inspirations bring on a sense of euphoria—frequently with hallucinations—as well as stimulation and loss of inhibition (which may lead to other dangerous behavior). Drowsiness and sleep may follow.

Like other drug users, inhalant abusers may display erratic behavior, poor self-care, and declining school performance. Parents may notice specific clues such as the aroma of the inhalant (which can persist in the breath for several hours), stains and odors in clothes, and an unusual stash of products (such as gasoline or aerosol cans) in a child's room. An adult who discovers children or adolescents in the act of inhaling should avoid surprise tactics or a sudden confrontation that might cause a startle reflex, since this could precipitate a sudden lethal heart-rhythm disturbance.

Beyond the Gateway—Dead-End Drugs

Beyond these gateway substances lies a dark world of more powerful drugs that assault bodies and minds more quickly and savagely. These may be grouped into four categories: **stimulants, sedatives/hypnotics, narcotics,** and **hallucinogens.**

Stimulants—the fast track downhill

Cocaine is one of the most addictive drugs on the street and in many ways the most dangerous. It directly stimulates pleasure centers in the brain, creating an overwhelming desire for the same experience again and again. Its powerful jolt to the central nervous system also triggers a rapid heart rate, constricted blood vessels, and elevated blood pressure. Even in young, well-conditioned bodies, these events can cause stroke, seizures, or cardiac arrest.

When the drug wears off, cocaine users become anxious, irritable, depressed, and desperate for the next dose. Bigger and more frequent doses are needed to produce the same effect, and progression from first use to desperate addiction can be rapid.

All of cocaine's routes of entry into the body pose unique hazards. Snorting cocaine up the nose can lead to destruction of the septum (the structure separating the two nasal passages) and eventual collapse of the bridge of the nose. Injecting cocaine into the veins can transmit dangerous microorganisms, including the viruses that cause hepatitis and AIDS, when needles or syringes are shared with other users. The cheapest form of cocaine, at five to fifteen dollars per dose, is **crack,** which produces a response so sudden and powerful that addiction frequently begins with the first dose. Crack is a form of freebase cocaine, a purified version of the drug that can only be smoked. (When heated, it produces a crackling sound; hence its name.)

Amphetamines ("speed") and their derivatives, whether swallowed, smoked, or injected, rev up the central nervous system and produce a sense of energy, excitement, and invincibility. But with this come a number of serious risks and consequences. Excitement may deteriorate into excitability, irritability, paranoia, delusions, and even violent behavior. When these drugs wear off, profound fatigue and depression are left in their wake. Tolerance results in a need for higher doses, and so addiction is not unusual. Chronic use leads to physical deterioration caused by malnutrition (from decreased interest in food) and loss of sleep. Heavy use can result in permanent brain damage, stroke, or heart attack.

The potential for abuse of these drugs has recently increased for two reasons. First, the widespread use of Dexedrine and Ritalin in treating attention deficit/hyperactivity disorder (ADHD) has placed more of these stimulants in circulation, thus increasing the likelihood of potential misuse through sharing with or selling to others. (Those with ADHD who receive proper doses of these drugs appear to have little risk of addiction to them.)

Second, and more important, the abuse of a form of amphetamine known as **methamphetamine** (also called "ice," "crank," "crystal meth," and "poor-man's coke," among other names) has reached epidemic levels. Methamphetamine is relatively cheap to manufacture in home laboratories, and an inexpensive dose gives users a more sustained high than cocaine. Teenagers and young adults use this drug to boost mood and self-confidence, suppress appetite to lose weight, and enhance sexual experiences. But ongoing use commonly leads to insomnia, agitation, psychosis, and violent behavior. Methamphetamine-induced emergency-room visits, crimes, and deaths have increased dramatically, and some experts fear use of this drug will become a plague dwarfing the cocaine epidemic that began in the 1980s.

Sedatives and hypnotics—escapes to the land of nod

These agents in small doses produce a pleasant sense of relaxation and sleepiness. In some cases they may be misused to offset the sleepless excitation from stimulants taken earlier in the day. Prolonged use usually leads to psychological and physical dependence. High doses of these medications, particularly when combined with other drugs (especially alcohol), can produce stuporous intoxication, depression of the drive to breathe, coma, and death. Withdrawal can be hazardous, with symptoms including anxiety, tremors, panic, and seizures.

A few decades ago, **barbiturates** were commonly prescribed by physicians as sedatives and sleeping pills. Because of problems with overdoses, abuse, and withdrawal, few doctors recommend them, so they are more widely marketed on the street than in pharmacies. Two exceptions are **phenobarbital,** used to treat seizure disorders, and **butalbital,** which is combined with caffeine and aspirin in headache remedies such as Fiorinal and Esgic. Despite their relative safety, both of these forms are still potentially habit-forming. **Benzodiazepines** (Valium, Librium, Xanax, Tranxene, Klonopin, and others) are widely prescribed to treat anxiety disorders. More sedating forms (Dalmane, Restoril, and Halcion) are often used to induce sleep. These drugs are not commonly sold on the street, but legitimate prescriptions can be misused or overused and lead to dependence.

An extremely potent, fast-acting benzodiazepine called **Rohypnol** produces significant short-term memory loss. This drug, which is sold legally in Europe, has been implicated in numerous date rapes in the United States. Sexual predators slip Rohypnol tablets (called "roofies") into an unsuspecting victim's drink; this leads to rapid onset of deep sleep and amnesia for whatever happens during the next few hours. Rohypnol has become the rapist's best friend—obliterating the victim's ability to resist or remember who did what.

Narcotics—painkillers with a hook

Derivatives of opium, known as **opiates,** such as **codeine, hydrocodone** (Vicodin, Lortab, and others), **oxycodone** (Percodan, Percocet, and others), and morphine are used widely in medicine to relieve pain. But they can also create a general sense of well-being and relief from psychological pain, leading to long-term use and dependence. Adults are more likely than teenagers to have problems with narcotic prescriptions for chronic problems such as headache or back pain.

Adolescents involved in high-risk drug behavior may be drawn into the snare of **heroin,** a derivative of morphine that is injected into the vein to produce an intense euphoria. Repeated use always leads to addiction, as well as to the perpetual risk for accidental overdose and transmission of hepatitis and AIDS viruses from contaminated needles and syringes.

Narcotic addicts deprived of their drug experience a host of unpleasant symptoms they will desperately seek to avoid. These include sweats, cramps, vomiting, and diarrhea. As miserable as narcotic withdrawal may feel, it is far less dangerous than abruptly stopping a long-term barbiturate or benzodiazepine habit, which can lead to convulsions.

Hallucinogenic drugs—checking out of reality

LSD (lysergic acid diethylamide), which seemed to be a faded relic of the psychedelic sixties, has made a disturbing comeback. Tiny amounts swallowed or licked off paper can produce intense hallucinations, which may be exhilarating or terrifying. The worst of the "bad trips" can bring on profound anxiety, confusion, panic, or self-destructive behavior, such as jumping off a building or stepping in front of oncoming traffic. **Mescaline, peyote,** and other hallucinogens have similar effects and risks. Long-term use can damage the brain, resulting in defects in memory and abstract thinking.

Phencyclidine (PCP, "angel dust"), originally formulated as an animal tranquilizer, is an extraordinarily dangerous hallucinogen. It can induce profound alterations of all sensory perceptions (sight, sound, touch, smell, and taste), essentially jerking its users far from normal consciousness. But this dissociation from reality can also provoke marked anxiety, depression, paranoia, and acts of horrific violence against oneself or others. An agitated PCP user may demonstrate incredible strength and no apparent sensation of pain, making him extremely dangerous to those who might try to restrain him.

Physical consequences of large doses of PCP can be severe—heart failure, seizures, coma, and lethal strokes. Users also risk direct brain damage, leading to alterations of speech, loss of memory and intellectual function, and in some cases, psychosis. PCP can be swallowed or smoked (if sprayed onto tobacco or marijuana). It can also be injected, at times with tragic results.

Designer drugs—the worst of all worlds

The incredibly misguided creativity of those who seek new and different drug experiences has led to the synthesis of a variety of powerful, addictive, and extremely hazardous substances. Most of these are spin-offs of other drugs such as PCP, amphetamines, or meperidine (Demerol, a potent painkiller). Those who experiment with **ecstasy** (the most well-known designer drug) and the other designer drugs literally play Russian roulette with their brains every time they swallow, snort, or inject. These drugs come aboard with the dangerous baggage of their parent compounds and then add unpredictable side effects. Irreversible brain damage, with long-term disabilities such as tremors, paralysis, and speech disturbances can be the pathetic legacy of a season of thrill seeking with designer drugs.

WHAT ARE THE STAGES OF INVOLVEMENT IN SUBSTANCE ABUSE?

Experts in adolescent substance problems have identified a common progression of alcohol- and drug-related behaviors that moves from bad to worse. While it is not a foregone conclusion that everyone who experiments with drugs will progress to the worst stages of involvement, a child can already have incurred a lot of damage before parents or others notice that something is wrong. Secretive adolescent behavior and skillful lying, combined with parental denial ("No one in *our* family could have a drug problem!"), may delay identification of the problem. While paranoia and daily inquisitions around the breakfast table are counterproductive, wise parents will keep their eyes and ears open and promptly take action if they see any signs that a problem may be developing.

Stage one: experimentation—entering the drug gateway
Characteristics:
- Use is occasional, sporadic, often unplanned—weekends, summer nights, someone's unsupervised party.
- Use is precipitated by peer pressure, curiosity, thrill seeking, desire to look and feel grown-up.
- Gateway drugs are usually used—cigarettes, alcohol, marijuana, possibly inhalant abuse.
- A drug high is easier to experience because tolerance has not been developed.

Parents may notice:
- Tobacco or alcohol on the breath or intoxicated behavior.
- Little change in normal behavior between episodes of drug use.

Stage two: more regular drug use—leaving the land of the living
Characteristics:
- Alcohol and other drugs are used not only on weekends but also on weekdays, not only with friends but when alone.
- Quantities of alcohol and drugs increase as tolerance develops; hangovers become more common.
- Blackouts may occur—periods of time in which drugs or alcohol prevent normal memories from forming; "What happened last night?" becomes a frequent question.

- More time and attention are focused on when the next drug experience will occur.
- Fellow drinkers/drug users become preferred companions.

Parents may notice:
- Son or daughter will be out of the house later at night, overnight, or all weekend.
- School performance worsens—unexplained school absences.
- Outside activities such as sports are dropped.
- Decreased contact with friends who don't use drugs.
- Disappearance of money or other valuables.
- Child withdraws from the family, is increasingly sullen and hostile.
- User is caught in one or many lies.

Stage three: waist deep in the mire of addiction—and sinking
Characteristics:
- Alcohol and drugs become primary focus of attention.
- Becoming high is a daily event.
- There is a use of harder, more dangerous drugs.
- More money is spent each week on drugs; theft or dealing may become part of drug-seeking behavior.
- Adolescent displays increasing social isolation; no contact with nondrug-using friends; more drug use in isolation rather than socially.

Parents may notice the behaviors listed above, plus:
- Escalation of conflicts at home.
- Loss of nearly all control of the adolescent.
- Possible discovery of a stash of drugs at home.
- Arrest(s) for possession of and/or dealing drugs or for driving while intoxicated.

Stage four: drowning in addiction
Characteristics:
- Constant state of intoxication; being high is routine, even at school or job (if there is any attendance at all).
- Blackouts increase in frequency.
- Physical appearance deteriorates—weight loss, infections, poor self-care.
- Injectable drugs are possibly used.
- Involvement in casual sexual relationships (at times in exchange for drugs).

- User will likely be involved with theft, dealing, and other criminal activity.
- Guilt, self-hatred, and thoughts of suicide increase.
- Adolescent abandons any apparent interest in spiritual matters.

Parents are likely to be dealing with:
- Complete loss of control of adolescent's behavior; escalation of conflict, possibly to the point of violence.
- Ongoing denial by user that drugs are a problem.
- Increasing problems with the law and time spent with police, attorneys, hearings, court officials, etc.
- Other siblings negatively affected because the family is preoccupied or overwhelmed by consequences of drug user's behavior.

This descent into drug hell is a nightmare that no parent envisions while rocking a newborn baby or escorting an eager five-year-old to kindergarten. But it can happen in any neighborhood, any church, any family, even when parents have provided a stable and loving home environment. In fact, it is often in such homes that a drug problem goes undetected until it's reached an advanced and dangerous stage. "This can't be happening, not in my house!" But if it does, parental guilt, anger, and depression can undermine the responses necessary to restore order.

WHAT CAN PARENTS DO TO REDUCE THEIR CHILD'S RISK OF DEVELOPING A SUBSTANCE PROBLEM?

Drug abuse is so widespread in our culture that you cannot expect to isolate your child from exposure to it. However, as with diseases caused by bacteria and viruses, you can institute infection-control measures. Specifically, take steps to reduce the likelihood of contact with drugs, and build your child's immunity to using them. These measures should be ongoing, deliberate, and proactive.

Model behavior you want your children to follow.

When it comes to drugs, two adages are worth noting: "Children learn what they live" and "What parents allow in moderation their children will do in excess." While not absolute truths, these maxims reflect the reality that kids are looking to their parents for cues as to what is acceptable behavior, while at the same time developing the discernment required to understand what moderation is all about.

If you smoke, your offspring will probably do likewise. But it's never too late to quit, and your decision to give up cigarettes will make an important statement to all the members of your family—especially if you are willing to hold yourself accountable to them.

If you consume alcohol at home, what role does it play in your life? Does it flow freely on a daily basis? Do you need a drink to unwind at the end of the day? Is it a necessary ingredient at every party or family get-together? If so, your children will get the picture that alcohol is a painkiller, tension reliever, and the life of the party, and they will likely use it in a similar fashion. For their sake (and yours), take whatever steps are necessary to live without alcohol.

If you drink modestly—an occasional glass of wine with dinner, a beer every other week, a few sips of champagne at a wedding—think carefully about alcohol's role in your family. Many parents decide to abstain while rearing their children in order to send an unambiguous message to steer clear of it. Others feel that modeling modest, nonintoxicated use of alcohol (while speaking clearly against underage drinking, drunkenness, driving under the influence, and other irresponsible behaviors) equips children and teenagers to make sensible decisions later in life.

Each family must weigh the options carefully and set its own standards. But if you or any blood relatives have a history of alcohol addiction (or *any* problem caused by drinking), make your home an alcohol-free zone and warn your adolescent that he or she may have a genetic predisposition toward alcoholism.

Also think about the impact of your family's habits on visitors or guests, including your teenager's friends. What might be perfectly harmless for you could prompt someone who has a potential for alcohol addiction to make a bad decision. All things considered, nothing is lost and much can be gained by abstaining.

What about the medicine cabinet? If you are stressed, upset, or uncomfortable, are d-r-u-g-s the way you spell r-e-l-i-e-f? Have you accumulated prescription narcotics and tranquilizers that you utilize freely when the going gets tough? Kids aren't blind. If they see the adults around them frequently taking "legitimate" drugs to dull their pain, why can't they use their own drugs of choice to do the same?

Even if you feel you have a legitimate need for painkillers (recurrent headaches, chronic back pain), you can become addicted to prescription drugs. Finding other ways to cope and working diligently to minimize the use of drugs for *symptom* relief should be priorities. Note: The appropriate use of antidepressants to treat the biochemistry of mood disorders does *not* represent a potential abuse situation. These medications are not addicting or habit-forming and are not sold on the street to create an artificial drug high (see Special Concerns, page 601).

Finally, if you use marijuana and other street drugs, whether for recreational purposes or because of an addiction problem, you are putting the parental stamp of approval not only on the drugs but also on breaking the law. For your own and your family's sake, seek help immediately and bring this dangerous behavior to an end.

Build identity and attitudes that are resistant to drug use.

This is an ongoing project, beginning during the first years of your child's life. Specifically:

- Create an environment that consistently balances love and limits. Children and teenagers who know they are loved unconditionally are less likely to seek "pain relief" through drugs, and those who have learned to live within appropriate boundaries will have better impulse control and self-discipline.
- Instill respect and awe for the God-given gift of a body and mind—even one that isn't perfect.
- Help children and adolescents become students of consequences—not only in connection with drugs but with other behaviors as well. Talk about good and bad choices and the logic behind them. "Just say no" is an appropriate motto for kids to learn, but understanding *why* it is wrong to use harmful substances will build more solid resistance.
- Build a positive sense of identity with your family. This means not only openly affirming and appreciating each member but putting forth the time and effort for shared experiences that are meaningful and fun. A strong feeling of belonging to a loving family builds accountability ("Our family doesn't use drugs") and helps prevent loneliness, which can be a setup for a drug experience.
- Encourage church-related activities (including family devotions) that build a meaningful, personal faith. *Reliance on God is the cornerstone of drug treatment programs, and it makes no sense to leave the spiritual dimension out of the prevention process.* A vibrant faith reinforces the concept that the future is worth protecting, stabilizes the emotions during turbulent years, and provides a healthy response to the aches and pains of life. In addition, an awareness of God's presence and a desire not to dishonor Him can be strong deterrents to destructive behavior.

Begin talking early about smoking, alcohol, and drugs.

Because experimentation with drugs and alcohol commonly begins during the grade-school years, start appropriate countermeasures in very young children. A five-year-old may not be ready for a lecture about the physiology of cocaine addiction, but you should be ready to offer commentary when you and your child see someone smoking or drinking, whether in real life or in a movie or TV program. If intoxication is portrayed as humorous (as in the pink-elephant sequence in the movie *Dumbo*, for example), don't be shy about setting the record straight.

Keep talking about smoking, alcohol, and drugs as opportunities arise.

Make an effort to stay one step ahead of your child's or adolescent's knowledge of the drug scene. If you hear about an athlete, rock star, or celebrity who uses drugs, be certain that everyone in the family understands that no amount of fame or fortune excuses this behavior. If a famous person is dealing with the consequences of drug use (such as being dropped from a team or suffering medical or legal consequences), make sure your kids hear the cautionary tale.

Be aware of current trends in your community and look for local meetings or lectures where abuse problems are being discussed. Find out what's going on—not only from the experts but from your kids and their friends. If you hear that someone is smoking, drinking, inhaling, or injecting drugs, *talk about it.* What are they using? What consequences are likely? Why is it wrong? What help do they need?

All this assumes that you are available to have these conversations. Be careful, because the time when you may be the busiest with career or other responsibilities may also be the time one or more adolescents at home most need your input. If you're too overworked, overcommitted, and overtired to keep tabs on the home front, you may wake up one day to find a major drug problem on your doorstep.

Don't allow your child or adolescent to go to a party, sleepover, or other activity that isn't supervised by someone you trust.

Don't blindly assume that the presence of a grown-up guarantees a safe environment. Get to know your kids' friends' parents, not just your kids' friends. Make certain your child knows you will pick him up anytime, anywhere—no questions asked—if he finds himself in a situation where drugs or alcohol is being used. And be sure to praise him for a wise and mature decision if he does so.

Have the courage to curtail your child's or adolescent's contact with drug users.

The epidemic of drug abuse spreads person to person. Whether a recent acquaintance or a long-term bosom buddy, if one (or more) of your teenager's friends is known to be actively using alcohol and/or drugs, you must impose restrictions on the relationship. You might, for example, stipulate that your adolescent can spend time with that person only in your home—without any closed doors and when you are around.

However, even with these limits in place, you will need to keep track of who is influencing whom. If your family is reaching out to a troubled adolescent and helping to move him toward healthier decisions, keep up the good work. But if there is any sign that the drug-using friend is pulling your teenager toward his lifestyle, declare a quarantine immediately. By all means, if your teenager feels called to help a friend climb out of a drug quagmire, don't let him try it alone. Work as a team to direct that person toward a recovery program.

Create significant consequences to discourage alcohol and drug use.

Teenagers may not be scared off by facts, figures, and gory details. Even the most ominous warnings may not override an adolescent's belief in her own immortality, especially when other compelling emotions such as the need for peer acceptance are operating at full throttle.

You may improve the odds by making it clear that you consider the use of cigarettes, alcohol, or illegal drugs a very serious matter. Judgment regarding punishments fitting crimes will be necessary, of course. If your adolescent confesses that he tried a cigarette or a beer at a party and expresses an appropriate resolve to avoid a repeat performance, heart-to-heart conversation and encouragement would be far more appropriate than summarily grounding him for six months.

But if your warnings repeatedly go unheeded, you will need to establish and enforce some meaningful consequences. Loss of driving, dating, or even phone privileges for an extended period of time may be in order. You can make the bitter pill less threatening by pointing out the following:

- He can easily avoid the penalty by staying clear of drugs and the people who use them.

- Consistent responsible behavior leads to more privileges and independence. Irresponsible behavior leads to decreased independence and more parental control.
- The drastic consequence can be used as a reason to get away from a bad situation. If a friend starts to exert pressure to smoke, drink, or use drugs, he can say, "Sorry, but I don't want to be stuck without transportation for the next six months."

WHAT IF A PROBLEM HAS ALREADY DEVELOPED?

Even in families that are closely knit, hold strong values, and practice ongoing drugproofing, there are no guarantees that substance abuse won't affect one or more of your children. The problems may range from a brief encounter with cigarettes to an episode of intoxication (perhaps with legal consequences) or even involve addiction. As you begin to cope with the chemical intruder(s) in your home, keep the following principles in mind:

Don't deny or ignore the problem.

If you do, it is likely to continue to worsen until your family life is turned inside out. Take the bull by the horns—but be sure to find out exactly how big and ugly the bull is. The marijuana cigarette you discovered may be a onetime experiment—or the tip of an iceberg. Talk to your child or adolescent about it—but also talk to siblings, friends, and anyone else who knows what he's up to. You may not like what you hear, but better to get the hard truth now than a ghastly surprise later.

Don't wallow in false guilt.

Most parents assume a great deal of self-blame when a drug problem erupts in their home. If you do carry some responsibility for what has happened (whether you know about it immediately or find out later on), face up to it, confess it to God and your family, and then get on with the task of helping your child. But remember that your child or adolescent must deal with his or her own responsibility as well.

Seek help from people experienced with treating drug problems.

Talk to your physician and pastor. They should be part of your team, even if in a supporting role. It is likely that you will receive a referral to a professional who is experienced in organizing a family intervention. This may include educational sessions, individual and family counseling, medical treatment, and long-term follow-up. When the user's behavior is out of control and he is unwilling to acknowledge the problem, a carefully planned confrontation by family members and others affected may need to be carried out under the supervision of an experienced counselor. The goal is to convince the drug user in a firm but loving way of the need for change—*now*. The confrontation should include specific alternatives for the type of treatment he will undergo and a clear-cut "or else . . ." if he is not willing to cooperate.

Be prepared to make difficult, "tough love" decisions.

If you have a drug-dependent adolescent who will not submit to treatment and insists on continuing the drug use and other destructive actions, you will need to take a stomach-churning step of informing him that he cannot continue to live in your home while carrying on this behavior. This will be necessary not only to motivate him to change but to prevent his drug-induced turbulence from destroying the rest of your family.

If you must take this drastic step, it would be helpful to present him with one or more options. These might include entering an inpatient drug-treatment center, halfway house, boot-camp program, or youth home, or staying with a relative or another family who is willing to accept him for a defined period of time. More ominous possibilities may need to be discussed as well, such as making him a ward of the court or even turning him over to the police if he has been involved in criminal activity. If you continue to shield him from the consequences of his behavior or bail him out when his drugs get him into trouble, he will not change, and you will be left with deep-seated anger and frustration.

Don't look for or expect quick-fix solutions.

It is normal to wish for a single intervention that will make a drug problem go away. But one conversation, counseling session, prayer time, or trip to the doctor won't be enough. Think in terms of a comprehensive response encompassing specific treatment and counseling and the gamut of your child's life—home, school, friends, and church.

Remember the father of the prodigal son.

"Tough love" means allowing the consequences of bad decisions to be fully experienced by one who is making them. It also means that he knows your love for him is so deep and secure that it will never die. Never give up hope, never stop praying, and never slam the door on reconciliation and restoration when he comes to his senses.

NOTES
1. U.S. Department of Health and Human Services, "Preliminary Estimates from the 1995 National Household Survey on Drug Abuse," *Advance Report No. 18* (Public Health Service, GPO, August 1996).

Recognizing Depression and Preventing Suicide in Children and Adolescents

DEPRESSION—AS COMMON AS THE COMMON COLD

Depression is by far the most common and important emotional health problem in America. In terms of its frequency among the population, depression could be compared to the common cold. But the similarity ends there.

- The sneezing and hacking of a cold is readily apparent to the person who has it, as well as to everyone around him. But depression can be manifested in a bewildering array of symptoms, many of them physical, but may not be recognized by the individual himself or by those closest to him.
- Cold viruses are usually vanquished by the immune system within a week, while untreated depression can continue for months or even years.
- Cold remedies are simple to use and readily obtained at the nearest supermarket. But appropriate treatment of depression is a prolonged process that nearly always involves one or more professionals and sometimes carefully chosen medication.
- A person with a cold isn't considered defective or weak-willed or in need of "getting his act together." But depression is a diagnosis no one wants to acknowledge or accept because of the stigma associated with having a mental disorder.
- While colds never have a fatal outcome except in the most physically frail individuals, depression can lead to the sudden and tragic ending of a life that would most likely have continued for many more years.

All of the difficulties and heartaches arising from depression apply not only to adults but also to children and adolescents, often with greater intensity. At any given time, nearly 2 percent of prepubertal children and 5 percent of teenagers are estimated to have a major depressive problem—not a brief case of "the blues" or a temporary mood swing—and that number may be conservative. What is more disturbing is that depression kills the young more frequently than it does adults. Suicide is the sixth leading cause of death in children between the ages of five and fourteen and the third leading cause of death among those between the ages of fifteen and twenty-four, claiming the lives of at least five thousand teenagers every year in the United States. The number may actually be higher, because many accidents (such as drug overdoses, drownings, or fatal automobile crashes involving a lone teenage driver) may in fact be suicides. The suicide rate among the young has risen dramatically since the late 1960s; among fifteen- to nineteen-year-olds, it has doubled, while among ten- to fourteen-year-olds it has tripled.[1]

A 1991 study by the Centers for Disease Control and Prevention found that 27 percent of the high school students surveyed had considered suicide, 16 percent had made a specific suicide plan, 8 percent had made a suicide attempt, and 2 percent had inflicted enough damage during a suicide attempt to require medical attention. Females attempt suicide four times more frequently than males. However, because young males are more likely to utilize violent methods (such as leaping from an overpass or using a gun), their suicide attempts are four times more likely to be fatal than those of females.

WHAT IS DEPRESSION?

In our culture the term *depression* is applied to a broad spectrum of situations in which a person feels unhappy. Here, however, we are dealing specifically with **clinical depression**—not a temporary emotional slump, such as after watching a sad movie or receiving a traffic ticket or even after a day in which one thing after another goes sour. Clinical depression involves a *persistent* and usually *disruptive* disturbance of mood and often affects other bodily functions as well. As we list the common characteristics of depression, it is important to note that these may manifest themselves quite differently in children and adolescents from how they appear in adults. In fact, because the behaviors provoked by depression are frequently confused with the normal emotional and physical upheavals of growing up, at one time it was erroneously assumed that this condition occurred rarely, if at all, before adulthood. In each symptom category we will mention some of the unique variations seen in young people who are depressed.

A persistent sad or negative mood

Most parents may at some point, if not frequently, complain that their teenager has a "lousy attitude." As described in chapter 13, it isn't at all unusual for adolescents to experience emotions and mood swings that seem out of proportion to the circumstances. But the depressed child or teenager seems to be in a perpetual slump.

Unfortunately, you won't hear a young person say, "In case you haven't noticed, I've been depressed for the past several weeks." Instead, you may see any of a number of the following signals that would appear disconnected:

- Continued overt sadness or moping, which may be accompanied by frequent episodes of crying.
- A loss of enthusiasm or interest in things that were once favorite activities.
- Increasing withdrawal and isolation from family and friends.
- Poor school performance: plummeting grades, loss of interest in schoolwork, and frequent absences.
- Outbursts of anger, arguing, disrespectful comments, or blatant hostility toward everyone at home.
- Repeated complaints about being bored or tired.
- Overt acting out: drug or alcohol use, running away, sexual activity, fighting, vandalism, or other antisocial activity.

This does not mean, of course, that all negative attitudes and actions are manifestations of depression. But a component of appropriate parental corrective action should be a willingness to entertain this possibility when a child or adolescent displays an unexpected and persistent disturbance in behavior.

Painful thoughts

If we compare depression to a very long, sad song, the mood disturbance just described is the mournful or agitated music. But accompanying the unhappy melody are painful lyrics—words that express, over and over again, a view of life that is anything but upbeat.

People who have experienced both depression and bodily injuries (for example, a major fracture) usually will confirm that physical pain is easier to manage than emotional pain. Usually one can expect physical pain to resolve or at least become tolerable. But no such hopeful expectation accompanies painful thoughts, which can roll into the mind like waves from an ocean that extends to a limitless, bleak horizon.

Painful thoughts, like a disturbed mood, can have several manifestations:

- *Relentless introspection.* Adolescents tend to be highly self-conscious during the normal (and necessary) process of establishing their identity during their transition into adulthood. But depression magnifies and warps this natural introspection into a mental inquisition. The inward gaze not only becomes a relentless stare, but it focuses exclusively on shortcomings. It can also move into some dangerous territory: "Wouldn't I and everyone else be better off if I weren't here? Why does it matter at this point whether I live or die?"

- *Negative self-concept.* Physical appearance, intelligence, competence, acceptance, and general worth are all subject to relentless and exaggerated criticism. This is not a healthy examination of areas that need improvement, nor repentance for wrongdoing that might lead to improvements in attitude and behavior. Instead, unrealistic self-reproach for whatever isn't going well in life—or, at the opposite extreme, spreading blame to everyone else—is likely to dominate a depressed child's or adolescent's thoughts and interfere with positive changes.

  A depressed teenager slumps into a lunchroom chair and moans, "I'm fat. I'm never gonna get a date. I'm stupid. I'll never pass algebra. I feel miserable. I'm never going to feel good again." Her friends, if they bother to hang around and listen to this litany of woe, may argue with her. "You're not stupid. Stop talking that way." If she persists in her lament, they may become fed up and agree with her, if only to end her complaints: "Okay, so you're fat and stupid. C'mon, we're gonna be late for class." Her parents might unwittingly make a similar mistake in trying to bolster her spirits: "What are you talking about? You look fine to us, and you're smart. That's enough of this negative talk!" Such responses only build feelings of rejection and a conviction that "no one understands me."

  This state of affairs will be drastically worsened for those who have been subjected to emotional, physical, or sexual abuse during childhood or adolescence. Whether these assaults attack the heart ("You're so stupid!" "Why can't you be like _____?") or the body, they create a sense of worthlessness that supplies powerful fuel for an ongoing depression.

- *Anxiety.* Persistent worry, whether focused on a specific issue or a free-floating apprehension that encompasses most daily activities, frequently accompanies depression. While a modest level of concern is not only normal but in fact necessary to motivate appropriate precautions for everyday activities, the anxiety associated with depression is disabling and actually interferes with effective responses to life's challenges.

- *Hopelessness.* This is particularly troublesome for children and adolescents, not only because they may feel emotions so strongly, but also because they haven't lived long enough to understand the ebb and flow of life's problems and pleasures. Most adults facing a crisis will think back to the last twenty-seven crises they have already lived through and will have gained enough perspective to know that this current trial will probably pass as well. But when young people collide with a crisis (or at least what appears to be one from their perspective), they usually have far fewer experiences with which to compare it and a limited fund of responses. If they can't see a satisfactory route past the current problem, it is no wonder they might begin to think that their "life is over" or "not worth living." This dark view of life isn't helped by some powerful voices in adolescent popular culture (especially in music) that focus on rage, alienation, despair, and death.

Physical symptoms

No emotional event occurs without the body participating, and it should come as little surprise that physical symptoms accompany depression. Common problems include:

- *Insomnia and other sleep disturbances.* Difficulty falling asleep at night, awakening too early in the morning, and fitful sleep in between are very common in depressed individuals. This may be accompanied by a desire to sleep during the day. Some have **hypersomnia** (sleeping for excessively long periods of time), in which sleep seems to serve as an escape from the misery of waking hours. An important sign that depression is improving is the normalization of sleeping patterns.
- *Appetite changes.* Loss of appetite and weight or nonstop hunger and weight gain are not uncommon during depression. Such changes can complicate an adolescent's normal concerns about appearance.
- *Physiological problems.* Depressed individuals often have a variety of physical complaints. Fatigue is almost universally present. Headaches, dizziness, nausea, abdominal cramps, episodes of shortness of breath, and heart palpitations are not at all unusual. Sometimes poor concentration, unusual pain patterns, or altered sensations in various parts of the body will raise concerns about a serious medical disorder. Very often an evaluation for an assortment of symptoms will uncover no evidence of

an underlying disease but will lead an attentive physician to suspect depression. The absence of a serious diagnosis may bring a sigh of relief to a young patient (and most certainly to his parents) but can also cause dismay. "Are you saying all of this is in my (my child's) head?" is a typical response. In fact, the symptoms are very real and a predictable component of depression. When depression improves with treatment, so do the physical symptoms.

Delusional thinking

Very rarely, a severe case of depression will also involve delusional thinking, in which the individual's beliefs and sensory experiences do not match with reality. He may hear voices or have hallucinations. He might believe that others are trying to harm him or entertain grandiose ideas about his identity or purpose in life. This is not merely a depression but a **psychosis,** a serious disorder of neurochemical function in the brain that must be treated with appropriate medication. (Hospitalization is often required at the outset.) Many psychotic individuals require lifelong medication to prevent a relapse.

WHY DO CHILDREN AND ADOLESCENTS BECOME DEPRESSED?

A complex blend of genetic, biochemical, personal, family, and spiritual factors can interact to cause depression. These include:

- *Genetics and biochemistry.* For a great many individuals, depression is primarily the result of a malfunction of **neurotransmitters,** compounds that participate in the electrochemical communication between nerve cells in the brain. Very often the vulnerability to a neurotransmitter disturbance appears to have a genetic origin, such that a number of members of the same family may be affected. This vulnerability, among other things, accounts for an individual becoming depressed for no apparent reason or struggling with depression throughout life.
- *Personal and family events.* A child who is brought up in an atmosphere of love, stability, encouragement, and consistent boundaries will usually see his world differently and interact with it more successfully than one who has lived with abuse, indifference, or chaos. For many individuals

depression is deeply rooted in early childhood experiences that taught them that the world is a dangerous place where no one can be trusted.

- *Recent stresses and reversals.* One or more major losses or traumatic events can set off a depressive episode (often referred to as a **reactive depression**) that is more prolonged and profound than the normal grieving process. Examples of such stressful events are a severe illness or death of a parent or other loved one (or even a pet); parental separation, divorce, or remarriage; a move from a familiar home; one or more episodes of physical or sexual abuse; a natural disaster; war or violence in the community; difficulty or failure in school or an athletic pursuit; the breakup of a close friendship or romantic relationship; a severe or chronic illness.

- *Personal and family faith.* A meaningful relationship with God and a sense of His love and involvement in an individual's life can have a significant stabilizing effect on mood and behavior. An ongoing personal commitment to God and positive connections with others who are caring and like-minded in faith serve to build a child's emotional world on a firm foundation, such that it will not crumble when the inevitable strains and storms of life arrive. Unfortunately, some religious situations involving intense legalism or an atmosphere of continuing condemnation can contribute to anxiety and depression.

What Can Be Done about Depression?

A parent's role in dealing with depression can be broken down into three key tasks:

Be alert for signs of depression.

These have already been listed, but it bears emphasizing that *parents are often caught off guard by their child's or adolescent's depression.* This disorder can occur even in the most stable home where children have been reared by devoted parents who provide consistent love and limits. Remember that for many individuals depression is caused primarily by a biochemical imbalance in the brain and not by bad parenting or a personal crisis. Don't assume that "it can't happen in our home" because in doing so, you might ignore or write off as a "bad attitude" significant changes in mood or behavior that desperately need your attention.

*If you suspect that your child or adolescent might be depressed or
suicidal (see page 602), seek appropriate help immediately.*

Depression is not a character weakness or a sign of parental failure. It is as important and *treatable* a problem as diabetes or asthma, and like those conditions,
it can lead to serious consequences—including death—if it is ignored. The approaches to this problem include:

**First and foremost, listen carefully to your child or adolescent, and take his feelings
and problems seriously.** One study of suicidal adolescents indicated that 90 percent felt that they were not understood by their families. Expressions of worry or
a sad mood should never be met with indifference or (worse) a shallow rebuff
("You'll get over it" or "Snap out of it!"). Sit down, shut off the TV, look your son
or daughter in the eye, and hear what he or she has to say—without judging, rebuking, or trivializing it. It might help enormously if you can say honestly that
you (or others you know and respect) have struggled with some of the same feelings.

Get a physician's evaluation. Usually a number of physical symptoms such as fatigue or headaches will need to be assessed, and rarely a specific disorder (for example, thyroid abnormalities) will be responsible for the entire gamut of
emotional and physical complaints.

**Get counseling with a qualified individual about the issues of life, including past
problems, family interactions, stressful situations, and other concerns.** This should
be carried out with someone who is trained to do this type of work with young
people and who also shares your basic values. Do not assume that a depression
can be "straightened out" in one or two counseling sessions. Normally several
weeks (sometimes months) of work will be necessary. Be prepared to become involved yourself at some point in the process. No depression occurs in a vacuum,
and family dynamics very often are part of both the problem and the solution.

Be willing to consider medication. This can play a very important role in the treatment of depression. **Antidepressants** can normalize disturbances in neurotransmitter function and are neither addictive nor an "escape from reality." On the
contrary, more often than not they allow the individual to tackle life issues much
more effectively, and they greatly accelerate the recovery process. The decision to
use medication and the choice of a particular agent will involve careful discussion with a primary-care physician or psychiatrist who can prescribe it and monitor its effects. Assuming that positive results are obtained, it is common to
continue medication on a maintenance basis for a number of months. (The neu-

rochemistry of depression is not like a streptococcal throat infection that can be resolved with ten days of treatment.)

Be willing to consider hospitalization. In severe cases, where the emotions have been extremely unstable or there has been suicidal behavior, hospitalization will usually be recommended in order to initiate treatment and ensure safety. The type of program utilized will vary considerably, depending on community resources, health insurance benefits, and the needs of the depressed individual.

Continue to support and pray for your depressed child. He needs to know that you are there for him and that you do not think of him as "crazy" or a colossal failure for having this problem. Prayer serves as an acknowledgment by parent and child that God alone has a complete understanding of this complex situation. Counseling and medication may serve as useful tools, but they are best used under His guidance.

Be on the lookout for risks of suicide and signs of suicidal behavior.

Many of the unique features of depression among young people also increase their risk of suicide. In particular, the intensity of their emotions and a shortage of life experiences that might allow them to imagine a hopeful future beyond an immediate crisis may give rise to self-destructive behavior, especially on an impulsive basis. In order to reduce the chance of a tragic loss of life, be aware of not only the signs of depression, which have already been listed, but also of the following risks and warning signs:

- *A previous suicide attempt.* This is considered the most significant predictor of a future suicide; more than 40 percent of adolescents who commit suicide have attempted it at least once in the past.
- *A family history of suicide.* Compared to their nonsuicidal peers, teenagers who kill themselves are five times more likely than their peers to have a history of a family member who has committed suicide.
- *Expressions of intense guilt or hopelessness.*
- *Threatening, talking, or joking about suicide.* It is important to have a heart-to-heart conversation with any child or adolescent who makes comments such as "I would be better off dead" or "Nothing matters anymore." Find out what is going on in his life and how he is feeling, and make it clear that you are committed to obtaining whatever help he might need to work through his problems. Broaching the subject of suicide does *not* encourage it, but rather increases the likelihood that a successful intervention can be started.

COMPLETE
BOOK OF BABY
& CHILD CARE
610

- *"Cleaning house."* You should be very concerned and should investigate immediately if a child or adolescent—whether your own or a member of someone else's family—begins to give away favorite possessions, clothing, entire CD or tape collections, etc. This is a common behavior among young people who are planning suicide.
- *A gun in the home.* Among young people, more suicides are carried out using firearms than by any other method. If anyone in your family—especially a teenager—is having a problem with depression, remove all guns from the home and keep them out.
- *Alcohol or drug abuse.* One frightening aspect of substance abuse is that it can trigger erratic, self-destructive behavior for which little or no warning was given. A mild depression can suddenly plummet to suidical intensity with the help of drugs or alcohol. Because of the unpredictable actions of chemicals on the system, a number of deaths occur among youngsters who did not intend to hurt themselves.
- *Suicide among other adolescents in your community.* Occasionally one or more suicides in a community or school will precipitate a disastrous "cluster" of self-destructive behavior among local teens.
- *A sudden, major loss or humiliation.* All of the stressful life events that were listed earlier in this section—death of a loved one, parental separation, failing an important test, etc.—not only can provoke a depressive episode but can also precipitate an unexpected suicide attempt.

If you feel that there is any possibility of a self-destructive act by your child, it is important that you not only express your concern but also *seek help immediately.* You may want to contact your child's/adolescent's physician for advice or referral. If anyone in your family has dealt with a counselor, this individual may be the appropriate initial contact. Many communities have a mental-health center that offers on-the-spot assessment of an individual's suicide risk or even an assessment team that will come to your home. *Stay with your child or adolescent* (or make certain that he or she remains in the company of a responsible adult) until you have reasonable assurance from a qualified individual and a clear commitment from your son or daughter that suicide is not going to be attempted. In situations where assurance cannot be obtained, the suicidal individual may need to be hospitalized for safety, further assessment, and the initiation of treatment. You will also need to take appropriate safety precautions, including removing any guns from the home and controlling access to medications.

What If a Child or Teenager Attempts Suicide?

Fortunately, the vast majority of suicide attempts by children and adolescents are unsuccessful. Some of these result in significant medical problems, while many are considered gestures or cries for help. *Any deliberate self-destructive act, whether planned or impulsive, should be taken very seriously, regardless of the severity of the outcome.* An evaluation at an emergency department should be carried out; subsequent hospitalization for medical treatment or observation is not uncommon.

After any medical problems have been resolved, a formal assessment by a qualified professional is mandatory. The course of action to be taken will depend upon a number of factors and may range from ongoing counseling while the child or adolescent remains at home to a formal treatment program in a psychiatric hospital setting. The latter approach is usually chosen both to ensure safety and to begin intensive treatment. While the details of treatment that might be used in such settings are beyond the scope of this book, it is important for parents to understand and approve of the approaches that will be used and to play an active role in their child's or adolescent's recovery process. As upset or guilty as you might feel under such circumstances, this is the time to draw close to your child who is in such pain and not to communicate shock and dismay ("How could you do such a thing?"). Above all, he will need loving and optimistic people on his team, and it will help immensely if his parents are at the top of the roster.

NOTES
1. Paul Meier, M.D., *Happiness Is a Choice for Teens* (Nashville: Thomas Nelson, 1997), 68.

CHAPTER 14

Passing the Baton

You don't raise heroes, you raise sons. And if you treat them like sons, they'll turn out to be heroes, even if it's just in your own eyes.
WALTER M. SCHIRRA, SR.

Passing the Baton: Instilling Values and Virtues in the Next Generation

If you think of parenting in the simplest of terms, it is in essence a twenty-year process of nurturing and guiding a precious human being from the utter helplessness of infancy to the independence and maturity of adulthood. Over time, it is easy to become buried in everyday concerns and lose sight of this sweeping perspective. This is unfortunate, because seeing the big picture often inspires mothers and fathers to commit themselves wholeheartedly to their parenting assignment as they grasp its profound significance and relative brevity.

Three other critical perspectives about parenting have been presented elsewhere in this book, but are worth repeating:

Children are a gift from God.

Children are, for a season, entrusted by their Creator, the perfect parent, to human fathers and mothers who are anything but perfect. At times—especially when the demands and details of child rearing seem overwhelming—this idea can be difficult to grasp. You may feel totally inadequate or even believe that parenthood was a mistake for you. But whether you are a single father/mother or a married couple, it is important to remember that your child is definitely a gift and that you are a gift to your child. Your acceptance, attention, values, and role modeling will have a profound influence on the person he or she becomes.

Parenthood is a process of working yourself out of a job.

While you will probably always *feel* like a parent, your role of guidance and authority has a very definite time limit and must eventually end. You should experience a major payoff when this occurs; instead of having a dependent child for the rest of your life, you will have an adult friend whose company and conversation you will savor and who can help *you* grow as an individual. One of the most important tasks of parenting will be working with your child, step by step, through this gradual release. Each child's pathway toward independence and each parent's willingness to grant it will be unique, and the process will not always be smooth. Judging your child's readiness for new freedoms and responsibilities is one of parenting's fine arts and should be shaped by awareness of your child's strengths and weaknesses, collaboration with your spouse (or a trusted adult if you are a single parent), soul-searching, and prayer.

MAKING MEMORIES

There are many simple things you can do as a parent to build memories and enhance special occasions with your child. However, when schedules are jammed with activities, some of life's simplest but most satisfying pleasures may be lost. But taking the time to create special memories can help cement a wonderful relationship with your children.

Below are some ideas that have been successful memory builders for many families. This is merely a list to help stimulate your own creative juices. Use these or add your own ideas to the list, but don't let years pass without creating some special times that your children will cherish and perhaps pass on to their own children.

Give the gift of time to your children.

- Schedule time with each of your children and make these "dates" as important on your calendar as any other commitment.
- If you are running errands, take one of the kids along and talk about what *she* finds interesting—her favorite game, toy, or book, for example.
- Make a special occasion of taking your child to work with you, and in so doing share this part of your life with him.

Record your thoughts, hopes, and dreams for your child in letters and journals.

- Letters can be written while you are pregnant and then given to your child later in life.

- Letters can be written for special occasions, such as a graduation from elementary school, public profession of faith, special birthday, first day of school, or first date.
- Letters can be written to celebrate a success or to console a discouragement.
- Even after the baton is passed, letters can be beautiful gifts at occasions such as engagements, weddings, births, achievements, and even failures.

Put special notes in your child's lunch box or on her pillow. Tell your child how much she means to you.

Take special family vacations. Follow the Santa Fe Trail if your family is into history. Scout out baseball stadiums. Go rafting. Or spend time at home camping in the backyard.

Make holidays special. Start new traditions, or re-create old ones.

On your child's thirteenth birthday take a moment, or an entire evening, to celebrate the transition to adolescence. Consider presenting a special gift (for example, a ring, necklace, or a "faith, hope, and love" charm) that can serve as a symbol of commitment to preserving the gift of sex for the wedding night.

When your son or daughter is ready to leave the nest for college or another destination, write a "release" letter (see page 633).

*Passing the baton: What will your children carry with them
into adulthood?*

In one very significant respect, parenting is like a relay race: One generation completes a very long lap and then passes a crucial baton to the runners in the next generation. In an Olympic relay, the gold medal usually hinges on the skill with which the baton is passed between the runners. If the baton is fumbled, the runner will still arrive at the finish line but probably with some disappointment over the final result.

Parents, grandparents, and others who are responsible for rearing the citizens of the next generation must repeatedly ask themselves some critical questions: Will this child carry with him into adulthood the values that are truly important? Will these values play a significant role in his life, his career, and his own family? Will they be passed on to his own children?

Jesus asked a question which has given pause to men and women for twenty centuries: "What good will it be for a man if he gains the whole world, yet forfeits his soul?" (Matthew 16:26). A similar question should be pondered regularly by parents: "What good is it if I achieve all my aspirations but my children reject the values I care about?"

THE BASIC GOALS

As a parent you have been entrusted by God to help mold your child's character, values, and spirituality, while preparing him for such practical matters as choosing a career, handling finances, and finding a husband or wife. This is a tall order, and we sometimes lose sight of these bigger issues while dealing with the daily details. But the important assignment of preparing your child for the future can be accomplished—one small step at a time.

The first step is to define what your specific goals should be. This chapter is intended to help with that process by serving as a basic road map, one that can be reviewed every year to gauge whether your race is still on course and your baton ready to be passed. You may find the length and breadth of this endeavor daunting. *How can I instill all of my values and virtues in my children? I'm still trying to develop them in my own life!* If you realize that you can't accomplish all of these goals perfectly and that you can't be an infallible guide to life for your child (because you're still figuring out a few things yourself), congratulations! Acknowledging this fact is the beginning of parental wisdom. You can be certain

Children can't grow without taking risks. Toddlers can't walk initially without falling down. . . . And, ultimately, an adolescent can't enter young adulthood until we release him from our protective custody.

DR. DOBSON
ANSWERS YOUR
QUESTIONS ABOUT
CONFIDENT,
HEALTHY FAMILIES

that God knew your shortcomings before entrusting you with a child, and you would be wise to seek His counsel on a regular basis.

As you think about these concepts, you may experience misgivings or even remorse. You probably haven't cherished every moment with your child (few parents do), and you may have felt burdened with—or even resentful of—the demands of parenting. Perhaps your children are already in the midst of stormy adolescence or are grown and gone, and you are painfully aware that you have not exactly been the world's best cheerleader, teacher, or coach. But it is never too late to make course corrections—and amends—as a parent. Even if your children are already grown, what you have learned (sometimes the hard way) can still benefit *their* children. What ultimately matters is that you ask for forgiveness where it is needed and then move forward, providing input and support that is appropriate for their current stage of life.

The following pages will focus on five key areas of your child's life: spiritual growth, character development, handling finances, choosing a vocation, and preparing for marriage.

SPIRITUAL GROWTH

It is a sad fact that some children who have been taken regularly to Sunday school and church will grow up to ignore God and reject the values their parents taught (or *thought* they had taught) at home. To their utter dismay, Mom and Dad learn too late that this training just didn't "take," and they wonder what went wrong.

The Old Testament story of Eli is an example. The devoted priest failed to influence the behavior of his own boys; both sons became profane and evil young men. Samuel—one of the greatest men in the Bible—witnessed Eli's parental mistakes and yet proceeded to lose his children too! The message the Bible communicates is loud and clear: Devotion to God is not inherited. God does not guarantee that our children will follow Him simply because we do. The reason, of course, is that every child must eventually decide *on his or her own* whether to follow, ignore, or reject God. If parents could lock in a child's commitment to God—if it were in fact impossible for the child to say no—then the child's love for God would not be love at all but the meaningless response of a preprogrammed machine.

Nevertheless, the fact that parents cannot preordain their child's faith does not mean that they shouldn't attempt to encourage it in a healthy way and to pray daily for his spiritual growth. Parents are admonished in the book of Proverbs to "train a child in the way he should go"—which means, among other things, that parents need some specific ideas about what that "way" should be. It is appropriate and desirable for a child to be exposed to a carefully conceived, systematic program of religious training. Yet many parents approach this project in a haphazard manner.

If a child is to be encouraged toward spiritual awareness and maturity, first provide him with clearly defined goals. Below is a checklist for parents, a set of targets that apply to both childhood and adulthood. Many of these require a level of maturity that cannot be expected of young children. But we can gently and consistently urge them toward these targets during their impressionable early years.

These scriptural concepts provide the foundation upon which all future doctrine and faith will rest. These should be taught deliberately and affirmed to children in a manner appropriate for their age.

Concept I: Loving God

One of the teachers of the law came and heard them debating. Noticing that Jesus had given them a good answer, he asked him, "Of all the commandments, which is the most important?"

"The most important one," answered Jesus, "is this: 'Hear, O Israel, the Lord our God, the Lord is one. Love the Lord your God with all your heart and with all your soul and with all your mind and with all your strength.'"

—*Mark 12:28-30*

- Is your child learning of God's love through the love, tenderness, and mercy of his parents?
- Is he learning to talk about the Lord Jesus and include Him in his thoughts and plans as part of his everyday experience?
- Is he learning to turn to God for help whenever he is frightened, anxious, or lonely?
- Is he learning to read the Bible?
- Is he learning to pray?
- Is he learning the meaning of faith and trust?
- Does he understand that God loved him so much that He sent His Son to die for him?
- Is he learning that loving and serving God is the ultimate source of joy and freedom in life?

Concept II: Loving others

"The second is this: 'Love your neighbor as yourself.' There is no commandment greater than these."
—*Mark 12:31*

- Is she learning to understand and empathize with others?
- Is she learning not to be selfish and demanding?
- Is she learning to share?
- Is she learning not to gossip and criticize others?
- Is she learning to serve others?

Concept III: Following God's rules

Fear God and keep his commandments, for this is the whole duty of man.
—*Ecclesiastes 12:13*

In addition to loving God and loving neighbors:

- Is he learning to honor God's name and not to misuse it?
- Is he learning that one day of the week—the Sabbath—is to be set apart from normal activities and dedicated to God?
- Is he learning to honor and respect his parents?
- Is he learning to value human life at all ages—from conception to advanced age—without regard to appearance, race, physical condition, or mental capacity?
- Is he learning to respect the gift of sex and the importance of preserving sexual experiences for marriage?
- Is he learning to respect the possessions of others: neither stealing nor borrowing without permission and making restitution if he damages another person's property?
- Is he learning to be truthful and honest?
- Is he learning the ultimate insignificance of material goods?

Concept IV: Following God's direction

Teach me to do your will, for you are my God.
— *Psalm 143:10*

- Is she learning that her primary purpose on earth is to serve the Lord?
- Is she learning to obey her parents as preparation for later obedience to God?

- Is she learning to behave properly in church?
- Is she learning a healthy appreciation for God's justice as well as His love?
- Is she learning that there are people in many types of benevolent authority roles—caregivers, teachers, coaches, police, youth leaders—to whom she must submit?
- Is she learning the meaning of sin and its inevitable consequences?

Concept V: Acquiring self-control

But the fruit of the Spirit is love, joy, peace, patience, kindness, goodness, faithfulness, gentleness and self-control.
—*Galatians 5:22-23*

- Is he learning to control his impulses?
- Is he learning to take proper care of the body that God has given him?
- Is he learning to work and carry responsibility?
- Is he learning to tolerate minor frustration?
- Is he learning to memorize and quote Scripture?
- Is he learning to give a portion of his allowance (and other money) to God?

Concept VI: Acquiring an appropriate self-concept

For everyone who exalts himself will be humbled, and he who humbles himself will be exalted.
—*Luke 14:11*

- Is she learning a sense of appreciation?
- Is she learning to thank God for the good things in life?
- Is she learning to forgive and forget?
- Is she learning the vast difference between self-worth and egotistical pride?
- Is she learning to bow in reverence before the God of the universe?

CHARACTER DEVELOPMENT

The development of positive, stable character traits should flow directly from spiritual growth. If a person's religious activities—Sunday school, Bible reading, prayer, and so on—are not accompanied by virtuous behavior, then his or her faith is shallow, false, or self-deluding.

My son, if your heart is wise, then my heart will be glad; my inmost being will rejoice when your lips speak what is right.

PROVERBS 23:15-16

What good is it, my brothers, if a man claims to have faith but has no deeds? Can such faith save him? Suppose a brother or sister is without clothes and daily food. If one of you says to him, "Go, I wish you well; keep warm and well fed," but does nothing about his physical needs, what good is it? In the same way, faith by itself, if it is not accompanied by action, is dead.

—James 2:14-17

Similarly, attempts to train a child to be "good" will have only limited success if the child does not have an understanding of God's love and justice as well as demonstrate personal repentance and submission to God's leadership.

Spiritual maturity and virtuous character will not develop during random lectures crammed into a few minutes every month. Parents need to plan ahead, focusing on the values they intend to instill. They must also take advantage of unscheduled "teachable moments," when a situation naturally lends itself to a discussion about positive (or negative) behavior. However this important task is carried out, the following are some important character traits, listed alphabetically, on which to focus.

Courage is frequently portrayed in movies and cartoons as the primary requirement for superheroes embroiled in daring exploits. But children need to understand that courage is also important for everyday life, both now and in the future. Indeed, one who learns courage as a child is more likely to be secure as an adult. Courage encompasses several elements:

- Daring to attempt difficult but worthy projects.
- Saying *no* to the pressure of the crowd.
- Remaining true to convictions, even when they are unpopular or inconvenient.
- Being outgoing and friendly, even when it's uncomfortable.

Courage can also apply to more highly stressful situations:

- Applying resources in creative ways when faced with overwhelming odds.
- Following difficult instructions in the face of danger.
- Confronting an opponent in an honorable way, confident that what is morally right will ultimately succeed.

Determination can help your child avoid becoming a pessimist. This trait helps a child:

- Realize that present struggles are essential for future achievement.
- Break down a seemingly impossible task by concentrating on achievable goals.
- Expend whatever energy is necessary to complete a project.
- Reject any distraction that will hinder the completion of a task.
- Prepare to handle hardships that lie ahead, whether the task is spiritual, physical, emotional, or relational.

Fidelity and chastity are rarely taught within our culture (by movies, television programs, popular music, etc.) and not as often by educators, coaches, or even church leaders as they were a generation ago. Therefore it is important that your children hear clearly from you about the benefits of reserving sexual activity for marriage. Children also need to grasp the serious potential consequences of sexual immorality: sexually transmitted diseases, infertility, crisis pregnancies, and a broken heart (see Special Concerns, page 541).

Honesty is not always rewarded in our culture, but it is a bedrock virtue. Without it, all of your child's most important relationships will be compromised and unstable. Children should be taught that truthfulness is critical when dealing with:

- Family members, friends, and acquaintances
- School
- Organizations, including future employers
- Governmental agencies
- God

Dishonesty must be discouraged in all its forms, whether it be outright lying to another individual, misrepresenting to an employer what one has (or hasn't) done, cheating on a test, plagiarizing, or doctoring an income tax return.

Humility arises from an honest assessment of one's own strengths and weaknesses, such that boasting is not necessary to gain acceptance or to feel contentment. Humility also involves submission to duly constituted authority, obedience to the law, and fairness in work and play. Most important, humility will keep your child on his knees in prayer.

Kindness and friendliness should be presented to a child as admirable and far superior to being "tough." Children need to be taught that it is usually better to understand than to confront, and that gentleness—especially toward those who are younger or weaker—is in fact a sign of strength. *Do not allow your child to become a bully.*

Love in many ways encompasses and surpasses other virtues, as stated by the apostle Paul nearly 2,000 years ago:

> Love is patient, love is kind. It does not envy, it does not boast, it is not proud. It is not rude, it is not self-seeking, it is not easily angered, it keeps no record of wrongs. Love does not delight in evil but rejoices with the truth. It always protects, always trusts, always hopes, always perseveres.
> —*1 Corinthians 13:4-7*

Children should be taught—and shown—how to love their friends, neighbors, and even adversaries.

Loyalty and dependability are traits needed for success in many arenas of life. A person who is flighty and cannot honor a commitment is unlikely to find true

---

HOW DO I ENCOURAGE SPIRITUAL GROWTH AND CHARACTER DEVELOPMENT?

The answer hinges on the little word *time*. These traits mature over many years of *time* as parents leave enough *time* in their busy lives to spend enough *time* with their children to talk about these subjects many, many *times*.

With enough time, you can encourage spiritual growth and character development in the following ways:

- *Be your child's primary role model.* Let him see the values you care about enacted every day in front of him. "Do as I say, not as I do" is a recipe for moral failure.
- *When you have done or said something that was mistaken, inappropriate, or just plain wrong, admit it.* Have the courage to apologize for what went wrong, and then explain why it was wrong. You will gain great respect from your children for doing so, and they won't forget what you say in these moments.

- *Read or tell stories that illustrate the values you care about.* The Bible is full of them. So is other literature, including dozens of passages that have been compiled by William J. Bennett in anthologies such as *The Book of Virtues, The Moral Compass,* and *The Children's Book of Virtues.*
- *Seize the teachable moment.* When a situation arises in which a moral example (good or bad) is before you, talk to your child about it. *This should not be limited to times during which you are correcting misbehavior.* It might occur, for example, while watching a video, a ball game, an erratic driver on the freeway, or another child's tantrum in the mall.
- *Praise your child—in front of others, whenever possible—when he does what is right.* When correcting him or administering disciplinary measures, do so in private.
- *Pray specifically for your child's spiritual and character development.*

happiness or success. Your children need to learn the importance of loyalty to family, employer, country, church, school, and other organizations and institutions to which they will eventually make commitments. If a child learns to be reliable and stand by his word, he will be trusted and see opportunities open before him throughout life.

Orderliness and cleanliness may or may not be "next to godliness," but they can increase a person's chances of success in many areas of life. While no one has ever died of dirty-room syndrome, a child who can learn to keep his possessions organized and in order will eventually be able to use his resources to their greatest efficiency. Personal cleanliness and good grooming speak of self-respect and project an important message to others: I care enough about those around me to try to appear basically pleasant.

Respect is a critical commodity in human relationships, whether within families, organizations, or entire nations. It encompasses basic courtesy, politeness, and manners toward others. It has largely been lost in our culture, and it desperately needs to be regained. When a person loses respect for life, property, parents, elders, nature, and for the beliefs and rights of others, a self-serving and destructive attitude will take its place.

Self-discipline and moderation are rare but valuable traits in a culture that claims that you can—and should—have it all. Children need to understand that, even if it is possible for them to do so, it is not necessary or wise to "have it all." Exercising self-discipline over physical, emotional, and financial desires can prevent illness, debt, and burnout later in life. Children should be taught the importance of the following:

- Controlling personal appetites
- Knowing the limits of body and mind
- Balancing work and recreation
- Avoiding the dangers of extreme, unbalanced viewpoints
- Engaging the brain before putting the tongue in gear

Unselfishness and sensitivity are universally appreciated and respected. A child who is more concerned about others than himself will be seen as mature beyond his years and can benefit himself and others.

MANAGING FINANCES

Teaching children how to manage money can be one of the greatest benefits parents provide for them before they leave home. Before you attempt to teach your child about money, however, determine how you are doing with your own finances. Do you set goals? Are you out of debt? Do you have long- and short-term savings? Have you begun investing in a college-education fund or your retirement? If so, you're definitely making wise decisions.

On the other hand, do you live from paycheck to paycheck? Do you have trouble keeping track of how much money is in your checking account? Is there always "too much month at the end of the money"? Are you an impulse buyer? Do you depend on your credit cards to make ends meet? If this is the case, before you start teaching your child how to manage money, you need to get your spending habits in order.

Whether you are a financial wizard or still struggling to balance your checkbook, the most important lesson your child needs to learn about money is that *God owns it all.* God is the creator and ultimate owner of every resource, and He has entrusted you to be a wise steward of whatever He has loaned to you.

It is important to realize that children begin shaping their views about money at an early age. Unfortunately, many families deal with this important topic haphazardly, offering their children little specific guidance while presum-

---

WHEN YOU PAY YOUR CHILD FOR WORK

- *Be clear about what you want done, and what you are offering.* Also, be sure to let your child know if there is a time frame involved ("I need this done by four o'clock").
- *Make sure that your child is capable of accomplishing the task.* If you tend to be a perfectionist, be careful that the standards you set for the work you want done aren't beyond your child's reach. On the other hand, don't make the mistake of lowering your expectations if your child is in fact capable of performing the task.
- *When possible, give your child some "on the job training."* Your child may be more open to learn how to use tools properly, for example, if the job helps earn money to buy something she wants.
- *Pay only for jobs that are completed.* Remind your

children that *you* as a parent aren't paid a salary unless you go to work every day, work all day, and perform your duties completely.
- *Pay for quality work.* If your child didn't do his best, you're only penalizing him by paying for laziness. Teach your child to strive to do a job right the first time.
- *Pay fairly within your budget, but don't overpay merely because you can afford it.* Even if you have a bountiful income, it doesn't make sense to pay your child fifty dollars for taking out the trash or doing the dishes. This only sets unrealistic expectations for the future. Pay according to the job description.
- *Reward extra effort.* If your child goes out of her way to do an outstanding job, reward her both emotionally and financially.

ing that they can learn the nuts and bolts of money management when they're older. But if you wait until your kids are ready to leave the nest before you begin to broach this subject, they may enter adulthood at a serious disadvantage when it comes to handling their finances wisely.

As a starting point, formulate coherent policies within your family for the following three issues. Keep in mind that there are several possible approaches and reasonable viewpoints for each issue.

Unpaid responsibilities. Each child over age five (some would say as young as three or four) should have certain jobs at home to do regularly without any specific pay. These might involve tasks related to her own possessions (e.g., cleaning up her room or helping with her laundry) as well as chores done for the good of the entire family (setting the table or feeding the dog). Obviously, the duration and complexity of the assignments should be appropriate for each child's age and capabilities. A child should learn that it is usual and customary for everyone in the family to pitch in and work for the common good without expecting a reward every time.

Allowances. Parents and financial advisors alike hold all sorts of divergent opinions about this subject. Some feel that giving a child a weekly allowance teaches her to expect a "free lunch," while others see it as part of a parent's appropriate expression of provision for a child. (Parents normally don't charge their grade-school children monthly rent or leave a food bill in their lunch box, for example, yet no one sees this as contributing to an expectation of free room and board throughout life.)

If you choose to give your child a weekly or monthly allowance, you should state clearly any guidelines you might have for the money you provide. For example, is the entire amount meant to be "mad money" for fun activities, or do you want your child to allocate amounts for certain expenses (such as school lunches), savings, and giving? As your child enters adolescence, you would be wise to give her the responsibility of managing funds designated for expenses such as clothing.

Opportunities to earn money. Both you and your child will benefit if she seeks opportunities to earn extra money in exchange for the satisfactory completion of a specific task (see sidebar, page 626).

In addition to setting basic policies about money and work, consider implementing the following ideas regarding money management:

Use visual reinforcement, especially for young children. Children love to track their progress visually. Keep a chart of your child's responsibilities; use color stars or stickers to indicate jobs she has completed. This provides an opportunity for you to praise your child for her accomplishments, and this in turn will motivate her for the next task.

Teach children to share their resources. As you provide money for your children, teach them the rewards of giving to others. Talk to them about the importance of giving back to God (who, don't forget, owns everything) by contributing regularly to church and other ministries. Encourage them by your own example.

Teach children to save. Even during the preschool years, it's not too early to teach your child to save for the future. As she gets older, she can also learn "the magic of compounding"—how money accumulates over time when left in an account that earns interest.

When your child becomes an adolescent, in addition to continuing the above principles, you need to begin preparing her to earn a living and releasing her from your financial supply line. Consider working on these preparations for greater financial responsibility:

Teach your teenager the principles of budgeting.

This will be important whether her future income is modest or abundant. Beginning at sixteen or seventeen, your adolescent should be allowed to make most of her own financial decisions. You may choose to provide her with a monthly allowance to be budgeted among several items such as clothing, toiletries, and other personal supplies you used to buy. Help her set up a budget, but she must also be given the freedom to fail—and in the process learn valuable lessons. For example, if she blows her entire clothing budget in the first six months of the year, she will have to forgo desirable purchases later on. Allocating cash between basic necessities, entertainment, savings, and giving to church and other worthy causes is a concept most teens do not understand without some guidance. But if you teach your child budgeting principles now, she'll benefit for a lifetime.

Checking account. Your adolescent should be given the opportunity to use and maintain her own checking account under your supervision. It is vitally important that you teach an older teenager how to balance a checkbook monthly. Many parents obtain a credit card (with a very modest spending limit) for an older child—perhaps in the senior year of high school—to train her to use it properly. Two warnings she must receive: (1) Never buy anything with a card that she would not have purchased with cash, and (2) pay off the total amount on the credit card each month without fail.

Personal expenses and bargain hunting. Your adolescent, whether living at home or away at college, should begin to deal with the amazing ability of "miscellaneous expenses" to derail her budget. Teach her to use self-control in her spending through your example. Show her where to shop and help her learn to seek the best values for her limited supply of dollars.

Career Preparation

Children begin thinking about "what I want to be when I grow up" early in life, as they play with their friends and watch their parent(s) go off to work every day. An ideal time to start career preparation is during the preteen years. Take the time to expose your children to a variety of occupations. If your daughter is interested in medicine, for example, let her spend time talking to her physician about the demands and rewards of this profession. The same approach can be taken for virtually any type of career that might interest your child.

Guiding and equipping your adolescent with skills to be gainfully employed is a major responsibility, one that must begin before he leaves home. The following are some ideas that might help in this process.

Equip your adolescent to discover his or her strengths and weaknesses.

- Expose him to job opportunities that fit his personality.
- Don't project your expectations on your child. Not all children follow in their parents' footsteps. If you're an accountant but your child has difficulty with math, don't push her into a career that would make her miserable. If you're an attorney but your son wants to be an artist, don't try to make him fit his artistic "square peg" temperament into the "round hole" demands of a legal career.
- Help your child discover his natural, God-given talents. During your child's formative years, he will excel in some areas and fail at others. Help him develop his strengths and identify possible career opportunities that might match them.

Equip your adolescent to think of vocation and career in spiritual terms.

- He is uniquely designed by God (Psalm 139:13-14).
- He has been given specific talents for a purpose (Romans 12:6-8).

- He must develop his God-given talents and strive for excellence (Proverbs 22:29).
- Work is a stage for his higher calling (Matthew 5:16).

Equip your adolescent to obtain guidance in the pursuit of education, training, and possible career fields.

You should be able to get some help in this area from the local school's professional guidance counselor.

- Identify your adolescent's likes and dislikes and expose her to fields she is interested in.
- Discover natural talents before college or vocational training. Work with your child (for example, by becoming involved with her in science class or in arts and crafts). Before spending thousands of dollars on college or vocational training, help your child find the path on which she is most likely to excel.
- Teach your child to pray for God's guidance and seek what He would have her do for a career.

Finally, consider seeking career-testing services that may help your older adolescent determine what career options fit his personality. These tests often help young adults hone in on their special talents, if they have not already done so, and they can also confirm whether a certain career choice is a logical path. Adolescents who are somewhat aimless might find that the test results point them in one or more specific directions. Others who are endowed with a number of definite interests might benefit from tests that help them focus on their areas of greatest strength. This might spare at least some from changing majors one or more times during college, which could prove both expensive and time-consuming.

PREPARATION FOR MARRIAGE

One of your most important goals when passing the baton to your child is to prepare him or her for marriage. If you have a strong and vibrant marriage, it is important to share with your children the principles upon which you have built and maintained this relationship. But if your marriage is less than ideal or you have experienced a divorce, lessons you have learned the hard way can still benefit your children, assuming that you are willing to be candid and transparent about your experience.

At a time when approximately 50 percent of marriages end in divorce and only 10 to 20 percent of the remaining marriages (5 to 10 percent of the total) are characterized by true satisfaction, parents face a formidable job educating their children about selecting a husband or a wife for life. Recent studies show that partners with similar interests have a better chance of achieving a fulfilling marriage. Because we are a mobile society, children from stable and loving homes often select partners with different backgrounds, customs, goals, interests, and beliefs. This does not mean that they cannot succeed in marriage, but in such cases both parties must enter the relationship with their eyes open and a willingness to work through their differences.

Early adolescence is a good time to begin discussing with your child characteristics and traits to seek in a future wife or husband. You may want to give him a list of twenty or thirty of these qualities and have him rank in order the ones he thinks are the most important. Quite often, children will discover that their mental image of their "dream partner"—very often a fantasy derived from movies and television shows—does not match with this ranking. It might be helpful to have your child save this list (or make a copy) and review it annually.

Also early in adolescence—perhaps on a special birthday such as the thirteenth—encourage your child to begin praying for a future spouse. As parents, you should be doing the same if you haven't started already. Toward the end of high school, however, give your adolescent some books that explore the process of selecting a partner and building a strong marriage. One excellent book is Dr. James Dobson's *Love for a Lifetime.* Another is *Finding the Love of Your Life,* by psychologist Dr. Neil Warren, which lists the following ten principles of mate selection, along with seven deadly mate-selection errors:

Principle #1: Eliminate the seven deadly mate-selection errors.

1. Don't get married too quickly. Longer courtships produce consistently healthier marriages.
2. Don't get married too young. Wait to get married until you know yourself well, and until you know well the kind of person with whom you can be happy. This usually means that first marriages will not begin until the mid to late 20s.
3. Don't be too eager to get married, and don't let anyone else who is overly eager push you into marriage. Make sure your mind is clear and settled.

4. Don't try to please someone else with your choice. You are the one who will profit or suffer from your choice for a lifetime.

5. Don't marry someone until you know him or her in a lot of different ways. You can make a far more accurate prediction about how much you will enjoy being married to a person if your experience is broad.

6. Don't get married with unrealistic expectations. Marriage isn't a panacea; it requires an incredible amount of hard work. Don't allow yourself to expect too much from your marriage.

7. Don't marry anyone who has a personality or behavioral problem that you're not willing to live with forever. These problems don't vanish; in fact, they often get worse. "Miracle cures" are far easier to come by before you are married. If the problem can be cured, make sure it is cured before you are married.

Principle #2: Develop a high degree of conscious clarity about the person you wish to marry, and filter this image through your conscious mind until you are completely comfortable with it.

Principle #3: Make sure the person you marry is very similar to you.

Principle #4: Get married only if both you and the person you want to marry are emotionally healthy.

Principle #5: Make sure you are passionately attracted to the person you want to marry, but wait until you are married to express the full intensity of your passion.

Principle #6: Decide to get married only after you have experienced a deeper, more stable kind of love. Passion may fade, but this kind of deeper love endures.

Principle #7: Develop mastery in the area of verbal intimacy. The love between two people who know how to be intimate with each other will grow dramatically.

Principle #8: Learn how to resolve differences before you get married. This will keep the road to love free and clear.

Principle #9: Get married only when you are ready to be absolutely committed to your partner—no matter what—for a lifetime.

Principle #10: If your parents, relatives, and close friends support your contemplated marriage, celebrate with them! If they don't, listen carefully to them before you make your final decision.

Encourage your adolescent or young adult to obtain counseling before an official engagement is announced, even if he is certain that he has found the "love of his life." Offer to pay for counseling if it is not furnished by the church. Many inventories are available to help counselors uncover any potential problem areas. The *Prepare* inventory, for example, identifies both strengths and weaknesses of each potential spouse and can predict which marriages are likely to succeed and which are at higher risk for divorce.

Inform your child that, even when married, he or she will need to work on this relationship for a lifetime. If you have grown children who are married, volunteer to pay for them to attend a marriage enrichment weekend (such as the Family Life Conference 1-800-FL-TODAY). You might even offer to baby-sit their children, if needed. (By the way, you might consider attending such a conference yourself.)

Finally, *warn your child once more about becoming sexually involved before marriage.* Among other things, premarital sex might lead him to marry the wrong person and rob him of a satisfying lifelong marriage. Children of divorce might be tempted to cohabit prior to marriage in hopes of avoiding their parents' mistakes. But statistics indicate that cohabitors have an even greater chance of divorce (approaching 75 percent).

The most important thing you can do for your children to help them develop a healthy concept of marriage is to *allow them to see you loving, cherishing, and respecting your partner.* If you are not married, allow your children to spend time with one or more families in which a nurturing, respectful marital relationship is modeled.

THE FINISHING TOUCH: RELEASING YOUR GROWN CHILD

In reality, you have been slowly releasing your child since birth, and, if he or she marries in the future, you will once again have to release your now-grown child—this time to become one flesh with a spouse. But there will come a time when you must pass the baton to your child. You, of course, will be a parent for life, but your role must change to that of a coach and friend, encouraging your grown child's progress—and perhaps, later on, watching your grandchildren take the baton to begin their lap.

But ready or not, shortly after your son or daughter graduates from high school, your formal job of parenting should be completed, and he or she will need to be released. *The fact that you are doing so should be specifically conveyed*

I have no greater joy than to hear that my children are walking in the truth.

3 JOHN 1:4

to your grown child, either verbally or in writing or perhaps both. The advantage of a letter is that it allows you time to organize your thoughts, it conveys a sense of permanence, and it allows your young adult to reread this important letter in the future.

Whether expressed in spoken or written words, your message of release may be communicated to a young adult who has given you a great deal more joy than grief and about whose future you feel confident. Or you may have to express sorrow and honest concern about your grown child's future health, safety, and financial stability. (Such a letter might have been written by the father of the prodigal son as the son was leaving home.) Regardless of the circumstances, however, the release must be given.

The specific wording of this conversation and/or letter will be different for each parent, but (among other things) it should communicate the following:

- Your job is done.
- You acknowledge that you have not been a perfect parent.
- You hope and pray that she will forgive you for your failings.
- You will continue to pray for her.
- If one day God allows her to marry and have children of her own, you hope that she will build on the positive traits of her parents and grandparents, avoid your mistakes, and improve in areas where you were weak.
- Whatever the future holds for her, you will always love her.
- You hope that she will hold fast to, and teach to her own children, the values that you care about.
- She should hold fast to her faith or strongly consider beginning her relationship with God if she has not done so already.

Reference Section

A

abdominal pain A child who complains that her stomach hurts could have any number of things wrong, ranging in severity from cramping caused by anxiety or constipation to a full-blown medical emergency. Very often the reason isn't obvious, and identifying the source of pain may require investigation by both parent and physician. This is particularly true for infants and toddlers, who can communicate very little, if any, specific information about their discomfort.

This section is not intended as a definitive explanation of all the causes of abdominal pain in children. Instead, we have provided a series of questions to help you narrow down the possibilities when your child complains of abdominal pain. If you need to call your child's doctor, the information you gather using these questions will make your conversation or office visit far more productive.

Where is the pain?
Pinning down the location of pain is sometimes easier said than done. When asked where it hurts, a child might make a broad gesture over the entire abdomen. Ask her to point to where it hurts the most or to trace the location if it hurts over a wide area.

Pain caused by cramping of the large or small intestine is usually felt over a broad area or will seem to the child to be centered at the navel (belly button). But if a specific area is inflamed, the pain will tend to be focused in one location. The usual pattern in **appendicitis,** for example, starts with cramping in the upper abdomen or around the navel and then gradually shifts to the right-lower abdomen as the appendix becomes more inflamed. If a child has **hepatitis** (a viral infection of the liver), pain will be in the upper-right side of the abdomen. Pain in the upper-middle abdomen, especially a burning sensation, frequently involves irritation of the stomach (**gastritis**).

In preteen and adolescent girls, pain in the lower half of the abdomen can be more difficult to sort out because it could involve the reproductive organs (uterus, fallopian tubes, and ovaries) or the urinary tract. If she needs to urinate often and has a burning sensation when urine is passed, a **bladder infection** is likely. This and most lower abdominal pain—especially in girls—usually needs a doctor's evaluation and treatment.

How long has the pain been present?
A pain that ends within ten or fifteen minutes usually involves a **spasm** (an intense contraction) of some part of the intestine. Many children, especially during the preschool and elementary school years, will complain about a stomach ache. This will usually disappear within a half hour or so. (Often a brief rest will help.) Constipation can also cause this type of pain; checking how often your child has a bowel movement may provide you with helpful information.

School anxiety can cause stomach aches that begin on Monday morning and miraculously disappear on weekends. Gentle questioning about progress at school—and, if needed, some troubleshooting about classwork or problems with other students—might help reduce both the anxiety about school and the weekday abdominal pain.

A

While pains such as these are not likely to be caused by serious disease, episodes that disrupt your child's activities or occur repeatedly over several weeks should be evaluated by a physician. If pain continues for more than an hour, especially if a child is obviously uncomfortable, call your child's physician.

Is there nausea and vomiting?

Nausea and vomiting can be caused by many types of problems in the abdomen. Often **gastroenteritis** (stomach flu) causes cramping or even constant pain, but vomiting is a more dramatic symptom. If your child vomits repeatedly, contact your doctor because ongoing fluid loss can lead to dehydration—especially in infants and small children. Listlessness, dry mouth, doughy skin texture, decreased production of urine (fewer wet diapers in infants) and, in more extreme cases, sunken eyes are symptoms of severe dehydration that should be evaluated immediately (see *vomiting*).

Is there diarrhea or constipation?

Diarrhea is often caused by an infection and is usually accompanied by cramping pains. A variety of viruses, bacteria, and parasites can cause diarrhea, and special tests may be needed to identify the organism that is involved (see *diarrhea*). The sudden onset of vomiting and diarrhea together is typical of gastroenteritis, a viral illness that often settles down after twelve to twenty-four hours. This combination, however, can cause dehydration more quickly than would either symptom alone. If diarrhea is the only problem and your child is alert and taking liquids satisfactorily, a call to the doctor's office can usually wait until office hours.

Constipation may also lead to cramping pains, often provoked by a meal and relieved by a bowel movement. When food enters the stomach, a reflex message is sent to the colon to contract and move the stool so it can be eliminated. Over time, stool can accumulate if the amount leaving the colon is less than the amount entering. If a day or two passes without a bowel movement—an event not uncommon in older children—the backup can become substantial. Furthermore, as the colon extracts water from stool, the contents tend to become harder with each passing day. When the stomach becomes full (especially after a large meal), the firm reflex squeeze of colon against a resistant collection of stool can produce major pain. If your child's doctor suspects that this is the cause of recurrent abdominal pain, simple measures to evacuate excess stool (see *constipation*) can produce dramatic improvement.

Is there fever?

If abdominal pain is accompanied by an oral temperature over 99.4°F (or rectal over 100.4°F), inflammation (usually involving an infection by bacteria or virus) is nearly always involved. Your child's doctor should be contacted for further directions, which will depend upon the other symptoms.

Is the pain affected by eating?

Pain in the upper abdomen that is relieved by small amounts of food or milk may be caused by inflammation of the stomach, which is aggravated by stomach acid and neutralized by some foods. While ongoing stomach irritation caused by acid (**peptic ulcer disease**) is uncommon in small children, it can definitely occur in older children and teenagers. In adolescents a history of burning discomfort that is worse when the stomach is empty but relieved by food or antacid suggests this possibility. In younger children the symptoms may be more vague. In general, if abdominal pain is severe, food should be withheld until you have contacted your child's physician.

In some situations, specific foods provoke abdominal pain. For example, children who cannot digest **lactose**—the sugar found in milk—may develop abdominal pain and diarrhea after eating dairy products. In **celiac disease,** gluten—the protein found in wheat—provokes an allergic reaction that damages the lining of the intestines and leads to foul-smelling diarrhea, cramping pain, irritability, and weight loss over a prolonged period of time. Because there is no immediate cause-and-effect relationship between a particular meal and the symptoms, the connection will not be obvious immediately. After other possible causes of these symptoms have been ruled out, your doctor may recommend a procedure in which a small amount of tissue is taken from the intestines for microscopic evaluation. If the diagnosis is celiac disease, your child will need a gluten-free diet.

How old is the child?

Certain problems are more specific to the young infant. **Colic,** for example, usually occurs in babies under three months of age. While a universal cause for this disturbance is not known with certainty, the classic theory holds that contractions in the intestines provoke pain and intense crying, pulling up of the legs, and often passing of gas. While not medically serious, the infant's crying can easily frustrate and discourage any parent. *If the baby has a fever or is vomiting, the problem is more serious than colic, and a doctor should be contacted.* Strategies for dealing with colic are outlined in detail in chapter 5.

Intussusception is an unusual event in which a segment of the intestine telescopes into another, producing a blockage. Although infrequent, this is still the most common cause of obstruction of a child's intestine before the age of six and is seen most frequently between three months and three years of age. The pain from this condition is severe and even more relentless than pain from colic. An X-ray procedure known as a **barium enema,** during which a thick liquid visible on an X-ray is introduced into the rectum, is usually necessary to make the diagnosis. (In some facilities, air is used rather than barium.) Very often this procedure solves the problem, pushing the displaced segment of intestine back where it belongs.

In older children, there are more possible causes of abdominal pain, but the child is usually able to communicate more detailed complaints. In addition to the conditions mentioned earlier (appendicitis, gastroenteritis, constipation), abdominal pain could be caused by the following:

- **Urinary tract infection.** In adults the discomfort of a urinary tract infection depends on its location. A bladder infection (**cystitis**) will cause stinging, burning, and the frequent need to urinate. A kidney infection (**pyelonephritis**) will cause fever and midback pain on one side of the body. In children specific symptoms are frequently absent; vague abdominal discomfort may be the only complaint. In a young child, especially a girl, a high fever and vague abdominal pain should always be evaluated for a possible kidney infection (see *urinary tract care and concerns*).
- **Strep throat.** Even though the typical symptoms of a streptococcal infection of the throat are fever, headache, and sore throat, in some children abdominal pain or vomiting is also present. If your doctor suspects strep throat, a straightforward test from a throat swab can help make the diagnosis (see *sore throat*).
- **Mesenteric adenitis.** This condition involves inflammation and swelling of lymph nodes located inside the abdomen. (Often lymph nodes in the neck are swollen and tender as well.) Because many of these nodes are found near the appendix, the pain they generate is often difficult to distinguish from that caused by appendicitis. However, unlike appendicitis, mesenteric adenitis resolves without specific treatment. (See *appendicitis*, as well as the comments about appendicitis earlier in this section.)
- **Pneumonia.** Even though infections of the lung rarely involve the intestinal tract, in some children pneumonia may cause abdominal pain.
- **Reproductive-organ disorders.** In adolescent girls, a number of problems involving the uterus and ovaries can produce abdominal pain, which is usually felt in the pelvic area. These disorders include such diverse conditions as infections (especially **sexually transmitted diseases** [STDs]), **ectopic pregnancy** (a pregnancy beginning to develop in the wrong location, most commonly the fallopian tube), **ovarian cysts,** pain related to ovulation (**Mittelschmerz**), **menstrual cramps,** and **endometriosis** (a condition in which the type of tissue that lines the inside of the uterus is also present in other parts of the body—most commonly on the outer surfaces of the uterus, ovaries, fallopian tubes, intestine, and/or bladder). For an adolescent girl, a doctor's evaluation of the pelvis will be extremely important, and further studies (such as an ultrasound examination) may be needed to make the diagnosis. (Detailed information about these conditions is provided in chapter 12.)
- **Stress,** especially in older children and adolescents, can cause abdominal pain in several locations, sometimes with baffling patterns. (See sidebar, page 401.)

abscess A collection of pus in the soft tissues of the body, forming a swelling that is warm, tender, and quite painful. Abscesses can occur in persons of any age and usually need to be drained surgically.

acetaminophen (Tylenol, Panadol, and generic forms) The nonprescription drug most frequently given to children in the United States. It helps reduce fever, aches, pains, and headaches in a variety of situations, including colds, sore throats, flulike illnesses, and minor bumps and scrapes. It is also commonly used to relieve discomfort that may follow immunizations. It has no specific effect on cold symptoms such as a runny nose or a cough, although some manufacturers combine it with other ingredients to create cold/cough syrups or tablets.

This medication can be given to infants as young as two months of age. However, if a baby under three months of age has a fever of 100.4°F or more taken rectally, acetaminophen should not be given without first contacting your child's doctor (see Special Concerns, page 267 and chapter 4, page 147).

Acetaminophen may be given every four hours with a maximum of five doses per day (see dosage chart). It comes in various forms, including drops, syrups, chewable tablets, suppositories, and adult-dose tablets. Be sure to read the label carefully to ensure that you have the right strength for your child. The dosage should be

A

ACETAMINOPHEN DOSAGE CHART

	SUSPENSION DROPS* AND ORIGINAL DROPS 80 MG/0.8 ML DROPPERFUL	CHEWABLE* TABLETS 80 MG TABS	SUSPENSION* LIQUID AND ORIGINAL ELIXIR 160 MG/5 ML	JUNIOR* STRENGTH 160 MG CAPS/ CHEWABLES	REGULAR** STRENGTH 325 MG CAPS/TABS	EXTRA** STRENGTH 500 MG CAPS/GELCAPS
0–3 mos/6–11 lbs/2.5–5.4 kg	$1/_2$ dppr† (0.4 ml)					
4–11 mos/12–17 lbs/5.5–7.9 kg	1 dppr† (0.8 ml)		$1/_2$ tsp			
12–23 mos/18–23 lbs/8.0–10.9 kg	$1^1/_2$ dppr† (1.2 ml)		$3/_4$ tsp			
2–3 yrs/24–35 lbs/11.0–15.9 kg	2 dppr† (1.6 ml)	2 tabs	1 tsp			
4–5 yrs/36–47 lbs/16.0–21.9 kg		3 tabs	$1^1/_2$ tsp			
6–8 yrs/48–59 lbs/22.0–26.9 kg		4 tabs	2 tsp	2 caps/tabs		
9–10 yrs/60–71 lbs/27.0–31.9 kg		5 tabs	$2^1/_2$ tsp	$2^1/_2$ caps/tabs		
11 yrs/72–95 lbs/32.0–43.9 kg		6 tabs	3 tsp	3 caps/tabs		
Adults & Children 12 yrs and over/ 96 lbs and over/44.0 kg and over				4 caps/tabs	2 caps/tabs	1 or 2 caps/gels

*Doses should be administered 4 or 5 times daily or as directed by your doctor. Do not exceed 5 doses in 24 hours.

Note: Since acetaminophen pediatric products are available without a prescription, parents are warned on the package label to consult a physician for use by children under 2 years or for use longer than 10 days and to consult a physician or poison control center immediately in case of accidental overdosage.

**No more than 8 dosage units in any 24-hour period. Not to be taken for pain for more than 10 days or for fever for more than 3 days unless directed by a physician.

†Dropperful.

based on current weight—not age. Typical doses are listed in the above chart.

Overdose warning

When taken properly, acetaminophen is safe, and allergic reactions to it are unusual. *But an overdose can produce serious—and occasionally fatal—liver damage.* The toxic dose is about 65 mg per pound of body weight—about ten times a single recommended dose. For a 22-pound one-year-old, this would be as little as a tablespoon of the pediatric drops, 18 of the 80 mg chewable tablets, or three adult extra-strength 500 mg tablets.

The severity of the overdose problem might not be apparent for three or four days. Within the first 24 hours after ingestion, symptoms which might occur (such as vague abdominal discomfort or mild lethargy) are not specific. (After a very large ingestion, however, altered consciousness or coma may be present.) Between 24 and 48 hours after the overdose, the child typically improves and may not have any symptoms at all. After 48 hours any liver damage will become apparent and may cause nausea, vomiting, confusion, or even coma.

To be effective, the antidote (a drug called N-acetylcysteine, or Mucomyst) should be given within eight hours of ingestion. *If you suspect that your child has taken too much acetaminophen, contact your doctor or local poison-control center immediately or go to the nearest emergency room— even if your child does not appear ill.* If there is any doubt as to how much the child has actually swallowed, a blood test can determine whether there is a risk of liver damage, and treatment can be started immediately.

Since acetaminophen is commonly given to young children, most liquid and chewable preparations have a pleasant taste, so keeping the supply out of a child's reach is extremely important.

acne Pimples, pustules, and the occasionally more serious cysts and scars of acne occur primarily during the teen years, when a child's self-consciousness is very often at an all-time high. Nearly 80 percent of adolescents experience acne to some degree. Girls tend to be affected at an earlier age, but acne occurs in boys more frequently and with greater severity. While in most cases acne clears up on its own eventually, it should be treated and not ignored, because some of the physical and emotional scars it leaves can last many years.

Acne originates in areas of the skin where there are large numbers of rudimentary hairs combined with large **sebaceous glands,** so named because they secrete a thick, oily material called **sebum.** The majority of these glands are present on the face, chest, upper back, and shoulders.

Causes

The hormonal surges of puberty stimulate the production of sebum, which normally passes uneventfully to the surface of the skin. Sometimes, however, the channels leading from sebaceous glands to the skin become blocked by dead cells. Sebum then accumulates into a visible bump commonly known as a pimple or **whitehead.** If the enlarging mass of sebum pushes outward to the skin surface, oxidation—not dirt—darkens the fatty materials, forming a **blackhead.**

Bacteria on the skin surface gain access to the buildup of sebum and multiply, releasing chemical by-products that not only irritate the skin but also attract white blood cells. The resulting inflammatory reaction produces more prominent irritated bumps called **pustules** or the larger (and more damaging) **acne cysts,** which in severe cases can leave disfiguring scars.

Factors that worsen acne

Why some teenagers develop a major acne problem while others are spared is not always clear, but a number of factors are known to aggravate acne:

- Tight-fitting clothing or headgear. Wet suits, helmets, headbands, and bras that rub skin may provoke changes in the skin area directly below them.
- Picking or scratching pimples and pustules.
- Hot, humid environments that cause heavy perspiration. Sunlight, however, can help some cases of acne, but beware of excessive sun exposure and the risk of burning.
- Some girls have a flare-up of acne before their menstrual periods, in response to hormonal fluctuations, when the outlet of the sebaceous gland becomes more obstructed.
- Medications, including **isoniazid** (used to treat tuberculosis), **phenytoin** (Dilantin) and **barbiturates** (used to control epilepsy), and **steroids** (whether forms prescribed by a physician or **androgens** used inappropriately by athletes to build muscles) may worsen acne. Some birth control pills improve it, while others will aggravate it.
- Oils and dyes in cosmetics and hair sprays can plug the sebaceous glands, so water-based products are better for people who are prone to acne. *Note: The impact of these factors on any given teenager's skin will vary a great deal.*

Effect of dirt and diet

Acne is not caused by dirt on the skin, and aggressive scrubbing (especially with abrasive materials) can actually make it worse. A mild, unscented soap should be used daily to remove oils from the skin surface.

The role of diet in acne has been more of a legend than reality. Despite persistent beliefs that greasy or sweet foods turn directly into pimples, dietary changes in fact have not been proven to cause or cure acne in the general population. However, anyone who notices a consistent relationship between a particular food and acne should consider avoiding that food.

Treatment

Medications commonly used for acne treatment include the following:

- **Benzoyl peroxide** kills the skin bacteria that cause inflammation and helps open the ducts through which sebum passes to the skin surface. It is available without a prescription in 2.5, 5, and 10 percent strengths in several forms. Liquids and creams are better for dry skin, while gel forms are more helpful for oily skin. Benzoyl peroxide can be applied once or twice daily after washing the affected area with mild soap and water. It will improve the majority of acne cases if used consistently. If using benzoyl peroxide for one or two months doesn't help, a doctor should be consulted. A family physician or pediatrician can manage most cases of acne, but for more severe outbreaks, a dermatologist may be needed.
- **Tretinoin** (Retin-A in various forms and strengths) is extremely effective in unplugging pores and even causing **comedones** (blackheads) to be expelled from the skin. This can be alarming at first, because the new appearance of comedones on the surface will suggest that the medication is making the acne worse. But this effect is only temporary. Tretinoin typically causes some redness and peeling of the skin. *Skin treated with tretinoin sunburns more easily, so avoiding the sun or using a strong sunscreen is important.* The combination of tretinoin applied at bedtime (thirty minutes after washing and drying the face) and benzoyl peroxide every morning should control 80 to 85 percent of acne in adolescents.
- Antibiotics applied topically or taken orally sometimes help by reducing the population of bacteria on the skin. Oral forms of **tetracycline** or **erythromycin** are particularly helpful when inflammation is intense. Tetracycline and similar drugs cannot be given to pregnant women or

children under twelve because these drugs discolor the teeth of a developing fetus or a child.

- **Isotretinoin** (Accutane), an extremely potent derivative of vitamin A, is used in the most severe cases of acne. Isotretinoin acts essentially like an enhanced version of tretinoin, and 90 percent of even the worst cases of acne will respond to treatment over a four- to five-month period.

  This drug has a number of potential side effects, including dry skin, itching, and changes in liver function. Most important, it can cause significant deformities in a developing fetus if taken during pregnancy. Any woman who plans to take isotretinoin must consider this fact very carefully. Some physicians will not prescribe isotretinoin to an adolescent or adult female unless she agrees to take oral contraceptives.

- **Azelaic acid** (Azelex) is a newer topical medication that is unrelated to the others listed above. Derived from cereal grains, it inhibits skin bacteria, decreases the sebum that blocks pores, and reduces inflammation. It is applied twice daily to skin that has just been washed and should be continued for four weeks before deciding whether or not it is helpful.

Whatever approach is taken, it is important to remember that (1) treatment can only control acne, not cure it. For most people, this problem will fade away before adulthood. (2) Once treatment is started, it might be several weeks before there is a visible change.

For the teenager who is agonizing over the latest crop of facial bumps, this news may bring little comfort. Parents (and a physician, when appropriate) will need to be empathetic and supportive. Sometimes support will involve a gentle reminder to be consistent with treatment.

adenoids Lymph tissue at the back of the throat (above the tonsils) that sometimes swells during childhood. In some children this swelling causes repeated ear infections, and it can obstruct nasal breathing. If a child experiences a number of adenoid-related ear infections, the adenoids may be removed.

allergen Any compound or material that can provoke an allergic reaction. Common allergens are grass, weed, and tree pollens; mold spores; dust mites; animal products such as **danders** (skin scales); insect venoms or other substances derived from animals that can gain entry to the human body; and substances such as foods, drugs, or other chemicals with which a person comes in contact (see *allergies in children*).

allergies in children Allergic disorders are extremely common in children and very diverse in their manifestations. These may involve the eyes (**allergic conjunctivitis**), the nose (**allergic rhinitis**), the skin (**atopic dermatitis**), the airways (**asthma**), the gastrointestinal tract (**food allergies**), or even the entire body (**anaphylaxis**).

An allergic reaction is the expression of an interaction between an agent called an **allergen,** which comes from the outside world, with **antibodies,** which are created by an individual's immune system. The most common allergens are grass, weed, and tree pollens; mold spores; dust mites; animal products such as danders (skin scales) or saliva; insect venoms or other substances derived from animals that can gain entry into the human body; and a variety of substances such as foods, drugs, or other chemicals with which a person comes in contact.

When allergens come in contact with antibodies, a variety of compounds may be released. These in turn can produce several types of reactions, including runny nose, sneezing, wheezing, hives, eczema, upset stomach, and, in severe cases, shocklike reactions. Some allergic events, such as the response to receiving the wrong type of blood in a transfusion, are common to all people. Most of the reactions that will be reviewed here, however, are the so-called **atopic disorders**—those that affect smaller numbers of individuals who are unusually sensitive to specific substances.

The tendency to develop allergies is frequently inherited. If both parents have allergies, their child has a 60 to 75 percent chance of developing an allergic disorder. If only one parent has an allergic syndrome, the percentage drops to between 25 and 50 percent. If neither parent has allergies, a child has less than a 10 percent chance of developing an allergic disorder. Children with allergies do not necessarily manifest the same reactions as their allergic parents. For example, a father with hay fever and a mother with allergic eczema might have a child whose primary problem is asthma. Allergic reactions to specific substances—for example, hives in response to penicillin—are not routinely passed from one generation to another. And when both parent and child have allergies, the responses in the child may be either milder or more severe than those of the parents.

The pattern of allergic reactions may change during childhood. For example,

- A baby might develop eczema before her first birthday, resolve it by the age of three, and then develop hay fever and asthma during her school years.

◆ Food allergies are usually outgrown, with the exception of reactions to peanuts and shellfish.
◆ Ragweed allergy may not develop until a child has lived through at least one ragweed season.
◆ A child might not be allergic to a pet at first, but later she might manifest a reaction because her immune system has become increasingly sensitized through repeated exposure to the animal.

In general, nobody can accurately predict whether a child will outgrow one or more allergies, but in many cases the reaction becomes less severe with the passage of time.

Symptoms
Allergic reactions can occur in so many ways that they are frequently confused with other problems or illnesses. For example, clear, watery drainage from the nose accompanied by sneezing and itching may suggest a cold, but in fact any or all of these symptoms could be allergic in origin. At the same time, allergies can predispose a child to frequent colds and ear infections. Even without allergies, infants and toddlers can have as many as six to ten colds every year in their first two years and three to four a year during their third and fourth years. When allergic symptoms are also present, it can seem impossible to tell where one problem leaves off and the other begins. Thus if a child's cold lasts more than two weeks or if she always seems to have a cold, allergies could be the reason.

Parents often think that a child's **sniffing, nose rubbing, snoring,** and **mouth breathing** are simply bad habits, but they could be signs of allergic activity. Constant mouth breathing caused by nasal congestion could even interfere with the proper alignment of a child's teeth.

Repeated **throat clearing,** especially when a child awakens in the morning, may be the result of allergies that cause the nose to swell and fill with mucus. The mucus drips into the throat, causing the child to clear it repeatedly. The throat can in turn become irritated, and a child might complain repeatedly of a **sore throat**. Distinguishing an allergic sore throat from one caused by an infection can at times be quite difficult.

Coughing is another common allergic symptom. It can arise from postnasal drainage into the throat or from spasm of the airway. If this spasm is more intense, **wheezing** could result. If coughing persists for more than a few weeks and is worse at night and aggravated by smoke, exercise, or cold air, asthma is a possible diagnosis.

Frequent **headaches,** especially in the forehead or face near the nose, may arise from pressure caused by allergic swelling in the nose. Allergic **eye symptoms** can include redness, itching, watery discharge, and swelling. Dark circles under the eyes are sometimes called "allergic shiners," but these may have other causes as well.

Many types of **skin rashes** are manifestations of allergies. **Eczema** is a patchy rash that is dry, slightly reddened, and very itchy. **Contact dermatitis** is an irritation of skin caused by an allergic reaction to a substance that comes in direct contact with the skin. Eruptions resulting from exposure to poison ivy, oak, or sumac are dramatic examples of contact dermatitis. **Hives** are a generalized allergic response involving raised, reddened, irregular itchy patches of skin that may blanch (turn white) when pressure is applied. They may vary from dime-size to much larger areas of skin, and they change size and location. Hives are sometimes associated with itchy swelling of the face, eyes, lips, hands, feet, and genitalia.

Evaluation
A doctor will use two primary tools to arrive at a diagnosis of allergies: the patient's history and a physical examination. In the vast majority of cases, the history alone will suggest the diagnosis. Results of the physical exam are also helpful, while laboratory testing is needed to clarify the diagnosis of an allergy only in a small percentage of cases. (Several tests might be necessary to determine the allergens to which a child is reacting.)

Since the history is so important, prior to a medical evaluation it would be helpful to think back over the past few months (or years) to recall specific details of your child's symptoms: When did the problem first start? How often does it bother her? What time of the day (or year) is it worse? Are symptoms more severe at home, outside, inside, in the city, out in the country, at the coast, or at high altitudes? Do the symptoms change with physical events or environmental factors such as cold, heat, dampness, exercise, or exposure to cigarette smoke? Have specific medications been used? Which of these has been most effective? Sometimes a diary can help you recall specific reactions, symptoms, and seasonal responses your child has experienced. Details about your child's environment, especially her bedroom, could be helpful. Stuffed toys, pillows, the furnace and its filter, knickknacks and blinds (which collect dust), and trees outside the window are all potential sources of allergens.

During the physical exam, the doctor will look for various signs of allergic activity. These might include pale, swollen mucous membranes, clear drainage from the nose, an allergic "crease" across the nose, or perhaps dark "allergic shiners" below the eyes. Wheezing or

A

coughing would of course be significant but may not necessarily occur during a scheduled office visit. The skin will be checked for evidence of eczema, including scratch marks and areas of thickening and redness, especially behind the knees, in the creases of the arms, and on the wrists.

Tests for allergies

While your child's history and physical examination provide evidence that she has an allergic disorder, they may or may not provide clues to the specific allergens that are provoking the reactions. This information can be very useful in suggesting whether or not changes in the home environment would reduce or eliminate allergic symptoms. It might also provide the basis for a form of treatment known as **immunotherapy** (see *immunotherapy*).

If your child's symptoms are particularly bothersome or persistent, unresponsive to medications, or severe (for example, wheezing episodes requiring repeated medical intervention), the physician or allergist might recommend **skin tests** to help identify what might be triggering these allergic responses. The testing involves pricking the skin on the back in several places, and in doing so, exposing these areas to substances that might provoke an allergic reaction. If your child is sensitive to a particular substance, a local reaction (redness and itching) will develop within several minutes. Occasionally certain substances may be injected directly into the outer layer of the skin, a process called **intradermal** testing. This is usually done when the child's history raises suspicions that one or more substances might be involved in her allergies but prick tests using those substances are negative.

Another option is the measurement of **immunoglobulin E (IgE)**, a specific antibody produced when an allergen enters the body. Blood tests can determine elevated levels of immunoglobulin E as well as the amount of antibody that has been produced against specific allergens such as grass, animal hair, or ragweed.

Common allergic syndromes

ALLERGIC RHINITIS An allergic reaction involving the lining of the nose is the most common of the atopic disorders, presumably because the nose is so often the first point of contact with airborne allergens. Symptoms occur with equal frequency among girls and boys and include a watery discharge and stuffiness of the nose, reddened lining of the lower eyelids, frequent clearing of the throat, mouth breathing, snoring, and the "allergic salute," an upward wiping of the nose with the palm of the hand. Many such wipes may result in the appearance of a line across the nose known as an "allergic crease."

There is often a history of repeated nosebleeds, headaches, earaches, dizziness, a nasal tone to the voice, and dark circles under the eyes.

There are two primary types of allergic rhinitis. **Perennial allergic rhinitis** causes symptoms throughout the year but especially during winter months when children spend more time indoors and have ongoing exposure to house dust or any indoor pets. **Seasonal allergic rhinitis,** more commonly known as **hay fever,** is brought on primarily by plant pollens that may be blown for miles by winds. While the seasons and local flora vary from region to region, troublesome pollens are typically produced by trees in the late winter and early spring, grasses in the spring and early summer, and weeds (especially ragweed) in the late summer and fall. Molds may also cause seasonal nasal allergy symptoms. Irritants such as dry air, tobacco smoke, pollution, rapid weather changes, humidity, cosmetics, and perfumes can also trigger episodes of allergic rhinitis.

The treatment of allergic rhinitis will depend upon the frequency and severity of the symptoms.

- **Antihistamines** interfere with the action of **histamines,** which are biochemical mediators in many (but not all) allergic reactions. In a best-case scenario, an antihistamine will reduce congestion, dripping, and sneezing for a few hours. However, side effects (most commonly drowsiness, especially in many of the nonprescription antihistamines) can limit the usefulness of these medications, and in some cases a trial-and-error approach is needed to find the best preparation for a particular child. Some of the newer antihistamines last longer (12 to 24 hours) and cause less drowsiness, but they require a prescription and are more expensive. Your child's physician can guide you to an appropriate antihistamine for your child with allergic rhinitis.
- **Decongestants** can shrink swollen membranes within the nose and ease breathing through congested nasal passages. As with antihistamines, effectiveness varies in children, and irritability is a potential side effect.
- **Decongestant nose drops and sprays** can be bought without prescription and may temporarily relieve congestion associated with allergic rhinitis. Local side effects can include stinging, burning, irritation, nosebleeds, and sneezing. When used regularly for more than a few days, "rebound" nasal congestion (which can be worse than the rhinitis) may develop each time the medication wears off. *If used at all, decongestant nose drops or sprays should be limited to occasional treatment of*

severe and disruptive congestion (for example, that which is interfering with sleep).

- **Cromolyn** or **steroid nasal sprays** may be prescribed for long-term use in a child who has extended bouts of allergic rhinitis. These do not provide immediate relief but may reduce the allergic activity within the nose for extended periods of time, without side effects such as sedation or irritability. To be effective, they should be used consistently on a daily basis.

- **Immunotherapy** (or **hyposensitization**), more commonly known as allergy shots, is a type of immunization in which small amounts of allergen are injected into the child at regular intervals and at gradually increasing doses. Eventually antibodies develop that can reduce or prevent the allergic response to the allergen. Typically the injections must be given regularly (usually weekly) for at least one to two years. If they are effective, the interval between them is gradually increased. Immunotherapy can be particularly helpful in treating allergic rhinitis caused by allergens that cannot be easily avoided, such as airborne pollens.

ASTHMA (reactive airway disease) A condition characterized by intermittent and reversible narrowing of the airways, producing bouts of coughing, wheezing, and difficulty breathing. Inflammation within the airways results in swelling, increased mucus secretion, and the spasmodic contractions that are experienced as wheezing. *Treating this underlying inflammation is as important in controlling asthma as stopping the wheezing episode itself.* (The characteristics, prevention, and treatment of asthma are described in detail on page 650.)

SKIN DISEASES There are three major forms of skin diseases caused by allergies.

Infantile eczema (also known as **atopic dermatitis,** see photos on page A27) is considered an allergic disorder for the following reasons:

- Many infants with this syndrome also develop allergic rhinitis and asthma later in life.
- In many cases the rash appears to be an allergic response to certain foods, especially egg white, milk, wheat, and corn. However, inhaling or direct skin contact with other allergens such as dust mites may also be involved.
- Infants and children with eczema are very prone to itching; the ongoing scratching that results plays an important role in perpetuating the rash. (Eczema has sometimes been called "the itch that rashes.")

Eczema usually develops when the child is two to six months old and may wax and wane over the next several months, often disappearing completely by the age of three. In some individuals this condition persists into later childhood or even adulthood. The rash of eczema is patchy, dry, slightly reddened, and very itchy. Intense scratching of the affected skin may lead to oozing, deep scratch marks called **excoriations,** bleeding, and infection. Irritation of the skin from chronic scratching may cause the formation of thickened plaques, a process called **lichenification.** During infancy, eczema often appears on the cheeks, scalp, neck, back of the arms, front of the legs, and the upper body. In an older child, the rash is commonly seen in the creases of the knees, elbows, neck, wrists, and face.

While foods and other allergens play a role in eczema, environmental factors also affect the skin. Cold, dry air causes the skin to become dry and scaly, while a hot, humid climate induces sweating, which may increase scratching. Skin irritants such as rough clothing, soaps, detergents, and fabric softeners can also worsen eczema.

A number of measures can help an infant or child with eczema. Try to maintain a stable temperature and humidity within the home. A child's skin should be protected from excessive dryness, which provokes itching and scratching. Because prolonged contact with water (especially very hot water) may actually dry the skin, use comfortably warm water for baths or showers and keep them short. Use a nonirritating brand of soap and pat lubricating oil on the affected skin while the skin is still damp. Moisturizing skin creams and softeners should be applied daily. Cotton clothing is preferable to wool, silk, and nylon. Clothes should be washed with a mild detergent and rinsed twice.

Check with your child's physician for recommendations regarding appropriate soaps and skin moisturizers for your child's age and skin condition. The physician may also recommend that a topical steroid preparation be applied to the most severely affected areas of skin. These can dramatically improve local inflammation and itching, but they should be used only as directed. Time limitations on the use of steroids—and the selection of the mildest form that will improve the rash—will help prevent steroid-induced local skin changes. An antihistamine such as diphenhydramine (Benadryl) may help prevent scratching at night, and keeping fingernails short will help prevent further irritation. Specific foods that are clearly linked to a child's eczema eruptions can be avoided, but determining which ones might actually be involved is usually not easy. Severe dietary restrictions are unlikely to help eczema. If you are concerned about

A

the number of foods that may be provoking a child's rashes, see a qualified allergist.

Contact dermatitis occurs when a substance that touches the skin causes local allergic reaction. The most familiar form of contact dermatitis is the eruption caused by poison ivy, oak, or sumac. Other potential causes of contact dermatitis include cosmetics, soaps, detergents, perfumes, dyes used in fabrics, rubber, metal (especially nickel, sometimes a component of jewelry or wristwatch casings), topical medications, and compounds used in the preparation of leather. Several days of exposure might be needed to provoke a reaction, but once a child is sensitized, a rash could appear within 24 to 48 hours after contact.

Usually the shape and distribution of the rash will suggest contact dermatitis to a parent or physician. Treatment involves, first and foremost, avoiding the irritating substances. A local eruption will usually respond to a topical steroid preparation, but in more extensive outbreaks (such as with poison oak or ivy) oral steroids may be prescribed for several days. Antihistamines such as diphenhydramine (Benadryl) sometimes help reduce itching.

Hives (also called **urticaria,** see photo on page A29) are a generalized allergic response involving raised, reddened, irregular itchy patches of skin that may blanch (turn white) when pressure is applied. They vary from dime-size to much larger areas of skin, and they constantly change size and location. When hives affect the deeper layers of the skin, the eruption is called **angioedema,** a change that can develop anywhere on the body but most commonly affects the mouth, eyes, tongue, genitals, and extremities.

Hives can last from minutes to days and may even recur in crops for weeks and months. An impressive number of allergens cause hives, and identifying the specific agent is sometimes quite difficult. Some possible causes and/or triggers of hives include the following:

- Foods such as milk, eggs, peanuts, berries, shellfish, and nuts
- Medications such as penicillin, sulfa drugs, and aspirin
- A variety of infections, including those caused by viruses (such as hepatitis or infectious mononucleosis), bacteria, fungi, and parasites
- Inhaled substances such as pollens, dust, and animal danders
- Physical events such as exposure to cold, heat, local pressure, vibration, and exercise
- Insect bites

If hives are a recurring problem or last for more than a few days, keeping track of foods, symptoms, or other events (including where the child has been) preceding their arrival could be useful. Skin testing is occasionally helpful. If there is a clear relationship to a specific food or drug, the provoking agent should be avoided. (The child's doctor and any others who care for him in the future should be notified of a suspected drug reaction.) In most cases, hives can be controlled with antihistamines such as diphenhydramine (Benadryl and others) or hydroxyzine (Atarax and others). Unless there is an underlying disease causing them, hives do not lead to other problems and will disappear without complications.

When hives are associated with sudden and dramatic swelling (especially around the face), difficulty breathing, or feeling faint, the child should be taken to the nearest emergency facility immediately. *If a child has had an extremely severe reaction to a particular drug, always remind the physician whenever any prescription is written and, as an extra safeguard, mention the reaction to the pharmacist when having it filled.* If a child has ever had an immediate and serious allergic reaction, ask the physician about obtaining a kit containing injectable epinephrine (adrenaline) for emergency use.

FOOD ALLERGIES Various symptoms and syndromes are commonly attributed to foods, but true food allergy is relatively uncommon. Many genuine reactions to food (such as lactose intolerance) do not directly involve the immune system, and many behaviors (such as fatigue or hyperactivity) are often provoked neither by food nor by allergy. As already noted, some foods such as shellfish, nuts, berries, chocolate, tomatoes, wheat, and milk products may be involved in eczema, hives, or more serious reactions. In some children certain foods consistently provoke vomiting, diarrhea, bloating, and/or "crampy" pain; whether or not the reaction is truly allergic or occurs on some other basis, the particular food in question should be avoided.

Food allergies (or other forms of intolerance) can be difficult to identify conclusively since foods are highly complex substances and the relationship between food and reaction may not be clear-cut. Keeping a diary of both foods and symptoms sometimes helps. Skin testing helps in some cases, but reactions in the skin do not always correlate with responses to foods. For many children a diagnosis can be made using an elimination diet; a child is first given simple foods that are unlikely to cause a reaction, and then others are added gradually. An elimination diet should be supervised by a physician or dietitian to reduce the risk of nutritional deficiencies.

BITES OR STINGS These may result in local or more widespread allergic reactions. An **immediate hypersensitivity** reaction (usually resulting from venom produced by bees, wasps, hornets, or fire ants) may be severe, involving hives, wheezing, and a rapid drop in blood pressure known as **anaphylaxis** (see Emergency Care). This is a medical emergency, and rapid treatment with epinephrine, intravenous fluids, and other measures will be necessary. These insects should not only be avoided in the future, but treatment kits containing an injection of epinephrine should be available at home, in the car, or in the gear taken on camping trips or other outings. Immunotherapy (allergy shots) may be recommended to prevent this type of reaction.

The more common **delayed hypersensitivity** reaction produces dramatic local swelling around the site of the bite or sting, but this occurs over one or two days and is accompanied more by itching than by pain. Antihistamines will reduce the swelling and itching, or a short course of oral steroids may be prescribed to resolve the reaction more quickly. Fortunately, someone who has this type of response is not destined to develop the more severe immediate hypersensitivity reaction in the future.

SPECIAL NOTE: Reducing a child's exposure to common household allergens
Dust mites are tiny, insectlike creatures that thrive in carpets, upholstered furniture, and bedding, especially when the air at home is warm and well humidified. The waste products of these microscopic animals can provoke a variety of allergic reactions, even after they have died. Encasing mattresses and pillows in special plastic covers can significantly reduce your child's exposure to dust mites. Treating carpets with mite-killing chemicals every few months may be necessary as well.

Molds thrive in warm, moist environments. A basement (especially if it has had any seepage or flooding), damp, dark closet spaces, or even a leaky toilet that invites mold to grow in the carpet surrounding it can breed these organisms. If your child definitely has a mold allergy, keeping the humidity at home less than 30 percent, using an air conditioner or dehumidifier, and monitoring your progress with a humidity gauge can be very helpful. Bathrooms, which obviously become warm and moist regularly, frequently harbor mold. Regular cleaning of tiles, bathtub, shower curtain or stall, walls, and ceilings with a mold-killing solution (such as an equal mix of bleach and water or a commercial spray) is a tedious but important job. Carpet should be taken out of the bathroom because water spilled from a shower or bathtub or a leaky toilet invites mold to grow both within and beneath the carpet.

Allergens are abundant in animal danders and may cause many different allergy problems. Dealing with pets in your home may become a highly emotional issue if animals are causing a child to have significant symptoms. An allergy evaluation might be necessary to settle the question of sensitivity, and if a pet is part of the problem, it will need to be kept outdoors. If symptoms are severe enough, the pet must be removed completely from the home for the sake of your child's health.

Every child deserves to live in a smoke-free environment, and for an allergic child exposure to tobacco smoke can be a hazard both to health and to life itself. Smoking should not be allowed in the home or any other environment (such as a car) in which an allergic child is present.

alpha-fetoprotein A protein produced in the liver and gastrointestinal tract of a fetus. The level of AFP can be measured in the mother's blood to screen for certain fetal abnormalities such as neural tube defects (see chapter 1, page 9).

altitude-related illness In order to function at altitudes higher than a few thousand feet above sea level, the human body must make several adjustments to compensate for the reduced availability of oxygen, especially when exertion takes place. People who begin strenuous exercise in the mountains without first becoming acclimatized may become very uncomfortable or in some cases seriously ill. Some individuals have difficulty even without exerting themselves.

Acute mountain sickness can begin a few hours or days after arrival at altitudes over 6,500 feet. Headache, loss of appetite, nausea, and fatigue are its primary symptoms. Irregular breathing patterns during sleep may cause frequent awakening, but with time sleep patterns return to normal. More severe cases are evidenced by changes in consciousness, **cyanosis** (a bluish discoloration of the skin, area beneath the nails, and lips), and a staggering gait.

Rapid ascent to higher altitudes (usually over 8,000 feet) followed by heavy exertion can lead to a serious disorder in which fluid leaks from small blood vessels into the air sacs of the lungs. Shortness of breath, cough, rapid heart rate, and fatigue develop over one to three days, and a characteristic gurgling sound may be heard if one listens to the chest. If untreated, this condition, known as **pulmonary edema,** can progress to cyanosis, changes in consciousness, coma, collapse of the cardiopulmonary (heart and lung) system, and even death.

Mild mountain sickness will usually improve with rest, increased fluids, and mild pain relievers for headache. A physician might prescribe the drug **acetazolamide** (Diamox) to help reduce symptoms. People who are more severely ill must be escorted or carried to a lower altitude as soon as possible. Improvement begins after the victim descends a thousand feet or more and receives oxygen by mask. *Never let the victim descend alone.* A thorough evaluation by a physician is mandatory before returning to a high altitude.

The most effective measure to prevent altitude-related illness is to allow enough time—two to four days, if necessary—for a child to become accustomed to the reduced oxygen concentration before beginning strenuous activities at a higher altitude. Increasing fluid intake will help, as will a high-carbohydrate diet. Teenagers or adults who have experienced acute mountain sickness (or worse) in the past may benefit from taking acetazolamide (Diamox) on the day of ascent and for two days after arrival. Teenagers involved in rock climbing or other mountain activities should be warned not to ignore symptoms because of peer pressure or a misguided desire to tough it out when they feel sick. Assume any illness at high altitude to be mountain sickness or one of its more serious variations until proven otherwise, and treat it accordingly.

amblyopia   Reduced vision from nonuse. (The eye is anatomically okay.) (See *eye care and concerns.*)

amenorrhea   Absence of menstrual periods.

amniocentesis   A prenatal testing procedure in which fluid is withdrawn from the amniotic sac surrounding the fetus. An analysis of the fluid can detect chromosomal abnormalities such as Down syndrome. This procedure is sometimes done late in pregnancy to determine the lung maturity of an infant (see page 102).

anal problems   By far the most alarming anal problem in infants and children is **bleeding,** and the most common cause of bleeding in this area is a **fissure,** a crack or tear in the sensitive skin of the anal opening. Fissures are nearly always caused by the passage of a hard stool, although scratching or sometimes irritation from cleansers in baby wipes can promote the formation of fissures. Typically the blood appears as a streak on the stool, and it may not be present the next time the bowels move. If blood actually flows after a stool, it will usually stop on its own in five to ten minutes.

Treatment involves eliminating any underlying cause of the fissure, if possible, since nearly all will heal on their own if they are not continually irritated. If stools are hard, increased amounts of fluid, dietary fiber (from fruit, vegetables, and bran), a mild stool softener, or even mineral oil may be helpful, depending upon the age of the child (see *constipation*). Multiple fissures and inflamed tissues may improve with warm soaks and the use of a mild cortisone cream. If there are other contributing factors such as infection or pinworms (see below), these should be treated. Your child's health-care provider should give you input in the diagnosis and management of this problem.

Hemorrhoids are dilated veins in the anal area that can bleed, itch, or clot. They are extremely uncommon in infants and children, and if discovered, a cause should be sought. While prolonged constipation and straining may be the cause, abnormalities in the venous system, which returns blood to the heart, must be considered.

Anal itching can be caused by irritated skin, a fissure, soaps and cleansers, or **pinworms.** If you discover your child intensely scratching this area during the night, pinworms might be the cause (see *pinworms*). A local infection involving the common yeast **Candida albicans** can be treated with antifungal cream. Occasionally a child with a bacterial infection in the nose will accidentally transfer the bacteria to the anal area. In this case, antibiotics will eradicate the eruption.

anaphylaxis   The most severe form of an allergic reaction. An allergen such as venom from a bee sting, medication, or food can set off a life-threatening reaction unless prompt medical attention is obtained. This can include severe difficulty in breathing, a drop in blood pressure, hives, and severe abdominal pain (see Emergency Care, page 764).

anemia   An abnormally low concentration of red blood cells, which are needed to carry oxygen to all tissues. Red blood cells are so vital to life that they are produced continually throughout the body in tissue called **marrow,** which lies protected within the bones of the skeleton. Red cells circulate within the bloodstream for about four months and then are removed by specialized tissues that recycle their contents. Anemia occurs when the production of red cells cannot keep pace with their loss or destruction. This condition is detected by a blood test that shows a low level of **hemoglobin,** the protein within red cells that transports oxygen, or by a low **hematocrit,** the percentage of whole blood that consists of red cells.

The significance and consequences of anemia will depend on a number of the following factors:

- The severity of anemia—whether the blood count is mildly or significantly reduced.
- How quickly the anemia has developed.
- The age and general condition of the infant or child.
- The presence of other medical problems.

The most common cause of anemia is **iron deficiency**, which results in a reduced production of hemoglobin. Deficiencies in vitamins and folic acid, which are much less common, can also cause a decreased production of red cells, along with other medical complications. Some forms of anemia, such as **sickle-cell disease,** arise from a change in the shape or rigidity of red cells, which leads to more rapid destruction.

The causes of anemia are numerous and may reflect minor or serious problems. It is important to diagnose anemia correctly and to determine the underlying cause, prescribe appropriate dietary and/or medical treatment, measure the result of that intervention, and prevent recurrences.

anterior fontanelle (see illustration on page 67) The diamond-shaped soft spot near the front of a newborn's skull, where the bones have not yet grown together. This will be replaced by solid bone by 18 months of age. The tough fibrous membrane covering the fontanelle is not easily injured, and parents need not fear touching or stroking this area when washing or combing a baby's hair.

antibiotic A drug that takes a specific action against one or several types of bacteria. Unlike viruses, which multiply only within the cells they invade, bacteria can live and reproduce on their own. Most bacteria are harmless to humans, but some are capable of damaging tissues, producing toxins that interfere with normal body functions, and even overwhelming the immune system—sometimes resulting in death.

Many antibiotics work by interfering with the multiplication of bacteria, while others kill them outright. Antibiotics do not interfere with the immune system but supplement the body's own defenses. Without an intact immune system, the most effective antibiotics would likely fail.

Use of antibiotics

Antibiotics can be effective in fighting infections under the following conditions:

THE INFECTION MUST BE CAUSED OR AGGRAVATED BY BACTERIA. This means that infections such as the common cold, influenza, most cases of the stomach flu, croup, and the majority of sore throats will not respond to antibiotics because they are caused by viruses. (Antibiotics are designed to affect specific structures and functions of bacteria that are not present in viruses, and thus viruses are not affected by antibiotics.) Skin problems such as ringworm or Candida (yeast) infections cannot be cured by antibiotics; specific antifungal medications can help resolve them.

Antibiotics are usually beneficial in treating:

- Prolonged upper-respiratory infections (lasting more than ten days), especially those involving the upper airways (**bronchitis**) or the sinuses (**sinusitis**). A sign of this type of infection is thick, persistent, discolored (yellow, green, or blood-tinged) phlegm from the chest or similarly colored drainage from the nose.
- **Ear infections**
- **Pneumonias,** which are infections of the lung tissue itself as opposed to the bronchial tubes. An exam and sometimes an X-ray are needed to make this diagnosis. In some cases, blood tests are necessary.
- **Wound and skin infections,** especially when pain, swelling, redness, and tenderness arise from a cut or scrape.
- Infections of the throat (**pharyngitis**) or tonsils (**tonsillitis**), if streptococcus or other disease-causing bacteria are involved. A throat swab for quick antibody testing and/or culture is necessary to make an accurate diagnosis of streptococcal infection. *The majority of sore throats, however, are caused by viruses and will disappear on their own.* If symptoms last more than a few days or if fever is persistent, contact your child's physician (see *sore throat*).
- **Urinary tract infections** in the bladder or kidney are usually caused by bacteria and should be treated with antibiotics. Cultures may be necessary to find the right medication. Follow-up is essential in treating a child because there could be an underlying problem with the anatomy or the function of the urinary tract (see *urinary tract cares and concerns*).
- The presence of a fever over 100.4°F (taken rectally) in an infant younger than three months may indicate a serious bacterial infection. A thorough evaluation will probably be necessary to make the correct diagnosis.

THE BACTERIA CAUSING THE PROBLEM MUST BE SENSITIVE TO THE ANTIBIOTIC. Not only must the antibiotic have the ability to affect the specific type of bacteria, but it must be effective in treating the particular strain of the bacteria. Many infections can be treated based on what is known about the bacteria that usually cause them. In serious, stubborn, or recurrent infections, however, a culture of the organisms and an evaluation of their sen-

A

sitivity to various antibiotics are necessary to determine further treatment.

THE ANTIBIOTIC MUST BE CAPABLE OF REACHING AN EFFECTIVE THERAPEUTIC LEVEL AT THE SITE OF THE INFECTION. Some antibiotics, for example, cannot be used to treat meningitis because they do not readily pass from the bloodstream into the central nervous system.

THE ANTIBIOTIC MUST BE APPROPRIATE FOR THE CHILD'S AGE-GROUP. Tetracyclines, for example, should not be given to a pregnant woman or to children younger than eight years of age, since these drugs may cause permanent discoloration of developing teeth.

THE DOSE, TIMING, AND RELATIONSHIP TO MEALS SHOULD BE ACCURATE. Obviously, it is up to the doctor to make an appropriate choice of antibiotic for your child's infection, but it is also important that you follow all the directions. Before you leave the pharmacy or the doctor's office, be sure that you understand the following:

- How much is to be given? Infants, toddlers, and school-age children will probably be taking liquid forms. A well-marked measuring device (such as an oral syringe) is more accurate than a kitchen spoon. If doses are given in terms of teaspoons, remember that

  > 1 tsp = 5 cc or ml
  > $^1/_2$ tsp = 2.5 cc or ml
  > $^1/_4$ tsp = 1.25 cc or ml
  > One cc (cubic centimeter) = one ml (milliliter)

- How often? Some antibiotics have convenient dosage routines of once or twice daily, but others must be given more often.
- With or without food? Some antibiotics must be taken on a full stomach to avoid nausea, while others won't be absorbed very well unless the stomach is empty.
- How long? This will depend on the type of infection and the antibiotic being used. Often a prescription must be continued for ten days or longer to bring the infection under control and prevent a recurrence. Be sure to complete the full course of antibiotic that has been prescribed— *regardless of how much the symptoms decrease or disappear.* (If an allergic reaction or other side effect is taking place, however, stop the antibiotic and contact your child's physician.)
- If the antibiotic is liquid, should it be refrigerated or left at room temperature? Some liquid preparations tend to dehydrate over the course of treat-

ment (especially when kept in the refrigerator), but this can be minimized by placing the container in a self-sealing plastic sandwich bag.
- Is a follow-up appointment needed? A recheck may be recommended by your doctor, even if things are going well. For example, if ear infections have been a problem, a follow-up on the appearance and functioning of the ear will be important. If your child has had any type of urinary tract infection, the urine may be rechecked to ensure that bacteria are no longer present.

SPECIAL NOTE: How to get the medicine down
Giving the proper doses of an antibiotic (or any other medication) at the right time can be challenging when the patient is an infant or toddler, especially if he isn't cooperating. Some ideas that may help this process include the following:

- Most liquid antibiotics are formulated in fruity flavors that are usually palatable to children. If the taste isn't appealing to your child, check with the pharmacist about disguising the flavor in food or liquid such as applesauce, pancake syrup, or juice (or, for an older child, peanut butter).
- Use the most effective delivery device for your child's mouth. For infants, calibrated droppers usually work the best; the medication can be inserted a little at a time into the space between the cheek and the gums. An alternative is to put a nipple (without bottle attached) into the baby's mouth and put the medication into the back of the nipple, or add the antibiotic to a small amount of juice or other liquid in a bottle. For toddlers and older children, most pharmacies or doctors' offices can supply a child-size spoon whose handle is a calibrated tube that measures the precise amount of medication.
- If an infant spits up immediately after taking an antibiotic, it is usually appropriate to try again. (This is not necessarily true for other types of medications.) If you are not sure about whether or not to do this or if your child is vomiting and cannot keep the antibiotic down, contact the physician for further directions.
- An older child can be rewarded for taking medicine pleasantly—perhaps with a gold star on a chart after each dose and a modest prize when the entire course of treatment is done. However, he must understand that the antibiotic must be taken whether he cares for it or not, and that you won't debate with him over every dose.

- If your child has a particular preference (such as chewable medications rather than liquid) or if he is able to swallow tablets, let the doctor know at the time the prescription is written.

Using antibiotics appropriately and effectively

- Don't assume that every infection has to be treated with antibiotics. If your doctor feels that your child's illness is caused by a virus, don't insist that antibiotics be given "just in case."
- Don't give one child's antibiotic to another, even if the illnesses seem very similar, without checking with the doctor first.
- Don't assume that if a little is good, more is better.
- Finish the full prescription.
- If cost is a concern, ask your doctor if there is a generic form of the medication that would be appropriate.

Allergic reactions and/or side effects

If you think an antibiotic may be causing a problem, contact your child's physician for further advice and clarification as to whether this might be an allergic reaction, a side effect, or something else entirely. Allergic reactions are a response of a child's immune system to a specific substance and are usually manifested as a rash or more serious conditions such as hives, swelling of face or tongue, or wheezing. If an allergic reaction to a drug has occurred, it is very likely that it will occur again—often more severely—if the same drug is given in the future. Antibiotics most commonly involved in true allergic reactions are derivatives of sulfa drugs (used most often to treat urinary infections) and certain forms of penicillin. Allergic reactions to specific drugs are not routinely passed from one generation to another. If one parent is allergic to penicillin, for example, this does not necessarily mean that the child will be.

Side effects, in contrast, are not brought about by the immune system and will not necessarily occur every time the same medication is given. A common side effect of some antibiotics is nausea, especially with erythromycin and its various derivatives such as clarithromycin (Biaxin) or the combination of sulfa and erythromycin known as Pediazole. Diarrhea can also be caused by any antibiotic that alters the normal assortment of bacteria in the colon.

It may be difficult to decide whether a problem is an allergic reaction or a side effect or whether it was caused by the antibiotic, the infection, an interaction between the two, or something entirely unrelated. Amoxicillin, for example, frequently provokes rashes during viral infections (especially acute mononucleosis) but not during subsequent uses. In this case, the reaction is not a true allergic response, and the antibiotic can be used in the future. If it is unclear whether or not an antibiotic caused a particular problem, the drug (and others similar to it) may have to be used with caution, if at all, in the future.

Your child's physician will record in the child's medical chart any reaction to a drug. Add this information to your child's health record at home. If you have phoned your child's physician about a reaction, remind him or her about it during your next office visit to ensure that it has been noted in the chart.

antibody A specialized protein that participates in the body's immune response to specific microscopic organisms (such as bacteria or viruses) or to foreign substances. A large number of specific antibodies have been identified and categorized into subclasses that are associated with diverse protective functions. Some antibodies, for example, appear immediately in response to a specific infection, while others participate in long-term immunologic "memory" that can protect against future infections by the same organism. In some situations an antibody response may cause mild or severe symptoms as in allergic reactions, or it may cause inflammation or damage to normal tissue as in autoimmune disorders such as rheumatoid arthritis.

antigen Any molecular structure, whether existing independently or as a component of an organism (such as a virus) or a cell, which brings about an immunologic response (see *allergen*).

Apgar score A scoring system on a scale from zero to ten that assesses the condition of a newborn at birth based on heart rate, breathing, reflexes, muscle tone, and color. Newborns are scored at one, five, and ten minutes after birth (see page 63).

apnea A temporary cessation (stopping) of breathing.

appendicitis An acute inflammation of the appendix, a narrow, worm-shaped structure positioned near the junction of the small and large intestines in the right-lower corner (called a quadrant) of the abdomen. Appendicitis is the most common reason for abdominal surgery in children.

The first symptom is usually cramping pain in the mid-upper abdomen that gradually moves downward and to the right while becoming more constant as inflammation intensifies. Loss of appetite, nausea, and vomiting commonly occur as well. Appendicitis has several different pain patterns, especially in children. Sometimes younger children do not pay attention to (or are unable to describe) the shift in location of pain from one area to the other, especially when they are not feeling well. Older children may be more cooperative and better able to describe the location and characteristics of the pain.

Fever may develop as infection and inflammation of the appendix become more severe. If the appendix is not removed, it will likely rupture. The infection contained within it can then spread into the abdominal cavity, resulting in inflammation of the inner lining of the abdomen—a condition called **peritonitis.** When this occurs, pain worsens and the child becomes increasingly ill.

In children with appendicitis, the time from the first symptom (typically, cramping pain and/or nausea) to rupture of the appendix is usually less than 36 hours. Because the symptoms of appendicitis are much more difficult to identify in children younger than two years of age, the likelihood of rupture in this age-group is almost 100 percent. The frequency of rupture is much lower among older children because they can usually communicate their symptoms more clearly, allowing for an earlier diagnosis.

No single test can establish or exclude appendicitis 100 percent of the time. The diagnosis is made by evaluating the child's history, a physical examination, laboratory results, and usually some form of imaging (X-ray and/or ultrasound). A blood count, urinalysis, and possibly other laboratory studies will be ordered. Standard X-rays of the abdomen may be taken, primarily to help rule out other conditions. Over the past few years, ultrasound has been very useful in diagnosing appendicitis.

If your child's doctor or an emergency-room physician suspects appendicitis, a surgeon will be consulted. (In some areas, family physicians perform appendectomies, in which case a surgeon would not be called.) If the surgeon agrees with the diagnosis, surgery is performed as soon as possible in an attempt to remove the appendix before it ruptures. This can prevent a much more severe illness, prolonged antibiotic treatment in the hospital, and longer postoperative recovery. If the doctor feels that the appendix has already ruptured, the operation might be delayed for a number of hours to allow for the administration of antibiotics and intravenous fluids. If the surgeon is not sure of the diagnosis, he or she may observe the child for a period of time.

Sometimes surgery for suspected appendicitis reveals a normal appendix. This is not evidence of bad medical judgment, because other conditions can mimic the pain of appendicitis. One common example is a condition called **mesenteric adenitis,** in which lymph nodes inside the abdomen (especially near the appendix) become enlarged, inflamed, and painful, in a manner strikingly similar to an inflamed appendix. Even if a normal appendix is found, it will be removed for three reasons: (1) the appendix has no proven function of importance to human health; (2) if it is left in the patient, it could become infected at some time in the future; and (3) if the appendix were left in and the patient's memory were faulty, a doctor evaluating the problem would see the scar and could mistakenly assume that the appendix was gone—leading to a potentially disastrous misdiagnosis.

If the appendix did not rupture, the child will usually leave the hospital in one to three days. If it did rupture, hospitalization may continue for another five to ten days or more to continue intravenous antibiotics and fluids. Usually normal activities can be resumed as soon as they are tolerated, with the exception of body-contact sports, which might cause pain in the event of a direct blow to the incision.

arthritis See Musculoskeletal Problems in Children, page 743.

ascariasis An infection caused by a large roundworm (ranging from five to fourteen inches in length) that is the most common human intestinal parasite worldwide. It is found most frequently in young children in tropical or subtropical climates, primarily in underdeveloped countries, and is uncommon in the United States. It is commonly transmitted by eating food that has been grown in soil contaminated by human feces. Symptoms if present may include vague abdominal discomfort, loss of appetite, or diarrhea. The diagnosis is made by examining a feces sample for microscopic-size eggs or by seeing adult worms passed in a bowel movement.

asthma Also called **reactive airway disease,** this condition may be an occasional annoyance or a disruptive, frightening, and at times life-threatening illness. During childhood as many as 10 percent of girls and 15 percent of boys will be affected at least once by this problem, which is the most common cause for children's admissions to hospitals in the United States. Of those affected, some will have had their first episode by the first birthday, and nearly 90 percent experience it by the age of five.

While the majority of children with asthma have occasional episodes that can be treated relatively easily, some develop severe and persistent symptoms that can be very stressful for everyone in the family. Usually the more seriously afflicted children have a family history of asthma and allergic disease and show signs of trouble during their first year of life. At least half of all asthmatic children become symptom-free eventually, at least in part because their airways enlarge as they grow. Unfortunately, despite more sophisticated treatments now available, deaths from asthma have risen over the past few years. *Treating this disease diligently should be a very high priority in any family in which one or more children are affected.*

Asthma is characterized by a tendency of the muscles surrounding both large and small airways to undergo spasmodic contractions, resulting in coughing, wheezing, or both. The events that trigger wheezing vary from person to person but can include illness (especially colds, bronchitis, and sinusitis), exercise, emotional upset, as well as exposure to smoke, dust, pollen, mold, air pollution, animal danders, cockroach infestation, or even certain foods. Some girls may wheeze during the days prior to their menstrual periods. Wheezing may also be provoked by certain medications such as aspirin. An important characteristic of asthma is that this spasm or constriction is *reversible;* with medication or time, the airway will return to normal.

Another important component of asthma is *inflammation.* Even when not in spasm, the inner lining of an asthmatic child's airways may be chronically inflamed with swelling, increased mucus production, and large numbers of inflammatory cells. Treating the wheezing while ignoring the inflammation will usually result only in temporary improvement.

Symptoms

Certain respiratory problems serve as signals that reactive airway disease is present. A dry, tight cough that occurs for no apparent reason or in patterns (such as during the night or after exertion) may be the only sign. In more intense episodes, overt wheezing may be audible from across the room. Some sounds that resemble wheezing, however, can actually arise from upper-airway infections such as croup, and a physician's exam may be necessary to make the distinction.

If the airways are particularly tight, the child may show more obvious signs of distress: rapid respirations, labored breathing with minimal exertion or when at rest, and noticeable use of muscles in the rib cage and neck with each breath. In severe cases, he may be unable to walk or talk, the skin may be pale or even dusky, and abdominal pain or even vomiting may occur. A child who is extremely short of breath should be seen by a physician immediately or taken to an emergency room.

Depending on the severity of the symptoms and the patterns of wheezing your child is showing, a variety of tests may be performed. Your child's doctor may ask you to obtain a **peak flow meter,** which measures the maximum rate of airflow your child can generate at a given time and can be used as a guide to adjust medications. This simple test can be extremely useful in keeping track of your child's progress on a day-to-day (or hour-to-hour) basis. A chest X-ray may be needed to rule out an underlying infection. Allergy testing may be appropriate to determine what is triggering wheezing episodes.

Prevention

This will depend to some degree on the specific triggers that provoke the airways to twitch and tighten. Some of these triggers will be clear-cut and others less obvious.

Dealing with **furry and feathered pets** in your home may become a highly emotional issue if animals are causing your child repeated bouts of breathlessness. An allergic evaluation might be needed to settle the question of sensitivity, and if a pet is indeed part of the problem, it may have to be kept outside. If symptoms are severe enough, the pet must be removed completely from the home for the sake of your child's health.

Dust mites are tiny, insectlike creatures that thrive in carpets, upholstered furniture, and bedding, especially when the air at home is warm and humid. The waste products of these microscopic animals can provoke all sorts of allergic reactions, including wheezing, even after the mites have died. Encasing mattresses and pillows in special plastic covers can significantly reduce your child's exposure to dust mites. Treatment of carpets with mite-killing chemicals every few months may be necessary. In some situations, it might be best for you to remove carpeting altogether.

Molds also thrive in warm, moist environments. A basement (especially if it has had any seepage or flooding), damp, dark closet spaces, or even a leaky toilet that invites mold to grow in the carpet surrounding it could breed these organisms and perpetuate asthma. Unfortunately, the humidifier you might have purchased to make your baby more comfortable can become a source of mold if it isn't cleaned and the water changed frequently.

If your child definitely has mold allergy, keeping the humidity at home at less than 30 percent, using an air conditioner or dehumidifier, and monitoring your progress with a humidity gauge can be very helpful. Bathrooms, which obviously become warm and moist regularly, frequently harbor mold. Regular cleaning of tiles, bathtub, shower curtain or stall, walls, and ceilings with a mold-killing solution (such as an equal mixture of bleach and water or a commercial spray solution) is a tedious but important job. Carpet should be taken out of the bathroom because water spilled from shower or bathtub or a leaky toilet invites mold to grow both within and beneath the carpet.

Every child deserves to live in a smoke-free environment, and for an asthmatic child **smoke exposure** can be a hazard both to health and to life itself. Any form of tobacco smoke will provoke and perpetuate wheezing; smoking should not be allowed in the home or any other environment (such as a car) in which an asthmatic child is present.

Reactions to **pollens** that appear at different times of the year (or year-round) may be more difficult to prevent because these particles are so tiny and can be blown for miles by the winds.

For the severely affected child, an evaluation by an allergist might be wise. The allergist can offer guidance regarding preventive measures, and when appropriate, treat with **immunotherapy** (allergy shots), which will cut down the child's reaction to specific triggers, especially pollens, that you can't easily control.

Treatment

A child of any age with asthma needs a team of attentive parents and health-care providers on his side. *Good rapport among all concerned is essential.* The specific approaches used for your child will depend upon the frequency and severity of the asthma episodes and the triggers that set it off. Treatment may be needed sporadically or year-round. *The most important intervention for asthma may be daily medication that prevents wheezing, not the sporadic treatment of flare-ups.*

Several types of medications are prescribed to treat asthma, but patients (or the parents of young children) must clearly understand their specific functions and when and how they should be used.

A family of medications called **bronchodilators**—for example, albuterol (Proventil or Ventolin) or terbutaline (Brethaire)—immediately relieve wheezing and usually maintain improved airflow for four to six hours. These are usually taken through **metered dose inhalers (MDIs),** which dispense measured bursts of medication. For very young children as well as older children with more severe asthma, a **home nebulizer device** may be more appropriate. This converts liquid medication into an aerosol form that is easily inhaled using a face mask or mouthpiece. Because bronchodilators are distantly related to adrenaline, they may cause tremors or rapid heart rate, especially if taken more often than prescribed. (These symptoms are more likely if the pill or syrup forms are used rather than an inhaler.) In children twelve years or older, the inhaled bronchodilator salmeterol (Serevent) may be used for maintenance to prevent attacks, since it is active for up to twelve hours.

However, salmeterol cannot be used to treat an acute asthma attack.

Because they help asthmatic children feel much better right away, bronchodilators are frequently overused. Repeated doses of this type of medication may cause enough temporary relief to delay more definitive care while the overall situation is actually deteriorating. If your child is using the bronchodilator four or five times a day regularly, his asthma is very likely out of control, and you should see his doctor about additional treatment. *Do not buy and use over-the-counter asthma inhalers as a substitute for proper medical care and supervision.*

Steroids in various forms more directly quiet down the inflammation that underlies the reactive airway response. Your child's doctor might prescribe a brief course of oral steroids to bring an intense wheezing episode under rapid control. Long-term oral steroid treatment can pose a major dilemma because of its combination of lifesaving benefits and major side effects. The same treatment given by inhaler does not risk the same side effects. *Using a steroid inhaler daily for weeks or months to prevent wheezing will generally be safer than intermittent doses of bronchodilators to stop acute asthma attacks.*

Cromolyn (Intal and other brands) is another option for long-term prevention, especially for a child with exercise-induced wheezing or a strong allergic component to his asthma. This medication is given by inhaler. While it is not as potent as a steroid, cromolyn can help prevent or minimize wheezing in a child who is already stabilized.

All inhalers are usually more effective in children if **spacers** such as the AeroChamber or InspirEase are used with them. A spacer is purchased separately (or provided by the physician), and the inhaler canister inserted into it prior to each use. (One steroid product, Azmacort, comes with a built-in spacer.) These devices eliminate the need for precise coordination of the child's deep inhalation and the actuation (firing the puff) of the inhaler. Spacers also prevent larger droplets of the medication from being deposited in the mouth and throat and improve the overall delivery of the drug to the lower airways. If your child is going to use a bronchodilator and a steroid and/or cromolyn inhaler at the same time, the bronchodilator should be given first because it will open up the airways and allow better distribution of the other medication. Holding the breath for a few seconds after inhaling a puff will help more of it arrive at its destination.

Theophylline has been used to treat asthma for years and may still be helpful for some children, though more often for maintenance than for acute care. Usually given in liquid, tablet, or powdered form (which is shaken into food such as cereal or applesauce), most theophylline given today is in timed-release forms that last for eight to twelve hours. Side effects can include nausea, vomiting, and jitteriness. Checking blood levels will usually be necessary to confirm that the right dose is being given.

Antibiotics may be needed at some point to treat a bacterial infection of the bronchial tubes or the sinuses. If your asthmatic child has a cold, check with the doctor before giving a decongestant and/or antihistamine formula. Some of these—especially certain antihistamines that can cause bronchial mucus to thicken—may interfere with the action of other medications.

Because so many medications are potentially helpful in treating wheezing, sometimes your asthmatic child may appear to be taking too many drugs. But if wheezing is intense, chronic, or difficult to control, a number of different medications might be needed, and it is extremely important that you understand how and when each is to be used.

If you feel confused about the mechanism of an inhaler or a spacer device, don't leave the pharmacy or doctor's office until you understand exactly what to do with whatever device you have been given, since your child's ability to breathe may depend on it. You may also need to learn how to use a peak flow meter, which will give everyone a better feel for how your child is doing.

Make sure you (and your child, if he's old enough) understand the purpose, dose, timing, and precautions for every medicine he is going to use. You should have *written* directions in your hand before you leave the doctor's office or pharmacy as well as an invitation to call back if you have questions. You should know whom to call and where to go in case the problem increases after office hours, since asthma has a tendency to worsen during the night.

You and your child's doctor should discuss the basic goals of therapy, which should not be limited merely to stopping acute wheezing episodes but should address preventing them as well. Ultimately, your child should be able to sleep through the night, feel normal during the day, and enjoy reasonable strenuous activity without coughing or wheezing. He should *not* think of himself as the sick kid who can't play ball or participate in sports because of his condition. Bronchodilators and cromolyn each have the capacity to reduce or prevent exercise-induced wheezing. A child or adolescent who coughs or wheezes during vigorous exercise may have less difficulty breathing and better endurance if one of these inhalers is used about a half hour before the activity begins.

astigmatism   An egg-shaped curvature of the cornea that prevents the eye from focusing correctly, resulting in blurry vision. Vision can usually be corrected through eyeglasses, contact lenses, or surgery.

athlete's foot (see photo on page A27)   A common skin infection caused by a type of fungus called a **dermatophyte** (literally, "skin plant"). It can live only in the outermost layer of skin where there are no living cells. Warm and humid conditions increase the likelihood of infection, as do shoes (especially those made of rubber or nylon) that do not allow the skin to dry or cool. Athlete's foot is more likely to occur after puberty.

The fungus itself does not penetrate into the skin, but substances generated by the fungus seep into the deeper (live) skin layers and provoke an allergic response. This commonly appears as a mild, scaly rash between the toes that may spread to the skin on the top or the sole of the foot. More intense reactions can occur, with bumps, blisters, burning, and itching.

A variety of antifungal creams, ointments, lotions, powders, and aerosols (many nonprescription) are effective in treating athlete's foot. Creams are often used because they are less greasy and easier to apply. A mild cortisone cream may also be used for a few days to relieve itching and irritation. A rapid improvement in symptoms does not mean that the fungus has been eradicated. Most antifungal medications must be continued every day for three to four weeks to bring about a cure. If symptoms do not improve after a week of treatment, the eruption should be evaluated by your doctor.

Unfortunately, someone with a healed case of athlete's foot is not immune to getting it again, and new contact with the fungus can restart the infection. Keeping the feet as clean and dry as possible can help prevent recurrences.

attention deficit/hyperactivity disorder (ADHD)   He is the toddler in perpetual motion, his throttle wide open every waking moment of the day (and a good deal of the night). He runs, jumps, climbs, opens, closes, pushes, shoves, and bulldozes over playmates, who seem nearly comatose by comparison.

He is the five-year-old whose kindergarten checkup is the major challenge of his doctor's afternoon. If the appointment is delayed for only a few minutes, he will rapidly investigate every surface and piece of equipment within reach. Despite his haggard mother's valiant efforts, permanent alterations of the room's contents are likely.

She is the third grader who fidgets, squirms, and taps her fingers through most of the school day. Anything and everything—the hair ribbons adorning the girl in front of her, the birds in the tree outside the classroom window, the sound of a passing truck, and a thousand other sights and sounds—distract her from whatever the teacher wants her to do. She can't seem to listen to directions, finish any assignment, or cooperate in any game. Her list of friends is as short as her attention span.

He is the young adult who dropped out of school, just lost his job, and can't maintain a relationship. His fuse is short (and he has a few scars to show for it), his moods are unpredictable, his apartment is a mess, and his calendar is empty. Depression and anger are his constant companions; drug and alcohol abuse could be waiting in the wings.

These vignettes illustrate variations on the theme called **attention deficit/hyperactivity disorder (ADHD)**, which is estimated to affect at least 5 percent of American children. (This includes approximately 2 million school-age children, nearly one per classroom.) Boys with ADHD outnumber girls at least four to one— some experts state as much as nine to one. No statistics can remotely estimate the depths of frustration, disappointment, resentment, and guilt that the parents of these children feel, at least at times. Despite a common belief that this problem disappears during adolescence, it usually doesn't go away, and millions of adults are probably affected as well. However, with help (and medication, when appropriate), adolescents and adults can learn to cope and live successfully with this condition.

Common features of ADHD

INATTENTION AND DISTRACTIBILITY An ADHD child cannot stay focused on any task that requires continuous attention, especially schoolwork. He may daydream or become distracted by any sight or sound in his vicinity. Completing an assignment can require much effort, but he is likely to misplace the final product between home and school. He cannot remember a sequence of directions: "Take out the trash, feed the bird, and pick up your clothes before you take your bath" might result in one or at most two of the commands being completed. The others will be forgotten or jumbled.

HYPERACTIVITY Perpetual motion has traditionally been the most striking trademark of ADHD, but in fact it is prominent in only about 30 percent of children who have the disorder. Experts now divide children with ADHD into subtypes based on their most overt characteristic: lack of attention, hyperactivity, or a blend of the two. While difficulty with attention may not be apparent until the child enters school, hyperactivity makes an im-

pact on everyone in his world from the time he is very young.

Some parents are aware that "something is different" from the first days of life with their demanding baby, who later turns into a turbocharged toddler. Most parents of small children wish they could acquire some of the energy of their offspring, but the hyperactive child is in a different league, living every day at top speed. Many children with ADHD also have volatile emotions. Whether they are joyful or angry—sometimes over what seems to be a trivial issue—everyone in earshot will hear about it. Just as rapidly, these feelings seem to pass as the child forgets the episode and moves on to something else.

IMPULSIVENESS The child with ADHD has little patience. He cannot wait his turn, stand in line, follow directions, or keep his hands off whatever he isn't supposed to touch. He talks before he thinks, acts before he analyzes, and leaps before he looks. As a result, he may suffer more than a few battle wounds and fractures.

ADHD has been given many names over the years, including Minimal Brain Dysfunction and Hyperkinetic Reaction of Childhood. It has been attributed to every cause imaginable: brain damage, birth trauma, poor parenting, lack of discipline, food additives, sugar, and pure willfulness. The best understanding presently is that the primary basis for ADHD is neurochemical, a subtle inherited malfunction of the intricate passing of messages between cells in the brain. So far, no specific medical finding, blood test, or X-ray is sensitive enough to detect the abnormality, although a doctor's evaluation is important in ruling out other causes of the troublesome behavior.

The child with ADHD exhibits difficulties in many areas of life (home, school, playground), but not always to the same degree, and parents may be confused and frustrated by some of the inconsistencies. Certain activities—usually ones that are highly intense such as video games—can hold his interest, at times to a striking degree. In some one-on-one situations, he may act quite normal. This variability is actually very typical of ADHD, but it gives the definite impression that the child's lack of attention is simple laziness or that his impulsivity is willful defiance.

One of the greatest challenges of parenting an ADHD child is discerning how much of a particular behavior arises from biology and how much from conscious decisions. As the child grows older, the causes may blend. For example, extreme difficulty with schoolwork, which requires prolonged concentration and mental effort, leads to dislike and then eventually to refusal to participate at all. Repeated rejection by others because of behavior he cannot control may push him toward more deliberately destructive acts.

Diagnosing ADHD

If you believe your child might have ADHD, it is very important to seek input from a qualified professional—better yet, from a team of professionals. Do not ignore the problems you see and assume that "he just needs more discipline" or that "he'll grow out of it"—because he probably won't. The diagnosis of ADHD should be made with a careful evaluation. Other learning disabilities, medical conditions, or problems at home may be causing the disruptive behavior.

The person who evaluates your child should be a properly licensed physician (usually a pediatrician, although family practitioners, neurologists, and psychiatrists who are experienced with ADHD may be involved) and/or a psychologist, social worker, or education specialist with training in ADHD and its management. Input from parents and school personnel, observation of the child, medical tests (if necessary), certain behavior-rating scales, tests of attention-related skills, and other measures may all be used, depending upon the evaluator's preference and experience.

Your child's doctor or teacher may suggest one or more preferred consultants. Local support groups such as Children & Adults with Attention Deficit Disorders (Ch.A.D.D.) can offer recommendations as well. Your school district is obligated by law to provide assessment services as its resources allow, even if your child is not enrolled in public school. The obvious advantage of this route is that it's affordable, especially if ADHD evaluation isn't covered under your health insurance or if you are uninsured. But, as is the case with some public services, you may have to wait several months for the work to be done.

Helping the ADHD child: first steps

Managing a child with ADHD requires participation from the entire family. Each member—including grandpa and grandma—needs to become educated about this problem, just as they would if a child had diabetes, asthma, or any other significant chronic condition. Input from the professional(s) involved and from books, tapes, and local support groups can be extremely helpful. The nonprofit organization Ch.A.D.D. provides a variety of services, including printed information (fact sheets, newsletters, educational materials for parents and teachers) and local chapters where parents—and adults with ADHD—can vent, support one another, and share ideas.

Parents of a child with ADHD must be unified and cooperative. The survival of your marriage will require your conscious decision to create a flexible team and firm support. If you are a single parent with an ADHD child, you will need to marshal all the support you can find—from relatives, friends, members of your church, even coworkers—to give yourself some breathing room. In all cases, prayers to God for wisdom and patience should be a vital part of each day.

The following can help restore and maintain order at home:

THE ADHD CHILD NEEDS STRUCTURE AND CONSISTENCY. A predictable routine every day, with specific times for meals, chores, homework, bathing, and bedtime, creates a stable framework for his life. The ADHD child most often *wants* to do what is right. External structure helps move him in the right direction.

House rules and expectations for behavior should be explicit, understandable and—very important—achievable. It would be unrealistic to expect a child with ADHD to sit quietly through a full-length sermon, go on an extended shopping trip, or dine in a formal restaurant without some difficulty—or total disaster.

GIVE INSTRUCTIONS SIMPLY AND CLEARLY; AVOID GIVING A CHAIN OF DIRECTIONS. A half hour after making a seemingly simple statement such as "Put the Legos away, let the dog out, and get your coat," you may find the ADHD child playing with another toy he spotted while putting away the Legos. The dog and the coat will have been long forgotten. If you have more than one thing you want him to do, tell him one item at a time.

ENFORCE RULES AND LIMITS CONSISTENTLY AND PREDICTABLY, WITH CONSEQUENCES APPROPRIATE FOR THE VIOLATION. For example, if he charges into a busy street on his bicycle despite being warned not to do so, bike-riding privileges should be suspended for a day. If he knowingly mistreats a toy and it falls apart, don't repair or replace it right away. If he has become too excited or aggressive playing with other children, give him a time-out in an uninteresting spot.

Remember, the child with ADHD may not seem to "get the picture," and he may actually repeat the behavior that you just punished him for. *It is important to make him suffer consistent consequences each time but to not yield to extremes: either giving up, which forfeits your right to be in charge, or reacting with increasingly harsh punishments.* As with all children, pick your battles carefully. Behaviors that put him or others at risk or are overtly destructive need your decisive response. But if you go to the mat with him over every minor annoyance, you'll be exhausted—and thoroughly depressed—every day.

OFFER PRAISE AND ENCOURAGEMENT. The child with ADHD needs to know he is loved and accepted as an important member of the family, especially because his disruptive behavior, difficulties with schoolwork, and lack of success in other areas such as games and sports will generate negative feedback from several directions. He needs to know that you and others are on his team and always will be.

When he does what he's told, accomplishes a task, plays well with another child, or makes progress at school, praise him. A special time of ten or fifteen minutes every day with one or both parents can allow some positive attention to be focused on him regularly.

Helpful approach at school

The demands of school are nearly always at odds with the natural bent of the child with ADHD. Often it is one or more problems in the classroom that bring the issue to a head. Many children are first diagnosed with ADHD as a result of a teacher's observations.

Some adjustments are usually necessary to prevent school from being the site of endless defeat, embarrassment, and disruption. Smaller, calmer, more structured classrooms are preferable to larger, more chaotic environments. Sitting at the front of the class where there are fewer distractions and closer supervision can be helpful. Giving him brief physical tasks, such as passing out papers or erasing the blackboard, will provide acceptable ways for him to get up and move around the room during the day.

In a best-case scenario, the teacher will be aware of his diagnosis and be sympathetic, tolerant, and willing to provide frequent, tactful reminders about assignments and appropriate behavior. Small-group and even individual instruction can be helpful. Just as in the home, the child with ADHD will need praise for his accomplishments and areas of strength to balance the negative feedback that invariably and frequently comes his way.

In the real world, not all of these helpful features will be readily available in the classroom. Parents may want to become advocates for special services for their child, which by law are to be provided by the local school district for those with educational handicaps, including ADHD. Advice from the professional who made the diagnosis or from a local support group might be necessary to guide parents in finding help within the system.

For some ADHD children, home schooling provides an environment that is more structured and conducive to learning. Taking this route obviously requires a fair amount of parental planning and effort, but it could pay off in the long run if it allows the child to complete his primary education more efficiently and with his self-esteem intact.

ADHD and medication

About 80 percent of children with ADHD will respond favorably to medications. This can be a sensitive subject for parents who worry about their child being "drugged" or controlled by mind-altering medications. But the appropriate prescription, adjusted by a physician attentive to the child's needs and schedule, can be very beneficial. Medication is only one component of a total approach to ADHD, not a magical quick fix for all the problems children have with this disorder.

Medications for ADHD might be likened to eyeglasses that correct blurry vision. While the glasses allow the child to see letters more clearly, they will not teach him to read. Similarly, medications for ADHD do not exert some mystical power over the child but merely enhance his own efforts to control himself and deal more effectively with daily events. Children under the age of five, however, are less likely to respond well to medical treatment and are more likely to have adverse side effects.

The medications that bring about positive changes are not sedatives and do not directly affect intellect or perception. Oddly enough, they are classified as stimulants, which would seem to be the last thing a hyperactive child needs. But rather than provoke turbocharged behavior, they most likely help normalize certain neurotransmitters (the chemical messengers within the brain). This causes increased attention span, better impulse control, less disruptive behavior at home and school, and more stable emotions.

The most commonly prescribed medications are **methylphenidate** (Ritalin), **dextroamphetamine** (Dexedrine), and various antidepressants. While Ritalin and Dexedrine are designated by the FDA as controlled substances, ADHD children do not become addicted to these medications, nor do they show any increased risk for substance abuse later in life. The specific choice and dosage must be determined for each child, usually by trial in which a low dose is started, behavior observed, and appropriate adjustments made. Feedback from the child himself, as well as from parents and teachers, is important in this process. Often the effects are obvious within an hour, although the final medication routine could take a few weeks to sort out.

Over the years, hundreds of studies have shown few problems with long-term side effects of these drugs. Some children will experience loss of appetite or difficulty sleeping, but changes in dose, timing, or type of medication will usually resolve these symptoms. Others may experience a "rebound" effect, in which disruptive behaviors or mood swings occur as a given dose wears off. Adjustments can usually minimize this effect.

Because of concerns over the effects of these medications on a child's long-term growth, many physicians have advocated drug "holidays" on weekends and during the summer. However, a child's ultimate height and weight rarely appear to be affected, and some children benefit from medication every day.

Since ADHD usually continues to be a problem into adulthood, it is possible that medications will play a role later in life. Each child's needs and responses must therefore be carefully considered over a period of years, not merely for a few months.

Diet, sugar, and food additives

Over the past several decades, a number of individuals have proposed that sugar, dairy products, preservatives, and artificial colors and flavors in foods trigger or aggravate ADHD symptoms. The most widely publicized theory has been from pediatric allergist Dr. Benjamin Feingold, who claimed in the mid-1970s that at least 50 percent of hyperactive behavior was caused by artificial colors and flavors. The Feingold diet thus involved the scrupulous avoidance of these items. Based on some success in individual cases, Dr. Feingold took his theory to the public, and his diet became the nutritional bulwark for thousands of parents of ADHD children. But subsequent controlled studies in larger numbers of children failed to support his claims. Similarly, a common belief that eating refined sugar triggers hyperactive behavior has not held up in large-scale studies.

It is quite possible that some children show a deterioration of behavior when they eat certain foods. If this happens consistently, those foods should be avoided. But proving cause-and-effect relationships can be very difficult, and some caution and skepticism are in order to prevent a child from becoming a "food cripple" who isn't allowed to eat anything but a handful of "safe" items.

Because a child with ADHD can create such havoc in a family, the desire for a magic formula to make the problem go away can become overwhelming. Several fringe therapies (e.g., the use of megavitamins) have attracted parents desperate for a cure, but the likelihood that these therapies will create lasting success without other measures being taken is remote.

ADHD resources

Children & Adults with Attention Deficit Disorders (Ch.A.D.D.)/499 Northwest 70th Avenue, Suite 408/ Plantation, Florida 33317-7588/954-587-3700

Martin, Grant, *The Hyperactive Child: What You Need to Know about Attention Deficit Disorder—Facts, Myths, and Treatment* (Wheaton, Ill: Victor Books, 1992).

autism An extremely complex neurological disorder with varying symptoms and signs. Among the most notable symptoms are nondeveloped or poorly developed verbal and nonverbal communication skills: abnormalities in speech patterns, impaired ability to sustain a conversation, abnormal social play, lack of empathy, and an inability to make friends. Autistic children often have a compulsive adherence to routines and rituals, and they usually lack interest in their peers.

The professional assistance provided for an autistic child will depend on various factors, including behavior and functional level, the availability of consultants and facilities in a given area, and the resources and stability of the family. Several professionals—physicians, psychologists, developmental specialists, speech therapists, and teachers—as well as ongoing programs, both in and out of the home, may be involved in the process of helping the autistic child reach his full potential.

B

bacteria (singular: bacterium) Microscopic single-cell organisms that are present in nearly every environment, including the human body. Unlike viruses, which can multiply only by taking control of the genetic equipment of cells they invade, bacteria live on the skin and in the mouth, digestive tract, and vagina. Of the thousands of different types of bacteria, most are harmless to humans. However, some are capable of damaging tissue, producing toxins that interfere with normal body functions, or even overwhelming the immune system. In most cases, bacterial infections can be treated with medications known as antibiotics (see *antibiotic*).

bad breath See *halitosis*.

bed-wetting (enuresis) Gaining consistent control of bladder and bowel during daytime hours is a significant milestone for a toddler or preschooler. For many children, keeping the bed dry at night is a more elusive goal, one that might not be reached until quite a bit later in life. Children who still wet the bed at night well into their grade-school years too often take an emotional beating (in some cases, a physical beating) because of this problem—*which is not under their conscious control.* One of the greatest problems faced by bed-wetting children is a parent with unrealistic expectations that every child should be completely dry, day and night, by the age of three. To deal with bed-wetting effectively and supportively, it is important to understand some basic realities of nighttime bladder function in children.

Definition

Enuresis is the involuntary passage of urine into the bed or clothes at least once or twice per month in a child who is at least five years of age. Although involuntary wetting may occur during the day, this discussion will be limited to nighttime enuresis.

A child with **primary enuresis** has never remained consistently dry through the night for more than six to twelve months. A child with **secondary enuresis** has achieved consistent nighttime bladder control for six to twelve months and then for some reason lost it.

Causes

Only about 1 percent of children with enuresis will be found upon medical examination to have an underlying disease or disorder such as a urinary tract infection, diabetes, significant constipation, a congenital abnormality of the urinary tract, or a disturbance in the central nervous system. When evaluating persistent bed-wetting, a child's physician will consider these physical possibilities (which usually have other manifestations) and carry out appropriate studies if necessary.

In the other 99 percent of children with enuresis, the problem may involve one or more of the following. (Clinicians are not in complete agreement about the relative importance of each of these factors.)

- *Delayed maturation.* During infancy, the bladder automatically empties six to eight times per day when a certain volume of urine is present. As a child matures, this emptying reflex is inhibited (held in check) by the central nervous system, so that he can hold larger amounts of urine and eventually release it voluntarily. In general, control is achieved earlier by girls than by boys. By the age of three, most children can consistently postpone urinating during waking hours. However, the ability of a child's central nervous system to inhibit emptying of the bladder during sleep may lag behind daytime control by months or even years. By the age of five, as many as 10 to 15 percent of children are not consistently dry in the morning.
- *Small functional bladder capacity.* A normal child can usually voluntarily hold urine in an amount of ounces equal to his age in years plus two. (A six-year-old child, for example, should be able to hold about eight ounces of urine.) If a child cannot hold at least the same number of ounces as his age, this decreased capacity may contribute to enuresis.
- *Increased formation of urine during the night.* A hormone called **vasopressin,** which is produced by the pituitary gland, reduces urine production by the kidneys. An increased amount of this hormone is normally secreted during the night, cutting the rate of urine production in half. Some bed wetters apparently do not secrete more vasopressin during the night and produce more urine than their non–bed-wetting peers. A similar result may occur, regardless of vasopressin levels, if a child consumes liquids before going to bed.
- *Difficulty awakening when the bladder is full.* While the general patterns of sleep are similar in both bed-wetting and non–bed-wetting children, many parents observe that their child with enuresis will "sleep through anything" and seems very difficult to awaken during the night.
- *A family history of enuresis.* Since so many of the factors contributing to bed-wetting have an inherent physiological basis, it should not be surprising that this problem often runs in families. Enuresis is seven times more common in children whose fathers were bed wetters and five times more common if the mother had this problem. If *both* parents were bed wetters, the likelihood that their child will have enuresis is greater than 75 percent, compared to a 15 percent chance if neither parent was a bed wetter.

Evaluation

If your child is wetting the bed repeatedly after the fifth or sixth birthday, an evaluation by your child's physician is a reasonable first step. (Very often this problem can be addressed during a routine checkup.) A careful history and a physical examination will be performed, along with any appropriate laboratory studies (such as a urinalysis). A culture of the urine will be taken if there is concern about an infection. In most cases elaborate diagnostic tests are not needed. But if the initial assessment raises concerns about the structure or function of the urinary tract, your child's physician will want to evaluate further.

If a child develops secondary enuresis—that is, he has been consistently dry in the morning for more than six months and then begins wetting the bed again—a specific explanation should be sought. Situations that are stressful to a young child (such as a move or a new baby in the house) very often play a role, although a medical problem such as a bladder infection or diabetes might also be manifested in this way.

Management

First and foremost, remember that for the vast majority of children enuresis will eventually resolve on its own as the central nervous system matures. (Each year after the age of six, 15 percent of children who still have enuresis will spontaneously stop wetting at night.) *Enuresis is not a sign of disobedience or weakness of character.* The child who wets the bed is already embarrassed and uncomfortable about it; ridicule or punishment for bed-wetting, including teasing by siblings, is cruel, unjust, and ineffective. Not only will it cause additional emotional problems, but it might actually delay the resolution of enuresis.

Unless an underlying medical problem has been discovered by the child's physician, it is unrealistic to expect the doctor to provide a specific treatment that will cure enuresis overnight. Steps can be taken to eventually achieve one of two satisfactory goals: Your child holds his urine through the night and then voids into the toilet or potty-chair in the morning, *or* your child awakens during the night when his bladder is full and voids into the toilet or potty-chair.

The following measures may help a child with enuresis:

- Encourage fluid intake during the day and discourage drinking liquids after the evening meal or within two hours of bedtime. If your child wants a drink before bed, limit intake to one or two ounces.
- Have your child empty his bladder just before he goes to bed.
- Encourage your child to get up during the night to urinate. A child who feels that his only goal is to delay emptying his bladder until morning may fail repeatedly. Giving verbal cues before bed ("Try to get up and use the toilet if your bladder feels full"), leaving the light on in the bathroom, or providing a potty-chair near the bed can help.
- To a degree that is appropriate for his age, let him participate in the cleanup process when the pajamas and bed are wet. *This should be presented not as punishment but as a matter-of-fact routine.* This can include rinsing out his pajamas and underwear and taking a quick bath or shower in the morning if he smells of urine. Sheets can be left open to air dry but should be washed when they have a disagreeable odor. A dry towel placed under the child's bottom may help reduce the amount of laundry. A school-age child who wakes up wet during the night can change his own pajamas and place a dry towel over the wet area of the sheet. (Dry pajamas and towel should be made readily available in his room.)
- Some experts believe that specific measures can increase the functional capacity of a child's bladder. Younger bed wetters who visit the bathroom frequently during the day can be encouraged to go less often. Children older than six or seven can be encouraged to try increasing the bladder's capacity by a simple exercise of waiting to use the toilet for at least ten or fifteen minutes after feeling the urge to go. *This should only be done if the child is a willing participant* and will be most helpful with a child who has a small bladder capacity. (To check his capacity, have him hold his urine as long as he can and then void into a measuring cup. Take the best of three measurements of his bladder capacity, which in ounces should equal his age in years plus one or two.)
- Protect the mattress with a plastic cover.
- Offer praise and perhaps a smiley-face sticker on the calendar when he has a dry night or awakens and uses the toilet.
- Avoid expressing dissatisfaction, dismay, or anger when he's wet in the morning.

Bed-wetting alarms

These devices might be helpful for a child with enuresis who is eight or older (or in younger bed wetters if they are highly motivated) and who has not succeeded with other methods. Unlike the older pad-and-bell systems, the newer alarms are compact, portable, simple to use, and relatively inexpensive (about $45 to $60). (Beware of aggressively advertised, expensive programs that promise to "cure" bed-wetting. Helping your child accomplish this goal may be labor-intensive, but it shouldn't be expensive.) A sensor attached to the child's underwear will cause the device to buzz or vibrate against the skin like a pager when very small amounts of urine are released. The child should be encouraged to wake up as quickly as possible when the alarm goes off, get to the toilet, and empty any remaining urine. Over a period of several weeks, most children begin to associate the full bladder with the alarm-awakening process, and then with awakening before the alarm goes off. Medical studies have demonstrated an overall success rate of about 70 percent of cases in which these alarm systems are used; they are most effective when both parent and child are motivated to use them every night for two to three months.

Difficulties may arise if the child does not readily awaken to the noise or vibration. Parents should be prepared to get up when the alarm sounds, gently rouse the child, and have *him* turn off the alarm and use the toilet after he is definitely awake. Patience and persistence on everyone's part will be needed to condition the child's central nervous system to awaken first to the alarm and eventually to the full bladder.

For those who want to try a less high-tech approach, a regular alarm (bell, buzzer, or radio) can be set to go off three or four hours after the child goes to bed. The alarm should be out of his reach so he must get up to turn it off. He should be encouraged to proceed from alarm to toilet to empty his bladder before returning to bed. The timing of this wake-up call will have to be determined by trial and error, of course, and will depend upon the hour that bed-wetting most commonly takes place. As with the bed-wetting alarms, this approach will require more effort if the child is extremely difficult to awaken during the night.

Drugs to stop bed-wetting

Two medications have been recognized as potentially helpful in controlling bed-wetting. The use of either requires a doctor's prescription and a thorough understanding of potential benefits, risks, and proper use. Consider these important points before using either of these drugs:

- They are best suited for children who are at least eight years old and for whom other methods have not been consistently successful.
- In many cases they provide temporary assistance rather than a permanent cure. Enuresis often resumes when a medication is discontinued (especially if done abruptly) unless other training methods have been utilized as well. Long-term use of medication might be considered in specific situations—for example, an older child or adolescent with persistent enuresis—depending upon the underlying cause.
- They can be very helpful for the child who wants to participate in activities such as camp-outs or sleepovers with friends or relatives without worrying about wetting the bed or sleeping bag.
- Either drug should be tried at home to check for effectiveness or side effects before being used on an overnight outing.

Imipramine (Tofranil and other brands) increases the bladder's functional capacity and reduces its tendency to empty spontaneously. It is inexpensive and usually well tolerated when given in the proper dose,

although it can cause anxiety and insomnia. The major problem with this drug, however, is its toxicity in case of an accidental overdose, which can lead to seizures, coma, or fatal heart-rhythm disturbances. For this reason, if your child is taking imipramine for enuresis, he must understand that *he should never take more than the doctor has recommended, and the bottle must not be accessible to any other child at home.*

Desmopressin (DDAVP) acts like the pituitary hormone vasopressin (described in the earlier section regarding causes of enuresis), reducing the amount of urine produced during the night. It is safe and relatively easy to take (it comes only in a nasal spray), but results obtained with it are inconsistent, and enuresis commonly recurs when the drug is discontinued. It is also expensive—well over $75 per month, compared with about $5 per month for generic imipramine. When it works, DDAVP can be particularly useful for the older child or adolescent who needs some protection from bed-wetting during an overnight outing with minimal risk of unwanted side effects.

In summary, bed-wetting can be a great source of ongoing distress and discouragement for a child. It is therefore very important that a child understands these points:

- He will eventually grow out of this problem.
- He is not the only child who has ever dealt with bed-wetting. (Perhaps Mom, Dad, or other relatives had enuresis as well. If this was the case, letting him know this will provide some reassurance.)
- His parents, siblings, and physician are all on his team.
- There may be some effort involved (appropriate for his age) in dealing with the wet pajamas and sheets and in bringing bed-wetting under control, but his participation is not a punishment.

Bell's palsy A sudden and usually temporary weakness affecting one side of the face. Movement of the mouth and eyelids (including the ability to close the eye) is most commonly affected. Bell's palsy often follows a viral illness, but many times the underlying cause is unknown. Most cases begin to improve within a week or two, and the vast majority resolve within two months. During that time, specific measures may be recommended to protect the cornea, which can become dry because of incomplete closure of the eyelids during blinking.

benign A term used to indicate that a condition is relatively mild or not likely to cause serious consequences. It is most commonly applied to a tumor that is not cancerous. (In contrast, a tumor that invades other tissue and/or spreads to other parts of the body is referred to as *malignant.*)

biceps (see illustration on page A7) Muscles that bend or flex the arms.

bilirubin A by-product of the breakdown of red blood cells, which normally circulate in the bloodstream for about four months until they literally wear out. The liver processes and excretes bilirubin. If the liver is diseased, as in hepatitis, or immature, as in newborns, the level of bilirubin in the bloodstream may become high enough to cause a yellow-orange discoloration of the skin known as **jaundice.**

Before birth a baby's bilirubin is largely managed through the mother's circulation. After birth it takes a newborn's liver a few days to take over this process, so the level of bilirubin in the baby's bloodstream will increase by a modest amount. If a significant backlog develops, the baby's skin will take on a yellow-orange hue, beginning with the head and gradually spreading toward the legs. Whether or not jaundice is significant will depend upon several factors, including the actual level of bilirubin, how soon and how fast it has risen, the suspected cause, and whether the baby is full-term or premature. In some instances, extremely high bilirubin levels can damage the central nervous system, especially in the premature infant. If you notice your new baby's skin color changing to bright yellow-orange, contact your baby's doctor.

If there is any concern, the baby's physician will order blood tests to check the bilirubin level, and if needed, other studies will be done to look for underlying causes. Sometimes high levels of bilirubin result from a difference between a mother's blood type and that of her newborn. For example, if the mother's blood type is O and the baby's is A or B, some anti-A or anti-B antibodies from the mother may cross the placenta into the baby's circulation before birth. These antibodies can destroy many of the newborn's red cells, leading to a high bilirubin level shortly after birth.

A more severe form of this process used to occur commonly in connection with a protein known as the **Rh factor,** which is either present on the surface of blood cells (making a person Rh-positive) or absent (Rh-negative). Whenever a mother with Rh-negative blood gave birth to an infant who was Rh-positive, the mother's immune system could become sensitized to the Rh factor. If she had another pregnancy with an Rh-positive baby, her Rh antibodies would cross the placenta and destroy significant numbers of the new baby's red cells. Babies born under these conditions were often jaundiced at birth and became quite ill, requiring immediate transfusions of antibody-free blood. Today Rh incompatibility problems are avoided by giving Rh-negative mothers a shot (called RhoGam) that prevents her immune system from developing Rh antibodies.

In most cases, a newborn's jaundice is the by-product of normal physiological processes and is not caused by an Rh or blood type incompatibility or other problems (such as infection). This so-called **physiologic jaundice** will eventually resolve on its own within 10 to 14 days.

In some situations (depending on various factors), the baby's doctor will recommend one or more of the following measures to help lower a bilirubin level that has become significantly elevated:

- Treat any underlying cause (such as an infection), if present.
- Increase the baby's fluid intake by feeding her more often.
- Expose the baby to *indirect* sunlight for periods of 20 to 30 minutes—dressed only in a diaper in a sunlit room *where the sun does not shine directly on her sensitive skin.* Since indirect sunlight has only a modest effect on clearing bilirubin, don't use this approach unless you are sure that your baby won't become too hot or too cold.
- Sometimes an enzyme found in the mother's milk interferes to a modest degree with the clearing of bilirubin. Your physician may ask you to stop breast feeding for a short time and use formula until the problem improves, after which nursing can resume. In such a case, it is important that you continue to express milk to maintain your supply. This should *not* be an occasion to stop nursing altogether. Some healthy breast-fed infants will have a slight orange hue for weeks.
- A treatment called **phototherapy** may be utilized if the bilirubin level needs to be treated. Under a physician's direction, the baby lies under a special intense blue light while wearing eyeshades like a sunbather at the beach. In addition, or as an alternative, a baby can lie on a thin plastic light source called a **Bili Blanket.** Whether carried out in a hospital or at home (using equipment provided by a home-health agency), phototherapy usually reduces bilirubin gradually within two or three days, if not sooner.

A newborn whose jaundice resolves and then reappears should be checked by a physician, as should an older infant or child who appears jaundiced for the first time. Some older infants who are taking solids and regularly enjoy carrots and other yellow vegetables may actually develop a slight orange hue, which is harmless and has nothing to do with bilirubin. This does not cause the whites of the eyes to become yellow. A more obvious yellow coloration of skin (as well as the whites of the eyes) in a child may indicate that the liver is inflamed or (far less commonly) that the drainage of bile from the liver is obstructed.

birthmarks Birthmarks occur where there is an overabundance of a particular component of normal skin such as tiny blood vessels (capillaries) or pigment cells. The cause of this local condition is unknown.

The flat, pink birthmarks commonly seen on the forehead, eyelids, back of the neck, and above the bridge of the nose are called **capillary hemangiomas,** also known as "stork bites" or "salmon patches." These are seen in about 50 percent of newborns. Eyelid patches will disappear by three to six months of age, while those on the neck will fade but may last for years.

Areas of dark or bluish gray pigmentation known as **Mongolian spots** (see photo on page A29) are common on the low back and buttocks of dark-skinned newborns, although these marks may be found in all racial and ethnic groups. These marks vary greatly in size and shape and usually disappear by two to three years of age.

A more permanent type of birthmark is the **café au lait spot,** a light brown flat patch that can occur anywhere on the body. While some are present at birth, others may appear later in life. While these markings are benign, the presence of six or more of them measuring more than 15 mm (about 5/8 inch) in diameter may indicate a more serious problem known as **neurofibromatosis** (see *neurofibromatosis*).

One or more dark brown, black, or blue-black spots known as **nevi,** which contain large numbers of pigmented cells, may be seen at birth in about one in one hundred Caucasian infants. While the vast majority of these spots never cause any trouble, on rare occasion (usually in adolescence or even later in adulthood), one or more may transform into a dangerous type of skin cancer called a **malignant melanoma.** You should become familiar with the appearance of any nevi on your child's skin and watch in particular for any of the following warning signs: significant change in size; crusting, oozing, or bleeding; the development of an irregular border or color pattern; and change from a flat to a raised or rough contour. Should any of these changes develop, ask your child's doctor or a dermatologist to examine the area.

A more troublesome (but also uncommon) birthmark is the **giant pigmented nevus,** an irregular raised dark brown patch over four inches in diameter. When this covers a large area of the lower trunk, it is called a "bathing trunk nevus." At a microscopic level this is structurally similar to the common moles (or **junctional nevi**), which become more common and widespread over the skin later in life. Unfortunately, giant pigmented nevi are much more likely than the smaller congenital pigmented nevi to transform into malignant melanomas. This change can occur during infancy or at any time later in life. For this reason a consultation with a dermatologist or plastic surgeon may be recommended at an early age.

blood poisoning Nonmedical term for the serious condition known as **septicemia,** in which a significant number of microorganisms (usually bacteria) are present in the bloodstream.

blood pressure The pressure of the circulating blood within the arteries is dependent on the strength of the heart's contraction, the elasticity of the walls of the arteries, and the volume of blood in an individual's body. Blood pressure is expressed as two numbers: the **systolic pressure,** which occurs at the peak of the heart's contraction, and the **diastolic** or minimum pressure in the blood vessels, which occurs when the heart is filling up with blood, preparing for the next beat.

High blood pressure (also called **hypertension,** which is no reflection on one's emotional state) is not unusual in adults and is a risk factor for coronary artery disease and stroke. Even though it is much less common in children, your physician will begin measuring your child's blood pressure routinely when the child reaches age three. Persistent high blood pressure in children should be investigated to find the cause.

body odors
Before puberty
Parents are usually aware of subtle (or at times strong) aromas emanating from their baby or young child during a typical day. Occasionally you may notice an unfamiliar odor that could indicate a specific problem.

Bad breath (**halitosis**) usually indicates that an infection is present somewhere—in the gums, throat, tonsils, adenoids, or sinuses. A child with nasal congestion who breathes through the mouth or a child with a chronic cough may also have bad breath. A trip to the doctor's office will probably be necessary to find and treat the cause.

An *extremely* foul odor emanating from a small child's face, worsening by the day and not improved by toothbrushing or bathing, is probably the result of an object that has been stuffed up the nose. Thick, discolored drainage from one nostril may be a more prominent symptom than the smell. A wad of paper, a pencil eraser, a piece of foam from the couch, a pea or bean, and a small body part from a stuffed animal are among the possibilities. In most cases, your child's doctor will be able to extract the foreign object with narrow forceps, but be prepared to help hold your child still while the object is removed.

A similar but less common scenario may occur if your daughter inserts a small object into her vagina. A strong odor from the genital area, with or without discharge, should be checked by her doctor. A bacterial infection can also generate a disagreeable odor that won't clear with simple bathing and will need medical attention.

Smelly feet can occur in a child of any age who wears poorly ventilated shoes. Heat, sweat, and bacteria are the main ingredients, and treatment isn't particularly complicated: Have the child wear well-ventilated footwear or sandals or let her go barefoot. Clean socks and a daily bath or shower will certainly help. Absorbent powder sprinkled into shoes may absorb some of the perspiration and help curb the aroma.

A sick child sometimes gives off unusual odors. An oddly sweet aroma (or one that resembles nail polish) can be caused by compounds called **ketones,** which accumulate when a child hasn't been eating because of a stomach upset. Rarely this smell heralds the onset of diabetes, but if so, the child will have other symptoms: thirst, frequent voiding, weight loss, and increasing listlessness. *This situation needs immediate medical attention* (see *diabetes mellitus*).

Unusual odors, such as a "maple syrup" or "sweaty feet" smell in an infant who isn't wearing shoes, may indicate metabolic disorders that are often serious but fortunately extremely rare. Usually other features of these diseases—failure to gain weight, lethargy, seizures, and delayed development, among others—will signal that something is drastically wrong well before anyone is concerned about unusual smells.

After puberty

With the onset of puberty comes a different set of odor problems. Sebaceous glands on the neck and upper body, under the arms, and in the genital area begin to produce material called **sebum.** Skin bacteria acting on this substance can generate very disagreeable body odor after one or two days. Interestingly, the watery perspiration that appears during exercise or stress has no odor at all.

Teenagers can fall into two extremes in dealing with body odors. Some are overly concerned about the social consequences of body odor and go to extremes using antiperspirants (which can irritate the skin under the arms), aftershave, cologne, vaginal douches, foot powders, or other products they have seen advertised in magazines or on TV. Other teens may need prompting to take care of even the very basic hygiene.

In dealing with adolescent odor issues, moderation and common sense should prevail. Daily showering or bathing, regularly using shampoo (every day for some teens), wearing clean socks and underwear each day, brushing teeth after meals, and laundering or drycleaning clothes—in other words, basic self-care—will prevent most body-odor problems.

Girls who have begun menstruating may worry about odor arising from this monthly event and be tempted to use "hygienic" measures such as douches or feminine sprays. Menstrual flow itself is not malodorous. Simple measures such as daily bathing or showering, changing saturated pads, or (most important) not leaving a tampon in the vagina for more than six hours will prevent or minimize unpleasant odors. Feminine-hygiene sprays can irritate delicate tissue, and douching is unnecessary to maintain cleanliness. Any persistent drainage that is discolored, itchy, painful, or foul-smelling could indicate the presence of an infection (or, rarely, a lost tampon). This should *not* be treated by douching but should be evaluated by a physician.

botulism (see also *food poisoning*) A rare but extremely dangerous form of food poisoning. It is caused by a toxin produced by the bacterium Clostridium botulinum, which may grow in improperly canned food. (Home-canned foods are the most common source of botulism.) **Infant botulism** may occur in babies younger than one year of age and is most commonly caused by the ingestion of honey contaminated with the spores.

breath-holding spells These are frightening but common events that occur in about 5 percent of children between six months and six years of age. There is a history of breath holding among parents or siblings in about one out of four families in which it occurs.

There are two types of breath-holding episodes. In the more common **cyanotic** type, crying occurs after a physical or emotional incident that provokes fear, anger, or frustration. Normally, most young children who suddenly become upset will release a long, continuous cry that finally ends just in time to take a big gasp of air and then cry out again. The breath holder extends her cry so long that she doesn't quite make it to the breath she

B

needs. She suddenly becomes stiff, arches her back, and turns blue in the face. She may lose consciousness for about 15 seconds (which can seem much longer to the first-time observer) and make brief jerking movements of the arms and legs that resemble (but are not) a brief seizure. Finally she will take a breath. When the episode is over she will be fully awake and aware, not confused or unresponsive as would be the case after a seizure.

The second type is the **pallid** breath-holding spell, in which the child becomes pale in response to a sudden painful stimulus (for example, getting her finger caught in a door or having blood drawn at the doctor's office). Aside from the child being pale rather than blue, this episode looks similar to the cyanotic breath-holding spell.

These spells ultimately arise from a brief lack of oxygen available to the brain. Although they are very dramatic and may appear life-threatening, breath-holding spells end spontaneously. They do not cause brain damage, nor are they a form of epilepsy. However, they can be very stressful to a parent or caregiver, especially if he or she has never seen one.

Once you have observed one or more breath-holding spells and know how they end, you can be calmer when one occurs in the future. While the term *breath-holding spell* implies that this event might be purposeful, be aware that it is not a performance or a deliberate, premeditated act. Nevertheless, don't let the potential of one of these spells become an indirect form of manipulation by your child. Some parents may give in to a child's demands to avoid seeing another spell ("We can't let Johnny get too upset, or he might turn blue again"). This is both unwise and unnecessary. If your child becomes upset over reasonable limits or appropriate disciplinary measures and has a breath-holding spell as a result, you should not feel guilty or alarmed. Stick to your principles. Children normally stop having these episodes on their own, and no specific intervention is needed.

breech   When a baby is born feet or buttocks first, instead of headfirst.

bronchiolitis   An acute respiratory illness that most commonly affects young infants, especially those between two and six months of age, although it can be seen in children as old as two. The viruses that cause this infection not only irritate the nose and upper airway (as seen in a typical cold), but they also provoke inflammation and narrowing of very small airways known as **bronchioles.** (This is a different illness from **bronchitis,** which affects the larger airways.)

Bronchiolitis is a seasonal illness, usually seen between November and April. While any of a number of viruses (including influenza) could be the cause, the **respiratory syncytial virus (RSV)** is usually involved. RSV is such an extraordinarily contagious virus that virtually all children have been infected with it by the age of two. Only about one in three develop lower-airway problems such as bronchiolitis or pneumonia, while the rest have more routine colds.

Bronchiolitis usually begins with typical cold symptoms—a runny nose, cough, and low-grade fever—for one to three days. Then comes a deeper, raspy cough, followed by more rapid, shallow, and noisy breathing (or in some cases wheezing), depending on the severity of infection. Infants with bronchiolitis frequently lack interest in feeding and often become restless and agitated.

For most infants, bronchiolitis is a self-limited illness that won't require special medication or hospitalization. The most important thing you can do for your child is to watch her activity, feeding, and breathing patterns. Calming and comforting her as much as possible can help, since fussing and crying can aggravate any breathing difficulty. Using a humidifier and encouraging her to take liquids will help her clear secretions and prevent dehydration. Because of the extra effort needed to breathe, she may nurse or take formula more slowly. Over-the-counter decongestants or cough mixtures are not usually recommended for infants with bronchiolitis, and antibiotics will not alter its course, although they may be used if a secondary infection (such as an ear infection) develops. Oral bronchodilators (medications that help open the airway) may be prescribed by your child's doctor.

Occasionally an infant with more severe bronchiolitis will need to be hospitalized. Oxygen and supplemental fluids are usually given, and inhaled bronchodilators may help as well.

A child with RSV sheds a large amount of virus from the secretions of the nose and upper airway, and these viruses (like many others) are easily passed from person to person by hands and inanimate objects. If you are caring for a baby or child with a runny nose and cough, remember to wash your hands after you have handled her (or anything she has touched or gummed) to reduce the risk of spreading the virus to other children. Infants and toddlers are contagious for two to three days before their symptoms begin and for one to two weeks after.

A baby with chronic medical problems who might have more difficulty with bronchiolitis might best be kept away from groups of small children (such as day care or the church nursery) during the winter and early spring, especially when RSV or influenza is known to be present in your community. Check with your baby's health-care provider for specific advice.

For most infants and children, there are no lasting effects of bronchiolitis. However, 30 percent or more will have problems with asthma later in life. It is unknown whether damage to the airways from RSV makes them more prone to wheezing or whether children who are destined to become asthmatic simply have more trouble with RSV.

bronchitis A common infection of the passages of the lungs known as the **bronchial tubes.** Typically a child with this illness will have a low-grade fever, cough, headache, and possibly wheezing. Symptoms usually last three to five days, although in some children coughing may persist for several days after the acute symptoms have subsided. If coughing continues for more than seven to ten days (especially if it is frequent) or if a child manifests any difficulty breathing prior to that time, she should be seen by a physician.

Many types of bacteria and viruses cause this illness. If ongoing coughing is accompanied by the persistent production of discolored (yellow, green, or gray) phlegm, infection from bacteria is more likely, and antibiotics may be helpful. Children with asthma and those exposed to tobacco smoke might have more severe or prolonged symptoms and may benefit from therapy utilizing inhaled medications.

bruxism Grinding or clenching of the teeth. This habit can develop at any age and usually occurs during sleep. If it continues over a prolonged period of time, abrasion of primary teeth can result.

bursa A fluid-filled sac found in various locations in the body where there is potential for friction to develop between two adjacent structures, such as a tendon and a bone. Typically a bursa is positioned to allow these structures to move freely in relation to each other. If a bursa becomes inflamed (a condition called **bursitis**), local pain, swelling, tenderness, and difficulty moving the affected area may result.

C

cancer Cancer is frightening for adults and even more frightening when discovered in an infant or child. Fortunately in children cancer is frequently not only treatable but often curable.

Cancer is not a single disease but a collection of different syndromes that have a common theme: the uncontrolled multiplication of a particular type of cell.

Because there are many types of cells, each having a different function and behavior, there are also many types of cancers. **Tumor** and **neoplasm** (literally, "new tissue") refer to abnormal growths, which may be further divided into **benign** and **malignant** subcategories. Benign (or "good") tumors arise in one place and stay there. They range in size from tiny warts (which are technically benign tumors caused by a virus) to rather bulky growths that may require extensive surgery to remove.

Malignant tumors not only grow at their point of origin but also tend to invade and disrupt surrounding tissue. (The term *cancer* is applied specifically to malignant tumors.) Worse, malignant cells may enter the lymphatic system. This system consists of tiny vessels that collect fluid from every part of the body and route it back into the bloodstream. Collections of cells known as lymph nodes, which assist in the body's immune response, are also found throughout the system. Unfortunately, cancer cells arising from a particular organ may invade nearby lymph nodes. When cancer enters the lymphatic system or the bloodstream it can spread to other parts of the body. This process is called **metastasis;** a tumor that has spread to a place distant from its point of origin is **metastatic.** Tumor cells multiply and spread so extensively that they disrupt normal body functions, eventually resulting in illness or even death.

Much research has been done to understand why certain cells rebel and override the normal processes that regulate their growth. Multiple factors may be involved, including genetic vulnerability, environmental exposure (for example, to radiation), and infection with certain viruses. It is usually not possible to determine why a particular individual has developed cancer at a young (or older) age.

The most common forms of cancer in children are actually not solid tumors but **leukemias,** in which certain types of white blood cells appear in the circulation in enormous numbers. These cells can not only interfere with normal immune function but can also overrun the bone marrow where normal blood cells are produced. Many cases of childhood leukemias are very responsive to medical therapy. Other common childhood tumors arise in the lymph tissue (**lymphomas**), kidneys, and central nervous system. Each type of cancer has its own characteristic patterns of growth, spread, symptom production, and response to treatment. (The most common adult cancers, which arise in the lung, breast, colon, or prostate gland, are very unusual in children.)

Symptoms that might suggest that a child has cancer are often vague or elusive and may not be evident until abnormal cells are disrupting normal body functions. These might include persistent fever, unexplained weight loss, fatigue, headache, or abdominal pain that is localized to one area. It is important to remember that such symptoms are not specific for cancer (or anything else) and should not lead to an immediate concern that a child has cancer. Occasionally a malignancy is discovered during a routine checkup when a doctor notices an unusual mass in the abdomen or perhaps skin changes that raise concerns over abnormalities in the blood.

The diagnosis of a tumor and identification of its particular cell type will require a formal medical evaluation and usually several tests and procedures. Some studies (such as blood tests) are relatively simple, while others, such as X-rays, CT scanning, or even surgical removal of tissue for diagnosis (**biopsy**) can be much more involved. Treatment options will depend upon the type of tumor, the extent of its spread, its cellular characteristics, the age of the child, and the experience of the physician. While detailed explanations of treatments such as radiation or chemotherapy are beyond the scope of this book, it is important that both parent and child (if the child is old enough) understand at each step what is going on, what the options might be, and what the benefits and potential risks of any proposed therapy are. Because of the anxiety and family disruption that childhood cancer can bring, a parent might not grasp all the information being presented and may need further explanations later. *Do not hesitate to ask for as much information as you need, as often as you need it, when dealing with a problem of this significance.*

Because medical treatments for cancer can be frightening to the child and the parents, the temptation to abandon standard therapy in favor of alternative or unconventional therapies is sometimes strong. But the search for such an approach could delay treatments that have proven response rates and much stronger validation from scientific research. Your child will be much better served by your emotional support and prayer in combination with timely administration of well-studied therapy.

candidiasis   An infection caused by the organism **Candida albicans** (a type of fungus) either on the skin surface or within the mouth or vagina. These so-called yeast infections are not uncommon in infants, appearing either as **oral candidiasis** (or **thrush**) or as **candida diaper dermatitis** (see photo on page A27). Occasionally, oral candidiasis is seen in children and adolescents who are using a steroid inhaler to treat asthma. This side effect may be avoided by rinsing out the mouth with water after each use of the inhaler.

Thrush appears as a white film or patches on the tongue, inner surfaces of the cheeks, or roof of the mouth. It may be confused with milk coating the mouth, but leftover milk can be scraped off easily with a cotton swab. Thrush is not harmful, but it can be a persistent annoyance, especially when Candida transferred to mother's breast causes a local eruption on her skin. Thrush can be treated with an oral antifungal solution such as **nystatin,** which the baby's physician will prescribe. Antifungal creams may also be applied to the areola and the nipple of breast-feeding mothers. Usually infant and mother are treated concurrently for several days to prevent the infection from being transferred back and forth between them. To prevent reinfection, nursing pads should be changed after every feeding. If the baby is bottle feeding or using a pacifier, the rubber nipples and pacifiers should be boiled every day until the infection clears. (Soaking these items overnight in a mixture of two tablespoons of vinegar in a quart of water is an alternative to boiling.)

Candida diaper dermatitis is intensely red, often with small extensions or "satellites" around the edges of the rash. This can be treated with an antifungal cream recommended by the baby's physician, as well as with other basic measures (see sidebar, page 161).

Candida vaginal infections can occur in postpubertal girls and adult women. These infections typically are manifested by an itchy vaginal irritation and discharge that contains white clumps resembling cottage cheese curds. The diagnosis can usually be established without difficulty in the physician's office and treated with one of several vaginal preparations (in cream or suppository form) or with oral medication. In some cases a yeast infection may occur in a child or adolescent after a course of antibiotics, since these drugs can temporarily reduce the population of oral or vaginal bacteria that normally help inhibit the growth of Candida. If yeast infections occur repeatedly, a search for a possible underlying cause may be carried out.

In recent years a small number of practitioners have claimed that a great variety of symptoms such as chronic fatigue, headaches, weight gain, depression, and intestinal disturbances can be linked to the presence of Candida albicans in the body. These assertions have not been validated by medical research and are not widely accepted in the health-care community.

canker sores   See *mouth care and concerns.*

caries   Decay or death of teeth and/or adjacent bone tissue (see also *teeth care and concerns*).

cataract A clouding or loss of transparency of the lens of the eye. Cataracts may be present at birth, or they may occur later in childhood, either as a result of an eye injury or as a component of certain conditions such as diabetes or Down syndrome.

cat scratch disease A bacterial infection with two components:

- A small, pimplelike eruption, usually on the arm or leg, where a child has had a recent cat scratch.
- Ten to 30 days later, a tender swelling of nearby lymph nodes (collections of cells that play an active role in the body's immune response). These lymph nodes can become quite large, sometimes measuring two inches in diameter. They are usually noticed in the armpit if the scratch was on the hand, in the groin if the leg or foot was involved, or in the neck if a cat scratched the child's face. Mild headache, low-grade fever, and fatigue may occur along with the swollen lymph nodes.

Cat scratch disease is a benign infection and will resolve on its own in about two months. In some cases, the antibiotic combination trimethoprim-sulfamethoxazole (Septra, Bactrim, or generics) may help.

Over 50 million homes in the United States have one or more cats; as a result this illness is fairly common (about 20,000 cases per year), though fortunately not contagious between humans. If you intend to keep one or more cats as a pet, you should teach your children how to approach, handle, and play with cats. In particular, children need to know that any rough play with a cat—and sometimes merely a gentle overture—can result in an unexpected clawing.

cellulitis A bacterial infection of the deep layer of skin (and at times the soft tissue directly beneath it), producing local redness, heat, swelling, and tenderness to the touch. Cellulitis should be treated with oral or, in severe cases, injectable antibiotics.

cerebral palsy A group of disorders involving posture and muscle tone resulting from a defect or localized damage in the developing brain. The symptoms will usually become evident within the first year or two of life. It is neither hereditary nor progressive, and its manifestations do not necessarily include mental retardation. The impairments of cerebral palsy can vary greatly in severity, and the cause may or may not be identifiable.

cerumen Brownish or yellowish, waxlike (or in some children, dry and granular) material secreted within the external ear canal. Also called **earwax.**

chalazion A round, painless (or slightly uncomfortable) swelling on the upper or lower eyelid, resulting from chronic inflammation of one of the glands (known as **meibomian** glands) that lubricate the inner surface of the eyelid (see also *eye care and concerns*).

chicken pox (varicella) (see photo on page A27) A common childhood viral illness characterized by the eruption of multiple red bumps, each with a small fluid-filled central blister.

New "crops" of pox erupt for three to five days. Gradually the blisters become crusted, form tiny scabs, and disappear, usually without leaving a scar. The rash is most prominent on the chest, abdomen, and face, but might cover the entire body, including the scalp, genital area, and inside the mouth. In some children, only a few scattered bumps will be visible, while other children are covered from head to toe. Adolescents or adults who develop chicken pox sometimes have a more severe case than do their younger counterparts. Fever may or may not be present. Itching is common and at times can be intense.

The incubation period for chicken pox can range from 11 to 21 days, but most often the time from exposure to onset of symptoms is 14 to 16 days. A child with chicken pox is contagious one or two days *before* the rash erupts and continues to be so until all the blisters have crusted. This will occur five to seven days after the rash first appears. Children should be kept out of school for about a week. An expectant mother who has never had chicken pox or is uncertain about her immunity to it should avoid exposure to this infection, especially during the first half of her pregnancy. (Chicken pox can cause congenital abnormalities in about 2 percent of newborns whose mothers become infected during the first 20 weeks of gestation. See chapter 1, page 22 .)

Most infants and children who develop chicken pox recover without any major problem. A few scars may remain, especially in areas where scabs have been repeatedly picked or scratched off. In some cases, bacteria such as streptococci or staphylococci infect a number of pox lesions. A child who suddenly worsens four or five days into the chicken pox outbreak, especially if fever recurs, should be seen by a physician to check for this complication.

Pneumonia is a rare but potentially serious complication of chicken pox. If a child develops a cough, shortness of breath, and rapid respirations during or shortly after chicken pox, contact a doctor as soon as possible. **Reye's syndrome,** a rare but potentially fatal illness affecting brain and liver, has been linked to the use of aspirin during chicken pox and other acute viral infections. *Aspirin should not be used to treat fever or aches for anyone, child or adult, who has chicken pox* (see *Reye's syndrome*). Persistent vomiting or a significant change in alertness or orientation could indicate this rare complication.

For most children and adolescents with chicken pox, treatment is supportive: rest, fluids, acetaminophen for fever and aches, and antihistamines such as diphenhydramine (Benadryl and other brands) as needed to relieve itching. Cool baths and calamine lotion also may relieve itching. These measures (along with gentle parental reminders and trimming the fingernails) can help a child resist the urge to scratch and pick at the blisters and scabs, minimizing the risk of scarring. If sores are present in the mouth, cool liquids (other than citrus or tomato juices, which may sting) and soft foods will be easier for your child to swallow than other foods.

There are specific measures for treatment and prevention of chicken pox:

- The prescription medication **acyclovir** (Zovirax) is sometimes given to reduce the severity of the illness. To be effective it must be started within 24 hours of the onset of the eruption.
- **Varicella-Zoster Immune Globulin (VZIG)** contains antibodies to the chicken pox virus. It is used in specific and very uncommon situations where immediate (although temporary) protection is needed. These situations might include a person with a severely impaired immune system who is exposed to chicken pox or a newborn whose mother develops this illness between five days before and two days after delivery. In the latter case, the newborn will be at risk for a more intense infection because of the immaturity of the immune system at this age combined with a lack of antibody protection from the mother.
- **Chicken pox vaccine** (Varivax) induces the body's immune system to create antibodies against the virus and can provide long-term protection. It is now commonly given to infants at the first birthday but may be used in older children and adults who have never had chicken pox.

cholesterol A fatty substance that is necessary in several biochemical functions in the body. It is both ingested in food and manufactured in the liver, and measurable levels of it are always present in the bloodstream. High levels of circulating cholesterol are associated with an increased risk of developing fatty plaques within blood vessels, a process that in many people begins early in life. The gradual thickening of these plaques, which is called **atherosclerosis,** can lead to partial or even complete obstruction of blood vessels. When one or more of the **coronary arteries** that supply blood to the heart become blocked, the muscle supplied by that artery will die. This is known as a **myocardial infarction**—often called a heart attack—and is frequently fatal. Coronary artery disease is one of the leading causes of death in the United States.

It is widely accepted medical practice to check the cholesterol level in adults as part of general health screening and to utilize diet, exercise, and in some cases medication to reduce it. Presently cholesterol screening in children is not a routine part of medical checkups because there is no clear consensus regarding the impact of childhood cholesterol levels on future health. The exception to this is in families where one or both parents (and perhaps a number of other relatives) have unusually high cholesterol levels—especially when coronary artery disease and other consequences of atherosclerosis occur before age 50. In such cases a genetic abnormality in fat metabolism might be transmitted to children, and high cholesterol levels will probably need specific treatment.

circumcision See chapter 3, page 74.

clavicle (see illustration on page A6) Collarbone.

colds (upper-respiratory infection, or URI) The most common acute illness in children, especially among infants and toddlers. Most are caused by one of a large assortment of viruses. (There are, for example, more than 100 types of the rhinovirus, which is but one of many viruses that can cause a cold.) Some URIs are caused by bacteria, but more often these organisms are secondary invaders that infect specific locations, such as the ears or sinuses, during or shortly after a cold caused by a virus.

Colds tend to be relatively uncommon during the first several weeks of a baby's life because an infant derives some protection against many viruses from antibodies transferred from the mother prior to birth. Breast-fed babies also receive protection from antibodies in mother's milk. Eventually infants must begin developing their own immunity through exposure to the numerous viruses (and occasional bacteria) that cause URIs.

After about six months of age it is common for infants and toddlers to have *six to ten colds every year.*

Some exasperated parents come to the doctor with small children who seem to have joined the Bug of the Month Club or whose colds seemingly overlap into nonstop illness lasting several months. Some of these situations may involve a child with allergies, which can cause a runny nose or cough to continue even when acute infections have resolved. However, an allergy is difficult to diagnose before the age of two. A careful medical evaluation is usually necessary to sort out the reasons for nonstop symptoms.

The frequency of colds is directly influenced by the opportunities for exposure to viruses—more specifically, exposure to other children (and adults) who are carrying and spreading the viruses. Children in day care or who are members of large families tend to have more frequent URIs. Colds can occur year-round, although they are more common during winter months—not directly as a result of frigid weather but as an indirect result of people gathering indoors during those months.

Symptoms

The familiar discomforts of a runny nose, sneezing, a dry hacking cough, and a low-grade fever (lower than 101.4°F) are the most common symptoms in children and adults. Mild irritation of the **conjunctiva**—the membrane that covers the surface of the eyeball and the inner eyelids—and increased tearing may also be present. Infants may, in addition, show signs of irritability.

The nasal drainage typically is clear and watery at first and then may become thicker and discolored (yellow or green). Usually it returns to a clear, thin consistency as the cold resolves. In an infant, mucus blocking the nasal passages could cause difficulty with nursing. Profuse or persistent discolored drainage may be an indication that a bacterial infection is present.

If present, fever tends to occur early in the illness and usually lasts for a few hours or up to three days. A fever that recurs after being gone for more than 24 hours may indicate that a secondary infection has developed. (Infants younger than three months may have no fever at all. In this age-group a rectal temperature higher than 100.4°F is significant and should prompt a call to your baby's physician. See Special Concerns, page 267, for further information.)

Additional cold symptoms may include a dry scratchy throat, headache, tiredness, and/or loss of appetite. When the throat is sore, lymph nodes in the neck may enlarge and become tender. An infection of the throat with group A beta-hemolytic streptococcus— more commonly known as strep throat—is a specific bacterial illness that should be treated with appropriate antibiotics (see *sore throat*).

Treatment

Since most colds are caused by viruses, they are usually self-limited, that is, they go away by themselves within two to seven days, although some symptoms may last as long as two weeks. *Unless there is specific evidence that bacteria are involved, antibiotics will not help a cold resolve more quickly.* The best approach is to provide supportive care and observe your child for any complications. Adequate or increased fluid intake (water or juice) might help keep drainage from becoming thick and difficult to clear. Breast or formula feedings can be maintained or even increased in frequency. Solids may be continued if your child is interested in them, but don't force the issue. Appetite sometimes decreases during a cold (especially when the body's temperature is elevated), and it is not uncommon for an infant or child to lose a little weight during a cold.

Acetaminophen (Tylenol and other brands) can be given as often as every four hours to reduce fever if your child appears uncomfortable. As an alternative, ibuprofen (Children's Motrin, Children's Advil, and other brands) can be given every six to eight hours to reduce fever and in some children appears to be more effective. (Aspirin should not be used during an acute illness because of its reported link with a rare but serious disorder of the liver and brain called Reye's syndrome.) Irritability will typically improve and activity will increase as the fever resolves.

Decongestants such as pseudoephedrine (Sudafed and several other formulations) may—or may not— reduce nasal congestion and help your child feel more comfortable. Their effectiveness varies widely with the particular child and illness. Similarly, antihistamines such as diphenhydramine (Benadryl and other brands) or chlorpheniramine (Chlor-Trimeton and many other formulations) may also be useful in keeping the nose dry, especially when allergies are involved. These and other antihistamines often cause sleepiness. In babies and children younger than two years of age, side effects can be more unpredictable, so it is wise to contact your child's doctor before using these medications. In very young infants, the use of saline nose drops and suctioning the nose with a bulb syringe is recommended to allow easier breathing. Some recent research has suggested that decongestants and antihistimines are unlikely to relieve cold symptoms in infants and young children.

Decongestant nose drops, which directly shrink the lining of the nose, are sometimes helpful in older children who are very congested, especially when it interferes with sleep. These drops should be used only for short periods of time. If used regularly for more than two or three consecutive days, the drops may not only lose their effectiveness but may create a rebound effect, in which the nose becomes even more congested when the last dose wears off.

If coughing is disruptive, especially at night, a cough syrup containing guaifenesin (an expectorant that tends to loosen secretions) and/or dextromethorphan (a cough suppressant) may provide a few hours of relief. If a nonprescription preparation is not effective, your child's doctor may prescribe a stronger formulation after seeing your child.

Potential complications
While most colds resolve without any great difficulty within seven to ten days, in some instances bacteria infect certain areas of the body during a cold, resulting in more serious or prolonged illness. Potential secondary bacterial infections (sometimes called superinfections because they are superimposed on the viral infection) can include:

- **Otitis media**—infection of the middle ear (the space behind the eardrum), usually manifested as pain and/or fever (see *ear infections*).
- **Sinusitis**—infection of one or more of the air-filled cavities within the head, usually manifested as localized headache and/or persistent discolored (yellow or green) drainage from the nose (see *sinusitis*).
- **Conjunctivitis**—infection of the linings of one or both eyes (known as the **conjunctivae**), causing irritation, redness, crusting, and discolored drainage (see *conjunctivitis*).
- **Bronchitis**—infection of the upper airway producing an ongoing cough, often accompanied by thick, discolored phlegm.
- **Pneumonia**—infection of a localized or widespread area in one or both lungs, manifested as fever, fatigue, coughing (mild or frequent and intense), and in severe cases rapid or labored breathing. (Note: pneumonia only rarely arises in connection with a cold. Most pneumonias develop suddenly and spontaneously, without prior symptoms.)

Prevention
No available vaccine will prevent infants and children from developing colds, so the most effective preventive measures are those that separate the child from viruses. Particular care should be taken to limit the exposure of infants younger than three months of age to people with colds because a baby's immune system is less effective at fighting infection during the first several weeks of life.

Infants in this age-group should spend little, if any, time in day-care settings, nurseries, and crowded public areas.

When one infant or child at home has a cold, frequent hand washing is perhaps the best way to reduce the risk of passing the infection to others, since viruses are often spread by direct touch. Infected droplets from the nose or chest may be present on a child's skin (especially if hands have contacted nose or mouth), or the droplets may become airborne during sneezing and coughing, eventually landing on clothes, toys, or other objects. When another child or adult touches any of these items (or the infected child himself), the virus can be picked up on the fingers and unwittingly introduced into the uninfected person's mouth, nose, or eyes if hands have not been washed.

Over the years there has been considerable discussion about the role of **vitamin C (ascorbic acid)** in cold prevention and treatment. While medical evidence does not suggest that vitamin C will prevent a cold, it may reduce the intensity or duration of symptoms. Using vitamin C for this purpose in children is not an established medical practice. Doses in great excess of the recommended daily allowance (RDA) are not advisable. Check dosage guidelines with your child's physician before using supplemental vitamin C.

When to call the doctor
Most colds can be managed at home without any specific input from or examination by your child's physician. However, there are a few exceptions to this general rule. Call your child's doctor, regardless of the hour, if

- a baby younger than three months of age has a fever of 100.4°F or higher (taken rectally);
- your infant or child appears unusually listless and unresponsive, or is extremely irritable and won't stop crying despite your efforts to comfort her;
- your infant or child appears to have difficulty breathing (beyond that produced by a stuffy nose). This would be manifested by noisy, labored breaths and in some cases by visible inward movement of the spaces between the ribs.

You should call your child's doctor during office hours if

- a cold lasts more than 7 to 10 days;
- nasal drainage is persistently thick and discolored;
- your older child complains of significant ear or throat pain;
- your older infant or child has a fever over 102°F for more than 24 hours;
- a cough persists for more than a few days or disrupts sleep and cannot be controlled using nonprescription cough syrup.

colic A particularly distressful pattern of crying that occurs in some infants between two weeks and three months of age. Several explanations for colic have been proposed (such as spasms of the bowel, a reaction to milk, a problem interacting with parents), but a universal cause has not been determined.

Infants with colic generally cry inconsolably for three or more hours, usually at the same time of day—most frequently between 6 and 10 P.M. During episodes of colic, the baby may draw his legs up, pass gas, thrash around, and generally appear extremely uncomfortable (which he probably is). When extended for hours, this can be very disruptive to a family, especially when it occurs with the first child.

Treatment

If your baby has prolonged crying spells, it is important to have him checked by his physician to rule out any medical problem. If he is in the age-group, his crying pattern is typical for colic, and he is developing and gaining weight appropriately and not suffering from an acute or chronic illness, the physician will probably diagnose colic. If so, your primary agenda during these episodes should be simply to comfort your baby as much as possible. Simple strategies can help, including gentle rocking (not jiggling too quickly), stroking the skin, singing or humming, wrapping him in a blanket, keeping the environment soothing and quiet, feeding him if he's hungry, or giving him a pacifier.

Remember that you are not a failure if you cannot quickly end the colic episode. Your goal is to be available to your baby and to survive the crying season the best you can. If you begin to feel frustrated or angry with your baby, it is very important that you not shake, swat, or otherwise physically harm him. If you are by yourself, lay him in the crib and let him cry for 15 or 20 minutes while you take a breather and calm down. This will not harm him, and he may be more responsive to your comforting measures when you pick him up again. If your spouse, another relative, or a good friend is with you, let that person relieve you for a while.

Chapter 4 (in the section Crybabies: What Happens When the Tears Won't Stop?) contains an expanded discussion about colic and the various measures that might help comfort a distressed infant.

colitis Inflammation of the lining of the large intestine that may result from an infection (usually bacterial or parasitic) or occur without an identifiable cause. The severity, duration, complications, and treatment of colitis vary considerably and will depend in part on the underlying cause. Manifestations commonly include abdominal cramping and frequent loose stools containing mucus and blood. A child with these symptoms should be evaluated and diagnosed so appropriate treatment can begin.

computerized tomography (also called a CT or CAT scan) A type of X-ray study that provides detailed cross-sectional views of an area of the body. A CT scan is not painful. In some cases a small amount of a liquid called a **contrast material** may be injected into the vein or taken orally to make certain structures more visible.

congestion A general term indicating the presence of abnormal fluid, mucus, or other material anywhere in the respiratory tract.

Congestion is a component in a number of illnesses. All of these syndromes have different causes, implications, and treatments. An infant with a stuffy nose, for example, will not need the same level of attention as one with noisy, rapid, labored breathing. When you call your doctor and mention your child's "congestion," it will help greatly if you can be specific about the location of the problem and any other symptoms such as fever, cough, wheezing, abnormal breathing patterns, or even something you can't quite pin down. Your observation that "she just doesn't look right" may be very important information, especially in an infant less than three months old.

For more detailed information about problems related to congestion, see the following topics:

Asthma, page 650
Bronchiolitis, page 664
Bronchitis, page 665
Colds, page 668
Croup, page 673
Epiglottitis, page 681
Laryngitis, page 706
Pneumonia, page 670

conjunctivitis (pinkeye) (see photo on page A28) Inflammation of the thin lining (the **conjunctiva**) that covers the white of the eyeball and the inner surface of the eyelids. Conjunctivitis may be caused by viral or bacterial infection, an allergic reaction, or chemical or physical irritants that come in contact with the eye. The most common symptoms of conjunctivitis are watering eyes, itching or irritation, and a diffuse pink or bloodshot appearance. In some cases there is puffiness of the eyelids and/or mild sensitivity to light. *Pain and extreme sensitivity to light are rarely seen in conjunctivitis and usually indicate a more serious problem.* If your child persistently complains that his eye hurts, he should be evaluated by his primary-care physician or an ophthalmologist as soon as possible.

Newborns can develop a **reactive conjunctivitis** from medicines that are put into the eyes at birth to prevent infection. During the first year of life, babies may also develop conjunctivitis because of obstruction of a tear duct, which prevents proper drainage of tears from the eye. Low-grade infection might persist until the tear duct opens spontaneously or (uncommonly) is probed and opened by an ophthalmologist.

In toddlers and older children conjunctivitis may accompany a bacterial or viral infection of the upper-respiratory tract. Hands that have wiped runny noses often wipe the eyes too, transferring the infection to one or both.

Conjunctivitis caused by bacteria usually produces a thick discharge that gathers on the lids. In the morning the eyelids may appear crusty or even stuck together. A warm, wet washcloth will remove the crust and unstick the lids. (Be sure to launder the washcloth before using it again to prevent spreading the bacteria to others.)

Bacterial conjunctivitis will usually respond to antibiotic drops or ointment within a few days. As you might suspect, instilling medicine into the eye(s) of a toddler or preschooler can be a major challenge. In fact, two adults may be needed—one to restrain the patient's head and body and the other to apply the medication. The best method is to gently pull the lower lid downward and place a drop or small amount of ointment into the outer corner of the eye, not directly onto the cornea.

Conjunctivitis caused by viruses tends to be accompanied by a more watery drainage than with bacterial infections, but in some cases the redness and swelling can be very intense. In severe cases an ophthalmologist may prescribe drops that calm the inflammation, but the medication won't stop the infection, which will run its course in 10 to 14 days. As with all viral infections, antibiotics will have no effect on this form of conjunctivitis.

The bacteria or viruses that cause conjunctivitis can be quite contagious through direct contact: little hands rub infected eyes then touch toys or other children, whose fingers then touch other eyes and noses, including their own. Toddlers and smaller children with these infections should be kept out of day-care or nursery situations until the problem is calmed down or at least until treatment is well under way. (Check with your child's physician.) You and any other caregivers should wash hands frequently when dealing with a child who has infectious conjunctivitis.

Allergic conjunctivitis is usually provoked by seasonal airborne pollens such as trees or grasses in the spring or weeds (especially ragweed) in the late summer. It often causes more itching and less inflammation than bacterial or viral conjunctivitis, and the drainage is invariably watery. In addition, nasal symptoms such as dripping and sneezing are likely. Any oral antihistamines used to treat nasal allergy may also improve allergic conjunctivitis, but in some cases your child's doctor might also prescribe antihistamine or anti-inflammatory eye drops.

constipation Constipation is present if any of the following occurs on a regular basis:

- Passing stool is painful.
- Stools are passed with difficulty or aren't passed at all, despite long straining efforts.
- Stools are passed fewer than two times per week, with the following exceptions: It is common for breast-fed infants older than six to eight weeks to pass painless, large, soft bowel movements only once a week. Infants younger than six months of age may strain to pass hard bowel movements, but the passage of stool occurs without pain.

  Occasionally an older child will pass a stool every three or four days without discomfort, although this is not usually felt to represent normal bowel function.

In addition, the following signs of constipation may be present:

- Small, hard, pebblelike stools
- Blood streaks on the stool or toilet paper when bowel movements are firm
- Resistance—even overt expressions of fear—when sitting on the toilet is suggested
- Soiling the pants with stool (called **encopresis**)
- Abdominal cramps and bloating, sometimes with loss of appetite

Causes
Constipation is often brought on by one or more of the following situations:

- *A diet that is short on fiber,* especially if it contains large amounts of dairy products. Fruits, vegetables, beans, and grain breads and bran cereals help keep stools soft and easier to pass.
- *Certain medications* such as codeine-containing cough syrups, methylphenidate (Ritalin), and iron supplements.
- *Resisting the urge to use the toilet.* An active child who is engrossed in play with friends or who is embarrassed about using the toilet at school where privacy may not be available may ignore or resist the signal from the colon that a bowel movement

is imminent. Eventually the urge will disappear, but the stool waiting to be eliminated will not.

- *A painful bowel movement,* usually arising from a small tear at the anal opening called a rectal fissure. Normally children do not want to repeat a painful experience and may not grasp the concept that bowel movements are not optional.

One or more of these factors—especially a painful bowel movement—can lead to an ever-enlarging wad of stool developing in the colon segments (the sigmoid and rectum) which are the last stop before release to the outside. The situation is compounded by the colon's continuous extracting of moisture from stool that isn't moving, causing it to become increasingly firm and difficult to pass. Eventually the final segments of colon become so distended that it becomes difficult for the anal sphincter to do its normal job of holding back stool, and small amounts may pass involuntarily and soil the child's underwear. Occasionally liquid stool will leak past the large, hardened stool, creating the paradox of diarrhea that is actually caused by constipation.

Evaluation and treatment

If constipation is ongoing, especially if it's associated with painful bowel movements, soiling, fear of using the toilet, or abdominal pain, your child's doctor should examine her to rule out any disorder that might require specific medical treatment. In some situations, removal of an impacted stool may be necessary (often through pediatric-size enemas), and your child's doctor will give you specific directions for doing so.

Continued home treatment of constipation will depend upon the child's age and dietary patterns. The following are general guidelines only and should not override any specific directions given by your child's physician.

Breast-fed infants who are not yet taking solids rarely develop true constipation (and may not have a bowel movement for 5 to 7 days), and additional water or juices are unnecessary unless specifically recommended by the physician. If a breast-feeding mother is taking medication that is constipating (for example codeine), alternative medications may need to be considered.

For bottle-fed infants younger than four months of age, usually juices (white grape, pear, and possibly prune) or Maltsupex (a barley extract) may be utilized twice daily, but you would be wise to contact your baby's physician for further input. Solids are not needed by infants younger than four months of age and might actually contribute to constipation. If one or more solids have been initiated in an infant this age who is now consti-

pated, it may be prudent to withhold them until she has passed the four-month mark.

For infants older than four months of age who are on solids, add juices and Maltsupex as noted above and utilize foods rich in fiber such as cereal, fruits (pears, peaches, apricots), and vegetables (peas or spinach) twice daily. Avoid applesauce, rice cereal, bananas, and carrots, which tend to be constipating.

For children who are eating table foods, adding foods containing higher levels of fiber or bran (oatmeal, bran cereals, whole wheat bread) and serving fruits or vegetables twice per day will often relieve constipation. Decrease constipating foods such as bananas, cooked carrots, applesauce, and dairy products (milk, ice cream, cheese).

Stool softeners such as Maltsupex (a barley extract), psyllium-seed derivatives (such as Metamucil or Citrucel), or mineral oil are sometimes beneficial, although approval from your child's physician would be wise before using any of these agents. You should also talk to the doctor before using any oral laxatives such as milk of magnesia or when considering the use of enemas.

A child refusing to use the toilet because of a painful anal fissure will probably need some local treatment along with stool-softening efforts. A 15- to 20-minute bath two or three times daily, mild (1/2 or 1 percent) cortisone cream or a topical anesthetic (21/2 percent lidocaine ointment) might ease the pain so a child can resume bowel movements without fear. Needless to say, a constipated toddler who is fighting use of the toilet is not a good candidate for toilet training. Postpone this project until she is pain-free and stools are moving more freely.

Call the doctor when

- recurrent or persistent rectal bleeding occurs (An occasional tiny dab of blood on the toilet tissue after a hard stool is not likely to indicate a major problem.);
- constipation is accompanied by abdominal pain;
- constipation persists despite dietary changes;
- definite rectal pain or a visible anal fissure is noted.

cornea (see illustration on page A12) The outermost clear, transparent layer of the central colored part of the eye. Trauma to this structure causes intense pain.

croup A variety of infections that involve the **larynx** (vocal cords) and **trachea** (the upper airway just below the larynx). When these structures become inflamed and irritated, they provoke a barking cough, noisy respirations, and in some cases labored breathing. Croup can be particularly difficult for a child under the age of three.

The most common version of this problem, and the one for which the term croup is normally reserved, is **viral croup** (also called **laryngotracheobronchitis,** indicating that the larynx, trachea, and bronchi are involved). This is caused most often by the parainfluenza virus and generally occurs in epidemics during the fall and early winter. If your child has croup, it is very likely that other children in your community have it as well. The illness usually lasts three to five days but may extend as long as a week.

Symptoms

Croup begins like a typical cold in a child between the ages of six months and three years. She then develops a seal-like barking cough that progresses to noisy congested breathing called **stridor.** Fever may occur, and acetaminophen may be given to reduce it and make the child more comfortable.

Croup frequently begins in the middle of the night. It can develop within a few hours after your child goes to bed. She may awaken frightened and distressed, with symptoms worsening when she is crying and agitated. As the illness progresses, the ongoing coughing and increased effort needed to breathe may cause her to lose interest in food or fluids and become mildly dehydrated. In more severe cases, she will appear to gasp for air when at rest.

Treatment

First, try to calm your child, because croup symptoms will worsen if she is upset. (This is one situation where it is appropriate to try to keep her happy, or at least comfortable, at all costs.) If she is breathing rapidly and noisily and appears to gasp for air even when at rest (that is, sitting quietly or lying down), take her *immediately* to the nearest emergency room. She may improve dramatically on the ride over (see below), but make sure she is evaluated anyway.

If she is not gasping when at rest, a time-honored home treatment for croup is steam, since moisture relieves congestion and opens the airways. The best way to create steam is to turn on a hot shower in your bathroom, close the door, and wait for the room to become foggy.

You can sit or stand with your child in the steam for 15 to 20 minutes. As an alternative, bundle her up and take her outside. Often the cool night air, especially when it is moist or foggy, will dramatically improve breathing.

If you don't see much improvement after 15 to 20 minutes, call the doctor (or take the child to the nearest emergency room if she appears to be getting worse). The doctor will want to know how rapidly your child is breathing (count the number of breaths in a minute before you call), whether the spaces between her ribs are moving in and out with each breath, and her general appearance.

If she improves, put a humidifier in her room while she sleeps. Because this cycle may repeat itself, it would be wise for you to stay with your child to monitor her breathing throughout the night. If your child relaxes and sleeps through the night, she probably won't need additional treatment except for steam and fluids. Over-the-counter cold and cough medicines are not particularly helpful for treating viral croup. Antibiotics are not effective unless a medical evaluation indicates that the symptoms are being caused by bacteria (see below). In some cases the doctor will recommend a short course of steroids, which decreases the severity of the symptoms in some children.

Severe croup might be treated in the emergency room (or in some offices) using medication called **racemic epinephrine** given as an inhaled aerosol. This usually helps the child breathe more easily for two or three hours. Some children with croup are sent home after one treatment and observation, while others who are more severely affected will be admitted to the hospital for further care, including frequent breathing treatments and oxygen as needed.

Other illnesses with croup symptoms

Bacterial tracheitis is an uncommon complication of viral croup in which bacteria invade the upper airway. A typical scenario is that of a child who develops symptoms of viral croup but fails to improve or actually worsens despite standard treatment. This infection is sometimes seen in children who are older than those who usually have viral croup. The child with bacterial tracheitis usually appears very ill, with high fever and increasingly severe shortness of breath. *Prompt medical care is very important,* because the upper airway can become so inflamed and swollen that the child is unable to obtain an adequate amount of air.

Epiglottitis is a rapidly progressive and very dangerous infection of the epiglottis, the soft tissue flap that covers and protects the airway whenever your child swallows. A child who has been well will rapidly develop a high fever and an extremely sore throat. Within a few hours she will be unable to swallow and may lean forward and actually drool rather than swallow. *This condition is a medical emergency because the swollen epiglottis can suddenly block the airway, leading to suffocation.* Fortunately, this disease has become extremely uncommon because most children are now routinely immunized against hemophilus influenzae type B, the bacteria that causes epiglottitis.

One final reminder: Whether croup symptoms involve the more common viral syndrome or the serious bacterial infections, all can significantly affect your child's ability to breathe—sometimes with rapid changes in her condition. *If you are at all uncomfortable with your child's breathing pattern (or her general appearance) during one of these illnesses, don't hesitate to take her to the nearest emergency medical facility, regardless of the time of day or night.* If her breathing appears significantly compromised and you don't feel you can transport her safely, call 911 to request emergency paramedic evaluation and transfer.

CT scan   See *computerized tomography.*

culture   A laboratory test in which a small sample of body fluid (such as urine or blood) or other tissue is evaluated for the presence of microorganisms that might be causing an infection. The sample is introduced into material called a culture medium, which enhances the growth of certain types of bacteria, viruses, or fungi. The choice of culture medium will vary depending upon the organism(s) suspected to be present.

cyanosis   Bluish discoloration of skin caused by lack of oxygen in the blood.

cystic fibrosis   An inherited disease characterized by abnormalities in the secretions of glands in many parts of the body. The respiratory tract, the pancreas, and the sweat glands of the skin are most commonly affected. Mucus secreted in the airways is abnormally thick and more difficult to clear, resulting in frequent and often serious respiratory infections. Deficiencies in pancreatic enzymes can cause inadequate absorption of nutrients (especially fats and protein), leading to slow growth and poor weight gain. Increased concentrations of salt in sweat may actually cause a parent to notice a salty taste when kissing a child with this disorder. There is no cure for cystic fibrosis, although advances in medical management have increased the life expectancy of children born with this disease. Treatment objectives include preventing and treating respiratory infections, supplementing digestive enzymes, and replacing salt lost through the skin.

cystitis   Inflammation of the bladder. The term is commonly used to refer to a bladder infection.

D

dacryocystitis   Inflammation of the tear (or **lacrimal**) sac located just below the inner corner of the eye, adjacent to the nose. This infection usually results from the blockage of the duct that carries tears from the lacrimal sac into the nose (see *eye care and concerns*).

dehydration   See *diarrhea* and *vomiting.*

diabetes mellitus   A disorder in which there is an impairment in the transfer of **glucose** (blood sugar) from the bloodstream into the body's cells. The accumulation of glucose in the blood, and its decreased availability within cells to serve as fuel for many biochemical functions, can result in a variety of short- and long-term consequences.

About 20 percent of all cases of diabetes—and nearly all cases in children—result from a failure of the pancreas to produce **insulin,** a hormone necessary to allow glucose to enter cells. Vulnerability to diabetes is inherited, and it appears that the disease develops when the pancreatic cells that produce insulin are destroyed. These children are said to have **insulin-dependent** (also called **Type 1** or **juvenile**) **diabetes,** because without daily injections of this hormone they will become severely ill. (Before insulin was available to treat diabetes, this form of the disease was uniformly fatal.) The other 80 percent of diabetics produce adequate amounts of insulin, but for a variety of reasons the hormone does not interact normally with cells, and glucose levels in the bloodstream rise. This form of the disease, called **non-insulin-dependent** (also called **Type 2** or **adult onset**) **diabetes,** nearly always occurs in adults and is treated with diet, exercise, and/or medications.

An infant or child who is developing diabetes will begin producing abnormally large amounts of urine and as a result will be continually thirsty. He may also be constantly hungry and yet lose weight. If the problem is not diagnosed and the metabolic consequences worsen, vomiting, dehydration, profound abnormalities in body chemistries—a condition called **diabetic ketoacidosis**—and eventually coma and death will follow. Diabetes might first be discovered during a routine exam when glucose is detected in a child's urine; during an evaluation for symptoms such as weight loss, increased hunger, or abnormal thirst; or during an acute and unexpected deterioration of a child's overall condition—usually an episode of diabetic ketoacidosis requiring intensive medical care.

D

Once diabetes is identified and stabilized, a comprehensive care plan will be needed. This will involve the combined skills of a physician, a dietitian, and frequently a specially trained diabetes educator. *This disease cannot be treated casually; it requires detailed understanding of dietary principles, monitoring of blood sugar using a glucose meter and test strips at home, and proper use of insulin to control day-to-day glucose levels.* Such detailed care is necessary for two reasons. First, it is important to prevent the immediate and sometimes dangerous problems that arise from extremely high or low levels of glucose. (Low blood sugar, or **hypoglycemia,** can result from a mismatch of insulin, food, and activity at a given point in time.) Second, ongoing elevation of blood glucose (or **hyperglycemia**) may not be high enough to cause acute symptoms but can nevertheless contribute to long-term disease in many organs or organ systems, including the eyes, kidneys, nervous system, and/or blood vessels. These potential complications and strategies to avoid them are normally explained in detail during diabetic-instruction sessions.

Depending upon age and maturity level, the child should gradually be given increasing responsibility for managing his diabetes. Continued education and troubleshooting by one or more experienced health-care providers will be necessary. Often emotional support is important for the child or adolescent who feels "stuck" with this disease. Despite all the extra effort involved in carrying out his everyday routines the diabetic child should not be restricted from participating in normal activities, including team sports and other athletic pursuits. It may be necessary to remind him from time to time that, with proper self-care (including diet and exercise) and attention to the details of managing glucose, he should be able to live a long and healthy life.

diaphragm (see illustration on page A9) The respiratory muscle that separates the chest from the abdomen.

diarrhea A common event in infancy and childhood, normally understood as a condition in which bowel movements (or **stools**) are looser than normal, occur too frequently, or both. In fact, the significance of a child's stool pattern will depend on two basic considerations.

First, *what is normal for the age-group and for the particular infant or child?* A normal breast-fed newborn will have as many as six to ten watery stools per day, which can vary in color from yellow to green to brown. Bottle-fed infants tend to have stools that are less watery and more mushy. After a few weeks, a breast-fed baby may absorb nutrients so efficiently that a stool is passed no more often than every few days. An older child may pass a stool every two or three days or two or three times a day on a routine basis without any problem. Some infants and children vary their pattern from week to week without any particular sign of trouble.

Second, and more important, *is the stool pattern causing any problems?* These problems could range from merely annoying to life-threatening and include the following:

- Irritation of the skin around the anus or over the entire diaper area
- Cramps or other discomfort
- Ongoing soiling of clothing, bedding, furniture, and carpeting
- Fluid losses serious enough to cause dehydration and, in severe cases, death

Increased frequency or volume of stools can occur for three reasons, any or all of which could apply to a given case of diarrhea:

- The intestinal tract is moving food more rapidly.
- Some or most of the food or fluids, as well as the substantial amount of liquid produced every day by the intestine, are not being absorbed normally.
- The intestine is secreting more fluid than usual.

To understand what might be happening to your child whose stools are more loose and frequent than you (or he) would like, it is helpful to think in terms of three basic types of diarrhea: acute diarrhea, chronic nonspecific diarrhea, and chronic diarrhea related to a pathological condition.

Acute diarrhea is usually infectious and accompanied by other signs of illness such as fever, nausea, and/or vomiting, and possibly dehydration if the infant's or child's intake of fluids is not keeping up with losses. Around the world, this is the leading cause of death among children under five years of age, causing more than 4 million deaths a year. In developed nations such as the United States, severe diarrhea leading to death is far less common (about 500 cases occur annually in the same age-group). The average American child has one or two episodes per year by the age of five. Diarrheal illness accounts for more than 10 percent of all hospitalizations in this age-group.

A variety of viruses and bacteria can cause acute infectious diarrhea (which is often referred to as **gastroenteritis** when nausea and vomiting occur). The most common offender is the **rotavirus,** which is seen most often among children between six months and two years of age. Bacteria that are transmitted in contaminated food (see *food poisoning*) or in unsanitary or crowded living conditions are also common causes of acute diarrhea, as are parasites such as **Giardia lamblia,** which may contaminate water supplies. Occasionally, an acute illness somewhere else in the body (for example, an ear infection) or medications (especially antibiotics) will provoke diarrhea.

Since acute diarrheal episodes will usually resolve without antibiotics, in most situations your greatest concern will be keeping track of the infant's or child's fluid intake and watching out for dehydration. When fluid losses are mild, you will see some increased thirst and a modest decrease in urine output (fewer wet diapers). If these occur, call your child's physician for advice, which may include a recommendation for a direct evaluation.

If the dehydration becomes more severe, an infant or child will manifest a number of the following signs:

- Constant thirst (in an older child who can express this need)
- Dry mouth and lips
- Fewer tears when crying
- No urine production for 8 to 12 hours, indicating that the kidney is conserving fluids
- Sunken eyes
- A sunken fontanelle (the soft spot in the skull, which is most readily felt during the first six months of life)
- Skin texture that is no longer elastic, but more like bread dough
- Persistent fussing in an infant, especially if it is more of a whine than a vigorous cry

With rare exception, these signs indicate a need for urgent evaluation.

Even more serious dehydration (with fluid losses of more than 10 percent of the child's normal body weight) will be suggested by the following symptoms:

- Cool and/or mottled skin
- Rapid, thready pulse
- Rapid respirations
- Moaning or grunting, or a weak, feeble cry
- Marked listlessness, with lack of interest in play or feeding, little response to being handled, and (in an infant) markedly reduced movements of arms and legs

A baby or young child with these symptoms is likely to be in serious trouble and should be evaluated immediately, usually in an emergency-room setting.

Other indications that medical evaluation should be sought sooner rather than later include:

- Bloody diarrhea, which may indicate that a significant bacterial infection or colitis (inflammation of the colon) is present
- Loose stools that are accompanied by vomiting and/or a temperature over 100.4°F (taken rectally) in an infant younger than three months of age
- Diarrhea is accompanied by significant pain in the abdomen

Your child's doctor will give you specific advice for preventing or correcting dehydration, which will depend to some degree on the age of your child and the severity of the problem. Traditionally, treatment of diarrhea involved an attempt to put the bowel "at rest" for a day or two while the infection runs its course. This involved giving the infant or child one or more forms of clear liquids—water, soft drinks, clear soup, clear juice, etc. — which are supposed to be absorbed more easily when the bowel is inflamed or damaged by the infection. *However, recent research has indicated that for a variety of reasons these liquids are not very effective and in some cases may make the diarrhea worse.*

One of the most significant advances in medical care during the past 50 years has been the discovery of an extraordinarily effective and inexpensive treatment for acute infectious diarrhea. Research into the physiology of the small intestine led to the development of a variety of **oral rehydration solutions (ORS),** which cooperate effectively with the body's mechanisms for absorbing fluid. These solutions contain specified amounts of sodium, potassium, and glucose mixed in water, can be safely used in infants and children of all ages, and are effective in treating both mild and severe dehydration.

Premixed ORS is available at drugstores in products such as Pedialyte, Rehydralyte, and Infalyte. *This type of solution, not the traditional clear liquids, is better suited to treat acute diarrhea, especially in infants and toddlers under two years of age.* ORS may be given by bottle, spoon, or even dropper, sometimes in frequent, very small amounts (especially if nausea and vomiting are present). Your child's doctor can recommend the type and minimum quantity of fluid you should give your child. If the rehydrating solution isn't flavored, its taste can be improved by adding one tablespoon of Jell-O powder to one tablespoon of boiling water and then adding this mixture to an eight-ounce bottle of the solution.

Breast-fed infants may continue nursing throughout an acute diarrheal illness. Infants who are formula-fed may also continue without stopping, although the physician might recommend switching temporarily to a lactose-free and/or non-cow's-milk formula. Children who have been taking other foods may continue doing so, although foods containing a lot of simple sugars (candy, soft drinks, fruit juices) might cause more water to enter the bowel and worsen diarrhea. Complex carbohydrates such as rice, bread, and potatoes are a better choice. Bananas and applesauce contain pectin that may help thicken loose stools. In general, recent research suggests that withholding food does not shorten the duration of diarrhea and may in fact lengthen it, because the lining of the intestine needs fuel to repair its damage.

Depending upon the duration and severity of the diarrhea, your child's physician may order stool tests to determine whether a specific, treatable bacteria or parasite is present. If this is found to be the case, appropriate antibiotic therapy may be recommended. Nonprescription products such as Kaopectate, which thicken stool, and drugs such as loperamide (Imodium), which reduce the frequency of bowel movements, are not recommended for young children.

Chronic nonspecific diarrhea is a common problem in which a child has ongoing loose stools that are not severe enough to cause dehydration, nor are they associated with weight loss, developmental problems, or other disease activity. They can vary greatly from day to day or week to week and may be associated with stress, an acute illness, a move, dietary changes, or nothing in particular. Throughout this process, the child does not appear ill.

A medical evaluation should be done if an unusual pattern of loose stools continues for more than three weeks in a child who does not otherwise appear ill. If no specific cause is found and the child is otherwise doing well, the diarrhea will eventually resolve on its own. Recent research indicates that many cases of chronic nonspecific diarrhea may be caused by excessive intake of fruit juices (especially apple juice). And, surprisingly, children on very low-fat diets may also have this problem. While maintaining conservative dietary habits regarding fat is important as a lifelong goal, younger children have a somewhat higher nutritional requirement for fat than adults do, and stringent restrictions on this (or any other) food group are not advisable. Your child's physician or a dietitian can give you further advice on this subject. (See Special Concerns, page 429.)

Chronic diarrhea related to a pathological condition (for example, a parasitic infection or a specific defect in absorption) will usually be manifested by a failure to gain weight as well as other signs of illness (for example, fever). During a medical exam for ongoing diarrhea, a number of these conditions will be considered and appropriate tests done to determine if one of them might be the cause.

diphtheria　An infectious childhood disease that causes sore throat, fever, and sometimes discolored membranes in the throat. Before immunizations were developed for this disease, it was one of the leading causes of death in children. It is rarely seen in the United States today because of immunization efforts.

diplopia　Double vision.

disc (disk)　Any round, flat, platelike structure in the body. It most commonly refers to the **vertebral discs,** the fibrous cushions between adjacent vertebrae in the spinal column.

dislocation　An injury in which the relationship between bones on either side of a joint is disrupted.

distal　Any point of the body that is farther away from the middle of the body. For example, the foot is distal to the knee.

diuresis　Increased elimination of urine.

dorsal　Toward the back.

dysentery　Any of several intestinal disorders characterized by inflammation and manifested by abdominal cramping and frequent (usually bloody) stools. Certain types of bacteria and parasites are the most common causes of dysentery (see *diarrhea* and *food poisoning*).

dysmenorrhea　Painful menstruation (menstrual cramps).

dyspepsia　Indigestion.

dysphagia　Difficulty in swallowing.

dyspnea　Difficult or labored breathing.

E

ear infections　Ear infections can involve any of three areas:

- **Outer ear**—the part of the ear you can see and the ear canal that extends to the eardrum
- **Middle ear**—space behind the eardrum that contains the tiny bones that conduct sound from the eardrum to the inner ear
- **Inner ear**—the balance center, located deep within the bony skull

Infection of the outer ear: otitis externa

More commonly known as "swimmer's ear," **external otitis** is common among school-age children, especially during the summer when swimming and water sports are in full swing. Bacteria invade the skin and soft tissue that line the ear canal, causing inflammation and swelling.

SYMPTOMS In mild cases a little irritation and itching will be noticed. But more commonly the child with external otitis will complain of nonstop pain—which can be very severe—in and around the ear. Discomfort may increase when the child chews. Even the gentlest tug on the earlobe will provoke pain. In some cases swelling and debris in the ear canal can be severe enough to cause a slight temporary decrease in hearing. A small amount of drainage may develop as the infection progresses.

CAUSES Water remaining in the ear canal after swimming can serve as a reservoir for bacterial growth and make the skin surface more vulnerable to bacterial invasion. Wax buildup contributes to this process by blocking the natural drainage of water from the canal. A second major cause is trauma to the canal from overzealous attempts to clean the ear using cotton swabs or other objects. Occasionally, chronic drainage from a perforated eardrum will result in external otitis.

TREATMENT Even if your child's history and complaints strongly suggest external otitis, a physician should confirm the diagnosis. If a large amount of wax and debris is present, the doctor will need to remove it. The infection is usually treated with eardrops that contain antibiotics to kill bacteria and cortisone to reduce swelling. The doctor may carefully place a soft "wick" in the ear canal to prolong the contact of the drops with the infected surface. In severe cases oral antibiotics may be prescribed as well. Swimming should be avoided until the infection has cleared.

Adequate pain control is important. Acetaminophen or ibuprofen and a warm compress placed over the ear can provide temporary relief, but your child may also need stronger prescription pain medication.

PREVENTION If excessive wax buildup is a recurrent problem (this often runs in families and is not a reflection of inadequate hygiene), your child's physician may need to remove this material periodically. The doctor might also suggest wax-clearing measures—other than rigorous use of cotton swabs—to try at home. In some cases, the use of soft molded earplugs when swimming is beneficial. Another approach is to instill a bacteria-inhibiting preparation (such as a 1 to 1 mixture of white vinegar and alcohol) into the ear canal after swimming.

Infection of the middle ear: otitis media

Otitis media (OM) is the most common acute illness, other than the common cold, in children younger than three years of age. Seventy-five percent of all children will experience at least one episode of OM, and 20 percent will have multiple recurrences.

SYMPTOMS Typically, an infant develops a cold, becomes irritable, cries persistently, sleeps fitfully (if at all), and loses his appetite; fever may or may not be present. Tugging at one or both ears is *not* a reliable indicator of an ear infection. An older child will complain specifically and continuously of ear pain. At times, fluid trapped behind the eardrum will build up enough pressure to rupture it. When this occurs, thick, discolored (usually yellow or green) material will drain from the ear—a reliable sign that an infection is present and a definite reason to contact the child's physician. Spontaneous perforation of the eardrum, which relieves pressure and results in a dramatic reduction of pain, usually heals in 7 to14 days as the infection resolves. (Before antibiotics were developed, deliberate incision of the eardrum with a tiny scalpel to drain the middle ear was the only specific treatment available for severe otitis media.)

CAUSES The underlying problem in most cases of OM is a malfunction of one or both **eustachian tubes,** the small passages that connect each middle ear to an area at the back of the throat, just above the **palate** (roof of the mouth). Normally the eustachian tubes drain secretions from the middle-ear cavities and prevent infected material from entering them. In infants and young children the tubes are shorter, narrower, and more nearly horizontal. As a result, any acute viral infection (specifically, a cold) can disrupt eustachian-tube function more easily. Fluid collects in the middle ear allowing bacteria also present in the nose to gain access to the ear. If an infection develops, inflammation and even more fluid in the middle ear increase pressure on the eardrum, causing pain and irritability.

A number of factors increase the risk of otitis media:

- Recurrent upper-respiratory infections (which can be a problem among children in day-care settings).
- Exposure to cigarette smoke at home.
- Chronic nasal allergy.
- Enlarged adenoids.
- Drinking from a bottle while lying flat.
- An inherited tendency for otitis media based on the shape and characteristics of the eustachian tube and middle ear. Typically, one or both parents will have had ear infections during childhood.

TREATMENT If your infant or child has the symptoms described above, she should be evaluated by a physician. If OM is present, antibiotics will be prescribed. *It is im-*

portant that your child take all the medication as pre-scribed and that any recommended follow-up be carried out. Usually symptoms will improve significantly within a day or two. Acetaminophen (Tylenol and other brands) or ibuprofen (Children's Motrin and other brands) can help relieve pain. Decongestants have not been shown to have a significant impact on OM, and drops (whether oil, pain relievers, or antibiotics) should be placed in your child's ear only if prescribed by the physician.

POSSIBLE COMPLICATIONS

♦ Persistence of fluid (called an **effusion**) in the middle ear that interferes with the conduction of sound. This can result in significant hearing loss, a particularly important problem in young children because it can delay language development. In older children, hearing problems caused by chronic middle-ear effusion can contribute to school and behavior problems.

♦ **Perforation** of the eardrum, as already mentioned. Occasionally this will fail to heal on its own, resulting in ongoing or intermittent drainage along with moderate hearing loss.

♦ **Mastoiditis,** an infection of the honeycombed, bony mastoid air cells directly behind the ear. Although mastoiditis can take place in any age-group, it is unusual before the age of two (see *mastoiditis*).

All of these complications require appropriate care by your child's primary-care physician and in some cases by an ear, nose, and throat (ENT) specialist. If there have been repeated bouts of otitis media and/or persistent fluid in the middle ear (especially with hearing loss), the physician may recommend a minor operation (called a **tympanostomy**) during which a small **ventilating tube** is placed in the eardrum. The initial procedure drains the fluid and improves hearing. The tube then continues to equalize pressure between the middle ear and the out-side atmosphere, preventing the reaccumulation of fluid, and usually reducing the number and duration of subse-quent ear infections. (The insertion of ventilating tubes is the second most common surgical procedure per-formed on children under the age of five.)

When dealing with otitis media, you should call your child's doctor if

♦ your child's pain or temperature persists after 48 hours of treatment;
♦ persistent drainage from the ear canal is noted;
♦ your child becomes increasingly ill;
♦ your child develops a stiff neck, severe headache, nausea, or vomiting.

Infection of the inner ear: labyrinthitis
Inflammation involving the inner ear (**labyrinthitis**) is uncommon in children and is also somewhat difficult to diagnose because it is not possible to see this area during an examination. More commonly seen in older children, labyrinthitis is characterized by sudden dizziness (or **vertigo**). There may also be nausea and vomiting.

CAUSES AND TREATMENT While labyrinthitis occasion-ally arises as a complication of otitis media, in most cases it is probably viral in origin; antibiotics are not helpful unless otitis media is present. Labyrinthitis normally re-solves on its own within a few days. However, this type of illness should be evaluated by your child's physician to rule out any other causes of vertigo and, if necessary, begin medication to relieve symptoms.

ecchymosis Collection of blood in the tissues causing a black, blue, or yellow discoloration of the skin; a bruise.

eclampsia A serious condition occurring late in preg-nancy or within 24 hours after delivery, characterized by convulsions (without any underlying seizure disorder). The cause is unknown. Increased blood pressure, water retention, and excessive loss of protein in the urine—a combination of symptoms referred to as **preeclampsia**—are usually observed beforehand, enabling the physician to take therapeutic measures in an effort to prevent eclampsia from occurring.

ectopic pregnancy A pregnancy that occurs outside the uterus, most commonly in a fallopian tube.

eczema (atopic dermatitis) (see photo on page A28) See *allergies in children.*

edema A diffuse abnormal accumulation of fluid within a particular tissue (for example, the lungs) or part of the body (such as the legs).

effusion A localized abnormal collection of fluid.

embolism The sudden blockage of an artery or vein by a clot or other obstructing material (such as fat, a tumor, or an air bubble), which has been carried through the bloodstream from another part of the body.

emesis Vomiting.

encephalitis Inflammation of brain tissue, usually caused by a virus.

encopresis Fecal soiling or leakage not due to illness or physical defect, which occurs past the age of normal toi-let training.

endocarditis An inflammation of the internal lining of the heart, usually caused by an infection.

endometriosis A condition in which the type of tissue (called endometrium) that lines the inside of the uterus is also present in other parts of a woman's body—most commonly on the outer surfaces of the uterus, ovaries, fallopian tubes, intestine, and/or bladder. Like its counterpart within the uterus, this tissue builds up each month in response to the normal hormonal cycle and bleeds at the end of that cycle. Blood accumulated in one or more abnormal locations can irritate the surrounding tissue, causing considerable pain as well as scarring that can lead to infertility.

enema Method of bringing about a bowel movement by inserting fluid into the rectum.

epiglottitis A life-threatening, rapidly progressive infection of the epiglottis, the leaf-shaped plate of elastic cartilage at the root of the tongue. In a typical case, a child who has previously been well will rapidly develop a high fever and an extremely sore throat. Within a few hours she will be unable to swallow and might lean forward and actually drool rather than swallow. *This condition is a medical emergency because the swollen epiglottis can suddenly block the airway, leading to suffocation.* Even a simple examination with a wooden tongue blade can precipitate closure of the airway.

Fortunately, this disease has become uncommon because most children are now routinely immunized against hemophilus influenzae type B, the bacteria that cause it.

epinephrine A hormone (also known as **adrenaline**), secreted by the adrenal glands, that prepares the body to respond to stress. Among its many physiologic effects, epinephrine raises blood pressure, increases heart rate, raises the output of the heart, and elevates the level of glucose (blood sugar) in the bloodstream. It has been synthesized for medical use and is commonly given as an emergency treatment for severe allergic reactions.

epistaxis Nosebleed.

erythema (see photo on page A28) Redness of the skin.

esophagus (see illustration on page A8) The hollow structure that transports food from the throat to the stomach.

eustachian tube (see illustration on page A13) The narrow pressure-equalization tube that allows air from the back of the nose and throat to travel to the middle ear.

exanthem A skin rash accompanied by an acute infection (for example, measles).

expectorant A compound included in many cough and cold preparations intended to loosen secretions and allow them to be cleared more easily from the respiratory passages.

eye care and concerns (see illustration on page A12) The eye is a marvel of engineering. Each eye is a compact but exquisitely sensitive biological camera that focuses images of the external world onto the **retina,** a ten-layer cellular membrane directly connected to the brain through the **optic nerve.** Before arriving at the retina (located at the back of the eyeball), light must pass through

- the **cornea,** a clear, highly sensitive structure that forms a domelike covering over the **iris,** whose pigment gives the eye its color;
- the **pupil,** the small black circular aperture (opening) in the center of the iris. The pupil dilates or constricts in response to the amount of light striking the eye;
- the **lens,** placed directly behind the iris, which focuses light on the retina;
- the **vitreous humor,** clear gelatinous material that fills the eyeball.

Vision disturbances can arise from abnormalities in the shape, function, or clarity of these structures.

Other important structures of the eyes are the **sclera,** the white surface of the eyeball; the **conjunctiva,** a membrane that covers the sclera and the inner surfaces of the eyelids; the **lacrimal gland,** which produces tears; and the **nasolacrimal duct,** through which tears travel from the inner corner of the eye into the nose.

Early developments
Even though a baby's eyes are not fully developed at birth, the intricate process of collecting visual information begins as soon as a newborn can open her eyes. The retina is not fully functional during the first few months, and the brain needs time to assemble visual images into meaningful patterns. Nevertheless, during the first few weeks of life, a baby will gaze intently at objects 8 to 15 inches from her face. She prefers to study plain, high-contrast, black-and-white images such as stripes, checks, or spirals, or a simple drawing of a face. But a newborn's favorite subject to scrutinize will be a person's face, about a foot away from hers. She will not respond directly to a smile for the first few weeks.

The iris in a light-skinned newborn contains little pigment and is usually blue gray or blue brown. The final color of a baby's eyes won't be known for at least six months or longer, during which time pigment gradually forms. The iris is brown from birth in most dark-skinned infants. The lacrimal gland does not become fully functional for about four weeks, so the crying newborn makes few tears. The sclera is relatively thin at birth and may have a slightly bluish tinge because of the dark color of the tissue lying just beneath it. A rise in bilirubin level shortly after birth may cause the sclera to appear yellow (see *bilirubin*).

By two or three months of age a baby will be able to coordinate her eye movements to stay locked on an interesting visual target that passes through a semicircle in front of her. She will also be interested in more complex shapes and patterns and will be able to hold her head steady enough to fixate on simple, high-contrast objects hung over her crib. By three months of age her depth of vision will have increased so that she will recognize you halfway across a room. Responses to color also develop over the first several weeks. At first, a newborn will pay attention to objects with bright, strongly contrasting colors. It will take a few months before the color vision has matured enough to distinguish a full palette of colors and shades.

All babies cross their eyes briefly as they develop their tracking skills. However, an infant who does not follow a face by the age of three months or whose eyes frequently wander or cross after five or six months may have a visual problem that should be addressed by the pediatrician or family doctor. The primary-care doctor will examine the eyes and, if appropriate, refer the patient to an ophthalmologist for evaluation. (Ideally this would be a **pediatric ophthalmologist**—a physician who specializes in children's eye problems—although many ophthalmologists deal with patients of all ages.)

By six months of age an infant is normally able to focus on people or objects several feet away and follow movement in all directions. **Visual acuity,** or ability to see objects, will improve from approximately 20/400 at birth to about 20/80. (The numbers used to express visual acuity are based on the ability to identify letters at a certain distance. A visual acuity of 20/80 means that the smallest letters a person can identify 20 feet away could be read by someone with normal (20/20) vision at a distance of 80 feet. Obviously infants cannot identify letters, but their visual acuity measured by other methods is still expressed in the 20/__ format.) A six-month-old will also show interest in more complex patterns and subtle shades of color.

By seven or eight months, a baby's visual capabilities will mature to the point that she can focus on people and objects across the room, though not quite with the clarity with which she sees whatever is directly in front of her. The average one-year-old can see well enough to spy small objects across the room or planes flying overhead, and by the age of two a child's visual acuity may approach 20/30 or 20/20, although this can be difficult to establish objectively. A child age two or older who squints a lot or brings objects close to her face to see them should have a formal eye exam, as should a child who is old enough to complain specifically of blurry vision or difficulty seeing the blackboard at school.

Routine infant and childhood exams include a brief check of the eyes: the clarity of each cornea, appearance of the eyelids, and responses of the pupils. Beginning at six months, the infant's ability to gaze at and follow an object, as well as the alignment of the eyes, will also be assessed. (Sometimes alignment can be difficult to judge because the skin adjacent to a baby's nose may partially cover the inner portion of the sclera, giving a misleading impression that one or both eyes are crossed.) Children as young as three can be screened for visual acuity using an appropriate eye chart or other testing methods that the child can comprehend.

Common eye problems during infancy

Chronic mucous drainage (nasolacrimal duct obstruction) is caused by a blockage of a baby's nasolacrimal duct, which normally drains tears into the nose after they have entered small openings in the inner corner of each eye. Six to 10 percent of infants are born with an obstruction of this duct. Within a few days or weeks after birth, tears will accumulate in and overflow from the affected eye. The small lacrimal sac located just above the obstructed duct may become infected, causing a constant backflow of discolored mucus into the eye. This usually bothers parents more than the baby, but more severe signs of infection such as inflammation and swelling may develop in the inner corner of the eye.

If the baby's primary-care physician diagnoses this problem, he or she might recommend warm soaks and massage of the tear duct up to six times per day. This is done by pressing the tip of a finger against the baby's nose just above the lacrimal sac (in the area where the upper and lower eyelids come together) and pushing downward toward the nasolacrimal duct. The pressure exerted against the obstruction may gradually open the drainage system. Antibiotic drops or ointment may be prescribed if an infection is present.

More than 70 percent of obstructed nasolacrimal ducts will open before the child is three months old, and 90 percent will open by nine months. If the problem does not resolve spontaneously, a probing, which involves placing a thin wire probe through the obstructed area, can be done in the office (or hospital) between three and nine months.

Strabismus is a misalignment of the eye. An eye may turn inward (esotropia), outward (exotropia), up (hypertropia), or down (hypotropia). Strabismus occurs in 4 to 5 percent of infants. Since eye movements are not fully coordinated until the child is three to six months old, temporary deviations in any direction before the age of three months usually do not require specific treatment. However, persistent deviation after the age of six months should be checked by the baby's physician, and usually the physician will refer the patient to an ophthalmologist. Appropriate treatment of strabismus is important because misalignment of the eyes causes ongoing double vision, causing the infant's brain to suppress information arriving from one eye or the other. This results in an impairment of vision called **amblyopia,** which develops in 2 to 4 percent of individuals. Depending on the extent of the strabismus, correction may require the use of special glasses or even muscle surgery on one or both eyes. The operation, usually done on an outpatient basis, modifies the attachment position of one or more of the muscles that control eye movements.

Common eye problems in childhood

By far the most common vision disorders in children are **refractive errors,** in which the retina does not receive a perfectly focused image. These affect 20 percent of children by the age of 16. Since genetic factors play a role in these disturbances, other family members may have similar problems. There are several types of refractive errors:

- **Myopia (nearsightedness)**—distant objects are out of focus. This condition usually develops as the eyeball grows and becomes longer than is ideal for focusing images on the retina. Normally myopia is not seen until a child is five to ten years of age, and it may become more pronounced during adolescence and early adulthood. A nearsighted child may squint because this helps bring distant objects into focus.
- **Hyperopia (farsightedness)**—distant objects are more easily brought into focus than those that are close. This condition is present in 80 percent of newborns, a consequence of the smaller size of a baby's eye. Normal alterations in the shape of the newborn's lens and cornea compensate for hyperopia early in infancy. Farsightedness may actually become more pronounced during the first few years of life, but a child's eye has a greater capacity than an adult's to adjust the shape of the lens (a process called **accommodation**), which effectively

brings a close object into focus. However, hours of this effort can cause eyestrain, headaches, and crossed eyes.
- **Astigmatism** is an abnormality in which the cornea is more egg-shaped than round, producing blurry or distorted vision. Squinting may improve a child's focus when astigmatism is present, but a severe distortion can cause eyestrain and headaches.

Refractive errors can be corrected with glasses or contact lenses. Mild hyperopia is usually not treated. Children who are highly active should use shatterproof lenses. Youngsters involved in sports can wear an elastic strap that attaches to the glasses and extends around the back of the head to keep them in place and prevent loss or damage.

Eye trauma, ranging from a scratch on the cornea to a severe injury that causes permanent visual impairment or loss, is not uncommon in childhood. According to the U.S. Public Health Service, more than 100,000 eye injuries occur every year in the United States, of which 90 percent are preventable. (Injuries due to darts, BB guns, and firecrackers are all too common. See Emergency Care, page 791.)

A **corneal abrasion** (see photo on page A28) is a scratch in the cornea's outer cell layers, often caused by a seemingly minimal incident such as being brushed by a leaf or twig. Since the cornea is very sensitive, the pain of an abrasion is usually intense. After the eye is examined by a doctor or ophthalmologist, an antibiotic is usually placed on the eye and a patch applied to prevent the eyelid from opening and closing over the injury. The antibiotic helps prevent secondary infection that could lead to more serious damage of the cornea. The surface of the cornea normally heals completely within 24 to 48 hours.

Sometimes trauma will cause internal bleeding of the eye, resulting in extreme pain and clouded vision. When blood appears in the clear space behind the cornea (a condition called a **hyphema**—see photo on page A29), the child should be taken immediately to an ophthalmologist or emergency room. To prevent further bleeding, the child must be kept at strict bed rest for up to five days. Enforcement of this low level of activity is critical. If the blood is not absorbed, an operation might be needed to remove it. A hyphema can cause scarring of the eye, which can in turn produce **glaucoma** (increased pressure within the eye). Further eye exams may be conducted to ensure that no additional damage has occurred.

If the eyeball has been penetrated or cut open, the child should be taken directly to the emergency room for immediate evaluation. If fluid is oozing from the eye, the child should be transferred while lying flat on her back so that additional fluid will not escape from the eye. A simple shield such as a small paper cup should be held over the eye (but without exerting pressure) to protect it.

A **chemical injury** to the eye, especially from an alkaline substance such as drain cleaner, can be very damaging and difficult to treat. It is important to flush any such material out of the eye with prolonged irrigation. Immediately place the face under a water faucet or hose and rinse the eye. Then promptly see an ophthalmologist or go to a hospital.

A **foreign object** (such as a piece of dirt) in the eye will cause irritation, pain, and tearing. Sometimes a parent can locate the foreign body under the upper or lower eyelid and gently remove it. If the object's size or location or the child's discomfort prevents removal at home, the child's doctor or an ophthalmologist should be contacted. Usually an anesthetic drop will be placed in the eye so the foreign body can be removed without pain.

Eye infections can be caused by viruses, bacteria, or fungal agents. Common symptoms of an eye infection are redness, tearing, watery or mucous drainage, and mild sensitivity to light. *Significant pain in one or both eyes, with or without sensitivity to light, should not be ignored.* In such cases, the child should be examined by her physician or an ophthalmologist, not only to relieve the discomfort but to treat conditions that might damage the eye if left alone.

Any virus or bacteria that infects the nose or throat can find its way into the linings of one or both eyes (or conjunctivae). Infections here, known as **conjunctivitis** (or pinkeye, see photo on page A28), produce a reddish discoloration and thick, discolored drainage. When this material dries overnight, the eyelids may stick together with crusty debris, which you will need to remove gently with a warm, wet washcloth. Your child's doctor will normally prescribe antibiotic drops or ointment for a few days. If the infection is caused by a virus (such as the common **adenovirus,** which is usually accompanied by an upper-respiratory-tract infection, fever, and sore throat), symptoms may not resolve for several weeks. Careful hand washing is a must for anyone handling a baby with conjunctivitis because the organisms involved can spread to others via contaminated fingers (see *conjunctivitis*).

Various forms of the **herpes virus** can on rare occasion cause problems on the surface of (or deeper within) the eye. **Chicken pox (varicella)** occasionally causes conjunctivitis if the virus forms one or more small blisters (similar to those on the skin surface) on the con-

junctiva of the eye. These normally resolve without damage. A reappearance of the chicken pox virus later in life, known as **herpes zoster,** or **shingles,** can also involve the cornea. In addition, the **herpes simplex virus,** which causes common cold sores of the lips, may affect the eye. Treatment of any herpes infection involving the eye will require an ophthalmologist to relieve discomfort and prevent rare complications that can cause scarring and long-term visual impairment.

Allergies can cause itchy and runny eyes, a condition known as **allergic conjunctivitis,** which often responds to antihistamines. In some cases eyedrops containing antihistamines or other anti-inflammatory substances can help reduce symptoms, although they do not provide a cure. Thick mucus, crusting, and pain are *not* a part of this problem, and causes other than allergy should be considered. In more severe allergic reactions, swelling of the conjunctival membrane occurs, producing a bubble on the surface of the eye or inner lids. This can look frightening, but it resolves without harming the eye.

Problems with the eyelids and the iris

The eyelids can be the site of both inflammation and infection. **Blepharitis** is a chronic condition that causes swelling and redness of the eyelids and a scaling of dandruff-like material from the eyelashes. Often blepharitis is caused by bacteria called **staphylococci,** but it may also be related to an inflammatory condition called **seborrhea.** Treatment involves removing the crust with a moist cotton applicator (which may be dipped in baby shampoo diluted with an equal amount of water). Antibiotic ointment may also be useful.

A **hordeolum,** better known as a **sty,** is a staphylococcal infection of a gland in the eyelid (see photo on page A31). This usually begins as a tiny red spot that grows into a pustule, which will eventually drain. Warm compresses may be applied three or four times a day, and antibiotic drops can be helpful. Inflammation of a different type of gland in the eyelid leads to a small lump called a **chalazion.** Warm soaks are also helpful, although this condition may take up to three months to resolve. Rarely, a chalazion will not disappear, and surgical removal under anesthesia becomes necessary. The persistence of blepharitis or a chalazion is often discouraging to parents, but most children will outgrow these problems.

As mentioned earlier, persistent pain in the eye, especially when discomfort is aggravated by light, should be evaluated as soon as possible. One condition that may cause this combination of symptoms is **iritis,** or inflammation of the iris. Frequently this is accompanied by redness of the sclera, which may give the misleading impression that a child has the more common conjunctivitis (pinkeye). But iritis must be treated quite differently to relieve pain and prevent scarring of the iris and other related structures. In children, iritis is often associated with medical conditions that affect other parts of the body (most commonly juvenile rheumatoid arthritis), and further evaluation to search for one of these disorders will probably be recommended.

For help with eye problems, contact your child's physician during daytime hours if your child

- has repeated episodes of crossing, wandering, or lack of alignment of the eyes after the age of three months, or persistent misalignment of the eyes at any age;
- has mild itching, discharge, or irritation of one or both eyes;
- complains of blurring or difficulty focusing (unless this is sudden and accompanied by other symptoms such as headache, in which case the physician should be contacted immediately);
- squints when looking at objects in the distance;
- repeatedly brings objects very close to the eyes to see them.

Contact your child's physician *immediately* if your child

- complains of persistent and significant pain in or around the eye;
- is struck in the eye by any object, especially if there is ongoing pain or visible damage;
- accidentally gets any chemical substance in one or both eyes (irrigation with water should begin *before* you call the physician).

Basic eye safety and reminders

- Never stare at the sun, especially when most of it is blocked during an eclipse, because of the risk of permanent ultraviolet damage to the retina.
- When spending extended hours playing on a sunny beach or in the snow, dark glasses that block ultraviolet light (which is reflected from sand or snow) can prevent a painful corneal burn.
- Always wear protective goggles when working with home or garden tools or in science labs where chemicals might splash into the eye.
- Protective eyewear should be worn at all times when playing racquetball or squash.
- Never aim flying toys (such as paper planes) at anyone's face.
- Playing with fireworks—especially those that fly, explode, or spew sparks—poses a significant risk to the eyes and is not an appropriate activity for children.
- Darts and BB guns are high-risk toys.

failure to thrive A medical term designating a perceptible decrease in the rate of growth and/or a persistent failure to gain weight (or actual weight loss) in an infant or child who previously has been developing normally. Possible causes include difficulty with nursing, inadequate or inappropriate food intake, a medical problem that interferes with the proper ingestion or utilization of food, chronic disease (for example, cystic fibrosis or diabetes), an ongoing infection, or in some cases social or emotional issues at home.

One of the many reasons routine checkups are important during infancy and childhood is that they provide an ongoing record of height and weight measurements, which may be the first indicators of failure to thrive. If these measurements raise any concerns, the physician may review a child's health history and dietary habits, carry out a physical examination, and possibly order other tests to help identify the cause. If no specific medical illness can be identified, it may become necessary to assess whether interactions within the family might be affecting the child's food intake or digestion.

fainting A relatively sudden and usually brief loss of consciousness caused by a temporary reduction in flow of blood to the brain (see Emergency Care, page 792).

femur (see illustration on page A6) The bone extending from the pelvis to the knee. It is the longest and largest bone in the body. (Also called the **thighbone.**)

fetal alcohol syndrome A specific pattern of abnormalities among infants born to alcoholic mothers. This pattern was first described during the late 1960s and given the name *fetal alcohol syndrome* in 1973. It is now estimated to occur in one out of every 1,000 births or approximately 5,000 cases per year. Common features include:

1. *Poor growth* before or after birth, with weight, height, and head circumference smaller than 90 percent of other newborns.
2. *Abnormalities of central-nervous-system function.* Of these, mental retardation is the most significant, seen in more than 80 percent of affected children. Fetal alcohol syndrome is one of the leading causes of mental retardation in the United States. Other problems include irritability during infancy, hyperactivity during childhood, and delays in development. In some infants, jitteriness

soon after birth is the direct result of alcohol withdrawal. Abnormalities in the central nervous system caused by alcohol may also affect development of bones and joints.

3. *Various defects of the face, eyes, and ears.* These are often more apparent during infancy and may become less obvious as the child grows into adulthood. Symptoms may include incomplete development of the facial bones, a thin upper lip, a short nose, prominence of the vertical skin fold on each side of the nose, and drooping upper eyelids. Various visual disturbances may be present also, including incomplete development of the optic nerve, misalignment of the eyes, nearsightedness, and astigmatism. Varying degrees of hearing loss are common in infants with this syndrome. These abnormalities frequently lead to delays in language development.

4. *Other birth defects* occur in infants with this syndrome, including a variety of congenital abnormalities of the heart (affecting approximately 30 percent) and the urinary tract (affecting about 10 percent).

Alcohol use during pregnancy

Warnings about the effects of drinking alcohol during pregnancy have been raised for centuries and are now more widely publicized than ever before. Nevertheless, recent estimates suggest that one in three pregnant women use alcohol.

Serdula, M., D. F. Williamson, J. S. Kendrick et al. "Trends in Alcohol Consumption by Pregnant Women: 1985 through 1988." *Journal of the American Medical Association* 265 (1991): 876–879.

Two basic facts about alcohol and pregnancy are extremely important:

◆ *There is no safe time to drink during pregnancy.* While the first three months of development after conception are usually when the growing baby is most vulnerable to drugs and toxins, alcohol can cause problems throughout the entire pregnancy.

◆ The toxic effects of alcohol on the fetus are known to be dose-dependent, that is, potentially more serious with higher levels in the bloodstream. Drinking a lot in a short period of time (as occurs during a binge) may be more hazardous than a steady intake of smaller amounts. Women who regularly consume more than eight drinks per week, whether all at once or spread evenly over seven days, run a 30 to 40 percent risk of having an infant with fetal alcohol syndrome.

The bottom line: It is impossible to know whether *any* amount of alcohol in any form can be considered safe

for a woman to drink while a baby is growing inside her. Therefore, *the best option is to abstain entirely from alcohol throughout the entire pregnancy.* It is wise for a woman to abstain or to consume no more than two alcoholic drinks per week if she is not yet pregnant but might become so in the near future.

While we know of no cure for fetal alcohol syndrome, infants who have it can be helped to reach their fullest potential. Particular attention should be paid to the child's vision and hearing to detect and treat problems that could impair normal development. Infants and children with fetal alcohol syndrome are also prone to develop ear infections and persistent fluid behind the eardrums, which should be treated to prevent hearing loss. Cavities in the teeth are more common in these children, so conscientious dental care is important. As these children approach school years, educational testing and special programs should be sought for them.

fever   See Special Concerns, page 267.

fibula (see illustration on page A6)   The smaller of the two bones that extend from the knee to the foot. It is located closer to the lateral, or outside, part of the leg, and it does not bear weight.

fissure   A slit or groove, which may be normal or abnormal, in tissue. Fissures often occur at a junction of skin and mucous membrane, such as at the anal opening.

flatfoot (see illustration on page 750)   A condition in which the normal arch of the foot has flattened out.

flatulence   Excessive production and passing of gas from the intestines.

fluorescein   Orange red dye used to detect certain types of abnormalities within the eye or to identify an injury on its surface.

fluorosis   A discoloration of the teeth, usually appearing as lacy white lines or specks, caused by excessive ingestion of fluoride. Supplemental fluoride helps strengthen the outer tooth enamel and may be present in the local water supply, in vitamin supplements, or in fluorinated toothpaste. Fluorosis sometimes develops if a child who drinks tap water is also given fluoride supplements exceeding the amount recommended for his area, based on the fluoride concentration in the local water supply. Some children swallow toothpaste when brushing their teeth. There is enough fluoride in a strip of toothpaste covering the length of the bristles to cause eventual discoloration of a child's teeth if a substantial amount is swallowed regularly (see *teeth care and concerns*).

folliculitis Inflammation of one or more follicles (tiny sacs or glands in the skin), typically as a result of bacterial infection. This occurs most often in hair follicles and in sebaceous glands, especially in the neck, thighs, buttocks, or armpits.

fontanelle See *anterior fontanelle*.

food poisoning (see chapter 1, page 197) A general term for a variety of illnesses occurring after a person has eaten food contaminated by certain types of bacteria; these bacteria either directly damage tissue or create toxins with far-reaching effects. Food poisoning often provokes a combination of intestinal symptoms: nausea, vomiting, abdominal cramps, and diarrhea; headache or fever may also occur, depending on the bacteria involved. One food-borne illness—**botulism**—affects the central nervous system and is sometimes life-threatening.

Very often food poisoning looks and feels like common viral gastroenteritis (stomach flu), and the only clue that food is the cause may be the simultaneous eruption of similar symptoms among family members or friends, especially if these people recently shared a meal or ate at the same restaurant. Unfortunately, food contaminated by these bacteria does not necessarily look, smell, or taste any different from uncontaminated food. As a result food poisoning usually catches its victims by surprise.

Staphylococcal food poisoning is the most common and often the most unpleasant food-related illness; fortunately it is the most short-lived. Staphylococci ("staph" for short) are best known for causing skin infections such as boils and impetigo. Someone with an infected wound or sore on the hands might introduce staph into food. If the food is warm—not hot or cold but about 100°F—the bacteria will multiply and produce a toxin that is resistant to cooking. (This is an important reason why warm foods should not sit for long periods of time. They should either be kept hot or directly refrigerated.)

Symptoms of staphylococcal food poisoning begin abruptly less than six hours after the meal and set off a combination of intense vomiting (usually the worst symptom), diarrhea, and severe abdominal cramps. The illness will end within 24 hours without specific treatment.

Campylobacter bacteria colonize wild, domestic, and farm animals, especially poultry. Undercooked chicken, turkey, and waterfowl are common food sources for this bacteria, along with raw (unpasteurized) milk.

Campylobacter infections begin with flulike symptoms: high fever and headache, nausea, vomiting, and abdominal cramps. Then comes diarrhea: frequent (up to twenty stools per day), usually watery, mucoid (containing mucus), or even bloody. Usually the illness subsides on its own, but relapses are possible. If a stool test identifies campylobacter as the cause of illness, appropriate antibiotic treatment will shorten the duration of the symptoms as well as the shedding of bacteria, which might infect someone else. (Outbreaks in day-care centers have been reported.)

Salmonella are bacteria that can cause not only food poisoning but more serious, widespread infections (especially in newborns and infants), as well as typhoid fever. While typhoid is far less common in North America than in developing countries, salmonella food poisoning has been on the rise over the past two decades. Animals, especially fowl and reptiles, are carriers of many salmonella species but do not transmit the specific form that causes typhoid (see *typhoid fever*).

Meats, dairy products (including ice cream), undercooked eggs, and contaminated egg products used in other foods (such as custards and mayonnaise) can contain salmonella. One or two days after ingestion, fever, vomiting, and diarrhea begin. Older children may complain of a headache and abdominal cramps. If all goes well, symptoms resolve in a few days without treatment. In fact, a child who is stable and showing no other signs of trouble probably should not be given antibiotics for salmonella food poisoning because these drugs may prolong the time that the bacteria remain in the intestinal tract.

Of all the bacteria that cause food poisoning, salmonella is the most likely to enter the bloodstream (although this is rare), through which it can travel and infect bones, kidneys, heart, lungs, or joints. Salmonella can also cause meningitis if it infects the linings around the brain and spinal cord.

Since widespread salmonella can be a serious problem, infants younger than three months of age, as well as children with chronic medical problems (such as sickle-cell disease, immune deficiency, or heart or kidney disease) should be treated with appropriate antibiotics if this bacteria is isolated from their stool. Young infants or children who are severely ill with salmonella will require treatment in the hospital with intravenous fluids and antibiotics.

Salmonella is known for its capacity to remain in the intestinal tract for weeks or even months after the acute symptoms are gone. The child in this "carrier state" won't be ill but can spread the bacteria to others, even after receiving antibiotics. Careful hand washing by adult caregivers and by the child himself (if he's old enough) is extremely important in the wake of a salmonella infection.

E. coli normally live in the intestinal tract of humans without causing disease, but some strains are associated with a variety of diarrhea syndromes. A common form is the mild but annoying **traveler's diarrhea,** which normally resolves on its own. Other forms are more serious and are accompanied by fever, cramping, and bloody diarrhea. (E. coli species are also commonly involved in urinary tract infections, and in infants they may cause meningitis or other serious illness. Most of these occur independently of the diarrhea syndromes discussed here.) One subtype can cause a serious combination of kidney failure, anemia, and clotting problems known as **hemolytic-uremic syndrome** (see page 697). This particular bacteria and other dangerous forms of E. coli are known to contaminate ground beef and other foods.

Two distinct types of infections are caused by species of the bacteria called **clostridium. Clostridium perfringens** resides in soil, sewage, and the intestines of humans and animals. It is best known for contaminating food produced in large quantities, such as that cooked in restaurants, institutional kitchens, or school cafeterias, where food may sit for hours slightly warm or at room temperature. Stews, casseroles, and gravies are particularly prone to transmit this organism. Symptoms are unpleasant—abrupt onset of vomiting and explosive diarrhea—but normally resolve without specific treatment within a few days.

Clostridium botulinum is another story. This bacterium produces a potent toxin that causes **botulism,** but only under conditions in which there is no oxygen plus the right mix of chemicals. This contamination can occur within improperly canned foods such as corn, beets, peas, and green beans, as well as in honey contaminated with clostridium botulinum spores. Unlike other food poisonings, botulism affects the central nervous system. After an 8- to 36-hour incubation, fatigue and headache begin, followed by visual symptoms (droopy eyelids, double vision, dilated pupils). A few hours later, swallowing and speech may be affected. Paralysis can develop, and if muscles necessary for breathing are affected, respiratory failure and death could follow.

Infant botulism often occurs when babies under twelve months of age are given contaminated honey. They become constipated and lethargic, with a weak suck and cry, floppy muscle tone, and in some cases sudden failure to breathe (apnea).

A specific antitoxin can be given with some success once the diagnosis is made, but long-term supportive care, including intravenous or tube feeding and respiratory support using a ventilator, might be necessary for several weeks. Botulism is less likely to be fatal in children than in adults, and eventually symptoms resolve completely. But without a doubt this is an illness that you want your child to avoid.

Treatment

If your child suddenly begins vomiting and having diarrhea, no one will be able to say whether food poisoning, viral stomach flu, or some other illness is the problem—unless, of course, other family members have the same problem and your doctor has made a specific diagnosis. If your child has a persistent high fever with diarrhea, the doctor may check stool cultures (or perform other lab tests) to find a treatable bacteria, especially if the diarrhea is bloody. While no single antibiotic is appropriate for any and all acute infections of the intestinal tract, some types of food poisoning will respond to the properly chosen antibiotic. In any case, your primary tasks will be:

PREVENT DEHYDRATION. If fluids lost through vomiting or diarrhea are not replenished, infants can become dehydrated within several hours and an older child after one or two days. Talk to your child's physician for specific directions, which will depend upon the child's age, general health, and the intensity of the illness. Be alert for signs of significant fluid loss that may need more aggressive medical care: decreased urine output (fewer than six wet diapers per day in an infant), fewer tears, dry mouth, and—most important—worsening listlessness (see *vomiting* and *diarrhea*).

KEEP THE CHILD COMFORTABLE. For this type of illness, you will be offering compassion and acetaminophen—and not much more. Medications that stop diarrhea (such as Imodium or Lomotil) should not be given to infants and toddlers under two years of age, and they should be given to older children only with your doctor's recommendation. While they might reduce the number of stools, they never cure the underlying disease. In some cases these medications prolong the stay of pathogenic bacteria in the intestine. In addition, they can mislead everyone about your child's condition, because fluids lost into the bowel may continue to accumulate while not appearing as stool. In other words, your child could become dehydrated without any visible fluid loss.

Similarly, medications that treat vomiting should be used sparingly and only as explicitly prescribed by your child's health-care provider *for this specific child's cur-*

rent illness. Antiemetic medications (drugs that control vomiting) tend to sedate small children, which can be problematic if you're concerned about worsening dehydration.

WATCH FOR SIGNS OF TROUBLE BEYOND THE INTESTINAL TRACT. Weakness, confusion, complaints of difficulty swallowing, or significant localized pain somewhere other than the abdomen should be reported to your child's physician. If your child's health is deteriorating and you cannot contact the doctor, take him to the nearest emergency room.

Prevention

Some basic precautions in the handling of food can prevent a great deal of misery and expense. The following measures will help keep food-borne disease away from your family:

- If you're preparing food, keep your hands clean. Wash after using the toilet, changing the baby, handling your pets, or touching any raw meat or eggs. Don't handle food if you are ill—especially if you have diarrhea or other intestinal symptoms—or if you have any infected cuts or sores on your hands.
- If raw meat or eggs have come in contact with any kitchen countertop, be sure to wash it thoroughly.
- Everyone must wash hands before eating.
- Cook meat thoroughly. Make sure that poultry and beef (especially hamburger) do not have any raw spots inside before they are served.
- Stay away from raw milk (even when it's "certified") or products made from raw milk.
- Don't let food sit at room temperature for more than two hours.
- If you prepare food today to be eaten tomorrow, put it directly into the freezer or refrigerator. Don't let it sit for hours to cool to room temperature.
- Never give honey to a baby before the first birthday.
- If you travel to a foreign country where you are not certain of the cleanliness of food preparation, stay away from salads and food sold by street vendors. Avoid water or ice unless you are certain that it came from a purified source.

foreskin (see illustration on page 74) A free fold of skin, also known as the **prepuce,** that covers the head of the penis. The foreskin is removed when a boy is circumcised. (See *genital care and concerns.*)

frenulum A fold of skin or membrane that limits the movement of a body part by attaching it to an adjacent nonmovable structure. (An example is the attachment of the tongue to the base of the mouth.)

G

galactosemia An inherited metabolic disorder characterized by an enzyme defect, present at birth, that prevents the body from breaking down galactose, a sugar derived from lactose (or milk sugar). If not detected and treated very early in life, accumulation of galactose in the liver and kidneys can damage these organs, and accumulation in the brain can lead to mental retardation. Newborns are routinely screened for this condition; when detected, a galactose-free diet can prevent these consequences.

gallbladder (see illustration on page A8) A sac, resembling a deflated balloon, that collects and concentrates **bile** secreted by the liver. Bile is a gold brown to greenish yellow liquid that serves several functions in the digestion and absorption of food; when food is eaten, the gallbladder contracts, releasing bile into the intestine to help digest it. In a small number of children (and more often in adults) hereditary and metabolic factors may lead to the formation of **gallstones,** which can range in size from tiny sandlike grains to an inch or more in diameter. If gallstones are present, contraction of the gallbladder may cause abdominal pain, often located in the upper-mid or right abdomen. Pain often (but not always) occurs after a large meal, especially if it contains a lot of fat. If gallstones provoke abdominal discomfort, treatment in most cases is surgical removal of the gallbladder.

gamma globulin A type of protein, present in the plasma (fluid portion) of human blood, that contains antibodies against many potentially harmful viral and bacterial organisms.

ganglion cyst A cystic swelling on the sheath of a tendon, usually on the back of the wrist.

gastritis Inflammation of the stomach lining.

gastroenteritis Inflammation of the stomach and intestinal tract, usually resulting from an acute viral or bacterial infection. Sometimes called stomach flu, gastroenteritis typically causes vomiting and diarrhea, often beginning abruptly and accompanied by abdominal cramps. Most viral gastroenteritis resolves within one or two days, but in some cases it leads to dehydration, especially among infants and young children (see *vomiting* and *diarrhea*).

generic A term designating a specific type of medication without reference to a brand name. For example, the drug ibuprofen is available in several generic preparations as well as in the brand-name forms Advil, Motrin, and Nuprin. Generic preparations are generally less expensive and theoretically contain the same medication as their brand-name counterparts. However, variations in manufacturing techniques may result in differences between generic and brand-name versions.

genital care and concerns (see illustrations page A10) Under normal circumstances, a newborn's genitals not only clearly identify the baby as male or female at the time of birth, but will show very few distinct changes until puberty a number of years later. (Genital developments during puberty are described in detail in chapter 12, page 480.) The baby girl's genital area—specifically the **labia,** or lips at the opening of the vagina—may appear swollen. In addition, a little mucus or even a small amount of blood may drain from the vagina during the first few days of life. Both are caused by sudden changes in hormone levels after birth and will disappear within several days without treatment. When the labia are gently spread apart, the **hymen,** a thin membrane that surrounds the opening of the vagina, will be visible.

Occasionally the labia will partially or completely grow together during the first or second year of life. Sometimes ongoing irritation of the labia from diaper rash or detergents will contribute to this condition, which is called **labial adhesions.** Normally no symptoms are present, but if the labia begin to obstruct the flow of urine, the child will be at risk for urinary tract infection. If you notice that your daughter's labia appear stuck together, tell her doctor. The physician may, with gentle manipulation, be able to pull them apart. If this cannot be done, a small amount of estrogen cream (obtained by prescription) can be applied to the edges of the labia for several days until they can be separated. Estrogen cream can also be used if adhesions form repeatedly. Eventually, a combination of physical growth and the body's own internal estrogen production will end this problem.

The **scrotum** of a newborn baby boy may appear puffy or swollen, a condition that normally resolves within a few days. Usually the **testes** (or **testicles**) will have arrived in the scrotum after their short but important journey from within the abdomen to the scrotal sac

during the final weeks of pregnancy. If the boy is born at full term (forty weeks), both testes should be easily felt in the scrotum, although they might move around inside the scrotum and may be felt as high up as the crease at the top of the thigh. This is normal as long as both testes can be felt in the scrotum most of the time.

Basic care and hygiene

If your son has not been circumcised, you need only bathe his genitals in soap and water along with the rest of the diaper area. At birth, the foreskin is firmly attached to the penis and cannot be retracted (pulled back). In fact, trying to do so can damage the sensitive tissues underneath. As your son grows, the foreskin will gradually separate from the head of the penis, and eventually it can be retracted. Once this has occurred, parents can begin gently pulling the foreskin back during bathing to clean the end of the penis. As your son grows older, he can do this himself as part of his normal bathing. Do not use cotton swabs to clean beneath a foreskin that will not retract. By one year of age, 50 percent of boys have foreskins that can be pulled back, and by five years of age 90 percent of boys have retractable foreskins.

If your son has been circumcised using a device called a Gomco clamp, a thin dressing such as gauze with Vaseline will be used to cover the tip of his penis. If the dressing becomes stuck to the penis, it can be soaked off with warm water. The edge of the circumcision may look quite yellow while it is healing. This appearance is sometimes confused with an infection. If you have any questions, call your physician. Many circumcisions are done with a Plastibell, and the baby will leave the hospital with the Plastibell still on his penis. The plastic ring should gradually fall off within a few days. If it does not or if you notice that the skin around it is becoming red, call your baby's physician.

No special care is needed for the genitals of infant girls. Tub baths, along with routine diaper changes, are sufficient. Occasionally spread her thighs and labia apart to wipe gently in the creases with warm water. (See chapter 5, page 161, for further details about bathing infants.)

Even when you change your baby's diaper frequently and keep the area clean, diaper rash may still develop. The first thing you might notice is redness or small bumps on the skin covered by the diaper. Usually the skin in the creases or skin folds is not affected. The most common cause of diaper rash is prolonged contact with a wet or soiled diaper, because chemicals in the urine and stool can irritate a baby's sensitive skin. Babies are more likely to develop diaper rash when they begin sleeping through the night, when they begin eating solid foods (probably due to the increased acids that are excreted), and when they have diarrhea. Other causes of diaper rash include chemical or fragrance irritants in baby wipes, detergents used to wash diapers, or soaps used during bathing. Some babies will even react to the material used in a specific brand of disposable diapers. Sometimes rashes are the result of a yeast infection (Candida) or, less commonly, bacteria. Yeast infections tend to cause a more intensely red irritation, often with small extensions or satellites around the edges of the rash.

Several measures can help prevent or heal diaper rash:

- Change the diaper as soon as possible after it becomes wet or soiled. Once a rash develops, ongoing contact with urine and stool can irritate it further.
- Try to eliminate other types of irritants. Change to fragrance- and alcohol-free wipes. If you wash your own cloth diapers, use soap rather than detergent, and double-rinse. If using disposable diapers, try another brand.
- Let your baby's bottom air dry after it is cleaned; leave it open to the air for a while before putting on a new diaper.
- Ointments such as Desitin or A&D can have a soothing effect. If the rash is severe, your baby's doctor may prescribe a mild cortisone cream to use for a few days. If yeast appears to be involved, an antifungal cream, either alone or blended with cortisone, will usually calm the rash within a few days.

Infections involving the genital area occur less frequently among older children. Uncircumcised boys occasionally develop an infection under the foreskin, manifested by local pain, swelling, and discharge. This should be evaluated and treated by a physician. Irritation at the tip of the **urethra** (the small tube through which urine passes) can also be a bath-time-related problem (see below) in boys.

Prepubertal girls sometimes develop irritation of the vagina and external genitalia (**vulva**), most commonly caused by prolonged exposure to bubble bath, soap, or shampoo in bathwater. Some simple preventive maneuvers include the following:

- Avoid bubble baths altogether.
- Keep bath times relatively short—15 minutes or less.
- If a child wants to play in the bath, let her do so before any soap or shampoo enters the water. As soon as the cleansing and hair washing is done, get her out.

If a prepubertal girl develops a distinct vaginal discharge, she should be seen by her physician. Occasionally during self-exploration a toddler or preschooler will insert a small object (such as a bead or a small wad of tissue) into her own vagina (or a child may insert an object into another child's vagina). This will cause a bacterial infection if not removed, but attempts to do so should not be made at home. Bacterial infections may also occur without a foreign object present. The doctor may collect a small amount of discharge on a sterile cotton swab to do a culture to identify the organism. Vaginal yeast infection is not typically seen before puberty. Using a nonprescription vaginal yeast remedy is not an appropriate substitute for a medical evaluation when a vaginal discharge is present in a prepubertal girl. If you are concerned about sexual abuse, it is imperative that the physician be notified, because this will significantly alter what tests are carried out, the treatment plan, and the follow-up (see Special Concerns, page 311).

Among adolescents who have had intercourse even once, any unusual discharge from the vagina or penis must be evaluated for sexually transmitted disease (see Special Concerns, page 573).

Specific genital problems in boys

HYDROCELE (see page 68) As the testes move from the abdomen to the scrotum during fetal development, they take with them a covering from the abdominal contents called the **processus vaginalis.** This covering produces a small amount of liquid that is normally undetectable. Sometimes, however, more fluid accumulates around one or both testes, forming a hydrocele.

A hydrocele will cause the scrotum to look larger and feel boggy to the touch, but it does not cause pain. (A flashlight beam placed directly behind the scrotum will cause the scrotum to glow red if this extra fluid is present.) A hydrocele on one or both sides of the scrotum may be present at birth, but if the genitalia are otherwise normally formed and both testes can be easily felt, no treatment is necessary. The fluid will gradually be absorbed, and in most cases, the hydrocele will disappear by one year of age.

A hydrocele can also develop later in life. Trauma, infection, tumor, and other illnesses can cause fluid to collect in the scrotum, but most often the cause is unknown. If your son has never had a hydrocele and you notice swelling in his scrotum, he should be evaluated by his physician, who may refer him to a general surgeon, pediatric surgeon, or urologist for further assessment.

VARICOCELE A **varicocele** is a dilation of the veins that drain the testes. This abnormality feels like a soft "bag of worms" above the testicle and occurs more commonly on the left side. It can cause a feeling of pressure in the scrotum, but it rarely produces pain unless it becomes quite large. A varicocele associated with a difference in size between testicles might impair fertility in the future. Surgery may be recommended in such cases, or if ongoing pain is a problem.

TESTICULAR TORSION Testes usually are firmly attached to the scrotal wall, so the testes cannot twist or rotate inside the scrotum. In some boys, however, the testes do not have normal attachments and are free to twist or turn. (Unfortunately, this cannot be diagnosed during a routine checkup.) When this happens, the blood supply to the testes is constricted and may be cut off, causing intense pain.

Testicular torsion (or twisting) can occur at any age, but the vast majority of cases are seen in teenagers. It usually causes sudden severe pain in the scrotum, most often on one side only. Some boys may also experience nausea, vomiting, or severe right-sided abdominal pain similar to that occurring with appendicitis.

Testicular torsion is a surgical emergency because the cells of the testes cannot survive without a constant supply of blood. Boys who have testicular torsion should be treated within a few hours of the onset of pain, so the normal functions of the cells within the testes (specifically, sperm and hormone production later in life) may be preserved. Even with appropriate and rapid treatment, it is possible that the testes may not function totally normally after torsion.

ORCHITIS AND EPIDIDYMITIS **Orchitis** is an inflammation of the testes, usually occurring in adolescents and young adults as a rare complication of a viral infection such as mumps or mononucleosis. (Mumps was the most common cause of orchitis before widespread vaccinations drastically reduced the number of cases.) Orchitis is manifested by swelling and tenderness of the testes and is sometimes accompanied by fever. A physician should confirm the diagnosis. Treatment of orchitis is usually limited to bed rest and appropriate pain medication.

Epididymitis is an inflammation of the **epididymis,** the tube that carries sperm from the testes to the urethra, and can occur at any age. Symptoms of epididymitis include pain and swelling in the scrotum, usually with marked tenderness just above the testicle. Viral and bacterial infections, as well as trauma, can cause epididymitis. In sexually active teens, infection with gonorrhea or chlamydia may cause the inflammation. Treatment for epididymitis will depend to some degree upon the cause, which is sometimes difficult to determine. Bed rest may be necessary, along with appropriate pain relief.

UNDESCENDED TESTES (see illustration on page 68) Testes are formed early in fetal development (beginning at six weeks gestation) and initially are located in the abdomen close to the kidneys. During the second trimester of the baby's development, the testes gradually move lower in the abdomen. By the twenty-eighth week of gestation, they begin migrating toward the scrotum through a tube called the **inguinal canal**. The movement of either testicle from the abdomen into the scrotum can be obstructed anywhere along its normal path, and if it fails to progress into the scrotum by the time of birth it is said to be undescended.

Three to 4 percent of normal, healthy newborn boys will have one (unilateral) or two (bilateral) undescended testes. In these infants, the scrotum may appear small and underdeveloped. Infants who are born prematurely, twin boys, and infants with spina bifida are more likely to have undescended testes. In most infants the undescended testicle(s) will move into the scrotum by the first birthday.

Sometimes a testicle that has descended normally will intermittently move into the upper end of the scrotum or even into the inguinal canal. This so-called **retractile testicle** may at times be difficult to feel—especially when the infant or child is cold, excited, or afraid. When the child is in warm water, which usually relaxes the muscles of the scrotal sac, the retractile testicle will usually drift (or can be gently maneuvered) downward into the scrotum, where it can be felt more easily.

If one or both testes cannot be felt by the first birthday, the child's physician may recommend an evaluation by a urologist or pediatric surgeon. To clarify the testes' location, an imaging study may be done or a **laparoscopy** advised. During a laparoscopy, performed under general anesthesia, a narrow scope is introduced into the abdomen through a small incision, allowing the urologist/surgeon to view the abdominal contents and locate the testes. This information can help plan future surgery, should it prove necessary.

For two reasons, evaluation and treatment are usually recommended if the testicle hasn't descended by the first birthday or (at the latest) the second birthday. First, there is a slight increase in the risk of developing cancer in a testicle that remains undescended. Second, testes remaining in the warmer environment of the abdomen may become less capable of producing healthy sperm and might contribute to infertility problems later in life.

germ A term once commonly applied to any microorganism that can cause disease. (This term no longer appears in medical literature.)

Giardia A protozoal (one-celled animal) parasite that commonly causes intestinal infection. Symptoms include abdominal cramps, bloating, and foul-smelling diarrhea and may extend over weeks or even months. Giardia infection is most commonly acquired by drinking contaminated water from streams, lakes, or (less often) city water supplies. The infection may also be spread through contaminated food. Because this parasite is present in stool, person-to-person spread may occur among those in close contact with an infected individual, primarily when hands are not washed adequately. Giardia infection is usually diagnosed through evaluation of stool specimens and treated with specific antibiotics.

gland An organ containing specialized cells that manufacture and release specific substances. Glands are classified into two primary types. **Endocrine glands** secrete biochemical compounds directly into the bloodstream; these chemical messengers affect one or more areas elsewhere in the body. The thyroid, the adrenal glands, and the gonads (testes and ovaries) are examples of endocrine glands. **Exocrine glands** excrete substances through a duct to a nearby location, which may be within or on the surface of the body. Examples of exocrine glands are sweat and salivary glands. The pancreas has both endocrine and exocrine functions because it secretes insulin directly into the bloodstream while manufacturing and releasing digestive enzymes (via the pancreatic duct) into the small intestine.

glaucoma A condition characterized by increased pressure within the eye. It can cause blindness if left untreated.

glomerulonephritis Inflammation of the filtering units (or **glomeruli**) of the kidneys. Glomerulonephritis may be manifested by fluid retention, diminished urine output, and elevated blood pressure. Loss of red blood cells from the kidneys into the urine may occur, causing reddish brown or tea-colored urine. The long-term outcome of this condition will depend upon its type and severity.

glucose The simple sugar that serves as the primary fuel for biochemical reactions within the cells of the human body.

goiter Enlargement of the thyroid gland that is chronic, diffuse, and noncancerous. Various metabolic and inflammatory conditions can cause a goiter, which is visible as a swollen area on the front of the neck.

groin Area of the body where the lower abdomen and upper thigh meet.

Guillain-Barré syndrome A nonhereditary, noncontagious, potentially life-threatening syndrome that follows a nonspecific viral illness. This condition primarily affects motor nerves and causes weakness and sometimes paralysis starting in the legs and moving upward to the upper body, including the arms and the respiratory muscles. In spite of its frightening and sometimes severe manifestations, Guillain-Barré syndrome resolves spontaneously and completely in most individuals within three weeks.

H

halitosis (bad breath) Halitosis can indicate that an infection is in progress in the gums, throat, tonsils, adenoids, or sinuses. Viral colds, sinus infections, tonsillitis, dental caries (tooth decay), poor oral hygiene, and even lung infections are common causes. A child with nasal congestion who breathes through his mouth or a child with a chronic cough may have bad breath. A trip to the doctor's office might be necessary to find and treat the cause of unusually intense or persistent halitosis.

hallucination A false perception involving any of the five senses, resulting from a disturbance in central-nervous-system function. In young children, transient visual hallucinations might occur during a high fever. In older children or adolescents, visual hallucinations are more commonly associated with the ingestion of a drug, whether an accidental overdose of a legitimate medication or the purposeful use of an illegal hallucinogenic drug. Recurrent auditory hallucinations are more characteristic of **schizophrenia.** A person (usually an adolescent) afflicted with schizophrenia might believe that he hears accusing or commanding voices, to which he may react with panic, self-protection, obedience, or even suicide.

Any hallucinatory sights, sounds, or other perceptions described by a child or adolescent should be discussed with your physician and an appropriate evaluation carried out.

hamstring The tendon located at the back of the knee and thigh. Also a group of muscles in the back of the leg commonly referred to as the hamstring muscles; a strain of these muscles is called a hamstring pull.

hand-foot-and-mouth disease (see photo on page A28) An annoying but self-limited illness caused by certain strains of virus known as **coxsackie.** It affects infants, toddlers, or preschool children, most commonly occurring during summer and fall, although it may be seen throughout the year.

After an incubation period of three to six days, ulcers appear on the tongue and the mucous membranes inside the mouth. Small blisters may also develop on the palms of the hands, on the soles of the feet, and occasionally on the buttocks. Discomfort from the mouth, tongue, and throat is usually more pronounced than that coming from the hands and feet. Fever sometimes accompanies this illness.

Hand-foot-and-mouth disease will clear up on its own in five to seven days. Creams, ointments, or any other topical medications will not help the healing process. Antibiotics are unnecessary and should not be used unless a secondary infection is present. Analgesic medications such as acetaminophen or ibuprofen may be used for pain. It is important to keep your child hydrated and nourished. Avoid spicy foods and acidic fluids that may irritate the mouth.

Because this infection can be transmitted from one person to another through oral secretions, your child should stay home from day care or school until the illness has run its course.

headache One of the most common problems seen by physicians who care for children. Very often headaches arise from infections such as colds or viral flulike illnesses; occasionally they follow an accidental blow to the head. Unless the illness or injury is severe, these acute headaches will resolve within a few days, if not more quickly. By age fifteen as many as 75 percent of children (in all socioeconomic and ethnic groups) experience headaches, often recurrent, that do not have an obvious immediate cause. Fortunately, only about one percent are a symptom of a serious disorder.

Most childhood headaches can be managed with relatively simple measures at home, but your child's physician should be consulted if they recur or if any headache is severe or prolonged for more than 24 hours.

Whenever a child is seen by a doctor for headache, an accurate assessment of the *history* and *pattern* of pain is extremely important. If your child complains about headaches, try to get a feel for the following characteristics; perhaps write them down for future reference if you seek medical help:

- How long has the headache been a problem?
- How often does it occur? Once a week or month? Daily?
- How long does it last? A few minutes? Several hours? A few days?
- Is there a pattern during the day? Is the headache in the morning, afternoon, evening, or all day long?
- Where does the head hurt? One side or both? Front or back?
- Does the head throb or pound, or is the pain more constant?
- Does the neck move easily, or is it tight or stiff?
- Is the pain increased by light, sound, body movement, or exertion?
- Are there other symptoms such as nausea, vomiting, abdominal cramps, or irritability? Is the child's skin cold and clammy?
- Does anything happen before the headache, such as visual changes (sparkling, flickering, blurring, or loss of vision), weakness of some part of the body, or dizziness?
- Does anything seem to provoke the headache?
- Does anything in particular help the headache go away?

It may not be easy to gather this information, especially if your child is very young and can't express what he is feeling. When headaches occur regularly, keeping notes can be very helpful as you, your child, and your child's doctor work to find the problem. Occasionally specific tests will be needed to rule out unusual causes of headaches.

Headaches caused by acute illness

Headaches associated with an acute infection will normally be accompanied by other symptoms such as fever, body aches, runny nose, sore throat, or cough. Very often the pain will wax and wane as fever rises and falls. Sinus infections sometimes produce pain localized above or behind one or both eyes, in the area of the cheekbone, or above the upper teeth. Typically this is accompanied by nasal drainage or postnasal drip that may continue for several days if not treated.

Headaches related to an acute illness can be treated with acetaminophen (Tylenol and other brands) or ibuprofen (Children's Motrin or other brands) in doses appropriate for your child's age and weight. *Aspirin should not be used because of its association with Reye's syndrome (a rare but serious disorder of the brain and liver) when taken during viral infections.* Other measures to relieve symptoms may also be appropriate, depending upon the illness (see *colds, sore throat,* and Special Concerns, page 267).

If your child has a headache during an acute illness, you should contact your physician if

- the headache is severe or unresponsive to treatment;
- your child complains of pain, stiffness, or difficulty moving the neck;
- pain is localized (on one side or in one area of the head);
- the headache continues for more than 24 hours;
- your child is confused, listless, or difficult to arouse.

Headaches caused by injury

Headache frequently follows an accident in which the head is struck, whether after a fall at home or on the playground, a spill from a bicycle, a collision during an athletic activity, or a more serious accident. If there are no obvious cuts, bumps, or bruises that need attention, you can observe your child afterwards for any changes in alertness and arousability. He may feel sleepy or even nauseated during the first few hours, and headache might occur as well. Since you need to keep track of your child's headache status after a blow to the head, don't give any pain relievers stronger than acetaminophen or ibuprofen unless specifically directed to do so by your child's physician. (Aspirin should not be used at all because it can increase the risk of bleeding.) You should contact your child's doctor after a head injury if

- your child lost consciousness or shows signs of disorientation, confusion, loss of memory, or other behavioral change immediately after the accident;
- crying continues without letting up for more than 15 minutes after the injury;
- the headache is progressively worsening;
- vomiting occurs more than one or two times;
- your child becomes increasingly difficult to arouse;
- your child displays any behavior that concerns you.

Recurrent headaches

Recurrent headaches will normally require a physician's evaluation to identify the cause or causes—some individuals have more than one type of headache—and a careful history can identify distinguishing characteristics.

Tension-type headache (also called **muscle-contraction headache** or **stress headache**) is by far the most common form of recurrent headache in children. One of these can last from 30 minutes to several days (or even weeks). Unlike migraine headaches (see below), no nausea, vomiting, or light sensitivity is present. This headache usually creates a vicelike pressure located "all over" the head, is constant (not pulsating with the heartbeat), and is not worsened by exertion. A tension

headache usually does not interfere with sleep or awaken the child during the night.

Assuming that your child has been diagnosed as having tension headaches, you should attempt to identify if possible any underlying stress or other psychosocial issues. This may or may not be a straightforward assignment. Children might not always express their feelings or may be reluctant to reveal the problems or cares they are facing. Open-ended discussion ("Tell me about how school is going") may provide some clues, although occasionally a more specific query ("Is there any particular person who is giving you a hard time right now?") will elicit more information.

It will take time and patience, but both parent and physician may need to explore concerns about school, friends (or enemies), or relationships within the family. Certainly major upheavals such as the death of a loved one, a move, or a family problem (especially separation or divorce) could play a role. It is common for children with tension headaches to also display symptoms of depression.

Sometimes the causes of a tension headache are more straightforward. Skipping a meal or eating erratically in general, getting too little sleep, getting overheated, or simply being worn out at the end of a long day can bring on headaches, sometimes daily. Some children routinely come home from school with a headache and simply need "quiet time" to bring it under control. A simple combination of a light snack followed by a 15- or 20-minute rest, perhaps with a cool washcloth across the forehead and calming music, may work wonders. An over-the-counter pain reliever (acetaminophen or ibuprofen) sometimes helps, but these medications should be used sparingly. Multiple doses on a daily basis can actually perpetuate headaches. Efforts to control the pace of life, along with exercise and more stable eating and sleeping patterns, can also be effective.

Migraine headaches are less common than tension headaches, affecting an estimated 5 percent of children at some point before the age of fifteen. In children, this type of headache is evenly distributed between genders, but after age fifteen it is three times more common in females. Up to 75 percent of patients with migraine headaches have a strong family history of this condition. The pain of migraine headaches is usually more intense than tension-type headaches and may last between 2 and 72 hours. Many people mistakenly believe that the term migraine designates any intense headache. The word actually is a French variation of the term hemicrania, which literally means "half of the head." Migraines commonly but not always occur on one side of the head. What specifically characterizes migraines is not merely their intensity, but any of the following specific and unique features:

- The headache is often located on one side of the head.
- Pain typically pulsates with the heartbeat.
- Headaches are worsened by physical activity.
- Nausea and/or vomiting are common; even abdominal pain may occur.
- There is sensitivity to light and/or loud noise.
- The headache may be preceded by an **aura**—a specific disturbance in the nervous system that lasts several minutes or longer and nearly always disappears as the headache arrives. The most common auras are visual: sparkling or shimmering light patterns, blurred vision, or even loss of part of the visual field. More unusual auras involve transient loss of sensation or weakness over part of the body, difficulty speaking, confusion, or dizziness. (Some children feel fatigued or irritable for hours or even days prior to a migraine, but this is not the same as an aura.)
- The headache is nearly always relieved by sleep. In many children with migraine headaches, there is marked improvement after vomiting.
- Between migraine episodes—even those that are severe—the child feels perfectly well.

The mechanism of migraines has traditionally been assumed to involve changes in blood vessels within the head, with constriction bringing about the aura if one is present, followed by a reflex dilation or widening that produces the pounding headache. More recent research suggests that migraines may also involve a disorder of chemical messengers within the brain known as neurotransmitters.

Even if your child has most or all of the typical symptoms of a migraine headache, the diagnosis should be established by a physician. This will involve a physical examination plus a discussion of the child's medical and family history; usually other studies will not be needed unless the headache pattern is very unusual. It is important for both you and your child to understand that these headaches, even when very uncomfortable, are not dangerous. The mechanism that causes them does not damage the brain, and in two out of three children who experience migraines, the headaches subside or disappear altogether later in life. (Migraines that begin late in the teen years, however, are more likely to continue into adulthood.)

Like tension headaches, migraines can be triggered by a variety of events including stress, erratic eating or sleeping patterns, exertion, the menstrual cycle, or a bump on the head. Specific foods (for example, nuts, chocolate, cola drinks, hot dogs, spicy meats, and foods containing monosodium glutamate) set off migraines in some children. Keeping track of the events leading up to these headaches may help you and your child identify and perhaps avoid such situations.

Migraine headaches in children are often surprisingly responsive to over-the-counter pain relievers such as acetaminophen or ibuprofen, especially if given early in the episode. Your child's doctor will review these options with you and consider other medications if necessary. Very often a process of becoming calm and relaxed (in some cases achieved simply by resting in a dark, quiet room) will reduce migraine pain, especially if the child can fall asleep for a while.

Other possible (but less common) causes of recurrent headaches

- Withdrawal from continued use of caffeinated foods and beverages.
- Sinus infections, which can produce acute headaches as already described, can continue for weeks and cause persistent headaches.
- Problems with vision that might cause squinting or straining are worth investigating, especially if headaches develop while the child is reading or doing schoolwork. A complete eye evaluation will be worthwhile, whether or not it uncovers a cause for headaches.
- Dental problems or inflammation of the jaw (**temporomandibular**) joint, or **TMJ,** are rare causes of headaches, which tend to be localized to the ear, face, jaw, or temple. TMJ pain can be aggravated by grinding the teeth during the day or night. It may begin after trauma to the face, or it can occur without any clear cause.
- Brain tumor—the diagnosis parents fear most when a child has recurrent headaches—is actually very uncommon. Headaches associated with a tumor tend to be persistent, relentless, and progressively more intense over several days or weeks. They may awaken a child from sleep or cause recurrent vomiting.
- Carbon monoxide exposure, usually from a leak in a gas furnace, can produce ongoing headaches. A clue to this possibility is the presence of headaches in other family members at the same time, especially if accompanied by nausea and vomiting. *If everyone in a home simultaneously develops severe headache and nausea, evacuate the house, call the gas company or fire department, and seek medical attention immediately.*

SPECIAL NOTE: Final cautions regarding headaches
Call your child's doctor if

- your child develops a sudden headache that's "the worst I've ever had";
- a headache is unresponsive to your doctor's recommended treatment;
- the headache is accompanied by abnormal weakness, difficulty with coordination, or unusual body or eye movements;
- headaches develop in the middle of the night or upon awakening;
- your child's level of alertness or consciousness changes with the headache.

heartburn A burning sensation in the chest arising from irritation of the esophagus (the hollow structure that transports food from the throat to the stomach). Heartburn is an uncommon complaint in children. In adolescents (and adults) it is often caused by reflux (or backflow) of acid from the stomach into the esophagus and may be aggravated by large meals, spicy foods, alcohol, chocolate, tobacco use, stress, or lying down less than an hour after eating.

A particularly intense burning sensation in the chest may occur if a medication (especially erythromycin or tetracycline, which may be used by an adolescent to treat acne) is swallowed immediately before lying down at bedtime without taking enough fluid to carry it into the stomach. If a tablet or capsule remains in contact with the lining of the esophagus for a prolonged period of time, severe pain may develop during the night or in the morning. This discomfort will resolve over the next day or two, although a doctor's evaluation may be necessary to confirm the diagnosis.

hemangioma A reddish purple birthmark caused by an abnormal distribution of newly formed blood vessels in the skin. The shape and size may vary. Treatment is rarely needed since most spontaneously disappear by two or three years of age.

hematemesis Vomiting of blood.

hematoma (see Emergency Care, page 803) A localized collection of blood that has escaped from one or more damaged blood vessels. (The term literally means "blood mass.") A hematoma can form in soft tissue (such as below the skin or in muscle) or within a specific area of the body (such as inside the skull). A hematoma near the surface of the body will feel like a smooth nodule. In contrast, blood that forms the discoloration of a black-and-blue bruise is usually spread diffusely through soft tissue and not necessarily collected into a hematoma.

hematuria Blood in the urine.

hemiplegia Paralysis of one side of the body.

hemoglobin Oxygen-carrying protein in red blood cells.

hemolysis The destruction or breakdown of red blood cells.

hemolytic-uremic syndrome A rare disorder characterized by damage to small blood vessels, especially within the kidneys, resulting in three significant problems:

- Acute kidney failure
- Anemia caused by destruction of red blood cells within the damaged blood vessels
- Low levels of platelets, the microscopic dislike bodies (smaller than red cells) in the blood that are important in the normal clotting process

The cause of this disorder is uncertain, but a combination of factors including genetics, a disturbance in immune function, and a precipitating infection (especially an intestinal illness caused by a certain strain of E. coli bacteria) is probably involved. Children under age two are most commonly affected. Initial symptoms typically include vomiting, diarrhea (which eventually becomes bloody), and abdominal pain, followed by decreased urine output. Significant fluid imbalances caused by kidney failure and intestinal fluid losses require intensive medical care, but more than 90 percent of children survive the acute phase. The majority regain normal kidney function.

hemophilia An inherited bleeding disorder, seen predominantly in males, caused by an inability to produce certain clotting factors. Manifestations of hemophilia vary greatly, depending upon the severity of the clotting defect. Infants and children with severe hemophilia are prone to frequent, spontaneous bleeding into skin, muscles, joints, and internal organs. Recurrent bleeding into joints, especially knees and elbows, can lead to a potentially crippling arthritis. In milder cases, excessive bleeding may occur only after injury or surgery.

hemophilus influenza A family of bacteria that can cause significant disease in infants and children. **Hemophilus influenza type A** causes ear infections, and **type B** causes several life-threatening diseases including pneumonia, epiglottitis, and meningitis. A vaccine for type B disease is now routinely given to infants along with DTaP and polio vaccines, so the most serious infections are now becoming rare.

hemorrhage Bleeding.

hemorrhoid A dilated vein in the anal or rectal area. Hemorrhoids vary in size and may cause itching, local pain (from inflammation), or bleeding.

hemostasis Control of bleeding.

hepatitis Inflammation of the liver, nearly always caused by a viral infection. (Inflammation of the liver caused by drugs or toxic substances may also be called hepatitis, but most commonly the term indicates an infectious origin.) Depending upon the type of virus involved and the individual's response to it, the inflammation may go undetected or at the other extreme produce profound illness. A child or adolescent with clinically significant hepatitis will typically experience fever, flulike symptoms, fatigue, jaundice (yellow orange skin and yellow color in the white area of the eyes), light or gray stools, and dark urine.

Many forms of viral hepatitis have been identified, and undoubtedly more will be discovered in the future. Of these, A and B are by far the most common.

Hepatitis A (previously called **infectious hepatitis**) is transmitted through contaminated food or water and is often acquired during foreign travel. The time from exposure to onset of symptoms is usually 15 to 40 days. The illness usually begins with five to ten days of nonspecific flulike symptoms, which may be followed by jaundice. (Fewer than 10 percent of children under age six who have hepatitis A develop jaundice. Among older children with hepatitis A infection, about half become jaundiced.) In the vast majority of cases, this infection resolves without complications in about a month, with rest as the primary treatment. Severe illness (or death) resulting from hepatitis A is extremely uncommon.

People who have ongoing close contact with the infected person may benefit from an injection of immune (gamma) globulin given within one or two weeks after exposure. This provides temporary protection that may prevent or minimize the impact of infection. Equally if not more important is good hygiene, including frequent hand washing, especially after any contact with stool from the infected individual. Children and infants may shed the virus in stool for several weeks after the illness has begun.

People who are planning to travel to high-risk areas (especially in developing countries) should consider obtaining specific hepatitis A vaccine, which is safe and nearly always effective, prior to departure.

Hepatitis B (formerly called **serum hepatitis**) is transmitted in ways similar to those that spread HIV/AIDS:

- From an infected mother to her baby before or at the time of birth.
- Through shared needles during intravenous drug use or through improperly cleaned tattoo needles that have been in contact with an infected person.
- Through contaminated blood products during transfusion. (Careful screening of donors and blood products has virtually eliminated this type of transmission.)
- Through an accidental needle stick of a health-care worker who is drawing or processing blood from an infected person.
- Through sexual contact with an infected individual.
- In as many as one in three cases, the source of the infection is unknown.

The incubation period for hepatitis B is longer—50 to 150 days—than for hepatitis A. The initial signs of illness may be minimal or nonspecific, such as fever, nausea, vomiting, and fatigue. In some cases, jaundice may be the first sign that the infection is present. Rarely, severe or life-threatening illness occurs at the outset. In about 90 percent of cases, the infection resolves in about two weeks without any specific treatment or long-term problems. However, one in ten individuals develops a chronic form of the infection, which after a number of years poses a risk for cancer or scarring (**cirrhosis**) of the liver. In addition, those with chronic hepatitis B can transmit the virus through sexual contact. They must never donate blood because even a tiny amount of it can infect another person.

Infants who acquire hepatitis B from an infected mother before birth are at higher risk for complications in the future. However, newborn hepatitis B infection can be prevented if an injection of hepatitis B immune globulin (or HBIG) is given within twelve hours after birth. To anticipate births at which this treatment might be necessary, pregnant women are now screened for hepatitis B virus as part of routine prenatal care.

Specific treatment for chronic hepatitis B is expensive and unpredictable in its effectiveness. However, a vaccine that is both safe and highly effective in *preventing* this infection has been available for the past few years. Because of the significant number of new cases of hepatitis B that continue to occur each year and its potential for causing serious long-term consequences, immunization of all children against this virus is now widely recommended and in many states required for school entry. The vaccine may be given at any age, starting at birth, and involves three injections—the second given one month after the first, and the third injection at least four months after the second.

In the past **Hepatitis C** was usually acquired from transfusions, but now sexual contact and the use of illegal intravenous drugs are the typical modes of transmission. Since blood products are now routinely screened for evidence of hepatitis C infection, the risk for acquiring the virus from a transfusion is now extremely low.

Hepatitis C causes acute symptoms such as fever, fatigue, and jaundice in fewer than 25 percent of cases. It is more likely to cause no immediate illness but smolder for years as a chronic infection. Fifty percent of infected adults develop chronic infection, and of these, 20 percent develop cirrhosis of the liver. Less is known about the long-term outcome in children. Very often the first indication of a prior hepatitis C infection is an abnormal blood test found during a routine physical later in life or (more often) noted among the screening tests done when an adolescent or young adult donates blood. Whenever such abnormalities are found, the donated blood is never given to a patient, and the potential donor is notified of his or her results so that further evaluation can be carried out.

hernia (see page 68) The protrusion of an organ or tissue through an opening in an adjacent body structure. This term is applied most commonly to defects in the abdominal wall, especially in the groin (**inguinal hernia,** see illustration on page 68) or at the navel (**umbilical hernia**). A small segment of intestine may push into one of these defects, forming a visible bulge that may be more obvious during crying or coughing, but may disappear when the child lies down. Inguinal hernias are normally repaired surgically to prevent the defect (and its associated bulge) from gradually enlarging. If a segment of intestine becomes trapped (or **incarcerated**) in the hernia, local pain and tenderness will develop, and immediate evaluation by a physician is necessary. Umbilical hernias normally resolve on their own without surgery (see *umbilical hernia*).

hiccup Involuntary spasm of the diaphragm.

hirsutism Excessive growth of body or facial hair, especially in women.

HIV infection/AIDS The immune system is a wondrously complex and efficient mechanism that continuously defends us from a formidable number of microscopic enemies. Most of its functions are carried out silently as would-be invaders are identified and destroyed before they multiply enough to cause any symptoms. Even when defenses are temporarily overcome, in the vast majority of cases the immune system mobilizes enough reinforcements to contain and eventually overcome the infection. Many infections provoke a complex biochemical "memory" called **immunity,** which helps prevent future invasions by the same organism.

One vital component of the immune system is the population of white cells called **lymphocytes** that play an important role in defending against viruses, fungi, parasites, and certain bacteria. A subgroup called **helper T cells** is necessary for the normal function of all lymphocytes. It is these cells that are gradually destroyed by the **human immunodeficiency virus,** or **HIV,** which results in a gradual deterioration of immune function. Eventually the affected individual develops unusual infections or severe cases of common infections, at which point he is said to have **AIDS,** or **acquired immune deficiency syndrome.**

HIV gains access to an uninfected person primarily through events in which blood or certain body fluids pass from one individual to another:

- *From an infected mother to her baby,* through contact with the mother's blood either before or at the time of birth. The majority of children with HIV/AIDS have acquired the disease this way. A pregnant woman infected with HIV has a 25 to 35 percent risk of transmitting the virus to her baby. (If she has active AIDS, the risk can be as high as 60 to 70 percent.) However, medical treatment can decrease the likelihood of transmitting the virus to her baby to less than 10 percent; **therefore, it is now widely recommended that every expectant mother be tested for HIV as part of routine prenatal care.**

- *From the breast milk of an HIV-infected mother to her baby.* Infants born to mothers with HIV should be fed formula.

- *Through sexual contact with an infected individual.*

- *Through shared needles during intravenous drug use,* or (much less commonly) improperly cleaned tattoo needles that have been in contact with an infected person.

- *Through contaminated blood products during a transfusion.* (Careful screening of donors and blood products has virtually eliminated this type of transmission.)

- *Through an accidental needle stick of a health-care worker who is drawing or processing blood from an infected person.* (This is also an extremely rare cause of HIV/AIDS transmission.)

It is important to note that HIV is *not* transmitted through everyday interactions—holding hands, hugging, sharing a meal, or other routine activities. It does not pass through the air. Tears, saliva, urine, and stool from an infected individual have not been proven to transmit HIV unless they are contaminated with blood. If blood—or body fluids that might contain it—from an HIV-infected individual must be handled or cleaned up, latex gloves should be worn to prevent direct contact with skin. The virus can be neutralized by a disinfectant such as 10-percent bleach solution (a given amount of bleach diluted by nine times that amount of water).

Initial contact with HIV may produce a mild flulike illness or no symptoms at all. For many months or years thereafter, there may be no unusual symptoms or signs of disease, but during this time the virus gradually destroys the T-cell population. The virus can be transmitted to others even while the affected person feels perfectly well. Eventually full-blown AIDS develops, during which a variety of infections become recurrent and disabling problems. These can include unusual pneumonias, chronic diarrhea, abscesses, bone and joint infections, unusually severe episodes of candidiasis or chicken pox, and central-nervous-system infections. The lymph nodes, spleen, and liver commonly become enlarged. An unusual form of cancer known as **Kaposi's sarcoma** may develop. HIV also causes damage within the central nervous system. In infants and children, this can result in delays in physical, intellectual, and behavioral development or in the loss of abilities that had previously been present. Inevitably death results from a combination of one or more infections or other complications.

Among infants who are infected with HIV at birth, about 20 percent develop AIDS within the first twelve months and die before the second birthday. In the other 80 percent the disease progresses at a slower rate, and AIDS develops in less than 10 percent of these children each year. HIV that is acquired later in life (most often through sexual contact or intravenous drug use) tends to progress more slowly toward AIDS, and a number of years may pass before any evidence of the disease is apparent.

HIV infection is diagnosed through a blood test that detects the presence of specific antibodies against the virus. If they are present, the individual is said to be **HIV positive.** Additional medical evaluation and ongoing follow-up are very important, even if no symptoms are present, in order to monitor the infected individual's immune status and general medical condition.

Management of HIV/AIDS is focused on four basic areas:

- *Slowing the virus's proliferation and its damage to the immune system.* While there is presently no cure for HIV infection, research continues to discover new treatment options that can help contain or slow the disease's progress. Because these medication regimes are constantly revised based on new research findings, they will not be described here. However, the physician(s) involved in the child's or adolescent's care will review the current options, including benefits, risks, and costs. Treatment protocols may require careful attention to proper dosing and timing of multiple medications to obtain the best results.
- *Reducing risk of infection.* Children with HIV will normally receive routine immunizations, including DTaP (diphtheria/tetanus/pertussis), MMR (measles/mumps/rubella), hemophilus influenza type B and hepatitis B, as well as pneumococcus and influenza vaccines. OPV (oral polio vaccine) should *not* be given to HIV positive individuals or their immediate family members because of the risk of developing vaccine-related polio. However, IPV (inactivated polio vaccine) may be used instead.

  While not isolating a child, prudent efforts should be made to minimize his exposure to people who have common infections such as colds, stomach flu, or cold sores (herpes simplex virus infections), or more unusual diseases such as tuberculosis. Ongoing use of antibiotics that prevent certain infections may be recommended for those with significantly reduced levels of helper T cells.
- *Treating infections that arise as a result of impaired immunity.* This can become a major challenge as AIDS progresses and more serious and complicated infections develop. Expert input from specialists, especially in infectious disease, will most likely be necessary.
- *General support.* Adequate nutrition, regular exercise, and attentive dental care for the infected individual, as well as continued emotional, social, and spiritual support for both patient and family, are all very important in the process of living with HIV. In many cases, one or both parents of an HIV-infected child have HIV and/or AIDS, complicating the process of providing care. Meeting the needs of both patient and family will usually require tapping into the resources of the

extended family, local church, and community at large. It is very important that HIV-positive children, adolescents, and adults not be cut off from these sources of support, especially out of misguided fear of contracting this infection from casual contact. As deemed appropriate by their physicians, HIV-infected children should be allowed to attend school and activities with other children. Like those with diabetes, asthma, cancer, and other chronic conditions, their life experiences should not be entirely defined by their medical condition.

SPECIAL NOTE: Who should be told about a child's HIV infection?

Despite more widespread public knowledge about HIV, for many reasons it is not easy to tell other people that one's child has this infection. Fear of negative reactions and uneasiness about disclosing the manner in which the virus was acquired (especially if one or both parents are also infected) can make discussing this disease an emotionally charged issue for many people. For this reason, revealing the diagnosis to just anyone may not be in the child's (or parent's) best interest. A child's doctor and other health-care providers who deal with HIV infection on a regular basis can provide valuable input on this subject. In general, the individuals who should be aware of the diagnosis are those who will be providing some form of care for the child, including:

- Physicians, dentists, nurses, and other health-care workers who will be involved in medical treatment, whether on a short- or long-term basis
- Caregivers, whether at home or in a day-care environment
- Teachers
- Relatives who are involved with the child on a regular basis

Relatives and friends who are not directly involved in the child's care may be made aware of the diagnosis if they are known to be trustworthy and supportive. Last, but not least, the child himself should be informed about his condition in a manner compatible with his age and maturity. For younger children basic facts can be explained on a need-to-know basis. An older child or adolescent will need more detailed information about his condition, its treatment, and his future prospects. In many ways, this subject should be approached the same as any other difficult topic: with respect for the child's need for truth, tempered by compassion and love, while avoiding secrets and misinformation.

hives (see photo on page A29) A generalized allergic response (also called **urticaria**) characterized by multiple raised, reddened, irregular patches of skin (often called welts). The patches are itchy, vary greatly in size, and continually change in size and location (see also *allergies in children*).

hoarseness A rough or raspy quality of the voice, brought about by conditions that alter the normal anatomy or function of the vocal cords. The following are the most common causes in children:

- **Laryngitis,** or inflammation of the vocal cords. Usually laryngitis is a component of a viral upper-respiratory infection and is accompanied by coughing and runny nose. In **croup,** hoarseness is accompanied by a barking cough and, in more severe cases, by labored breathing (see *croup*). Sometimes the child's voice will be reduced to a whisper. With rare exception, as the infection resolves, the voice will gradually return to normal over one to two weeks.
- **Overuse of the vocal cords,** from continual loud talking and yelling. (Among teenagers, this sometimes occurs following overzealous cheering at sporting events or concerts.) Persistent abuse of the vocal cords could lead to thickening or the development of nodules on them, which could perpetuate hoarseness. Speech therapy may be necessary to help a child or adolescent change vocal patterns that are causing this problem.

Less common causes of hoarseness in children include:

- The presence of one or more **papillomas,** warty growths on the vocal cords caused by the human papilloma virus (HPV). This virus can be acquired during birth if a child's mother has a genital HPV infection, although hoarseness is typically not noted until two to four years of age.
- **Vocal cord paralysis,** which usually results from injury to nerves in the neck that control vocal-cord movement. This can occur at birth or from trauma or surgery.

Acute hoarseness, whether brought on by infection or by overuse of the vocal cords, will normally resolve on its own if the voice is allowed to rest for a few days by whispering or maintaining quiet conversations. But any acute hoarseness associated with difficulty in breathing, especially when bursts of harsh coughing leave a child gasping for air, should be evaluated by a physician. If a child is clearly in distress, he should be taken to an emergency center *immediately*.

H

If hoarseness continues for more than a few weeks, the child's doctor should be contacted. In some cases, an **ear, nose, and throat (ENT) specialist** will be asked to evaluate the problem, especially if there is concern about a possible abnormality of the vocal cords.

homeopathy System of alternative medicine based on the theory that certain diseases can be treated or cured by giving extremely small doses of substances (chemicals, minerals, or even poisons) that in larger quantities would produce the symptoms of the disease being treated. Homeopathy's theory of disease causation and treatment is not recognized as valid in the mainstream scientific community, and the effectiveness of homeopathic treatments remains controversial.

hordeolum A bacterial infection of sebaceous glands in an eyelid. Also called a **sty** (see also *eye care and concerns*).

humerus The bone of the upper arm that extends from the shoulder to the elbow.

hydrocele (see illustration on page 68) A painless swelling of the scrotum caused by accumulation of fluid in the space surrounding one or both testes (see also *genital care and concerns*).

hydrocephalus An abnormal increase in the amount of fluid (specifically called **cerebrospinal fluid,** or **CSF**) that normally circulates within the central nervous system and cushions the brain within the skull. During infancy, hydrocephalus is associated with unusual enlargement of the head. It is often associated with congenital abnormalities.

hymen A thin membrane that surrounds the opening of the vagina.

hyperglycemia High blood sugar.

hyperventilation Abnormally rapid and deep breathing that most commonly arises from emotional stress. The person with this problem (usually an older child or adolescent) experiences a compelling hunger for air, often described as a feeling that "the air isn't going all the way into my lungs." Hyperventilation is sometimes accompanied by tightness in the chest, a racing heart, anxiety, or panic. Continued rapid and deep breathing can cause changes in the body's internal acid-base balance, which in turn leads to light-headedness, weakness, numbness, and tingling of the fingers and mouth, all of which may provoke even more anxiety and heavy breathing.

Any child or adolescent who complains of shortness of breath or appears to be breathing more rapidly or deeply than usual should be evaluated by a physician to rule out a medical disorder. If hyperventilation is diagnosed, the child will be instructed to breathe more slowly. Cupping a paper (not plastic) bag over the mouth and "rebreathing" his exhaled air will normalize his acid-base balance and improve his sense of well-being within a few minutes.

If hyperventilation episodes are recurrent and disruptive, counseling or even medication may be necessary to control the underlying causes.

hypoglycemia Low blood sugar.

hyposensitization See *immunotherapy*.

hypospadias Abnormal position of the opening of the urethra on the underside of the penis.

hypoxia Condition in which an inadequate supply of oxygen is delivered to the tissues.

ibuprofen (Motrin, Advil, and other brands) An anti-inflammatory medication, available without prescription, that may be helpful in reducing fever and relieving minor pain. It may be given to infants as young as six months of age, with dosing based on weight (see chart). Higher doses may be utilized for reducing fever greater than 102.5°F. Ibuprofen is available in a variety of dosage forms (liquid, chewable tablets, and caplets) and may be given every six to eight hours as needed. It should not be given to children with kidney disease, asthma, nasal polyps, or dehydration unless specific direction to do so has been given by a physician who is aware that one or more of these conditions are present.

idiopathic Arising from an unknown cause.

IM Abbreviation for *intramuscular,* literally meaning "within muscle." This word and its abbreviation are normally applied to injections given directly into muscle.

immunity Resistance to a potential disease-causing organism. Immunity may be inherited, acquired from contact with the organism, induced through immunization, or passed temporarily to a newborn from the mother.

IBUPROFEN DOSAGE CHART FOR CHILDREN

AGE	WEIGHT IN LBS (APPROX. KG)	LOW FEVER 5 MG/KG (FEVER ≤ 102.5° F)		HIGH FEVER 10 MG/KG (FEVER > 102.5° F)	
		(MG)	(TSP)	(MG)	(TSP)
6–11 mos	13–17 (6–7)	25	1/4	50	1/2
12–23 mos	18-23 (8–10)	50	1/2	100	1
2–3 yrs	24–35 (11–15)	75	3/4	150	1 1/2
4–5 yrs	36–47 (16–21)	100	1	200	2
6–8 yrs	48–59 (22–26)	125	1 1/4	250	2 1/2
9–10 yrs	60–71 (27–32)	150	1 1/2	300	3
11–12 yrs	72–95 (33–43)	200	2	400	4

One dose may be given every 6 to 8 hours as needed (see chart). For fever control, do not exceed 4 doses per 24 hours.

immunotherapy (hyposensitization) A form of treatment for allergy commonly known as allergy shots. It is a series of immunizations designed to reduce or eliminate an individual's allergic response to a particular substance (called an **allergen**). Small amounts of selected allergens are injected into a person at regular intervals and in gradually increasing doses. When the treatment is successful, the immune system produces antibodies to the allergen that can reduce or prevent the body's allergic response. The injections are usually given weekly for at least one to two years. If they are effective, the interval between them is gradually increased. Immunotherapy can be helpful in treating allergic nasal congestion caused by allergens such as airborne pollens, which cannot be easily avoided.

impetigo (see photo on page A29) A bacterial skin infection, usually caused by common strains of streptococcus or staphylococcus, in which an irregular honey-colored crusted eruption spreads over the face and/or upper body. The affected child usually has no pain, itching, or other signs of acute illness (such as fever). In a less common type of impetigo caused by certain strains of staphylococcus, the eruption appears as large blisters containing a discolored, puslike material.

Impetigo responds rapidly—often as quickly as it appeared—to topical and/or oral antibiotics, which are normally continued for one week. Crusts can be gently soaked off with a warm, wet washcloth, and the areas beneath them cleansed with soap and water. Because the bacteria that cause impetigo can easily spread by direct touch, the child's fingernails should be kept short and his hands washed frequently with antibacterial soap. He should be kept away from group-care situations until the infection has resolved.

incontinence Uncontrollable or involuntary loss of urine and/or stool.

induration A localized hardening of skin or other tissue.

inflammation The response of body tissue to injury or infection, usually identifiable by local redness, swelling, pain, and warmth.

influenza Better known as flu, an acute infection that frequently occurs in epidemics or occasionally in worldwide outbreaks known as **pandemics.** Three types of influenza virus, known simply as types A, B, and C, have been identified; A and B are responsible for nearly all epidemics. Unfortunately, each of the three types has a number of different strains, and the virus undergoes subtle biochemical changes on an ongoing basis. As a result, someone who catches the flu or is vaccinated this year usually will not be immune during next year's outbreak. That is why those who need flu shots must get a new one each year. Influenza is typically seen in the United States and Canada in the fall and winter, usually involving strains that have been identified a few months earlier in Asia. These outbreaks develop quickly, spread rapidly, and may involve sizable numbers of people in a

I

given community. While complications and mortality are uncommon in healthy individuals, influenza can be serious for children who have chronic illnesses.

Symptoms

Influenza is characterized by the sudden onset of chills, fever, muscle aches, headache, lack of appetite, and a dry cough. Nausea, vomiting, and abdominal pain sometimes occur in younger children but are less common in adolescents or adults. (Acute gastroenteritis, often called stomach flu, is an entirely different type of infection.) In some children, influenza can appear to be a simple respiratory-tract infection or an illness with fever but without any cold or cough. Influenza does not cause a rash or intense inflammation of the throat (pharyngitis). If bacteria become involved as secondary invaders, complications such as bronchitis, sinusitis, middle-ear infection, and pneumonia could develop.

Flu is spread via respiratory secretions that become airborne with coughing or are passed person to person by unwashed hands. A child or adult is most contagious for a period extending from 24 hours before the onset of symptoms through the time they show signs of resolving. The incubation period (the time from exposure to onset of symptoms) is one to three days.

Treatment

Treatment of influenza is usually focused on relief of symptoms. Acetaminophen (Tylenol and other brands) or ibuprofen (Children's Motrin and other brands) can be used to relieve fever and aches, but aspirin should be completely avoided because of the risk of Reye's syndrome. The child should drink a lot of fluids. (There is usually not much appetite for solids until symptoms begin to abate.) Until the fever, aches, and cough have calmed down for 24 hours, the child should remain at home and quiet. Antibiotics will have no effect on the course of the illness, although they can be helpful if secondary bacterial infections develop.

Two drugs, amantadine and rimantadine, may reduce the severity of symptoms if given within the first 48 hours of the onset of a type A influenza virus infection. (The type of virus involved in a local epidemic may be identified by the local health department.) They can also prevent influenza from spreading to other family members. These drugs are not routinely given to children, since influenza normally resolves without treatment in two to five days. Your child's doctor can advise you whether one of these medications might be helpful or necessary.

A flu vaccine is developed each year and given every fall. It is not recommended for all children but should be considered annually for those with chronic conditions such as heart disease, asthma, kidney failure, and disorders of the immune system. For children with these and other long-term medical problems, influenza can be a much more serious (or even fatal) illness. Other family members in the home of a high-risk child should be vaccinated as well. Flu vaccine can be given to infants as young as six months of age, although it is less effective in younger children.

Some parents may choose to vaccinate children who do *not* have chronic illnesses to minimize the risk of their missing school or other important activities. (See also *Reye's syndrome.*)

intussusception A condition in which one segment of the intestine telescopes into another, usually causing an obstruction and abdominal pain (see *abdominal pain*).

iron A mineral necessary for the production of **hemoglobin,** the protein within red blood cells that transports life-sustaining oxygen throughout the body. Without adequate amounts of iron, an infant or child can develop iron-deficiency anemia, characterized by small red blood cells containing abnormally small amounts of hemoglobin. Depending upon the severity of the anemia, the child may appear pale and be irritable and easily fatigued. (Children who are iron deficient sometimes display a behavior called **pica,** in which they feel compelled to eat ice, clay, or dirt.) Prolonged anemia can interfere with growth. In addition, iron deficiency can have adverse effects on a child's behavior, intellectual development, and school performance.

Normal infants are born with enough iron to prevent deficiency through the first few months of life, even if dietary iron intake is inadequate. After the age of six months, however, consistent iron intake is necessary to prevent anemia. Breast milk normally provides enough iron for a growing infant, while bottle-fed infants should receive iron-fortified formula. Cow's milk from the dairy case should not be given to infants younger than twelve months of age because what little iron it contains is poorly absorbed by children. Cow's milk may irritate the intestinal tract and cause small amounts of blood loss when given to infants before their first birthday. Once the baby is eating solid food, iron-enriched cereals should be a regular part of the diet. Green and yellow vegetables, potatoes, red meat, and egg yolks also supply iron.

If iron deficiency is diagnosed in an infant or child during routine screening or an evaluation for another problem, the physician will look for possible causes. Before 24 months of age, inadequate dietary iron intake is the most common explanation. In children older than two, a possible chronic loss of blood (usually from the intestinal tract) may need to be investigated. In addition, an appropriate iron supplement (drops, liquid, or tablets) will be recommended, with the amount determined by the child's weight and the severity of the anemia. It is important to follow the directions carefully, since inadequate dosing can delay the resolution of anemia, while excessive doses can be toxic. Taking the iron supplement with milk might interfere with its absorption, but vitamin C will enhance it. (For a child older than twelve months of age, orange juice would be a useful accompaniment to the iron.) *Keep iron supplements away from young children; accidental ingestion of iron preparations is one of the most common and serious types of poisoning in children under five.*

The physician who is treating the iron deficiency will eventually request a follow-up blood test (which usually can be performed as a simple finger-stick) to confirm that the problem is resolving.

J

jaundice See *bilirubin.*

jock itch (tinea cruris) A fungal skin infection of the groin, inner thighs, and in some cases the lower abdomen. It is more common in adolescent males, especially during hot weather, and is characterized by a pink, scaly, itchy rash. Jock itch can be treated with antifungal cream, powder, or spray (nonprescription) for several days. Keeping the affected areas clean and dry improves this condition and can help prevent recurrences. Daily showering or bathing followed by careful drying, wearing loose-fitting cotton underwear, and washing shorts and athletic supporters after each use will aid recovery.

jugular Having to do with the neck or throat. The term is used most often in connection with the large veins in the neck.

K

Kawasaki disease An illness that most commonly affects children of Asian descent under age four. The cause is unknown, but it is clearly not contagious.

Kawasaki disease is characterized by a fever (typically over 103°F) that rises and falls repeatedly for five or more days, followed by a cluster of at least four of the following symptoms:

- Enlarged lymph nodes in the neck
- Inflammation in and around the mouth—a rough, "strawberry" tongue, redness of the mouth and throat, and cracking and peeling of the lips
- Swelling (**edema**) of the hands and feet, with peeling skin as the disease progresses
- Redness of the membranes over the eyes, but without pus
- A diffuse rash over the upper body and possibly the arms and legs

Fever may continue for 10 to 14 days, during or after which a number of heart abnormalities may develop. The most serious of these is damage to the coronary arteries, which supply blood to heart muscle. Coronary artery disease may occur in 20 to 25 percent of untreated cases, but prompt treatment can reduce the likelihood of this potentially serious complication.

Treatment of Kawasaki disease includes a single dose of intravenous gamma globulin and high doses of aspirin. Depending on the course of the illness, aspirin may be continued for a prolonged period of time. (This is one of the few situations in which aspirin is given to a small child with a fever. In viral illnesses such as chicken pox and influenza, aspirin is to be avoided because of the risk of Reye's syndrome [see *Reye's syndrome*]). Follow-up by a pediatric heart specialist is important until it is certain that no abnormalities of the heart are present.

keloid An excessive formation of scar tissue where a wound (traumatic or surgical) has healed. Keloid formation is more common in dark-skinned individuals. A keloid may enlarge over months or even years. Local injection of cortisone into the scar tissue may help decrease its size.

knock-knee (see illustration on page 753) A common deformity of the legs seen in children after the age of two, in which the knees are unusually close together when the child is standing or walking. Normal alignment of the knees typically takes place by the age of eight. (See Musculoskeletal Problems in Children, page 743.)

kyphosis (see illustration on page 759) An excessive backward curvature of the upper (thoracic) spine, resulting in a humpback or rounded appearance when viewed from the side.

K

L

labia Lip-shaped structures or outer folds that protect the female genitalia.

labyrinth The fluid-filled chambers in the inner ear.

laceration (see Emergency Care, page 804) A cut or tear in the skin.

lacrimation The secretion and discharge of tears.

lactose Type of sugar found in breast milk, cow's milk, and most nonsoy infant formulas.

lactose intolerance The inability to digest **lactose,** one of the two most common sugars in the human diet and the primary sugar in cow's milk. Variable amounts of it are found in many products (such as cheese, ice cream, and yogurt) that are derived from milk. Lactose intolerance occurs when there is a deficiency of the enzyme **lactase,** which is necessary to convert lactose into simpler sugars that can be absorbed into the bloodstream.

An affected person who consumes foods containing lactose may develop bloating, cramping, diarrhea, increased bowel gas, and general abdominal discomfort. This type of reaction to lactose may be a lifelong tendency or a temporary problem. Lactose intolerance is very common in both African-Americans and Asians after the age of five. Because lactase is found in the outer cell layer of the small intestine, it may also be lost temporarily during infections or other disorders that damage the intestinal lining. After a child has had gastroenteritis (stomach flu), intestinal lactase may be reduced for days or even weeks; it is sometimes recommended that milk products be avoided for several days after a child has had this type of infection.

Avoidance of foods containing lactose will prevent symptoms in a child with lactose intolerance. In addition, nonprescription lactase preparations (Lactaid, Lactrase, and others) may be added to milk products or swallowed along with lactose-containing foods to prevent symptoms.

laryngitis Inflammation of the vocal cords, characterized primarily by hoarseness or even a temporary complete loss of the voice. Most cases of laryngitis are caused by viruses and are commonly associated with a dry cough. With rare exception, the voice returns to normal in one to two weeks without specific treatment (see *hoarseness*).

lateral A term indicating a position away from the midline of the body. For example, the ear is lateral to the cheek, and on each foot the little toe is lateral to the big toe.

lavage The washing out of an organ such as the stomach or bowel.

lead poisoning Depending upon the amount of lead ingested and the time span during which it enters the body, lead poisoning can cause many symptoms: weakness, irritability, weight loss, vomiting, personality changes, staggering gait, constipation, headache, and abdominal pain. In extreme cases, mental retardation, convulsions, and coma develop. More commonly, small amounts of lead are continually ingested and may not cause obvious symptoms in early childhood but sometimes become evident later in the form of learning disorders.

Young children—especially toddlers who are prone to put everything they find into their mouths—are at risk of lead poisoning if they live in homes or apartments built prior to 1977. (In that year, federal regulations reduced the amount of lead that could be added to house paint.) Paint chips and flakes on windowsills, paint peeling from walls, and dust-size particles can be picked up by exploring hands and swallowed.

The level of lead in the bloodstream can be screened during an evaluation for the above symptoms. In some neighborhoods where a significant percentage of homes are older, such screening might be part of a routine checkup. Based on the result of this screening, the child may be treated with a medication (known as a **chelating agent**) that binds to the lead and increases its rate of elimination from the body.

An obvious means of preventing further exposure to lead is to repaint old houses and furniture, after first removing the lead-containing paint. Sanding or scraping old paint can generate dust containing lead, however, so care must be taken to avoid exposing the family to this material. (This job is best done by workers who are experienced in removing lead-containing paint.)

lens (see illustration on page A12) The transparent body, located just behind the iris of the eye, which focuses light on the retina (see also *eye care and concerns*).

lesion A wound, injury, or pathological change in any tissue, especially the skin.

lethargy Lack of energy; feeling of tiredness or listlessness.

leukemia A form of cancer involving uncontrolled production of immature white blood cells. Depending on the type of cells involved, there can be a number of significant consequences:

- The increased numbers of abnormal cells in the bone marrow interfere with the production of red blood cells (which carry oxygen) and platelets (which begin the clotting process if blood vessels are damaged), as well as other types of white cells. This can cause anemia (a low number of red cells), as well as bruising and clotting abnormalities.
- The immature white cells do not carry out immune functions as well as their normal counterparts, resulting in susceptibility to infection.
- The abnormal white cells may proliferate in other tissues, such as those in the central nervous system.

Leukemia can cause a variety of symptoms including recurrent fever, lymph-node enlargement, joint swelling, unusual bruising, fatigue, and irritability. The disease is usually detected when a blood count reveals significant abnormalities, including an extremely high white cell count. Further studies are then necessary to clarify the type and extent of the leukemia.

Acute lymphoblastic leukemia (ALL) is the most common form, accounting for one out of every four cases of all cancers occurring before the age of fifteen. About 2,500 children are affected every year in the United States, and of those, 85 percent are diagnosed between the ages of two and ten. The good news about this type of leukemia is that with chemotherapy over 95 percent of cases go into remission (in which the cancer is brought under control), and over 70 percent can be cured completely. Other forms of leukemia may be more difficult to treat and bring into remission. Some cases respond to more sophisticated treatments such as bone-marrow transplantation.

leukopenia A reduction in the number of **leukocytes** (white blood cells) in the blood.

lice (pediculosis) (see photo on page A28) One of the most aggravating health problems faced by parents is dealing with head lice in their children. If you or perhaps a school nurse has discovered one or more of these tiny, wingless parasites in your child's hair, you need not panic or feel embarrassed. This common infestation occurs in 8 to 10 million schoolchildren each year.

Three different kinds of lice live on the human body: head lice, body lice, and pubic or "crab" lice. **Head lice,** which commonly infect people (especially in child-

hood), are about the size of a sesame seed. They live on the scalp, biting and sucking small amounts of blood, and cannot survive more than a few hours away from a human host. Since they cannot fly or jump from person to person, they are usually passed by sharing clothing, combs, or hairbrushes, or sometimes by cuddling with someone who has lice. They are not found on dogs, cats, or other pets.

Head lice hatch from eggs called **nits,** which are tiny, grayish white, and teardrop shaped. Nits are attached to the hair by a gluelike substance produced by the female louse. They will not wash out or blow away but must be fine combed or picked out of the hair with tweezers. (This tedious process gives us the term *nit-picking*.) Nits hatch in about a week to produce mature lice, which then lay more eggs.

Detection of lice
The most common symptom of infestation with head lice is itching caused by their bites. Intense scratching of the infested area may lead to a secondary bacterial infection if the child's hands are contaminated. A child who repeatedly scratches the head should be checked for lice, especially if there is a known epidemic in the school or neighborhood.

Lice, which are grayish in color, can be difficult to locate because they move surprisingly fast and tend to shy away from light. The nits, which are lighter, are easier to see. Using a magnifying glass in natural light, look for small, grayish white eggs firmly attached to the hair shafts near the scalp. Nits can sometimes be mistaken for dandruff flakes, but since they are firmly anchored to hair they do not brush away.

Treatment
Lice can be safely and effectively treated by shampooing the hair with agents that destroy both lice and nits. Two effective nonprescription treatments for head lice are permethrin cream rinse (Nix) and pyrethrin shampoo (Rid). As an alternative, 1-percent lindane is available only by prescription. Because central-nervous-system toxicity from absorption of lindane through the skin has been reported in infants, it is not recommended for use on infants and toddlers, nor on pregnant women or nursing mothers. It should be left on the skin for only five minutes and then thoroughly rinsed. Lindane shampoo should be applied once when the head lice are identified, then reapplied in 7 to 10 days to ensure that all nits are destroyed.

An effective way to remove nits is to use a 10-minute pretreatment of the hair with a one-to-one mixture of water and white vinegar followed by regular shampooing. This will help loosen nits from hair shafts and make their removal easier.

Bedclothes, blankets, or clothing that has been in contact with your child during the 48 hours prior to discovery of the lice should be dry cleaned or washed in hot water (130° for 20 minutes). Hair accessories should be soaked in hot water. If an item (such as a stuffed animal) cannot be washed, it may be run through the dryer on a hot setting for 30 minutes (which will kill the lice) or sealed in a plastic bag and left alone for two weeks (which will cause the lice to die out).

Head lice can infest anyone, rich or poor, even in immaculate homes. Even after appropriate measures have been taken to eliminate lice, they can appear later because of reexposure. This can be extremely frustrating and demoralizing, especially after a lot of time and effort have been spent shampooing, nit-picking, and cleaning. To avoid reinfestation, all affected family members must be treated, and all infested children in a school or camp should be excluded from playing with others until they are nit-free. To end a local epidemic, a coordinated effort to check all children will be needed.

Body lice and **pubic lice** are less common in the pediatric age-group. Body lice are more commonly associated with crowded living conditions with limited access to laundry facilities. The lice might be found in the seams of children's underwear, rather than directly on the skin. Body lice can be eradicated by washing clothes in boiling water and then applying a hot iron to the seams. In adolescents and adults pubic lice are usually discovered crawling among the pubic hairs and may have been transmitted during sexual activity. They can be eliminated by topical application of the same medication used to treat head lice.

ligament (see Emergency Care, page 791) Strong but flexible fibrous bands that are attached to adjacent bones to keep them in proper alignment. A sudden and forceful twisting motion can stretch or tear a ligament, resulting in a sprain.

lingua The tongue.

lipoma A benign growth of fatty tissue.

lockjaw Lay term for tetanus, which (among other symptoms) can cause spasm of the muscles involved in chewing and make it difficult for the victim to open his mouth (see *tetanus*).

lordosis An excessive forward curvature of the lower (**lumbar**) spine, resulting in a swayback appearance when viewed from the side.

lumbar A term referring to the lower part of the back located between the ribs and the pelvis.

Lyme disease (see photo on page A29) The most common disease spread by tick bites; about 7,000 cases are reported annually in the United States. It is caused by a corkscrew-shaped bacterium called a **spirochete** carried by the pinhead-size deer tick. Only 2 percent of these ticks carry the disease in most states, but in New England, Wisconsin, and Minnesota, more than 50 percent of deer ticks are infected. Not surprisingly, Lyme disease is seen most commonly in these areas and in the Pacific Northwest, but cases have been reported in every state. (The disease was named for the town of Lyme, Connecticut, where an unusual cluster of children with arthritis in 1975 first led to its discovery.)

The ticks that carry the Lyme disease bacteria have a prolonged (two-year) life cycle involving large mammals, including deer and humans, as well as rodents and birds. The bacteria are normally transmitted when the ticks are at the nymph stage (midway between larvae and adults). Nymphs are so small that they may not be noticed when they attach to the skin. They are more active in the summer, increasing the odds of contact with campers and hikers. The spirochetes are not transmitted through contaminated food or water, or by insects such as mosquitoes or fleas, nor can they be caught from another person with Lyme disease.

Nymph (or less commonly, adult) ticks are picked up when animals or humans brush against shrubs or grasses that harbor them. The ticks cannot fly or jump but can crawl and eventually attach anywhere on the body, favoring hidden areas such as the groin, armpits, and scalp. Once the tick's head is embedded in a person's skin, it begins a long process of sucking a blood meal. This process can take days, during which the body of the tick slowly enlarges. The spirochetes that cause Lyme disease are usually transmitted after the tick has been feeding for about one to two days.

Symptoms

A telltale rash will develop in three days to a month in 80 percent of the people who have been infected with the Lyme disease spirochete. This rash, called **erythema migrans** (literally, "migrating red"), typically has the appearance of a bull's-eye that appears at the site of the bite and then slowly expands. Other smaller lesions may also occur. The rash does not itch, is not painful, and may last as long as two months. Flulike symptoms (such as chills and fever, headache, fatigue, and pains in muscles and joints) sometimes occur in the early stages of the disease. Any rash that develops within 48 hours of a tick bite is *not likely to be Lyme disease but rather an allergic reaction to the bite.*

If untreated, up to 20 percent of people with Lyme disease may progress to a second stage in two to twelve weeks, during which a stiff neck, facial-nerve paralysis, abnormalities of heart rhythm, and weakness or numbness of extremities develop.

The final stage occurs six weeks to two years after the tick bite in many people who go untreated. Symptoms primarily involve painful, swollen joints (arthritis)—especially of the knees—which could become chronic in 10 percent of children.

Similarity to other diagnoses

Lyme disease can be difficult to identify because the symptoms are either vague or similar to those of other disorders. In addition, many people will not have seen or felt the tiny deer tick that transmitted it, and one in four will not have the distinctive circular rash. The spirochete that causes Lyme disease is difficult to culture from blood or body tissue. Blood tests might be utilized to identify antibodies the body has produced against the spirochete, but the antibodies may not be detectable within the first few weeks of infection. To confuse matters further, someone with vague symptoms of fatigue and joint aches might show a positive antibody response to the Lyme disease spirochete but in fact have another type of infection.

Ultimately, a combination of history, symptoms, exam, and laboratory findings will lead a physician to suspect Lyme disease.

Treatment

In its early stages Lyme disease is treated with two to three weeks of antibiotics, usually amoxicillin, erythromycin, or a tetracycline derivative called doxycycline. (Doxycycline should not be given to children younger than eight because it can cause staining of the teeth, or to a pregnant woman.) If not treated until the later stages, more prolonged treatment with antibiotics may be necessary.

Prevention

Appropriate clothing—especially light-colored slacks tucked into boots—as well as insect repellents and frequent tick-checks are necessary to avoid transmission of the disease. (See *ticks* for additional measures to reduce the likelihood of tick bites.)

lymphadenopathy Swollen lymph nodes.

lymph nodes Small collections of cells that assist in the body's immune response. They are found throughout the lymphatic system, which is composed of tiny vessels that collect fluid from every part of the body and route it back to the bloodstream. Lymph nodes are commonly enlarged when reacting to an infection, such as when the nodes in the neck become swollen and tender in response to a sore throat. They may also become enlarged when invaded by cancer cells, a rare event in children and adolescents. Lymph nodes are frequently but inaccurately called glands.

M

macula (of the eye) (see illustration on page A12) Central part of the retina responsible for detailed vision.

macule (of the skin) General term for a discolored flat spot on the skin.

magnetic resonance imaging (MRI) A type of imaging study that utilizes a strong magnetic field to create detailed cross-sectional views of an area of the body. An MRI study is not painful and does not involve X-ray exposure.

malaria A tropical infectious disease caused by a parasite that is carried and transmitted by mosquitoes. Malaria remains a major health problem in developing countries, killing an estimated one million children worldwide every year. Travelers to foreign countries where malaria may be present (especially Africa, Asia, Central and South America) should check with their physicians and/or local public-health departments for advice regarding preventive medication, which should be started prior to departure.

malignancy Cancer.

malleolus Either of the rounded, prominent ends of the bones of the lower leg (the tibia and fibula) that protrude on each side of the ankle.

malocclusion Failure of the upper and lower teeth to align properly when a person bites down or chews.

malunion Failure of the pieces of a broken bone to heal in proper alignment.

mandible The lower jaw.

marrow The soft tissue that fills the central cavities within bones. Red and white blood cells are produced continuously within bone marrow, as are platelets (the tiny, disclike structures within the blood that participate in the clotting process).

mastitis   Inflammation of the breast tissue, usually caused by a bacterial infection.

mastoiditis   An infection of the honeycombed, bony mastoid air cells located just behind the ears. Over the past 25 years a number of potent antibiotics (and, when needed, surgical procedures) have greatly reduced the number of serious complications, including mastoiditis, which can arise from middle-ear infections (see *ear infections*).

Although mastoiditis can take place at any age, it is unusual before the age of two, since the mastoid air cells usually have not started to develop until that age.

Symptoms
The child who develops mastoiditis typically has been fighting an ear infection that has not improved over a two-week period. He is still feverish and has persistent pain and a red, inflamed eardrum. He also develops a characteristic swelling and tenderness behind the ear, typically displaced outward and downward.

Just as mastoiditis can be a complication of otitis media, **meningitis** may complicate mastoiditis in some cases. Fever, severe headache, and stiff neck will typically be present, and a lumbar puncture (spinal tap) will be needed to make this diagnosis (see *meningitis*). Two percent of children with mastoiditis will develop an intense, localized pus-forming infection called an **abscess** in the brain. This is manifested by persistent headache, fever, and confusion and is diagnosed using **computerized tomography (CT)** scanning.

Treatment
When acute mastoiditis is diagnosed, a child will usually be hospitalized for further evaluation, intravenous antibiotics and, when necessary, surgery to drain the infected area. Once therapy has begun, the child should be free of pain in four or five days. After discharge from the hospital, oral antibiotics will probably be continued for an additional four to six weeks.

masturbation   Self-stimulation of the genitalia for sexual gratification. (For information about discussing this topic and other aspects of sexuality with children, see chapter 10, page 373, and chapter 11, page 423.)

maxilla   The irregularly shaped bone that forms the upper jaw, the hard palate, part of the nasal cavity, and the floor of the eyeball. The upper teeth are implanted in the maxilla.

measles (rubeola)   A highly contagious viral infection that begins with high fever and malaise (lethargy or fatigue), followed by a harsh cough, intense runny nose, and watery, inflamed eyes. Severe conjunctivitis may be present along with sensitivity to light. White specks on a red base, known as **Koplik's spots,** may develop on the inside of the cheek. Finally, a rash begins near the hairline and progresses downward, disappearing from the face as it involves the arms and legs. The rash disappears within six days, after which the affected skin may peel.

Secondary bacterial infections of lungs, ears, sinuses, and lymph nodes or respiratory complications such as wheezing, croup, or pneumonia may occur in as many as 15 percent of cases. A rare but much more serious inflammation of brain tissue known as **measles encephalitis** occurs in one out of 2,000 cases, and half of those affected may suffer severe neurologic consequences or even death.

Fortunately, measles is far less common now than it was half a century ago because of the widespread use of measles vaccine, which is typically given as part of the **MMR (measles/mumps/rubella)** combination. The first dose of MMR is normally given when the child is 12 to 15 months of age; a second dose is now recommended after the age of four. Sporadic outbreaks of measles have occurred in areas where significant numbers of children have not been vaccinated or have not received a second dose of MMR (see also *rubella*).

melanin   Brownish black pigment that gives color to hair, eyes, and skin.

meninges   The membrane that covers and protects the brain and spinal cord.

meningitis   An inflammation of the membranes that cover the brain and spinal cord, usually caused by a viral or bacterial infection. This condition can develop at any age, although young infants are the most susceptible to it.

Bacterial meningitis is the most serious form of this illness and may lead to such complications as impairments in hearing and/or vision, mental retardation, and seizures. The bacteria that most commonly cause meningitis during childhood are pneumococcus and meningococcus. Some strains of meningococcus are quite contagious, so those who have had household and day-care contact with a child who develops meningococcal meningitis are usually given a preventive antibiotic. For many years hemophilus influenza was the most common cause of childhood bacterial meningitis, but a vaccine now given during infancy has drastically reduced the number of cases involving this organism.

Symptoms

A child with meningitis will commonly have dramatic symptoms: headache, irritability, lethargy, stiff neck, vomiting, and sensitivity to light (**photophobia**). An infant or toddler with meningitis may have only a fever and possibly a seizure. Distinguishing a harmless **febrile (fever) convulsion** from one caused by meningitis may not be easy. *In infants younger than three months of age, the signs of meningitis may be much less obvious.* A fever, poor feeding, and perhaps an episode or two of vomiting might be the only signs of this serious infection. An infant this age with a fever over 100.4°F (taken rectally) should be evaluated thoroughly by a physician.

If your doctor is concerned about the possibility of meningitis, it is likely that he or she will order blood tests and perform a **lumbar puncture (spinal tap)**. Parents often believe that this procedure is extremely painful and/or dangerous, especially on a tiny baby, but this is not so. To make the proper diagnosis, a small amount of the fluid that surrounds the spinal cord must be extracted and sent to the laboratory for a variety of tests, including bacterial culture. Your doctor will explain the procedure to you in detail if it needs to be done.

Treatment

Bacterial meningitis is a serious condition. To prevent significant complications (or even death), intravenous antibiotics are usually given for one to two weeks. When it is uncertain whether or not the infection is bacterial, antibiotics are started and continued for 48 to 72 hours until the results of spinal fluid and blood cultures become available. Viral meningitis (also called **aseptic meningitis**), which is more common in the summer and fall, resolves without antibiotics; frequently patients do not need hospitalization once the diagnosis is clear.

meniscus   Crescent-shaped cartilage tissue found within the knee joint, which serves as a cushion between the two bones (the femur and the tibia) that form the knee.

menorrhagia   Heavy bleeding during menstruation.

metatarsal   A term referring to the five long bones in each foot that are adjacent to, and form a joint with, each of the toes.

microcephalic   Having an abnormally small head.

milia (see photo on page A29)   Small white bumps that appear on the face of up to 50 percent of newborns.

These tiny cysts arise from structures known as sebaceous glands whose ducts are temporarily blocked. The glands are not infected, and milia will disappear without treatment during the first two months of life.

miliaria (heat rash, prickly heat) (see photo on page A29) White rash caused by blocked sweat glands. The small, white, fluid-filled bumps can occur in infants who are dressed too heavily, especially in a warm humid environment. The rash will disappear when the infant is placed in dry, cooler surroundings or dressed in lighter clothing.

Mittelschmerz   Pelvic pain that occurs approximately two weeks prior to a menstrual cycle. The pain arises from the release of an ovum (egg) from one of the ovaries (see chapter 12, page 485).

mole   A pigmented spot or bump on the skin.

molluscum contagiosum (see photo on page A29)   A common, somewhat contagious skin condition caused by a virus. The rash is characterized by small, discrete, pearly white or skin-colored, dome-shaped papules with sunken tops from which a plug of cheesy material can easily be expressed. They are found most commonly on the face, neck, and thighs. It is a self-limited disease but can persist for months.

mononucleosis (mono)   Acute infectious viral illness that occurs most commonly during adolescence. The vast majority of cases are caused by the **Epstein-Barr virus** (**EBV**), which infects virtually all individuals by the time they reach adulthood. In most people, however, infection with EBV occurs during childhood when it either goes unnoticed or causes symptoms identical to those of other common illnesses. If the first encounter with this virus occurs after puberty, the results are often much more dramatic.

Symptoms

After a prolonged incubation period of 30 to 50 days, the virus may cause fatigue, headache, and a low-grade fever for a few days, followed by a severe sore throat, higher fever, and marked enlargement of lymph nodes in the neck. Tonsils sometimes become very inflamed, with swelling, redness, and white patches (called **exudate**). Nausea and even vomiting might also occur. This phase of the illness may last for one or two weeks, and the fatigue quite a bit longer. During this time the spleen might enlarge, causing vague upper-left abdominal discomfort.

If your adolescent (or any child) has these symptoms, contact the doctor. A blood count and a more specific test for mononucleosis can help confirm the diagnosis,

M

although these tend to be more accurate if the illness has been under way for a few days. The doctor may swab the throat to check for infection with **group A beta-hemolytic streptococcus** (strep throat), which may occur at the same time, causing similar symptoms, and will normally be treated with antibiotics. There is no antibiotic that treats EBV specifically.

Treatment
Mononucleosis will usually run its course with treatment consisting only of comfort measures: rest, liquids, acetaminophen or ibuprofen for pain relief and fever reduction as needed, and more rest. Do *not* give aspirin, because it has been linked to a rare but serious disorder called Reye's syndrome when given during acute viral infections. More intensive medical intervention could become necessary to manage two uncommon complications:

- Swelling of tonsils so severe that swallowing or even breathing is difficult.
- Rupture of an enlarged spleen, a rare event that is manifested by sudden and persistent pain in the upper-left abdomen. This may in some cases be the first manifestation of mono. If rupture is diagnosed, the spleen is removed or repaired surgically to prevent significant blood loss.

Short- and long-term outlooks for someone with mononucleosis
Light activities may resume as tolerated after the fever and sore throat resolve, but several more days or even weeks of fatigue could limit participation in school or other pursuits. Contact sports or rough-and-tumble play should be avoided for three or four weeks to reduce the risk of rupturing the spleen. (However, in half the cases in which the spleen ruptures there is no history of trauma to the abdomen.) Your teenager's physician will provide more specifics about returning to athletic activities.

Because of the striking fatigue associated with acute mononucleosis, there was at one time speculation that EBV might be the cause of long-term chronic fatigue in teenagers and adults. The diagnosis of chronic Epstein-Barr syndrome was in fact given to many people suffering from fatigue, but further research has not validated the existence of this disease. Only very rarely does an individual have persistent symptoms that can be attributed to ongoing active mononucleosis, usually involving a disturbance in immune response. In general, anyone who has disabling fatigue for more than a few weeks, whether or not it is preceded by mononucleosis, should be evaluated for other possibilities. (This statement applies to light, everyday activities. For athletes, stamina and conditioning may be hampered much longer; peak performance may not be restored for many months following acute mononucleosis.)

Prevention
EBV is known to be transmitted through saliva (thus earning its popular distinction as the "kissing disease"), but it is actually not highly contagious. Only those who have never been infected with EBV by the time they reach puberty are at risk for mononucleosis. (A large number of people acquire EBV during childhood without developing major symptoms and are thus immune without knowing it.) As a result, widespread epidemics of mononucleosis do not take place. Nevertheless, if you have someone at home with this illness, others should avoid sharing utensils or anything else that would bring them into contact with the infected person's saliva (including mouth-to-mouth kissing). Unfortunately, unless a person had mononucleosis that was confirmed by a physician, there is no way to be certain of one's immunity to it without doing expensive antibody tests.

motion sickness Nausea (and in some cases vomiting) that develops in susceptible individuals during automobile, airplane, train, or boat travel, as well as on certain types of amusement-park rides. This common problem can often be alleviated in a grade-school child or adolescent by teaching him to focus on the horizon rather than reading or watching objects that are at close range while in a moving vehicle. Providing adequate fresh air in the car can also be helpful.

Sitting in the front seat can reduce motion sickness, but for safety reasons this approach should be restricted to children over 12 years of age who can be properly secured with both lap and shoulder belts. (*In general, children are safer in the backseat, and if the car is equipped with a passenger-side air bag, no child younger than 12 should ride in the front seat.*) Dramamine sometimes reduces motion sickness if taken prior to a long auto trip or before an airplane or boat ride.

mouth care and concerns The mouth serves as the entrance for a baby's life-sustaining nourishment and the exit for his cries and laughter, and later in life for his speech. It is bordered by the **mandible** (lower jawbone) and the **maxilla** (upper jawbone). Structures contained within the mouth include the **tongue, soft palate, hard palate** (roof of the mouth), **tonsils,** and **adenoids.** At birth, the muscles surrounding the mouth are remarkably strong, allowing babies to suck firmly enough to acquire adequate nutrition.

Mouth infections

As the point of entry for food and often other objects (none of which are sterile), the mouth is continually exposed to a variety of bacteria, viruses, and other microscopic organisms. In fact, the mouth is continuously colonized by enormous numbers of bacteria, but as long as the tissues (especially the gums, teeth, and tonsils) are healthy, these bacteria normally do not cause problems. A significant exception is a human bite (or accidental puncture by a tooth), which creates a contaminated wound if the skin is broken. In such cases, the one who was bitten should be evaluated by a physician to ensure that the wound is properly cleansed. Antibiotics are usually prescribed in such cases.

Bad breath

Bad breath can occur in children of all ages but is more common in older children with a full set of teeth. If your child has bad breath, make sure he is brushing and flossing his teeth often and regularly. Bad breath can be a sign of infection in the throat, tonsils, adenoids, gums, or sinuses. If brushing alone doesn't help, a trip to the doctor's and/or dentist's office will probably be necessary to find and treat the cause.

Candida

Known commonly as **thrush,** this infection is caused by the common yeast **Candida albicans.** It is seen most often in newborns. Thrush appears as a white film over the tongue, inner surfaces of the cheeks, or roof of the mouth. It may be confused with milk coating, but unlike thrush, milk can be easily dabbed off with a cotton swab. Thrush is not harmful, although candida transferred to a mother's breast may cause a local eruption of her skin.

Thrush can be treated with an antifungal solution such as nystatin, which your physician will prescribe. You can use an ordinary cotton swab or a device known as a toothette (which looks like a lollipop stick with a small sponge on the end) to apply the medication. Dip the toothette in the solution and gently scrub the affected areas inside the mouth. If you don't scrub, the thrush will still resolve with repeated applications of the medicine, but the process may take longer. Be patient, because even with diligent efforts the infection might not disappear for weeks. (Don't worry if your baby swallows some of the nystatin because it is not harmful.)

Some oral candida infections don't clear with nystatin, or they return in spite of repeated treatments. An alternative treatment is one percent gentian violet, a dye that can be purchased from the pharmacist without prescription. Gentian violet is applied with a cotton swab to the inside of your baby's cheeks twice daily for three days. Though harmless, it can stain everything in sight a vivid purple unless you are very careful with the swabs.

Canker sores

Also known as **aphthous ulcers,** these small, painful sores appear inside the mouth, either singly or a few at a time. They may occur on the gums, inner surfaces of lips or cheeks, tongue, palate, and in the throat. They have a well-defined, depressed whitish center surrounded by redness. They may arise during an acute illness, although no specific virus or bacteria is known to cause them, or they may form in an area that has been traumatized (for example, where the inner surface of a lip or cheek has been accidentally bitten). They tend to recur throughout the lifetime of susceptible individuals.

The sores are usually preceded by burning, itching, or pain for a day or so before they actually appear in the mouth. They can be painful enough to interfere with eating; avoid foods that are hot, spicy, and acidic (such as citrus fruits and tomatoes). Cold foods, particularly liquids, are usually better tolerated.

There is no specific cure for canker sores, which will eventually disappear without treatment in 10 to 14 days. Over-the-counter analgesics such as acetaminophen (Tylenol and others) and ibuprofen (Children's Motrin, Children's Advil, and others) may relieve some of the discomfort. Check with your child's physician about topical medications. If the sores persist for more than 15 days, the child should be seen by a physician.

Hand-foot-and-mouth disease (see page 693 and photo on page A28)

This annoying but self-limited illness is caused by certain strains of a virus known as **coxsackie.** It affects infants, toddlers, and preschool children, most commonly during summer and fall, although it may be seen throughout the year. After a short incubation period of three to six days, small sores appear on the tongue and sides of the mouth. Small blisters may also develop on the palms of the hands, the soles of the feet, and occasionally the buttocks. Discomfort from the mouth, tongue, and throat is usually more pronounced than that coming from the hands and feet. Fever may accompany this illness.

Hand-foot-and-mouth disease will clear up on its own in five to seven days. Creams, ointments, or any other topical medications will not assist in the healing process. Antibiotics are not needed and should not be used unless a secondary infection is present. It is important to keep your child hydrated and nourished. A soft bland diet is best until the ulcers clear up. Citrus and tomato juice might cause stinging in the mouth. Analgesic medications such as acetaminophen or ibuprofen may be used for pain.

M

Because this infection can be transmitted from one person to another through oral secretions, your child should stay home from day care or school until the illness has run its course.

Pharyngitis (sore throat) and tonsillitis

These common infections in children and adolescents are discussed in detail beginning on page 728.

Other mouth problems

Newborns can be born with a condition historically referred to as **tongue-tie,** in which the **frenulum**—the piece of tissue connecting the tongue to the floor of the mouth—extends too far forward. Parents may notice a dimple on the tip of the tongue as the child grows. Doctors used to snip the frenulum at birth, but this is an uncommon procedure now. Most children with this condition suffer no significant consequences. However, if tongue-tie seems to cause feeding or speech difficulties, you should talk to your child's physician about treatment options.

About one in 1,000 children is born with **cleft lip** or **cleft palate** (or both), a defect in the development of the central part of the lip or palate (roof of the mouth). The cause of this condition is unknown, but it occurs during weeks seven to twelve of pregnancy when the middle of the mouth fails to form properly. It is seen more commonly among Native American and Asian infants and least frequently in African-Americans.

Cleft lip and palate are not life-threatening conditions, although their appearance may provoke anxiety or other negative responses in adults or older siblings. The bonding process between parent and child may be impaired as a result, but it is very important that these infants receive all the cuddling, cooing, and other signs of affection that all babies need to thrive. (It is equally important not to overcompensate by becoming overly attentive to the child with the defect, and in so doing, deprive other children at home of time and attention they need.) While some infants with this problem are able to breast-feed easily, others have sucking difficulty and require a specialized soft nipple. Depending upon the extent of the problem and the timing of surgical repair (see below), speech development and socialization may be affected.

Because of the breadth of problems associated with cleft lip and palate, caring for an infant with this condition usually requires an experienced medical team consisting of a plastic surgeon, ENT specialist, pediatrician, dentist, orthodontist, and speech therapist. A psychologist and/or social worker can help the family work through emotional and practical issues, both before and after the corrective process. The good news about cleft

lip and palate problems is that they are surgically correctable, a process that may begin as early as four months or as late as eighteen months.

Future siblings of a child with cleft lip or palate are at higher risk of being affected. If the parents are normal and no other siblings have it, the risk of cleft lip or palate occurring again is about 2 percent. If either parent or another sibling is affected, the future risk could be as high as 7 percent, and if both a parent and a sibling are affected, the risk is 14 to 17 percent. Children with this condition may have associated problems such as congenital heart disease and spinal abnormalities. If your child has a cleft palate, don't be alarmed if your pediatrician orders extra tests to ensure that he does not have other medical conditions.

The care of the teeth and common dental problems in children are discussed in *teeth care and concerns.*

MRI See *magnetic resonance imaging.*

mucosa The mucous membrane covering canals and cavities that open to the outside of the body (e.g., the mouth, the rectum).

mumps A childhood viral infection of the **parotid (salivary) glands** located in front of the ears. This disease has almost been eliminated by childhood MMR immunizations.

muscular dystrophy An inherited disease of progressive muscle weakness, most commonly found in males.

mute Unable to speak.

myalgia Muscle pain.

myopia Nearsightedness; the inability to see distant objects clearly (see also *eye care and concerns*).

myositis Inflammation of one or more muscle groups, resulting in pain, tenderness, and/or weakness.

N

nail care and concerns Because an infant's fingernails grow quickly and may accidentally scratch the face, they should be gently trimmed once or twice a week using infant nail clippers. Toenails, which do not grow as quickly (and can't cause any injury) need only be trimmed once or twice a month.

The hands of a young child are constantly exploring the world around him, and thus both fingers and fingernails are at risk for a variety of injuries. If a child is barefoot much of the time, toenails could occasionally be injured as well. If a nail becomes cracked without rough edges, no special care is needed. If a nail is nearly torn off, however, use clippers or scissors cleansed with rubbing alcohol to cut off the loose fragment. Each day soak the hand or foot for twenty minutes in a solution of warm salt water ($1/2$ tsp salt in 2 cups water), then apply antibiotic ointment and a small adhesive bandage. Within about a week the raw nail bed will be covered with new skin, and this routine can be stopped. A new nail will eventually grow out.

Occasionally a crush injury (as occurs when a finger is caught in a closing door) will cause bleeding under a fingernail. This will be manifested by a deep blue discoloration of the nail and a great deal of pain. This injury should be seen by the child's physician, who may use a special tool to poke a hole in the nail to release the blood and relieve pain immediately. If the nail bed is cut as the result of a crush injury, it may need to be sutured (stitched) under local anesthesia.

Nail biting is a common self-comforting, unconscious habit among children. Attempts to stop it through nagging, ridicule, or punishment will cause more harm than good. A child who wants to break the habit can be assisted in a variety of ways:

- Offer a reward for a certain number of days or weeks of "biteless" nails.
- Devise a simple, nonjudgmental signal (such as saying the child's name in a friendly tone and pointing to your hand) you can use when you see him biting his nails.
- Sour-tasting solutions painted on the nails may serve as a reminder to keep fingers out of the mouth.

An infection of the soft tissue at the junction of the cuticle and the fingernail is called a **paronychia** (see photo on page A30). This usually involves common staphylococcal or streptococcal bacteria, although the herpes virus can also cause this problem. The infection usually arises from a break in the skin resulting from thumb-sucking or chewing or pulling on a cuticle. Occasionally pus will drain from the red, tender, swollen tissue. If a pus pocket is clearly visible, your child's doctor might lance it, which will relieve pressure and reduce pain. The doctor might recommend 10- or 15-minute soaks in a solution of a little antibacterial soap in 6 to 8 ounces of warm water, along with the application of an antibiotic ointment. In more severe cases, oral antibiotics might be prescribed.

Ingrown toenails are caused by improper cutting of the toenails and/or wearing tight shoes, and the nail becomes embedded in the flesh. Always cut a toenail straight across rather than curve it down on the sides. If an ingrown nail develops, soak the foot daily in a solution of soap and water as just described. Massage the swollen part of the toe away from the nail. Frequently, ingrown toenails (especially on the big toe) become infected, causing pain, redness, and swelling where the nail joins the infected skin. While gentle cleansing and warm soaks may help to some extent, your child's doctor might recommend antibiotics and/or removal of the segment of nail that has become embedded in the skin. (A local anesthetic is given to numb the toe before this is done.)

narcolepsy A disorder characterized by profound difficulty maintaining wakefulness during the day regardless of surrounding activity or noise. Increasing sleep at night does not improve this condition, which begins after puberty in the majority of cases (but may be seen as early as three years of age). Narcolepsy can be highly disruptive to normal activities but can be treated on a long-standing basis with central-nervous-system stimulants.

nausea Queasiness or unpleasant sensation in the stomach that makes a person feel like vomiting.

nebulizer A device used to administer medication in an aerosol form through a face mask.

neoplasm A tumor.

neuralgia Pain along the course of a nerve.

neuritis Swelling or inflammation of a nerve.

neurofibromatosis An inherited disorder characterized by soft, fibrous tumors that may be found over the entire body. Associated areas of brownish skin pigmentation are called **café au lait spots.**

neuroma A benign tumor growth that arises from a nerve.

neutrophil A type of white blood cell that is specifically associated with the body's immune response.

nevus A birthmark or a mole (see *birthmarks*).

nocturia Urination at night.

node A collection of lymph tissue (see *lymph nodes*).

nonunion The failure of the broken ends of a fractured bone to reunite.

nosebleed (epistaxis) See Emergency Care, page 796.

O

obsessive-compulsive The need to repeatedly perform a certain behavior and/or obsess over certain thoughts.

occiput The lower portion of the back of the head where it merges with the neck.

ocular Having to do with the eyes.

oligomenorrhea Abnormally infrequent and/or scanty menstruation.

orifice Entrance or exit of a body cavity (e.g., the mouth).

osteoma A tumor arising from bone tissue.

osteomalacia Softening of the bone due to a calcium or vitamin D deficiency or kidney disease.

osteomyelitis A serious bacterial infection of bone. It requires prolonged antibiotic treatment and in some cases splinting of the affected area. Surgical intervention is sometimes necessary to remove pus and diseased tissue.

osteoporosis Abnormal loss of bone density. This condition is normally associated with postmenopausal women, but it can also occur among adolescent females who have stopped menstruating because of severe weight loss (as in **anorexia nervosa**) and/or extreme levels of exercise (see Special Concerns, page 429).

otitis externa Inflammation or infection of the outer ear canal, commonly called "swimmer's ear" (see *ear infections*).

otitis media Inflammation or infection of the middle ear (see *ear infections*).

P

palate (see illustration on page A14) The roof of the mouth.

pallor Pale appearance of the skin.

palpate To feel with the fingers.

palpebra The eyelid.

palpitation The sensation that the heart is beating too rapidly, irregularly, or strongly.

papilloma A wart.

papule A small, solid, raised skin lesion.

paraplegia Paralysis of the legs and lower part of the body, with impairment of both motion and sensation.

parasite An organism that lives on or within another living creature (called the host) and draws nourishment from its host's body.

parenteral A term applied to medications or fluids that are not given by mouth or suppository, but by injection into a vein, muscle, or fatty layer below the skin.

paresis Partial paralysis or weakness of a specific muscle.

paresthesia Abnormal burning, prickling, or tingling ("pins and needles") sensation on the skin.

paroxysm A sudden attack (such as coughing).

patella (see illustration on page A6) The kneecap.

pediculosis Infestation of lice (see *lice*).

peptic ulcer A crater resulting from digestion (by stomach acid and the enzyme **pepsin**) of a localized area of the tissue that lines the stomach or first segment of the small intestine. This can also be associated with a bacterial infection.

perforation A hole or breakthrough in the membrane or wall of an organ.

pericarditis Inflammation of the sac that surrounds the heart.

periosteum (see illustration on page 66) The tough fibrous tissue that covers the bones.

peripheral Located at or near the surface or an outward part of the body.

pertussis (whooping cough) A highly contagious bacterial infection that primarily affects infants and children. Pertussis causes severe paroxysms of coughing, characterized by 10 to 30 intense coughs ending with a loud inspiration (which produces the *whoop* sound). These episodes may continue for months. In severe cases, pneumonia, seizures, and death may result. About 4,000 cases are reported each year in the United States, half of which involve children less than a year old. Before the development of a vaccine for this disease, pertussis was a leading cause of serious illness and death among infants and small children. Children who are not immunized against pertussis (the *P* in the DTaP vaccine) are at risk of contracting this disease.

petechiae Flat, purple to red, pinhead-sized spots that appear in the skin or mucous membranes as a result of leakage of blood from tiny blood vessels.

phlegm Mucus produced in the lungs, especially during an infection.

photophobia An abnormal intolerance of light.

pigeon toes (in-toeing) (see illustration on page 756) A minor abnormality in which the leg or foot is rotated, causing the foot or toes to point inward (see Musculoskeletal Problems in Children, page 743).

pinna (see illustration on page A13) The fleshy, projecting part of the ear on the outside of the head.

pinworms The most common type of parasitic worm that infects children in developed countries. While certainly annoying, they are essentially harmless. Pinworms are white or gray, thin, and $1/4$ to $1/2$ inch long. They may easily be mistaken for a vegetable fiber or a piece of lint—until they move.

Their 35-day life cycle begins when eggs are unknowingly swallowed. Pinworms hatch in the small intestine and migrate to the colon (large intestine). After mating, the females move to the anal area to lay their eggs on the surrounding skin, usually late in the evening. While this is taking place, children may awaken with itching (or in girls, pain in the genital area). The eggs around the anus are picked up when a child scratches this area and may be returned to the body when he sucks on a finger or puts his hands in his mouth. The eggs can also be transferred to toys or other objects, where they may be picked up by someone else. Pinworm eggs can survive outside a human body for approximately two weeks.

If you notice your child frequently scratching his anal area or if your young girl has pain in the genital area (which may increase with passing urine), check for pinworms. You may be able to spot them if you check your child's anal area with a flashlight a few hours after the child has gone to bed or in the early morning. If you suspect that your child has pinworms but don't see them, contact your doctor, who may ask you to collect a specimen using clear cellophane tape. You can press the sticky side of the tape against your child's anus a few hours after bedtime or in the early morning and reapply it to a glass slide the doctor may give you. Your doctor will then examine the slide under a microscope for pinworm eggs to confirm your suspicions.

Pinworms can be treated relatively easily with a single dose of an oral prescription medication called mebendazole (Vermox). This is sometimes repeated a week or two later. Your doctor may recommend that the entire family be treated.

Pinworm eggs are so tiny (invisible to the naked eye) and so easily spread that it can be difficult to make your home completely worm free. You can reduce your child's chances of reinfection by

- reminding him to wash hands after using the bathroom, or doing it for him if necessary, and keeping his fingernails short and clean;
- regularly cleaning his toys and any surfaces he has touched.

You may also want to wash your child's clothes and bedding or clean his room to prevent reinfection or the spread of pinworms to the rest of the family. But if the worms return even after a thorough cleaning, don't despair. Ask your doctor for another round of pinworm medication (this time treating the entire family if it wasn't done before), keep everyone's hands as clean as possible, and eventually you will be rid of these unwelcome parasites.

pityriasis rosea (see photo on page A30) A common, benign skin eruption that most often occurs between the ages of 10 and 35, although it can appear at any age. The cause is thought to be a virus, but this condition is not contagious. The rash tends to occur more often during the colder months. About 20 percent of those with pityriasis rosea may have coldlike symptoms: fatigue, headache, sore throat, and fever.

Most cases begin with the sudden appearance of what is called a "herald patch," usually on the upper body or the neck. This patch is typically oval, usually one to two inches long, slightly raised, and may be reddish purple in color. More eruptions develop over a period extending from a few days to several weeks. These patches are smaller than the herald patch and are typically located on the upper body, neck, and upper portions of the arms and legs. The patches have a wrinkled, tissuelike scale, and their oval shapes tend to lie parallel to skin creases. This is most noticeable on the back, where the rash will vaguely resemble a Christmas tree—a pattern that is classic for pityriasis rosea.

The rash, which may be accompanied by itching, disappears after a few weeks without any specific treatment. An oral antihistamine such as diphenhydramine (Benadryl) may provide some relief if itching is a problem. Moisturizing lotion is sometimes soothing. While the rash is essentially harmless, sometimes the patches may leave behind a darker coloration of the skin. This is called **postinflammatory hyperpigmentation** and is especially prevalent in African-Americans.

placebo   A substance that has no biological effect in the body. Placebos are used in research studies to evaluate the effectiveness and side effects of a drug.

plantar   Referring to the bottom of the foot.

plasma   The fluid portion of human blood.

platelets   The tiny, disclike structures in the blood that participate in the clotting process.

plumbism   Chronic lead poisoning (see *lead poisoning*).

pneumothorax   The presence of air or gas in the pleural cavity (the space between the lungs and chest wall), which may compress the lungs and cause difficulty breathing.

poison ivy/poison oak/poison sumac   (see photo on page A30)   The most common causes of allergic contact dermatitis among both children and adults. When the leaves of these plants are broken or crushed, they release an oily substance that can provoke a significant allergic response in many (but not all) people. When this substance penetrates the skin, it stimulates the immune system to respond more vigorously to it in the future. The person is now sensitized to the plant, and the next time it touches his skin an intense, itchy inflammation of the skin (or **dermatitis**) erupts at the point of contact. This rash is an internal response of the allergic individual and is not contagious. (However, if the oil from one of these plants has not been washed from one person's skin or clothing, it can be transferred accidentally to some-one else by direct contact. This can give the misleading impression that a plant dermatitis is contagious.) Despite their dangerous-sounding names, these plants do not contain any poisons or toxins that directly damage skin.

Reactions to one of these plants will vary from person to person and will depend on the size of the exposed area and the thickness of the skin involved. (Thick-skinned areas such as the palms and soles tend to suffer little reaction, while thin-skinned areas such as the forearm and face develop a rash more quickly and severely.)

In the sensitized person, a skin rash will break out within a few hours of new contact with the plant. Itching is common and often intense, and blisters may form on the involved areas. There is often an oozing of yellowish liquid, which can become crusted. Contact of the plant with eyelids or with male genitalia may provoke marked swelling in these areas. Areas exposed to less of the plant allergen may respond several days later, giving the misleading impression that the eruption is spreading. In the absence of complications or continued exposure, the eruption rarely lasts longer than 10 days.

Because it takes about 10 minutes for the plant allergen to penetrate the skin, rinsing the affected area with water immediately after exposure may prevent initial sensitization or an allergic response. *Don't use soap, which removes protective oils from the skin and may increase the allergen's penetration.*

Once the rash develops, nothing will reduce its duration. However, if the area of skin involved is relatively small, early application of a steroid cream can reduce the severity of the dermatitis. One percent hydrocortisone cream (nonprescription) may be used, or a stronger preparation may be prescribed by a physician. If the rash is widespread, the doctor may prescribe oral steroids. When used as directed for several days, this medication can help calm an intense allergic response.

Cool, moist compresses and calamine lotion can reduce itching and irritation. Oral antihistamines such as diphenhydramine (Benadryl) can reduce itching, and their sedative action may promote sleeping.

polio   An acute viral infection of the central nervous system with serious complications such as muscle paralysis and the inability to breathe. Polio has been eradicated in the United States through widespread immunizations.

polydactyly   An abnormality in which one or more extra fingers or toes are present.

polydipsia Excessive thirst.

polyp A growth arising from a mucous membrane, such as the inner surface of the nose or the lining of the colon (large intestine).

polyuria Excessive urination.

precocious puberty Sexual development that occurs earlier than normal.

prepuce The fold of skin covering the head of the penis.

prolapse Displacement (usually downward) of an organ or other body part from its original anatomical position.

proteinuria Protein in the urine.

ptosis Drooping of the upper eyelid.

pubis (see page A6) The lower front portion of the pelvis.

pupil (see illustration on page A12) The opening in the center of the iris of the eye.

purpura A hemorrhage into the skin that looks like a bruise.

purulent Containing, or consisting of, pus.

pustule (see photo on page A30) A small nodule, cyst, or blister that contains pus.

pyloric stenosis This condition is found in infants between two weeks and three months in age and is more frequently seen in firstborn males. The muscle surrounding the stomach's outlet thickens so the channel becomes extremely narrowed or obstructed, possibly resulting in projectile vomiting. The infant soon becomes dehydrated and malnourished. Intravenous fluids are needed to restore hydration and electrolytes to normal. Surgery is done to correct the condition.

Q

quadriceps The four thigh muscles that meet at the tendon below the kneecap.

quadriplegia Paralysis and impaired sensation of both the arms and legs.

R

rabies (see Emergency Care, page 767) A viral illness affecting the central nervous system that is virtually always fatal. Rabies is transmitted to humans through the bite of an infected animal, most commonly wild animals such as bats, foxes, skunks, and raccoons. Transmission by domestic dogs and cats is extremely uncommon, and the disease is not spread by mice, rats, gerbils, or hamsters acquired from pet shops.

radius The shorter of the two bones in the forearm on the thumb side of the hand.

rectum (see illustration on page A8) The last segment of the large intestine. The rectum carries stool to the outside of the body through an opening called the anus.

reflux A backflow of liquid caused by a valve or sphincter failing to close.

retina (see illustration on page A12) The cellular membrane covering the back inner surface of the eyeball. The retina contains the light-sensing cones and rods that are necessary for vision and connects directly to the brain via the optic nerve.

Reye's syndrome A rare but potentially fatal illness of preschool and school-age children. A number of organs may suffer damage, but the brain and liver are typically the most severely affected. The most worrisome feature of this disease is **edema** (increased fluid) within the brain, which can cause a dangerous increase in pressure within the skull. At least 70 percent of children diagnosed with Reye's syndrome survive, but they may have neurological defects, depending upon the severity of the illness. Younger children appear to be at greatest risk; very rarely has Reye's syndrome been reported in adults.

Symptoms
This syndrome is usually preceded by a viral infection such as chicken pox or influenza. The exact cause is unknown, but it is believed to be associated with taking aspirin (or products containing aspirin) during the infection.

The following is a typical scenario of Reye's syndrome:

1. A child has the chicken pox, flu, or other viral illness, during which she receives a product containing aspirin to reduce fever and aches.

2. At first she seems to improve, but five to seven days after the beginning of the illness, she begins to vomit repeatedly.
3. After the vomiting ceases, she becomes listless, inattentive, irritable, and delirious.
4. As the disease progresses the child may become confused, and within a few hours, seizures and a deep coma may develop.

Treatment

It is important that you seek medical attention immediately if your child is manifesting the above symptoms, especially listlessness or confusion that follows vomiting. If Reye's syndrome is suspected, blood tests and a spinal tap will usually be necessary to make the correct diagnosis. Treatment is supportive and requires admission to a hospital equipped to deal with life-threatening situations involving increased pressure within the skull and abnormalities of liver function.

Prevention

No one understands why Reye's syndrome affects some children and not others. Over the past several years physicians and other health resources have warned parents not to give aspirin to their children during viral infections (or, for that matter, most other acute conditions), and this has decreased the number of reported cases of this disease. *If your child develops a fever and/or aches during an illness, you should use acetaminophen or ibuprofen instead of aspirin to relieve it.* Check the label of any product you give your child during an acute illness to be sure that it does not contain aspirin. (The label should include a specific warning about Reye's syndrome.)

rheumatic fever A serious but uncommon disease in which an infection involving bacteria known as Group A beta-hemolytic streptococcus provokes an exaggerated response by the immune system, which in turn attacks heart, joints, and other tissues.

Rheumatic fever is more common in winter and spring. In general, children between the ages of five and 15 are most susceptible to it. This disease has become uncommon in recent decades, probably because fewer streptococcal infections go untreated. Across North America rheumatic fever occurs in fewer than one in 10,000 people each year.

Rheumatic fever involves many systems and tissues; distinguishing it from other conditions can be difficult. The American Heart Association has developed criteria that help determine if an illness is in fact rheumatic fever. Usually finding two of the following symptoms (or

one of the following along with other evidence) is necessary to make this diagnosis:

- **Heart disease.** Rheumatic heart disease, the most serious component of rheumatic fever, occurs in one-half to two-thirds of all cases. The most significant problem is damage to one or more heart valves, although the heart muscle is frequently affected (myocarditis), as is the fibrous covering of the heart (pericarditis).
- **Arthritis.** Pain, swelling, redness, and tenderness occur in multiple joints, either simultaneously or in a migratory fashion (literally appearing to move around to different parts of the body). Arthritis results in limitation of motion of joints and the inability to support weight.
- **Rash.** Called **erythema marginatum,** this characteristic rash has an elevated, reddened margin. It typically appears only in severe cases of rheumatic fever.
- **Sydenham's chorea.** This neurological disturbance (once called St. Vitus' Dance) is characterized by involuntary facial grimacing, clumsiness, abnormal movements of the extremities, and irritability.
- **Lumps under the skin.** These nodules, which are not tender to the touch, occur on the arms, legs, or skull, usually only in severe cases.

Other findings that support the diagnosis of rheumatic fever include a persistent fever above 101.4°F, joint pain without signs of inflammation or swelling, an abnormal electrocardiogram, or the history of a previous episode of rheumatic fever. In about 80 percent of cases there will be clinical and/or lab evidence of a recent streptococcal infection.

All the signs of rheumatic fever, including arthritis, chorea, and skin rash, will eventually disappear, but effects of damage to one or more heart valves may last a lifetime. Severely affected valves, which do not close properly during the heart's normal cycle of contracting and then refilling with blood, may cause congestive heart failure, a condition in which a child's heart cannot keep up with the demands of exertion or even quiet activities. In such cases, valve replacement may be necessary.

Children who develop rheumatic fever must be treated with antibiotics to prevent any future streptococcal infection and regular doses of aspirin for two to six weeks to reduce arthritis and fever. (This is one of the few instances where aspirin is used to treat a child with an acute illness involving fever.) Rarely, cortisone is used in cases with severe heart involvement. Additional medications will be required to control heart failure, if it occurs.

Rh factor An antigen (substance that can produce an immune response) present on the surface of red blood cells in some individuals. When present, the person is said to be Rh-positive. Rh status is routinely determined when blood is donated and will be appropriately matched (along with blood type) to that of the recipient. In the past, differences in Rh status between mother and baby led to significant jaundice in some newborns (see *bilirubin*).

rhinitis Inflammation or swelling of the mucous membranes of the nose.

rhinorrhea A runny nose.

ringworm (see photos on page A30) A common and easily treated skin infection caused by a fungus called a **dermatophyte** (literally, "skin plant"), which invades only the outermost layer of skin. (This condition is not caused by worms.)

Ringworm is mildly contagious through direct contact. Poor hygiene increases the likelihood of infection, but anyone who comes in contact with the fungus can become infected. House pets such as cats and dogs can pass dermatophytes to children via direct contact with skin.

Ringworm usually begins as one or more small, round, somewhat itchy, scaly, reddish spots that gradually increase in size. As each spot grows, its center usually begins to clear while the outer rim becomes raised. (The circular shape of the eruption and the wormlike appearance of the outer rim are the inspiration for its name.)

Your child's doctor can often diagnose ringworm simply by its appearance. He or she may scan the skin with an ultraviolet light, since areas infected by some dermatophytes may glow slightly, or gently take scrapings from the affected skin and look for signs of the fungus under a microscope.

Once the diagnosis is made, ringworm can usually be treated with over-the-counter or prescription antifungal medication (creams). Depending upon the type used, the cream should be applied for two to three weeks to be effective. In severe cases oral medications may be prescribed. Skin-to-skin contact with infected individuals or pets should be minimized to avoid spreading the infection.

Rocky Mountain spotted fever A potentially fatal tick-borne infectious disease that is rarely found in the Rockies. Rather, it is prevalent in the tick-infested woods in the mid-Atlantic and southern states. It is characterized by a rash, low-grade fever, headache, muscle aches, nausea, and vomiting beginning approximately seven days following a tick bite.

roseola A viral illness most commonly seen in children younger than two years of age. It is characterized by an average of three to five days of high fever—ranging from 103°F to 105°F and occasionally as high as 106°F—accompanied by very few specific symptoms. A mild runny nose, an occasional cough, a little drowsiness, and at times irritability may be noted, but overall the child with roseola does not appear as ill as the temperature might lead you to expect. (In fact, a child may seem to be in surprisingly good spirits.) After the temperature abruptly returns to normal, a rash appears. Fine red spots or bumps first appear on the upper body and then spread to the upper arms and neck, with little involvement of the face and legs. The rash fades quickly.

If your child experiences a high fever for more than 24 hours, check with his physician, who may want to evaluate him. Typically there will be no findings from examination or laboratory tests (such as a blood count or urinalysis) to suggest a specific treatable cause of the fever. Supportive measures such as acetaminophen (Tylenol) to reduce fever, extra fluids, and light clothing are the only necessary treatment. Since roseola is caused by a virus, antibiotics will not affect its course. The illness is contagious until the fever has disappeared.

Roseola is not considered dangerous, although the high fevers it often generates can be worrisome to parents. Remember that, with very rare exception, the main purpose of cooling measures is to keep the child comfortable. If he is responsive and appears relatively content, the fever can be left to run its course.

In some children with roseola, a rapid upswing of temperature may provoke a **febrile seizure.** This will require consultation with the child's physician to rule out a more serious illness. Aggressive cooling measures for a child who already has a high fever will do little to prevent febrile seizures. (For more information about fever and febrile seizures, see Special Concerns, page 267, and *seizures*.)

rubella (German measles) (see photo on page A31) A mild viral illness, lasting three to four days and occuring in children who have not been immunized with the rubella vaccine. It is characterized by a widespread rash of pink-red spots that begin on the face and move rapidly down the body. Rubella in early pregnancy may cause severe congenital abnormalities in the developing fetus.

S

scabies (see photo on page A31) Scabies has been described by physicians for more than 2,000 years and was the first infection in humans for which a responsible organism was specifically identified. The cause of scabies is a tiny, eight-legged arthropod called a **mite,** which carries out its life cycle on and within human skin. Female mites (twice the size of males) are only about 3/10 of a millimeter long and barely visible to the naked eye. They cannot hop or fly, and thus transmission from one person to another nearly always involves skin-to-skin contact.

The female mite burrows below the skin in a meandering pattern, laying a few eggs each day. After two to four weeks, she dies. Her eggs hatch, and new mite larvae grow, molt, and eventually emerge on the skin surface. The itching and rash of scabies don't begin until 10 to 30 days after the first mites crawl under the skin, since itching is actually an allergic reaction to the mites, their eggs, and their waste products.

Scabies infections are more common in crowded living conditions where there is more opportunity for skin-to-skin transmission. They tend to be worse among those who cannot bathe very often, in which case hundreds or even thousands of mites may infest one individual. (Normally, fewer than 15 active mites are enough to cause symptoms.)

Symptoms

If your child or anyone in your family experiences intense itching, especially at night, you should suspect scabies. In older children, numerous itchy, fluid-filled bumps may be visible next to a reddish burrow track on the hands, feet, face, elbows, waist, wrists, and/or genitalia. In younger children, the bumps appear more often on the upper half of the body.

Unfortunately, burrow tracks aren't always evident without a close look at certain areas (such as the spaces between the fingers or the toes). The severe itching provokes equally intense scratching, which may damage skin. This in turn may become infected by bacteria. As a result, scabies can look like nearly any other skin disease, a problem that could delay the correct diagnosis.

Treatment

If your child's doctor suspects scabies, he or she will examine the rash and may gently scrape the skin of the affected area to examine it for mites or eggs. If mites are found or if the rash is highly suspicious even when mites are not visible, one of the antiscabies medications (usually permethrin or lindane) will be prescribed. The medication is usually a lotion. It must be applied to the entire body, left on for a number of hours, and then rinsed off. Your child should shower and wash his body and hair completely when rinsing. Since scabies is so contagious, it is likely that your doctor will choose to treat everyone in your household so your child does not become reinfected.

It is important to follow your doctor's directions precisely. Concerns have been raised about the possibility that lindane might cause seizures in children, and thus this medication should be avoided in children with pre-existent epilepsy. It is also not recommended for use in infants and toddlers nor in pregnant women or nursing mothers. In addition to the antiscabies medication, your doctor may prescribe anti-itch medication (such as cortisone cream or calamine lotion). Antibiotics may be needed if any areas of skin have become infected with bacteria.

Once the first round of medication is applied, your child is no longer contagious. However, the rash will continue to be visible and itchy for up to four weeks. *You should not repeatedly treat your child with antiscabies medication to stop the itching.* If the itching does not go away after a month, it is possible that your child has become reinfected, but you should not use another round of medication until specifically told to do so by your child's doctor.

Since scabies is transferred through close contact, it is important to treat anyone who has had repeated direct contact with your child. In a few cases mites are spread indirectly via clothing and linens, so wash these items in hot water after everyone has received the antiscabies medication.

scarlet fever A **strep throat** infection with a rash. It is more common in children between the ages of 3 and 12. Its symptoms are often headache, nausea, and high fever. Within 48 hours a fine red rash appears on the skin, leaving a sunburned effect. The rash often feels like coarse sandpaper and is often more intense on the lower abdomen.

schizophrenia A hereditary mental disorder (a type of **psychosis**) characterized by a significant disturbance in thought processes. Symptoms may include random and illogical speech, hallucinations (usually auditory), delusions, and withdrawal into internal fantasy. Schizophrenia is rare before the age of 15 but affects one percent of adults. It is more often first manifested during adolescence. Treatment includes ongoing antipsychotic medication, which can significantly help normalize thought patterns, and efforts to teach and maintain social and learning skills.

sclera (see illustration on page A12) The white covering of the eyeball.

scrotum (see illustration on page A10) The skin-covered sac that contains the testes.

sebaceous cyst A saclike nodule that arises from a sebaceous gland.

sebaceous glands Glands in the skin that release sebum (an oily substance) through the hair follicles.

seborrhea Excessive production of sebum usually resulting in an oily or scaly face and scalp.

seizures *If your infant or child is having a seizure now:*
- Gently lay him on a soft surface such as a bed or carpet, away from any hard objects. Position the head to the side so that any saliva (or any material that comes up if he vomits) can drain from the mouth.
- If his mouth is empty, don't put a finger, stick, or spoon in the child's mouth because this may damage his teeth or cause him to vomit. If he has anything in his mouth, gently remove it with your finger. Do not try to pour a liquid into his mouth.
- Since he cannot swallow his tongue, don't try to grab it with your fingers.
- Don't restrain the child.
- Do not immerse him in a tub of water, even if he has a high fever.
- If you can, time the seizure's length and carefully observe your child's movements during the episode.
- If the seizure lasts for more than five minutes, call 911 for emergency medical assistance. Even if the seizure ends before help arrives, allow the paramedics to assess your child.
- If the seizure ends within five minutes, call your child's physician immediately for further advice.

A **seizure** is a sudden abnormal surge of electrical activity in the brain, with manifestations that may range from subtle lapses in attention to terrifying convulsions. The word *seizure* is well chosen; during an episode it seems as if the affected child's thoughts and activity have been abruptly seized or taken over by a hostile force.

Each of us has a seizure threshold. Given the right (or wrong) set of circumstances—an infection or tumor involving the brain, a low level of sodium in the bloodstream, or a sudden withdrawal from certain types of medications—anyone can have a seizure. But some people, particularly in childhood, are much more vulnerable to this disturbance.

A seizure is a specific event. When seizures occur more than once without an immediate precipitating cause (such as a fever or injury), the condition is called **epilepsy.** The term *epilepsy* (derived from a Greek word meaning "seizure") is synonymous with the term **seizure disorder.** Epilepsy is not truly a disease, but rather a complex of symptoms arising from disordered brain function, which itself may have a variety of pathological causes. In about 60 percent of diagnosed epileptics, no specific cause for the seizures is ever found, and the condition is referred to as **idiopathic epilepsy.** (*Idiopathic* is a medical term used when the cause of a condition is unknown.)

There are different kinds of seizures, each with characteristic behavioral patterns and usually specific brainwave abnormalities that accompany it. It will be important for your doctor to classify them accurately because the type of seizure will often dictate which treatment approach (usually one of the antiepileptic or anticonvulsant medications) is appropriate to control the problem. Details of a given episode can help distinguish a true seizure from events and behaviors that are not seizures.

In the more common **generalized** seizures (sometimes identified by the older term **grand mal**), there is an abrupt loss of consciousness. The individual falls to the floor with both stiffness (or increased **tonicity**) and jerky (**clonic**) movements. Uncontrolled jaw movements may cause injury to the tongue. Loss of control of the autonomic nervous system may cause the seizure victim to urinate or have a bowel movement.

This type of seizure may be preceded by an **aura,** an odd sensation (such as tingling or a strange aroma that no one else can smell) which the child may come to recognize. After the seizure there is nearly always a prolonged state (referred to as **postictal**) during which the child sleeps, is very sluggish, or has transient weakness of an arm or leg.

A generalized seizure is, without a doubt, extremely dramatic. Children seeing one of their classmates suddenly writhing on the floor may literally panic. Parents first observing their child in the throes of a full-blown convulsion are usually horrified and may be convinced that he is going to die before their eyes. But the seizure itself is not dangerous unless

- food or vomited material is aspirated into the airway during the episode;

♦ it occurs in a situation where sudden loss of consciousness would be dangerous, such as while swimming or driving a car;

♦ it is extremely prolonged (more than 30 minutes).

If a single seizure (or multiple seizures without full recovery) lasts more than 30 minutes, a child is said to be in **status epilepticus.** This frightening situation occurs more commonly in children younger than five years of age. If not brought under control, status epilepticus can have serious consequences (including brain damage or even death); emergency medical assessment and treatment are very important.

Absence (also called **petit mal**) seizures are momentary lapses of awareness with no recollection of the event after it happens. The child may stop and stare for a few seconds. In some cases there may be brief jerks or fluttering of the eyelids. Absence seizures may occur frequently and be so brief that they escape detection. All children occasionally stare or daydream, but they can be aroused or spoken to during the lapse. In a true absence seizure, the child will be out of contact and cannot recall the event after it ends.

Myoclonic seizures are jerking or rhythmic muscle contractions involving a few (or many) muscle groups and are sometimes accompanied by a fall. **Complex partial** seizures (previously known as psychomotor or temporal lobe seizures) begin with an aura that may involve a vague sensation of fear, an odd and usually unpleasant taste or smell, or hallucinations. Then comes the seizure, which may involve a minute or more of blank staring, chewing, or swallowing movements or purposeless activity, followed by a period of confusion.

In **akinetic** seizures (also called **drop attacks**) the child falls but does not shake or become stiff. Physical injuries (such as cuts on the head or face) occur more frequently as a direct consequence of this type of seizure than from any other.

Febrile seizures

Febrile seizures are a type of generalized seizure precipitated by a fever. (Because there is a specific reason for febrile seizures, they are not considered a form of epilepsy.) They are estimated to occur in 2 to 5 percent of children between the ages of four months and five years. The majority take place between six months and three years, with a peak incidence between 14 and 18 months. They become less common after three years of age and are very unusual after age five.

The setting for a febrile seizure is most commonly an upper-respiratory infection, although other situations that induce a fever may provoke it as well. The seizures often begin early in an illness, usually during the rapid upswing of a fever (which doctors refer to as a spike). In fact, an infant or child whom you find hot and cranky with a temperature of 104°F is *not likely to have a seizure in the immediate future, since he has already arrived at the high temperature without incident.*

Febrile convulsions normally last less than five minutes (which may seem like an eternity) although rarely they continue as long as 15 minutes. During one of these episodes a child typically will roll the eyes backward, then stiffen and rhythmically shake both arms and both legs. After the seizure subsides, he will still have a fever, but other than experiencing a little sleepiness, he should feel and act relatively normal.

If your child experiences febrile convulsions, first and foremost you should try to stay calm and let the seizure run its course. Panicky efforts to stop the seizure or otherwise help your child may do more harm than good.

After the seizure is over and while your child is resting, take his temperature rectally, then call your doctor and describe what happened. If this is your child's first seizure, he should be evaluated in the office or the emergency room. Further tests may be necessary, depending upon his age, his appearance when examined, and other features of his illness. It will be very important to determine whether this episode was a febrile seizure or a manifestation of a more significant problem. In infants and children under the age of two, there may be particular concern about the possibility of meningitis.

If your child has had a febrile convulsion, he has a 20 to 40 percent chance of having at least one similar episode before the age of five. But only 2 to 4 percent of children who have a febrile convulsion will continue to have seizures that are not related to fevers during late childhood or adulthood. Children who are at risk for this long-term seizure problem are those whose febrile convulsion was more complex in some way—for example, lasting more than 15 minutes, involving only one side of the body, or occurring more than once in a day—or those for whom there is a family history of seizures.

It is important to understand that febrile seizures are not actually harmful to a child, even though they can be very upsetting to the parents. Repeated episodes do not damage the brain or cause behavior or learning problems later in life, and parents need not live in terror every time their child has a fever. For this reason, children with febrile seizures are typically not given ongoing anticonvulsant medications to reduce the likelihood of recurrences. However, after the first occurrence and evaluation, it is a good idea to notify the doctor whenever one takes place. During an illness in which fever is present (or might occur), it is reasonable to give acetaminophen every four to six hours or ibuprofen every six to eight hours to a child who has had a febrile seizure in the past, although this may or may not be a successful measure in preventing one of these episodes.

Four important (and reassuring) facts about seizures

- A seizure is a complex neurological symptom, not a disease in and of itself. It is also *not an indication of an emotional or spiritual disturbance.* If your child witnesses a seizure, he may be frightened, especially if the person is someone he knows. Explain to him what has happened and reassure him that he does not need to be afraid of that individual.
- With the rare exception of an extremely prolonged (more than 30 minutes) uncontrolled seizure, these episodes do not cause brain damage or mental retardation. While it is true that some children who are mentally retarded or who have brain abnormalities may have convulsions, an underlying condition is likely to be the cause of both the retardation and the seizures.
- The vast majority of children with convulsions have normal intelligence and should not be put in special-education classes merely because they have seizures. Most epileptic children will be completely normal except for a few minutes (if that much) during a given year.
- Most people who have seizures during childhood will not continue to have them for the rest of their lives.

Diagnosis and treatment

If your baby or child appears to have had a seizure, it will be important for the physician to know as accurately as possible what actually took place, determine whether any underlying problem(s) provoked the episode, and decide whether further studies should be done and/or medications given. Some important elements of the medical evaluation will include the following:

- *The history.* What actually happened? Did the episode begin gradually or suddenly? Was the whole body or only a limited area (such as a twitching arm or leg) involved? How long did it last? (Keep track of the time because seizures always seem to last longer than their true duration.) Did the child lose consciousness? If so, how quickly did he return to normal? If he is old enough to describe what happened, did he notice anything before the episode? Was he incontinent of urine or stool? Did he bite his tongue or sustain any other injury? Was he ill at the time, or was

there any injury (such as a blow to the head) prior to the episode?

It may be difficult to keep track of such details during an event as terrifying as a seizure, but all of this information is extremely important for the physician who is evaluating the problem. It will be necessary to decide whether a seizure has actually taken place. (See SPECIAL NOTE at the end of this definition.)

- *Physical examination.* This may not be terribly revealing if the episode in question happened last week. But immediately after a lapse in consciousness or in an infant who has just had a febrile convulsion, the physical exam might offer important clues to the diagnosis.
- *Laboratory tests.* The physician may request that certain blood tests be performed to rule out a metabolic cause for the seizure or to help evaluate any infection that might be in progress.
- *A lumbar puncture (spinal tap).* This may be recommended if there is any question that a seizure might involve an infection in the central nervous system, most commonly meningitis. It is more likely to be requested in infants and young children (under two years of age) who have had their first febrile seizure, especially when they are younger than three months of age. In this age-group a fever and a seizure may be the only indications that meningitis is present. While it might sound frightening and dangerous, a lumbar puncture is not a highly risky procedure, even in an infant.
- *An electroencephalogram (EEG).* This study of electrical activity in the brain is a very helpful tool in the investigation of a seizure disorder. It can be particularly useful in distinguishing certain behavioral or physical abnormalities (such as those mentioned below under the SPECIAL NOTE) from true convulsions. Unfortunately, at times the EEG can appear normal in a child who in fact has a seizure disorder.

  The most important use of the EEG, however, is to identify characteristic brain-wave patterns that, when correlated with the child's symptoms during a seizure, allow the physician to classify the seizure disorder. This helps determine which medication(s) will be most effective in controlling the seizures. An EEG involves attaching electrodes to the scalp but does not deliver any electrical shock and is not painful. In some cases the child may be sedated for the procedure, while in others he will be studied

S

after he has been kept awake all night (a tactic that increases the odds of seeing abnormal activity).

- *CT, MRI, or other imaging of the brain.* This may be needed if there is a history or evidence of trauma to the head or any concern about other physical abnormalities within the brain that might be causing seizures.

Not all of the tests just described will necessarily be done as part of an evaluation of possible seizure activity. After a classic febrile seizure, for example, a child may simply be observed for a while in the doctor's office or emergency room and then sent home. Depending upon the entire picture, however, some or all of these studies may need to be done.

If the diagnosis of a particular type of recurrent seizure disorder is confirmed, it is likely that the physician will recommend that one or more anticonvulsant medications be given over a period of time. These drugs will decrease the likelihood of further seizures (or eliminate them altogether), hopefully without interfering with normal activities or school performance. Febrile convulsions are an exception to this approach and normally are not treated with ongoing preventive medication.

Details regarding specific drugs and their potential side effects are beyond the scope of this book but should be carefully reviewed with the prescribing physician. *It is very important to take the medications consistently as they have been prescribed.* Some children may require periodic blood tests to confirm that drug levels are appropriate and that certain adverse effects are not taking place. All these measures may seem burdensome for children and parents alike, but haphazard use of these medications may allow more seizures to occur or increase the risk of side effects. If your child with seizures is taking one or more medications that you feel are adversely affecting his life (for example, causing excessive drowsiness or poor school performance), you should not change the dose or discontinue any drug without discussing the problem with his physician.

Occasionally seizures that are disruptive and not adequately controlled with medication may be improved with surgery. Extensive evaluation and highly technical procedures are required for this type of treatment, which typically is carried out by a team of specialists at a regional children's hospital.

Epilepsy and lifestyle

Most children with epilepsy can lead normal lives and participate in most activities, including sports. Some physicians prefer to exclude children with convulsive disorders from collision sports such as football and hockey. However, unless seizures resulted from head trauma or tended to occur following blows to the head, it is likely that most children can compete while wearing protective headgear. Boxing is not recommended as an athletic activity for any children because of its potential for causing damage to the brain. It is definitely not appropriate for a child with a seizure disorder.

Children with well-controlled seizures may swim, but when doing so, they should be on a buddy system with someone else in the pool. High diving, rock (or tree) climbing, and scuba diving are activities that should be off-limits to a person with a history of seizures.

Some convulsions can be provoked by flickering light patterns, and children with this tendency may experience a flare-up of seizures if they spend long periods of time playing video games. Loss of sleep, erratic eating habits, and alcohol use—behaviors that sometimes occur during adolescence—are also risky for the person with epilepsy and should definitely be avoided.

Of great concern for the teenager with a history of seizures is whether driving will be allowed. Laws vary from state to state, but most require evidence of an extended seizure-free period (for example, two years) before a learner's permit or driver's license will be granted. Medications that are being taken to prevent seizures should not impair the teenager's ability to operate a car safely. It is important for parents to follow these guidelines explicitly. Failing to report an adolescent's recent seizure activity because of fear of losing driving privileges could be a major, if not fatal, mistake. These regulations exist for your child's protection, as well as for the safety of everyone else on the road.

SPECIAL NOTE: Was that a seizure?

Many unusual or even frightening behaviors of infants or children may appear to be seizures, but are in fact other types of episodes. Some of the more common of these include:

- *A fainting episode.* Usually a child or adolescent who is about to faint feels dizzy, weak, or lightheaded beforehand. Several circumstances could precede the episode: a hot and/or crowded environment, lack of fresh air, hunger, an acute illness, an emotional incident, or a medical procedure (such as having blood drawn). Sweating, paleness, and a slow heartbeat are usually present also. Most important, the episode resolves quickly when the individual lies down, elevates the feet, and breathes fresh air. After a generalized seizure, on the other hand, there is a prolonged time during which the individual is first unconscious and then dazed and confused.

◆ *Shuddering or shivering episodes in infants.* These may occur frequently but without any apparent change in consciousness. Often there is a history of tremors among family members.
◆ *Breath-holding spells.* These incidents are frightening but harmless and are invariably brought on by physical or emotional incidents that provoke fear, anger, or frustration. They occur most commonly in children six months to three years of age.

During the spell, the child may stiffen, make jerking movements of the arms and legs that resemble a brief seizure, and appear pale or blue in the face. Finally he will take a breath and very quickly regain color and responsiveness, after which there may be a brief period of inactivity or even sleep. When the episode is over he will be fully awake and aware, not confused or unresponsive as seen after a seizure (see *breath-holding spells*).
◆ *Night terrors.* During the early hours of sleep, a child may display intense crying, thrashing, sweating, and no apparent recognition of parents. After several minutes, he falls back to sleep and has no memory of the episode the following morning (see chapter 9, page 336).
◆ *Tics* or *Tourette's syndrome.* These are syndromes of involuntary muscle jerks, grunts, or vocalizations, which may worsen under stress. They are notable for being stereotyped—that is, the same over and over (see *tics* and *Tourette's syndrome*).
◆ *Staring episodes.* A parent or teacher may notice that a child is so preoccupied that he seems temporarily unresponsive as he stares into space. Distinguishing this from a petit mal seizure may be difficult.

When in doubt about any of these behaviors or any other situation in which an infant or child shows sudden unusual body movements or changes in consciousness, a medical evaluation is in order. Carefully describing the event to the physician is the first, but in many ways the most important, step in arriving at a diagnosis.

sepsis   A life-threatening condition involving the presence of large numbers of microorganisms (usually bacteria) in the bloodstream.

septum   A thin dividing wall within or between parts of the body.

serum   The liquid portion of blood that does not contain blood cells or the protein fibrinogen, which is involved in clotting.

sickle-cell disease   A worldwide health problem that primarily affects people of African descent but also occurs in people of Mediterranean, Asian, and Central and South American heritage. About one in 500 black children is affected, and one in 12 carry the gene for this disease. (Carriers are said to have **sickle-cell trait** and may at times have mild symptoms of the disease.)

The underlying problem in sickle-cell disease is a slight but critical change in **hemoglobin,** the oxygen-carrying protein within red blood cells. Under certain conditions, "sickle" hemoglobin aggregates into elongated crystals that distort the shape of red cells. These crescent- or sickle-shaped cells do not survive as long as normal (round) red cells do, leading to chronic anemia. (This aspect of the disease led to its being called sickle-cell anemia in the past, but this term does not adequately convey the wide variety of medical problems that can result from this condition.) These cells can also obstruct small blood vessels, causing repeated episodes of severe pain, especially in the abdomen, bones, and joints. Damage or functional problems involving bone, spleen, kidneys, lungs, or other organs may occur. In addition, children with sickle-cell disease are at significant risk of serious infections from certain types of bacteria.

Sickle-cell disease is normally not manifested at birth, and the first symptoms typically do not appear until the latter part of the first year of life. However, infants with this problem can be identified by blood screening after birth. Appropriate immunizations and daily preventive doses of penicillin during the first five years of life can help prevent a variety of infections.

While these basic measures substantially reduce the risk of serious disease and mortality during childhood, there is no specific treatment that will normalize the sickle hemoglobin. Therefore, a thorough understanding of this disorder by parents and other family members and ongoing comprehensive medical care—including treatment of pain crises, anemia, infections, and other complications—will be necessary to protect the life and health of a child born with sickle-cell disease.

sinusitis   Inflammation of one or more of the air-filled cavities within the head, which is sometimes a complication of an upper-respiratory infection or allergic rhinitis (see *colds* and *allergies in children*). Any of several types of bacteria may be involved in this process, and these organisms may be difficult to eradicate if there is poor drainage from the affected area(s).

The most common symptom of sinusitis is persistent nasal drainage and/or postnasal drip for more than 10 days. The drainage is often discolored and may be ac-

S

companied by low-grade temperature, coughing, and/or bad breath. Specific sinuses sometimes generate localized symptoms. The **ethmoidal** sinuses—the only sinus cavities developed at birth—may produce pain behind one or both eyes if infected. Infected **maxillary** sinuses, located between the eyes and the upper teeth, produce facial pain or aching in the upper molar teeth. Maxillary sinusitis usually does not occur before the first birthday. **Frontal** sinusitis, which is rare before the age of ten, typically produces pain above one or both eyebrows.

Treatment of sinusitis usually requires at least 10 days of oral antibiotics. Additional measures such as decongestants, antihistamines, and/or prescription nasal sprays containing cortisone or cromolyn may be recommended by the physician, depending on the specific conditions of the infection. In rare cases, severe sinusitis or complications such as **periorbital cellulitis** (an infection of the soft tissue surrounding the eye) require hospitalization for intravenous antibiotics and close observation.

Chronic or recurrent sinusitis is caused or aggravated by a variety of factors including allergies, anatomical abnormalities, repeatedly diving or jumping into water feetfirst, cysts within a sinus cavity, and immunity disorders. Evaluation by an allergist or ENT (ear, nose, and throat) specialist will be recommended in some cases.

sitz bath A bath taken to relieve rectal or vaginal discomfort; only the lower body is immersed.

smallpox An acute, highly contagious viral illness that was characterized by an extensive eruption of tiny nodules that subsequently formed pus-filled blisters. Victims were often left with hundreds of pitted scars or pockmarks. Because of worldwide vaccination efforts, this disease has been completely eradicated. Smallpox vaccine is no longer necessary (or given) anywhere in the world.

snoring A harsh noise produced by vibration of the soft palate and uvula of a sleeping child who is breathing predominantly through the mouth. Not all noisy breathing is snoring. Nasal congestion and wheezing, for example, also generate sounds during sleep, but these are often heard during waking hours as well.

Snoring occurs for a number of reasons, most of which are not causes for concern. One of the most common causes is relaxation of the muscles and tissues in the back of the mouth, which allows them to vibrate while the child is inhaling or exhaling. Since the position of the head affects the vibration of these structures, simply moving the child can reduce or eliminate the snor-

ing. This type of snoring can occur whether a child is breathing through the mouth or the nose.

Children with nasal congestion, whether caused by upper-respiratory infection or allergy, will breathe through the mouth at night and thus be more likely to snore. Over-the-counter decongestants and antihistamines are often not effective in children, but if one of these preparations helps a child breathe more easily through the nose, a bedtime dose could help alleviate the snoring. Unfortunately, decongestants (such as phenylephrine or pseudoephedrine) sometimes have a stimulant effect and actually interfere with sleep. While antihistamines (such as diphenhydramine or chlorpheniramine) usually make children drowsy, occasionally these drugs cause an increase in activity. You may want to give a test dose during the day to see how your child responds.

If a child's tonsils are unusually large (hypertrophied), they may actually touch each other in the back of the mouth. This can cause not only loud snoring during sleep but also short periods of **apnea,** or cessation of breathing, lasting for several seconds. If your child has a pattern of continuous loud snoring and episodes of apnea, have him checked by your primary-care physician or an ENT (ear, nose, and throat) specialist. Tonsils and/or adenoids large enough to cause snoring and obstruct breathing at night can lead to more serious problems involving the heart and lungs. Tonsillectomy and/or adenoidectomy may be necessary to correct this condition.

sore throat In most cases a sore throat results from inflammation of the **oropharynx**—the area at the back of your child's mouth that is directly visible when the doctor looks with a light and tongue depressor. Inflammation of this area is called **pharyngitis,** and if the tonsils are involved the illness is called **tonsillitis.** Most acute sore throats are caused by viruses and are often associated with postnasal drainage from colds. A small percentage (about 10 percent) of all sore throats are caused by the bacteria known as group A beta-hemolytic streptococci. These infections are commonly called strep throats. Chronic throat pain may also be caused by allergy.

Viral sore throat
Most acute sore throats are caused by viruses, usually in the setting of a cold. Throat discomfort tends to be scratchy or raw rather than severely painful and is but one of several complaints, including runny nose, cough, aches, and fever. These symptoms will normally resolve on their own—without antibiotic treatment—in three

to five days, although occasionally they may last as long as one to two weeks. If you are concerned about the severity or duration of your child's sore throat, don't hesitate to seek advice from her physician.

Some special forms of viral sore throat include:

- **Acute infectious mononucleosis.** This illness is seen primarily among teenagers and is often more prolonged and severe than the sore throat associated with a cold. The tonsils are inflamed with swelling, redness, and white patches called **exudate;** lymph nodes (or "glands") in the neck are usually swollen and tender as well (see *mononucleosis*).
- Coxsackie virus can cause **herpangina,** an illness in which painful blisters form in the throat and on the palate. This virus also causes hand-foot-and-mouth disease, in which small blisters appear in the mouth and on the tongue, as well as on the palms and soles. Both of these syndromes, while quite uncomfortable, resolve without treatment.
- Herpes simplex, the virus that causes **cold sores** (fever blisters) on the lips, may erupt in the mouth or throat with a cluster of painful sores that resemble tiny blisters. These occur in approximately one percent of children having their first encounter with the herpes virus and will disappear within a week without specific treatment. The herpes virus is known for causing recurrent eruptions, but these will occur only in the form of the more familiar cold sores on the lip.

Strep throat

Streptococcal sore throats are usually more severe and focused; children have more difficulty swallowing and there is an absence of typical cold symptoms (such as runny nose, cough, or laryngitis). A sudden onset with high fever and swollen neck glands is not unusual. The tonsils may be inflamed, with swelling, redness, and white patches of pus (also called exudate). Occasionally abdominal pain, vomiting, rash, and headache are also present. Strep throat is unusual in children younger than three years of age. In this age-group streptococcus more commonly causes chronic nasal infections with thick, discolored drainage.

When a child or adolescent develops an uncomfortable sore throat, it is important to determine whether or not streptococcus is the cause, especially when fever is present. This may be done in the doctor's office or another laboratory by gently swabbing the throat with a cotton swab and performing a rapid strep test, throat culture, or both. If strep is identified, your child's doctor will prescribe an appropriate antibiotic. In most cases this will need to be continued for 10 days, although some newer antibiotics require shorter courses.

Whatever medication is prescribed, *follow the directions and give your child the entire course of medication, which may extend for a few days after she feels well.* Failure to do so might result in a recurrence of illness. Proper treatment tends to shorten the course of the illness and prevents more serious complications. It may also reduce the spread of streptococcal infection to other people and allow an earlier return to school or day care. Most physicians feel that after 24 hours of antibiotic therapy, a child will no longer be contagious.

Occasionally streptococcal infections are accompanied by a sandpaper-textured rash. This syndrome, known as **scarlet fever,** is treated in the same manner as the more common strep throat and will be equally responsive to antibiotics (see *scarlet fever*).

Allergen-induced sore throat

Many children develop seasonal allergic complaints, especially in the spring or fall. Swollen nasal passages often lead to frequent mouth breathing that, when accompanied by postnasal drip, results in a sore throat, especially upon awakening. The child with this type of sore throat is not acutely ill and will lack fever and swollen lymph nodes in the neck. Specific treatment options can be reviewed with your child's physician (see *allergies in children*).

Less common causes of sore throat

CANKER SORES (aphthous ulcers) When one or more of these develop toward the back of the mouth, a child will complain of an intense sore throat. Other signs of illness are typically absent. Canker sores do not require antibiotic treatment and gradually resolve over several days (see *mouth care and concerns*).

ACUTE EPIGLOTTITIS See *epiglottitis.* Fortunately, this disease has become uncommon because most children are now routinely immunized against haemophilus influenzae type B, the bacteria that causes it.

LARYNGITIS/TRACHEITIS When the larynx (vocal cords) and/or the airway just beyond it are inflamed, a child may complain of sore throat. Usually she will point to the midportion or lower neck if asked where she feels uncomfortable. Hoarseness and coughing (often with a barking quality) are usually present also. If your child is very uncomfortable or has noisy or labored breathing, her physician should be called.

Home treatment for sore throat

Whatever might be the cause of your child's sore throat, much (if not all) of your treatment at home will involve measures to keep her comfortable and prevent the spread of the infection to others:

- Rest. When the child is feeling better and the fever has subsided for at least 24 hours, the worst has probably passed.
- Give liquids of all kinds—either chilled or warm. Acidic juices (orange, lemon, tomato) may cause a stinging sensation in an inflamed throat.
- Feed her soft foods that won't irritate the throat.
- Warm saltwater gargles every few hours may be soothing, if your child is old enough to cooperate. (Mix about $1/2$ teaspoon of salt in 4 ounces of water.)
- Acetaminophen (Tylenol and other brands) or ibuprofen (Children's Motrin and other brands) in doses appropriate for your child's age and weight can be very helpful in relieving throat pain, fever, headaches, and body aches. *Aspirin should not be used to treat sore throats or other acute childhood infections because of its link to Reye's syndrome, a serious illness affecting both brain and liver tissue* (see *Reye's syndrome*).
- *Don't start treating your child with any leftover antibiotics unless specifically instructed to do so by her doctor.* Most sore throats do not respond to antibiotics, and diagnostic tests for strep throat may not be valid if an antibiotic has been taken beforehand. If you feel that your child needs specific treatment for a sore throat, call her doctor for further advice.

Some symptoms require a doctor's examination; contact your physician if your child has any of the following complaints:

- A sandpaper-textured rash
- Drooling or difficulty swallowing
- Severe pain
- Persistent fever higher than 102°F
- Sudden onset of severe symptoms
- Sore throat lasting more than three to five days, especially if fever is present

spasm An involuntary contraction of a muscle that is more prolonged than a twitch.

sphincter A circular-shaped muscle that constricts a passage within the body (such as the junction between the esophagus and the stomach) or an opening leading to the outside of the body (such as the anus). Depending upon its location, a sphincter may open automatically as part of a specific function (such as passing swallowed food into the stomach) or it may be under voluntary control.

sputum Mucus secreted by the respiratory tract; phlegm.

steroid abuse Competitive athletes and bodybuilders of both sexes may be tempted to boost their physical prowess by using anabolic steroids. These compounds are chemically distinct from the corticosteroids (for example, prednisone) prescribed by physicians to treat allergic reactions, asthma, and many other conditions. While some forms of anabolic steroids are available to treat specific medical problems, prescribing them for athletic or bodybuilding purposes is illegal.

Anabolic steroids are readily available to adolescents through underground sources. Abusers of these drugs may "stack" them (take more than one type at once) or utilize "pyramiding" (increasing the dose, sometimes to massive levels, over time). Their effects include rapid muscle growth, increased strength, and endurance for longer and more vigorous workouts. In the long run there are numerous drawbacks for both men and women.

Male users may develop acne, reduction in size and function of the testicles, impotence, purplish skin marks called **striae,** and male-pattern baldness. Women risk developing a permanently low-pitched voice, thinning hair around the temples, enlargement of the clitoris, striae, and increased facial hair. Adolescent users may retard their growth or end it prematurely, resulting in a shorter stature than they would have otherwise attained. All users risk liver disease, elevated blood pressure, and heart disease. In addition, aggressive behavior, impaired judgment, abuse of alcohol and other drugs, and in some cases significant psychiatric disturbances including psychosis (losing touch with reality) may be associated with the use of anabolic steroids.

School programs are now more actively addressing the issues surrounding steroid abuse. Adolescent steroid abuse should be taken as seriously as any other illicit drug problem. A medical evaluation and ongoing counseling should be carried out to address dependence, withdrawal symptoms, and the underlying causes of this drug-seeking behavior.

steroids A group of compounds that are biochemically related but have several physiologic effects. Because anabolic steroids build muscle mass, they may be used—inappropriately and illegally—by athletes and bodybuilders, but these steroids have numerous adverse reactions (see *steroid abuse*).

Corticosteroids, which inhibit the body's inflammatory response, may be prescribed by physicians for several therapeutic purposes. Potential uses of systemic steroids (which are taken by mouth or injection) include the treatment of severe allergic reactions, acute asthma attacks, and widespread poison oak/ivy. Corticosteroids are also prescribed in cream, lotion, or ointment for certain types of skin eruptions; in nasal inhalers for allergic rhinitis (see *allergies in children*); and in oral inhalers for controlling or preventing asthma (see *asthma*). Steroids can have multiple side effects with long-term usage. Short-term usage (less than two weeks) usually has no significant side effects.

stomatitis Inflammation of the inner surface of the mouth.

strabismus Misalignment of the eyes; the eyes are not straight. (One may go up or down, or move in or out in respect to the other. See *eye care and concerns.*)

strawberry hemangioma (see photo on page A31) A bright red benign skin growth consisting of newly formed capillaries (tiny blood vessels) whose color and surface texture suggest a strawberry. In some cases this marking is present at birth, while in others it appears during the first month of life. All typically grow rapidly over the next few months. They usually undergo a significant reduction in size between the second and third years of life, and the vast majority disappear by the age of nine. Consequently, this growth may appear unsightly for several months or even years, but surgical removal is rarely needed.

stridor Harsh, raspy breathing usually caused by the narrowing of the larynx or trachea.

sty (see photo on page A31) An infection of the sebaceous glands on the edge of the eyelid (see *eye care and concerns*).

subluxation Incomplete or partial dislocation of a bone.

subungual Under the nail.

sudden infant death syndrome (SIDS) The sudden, unexplained death of an infant. This syndrome is explained in detail in the sidebar on pages 172–173.

suppository Bullet-shaped medication that is placed in either the vagina or the rectum and is absorbed through the mucous membranes into the bloodstream.

suture A surgical stitch.

syncope Passing out; loss of consciousness. Medical term for fainting episode.

T

tachycardia A rapid heart rate.

tachypnea A rapid rate of breathing.

teeth care and concerns (See also Emergency Care, page 787.)

The debut of teeth
One of the memorable milestones in parenting is seeing the first white nubbin poking though a pink gum line, nearly always between six and ten months of age. This is the first of the **primary** (temporary) teeth, which allow children to chew and speak until the secondary, or permanent, teeth appear.

Between six and nine months of age (or in some infants as late as fifteen months), the lower **central incisors** (middle teeth), the upper **central** and **lateral incisors** (the teeth to the side of the middle teeth), and the lower lateral incisors will erupt—usually in that order. Between twelve and sixteen months, look for the first top and bottom **molars** (jaw teeth used for chewing), along with the lower **cuspids** (the pointed teeth on the sides). Between eighteen and thirty months, the primary teeth will be completed with the appearance of the upper cuspids and the upper and lower second molars.

See Atlas of Body Systems insert for diagrams of the teeth and mouth (page A15).

Many children experience discomfort with the eruption of teeth. They drool more than usual and may try to gum the nearest firm object. Contrary to popular belief, teething does *not* generate a temperature over 100.4°F (rectally). (A baby or toddler with a higher fever should be assumed to have another problem.) Rubbing a finger against the gum through which the tooth is erupting sometimes helps; some infants prefer teething rings. Acetaminophen (Tylenol and others) can help, but topical preparations that are supposed to numb the gums usually do not provide dramatic relief because they don't remain in place very long.

The general order and appearance of the permanent teeth are as follows:

ages 4 to 6   Primary teeth begin to fall out and be replaced by permanent teeth

ages 6 to 8	Arrival of upper first molars, lower central incisors, lower first molars, and upper and lower central incisors
ages 8 to 10	Lateral (side) incisors erupt on the top; lower cuspids appear
ages 10 to 13	Upper first and second bicuspids, lower first and second bicuspids, second molars appearing on the upper and lower gums
ages 17 to 22	Wisdom teeth

The timing of tooth eruption can vary greatly from child to child.

Dental care in the young child

Dental care at home can begin before the first teeth erupt. Infants begin collecting plaque on their gum pads even before the teeth break through them; this material can accumulate on the emerging dental surfaces. The gums can be gently cleaned of milk curds and other food debris using a clean washcloth moistened only with water. After the first teeth have erupted, a small soft toothbrush may be used. Teeth should be brushed within five or ten minutes after a meal. You can use a very small (pea-sized or less) dab of fluoride toothpaste, but if a young child objects, this can be postponed until he is older. When he is using a fluoride toothpaste regularly, be sure that only a small amount is placed on the brush. (Fluoride helps strengthen the outer enamel, but there is enough in a strip of toothpaste covering the length of the bristles to cause eventual discoloration of a child's teeth if he swallows the toothpaste regularly.)

Continue to supervise toothbrushing as your child matures: he starts, you finish. Many parents allow their toddlers to do the majority of the brushing, but if your child insists that he wants to "do it himself," find creative ways to encourage him to let you help. You should continue this supervision through seven to ten years of age, until you are convinced that your child is adequately brushing all of his teeth.

Fluoride taken by mouth is important to the development of strong teeth. To determine whether your child is receiving an adequate amount, find out how much is present in your water supply. If you are breast-feeding, you should discuss with your baby's doctor whether or not fluoride supplementation is necessary. Children drinking tap water containing fluoride in a concentration of 0.6 parts per million (abbreviated ppm) do not need any supplementation. If you have a private well, call your local water or health department, which may offer free fluoride-level testing. For areas in which the water supply contains less fluoride, the American Academy of Pediatrics' Committee on Nutrition recommends that fluoride be supplemented each day according to the following schedule:

DAILY FLUORIDE SUPPLEMENT

Ages	WATER FLUORIDE CONTENT		
	0 ppm–0.3 ppm	0.3 ppm–0.6 ppm	>0.6 ppm
6 mo–3 yrs	0.25 mg	0	0
3–6 yrs	0.5 mg	0.25 mg	0
6–16 yrs	1.0 mg	0.5 mg	0

Conforms to new ADA guidelines for fluoride supplementation.

First trip to the dentist

Most dentists who see children recommend that a child's first visit be shortly after the first birthday, but definitely by the age of three, followed by dental checkups and cleaning every six months. You may wish to utilize a pediatric dentist, who will be well prepared to work on younger patients and will often have an office setting that is inviting and relaxing for children.

The welfare of the primary teeth should not be ignored merely because they will eventually be replaced by permanent teeth. If primary teeth become damaged or decayed or lost prematurely, the alignment of the permanent teeth could be adversely affected.

Dental caries (tooth decay)

According to the National Institute of Dental Research, half of all American children have had at least one cavity by the age of seven. By the age of 17, 80 percent have had at least one decayed, repaired, or missing tooth.

The development of a cavity requires the following ingredients:

- cariogenic (cavity-producing) bacteria, which can produce tooth-eroding acid
- accumulation of plaque on the surface of one or more teeth, which provides a place for bacteria to grow
- prolonged contact between the teeth and carbohydrate food materials (especially simple sugars found in sweets)
- a susceptible tooth surface; while any surface can be the site of a cavity, pits and fissures in the teeth are particularly vulnerable

Much of the pain, inconvenience, and cost resulting from dental caries is preventable through a combination of everyday measures at home and regular screening and appropriate intervention at the dentist's office:

- Regular brushing at home and periodic cleaning by a dentist/dental hygienist to remove accumulated plaque.
- Fluoride, whether as a supplement or as an ingredient in toothpaste, strengthens enamel and reduces bacterial activity.
- Avoid contact of sugars with teeth for prolonged periods of time (see below).
- Along with cleaning, appropriate screening, X-rays, and any necessary repair work, your child's dentist may recommend the use of sealants, thin plastic coverings for the molars that effectively prevent the formation of plaque and cavities.

SPECIAL NOTE: Reducing fuel for tooth decay
While sugary foods have traditionally been associated with dental caries, the primary issue is *how long* these simple carbohydrates remain in contact with the teeth. Particularly troublesome situations to avoid include:

BOTTLE CARIES These cavities of the upper front teeth develop when babies repeatedly fall asleep with a bottle of milk or juice in the mouth, allowing the liquid to bathe the teeth. Once bottle caries appear, a pediatric dental specialist may be needed to correct the problem.

The best way to prevent this condition is to resist the temptation to give a fussy baby a bottle in bed. If a baby has already become used to a bedtime bottle and parents are not ready to deal with the unhappy response to an abrupt withdrawal, a little water in the bottle is safer than milk or juice. Even when a child is in an upright position, the simple carbohydrates in juices sucked from a bottle tend to remain in contact with the teeth longer than when they are sipped from a cup. Therefore, hold off on juices until he can drink from a cup, and work toward weaning him off bottles altogether by the age of 15 months (see chapter 8, page 252).

FOODS THAT ARE BOTH SWEET AND STICKY The regular consumption of chewy, sticky candies and other sweet concoctions that are not easily removed from the teeth increases the odds of decay.

EATING SWEET FOODS BETWEEN MEALS Unless a child brushes after every snack, these foods will remain in contact with teeth for prolonged periods of time.

Discoloration of the teeth
A variety of situations can lead to discoloration of the teeth:

- Trauma to the pulp (soft tissue that fills the center of the tooth) may result in a grayish discoloration.

- Ingestion of excessive fluoride may cause a whitish discoloration. Larger amounts may create a mottled or dotted appearance.
- Tetracycline antibiotics and their derivatives (including minocycline and doxycycline) can cause brown staining of the teeth in children if given to them before the age of eight or if taken by their mothers during pregnancy.

Injuries to the teeth
(See also Emergency Care, page 787.)
About 10 percent of children will experience significant dental trauma at some time before age 18, most commonly as a result of falls, bicycle and motor vehicle accidents, fights, and sporting events. **Dental fractures, tooth loss (avulsion),** and **gum lacerations** comprise the majority of injuries. Because these are often associated with other more serious injuries (such as blows to the head), the significance of tooth injuries can be overlooked. Besides damage to the tooth itself, periodontal tissues can be damaged and need attention as well.

To minimize the likelihood of dental injuries, each child who participates in contact sports should wear a mouth protector. Children with protruding teeth should have them properly aligned. Those with neuromuscular disorders should wear the appropriate headgear if their condition causes frequent falls. Using seat belts can also prevent dental injuries resulting from car accidents.

Orthodontics
Occlusion of the teeth (the way they come together when the mouth is closed) is important not only for cosmetic purposes but also for speech and eating. If your child has an **overbite** (the upper teeth protrude in front of the lower teeth), an **underbite** (the lower teeth protrude in front of the upper teeth), or a **crossbite** (upper teeth over the bottom teeth on one side, and vice versa on the other), and the misalignment significantly impairs speech or appearance, ask your dentist to refer you to an **orthodontist** (a dentist who specializes in correcting the alignment of the teeth and the bite).

Since orthodontic practice now focuses on preventive care, many appliances can be used to mold the bones of the mouth while they are still forming (between ages seven and twelve). But even if your child has passed puberty and is well into his teens, corrective orthodontics can still be done effectively.

temporal Referring to the side of the head.

tendon (see illustration on page A7) The tough white fibrous tissue connecting muscle to bone.

T

tendonitis Inflammation or swelling of a tendon.

tetanus A serious and frequently fatal disease of the central nervous system caused by a potent toxin produced by bacteria known as Clostridium tetani. In an unvaccinated individual, the toxin may be produced in a wound (especially a puncture) that has been contaminated by soil containing spores of this bacteria. After an incubation of 4 to 14 days (or longer), severe muscle spasms develop throughout the body. (The stiffness and spasm commonly seen in the neck and jaw muscles led to tetanus receiving the nickname "lockjaw.") Because of widespread routine tetanus immunizations, this disease is rarely seen in the United States, but worldwide it is estimated to cause 500,000 deaths per year.

Tetanus immunization is typically given to infants at 2, 4, and 6 months of age, with boosters at 15 to 18 months and 4 to 6 years. Thereafter, boosters are recommended every 10 years, or after 5 years if a person sustains a wound significantly contaminated by dirt or other debris (especially animal manure).

thrush See *candidiasis*.

thumb-sucking All infants are born with a sucking reflex; it is both satisfying and necessary for survival. Ultrasound studies have shown babies sucking their thumb before birth; after birth it is quite normal for babies to suck their fingers, thumbs, and even toes! The majority of children give up thumb-sucking on their own as they pass through infancy and toddlerhood. One study found that thumb-sucking persisted in 45 percent of three- to four-year-olds, nearly 15 percent of five-year-olds, and 6 percent of six-year-olds.

Thumb-sucking becomes a problem only when it continues long enough into childhood to cause **malocclusion**—an improper fit between the upper and lower teeth when biting down.

Children who don't want to stop sucking won't. Once they wish to stop, a few simple measures can help them:

- Stop-zit is a substance whose bitter taste can discourage thumb-sucking when it is applied to the thumbs.
- A grapefruit skin kept in a plastic bag in the child's pocket and frequently rubbed on the fingers is sometimes helpful.
- Positive rewards for hours or days without thumb-sucking are sometimes effective.

Since thumb-sucking is an unconscious self-comforting measure, it should not be treated as a punishable offense. Parents may wish to devise a simple, nonjudgmental signal (such as a wink or saying the child's name in a friendly tone and then pointing to your hand) that can serve as a reminder when you see him sucking his thumb. Whether family members ignore or actively try to discourage thumb-sucking, a child will eventually outgrow this habit.

thyroid An endocrine gland at the front of the neck. Thyroid hormone, which is manufactured and released into the circulatory system by this gland, plays a key role in setting the body's basic metabolic rate.

The thyroid gland occasionally becomes either overactive or underactive. **Hyperthyroidism** is a condition in which excessive amounts of thyroid hormone circulate in the bloodstream. Symptoms can include tremors, anxiety, rapid heart rate, weight loss, weakness, and sweatiness. Hyperthyroidism may occur when a portion of the thyroid gland produces excessive hormone. It may also develop when an inflammatory or infectious process damages the gland, causing injured cells to release thyroid hormone into the bloodstream. Treatment of hyperthyroidism will depend upon the underlying cause. Medication may be given to minimize the symptoms or to reduce the gland's output. More involved measures, such as radioactive iodine that effectively terminates the thyroid's activity, may be needed in rare cases.

Hypothyroidism is a condition in which too little thyroid hormone is in circulation. In infants, hypothyroidism is a serious problem that usually leads to mental retardation and developmental delays if not treated. Because hypothyroidism often does not cause any symptoms in the newborn, screening tests are done at birth in an effort to detect this problem and treat it as early as possible. In older children and adolescents, hypothyroidism may be manifested by delayed growth, intolerance to cold, constipation, brittle hair, sluggishness, and a lack of menstrual periods. When supplemental thyroid hormone is taken in appropriate doses, these symptoms gradually resolve.

tibia (see illustration on page A6) The larger of the two bones that comprise the lower leg.

ticks (see photo on page A31 and illustration on page 771) Insects that can attach themselves to the skin of birds or mammals, including humans, and feed off their blood for many hours. Usually tick bites are neither painful nor itchy, so a child or adult is usually unaware of their presence. The amount of blood ticks remove is not significant, but many species can transmit microscopic organisms that cause serious human illnesses.

Ticks vary greatly in size and are usually brown or black. The tiny deer tick that can transmit Lyme disease is the size of a pinhead. Wood or dog ticks, which carry the organisms that cause Rocky Mountain spotted fever, may grow to half an inch in diameter. Ticks cannot jump or fly, so they come in contact with humans only when a person brushes against grass, bushes, etc., where ticks are present.

Once on the skin, a tick can crawl to any part of the body, although many prefer hidden areas such as the groin or armpit. A tick firmly attaches its head deeply into the skin. The tick's body gradually swells as it feeds. Diseases carried by ticks are not transmitted until the ticks have been attached for approximately 24 hours.

Prevention

If you live or vacation in a tick-infested area, there are several precautions you can take. Dress your child in light-colored clothing (which will make a tick easy to spot) and if possible cover his entire body. If he is wearing long pants, tuck them into socks and use insect repellent on the shoes and socks.

While outside, use a buddy system in which two people check each other for ticks. After returning from outdoor excursions, inspect every family member (including infants) thoroughly. Since ticks tend to hide in hairy places, be sure to look through the scalp.

If your child plays outdoors alone, teach him to identify ticks and make sure he comes to you immediately for removal if he finds one. If you discover a tick attached to your child or any family member, don't be alarmed, but carefully remove it (see below) as soon as possible. Remember that disease transmission is unlikely if the tick has been attached for less than 24 hours.

Removal of ticks

Ticks must be removed *gently* and *completely*. Do not squeeze, crush, or squash ticks that are on your child's body. Instead, use a pair of tweezers to pull the tick off with a gentle, outward motion. Do not twist while pulling, because this may cause the head to break off and remain within the skin. If you don't have tweezers, use your fingertip—covered with tissue or a latex glove if available—and some thread. Place the thread around the tick and pull gently. If the head remains under the skin, use a sterilized needle to remove it as you would a splinter or sliver.

Applying rubbing alcohol, fingernail polish, or petroleum jelly to the tick is not likely to cause it to release its grip. Once the tick is removed, wash the area thoroughly with soap and water.

Call your doctor if

- you can't remove the tick completely;
- a fever or rash develops a week or so after the tick has been removed;
- you think your child has been bitten by a deer tick, especially if it remained attached for more than 24 hours.

tics Quick, repetitive but involuntary movements of specific muscle groups occuring in 12 to 24 percent of school-age children. Tics are often hereditary. Common tics include grimaces, twitches, eye blinking, and squinting. Twisting or flinging movements of the extremities can occur. Vocal tics such as throat sounds or other noises are less common. Boys are more commonly affected than girls, and the behavior may be more obvious during periods of excitement or fatigue. However, tics disappear during sleep.

In most cases tics gradually resolve without specific treatment over a period of a few weeks to a few months. For some individuals, however, they can be an ongoing or even lifelong problem. If tics are persistent, severe, or disruptive, neurological or psychiatric evaluation may be appropriate, and sometimes medication is recommended.

tinea versicolor A rather common fungal skin infection that produces patches of flaking skin with varying colors ranging from white to salmon to brown; they are located primarily over the neck, upper chest, back, and upper arms.

tinnitus A noise heard in the ear described as a ringing, buzzing, or clicking sound.

tonsils Paired structures located in the back of the throat that are composed primarily of lymph tissue and are strategically placed to serve as a defense against infection. Unfortunately, they themselves can become acutely or chronically infected, a condition called **tonsillitis.** While any number of viruses or bacteria can cause tonsillitis, two of the most important types of infection are **streptococcal tonsillitis** and acute **infectious mononucleosis** (see *sore throat* and *mononucleosis*).

In previous generations, tonsillectomy (removal of the tonsils) was an extremely common surgical procedure, but it is done much less frequently today. Reasons for tonsillectomy that are widely accepted at this time include:

- Severe, persistent enlargement of tonsils causing repeated difficulty with swallowing, sometimes accompanied by drooling. (The tonsils may appear to touch each other in the back of the mouth [see *sore throat*].)

+ Recurrent **peritonsillar abscess,** a severe infection involving the soft tissue adjacent to one of the tonsils. This infection not only causes serious illness but also indicates that the tonsil is no longer preventing the spread of infection.
+ Recurrent **cervical adenitis,** a significant bacterial infection of lymph nodes in the neck (also indicating that the tonsil is not inhibiting the spread of infection).
+ Suspected tumor of a tonsil, an extremely rare situation.
+ Severe snoring accompanied by multiple episodes of **apnea** (a few seconds of interrupted breathing) during the night. This condition disrupts sleep and is associated with both daytime drowsiness and worsening school performance.

Tourette's syndrome (see also *seizures*) A chronic disorder characterized by a variety of muscular and vocal tics: quick, involuntary, repetitive movements of the face, arms, or legs, or sounds such as grunts, sudden exclamations (sometimes using vulgar language), or other noises. Like other forms of tics, Tourette's syndrome is hereditary. In most cases it is first manifested between the ages of 2 and 15. Stress, excitement, or fatigue may aggravate symptoms, as may stimulants such as methylphenidate (Ritalin) or dextroamphetamine (Dexedrine), medications frequently prescribed for attention deficit/hyperactivity disorder (ADHD)—which often coexists with Tourette's syndrome. If tics are persistent, severe, or disruptive, neurological or psychiatric evaluation may be appropriate, and one or more specific medications may be recommended.

toxin Poisonous substance produced by a living organism.

triceps (see illustration on page A7) The muscle used to extend or straighten the forearm.

trisomy Presence of an extra chromosome in addition to the usual pair.

tuberculosis (TB) An infectious disease caused by the bacteria known as Mycobacterium tuberculosis. In previous generations this disease was a common cause of death in the United States, and it remains so in many parts of the world. Effective antituberculosis antibiotics, as well as public-health measures and effective screening procedures, led to a gradual decline in the number of TB cases and the deaths they caused. Unfortunately, that trend changed after 1986, as the number of cases in the United States began to rise again, often involving strains that have developed resistance to drugs that were previ-

ously effective. Among young people, children under three and adolescents are the most susceptible to infection.

Those at greatest risk for TB include certain ethnic minorities, indigent and homeless people, individuals infected with HIV, migrant workers, and health-care workers who care for TB patients. The most common risk factor for a child becoming infected with TB is household exposure to an infected adult.

In a child whose general health and immune function are intact, contact with TB bacteria usually does not lead to active disease. The bacteria is typically inhaled into the lungs and then literally walled off by an immune response that prevents future activity, often for the rest of the child's life. The only evidence that the exposure took place may be a positive response to a skin test applied to the forearm during routine screening (most commonly during a checkup prior to entering kindergarten).

If the test is positive, a chest X-ray will normally be done to confirm that active TB is not in progress. If active disease is not present, usually the child will be given prophylactic (preventive) antibiotics for six to nine months to prevent disease in the future. If active infection is under way, additional long-term drug therapy will be necessary to contain it. Both of these measures are necessary to prevent much more severe or even fatal consequences such as diffuse and severe disease throughout one or both lungs or involvement of other tissues such as bone or kidney or even meningitis.

Turner's syndrome A female genetic disorder caused by having only a single *X* chromosome, rather than the usual pair of *X* chromosomes. It is characterized by a small jaw, a high-arched palate, the appearance of widely spaced nipples, and a deformity of the forearms that causes the palms to face outward. In infants swelling of the hands and feet, loose skin folds at the back (nape) of the neck, and significantly low birth weight and decreased length are common. In adults it is characterized by short stature.

typhoid fever A bacterial infection caused by a type of salmonella (Salmonella typhi) and transmitted by contaminated water, milk, or foods (especially raw oysters and other shellfish). Symptoms include a prolonged fever, abdominal pain, diarrhea, and (in some children) a rash with rose-colored spots. Intestinal bleeding and perforation are significant but relatively uncommon complications. Typhoid fever is treatable with appropriate antibiotics and supportive care. A vaccine is available for those planning travel to foreign countries where exposure to Salmonella typhi might occur.

U

ulcer A sore on the skin or mucous membrane resulting from the destruction of surface tissue.

ulna (see illustration on page A6) The longer of the two bones of the forearm.

umbilical hernia A protrusion of abdominal contents (usually intestines) through the **umbilicus** (belly button) caused by imperfect closure of the muscles of the abdominal wall, where a natural widening was present before birth to accommodate the umbilical cord. The hernia appears as a soft swelling covered by skin that bulges from the umbilicus during crying, coughing, or straining. The swelling can be gently pushed back through the fibrous ring of the umbilicus.

Most umbilical hernias appear before the child is six months old, and they will disappear spontaneously by the age of 12 to 18 months as the structures of the abdominal wall fuse together and close the defect. Surgery is rarely needed, but it may be considered if the hernia is persistent and still enlarging at the age of two, or if it remains in a child three to five years of age.

Surgery will be necessary on an emergency basis if a rare condition called **incarceration** develops: a small segment of intestine becomes caught in the hernia defect, producing significant pain and local swelling. Reduction of blood flow to intestinal tissue can cause significant damage if the incarcerated intestine is not released. Normally a repair of the hernia defect is also done during the emergency surgery.

ungual Having to do with the nails.

ureter (see illustration on page A10) The narrow tube that carries urine from the kidneys to the bladder.

urethra (see illustration on page A10) The tube that carries urine from the bladder and out of the body.

urethritis An inflammation of the urethra.

URI Upper-respiratory infection. See *colds*.

urinary tract care and concerns The kidneys produce urine and serve a number of important functions, including maintaining fluid balance and blood pressure and eliminating waste products. They are very complex and efficient filters of the blood, allowing unnecessary compo-

nents to pass into the urine while returning 99 percent of the filtered fluid to the circulatory system.

The kidneys adjust to the body's fluid needs. For example, a dehydrated individual will produce less urine, allowing the body to conserve water. The kidneys also adjust the salt and mineral composition of the blood. When a kidney is damaged, diseased, or receiving an inadequate supply of blood, it cannot carry out its filtering functions properly. When this occurs, certain components of blood such as protein, sugar, and red blood cells may leak into the urine.

Normally the clear yellow urine produced by each kidney flows continuously through a narrow, muscular tube called the **ureter** to the bladder, where it is stored until automatic or voluntary input from the nervous system causes it to be eliminated. This process involves simultaneous contraction of muscles within the bladder wall and relaxation of muscles (called the **sphincter**) at the bladder's outlet.

Painful urination (dysuria)
Discomfort while passing urine can be caused by one of the following situations:

- Infection (see below)
- Irritation from something coming in direct contact with the genital area, such as bubble bath or other soapy material in the tub, new laundry soap, creams, or lotions
- Trauma
- A foreign body in the vagina or urinary tract (see *genital care and concerns*)

Any time your child complains of painful urination or if you notice a distinctly abnormal color of the urine (especially a reddish tinge that could indicate that blood is present), contact your child's physician as soon as possible. If a child is having difficulty urinating because of pain, you can help by placing her in a bathtub of warm water and allowing her to urinate there.

Urinary tract infections
Urinary tract infections are common in children but may be difficult to diagnose because of the unpredictable and variable symptoms that accompany them. Infants with urinary tract infections may have fever, irritability, poor feeding, vomiting, or diarrhea. An older child may have the more familiar symptoms of frequent, burning urination but may also have abdominal pain, bloody or cloudy urine, or incontinence.

To diagnose a urinary tract infection (**UTI**) a doctor must have a urine sample. In younger children this may be obtained by placing a specially designed sterile plastic bag over the genitalia. When an uncontaminated specimen (such as in a very young infant with a fever) is needed, a catheter may be inserted directly into the infant's urethra, or the doctor may perform a suprapubic tap. In this procedure, urine is aspirated directly from the bladder through a thin needle inserted briefly through the infant's lower abdominal wall. Older children will normally be able to void into a sterile container after the genitalia are cleansed with an antiseptic solution.

Once the specimen is obtained, a urinalysis is performed. This will include an examination under the microscope to look for white and red blood cells as well as bacteria. If it appears that an infection is present or if there is concern about infection even when the urine appears normal, a portion of the specimen will usually be sent to a laboratory for culture to confirm that bacteria are present in significant numbers. If so, the sensitivity of the bacteria to various antibiotics will also be evaluated to ensure that an appropriate medication is prescribed. (Often an antibiotic is started while results of the culture are awaited.)

A bacterial infection can occur virtually anywhere along the pathway of the urine flow. An infection involving the kidney is called **pyelonephritis** and is a serious illness. Infection of the bladder, which is much more common but fortunately also far less serious, is called **cystitis. Urethritis** is an infection of the urethra (the tube through which urine exits the body) and is most often seen in sexually active adolescents, especially males with gonorrhea or chlamydia.

Urinary tract infections in infants are more common in boys, particularly those who are not circumcised. About one percent of uncircumcised male infants younger than one year old will develop a urinary tract infection, which is ten times the rate for circumcised males. An infant younger than three to six months of age with a urinary infection is also more likely to have bacteria present in the bloodstream than an older child. Treatment may thus involve hospitalization for closer observation and intravenous antibiotics.

An infant who develops a urinary tract infection may have a malformation of one or both kidneys, ureters, or the bladder. After the infection has been treated, it is important that she also have an ultrasound of her kidneys, as well as a **voiding cystourethrogram (VCUG).** A VCUG is performed by placing a catheter in the urethra, filling the bladder with water-soluble contrast, removing the catheter, and then watching the infant void while X-rays are taken. This allows the physician to evaluate the location, size, and shape of the bladder and to determine whether emptying the bladder is associated with a backward flow of urine (called **reflux**) through one or both

ureters toward the kidneys. These results will help the doctor plan proper management, which may include prophylactic (preventive) antibiotics or possibly surgery if a malformation is found.

Urinary tract infections in older children may occur either in the bladder or the kidneys. A kidney infection is likely to cause a more severe illness, with fever, nausea, vomiting, and abdominal or back pain on the same side as the infection. Bladder infections usually cause frequent or painful urination, a sense of urgency (the child feels the need to pass urine immediately), and bloody or cloudy urine. If the infection appears to involve the kidney and the child is definitely ill (especially if vomiting), it may be necessary to admit her to the hospital for intravenous antibiotics and fluid replacement. Infections in the bladder can usually be treated with oral antibiotics.

Girls who have their first urinary tract infection after the age of five are less likely to have underlying structural abnormalities. The decision to recommend ultrasound and X-ray examinations in this age-group will depend a great deal on the circumstances and severity of the infection. Many physicians feel that any boy who has a urinary tract infection, regardless of age (except for an adolescent with a sexually transmitted disease), should be evaluated to look for an underlying cause.

Recurrent urinary tract infections are occasionally seen among children, and especially in girls, usually because of the relatively short distance from the female bladder to the outside. After she has been evaluated for any underlying problem that might predispose her to infection, it is important that a child with recurrent UTIs be followed carefully by her physician, since ongoing untreated infection could lead to kidney damage. The overall recurrence rate for urinary tract infections is about 25 percent for all children but much higher for girls. After two or three infections, a young girl's chance of experiencing another episode within one year is as high as 60 to 75 percent. In such cases, the physician may decide to prescribe a prophylactic antibiotic to prevent further infections. Usually this medication is taken only once a day and is not likely to cause any long-term problem.

Kidney disease

Changes in the characteristics or amount of urine may result from a disorder of the kidney itself or from a problem in the ureter or bladder. Decreased urine production may be caused specifically by dehydration, kidney disease, or obstruction to the flow of urine. There are many types of kidney diseases, but they cause only a limited number of symptoms:

- Decreased or (more rarely) increased urine production
- Passage of blood, which may be visible to the naked eye or detected only by chemical tests or microscopic examination
- Sugar (glucose) in the urine, which is virtually always associated with a high level of glucose in the blood (diabetes)
- Increased amounts of protein in the urine, which can usually be detected by a simple chemical test in the physician's office
- Swelling of the hands, ankles, feet, scrotum, or eyelids (called **edema**)
- Pain in the midback or flank area on one side of the body
- Fever, which may be a sign of infection within or adjacent to a kidney

Increased urine production (polyuria)

Increased urine production can be a normal response when a child drinks a lot of fluid, or it can indicate a more serious problem. Kidneys will produce an abnormal amount of urine for three basic reasons:

- Kidney damage prevents the kidneys from concentrating urine.
- The hormones that control the kidneys' concentrating abilities are not being produced or are not functioning properly.
- A disease such as diabetes causes a marked elevation of certain substances (especially glucose or blood sugar) in the bloodstream. When the concentration of glucose in blood exceeds a certain level, the kidney can no longer prevent some from spilling into the urine. This results in a higher volume of urine and can eventually lead to a substantial fluid loss.

Blood in the urine (hematuria)

Seeing blood in the urine can be frightening for both parent and child. But not everything that makes the urine look red is blood. It is not uncommon to see a small amount of pinkish red, pastelike material in a newborn's diaper. This is usually caused by urate crystals that form in concentrated urine. If these are seen in a breast-fed baby, it may be helpful to nurse more frequently. If you are bottle-feeding, consider giving a few ounces of additional water. Urate crystals will usually disappear by the second week of life.

Some foods such as beets and certain medications can cause a child's urine to change color. You should consult with your child's physician if this occurs.

Blood in an infant's diaper area may come from the urinary tract, from the vagina in little girls, or from the gastrointestinal tract. If you notice blood in the diaper, take the diaper with you to your physician.

Blood in the urine is sometimes clearly visible but at other times may be present in quantities so small that it can be detected only by a microscopic evaluation and/or a dipstick—a thin test strip that identifies a variety of substances in the urine. The following conditions cause red blood cells to be present in the urine, and it is important that the underlying cause be determined if at all possible:

- Urinary tract infection
- Trauma, including injuries to the kidneys or genitalia
- Kidney diseases, including hereditary kidney problems, that leak small amounts of blood into the urine
- Kidney stones
- Blood-clotting problems
- Abnormalities of immune function
- Exposure to toxic substances
- Tumor, which in children would nearly always involve the kidney rather than ureter, bladder, or external genitalia
- Vigorous exercise—running, jumping, etc.

Your physician will examine your child and ask questions to sort through these possibilities. A urine specimen will be evaluated. If a urinary tract infection does not appear to be the problem, the physician will probably do a careful evaluation of the genital area and order special blood and/or imaging tests (X-ray or ultrasound) to help determine the cause of the hematuria.

Obstruction: hydronephrosis

Malformations of any portion of the urinary system can occur during fetal development. The most common of these in both girls and boys is an obstruction that decreases or completely stops the flow of urine. The resulting increase in pressure causes swelling within the urinary tract. When one or both kidneys are involved, the condition is called **hydronephrosis** (literally, "water kidney"). Sometimes this type of obstruction can be diagnosed during pregnancy through an ultrasound. One of the first surgeries developed for preborn babies was the treatment of hydronephrosis by removing the obstruction while the kidneys still had time to grow.

Obstruction: persistent urethral valves

In boys, the urine flows through the urethra inside the penis. During fetal development, small flaps called valves stop the flow of urine. Before the baby is born, these valves normally disappear, allowing urine to pass freely. If the flaps of tissue remain after birth, they can obstruct the urine flow and cause bladder distention. One clue that a baby may have urethral valves is that the urine stream is weak and dribbling rather than forceful. (Most parents of boys have been sprayed during diaper changes, an indication that the flow of urine is not obstructed.)

Obstruction: meatal stenosis
The opening at the end of the penis through which urine passes is called the **meatus.** If the baby boy is circumcised at birth, the head of the penis (glans) is exposed to urine and stool in the diaper. The sensitive cells of the meatus may become irritated and heal with scar tissue, which can cause a narrowing known as **meatal stenosis.**

If the boy's urine stream appears narrowed—a thin, jetlike stream as if coming from a nozzle—or if it deviates to one side so much that he must deliberately aim his penis to keep the urine stream within the toilet bowl, he should be examined by a physician. If meatal stenosis is severe, a urologist may perform minor surgery to dilate the meatal opening.

urinary urgency   The sensation of needing to urinate immediately.

UTI   Urinary tract infection.

uvula   The fleshy mass that hangs down from the roof of the mouth at the back of the throat.

V

vertigo   A spinning sensation that often results in nausea.

viruses   Small particles capable of reproducing themselves but only within living cells. They cause many diseases, some common and some rare, such as colds, influenza, measles, mumps, chicken pox, herpes, AIDS, and rabies. At the present time there is no cure for a virus; antibiotics are totally ineffective. There are certain antiviral agents that can modify, shorten the course of, or even temporarily keep some viruses under control, but none can cure the body of a virus once it is present. Most viral infections spontaneously resolve on their own; however, some such as HIV do not. Vaccines are available for a few viruses that will prevent a virus from causing disease in a person who is exposed to it (e.g., polio).

vitiligo   A skin condition identified by patches of skin that don't contain pigment, thus appearing white.

vomiting   The forceful ejection of stomach contents through the mouth. Vomiting is not the same as spitting up or regurgitating, when a small amount of previously swallowed material (usually breast milk or formula) reenters an infant's mouth without force. Spitting up is not uncommon during the first year of life because the sphincter (a ringlike muscle) between the esophagus and the stomach does not always close tightly or may remain open much of the time at this age. During the first year, the sphincter gradually matures and tightens, reducing the number of spitting-up episodes.

Forceful vomiting is always a significant symptom in an infant younger than three months of age. It may be related to milk protein intolerance and could require formula substitution. It may also be a symptom of a partial or complete obstruction of the gastrointestinal tract.

The most common such obstruction in infants is **pyloric stenosis,** a condition in which the muscles that line the segment of small intestine just beyond the stomach thicken and block the outlet of the stomach. The vomiting associated with this condition is so forceful that it is called **projectile vomiting.** Additional symptoms will include failure to gain weight and a general look of undernourishment. This condition is most common in boys who are the firstborn in their family. It requires surgical correction (see chapter 4, page 153).

The most common cause of vomiting in older infants and children is infection. Vomiting of this type is frequently accompanied by nausea, abdominal cramps, and in some cases fever. The infection may be in the stomach and bowel (**gastroenteritis,** also called **stomach flu**), in which there can be both diarrhea and vomiting. Vomiting is sometimes caused by stimulation of the brain's vomiting center by toxins that circulate as the result of infections elsewhere, such as in the throat, ear, or lung.

Sometimes vomiting is so forceful it produces a tear in the esophagus. In such instances there may be streaks of blood in the vomited material. *The presence of large amounts of vomited blood is a serious concern that should be evaluated by a physician immediately.*

The danger of dehydration
The main concern with repeated vomiting, especially if accompanied by diarrhea, is that the infant may become dehydrated from fluid loss. When these losses are mild, increased thirst and a modest decrease in urine output (fewer wet diapers) will occur. If so, call your child's physician for advice, which may include a recommendation for a direct evaluation.

The following symptoms indicate more severe dehydration and, with rare exception, call for immediate evaluation:

- Constant thirst (in an older child who can express this need)
- Dry mouth and lips
- Fewer tears when crying
- No urine production for 8 to 12 hours, indicating that the kidney is conserving fluids
- Sunken eyes
- A sunken fontanelle (the soft spot in the skull, most readily felt during the first six months of life)
- Skin texture that is no longer elastic but more like bread dough
- Persistent fussing in an infant, especially if it is more of a whine than a vigorous cry

Even more serious dehydration (with fluid losses of more than 10 percent of the child's normal body weight) will be suggested by the presence of these symptoms:

- Cool and/or mottled skin
- Rapid, thready pulse
- Rapid respirations
- Moaning or grunting, or a weak, feeble cry
- Marked listlessness with lack of interest in play or feeding, little response to being handled, and (in an infant) markedly reduced movements of arms and legs

A baby or young child with these symptoms is likely to be in serious trouble and should be evaluated immediately, usually in an emergency-room setting.

Prevention and treatment of dehydration

Your child's doctor will give specific advice for preventing or correcting dehydration, which will depend to some degree on the age of your child and the severity of the problem. Usually some effort will be made to rest the bowel for a day or two while the infection runs its course. Traditionally, this has involved giving the infant or child one or more forms of clear liquids—water, soft drinks, clear soup, clear juice—which are supposed to be absorbed more easily when the bowel is inflamed or damaged by infection. However, research into the physiology of the small intestine has led to the development of a variety of **oral rehydrating solutions (ORS),** which cooperate more effectively with the body's mechanisms for absorbing fluid. These solutions contain specified amounts of sodium, potassium, and glucose mixed in water, can be safely used by infants and children of all ages, and are effective in treating both mild and severe dehydration.

Premixed ORS is available at drugstores in products such as Pedialyte, Rehydralyte, and Infalyte. *It is this type of solution, not the traditional clear liquids, that is best suited to treat acute gastroenteritis, especially in children under two years of age.* ORS may be given by bottle, spoon, or even dropper, usually in frequent small amounts. (If the rehydrating solution isn't flavored, its taste can be improved by adding one tablespoon of Jell-O powder to one tablespoon of boiling water, and then adding this mixture to an eight-ounce bottle of the solution.)

Your doctor will specifically recommend the type and minimum quantity of solution you should give to your child. A typical routine is to give a teaspoon to a tablespoon (depending on the child's size) every ten minutes for an hour and then doubling the amount each hour if vomiting does not occur.

Breast-fed infants can continue nursing but with frequent shorter feedings (for example, ten minutes every hour or two, using one side at a time). If vomiting persists in a nursing infant, the doctor may recommend using a rehydrating solution for a few hours.

In most cases of gastroenteritis, after eight hours without vomiting, foods such as rice cereal or applesauce for infants, or bread, rice, mashed potatoes, or crackers for older children can be eaten in small amounts. If vomiting recurs, oral intake should be ceased for an hour, and rehydrating fluid can be started again.

Vomiting accompanied by significant pain in the abdomen, whether generalized or localized, may indicate the presence of an acute medical problem such as appendicitis. Vomiting accompanied by intermittent abdominal pain and blood in the stool may indicate an obstruction or a bacterial infection. If vomiting and abdominal pain persist for more than a few hours, the child should be examined by a physician.

vulva   External parts of the female reproductive tract surrounding the opening of the vagina.

warts   (see photo on page A31)   Small, benign skin tumors caused by various strains of the human papilloma virus. They are a common affliction of children and teenagers. The virus enters the skin through direct contact with another infected person or with a warm, moist surface (such as a locker-room floor) where infected skin has been shed. Warts eventually disappear as the immune system recognizes and eliminates the papilloma virus, but this process may take many months or even years. If not treated, the virus—and the warts it causes—may spread from its initial location (usually the hands) to other parts of the body or (less commonly) to other people.

Warts come in three basic forms:

Common warts appear as round, firm bumps on the skin with a sharply defined margin and a slightly roughened surface. If picked or pared with a scalpel, they will bleed actively. Common warts are generally found on the hands (especially around the edges of fingernails) and occasionally on the legs (most frequently around the knees).

Plantar warts (see photo on page A30) occur on the soles of the feet, virtually always over pressure points (particularly on the heel or ball of the foot). They can be bothersome or even painful, since a callus can build up around the wart and create uncomfortable pressure, which is particularly noticeable while walking or running.

Flat warts, which are flat-topped and flesh colored, are seen most often on the backs of the hands or on the face, sometimes in small clusters or in a line.

(Genital [or venereal] warts, which are also caused by strains of the human papilloma virus, behave and are treated differently from the other types of warts mentioned here. They can have more serious long-term consequences. They are discussed in detail in the section on sexually transmitted diseases on page 576 .)

While warts eventually go away on their own, removing them when possible to prevent them from spreading is wise. The method chosen will depend on the size and number of warts, their location, and the age (and level of cooperation) of the child. Whatever method is used, it is important to encourage your child *not* to pick or pull at the warts to prevent them from spreading.

Various weak acid formulations, available in both over-the-counter and prescription varieties that can be applied at home, are a slow but painless approach for both common and plantar warts. The medication will work best if the wart has first been pared down to remove the thick outer layer of dead skin. A physician can do this with a scalpel, or you can use an emery board at home (one not used for any other purpose, in order to prevent the virus from spreading). If the wart bleeds a little, don't pare any further but don't worry. This may actually allow white blood cells to interact with the wart virus and speed up the immune response.

The wart site is soaked in warm water for a few minutes, and then a drop of the acid solution (for example, Duofilm) is applied onto the wart surface, allowed to dry into a film, and then covered for 24 hours. A variation of this is the **salicylic acid plaster,** which contains medicine and self-adhering covering in one package. These are usually left in place for 8 hours out of the day. Either format will require 6 to 12 weeks of daily use.

For a more rapid response, your child's primary-care physician or a dermatologist may be able to destroy one or more warts directly. **Liquid nitrogen** applied directly to a wart with a cotton swab feels very cold and stingy while the wart is being frozen, after which the area turns pink and aches for several hours. Eventually a dark blister will form, and the wart will peel away on its own. (Your child should be encouraged not to do this himself.) This method is appropriate for a few warts on areas of skin that aren't too sensitive (such as the back of the hand), but after the first experience your child may balk at having freezing done repeatedly, especially if fingertips (where there is an abundance of nerve endings) are involved.

An even more direct approach in the doctor's office involves a shot of local anesthetic under the wart, followed by **curetting** (scraping the wart out of the skin with a sharp instrument) and then using an electrical instrument to **cauterize** the base. The dark crater that remains must be protected with a small dressing to prevent infection. Flat warts can be managed with topical medications (such as Retin-A) rather than acids, freezing, or burning. This is particularly important when they are present on the face.

whiplash An injury to the soft tissues of the neck and/or upper back caused by sudden, unintended bending of the neck.

W

Musculoskeletal Problems in Children

The human body is designed with an elaborate system of approximately 700 muscles and more than 200 bones. Like all other components of the body, the musculoskeletal system functions very well most of the time, but problems can develop at any age.

This section is not intended as a comprehensive textbook of pediatric orthopedics.[1] Its purpose is to help you become somewhat familiar with the more common musculoskeletal problems of infancy, childhood, and adolescence. These will be divided into three major groupings: injuries (the most common); inflammatory and infectious diseases; and structural disorders, a number of which are congenital.

FRACTURES, SPRAINS, DISLOCATIONS, STRAINS, AND TENDONITIS

A child's bone is generally much more flexible than an adult's. It is covered with a fairly thick layer of fibrous tissue called **periosteum,** which contributes to healing if the bone should fracture. At each end of long bones (such as the shinbone) there is an area known as the **growth plate,** where growth in length and width of the bone takes place. The fastest growing growth plates are the lower end of the femur (thighbone) and the upper end of the tibia (shinbone). Growth plates disappear completely during adolescence.

Fractures

As a child grows, gains weight, and becomes more mobile, falls and other accidents can exert enough stress on a bone to cause a **fracture,** or break. There are several types of fractures.

Nondisplaced fracture. Sometimes a bone breaks completely but the pieces are not separated. Depending upon the location of the fracture, it will be straightened (if necessary) and then immobilized in a splint or cast for a period of time recommended by the treating physician.

Greenstick fracture. If you have ever taken a fresh branch off a tree and tried to break it, you may have noticed that one side of the branch may break while the other side bends. The same phenomenon can occur in a child's bone; this is called a **greenstick fracture.** The treatment is the same as for a nondisplaced fracture.

Displaced fracture. This occurs when the bone breaks completely, and the broken ends move away from one another. This will be treated in one of three ways:

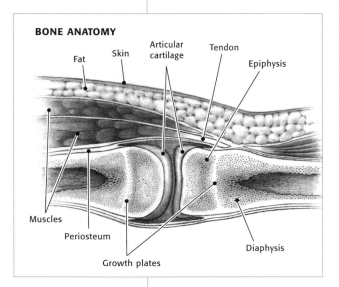

BONE ANATOMY

Fat · Skin · Articular cartilage · Tendon · Epiphysis · Muscles · Periosteum · Growth plates · Diaphysis

- In a **closed reduction,** the child is usually sedated or given a general anesthetic, and the doctor then attempts to move the broken pieces into proper alignment. If the procedure is successful, a cast is applied for stabilization until the fracture heals.

- Sometimes the broken ends of the bone can be brought together, but they are so unstable that they will not remain in proper alignment, even with a cast. In such cases **metal pins** are inserted into the bone to hold the pieces together. This is done under anesthetic, and usually a splint or cast is applied afterward. Depending upon the location of the fracture, the pins will be left in place for a few weeks and then removed.

- If the ends of the fractured bone cannot be brought together by a closed reduction, an **open reduction** will be performed to accomplish this goal. In this case, the surgeon has to make an incision in the region of the fracture to be able to see the bone ends directly. The alignment is corrected and is often held in place with pins or a plate and screws.

Open fracture. This injury, in which one end of a fractured bone protrudes through the skin, is an urgent situation. The wound should be covered and the child taken immediately to the nearest emergency room. Often, open fractures are contaminated with dirt, grass, clothing, etc. The surgeon will attempt to remove all of the debris to reduce the chance of infection. Antibiotics should be given. Usually the wound is not sutured together right away, but it may be closed later if there is no sign of infection.

FRACTURES

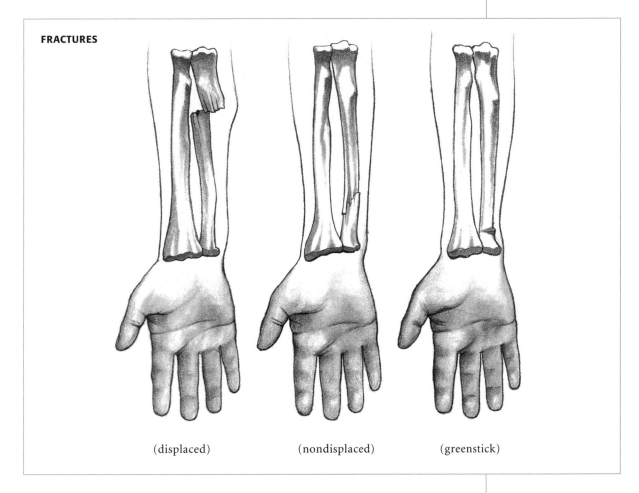

(displaced)　　　　(nondisplaced)　　　　(greenstick)

Sometimes weeks after a child has suffered a fracture, the bone will appear crooked, even though the healing process is going well. Because bone is a living tissue, it not only heals but also undergoes **remodeling,** a process by which the growth plate and periosteum gradually correct the deformity. If you see an X-ray of the same bone years later, you may find it hard to tell that it was ever broken.

Remodeling cannot correct all deformities, however, and the ability of bones to remodel decreases as a child gets older. If a fracture involves the growth plate, a crooked and/or short limb occasionally results, and surgery may be required to correct this problem.

Sprains

To move properly in relation to each other, the joint between adjacent bones is bridged by strong but flexible fibrous bands called **ligaments** that help keep the bones in proper alignment. A sudden, forceful twisting motion can cause stretching or tearing of a ligament, better known as a **sprain.** This will typically produce pain when a child attempts to move or put weight on the affected area, as well as swelling and often a bluish discoloration. Since sprains are more common in adults than in children and since it may be difficult to determine if a fracture is present merely by looking at an injured arm or leg, a child with these symptoms should be evaluated by a physician.

The simple acronym **RICE** can help you remember the steps to take following a sprain:

◆ **R**est the injured area.
◆ **I**ce or cold packs can decrease swelling and pain, but their contact with skin should be limited to 20 minutes three to four times a day.
◆ **C**ompression, such as an elastic wrap around the affected area, can also reduce swelling and pain. (This should not be tight enough to cause discomfort, numbness, or tingling.)
◆ **E**levate the injured area as much as possible for 24 hours to help reduce uncomfortable swelling.

Dislocations

When this happens, the relationship of the two bones that make up a joint is disrupted. In a dislocation of the hip, the ball comes out of the socket. The areas most commonly affected are the shoulder, elbow, kneecap, and fingers. Frequently, there is an associated fracture. Dislocations are best treated by a physician (not by untrained bystanders) and will likely require sedating medication or a general anesthetic to relax surrounding muscles before the bones are put back in their proper relationship. The injured area is usually protected for a few weeks and followed by a gradual return to normal activities. Shoulder and kneecap dislocations often occur repeatedly after the initial episode; sometimes surgery is needed to prevent further episodes.

A common dislocation in younger children is the so-called **nursemaid's elbow,** which occurs when a toddler or preschooler is tugged forcefully by one arm. Often the injury takes place when an adult is holding the hand of a child who trips while walking. The adult may actually pull upward in an effort to stop the fall. This causes the upper end of the radius (one of two bones in the forearm) to slip through a ring of fibrous tissue that normally holds it in place. Afterwards, the child's arm may hang limp at his side, and the child will protest loudly if anyone attempts to move it. Often a doctor can resolve this type of dislocation with a simple maneuver. Normally this quickly resolves the pain, and soon afterward the child will begin using the arm again.

Strains

During vigorous exercise, muscles may be stretched or even torn, resulting in a **strain.** This will cause pain and tenderness of the muscle itself—for example, the front of the thigh following repetitive jumping or a day of skiing—rather than pain in a joint that a sprain would cause. Most strains can be treated at home with rest, ibuprofen, acetaminophen, and gentle ice massage for 20 minutes three or four times a day. If the pain is severe or does not improve after 48 hours, the child should be evaluated by the physician. A child or adolescent who has had problems with strained muscles should be taught to do gentle stretching exercises prior to any strenuous exertion.

GENERAL FIRST-AID PRINCIPLES FOR BONE AND JOINT INJURIES

Some fractures are obvious, and others are suspected when significant pain, swelling, or discoloration follow an injury. If you know or suspect that your child has fractured a bone, do the following:

- Make sure he avoids putting pressure or weight on it.
- Gently splint the affected area to reduce pain and the risk of further damage. For an arm injury, a simple sling or a magazine held against the arm with an elastic wrap will usually be adequate. A leg may be splinted by carefully binding it to the other leg with a towel placed between them.
- Don't try to manipulate fractures or dislocations unless you are trained to do so and you are certain of the nature of the injury. Significant additional injury can occur through inappropriate movement of an injured limb.

- If possible, cover any open wounds to prevent further contamination.
- Don't give the child anything to eat or drink until the injuries have been evaluated and it is clear that surgery will not be needed.
- Take the child to the nearest emergency department for treatment.
- If the neck appears to be injured it is *very important* that the child only be moved by people trained to deal with this type of injury. This is an emergency, and assistance should be sought immediately by calling 911. While waiting, keep the child from moving as much as possible. The transport team will carefully apply a neck brace and place the child on a spine board.

Tendonitis

Tendons are fibrous tissues that attach muscle to bone. Some tendons, such as those extending to the fingers, are quite long. Repetitive use of certain muscles may cause local inflammation known as **tendonitis** at or near the attachment site. If your child's doctor diagnoses this problem, avoidance of activities that provoke pain and possibly the use of anti-inflammatory medications such as ibuprofen may be recommended until the pain resolves.

INFLAMMATORY DISEASES

Arthritis

In **arthritis** one or more joints become inflamed, resulting in local tenderness, swelling, redness, and pain with movement. Arthritis is much less common in children than in adults. Its occurrence is nearly always an acute condition and not the result of the long-term wear and tear that goes with aging.

Juvenile rheumatoid arthritis (JRA)

This is the most common cause of chronic arthritis in children, occurring generally between the ages of three and six or early in puberty. (It is uncommon before the age of one or after the age of sixteen.) In JRA, for reasons not clearly understood, the child's own immune system begins to damage joints and in some cases other tissues as well. There are a number of different forms of JRA:

- The **polyarticular** form involves multiple joints.
- The **pauciarticular** form, which is more common, involves only one or two joints. It may be associated with inflammation of structures within the eye that can lead to glaucoma or cataracts.
- The **systemic** form involves not only joints but also other tissues such as the lungs or heart or the fibrous linings that surround them.

A combination of persistent swelling and pain within one or more joints, often accompanied by fever, may lead a child's physician to consider this diagnosis and order laboratory tests. If JRA is diagnosed, treatment will focus on containing the inflammation for prolonged periods of time. Because it is effective and inexpensive, aspirin is sometimes used on an ongoing basis—one of the few occasions when aspirin is specifically recommended in childhood, although it must be discontinued during any flulike illness or chicken pox because of its association with Reye's syndrome. Other anti-inflammatory medications such as ibuprofen may be used as an alternative, and in severe cases more unusual drugs are given (often under the supervision of a rheumatologist).

Lyme disease

This is the most common disease spread by tick bites. It is caused by bacteria carried by the pinhead-size deer tick. In untreated cases, arthritis may develop weeks or months after the initial infection. Symptoms primarily involve painful, swollen joints—especially of the knees—that become chronic in 10 percent of children (see *Lyme disease*, Reference, and photo on page A29).

Transient synovitis

This inflammation occurs most commonly in the hip and much more frequently than septic arthritis. The child may have all the symptoms of septic arthritis—especially a limp or unwillingness to walk because of pain, and a slight fever—but she does not appear as ill as a child with septic arthritis. Medical evaluation will be necessary to make a diagnosis. If the physician is confident that the child does not have an infected joint, he or she may recommend rest, quiet activities, and ibuprofen.

INFECTIOUS DISEASES

Septic arthritis

A bacterial infection of a joint, or **septic arthritis,** can be very serious and could potentially cause permanent, major damage if not detected early and treated appropriately. The hip and the knee are most commonly involved. The cause may be obvious (for example, a puncture wound from a nail), but more often the source of the infection is unknown. Most likely bacteria are carried through the bloodstream and deposited in the lining of the joint. Septic arthritis may also begin when a bone infection (**osteomyelitis**) extends from bone into a joint (see page 750).

Symptoms of septic arthritis vary, depending on the age of the child. In young infants, the only sign may be irritability until it becomes clear that the baby does not tolerate movement of the affected joint. The toddler might develop a limp and within a short time refuse to walk. She may appear quite ill with a high fever, and any attempt to move the joint produces severe pain. The school-age child might complain of pain in a joint after playing sports or other vigorous activity, and by the next day the affected joint is hot and swollen.

A child who has a hot, tender joint should be evaluated by a physician as soon as possible. If the diagnosis of septic arthritis is confirmed, the joint will need to be drained and washed out. This is usually done in the operating room with the child anesthetized. The child will also need to be treated with antibiotics, which will first be given intravenously. After several days the antibiotic may be given orally.

Osteomyelitis

This bone infection may produce symptoms similar to those in septic arthritis. The child will be acutely ill and irritable, with fever and a sore, tender limb that she may refuse to use. The doctor may do special tests in addition to routine blood work to confirm the diagnosis and identify the specific bacteria causing the infection. Because X-rays taken early in the disease may appear completely normal, the physician may order a more sensitive test called a **bone scan.** This study may identify any area of bone that is inflamed or has been recently damaged. If an area of redness and swelling is visible, the physician may also attempt to aspirate a sample of infected material through a needle after numbing the area with local anesthesia.

When osteomyelitis is diagnosed, it will be treated with a prolonged course of intravenous antibiotics followed by a longer course of oral antibiotics. In some cases, surgical removal of infected material is necessary.

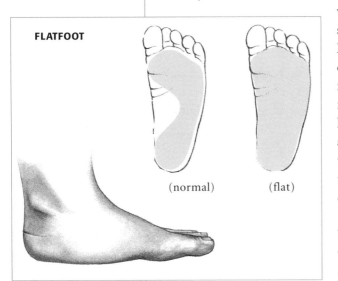

FLATFOOT

(normal)   (flat)

STRUCTURAL PROBLEMS AND PAIN SYNDROMES OF THE LIMBS

Parents are often concerned about the appearance of a child's feet and specifically whether **flatfeet** might be present. When children begin walking, it appears that many have flatfeet because of increased fat deposits in the arch. As a child grows, it becomes apparent that, in most instances, the feet are not flat at all; an arch becomes evident by age ten. There is little justification for prescribing expensive "orthopedic" shoes or custom-molded inserts, since there is no proof that they help to correct flatfeet. Similarly there is no evidence that high-top shoes are better for a child with flatfeet than low-cut shoes.

Children with obvious flatfeet may develop aching in their feet, particularly when they have been on them for much of the day. In such cases it may be helpful to provide a support within the shoe. For some, a good pair of running shoes with an arch support already in place will be adequate. For others a custom-molded insert may be helpful in providing relief. Surgery is needed only very rarely to treat flatfeet and is usually reserved for severe cases that have not responded to simpler measures. Before agreeing to such surgery, a second and possibly even a third opinion should be sought. At least one of the consultants should be an orthopedic surgeon with a lot of experience treating children's feet.

Banana foot (calcaneovalgus)

This is a common deformity found at birth. The top of the foot lies directly against the front of the leg. This occurs as a result of positioning within the uterus, and in 90 percent of cases involves both feet. Fortunately the deformity starts to correct spontaneously after delivery, and gentle stretching can help speed up the correction. These children often walk with their feet pointing out, or turned out more than normal. This will usually correct without treatment.

BANANA FOOT

Curved foot (metatarsus adductus)

This deformity is common at birth and often mistakenly called clubfoot, but it does not have all the features of clubfoot and generally causes fewer problems. The curved shape of the foot spontaneously corrects itself in 85 to 90 percent of cases, and because of this, treatment is deferred until the age of three months. Treatment of a persistent deformity usually involves stretching and casting or using special braces or shoes. In very few cases will the deformity persist or be severe enough to warrant surgery. Occasionally there is an association between metatarsus adductus and hip dysplasia (see page 755).

CURVED FOOT
(Metatarsus Adductus)

Clubfoot

Clubfoot is a deformity easily recognized in newborns, but the cause is unknown in most cases. The severity of the deformity can range from a very flexible clubfoot to one that is very rigid. Most fit somewhere in between. The affected foot will be smaller than normal; the calf above the clubfoot will often be significantly smaller, and the entire leg slightly shorter than normal. These differences will continue throughout the child's growth process. Treatment should be started as soon as possible by a physician who has a lot of experience treating clubfeet. The initial treatment includes frequent stretching of the foot by the physician fol-

CLUBFOOT

(normal)   (club)

lowed by the application of a cast. In some instances the deformity will be corrected, and the casting will be replaced by bracing or special shoes for several months. Eventually the child can wear regular shoes and should be checked regularly as he grows.

In a significant number of cases, the clubfoot will not completely correct with stretching and casting, and surgery will be recommended—some may even require multiple surgeries. Surgical correction in most cases results in nearly normal function of the foot, although some stiffness and discomfort may occur, especially after vigorous activity.

High-arched foot (cavus)

This condition may be an indication of an underlying disease. If your child's feet appear normal during childhood but develop high arches in later childhood or adolescence, have him assessed by a physician, who will look carefully for evidence of a neurologic problem.

Bunions (hallux valgus)

HIGH ARCH

Bunions can occur in older children and adolescents. Often the appearance of the deformity and the pain that accompanies it bring an adolescent to the doctor. In some cases finding shoes that are wide enough to fit comfortably is difficult. Occasionally, a **foot orthosis** (such as an arch support) may help slow down the deformity's development, but usually acceptable correction is achieved only through surgery. While surgery is successful much of the time, sometimes subsequent surgeries become necessary. If pain is tolerable and appropriate footwear can be found, it is best to postpone surgery as long as possible. There is a very high recurrence rate after surgery for this deformity in an adolescent. The likelihood of recurrence declines as the adolescent becomes an adult.

Heel pain

Often seen in very active children, heel pain probably represents an "overuse" syndrome. One of the most common causes is **Sever's disease,** which occurs where the Achilles tendon attaches to the heel bone. The heel is often quite tender to the touch at this site. In most instances, restricting activities that cause the greatest discomfort, as well as an exercise program to stretch the heel cord, and heel cups added inside the shoes, are of greatest benefit. Icing the heel before and after activity can also help. Very rarely is it necessary to immobilize the leg in a cast. Surgery does not help this problem. In most cases this condition disappears on its own in ten to twelve weeks.

Knee pain and disorders

Knee pain is a common complaint in children and adolescents. A number of conditions can cause this, including significant hip problems that produce pain near the knee. (See "Slipped capital femoral epiphysis," page 757). Most often pain in the knee occurs during activity rather than when the knee is at rest.

Pain in the region of the kneecap is very common in teenage girls, although the underlying cause is often not clear. Frequently the best approach is to start a program of thigh-muscle (quadriceps) strengthening and hamstring-stretching exercises with occasional use of a nonsteroidal, anti-inflammatory drug. Sometimes it's advisable to restrict participation in physical education and sports until the pain resolves.

An extremely tender area, often with an obvious bump, may be present about an inch below the kneecap where the large tendon from the kneecap attaches to the shinbone. This condition is known as **Osgood-Schlatter's disease** and is similar to Sever's disease of the heel. It is best treated by rest, application of ice packs, ibuprofen, thigh exercises, and, rarely, immobilization. This condition usually resolves on its own as the child passes through adolescence.

BOWLEG (Genu Varum)

KNOCK KNEE (Valgum)

A condition called **osteochondritis dissecans,** which produces a softening of bone under the cartilage, can cause pain deep within the knee. With restriction of running and jumping activities, this condition usually heals slowly on its own. Occasionally, the affected area of bone and/or cartilage separates partially or completely from the rest of the bone and requires surgery.

If your child complains of a sore swollen knee, has no history of injury or infection, and the symptoms persist for several weeks without improvement, he may have juvenile rheumatoid arthritis (see page 748).

As children grow, their legs usually progressively change in shape. Toddlers are most commonly quite **bowlegged.** Between the ages of two and eight, children typically appear **knock-kneed** and may become more so during this period. After the age of eight, the legs gradually become more straight, although they don't always correct completely.

If your child's legs seem excessively crooked and don't seem to be following the basic pattern described above, it is important that you consult your child's doctor. Occasionally, severe bowlegs or knock-knees are signs of underlying disease. Leg braces have not proven very effective in correcting these deformities, and surgery becomes necessary in some cases.

In-toeing, out-toeing, and toe-walking

A common reason for a child to be brought to an orthopedic surgeon is to be evaluated for **in-toeing** (or a pigeon-toed appearance of the feet), which occurs in 10 percent of children between the ages of two and five. The complaint most frequently expressed by parents is that the child seems to trip and fall a lot.

The source of in-toeing varies. Younger children may have a curved deformity of their feet (metatarsus adductus, see page 751) that gives the appearance of in-toeing. Children most commonly in-toe because they have a **torsion** or twist in the tibia (shinbone) or the femur (thighbone) or sometimes both. Torsion of the tibia is usually responsible for in-toeing in a child younger than age two or three. If the problem begins when the child is over age three, the location of the torsion is more often in the femur.

Most in-toeing will correct on its own. A slight degree of persistent in-toeing is not a serious problem. (Some of the fastest runners in the world have this condition.) There is no clear evidence that persistent in-toeing leads to increased incidence of degenerative arthritis in the hip in adulthood. Several methods have been used in children to try to correct torsional problems, including wedges on the sides of the shoes, braces, various night splints, and casting. There is little evidence that any of these methods directly improves the degree of in-toeing.

Many children toe out when they start to stand. In most children this condition will also correct itself in time. A persistent **out-toeing** deformity is much less common than in-toeing. If the problem is severe, it may require corrective surgery.

Occasionally a child will continue **toe-walking** (walking on tiptoes, which is often seen when a toddler is learning to walk) through the first few years of life or even later into the school years. This usually results from one of the following:

- A persistent habit, which can be altered by having the child practice a normal gait
- Congenital tight heel cords, which may need gentle stretching
- Cerebral palsy, in which case other manifestations of this disorder will be present as well

If your child toe-walks all or most of the time, your physician or an orthopedist can evaluate his gait and recommend an appropriate approach for correcting it.

Growing pains

Children commonly experience growing pains. A typical scenario is that of a healthy five-year-old who is very active during the day and has no noticeable problems. He goes to bed but sometime later awakens, screaming about pain in one leg or occasionally in both. (The pain might develop before he falls asleep.) There is no history of injury, and the child is not sick. The parents do what they can—rubbing the leg, applying heat, giving him a warm bath or a pain reliever—and in 30 to 60 minutes the pain resolves and the child goes back to sleep. In the morning it appears that nothing has happened. There is no pain, limp, or any other evidence of a problem. This may recur frequently, at which point the child is taken to the doctor, who can find absolutely nothing wrong with him. The physician says the child has **growing pains.**

Nobody really knows what causes these pains, nor does there appear to be any way to prevent them. The pain is reasonably short-lived, and there are no long-term consequences. The best advice is to be patient because the pains will eventually stop.

On the other hand, if a child screams with pain at night and then limps and complains of pain during the day, he needs to be evaluated by a physician.

Dislocated hip

A physician may uncover some form of unstable hip in an infant shortly after birth. If the hip is completely out of place, it is **dislocated.** Sometimes the hip is in its proper position, but with a little pressure it can be moved out of joint and then back into place. This hip is called **dislocatable.** In other instances, the hip-joint socket is too shallow, in which case the hip is called **dysplastic.**

The most serious infant hip problem is a dislocated hip, which should be diagnosed and treated as soon as possible. Generally a splint, harness, or cast will be required for several weeks, with frequent progress checks by the physician.

The most common problem is a dislocatable hip. In many cases, it corrects itself within a few days. If the problem is detected at birth, the physician may decide to use some form of splint, harness, or brace to hold the hips in the best position for healing. In most cases, the hip will eventually develop normally.

A dysplastic hip can be extremely difficult to diagnose, even in the most experienced hands. It may become apparent only after the hip eventually dislocates. In milder forms it may not become apparent for many years and then manifest itself as a painful hip with early arthritis.

Some babies' hips will appear normal during the examination at birth but will later dislocate. You may notice when changing the baby's diaper that you cannot spread one leg as far as the other. This should be pointed out to the doctor. An X-ray or sonogram will probably be performed, and if a dislocated hip is found, treatment will begin.

PIGEON TOES

(internal femoral rotation)   (internal tibial rotation)

Occasionally a dislocated hip will not be diagnosed until the child begins to walk. The child may be observed walking on tiptoes on one leg, which will appear shorter than the other. See a doctor immediately; an X-ray will probably be taken. The older the child is before the diagnosis is made, the more likely that surgery will be required to replace the hip back in the socket.

Legg-Calvé-Perthes Disease

This occurs in children as young as eighteen months and as old as fourteen years of age, with a peak incidence between ages four and seven. The condition develops when, for reasons that are uncertain, the blood supply to the ball-shaped head of the femur (thighbone) is interrupted. As a result, part or all of the head of the femur dies. At first there may be little or no indication of this. Over time, however, the hip will begin to hurt, causing the child to limp and decrease movement of the hip joint. An X-ray of the hip usually confirms the diagnosis.

While the body is removing the dead bone and replacing it with new live bone, the tissue at the head of the femur is somewhat soft and pliable. This tissue can become deformed, and if uncorrected, the deformity can become permanent as the soft tissue transforms to bone.

Once Legg-Calvé-Perthes Disease is diagnosed, treatment focuses on keeping the ball of the femur positioned properly in the hip socket and moving the hip as much as possible to help mold the pliable tissue into the appropriate round shape. Casting, bracing, exercise, and surgery may be used.

Slipped capital femoral epiphysis

This most commonly occurs in overweight teenage boys, but it can occur in girls as well. The ball of the hip joint gradually slides off the neck of the femur (thighbone) and through the growth plate. The child will begin to experience groin pain or sometimes knee pain, which worsens with activity. One foot may turn out more than the other when the child walks. Diagnosis and treatment must be carried out as early as possible. If there are delays, the ball of the hip may slide further off the neck, making the prognosis worse. Sometimes a fall causes further slippage, in which case pain is usually more severe. In either case, surgical treatment is necessary.

SLIPPED CAPITAL FEMORAL EPIPHYSIS (normal hip) (abnormal hip)

A final note about pain and limping

From time to time, a child may complain that an arm or leg hurts and then become absorbed in play without any apparent discomfort. If so, it is reasonable to wait and watch for further reports of pain. However, any complaint about pain in a particular area that lasts for more than a day or two should be investigated by a physician. In a child of any age *a limp or unwillingness to walk because of leg pain may indicate a significant problem and should be reported to the doctor immediately.*

PROBLEMS INVOLVING THE NECK AND BACK

Torticollis is sometimes referred to as "wry neck." The child's head is tilted to one side with the face turned slightly to the other side. When it occurs during infancy, torticollis is usually not visible at birth but appears a week or so later. The cause is not clear but the problem is usually an excessive tightness in one of the neck muscles. The treatment is usually a careful stretching program. In many cases the deformity will correct with this treatment. If the problem is ignored until the child is older than one year, a stretching program is not likely to be effective, and surgery is usually necessary.

A similar condition may develop acutely in an older child, and it will typically disappear over a few days. Rest, local heat, pain relievers, and possibly physical therapy may be helpful once a physician has confirmed the diagnosis. There are a number of possible causes of this condition, including inflammation or infection in the neck and throat, as well as injury. It is important to have the child checked by a physician to make a diagnosis and initiate appropriate treatment.

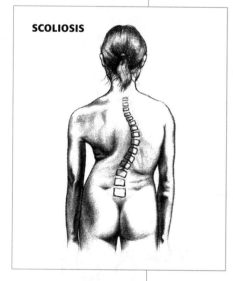

SCOLIOSIS

Scoliosis is an abnormal curvature (usually sideways) of the spine, most commonly seen in adolescent girls but occasionally found in boys. The cause of this curvature is not known, but it seems to be associated with the growth spurt that takes place around puberty. Often the problem is picked up in school screening programs when the child bends forward at the hips while the examiner looks along the spine. If the ribs on one side appear higher than those on the other, scoliosis may be present. An X-ray is the best way to confirm the presence of a spinal curvature, from which the doctors can measure the degree of curvature.

Usually more than one curve is present. One of the curves is considered the main or primary curve, and the other is called the compensatory or secondary curve. If the primary curve is less than 25 degrees, the child is watched carefully, and an X-ray is usually taken every six months during the growth spurt. Curves greater than 25 degrees may require a brace to prevent the curve from worsening. (It is not intended to reduce the size of the curve.) Bracing is not always effective, however, and sometimes the curve continues to worsen. If the curve exceeds 40 to 50 degrees, surgery is usually recommended. The surgery is designed to decrease the size of the curve and fuse the spine to prevent the curve from increasing again. Steel rods are usually inserted along the spine to hold it straighter while the fusion becomes solid. After the fusion is solid (usually twelve months or more after surgery), the child can return to most activities.

Kyphosis (or "roundback") is an accentuation of the normal curvature of the upper (thoracic) spine. Usually this is first noted during early adolescence (between ages ten and fifteen) and often simply results from bad posture. More severe cases are associated with wedge-shaped vertebrae, a condition known as **Scheuermann's disease.** This is treated with an approach similar to that taken with scoliosis. If the deformity is less than 45 degrees the child is taught specific exercises and watched carefully. If the curve is between 45 and 70 degrees, bracing is used. Once the curve exceeds 70 degrees, surgery is usually needed to correct it.

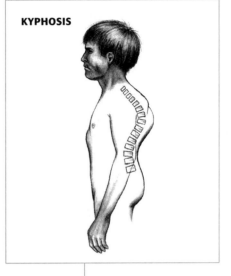

KYPHOSIS

Unlike back pain in adults, **back pain in children** normally should not be assumed to be the by-product of a mechanical strain (simple wear and tear) of ligaments and muscles, unless there is a particular injury that might explain it. *Ongoing back pain in a child or adolescent usually has a specific cause, such as inflammation, structural abnormality, infection, or (rarely) tumor, and should be thoroughly assessed by a physician.*

One of the more common causes of back pain in children is **spondylolysis,** a bony defect in a vertebra that may allow it to slide forward onto the one below it (a condition called **spondylolisthesis).** Treatment is directed toward relieving symptoms and may include rest, anti-inflammatory medication, and perhaps bracing. If pain persists despite conservative treatment or if the gradual slipping of one vertebra onto the other worsens, surgery may be necessary to stabilize that short segment of the spine.

NOTES
l. **Orthopedics** (a term derived from the Greek words for "correct" and "child") is the surgical specialty that deals with problems of the musculoskeletal system. Its practitioners, known as **orthopedists** or **orthopedic surgeons,** have completed a number of years of training in this field following graduation from medical school. Physicians who specialize in metabolic and inflammatory bone, joint, and muscle disorders that are not treated surgically (for example, arthritis syndromes) are called **rheumatologists.**

Emergency Care

TABLE OF CONTENTS

IF YOU DIAL 911 . . .

- Tell the dispatcher that you have a medical emergency, and then state briefly what has happened (including the age of the child), where you are, and the number from which you are calling.
- *Stay on the line* so you can answer any questions the dispatcher might ask. He or she may also give you specific instructions for emergency care prior to the arrival of emergency personnel. Do not hang up until the dispatcher indicates it is time to do so. (He or she should hang up first.)
- If it is nighttime, turn on your outside lights—especially those that illuminate your address.
- If possible, have someone stand outside to direct the emergency personnel to the victim.

THE MEDICINE CABINET

- appropriate thermometer for age. Know how to read it. (See "When your child has a fever," page 267.)
- petroleum jelly (Vaseline)
- antiseptic wipes
- Band-Aids and gauze pads with adhesive tape for cuts and scrapes
- Steri-strips or butterfly closures
- antibacterial ointment
- elastic (Ace) bandages: 2-inch width for children under 12 months; 3-inch width for

children ages 1 to 5; 4-inch width for children over age 5

- Popsicle stick for finger splinting
- acetaminophen drops, liquid, or chewables, appropriate for age (Tylenol and other brands)
- ibuprofen liquid or tablets, appropriate for age (Children's Advil, Children's Motrin, and others)
- instant cold packs (small plastic bags that become cold when squeezed to mix the chemicals inside them)
- tweezers

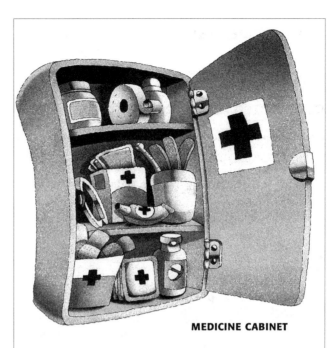

MEDICINE CABINET

FIRST AID KIT

Prepare a first aid kit for each car and a smaller version for hiking or biking. Include the following items:

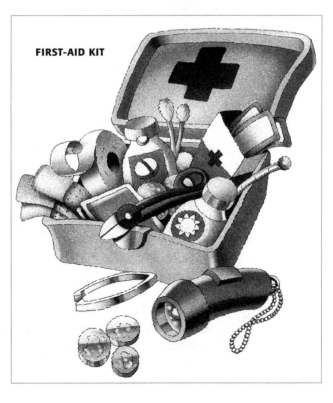

FIRST-AID KIT

- antiseptic wipes for cleaning cuts
- antibacterial ointment
- Band-Aids
- gauze pads and adhesive tape for larger scrapes
- sunblock
- instant cold pack
- elastic bandage—3-inch width
- acetaminophen (Tylenol) or ibuprofen (Children's Advil, Children's Motrin, or others)
- tweezers
- Steri-strips or butterfly closures
- money for a phone call

Emergencies *(listed alphabetically)*

ALLERGIC REACTIONS   *See also* Allergies in Children, Reference.

GENERALIZED ALLERGIC REACTIONS

Generalized allergic reactions can vary greatly in severity, from mild itching to life-threatening anaphylaxis, and may occur in response to:

- foods (especially strawberries, nuts, chocolate, shellfish)
- medications
- substances called **contrast materials** that are injected into the body during certain X-ray procedures
- insect stings

Symptoms   **of mild reactions**

- rash—typically scattered widely over the body. Raised, itchy welts called **hives** are a common manifestation of a generalized allergic reaction.
- generalized itching

Symptoms   **of moderate reactions**

- All of the above, and
- swelling of the face, tongue, or throat
- wheezing/coughing
- light-headedness

Symptoms   **of anaphylaxis (anaphylactic shock)**

In the more severe, life-threatening reaction known as **anaphylaxis,** these symptoms may develop very rapidly and be very intense. In addition to the above, the following may occur:

- difficulty swallowing or breathing
- nausea/vomiting
- abdominal cramps
- sudden drop in blood pressure, manifested by pale, clammy skin; altered consciousness or unconsciousness; and rapid, weak pulse

Anaphylaxis may lead to cardiac arrest and death if not treated promptly.

Treatment

For mild reactions:

- Use antihistamines—especially diphenhydramine (Benadryl and others) or clemastine (Tavist)—to help relieve itching, swelling, and hives.
- Lie down if feeling light-headed.
- If you think the reaction involves a medication, withhold further doses until you consult your child's physician.
- When a drug reaction (of any kind—see below) has occurred, remind your child's doctor during the next office visit to ensure that the information about the reaction is recorded on the child's permanent medical record.

Treatment

For moderate reactions:

- All of the above. In addition, contact your child's physician immediately or go to the nearest emergency room.

Treatment

For severe reactions (those involving rapid swelling of face/throat/tongue or difficulty breathing):

- Call 911.
- If the child has been bitten, stung, or has ingested a substance, any of which have caused severe reactions *in the past,* call 911, even before symptoms are evident.
- Try to keep yourself and your child calm.
- If the child is wheezing and has an inhaler available that is intended for acute (not maintenance, such as Serevent) treatment of wheezing, have him use it as directed.
- If the child has an emergency kit (for example, EpiPen or Ana-Kit) containing syringes prefilled with epinephrine (adrenalin), follow the instructions for giving this injection.
- Check the ABCs—airway, breathing, and circulation. If necessary, begin CPR (see page 806).
- If the episode follows a bee sting, remove the stinger. Scrape it off with a credit card or other flat object—*do not use tweezers, since this may squeeze more venom into the skin.*
- If the child feels faint, have him lie down on a flat surface, cover him with a blanket or a coat, and elevate his feet 8 to 12 inches (to help maintain his blood pressure).
- DO NOT elevate the head if there is a breathing problem; this may aggravate a blockage of the airway.
- After your child has had an anaphylactic reaction, talk to his doctor about obtaining emergency treatment kits containing an injection of epinephrine (for example, EpiPen or Ana-Kit) that can partially or

completely reverse the reaction. These should be available at home, in the car, and in the gear taken on camping trips or other outings.

◆ A child who has had an anaphylactic reaction should wear a medical ID tag with this information, especially if he may need an emergency injection of epinephrine.

A child can have an allergic reaction to a substance that has never caused problems before, even with many prior contacts. If a reaction occurs, every reasonable effort should be made to prevent contact with that substance in the future because reactions that were initially mild can become more severe with further exposure.

ALLERGIC REACTION OR DRUG SIDE EFFECT?

Some children (and adults) experience side effects from over-the-counter (OTC) or prescription medications. Examples of common side effects are drowsiness with many antihistamines, nausea and/or diarrhea from certain antibiotics, and dry mouth from some forms of antidepressants. These reactions can vary considerably from person to person, and over time they can also change in a given individual using the same drug. Usually the potential side effects of a medication are listed on the label of an OTC drug. For prescription drugs, the physician will often review possible side effects, or the effects will be noted by the pharmacist when the prescription is filled.

Side effects are not the same as allergic reactions, which involve a specific response of the immune system. Distinguishing between side effects and allergic reactions is important: if a true allergic reaction has occurred, repeated doses of the same or a related drug might cause a more serious reaction in the future. By contrast, side effects may or may not occur if the drug is taken in the future. Sometimes a symptom that might seem like a drug reaction actually has no relationship to the medication, and the timing of its appearance is purely coincidental. Deciding whether or not a drug has caused a particular problem and whether it may be safely taken in the future can often be difficult and should be discussed with your child's physician.

BITES AND STINGS

ANIMAL BITES

Treatment

If your child has been bitten by any animal, wild or domestic, do the following:

◆ Clean the wound at once with water and mild soap.
◆ If the wound is severe—with large tears or perforations, handle it as you would any large wound (see Wounds and Wound Care).
◆ Contact your child's doctor as soon as possible.

CONCERNS ABOUT RABIES

The major concern after the bite wound is treated is whether or not the child will need specific treatment to prevent rabies (a viral infection that is nearly always fatal). If the wild animal has been caught, it will be killed and its brain examined microscopically for evidence of this disease. While awaiting the results of this examination—or more commonly, if the animal is not captured and its brain cannot be evaluated—a decision must be made whether or not to begin a rabies vaccination series. This will depend to a large degree on the type of animal involved and the circumstances of the bite.

In most parts of the United States, bites from wild rodents such as squirrels, rats, chipmunks, mice, and rabbits usually will not be treated with rabies vaccination. However, your child's doctor may consult the local public-health authority for specific advice. On the other hand, skunks, raccoons, opossums, bats, and all wild carnivores should always be considered potentially rabid (rabies carrying) and should never be touched, even in a park or other setting where they are accustomed to receiving food from human hands. A bite from one of these animals—especially if the animal was not provoked or defending itself—is more likely to raise concerns about rabies.

Bites from domestic animals (dogs, cats, etc.) are more common but rarely cause rabies. If someone is bitten by a domestic animal, treat the wound as described above. The animal will usually be available for observation, and public-health officials may quarantine it for ten to fourteen days. If the animal appears normal at the end of the quarantine, no rabies vaccination is required. But if the animal becomes ill, it will be promptly sacrificed and its brain examined microscopically for rabies. Rabies treatment and vaccination should be started as soon as a quarantined animal is found to be ill, and not delayed while awaiting results of the brain examination.

When purchased from pet stores, **mice, rats, gerbils,** and **hamsters** are not known to transmit rabies.

Wild animals that have been raised as pets—such as raccoons, skunks, foxes, wolves, ferrets, and small wildcats can carry rabies even if they have appeared healthy in captivity for long periods. This is particularly true of skunks, which have had rabies virus isolated from their saliva even when born in captivity.

PREVENTING DOG BITES

- Before you get a dog, consider the breed and gender. Female dogs and neutered males are less likely to bite than non-neutered males. Some breeds of dogs are more aggressive than others.
- Teach children how to treat a dog properly. Prodding, poking, and tail pulling may provoke a bite even from the most mild-mannered canine. This also can occur if a sleeping dog is jolted awake by a child or if a child tries to play with a dog who is eating. If you have one or more active toddlers who might not understand these ground rules, you might consider waiting until they are more mature before getting a dog.

- Don't leave infants or small children unattended with a dog.
- Obedience training for dogs—which should not involve harsh physical punishment—is a worthwhile investment. Teach children to use dog commands ("Down," "No," etc.) appropriately.
- When walking your dog, observe local leash laws. Do not let your dog approach a child it does not know.
- Do not let your child approach a strange dog.
- Teach your child to stand still and stay calm if approached by a strange dog. Running away may arouse a dog's instinct to chase and bite.
- Teach your children never to try to break up a dogfight.

HUMAN BITES

These bites commonly become infected because they are likely to be heavily contaminated by bacteria, which are abundant in saliva. In addition, the victim may be reluctant to seek medical help because of legal concerns or embarrassment.

Treatment — Treatment for a human bite is the same as that outlined for animal bites. Human bite wounds are rarely sutured because of the contamination risk noted above. These wounds should be vigorously irrigated and then left open. Antibiotics are usually required for all but the most minor wounds.

BEE AND WASP STINGS

Honeybees almost always leave the stinger (with attached venom sac) in the skin. This should be removed as quickly as possible by scraping the skin at the stinger base with a credit card or other flat object. Do not grasp the venom sac with fingers or tweezers because this will inject the venom remaining in the sac into the skin. (Wasp stingers are smooth and do not remain in the skin.)

HONEYBEE

WASP

Symptoms — **of response to venom**

- pain, redness, and swelling at the sting site
- itching, sometimes intense, 12 to 24 hours later

Treatment
- avoid scratching to reduce risk of infection
- apply ice to affected area
- elevate affected area

Symptoms   **of hypersensitivity reaction**
- significant swelling, usually beginning one or two days after the sting and spreading past one or more neighboring joints
- mild itchiness
- usually very mild pain, or no pain at all

Treatment
- Take antihistamines such as diphenhydramine (Benadryl and others) to relieve itching and swelling.
- For more severe local reactions, contact your child's physician. Sometimes oral steroids (prednisone) are prescribed.
- Antibiotics are rarely necessary.

Symptoms   **of multiple stings**

A toxic reaction may occur when a person is stung multiple times, often 10 or more.
- moderate swelling
- vomiting
- diarrhea
- light-headedness

Treatment   Go to an emergency facility immediately or call 911. Severe symptoms can develop quickly, and the emergency room is better equipped to treat a serious reaction to bee or wasp venom.

Symptoms   **of life-threatening or anaphylactic reaction**

This reaction affects the entire body and can result from one or multiple stings. Initial symptoms occur shortly after the sting. For symptoms and treatment, see anaphylaxis, page 764.

PREVENTION

If your child has had a severe reaction to an insect sting in the past, talk to his doctor about obtaining emergency treatment kits containing an injection of epinephrine (for example, EpiPen or Ana-Kit) that can partially or completely reverse a similar reaction in the future. These should be available at home, in the car, and in gear taken on camping trips or other outings. The child should wear a medical ID tag indicating that he is at risk for this type of reaction, especially if he may need an emergency injection of epinephrine. You might also want to see an allergist about giving your child immunotherapy injections to prevent this potentially life-threatening problem in the future. Even after completing an allergy-shot series, emergency kits containing epinephrine should still be available.

SPIDER BITES

In the continental United States and Canada only the bites of brown recluse and black widow spiders inject venom that can cause serious problems. However, any spider bite can cause significant swelling.

BROWN RECLUSE

Symptoms

Often the brown recluse bite is at first painless or causes only a brief stinging. Several hours later pain begins around the site and can become severe. The involved area often has a "red, white, and blue" appearance: a wide area of reddened skin, within which is a smaller patch of white-appearing skin, and finally a central bluish discoloration around the fang marks. The central (blue) area usually forms an ulcer that may take weeks or months to heal and occasionally requires skin grafting. This procedure is generally done about two months after the bite because the graft may slough off if applied to the poisoned area too early. Other possible symptoms of brown recluse bites include fever, skin rash, nausea or vomiting, joint pain, and bloody urine.

Treatment

There is no specific treatment or antidote for brown recluse bites. Many treatments have been tried and found to be ineffective. Cleanse and elevate the wound. Antibiotics are occasionally prescribed, and a tetanus booster is given if needed. In general the best approach is a combination of effective pain relief and keeping the bite site clean and dry to prevent secondary infection.

PREVENTION

Brown recluse spiders prefer warm, dry, and abandoned locations—for example, vacant buildings, woodpiles or sheds, or seldom-used closets. The spider is brown with a violin-shaped marking on its back. Active primarily at night, they usually bite when trapped in clothing or shoes. Be careful when delving into closets and other spaces that have been undisturbed, and shake out clothes and shoes that have been stored awhile or that are kept in areas where brown recluse spiders have been seen.

BROWN RECLUSE
SPIDER

BITES AND STINGS
771

E
M
E
R
G
E
N
C
Y

BLACK WIDOW

Symptoms A black widow bite is generally unnoticed at first but then becomes painful—often severely so—within 15 minutes to 4 hours. Pain will usually reach a peak in 2 or 3 hours, but it can last up to 48 hours. Associated muscle spasm, which may be very severe, contributes to the pain. Usually only two tiny red spots are visible at the bite site, or no local reaction may be seen at all.

BLACK WIDOW

Treatment The primary goal of treatment for a black widow bite is to relieve pain and muscle spasm. An antivenin is available, but it is generally reserved for severe cases, which are more commonly seen in young children.

PREVENTION

The black widow is a shy, coal black spider with a red or yellow hourglass marking on the underside of the abdomen. Only the female spider bites. She builds a chaotic, irregular-shaped web that is easy to recognize when compared to the highly symmetrical webs of other spiders. The black widow is found throughout the United States, preferring warm, dry environments, both indoors and out.

TARANTULAS

These spiders attack only when handled roughly. Their bite can be painless or can cause a deep, throbbing discomfort that generally stops after about an hour. The only treatment needed is elevation and possibly a pain reliever, although most of the discomfort usually subsides before the medication takes effect.

TICK BITES See also *ticks,* Reference.

While tick bites are generally insignificant in and of themselves, some ticks transmit infections that can be serious, including Lyme disease (see *Lyme disease,* Reference, and see photo on page A29) and Rocky Mountain spotted fever (see *Rocky Mountain spotted fever,* Reference). Generally, most tick-borne diseases are transmitted only after the tick has remained attached to the skin for many hours (see photo on page A31). For example, transmission of Lyme disease is unusual if the tick remains attached less than 24 to 48 hours.

TICK

Another, less common tick-borne illness is tick paralysis,

which usually afflicts children. Weakness and paralysis begin in the legs and progress upward with increasing severity as long as the tick is attached. Eventually difficulty with speech and swallowing and respiratory problems occur; rarely, death may result. Tick removal reverses this disorder (see *ticks*, Reference).

PIT VIPER

SNAKEBITES

Pit vipers—rattlesnakes, cottonmouths, and copperheads—inject venom through two hollow needlelike fangs.

Coral snakes are also poisonous, but they are much less common than pit vipers. Unlike pit vipers, coral snakes do not have hollow fangs, but rather short (less than 1/8 inch) rigid grooved pegs. Therefore, they must gnaw on their victim to inject venom.

CORAL SNAKE

If a child has been bitten by a snake, identifying the particular type is important but not critical. Even if the snake has been killed, the head should be preserved to make identification easier. Be very careful when handling dead poisonous snakes because their strike reflex can cause a venom-injecting bite up to an hour after they are killed.

Symptoms

When a pit viper strike has injected venom, swelling and/or pain almost always occurs within 30 minutes. Anyone who has been bitten by one of these snakes should be en route to the hospital before this much time has elapsed.

Treatment

First aid for a snakebite victim is quite simple:

◆ Don't panic; keep the victim as calm as possible. Activity speeds the spread of venom.
◆ Splint the bitten part and keep it slightly below heart level if possible.
◆ Transport the victim to the nearest hospital immediately.
◆ There is almost no evidence that cutting the bite site and applying suction will remove much venom. There is clear evidence that in untrained hands this practice can lead to tissue damage and infection. There may be some benefit from removing venom from a wound, without incision, using newer suction devices.
◆ The use of tourniquets is not recommended because they are difficult to apply correctly and can cut off blood supply to the affected limb. A lightly constricting band six to ten inches above the bite site, in conjunction with the first aid measures above, may slow the spread of venom. Application of an ice pack may also be helpful.

The victim should be observed in the emergency department for at least four hours before a "dry strike" is diagnosed. Any symptoms of envenomation (venom injection) will be treated with **antivenin,** and the child will be admitted to the hospital. Antibiotics are frequently used even in dry strikes because these puncture wounds are easily infected. A tetanus booster is usually given if the victim has not had one in the past five years.

PREVENTION

Prevention of snakebites lies mainly in recognizing poisonous snakes and staying clear of them. Pit vipers are readily identified by their triangular/arrow-shaped heads and oblong pupils (like a cat's). All native North American snakes with oblong pupils are poisonous.

Coral snakes have round heads and bright red, black, and yellow bands around their body. They always have a black-tipped head, which has given rise to the warning "If the head is black, get back." About 15 nonpoisonous snakes mimic the coral-snake color pattern, but the coral snake is unique in having its red bands next to yellow bands. If the red band is next to a black band, the snake is a nonpoisonous mimic. (An easy way to remember the color patterns is the rhyme "Red on yellow kills a fellow; red on black, venom lack." However, in some parts of the world, including Mexico, coral-snake color bands do not follow this pattern.)

SCORPION STINGS

Scorpions inject venom through a single stinger in the tail. They rarely inject enough venom to be lethal, although small children and the elderly are at risk for severe reactions.

Symptoms   Immediate pain with minimal redness and swelling but increased sensitivity to touch at the injured area. In severe cases, muscular paralysis and respiratory failure can occur. Symptoms last for about four hours in most healthy individuals.

SCORPION

Treatment   First aid includes the application of ice to the injured area. Most patients with symptoms should see a doctor and will probably be observed for several hours. Oral pain medication is usually effective, but occasionally stronger pain-relief measures are necessary.

PREVENTION

Scorpions are found almost exclusively in the southwestern states and hibernate from about October through April. They feed at night, hiding during the day—often in sleeping bags or boots. Stings can be prevented by shaking out sleeping bags or boots prior to using them.

Scorpions also hide under rocks and on ledges, so caution is advisable when hiking or rock climbing.

MARINE ANIMAL STINGS
STINGRAYS

Symptoms A jagged wound that is immediately and intensely painful; the worst pain occurs after about an hour and then gradually subsides over a period of up to two days.

Treatment Stingray venom breaks down when warm but is stable and persistent when cool. First aid consists of applying hot water from the faucet—as hot as one can tolerate without causing a burn—to the affected area. This will promptly decrease the pain, but discomfort will recur as soon as the area (generally the leg or foot) is allowed to cool. Frequent heat application is necessary for a day or two to control the pain.

STINGRAY

Infection may occur if the venom and barb fragments (or the entire spine) remain in the wound. Usually these are removed by irrigating with hot water, and most wounds do not become infected. A tetanus booster is recommended if none has been given during the previous five years.

PREVENTION

Stingrays partially submerge themselves in sandy shallow water in sheltered bays, lagoons, and river mouths. The animal's whiplike tail has several (one to four) barbs (spines) that are covered with a mucous venom. The tail reflexively whips upward when the ray is touched.

To prevent being stung, bathers should shuffle (not step) when walking in shallow water. This disturbs the stingray, and it will flee before one has a chance to step on it.

JELLYFISH AND FIRE CORAL

JELLYFISH

These two marine animals have a tiny venom-containing capsule (nematocyst) on the outer surface of their tentacles or near the mouth. Contact with a swimmer causes the capsule to penetrate the skin and diffuse venom into it. The attached capsule can discharge repeatedly when it's exposed to water.

Symptoms
: The nematocyst sting is generally quite painful but rarely causes serious medical problems. However, a person who is stung multiple times may develop symptoms such as vomiting, extreme weakness, bloody urine, or fainting.

Treatment
: For treatment of a severe reaction resulting from multiple stings, go to an emergency facility for prompt medical attention.

   Less severe stings can be managed at home. The best way to neutralize the nematocysts is to apply liberal amounts of vinegar for 30 minutes. Large tentacles should be removed using gloves. Remaining nematocysts can be removed by applying shaving foam and gently shaving the area.

STARFISH

Starfish have thorny spines that are coated with a slimy venom. When the spines penetrate a victim's skin, the venom seeps into the wound.

STARFISH

Symptoms
: Immediate, intense burning pain at the wound site; the venom rarely causes a more serious reaction.

Treatment
: As with stingray venom, heat will hasten pain resolution.

SEA URCHINS

These creatures have venom-bearing spines that are long, sharp, and brittle and can break off in the skin. Purple pigment from the spine can leach into skin and appear to be a retained spine fragment.

SEA URCHIN

Symptoms
: Intense burning pain where the skin has been penetrated.

Treatment
: If a spine fragment remains in the skin, it should be removed by a physician, because unnecessary pain and further tissue damage can result from attempts to take it out without adequate local anesthetic.

   Immersion in hot water will decrease pain, as previously described for stingrays and starfish. X-rays may be needed to determine whether any spine fragments remain in the skin. Antibiotics and a tetanus booster will be given if necessary.

E
M
E
R
G
E
N
C
Y

BLEEDING   *See also* Wounds and Wound Care.

Bleeding can arise from two sources:

- veins, which carry a slow and steady supply of blood back to the heart, or
- arteries, which carry blood under higher pressure from the heart to the rest of the body

An arterial injury is potentially more serious because blood escaping under pressure may be lost in large amounts in relatively little time. The amount of blood directly visible is not necessarily a reliable sign of the severity of an injury and may not reflect how much blood a person has lost. For example, some serious injuries do not bleed heavily or may bleed internally. Some minor wounds, such as scalp lacerations, may appear to bleed profusely, but in fact the amount of blood lost is relatively insignificant.

Treatment

- If possible, wear latex gloves or keep several layers of cloth or bandage between you and the blood. This is a good idea even if you have no reason to believe the bleeding person has an infectious disease that could be transmitted through blood.
- If time permits, wash your hands before tending a wound. This will help prevent infecting the wound with any bacteria on your hands.
- If there is severe external bleeding or evidence of major trauma, CALL 911.
- Try to keep the child (and yourself) calm.
- Remove any loose debris from the wound.
- Apply direct pressure to the wound using a sterile dressing or a clean cloth unless there is an eye injury, skull fracture, or an embedded object. In these cases do not apply direct pressure.
- If an arm or a leg is bleeding, elevate it above the level of the heart unless movement causes increased pain or you suspect the arm or leg is fractured.
- If direct pressure has stopped the bleeding but it starts again, reapply pressure.
- If you must free your hands, apply a pressure bandage (see next page).
- If the wound is large enough to make direct pressure ineffective or if direct pressure has not stopped the bleeding after 15 minutes, pressure-point bleeding control may be necessary (see next page).
- If there is no indication of neck, head, or back injury and the bleeding is severe, take steps to prevent shock (a severe drop in blood pressure). Signs of shock include bluish color of the fingernails or lips, clammy skin, pale skin color, weakness, confusion, and decreasing alertness. If one or more of these occur, be sure that someone has called 911. Lay the person flat, and if possible elevate the feet about 12 inches. Cover the victim with a blanket or coat.
- DO NOT move a child who may have an injury to the head, neck, or back.

- DO NOT attempt to clean a large wound because this could aggravate bleeding that would otherwise slow down.
- DO NOT probe, explore, or pull any embedded object out of a wound. This also may increase bleeding.
- DO NOT apply ice directly to a wound.
- DO NOT use a tourniquet.
- DO NOT remove a dressing that becomes soaked with blood or attempt to peek at the wound to see if bleeding has stopped. These actions can disturb the wound surface and may actually increase bleeding. If necessary, add more dressings.

Even when bleeding is controlled, many wounds require medical attention, including:

- gaping wounds
- animal or human bites
- wounds located directly over joints
- wounds associated with a broken bone, loss of muscular function, or loss of sensation

Treatment

applying a pressure bandage

If you need to free your hands to move the child or attend to other injuries (whether or not the bleeding has stopped), a pressure bandage can be applied. This holds the dressings in place while maintaining direct pressure on the wound.

1. Apply a dressing of sterile gauze to the wound or clean cloth if gauze is not available. Wrap long strips of cloth or a long bandage around the area where the wound is located to hold the dressing in place.
2. Cut or split the end of the bandage or cloth into 2 strips and tie these together to secure the bandage in place. The knot should be tied directly over the wound.
3. Make sure the pressure dressing is not too tight! It should be tight enough to maintain pressure on the wound, but not so tight that it prevents the tissue beyond the wound (that is, more distant from the heart) from receiving the blood it needs. If the area beyond the dressing is throbbing with pain and/or becoming blue and cold, the bandage should be loosened.

Treatment

pressure-point bleeding control

Important: If you need to use this technique, be sure that someone has called 911 and medical help is on the way.

This technique is used to control bleeding from an extremity only when other methods have not worked. First try using direct pressure combined with elevation of the extremity. Pressure-point bleeding

EMERGENCY

control is a last resort because areas of the body that are not bleeding will also have their blood flow reduced.

Each arm or leg has a major artery supplying it. When bleeding cannot be controlled by other means, pressure on that specific artery can reduce blood flow. When this approach is accompanied by direct pressure to the wound and (if possible) elevation of the injured area, bleeding can usually be controlled.

When the bleeding is coming from the leg, the pressure point is over the **femoral artery.** If there are no suspected injuries to the head, neck, or spine and the child can be moved, place her on her back. Locate the femoral artery at the point where the leg and the groin meet, a little toward the groin side. Use four fingers to feel for a pulse. Once the pulse has been located, apply firm pressure with the heel of the hand to compress the artery against the underlying bone.

When the bleeding is coming from the arm, the pressure point is over the **brachial artery.** This can be found at the middle of the inner aspect of

WRAPPING A WOUND

PRESSURE POINT BLEEDING CONTROL

Brachial

Femoral

the arm, just underneath the biceps muscle on the top of the arm. After you have found the pulse, use four fingers along the path of the artery to apply pressure and compress the artery against the underlying bone.

Remember: Elevation of the limb and direct pressure on the wound should be continued along with pressure-point bleeding control. When performed correctly, this technique will stop or significantly reduce major bleeding.

BLEEDING WITHOUT A VISIBLE WOUND

Symptoms Bleeding can occur without visible wounds. Bleeding can be significant in these situations:

- Blood in the stool. This can be bright red, which indicates bleeding from a source at or near the anal opening, or a deep purplish black, which usually is more characteristic of blood lost from the upper intestinal tract.
- An abnormal amount or duration of menstrual bleeding. Note: Any vaginal bleeding in a child who has no other signs of puberty (such as breast development) is abnormal and should be evaluated.
- Blood in the urine. This may be bright red, which usually occurs with bleeding from the bladder or urethra (the tube through which urine exits the body) or a darker (tea) color, which suggests an origin within the kidney. Blood in the urine should be fully investigated by your child's doctor.
- Vomited blood. This may arise from bleeding within the stomach or esophagus (the passage between the throat and stomach), but more commonly in children and adolescents vomited blood arises from a nosebleed that drained down the throat rather than out the nose. An acute illness such as gastroenteritis (stomach flu) may produce blood-tinged vomited material but not blood itself. In general, any vomiting of bright red material should prompt an immediate call to your child's physician.

Treatment Any of the above situations calls for medical evaluation or consultation.

BONE AND JOINT INJURIES *See also* **Musculoskeletal Problems in Children.**

FRACTURES AND DISLOCATIONS

A fracture (or broken bone) occurs when enough force is applied to a bone to disrupt its structure and break it.

A dislocation occurs when the bones on either side of a joint move out of their normal alignment with one another. Either of the bones involved in a dislocation may also be fractured.

E
M
E
R
G
E
N
C
Y

Symptoms   One or more of the following may indicate that a fracture or dislocation has taken place:

+ swelling
+ deformity
+ moderate to severe pain
+ localized tenderness
+ poor function or movement of the involved area

Treatment   + Avoid putting pressure or weight on the affected area.
+ Gently splint the affected area to reduce pain and prevent further damage. Splints should be applied across at least one joint above and below the suspected fracture. Elbows should be supported on a pillow, and suspected arm or shoulder injuries should be placed in a sling while the person is taken to the emergency room. A leg may be splinted by carefully binding it to the other leg with a towel placed between them. Toes and fingers usually do not require splinting but should be protected until they're examined by a doctor.
+ If the neck appears to be involved, the person should not be moved without a backboard and neck brace, which will normally be provided by an emergency transport team.
+ Don't try to set or realign fractures or dislocations. Significant additional injury can occur through inappropriate movement of an injured limb.
+ If possible, cover any open wounds to try to prevent further contamination.
+ Take your child to his physician or the nearest emergency room for treatment.

OPEN FRACTURES

With this type of injury one end of a fractured bone is protruding through the skin.

Treatment   Cover the wound (using a sterile dressing, if available) and take the person to an emergency facility immediately. Don't give the person anything to eat or drink, because surgery will likely be required.

SPRAINS

In order for bones to move properly in relation to one another, the joint spaces between adjacent bones are bridged by strong but flexible fibrous bands called ligaments that help keep the bones in proper alignment. A sudden and forceful twisting motion can cause a sprain, the stretching or tearing of a ligament.

Symptoms
- pain when moving or putting weight on the affected joint
- swelling and often a bluish discoloration

Since sprains are more common in adults than in children and since it may be difficult to determine if a fracture is present merely by looking at an injured arm or leg, these symptoms should be evaluated by a physician.

Treatment
The simple acronym RICE can help you remember what to do following a sprain:
- **R**est the injured area.
- **I**ce or cold packs can decrease swelling and pain, but their contact with skin should be limited to 20 minutes out of every hour.
- **C**ompression, such as an elastic wrap around the affected area, can also reduce swelling and pain. This should not be tight enough to cause discomfort, numbness, or tingling.
- **E**levate the injured area as much as possible for 24 hours since this will also help reduce uncomfortable swelling.

BURNS

The most widely used classification system for burns categorizes them according to size and depth. Since first aid treatment depends on a burn's severity, it is important to check the center of the wound. This is usually where the burn will be deepest, and its appearance will give an indication of the type of treatment the burn needs.

WHAT NOT TO DO FOR A BURN

- Do not open blisters. When sealed, they normally provide excellent protection for the underlying skin. However, in some situations a physician may rupture and remove the covering of a blister using a sterile technique, especially if infection is evident.
- Do not attempt to remove clothing that is stuck to a burn because this could peel away the skin.
- Do not use butter, antiseptic creams, or any other folk remedies on burns. These items may significantly slow the healing process and can actually cause or contribute to infection.

FIRST-DEGREE (SUPERFICIAL) BURNS

These burns are the most common and the least severe. They can be caused by sun exposure or brief contact of skin with hot water or a hot surface such as the burner on a stove.

Symptoms
- bright redness of the affected area, but no blisters
- mild swelling
- minor pain—because first-degree burns irritate nerve endings

Treatment	◆ Hold the affected area under cold running water for several minutes. ◆ Do not use ice, which might reduce the local blood supply. ◆ To soothe the pain, use a nonprescription pain reliever.

SECOND-DEGREE (PARTIAL-THICKNESS) BURNS

These are generally caused by contact with hot liquid and occasionally by sunburn.

Symptoms	Second-degree burns are characterized by blisters that form because the burn penetrates more deeply into the skin, causing body fluids to be released.
Treatment	◆ Immediately submerge the burned area in cold water. ◆ Keep cold water in contact with the burn for at least five minutes or until medical help is given. ◆ If the burn is minor, treat it the same as a first-degree burn. ◆ If the burn is more widespread, apply cool, wet cloths to the affected areas and see a doctor immediately. A sizable burn will require medical follow-up, including regular dressing changes, topical medication if appropriate, adequate pain relief, and possibly antibiotics. ◆ Extensive partial-thickness burns can be serious or even fatal and may require specialized medical care. Very often this is carried out at a regional burn center.

THIRD-DEGREE (FULL-THICKNESS) BURNS

These are the most serious and, if extensive, can be fatal. All skin layers are destroyed, and the surface will usually appear charred or white. Paradoxically, full-thickness burns do not hurt as much as the others because the nerve endings in the skin are no longer functioning.

Treatment	Do not attempt to treat this type of burn; call for medical attention immediately.

Burns of varying size and depth can occur in the following ways:

THERMAL BURNS

Scalds, the most common thermal burns, are usually caused by contact with hot water. Exposing skin to water at 140°F for three seconds or 156°F for one second will result in a scald. (Coffee is usually about 180°F when freshly brewed.) Immersion burns (such as occur in a hot bathtub) involve longer contact and usually burn a wider area. Because grease or hot oil is around 400°F and may not run off of skin as quickly as water does, it tends to cause deeper burns.

Flame or **flash burns** are the next most common thermal burns, and these result from fires or explosions. It is important to remove the person immediately from the heat source and take off burning or smoldering clothing. A person with flash burns should be observed for wheezing or difficulties breathing.

Contact burns are often deep and are caused by touching hot surfaces such as curling irons, stoves, hot coals, etc.

Treatment Treatment for any thermal burns includes immediate application of cool water, which will decrease pain and may reduce the extent of skin damage. Do not apply sprays, creams, or butter to this (or any other) type of burn.

ELECTRICAL BURNS   *See also* **Electric Shock.**

Electrical burns can cause more damage internally than might be suspected from the appearance of the skin surface.

Treatment
◆ Separate the victim from the electrical source. Do not touch the victim until it is certain that she is no longer in contact with the source of electricity.
◆ Check for a pulse and administer CPR if necessary.
◆ Because of the possibility of internal damage, a person who has sustained an electrical burn should see a physician even if she does not feel any immediate discomfort.

CHEMICAL BURNS

Chemical burns are commonly caused by household cleansers and solvents. Alkali burns tend to be more serious than acid burns.

Treatment
◆ Carefully remove contaminated clothing.
◆ Flush thoroughly with water for at least 10 minutes.
◆ Call your child's physician or take the child to the nearest emergency facility.

CARBON MONOXIDE POISONING

Carbon monoxide poisoning is likely to occur

◆ wherever there is fire or smoke, especially in enclosed places
◆ in poorly ventilated rooms that are heated by wood-burning stoves or kerosene-type space heaters
◆ in closed garages where gasoline engines are running
◆ in cars that have faulty exhaust systems

E
M
E
R
G
E
N
C
Y

Symptoms

Early signs of carbon monoxide poisoning include

- headache
- dizziness
- distorted vision
- mild difficulty breathing

Signs of more severe poisoning are

- intense headache
- nausea/vomiting
- reddening of the skin
- sleepiness
- poor coordination
- unusual behavior
- loss of consciousness

Carbon monoxide poisoning should be *strongly* suspected if several individuals in the same house develop these symptoms simultaneously.

Treatment

- Move everyone to fresh air immediately.
- If someone is unconscious, begin rescue breathing or CPR if necessary (see page 806).
- Whether there is one or many victims, seek medical evaluation as quickly as possible. If no one can drive or a victim is unconscious, call 911 for emergency treatment and transportation.
- After each person has received treatment, contact the local gas company or fire department so they can check for carbon monoxide in the home.
- The primary treatment for carbon monoxide poisoning is 100 percent oxygen given by mask for several hours.

CHOKING

See also Cardiopulmonary Resuscitation (CPR) and Choking Emergencies, page 806.

Symptoms

- gasping for breath
- grabbing the throat
- turning blue
- unable to talk

Treatment

If a choking person is making noise or coughing forcefully, do not interfere but stay with him until the episode ends and the object is expelled. If he is unable to cough or move air in any way, quickly look into his mouth. If you see the object and can easily retrieve it, do so cautiously, being careful not to push the object farther down the throat.

If it is not easily removable, do not attempt to grasp it. Call for emergency help. Then proceed to the following measures (see page 814).

For an infant or small child try the **back blow approach:**

◆ Place the child face down across your leg or lap with the head lower than the rest of the body.
◆ Support the child's chin with one hand.
◆ Firmly and deliberately slap the back between the shoulder blades four times.

If this technique proves unsuccessful in expelling the foreign object, then proceed with the **chest thrust approach:**

◆ Place the child face up across your leg, keeping the head lower than the body.
◆ Support the head and neck with one hand.
◆ Place two fingertips for a newborn or the heel of the hand for an older baby on the lower sternum (just above the stomach area) and push in and up four times in rapid succession.

Alternate these approaches until the object is dislodged and the child begins to breathe.

For an older child (over 40 pounds), use the Heimlich maneuver:

◆ Stand behind the child, wrapping your arms around the child's waist (between the navel and the rib cage).
◆ Make a fist with one hand and place your free hand over the fist.
◆ Thrust your fist in and upward (into the upper abdominal area) in four separate and distinct motions.

Once the object is freed, begin rescue breathing or CPR if the child is not breathing. Remember: CPR is of no value until the object is dislodged.

For the older child who is unconscious, the standard upright Heimlich maneuver will not work. In that case, follow these instructions:

◆ Place the child on his or her back on the floor.
◆ Kneeling over (or straddling) the child, place the heel of one hand on the child's abdomen and place the free hand on top of the first hand, fingers interlocking.
◆ Push the heel of the bottom hand into the child's upper abdomen with four quick, upward thrusts.

PREVENTION

◆ Keep small, hard objects away from small children. This includes hard candy, nuts, popcorn, hot dogs, chewing gum, and hard fruits and vegetables.
◆ Cut food into small pieces.
◆ Remove small toys or hanging mobiles from the crib before the baby is able to reach them.
◆ Use only unbreakable toys that have no sharp edges or small parts that can come loose.
◆ Do not allow electrical or hanging cords within reach of a crib or a toddler's play area.

◆ Do not allow an infant to wear a necklace or a young child to play with any cord or string around the neck.
◆ Keep plastic bags and balloons out of reach of all children. A popped or deflated balloon in a small child's mouth, if inhaled, could easily obstruct his airway.

SWALLOWED OBJECTS

It is not uncommon for children to swallow nonfood objects, either deliberately or accidentally. Toddlers, who are prone to place small items into the mouth, are at particular risk for this type of accident. Fortunately, once the object passes through the esophagus (the tube that carries food from the throat to the stomach), it will usually progress through the rest of the intestinal tract without difficulty. As this occurs, the child will not show any signs of distress, except in rare cases where an odd-shaped (and usually pointed) object such as a toothpick becomes stuck or perforates the bowel.

Treatment

An X-ray may be done to try to confirm the object's location (although not all objects will be visible on an X-ray), and the child's stools may be examined for the next few days until the object passes. If it is not found after 4 to 7 days, a second X-ray may be performed. (If the object is metallic, some emergency facilities use a metal detector to track its progress.) Seek immediate medical attention if abdominal pain develops before the object has passed out of the child's body.

Symptoms

of object lodged in esophagus

A small percentage of swallowed objects become lodged in the esophagus. When this occurs, a mild pain will usually develop in the chest below the sternum (breastbone), along with increased salivation caused by the inability to swallow.

Treatment

◆ The child will be frightened, so keep him as calm as possible.
◆ DO NOT attempt to force the object into the stomach by giving fluids or food.
◆ In most cases the object will pass into the stomach within 10 minutes. But if pain or difficulty in swallowing persists, the child will need emergency medical attention.

An X-ray of the chest/abdomen will usually disclose the location of the object. A specialist may be consulted and an **endoscopy** done. In this procedure a narrow, flexible fiber-optic device, known as an endoscope, is passed into the sedated child's esophagus in an attempt to dislodge or remove the foreign body.

Treatment   *for swallowing small batteries*

If a child swallows a small "button battery"—the small, round battery used in watches, hearing aids, and other electronic devices—see a doctor immediately. A button battery that does not pass through the esophagus must be removed (usually using an endoscope) because it can cause a serious local erosion or even a perforation within a matter of hours.

DENTAL EMERGENCIES

AVULSION—LOSS OF A TOOTH

Treatment   If an avulsed permanent tooth is reimplanted within 30 minutes of the injury, the tooth will survive over 90 percent of the time. (Primary or baby teeth cannot be successfully reimplanted.) If the delay exceeds two hours, the chances of success are less than 5 percent. Therefore, the tooth must be replaced in its socket almost immediately.

If your child has lost a tooth, do the following:

◆ Find the tooth.
◆ Rinse the tooth under tap water; do not touch the dental roots.
◆ Gently reinsert the tooth, making sure it is facing the right direction.
◆ Go directly to the dentist while gently holding the tooth in place.
◆ Note: If the parent or child is unable (or afraid) to replace the tooth, place it in cow's milk while seeking emergency dental care.

DISPLACED TOOTH

A displaced tooth has not been completely knocked out of the mouth but has been seriously dislodged—usually inward toward the tongue, as when the child has fallen on his face or been hit in the mouth.

Treatment   ◆ Control bleeding with direct pressure and ice as long as this does not increase pain.
◆ Reposition the tooth, if possible, and gently hold it in place.
◆ Seek dental care immediately. Delaying treatment decreases the likelihood that the tooth will survive.

LOOSE TOOTH

In this case, the tooth is loose but not displaced from its socket. The tooth can be moved backwards and forwards (or sometimes up and down).

Treatment If your child's tooth becomes loose:

- ◆ Control bleeding if present.
- ◆ Try to avoid repeated movement of the tooth. Remind your child not to wiggle the loose tooth or chew food until you have spoken with the dentist.
- ◆ Contact a dentist as soon as possible for further advice.

SENSITIVE OR CHIPPED TOOTH

Minor injuries to the mouth or teeth often result in a chipped tooth or increased sensitivity to gentle tapping on the tooth—but the position of the tooth has not changed. In this situation, consult your dentist as soon as possible for further advice.

BEWARE OF OTHER INJURIES

Children with dental trauma often have other head and facial injuries. Appropriate medical treatment should be given in addition to any emergency dental care. A tetanus booster may be considered if one has not been given within the last five years. Do not use aspirin to control pain because it may prolong bleeding.

DROWNING

Treatment
- ◆ Prolonged lack of oxygen from being submerged under water leads to cardiac arrest, so it is important that rescue breathing or CPR (either mouth-to-mouth or mouth-to-nose ventilation) be started immediately—even in the water if necessary.
- ◆ Call 911 for medical assistance and a quick transfer to the nearest emergency center.
- ◆ If you know what happened prior to the accident, tell the rescue workers, particularly if head and neck injuries are likely (as would be the case if the child was diving when the accident occurred).
- ◆ Keep the child warm, especially if he was in cold water. Wrap him in towels or a blanket until medical personnel arrive.

PREVENTION

Studies show that 70 percent of drowning accidents could be avoided if self-closing, self-latching doors were installed in homes and on gates in the fences around pools. Sturdy, childproof pool covers and alarms on doors leading to the pool area—or even an alarm that sounds when someone enters the water—are also appropriate safety measures. Parents need to teach their children the importance of swimming only when supervised and the necessity of life jackets when boating. Older children and adolescents should be warned explicitly of the risks of alcohol and/or drug consumption while swimming or boating.

When young children are around water, they must always be supervised by an adult. Parents and teens should strongly consider becoming certified in CPR. Poolside telephones are helpful because they allow adults to answer the phone while continuing supervision. They also can speed the process of calling for help if an accident occurs.

RATES OF SURVIVAL

The chances of surviving submersion are not significantly affected by the type of water (salt, fresh, or pool water with chemicals). How long a child can survive without oxygen depends on many other factors, including age, previous health, the water temperature, and the speed and effectiveness of the rescue effort. Children under age five have an advantage because of a nerve reflex that causes the heart to slow down and blood to be diverted to the brain and heart. Younger children usually survive if submersion lasts less than 3 minutes and may survive a submersion lasting up to 10 minutes if the water temperature is 50° to 60°F (10° to 15°C). In general, cold water temperatures improve survival chances.

EAR PAIN AND INJURY

A blow to the side of the head that results in significant swelling or bleeding from the outer ear, bleeding from the ear canal, or loss of hearing should be evaluated by a physician as soon as possible. Ear pain that is not associated with trauma usually arises from infection of the ear canal or middle ear and will also need medical assessment (see *ear infections*, Reference).

REMOVING OBJECTS FROM THE EAR

Occasionally a child will insert a small object (such as a bead or a small bean) into an ear and cannot remove it. Less commonly, a small insect may crawl into a child's ear canal. While the sensations experienced by the child can be annoying, neither of these situations poses a threat to hearing, and both parent and child should try to remain calm.

Treatment   It may be possible to remove the object/insect at home by following these steps:

- ◆ If an insect has entered the ear canal, put a few drops of oil (mineral, baby, or vegetable) or peroxide in the ear canal.
- ◆ If you can see the object or insect in the ear, carefully remove it with tweezers—but only if it is clearly visible at the opening of the ear canal.

- If you cannot see the object clearly or if it is deeper within the ear canal, tilt your child's head to the side of the injured ear.
- If this doesn't work, leave the child alone. Attempting to remove the object may damage the ear. Seek medical attention as soon as possible.

ELECTRIC SHOCK

Most electric-shock incidents involving children occur in the home through contact with electrical outlets, cords, or appliances. Infants and toddlers are particularly at risk of shock from biting electrical cords or inserting objects into electrical sockets. Most of these shocks cause minor injuries or burns unless the child is standing in water when the electrical contact is made.

Serious injuries or death from electric shock (electrocution) usually results from direct contact with high-voltage wires that have fallen during storms or may occur when children climb a power pole and touch an electric box or wire. Electric shock is always possible during an electrical storm, particularly if persons are on or in water or take shelter under trees or near any other structures that will conduct electricity from a lightning strike.

Treatment
- Break the child's contact with the electrical source using a nonconducting object such as a wooden stick. Do not touch the victim until you are certain he is no longer in contact with the source of electricity.
- If the child is not breathing or has no pulse, begin rescue breathing or CPR (see page 806).
- Call for emergency help immediately.

PREVENTION
- Cover all electrical outlets with safety plugs when infants and toddlers are in the house.
- Unplug bathroom and other small appliances when they are not in use.
- Keep electrical cords out of children's reach.
- Teach children to never touch any electrical equipment while in the bathtub or use any electrical appliance or equipment when standing on a wet surface.
- Warn older children to stay away from outdoor electrical wires. This includes avoiding any fallen wires and staying off poles that hold power lines or electric boxes.
- Keep children inside during electrical storms. *At the first sign of lightning, get them out of swimming pools, rivers, or ponds, whether they are swimming or in a boat.* Teach children not to seek shelter under trees when there is lightning, but to go to the nearest indoor shelter.

EYE INJURIES   *See also* Eye Care and Concerns, Reference.

In general, any direct injury to the eye—cut or puncture, blow with a ball or fist, or debris in the eye—should have immediate medical attention if there is significant pain, blurring, and/or loss of vision. If pain is minor and no serious injury is obvious, contact the doctor to determine whether your child should be seen in an emergency facility or the doctor's office.

Treatment
- Until it is seen by a doctor, keep the eye closed. This is a natural response to eye injury and helps reduce discomfort.
- If the eye has been penetrated or cut open, take the child directly to the emergency room. If there is fluid oozing from the eye, transfer the child lying flat on his back so additional fluid will not escape.
- Hold a simple shield, such as a paper cup, over the eye to protect it— but don't exert any pressure on the eye.

CHEMICALS IN THE EYE

Treatment
Take prompt action whenever any chemical has splashed into the eye. Although many materials will cause only minor irritation, some can result in serious injury or blindness if not attended to immediately.

Start immediate and continued flushing with lukewarm water. A gentle flow of water should run into the affected eye(s). Hold the child under a tap or hose or carefully pour water from a glass or pitcher into the eye(s) with the child lying down. If only one eye is involved, hold the child on her side with the affected eye down so none of the chemical can accidentally flow into the other eye. You will probably need to have another adult hold the eye open while you pour the water. Use the following formula guidelines to determine how long to irrigate the eye:

- alkaline materials: 20 minutes
- acids: 10 minutes
- less reactive chemicals: 5 minutes

After the eye(s) has been irrigated, seek medical attention as soon as possible.

Alkaline materials can penetrate deeply and cause serious damage. Examples of alkaline materials are drain cleaners, oven cleaners, and bleach. Look for these words on product labels:

- lye
- sodium hydroxide
- potassium hydroxide
- ammonia

◆ calcium oxide
◆ trisodium phosphate
◆ wood ash

Acids tend to cause more localized tissue damage but can still cause significant injury. Examples of acids are automobile battery fluid, toilet bowl cleaners, and swimming pool acid. Look for these words on product labels:

◆ sulfuric acid
◆ hydrochloric acid
◆ phosphoric acid
◆ hydrofluoric acid
◆ oxalic acid

Less dangerous chemicals should be washed out of the eye also. Most of these materials will cause only mild redness, stinging, and temporary swelling involving the conjunctiva (the thin, clear tissue lining the white surface of the eyeball and inner surfaces of the eyelid). Irrigation will lessen the irritation and probably prevent the child from rubbing the eye and aggravating the soreness. Examples of less dangerous chemicals include food, alcohol, and household soaps.

FAINTING   *See also* **Loss of Consciousness.**

Common situations in which fainting might occur include

- ◆ a traumatic or anxiety-provoking situation—such as having blood drawn or witnessing an alarming event
- ◆ standing for long periods of time with the knees locked, especially on a hot day
- ◆ an acute illness, especially when there has been loss of fluid through vomiting and/or diarrhea
- ◆ standing up suddenly after lying down or squatting, especially when a person is hot or mildly dehydrated
- ◆ standing in a hot, crowded area where there is little fresh air

Symptoms   Warning signs for fainting include the following:

◆ paleness in the face
◆ cold, clammy skin
◆ dizziness
◆ nausea
◆ blurred vision
◆ unusually rapid or slow pulse
◆ feelings of anxiety or panic
◆ numbness or tingling in the fingers or toes

Treatment   If you notice these warning signs or your child feels that she is about to pass out, have her lie down immediately and, if possible, elevate her feet. Do not allow her to stay upright because this can deprive her brain of needed oxygen. If she loses consciousness:

◆ Lay the child on the floor on her back.
◆ Make sure that her airway is clear and that she is breathing.
◆ Loosen any clothing to make certain she is comfortable and able to breathe easily.
◆ If you are inside a building, open the windows to circulate fresh air.
◆ If your child vomits while unconscious, turn her head to the side and wipe out her mouth.
◆ Keep the chin up to prevent the tongue from obstructing her throat.
◆ If the child remains unconscious for five minutes or longer or if she displays any unusual movements or behavior during or after the episode, call for medical help.

If the episode passes within 15 minutes, emergency medical attention may not be necessary. However, fainting may be a sign of a more significant condition (for example, anemia or pregnancy). If your child has fainted for no apparent reason or has repeated fainting episodes, contact her physician for further advice. In addition, a sudden loss of consciousness without any of the symptoms described above is *not* likely to be a fainting episode and should be evaluated immediately.

HEAD AND NECK INJURIES

Most childhood bumps on the head do not cause significant damage, although many result in a lump or "goose egg," which may alarm parents when it appears soon after the accident. This localized collection of blood, called a hematoma, is not unusual because of the abundant blood supply in the scalp. The lump will gradually decrease in size over the next few days, although local discoloration may persist for weeks.

Treatment   ◆ Typically a child will cry for a few minutes after bumping his head. He will need comforting and reassurance; a cold pack gently applied to the point of impact may help reduce local swelling.
◆ If the pain continues after 15 or 20 minutes, acetaminophen (Tylenol) in a dose appropriate for his size may help. Do not give aspirin because it inhibits blood clotting. Stronger pain medication (such as codeine) might cause drowsiness, which could make evaluation of his condition more difficult later on.
◆ Over the next few hours he may complain of a little dizziness, nausea, and fatigue. He may throw up once or twice and want to lie down or nap. It is not necessary to try to keep him awake, but after an hour or so make sure he can be awakened without difficulty.

♦ Watch his progress over the next 24 to 48 hours because in very rare instances a blow to the head results in bleeding within the skull. This complication is commonly associated with increasing headache, repeated vomiting, and/or (most important) difficulty arousing the child. Observe his daytime behavior for possible signs of trouble (see below) and awaken him when you go to bed and once again three or four hours later. Make sure that he can be fully awakened, that he has normal strength and movement of arms and legs, and that he talks appropriately with you (or, if he is too young to talk, that he interacts normally in other ways).

Symptoms   *of more serious injury*

While most bumps on the head will not need medical attention, you should contact your child's doctor if one or more of the following occur:

♦ There is loss of consciousness, even if it lasts only a few seconds. A child who remains unconscious for more than a few minutes after a head injury should be seen by a doctor immediately. If there is any possibility of a neck injury, he should not be moved until he has been properly immobilized using a backboard and neck brace provided by an emergency transport team.

♦ The child is confused or disoriented following the accident or cannot remember what happened. If any alteration or loss of consciousness occurs following a blow to the head, the child is said to have a concussion. While a concussion does not necessarily indicate permanent damage to the brain or skull, closer observation in the hospital and/or at home will usually be recommended for at least one to two days following the injury.

♦ The child becomes increasingly difficult to arouse.

♦ The child is younger than 12 months of age.

♦ Crying continues for more than 10 minutes after the injury.

♦ The child complains of persistent or worsening headache. In an infant or a toddler who is too young to say what is bothering him, this may be manifested by ongoing irritability.

♦ The child vomits more than 3 times during the 24 hours after the accident.

♦ A seizure occurs (see *seizures,* Reference).

♦ There is a cut on the head (or elsewhere) that may require suturing.

♦ Clear or bloody fluid is draining from the nose or ears.

♦ You have any questions or concerns about the injury or your child's behavior.

Treatment   *for more severe head or neck injury*

If your child appears to have had a more severe head or neck injury, keep him as still as possible, especially his head and neck. Check for loss of consciousness by calling the child's name or tapping his chest. If he has lost consciousness, check his breathing and pulse as well. If they are absent, start rescue breathing or CPR immediately (see page 806).

If the child was not unconscious for more than a few seconds and if he is not complaining of any headache or neck pain, it is probably all right to let him move. However, if he complains of neck pain, or if you are concerned that he might have hurt his neck, do not move him because a neck injury that might not be apparent could lead to paralysis if he is improperly moved. Call 911 and have medical personnel evaluate and transport him to the hospital using appropriate immobilization techniques.

LOSS OF CONSCIOUSNESS   *See also* Fainting *and* Head and Neck Injuries.

Loss of consciousness in infants and children is most commonly caused by direct trauma to the head. But other conditions and illnesses can cause this event, including fainting episodes, seizures, severe allergic reactions, accidental or intentional drug ingestion, and diabetes. Losing consciousness is potentially very significant, even if it is brief and appears to resolve completely, and it should be discussed with (and possibly evaluated by) a physician.

Treatment   Check breathing and pulse. If they are absent, start rescue breathing or CPR immediately (see page 806). Any apparent loss of consciousness can be confirmed by calling the child's name, gently shaking him (unless there is concern about head or neck injury), or tapping his chest. An unconscious child will not respond.

Whenever a child has lost consciousness, it is important to consider the possibility of a head injury. If there is any evidence that this has occurred (for example, bleeding or visible swelling), keep the head and neck immobilized and call 911 for transport to an emergency facility.

MUSCLE STRAINS AND CRAMPS

Muscle strains and cramps can result from vigorous physical activity and exercise.

STRAINS

A strain is an injury in which muscle fibers are pulled, stretched, or torn during physical activity.

Treatment   ◆ Do not massage the muscle; let it rest.
◆ Elevate a strained arm or leg to prevent swelling.
◆ Apply a cold cloth or compress to the muscle. To "ice" the injury,

wrap ice in a clean cloth and apply to the injury for a maximum of 20 minutes every hour. Repeat intermittently for 24 hours.
◆ After 24 hours, use a warm wet compress to soothe the muscle.
◆ Ibuprofen and/or acetaminophen can help ease pain and reduce swelling.

CRAMPS

Cramps—painful and usually sudden spasms of one or more muscles—can occur following overworking of a muscle or may happen spontaneously during sleep.

Treatment
◆ If your child has a cramp, help him gently stretch out the muscle immediately.
◆ Massage the knotted muscle for several minutes.
◆ Follow the massage with a warm bath, a warm wet compress, or a heating pad.

NOSEBLEEDS

Nosebleeds can have a variety of causes, including nose picking, dry weather, or trauma (such as being hit in the nose).

Treatment
Nosebleeds usually do not require medical attention. If your child gets a nosebleed, follow these steps:
◆ Have the child lean over a sink or sit in a chair with his head bent slightly forward to prevent the blood from running down the throat.
◆ Have the child blow the nose once into tissue or toilet paper to remove any clotted blood. If any blood has run into the mouth, have the child spit it out. (Swallowing the blood can irritate the stomach.)
◆ Apply pressure with the child's thumb and forefinger, pinching the nose near the opening of the nostrils (not high on the bridge of the nose) for five minutes or more. If your child cannot apply pressure, do it for him.
◆ After five minutes slowly remove your fingers. If the nose continues to bleed, repeat for 10 more minutes.
◆ If the nose continues to bleed, contact your physician.

OBJECTS IN THE NOSE

If you have small children, it may only be a matter of time before you will be called upon to remove a toy or other small object from your child's nose.

Treatment   Before seeking medical treatment, try to remove the object following these steps:

◆ Calm the child, and ask her to breathe through her mouth.
◆ Hold a tissue up to your child's nose and have her blow her nose.
◆ If the object doesn't come out, contact your physician. Do not try to remove it with tweezers or a cotton swab. This could damage the inside of the nose.

OVEREXPOSURE TO HEAT OR COLD

HYPOTHERMIA

Hypothermia, or low body temperature, results from prolonged unprotected exposure to a cold environment. Immersion in cold water causes much greater loss of body heat than exposure to air the same temperature and thus can cause hypothermia within minutes. (Wearing wet clothes in a cold environment also increases heat loss and the likelihood of hypothermia.) Small children and infants are especially prone to hypothermia.

Our physiological functions, metabolism, and central nervous system can function only within a very narrow temperature range. As the body loses heat, several internal responses attempt to maintain the internal or core temperature as close to 98.6°F (37°C) as possible. Blood flow is diverted to the upper body to preserve heat within the brain, heart, lungs, and other vital organs. The hands, feet, arms, and legs become cold first, but our limbs are designed to tolerate this decrease in temperature fairly well. Shivering (rapid involuntary contractions of muscles) generates heat to preserve core body temperature.

Symptoms
◆ numbness and/or weakness
◆ lethargy
◆ sleepiness
◆ confusion
◆ loss of coordination
◆ staggering
◆ inappropriate behavior

Treament
◆ Move victim to a warm area. If this is not possible, shelter her from the wind, change any wet clothing, and put her in a sleeping bag if one is available. An adult lying in the same sleeping bag may provide additional heat for a child. Give the victim something warm to drink, if she is able to drink and it is available.
◆ If symptoms persist, if there is any loss of consciousness, or if there has been an immersion in near-freezing water, take the victim to the nearest emergency room immediately.

FROSTBITE

This freezing injury to skin occurs most often in windy or wet conditions. It typically affects areas of the body that are exposed or have a limited blood supply, such as the nose, ears, fingers, and toes. Frostbitten fingers or toes are usually flushed. If the frostbite is severe, the affected skin will become hard, white or mottled, and numb.

Treatment   As soon as you recognize any change in local skin color (especially in a vulnerable area) after being outdoors, take the following steps:

- Bring the person in from the cold as quickly as possible and remove any wet clothing.
- "Thaw" out the frostbitten part of the body by immersing it in warm (but not hot) water or applying warm moist compresses to it. (Use a bathtub if multiple areas are involved.) Do not use a heat lamp or electric heater, which might overheat and actually burn frostbitten skin.
- Numbness will usually disappear, and the normal skin color will return within a half hour. Pain may be felt as the affected areas rewarm; acetaminophen may be given if needed.
- Keep the rest of your child's body comfortable with blankets or other warm clothing.
- Do not massage or rub snow on frostbitten areas of the body—this can cause damage to local tissue.
- If skin color and sensation are not normal within 20 to 30 minutes or if blisters develop in the frostbitten areas, seek medical attention.

PREVENTION

The primary means of preventing hypothermia or frostbite is to dress appropriately for cold weather. Additional helps include the following:

- Because a significant amount of heat is lost from the surface of the head and because ears and fingers are particularly vulnerable to frostbite, make sure your child wears a hat or ear protection and mittens outdoors in cold weather.
- Multiple layers of clothing help prevent loss of body heat. Since wet clothing significantly increases heat loss, the outermost layer should be waterproof.

HYPERTHERMIA

Hyperthermia is an increase in the internal or core body temperature resulting from circumstances such as strenuous exercise or exposure to high environmental temperatures. (Fever, which is by far the most common cause of temperature elevation, is discussed in Sepecial Concerns, page 267.) The body responds to this heat stress with mechanisms designed to maintain core temperature close to 98.6°F (37°C). The respiratory rate will increase (which causes heat to be lost from the lungs), and sweat will evaporate from the skin (which helps the body cool).

If the environmental temperature is higher than body temperature, the only way heat can be lost from the body is through evaporation. In high humidity conditions sweat does not readily evaporate, thus slowing the cooling process even more. Dehydration increases the risk of hyperthermia, as do certain medications that may reduce the body's ability to sweat.

Hyperthermia can take the following forms.

HEATSTROKE

This is the most severe form of hyperthermia, occurring during extremes of temperature and very strenuous exercise. The body temperature often climbs above 105°F, sometimes with an absence of sweating.

Symptoms
- confusion
- impaired coordination
- loss of consciousness

Treatment
Heatstroke is a medical emergency that should be treated immediately.
- Remove the victim's clothing.
- Move him to a cooler environment.
- Blow air on him with a fan while spraying him with a mist of water.
- Give him liquids. (If the person cannot take enough liquid by mouth, he will need intravenous fluids.)
- Apply cold packs to the groin or the armpits.

HEAT EXHAUSTION

Milder than heatstroke, the body temperature may or may not be elevated.

Symptoms
- nausea
- vomiting
- fatigue
- headache

Treatment
Heat exhaustion can progress to heatstroke if not treated properly, but symptoms should resolve within one hour with proper treatment. Follow the same treatment as given above for heatstroke.

HEAT SYNCOPE, OR HEAT FAINTING

This is fairly common and typically occurs when a person must stand for a prolonged period in a hot environment. (A band member standing at attention for an extended time on a hot day is a candidate for this problem.) In this case, blood pools in the legs, causing blood pressure to drop until the person feels faint.

Treatment
- ◆ Move to a cooler location.
- ◆ Have the person lie down.
- ◆ Elevate the legs.
- ◆ Give liquids.

POISONING

A child who has ingested a toxic substance or an excessive amount of a therapeutic medication may or may not be able to tell you what has happened; this will depend on the child's age, her condition after the episode (that is, alert, drowsy, or unconscious), and her emotional state.

Symptoms
Indications that your child has swallowed a toxic substance (or an overdose of medication) could include the following:

- ◆ sudden illness for no apparent reason
- ◆ close proximity to a potentially toxic substance such as a household cleaning product or a medication—especially if the container is open and pills or liquid are spilled
- ◆ unusual behavior
- ◆ unusual liquids, stains, or powder on the skin, clothing, or around the mouth
- ◆ dizziness, weakness, stupor, confusion, or coma
- ◆ blurry vision, double vision, or a change in the normal size of the pupils
- ◆ rapid heart rate
- ◆ fever, headache, irritability
- ◆ rash or changes in skin color (blue, flushed, or pale)
- ◆ depression or unusual shifts in mood
- ◆ ringing in the ears
- ◆ coughing, chest pain, or difficulty breathing—with or without increased noise during breathing
- ◆ nausea, vomiting, abdominal pain or cramping, or diarrhea
- ◆ twitching muscles or unexplained muscle pain or cramping
- ◆ excessive saliva
- ◆ inability to control urination or bowel movements

◆ loss of appetite
◆ abnormal breath odor

Treatment
◆ Check the ABCs—airway, breathing, and circulation—and begin rescue breathing or CPR if necessary (see page 806). If CPR has been initiated, have someone call 911. (If you are alone, call 911 after you have carried out CPR for approximately one minute.)
◆ If CPR is not needed, call your child's physician, the nearest emergency room, or a local poison-control center. If you can't find a number for a poison-control center, call 1-212-POISONS.
◆ If the child is having seizures, protect him from injury (see next page).
◆ If the child vomits, try to protect the airway. Position him so that whatever is vomited will exit away from the mouth and not accidentally be inhaled into the airway. If necessary, gently remove any remaining material from his mouth.
◆ If the exposure was a skin contamination, remove all contaminated clothing and wash skin, hair, and nails.
◆ If he has been exposed to fumes, remove him from the area in which the fumes are present.
◆ If the material went into the eye, irrigate it thoroughly with tap water (see Chemicals in the Eye, page 791).
◆ Take the substance and its container with you to the doctor's office or emergency room and be prepared to answer some questions: Where was the child found? What and how much was ingested? When did symptoms (if any) begin? Did symptoms begin gradually or abruptly? What treatment was done at home and when?
◆ DO NOT wait for dramatic signs of illness before seeking medical assistance.
◆ DO NOT give anything as an antidote or attempt to neutralize a poison unless you have been told to do so by a physician or poison-control center.
◆ DO NOT attempt to give the child anything by mouth if he is unconscious.
◆ DO NOT induce vomiting unless directed to do so by a physician or a poison-control center.
◆ DO NOT rely on the label of a medication or other substance to tell you whether or not it is potentially hazardous.

USING IPECAC

Ipecac is a medicine used to induce vomiting, thereby reducing the amount of toxic material available to be absorbed into the bloodstream.

Some substances should not be vomited because they will cause even more damage to body tissues on their way up. *Do not use ipecac unless you know what has been swallowed and you have been instructed by a doctor or poison-control center to use it.*

The best results are obtained if ipecac is given within 30 minutes of the ingestion. If a number of hours have passed since the material was swallowed, in most cases it is not likely that any of it will still be present in the stomach.

DO NOT use ipecac when the child has swallowed the following:

- alkaline materials: detergents, drain cleaners, oven cleaners, bleach, and flat circular batteries. Chemical names to look for include lye, sodium hydroxide, potassium hydroxide, ammonia, calcium oxide, trisodium phosphate, and wood ash.
- acids: automobile battery fluid, toilet-bowl cleaners, soldering fluxes, antirust compounds, and slate cleaners. Chemical names include sulfuric, hydrochloric, phosphoric, hydrofluoric, and oxalic acids.
- petroleum products: cleaning fluid, gasoline, kerosene, coal oil, fuel oil, or paint thinner.
- sharp or solid objects: glass, nails, razors, a thermometer.

DO NOT use ipecac when a toxic substance is swallowed by

- a child less than 6 months of age
- a child who has a hereditary tendency to bleed (i.e., hemophilia)
- a child who has had significant vomiting already
- a child who is stuporous, unconscious, or having a seizure

Directions for giving ipecac:

- For a child between 6 and 12 months of age, give one to two teaspoons (5 to 10 ml).
- For a child 1 to 12 years of age, give one tablespoon (15 ml).
- For a teenager, give one to two tablespoons (15 to 30 ml).
- Give the dose with one or more glasses of water or juice (no milk products).
- If vomiting does not occur in 20 to 30 minutes, repeat the dose.
- If vomiting does not occur after a second dose, contact your doctor or emergency facility for further advice.

SEIZURES

A seizure is a sudden abnormal surge of electrical activity in the brain, with manifestations that may range from subtle lapses in attention to terrifying convulsions.

Symptoms   These vary according to the type of seizure. See *seizures,* Reference.

Treatment   If your child is having a seizure

◆ Gently lay him on a soft surface such as a bed or carpet, away from any hard objects. Position the head to the side so that any saliva (or any material that comes up if he vomits) can drain from the mouth.
◆ If his mouth is empty, don't put a finger, stick, or spoon in it because this may damage his teeth or cause him to vomit. If he has anything in his mouth, gently remove it with your finger. Do not try to pour a liquid into his mouth.
◆ Since he cannot swallow his tongue, don't try to grab it with your fingers.
◆ Don't restrain the child.
◆ Do not immerse him in a tub of water, even if he has a fever.
◆ If you can, time the seizure's length and carefully observe your child's movements during the episode.
◆ If the seizure lasts for more than five minutes, call 911 for emergency medical assistance. Even if the seizure ends before help arrives, allow the paramedics to assess your child.
◆ If the seizure ends within five minutes, call your child's physician immediately for further advice.

WOUNDS AND WOUND CARE

BRUISES AND HEMATOMAS

Bruises (also called contusions) usually form a bluish discoloration at the site of the injury and fade from blue to green to yellow over one to two weeks.

A hematoma (goose egg) is a collection of blood and swelling in the skin or just underneath it. Depending upon its size and location, this swelling will go down in one to ten days.

Treatment   ◆ Rest the injured area for a few days.
◆ Apply ice intermittently to the injured area for a few days. The ice can be applied for 20 minutes every two to four hours and will help to limit bleeding into the tissues. If your child won't allow you to put ice on the bruised area, it will still heal fairly quickly in most cases.

ABRASIONS

Abrasions (or scrapes) are broad areas of superficial skin damage; they seldom result in any deep underlying damage and rarely leave a significant scar. They heal quickly and usually do not become infected.

Treatment
- ◆ Cleanse the wound gently with warm soapy water to remove any dirt and debris. A painless antiseptic such as hydrogen peroxide can help cleanse an abrasion.
- ◆ Apply an antibiotic ointment such as a neomycin-polysporin mixture (Neosporin) or one prescribed by your child's physician. Cover with a nonstick wound dressing to keep it clean.
- ◆ Change the dressing once or twice daily until the wound is no longer moist and sensitive.

LACERATIONS

A laceration can range from a minimal break in the skin surface, requiring only a brief cleansing and a day or two of a simple dressing, to a long, gaping wound requiring extensive repair. A deep laceration may damage tendons, nerves, joints, or other underlying tissues. It may also contain dirt or other foreign material that can lead to infection. Because of these potential complications, most wounds deeper or wider than 1 or 2 mm should be examined by a physician to determine appropriate treatment.

Treatment
First aid for lacerations that might require sutures (stitches) includes the following:

- ◆ Apply steady pressure with clean gauze or washcloth to stop bleeding.
- ◆ Keep the area clean.
- ◆ Rinse with clean water if available.
- ◆ Keep covered with a sterile bandage, or at least a clean cloth, until the wound can be examined by a medical professional.
- ◆ A laceration should be closed within 24 hours. The sooner the wound is treated, the less likely it will become infected. If a laceration is not sutured, the consequences are usually not serious, but healing could take longer and the resulting scar is likely to be wider or more prominent.
- ◆ Sometimes lacerations are deep enough to involve injury to a nerve or tendon. For this reason, any laceration that looks deep at all should be examined and cleaned by your child's physician or another medical professional.

WHEN SUTURES ARE NOT USED

With some contaminated lacerations or certain types of animal or human bites, the physician may not use sutures because closing the wound could increase the risk of infection. In such cases the wound will be left open, but it will gradually heal as the body's repair processes close the defect.

CONCERNS ABOUT TETANUS

Any laceration, puncture, bite, abrasion, or burn should prompt a review of a child's tetanus immunization status. Tetanus is a potential threat following any wound, but it is a greater concern following punctures or contaminated wounds. If a child is on schedule for his or her immunizations or is fully immunized, no tetanus update will be needed. Otherwise a tetanus booster should be given.

SIGNS OF INFECTION

Signs and symptoms of infection include local pain, swelling, and redness, which may spread over a large area around the wound. There may also be fever. Inflammation of local lymph channels may form a red streak that extends away from the wound. Some bacteria cause the production of discolored drainage (or pus). If a wound appears to be developing an infection, show it to a physician. Mild heat on the affected area, rest, elevation of the affected area (if an arm or leg), and antibiotics will most likely be recommended.

THE IMPORTANCE OF FOLLOW-UP

Be sure to obtain specific wound-care instructions before leaving the office or emergency facility. In general, if sutures or sterile strips have been used, the wound should be kept dry for a few days. This will mean that the child should not go swimming or soak the wounds while bathing. In some cases, the physician may instruct you to clean the wound and apply fresh dressings. He or she should also tell you when the strips or bandages should be removed. A follow-up appointment is usually required when stitches need to be removed.

Cardiopulmonary Resuscitation (CPR) and Choking Emergencies

It is highly recommended that parents and teenagers take a Red Cross class in first aid and cardiopulmonary resuscitation (CPR), and then take a refresher class every 2 years. For those who have completed this training, the following material is a review of the basic steps for assisting a choking victim and for performing CPR.

CARDIOPULMONARY RESUSCITATION (CPR): NINE-YEAR-OLD TO ADULT

1. Check to see if the victim is conscious.
   - Tap his chest or shoulder, or give his body a gentle shake.
   - Do not shake his head and neck.
   - Call out to him, "Are you OK?"

2. If there is no response, shout for help.
   - As soon as someone is available, have him or her call 911.

3. Roll the person onto his back if he is not in that position already.
   - Support his head and neck, keeping them in a straight line with his back.
   - Lay the victim on a firm surface.

4. Check to see if he is breathing.
   - Kneel next to his head.
   - Tilt his head back and lift his chin to open the airway.
   - Put your head near the person's mouth and nose.
   - For 5 seconds, look, listen, and feel for breathing.
     (a) Is the chest rising?
     (b) Can you hear breathing sounds?
     (c) Can you feel air moving against your face?

Tilt head back and lift chin. (See 4.)

Make tight seal over victim's mouth. (See 5.)

5. **If you can't see, hear, or feel the victim breathing, you must immediately begin breathing for him (rescue breathing).**
   - Pinch his nose shut using 2 fingers.
   - With your lips make a tight seal around the victim's mouth.
   - Give 2 full breaths.
     (a) Breathe into the victim for about 1 to 1½ seconds, watching for the chest to rise.
     (b) Pause to let the air flow out, and then give another breath.

6. Check the victim's pulse.
   - Feel for a pulse at the side of his neck for 5 to 10 seconds.
   - If you feel a pulse but he is not breathing:
     (a) Give 1 breath every 5 seconds.
     (b) Recheck the pulse every 10 to 12 breaths.
     (c) Continue breathing for the victim until
        —the victim begins to breathe without help, or
        —another rescuer takes over, or
        —you do not feel a pulse.

7. **If there is no pulse, begin CPR.**

Have someone call 911 for help, if this has not been done already.

Feel for pulse at side of neck. (See 6.)

8. Kneel beside the victim, halfway between his head and chest, so you can move quickly between giving breaths and compressing the chest.

9. Position your hands on the victim's chest.
   - Place the middle finger of 1 hand at the lower end of the breastbone (where the lower border of the rib cage meets the breastbone).
   - Place the heel of your other hand on the breastbone, 2 finger widths above the end of the breastbone (where you placed your middle finger).
   - Remove your finger from the lower end of the breastbone and place the heel of that hand over the hand that is on the breastbone.

Position hands on victim's chest. (See 9.)

♦ Don't allow your fingers to rest on the victim's chest.
  (a) Point your fingers upward (away from the body), or
  (b) mesh the fingers of your 2 hands.

10. Compress the chest by pressing straight downward.
    ♦ Use your body weight, not your arm muscles.
    ♦ Keep your arms straight, with elbows locked.
    ♦ Lean with your shoulders over your hands.
    ♦ You should move straight up and down, not rock back and forth.
    ♦ The breastbone should depress 1½ to 2 inches.
    ♦ Give 15 compressions in 10 seconds. (Count 1 and 2 and 3. . . .)

Compress chest, using body weight. (See 10.)

11. After you have given 15 compressions, give 2 full breaths.
    ♦ Gently tilt the victim's head back.
    ♦ Pinch the nose shut with your fingers.
    ♦ With your lips make a tight seal around the victim's mouth.
    ♦ Give 2 full breaths for 1 to 1½ seconds each.
    ♦ Check the pulse.

If there is no pulse:

12. Repeat the cycle of 15 compressions and 2 breaths for 4 cycles.
    ♦ After 4 cycles (about 1 minute), check for a pulse.
    ♦ If there is no pulse, continue CPR.
    ♦ If a pulse is present, check for breathing.
      (a) Carry out rescue breathing if the victim is not breathing.
    ♦ Continue CPR or rescue breathing until
      (a) the victim is breathing and has a pulse, or
      (b) another rescuer takes over.

CARDIOPULMONARY RESUSCITATION (CPR): YOUNG CHILD—AGES 1 TO 8

1. Check to see if the child is conscious.
   - Tap her chest or shoulder, or give her body a gentle shake.
   - Do not shake her head and neck.
   - Call out to her, "Are you OK?"

2. If there is no response, shout for help.
   - As soon as someone is available, have him or her call 911.

3. Roll the child onto her back if she is not in that position already.
   - Support her head and neck, keeping them in a straight line with her back.
   - Lay the child on a firm surface.

4. Check to see if she is breathing.
   - Kneel next to her head.
   - Tilt her head back and lift her chin to open the airway.
   - Put your head near the child's mouth and nose.
   - For 5 seconds, look, listen, and feel for breathing.
     (a) Is the chest rising?
     (b) Can you hear breathing sounds?
     (c) Can you feel air moving against your face?

5. **If you can't see, hear, or feel the child breathing, you must immediately begin breathing for her (rescue breathing).**
   - Pinch her nose shut using 2 fingers.
   - With your lips make a tight seal around the child's mouth.
   - Give 2 full breaths.
     (a) Breathe into the victim for about 1 to 1½ seconds, watching for the chest to rise.
     (b) Pause to let the air flow out, and then give another breath.

Tilt head back and lift chin. (See 4.)

Make tight seal over victim's mouth. (See 5.)

6. Check her pulse.
   - Feel for a pulse at the side of her neck for 5 to 10 seconds.
   - If you feel a pulse but she is not breathing:
     (a) Give 1 breath every 5 seconds.
     (b) Recheck the pulse every 10 to 12 breaths.
     (c) Continue breathing for the child until
         —she begins to breathe without help, or
         —another rescuer takes over, or
         —you do not feel a pulse.

7. **If there is no pulse, begin CPR.**

Have someone call 911 for help, if this has not been done already.

8. Position your hands on the child's chest.
   - Place the middle finger of 1 hand at the lower end of the breastbone (where the lower border of the rib cage meets the breastbone).
   - Place the heel of your other hand on the breastbone, 2 finger widths above the end of the breastbone (where you placed your middle finger).
   - Remove your finger from the lower end of the breastbone and place the heel of that hand over the hand that is on the breastbone.
   - Don't allow your fingers to rest on the child's chest.
     (a) Point your fingers upward (away from the body), or
     (b) mesh the fingers of your 2 hands.

9. Compress the chest by pressing straight downward.
   - Use your body weight, not your arm muscles.
   - Keep your arms straight, with elbows locked.
   - Lean with your shoulders over your hands.
   - You should move straight up and down, not rock back and forth.
   - The breastbone should depress 1 to 1½ inches.

Feel for pulse at side of neck. (See 6.)

Position hands on victim's chest. (See 8.)

- Give 5 compressions over about 4 seconds. (Count 1 and 2 and 3. . . .)

10. After you have given 5 compressions, give 1 full breath.
    - Gently tilt the child's head back.
    - Pinch her nose shut with your fingers.
    - With your lips make a tight seal around the child's mouth.
    - Give 1 full breath for 1 to 1¹/₂ seconds.
    - Check the pulse.

If there is no pulse:

11. Repeat the cycle of 5 compressions and 1 breath for 10 cycles.
    - After 10 cycles (about 1 minute), check for a pulse.
    - If there is no pulse, continue CPR.
    - If a pulse is present, check for breathing.
      (a) Carry out rescue breathing if the child is not breathing.
    - Continue CPR or rescue breathing until
      (a) the child is breathing and has a pulse, or
      (b) another rescuer takes over.

Compress chest, using body weight. (See 9.)

CARDIOPULMONARY RESUSCITATION (CPR): NEWBORN TO 1 YEAR

1. Check to see if the baby is conscious.
   - Tap his shoulder, or give his body a gentle shake.
   - Do not shake his head and neck.

2. If there is no response, shout for help.
   - As soon as someone is available, have him or her call 911.

3. Roll the baby onto his back if he is not in that position already.
   - Support his head and neck, keeping them in a straight line with his back.
   - Lay the baby on a firm surface.

4. Check to see if he is breathing.
   - Gently tilt his head back and lift his chin to open the airway.
   - Put your head near the infant's mouth and nose.
   - For 3 to 5 seconds, look, listen, and feel for breathing.
     (a) Is the chest rising?
     (b) Can you hear breathing sounds?
     (c) Can you feel air moving against your face?

5. **If you can't see, hear, or feel the infant breathing, you must immediately begin breathing for him (rescue breathing).**
   - With your lips make a tight seal around the baby's nose and mouth.
   - Give 2 slow breaths.
     (a) Breathe into the infant for about 1 to $1\frac{1}{2}$ seconds, watching for the chest to rise.
     (b) Pause to let the air flow out, and then give another breath.

6. Check his pulse.
   - With 1 hand, keep the baby's head tilted back.
   - With your other hand, check for a pulse.
     (a) Feel for 5 seconds on the inside of the baby's upper arm, between the elbow and shoulder. Also listen for a heartbeat by placing your ear next to the baby's chest.
   - If you feel a pulse but he is not breathing:
     (a) Give 1 breath every 3 seconds.
     (b) Recheck the pulse every 20 breaths (about once per minute).
     (c) Continue breathing for the infant until
         —he begins to breathe without help, or
         —another rescuer takes over, or
         —you do not feel a pulse.

7. **If there is no pulse or heartbeat, begin CPR.**

Have someone call 911 for help, if this has not been done already.

Tilt head back and lift chin. (See 4.)

Make tight seal around nose and mouth. (See 5.)

Feel inside upper arm for pulse. (See 6.)

8. Position your fingers on the baby's chest.
   - With 1 hand, keep the baby's head tilted back.
   - Place the index finger of your other hand on the center of the breastbone, just below the level of the nipples.
   - Place your next 2 fingers (the middle and ring fingers) right next to your index finger (slightly farther down the baby's breastbone). Then lift your index finger.

9. Compress the baby's chest using your 2 fingers.
   - Push the breastbone straight down ¹/₂ to 1 inch.
   - Give 5 compressions over about 3 seconds.

Compress chest using 2 fingers (See 9.)

10. After you have given 5 compressions, give 1 full breath.
    - With your lips make a tight seal around the baby's nose and mouth.
    - Give 1 full breath for 1 to 1¹/₂ seconds.
    - Check the pulse.

If there is no pulse:

11. Repeat the cycle of 5 compressions and 1 breath for 10 cycles.
    - After 10 cycles (about 1 minute), check for a pulse.
    - If there is no pulse, continue CPR.
    - If a pulse is present, check for breathing.
      (a) Carry out rescue breathing if the baby is not breathing.
    - Continue CPR or rescue breathing until
      (a) the baby is breathing and has a pulse, or
      (b) another rescuer takes over.

Make tight seal around nose and mouth. (See 10.)

CHOKING EMERGENCIES: ONE-YEAR-OLD TO ADULT

1. Determine if the person is choking.
   - If there is forceful coughing or the person can speak, do not interfere.
   - Ask the person if he is choking.
   - If he is unable to speak or cough, have someone call 911 and take immediate action (step 2 and following).

2. Get behind the victim and position your hands.
   - Wrap your arms around the victim's waist.
   - Make a fist with 1 hand.
   - Place the thumb side of your fist against the middle of the victim's abdomen—just above the navel but below the rib cage.
   - Grab your fist with your other hand.

3. Give abdominal thrusts.
   - Quickly pull your fist inward and upward into the abdomen.
   - **If the victim is pregnant or too big to reach around the abdomen, give chest thrusts instead.**
     - **(a) Place your fist against the center of the breastbone.**
     - **(b) Grab your fist with your other hand, and give thrusts into the chest.**
   - Continue thrusts until
     - (a) the object is forced out of the victim's airway, or
     - (b) the victim becomes unconscious.

Wrap arms around victim's waist. (See 2.)

If the victim is unconscious:

4. Have someone call 911 for help, if this has not been done already.

5. Roll the person onto his back if he is not in that position already.
   - Support his head and neck, keeping them in a straight line with his back.

- Lay the victim on a firm surface.
- Clear any material out of the mouth.
   (a) **Be careful not to push any object or food farther down.**

6. Check to see if he is breathing.
   - Kneel next to his head.
   - Tilt his head back and lift his chin to open the airway.
   - Put your head near the person's mouth and nose.
   - For 5 seconds, look, listen, and feel for breathing.
      (a) Is the chest rising?
      (b) Can you hear breathing sounds?
      (c) Can you feel air moving against your face?

Tilt head back and lift chin. (See 6.)

7. **If you can't see, hear, or feel the victim breathing, you must immediately begin breathing for him (rescue breathing).**
   - Tilt the victim's head back.
   - Pinch his nose shut using 2 fingers.
   - With your lips make a tight seal around the victim's mouth.
   - Give 2 full breaths.
      (a) Breathe into the victim for about 1 to 1½ seconds, watching for the chest to rise.
      (b) Pause to let the air flow out, and then give another breath.

Make tight seal over victim's mouth. (See 7.)

If the breaths will not go in:

8. Tilt the head farther back, and try again.
   - Pinch his nose shut using 2 fingers.
   - With your lips make a tight seal around the victim's mouth.
   - Give 2 full breaths.

If the breaths still will not go in, the airway is probably blocked.

9. Give abdominal thrusts.
   - Straddle 1 of the victim's upper legs.

- Place the heel of your hand on the victim's abdomen, just above the navel and below the rib cage.
- Place your other hand on top of the first, and point your fingers toward the victim's head.
- Give 5 quick thrusts toward the head and into the abdomen.

10. Sweep the victim's mouth with your finger.
    - Use your fingers and thumb to grasp and lift the victim's lower jaw and tongue.
    - Slide 1 finger into the mouth, down the victim's cheek to the base of his tongue.
    - Try to hook or sweep the object out.
      (a) **Be careful not to push any object or food farther down.**

    If the person is still not breathing, repeat steps 5 through 8.
    - Tilt the head back.
    - Give 2 slow breaths.
    - Retilt the head.
    - Give 2 slow breaths.
    - Give 5 abdominal thrusts.
    - Do finger sweep.

11. Continue this sequence until the object is removed and you can inflate the victim's lungs.

12. Once you are getting air into the victim, check for breathing and pulse. (See CPR, page 806.)
    - If he is not breathing, begin rescue breathing. (See CPR, page 807.)
    - If he does not have a pulse, begin CPR. (See CPR, page 807.)

CHOKING EMERGENCIES: NEWBORN TO 1 YEAR

1. Determine if the baby is choking.
   - If there is forceful coughing or the baby can cry, do not interfere.
   - If she is unable to cry, cough, or breathe or if she is coughing very weakly, have someone call 911 and take immediate action (step 2 and following).

2. Position the baby face down on your forearm.
   - Support the baby's head and jaw as you turn her face down.
   - Position her so that her head is lower than her chest.

3. Give 4 back blows.
   - Use the heel of your free hand.
   - Strike forcefully between her shoulder blades.

4. Turn the baby onto her back.
   - Support the baby's head and jaw as you roll her over.
   - Rest her back on your thigh.

5. Give 4 thrusts to the chest.
   - Place 2 or 3 fingers in the center of her breastbone (just below the level of the nipples).
   - Thrust downward quickly about $\frac{1}{2}$ to 1 inch.

6. Repeat steps 2 through 5.
   - Turn the baby face down.
   - Give 4 back blows.
   - Turn the baby on her back.
   - Give 4 chest thrusts.

7. Repeat this sequence until the baby begins to cough or breathe, or until she coughs up the object.

If the baby is unconscious:

8. Have someone call 911 for help, if this has not been done already.

Position baby face down on forearm. (See 2 & 3.)

Give chest thrusts using 2 or 3 fingers. (See 5.)

E
M
E
R
G
E
N
C
Y

9. Roll the baby onto her back.
   - Support her head and neck, keeping them in a straight line with her back.
   - Lay the baby on a firm surface.

10. Clear any material from the baby's mouth.
    - Use the fingers and thumb of 1 hand to grasp and lift the baby's lower jaw and tongue.
    - Use the little finger of your other hand to sweep the object or food out.
    (a) **Be careful not to push any object or food farther down.**

Clear material from baby's mouth. (See 10.)

11. Check to see if she is breathing.
    - Gently tilt her head back and lift her chin to open the airway.
    - Put your head near the infant's mouth and nose.
    - For 3 to 5 seconds, look, listen, and feel for breathing.
    (a) Is the chest rising?
    (b) Can you hear breathing sounds?
    (c) Can you feel air moving against your face?

12. **If you can't see, hear, or feel the infant breathing, you must immediately begin breathing for her (rescue breathing).**
    - With your lips make a tight seal around the baby's nose and mouth.
    - Give 2 slow breaths.
    (a) Breathe into the infant for about 1 to 1½ seconds, watching for the chest to rise.
    (b) Pause to let the air flow out, and then give another breath.

If the breaths will not go in:

Check to see if baby is breathing. (See 11.)

13. Tilt the head farther back, lift the chin, and try again.

If the breaths still will not go in, the airway is probably blocked.

14. Repeat the sequence of back blows and chest thrusts until the baby is breathing on her own or you are able to inflate her lungs.

- Turn the baby face down.
- Give 4 back blows.
- Turn the baby on her back.
- Give 4 chest thrusts.
- Check the mouth for any object or food.
- Tilt the head back.
- Give 2 slow breaths.
- Retilt the head.
- Give 2 more small breaths.

15. Once you are getting air into the victim, check for breathing and pulse. (See CPR, page 812.)
    - If she is not breathing, begin rescue breathing. (See CPR, page 812.)
    - If she does not have a pulse, begin CPR. (See CPR, page 812.)

Make tight seal around nose and mouth. (See 12.)

Safety—Indoors and Out

HOME SAFETY: INDOORS

- Never step away when your baby is on a high surface such as a changing table or countertop.
- Keep the sides of a baby's crib raised.
- If an infant seat is used outside the car, place it on the floor.
- Avoid infant walkers.
- Install safety gates (*not* accordion-style) to guard stairways.
- Lock doors to dangerous areas such as the basement and garage.
- Check the stability of drawers, tall furniture, and lamps before a baby becomes mobile.
- Remove tablecloths that might be within the reach of a toddler.
- Make sure any windows above the first floor of a multistory house are closed or have screens or guards that cannot be pushed out.
- Don't underestimate the climbing ability of a toddler.
- Remove or pad low furniture with sharp corners, such as coffee tables, in your child's living area.
- Place safety latches on all drawers and cupboards that are off-limits.
- Move anything dangerous—cleaning products; plumbing, gardening, painting,

refinishing, and agricultural chemicals and supplies; knives or other sharp utensils; and medicines—to high cabinets that are latched.

- Make knives off-limits to a child until he is old enough to learn (and demonstrate) how to use them correctly.
- Put covers on unused electrical outlets.
- Keep electrical cords out of the reach of children.
- Remove all poisonous plants from the home.
- Put the number of the nearest poison center on all phones. Call if a child puts something in his mouth that might be poisonous.
- Buy syrup of ipecac, but use only if directed to do so.
- Purchase all medicines in containers with safety caps.
- Do not transfer toxic substances to bottles, glasses, or jars, especially if those containers originally contained familiar liquids for drinking (such as juice).
- When leaving your children with a baby-sitter, leave emergency phone numbers, a permission slip for emergency care, and insurance information. (Or designate whom the sitter should call.) Make certain the sitter knows the address and phone number of your home, in case she needs to provide this information to emergency personnel.

FIRE AND BURN PREVENTION

- Never eat, drink, or carry anything hot near or while holding a baby or a small child.
- Don't cook when your child is at your feet. Use a playpen, high chair, or crib as a safety area for small children while you are preparing food.
- Use the rear burners on your stove, and keep the pan handles out of reach.
- Check formula, food, and drink temperatures carefully.
- Keep hot appliances and cords out of the reach of children.
- Do not allow your child to use the stove, microwave, hot curlers, curling iron, or steam iron until he or she is old enough to learn how to do so safely.
- Install and maintain smoke detectors in accordance with fire regulations in your area. If they are not wired directly into your home's electrical system, check smoke detector monthly and replace batteries annually.
- Provide nonflammable barriers around heating surfaces and fireplaces.
- Teach your child to drop and roll on the ground if his clothing catches fire.
- Have your heating system checked annually.
- If there are one or more tobacco smokers in the family, they should not be allowed to smoke inside the home.
- Keep matches and lighters out of the reach of children.
- Have a working fire extinguisher near the kitchen, but instruct your child not to play with it. However, older children and adolescents should be taught how to use it in an emergency.
- Do not permit your child to possess or play with fireworks.

SMOKE DETECTORS

Residential fires kill about 5,000 people every year in the United States, and the majority of these fatalities result not from burn injuries but from inhalation of smoke and toxic gases. Death usually occurs at night, when the victim is sleeping. Properly installed and maintained home smoke detectors could prevent many of these deaths.

Smoke detectors are considered the best and least expensive early-warning systems because they can alert people in a home *before* the fire ignites, *before* the concentration of smoke reaches a dangerous level, or *before* a fire becomes extremely intense. The risk of dying from a fire-related incident is twice as high in a home without functioning smoke detectors as in a home with them.

Smoke detectors can be wired directly into a home's electrical system, or they may be battery powered, in which case fresh batteries should be installed at least once a year. Each smoke detector should be tested regularly in accordance with the manufacturer's recommendations to ensure it is operating properly.

SMOKE DETECTOR

At least one detector should be installed on each floor of a multistory home, preferably near a bedroom so that sleeping residents will be given early warning in the event of a fire. Local fire regulations and/or building codes may specify that more smoke detectors must be installed for a particular home's floor plan.

FIRE AND DISASTER PREPARATION

Hopefully you will never have to deal with a major fire in your home, but some basic preparation can prevent confusion and panic should one occur. Cover the following details with your children:

♦ Using 911. (Call only after you've left the burning building.)

- Staying low to the ground when smoke is present.
- Avoiding opening any doors that are hot to the touch.
- Escaping through a window (including the use of a chain ladder in a multistory home).
- Discussing what firefighters may look like in their full gear. (Unless prepared ahead of time, children might be frightened by the bulky shapes with face masks and axes or other tools; hiding from the firefighters could be disastrous.)

FIRE ESCAPE ROUTE

- Getting help from neighbors.
- Agreeing on a meeting place if family members have different escape routes.
- Practicing family fire drills.

Make sure that your home address is clearly visible from the street. If possible, have the numbers neatly painted on the curbside as well.

While you are talking about your family's response to a fire, you should also go over contingency plans for any possible natural disaster (earthquake, flood, tornado, hurricane) that might occur where you live. Include instructions as to whom you or your children might contact in case communications are disrupted. (It may be easier to get in touch with a relative across the country, who could serve as a communication center for the family.)

WATER AND TUB SAFETY

- Turn down your water heater to 120°F or less.
- Make sure that an adult—not another child—bathes a baby.
- Remain in the room during every second of a child's bath. Have everything you'll need available at the tub before you start.
- Install strips with a roughened surface or lay a rubber mat in the bathtub to prevent slips and falls.
- Provide a barrier around any pool or spa. This should consist of a tall, hard-to-climb fence (which can be locked) extending around all four sides of a pool or an approved pool or spa cover.
- Do not leave buckets filled with water in any area where a toddler might play.

- Prohibit swimming in fast-moving water such as a creek, river, or canal.
- Permit diving *only* after the depth has been checked and your child has been taught how to dive correctly.
- Never leave your child unsupervised when he is in, on, or around water.
- Keep rescue equipment at the waterside, and take CPR training.

FIREARMS

- Any guns kept in the home should be unloaded and locked up, with ammunition locked in a separate location.
- Keeping a handgun for protection is dangerous to your family.
- Teach your children never to touch any gun they might find. If they see or hear about a gun at school, tell them they should tell an adult immediately.
- Non-gunpowder firearms (BB or pellet guns) should not be considered toys and are not recommended for children.

HOME SAFETY: OUTDOORS

- Before allowing your mobile child to explore the great outdoors around your home, take a child's-level survey of any area she might reach. If she's a skilled crawler, keep in mind how fast she can move while your attention is diverted.
- If you have a swimming pool, make sure that a childproof fence surrounds it. (Some states require this safety barrier by law.) If your yard contains a spa, it should be securely covered when not in use.
- Check the lawn for mushrooms—if you are not absolutely certain that they are nontoxic, get rid of them because anything a young child finds will likely go straight into her mouth.
- Make sure that potentially hazardous items such as garden tools, insecticides, or fertilizer are not accessible to children.
- Older children should not use garden, hand, or power tools until you teach them to use them correctly and safely. Give them detailed instructions (including demonstrations, if appropriate) and safety precautions; they should repeat back to you both directions and cautions before they are allowed to handle any potentially hazardous equipment.
- Protective eyewear must be worn if the use of any tools will produce flying debris. In addition, ear protection should be used when using loud power tools.
- Don't forget to apply sunscreen with a sun protection factor (SPF) rating of 15 or more if a child is going to be outdoors for any length of time, especially between the hours of 10 A.M. and 3 P.M.—even on a hazy or overcast day. This is particu-

larly important at higher altitudes or around lakes and seashores where the sun's ultraviolet light (which provokes the burn) can reflect off of water and sand. Special caution is needed for infants, because *a baby's skin can become sunburned after as little as 15 minutes of direct exposure.* Sunscreens containing PABA shouldn't be used on a baby's skin before six months of age. If you take your baby outdoors for any length of time, keep her in the shade or use an umbrella, and make sure that her skin is covered with appropriate clothing (including a hat or bonnet) if some sun exposure is unavoidable.

WEATHER SAFETY

- Dress your child appropriately for the outing, allowing for adjustments if the weather changes.
- Carry rain gear in your car.
- Apply sunblock (SPF 15 to 45, depending on skin type) before you or your child go outside.
- Take and use hats and sunglasses.

BICYCLE SAFETY

- Make sure your child takes a bike-safety class or teach him the rules of the road yourself.
- Stick to bicycle paths whenever possible.
- Children under age six should not ride on the street.
- Make sure that the bicycle is the right size (take the child along when you buy it). When sitting on the seat with hands on the handlebars, the child should be able to touch the ground with the balls of his feet. When straddling the center bar with both feet flat on the ground, there should be at least one inch of clearance between the bar and the child's crotch.
- Do not buy a bicycle with hand brakes until the child is able to grasp with sufficient pressure to use them effectively.
- Keep the bicycle in good repair and teach your child how to fix and maintain it.
- Insist that your child wear a bicycle helmet and always wear one yourself.
- Discourage your child from riding at night. If it is necessary for him to do so, be sure that the bicycle is properly equipped with lights and reflectors and that your child wears reflective (or at least bright) clothing.

SAFETY GEAR

* Provide the protective equipment appropriate for any sport in which your child participates. Make sure it is worn at practices as well as at games.
* Your child must wear a properly fitting helmet that meets the standards of the American National Standards Institute (ANSI) or the Snell Memorial Foundation when riding a bike or when sitting in a carrier seat on your bicycle. Wear your own helmet as well, both for self-protection and to set a good example. Critical injuries to the skull and brain can occur during a bicycle accident, and a helmet can reduce the severity of damage by as much as 90 percent. As your child grows, the helmet will need to be sized upward accordingly.
* Make sure that your child uses wrist guards, elbow and knee pads, and a helmet for rollerblading and skateboarding.

PEDESTRIAN SAFETY

* Fence off and/or supervise any outside play area.
* Provide a play area that prevents balls and riding toys from rolling into the street.
* Prohibit riding of Big Wheels, tricycles, and bicycles in or near traffic or on driveways.
* Hold a young child's hand when walking around traffic.
* When crossing the street, teach and model safety measures: Stop at the curb, then look—left, right, then left again—before entering the street.
* Plan walking routes that minimize crossing heavy traffic.

MOTOR VEHICLE SAFETY

SEAT BELTS AND CAR SEATS

Over the last 20 years, widespread use of seat belts has led to a steady reduction in traffic fatalities. Proper use of seat belts and car seats decreases the risk of serious injury or death by as much as 50 percent. But in the United States, the leading cause of death in people under age thirty-five continues to be motor-vehicle-related injuries. Most of these individuals were not properly restrained by seat belts or car seats.

SAFETY ON THE ROAD

* Parents and children should wear their seat belts. *Do not start the car until everyone is secured in an infant or child seat or properly belted.*

EMERGENCY

- *Never hold a child in your lap when you are riding in a car.*
- *A child under twelve should never be placed in the front seat of an automobile with a passenger-side air bag because deployment of the bag can cause fatal injuries in a young passenger—even during a minor accident.*
- For children under 40 pounds (18 kg), use a car safety seat approved for your child's age and weight in accordance with the manufacturer's directions. (Make sure you have a safety seat for your infant's first important ride home from the hospital.) *The seat should be secured in the rear seat of the vehicle.* For an infant who weighs less than 20 pounds (9 kg), the seat should face backwards. Buy or rent the next size up as your child grows larger.
- Toddlers 40 to 60 pounds should be properly secured in a booster seat.
- When the child reaches 60 pounds, lap and shoulder belts should be used. The lap belt should be low and tight across the pelvis, not the abdomen. The shoulder harness should be placed snugly over the collarbone and breastbone, not the shoulder.
- If your child takes off his seat belt or gets out of the car seat while you are driving, pull over safely and stop the car. Do not attempt to deal with this (or any other) problem while driving.
- Insist that your child wear a seat belt, no matter whose car he rides in.
- Never leave your child unattended in a car.
- Never transport a child in a cargo area that is not properly equipped to carry passengers (specifically, the back of a station wagon, van, or pickup truck).
- Do not allow your child under age twelve to operate a motor vehicle, including a motorcycle, motorbike, trail bike, or other off-road vehicles. An adolescent should operate one of these vehicles only if he is licensed and properly trained, and has demonstrated appropriate responsibility.
- Be very cautious about allowing your child to ride as a passenger on a motorcycle, motor bike, trail bike, or off-road vehicle. Insist on a proper helmet, slow speed, and a mature, sober driver.

Additional Resources

Books, journals, and organizations are listed alphabetically and in categories.

Some organizations listed are secular. These are marked with an asterisk (*). Inclusion on this list does not necessarily constitute an endorsement by Focus on the Family of an organization's material content or viewpoint. It would be wise to investigate any organization prior to using it as a resource.

For more information on resources or materials call 1-800-A-FAMILY.

Abuse

Boundaries: Gaining Control of Your Life by Dr. Henry Cloud and Dr. John Townsend. Grand Rapids, Mich.: Zondervan, 1992.

Child SHARE
Joanne Seldmeth, Executive Director
5400 Van Nuys Blvd., Ste. 412
Van Nuys, CA 91401
(818) 957-4452
This agency was set up to recruit, train, and support families or individuals who will provide quality care for abused, neglected, or abandoned children. They also have a monthly newsletter, videos, and other materials.

Door of Hope: Recognizing and Resolving the Pains of Your Past by Jan Frank. Nashville, Tenn.: Thomas Nelson, 1995.

Healing for Damaged Emotions by Dr. David Seamands. Wheaton, Ill.: Victor Books, 1981.

Love Must Be Tough by Dr. James Dobson. Dallas, Tex.: Word, 1983.

National Child Help Hotline
Child Help International Order of Foresters
(800) 422-4453
Provides counseling, referral and reporting services concerning child abuse.

Pain and Pretending by Rev. Rich Buhler. Nashville, Tenn.: Thomas Nelson, 1990.

When Love Is Not Enough: Parenting through the Tough Times by Stephen Arterburn and Jim Burns. Colorado Springs, Colo.: Focus on the Family, 1992.

Addictions
see also Substance Abuse
see also Drug Abuse

Healing Life's Hidden Addictions by Dr. Archibald Hart. Ann Arbor, Mich.: Servant, 1992.

Love Hunger: Action Plan by Dr. Sharon Sneed. Nashville, Tenn.: Thomas Nelson, 1993.

Love Hunger: Recovery from Food Addiction by Dr. Frank Minirth, Dr. Paul Meier, Dr. Robert Hemfelt, and

Dr. Sharon Sneed. Nashville, Tenn.: Thomas Nelson, 1990.

Adoption, Infertility, and Miscarriage

The Ache for a Child by Debra Bridwell. Wheaton, Ill.: Scripture Press, 1994.

Adoption Resources Information Sheet
This information sheet lists organizations that provide assistance to potential adoptive parents, including those who want to know about adopting special-needs children. Also listed are adoption search organizations, Canadian and international adoption information, and helpful resources.

Adoptive Families of America*
2209 Como Ave.
St. Paul, MN 55108
(612) 645-9955
This national adoptive parent organization serves parents who have adopted, or who are waiting to adopt, children from all countries. It is a national umbrella organization for over 300 adoptive parent support groups. A helpline is available 24 hours a day for families in crisis. The group does not discuss adoption in general, but it can provide information about adoption issues, health insurance equity, and adoption procedures. A free general information booklet for prospective adoptive parents is available as well as a bimonthly magazine called *Adoptive Families*.

Baptist Children's Homes and Family Ministries
354 West St.
Valparaiso, IN 46383
(219) 462-4111
This organization exists to assist churches and communities through the care and counseling of children and adults, "setting the solitary in families" (Psalm 68:6). It sponsors eight group homes for children and a home for unwed mothers; it also offers adoption and foster care services.

Bethany Christian Services
901 Eastern Ave., NE
P.O. Box 294
Grand Rapids, MI 49501

(616) 224-7617—Main office
(562) 803-3454—Los Angeles County
(616) 224-7540—Refugee Service Center
(800) BETHANY (238-4269)—Bethany Life Line
   (24-hour Crisis Pregnancy Hotline)
   http://www.bethany.org—Internet Web site
This privately licensed Christian Child Welfare and Adoption Agency offers pro-life pregnancy counseling, temporary foster care, help with international adoptions, and alternative living arrangements for pregnant women. A listing of locations in different states is available. Also, Spanish literature is available directly from Bethany Christian Services, 9928 Flower, Ste. 202, Bellflower, CA 90706.

Brian Was Adopted by Doris Sanford. Sisters, Oreg.: Multnomah, 1989.

Christian Family Care Agency
3603 North Seventh Ave.
Phoenix, AZ 85013
(602) 234-1935
C.F.C.A. serves families in crisis through counseling, pregnancy assistance, foster care, and adoption. Video and slide presentations, speakers, and brochures are available upon request. This group publishes a semi-annual newsletter called *CFCA Update*.

The Family Network, Inc.
307 Webster St.
Monterey, CA 93940
(800) 888-0242
(408) 655-5077

Or: (for Spanish materials)
Mrs. Rosario Gasquet
4945 Barbara
Maryland Heights, MO 63043
(314) 291-4577
This ministry assists with home studies and family assessment for adoption, placement services for domestic (U.S.) and foreign children, professional pro-life pregnancy counseling, postplacement supervision, and services in Spanish.

Holt International Children's Services
P.O. Box 2880
Eugene, OR 97402
This nonprofit organization works to unite homeless children from foreign countries with adoptive families

in the United States. Holt is one of two American agencies currently approved by the Romanian government to handle Romanian adoptions; the other is Bethany Christian Services.

How to Adopt a Child by Connie Crain and Janice Duffy. Nashville, Tenn.: Thomas Nelson, 1994.

Major League Dad by Tim and Christine Burke. Colorado Springs, Colo.: Focus on the Family, 1994.

National Council for Adoption
1930 17th St., NW
Washington, DC 20009
(202) 328-1200
(202) 328-8072—Hotline
This secular organization, able to process Spanish correspondence, serves as a clearinghouse of information on the issue of adoption.

SHARE* (Pregnancy and Infant Loss Support, Inc.)
St. Joseph Health Center
300 First Capitol Dr.
St. Charles, MO 63301-2893
(314) 947-6164
This Catholic organization provides a strong, supportive atmosphere through mutual self-help groups, where people can share their experiences, thoughts, and feelings regarding the loss of an infant through miscarriage or to some other reason after birth. It publishes a newsletter 3–4 times a year and offers some materials in Spanish.

Stepping Stones
Dr. and Mrs. Van Regenmorter
1804 S. Emerson
Denver, CO 80210
Stepping Stones, a bimonthly newsletter concerning infertility and miscarriage, is offered for a suggested donation of $5 a year. Dr. and Mrs. Van Regenmorter are also available for speaking.

The Whole Life Adoption Book by Jayne E. Schooler. Colorado Springs, Colo.: Pinon Press, 1993.

Death

Caring for Your Aging Parents, When Love Is Not Enough by Barbara Deane. Colorado Springs, Colo.: NavPress, 1989.

Empty Arms by Pam Vredevelt. Sisters, Oreg.: Multnomah, 1995.

How to Help a Heartbroken Friend by David Biebel. Nashville, Tenn.: Thomas Nelson, 1993.

Sunrise Tomorrow: Coping with a Child's Death by Elizabeth Brown. Grand Rapids, Mich.: Fleming H. Revell, 1992.

When God Doesn't Make Sense by Dr. James Dobson. Wheaton, Ill.: Tyndale House, 1993.

When Is It Right to Die? by Joni Eareckson Tada. Grand Rapids, Mich.: Zondervan, 1995.

Depression

Beyond the Hidden Pain of Abortion by Patricia Bigliardi. Aglow Communications, 1994.

Dark Clouds, Silver Linings by Dr. Archibald Hart. Colorado Springs, Colo.: Focus on the Family, 1994.

Don't Let Jerks Get the Best of You by Dr. Paul Meier. Nashville, Tenn.: Thomas Nelson, 1993.

A Door of Hope: Recognizing and Resolving the Pains of Your Past by Jan Frank. Nashville, Tenn.: Thomas Nelson, 1995.

Living through the Loss of Someone You Love by Sandra Aldrich. Ventura, Calif.: Regal, 1990.

NewLife Treatment Centers
Corporate Office
820 W. Spring Creek Parkway
Ste. 400
Plano, TX 75023
1-800-NEW LIFE

Disabilities and Diseases

American Association Deaf-Blind*
814 Thayer Ave., Ste. 302
Silver Spring, MD 20910

American Cancer Society*
1599 Clifton Rd., NE
Atlanta, GA 30329-4251
(800) 227-2345
(404) 320-3333

American Council of the Blind*
1155 15th St., NW, Ste.720
Washington, DC 20005
(800) 424-8666
(202) 467-5081

American Diabetes Association*
(800) 342-2383
(703) 549-1500 in Virginia and the District of
    Columbia metropolitan area
Provides free literature, newsletters, and information on
diabetes health education and support-group assistance.

American Epilepsy Society*
638 Prospect Ave.
Hartford, CT 06105-4298
(860) 586-7505

Association for Children with Down Syndrome*
2616 Martin Ave.
Bellmore, NY 11710
(516) 221-4700

Asthma and Allergy Foundation of America*
1125 15th St., NW, Ste. 502
Washington, DC 20005
(800) 727-8462
(202) 466-7643

Autism Research Institute*
4182 Adams Ave.
San Diego, CA 92116
(619) 469-6618

Blind Children's Center*
4120 Marathon St.
Los Angeles, CA 90029-0159

(800) 222-3566
(213) 664-2153
This organization deals primarily with blind children
from birth through elementary school.

**CHADD: Children & Adults with Attention Deficit
Disorders**
499 N.W. 70th Ave., Ste. 101
Plantation, FL 33317
(800) 233-4050
(954) 587-3700

Christian Services for the Blind
Dr. Franklin Tucker, Director
P.O. Box 26
South Pasadena, CA 91031
(818) 799-3935
This ministry was set up to evangelize and expand the
lives of the blind and partially sighted. Four monthly
magazines, *Decision, Power for Living, Focus on the
Family,* and *Our Daily Bread* are offered, as well as free
Braille books, Bibles, and cassettes. *Focus on the Family*
and Focus on the Family's *Citizen* magazines are also
available on tape.

(Chronic Fatigue Syndrome)
CFIDS Association of America
P.O. Box 220398
Charlotte, NC 28222-0398
(800) 442-3437
(704) 365-9755

Deaf Missions
21199 Greenview Rd.
Council Bluffs, IA 51503-9500
(712) 322-5493
This organization, set up to provide visuals and
train workers to help bring the gospel to deaf
people, has Bible camps and college extension
classes. It offers a monthly newsletter, *Deaf Missions
Report,* and the devotional *Daily Devotions for the
Deaf.*

Direct Link*
P.O. Box 1036
Solvang, CA 93464
(805) 688-1603 (Monday–Friday, 8:00 A.M.–
    1:00 P.M., PST)
Set up as a nonprofit information referral service, this
organization links the disabled with the providers of

direct services, both Christian and secular. Direct Link does not provide direct services such as financial assistance or personal counseling.

Exceptional Parent: The Magazine for Families and Professionals, 1997 Resource Guide*
P.O. Box 3000, Dept. EP
Denville, NJ 07834
Provides addresses and phone numbers for organizations nationwide and by state for many disabilities and diseases.

The Food Allergy Network*
10400 Eaton Pl., Ste. 107
Fairfax, VA 22030-2208
(703) 691-3179

Friendship Ministries
Mrs. Cecilia Mereness
Mrs. Elsa Prince
2850 Kalamazoo Ave., SE
Grand Rapids, MI 49560
(616) 224-0842
(800) 333-8300 (U.S. only)

Or:
P.O. Box 5070
Burlington, ON L7R 3Y8
Canada
(800) 263-4252 (Canada only)
Organized to promote spiritual development for people with mental disabilities, this ministry offers religious educational curriculum and provides assistance to churches to reach and teach people with mental disabilities.

Handi•Vangelism
Timothy D. Sheetz, Director
237 Fairfield Ave.
Upper Darby, PA 19082
This ministry to disabled individuals provides seminars, conferences, literature, periodicals, support groups, and counseling. It helps the local church include the disabled in their programs and operates Handi•Camp, an overnight camping program for physically or mentally disabled children, teens, and adults.

Heartline*
A service of the American Heart Association
(804) 965-6464

Answers questions and provides free literature on heart, health, cardiovascular diseases, and strokes.

I'll Love You Forever by Dr. Norman and Joyce Wright. Colorado Springs, Colo.: Focus on the Family, 1993.

Joni Eareckson Tada
c/o JAF Ministries
P.O. Box 3333
Agoura Hills, CA 91301
(818) 707-5664
The purpose of this Christian ministry is to bring together disabled people and local congregations through evangelism, encouragement, inspiration, and practical service. Joni Eareckson Tada offers seminars and conferences for churches and has her own radio show. Resources and referrals for families with disabled members are available, as well as a special deaf ministries outreach that includes deaf-awareness classes, evangelism, and discipleship through camping and curricula.

Juvenile Diabetes Foundation International
(800) 533-2873
(212) 785-9500
Answers questions and provides brochures on juvenile diabetes; gives referrals to physicians and clinics.

Lung Line*
National Asthma Center
A service of the National Jewish Center for Immunology & Respiratory Medicine
(800) 222-5864
(303) 355-LUNG in Denver
Answers questions about asthma, emphysema, chronic bronchitis, allergies, juvenile rheumatoid arthritis, smoking, and other respiratory and immune system disorders; callers' questions are answered by registered nurses.

National Association for Down Syndrome
P.O. Box 4542
Oak Brook, IL 60522
(630) 325-9112
This organization offers resources on Down syndrome in both English and Spanish. Additional services are provided for the local Chicago area.

National Association for Parents of the Visually Impaired*
P.O. Box 317
Watertown, MA 02272-0317
(800) 562-6265

National Attention Deficit Disorder*
P.O. Box 1303
Northbrook, IL 60065-1303
www.add.org

National Captioning Institute*
5203 Leesburg Pike
Falls Church, VA 22041
(703) 917-7600
(800) 533-9673
This secular organization provides information on telecaption decoders that pick up closed-captioned messages for the hearing impaired on videos and television. They also provide information on audio-link, an infrared system that greatly enhances sound.

National Center for Youth with Disabilities*
University of Minnesota
Box 721
420 Delaware St., SE
Minneapolis, MN 55455
(612) 626-2825

National Organization of Parents of Blind Children*
1800 Johnson St.
Baltimore, MD 21230
(410) 659-9314
(800) 638-7518 (job opportunities for the blind)
This national federation was set up to integrate the blind into society on a basis of equality by removing legal, economic, and social discrimination and by educating the public. It publishes a monthly newsletter on issues related to the blind.

**National Sudden Infant Death Syndrome *
Resource Center**
2070 Chain Bridge Rd.
Vienna, VA 22182
(703) 821-8955

NORD: National Organization for Rare Disorders*
100 Rte. 37, P.O. Box 8923
New Fairfield, CT 06812-8923
(800) 999-6673
(203)746-6518

Sudden Infant Death Syndrome
National SIDS Foundation
(800) 221-SIDS
(410) 653-8226
Provides literature and referrals on SIDS as well as information on support groups.

Tourette Syndrome Association
42-40 Bell Blvd.
Bayside, NY 11361
(718) 224-2999
The purpose of this national association is to educate patients and their families about the disease called Tourette's syndrome and to provide support groups. They publish a quarterly newsletter.

When God Doesn't Make Sense by Dr. James Dobson. Wheaton, Ill.: Tyndale House, 1993.

Drug Abuse
see also Addictions
see also Substance Abuse

National Clearinghouse for Alcohol & Drug Information*
(800) 729-6686
(301) 468-2600 in Maryland
Offers information and technical assistance to schools, parent groups, business and industry, and national organizations in developing drug abuse prevention activities. Does not provide crisis counseling, intervention, treatment, referral, or information on the pharmacology or criminal aspects of drugs.

National Institute on Drug Abuse Helpline*
(800) 662-HELP
Provides general information on drug abuse and on AIDS as it relates to intravenous drug users; also offers referrals.

Family Life—Spiritual

Faithful Parents, Faithful Kids by Greg Johnson and Mike Yorkey. Wheaton, Ill.: Tyndale House, 1993.

Family Shock: Keeping Families Strong in the Midst of Earthshaking Change by Gary R. Collins. Wheaton, Ill.: Tyndale House, 1996.

Habits of a Healthy Home by Bill Carmichael. Wheaton, Ill.: Tyndale House, 1997.

Home with a Heart by Dr. James Dobson. Wheaton, Ill.: Tyndale House, 1996.

Parents Resource Bible (TLB). Wheaton, Ill.: Tyndale House, 1995.

Together at Home by Dean and Grace Merrill. Wheaton, Ill.: Tyndale House, 1996.

Finances

Christian Financial Concepts
P.O. Box 2377
Gainesville, GA 30503-2377
(770) 534-1000
(800) 772-1976
Provides a network of approximately one thousand financial advisers. Write for a list of local referrals, speaking requests, or information on seminars. You may also call for referrals to local financial counselors or to order books and tapes.

Ron Blue & Co.
1100 Johnson Ferry Rd., Ste. 600
Atlanta, GA 30342
(404) 705-7000
Offers advice about investments and handling money.

Home Schools

Christian Home Educators Association (CHEA)
Philip Troutt, Executive Director
P.O. Box 2009
Norwalk, CA 90651-2009
(310) 864-2432

Or: Christian Home Educators of Colorado
3739 East 4th Ave.
Denver, CO 80206
(303) 388-1888
This organization provides training and resources to home-schooling parents, support groups and seminars, a monthly magazine, curriculum manual, and updated information on legislative and legal issues through a monthly newsletter.

The How & Why of Home Schooling by Ray E. Ballman. Wheaton, Ill.: Crossway, 1987.

Raising Achievers: A Parent's Plan for Motivating Children to Excel by Dr. Nita Weis. Nashville, Tenn.: Broadman & Holman, 1995.

Survivor's Guide to Home Schooling by Luanne Shackelford and Susan White. Wheaton, Ill.: Crossway, 1989.

Love and Marriage

FamilyLife Marriage Ministry
P.O. Box 8220
Little Rock, AR 72221
800-FL-TODAY
This organization presents marriage and parenting weekend seminars throughout the United States.

The Gift of Sex by Dr. Clifford and Joyce Penner. Dallas, Tex.: Word, 1981.

Holding on to Romance by Dr. H. Norman Wright. Ventura, Calif.: Regal, 1992.

How to Change Your Spouse (without Ruining Your Marriage): Healthy Ways to Bring Out the Best in Your Mate by Dr. H. Norman Wright and Dr. Gary J. Oliver. Ann Arbor, Mich.: Servant, 1994.

Incompatibility: Grounds for a Great Marriage by Chuck and Barb Snyder. Sisters, Oreg.: Questar, 1994.

The Language of Love with Study Guide by Gary Smalley and Dr. John Trent. Colorado Springs, Colo.: Focus on the Family, 1991.

Marriage Savers: Helping Your Friends & Family Stay Married by Michael McManus. Grand Rapids, Mich.: Zondervan, 1993.

Men: Some Assembly Required by Chuck Snyder. Colorado Springs, Colo.: Focus on the Family, 1995.

More than You and Me by Kevin and Karen Miller. Colorado Springs, Colo.: Focus on the Family, 1994.

Powerful Personalities by Tim Kimmel. Colorado Springs, Colo.: Focus on the Family, 1993.

Romancing the Home: How to Have a Marriage That Sizzles by Dr. Ed Young. Nashville, Tenn.: Broadman & Holman, 1993.

The Second Decade of Love by Greg Johnson and Mike Yorkey. Wheaton, Ill.: Tyndale House, 1994.

The Triumphant Marriage by Dr. Neil Clark Warren. Colorado Springs, Colo.: Focus on the Family, 1995.

The Two Sides of Love with Study Guide by Gary Smalley and Dr. John Trent. Colorado Springs, Colo.: Focus on the Family, 1992.

What Wives Wish Their Husbands Knew about Women by Dr. James Dobson. Wheaton, Ill.: Tyndale House, 1975.

Materials for Men

Developing the Leader within You by John Maxwell. Nashville, Tenn.: Thomas Nelson, 1993.

Fatherless America: Confronting Our Most Urgent Social Problem by David Blankenhorn. New York, N.Y.: Basic Books, n.d.

The Five Key Habits of Smart Dads by Paul Lewis. Grand Rapids, Mich.: Zondervan, 1994.

God of My Father: A Son's Reflections on His Father's Walk of Faith by Dr. Larry Crabb Jr. and Lawrence Crabb Sr. Grand Rapids, Mich.: Zondervan, 1994.

The Hidden Value of a Man by Gary Smalley and Dr. John Trent. Dallas, Tex.: Word, 1994.

If I'm Not Tarzan and My Wife Isn't Jane, Then What Are We Doing in the Jungle? by Steve Farrar. Sisters, Oreg.: Questar, 1992.

The Sexual Man: Masculinity without Guilt by Dr. Archibald Hart. Dallas, Tex.: Word, 1993.

Parenting—General

1001 Ways to Help Your Child Walk with God by Kathie Reimer. Wheaton, Ill.: Tyndale House, 1992.

As You Leave Home by Jerry Jenkins. Colorado Springs, Colo.: Focus on the Family, 1993.

The Book of Virtues by Dr. William J. Bennett. New York, N.Y.: Simon and Schuster, 1994.

Books That Build Character by William Kirkpatrick, Gregory Wolfe, and Suzanne M. Wolfe. New York, N.Y.: Simon & Schuster, 1994.

Bringing Up Kids without Tearing Them Down by Dr. Kevin Leman. Colorado Springs, Colo.: Focus on the Family, 1994.

Children of Divorce by Debbie Barr. Grand Rapids, Mich.: Zondervan, 1992.

Daddy, I'm Pregnant by a dad named Bill. Sisters, Oreg.: Questar, 1988.

Decent Exposure: How to Teach Your Children about Sex by Connie Marshner. Wolgemuth & Hyatt, 1988.

Dr. Dobson Answers Your Questions by Dr. James Dobson. Wheaton, Ill.: Tyndale House, 1982.

Faithful Parents, Faithful Kids by Mike Yorkey and Greg Johnson. Wheaton, Ill.: Tyndale House, 1993.

FaithTraining by Joe White. Colorado Springs, Colo.: Focus on the Family, 1995.

Family University
15110 Avenue of Science
San Diego, CA 92128
(619) 487-7099

This organization, which offers a variety of resources, is designed to attract men into fellowship and to equip fathers for successful family living.

The Five Key Habits of Smart Dads by Paul Lewis. Grand Rapids, Mich.: Zondervan, 1994.

Guiding Your Family in a Misguided World by Dr. Anthony Evans. Colorado Springs, Colo.: Focus on the Family, 1991.

Hide or Seek by Dr. James Dobson. Old Tappan, N.J.: Fleming H. Revell, 1979.

How to Parent Your "Tweenager": Understanding the In-Between Years of Your 8- to 12-Year-Old by Dr. Mary Manz Simon. Nashville, Tenn.: Thomas Nelson, 1995.

The Hurting Parent by Margie Lewis and Gregg Lewis. Grand Rapids, Mich.: Zondervan, 1980.

Keeping Your Family Together When the World Is Falling Apart by Kevin Leman. Colorado Springs, Colo.: Focus on the Family, 1993.

The Key to Your Child's Heart by Gary Smalley. Dallas, Tex.: Word, 1984.

Let's Hide the Word by Gloria Gaither and Shirley Dobson. Dallas, Tex.: Word, 1994.

Let's Make a Memory—Revised by Shirley Dobson and Gloria Gaither. Dallas, Tex.: Word, 1986.

Life on the Edge by Dr. James Dobson. Dallas, Tex.: Word, 1995.

The Mommy Book by Karen Hull. Grand Rapids, Mich.: Zondervan, 1986.

MOPS International (Mothers of Preschoolers)
1311 S. Clarkson St.
Denver, CO 80210
(303) 733-5353
(800) 929-1287—To find a chapter near you
This outreach organization gives support to mothers of toddlers. Local groups in many states affirm mothers and provide them with information on important mothering issues.

Mothers at Home
8310A Old Courthouse Rd.
Vienna, VA 22182
(703) 827-5903
(800) 783-4MOM (783-4666)—To order resources
Set up to support mothers who choose to stay at home, this group offers a secular monthly newsletter, *Welcome Home,* which includes helpful material submitted primarily from its subscribers.

A Mother's Manual for Holiday Survival by Kathy Peel and Judie Byrd. Colorado Springs, Colo.: Focus on the Family, 1991.

A Mother's Manual for Schoolday Survival by Kathy Peel and Joy Mahaffey. Colorado Springs, Colo.: Focus on the Family, 1990.

A Mother's Manual for Summer Survival by Kathy Peel and Joy Mahaffey. Colorado Springs, Colo.: Focus on the Family, 1989.

National Center for Fathering
Ken Canfield, Director
10200 West 75th St., Ste. 267
Shawnee Mission, KS 66204
(913) 384-4661
http://www.fathers.com—Internet Web site
This group helps organize seminars for fathers on a local-church level. It also provides Bible study materials, curriculum, and a free bimonthly newsletter entitled *Today's Father.*

National Organization of Mothers of Twins Club, Inc.
P.O. Box 23188
Albuquerque, NM 87192-1188
(505) 275-0955
The purpose of this organization, with 361 local chapters across the country, is to offer support to parents and to research and educate the public about twins. It offers a quarterly newsletter and free brochure.

The New Dare to Discipline by Dr. James Dobson. Wheaton, Ill.: Tyndale House, 1992.

Parenting Isn't for Cowards by Dr. James Dobson. Dallas, Tex.: Word, n.d.

Parenting Passages by David Veerman. Wheaton, Ill.: Tyndale House, 1994.

Parents in Pain by Dr. John White. Elgin, Ill.: InterVarsity, 1979.

Preparing for Adolescence by Dr. James Dobson. Santa Ana, Calif.: Vision House, 1978.

Raising Them Right edited by Mike Yorkey. Colorado Springs, Colo.: Focus on the Family, 1994.

Right from Wrong by Josh McDowell. Dallas, Tex.: Word, 1994.

Solid Answers by Dr. James Dobson. Wheaton, Ill.: Tyndale House, 1997.

Stress and Your Child by Dr. Archibald Hart. Dallas, Tex.: Word, 1992.

The Strong-Willed Child by Dr. James Dobson. Wheaton, Ill.: Tyndale House, 1978.

The Way They Learn by Cynthia Ulrich Tobias. Colorado Springs, Colo.: Focus on the Family, 1994.

When Love Is Not Enough: Parenting through Tough Times by Stephen Arterburn and Jim Burns. Colorado Springs, Colo.: Focus on the Family, 1992.

When You Feel Like Screaming by Dr. Grace Ketterman and Pat Holt. Wheaton, Ill.: Harold Shaw, 1988.

Pro-Life Materials

Bethany Christian Services
Mr. Glen DeMots, Associate Executive Director
901 Eastern Ave., NE
P.O. Box 294
Grand Rapids, MI 49501
(616) 224-7617
(562) 803-3454—Los Angeles County number
(616) 224-7540—Refugee Service Center
(800) BETHANY (238-4269)—Bethany Life Line
(24-hour Crisis Pregnancy Hotline)
A listing of locations in different states is available. This private licensed Christian Child Welfare and Adoption Agency also offers pro-life pregnancy counseling in person or by telephone, temporary foster care, alternative living arrangements for pregnant women, and help with international adoptions.

CareNet (formerly the **Christian Action Council**)
109 Carpenter Dr., Ste. 100
Sterling, VA 20164
(703) 478-5661
http://www.goshen.net/CareNet—Internet Web site
CareNet is a network of more than 450 crisis pregnancy centers (CPCs) in the U.S. and Canada. This organization provides a newsletter every other month and offers a postabortion Bible study entitled "Women in Ramah."

Safety

Auto Safety Hotline*
National Highway Traffic Safety Administration
(800) 424-9393
(202) 366-0123 in the District of Columbia
Provides information and referrals on the effectiveness of occupant-protection devices such as safety belts and child safety seats; also gives information on auto recalls, auto-crash test results, tire quality reports, and other auto safety topics. Staffed by experts who investigate consumer complaints and provide assistance to resolve problems; reports safety defects and gives referrals to other government agencies for consumer questions on warranties, service, and auto safety regulations.

Consumer Product Safety Commission*
(800) 638-CPSC
Answers questions and provides materials on consumer product safety, including product hazards, product defects, and injuries sustained while using product; covers only products used in and around the home, excluding automobiles, foods, drugs, cosmetics, boats, firearms, and pesticides.

National Fire Protection Association*
(800) 344-3555
Provides literature on fire safety and fire codes and standards.

National Safety Council*
(800) 621-7619—for placing orders
Provides posters, brochures, and booklets on safety and the prevention of accidents.

Schools and Related Issues

Association of Christian Schools, International
Dr. Paul Kienel, President
P.O. Box 35097
Colorado Springs, CO 80935-3509
(719) 528-6906
(800) 367-0798—orders only
The largest Christian school organization in the world holds yearly conventions nationwide for educators, administrators, and parents, in addition to providing a wide variety of services for teachers and administrators. Referrals for Christian boarding schools are listed.

Blind Children's Center
4120 Marathon St.
Los Angeles, CA 90029-0159
(800) 222-3566
(213) 664-2153
This secular organization deals primarily with blind children from birth through elementary school.

CHADD: Children & Adults with Attention Deficit Disorder
499 N.W. 70th Ave., Ste. 101
Plantation, FL 33317
(954) 587-3700
This secular, nonprofit, parent-based organization was formed to help parents and teachers with ADD children. There are 50 chapters in the U.S. The organization has a yearly national conference and offers a monthly newsletter and additional resources on the subject.

Choose a Christian College by the Christian College Coalition. Peterson's Guides, Inc., 1992.

Christian Educators Association
P.O. Box 41300
Pasadena, CA 91114
(818) 798-1124
(818) 798-2346—fax
ceaieduca@aol.com—E-mail
This national organization has local chapters for educators and parents and keeps members informed on issues affecting education. They offer a nationwide prayer network, conferences, curriculum, and liability coverage comparable to NEA. Legal advice is available to members.

Christian Schools International
Mrs. Sheri Haan, Executive Director
P.O. Box 8709
3350 E. Paris Ave., SE
Grand Rapids, MI 49518
(616) 957-1070
An extended catalog of resources and publications for curriculum and administration of schools is offered.

Coalition for Christian Colleges and Universities
329 8th St., NE
Washington, DC 20002
(202) 546-8713
coalition@cccu.org—E-mail
http://www.cccu.org—Internet Web site
A complimentary list of and general information on Christian colleges and universities are available for those interested in Christian higher education.

Creating a Positive Public School Experience by Eric Buehrer. Nashville, Tenn.: Thomas Nelson, 1994.

Eagle Forum Education & Legal Defense Fund
Phyllis Schlafly, President
Box 618
Alton, IL 62002
(314) 721-1213
http://www.eagleforum.org—Internet Web site
This well-known national pro-family organization is concerned with legislation and policy making at the local, state, and national levels.

Educational Guidance Institute
Onalee McGraw
188 Berbusse Ln.
Front Royal, VA 22630
(540) 635-4420
Offerings include a support system to parents, educators, community leaders, and policy makers; seminars and conferences; and the "Foundations for Family Life Education" abstinence-based sex education curriculum.

The Foundation for American Christian Education
P.O. Box 9588
Chesapeake, VA 23321
(757) 488-6601
This organization provides research, documentation, and a publication of America's Christian history and government. Seminars and conferences are also offered.

Foundation for Thought and Ethics
Jon Buell
P.O. Box 830721
Richardson, TX 75083-0721
This is a Christian ministry that develops public school curriculum and textbooks, publishes a periodic newsletter, and holds seminars and conferences.

Gateways to Better Education
Mr. Eric Buehrer
P.O. Box 514
Lake Forest, CA 92630
(714) 586-5437
Public school parents will find assistance in evaluating programs and school curricula. The Parent Education Network (PEN) links parents who deal with similar issues in their schools. A complimentary bimonthly newsletter is available, and seminars and conferences are offered.

Helping Your Child Succeed in Public Schools by Cheri Fuller. Colorado Springs, Colo.: Focus on the Family, 1993.

How to Survive Middle School by Rick Bundschuh. Grand Rapids, Mich.: Zondervan, 1991.

Learning Disabilities Association of America (LDA)
4156 Library Rd.
Pittsburgh, PA 15234
(412) 341-1515
(412) 341-8077
Formerly the Association for Children and Adults with Learning Disabilities, this organization is set up to define and provide solutions for learning problems such as dyslexia and ADD. It also provides a state newsletter and referral information and offers several publications regarding learning disabilities. Conferences for parents, teachers, and other professionals are available as well.

Moms In Touch International
P.O. Box 1120
Poway, CA 92074-1120
(800) 949-6667 (949-MOMS)
(619) 486-4065
(619) 486-5132—fax
mitihqtrs@aol.com—E-mail
http://www.europa.com/~philhow/
moms_in_touch.html—Internet Web site

Set up as a support base for schools, mothers meet weekly to pray for their children, teachers, and administrators. They publish a monthly newsletter.

National Right to Read Foundation
P.O. Box 490
The Plains, VA 20198
(800) 468-8911
This is a nonpartisan organization dedicated to the elimination of illiteracy through the use of phonics and values-based literature. In addition, they offer a monthly newsletter for $25 a year.

Teachers Saving Children
P.O. Box 125
Damascus, OH 44619-0125
(330) 537-2546
Instituting positive changes in the National Education Association is the purpose of this organization for teachers.

The Way They Learn by Cynthia Ulrich Tobias. Colorado Springs, Colo.: Focus on the Family, 1994.

Welcome to High School by Diane Eble, Chris Lutes, and Kris Bearss. Grand Rapids, Mich.: Zondervan, 1991.

Sex Education

Almost 12 by Kenneth N. Taylor. Wheaton, Ill.: Tyndale House, 1995.

Decent Exposure: How to Teach Your Children about Sex by Connie Marshner. Wolgemuth & Hyatt, 1988.

Sex, Lies, & . . . the Truth by Rolf Zettersten. Wheaton, Ill.: Tyndale House, 1994.

Sex: What You Don't Know Can Kill You by Joe S. McIlhaney, Jr., M.D., with Marion McIlhaney. Grand Rapids, Mich.: Baker, 1997.

Single Parenting

Boundaries: Gaining Control of Your Life by Dr. Henry Cloud and Dr. John Townsend. Grand Rapids, Mich.: Zondervan, 1992.

Changes That Heal by Dr. Henry Cloud. Grand Rapids, Mich.: Zondervan, 1995.

Children of Divorce by Debbie Barr. Grand Rapids, Mich.: Zondervan, 1992.

The Complete Financial Guide for Single Parents by Larry Burkett. Scripture Press, 1993.

Faithful Parents, Faithful Kids by Greg Johnson and Mike Yorkey. Wheaton, Ill.: Tyndale House, 1993.

Spiritual Training

1001 Ways to Help Your Child Walk with God by Kathie Reimer. Wheaton, Ill.: Tyndale House, 1992.

Discipleship Journal
   P.O. Box 54470
   Boulder, CO 80323-4470
   (800) 877-1811
This Christian growth periodical, published by NavPress, challenges believers to develop a deeper relationship with the Lord. Call or write for subscription information.

FaithTraining by Joe White. Colorado Springs, Colo.: Focus on the Family, 1995.

(Christian Parenting)
The Family Book of Christian Values by Stuart and Jill Briscoe. Elgin, Ill.: David C. Cook, 1995.

   Familywalk or *Youthwalk*
   Walk Thru the Bible Ministries
   4201 N. Peachtree Rd.
   Atlanta, GA 30341-1207
   (770) 458-9300
   (800) 877-5604—for *Familywalk*
   (800) 877-5286—for *Youthwalk*
The *Familywalk* devotional offers stimulating, entertaining devotions, suggested for parents with children ages 6–11. It is available in magazine and book format. *Youthwalk* is a daily devotional for junior high and high school age teens.

Guiding Your Family in a Misguided World by Dr. Anthony Evans. Colorado Springs, Colo.: Focus on the Family, 1991.

Stress

How to Beat Burnout by Dr. Frank Minirth, Dr. Paul Meier, Don Hawkins, and Dr. Richard Flournoy. Chicago, Ill.: Moody, 1986.

Margin: How to Create the Emotional, Physical, Financial, & Time Reserves You Need by Dr. Richard Swenson. Colorado Springs, Colo.: NavPress, 1992.

When You Feel Like Screaming: Help for Frustrated Mothers by Dr. Grace Ketterman and Pat Holt. Wheaton, Ill.: Harold Shaw, 1988.

Substance Abuse
see also Addictions
see also Drug Abuse

Al-Anon and Alateen*
   (800) 356-9996
Provides printed materials on alcoholism, aimed specifically at helping families.

Alcoholism & Drug Addiction Treatment Center
   (800) 382-4357
Refers adolescents and adults to local facilities for help.

Healing Life's Hidden Addictions by Dr. Archibald D. Hart. Ann Arbor, Mich.: Servant, 1992.

Mothers Against Drunk Driving (MADD)*
   P.O. Box 541688
   Irving, TX 75062
   (214) 744-MADD (744-6233)
   (800) 438-MADD (438-6233)
This well-known group offers resources on alcoholism, drunk driving, and victim assistance.

National Council on Alcoholism & Drug Dependence
   (Hope)line
   (800) NCA-CALL
Refers people to local affiliates and provides written information on alcoholism and teenage drinking problems.

National Clearinghouse for Alcohol & Drug Abuse Information
   P.O. Box 2345
   Rockville, MD 20847-2345
   (800) 729-6686

This organization provides information and referrals upon request.

National Runaway Switchboard*

(773) 880-9860
(800) 621-4000

This 24-hour service allows runaway children to leave messages for parents, and parents to leave messages for children. Materials and referrals are available.

Overcomers Outreach, Inc.

Judy Turnbull
520 N. Brookhurst, Ste. 121
Anaheim, CA 92801
(714) 491-3000

This organization is designed to address problems of alcoholism and drug dependency within churches.

Parents in Pain by John White. Downers Grove, Ill.: InterVarsity Press, 1979.

PRIDE (Parents' Resource Institute for Drug Education)*

3610 Dekalb Technology Parkway, Ste. 105
Atlanta, GA 30340
(404) 577-4500

This secular organization offers helpful resources regarding drug problems. Parents may become better informed about the biological impact of drugs.

Teen Challenge

P.O. Box 1015
Springfield, MO 65801
(417) 862-6969

Well known for its effectiveness, this organization provides a broad scope of help and information in every area of drug and alcohol abuse.

When Love Is Not Enough by Stephen Arterburn and Jim Burns. Colorado Springs, Colo.: Focus on the Family, 1992.

Teen Materials

Answers to Tough Questions Skeptics Ask about the Christian Faith by Josh McDowell and Don Stewart. Nashville, Tenn.: Thomas Nelson, 1980.

Cars, Curfews, Parties and Parents . . . 77 Pretty Important Ideas on Family Survival by Susie Shellenberger and Greg Johnson. Minneapolis, Minn.: Bethany House, 1995.

Guys and a Whole Lot More: Advice for Teen Girls on Almost Everything! by Susie Shellenberger. Grand Rapids, Mich.: Fleming H. Revell, 1994.

How to Live with Your Parents without Losing Your Mind by Ken Davis. Grand Rapids, Mich.: Zondervan, 1988.

I Only See My Dad on Weekends: Kids Tell Their Stories about Divorce & Blended Families by Beth Matthews, Andrew Adams, and Karen Dockrey. Elgin, Ill.: Chariot Family Publishing, 1994.

Life on the Edge by Dr. James Dobson. Dallas, Tex.: Word, 1995.

Index

Marriage maintenance 361
  during children's adolescence 523
Marrow 646, 709–710
Martial arts 403
Mastitis 134–135, 710
Mastoiditis 680, 710
Masturbation 423, 710
Maternal-fetal medicine specialist 36
Maxilla 710, 712
Maxillary sinuses 728
Mealtimes 233, 253–254
  ages 3 to 4 years, 371
Measles 710
Measles encephalitis 710
Measles immunization 21–22, 265
Meatal stenosis 740
Meatus 740
Meconium 63, 132
Media concerns, ages 5 to 11 years
  413–417
  and adolescents 527–531
Medication, and breast feeding 124
  during labor 70–71
Meibomian glands 667
Melanin 710
Melanoma 662
Memories, making with children 616
Menarche 482
Meninges 148, 710
Meningitis 145, 398, 710–711
  in newborns 148
Meniscus 711
Menorrhagia 711
Menses 486
Menstrual cramps 487–491
Menstrual cycle 482–494
Menstrual period 486–494
  absence of, in anorexia nervosa
    433–434
  first 422
  irregular 491–492
Meperidine, after cesarean delivery 73
Mesenteric adenitis 637, 650
Metastasis 665
Metastatic tumor 665
Metatarsal 711
Metatarsus adductus (see Curved foot)
Metered dose inhalers (MDIs) 652
Methadone, use during pregnancy 16
Methamphetamine 587
Methylphenidate (Ritalin) 656
Microcephalic 711
Middle ear 152, 679
Midol, for menstrual cramps 489
Migraine headache 398, 695–696
Milia 68, 711, A29

Miliaria 711, A29
Milk consumption, age 2 years 340
  ages 12 to 24 months 250–251
Minerals, in breast milk 122–123
Mite 722
Mittelschmerz 485, 637, 711
MMR immunization 21–22, 265, 368,
  710
  booster 396
  booster, during adolescence 498
Molars 731, A15
Molding 65
Molds
  and allergy 645
  and asthma 651
Mole 711
Molluscum contagiosum 711, A29
Moms In Touch International 442
Money, teaching children and
  adolescents about 626–629
Mongolian spots 67–68, 662, A29
Mononucleosis (mono) 711–712
Monsters, fear of 377
MOPs (see Mothers of Preschoolers)
Moral values 411–417, 615, 621–625
Moro reflex 69
Mothers Against Drunk Driving
  583–584
Mothers of Preschoolers (MOPs) 259,
  384
Mother-son relationship 526
Motion pictures (see Movies)
Motion sickness 712
Motorbikes 407
Motorcycles 407
Motor vehicles, safety concerns
  406–407, 825–826
Mountain sickness, acute 645
  mild 645
Mouth breathing 641
Mouth care and concerns 712–714
Movement, age 2 years 332–333
  of newborns 183–184
Movies, and adolescents 528–529
  ages 5 to 11 years 415–416
MRI (see Magnetic resonance imaging)
Mucosa 714
Mumps 714
Mumps immunization 21–22, 265
Muscle strains and cramps 795–796
Muscular dystrophy 714
Mushrooms 224
Music, and adolescents 527–528,
  536–537, 539
Music lessons, ages 5 to 11 years
  405–406

Myalgia 714
Myocardial infarction 668
Myoclonic seizures 724
Myopia (nearsightedness) 683, 714
Myositis 714

N

Nail biting 715
Nail care and concerns 714–715
Naproxen, for menstrual cramps 488
  use during pregnancy 17
Naps, ages 12 to 24 months 257
  age 2 years 335
Narcolepsy 715
Narcotics 588
  after cesarean delivery 73
  use during pregnancy 16
Nasal sprays, use during pregnancy 18
Nasolacrimal duct 681
Nasolacrimal duct obstruction 682–683
  (see Chronic mucous drainage)
Natural childbirth 44–46
Nausea 715
  and vomiting 740–741
Nebulizer 715
Neck injuries 793–795
Negativism, age 2 years 355
  in toddlers 259–262
Neglect, of children 317
Neonatologist 37
Neoplasm 665, 715
Neuralgia 715
Neural tube defects 9, 10, 19, 99
Neuritis 715
Neurofibromatosis 662, 715
Neuroma 715
Neutrophil 715
Nevus 715
  giant pigmented 662
  junctional 662
Newborn, behavior of 165–166
  body movements of 183–184
  body temperature of 159
  bonding with 70–73
  clothing for 46–49
  colic 176–180
  crying in 175–180
  daily routines 120–121
  dressing and undressing 159
  examination of 73–74
  feeding 121–143
  growth of 183
  head support for 158
  hearing in 181–182

Table of Contents

Fetal Development

APPROXIMATELY 5 WEEKS

APPROXIMATELY 6 WEEKS

Six weeks after the union of father's sperm and mother's egg, the baby's heart is beating 140 to 150 times per minute. Small buds, which will soon become arms and legs, have sprouted. The large blood vessel in the umbilical cord is carrying oxygen-rich blood from the placenta to the baby, while the two smaller vessels take waste products back to the placenta.

APPROXIMATELY 8 WEEKS

Two weeks later (8 weeks after conception), fingers and toes have formed; bones, hair, and nails have yet to develop. Tiny muscles are beginning to create body movements, but these cannot be felt by the mother. New nerve cells in the brain are being produced at the astonishing rate of 100,000 per minute.

APPROXIMATELY 12 WEEKS

At 12 weeks after conception, all the internal organs and tissues are formed, and the heartbeat may be heard using an electronic listening device. The baby is seen here suspended in amniotic fluid. The irregular tissue surrounding the baby is called the *chorionic sac,* which attaches to the placenta.

APPROXIMATELY 16 WEEKS

APPROXIMATELY 16 WEEKS

APPROXIMATELY 16 WEEKS

Sixteen weeks after conception, the baby is kicking, turning the head, making facial movements, swallowing, hiccuping, sleeping, and waking. Within the next two weeks the mother will begin to feel movements within her. These will feel faint and almost fluttery at first but will become much stronger in the coming weeks.

APPROXIMATELY 18 WEEKS

By 18 weeks the baby is approximately 9 inches long and is stretching, turning, and grasping. A finger touching the lips may set off a sucking reflex.

APPROXIMATELY 18 WEEKS

8TH MONTH

As the time of birth approaches, the baby's weight is rapidly increasing, and space within the amniotic sac is becoming more cramped. Stretching and kicking movements are much more forceful. The eyes are now opening and closing. Within a few more weeks, this new person will be ready to be welcomed into the world.

Skeletal System

Temporal

Frontal

Maxilla

Mandible (jaw)

Scapula (shoulder bone)

Clavicle (collarbone)

Sternum (breastbone)

Ribs

Costal cartilage (rib cartilage)

Xiphoid process

Humerus

Radius

Illiac crest

Ulna

Ilium

Acetabulum (socket)

Carpals (wrist bones)

Sacrum

Pubis

Ischium

Metacarpals (handbones)

Pubic symphysis

Phalanges (fingers)

Femur (thighbone)

Fibula

Patella

Tibia (shinbone)

Medial malleolus (anklebone)

Metatarsals (foot bones)

Lateral malleolus (anklebone)

Phalanges (toes)

ANTERIOR VIEW

Parietal

Occipital

Cervical vertebrae (1–7) (bones of the neck)

Clavicle

Thoracic vertebrae (1–12) (bones of the upper back)

Scapula

Humerus

Lumbar vertebrae (1–5) (bones of the lower back)

Radius

Ulna

Carpals

Metacarpals

Ischium

Phalanges

Tailbone — Sacrum / Coccyx

Femur

Tibia

Fibula

Calcaneus (heel bone)

Phalanges

POSTERIOR VIEW

Muscular System

Temporalis

Frontalis

Orbicularis oculi

Orbicularis oris

Masseter

Sternocleidomastoid

Trapezius

Deltoid

Pectoralis major

Linea alba

Biceps brachii

Rectus abdominis

Brachioradialis

Externus oblique

Flexors of the wrist and fingers

Sartorius

Tensor facia latae

Rectus femoris

Tendons of quadriceps extensor

Vastus lateralis

Pantellar tendon

Vastus medialis

Gastrocnemius

Tibialis anterior

Peroneus longus

Extensor digitorum longus

ANTERIOR VIEW

Occipitalis

Splenius capitis

Infraspinatus

Trapezius

Deltoid

Rhomboideus major

Teres minor

Triceps brachii

Teres major

Latissimus dorsi

Extensors of the wrist and fingers

Gluteus medius

Gluteus maximus

Vastus lateralis

Semitendinosus

Biceps femoris

Semimembranosus

Popliteal fossa

Gastrocnemius

Hamstring tendons

Soleus

Achilles tendon

Flexor digitorum brevis

POSTERIOR VIEW

Digestive System

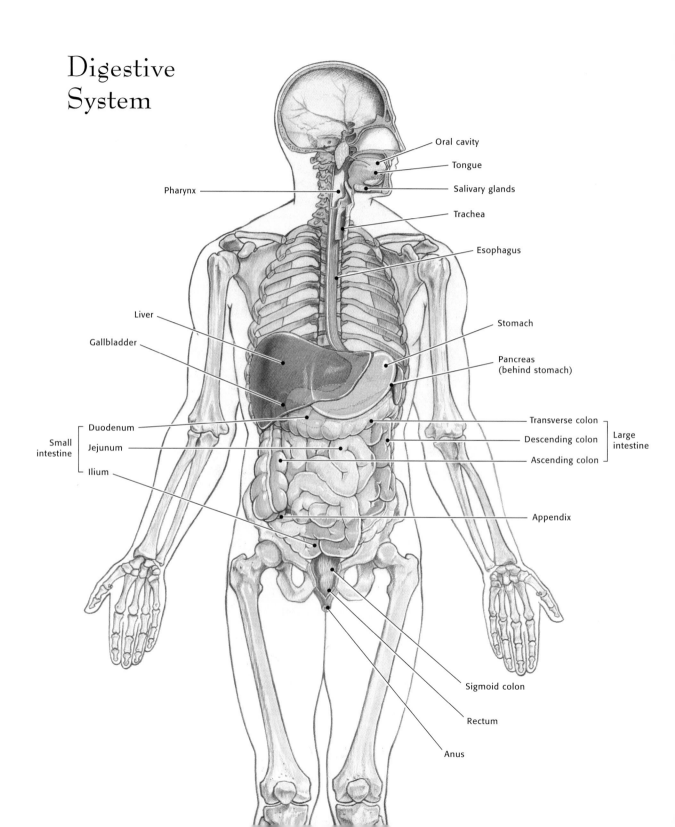

Oral cavity

Tongue

Salivary glands

Pharynx

Trachea

Esophagus

Liver

Stomach

Gallbladder

Pancreas
(behind stomach)

Transverse colon

Duodenum

Descending colon

Large
intestine

Small
intestine

Jejunum

Ascending colon

Ilium

Appendix

Sigmoid colon

Rectum

Anus

Respiratory System

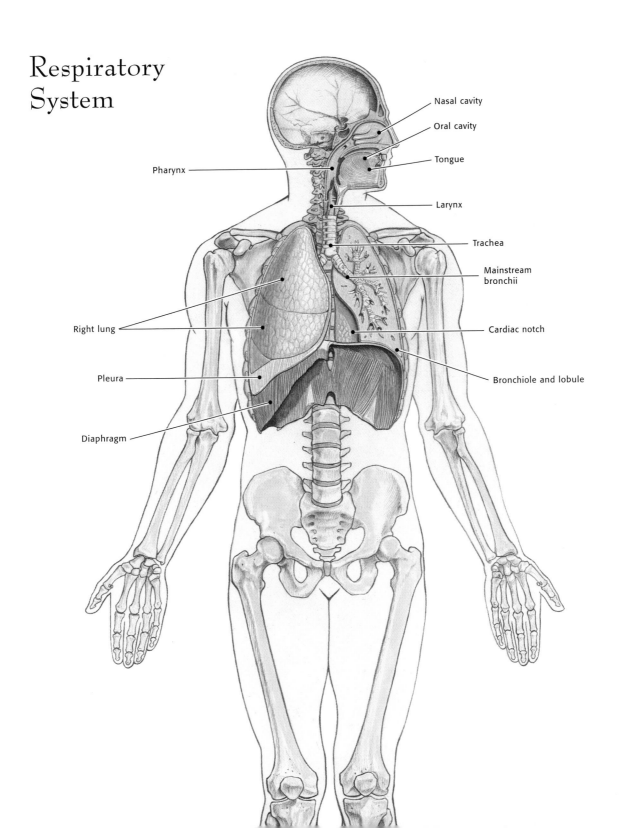

Nasal cavity

Oral cavity

Tongue

Pharynx

Larynx

Trachea

Mainstream bronchii

Right lung

Cardiac notch

Pleura

Bronchiole and lobule

Diaphragm

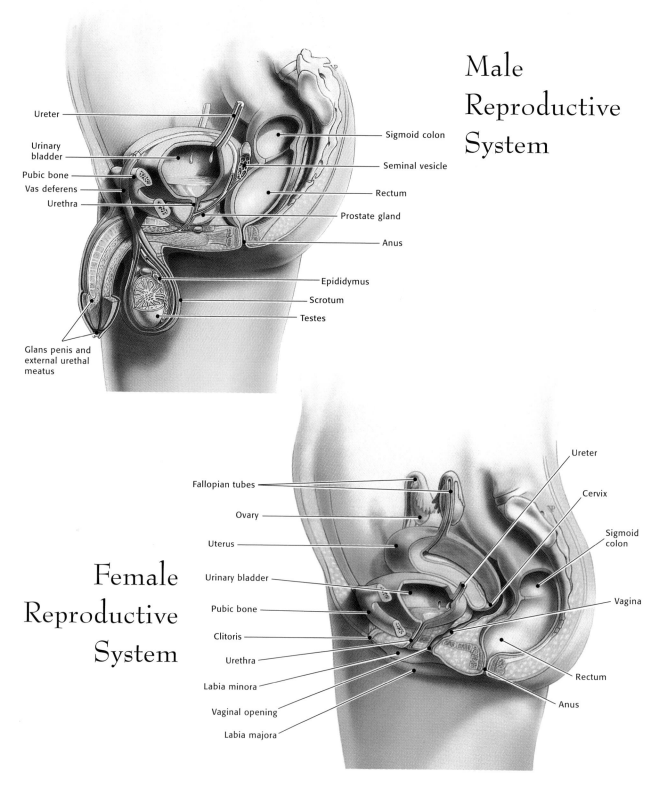

Male Reproductive System

Ureter

Urinary bladder

Pubic bone

Vas deferens

Urethra

Sigmoid colon

Seminal vesicle

Rectum

Prostate gland

Anus

Epididymus

Scrotum

Testes

Glans penis and external urethal meatus

Female Reproductive System

Fallopian tubes

Ovary

Uterus

Urinary bladder

Pubic bone

Clitoris

Urethra

Labia minora

Vaginal opening

Labia majora

Ureter

Cervix

Sigmoid colon

Vagina

Rectum

Anus

The Skin

Hair shaft

Sweat duct

Epidermis

Sebaceous gland

Arrector pili muscle

Dermis

Hair follicles

Subcutaneous tissue

Sweat gland

Blood vessels

Fat cells

The Eye

Conjunctiva

Lateral rectus muscle

Lens

Iris

Sclera

Lens capsule

Vitreous body

Pupil

Retina

Cornea

Choroid

Macula

Lamina cribosa of sclera

Trabecular network

Suspensary ligaments of the lens

Optic nerve

Central artery and vein of retina

Medial rectus muscle

The Ear

Pinna

Nerves carrying
impulses to
brain

Semicircular
canals

Vestibule

Stapes
(stirrup)

Vestibular

Facial

Malleus
(hammer)

Incus
(anvil)

Cochlea

Cochlear

Tympanic membrane
(eardrum)

Tympanic cavum
(middle-ear cavity)

External acoustic meatus
(ear canal)

Eustachian
tube

The Head

Parietal lobe

Frontal lobe

Occipital lobe

Temporal lobe

Cochlea/
semicircular
canals
(inner ear)

Olfactory bulb
(nasal sensory nerves)

Frontal sinus

Tympanic
membrane
(eardrum)

Optic nerves

Nasal bone

External ear canal

Sphenoid sinus

Temperomandibular
joint and capsule

Auditory tube
(eustachian)

Head of the
mandible

Hard palate

Cerebellum

Soft palate

Tonsil

Tongue

Spinal cord

Mandible

Cervical
nerves

Epiglottis

Vocal cord

Esophagus

Trachea

The Teeth

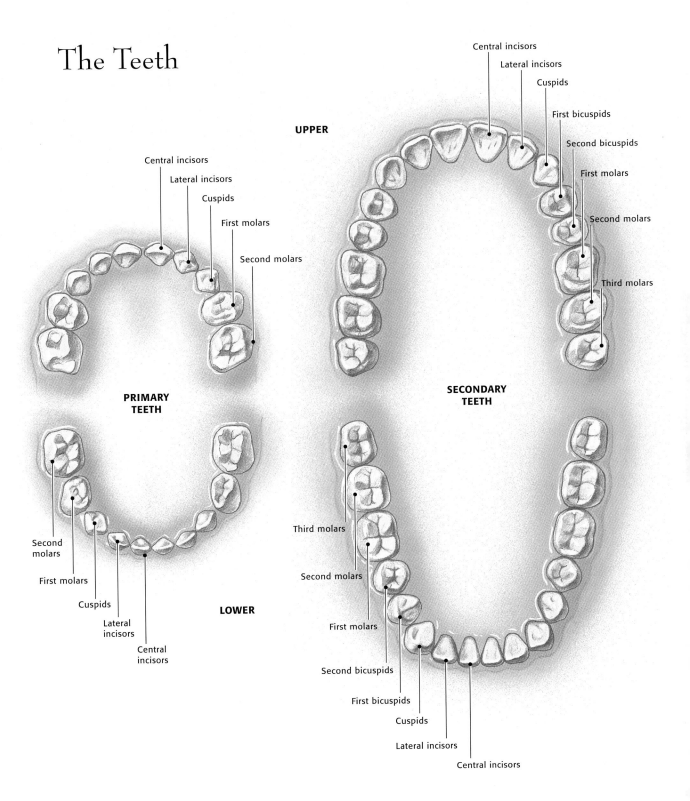

UPPER

Central incisors
Lateral incisors
Cuspids
First bicuspids
Second bicuspids
First molars
Second molars
Third molars

Central incisors
Lateral incisors
Cuspids
First molars
Second molars

PRIMARY TEETH

SECONDARY TEETH

Third molars
Second molars
First molars
Second bicuspids
First bicuspids
Cuspids
Lateral incisors
Central incisors

Second molars
First molars
Cuspids
Lateral incisors
Central incisors

LOWER

Baby Products

HIGH CHAIR

PLAYPEN

STROLLER

SWING

SMALL
OBJECT TESTER

CABINET
SAFETY STOPS

NASAL
ASPIRATOR

SAFETY
SCISSORS

CORNER
CUSHIONS

NAIL
CLIPPERS

OUTLET
PLUGS

ORAL
SYRINGE

CABINET
SLIDE LOCKS

MEDICINE
SPOON

RECTAL
THERMOMETER

ORTHODONTICALLY
APPROPRIATE
PACIFIERS

INFANT
CAR SEAT/CARRIER

REVERSIBLE
BABY
PACK/CARRIER

BABY BACKPACK
(for infants who
have achieved
head control)

Food Guide Pyramid

WITH SUGGESTED
DAILY SERVINGS

FATS, OILS, AND SWEETS (use sparingly)

MILK, YOGURT, AND CHEESE (2–3 servings)

MEAT, POULTRY, FISH, DRY BEANS, EGGS, AND NUTS (2–3 servings)

VEGETABLES (3–5 servings)

FRUITS (2–4 servings)

BREAD, CEREAL, RICE, AND PASTA (6–11 servings)

Servings are for adolescents or adults. Keep in mind a serving size for
a toddler or young child is much smaller than a normal adult serving.

FATS/OILS/SWEETS

Better:
gelatin dessert
fruit rolls
frozen pops
soft drinks
punch
fruit drinks
hard candy
reduced-fat
  mayonnaise or
  salad dressing
catsup
taco sauce

mustard
pickle relish,
  pickles
barbecue sauce
soy sauce
jam, jelly
syrup, honey
sugar

Worse:
cookies
cake, pie
granola bar

toaster pastry
donut, pastry
chocolate candy
chips
sour cream
gravy
cream sauce
whipped cream
cream cheese
mayonnaise
salad dressing
butter, margarine

VEGETABLES
*A serving is about 1 cup of raw leafy
vegetables, 1/2 cup of other vegetables, or
3/4 cup of vegetable juice.*

Better:
carrots, corn
green beans, peas
collards, kale
broccoli, okra
cauliflower
potato, sweet
  potato
spinach, mustard
  greens
peppers
spaghetti sauce,

salsa
tomato
cucumber
zucchini or other
  squash
mushrooms
cabbage, bok choy
coleslaw
green salad,
  lettuce
bean sprouts
mixed vegetables

vegetable soup,
  juice

Worse:
avocado
hash browns
potato salad
fried vegetables
tempura
  vegetables
french fries
potato puffs

MILK/YOGURT/CHEESE
*A serving is about 1 cup of milk or yogurt,
1 1/2 ounces of natural cheese, or 2 ounces
of processed cheese.*

Better:
nonfat milk
nonfat yogurt
low-fat milk
low-fat yogurt
low-fat chocolate
  milk
low-fat pudding

low-fat cheese
mozzarella cheese
string cheese
low-fat cottage
  cheese
soft-serve ice
  cream
frozen yogurt

Worse:
whole milk*
milk shake
hot chocolate
pudding
flan or custard
cheese
ice cream

recommended for children under 2 years

FRUITS
*A serving equals 1 medium-sized piece of
fresh fruit or 1/2 cup of canned fruit.*

apple, grapes
peach, nectarine
plum, pear
orange, tangerine
grapefruit
banana

apricots
berries, kiwi
mango, papaya
pineapple
cantaloupe
watermelon

other melon
dried fruit, raisins
fruit cocktail
100% fruit juice

MEAT/POULTRY/FISH/
DRY BEANS/EGGS/NUTS
*A serving equals 2–3 ounces of cooked meat
or 1/2 cup of cooked dried beans. 1 egg
or 2 tablespoons of peanut butter equal
1 ounce of meat.*

Better:
dried beans, peas,
  lentils
tuna
fish (baked or
  broiled)
refried beans
  (canned)
chicken or turkey
  (no skin)
tofu

lean beef
lean ham
lean pork, lamb

Worse:
eggs
chicken or turkey
  (with skin)
beef
pork chop
ham

fried fish
fish sticks
fried chicken
chicken nuggets
peanut butter
nuts and seeds
ground beef
frankfurters
ribs
lunch meat
sausage

BREAD/CEREAL/RICE/PASTA
*A serving is equivalent
to 1 slice of bread or a
small roll; 1 ounce
of cold cereal; 1/2 cup
of cooked cereal,
rice, or pasta; or 3–4
small crackers.*

Better:
rice, grits
spaghetti, maca-
  roni, noodles
bagel, English
  muffin
pita bread
whole grain,
  enriched bread
raisin bread
tortillas
hot dog,
  hamburger bun

oatmeal
hot cereal
dry cereal
whole grain cereal
saltine crackers,
  rice cakes
whole wheat
  crackers
graham crackers
roll
pizza crust
ramen noodles

Worse:
pancake
waffle
French toast
granola
biscuits
Mexican sweet
  bread
muffins
corn bread
snack crackers
pasta salad

Physical Growth Girls: Birth to 36 months

NCHS PERCENTILES*   NAME _____ RECORD # _____

MOTHER'S STATURE _____ GESTATIONAL

FATHER'S STATURE _____ AGE _____ WEEKS

DATE	AGE	LENGTH	WEIGHT	HEAD CIRC.	COMMENT
	BIRTH				

*Adapted from: Hamill PVV, Drizd TA, Johnson CL, Reed RB, Roche AF, Moore WM: Physical growth: National Center for Health Statistics percentiles. AM J CLIN NUTR 32:607-629, 1979. Data from the Fels Longitudinal Study, Wright State University School of Medicine, Yellow Springs, Ohio.

© 1982 Ross Products Division, Abbott Laboratories

Physical Growth Boys: Birth to 36 months

NCHS PERCENTILES*   NAME_____   RECORD #_____

*Adapted from: Hamill PVV, Drizd TA, Johnson CL, Reed RB, Roche AF, Moore WM: Physical growth: National Center for Health Statistics percentiles. AM J CLIN NUTR 32:607-629, 1979. Data from the Fels Longitudinal Study, Wright State University School of Medicine, Yellow Springs, Ohio.

Physical Growth Girls: 2 to 18 Years

NCHS PERCENTILES*

*Adapted from: Hamill PVV, Drizd TA, Johnson CL, Reed RB, Roche AF, Moore WM. Physical growth: National Center for Health Statistics percentiles. AM J CLIN NUTR 32:607-629, 1979. Data from the National Center for Health Statistics (NCHS) Hyattsville, Maryland.

© 1982 Ross Products Division, Abbott Laboratories

Physical Growth Boys: 2 to 18 Years

NCHS PERCENTILES*

NAME _____ RECORD # _____

*Adapted from: Hamill PVV, Drizd TA, Johnson CL, Reed RB, Roche AF, Moore WM. Physical growth: National Center for Health Statistics percentiles. AM J CLIN NUTR 32:607-629, 1979. Data from the National Center for Health Statistics (NCHS), Hyattsville, Maryland.

Physical Growth Girls: Prepubescent

NCHS PERCENTILES*   NAME _____   RECORD # _____

*Adapted from: Hamill PVV, Drizd TA, Johnson CL, Reed RB, Roche AF, Moore WM: Physical growth: National Center for Health Statistics percentiles. AM J CLIN NUTR 32:607-629, 1979. Data from the National Center for Health Statistics (NCHS), Hyattsville, Maryland.

© 1982 Ross Products Division, Abbott Laboratories

DATE	AGE	STATURE	WEIGHT	COMMENT

Physical Growth Boys: Prepubescent

DATE	AGE	STATURE	WEIGHT	COMMENT

Recommended Childhood Immunization Schedule

UNITED STATES, JANUARY–DECEMBER 1997

VACCINE / AGE	Birth	1 mo	2 mos	4 mos	6 mos	12 mos	15 mos	18 mos	4–6 yrs	11–12 yrs	14–16 yrs
Hepatitis B[2,3]	Hep B-1		Hep B-2		Hep B-3					Hep B[3]	
Diphtheria, Tetanus			DTaP or DTP	DTaP or DTP	DTaP or DTP		DTaP or DTP[4]		DTaP or DTP	Td	
H. influenzae type b[5]			Hib	Hib	Hib[5]	Hib[5]					
Polio[6]			Polio[6]	Polio		Polio			Polio		
Measles, Mumps, Rubella[7]						MMR			MMR[7] or	MMR[7]	
Varicella[8]							Var			Var[8]	

Vaccines[1] are listed under the routinely recommended ages. Bars indicate range of acceptable ages for vaccination. Bars with heavy borders indicate catch-up vaccination: at 11–12 years of age, hepatitis B vaccine should be administered to children not previously vaccinated, and varicella virus vaccine should be administered to unvaccinated children who lack a reliable history of chicken pox.

[1]This schedule indicates the recommended age for routine administration of currently licensed childhood vaccines. Some combination vaccines are available and may be used whenever administration of all components of the vaccine is indicated. Providers should consult the manufacturer's package inserts for detailed recommendations.

[2]**Infants born to HBsAg-negative mothers** should receive 2.5 mg of Merck vaccine (Recombivax HB) or 10 mg of SmithKline Beecham (SB) vaccine (Engerix-B). The second dose should be administered ≥ 1 month after the first dose.

Infants born to HBsAg-positive mothers should receive 0.5 mL hepatitis B immune globulin (HBIG) within 12 hours of birth and either 5 mg of Merck vaccine (Recombivax HB) or 10 mg of SB vaccine (Engerix-B) at a separate site. The second dose is recommended at 1–2 months of age and the third dose at 6 months of age.

Infants born to mothers whose HBsAg status is unknown should receive either 5 mg of Merck vaccine (Recombivax HB) or 10 mg of SB vaccine (Engerix-B) within 12 hours of birth. The second dose of vaccine is recommended at 1 month of age and the third dose at 6 months of age. Blood should be drawn at the time of delivery to determine the mother's HBsAg status. If it is positive, the infant should receive HBIG as soon as possible (no later than 1 week of age). The dosage and timing of subsequent vaccine doses should be based upon the mother's HBsAg status.

[3]Children and adolescents who have not been vaccinated against hepatitis B in infancy may begin the series during any childhood visit. Those who have not previously received three doses of hepatitis B vaccine should initiate or complete the series during the 11–12-year-old visit. The second dose should be administered at least one month after the first dose, and the third dose should be administered at least four months after the first dose and at least two months after the second dose.

[4]DTaP (diptheria and tetanus toxoids and acellular pertussis vaccine) is the preferred vaccine for all doses in the vaccination series, including completion of the series in children who have received ≥ 1 of whole-cell DTP vaccine. Whole-cell DTP is an acceptable alternative to DTaP. The fourth dose of DTaP may be administered as early as 12 months of age, provided 6 months have elapsed since the third dose, and if the child is considered unlikely to return at 15–18 months of age. Td (tetanus and diphtheria toxoids, absorbed, for adult use) is recommended at 11–12 years of age if at least 5 years have elapsed since the last dose of DTP, DTaP, or DT. Subsequent routine Td boosters are recommended every 10 years.

[5]Three H. influenzae type b (Hib) conjugate vaccines are licensed for infant use. If PRP-OMP (PedvaxHIB [Merck]) is administered at 2 and 4 months of age, a dose at 6 months is not required. After completing the primary series, any Hib conjugate vaccine may be used as a booster.

[6]Two polio virus vaccines are currently licensed in the U.S.: inactivated polio virus vaccine (IPV) and oral polio virus vaccine (OPV). The following schedules are all acceptable by the ACIP, the AAP, and the AAFP, and parents and providers may choose among them:

1. IPV at 2 and 4 months; OPV at 12–18 months and 4–6 years
2. IPV at 2, 4, 12–18 months and 4–6 years
3. OPV at 2, 4, 6–18 months and 4–6 years

The ACIP routinely recommends schedule 1. IPV is the only polio virus vaccine recommended for immunocompromised persons and their household contacts.

[7]The second dose of MMR is routinely recommended at 4–6 years of age or at 11–12 years of age but may be administered during any visit, provided at least one month has elapsed since receipt of the first dose and that both doses are administered at or after 12 months of age.

[8]Susceptible children may receive varicella vaccine (Var) during any visit after the first birthday, and unvaccinated persons who lack a reliable history of chicken pox should be vaccinated during the 11–12-year-old visit. Susceptible persons ≥ 13 years of age should receive two doses at least one month apart.

Approved by the Advisory Committee on Immunization Practices (ACIP), American Academy of Pediatrics (AAP), and American Academy of Family Physicians (AAFP).

Skin Condition Photos

ABRASION

ATOPIC DERMATITIS

Hand

ALOPECIA

In an infant

CANDIDA DIAPER DERMATITIS

(diaper rash)

ATHLETE'S FOOT

CHICKEN POX

(varicella)

ATOPIC DERMATITIS

Face

CONGENITAL NEVUS

A28

CONJUNCTIVITIS
(pinkeye)

FLEA BITES

CORNEAL ABRASION

Fluorescent dye accumulates in abraded area.

HAND-FOOT-MOUTH DISEASE
(Coxsackie)

ECZEMA

HEAD LICE

Note: The nits are attached to the hair.

ERYTHEMA MULTIFORME
(blisters)

HERPES
Lip

HIVES
(urticaria)

MILIA

HYPHEMA
Blood collected in
clear space behind
cornea

MILIARIA
(heat rash,
prickly heat)

IMPETIGO

**MOLLUSCUM
CONTAGIOSUM**

LYME DISEASE

MONGOLIAN SPOTS

NEONATAL ACNE

POISON OAK
(Blisters)

PARONYCHIA
(ingrown toenails)

PUSTULE

PITYRIASIS ROSEA

RINGWORM
(Tinea Capitis)
Face

PLANTAR WART
Recently treated

RINGWORM
Head

RUBELLA

(German measles)

STY

SCABIES BITES

SUBCONJUNCTIVAL HEMORRHAGE

SEBORRHEIC DERMATITIS

(cradle cap)

TICK BITES

(actual tick on skin)

STRAWBERRY HEMANGIOMA

WART

Metric Conversion Charts

VOLUME	
1/4 tsp.	1.25 ml
1/2 tsp.	2.5 ml
1 tsp.	5 ml
1 Tbsp.	15 ml
1/4 cup	50 ml
1/3 cup	75 ml
1/2 cup	125 ml
2/3 cup	150 ml
3/4 cup	175 ml
1 cup	237 ml

WEIGHT	
1 oz.	30 g
2 oz.	55 g
3 oz.	85 g
4 oz.	115 g
5 oz.	140 g
6 oz.	170 g
7 oz.	200 g
8 oz.	250 g
16 oz.	500 g
32 oz.	1000 g

TEMPERATURE CONVERSION: Fahrenheit/Centigrade			
°F	°C	°F	°C
97.0	36.1	101.4	38.6
97.5	36.4	101.6	38.7
98.0	36.7	101.8	38.8
98.2	36.8	102.0	38.9
98.4	36.9	102.2	39.0
98.6	37.0	102.4	39.1
98.8	37.1	102.6	39.2
99.0	37.2	102.8	39.3
99.2	37.3	103.0	39.4
99.4	37.4	103.2	39.6
99.6	37.6	103.4	39.7
99.8	37.7	103.6	39.8
100.0	37.8	103.8	39.9
100.2	37.9	104.0	40.0
100.4	38.0	104.2	40.1
100.6	38.1	104.4	40.2
100.8	38.2	104.6	40.3
101.0	38.3	104.8	40.4
101.2	38.4	105.0	40.6

Quick Medical Reference Sheet

Photocopy this chart for each child in your family

CHILD'S NAME _____

Birth date _____ Blood type _____

Any allergies or ongoing medical conditions _____

_____

_____

Child's physician _____

Long-term prescriptions used by the child:

    Medication _____ Prescription # _____

    Medication _____ Prescription # _____

    Medication _____ Prescription # _____

    Pharmacy phone # _____

Illness _____

    Year and month _____

    Physician treating _____

    Severity of illness/specific problems _____

    _____

    Treatment/medications used _____

    _____

Illness _____

    Year and month _____

    Physician treating _____

    Severity of illness/specific problems _____

    _____

    Treatment/medications used _____

    _____